THE MISSING PEACE

THE MISSING PEACE

•

The Inside Story of the Fight for Middle East Peace

DENNIS ROSS

FARRAR, STRAUS AND GIROUX

NEW YORK

Farrar, Straus and Giroux
19 Union Square West, New York 10003

Distributed in Canada by Douglas & McIntyre Ltd.
Printed in the United States of America
First edition, 2004

Library of Congress Cataloging-in-Publication Data
Ross, Dennis
  The missing peace : the inside story of the fight for Middle East peace / Dennis Ross.— 1st ed.
  p. cm.
  Includes bibliographical references and index.
  ISBN-13: 978-0-374-19973-9
  ISBN-10: 0-374-19973-6
  1. Arab-Israeli conflict—1993—Peace.   2. Israel—Politics and government—1993–
3. Palestinian Arabs—Politics and government.   4. Ross, Dennis.   5. Middle East—Foreign
relations—United States.   6. United States—Foreign relations—Middle East.   I. Title.

DS119.76.R68 2004
956.05'3—dc22
                                                                          2003027827

Designed by Lisa Stokes
Maps designed by David Swanson, International Mapping Associates

www.fsgbooks.com

10 9 8 7 6 5 4 3 2 1

Jacket photograph credits
Front jacket, from left: Dennis Ross and Yasir Arafat, 1994, author's personal collection. Hosni
Mubarak (Egyptian President), Shimon Peres (Israeli Foreign Minister), Andrei Kozyrev (Russian Foreign Minister), Nabil Sha'ath (Palestinian Authority), and Yasir Arafat, 1994, author's
personal collection. Dennis Ross, Yasir Arafat, and Yitzhak Rabin outside the President's Oval
Office, 1995, Official White House photograph. Dennis Ross and President Bush, 1992, Official White House photograph. President Clinton, Secretary of State Warren Christopher, and
Dennis Ross, 1995, Official White House photograph. Dennis Ross and Warren Christopher,
1993, Official White House photograph. Dennis Ross and Ehud Barak (Prime Minister of Israel), Office of Public Affairs American Embassy, Tel Aviv, Israel, Secretary of State visit to the
Middle East, 1999.
Spine: Dennis Ross and James Baker, author's personal collection. Dennis Ross, President Clin-
ton, and Madeleine Albright, 1998, Official White House photograph.
Back jacket, from left: Dennis Ross with Binyamin Netanyahu, United States Information Service
photograph by Matty Stern. Dennis Ross, Abu Ala, and Abu Mazen, United States Information
Service American Embassy, Tel Aviv, Israel, Secretary of State visit to Israel and the PA, 1998.
Dennis Ross and Hafez al-Asad, President of Syria, author's personal collection.

The opinions and characterizations in this book are those of the author, and do not necessarily
represent official positions of the United States Government.

To the children of the Middle East

Contents

Dramatis Personae

Egypt

Osama al-Baz	National Security Advisor and senior advisor to the President
Nabil Fahmy	Senior advisor to the Foreign Minister; currently ambassador to the United States
Esmat Abdel Meguid	Foreign Minister (1984–91)
Amre Moussa	Foreign Minister (1991–2001)
Hosni Mubarak	President
General Omar Suleiman	Head of military intelligence

Jordan

Crown Prince al-Hassan	Crown Prince of Jordan
King Hussein	King of Jordan
Abdul Salam Majali	Prime Minister (1993–97)
Fayez Tarawneh	Ambassador to the United States (1992–97); Prime Minister (1998–2000)

Syria

Moufak Allaf	Syrian negotiator
Hafez al-Asad	President of Syria
Riad Daoudi	Syrian lawyer used by Asad as negotiator

Walid al-Moualem   Chef de cabinet to the Foreign Minister, Syrian
                            ambassador to the United States, and chief
                            negotiator
Ibrahim Omar   Syrian general attached to negotiations
Butheina Sha'aban   Asad's trusted interpreter and later foreign policy
                            advisor
Farouk Shara   Foreign Minister
Hikmat Shihabi   Chief of Staff of Syrian military

Saudi Arabia

Crown Prince Abdullah   Crown Prince of Saudi Arabia and de facto leader
                            since 1995
King Fahd   King of Saudi Arabia
Prince Saud al-Faisal   Saudi Foreign Minister
Prince Bandar bin Sultan   Saudi ambassador to the United States and
                            frequent informal mediator

Palestinians

Hussein Agha   Academic and advisor to Abu Mazen
Abu Ala (Ahmed Qurei)   Lead negotiator at Oslo, Fatah Central Committee
                            member, and Speaker of the Palestinian Legislative
                            Council
Yasir Arafat   Chairman of the PLO
Hassan Asfour   Palestinian negotiator and aide to Abu Mazen
Hanan Ashrawi   Palestinian spokeswoman
Mohammad Dahlan   Head of Palestinian security in Gaza and
                            negotiator
Saeb Erekat   Palestinian negotiator and Minister of Local
                            Government
General Amin al-Hindi   Head of the Palestinian secret police
Abu Mazen (Mahmoud Abbas)   Secretary-General of the PLO and top Palestinian
                            negotiator
Yasser Abed Rabbo   Minister of Information and Culture and negotiator

Jibril Rajoub — Head of the Palestinian Security Organization in the West Bank

Mohammad Rashid — Finance advisor to Arafat and negotiator

Nabil Abu Rudeina — Arafat's chief of staff and spokesperson

Nabil Sha'ath — Minister of Planning and International Cooperation and close aide to Arafat

Israelis

Moshe Arens — Foreign Minister (1983–84); Defense Minister (1988–90)

Ami Ayalon — Head of Shin Bet security service (1996–2000)

Ehud Barak — IDF Chief of Staff (1991–94); Foreign Minister (1995–96); Prime Minister (1999–2001)

Yossi Beilin — Deputy Minister of Foreign Affairs (1992–95) and driving force behind Oslo

Shlomo Ben-Ami — Minister of Internal Security (1999–2001) and acting Foreign Minister (2000–2001)

Uzi Dayan — General and military advisor to negotiations and National Security Advisor

Oded Eran — Negotiator during Oslo and Barak's tenure

Yossi Ginossar — Secret channel to Arafat used by Rabin and Barak

Dore Gold — Senior foreign policy advisor to Netanyahu and later ambassador to the UN

Ephraim Halevy — Deputy head of Mossad and later head of Mossad

Avigdor Kahalani — Minister of Internal Security (1996–99)

David Levy — Foreign Minister (1996–98)

Dan Meridor — Minister of Justice (1988–92); Likud member of Knesset and later Minister without portfolio from the Center Party in Barak's Coalition

Salai Meridor — Principal aide to Moshe Arens

Shaul Mofaz — IDF Chief of Planning (1996–97); IDF Chief of Staff (1998–2002)

Yitzik Molho — Advisor to Netanyahu and negotiator

Yitzhak Mordechai — Defense Minister (1996–99)

Dani Naveh	Advisor to Netanyahu and negotiator
Binyamin Netanyahu	Likud party leader (1993–96); Prime Minister (1996–99)
Shimon Peres	Prime Minister (1995–96); Foreign Minister (1986–88; 1992–95); key sponsor of Oslo
Yitzhak Rabin	Prime Minister (1974–77; 1992–95); Defense Minister (1984–90)
Itamar Rabinovich	Ambassador to the United States and Rabin's negotiator on the Syrian track
Daniel Reisner	IDF legal advisor
Elyakim (Eli) Rubinstein	Attorney General and key negotiator on treaty with Jordan
Uri Saguy	Barak's chief negotiator on Syria and former IDF chief of military intelligence
Uri Savir	Director General of Israel's Foreign Ministry (1993–96) and Israel's chief negotiator with the PLO and, in 1996, with Syria
Amnon Shahak	IDF Deputy Chief of Staff (1991–95); IDF Chief of Staff (1995–96); Minister of Tourism (1999–2001); frequent informal envoy
Yitzhak Shamir	Prime Minister (1983–84; 1986–92)
Natan Sharansky	Head of the Ysrael Ba'aliyah Party and minister in Netanyahu and Barak governments
Ariel Sharon	Foreign Minister (1998–99)
Gilad Sher	Barak's lead negotiator with the Palestinians
Yoel Singer	Legal advisor to the negotiations
Ezer Weizman	President of Israel (1993–2000)
Shlomo Yanai	IDF chief of planning during Syrian and Palestinian negotiations (1997–2001)
Dani Yatom	Military Secretary to Rabin and Peres; head of the Mossad; key advisor to Barak

United States

Madeleine Albright	Secretary of State (1997–2001)
James A. Baker, III	Secretary of State (1989–92)

Samuel (Sandy) Berger	Deputy National Security Advisor (1993–97); National Security Advisor (1997–2001)
Warren Christopher	Secretary of State (1993–97)
Thomas (Tom) E. Donilon	Assistant Secretary of State for Public Affairs and Chief of Staff to Secretary Christopher (1993–96)
Lawrence Eagleburger	Deputy Secretary of State (1989–92); Secretary of State (1992–93)
Rahm Emanuel	Chief White House advisor (1993–98)
Gamal Helal	Special advisor to the special Middle East coordinator and translator
Martin Indyk	Special assistant to the President for Near Eastern Affairs, National Security Council (1993–95); ambassador to Israel (1995–97); Assistant Secretary of State for Near Eastern Affairs (1997–99); ambassador to Israel (1999–2001)
Patrick (Pat) Kennedy	Assistant Secretary of State for Administration (1993–2000)
Anthony (Tony) Lake	National Security Advisor (1993–97)
Rob Malley	Special assistant to the President, director for Near Eastern Affairs, National Security Council (1999–2001)
Aaron Miller	Member, State Department Policy Planning Staff (1989–93); Deputy Special Middle East coordinator (1993–2001)
Mark Parris	Special assistant to the President, senior director for Near Eastern Affairs, National Security Council (1995–97)
Robert Pelletreau	Assistant Secretary of State for Near Eastern Affairs (1994–97)
John Podesta	White House Chief of Staff (1998–2001)
Nick Rasmussen	Assistant to the special Middle East coordinator
Bruce Riedel	Special assistant to the President, senior director for Near Eastern Affairs, National Security Council (1997–2001)

James (Jamie) P. Rubin   Assistant Secretary of State for Public Affairs and key advisor to Secretary Albright (1997–2001)

Jon Schwartz   Deputy Legal advisor to the State Department

George Stephanopoulos   Senior White House advisor for Policy and Strategy (1993–96); key political advisor to President Clinton

Toni Verstandig   Deputy Assistant Secretary of State for Near Eastern Affairs (1994–2001)

Edward (Ned) S. Walker, Jr.   Assistant Secretary of State for Near Eastern Affairs (1999–2001); ambassador to Israel (1997–99); Ambassador to Egypt (1994–97)

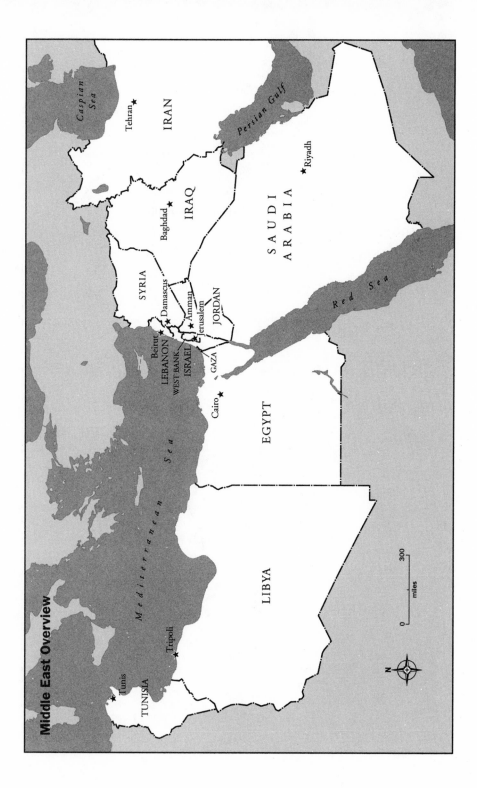

Middle East Overview

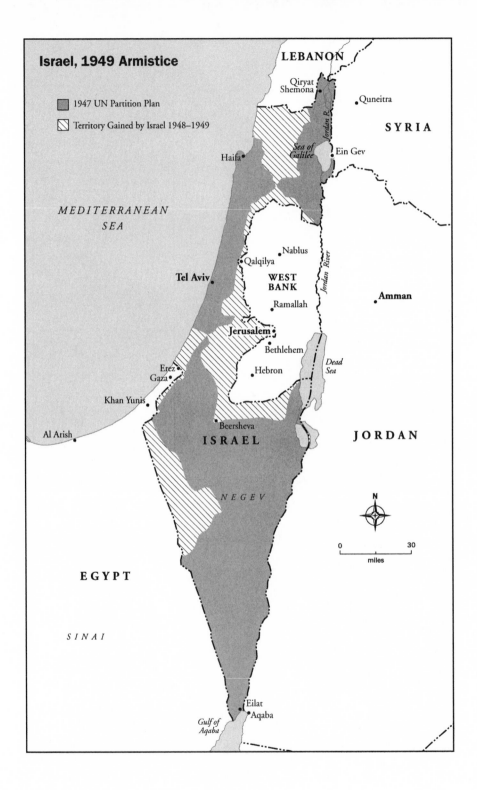

Israel, 1949 Armistice

- ■ 1947 UN Partition Plan
- ⬚ Territory Gained by Israel 1948–1949

LEBANON

Qiryat Shemona

Quneitra

SYRIA

Jordan R.

Sea of Galilee

Ein Gev

Haifa

MEDITERRANEAN SEA

Nablus

Qalqilya

Tel Aviv

WEST BANK

Jordan River

Amman

Ramallah

Jerusalem

Bethlehem

Dead Sea

Erez
Gaza

Hebron

Khan Yunis

Beersheva

JORDAN

Al Arish

ISRAEL

NEGEV

N

0   30
miles

EGYPT

SINAI

Eilat
Aqaba

Gulf of Aqaba

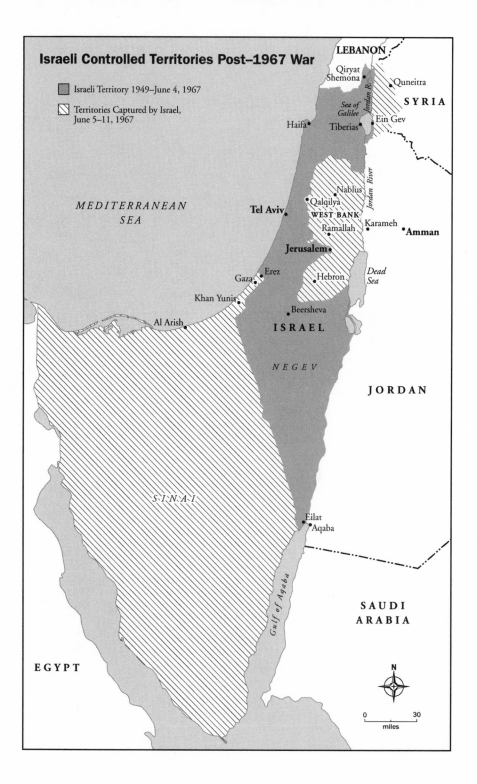

Israeli Controlled Territories Post–1967 War

Israeli Territory 1949–June 4, 1967

Territories Captured by Israel,
June 5–11, 1967

LEBANON

Qiryat
Shemona

Quneitra

SYRIA

*Sea of
Galilee*

Jordan R.

Haifa

Tiberias

Ein Gev

*MEDITERRANEAN
SEA*

Nablus

Qalqilya

Tel Aviv

WEST BANK

Jordan River

Ramallah

Karameh

Amman

Jerusalem

Gaza

Erez

Hebron

*Dead
Sea*

Khan Yunis

Al Arish

Beersheva

ISRAEL

NEGEV

JORDAN

S I N A I

Eilat
Aqaba

Gulf of Aqaba

**SAUDI
ARABIA**

EGYPT

N

0   30
miles

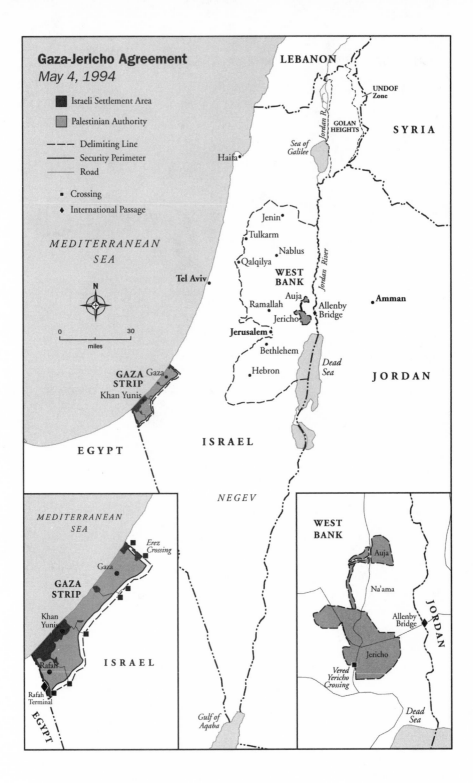

Gaza-Jericho Agreement
May 4, 1994

■ Israeli Settlement Area

■ Palestinian Authority

– – – Delimiting Line

——— Security Perimeter

——— Road

■ Crossing

◆ International Passage

LEBANON

UNDOF Zone

Jordan R.

GOLAN HEIGHTS

SYRIA

Sea of Galilee

Haifa

MEDITERRANEAN SEA

N

0   30
miles

Jenin

Tulkarm

Nablus

Qalqilya

WEST BANK

Jordan River

Tel Aviv

Ramallah

Auja

Allenby Bridge

Jericho

Amman

Jerusalem

Bethlehem

Dead Sea

JORDAN

Hebron

GAZA STRIP   Gaza

Khan Yunis

ISRAEL

EGYPT

NEGEV

MEDITERRANEAN SEA

Erez Crossing

Gaza

GAZA STRIP

Khan Yunis

ISRAEL

Rafah

Rafah Terminal

EGYPT

Gulf of Aqaba

WEST BANK

Auja

Na'ama

JORDAN

Allenby Bridge

Jericho

Vered Yericho Crossing

Dead Sea

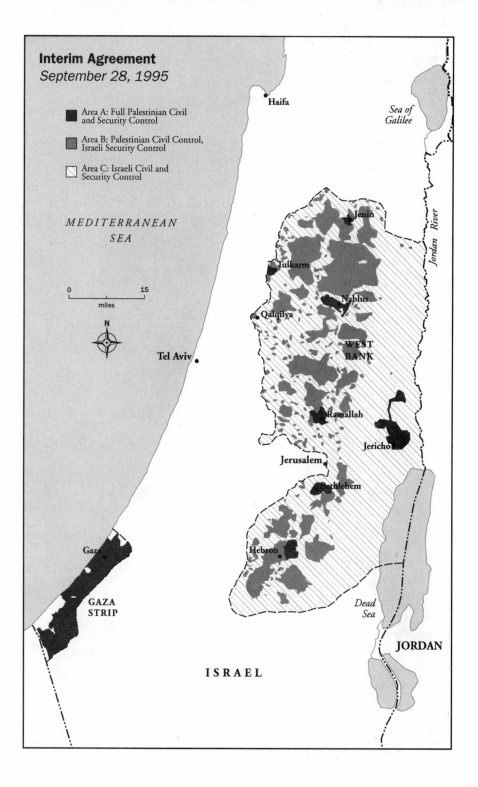

Interim Agreement
September 28, 1995

Area A: Full Palestinian Civil and Security Control

Area B: Palestinian Civil Control, Israeli Security Control

Area C: Israeli Civil and Security Control

MEDITERRANEAN SEA

0   15
miles

N

Haifa

Sea of Galilee

Jordan River

Jenin

Tulkarm

Nablus

Qalqilya

WEST BANK

Tel Aviv

Ramallah

Jericho

Jerusalem

Bethlehem

Gaza

GAZA STRIP

Hebron

Dead Sea

JORDAN

ISRAEL

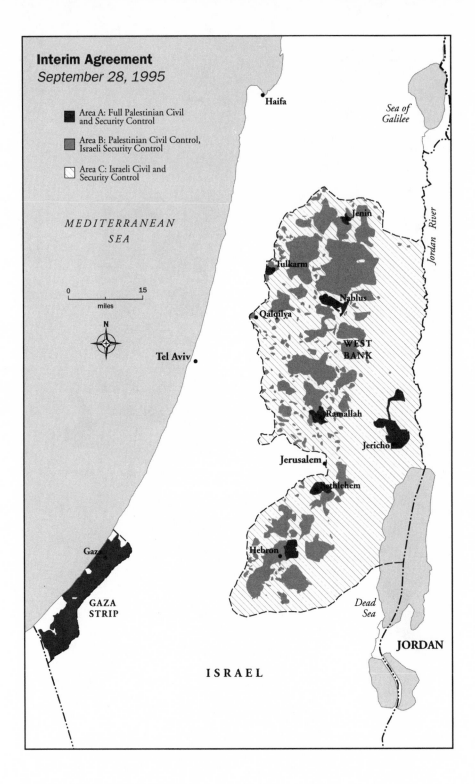

Interim Agreement
September 28, 1995

■ Area A: Full Palestinian Civil and Security Control

■ Area B: Palestinian Civil Control, Israeli Security Control

□ Area C: Israeli Civil and Security Control

MEDITERRANEAN SEA

0   15
miles

N

Haifa

Sea of Galilee

Jordan River

Jenin

Tulkarm

Nablus

Qalqilya

WEST BANK

Tel Aviv

Ramallah

Jericho

Jerusalem

Bethlehem

Gaza

GAZA STRIP

Hebron

Dead Sea

JORDAN

ISRAEL

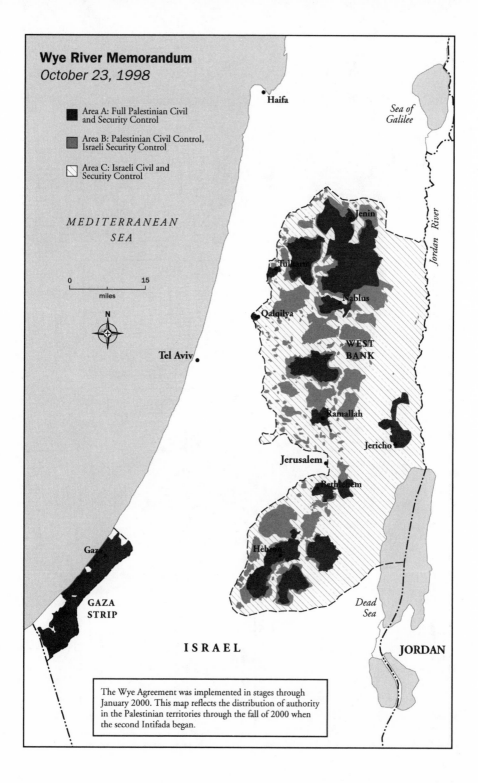

Wye River Memorandum
October 23, 1998

- Area A: Full Palestinian Civil and Security Control
- Area B: Palestinian Civil Control, Israeli Security Control
- Area C: Israeli Civil and Security Control

MEDITERRANEAN SEA

0   15
miles

N

Haifa

Sea of Galilee

Jenin

Tulkarm

Nablus

Qalqilya

Jordan River

WEST BANK

Tel Aviv

Ramallah

Jericho

Jerusalem

Bethlehem

Gaza

Hebron

GAZA STRIP

Dead Sea

ISRAEL

JORDAN

The Wye Agreement was implemented in stages through January 2000. This map reflects the distribution of authority in the Palestinian territories through the fall of 2000 when the second Intifada began.

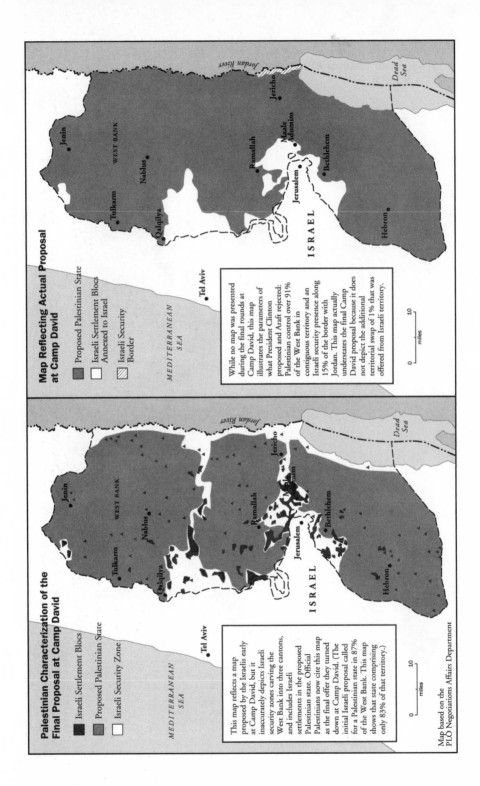

Map Reflecting Actual Proposal at Camp David

Legend:
- Proposed Palestinian State
- Israeli Settlement Blocs Annexed to Israel
- Israeli Security Border

MEDITERRANEAN SEA

Tel Aviv

WEST BANK

Jenin
Tulkarm
Nablus
Qalqilya
Ramallah
Maale Adumim
Jerusalem
Bethlehem
Hebron
Jericho

Jordan River

Dead Sea

ISRAEL

0 — 10 miles

While no map was presented during the final rounds at Camp David, this map illustrates the parameters of what President Clinton proposed and Arafat rejected: Palestinian control over 91% of the West Bank in contiguous territory and an Israeli security presence along 15% of the border with Jordan. This map actually understates the final Camp David proposal because it does not depict the additional territorial swap of 1% that was offered from Israeli territory.

Palestinian Characterization of the Final Proposal at Camp David

Legend:
- Israeli Settlement Blocs
- Proposed Palestinian State
- Israeli Security Zone

MEDITERRANEAN SEA

Tel Aviv

WEST BANK

Jenin
Tulkarm
Nablus
Qalqilya
Ramallah
Maale Adumim
Jerusalem
Bethlehem
Hebron
Jericho

Jordan River

Dead Sea

ISRAEL

0 — 10 miles

This map reflects a map proposed by the Israelis early at Camp David, but it inaccurately depicts Israeli security zones carving the West Bank into three cantons, and includes Israeli settlements in the proposed Palestinian state. Official Palestinians now cite this map as the final offer they turned down at Camp David. (The initial Israeli proposal called for a Palestinian state in 87% of the West Bank. This map shows that state comprising only 83% of that territory.)

Map based on the
PLO Negotiations Affairs Department

Map Reflecting Clinton Ideas

■ Proposed Palestinian State

□ Israeli Settlement Blocs Annexed to Israel

Haifa

Sea of Galilee

MEDITERRANEAN SEA

0   15

miles

N

Jenin

Tulkarm

Nablus

Qalqilya

Tel Aviv

WEST BANK

Jordan River

Ramallah

Jericho

Jerusalem   Maale Adumim

I S R A E L

Bethlehem

Hebron

Gaza

GAZA STRIP

Dead Sea

JORDAN

E G Y P T

No formal map was presented to the Israelis and Palestinians in December 2000 by President Clinton, but this map illustrates the Clinton ideas—a Palestinian state in 95% of the West Bank and 100% of Gaza. This map actually understates the Clinton ideas by not showing an additional 1 to 3% of territorial swaps to the Palestinian state from areas within Israel.

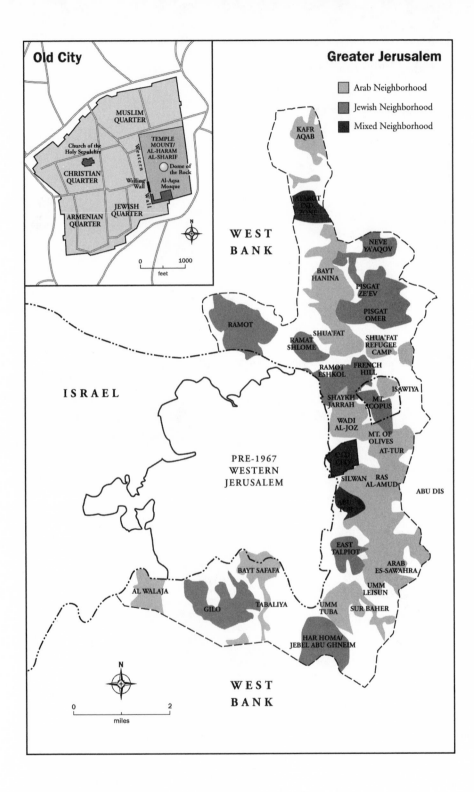

Old City

MUSLIM QUARTER

Church of the Holy Sepulchre

TEMPLE MOUNT/ AL-HARAM AL-SHARIF

Dome of the Rock

CHRISTIAN QUARTER

Wailing Wall

Al-Aqsa Mosque

Western Wall

ARMENIAN QUARTER

JEWISH QUARTER

N

0   1000
feet

Greater Jerusalem

Arab Neighborhood

Jewish Neighborhood

Mixed Neighborhood

KAFR AQAB

WEST BANK

ATAROT IND. ZONE

NEVE YA'AQOV

BAYT HANINA

PISGAT ZE'EV

PISGAT OMER

RAMOT

SHUA'FAT

RAMAT SHLOME

SHUA'FAT REFUGEE CAMP

RAMOT ESHKOL

FRENCH HILL

ISAWIYA

ISRAEL

SHAYKH JARRAH

MT. SCOPUS

WADI AL-JOZ

MT. OF OLIVES

AT-TUR

OLD CITY

PRE-1967 WESTERN JERUSALEM

SILWAN

RAS AL-AMUD

ABU DIS

ABU TOR

EAST TALPIOT

ARAB ES-SAWAHRA

BAYT SAFAFA

UMM LEISUN

AL WALAJA

GILO

TABALIYA

UMM TUBA

SUR BAHER

HAR HOMA/ JEBEL ABU GHNEIM

N

0   2
miles

WEST BANK

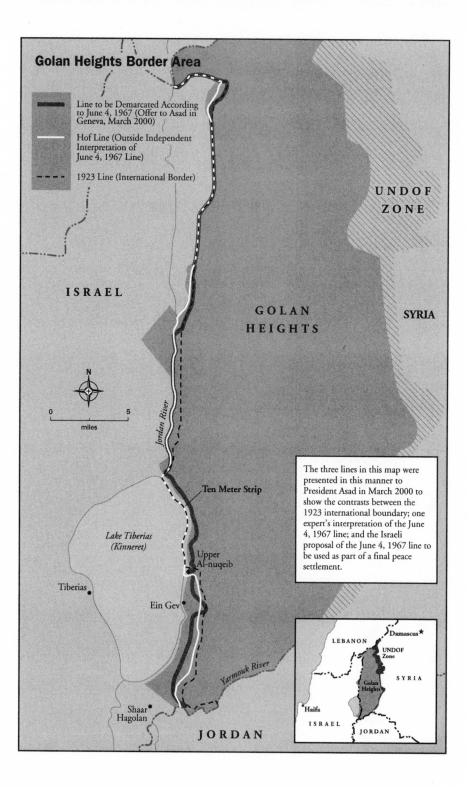

Golan Heights Border Area

- **Line to be Demarcated According to June 4, 1967 (Offer to Asad in Geneva, March 2000)**
- **Hof Line (Outside Independent Interpretation of June 4, 1967 Line)**
- - - **1923 Line (International Border)**

UNDOF ZONE

ISRAEL

GOLAN HEIGHTS

SYRIA

N

0 — 5 miles

Jordan River

Ten Meter Strip

Lake Tiberias (Kinneret)

Upper Al-nuqeib

Tiberias

Ein Gev

Shaar Hagolan

Yarmouk River

JORDAN

The three lines in this map were presented in this manner to President Asad in March 2000 to show the contrasts between the 1923 international boundary; one expert's interpretation of the June 4, 1967 line; and the Israeli proposal of the June 4, 1967 line to be used as part of a final peace settlement.

LEBANON
Damascus ★
UNDOF Zone
SYRIA
Golan Heights
Haifa
ISRAEL
JORDAN

The End

It was January 2, 2001. Yasir Arafat was due at the White House in thirty minutes, and I was about to go into the Oval Office to brief the President. No matter how many times I had done this, no matter how many times Arafat had come, there was always a sense of anticipation. Each time the objective had been to advance the process, to move the ball down the field.

But it was different this time. This time we faced the moment of truth. It was too late to think in terms of process. President Clinton had seventeen days left in office. Now we had to know: Could Yasir Arafat end this conflict? Could he accept the ideas, the proposals, the President had presented ten days ago?

Already he had missed the deadline we had sought to impose on both sides for a response to the President's ideas. As usual, Chairman Arafat had equivocated. He had questions. He sought clarification. He wanted further discussions. He hoped that I would meet with the negotiators on each side and clear up misunderstandings, and he even succeeded in getting President Hosni Mubarak of Egypt to make this request to President Clinton.

All this in response to an unprecedented set of ideas that would have produced a Palestinian state in all of Gaza and nearly all of the West Bank; a capital for that state in Arab East Jerusalem; security arrangements that would be built around an international presence; and an unlimited right of return for Palestinian refugees to their own state, but not to Israel.

The ideas represented the culmination of an extraordinary effort to reach a final Israeli-Palestinian peace deal. Thousands of miles had been covered, figuratively and literally. Thousands of hours of discussions had taken place. And, without exaggeration, thousands of arguments had been made, dissected, and examined in trying to understand what each side could and could not live with. The Clinton ideas were not about what each side wanted; they were about what each side needed.

The Clinton ideas were a "first" and a "last." Never before had the United States put a comprehensive set of proposals on the table designed to end the conflict between Israelis and Palestinians—or at least shrink the differences on all the core issues to a point where a final deal could be hammered out quickly. We had come close to doing so in July five months earlier at the Camp David summit. But there, our ideas were not comprehensive—as we presented proposals neither on security arrangements nor on Palestinian refugees. Moreover, the ideas at Camp David were a mix of what Ehud Barak told us he could accept on withdrawal from the West Bank and Gaza and what we thought might resolve the sensitive issue of Jerusalem.

Now, while our ideas should have come as no surprise to either side, they represented our best judgment of what each side could accept in the end. We could not do better. Painful concessions were required on each side. Historic myths would have to give way to political necessity and reality on each side—with Israel giving up two core beliefs: that all of Jerusalem, including the Arab neighborhoods of East Jerusalem, would be Israeli, and that the Jordan Valley must never be surrendered. For their part, the Palestinians had to give up the myth of "right of return" to Israel—the animating belief of the Palestine Liberation Organization (PLO) and the Palestinian diaspora throughout their history.

There could be no more haggling. Discussion within the parameters of the President's ideas was acceptable; trying to redefine these parameters was not.

That is what President Clinton had told both Israeli and Palestinian negotiators on December 23, 2000, when he presented the ideas to them. He told them if either side could not accept the ideas, they would be withdrawn and would leave with him when he left office. By December 27, he needed to know whether they were prepared to accept his ideas.

Yet here we were on January 2, 2001, having received Barak's affirmative answer on the twenty-seventh, but still not having heard anything but evasions from Arafat. Notwithstanding Arafat's efforts to engage us on "clarifying" the ideas, we had held firm and not done so. But we had also not withdrawn the President's proposal. We had not pulled back from this process, fearing, as we had so often during the Clinton years, that to do so would trigger a crisis, or an explosion, or a serious deterioration into violence. By not pulling back, we continued to keep alive the hope that a final agreement might yet be possible by January 20.

By this time, however, I had grave doubts that an agreement remained possible.

After all, Arafat was equivocating in circumstances in which there was no more time, at least for Clinton; in which he had the backing for accepting the Clinton proposal from nearly every significant Arab leader, President Mubarak of Egypt, Crown Prince Abdullah of Saudi Arabia, King Abdullah of Jordan, President Ben Ali of Tunisia, and King Mohammad of Morocco; and in which Barak's acceptance of the Clinton ideas would disappear in the near certainty of his looming electoral defeat—a defeat that might only be averted by Palestinian acceptance of the President's ideas and the conclusion of a peace agreement. The stakes were clear and the choices stark, or so they should have been to Yasir Arafat.

This was my message to the President as I entered the Oval Office. If Arafat was posturing to try to get more, he had to be told that he was in danger of losing everything, and, I told the President, he must "hear that from you . . . and he must have no doubts that you have taken it to the limit and this is it." He must hear from you that "you worked your ass off" and presented something that no other U.S. president had ever been willing to propose—namely, a balanced package designed to end the conflict that tilted toward the Palestinians on territory and Jerusalem and tilted toward the Israelis on security and refugees. You had done your best, and there was nothing more you could do. It was now time for the Chairman to decide.

In closing, I reminded the President that Arafat never made a decision before he had to. He always waited until one minute to midnight. Unfortunately, I said, it was now three in the morning, and you need an answer in this meeting: Is it yes or no? Anything else, and Arafat was telling you he could not do a final deal, and he must know that is the conclusion you will draw.

"I got it," the President said.

| MY JOURNEY TO THIS POINT |

Preparing the President of the United States for his moment of truth with Yasir Arafat was not exactly what I had envisioned growing up in Marin County, just across the Golden Gate Bridge from San Francisco. I grew up with a Jewish mother and Catholic stepfather in a nonreligious household. It was only after getting married and having children that I became a more observant Jew and began to attend synagogue regularly.

I came of age politically in the 1960s, energized by the civil rights movement, mobilized by the agony of the Vietnam War, and instilled with a belief in public service by President Kennedy and his brother Robert. My first serious political campaign experience was in 1968 working for Bobby Kennedy in Los Angeles, first registering Hispanic and African-American voters in east and south-central L.A. and then canvassing precincts in L.A.'s predominantly Jewish district of Fairfax.

Later, I was to spend two years working for George McGovern in his campaign for the presidency. After that experience, I wanted to be less involved in politics and more capable of affecting policy. With that in mind, I returned to graduate school at UCLA determined to build an expertise in international relations. I focused most heavily on Soviet studies, arms control, and the Middle East. For three years I was the teaching assistant of Malcolm Kerr, perhaps the leading scholar on politics in the Arab world at that time. Professor Kerr opened doors for me in the Arab world, making possible a series of interviews in Egypt and Jordan in 1975 that gave me greater insight into the psychology and sense of grievance embedded in the Arab Middle East.*

By this time I had been to Israel twice. My interest in Israel had been very much awakened by the Six-Day War in 1967; Israel's survival seemed at stake before the war with Egypt's leader, Gamal Abdel Nasser, boasting of Israel's destruction. But its stunning victory revealed Israel's strength and the gap between Arab rhetoric and reality.

I found Israel to be dynamic, with an intellectual vibrancy and an impulse to debate every imaginable issue. I identified with its people, and my own Jewish identity became more important to me as a result. Intrinsically, I believed Israel had a right to exist and that the Jewish people needed and deserved a homeland, a place of refuge. In Israel, I saw a country that was filled with pride and vulnerability, hope and fear, and a craving for peace combined with a constant preparation for war.

In the Arab world, I saw less uniform hostility to Israel's existence than was portrayed in its media or ours. But I also found a profound belief that a grave injustice had been done to the Palestinian people and that it must be corrected if anything was to change in the area. There was, to be sure, no more than a grudging acceptance of the reality of Israel, and even from those most ready to accept a two-state solution to the conflict—Israel and Palestine coexisting side by side—there was no real readiness to accept the legitimacy of Israel's existence. Acknowledging Israel as a fact was one thing; having to accept its legitimacy was quite another.

For me, this meant that it might be possible to end the Arab-Israeli conflict. But it also meant that any effort at peacemaking must be premised on a strong U.S.-Israeli relationship. Israel, given its small size and vulnerability, must feel secure if it was to make concessions for peace. Could or would Israel feel safe enough to contemplate giv-

---

*Professor Kerr, an extraordinary human being and teacher, left UCLA to become the president of the American University in Beirut; in January 1984, while I was working in the Pentagon, Islamic fundamentalists assassinated him—assassinated a man they saw as a symbol of America, and a man I knew to embody so much that was good about our country.

ing up territory—and inherently more defensible borders—if it questioned the U.S. commitment to its security? I doubted it. Similarly, would the Arab world even believe it had to accommodate itself to Israel's existence if it had reason to question the staying power of the U.S. commitment to Israel? I also doubted that. When Anwar Sadat of Egypt made peace with Israel, he explained that he could have fought Israel, but he could not fight the United States. Peacemaking required that the Arabs understand that no wedge would be driven between the United States and Israel, and that Israel was not going to disappear.

This did not mean that we could never question or criticize Israeli policies. We could, and from the time I was a graduate student at UCLA I believed that Israel's policy of building settlements in the West Bank and Gaza was wrong and misguided. Criticism was legitimate, but creating a breach in the relationship was not.

Along with believing that peace must ultimately be between the two parties and therefore must be negotiated directly by them, my approach to the peace process was shaped by the conviction that Israel must feel secure if it was to take risks for peace.

Since I was to emerge as the architect of our policy toward the Arab-Israeli conflict in the first Bush administration and the lead negotiator in the Arab-Israeli peace process throughout the Clinton presidency, my assumptions were important. While some, especially in the Arab world, raised not so subtle questions about my being Jewish and its effect on my fairness as a negotiator, my faith was never an issue with Presidents Bush or Clinton. Nor was it an issue with Secretaries Baker, Christopher, and Albright—the three Secretaries of State with whom I worked most closely.

Did being Jewish create a problem for me with Palestinian or Arab negotiators and leaders?

At Camp David, Hassan Asfour, one of the Palestinian negotiators, asked me if I knew "why we criticize you." I nodded, saying I did understand. But that did not satisfy Hassan. He wanted to tell me. He wanted me not to assume I knew the answer but to hear it from him. In fact, he told me what I knew: it was easier and safer to criticize me than either the President or the Secretary of State. Criticize them, and maybe America walks away. Criticize me, and it goes with the territory. Negotiators can be fair game for criticism; leaders cannot be.

But I also knew this was not the whole story. My being Jewish gave Palestinians, and Arabs more generally, a ready-made handle to explain *publicly* why America was not following its "interests" in the Middle East. One myth that permeated the Arab media—no doubt because Arab regimes mandated this—was that absent the power of the Jewish lobby or Jewish officials, America would not support Israel. In Arab eyes there had to be a reason for such support, especially when U.S. dependency on Arab oil should dictate a different posture. It was difficult for many in the Arab world ever to accept that there could be anything wrong with their cause or the way they presented it. Nor could they acknowledge the importance of Israel being a democracy and having shared values with the United States lest they have to explain their own lack of democracy. Thus bias must explain the American posture—and of course I was the visible manifestation of it.

Being Jewish, however, was also an issue with some in Israel and some in the Jewish community in the United States. There were those who felt Israel to be in such danger—and the Arabs to be so untrustworthy—that Israel should never be subject to criticism or pressure. During the Bush administration of 1989–92—especially given President Bush's very clear pressure on the Shamir government—I received hate mail labeling me a self-hating Jew.

Much like with the public Arab criticism of me, there was a presumption: my Jewishness meant by definition that I must adopt certain positions and attitudes. With the Arab world, I must be unfairly biased. With what was primarily the right wing of the Jewish community, I should be unquestioning in my support of Israel.

In order to take some of the abuse I did, I had to believe strongly in what I was doing. Even with periodic bouts of self-doubt, I did. I was firmly convinced that what I was doing was just. Right, from the standpoint of America's interests—because peace and stabilization in a region laden with weapons and petrochemicals was important to us. Right, from the standpoint of Israel's interests—because Israelis would never know true security without peace. Right, from the standpoint of the Arabs, and especially the Palestinians—because reform in the Arab world and freedom and hope for the Palestinians would only come with the advent of peace.

In the Jewish tradition, there are few higher callings than to be a seeker of peace—a Rodef Shalom. My supporters in the Jewish community often described me as a Rodef Shalom, and few descriptions meant more to me.

In truth, being a "seeker of peace" gave me credibility with the Palestinians, the Syrians, and Jordanians—and all those I worked with to negotiate agreements on the Arab side. They got to know me in the good times and bad, in the periods of breakdown and breakthrough, and in the endless moments of arcane discussion on the minutiae of the negotiations.

I was predictable, always trying to come up with the pathway around a problem; determined to find the way out of stalemate; pressing to have each meeting advance where we were. They might not like my ideas, but they always knew I would come up with ideas. They might not like what they would hear from me, but they always knew it was what I believed and not a manipulation. They might feel I was too sympathetic to the Israeli needs, and insufficiently attuned to theirs, but they always knew I would listen to their concerns. Whether they agreed with me or whether they thought I was too demanding of them, they appreciated my commitment to peace. They saw my passion and determination. That is what mattered, not my being Jewish.

It was also that passion and determination that sustained me through the highs and lows of the effort. The breakthroughs—breaking the taboos on direct negotiations at Madrid, the "handshake" at the White House ending an era of mutual rejection between Israelis and Palestinians, the Israeli-Jordanian peace treaty, the "nonpaper" agreement between Israelis and Syrians on the principles of security arrangements, the Hebron agreement after two twenty-three day shuttles, the Wye River agreement between a Likud-led government and the Palestinian Authority at the end of eight days of summitry—were exhilarating. The breakthroughs were never easy, always exhausting, and nearly always the result of going to the brink of failure before succeeding.

But there were many more deflating setbacks. The acts of terror that always seemed to occur whenever we were making progress; they were not only sickening but tended to destroy whatever tentative steps forward we were taking. The assassination of the architect of the process in Israel—a body blow to those who saw Yitzhak Rabin as the one clearly credible champion of peace and security in Israel. The electoral defeat of those in Israel ready to make far-reaching concessions for peace, combined with the Palestinian resort to violence that raised a fundamental question about the premise of the peace process and Yasir Arafat's commitment to ending the conflict.

Having labored through the highs and lows of this process in a leading position for twelve years of the Bush and Clinton terms, having seen the eruption of a Palestinian uprising (the Intifada) two months after the disappointing conclusion of an extraordinary fifteen-day summit at Camp David, and yet now having seen an Israeli government accept unprecedented concessions to end the conflict, I knew that Arafat's visit to the White House on January 2, 2001, was our last chance. President Clinton's term was about to end. If there was no deal now, I knew the pendulum would swing away from dealing with solutions to the Arab-Israeli conflict and back to crisis management. Without a deal, the Israelis would see the violence and the rejection of the Clinton ideas as proof that they had no Palestinian partner. A new government would be elected in Israel, with a mandate not to make Barak-style concessions but to prove to the Palestinians and Arafat the futility of violence and terror.

In November, I had announced my decision to leave at the end of the Clinton term. I believed the new Bush administration would disengage from the process, presuming that it was a mistake to invest in peacemaking in the Middle East the way Clinton had. I understood that only limited agreements would now be possible, and that it would take the kind of effort I had made during the Netanyahu years even to produce very limited understandings. Personally, I was not prepared to revert to the fireman role that had me staying in the Middle East merely to keep everything together. I had be-

come invested in a solution, and was not emotionally prepared to revert to simply trying to manage Israeli-Palestinian talks that existed largely for their own sake. Someone
else could and should assume that responsibility if we were now unable to do the deal
on permanent status.

We would now find out if Arafat was up to ending the conflict. He had played out
the string and he would risk losing everything he had gained if he now said no. Even at
Camp David, given the six months remaining in the administration and an Israeli government that he perceived was still stable, he had not believed he was out of time. Now, by
any measure, there was no more time. If his purpose was to reach agreement, this was it.

| ARAFAT'S MOMENT OF TRUTH |

President Clinton knew the stakes. He had been explaining them to every Arab
leader he spoke to following his presentation of the ideas on December 23. Following
a plea from the Tunisians to see Arafat—a plea that the Foreign Minister Habib bin
Yahya had communicated to me, stating that Arafat can only say "yes in the presence
of President Clinton"—the President agreed to have Arafat come to the White House
provided Arafat would come immediately. Arafat had agreed less than twenty hours
earlier. Now, as we awaited his entry into the Oval Office, I knew the question was not
whether President Clinton "got it," as he had said to me, but whether Arafat got it.

As Arafat entered the Oval Office, I whispered to Secretary Albright that we would
now see whether Arafat was maneuvering to respond favorably or whether he was maneuvering for the sake of avoiding a decision. She nodded, basically sharing my doubts.

We had decided that the meeting should be very small to avoid any posturing on
Arafat's part and ensure that we got down to business. Following the "photo op" with
the press, the President asked the Chairman to limit the meeting to the leaders and a
note-taker on each side. In the event that the Chairman wanted Saeb Erekat—the lead
Palestinian negotiator—to join them, I would sit in as well. As it turned out, the Chairman wanted Nabil Abu Rudeina, his chief of staff, to be his note-taker and Saeb to be
there for support on the details. As a result, Rob Malley, who worked on the National
Security Council staff, stayed as the note-taker and I joined as well.

Arafat's approach to the meeting was initially to play to the President's vanity. He
had often done that, but his comments had become increasingly generous and emotional. In a phone conversation with the President on December 19, perhaps with an
eye to the ideas the President was shortly to present, Arafat had spoken of the "blind
trust in you" that we have and noted that "your contributions to my people and to the
process will never be forgotten." He now echoed those words, and then said that the
President's ideas represented a "tremendous advance for the peace process."

At this moment, I was beginning to think that Habib bin Yahya might be right. Maybe Arafat needed to be in the President's presence in order to say "yes." My hopes were raised further when Arafat told the President that he "accepted [your] ideas." Then my fears materialized. He was accepting the ideas, but he had reservations. And the reservations, unfortunately, revealed his real answer.

On Jerusalem, he said when it came to the religious holy sites the Israelis could not have sovereignty over the Western Wall. Why, he asked, was the Western Wall being raised now? He knew that the Wailing Wall mattered to the Jews, nothing else. No one had ever spoken of the Western Wall before; the British, during the mandate period, had only spoken of the significance of the Wailing Wall. He could not accept the Western Wall, particularly because it ran into the Muslim Quarter. Similarly, he had basic problems with the security provisions, declaring that the Israelis could not operate in Palestinian airspace. The Arab League, he claimed, would never accept this. And on refugees, he simply rejected our formula, stating that there was a need to come up with a different, although unspecified formula.

We had developed a finely tuned package designed to conclude negotiations, not begin them. With great effort we sought to respond to the essentials of each side on each issue. Arafat was taking those parts of the package that gave the Israelis something and he was seeking to emasculate them. To balance giving the Palestinians sovereignty over the Haram al-Sharif, we had a formula designed to address Israeli needs in the area below the Haram, and it spoke of the Western Wall and the "Holy of Holies" or the holy space of which it was a part. Arafat's position would undo that, not to mention that his comments on the wall were factually and historically wrong. On security, his position on airspace, given the small space and the size of the Israeli air force, was simply impractical and signaled he would not countenance any of the essential parts of the security provisions. On refugees, we had presented a multipart formula that was an integral part of the whole package and Arafat was simply dismissing it, telling us, in effect, "to give me more." In other words, he was prepared to take the good part of the package for him, and redo the parts that required him to give.

The President's initial response was not strong. Rather than rebutting Arafat's reservations or making clear that they constituted a rejection, not an acceptance, of his ideas, the President turned to me and asked, "Why did we say the Western Wall" instead of the Wailing Wall? In doing so, he immediately signaled the ideas were more mine than his, and that we might well be open to reconsidering them.

I responded to the President's question, saying that we had put together a package designed to meet each side's needs. We had addressed what the Palestinians told us they needed on the Haram. But Israel also had needs and interests and we had tried to accommodate those in a way that preserved what the Palestinians needed. Sovereignty over the Western Wall did not undercut Palestinian sovereignty over the Haram, but did meet a minimal Israeli requirement.

I then turned to Chairman Arafat and, using my hands, illustrated the purpose of the President's proposals and the consequences of Arafat's response. Holding my hands an inch apart, I said, "Mr. Chairman, the President's ideas shrink the gap between you and the Israelis to this small space. You want to move the side that is hard for you back." And at this point, I pulled my right hand away from my left, opening up a space of about five inches. I continued, saying, "If we do that, we will lose the Israeli yes, and they will insist on backing away from the things in our package that are hard for them." I then proceeded to move my left hand away, leaving a space of almost a foot between my two hands. "As you can see, if we do that we will be right back to where we started, with a gap that is too wide to bridge."

He had watched and listened carefully to what I had said. He then slowly but forcefully stated that "you are the one—you are the one—who has always told me we must talk directly to the Israelis to resolve our differences. We have reservations, they have reservations, let us talk about our reservations."

I told him that was perfectly reasonable, and we would never block such a discussion, but they did not need the President's ideas to do that. You are, I noted, trying to redefine the President's ideas; Barak is not.

President Clinton at this point looked at Arafat and said, "Dennis is right. We cannot open up the package without undoing it."

But knowing Arafat as I did, I was sure he had not gotten the message. He had heard nothing that required him to give an unmistakable answer now or know that we would desist with our efforts. At this point, I asked the President if I could have a private word with him.

We walked across the Oval Office to an area near his desk and the double-doors that opened onto the portico leading to the Rose Garden, and I said: "Arafat is not getting the message. I believe you need to sit with him alone, or at most with only a note-taker, and tell him you have to have an unequivocal answer. Right now he does not think he has to give one. You should make sure Arafat does not leave here with a misunderstanding about you or your willingness to do anything more for him absent a clear and positive answer. This is better done without Saeb and me in here."

The President asked if I really thought Arafat was not getting it, to which I replied, "He ain't getting it." He nodded and went back to Arafat, telling him he wanted to have a more private and personal discussion, and Saeb and I left. In the private meeting, the President became far more blunt with Arafat. As I found out later, President Clinton did so by telling Arafat that by not responding to the "ideas," he was killing Barak and the peace camp in Israel. Having said "yes," Barak was now "hanging out there" and looking like a fool. In such a circumstance, the President told Arafat there was nothing more that we could do without a clear answer from him.

Arafat listened but did not budge. He again said he had reservations, the Israelis did as well, and they should discuss them. While the President made clear that the Israeli reservations were within the parameters and Arafat's were outside, Arafat said the discussions should continue with our help. And that is the way the meeting ended, with the two agreeing to talk on the phone before Arafat left town in the morning.

If there had been any hope of an agreement, it was gone now. It mattered little that President Clinton focused on what Arafat was doing to Barak and not to him. Arafat was not going to say yes under any circumstances. Seeing the President had made no difference. As he had so often in his career, Arafat was seeking to have it both ways, creating the illusion of being positive by accepting the ideas, but practically rejecting them with his reservations. We were seeing a variant of what Arab leaders had always referred to as "the Arafat answer": *La-Na'am* (no and yes in Arabic).

This was not a case of tactics or bargaining. President Clinton had put unprecedented ideas on the table. Arafat had the best deal he could ever get. He could not get more and he had hit the proverbial wall. He could not wring out one more concession or gain one more tactical advantage. We had left the realm of tactics and we now had to face a strategic reality: Arafat could not do a deal that ended the conflict. Partial deals were possible because they did not require him to adopt any irrevocable positions. But a comprehensive deal was not possible with Arafat. Too much redefinition was required. He was not up to it. He could live with a process, but not with a conclusion.

As if to prove this point, the next morning in his call with the President he was content with our declaring that he had accepted our ideas with reservations and that the two sides would continue their discussions. The President, given his eye on the upcoming Israeli elections and his understanding that should he now announce the failure of our efforts, he would be putting the nail in Barak's electoral coffin, agreed to put a positive face on Arafat's answer. But we all knew the reality now.

The game was over. For the foreseeable future, it would be necessary to switch gears; we would be out of the peacemaking business and back to a preoccupation with crisis prevention and the defusing of conflict. Ariel Sharon would be the new Israeli Prime Minister, the peace camp in Israel would be discredited for some time, and it would take years to get back to the point where the existential issues of this conflict could be addressed, much less resolved.

Arafat should have known all this; he was certainly getting this message from many European and Arab leaders in the days prior to his meeting with the President. Yet he was unable to accept an independent Palestinian state that was territorially viable and had Arab East Jerusalem as its capital.

How did we get to this point? Shouldn't we have known by then that Arafat could not do a permanent deal? Were we really as close to resolving the Israeli-Palestinian and the Arab-Israeli conflict as we thought?

Only by knowing the full story of what had transpired over the preceding decade of peace-seeking is it possible to answer these and other questions about the Arab-Israeli peacemaking process. Only by telling this story can we debunk the myths that prevent all sides from seeing reality and adjusting to it. Indeed, only by telling the story can we hope to learn the lessons from the past and make it possible to shape a different future.

Ultimately, that is why I have chosen to tell this story. I want those in (and outside) the Middle East to understand what have been the critical "missing pieces" that have perpetuated the conflict with all its victims and suffering. The lack of public conditioning for peace, the reluctance to acknowledge the legitimacy of the other side's grievance and needs, the inability to confront comfortable myths, the difficulty of transforming behavior and acknowledging mistakes, the inherent challenge of getting both sides ready to move at the same time, the unwillingness to make choices, and the absence of leadership, especially among Palestinians, are all factors that have made peace difficult to achieve.

Nevertheless, I remain an optimist. The building blocks for peace were put in place in the last decade. The terms for producing peace agreements are no longer a mystery. They emerge in the following pages. Unfortunately, the psychological inhibitions that still make peace only a distant hope also emerge in the following pages. If there is one overriding lesson from the story of the peace process, it is that truth-telling is a necessity, not a luxury. All parties must face the facts of the past honestly and learn from them. All parties must face up to reality, not continue to deny what they must concede in order for peace to be possible. When they are finally ready to do so, we may no longer have to lament the pain and sorrow of the missing peace.

Why Israelis, Arabs, and Palestinians
See the World the Way They Do

THERE IS LITTLE PROSPECT of mediating any conflict if one does not understand the historical narratives of each side. I say this not because it is important to perpetuate the historical debate or because one side can convince the other that it is wrong, but rather because both sides in any conflict must see that a third party understands why it feels the way it does, why it values what it values, why its symbols say so much about its identity.

Peacemaking in the last decade emerged from a historical context of deep-seated grievances and desire for justice on both sides. Arabs and Israelis each have a narrative that tells their story and interprets their reality, and these narratives were lurking in every discussion. To understand these narratives, one needs to know what shaped them; how they evolved; and how particular historical developments affected attitudes and beliefs. Only then can one appreciate what we had to contend with in trying to promote peacemaking.

| THE ISRAEL NARRATIVE |

For the Israelis, their national movement, Zionism, is a natural response to the tragedies of Jewish history. Ever since the destruction of the Second Temple in Jerusalem in 70 A.D., Jews had been dispersed and without a homeland. Dispersal had made Jews weak and vulnerable, and led to repeated expulsions and devastations. Weakness had become a way of life. Zionism meant a cultural, psychological, and political renaissance. It meant creating a homeland for Jews that could be a safe haven. It meant creating a new "man" who was strong, close to the earth, able to defend himself or herself. A history of meekness and disaster would give way to strength and never again turning the other cheek.

The philosophy of Zionism began emerging in the 1860s, but it took the pogroms in Russia, the Dreyfus trial in Paris, and the emergence of leading figures like Theodor Herzl, Chaim Weizmann, Ahad Ha'am, and Nahum Sokolow to transform it into a political movement with deep national yearnings. The Dreyfus trial convinced Herzl, a Hungarian Jew living and working in France as a journalist, that even in an enlightened place like France there was no refuge from anti-Semitism. It was not only that Captain Alfred Dreyfus, a French officer who was Jewish, had been arrested on trumped-up charges of spying for Germany. It was hearing a French crowd outside the trial chant "Death to the Jews" that left Herzl certain that there was no hope for assimilation of Jews in their host countries: the only answer was Jewish sovereignty. For Herzl, Jews could never be secure without a state of their own.

Herzl authored a book, *The Jewish State*, in 1896 and founded the World Zionist Organization the following year, even while remaining largely unaware of the activities of Russians beginning to immigrate to Palestine—activities that included reintroducing Hebrew as the national language. Herzl lobbied world leaders to gain support for a Jewish state. He pressed the leaders of the Ottoman Empire, including the Sultan, to lift the restrictions they had imposed on Jewish immigration and land purchases in Palestine.

When Herzl died in 1904 at the age of forty-four, he left behind a legacy that put the Zionist agenda on the world stage. And others like Chaim Weizmann were continuing to have a major impact on the world outside of Palestine. From the first wave of immigration, referred to as the first *aliyah* (ascent) to Palestine in the 1880s, there was a split between those actually settling the undeveloped land and those representing the Zionist movement to the outside world. For those in Palestine the hardships were great, the life extremely difficult and austere, and the dangers quite real. Those trying to reclaim a Jewish land had little patience with political niceties; those trying to win favor internationally felt compelled to be patient and not overplay their hand.

The London leaders of the Zionist movement, led principally by Weizmann, made tremendous efforts to gain British endorsement of the Jewish right to Palestine. They succeeded ultimately in November 1917, when the British government issued the Balfour Declaration. While not explicitly supporting Jewish statehood, the Balfour Declaration called for the establishment of a Jewish national home in Palestine. A historic threshold had been crossed. The effect on world Jewry was electric, with over 200,000 enthusiastic Jews turning out in Odessa to welcome a visiting Zionist delegation shortly after the issuance of the declaration.

The Balfour Declaration married the symbolic with the practical. By making the Zionist dream seem like something other than a distant hope, it inspired activism. It spurred immigration, especially after the armistice ending World War I. It became a more formal promise when recognized internationally at the Paris Peace Conference and made a part of the British Mandate for Palestine after the war.

The leaders of the Jewish community in Palestine, the Yishuv (literally, "settlement"), understood and appreciated the significance of the Balfour Declaration, but as David Ben-Gurion made clear at the time, it was Jewish pioneers in Palestine, not the British, who would determine the Zionist future: "Britain has made a magnificent gesture; she has recognized our existence as a nation and has acknowledged our right to the country. But only the Hebrew people can transform this right into a tangible fact; only they, with body and soul, with their strength and capital, must build their National Home and bring about their national redemption."

Those in Palestine focused on creating facts on the ground. Those on the outside focused more on symbols of acceptance and legitimacy. Their efforts were complementary, but presaged divisions in the movement. Division and debate were constant hallmarks of the Zionist movement—both within the growing Jewish community in Palestine and between the leaders of the Yishuv and the leaders of the Zionist movement on the outside.

Every conceivable question was subject to discussion in a movement that was secularist, socialist, and egalitarian to its core. Should Arab labor be used? Could Jews develop the land and create a new ethos if they depended on Arab workers? Was it right to depend on them? Shouldn't the Jews be completely self-reliant, both to become completely independent and to avoid any exploitation of others? Should there be cooperation with the Arabs or separation from them? Should areas bought from absentee or rich Arab landowners, so essential for gaining control of the land, be pursued without regard to Arab tenant farmers who were being displaced? Should immigration be limited to numbers the Arabs could tolerate or should there be an all-out effort to bring as many Jews to Palestine as quickly as possible? Should the Jews limit themselves only to self-defense or be prepared to preempt possible attacks by hitting first? Was it possible to reach agreement with the Arabs of Palestine, or was conflict inevitable?

While the predisposition was, in Weizmann's words, to make Palestine as Jewish as France was French and Britain was British, the answers to these questions were not a given until violent Arab resistance to Jewish immigration and Jewish presence began to manifest itself with the deadly riots of 1920 and 1921. The 1921 riots in particular had a devastating effect, beginning as they did with brutal attacks on new Jewish immigrants in Jaffa and then spreading throughout the country over the next several days. Scores were killed, and the British were largely powerless to prevent the carnage. For the Yishuv, there were a number of lessons drawn: separation made more sense than co-operation; segregation, not commingling with the Arabs, became a new focus leading to an exodus from Jaffa and the development of Tel Aviv; acquiring large swaths of contiguous territory took on a new urgency; and self-reliance, especially with regard to defense, became an article of faith.

As would happen so often in this conflict, violence and the resulting sense of vulnerability would harden attitudes and limit choices. It led to a mind-set among the Jews of Palestine that security was not only a necessity but a way of life. The threats did not alter the resolve to build the Jewish presence; if anything, they fueled the desire to achieve a Jewish majority in Palestine—a majority that could make them more secure and ensure a state.

Arab resistance to Jewish immigration increased, but even leaders in the Arab national movement often surreptitiously sold land to the Jewish National Fund for Jewish settlement, feeding the Jewish perception that Arab hostility was being manipulated for the purposes of gaining advantage over rivals for power. But regardless of whether the hostility was being manipulated, it became far worse and the violence far more systemic in the 1930s. Beginning with the riots of 1929, which triggered a massacre of the Jews in Hebron and led to the evacuation of a Jewish community that had lived continuously in Hebron for eight hundred years, the violence reached a new level during the Arab revolt of 1936–39.

Struggle within Palestine was intensifying at the very time that the need for a haven for Jews was becoming more acute. Hitler's rise to power threatened first Germany's Jews and then all the Jews of Europe. The reluctance of the world to take in Jewish refugees combined with the British restriction on Jewish immigration to Palestine (the response to the Arab revolt) to make escape impossible for the vast majority of European Jewry.

The Holocaust, an unimaginable evil for the rest of the world, was an unspeakable reminder for the Jews of Palestine that the worst can happen; that weakness begets tragedy; that others can never be relied upon; and that they must have a state of their own—for themselves and the survivors. While pragmatism, facts on the ground, and creating realities on which to build reflected core beliefs that guided the mainstream leadership of the Yishuv, they took on new urgency after the Holocaust. Even prior to it—as the threat to European Jewry became more apparent and the threat from the Arabs escalated—a hardheaded approach to getting what one could took on new meaning. When the Peel Commission in 1937 responded to the Arab revolt with the recommendation of partition of Palestine into a Jewish state and an Arab state, David Ben-Gurion, the elected leader of the Yishuv, accepted the recommendation—even though the boundaries of the Jewish state would have made it small and seemingly untenable. As he said at the time, "A partial Jewish state is not the end but the beginning, a powerful impetus in our historic effort to redeem the land in its entirety."

Others like Ze'ev Jabotinsky, the leader of the opposition Revisionists, were far more dogmatic; they fought, especially after World War II, against surrendering any part of biblical Palestine, fearing the practical and ideological consequences of giving up any claims. However they were in the minority. Again, Ben-Gurion's pragmatic attitude governed the Yishuv's response to the UN partition plan that was ultimately adopted on November 29, 1947.

Once again the Jewish leadership accepted the partitioning of Palestine into two states: one Arab, one Jewish. Only now, with the British having turned the Palestine problem over to the UN to resolve, and having announced their own withdrawal in six months' time once the partition plan was adopted, the fighting in Palestine became far worse. Much as with the response to the Peel Commission recommendations, the Arabs again rejected the partition plan and the very concept of a Jewish state.

For the Jews of Palestine, enduring Arab opposition and hostility had become a given. In response, a distinct mind-set took root: create an unmistakable reality that would leave the Arabs no choice but to accept and to adjust to that which they opposed. Here again, there was the mainstream or Labor establishment sentiment and the minority or Revisionist school of thought. While both believed that Arab rejection could only be combated by unmistakable strength and by creating immutable realities, the mainstream believed that the Arabs would accommodate themselves to the new state of Israel when it became clear to them that it could not be defeated and would never disappear. Peace was therefore possible, but not until the Arabs adjusted to Israel as a fact that could not be undone. The Revisionists were basically more pessimistic. Some felt the Arabs would never accept a Jewish state in their midst, and that, in the words of Jabotinsky, an "iron wall" would need to be erected to separate the Jews from their neighbors. Living under siege was an unfortunate reality, but one that could be endured.*

Unquestioned strength, creating facts, and self-reliance became part of the Israeli sociology. The Zionist view of the disasters of Jewish history put a premium on self-reliance. Israel's early experiences as a state cemented that viewpoint. While the fighting with the Arabs of Palestine had intensified after the partition plan was approved,

---

*Later some from the Revisionist school, like Menachem Begin and Yitzhak Shamir, came to believe that peace was possible but that it would take far longer than the Labor party leaders believed and much less could be given up to the Arabs; otherwise the Arabs would see signs of Israeli weakness and lose their interest in making peace.

invasion from all of its Arab neighbors followed immediately upon the declaration of the state of Israel on May 15, 1948.

The 1948 war, what the Israelis call the War of Independence, took an extraordinarily high toll on the new State of Israel. The Jewish population in Palestine at the time was 650,000. Israel lost nearly 1 percent of its population, or more than 6,300 dead, during the 1948 war. No benefactors or allies were on the outside to come to the new state's assistance. The United States, though recognizing the new state fourteen minutes after its declaration, provided no assistance during the conflict. (It allowed private assistance to flow to Israel, but would not provide direct military assistance for more than twenty years after Israel's founding.)

Israel was largely on its own. The Soviets permitted Czechoslovakia to supply arms to the Yishuv in April of 1948, but otherwise the new state had no consistent or reliable source of arms supply through the course of the war. It was not only the absence of help from the outside that cemented the ethos of self-reliance. It was the relatively successful, if costly, experience in the war. As a result of the war, Israel, while unable to hold all of Jerusalem, was able to create borders that exceeded what the partition plan had called for. Once again, establishing facts on the ground created a new reality for the new state—with the Negev Desert, more extensive parts of the Galilee, and the central areas around Ramle and Lod being incorporated into Israel.

Armistice agreements ended the war, but brought Israel no recognition. The agreements set up Mixed Armistice Commissions bringing Israelis into regular contact with representatives of their neighbors for several years. With Transjordan* and with Syria, diplomatic openings that appeared after the 1948 war closed quickly with the assassination of King Abdullah of Transjordan in 1951 and with a series of coups in Syria in 1949 and the early 1950s that removed Israel's potential partners. Peace was not in the offing. While France became a covert supplier of arms, the Israelis understood that they could rely on no one else to come to their defense in a region in which from the mid-1950s onward they faced the unrelenting hostility of their neighbors.

Indeed, Ben-Gurion's efforts to have the United States include Israel in its efforts to organize the Middle Eastern states into an anti-Soviet alliance in the 1950s were rebuffed. The Eisenhower administration was eager to forge an alliance in the Middle East that would, in effect, join NATO in Europe and SEATO in Asia to close the ring of containment around the Soviet Union. Knowing that Arab states would not be part of any alliance that included Israel, the Eisenhower administration rejected Israel's request to be included either in the Baghdad Pact or in NATO. Ben-Gurion hoped to

---

*Transjordan officially became the Hashemite Kingdom of Jordan in 1949, but had obtained its independence from the U.K. in 1946.

find some enduring base of support from the outside. But Israel was left largely on its own while President Eisenhower sought to organize the world into an anti-Soviet bloc.

A bitter experience with the events leading to the Six-Day War in June 1967 solidified the deeply ingrained Israeli conviction that it could never count on anyone but itself for its security and defense. Israel, under pressure from President Eisenhower, had withdrawn from the Sinai Desert in March of 1957; the Israelis had seized the Sinai Peninsula as a result of the Suez war in October–November of 1956. In collusion with the British and French—who sought to undermine Egypt's President Gamal Abdel Nasser—the Israelis invaded the Sinai. The plan called for the British and French to interpose themselves between the combatants in order to safeguard the Suez Canal. But things went awry when the Israelis advanced too quickly and Nasser retreated before the British and French could get to the canal. Though having lost their ostensible reason for seizing the canal, they went ahead and did so anyway. Seeing this as a gross violation of international law, President Eisenhower opposed the British and French, and forced them to withdraw from the Suez Canal.

The Eisenhower administration also insisted that Israel withdraw from the Sinai, but acknowledged that the Egyptian blockade of Israel's port on the Red Sea, Eilat, was wrong, and committed the United States to preventing any reimposition of that blockade. In addition, to preserve a buffer between Egypt and Israel in the Sinai the United Nations General Assembly mandated the deployment of the United Nations Emergency Force (UNEF) to the Sinai in the aftermath of the Israeli withdrawal. Thus, Israel withdrew, believing it had firm commitments that addressed its security concerns.

But in May 1967 these commitments proved to be hollow. Nasser, after being taunted by the Syrians and Jordanians for not doing enough to protect Syria in the face of escalating tensions and military engagements with Israel, demanded that UN Secretary-General U Thant pull the UNEF out of the Sinai. U Thant complied. Nasser moved Egyptian forces back into the Sinai. While probably not originally intending to do so, he acted to reimpose the blockade on the Israeli port of Eilat when he declared on May 22 that the Straits of Tiran were mined. In addition, he moved six Egyptian divisions to the Israeli border, threatening to inflict a final defeat on Israel once and for all.

Israel, with no strategic depth and facing six divisions on its borders, mobilized its forces. It also asked the United States to fulfill the Eisenhower commitments of 1957. Being bogged down in Vietnam, the Johnson administration offered only to try to put together an international flotilla to open the Straits of Tiran to Israeli shipping from Eilat. The United States did not address the Egyptian threat in the Sinai, and in any case showed little capability or will to break the blockade of Eilat. After nearly two weeks of uncertainty—with bloodcurdling threats about the destruction of Israel coming from Egypt and ineffectual U.S. efforts still under way—Israel launched a pre-emptive attack against the Egyptian air force, destroying it in the first three hours of the war. In six days Israel went on to defeat Egypt, Jordan, and Syria, seizing consider-able territory from all three: the Sinai Desert and the Gaza Strip from Egypt; the West Bank from Jordan; and the Golan Heights from Syria.*

The war had several legacies for Israel and the area. First, the Israeli belief that they could never count on anyone else was not only confirmed but also reinforced with the conviction that they need not do so. The precipitous UN withdrawal from the Sinai made them doubt the value of any UN presence, particularly if it was designed to ad-dress Israeli security needs. Similarly, the U.S. failure to live up to the Eisenhower com-mitments confirmed that Israel must always be responsible for its own defense and be the sole arbiters of what was needed for its security.

Second, the Israelis controlled vast amounts of Arab territory now, and in the West Bank and Gaza, that meant having responsibility for more than one million Palestin-ian Arabs. In the initial euphoria after the war, there was a great expectation that peace would now be possible. No victory could be more decisive. Israel's staying power could no longer be in question. The fact of Israel now had to be clear to the Arabs. Surely, now they would adjust to the reality, and accept Israel. Moshe Dayan put this expecta-tion into words when he said, "We are waiting for a telephone call from the Arabs."

But that call never came. This expectation, this assumption, was not fulfilled, even though the Israelis were also prepared to act on it. The national unity government adopted a secret resolution in the cabinet on June 19, 1967; it would have authorized Israel to withdraw to the international borders with Egypt and Syria in exchange for peace treaties with each of its neighbors. While discussion on what to do with Jordan and the issue of refugees was deferred, Jerusalem was simply excluded from this formula for peace.[†]

---

*The best single book on the 1967 War is Michael Oren's *Six Days of War*, Oxford: Oxford Uni-versity Press, 2002.

[†]Government Secretariat
Decision No. 563, the government from 19/06/1967

Deciding:
To authorize the suggestions that were summarized by the Minister's Committee that was ap-pointed by Decision No. 561 as follows:

I. Israel's position with regards to the territories held by the IDF

   a. Egypt:
      Israel suggests the signing of a peace agreement with Egypt on the basis of the inter-national boundary and the security interests of Israel. In accordance with the interna-tional boundary, the Gaza strip is within the territory of the State of Israel.

In the 1948 war, the Arab Legion of Transjordan had won the battle for East Jerusalem, dividing the city east and west. The Old City, or the walled part of Jerusalem, was thus controlled by the Jordanians, and from 1948 to 1967 Israelis were prevented

---

This peace agreement will require:
1. A promise of freedom of navigation in the Straits of Tiran and in the Gulf of Shlomo.
2. A promise of freedom of navigation in the Suez Canal.
3. A promise of freedom of overflight over the Straits of Tiran and the Gulf of Shlomo.
4. Demilitarization of the Sinai Peninsula.

Until the signing of a peace agreement with Egypt Israel will continue to hold onto the territories that it is currently holding.

b. Syria:
Israel suggests the signing of a peace agreement with Syria on the basis of the international border and the security needs of Israel.
The peace agreement will require:
1. Demilitarization of the Syrian heights currently held by IDF forces.
2. A final promise of non-interference in the flow of water from the Jordan River's sources to Israel.

Until the signing of a peace agreement with Syria, Israel will continue to hold onto the territories it is holding currently.

c. To push off the discussion on the stance that will be taken in relation to Jordan.

d. Refugees:
1. Preparations for peace in the Middle East and the regional coordination that will come with it will open up chances for a regional and international settlement on a solution for the problem of refugees.
2. Push off the discussion of ways to settle the problem of refugees.

II. Israel's stance with regards to the United Nation's Assembly Special Session on the Middle East Crisis:

a. In the speech of the Foreign Minister in this Assembly only the request for the signing of a peace agreement with the neighboring countries will be mentioned and it will be pointed out that it is a fact that there will be no consideration of a return to the situation before the date of 5/6/67.

b. If the Foreign Minister will find it right to do so he is authorized to bring up the subject of the refugees in accordance with the decision summarized in paragraph I (d) above.

c. In secret discussions with United States representatives, the Foreign Minister is authorized to explain in detail Israel's stance with regards to the territories it holds in accordance with decisions I (a and d) listed above.

from being able even to visit the holiest site in the Jewish faith—the Western Wall, the only remnant of the Second Temple. For even the most secular Israelis, the liberation of the Wailing Wall, the visible part of the Western Wall, was a unique moment of overwhelming emotion, poignancy, and faith. Even the nonreligious were connected again to the core of Judaism, to the cornerstone of Jewish identity. To remove any doubt that any Israeli would ever again be denied access to the Western Wall, the Jewish cemetery on the Mount of Olives, or the other holy or historic sites in Jerusalem, Israel annexed East Jerusalem after the 1967 war.

While Jerusalem was thus excluded from the June 19 cabinet formula, the Sinai Desert and the Golan Heights, both seized during the war, would have been returned to Egypt and Syria in return for peace. Had Egypt and Syria responded, it would have been difficult for Israel to continue, in the words of the cabinet decision, "to push off the discussion on the stance" to be taken "in relation to Jordan." Well before the principle of "land for peace" was adopted in November of 1967 in UN Security Council resolution 242, an Israeli government of national unity, a government that included Menachem Begin of Likud, was, in effect, adopting this very principle.

Unfortunately, as has been the case all too often in the history of this conflict—and we will see it clearly in the story that unfolds in the 1990s—the parties were out of sync. The Israelis, believing that the Arabs would now see the reality, adjust to it, and make peace, were not seeing the territory seized as having a value other than as leverage to be used in exchange for ending the conflict with their neighbors. But the shock of defeat had been too great for the Arabs, and they were not yet ready to accommodate Israel.

When this became apparent, especially with Nasser's declaration of "three no's" at the Arab summit in Khartoum in September 1967—no to recognition of Israel, no to negotiation with Israel, and no to peace with Israel—the land began to be viewed differently by the Israelis. The Labor-led government began to build military settlements in strategically important areas of the West Bank and Gaza. The principal consideration was security.

Security, while always a preoccupation, became a more paramount consideration in the aftermath of the 1973 war. On the holiest day of the year for Jews, Yom Kippur, Israel suffered a colossal strategic surprise. The Six-Day War in 1967 had transformed the Israeli psyche, convincing many in the military and intelligence establishment that the Arabs knew and accepted that they did not have a credible military option. Indicators that should have given warning of preparations for attack were ignored. Confidence that Israel could absorb any attack—bound to be limited—and repulse it quickly became a conventional wisdom.

Convictions of relative invincibility were soon to give way to profound feelings of self-doubt as the coordinated surprise attack by Egypt and Syria—though eventually overcome—cost Israel very dearly in blood and treasure. Unlike either the 1956 or 1967 wars, in which the Israeli casualties measured in the hundreds and were over within days, the 1973 war cost nearly three thousand Israeli lives and took nearly three weeks—a frightful cost for a nation extraordinarily sensitive to casualties with an economy that depended on a small standing army, not a country mobilized for war.

If there was euphoria after 1967, there was depression after 1973. Arab military prowess was far greater than the Israelis had come to believe after the Six Day War, and it seemed bound to grow, especially with seemingly unlimited backing from the Soviet Union. The Saudi withholding of oil shipments during the war—and the resulting gas lines in the United States—raised fears that Arab leverage would lead to U.S. pressure on Israel to satisfy Arab interests. And this concern about the United States came at the very moment when America for the first time had provided military support and weapons resupply during a war that had proved pivotal to Israel's ultimate success.

Israel suffered a crisis of confidence after the 1973 war. Its relationship with the United States became one of greater dependence, despite the instinctive Israeli belief that it could never rely on anyone for its security. It knew it could no longer take comfort in the status quo. It had to reconcile its need to guard against greater threats with the reality that pressures to negotiate territorial concessions were bound to grow with active U.S. diplomacy.

And U.S. diplomacy became active. Initially, the war itself, with its potential for escalation between the United States and the Soviet Union, triggered our diplomacy. The Soviets were the main suppliers of arms to the Egyptians and Syrians, and the Soviets saw the initial successes in the war as vindication of their weaponry—weaponry that had been overwhelmed and criticized during and after the 1967 war. After an initial delay, we had rushed resupplies to Israel, not only to meet critical shortfalls of material but also to counter Soviet resupply of the Egyptians and Syrians.

However, when the Israeli army succeeded in crossing the Suez Canal and in a pincer move was poised to destroy the Egyptian Third Army, it was American, not Soviet, pressure that stopped the Israelis and produced a cease-fire. Secretary of State Henry Kissinger believed that destruction of the Third Army would make a political process between Egypt and Israel impossible, and he and President Nixon insisted that the Israelis accept a cease-fire. (The Israeli government, believing it could not say no to the United States at this point, reluctantly complied.)

Egypt, in Kissinger's eyes, needed to preserve its dignity if it was to begin to negotiate with Israel. Indeed, he believed that Egypt's President, Anwar Sadat, could negotiate, but only if his representatives could go to the negotiating table with their honor intact.

Kissinger proved correct, and negotiations between Israeli and Egyptian military representatives began after the war. These negotiations set in motion a process of disengagement agreements. There were two between Israel and Egypt in 1974 and 1975, which were brokered by Secretary Kissinger and which led to Israel's withdrawal from nearly half of the Sinai Desert. Kissinger also brokered a disengagement agreement between Israel and Syria; these negotiations were indirect, with Kissinger shuttling between the Israelis and Syrians for thirty-two days to work out an agreement in which the Israelis withdrew from their forward positions only twenty-five kilometers from Syria's capital, Damascus, to a line in the Golan Heights adjacent to the city of Quneitra and with limited-deployment zones for the Israeli and Syrian forces on either side of Quneitra.*

While the disengagement agreements were not peace agreements but rather agreements designed to cement and make more stable the cease-fire that ended the 1973 war, they were seen as setting important precedents. After all, they involved Israeli withdrawal from Arab territories in return for obligations on security.

In the final days of the 1973 war, the UN Security Council adopted UNSC Resolution 338. Resolution 338 called for negotiations between the Arabs and Israelis to implement UNSC Resolution 242. Resolution 242 established the principles that should guide an agreement: withdrawal of Israeli armed forces from territories occupied in the recent conflict; termination of all claims of belligerency; respect for and acknowledgment of the sovereignty, territorial integrity, and political independence of every state in the area and their right to live in peace within secure and recognized borders; a just resolution of the refugee problem. The principles were general, certainly not precise. (The Palestinians were treated only indirectly and even then as a refugee, not political, problem.) Resolution 338 was the resolution whose purpose was to establish the negotiations, based on the principles outlined in 242, that would lead to a final peace settlement.

Though general, these resolutions were reduced to the formula of "land for peace." This basic formula had been acceptable to Labor governments. But there was a growing bloc of nationalist and religious groups in Israel that were tied to the Likud Party and rejected the idea of giving the land back.

By the mid-1970s, pressure was building from this bloc—"the bloc of the faithful," the Gush Emunim—to build Israeli settlements in the West Bank, Gaza, and Sinai. Those who had not been happy with the original acceptance of the partition plan in 1947—and those who felt this area was part of God's patrimony—were determined to settle the land to ensure it could never be given back. They saw themselves as

---

*Kissinger sought agreements over all the Arab areas that Israel had occupied during the 1967 war. Though Jordan had stayed on the sidelines during the 1973 war, Kissinger also saw value in at least a limited agreement on the West Bank, proposing a partial Israeli pullback and giving Jordan a renewed foothold in Jericho. This was never seriously pursued.

the latter-day Zionist pioneers, continuing the spirit of those who had fought and set-tled the land, ensuring there could be a state of Israel. They were creating facts on the ground, and when the Likud Party—for the first time in Israel's history—upset the La-bor Party in the elections of 1977, they had a government committed to their ideology.

That ideology was based on the principle of "peace for peace," not land for peace. It was an ideology guided by a belief that the issue was not the land, but rather accep-tance of Israel by the Arab world. Arab reluctance to accept Israel in their midst ex-plained their demand for the land. If the Arabs truly accommodated themselves to Israel's reality, they would accept Israel's need for defensible borders—or so the think-ing went.

Others in Israel, principally in the center-left groups led by the Labor Party, saw a different reality. They saw an Arab world that had a need to make peace with their honor intact. With the disengagement agreements, they began to see the possibility of peace.

In November 1977, the President of Egypt, Anwar Sadat, the leader of the largest Arab country, decided in a bold, unprecedented stroke to travel to Israel. His trip was a transforming experience for Israelis.* All of Israel, not only the center-left, saw peace as possible for the first time. The effect on Israelis of all stripes was nothing short of electric. Israelis had lived with their basic existence denied; with their legitimacy as a nation rejected; with their day-to-day security threatened by their neighbors.

By coming to Israel, President Sadat broke the ring of isolation and rejection of Is-rael in the region. He demonstrated acceptance of Israel. It mattered little to Israelis that the terms he outlined in his speech to the Knesset in Jerusalem were maximal with regard to the principle of land for peace. What mattered was that he was serious about acceptance of, and peace with, Israel—something he demonstrated before the eyes of the world by coming to Jerusalem and declaring, No more wars, no more bloodshed.

Sadat's trip produced a psychological breakthrough. But psychological break-throughs have to be translated initially into political understandings and then formal agreements. Sadat's trip set in motion bilateral negotiations between Israel and Egypt at different levels. When the negotiations bogged down in the summer of 1978, Presi-dent Jimmy Carter intervened and at his invitation the leaders and their delegations met at Camp David that September. For thirteen days they wrestled with the issues of

---

*Secret meetings in Morocco between the Israeli Foreign Minister Moshe Dayan and Egyptian Deputy Prime Minister Hassan Tuhamy in September paved the way for Sadat's dramatic visit two months later. The most thorough account of the diplomatic efforts that led to the Egyptian-Israeli peace treaty is William Quandt, *Camp David: Peacemaking and Politics*, Washington, D.C.: Brookings Press, 1986.

Israeli withdrawal and also Palestinian rights. Sadat, who had not been prepared to let the Syrians or others determine whether Egypt could get its land back, was also determined to show that he had not forgotten the Palestinians as he negotiated a peace treaty with Israel.

But that was the essential point: to negotiate a peace agreement with Israel after having demonstrated his seriousness by going to Jerusalem.

In such circumstances, Israeli Prime Minister (and Likud leader) Menachem Begin, notwithstanding the ideology of his party, was prepared to do what few expected: withdraw Israeli troops and settlements from the entire Sinai and accept an autonomy plan for the Palestinians in the West Bank and Gaza in return for a peace treaty with Egypt. Even the Labor Party's political establishment at this time had not been willing to address the political needs of Palestinians apart from dealing with Jordan, and many in Labor opposed Begin's support for autonomy on the grounds that it would eventually lead to independent statehood. Yet Sadat demonstrated his seriousness as a partner, and Israelis made concessions (in difficult negotiations) that exceeded expectations and predictions.

This, too, is part of the Israeli ethos: a readiness to make serious, far-reaching concessions when it is clear they have a real partner—one that is prepared to acknowledge Israeli concerns directly, run demonstrable risks for peace, and reach out to the Israeli public.

This Israeli ethos reflects the deep-seated desire for peace in Israel—a desire that is commingled with fear and doubt about Arab intentions. President Sadat made peace—seemingly unattainable because of Arab rejection—thinkable.

To be sure, a broader peace with the Arab world was not at hand. Not only did no other Arab leaders follow Sadat's lead, but Saddam Hussein organized a summit in Baghdad to isolate Egypt for its peace with Israel. "Rejection" of Israel was still politically correct in the Arab world. But Israelis also knew an Arab world without Egypt was far less capable of waging war against Israel. And they also knew that while they would continue to face terror and regional isolation, it would be difficult for the Arab world to isolate Egypt, its largest and most influential country, forever, and other Arab leaders like King Hussein might feel more able to make peace at some point. In any case, peace was now possible, and Israelis did not want to live without hope.

They did not want to live under siege, or behind an "iron wall," if there was an alternative. They believed there was no alternative to their own strength, and the importance of the Arabs fully appreciating that strength, but they did not want to forgo opportunities for peace. They believed they had little room for error, and that their concerns about security would always have to be kept paramount. At the same time, the Israeli perception of their needs could clearly be influenced by Arab behavior—by the perception that they had a genuine partner for peace. Alternatively, when they saw no partner for peace, unilateral impulses to ensure security came to the fore.

This was the Israeli ethos I came to know so well in the years of working with Israelis of different ideologies, parties, and generations. Some Israelis were more inclined toward caution and suspicion toward the Arabs; some were more hopeful and empathetic toward the Arabs generally and the Palestinians specifically. (Those Israelis who had been born in Israel and who never questioned their own right to their state tended to be more understanding of the Palestinians than an older generation of Zionists who seemed to worry that acknowledgment of Palestinian rights could somehow undercut their own.) Regardless of the difference in orientation and emphasis, there was a basic ethos and a basic set of concerns that Israelis brought to the negotiating table. Naturally, the Arabs brought theirs as well.

| THE ARAB AND PALESTINIAN NARRATIVE |

The Arab and Palestinian narrative is actually two narratives, which have similar roots and converge in certain respects. But the Palestinian narrative is ultimately distinct, and informed by a different set of experiences.

The term "Arab" has been used to describe those living in the Middle East, embracing a common culture, history, and traditions heavily—but not solely—influenced by Islam, and being bound by the use of the Arabic language. As we will see, the language—as opposed to religion—became an important vehicle for building a sense of identity and shared destiny. Understandably, religious and ethnic minorities such as Christians in Lebanon and Palestine, and Alawis and Druze in Syria, tended to be the most zealous in promoting Arab nationalism, especially secular Arab nationalism.

In its essence, Arab nationalism responded to a profound yearning to overcome divisions and weakness in the Arab world. While exile and dispersal had made Jews weak throughout their history in the eyes of the Zionists, sectarian, tribal, and clannish differences had subjected Arabs to constant conflicts; had led to foreign domination; and had robbed them of the glory that had once been theirs in history. The Arab revival could end the internal conflict; it could foster a unity of all Arabs, restoring their strength, their dignity, their self-respect, their identity, and their independence—or so it was believed.

| THE "ARAB AWAKENING" |

George Antonius's historic work *The Arab Awakening* argues that the emergence of a uniquely Arab consciousness began in the mid-nineteenth century. Arab nationalists in the twentieth century, seeking to demonstrate that Arab nationalism had deeper historical roots, embraced the Antonius narrative. More recent historiography suggests that Antonius exaggerated the impact of those who began to develop an Arab identity—

an identity designed to submerge the regional and clannish loyalties that had characterized so much of the Middle East throughout history. No one claims that the sentiments Antonius portrays as emerging in the nineteenth century did not exist. Rather that the numbers of actual adherents to this Arab revival remained very small in number, primarily Christian, and largely limited to Damascus.

For Antonius, it is the resurrection of the Arabic language that marked a starting point for the Arab revival. The Turkish language was the official language of the Ottoman Empire, which by the mid-nineteenth century had dominated the Arab world for 350 years. Books had been in rare supply, and the installation of a printing press in the Arabic language revolutionized the educational system. The arrival and competitive impulses of American and French Christian missionaries in Syria (and in what is today Lebanon) put a new premium on education, and contributed to the surge of interest in Arabic language, literature, ideas, and culture. The founding of the Syrian Protestant College in Beirut in 1866—which later became the American University of Beirut—provided a focal point for the promotion of national consciousness.

Antonius notes that secret societies in Greater Syria began to emerge in the late 1800s with the credo of promoting such Arab independence. But C. Ernest Dawn, the scholar who effectively coined the term "Arabism," points out that these societies were limited to a very small band of extreme Arab nationalists in Syria. Most of those in the Arab provinces favored decentralization and reform, not independence.

Paradoxically, it was the Young Turk movement and the revolution of Turkish military officers in 1908 who insisted on creating a constitution and ending autocratic rule that gave the Arab nationalists a new impetus. While the Young Turks were not yet ready to end the empire or remove the Sultan, their demand for reform also included a call for "equality" among Turks and the others in the empire. For the Arabs, this meant a new status and the chance to build their identity. For many, even the promise of autonomy was sufficient as a starting point.

This was especially true for leading Arab officers in the Turkish military. Officers like Aziz Ali had joined one of the secret societies not because they sought independence, but because they favored autonomy for the Arab provinces of the empire.

But the commitment to autonomy and equality went unfulfilled. The Committee of Union and Progress (CUP), the group that dominated Ottoman politics in the decade after the emergence of the Young Turk movement, ended up promoting far more "Turkification" than decentralization for the Arabs. Worse still, in 1914 Aziz Ali was arrested and sentenced to death for his membership in the secret society, al-Ahd. While Ali was ultimately pardoned and allowed to go to Egypt, he became a symbol of Turkish oppression of the Arabs.

With the advent of World War I in 1914, the secret societies in Damascus—

though fearing European, especially French, designs on the Arab provinces—formulated conditions under which the Arabs could offer to align with the British against the Turks. Amir Faisal, the son of Sharif Hussein of Mecca, was given these conditions and told that if the British would agree to them, those leaders of the Arab movement in Greater Syria would recognize the Sharif as the Arab spokesman and would heed his call for an uprising against the Turks. What the secret societies were asking, what Amir Faisal gave to his father, and what his father communicated to the British was a simple proposition: commit to independence in all the Arab provinces of the Ottoman Empire (Syria, Mesopotamia, the Arabian Peninsula), and recognize an Arab caliphate if one was created, in return for an Arab uprising against the Turks.

The Sharif's communication with the British took the form in 1915–16 of an exchange of letters with the British High Commissioner in Egypt, Sir Henry McMahon. These letters and the commitments embodied in them, the Sykes-Picot agreement that followed these letters, and the Balfour Declaration have come to form an important part of the Arab narrative—a narrative of perceived broken promises, betrayal, and efforts to deny the Arabs their rightful destiny.

For the Arabs, Sharif Hussein was crystal-clear: he was offering alignment and an uprising against the Turks in return for independence in all the Arab territories of the Ottoman Empire, being quite precise in his definition of the territories and boundaries to be included. In terms of today's geographic definitions, that meant Syria, Lebanon, Israel and Palestine, Iraq, Saudi Arabia, and the United Arab Emirates. He replied sharply and unmistakably to McMahon's efforts initially to avoid a discussion of the "frontiers and boundaries," saying the "boundaries represent not the suggestions of one individual . . . but the demands of our people." No commitment on the boundaries of the areas that would gain independence, and there would be no Arab uprising against the Turks.

In the subsequent exchanges when McMahon committed to supporting independence in the areas the Sharif had outlined, with some exceptions where the "French had interests west of Damascus," the Sharif made clear that "any concession designed to give France or any other Power possession of a single square foot of territory in those parts is quite out of the question."

Not surrendering a single square foot—something I was to hear often seventy years later from President Asad—reflected, in Arab eyes, that the land had almost a sacred quality. While the British felt they had qualified their promise at least with regard to the areas west of Damascus, the Sharif of Mecca believed he had a firm promise of independence in return for the uprising. Whatever the qualifiers in the McMahon letters, they did not cover the Sykes-Picot agreement—an agreement that was worked out in 1916 after the McMahon-Hussein letters. It was an agreement between the British,

French, and Russians, and it divided up the Ottoman Empire into different spheres of influence, with the French sphere in most of Syria, the British sphere in Mesopotamia (Iraq) and the ports of Palestine, and the Russian sphere in parts of Turkey and the Bosporus. (For Palestine, there would be an international regime.)

The needs of the alliance on the one hand conflicted with the needs of the Arabs on the other. The British may have felt that spheres of influence and independence could be reconciled after the war, and in the interim, they needed to assuage the interests of the French and the Russians for the sake of the war effort in Europe. However, when the terms of Sykes-Picot became known, the Arabs not only saw a betrayal of the promise on independence, but also a specific design, using spheres of influence, to carve up the Arab world and prevent Arab unity. To make matters worse, the Balfour Declaration appeared to give Arab land away to Jewish outsiders. In Arab eyes, they had acted in good faith, and in return they confronted a world of contradictory promises that undercut everything Faisal and those around him were trying to cultivate: a new national consciousness emphasizing the sanctity of the land, independence, and unity.

The contradictory promises might have meant little if the Arabs had been permitted to establish their independence after the war. But they were not. Faisal returned to Damascus in October 1918 amid a surge of nationalist fervor. He presided over elections to a national assembly that convened in July of 1919. The assembly, which came to be called the Syrian General Congress, passed resolutions calling for recognition of a sovereign Syrian state under the leadership of Amir Faisal and repudiation of the Sykes-Picot agreement, the Balfour Declaration, and any partition of Syria or the creation of a Jewish commonwealth. While Faisal set about creating a governmental administration and attracting nationalists to his cause, he was evicted from Damascus by the French in July 1920. (The British would install him as King in what became Iraq, and his brother Abdullah would become King in what became Transjordan. Faisal's government became home to the first real ideologists of Pan-Arabism, with his minister of education, Sati al-Husri, becoming the standard-bearer of Arab unity—the answer to Arab weakness and the prescription for strength and greatness.)

Divisions and colonialism, not independence and unity, were the legacy of the British promises. It is this history of betrayal and the arbitrary division of the former Ottoman Empire that has led many in the Arab world, including Osama bin Laden, to speak of the humiliations of the past. (Bin Laden in his first videotape after 9/11 referred specifically to this period in speaking of "the last eighty years of humiliation and disgrace.") Outsiders imposed their borders. Outsiders were free to break promises. Outsiders were never held accountable. Consequently, defying outsiders and standing up to those who inflict humiliation have come—as we will see—to be embedded in the broader psychology of the Arab world.

| THE BEGINNINGS OF PALESTINIAN NATIONALISM |

Following Faisal's eviction, particular nationalisms began to emerge with localized resistance to French rule in Syria, an uprising in Iraq against ongoing British presence and tutelage and turmoil in Palestine. For the Arabs of Palestine, a more distinctly Palestinian consciousness began to emerge. The Zionist program had already energized the determination to protect the Arab identity of Palestine. In Jaffa in May 1919, a Christian-Muslim assembly had convened and demanded a cessation of Jewish immigration, a prohibition on Jewish land purchases, and a representative government of Muslims, Christians, and Jews—something that would preserve a permanent Arab majority and Jewish minority. But the assembly was not calling for an independent Palestine; on the contrary, its resolution declared that Palestine was part of Syria and that the government should have autonomy in "Greater Syria under the rule of Prince Faisal."

With Faisal's eviction, with the return of intellectuals from Damascus who had been part of Faisal's administration and army, with the dream of a Greater Syria shelved, and with increasing Jewish immigration constituting a threat in Arab eyes, Palestinian nationalism began to express itself. Associations and clubs were formed; though literacy was limited, periodicals were established; debate over whom to struggle against, the British or the Jews, became increasingly vocal. Soon thereafter, active resistance and violence began to be used against the Jewish presence and Jewish immigration, leading in particular to the bloody riots of 1921.

Few factors are more likely to lead to a nationalist identity than a shared sense of threat. One of the leading Arab thinkers, writers, and educators in Palestine at the time, Khalil Sakakini acknowledged the Jewish desire for Palestine, but wrote that you cannot kill "an entire nation in order to live." Similarly, the British commission investigating the riots of 1921 blamed the violence on the Arabs, but noted that they had genuine fears of being expelled.

Dispossession became a national symbol and driving force of the Arabs of Palestine. The visible sign of this was tenant farmers being evicted, often forcibly resisting, but being evicted nonetheless from the land they had worked and lived on for generations. It mattered little to the Arabs of Palestine that the land had been purchased by the Jews from Arab landowners. What mattered was that Arabs were being dispossessed, and that the Jewish presence was growing at the expense of the Arabs.

Trying to prevent Jewish immigration and Jewish land purchases became the constant themes of the Arabs of Palestine. However, this unity of theme and emerging Palestinian identity did not forge a unity of purpose or action. The divisions and rivalries between the leading families—Husseinis, Nashashibis, Nusseibehs, Deganis, Masris, Shawaas—were but one factor dividing the Arabs of Palestine; the religious divide between Muslims and Christians another; village versus city dwellers another of importance, with seven out of ten living in villages with a more traditional focus and only limited education.

The divisions fostered competition and militated against moderation or compromise with the Jews. Rivals could always outbid, always accuse moderates of betraying Arab interests. The Mufti of Jerusalem, Haj Amin al-Husseini, used Islam to build his base of support. He used perceived threats to Islam, especially in Jerusalem, to mobilize passions and resistance to the Jews—leading to an explosion of violence in 1929. But he, too, faced more extreme and charismatic religious figures like Sheikh Izz al-Din al-Qassem, who in the mid-1930s called for violence and terror against the Jews and the British. While the Mufti initially resisted his calls, the frustration level among the Arabs rose with the dramatic growth of Jewish immigration in the 1930s. Resistance and violence escalated and reached a peak in the Arab revolt of 1936–39.

Even here, however, the divisions eventually led to the revolt turning inward. The search for collaborators—a phenomenon seen again in the first and second Intifadas—combined with score-settling between rival families and clans to inflict great pain on the very people struggling against what they saw as formidable odds. Internal division fed the desire for unity but typically blocked its achievement. It also blocked what might have been more pragmatic impulses.

Unlike the Jews of the Yishuv who focused on creating facts and getting what they could, the Arabs of Palestine remained riveted on principle and the strength of their claims. To be more pragmatic meant to be willing to surrender claims. Unfortunately, focusing only on the strength of their claims, especially in the aftermath of the Holocaust and given the sense that the Jewish people were owed a great debt, generated little international sympathy for the Arabs.

While the Arabs at the time did not deny the great crime committed against the Jewish people, they did not see why they should pay for it. When President Roosevelt saw Ibn Saud, the King of Saudi Arabia, in 1945 and tried to persuade him that the extraordinary suffering of the Jews should make the Arabs open and hospitable to the Jewish interests in Palestine, the King was unmoved, emphasizing that the Germans, not the Arabs, should pay: "Make the enemy and the oppressor pay . . . Amends should be made by the criminal, not by the innocent bystander. What injury have Arabs done to the Jews of Europe? It is the Christian Germans who stole their homes and lives."

For the Arabs of Palestine, it was the Jews who were "stealing" their homes. In their eyes, they were not responsible for what was done to the Jews in Europe. But in Palestine, it was the Arabs who were being victimized; it was the Arabs who were suffering from a great injustice. It was the Arabs of Palestine who, in the words of George Antonius (himself a Palestinian Arab), had "the natural right of a settled population . . . to remain in possession of the land of its birthright." Their deep and abiding sense of injustice instilled in the Arabs of Palestine a belief in entitlement. They were entitled to the land—it was theirs, they had been promised independence over it, they need not surrender it to those coming from the outside.

Entitlement and the politics of rivalry ruled out compromise. There was no constituency among the Arabs of Palestine prepared to argue publicly for partition. There was no constituency that was prepared to surrender any claims—or acknowledge Jewish claims. And, fundamentally, there was no constituency that felt there was any practical need to do so. The Arabs within Palestine and those on the outside felt that the Jews without British protection would be swiftly defeated. Who needed to worry about creating facts vis-à-vis the Jews on the land when Arab power would create its own facts on the battlefield?

But the reality of division and competition was far more potent than the illusion of unity among the Arabs within Palestine or with their Arab brothers outside. The personal, family, and political rivalry between Abd al-Kader al-Husseini, who led the fighting around Jerusalem until he was killed in March of 1948, and Fawzi al-Qawuqji, who led the Arab forces in the northern part of the country, precluded effective cooperation against the Jewish forces. There was no more unity among the Arab states that invaded the newly declared state of Israel. Anwar Nusseibeh, in describing the attitudes of the invading Arab states, wrote: "Obviously, they thought of the Palestine adventure in terms of an easy walkover for the Arabs, and the only point that seemed to worry them was credit for the expected victory."

Apart from grossly underestimating the determination and staying power of the Jews of Palestine—who now had a state—the Arab states were all looking to deny their rivals an advantage in Palestine. And the Arabs of Palestine were very quick to confer the responsibility of dealing with the Jews on the Arab states. The Palestinian Arabs had succeeded in creating a distinct national identity, but they had not been able to translate this into a meaningful reality on the ground and they had been too quick to defer to others. Again, in the words of Anwar Nusseibeh, himself a Palestinian who lost a leg in the 1948 war, "I underestimated the strength of my enemy and overestimated the strength of my own people." And, of course, the Palestinians were lacking in leadership, with Nusseibeh commenting that the Mufti succeeded as a symbol, but failed as a leader.

The Palestinians were to pay dearly for the lack of leadership not only in the period leading up to 1948 but repeatedly in the future. The advent of Israel and the 1948 war produced what the Palestinians call the Nakba, the catastrophe. Nearly 750,000 Arabs fled Palestine, demoralized, disoriented, homeless, and with no clear place to go. It is part of the Palestinian narrative that the refugees were forced by the Israelis to leave their homes.

Naturally, the Israeli narrative is different, with far greater emphasis put on refugees fleeing because they thought the Arabs would, as Nusseibeh said, make quick work of the Jews—and that once done they could return. While there is some truth to this, there is no denying that in many places the Israelis did force Arabs to leave and, with the exception of Haifa, the Israelis shed no tears over the Arab departure from their new state.

Regardless of why 750,000 Arabs fled, it was a disaster for the Palestinian people. They were stateless and with no status. The camps that became home to so many of the refugees were designed to keep the cause of Palestine alive, not resolve their problem. While the Palestinians in them lived with the hope of returning to their homes, their Arab hosts did very little for them—politically, economically, or socially. In the words of Fawaz Turki, a Palestinian refugee, the Palestinians were the "disinherited." Their cause was used by a new generation of Arab leaders who for their own inter-Arab purposes and ambitions claimed they would avenge the disaster of 1948.

The 1948 defeat swept away an older generation of leaders in the Arab world. Middle-class nationalists, rooted in the militaries, overthrew corrupt leaders "disconnected from the aspiring social classes." These new leaders, it was believed, would build modern states and armies and "arrest the political decline and stagnation" that had produced defeat. The doctrine of Arab nationalism, of Pan-Arabism, was embraced and emphasized as the only salvation for the Arab world. Only Arab unity would make it possible to progress and recover past glories—and only Arab unity would make it possible to liberate Palestine.

The Palestinians as a people were submerged in the service of the cause. Once again it was up to others, not to them, to deal with the issues affecting their destinies. While the "cause" of Palestine was universally accepted, it became a tool in inter-Arab rivalries. Much as the Arabs of Palestine constantly outbid each other prior to 1948, so, too, did the competing Arab nationalists use the Palestine issue to gain advantage over their rivals and put them on the defensive. Moderation was a danger in this context. And as my professor, Malcolm Kerr, wrote, Palestine, far from being a vehicle for Pan-Arabism, had become a "stick" with which to beat one's Arab rivals.

No one was better at this than Gamal Abdel Nasser. No one spoke the idiom of Arab nationalism better than Nasser. He had assumed a hero status in the Arab world by seemingly defying those who had humiliated the Arabs for so long. He had broken the West's monopoly on arms supplies to the area by turning to the Soviets for arms in 1955. He had overcome the aggression of the British, French, and Israelis in the 1956 Suez war—and only one with mystical powers could have done so. That his victories were actually the work of others—the Soviets competing in the Middle East with the West and President Eisenhower undoing the British, French, and Israeli actions—did nothing to alter the perceptions of his heroic achievements.

While he became an enormously appealing figure to the Arab publics throughout the Middle East, Nasser's plans for unity came to naught. Rather than fostering Arab unity, he was constantly embroiled with the Arab nationalist regimes and monarchies alike, and he became bogged down in the 1960s in a war in Yemen—Egypt's Vietnam. And his rivals in the area lost no opportunity to try to embarrass him—a reality that led him to take the steps that produced the war in June 1967.

If the loss in 1948 produced upheaval, the crushing defeat in 1967 produced depression and doubt. Nasser lost his hero status. The Arab nationalists had failed. Some in the Arab world looked to Islam for salvation. But the Palestinians knew they must look to themselves for salvation. They could no longer count on the Arabs to do for them, to achieve for them.

Before 1967, the Arabs knew best what was good for the Palestinians. After the Arabs failed so clearly, not only did the Palestinians know what was best for themselves, but the Arab world, for the time being, seemed willing to acknowledge this as well.

The Palestine Liberation Organization, which had been established in 1964 and headed by Ahmed Shuqayri, had been perceived as Nasser's instrument. After the war, Shuqayri was forced out. Palestinians would develop a meaningful resistance organization, serving Palestinian interests and making it clear that the world could no longer ignore the plight of the Palestinian people.

To gain credibility, the Palestinians needed their victory and their heroes. They created both in the battle of Karameh in March 1968. Israeli forces attacked fedayeen bases across the Jordan River in Jordan. In a battle that dragged on for hours, with the Jordanian army joining the Palestinians and casualties high on all sides, a new myth was born. Palestinian fighters were seen as heroes. They would stand up to the Israelis. They would not be defeated the way the Arabs had been. For many Arab intellectuals and writers who had been demoralized by the 1967 defeat, the Palestinian fighters, especially after Karameh, restored their sense of pride and as such were given exalted status.

But for the Palestinians, Karameh and increasing commando raids meant much more. It gave them stature; it gave an identity; it gave them a reason to be respected. It is hard to exaggerate the Palestinian feeling of being ignored, humiliated, and considered a nonpeople. And here it was not just the Israelis or the international community who fostered this reality. It was their existence in the Arab world. Only in Jordan were they considered citizens. Everywhere in the Arab world they were subjected, in Fawaz Turki's words, to "indignities." They required work permits to work; they required special documents to be able to travel; and the caprice of local Arab officials could determine whether they could get such documents. The "enervating and degrading existence" was of "no concern to those who spoke on their behalf. Pawn politics and indifference" shaped the Arab treatment of the Palestinians in Palestinian eyes. The Palestinian resistance movement and especially Fatah, Yasir Arafat's organization, captured their imagination.

Arafat became the head of the PLO in February 1969. He founded Fatah in 1962. Operating initially out of Kuwait in the early 1960s, Arafat and Fatah were the masters of the communiqué, first declaring operations against the Israelis and then later actually carrying out attacks beginning in 1965. Even before 1967, his focus was uniquely Palestinian. He was not focused on what was good for the Arabs; he was riveted on what the Palestinians needed. Through guile and his readiness to work with all groups, he gradually built his strength among differing Palestinian organizations, becoming the leader of the PLO by the end of the decade. His faction might be Fatah, but now he headed the PLO, which remained an umbrella organization drawing together many armed Palestinian groups of diverse ideologies, revolutionary credentials, and continuing attachments to different Arab regimes.

Terror and violence were seen as legitimate tools to force the world to pay attention to the Palestinians and address their grievances. Terror and violence were designed as well to tie the hands of key Arab states like Egypt and Jordan. Notwithstanding Nasser's "three no's" at Khartoum, there was great suspicion among Palestinians (and militant regimes in Syria and Iraq) that at the first opportunity Nasser and Hussein would sell out the Palestinians and do a deal with Israel to get their land back. It is not that Moshe Dayan was wrong to sit by the phone waiting for the Arabs to call after the war; it is that he was sitting too soon.

Palestinian fears were driven by a perception that Egypt and Jordan believed they could not defeat Israel, and it was therefore only a matter of time before they would turn to diplomacy and away from conflict.*

---

*In truth, Palestinian fears had a basis. Both Egypt and Jordan began at least privately to contemplate the possibility of a settlement. Neither was in a rush to embrace publicly the "land for peace" formula as embodied in UNSC Resolution 242 in November 1967. But that changed by 1970, notwithstanding Palestinian efforts to maintain resistance—not negotiation—as their only strategic approach to the conflict with Israel.

The year 1970 was not good from the Palestinian point of view. They suffered two blows: one political and one territorial. Nasser, who had engaged in a war of attrition with Israel along the Suez Canal, agreed to a cease-fire plan formulated by Secretary of State William Rogers. The plan was based on acceptance of UNSC Resolution 242, and signaled a readiness to consider a diplomatic solution to the conflict. At this point, Nasser acted to pursue Egyptian interests, notwithstanding the desires of the Palestinians. King Hussein's blow to the Palestinians was far more direct and brutal. In a bloody showdown, his army defeated and expelled the Palestinian resistance forces—most of whom ended up in Lebanon. No longer would Fatah or the other groups have a base in Jordan.

The precipitating event was the hijacking of three airliners by one of the PLO's constituent groups—the Popular Front for the Liberation of Palestine. The PFLP was always in the forefront of dramatic acts of terror designed to maximize attention on the Palestinians. Perhaps driven by a desire to polarize the region further and make it difficult for Nasser to pursue the Rogers Plan, the hijacking of three passenger aircraft and the parking and eventual destruction of them in the Jordanian desert was an event condemned by the international community. It was also a source of profound embarrassment to King Hussein. In fact, a showdown between Hussein and Arafat was almost inevitable.

After Karameh and their new standing in the Arab world as committed resistance fighters, the Palestinian forces had increasingly acted as if they ruled Jordan. The Palestinians saw little need to keep the understandings that Arafat would work out with King Hussein on how the commandos were to behave. There were constant challenges to Jordanian authority and sovereignty, with the Jordanian army becoming increasingly restive. When the King acted against the Palestinians, it is clear, that he had the sanction of many other Arab leaders to do so. In the words of Fouad Ajami, the "dominant Arab order" was not about to let the Palestinians dictate what was and was not permissible in the area.

The King's crackdown also led to a change of regime in Syria. The President of Syria, Salah Jadid, sent the Syrian army across the border into Jordan to assist the Palestinians against the Jordanian army. Hafez al-Asad, commander of the Syrian air force, refused to commit the air force—after seeing Israeli mobilization of forces and the U.S. backing of King Hussein. Rather than coming to the aid of the Palestinians, he launched a coup against Jadid a short time later and became the President of Syria— an office he maintained until his death in June 2000. This was also bad news for Yasir Arafat. From 1970 onward, President Asad would consistently back Arafat's rivals in the Palestinian movement. (As President Asad was to tell me later, he had arrested

Arafat in Damascus in the early 1960s, but because of pressure from others had reluctantly—and with obvious regret—released him.)

A pattern of maneuvering between rival forces, groups, and Arab leaders became the necessary hallmark of Arafat's rule of the PLO. While Algeria's liberation movement against the French was the reputed model for the Palestinian leadership, the discipline and coherence of the FLN was never seen in the PLO. On the contrary, consensus-building and persuasion—not force—was used to deal with the differing groups living under the PLO's umbrella. Political disputes were never pushed to the breaking point, particularly because that would mean foreclosing options and making permanent enemies of other Palestinians.

Whether dealing internally or with Arab leaders, "maneuvering" described the style and the purpose of Arafat's leadership of the Palestinians. Maneuvering between those who sought to control the Palestinian cause or do it harm or who threatened Arafat's dominance of the movement became his guiding principle. For Arafat, if there was a governing ethos, it was never erase an option, never close a door, and never commit to anything that was irrevocable—indeed, never regard any commitment as binding. Weakness, not strength, produced such a mode of thinking and operating. Whatever the claims after 1967, whatever the centrality of the "cause" in the psychology of the Arab world, the Palestinian leadership was governed by the reality of weakness and dependency. The blows of 1970 brought them back to that reality.

It should come as no surprise that those who feel they are weak will not weaken themselves further by dividing their ranks or foreclosing options. That is why a habit of maneuvering and evading, but not deciding, governed the movement and its leader. Unity in Palestinian eyes needed to be maintained at all costs. Fights between Palestinians could only serve Israeli interests. Better to avoid decisions that would provoke internal opposition; better to paper over possible disagreements and better to ensure consensus than to let Israel exploit divisions among Palestinians—or so Palestinian thinking went.

Yasir Arafat kept the movement together. He succeeded in the aftermath of the 1973 war, at the 1974 Arab summit in Rabat, in getting the Arab world to recognize the PLO as the "sole, legitimate representative" of the Palestinian people. But this too was part of a deal: he would "control" the genuine revolutionaries in his movement—those who believed that the liberation of Palestine must be part of a broader revolution against the existing political order in the Arab world—and not intervene in the internal politics of the Arab states; in return the PLO would be given this standing. (With the important exception of Lebanon, Arafat basically hewed to this bargain; his maneuverings in Lebanon eventually led to an alliance between the Christian forces and the Israelis and the expulsion of the PLO's forces following Israel's invasion in the summer of 1982.)

Arafat had to maneuver to build Palestinian leverage, to keep the "cause" alive before the Arabs and the world, and to limit what might be done to the Palestinians by the Israelis or other Arabs. Hopes for Arab leverage soared after the 1973 war, given its successes on the battlefield and the use of the oil weapon. But Arab leverage required real unity, and what became increasingly apparent was that each Arab country—while obliged to speak the idiom of Arab unity—pursued and protected its own interests.

The Saudis and other oil states would not let the Palestinians or the Egyptians gain control over their precious resource and use it for their purposes. President Sadat, who had succeeded Nasser, would not let the Palestinians or the Syrians determine whether Egypt could get its land back. King Hussein, notwithstanding the Rabat summit decision on the PLO, would not simply let Arafat build a base in the West Bank at the expense of Jordan's role and influence there. Indeed, until the late 1980s, the King continued to harbor hopes that at some point he might yet regain responsibility for the West Bank and a leadership role among the Palestinians. Whatever the ability of the Palestinians to appeal over the heads of Arab leaders to the wider Arab street, Arafat understood his limitations—telling me at Camp David in July 2000 that he had wanted to go with Sadat to the original Camp David but was prevented by the Syrians and the Soviets from doing so.

Maneuvering between conflicting forces and carrying out acts of terror may have kept the PLO together and reminded the world and the Israelis that the Palestinians would not go away without their grievances being addressed, but it did nothing to end the growing Israeli settler presence in, and the Israeli military's rule of Palestinians in the West Bank and Gaza. As the Israeli occupation took on deeper roots, and as Likud-led national unity governments in the 1980s promoted more building of Israeli settlements throughout the territories, Palestinian frustration with Israeli control became more pronounced.

Violent flare-ups between Israeli forces and Palestinian youth, especially in and around the refugee camps in Gaza, became a more frequent occurrence. And then, in December 1987, an accident in which an Israeli driver in Gaza lost control of his vehicle and killed a number of Palestinians triggered riots initially in Gaza and subsequently in both Gaza and the West Bank. The riots did not stop. Strikes and stone-throwing at Israeli soldiers and settlers became a daily reality, and the Palestinians soon gave this reality a name: the Intifada, the uprising.

This first Intifada was unquestionably an expression of Palestinian frustration and anger. It came from within the territories, not outside. The "children of the stones" captured the imagination of the Arab intellectuals; it responded to a need not to submit but to defy. It was a statement, in effect, that the Palestinians in the territories would not settle for occupation. Whatever the Israeli intentions, the Palestinians felt degraded and humiliated under occupation. Israeli actions used to try to prevent Palestinian acts of terror—preventive detention, physical intimidation and abuse, demolition of houses of the families of the terrorists—deepened Palestinian resentment, and fostered their sense of victimization.

Victimization has deep roots in the Palestinian mind. Whereas the preoccupation with security governed the Israeli approach to negotiations with all of its neighbors, the need to end victimization and to be accorded dignity, respect, and genuine independence governed the Palestinians. Every position or issue in the talks would be evaluated in terms of how it limited Israeli control or gave the Palestinians greater standing or independence.

The Palestinians' sense of being victims also fostered a sense of entitlement. They were entitled to the land. It was theirs, and it had been taken. They did not have to prove anything to the Israelis; it was the Israelis who must prove themselves to Palestinians—who were, after all, the victims of the conflict. As victims, the Palestinians felt (and emphasized throughout the negotiations) that it was the Israelis who were always required to take the first step or make the first concession in the talks. Similarly, the United States, as the principal sponsor of the peace process, had a responsibility to the victims to level the playing field. In turn, little was required of the Palestinians because as victims, they were owed much. Responsibility was not part of the Palestinian political culture. Rather, it was the Israeli responsibility or the American responsibility or the international community's responsibility or even the Arab responsibility to redress the wrongs or take steps to end the conflict.

Naturally, seeing themselves as victims, Palestinians found it difficult to feel empathetic to Israeli needs. It was not just that Israelis had taken by force what had been theirs, and now kept them under occupation; it was also that Palestinians genuinely saw great Israeli strength and their own weakness. The Israelis spoke of security, but from the Palestinian perspective, they were the ones in need of security from the uses and abuses of Israeli force.

Being victims also created one other reality for Palestinians: they became attracted to those who might stand up to and threaten Israel or its benefactor. In 1990, when Saddam Hussein threatened to burn half of Israel with chemical weapons; when he claimed he had invaded Kuwait for the Palestinians cause, when he fired Scud missiles against Israel, Palestinians were among Saddam's biggest supporters. No one else seemed prepared to defy the Western world on the Palestinians' behalf. No one else seemed so prepared to humiliate those who had humiliated all the Arabs. No one else seemed so prepared to demonstrate that the Arabs were not powerless.

But much like Nasser, Saddam produced disaster, not salvation. His defeat, however, helped to set in motion events that would lead for the first time since the advent of Israel to a serious process for negotiating an end to the Arab-Israeli conflict. President Bush had promised repeatedly that once we had ended Iraq's aggression against Kuwait, we would work to promote a comprehensive peace in the Middle East. Our strongest Arab allies in the war against Iraq—Saudi Arabia and Egypt—were eager for us to launch such an initiative, feeling more secure from radical threats and wanting to demonstrate their continuing fealty to broader Arab causes, like the Palestinian cause, notwithstanding their having joined in the fight against an Arab leader.

Palestinians and many in the Arab world continued to see an American double standard when it came to this peace initiative. They asked why was Israel permitted to effectively ignore Security Council resolutions while Saddam was forced to comply? They did not see the difference between the Security Council resolutions. Those against Iraq came as a response to Saddam's eradication of a member state of the UN; the resolutions required his compliance, not his acceptance. Noncompliance carried sanctions, and led to the use of force against his absorption of Kuwait. The resolutions that Palestinians and Arabs more generally focused on with regard to Israel were resolutions 242 and 338. They were adopted after the 1967 and 1973 wars. They provided the guidelines or principles that should shape negotiations to resolve the conflict between Arabs and Israelis. The terms of a final peace settlement were not established in these resolutions and they could not be mandatory on either side.

But drawing distinctions between Security Council resolutions involving the Iraqis and the Israelis was not satisfying. The Arab world generally rejected the idea that Iraq faced pressure to implement Security Council resolutions while Israel did not. They wanted equal treatment. They wanted to portray all Security Council resolutions as having the force of international law.

For the Arab world generally, the resolutions were their face-savers. They would resolve the conflict with Israel, but only on the basis of international law, "international legitimacy," as they called it. Here was their explanation, their justification for ending the conflict. If Iraq had to follow international legitimacy, so too, must Israel. Messy, difficult negotiations made it look like the Israelis were trying to avoid their responsibilities, not fulfill them. Land for peace—what UNSC resolutions 242 and 338 came to mean—was simple. The Israelis should simply withdraw; there should be no need for complicated negotiations. If Israel would withdraw, there would be no more reason for war, no more reason for conflict. Indeed, the Arab and Palestinian concept of peace was the absence of conflict; it was not acceptance, not reconciliation, not cooperation, and not warm relations. This was, of course, in keeping with the basic belief that Israel was not entitled to be there. Arabs would acknowledge Israel's existence and end the conflict but they would minimize relations with it.

| GAPS IN THE NARRATIVES, GAPS IN PERCEPTION |

The Israeli concept of peace was very different. Israelis wanted more than an acknowledgment of their reality. They wanted acceptance of it. They wanted proof of the commitment to living in peace. They feared giving up tangible assets like land that gave Israel a more defensible territorial position in return for intangible and highly reversible promises—promises that meant little if the fundamental reality remained one characterized by hostility that justified either war or continued terror against Israel.

That is why Israelis wanted to see concrete signs of peace and normalization. With Likud, withdrawal from land was difficult in any case; however, with demonstrations of a serious commitment to peace—by taking risks, by dealing directly with Israelis, by showing a readiness to address Israeli security concerns seriously, by accepting normal relations and cooperative ventures, and by being willing to engage in tough, practical, detailed negotiations—the land part of the equation could be dealt with by the Israelis. Ultimately, Israelis needed assurance that the formula was land for peace, not land for nothing.

Conversely, in Arab and Palestinian eyes, the land was theirs, they were doing the Israelis a favor by ending the conflict and agreeing to live with Israel's presence. As President Asad of Syria was to say to me on several occasions, "Don't the Israelis understand what I am offering them?" (Asad, given his Arab nationalist credentials, felt the Israelis should have been grateful for his readiness to give up the fight and acquiesce in Israel's existence; in return, they needed, in his eyes, to satisfy him completely on the land, on the timing of withdrawal, and on limiting the content of normal relations.)

Once again we see the Israeli mind-set focused on the practical, the detailed, and the security dimensions of relations and intentions—all of which would prove that the Arabs were actually transforming their attitude toward Israel and would genuinely accept its presence. By contrast, the Arab and Palestinian mind-set was drawn to the principles, the generalities, and their broad claims. Satisfy their basic claims, and peace—the absence of conflict—would result. The responsibility was all Israel's, not theirs.

Over time, the negotiations that emerged from the Madrid and Olso processes were very detailed on all issues. But the points of departure were very different. The Arabs and Palestinians always sought acceptance of their principles while the Israelis always sought recognition of the practicalities. The gaps on the issues bore not just disagreements but very different attitudes about the negotiations, their purpose, and the tactics that should be employed.

This is the world that shaped each side's approach to negotiations when we finally got to the point where negotiations between Israel and all of her neighbors, including the Palestinians, became possible. To be sure, getting negotiations launched meant crossing a major historic threshold. Knowing how important recognition was to the Israelis, the Arabs sought to withhold it in order to gain Israeli concessions first. The Israelis wanted direct negotiations, but did not want to have to pay for them by conceding on the points of substance.

President Sadat had understood that. The Arab world had sought to isolate Egypt for reaching a peace treaty with Israel. By the middle 1980s, that effort ended, and the Arabs were willing to consider diplomatic approaches, provided they did not have to deal directly with Israel. They sought indirect negotiations through the United States, or, in time, through an international conference that would present the Israelis with a collective Arab position. Israel wanted the Arabs to demonstrate their commitment to peace by being willing to meet bilaterally and directly—as Sadat had done—and opposed indirect negotiations or an international conference.

This is where the story of my involvement in peacemaking efforts began. Prior to the Madrid peace conference, the question was: Could negotiations ever take place? Afterward, it was, Could the negotiations ever produce peace?

The Road to Madrid

THROUGHOUT THE 1980S, THE Reagan administration intervened actively in the Middle East. Unfortunately, few of the initiatives bore fruit. Some failed outright, like the effort to stabilize Lebanon in the aftermath of the Israeli invasion of 1982, which led to the introduction of U.S. troops, the loss of 241 marines in the suicidal bombing of their barracks in Beirut, and an American withdrawal by early 1984. Others, like the Reagan plan—an effort to present a broader vision for Middle East peace following the Israeli siege of Beirut and our brokering of the PLO's exit from Lebanon—consumed time and effort but yielded no results.

With the failures of the Lebanon intervention and the Reagan plan, Secretary of State George Shultz scaled back U.S. diplomacy in the region. We would not send troops into Middle East trouble spots or outline comprehensive plans for resolving the Arab-Israeli conflict. Rather, we would focus on getting peace talks started, for if the Arabs and Israelis could not even talk, the conflict would never end. Instead it would threaten both to escalate dangerously and to disrupt the world oil market and the U.S. economy.

Unfortunately, the U.S. diplomatic efforts were unable to overcome the Arab reluctance to negotiate directly with the Israelis. Arab leaders, still trying to withhold direct recognition of Israel, would hold talks only at an international conference, while the Israelis continued to insist on direct, bilateral negotiations.

There was also the question of who would represent the Palestinians in negotiations.

Having designated the PLO as the sole, legitimate representative of the Palestinian people, Arab leaders were emphatic: the PLO. For the Israelis, this was unthinkable. The PLO was a terrorist organization. They would not sit with its representatives.

If nothing else, sitting with the PLO would signal that Israel accepted the PLO agenda of independence and statehood. So the Israelis did not want to deal with the Palestinians as a discrete issue.

By the mid-1980s, few Israelis would have been willing to embrace Golda Meir's 1969 assertion that the Palestinians did not exist as a people. Nonetheless, most influential Israelis hoped to deal with them in connection with the Jordanians. Solve the problem of the West Bank with Jordan, they reasoned, and the Palestinian problem would be solved as well.

The PLO had its own policy of denial and rejection. Its charter called for the eradication of the Zionist entity (i.e., Israel); the departure from Palestine of all Jews who arrived after the Balfour Declaration; and the creation of a binational democratic state in which Palestinians would be the decisive majority and Jews a distinct minority.

Given the PLO's rejection of Israel and its commitment to terror, the United States was not willing to deal directly with Arafat or lesser representatives of the PLO at this time. Nonetheless, throughout the 1980s the State Department pressured Arab states (in particular Egypt, Saudi Arabia, Morocco, and Jordan) to persuade the PLO to accept UNSC resolutions 242 and 338—the essence of which was the call for negotiations on the principles of withdrawal from territories occupied in the 1967 war in return for peace for all states within secure and recognized borders. Those efforts typically came to naught as Arafat would hint at being ready to accept 242 and 338 only to retreat into ambiguity (indeed, the ambiguity that would allow him to tell his own constituency that he had not truly recognized Israel and its right to exist).

In 1985, Arafat, still politically weakened by the PLO's forced expulsion from Lebanon in 1982, agreed with King Hussein to form a joint Jordanian-PLO peace delegation based on three conditions: accept resolution 242; renounce terror; and explicitly recognize Israel's right to exist. Secretary of State Shultz was prepared, at least initially, to have the United States act as an intermediary between the joint Jordanian-PLO delegation and the Israeli delegation to open negotiations, but Arafat refused to fulfill the commitment he made to the King on these three conditions. As a result, King Hussein renounced his understanding with Arafat, talks were postponed indefinitely, and the stalemate on peacemaking deepened. However, three developments—the demise of the Soviet Union, the Gulf War, and the first Palestinian Intifada—combined to break the stalemate and create a new context for U.S. diplomacy.

| THE NEW CONTEXT FOR DIPLOMACY |

With the demise of the Soviet Union, the Arab world lost its principal military patron and its chief military option. The Syrians and others doubted—even during the period of perceived Soviet strength—that they could defeat Israel in war, especially with Egypt out of any coalition. But the possession of advanced Soviet arms and Soviet backing gave them leverage against Israel, and of course against the United States, and the threat of Arab force remained credible. During President Asad's trip to Moscow in 1987, however, President Gorbachev, as part of his "new thinking," declared that the Soviet Union would not back the Syrian military concept of "strategic parity" with Israel.

President Asad got the message. Only the Soviet Union had the wherewithal to make Syria's strategic military parity with Israel even a theoretical possibility.

It is here that one can see the roots of Asad's decision to join the Gulf coalition against Saddam Hussein and Iraq. Asad seemed to see the geopolitical trend: the Soviet Union was in decline, and the United States in the ascendancy.

To be sure, Saddam Hussein was Asad's rival, competing for the mantle of Arab nationalist leader as the two incessantly plotted against each other. But in meetings with Secretary of State James Baker in 1990 after the Iraqi invasion of Kuwait, Asad was at pains to say that it was not a simple thing to join the coalition arrayed against Saddam, especially if it meant the use of force by outsiders against a "brother Arab." Surely, by emphasizing the difficulties with his public, Asad hoped that the United States (and the wealthy Gulf states) would feel obliged to reward him financially for joining the coalition. But that could not have been the whole story.

A reward alone would have been unlikely to persuade Asad to run potential risks internally—particularly given his allergy to even hints of unrest then appearing in Damascus. He sought something more: a relationship with the United States so that we might use our leverage to get his country's land back from Israel.

In the meetings we had with Asad after the Iraqi invasion and before the war in January 1991, Asad stressed the U.S. duty to address Arab-Israeli peace after reversing Iraqi aggression. He was not alone in arguing that if we forged a coalition for war, we should also have a coalition for peace after the war. Indeed, this became part of the U.S. mantra in justifying the coalition against Saddam. Once we had reversed Saddam's aggression, the thinking went, we would be able to tackle the Arab-Israeli issue.

Arafat, ever the one to focus on the pressures of the moment and the politics of the street, did not see the larger geopolitical trends. Unlike Asad, he supported Saddam— seeing his popularity among Arab publics for his defiance of the West. But his choice had devastating consequences for the Palestinians. Feeling betrayed, the Kuwaitis, Saudis, and others expelled hundreds of thousands of Palestinians from the Gulf. Once again Palestinians faced the upheaval of exile, with lost homes, jobs, and security. Arafat, too, lost his main financial base and political support.

Asad's choice put him in the center of post–Gulf War diplomacy. Arafat's choice relegated him to the sidelines. Even prior to the war, Arafat was not riding a winning streak.

The first Intifada, which began at the end of 1987, took Arafat by surprise. Here were Palestinians in the territories resisting Israeli occupation and capturing the attention—and sympathy—of the world. Here were the Palestinians in the West Bank, Gaza, and East Jerusalem organizing, planning, and guiding the resistance. Where was Arafat? Where was the PLO?

Naturally, Arafat tried to translate what was happening on the ground into at least a symbolic gain for the Palestinians. Ironically, his need to prove his relevancy led him to act out of character: he made a decision that was controversial in the world of the Palestinians who lived outside the territories. In November 1988, he engineered the PLO's adoption of the Algiers Declaration, which called for a two-state solution to the conflict with Israel. Forty years after rejecting the partition plan, the Palestinians were now ready to accept a Jewish state alongside an Arab state. With this threshold crossed, it was not a great leap for Arafat to accept American terms for the opening of a dialogue with the United States.

For the Reagan administration, this was a long-sought opening, and Secretary of State Shultz, in the waning days of the Reagan administration, seized it. In return for the PLO's recognition of UNSC resolutions 242 and 338, Secretary Shultz in December 1988 authorized a dialogue with the PLO. But Shultz circumscribed the dialogue, restricting U.S. contact with the PLO to our embassy in Tunis and forbidding contact with Arafat or other leading members of the PLO Executive Committee. We might now be able to talk to the PLO officially, but political-level meetings were not yet "kosher."

The Intifada clearly affected Arafat. But it also affected the Israelis; for the first time they saw the high cost of continued occupation. Not only did the anti-Intifada mission blacken Israel's image internationally; the Israeli military also did not like the mission—reservists did not like firing on Palestinian youth, did not like serving in Palestinian cities, and saw themselves as preserving occupation, not defending Israel. Accordingly, Israel Defence Forces (IDF) officers began to tell the Israeli press that there was no military answer to the Intifada. There could only be a political answer.

| MY ROLE |

As the days of the Reagan administration wound down, I saw the IDF attitude presaging a change in Israel's approach to the Palestinians. I saw the Arafat acceptance of 242/338 as indicating new possibilities with the Palestinians. And I saw Gorbachev's "new thinking" as likely to reduce competition with the Soviets in the Middle East, in-evitably removing one of the major impediments to making progress between Arabs and Israelis. These were not simply abstract or academic perceptions on my part. I was deter-mined to find ways to act on them. And, as someone about to play a leading role in pol-icymaking in the incoming Bush administration, I would soon be in a position to do so.

How did I come to assume such a role? I had gotten to know then Vice President George Bush while working on the National Security Council (NSC) staff. My initial positions in the government were in the Defense and State Departments. I had left the government in 1984 for the University of California, where I ran a joint graduate stu-dent program between Berkeley and Stanford on Soviet International Behavior. But I was offered the senior Middle East position on the NSC staff and joined the White House in June 1986.

The NSC staff plays a coordinating role between the government agencies on pol-icy and supports the President directly in preparing him for meetings with foreign lead-ers or for foreign trips. Naturally, it also supports the Vice President. When Vice President Bush took a trip to Egypt, Israel, and Jordan in July 1986, I accompanied him.

The State Department traditionally looks to the Vice President to perform cere-monial tasks on such trips. But this Vice President felt he had something to contribute in foreign policy. His leading staff members—Craig Fuller, Fred Khedouri, and Mar-lin Fitzwater—were thinking in terms of the elections in 1988 and wanted him to look presidential. And I saw the potential for a limited but real diplomatic achievement.

As I first explained to Fred Khedouri, Bush's Deputy Chief of Staff, the unique po-litical situation in Israel had created an interesting confluence of interests among Israel, Egypt, and Jordan. Within weeks the Israeli Prime Minister, Shimon Peres, would ex-change offices with Foreign Minister Yitzhak Shamir as part of a rotation agreement that resulted from a dead-heat election and the formation of a national unity govern-ment in 1984. President Mubarak and King Hussein saw Shamir as an Israeli extrem-ist and would wish to constrain him as Prime Minister. So would the moderate Peres, who would also want guidelines for peace negotiations that would allow him to play an active role as Foreign Minister. Because Shamir was convinced that Peres was loath to exchange offices, I argued that he would not want to give Peres an easy pretext for void-ing the rotation agreement (such as allowing Peres to claim that Shamir was blocking an opportunity for peace).

In light of this, I suggested that the Vice President should try to put together a statement of common principles that Israel, Egypt, and Jordan would accept. Such a statement would bring Jordan openly into an agreement with Israel for the first time, and set guidelines for any future Arab-Israeli negotiations. Fred was convinced and arranged for me to make my case to the Vice President on the flight.

Vice President Bush liked the idea, but doubted that it would be possible. Nonetheless, he agreed to pursue it, and in fact made it a centerpiece of his discussions with each leader. Sure enough, we reached agreement on a common statement.

From that point, the Vice President asked me to brief him periodically; Craig and Fred asked me to write themes for general foreign policy speeches; and Bob Teeter, the Vice President's pollster and chief political advisor, asked me to outline what I believed were the big issues facing the United States in foreign policy in the years ahead.

In June 1988, with the Vice President certain to be the Republican nominee for President, Craig and Bob asked me to join the Bush campaign as the chief foreign policy advisor. Leaving aside the fact that the Vice President was trailing Michael Dukakis badly in the polls, I was ambivalent. Though I was in the Reagan White House as the senior advisor on Arab-Israeli issues—a position seen as more professional than partisan—I was a lifelong Democrat. All my campaign experiences had been working for Democrats. I had met many of my best friends in those campaigns. I had even met my wife, Debbie, in one such campaign.

My closest friends from my earlier political days—Terry Friedman, then a Democratic state legislator in California, and Harley Frankel, then a businessman active in Democratic politics—both said it would be a big mistake, and argued: "Bush is going to lose. Don't do it."

But I felt differently. I liked the Vice President. I thought highly of him. I was comfortable with his views on foreign policy, and I was not convinced he was going to lose. Should he win, I would have my pick of jobs, and would also be able to bring good people into key foreign policy positions.

That is what happened. After Bush's victory, both Brent Scowcroft, who would be the National Security Advisor, and James Baker, who would be the Secretary of State, each wanted me to go with them: Scowcroft as Deputy National Security Advisor; Baker as head of his Policy Planning Staff. The President-elect told me I should take whichever job I wanted most. While the position with Scowcroft was more prestigious, I wanted to be with Baker at the State Department.

It controlled all the day-to-day mechanisms of diplomacy. Cables drafted in the department would convey instructions to ambassadors. Cables sent to the envoys shaped negotiations. From the White House, one might be able to influence those cables and might even be added to a State Department delegation for negotiations—as I was when I was at the NSC—but it was clear the real work of diplomacy was done at State.*

---

*There, of course, had been one area during the Reagan administration in which the NSC staff had assumed an operational responsibility. That had produced the disaster of the Iran-contra af-

Moreover, James Baker promised to be a force in international diplomacy. While I knew that President-elect Bush would be far more engaged in foreign policy than President Reagan (and that this would make the Deputy National Security Advisor a vital figure), I believed that Baker would drive foreign policy. I had seen him operate in the campaign. He exuded authority. He quickly brought order to most discussions. He put a premium on identifying clear and practical objectives. He asked the right questions, and he had good intuitive judgment.

No one would be closer to the President than Baker. That would give him great authority within the administration and internationally. And he was a doer. While clearly tough-minded, he was not dogmatic and would be open to new thinking—something I felt was required at a historical point in which great changes in the international system seemed likely.

Robert Zoellick, who had served under Baker when he was the Secretary of the Treasury and then in the Bush campaign, told me that Baker operated by investing great trust and responsibility in a very few aides. While it was rare for people to win Baker's trust quickly, Bob told me that I had done so.

Still, before signing on with Baker, I had one question: Would I be free to shape U.S. policy in the two areas that mattered most to me: the Arab-Israeli conflict and the Soviet Union? Baker was quick to tell me I would have the lead on these issues—and whatever else I felt was important.

And he was true to his word. While he was Secretary, two behaviors were certain to trigger his legendary anger: questioning his word or going back on yours.

Baker was also extremely sensitive to avoiding any appearance of a conflict between himself and the President, and would overreact to dispel even the suggestion of a conflict. This is what produced Baker's notorious declaration that when the Israelis were serious about peace, "the telephone number is 1-202-456-1414," the number for the White House switchboard. At a session of the House International Affairs Committee, Congressman Mel Levine lauded Baker for his efforts to bring about an Israeli-Palestinian dialogue, but then went on to fault President Bush for derailing our initiative with his public criticism of Israeli settlement building in East Jerusalem. I was sitting behind Baker, and I knew how he might respond; hoping to preempt that, I gave the Secretary a note suggesting he say that Mel was wrong and that it was the parties, not the President, who had failed to do what was needed. But that was not nearly strong enough for the Secretary. He would make sure that no one could say he did not

---

fair; recommendations for keeping the NSC staff out of operational matters had been put in place as a result.

stand with the President—and would do so by making a statement bound to produce headlines that would divert the attention away from the President and onto the Israelis.

In the world of Washington policymaking, where jealousy is part of the culture and knocking people off their pedestals seems to be relished, Baker would never allow a gap to appear between himself and his boss. That was a good object lesson, and one I applied for the rest of my tenure. This did not mean one could not argue with the boss. Indeed, Baker had surrounded himself with strong-minded aides who were expected to tell him when he was wrong.

As the Bush administration took charge, Baker counted on me to educate him on the Soviet Union, arms control, and the Middle East. Over time, he was to educate me in the art of negotiating. I could not have had a better teacher.

| SHAPING THE BUSH ADMINISTRATION STRATEGY FOR ARAB-ISRAELI PEACE |

From the beginning, Baker had one proviso for Middle East policy: he didn't want to be "flying around the region the way Shultz did." He would not go to the Middle East unless there was a chance of real progress—a point he made to every Middle Eastern leader who came to Washington in the spring of 1989.

Given the circumstances, there was little point in Baker visiting the area. While the Intifada had created pressures for a diplomatic solution, the Israelis and Palestinians still had fundamental disagreements on Jerusalem, borders, sovereignty, and refugees; and their views of the shape of any negotiating process were also completely at odds. As if that were not enough, the daily violence spoiled the environment for peacemaking. As I told Baker, you need "heroes for dramatic breakthroughs"—Sadat, for example—and there were no heroes in the region.

In a strategy paper, I proposed a two-phased approach: first, a prenegotiation phase designed to change the environment, and then a negotiation phase focused on how to devolve Israeli responsibility to the Palestinians in the West Bank and Gaza. Once the Israeli military government had been dissolved and Palestinian self-rule had been established, it would become possible to negotiate the core issues of Jerusalem, borders, and sovereignty.

Fundamentally, I was trying to get away from the grandiose and focus on the practical. Real people were suffering in the West Bank and Gaza. Palestinians had to see their day-to-day conditions change. While Shamir would not deal with Arafat or the PLO, he had an interest in showing that he could work out new arrangements with the Palestinians in the territories. Conversely, Arafat had an interest in being able to take credit for any positive changes in the territories. Each of them, I argued, faced a risk in our approach, but a bigger risk in letting the situation get any worse.

With this in mind, I proposed a "mutually reinforcing set of steps" in the territories. We should ask the Israelis to release teenage prisoners from the Ketziot jail, lift the military sieges and sweeps of villages, and relax restrictions on commercial activity. We should ask the Palestinians to establish local cease-fires, engage in regular discussions with Israeli officials, and end the strikes called in the Palestinian cities that inevitably led to clashes with the Israeli military. These measures, I wrote the Secretary, "not discussion of abstract principles or a vague international conference, will determine the value of our dialogue with the PLO."

I had not ruled out an international peace conference. In fact, I suggested that the prenegotiation phase might conclude with elections in the territories, which would produce a delegation of Palestinians elected to negotiate with the Israelis at "a properly structured international conference."

I describe this strategy paper in some detail not only because many of its concepts were embodied in the subsequent agreements but because of its emphasis on changing the realities on the ground: reducing violence, transforming attitudes, building confidence, and showing that each side could make commitments and deliver on them. Throughout my tenure, I was constantly preoccupied with dealing with the practicalities and conditions of the Israeli-Palestinian relationship—and improving them.

Baker accepted the strategy and began in early February to seek the support of European leaders. Meanwhile, with Prime Minister Shamir coming to Washington in March, the Secretary authorized me to open a "private channel" to the Israelis, and I saw Eli Rubinstein in February.

In February 1989, Eli was an aide to Shamir, and there was no one closer to the Prime Minister. I had first met him the 1980s when he was the deputy chief of mission in the Israeli Embassy in Washington. He was a disciple of Moshe Dayan and was part of the Israeli team at Camp David with Prime Minister Begin. Twenty-two years later, he went with Prime Minister Barak to Camp David again. He is a man of many parts: a lawyer, religiously observant, instinctively conservative, a family man with four daughters, never at a loss for words, with an enormous capacity for work—and a wonderful sense of humor.

We met alone in my office in the State Department. In diplomacy, it is a good idea to learn your interlocutor's position before revealing your own—so as to keep something in reserve. Not surprisingly, Eli was reluctant to talk about Israeli plans, but with prodding, he relented and explained that the Prime Minister was prepared to relax some restrictions on the Palestinians in the territories, and to think about ways to give Palestinians some greater role in their own governance, if the Palestinians would stop the Intifada and the United States would promise not to stage an international conference.

I addressed the last point first. "Look, Eli," I said, "taking steps on the ground that ease the conditions is good, but the Intifada is not going to stop unless there is a political pathway."

What did I have in mind? Eli asked. I went over the elements (the prenegotiation and negotiation phases) I had discussed with Baker, stressing that we needed the Israelis to show they were prepared to try to "address Palestinian rights." I added that we could not beat something with nothing. If you don't like the international conference idea, if you don't like our approach, I said, make sure the Prime Minister comes to Washington with a credible initiative.

Eli got the message, and Shamir came with an initiative. It had several parts: strengthening Egyptian-Israeli peace; initiating direct negotiations with the other Arab states and ending the state of war; planning an international "endeavor" to deal with the refugee issue by improving their "living conditions" in the territories; and planning elections for Palestinians who would negotiate with them.

From our standpoint, the elections component of Shamir's initiative was the most useful; from theirs, the Arab states and refugee components were. They sought to shift the agenda to Arab state recognition of Israel and to transform the refugee issue into a humanitarian, not political, problem. Understandable; however, after telling Shamir we would make an effort to push all the elements of the initiative, I told him we would have few takers for the items he most wanted, but we could sell elections.

"Selling" became part of our modus operandi—beginning a pattern that would characterize our approach throughout the Bush and Clinton years. We would take Israeli ideas or ideas that the Israelis could live with and work them over—trying to increase their attractiveness to the Arabs while trying to get the Arabs to scale back their expectations. Why did this pattern emerge? The realities dictated it.

Because the Israelis held the territories, they were on the giving end; as Rabin would tell me later, "We give, they get." The Arabs, for their part, believed they were getting what was rightfully theirs, so they wanted the Israelis to give and they wanted us to produce the giving.

This tended to make two-way negotiations difficult. The Israelis would try to minimize the scope of any idea, assuming correctly that we would inevitably build on the idea, even transform it, as we tried to sell it to the Arabs or the Palestinians, who constantly tried to maximize whatever we offered.

That was the case on the elections initiative that we pursued from the spring of 1989 until the Israeli national unity government collapsed in March 1990. Shamir wanted to hold elections among Palestinians in the territories, and whoever was elected could then talk to Israelis about limited autonomy. We wanted to create an engagement between Israelis and Palestinians, using a dialogue on elections to focus not only on the conditions under which elections would be held but also to address the agenda for postelections negotiations. We had in mind the beginnings of a political process that could affect the realities on the ground—otherwise there would not be an environment for elections—while also involving the Shamir government in discussions on responding to Palestinian needs and devolving Israeli control.

If we were trying to expand the Shamir initiative to give it much more political content, the PLO in Tunis was trying to transform it entirely: the PLO representatives in Tunis offered to accept the elections initiative only if the Israelis withdrew from the territories and accepted Palestinian statehood before the elections. In other words, forget negotiations, meet our strategic objectives, and we will accept elections—not peace.

This was ridiculous and we told the PLO representatives in Tunis so. There was little point in having a dialogue with them if they were not going to respond realistically to ideas that we raised. No doubt the PLO approach was motivated, in part, by the desire to put pressure on Palestinians in the territories not to get out front of them.

In May, the Secretary sent me to the area. I met with an impressive group of Palestinians from the West Bank, Gaza, and East Jerusalem. They were quick to say that only "Tunis" (the PLO) could speak for them, but changed their tune when I said that was a prescription for leading nowhere. Then they began to engage seriously: What would have to happen on the ground before elections could be held? Would the Israelis change their behaviors before or during the election period? Would East Jerusalemites be able to vote and to run for office, especially given Israeli claims on all of Jerusalem?

Their very questions proved that the elections initiative could launch a meaningful process, provided I told them that they were prepared to engage first with the Israelis on the basis of the elections initiative itself. In doing so, I hoped to build pressure on Arafat and the PLO by letting those in the territories know what they had to gain.

Although I saw Prime Minister Shamir on this trip, the most important meeting I had in Israel was with Dan Meridor, the Minister of Justice. Dan's father, along with Menachem Begin, had been one of the founders of the Herut Party, the forerunner of Likud. Dan was anointed as one of the "princes" of Likud, was close to Begin, and served as his cabinet secretary. He was known in Israel as a man of principle; though he was ideologically a product of the Revisionist school, he was practical and a problem-solver.

We met, just the two of us, at the King David Hotel, not to negotiate but to informally exchange views. I told Dan what I had done with the Palestinians.

I was surprised by his response. It was not the PLO that was the problem per se, he said, it was the difference in agenda between the PLO in Tunis and the Palestinians who lived in the territories: "We can deal with the internal PLO; indeed, we must be able to live with them. But we cannot deal with the external PLO because their aim is to eradicate Israel. They can never give up the 'right of return' for the refugees and that is the end of the state of Israel. If you legitimize the external PLO in your dialogue or you give them a role in this process, you will legitimize their agenda."

Dan's position raised two questions. First, would the "internal PLO" be prepared to engage in the search for a political solution without the external PLO's sanction— and if not, wouldn't we have to find a way to gain the PLO's approval? Second, did Shamir really share this view? Dan had no clear answer; the only possibility he saw was that elections and negotiations would produce meaningful responses to Palestinian needs, thus building the insiders' authority. Negotiations, of course, would require Shamir to address Palestinian political aspirations. Here Dan, at least implicitly, was accepting Palestinian statehood. Dan left no doubt that he was way out in front of Shamir. Nonetheless, this told me that in Likud—the right wing in Israel—there were those who might be ready to move further than I had thought.

| EGYPT ENTERS THE FRAY |

We now had an initiative, but we could not get the PLO leaders to "authorize" the Palestinians in the territories to embrace it. Instead, they insisted that the PLO take part in any preelection dialogue; that the dialogue take place under the UN's aegis; and that statehood be on the agenda.

After working on the elections initiative throughout the spring, Secretary Baker informed the Egyptians in June that without a credible response by the Palestinians, there was little point in our proceeding. Should the PLO think they could kill this initiative and get an international conference, they were wrong. We would oppose it.

President Mubarak said he would work to change the PLO's position, and sent Osama al-Baz, his chief aide, to Tunis to work with the Palestinians. Osama, who had been with Sadat at Camp David, was brilliant, capable of anticipating any argument one might make. He knew Arafat and the PLO leadership better than any other senior Egyptian official. I saw Osama before he went to Tunis, and told him that if he wanted us to persist he needed "to get us something to work with."

Quietly, Osama began to work not only with the Palestinians but also with some on the Labor side of the Israeli unity government, such as Nimrod Novik, who were more forward-leaning on Palestinian needs than Shamir.

His efforts led after nearly two months to Egypt declaring a "ten-point" plan setting down the conditions in which the elections should be conducted. They spelled out who was eligible to vote and run in the elections, namely, all Palestinians in the West Bank, Gaza, and East Jerusalem. They called for international super-vision of the elections. They called for the elections to be part of efforts based on key principles, including "territory for peace." They called for a "halt to settlement con-struction."

Each of these points was neuralgic for Shamir, but not necessarily for all his Labor partners in the government. The aim of some like Nimrod Novik was to "expose" Shamir on peace as either for or against. Either real progress would be made or the unity government would fall over Shamir's opposition to peace, something likely to benefit the Labor Party.*

I wanted Osama to produce a response, and he had. Even so, collusion with some in Labor—which would become a pattern of Egyptian behavior—confronted us with a dilemma.

Shamir, given his access to Israeli intelligence reports, would know of Labor's role in producing the ten points. Were we to embrace them, he would see us as part of a ca-bal to trap him, and we would lose the ability to move the Israeli Prime Minister. Were we not to embrace them, the Egyptians would be left hanging.

We took the only position we could: that there should be discussion on how to reconcile the ten points with the Israeli initiative. That proved difficult, but the ten points did make the elections—and not an international conference—the focal point of all diplomatic efforts.

| COULD WE GET TO ELECTIONS? |

Now we—with me in the lead on the U.S. team—turned to creating a preelection dialogue between the Israelis and Palestinians in the territories. Mubarak, again, cre-ated an opening in a message to President Bush; in early September he conveyed that the PLO was ready to soften its terms dramatically and authorize, with a few condi-tions, a delegation of Palestinians from the territories to meet with an Israeli delegation to discuss the elections proposal.

This looked promising, and Secretary Baker told the Egyptian Foreign Minister, Esmat Abdel Meguid, that we would try to get the Israelis to accept it, provided we pre-served the fiction that the PLO was not responsible for the dialogue.

---

*I say some because Yitzhak Rabin, the Labor Minister of Defense, sent me a private message at the time saying he did not believe Israel could accept the ten points "as drafted." He, for one, did not like including East Jerusalemites as candidates in the election—it would open the Jerusalem issue and he felt it was premature to do so.

At the same time, Baker told Moshe Arens, the Israeli Foreign Minister, that a dialogue with the Palestinians from the territories required PLO acquiescence. The critical questions to resolve became: Would the Israelis accept some Palestinians expelled from the territories in the delegation? Would the Palestinians be able to raise the ten points in the discussions? Would Egypt be able to play a role in the conduct of the talks? And would the United States be present in the talks as an observer?

While not enthusiastic, Arens was ready to respond favorably to each of these questions, with the exception of the composition of the Palestinian delegation. He needed reassurance that the Palestinians would neither include terrorists in the group nor insert known PLO figures from the outside—transforming the delegation into a PLO delegation.

With both Arens and Meguid coming to New York for the UN General Assembly session in late September, I suggested a trilateral meeting to reach agreement on all the issues, including especially Arens's concerns on the composition of the Palestinian delegation. I joined Baker and each issue was resolved, with an understanding that we would work actively with Egypt and Israel to come up with a list of Palestinians that Israel could accept.

Then Arens raised the issue of Egypt's work with the Labor side of the Israeli government. "This cannot continue," he said. "It is wrong, it is counterproductive, and it is complicating the political situation in Israel." There was a very pregnant pause—with Baker and me exchanging glances, wondering how Meguid would respond. Meguid simply said, "Misha, we will work with all the parts of the Israeli government," and Arens responded: "You say it, I accept it."

Arens had made his point. If this initiative was to have any chance of working, neither he nor Shamir could be excluded.

We left the meeting hopeful. But Meguid soon found that the PLO had its own ideas. Arafat wanted to choose the delegation, not subject it to Israeli veto, although Baker had made it clear—and Meguid had accepted— that Israel would be allowed to vet the list.

The process was gridlocked again. To overcome this latest deadlock, I proposed that we would allow Israelis to choose from a pool of Palestinian names. (The pool would consist of Palestinians we had met with, Israeli officials had met with, and those the Egyptians suggested.)

Even as this seemed to clear one hurdle, we were soon confronting another: notwithstanding Meguid's promise, the collusion between the Egyptians and Labor Party members had not stopped and now produced a crisis in the Israeli government. When Shimon Peres's colleagues suggested to Osama al-Baz that Egypt simply issue an invitation for the beginning of the dialogue in Cairo, Mubarak did so, inviting the Israelis to come and begin a dialogue with a ten-member Palestinian delegation that included a small number of Palestinians from outside the territories. Peres, as leader of the Labor faction in the government, insisted that the cabinet vote on the invitation.

But the Cabinet deadlocked 6 to 6 on the Egyptian invitation. The tie constituted a rejection and triggered a coalition crisis, not the beginning of a dialogue. Now Arens, fearing the breakup of the unity government, called Baker and pleaded with him to present a plan based on our discussions in New York. He believed that Labor would not be able to quit the government if there were an active peace initiative.

I drafted five points, drawing on the New York discussion and reflecting what I believed each side could accept. These became known as the Baker "five points":

—Egyptian-Israeli agreement that an Israeli delegation should conduct a dialogue with a Palestinian delegation in Cairo;
—U.S. recognition that Egypt could not substitute itself for the Palestinians and would consult with the Palestinians on all aspects of the dialogue;
—U.S. understanding that Israel would attend the dialogue only after a satisfactory list of Palestinians had been worked out;
—U.S. understanding that Israel would come to the dialogue based on its "initiative."* The Palestinians would come to the dialogue prepared to discuss elections and negotiations in accordance with the Israeli initiative, but would be free to raise issues for how to be successful in each;
—U.S. hosting of a meeting of the Israeli and Egyptian Foreign Ministers in Washington to facilitate the process.

We thought the five points gave each side an explanation and plenty of cover. But Shamir was not happy with them, feeling they were vague and open-ended—and he said so to the Israeli press. At Baker's urging, President Bush called Shamir, challenging him to stand by his own initiative. Shamir told the President that he wanted to proceed but wanted some modifications to the points. Baker was not willing to work with the Israeli modifications until he knew whether the Egyptians would also ask for changes.

Sure enough, Meguid did. We were back in the souk, operating it from long distance over the phone. I knew we would be stuck unless we could get one side to say yes

---

*Shamir presented to his cabinet the initiative he had outlined to us in Washington. This became known as the May 14 initiative—referring to the day it was adopted by the Israeli cabinet.

to the five points, thus putting pressure on the other side. I focused on getting a yes from the Israelis.

One thing I had found: getting things done required my own private channel. The keys to such a channel were trust and delivery. Each had to protect the confidences of the other, and each had to be able to deliver something on behavior. With the Soviets, I had one with Sergei Tarasenko, the Soviet Foreign Minister's closest advisor. With the Israelis, I was to develop several. I turned to Salai Meridor, Dan's younger brother and Arens's right-hand man.

Fearing that both Baker and the President were about to give up on the dialogue— in no small part because they had become fed up with Shamir—I told Salai we needed an Israeli "yes" to the Baker points. "Don't try to negotiate on them; if you need some assurances on the side about how we interpret the points, that's something we can probably do."

Salai promised to see what he could do, saying the best we could hope for was cabinet approval with reservations. I felt we could manage that.

We needed Shamir to know that he was on the verge of losing both the President and the Secretary, and he needed to hear that from someone he trusted. Consequently, I worked one other channel. Max Fisher was a leading Jewish philanthropist who had given and raised large amounts of money for projects in Israel. A Republican, he had served Presidents Nixon and Ford as a channel to Israeli leaders, particularly Prime Minister Rabin during the tense period of the "reassessment" in 1975.* Max was discreet, and spoke nearly every Saturday to Shamir. I told him what we were thinking. And he did convey the message—and I believe Shamir got it. The result: the Israeli cabinet voted to approve the Baker proposals with reservations.

Now the Egyptians went back to work on the PLO, but in a way that almost stopped the process. It happened at a press conference in Cairo. Ignoring the fact that the PLO could not be seen publicly as the arbiter of the five points, President Mubarak, asked to comment on them, said: "It is not up to Egypt to decide on Baker's proposals, but to the PLO. . . . It is, therefore, up to the PLO to approve or disapprove these proposals. . . . Once they come up with a view or an opinion, we adopt it in our talks with the United States and Israel."

---

*When Rabin was unwilling to accept Kissinger's terms for brokering a second interim agreement in the Sinai, Kissinger persuaded President Ford that we would need a "reassessment"—a term read as a reassessment of our relationship with Israel. The reassessment was designed to pressure Rabin to be more flexible, and within a relatively short time Kissinger was able to mediate the second disengagement agreement between Egypt and Israel.

This may have been Mubarak's way of putting pressure on Arafat to say yes or no. But Shamir saw it as proof of Egypt's bad faith. Several weeks later, when providing the answer to the five points, the Egyptians again sought to do so in unacceptable terms— revealing, I suspected, less their desire to be seen as putting pressure on the PLO and more their interest in avoiding responsibility.

We were in Malta for a summit between President Bush and President Gorbachev. At 2 a.m., Frank Wisner, the U.S. ambassador to Egypt, cabled me Meguid's response on the five points—again, it was not an Egyptian response but a PLO response, literally quoting a full text of a decision by the PLO Central Committee. Without waking Baker, I instructed Ambassador Wisner to tell Meguid there were only two choices now: either say that "Egypt, having consulted with the Palestinians, accepted the Baker proposals," or simply let us announce that we had agreement from Egypt and make no statement. Meguid chose the latter.

We now had two "yeses" to the Baker proposals. But one thing I was beginning to learn about dealing in this process—about dealing with Middle Eastern parties—was that every advance brought new problems. The Israelis did not want outsiders in the delegation. The Palestinians insisted on both outsiders and an East Jerusalemite on the delegation. The East Jerusalemite represented the Palestinian claim to East Jerusalem; his exclusion implied, in their eyes, that they were surrendering their right to East Jerusalem. For the Israelis, such inclusion suggested that they might compromise on the unity of Jerusalem.

We overcame this problem with the help of Yitzhak Rabin, who traveled to Washington in January 1990. Prior to seeing Secretary Baker, he floated two solutions in a private meeting with me: one was to solve the outsider issue by allowing two deportees to return and be on the Palestinian delegation. The other was to invite a "dual addressee"—one of the many Palestinians who lived in East Jerusalem but maintained an address outside of the city. What did I think?

I liked both ideas, but I doubted Shamir would. Rabin told me Shamir would, but he did not want to raise them with Baker if I thought they would not fly. Now I had an idea. Osama al-Baz, the Egyptian, also happened to be in town. Why not raise them with him?

Rabin was fine with this, but Baker was not. He did not trust Shamir. Before having me go to Osama, he wanted to know that Shamir accepted the Rabin ideas. So Baker called Shamir to ask whether he was familiar with the ideas Rabin had raised with us. He was. Did he have a problem if we tried them out on the Egyptians? He did not.

I went to see Osama, and he, too, liked the ideas, but asked for two or three days to find out if the Palestinians would accept them. Three days later he called me and in his high-pitched voice said: "Dennis, we persuaded them. But Arafat is under a lot of pressure, and we need to move now."

I took this to mean that Arafat's acceptance was tenuous and easily undone. Now I joined Baker as he called Israel. When Baker told Shamir the "good news"—the Egyptians had agreed—"and I believe we can move quickly now," Shamir said he needed to wait until after an upcoming Likud Party conference. Let's "not rush," he said. Instead he proposed to have Misha Arens come to Washington to work out the ideas with the secretary.

To make sure the Baker-Arens meeting would succeed, I suggested that Salai come to Washington the day before Arens so we could work on a precise formula to embrace the Rabin ideas. He agreed and we met at my house in Bethesda the evening before the meeting.

I was to use my house frequently for meetings. It created privacy and informality. More importantly, it made everything more personal. Somehow it was impolite to be combative in someone's home—both for the guest and for the host.

While not wasting much time going over how we had arrived at this point, Salai made it clear that Arens wanted the meeting with Baker to succeed. That meant agreeing on a formula for representation on the Palestinian delegation that would not expose Israel.

Salai then shocked me, telling me that he was not so sure that Shamir accepted the Rabin ideas. How could that be? I said, incredulous. Why would Shamir acknowledge the ideas and then let us raise them with the Egyptians?

Salai was not sure, but wanted me not to take Shamir's acceptance as a given. But that created a problem: our formula had to be able to cover the Rabin ideas or we were nowhere and "Misha will have come for nothing and is likely to take the heat from Baker."

With this in mind, we fashioned a formula posed in the form of a question that met Arens's criterion of not exposing Israel while being consistent with what Rabin had raised and we had conveyed to Egypt: "As regards the participants in the Israeli-Palestinian dialogue, would the government of Israel be ready to consider on a name-by-name basis any Palestinian who was a resident of the territories?" This formula ensured that Israel would not be surprised. Moreover, "resident of the territories" covered both the outsider and East Jerusalemite issues: the deportees allowed to return would be residents again, but a Palestinian resident of the territories would not have a Jerusalem identity card, and thus would not be, in Israeli eyes, a resident of East Jerusalem. (For the Israelis, East Jerusalem was formally part of Israel, not part of the West Bank; Palestinians in Jerusalem were thus treated differently and given Jerusalem identity cards.) There clearly were prominent Palestinians who worked in East Jerusalem but maintained an address outside of Jerusalem—and so did not have an East Jerusalem identity card. If challenged on having a Jerusalemite on the Palestinian delegation, Shamir could say that person did not have a Jerusalem identity card and Palestinians could say "everyone knows that person is a Jerusalemite."

Salai and I concluded our evening with the pledge that we would get our respective bosses to accept this formula. While Arens personally accepted it, he said he had to consult with the big three in the unity government—Shamir, Peres, and Rabin—and would let Baker know once he had done so.

As it turned out, Arens could not deliver Shamir. Shamir was shortly to use President Bush's criticism of Israeli settlement activity in East Jerusalem as a pretext for announcing that he could not support the American proposals. Peres pushed for a cabinet vote, and given Arens's support, Likud split; the cabinet approved the formula while Prime Minister Shamir voted against it.

In response, Peres pushed for a vote of no confidence in the Knesset, and when the Shas religious party abstained in the vote, the unity government under Yitzhak Shamir fell.

There were no tears in Washington over its demise. Shamir's opposition to the dialogue confirmed what Bush and Baker believed—namely, that he had been stringing us along. Peres was much more in favor of taking steps for peace, and had the votes to form a government. We believed that real progress could be made now.

There was only one problem. Peres failed to put together a new government. On the day of the scheduled Knesset vote to install the new government, ninety-six-year-old ultra-orthodox Rabbi Shach inveighed against joining a Peres-led government, and two of the members of the Aguda Party (an Orthodox religious party) said they would not vote for Peres—and he lost his majority. After three months of wrangling, Shamir, not Peres, was able to form a new government, one dominated by rightist and religious parties and once again led by Yitzhak Shamir—a man no longer trusted in Washington.

Shortly after taking office again, Shamir sent messages to the White House and the State Department emphasizing that he was serious about pursuing peace. No one in Washington—no one in the State Department or the White House—believed him. On August 2, 1990, however, Saddam Hussein shifted our attention from peace to war.

| A COALITION FOR WAR BECOMES THE COALITION FOR PEACE |

Secretary Baker was in Irkutsk, Siberia, holding a ministerial meeting with Soviet Foreign Minister Eduard Shevardnadze when we received word that Iraq had invaded Kuwait. When Baker told him that the invasion was under way, Shevardnadze was initially disbelieving and later embarrassed to be caught unawares, particularly given the significant Soviet presence in Iraq.

Baker flew on to Mongolia as planned and I returned to Moscow on Shevardnadze's plane. There are times in life and in foreign policy when serendipity counts for more than planning. I had previously arranged to return to Moscow on Shevardnadze's plane so I could avoid going to Mongolia, and thus make it home for a weekend with my family.

But the flight and my presence in Moscow proved fortuitous. Based on a suggestion from a member of my staff, Peter Hauslohner, I decided to see if we could forge a common U.S.-Soviet response to the Iraqi invasion. Doing so would make it impossible for Saddam Hussein to play us off against each other and would deny others the opportunity to point to our differences as an excuse for not taking a position on the invasion.

Though it proved far more difficult than I had imagined, I was able to negotiate a joint U.S.-Soviet statement condemning the Iraqi invasion and declaring an embargo to undo it. Baker returned to Moscow and he and Shevardnadze issued it the day after the invasion. It put the United States and the Soviet Union on the same side against Iraq—a country that had been a leading Soviet client. It established the basis for the international and regional coalition against Iraq.

Over the next months of coalition building and maintenance—and through the weeks of the war itself—we built the consensus not only for war but also for the launching of a Middle East peace initiative following the conflict. Indeed, it became a given that once the Iraqi invasion and occupation of Kuwait was undone, we would make a serious effort to launch a peace process between Arabs and Israelis.

| SHAPING A NEW INITIATIVE, A NEW BEGINNING ON PEACE |

Even before we went to war with Iraq in January 1991, I began to think about how to shape an American initiative to launch a serious peace process afterward. It was not just that the United States had taken on an obligation to do so; it was also that I expected circumstances in the region to give us a fleeting opportunity to accomplish something once we defeated Iraq. Radicals would be discredited, Arafat would be weak, regional moderates would be ascendant, our standing and authority in the region would be unprecedented, and the Soviets would be on our side.

With my senior deputy, Bill Burns, and others, I wrestled with two questions: What should be done while these circumstances prevailed, and how should we go about it? In time, the "what" became "breaking the taboo on direct negotiations." After all, to make peace we had to overcome the prohibition against Arabs talking to Israelis. The "how" became a two-track approach to negotiations: parallel sets of talks between the Israelis and Palestinians from the territories on the one track and between Israel and the neighboring Arab states on the other.*

Once the war on Iraq was over, the logic of the two-track approach seemed overwhelming. Israel could not be expected to negotiate with Palestinians—who had cheered Iraqi Scud missile attacks on Israel—if it did not have the chance to achieve a broader peace with the Arab states; similarly, the Arab states could not be expected to negotiate with Israel unless Israelis were willing to do likewise with the Palestinians.

As important as it was to break the taboo on negotiations, we also needed to shape an environment that could either be conducive to negotiations or be destructive to them. In preparation for Secretary Baker's first trip to the region in early March 1991, I wrote a strategy paper for the Secretary that outlined steps that each side could take to signal the other that it was a new day.

The Arabs might:

—help to promote credible Palestinian leaders in the territories as negotiating partners with Israel;
—consider confidence-building measures in security (e.g., notification of exercises, changes in alert levels of forces, and troop movements);
—allow covert exchanges of intelligence with Israel on terrorism;
—permit meetings with unofficial Israelis (e.g., scholars, journalists);
—convey to countries like Japan that the secondary boycott of Israel would be dropped, and, in time, be ready to drop the primary economic boycott of Israel;
—drop credential challenges of Israel at the UN and in other international agencies, and be ready to reject the UN General Assembly resolution declaring that Zionism is racism;[†]
—declare that they no longer considered themselves in a state of war with Israel and were ready to normalize relations fully when a peace treaty was concluded.

---

*As early as the fall, I had held separate discussions with Tarasenko and Eitan Bentsur, who was Director General of the Israeli Foreign Ministry at that time. Both had agreed that we had to broaden the scope of our efforts on peace beyond creating a dialogue between Israelis and Palestinians from the territories. The genesis of the two-track approach came from these discussions.

[†]In November 1975, the United Nations General Assembly passed Resolution 3379 by a vote of 72 to 35, with 32 abstentions. The resolution, thereafter cited by Arabs as an international ruling against Israel's right to exist, declared that "Zionism is a form of racism and racial discrimination." Resolution 3379 was ultimately repealed in December 1991.

The Israelis might:

—ease conditions on the Palestinians in the West Bank and Gaza (e.g., end
deportations, halt administrative detention, relax travel restrictions, reopen
universities, withdraw the IDF from certain villages and towns, etc.);
—declare readiness to withdraw from South Lebanon after a six-to-twelve-month
period of tranquillity on Israel's border;
—make a commitment to a comprehensive settlement based on the principles
embodied in 242/338, stating a willingness to negotiate on the Golan Heights and
to negotiate a permanent status agreement providing for confederal solutions for
the West Bank/Gaza. (Confederal solutions could include joining Jordan, the
West Bank, and Gaza together—with the Palestinians having a separate state in
a union with Jordan; Israeli openness to such possibilities would signal that Israel
did not see autonomy for Palestinians as the end of the road.)

I did not expect that either side would be prepared to take many of these steps initially. But I was hoping that our new weight and authority—and the difficulty of saying no to us in the afterglow of the war—might make the negotiations easier to launch,
and if launched, more productive.

| THE BAKER MIDDLE EAST TRIPS FROM MARCH TO
OCTOBER: RIDING AN EMOTIONAL ROLLER COASTER |

After the war, our Arab friends felt a great weight had been lifted off their shoulders. In the Arab Middle East, there is what might be described as a "bandwagon culture": one goes with the winners—or those who look to be the winners—and stays far
away from the losers.

Saddam Hussein, much like Nasser in Egypt before him, had sought to seize the
mantle of the defier who would stand up for the powerless against the powerful, for the
have-nots against the haves. It mattered little that he was a horrific oppressor of his own
people. He portrayed himself as serving the larger cause of restoring greatness to the
Arab world were he to prevail. His first casualties would be many of the existing Arab
regimes, especially those in the Arabian Peninsula. Thus our Arab friends needed Saddam to be defeated.

For King Fahd of Saudi Arabia and President Mubarak of Egypt—having aligned
themselves with us against Saddam—our victory was their victory, and they reveled in
it. President Bush had said that Saddam's aggression would not stand. He had deliv-

ered. Now, when he told the Congress that we would work to produce Arab-Israeli peace, no one in the Arab world seemed to doubt him.

The Israelis, who had taken Scud missile attacks and not retaliated because of U.S. pressure, had a different view. The U.S. defeat of Iraq dramatically reduced perhaps the greatest threat Israel faced. Yet Israelis worried that their deterrent policy, a policy based on the vow that they would hit back tenfold for any loss, would be eroded by their failure to respond.

This was the situation when the Baker delegation arrived in Saudi Arabia on March 8, 1991, a week after the war ended. Why begin in Riyadh? If there was ever a time when the Saudis might be responsive on peace, this was it. And our best chance to affect the Shamir government would be to have something in hand from the Arabs, creating pressure on Shamir to respond.

Our initial meeting included only Baker and me and King Fahd and Prince Bandar, with Bandar serving as the interpreter. When Baker laid out the concept of a two-track approach to the negotiations, the King approved. He went further, telling us he had recently told a visiting American congressman, who happened to be Jewish, that he foresaw the day when Israel would be at peace with all of its Arab neighbors and that peace would include full diplomatic and commercial relations. "The congressman told me that he never heard me speak this way. And I said let us reason and be logical. . . . We know there is a state called Israel; no one is denying it and no one should deny it."

Baker asked whether the Saudis, as regional leaders, would be prepared to take confidence-building steps either unilaterally or collectively? A yes, he said, would help him move Shamir. He did not need to know tonight, but he did need to know before he saw Shamir. The King promised to have Bandar contact us before we got to Israel.

Bandar did so, telling me that the King would send him to gain Mubarak's and Asad's support for the process, including the importance of accepting confidence-building steps. But he offered no specifics, saying only that the Saudis would work with the Palestinians in the territories to come up with possible partners for the negotiations.

At every stop we made in the Gulf, in Egypt, and even in Syria, we got essentially the same message with varying degrees of warmth. The desire for an American initiative was very strong, and in every capital we heard the same thing: We will support your initiative.

I suspected the mood in Israel would be different. Shamir's government still had little enthusiasm for the process. This would be Baker's first visit to Israel even though he had been secretary for over two years at this point.

His diplomacy prior to the Iraqi invasion had been conducted over the phone or in the States. Baker had given a blunt speech to AIPAC, the American Israel Public Affairs Committee (America's pro-Israel lobby) in the spring of 1989, calling on Israel to give up the dream of a "greater Israel," and before the Congress a year later had made the disparaging remark about Israel suggesting it call the White House when it was serious about peace. After the Iraqi invasion of Kuwait, Baker had visited the Middle East but not gone to Israel, given Arab sensitivities and his desire to avoid creating a linkage between our sanctioning Saddam and our support for Israel. I had failed to convince him that we might pay a price later with the Israeli public if we excluded Israel on all regional trips, even if the trips were related to trying to reverse Iraq's invasion of Kuwait.

Now confronting a legacy of suspicion in Israel, Baker sought to reach out to the Israeli public, emphasizing Israel's need for security and the American commitment to that security. At the same time, he also called attention to the new possibilities in the Arab world after Saddam's defeat. He told Shamir that the Arabs were ready for negotiations with Israel, provided that Israel was ready to negotiate with the Palestinians. Furthermore, none of the Arab leaders he had spoken with had raised the PLO in this context.

He also reported that the Arabs had been willing to consider mutual confidence-building measures (CBMs). Baker summarized the CBMs on the Arab side and asked Shamir to accept the steps for Israel that I had outlined in the memo. As if he were a mirror image of Asad, Shamir was far more open to the steps the Arabs would take than to any that Israel would take.

Nonetheless, Shamir did not want to appear opposed to a U.S. peace initiative. At a private dinner with Baker that evening, he was unusually forthcoming about the future, telling Baker in confidence that a confederal arrangement with Jordan, the Palestinians, and Israelis might work. And when Baker raised the idea of a U.S. guarantee for Israeli security and U.S. troops on the Golan in exchange for Israeli withdrawal, Shamir seemed willing to consider it. Baker was pleasantly surprised.

While Baker was dining with Shamir, I was having dinner with the "princes" of Likud: Dan Meridor, Bibi Netanyahu, Benny Begin, and Ehud Olmert. They wanted to know what we had heard especially from the Saudis, and when I reported what Fahd had to say about eventual full relations with Israel, they wanted to move quickly to negotiations. It was my turn to be surprised.*

*Shamir had hosted the Secretary and Mrs. Baker at his residence for dinner. Oded Eran was the number two in the Israeli embassy in Washington, but returned to Israel for the Baker visit and hosted the dinner for me at his home with the "princes." Oded and I had become close, especially during Rabin's tenure as Defense Minister; Rabin frequently used Oded to transmit private messages to me, and I found Oded not only trustworthy but also a very creative partner in problem-solving.

THE APRIL TRIPS · We left the region hopeful, but that hope was premature. Once the good feelings and generalities had to be translated into concrete steps and commitments, the going became far more difficult. Both sides resisted taking their own steps on CBMs, each side arguing it was up to the other side to prove its good intentions. Our arguments on mutuality had little effect, and inevitably we began to focus instead on getting negotiations launched.

We were to return to the region in April. From the March trip, we knew we had a general convergence toward a two-track approach to negotiations; that working groups between Israelis and Palestinians and Israelis and the Arab states could conduct the negotiations, perhaps launched at a regional conference; and that the PLO would not be representing the Palestinians in the negotiations. Knowing that Shamir would seek to limit whom he would talk to among the Palestinians, what they would talk about, and how they would go about it, we decided—in a "selling mode" again—to find out what he could live with and then take this to the Arabs.

Shortly before we left for the region, Dan Meridor came to Washington and I convinced the Secretary that we could use a private meeting with him to convey questions to Shamir. At the Secretary's residence on Foxhall Road in Washington, we asked Dan three questions: Would Shamir accept a regional meeting or conference cosponsored by the United States *and* the Soviet Union to initiate direct negotiations? Would he accept a list of seven Palestinians from the territories whom we considered credible as partners for negotiations? Would he accept a comprehensive settlement of the Arab-Israeli conflict based on UNSC resolutions 242/338?

Dan promised to convey these questions to Shamir, along with our view that positive answers would give us something to take to the Arabs. Then he previewed Shamir's likely concerns. With regard to the conference, he would need Soviet recognition of Israel. It was hard to envision the Soviets being a cosponsor of such a conference without that. As for the Palestinians, Shamir would want a clear firewall between our Palestinian "partners" and the PLO. Finally, on resolutions 242 and 338, Shamir would be uncomfortable with the implication of land for peace. In Jerusalem the next week, Shamir echoed Dan's concerns almost exactly. He also wanted ironclad guarantees that the conference would have no decision-making power or authority, no capacity to reconvene itself, and would have no reason to meet except to launch direct negotiations. He was willing to accept 242 and 338 as the basis "as agreed at Camp David" so that he could tell his constituency he was not agreeing to anything new.*

---

*Moreover, by saying "as agreed at Camp David," he could also argue that Israel had already met its obligations on 242/338 as it related to withdrawal: since the Sinai Desert constituted more than 90

With regard to the Palestinians, we suggested criteria that, in Baker's words, would allow us to "fence out the PLO": Palestinians who were prepared to accept the two tracks of negotiations, who would agree to a phased approach to negotiations (transitional arrangements first, permanent status later), and who would live in peace with Israel would be acceptable partners for talks whether or not they were on our list of seven.

Shamir wanted more. He wanted the Palestinians to renounce the PLO; he wanted us to declare a violation if the PLO in Tunis claimed that they were giving instructions to the Palestinians. He wanted the Palestinians to be part of a joint delegation with the Jordanians, not a delegation on their own.

Of these requests, we were only prepared to consider the joint delegation with Jordan, which might be useful for finessing certain issues, especially Jerusalem. But no Palestinian would negotiate with the Israelis on condition of renouncing the PLO. We could not qualify 242 and 338—lest the Arabs insist on an explicit reference to "land for peace"— and we could not respond to every PLO statement coming out of Tunis. "We would be doing nothing else," I told Shamir. We also told him that if the Palestinian delegation acted as if it was simply representing the PLO, we understood that Israel would walk out.

After considerable effort on our part, Shamir reluctantly accepted our criteria, and Baker used the prime minister's readiness to accept a regional conference, our criteria for Palestinian participation, and our view on 242 and 338 as the basis of negotiations to demonstrate to Mubarak and Fahd that Shamir was ready to launch the two-track negotiations. Given the PLO's weakness at this point, we believed that if Asad would do likewise, we could move all parties to negotiations.

Both Mubarak and Fahd agreed to press Asad. But Asad, it turned out, was unimpressed, and instead imposed four conditions of his own; the most unacceptable being that the conference should be continuous—and that it should be held under the aegis of the United Nations.

Naturally, a continuous conference under the aegis of the UN was completely unacceptable to Shamir. In his eyes and in the eyes of most Israelis, a continuous UN-led conference would not only preempt bilateral negotiations but also do so in a forum bound to be biased against Israel. After all, the UN was a body that had adopted the resolution equating Zionism with racism—and its forces in southern Lebanon (UNIFIL) had allowed terrorists to operate out of their areas against Israel with impunity.

Arafat might be in a weak position after the Gulf War, but Asad was not. We could finesse the Palestinian representation issues, but Asad's conditions were not so easy to

---

percent of the territory Israel occupied as a result of the 1967 war, Shamir could say Israel had withdrawn from the territories.

handle. We tried to forge a compromise between Asad's view of a conference (continuous and under UN auspices) and Shamir's (a onetime meeting and no UN role).

In the meantime, one other procedural issue emerged. The Europeans wanted to be represented at the conference. This was fine with Asad and the Arabs, but not with Shamir, who deeply mistrusted the Europeans because of their long support for the PLO. We suggested that the European Community could be represented at the conference by an observer. To deal with the UN, we proposed that any agreement that emerged from the talks be registered with the UN and endorsed by the Security Council; the UN Secretary-General be regularly briefed on the status of talks; and a representative of the Secretary-General be permitted to attend the conference as a nonspeaking observer. With regard to the conference specifically, we suggested that it could reconvene but only if there was a consensus for it to do so—one the Israelis could block.

In framing these formulas, we were trying to produce something symbolic for Asad while protecting Shamir on the substance. But neither Shamir nor Asad was prepared to budge. They dug in, treating these procedural questions as if they would affect the heart of the negotiations themselves. Perhaps they feared that losing on procedure would presage losing on substance; or perhaps they were far less keen to negotiate than we thought.

Whatever the reason, we went from hopeful in March to despairing in April. The Saudis compounded our despair when, during our third trip, Foreign Minister Saud told us that Saudi Arabia, not having a border with Israel, would not attend any peace conference. This clearly contradicted what the King had told us. Baker responded angrily: "I guess that it was okay to be partners in war, but not in peace." In a subsequent meeting with King Fahd, Baker made his disappointment clear, but the King did not alter their position.*

When we arrived in Israel following the meetings in Saudi Arabia, Shamir was able to use the Saudi retreat and Asad's insistence on a UN presence at an ongoing conference to argue that the Arabs were not prepared to talk peace directly with Israel. As a result, he would not think about embracing the compromise formula I had crafted.

We had leverage on Shamir so long as it appeared that there were Arab partners for peace and that the prime minister was resisting our efforts to take advantage of a clear opportunity. Now we did not have that. So we resolved to try to produce an Arab move, and Asad was clearly the most important actor in this regard. In a nearly ten-

---

*I suspected that the traditionalists in the royal family had resisted Saudi Arabia doing anything on peace and that the King had, at least for the moment, acquiesced.

hour meeting in Damascus, Baker came up with a proposal: he would propose to President Bush that the U.S. guarantee the border between Israel and Syria in both directions after peace, assuring the Syrians that Israel would not attack and the Israelis that Syria would not attack. Because Syria would never get the Golan Heights back if the Israelis felt a security threat there, Baker explained, the U.S. guarantee offered Asad his only real chance to recover them. But Baker would raise this proposal with President Bush only if Asad would accept our compromises on the UN and the conference. Asad initially demurred and Baker grew exasperated. Finally, Baker told Asad that in all their meetings he had not shown any flexibility whatsoever. To which Asad, sounding much like Sharif Hussein in his letter to High Commissoner McMahon, replied, "The land is important. It connotes dignity and honor. A man is not chosen to go to paradise unless he can do so in a dignified way. We don't want anyone to say we have given up what we have been talking about for twenty years."

Baker told him you can keep saying that for another twenty years and you won't get the land back. This is your chance. But Asad said only that he would consult with the Syrian leadership and come back to the Secretary.

Baker had sought to break the deadlock using a substantive proposal to gain a compromise on process. Asad had equivocated; we returned to Washington on a decidedly down note. Soon our outlook was to improve.

THE MAY TRIPS · On May 3, Ed Djerejian, our ambassador to Syria, conveyed that Asad would accept our compromises on the UN and the conference, provided that President Bush fulfilled Baker's promise on the U.S. guarantee of the border. For the first time, we had flexibility from Asad.

But I had no illusions about Shamir: he would try to dismiss the meaning of Asad's procedural move. So I decided that we needed to arrive in Israel with something more from the Arabs—thereby leaving Shamir with little room to escape a move on the nonsubstantive issues. So I went to see Prince Bandar at his American residence in McLean, Virginia.

Bandar bin Sultan, known by everyone in Washington as Bandar, was the Saudi ambassador to the United States. His father was the Defense Minister in Saudi Arabia, the third-ranking figure of power in the royal family behind the King and the Crown Prince.

Bandar cut a dashing figure—gregarious, outgoing, and confident. His time in the States—having trained as a fighter pilot and then become the Saudi ambassador early in the Reagan administration—not only gave him a feel for the country but also Americanized him in many ways. He became a huge Dallas Cowboys fan, even having a replica of one of their Super Bowl trophies in his house. He bought a breathtaking estate in McLean, with indoor and outdoor pools, an extensive garden, and a tennis court, as well as a 55,000-square-foot "chalet" in Aspen. When he threw a going-away party in McLean for Sir Anthony Acland, the departing British ambassador, who had been instrumental in supporting the effort against Iraq, he modestly announced to the guests that there would be after-dinner entertainment in his library. Little did I suspect that Roberta Flack would perform for us.

I first got to know Bandar when the Reagan administration decided to sell F-15 fighter planes to Saudi Arabia, the first such sale to an Arab state. When some congressmen worried that the F-15s posed a threat to Israel, Bandar worked closely with the administration to try to address these concerns, and I was impressed by his ability to operate on the Hill.

I began to work with him closely when I returned from Berkeley to the NSC in 1986, and Bandar would jokingly refer to me as his "radical Berkeley friend." After the Iraqi invasion of Kuwait, he and I would talk every day when we were both in Washington. It was he who convinced King Fahd to allow U.S. forces to be stationed in Saudi Arabia. In his eyes, merely containing Iraq was not an option, as Iraq would remain a threat, yet the U.S. presence in Saudi Arabia would stir up nationalists and Islamists within the country. For Bandar, then, there was no alternative to defeating Iraq—and he knew that I shared that view.

So Bandar worried when Secretary Baker led a delegation to meet the Iraqi Foreign Minister, Tariq Aziz, in Geneva on January 9—six days before the deadline the UN Security Council had imposed for Saddam to withdraw from Kuwait. The meeting grew out of President Bush's desire to demonstrate that he had exhausted all options before resorting to force. But Bandar was nervous. As he said to me before we left, "Jimmy Baker is too good at producing deals, don't let him do one that we will all regret."

He need not have worried. Baker was not going to let Saddam off the hook. But now we were in danger of losing the moment for pursuing Arab-Israeli peace. In his many meetings with congressmen in the pre-war period, Bandar stressed that once Saddam was defeated, Saudi Arabia would take the lead in making peace with Israel. Now I chose to remind him of this.

Whenever either of us had something important to discuss, we would do it at his house—either late at night or on the weekend. This time we sat together in the garden room on a Saturday afternoon. "Bandar, you have a problem," I told him. "In this country there is a collective sense that we did not just liberate Kuwait, we saved your butt. No one can understand, especially on the Hill, that Saudi Arabia is now doing nothing for peace. I am getting members of Congress calling me. Your own credibility is at stake, and I am afraid that we are going to see a very strong anti-Saudi campaign emerge soon unless we can do something."

Few were better than Bandar at parrying an argument. Today, though, he was not defensive; he simply asked: "What's your idea?"

My idea, I told him, was twofold: have the Gulf Cooperation Council attend the peace conference not as participants but as observers. Following the conference, which would initiate bilateral negotiations, have them attend the subsequent multilateral talks as participants. Attending as observers would allow them to draw a distinction between themselves and Israel's immediate neighbors. Their attending as participants would demonstrate their desire to deal with the broader issues of instability that would be the focus of the multilateral working groups: regional economic development, arms control, water, environment, and refugees. "Bandar," I said, "since Saudi Arabia dominates the Gulf Cooperation Council, everyone will know this is a Saudi idea to bring the six countries of the Arabian Peninsula into a negotiating process with Israel."

Bandar loved the idea and promised to make it happen. I asked only one thing: that the GCC announce the idea on the eve of our next trip to the region. This way, I explained, Baker would meet Shamir having produced Asad's flexibility and an unmistakable Arab readiness for dealing with Israel. Bandar agreed.

Baker, too, was pleased and very much liked the prospect of arriving in Israel with two cards in his pocket. Once again, however, our best-laid plans went awry.

The Saudis made the announcement that Bandar had promised as we were en route to the region. Once in Damascus, however, we discovered that Asad had retreated from the position Ed had conveyed to us. Asad told Baker he had agreed to compromise based on Baker's "guarantee" that Israel would withdraw from the Golan Heights. Baker was livid. He had guaranteed no such thing. Why would he guarantee Israeli withdrawal in exchange for two procedural concessions by Asad? He promised to guarantee the border once agreed; that was all. But Asad would not budge.

Obviously, he had had a change of heart. Baker thought Asad did not want to move before Shamir. I thought he was testing us, hoping for more. Meanwhile, he had preserved deniability by claiming there was a misunderstanding.

But there was no misunderstanding, and Baker, on our flight from Damascus to Jerusalem, decided to vent his anger to the press traveling with us. On "background"—meaning his words could be attributed only to a "senior official"—he said that Asad was the impediment to progress and that we might consider pursuing the process without Syria.*

---

*That his words stung the Syrians was clear when Syrian Foreign Minister Farouk al-Shara—two weeks later at a meeting in Lisbon—came up to me thinking I had been responsible for the backgrounder and pleaded with me to never say such things about Syria again. My reply: Don't walk away from commitments and we won't.

Arriving in Israel with a Saudi commitment but none from Asad, we had little leverage with Shamir, and—not surprisingly—he refused to modify his position. To save face, we decided to produce a nonpaper summarizing all the points Israel was prepared to accept in order to launch the negotiations. We hoped this might help us to move Mubarak and King Hussein of Jordan.

Hosni Mubarak pleaded with Baker not to give up on Asad, describing him as a "rug merchant" who would always try to see how much more he could get. In reply, Baker, genuinely frustrated but also mindful that his readiness to walk away might motivate Mubarak to do more to affect Asad, bluntly told his host that he did not intend to just keep flying around the Middle East—and, using one of his favorite phrases, said he was ready to go home and leave "the dead cat" on Asad's doorstep.

As we concluded our May trips, we were at a dead end. Baker and I had discussed the possibility of forcing the issue by simply issuing an invitation to the conference and seeing who was prepared not to show, but decided it was too risky: if either the Syrians or Israelis decided not to come, the initiative would be over. Repeatedly over the coming years, I would have to resist the temptation to force the parties to make decisions for or against the peace process—because if the process lapsed, the potential for violence and terror would increase dramatically; absent diplomacy, the extremists, especially in the Arab world, would emphasize that armed struggle was the only answer.

Still, we knew we had to change the dynamic. Instead of issuing formal invitations, we sent a letter from the President to all the leaders in the area detailing our ideas for launching negotiations and asking each leader if he was prepared to attend a conference based on them. Shamir answered "no, but," leaving a little room for ongoing discussion. Asad did not respond. Initially, the Syrians told us they did not believe it was necessary to respond because the Israelis had said no.

Regardless of the Israeli reply, this was unacceptable to us. A letter from President Bush required a response.

We applied pressure directly and via the Egyptians and Saudis. Still, for six weeks there was no response from Asad—just a drumbeat from us on what he could gain by responding affirmatively. Finally, on July 14, Asad, in a letter to President Bush, provided an unqualified "yes." He may not have been eager to negotiate with Israel, but he clearly wanted an ongoing relationship with the United States. And if that meant dealing with Israel, he would do so.*

---

*Interestingly enough, when we met Shamir a short while later, he said Asad said yes because "he thinks I will say no." To which I said, "Mr. Prime Minister, you may be right, but he knew by accepting our terms, he ran the risk that you might say yes. That tells me that he was ready to accept the direct negotiations with you and that is a real departure."

THE ROLLER COASTER CONTINUES · With Asad's yes in hand, we made a plan to return to the Middle East immediately after the G-7 summit in Paris. We sought to get Shamir to transform his "no, but" into a "yes, but." Knowing Asad's yes would put Shamir on the defensive, I wanted also to demonstrate to the Israeli public—always the source of real pressure on Shamir—that his enthusiasm for new settlements in the territories was costing Israel the benefits of Arab changes of heart. Once again I turned to Bandar. Could he get the King to endorse a suspension of the Saudi economic boycott of Israel in return for an Israeli suspension of settlement building? As I explained to Bandar, such an act would demonstrate that the Arabs envisioned a new day with Israel, while also exposing as fiction Shamir's familiar argument that settlement activity cost nothing. Bandar liked the idea and persuaded King Fahd to endorse it. So did the Europeans and Japanese at the G-7 summit, as did the Saudis and Egyptians once we arrived in the region.

Suddenly it appeared that there were partners for peace and Shamir was the reluctant one. Knowing that was not tenable in Israel, Shamir told us he was prepared to make the necessary concessions on the UN and the reconvening of the conference if the joint delegation of Jordanian-Palestinians met with his satisfaction. Following a Bush-Gorbachev summit in Moscow on July 30–August 1, Shamir agreed to our terms, provided we would ensure that there would be no one on the joint delegation whom Shamir could not sit with. When Yossi Ben-Aharon, Shamir's Chief of Staff, protested that would not be good enough for the Prime Minister, Shamir cut him off and said that Secretary Baker's word was good enough for him.

| LETTERS OF ASSURANCES |

Unfortunately, Yasir Arafat was in no hurry to see a joint Jordanian-Palestinian delegation formed. Though under pressure from Egypt, he began stalling, and also encouraged the Palestinians to try once more to get an East Jerusalemite on the delegation.

This issue was particularly difficult for Faisal Husseini, the Palestinian who met with Secretary Baker in West Jerusalem on each of our trips. Faisal was the son of Abd al-Kader al-Husseini, a charismatic Palestinian leader who was killed near Jerusalem in the spring of 1948, and nephew of the Mufti of Jerusalem. There was no Palestinian with a stronger tie to Jerusalem than Faisal. (Even Arafat tried to embellish his ties to Jerusalem by claiming he was a cousin of Faisal—thereby claiming he was a Husseini.)

In August Faisal came to see me for an off-the-record discussion, wanting assurances that if Arafat and the PLO were kept out of the conference, Palestinians would be able to announce their side of the Jordanian-Palestinian delegation. They, like the Israelis, would not have to sit with anyone unacceptable to them, and they would be able to raise issues of concern to them in their conference speeches, including their objective of having a state at the end of the process.

I was able to assure him, and he was very pleased. But it was clear that Faisal was counting on going to the conference himself, as a dual-address East Jerusalemite and as the leader of the delegations that had been seeing Baker. Now I had to tell him otherwise—that the Jerusalemites on the joint delegation could only be Jordanians, not Palestinans. As I did so, tears welled up in his eyes and he fell silent. I tried to comfort him, saying I knew this was painful but we had come a long way, here was a chance to launch negotiations, and negotiations offered the best, indeed only, chance for Palestinian salvation. I knew that he wanted what was best for the Palestinians. I knew this was a bitter pill for him, but I owed him the truth, and the truth was that there would be no conference any other way.

It took a few moments before Faisal regained his composure. When he did, he told me this was very hard to swallow: it would look like the Palestinians were conceding Jerusalem to begin negotiations and no Palestinian could do that.

In response, I told him that there were different ways we could make it clear that this was not the case. As I spoke, he refocused, and allowed that something might be possible; and as it happened, my next several meetings with Faisal and Hanan Ashrawi focused almost exclusively on the terms of our assurances.

Meanwhile, Shamir, too, now wanted certain assurances in writing about exclusion of the PLO, the Israeli position on the Golan Heights, U.S. support for Israel at the UN Security Council, and being able to vet U.S. peace ideas before they were presented to the Arabs. When the Shamir government leaked that we had begun discussions on a letter of assurances, all the Arab participants sought such letters as well.

Through the remainder of August and into September, we crafted draft letters of assurances for the Israelis, Jordanians and Palestinians, and the Syrians. Secretary Baker told the parties that certain principles would guide this exercise and the terms of reference for the conference. There would be no secret assurances. All parties would be briefed on the content of, but not actually shown, the letters of assurances sent to others. And we would not break new ground or change existing U.S. policy in these letters or the invitation to the conference.

Sound principles, but this proved to be a most difficult and delicate exercise of diplomacy. Moreover, it meant we were thrust again into a bargaining process in which every party would try to get something else before agreeing to go to the conference.

In retrospect, the conference was probably too far along to be undone. Asad had decided to go; that left both Shamir and the Palestinians no choice but to go as well.

But what appears so clear now certainly did not seem that way at the time. In the last month before getting to the Madrid conference, there were some moments of great drama and uncertainty.

| GETTING TO MADRID AND CONVENING THE CONFERENCE |

While Asad may have decided to go, he was not about to make it easy for us. He used the letter of assurances and the invitation to the conference as vehicles to reopen basic questions. He sought to get us to walk away from the multilateral talks, claiming they represented normalization with Israel before he had recovered his land. He saw other Arabs engaging Israelis as reducing his leverage, not as convincing Israelis that the region was changing in a way that offered Israel genuine peace if it withdrew from Arab territory. Thus, he wanted the multilateral talks to be postponed until much later in the process. Over my opposition, Baker—fearing that Syria might block all negotiations with Israel—was prepared to trade away the multilateral talks if it would preserve the bilateral negotiations. But Asad overplayed his hand, angering Baker as he seemingly backed off of earlier understandings in two days of enervating talks in Damascus on the letter of assurances and the invitation on October 15 and 16. Finally, at a point when Baker was literally ready to walk out on Asad, the Syrian President called the negotiation to an end, accepting that we would agree to disagree about the multilaterals and that when they were held Syria would not attend.

The Palestinians also drove Baker to distraction, not living up to their promises to provide the list of Palestinians for the joint delegation even after we stretched very far (in their letter of assurance) to meet their concerns on East Jerusalem—stating that the status of Jerusalem could not be prejudged and could be resolved only by negotiations; acknowledging that we did not recognize Israel's annexation of East Jerusalem; agreeing to meet a Faisal Husseini-led delegation in East Jerusalem, and inviting Faisal to see President Bush in the White House. These moves were designed to signal our understanding of the significance of East Jerusalem to Palestinians, and they were supposed to be reciprocated by the Palestinians. When they were not and when Faisal (accompanied by Hanan Ashrawi) suddenly tried to press for additional U.S. concessions on East Jerusalem, during a meeting with Baker and me, the Secretary again exploded, shouting that "the souk never closes with you people," and stalked out. Faisal was stunned, and asked me to persuade Baker to return. I was only prepared to do so if Faisal would drop any additional requests. He did so. But subsequently, Arafat's manipulations and the personal rivalry among Palestinians in the West Bank and Gaza prevented Faisal from being able to provide more than half of the fourteen names he had promised for the joint delegation.

Now we were ready to force the issue. Knowing that the Syrians, Jordanians, Egyptians, Saudis, and Israelis were ready to go at this point, Baker made a joint announcement in Jerusalem with the new Soviet Foreign Minister, Boris Pankin. The conference would be convened in ten days in Madrid, lasting from October 30 to November 2. (Interestingly, the next morning the Palestinians submitted the full list of names. It was acceptable, and they asked if we would announce they had been the first to agree to attend.)

This was one of those times when forcing the issue worked. But the circumstances were unique, with nearly every Arab leader ready to go to the conference and the Palestinians in a weakened condition after the Gulf War.

In many ways the Madrid conference was more about symbolism than practicality. We were breaking the symbolism of denial—a taboo on direct talks between Arabs and Israelis. We were launching a peace process based on Arab states talking to Israel, with UNSC resolutions 242 and 338 serving as the guiding principles. Israelis would also talk to Palestinians with an incrementalist logic guiding these negotiations—transitional arrangements for Palestinian self-government would be negotiated initially, with the permanent status issues of Jerusalem, borders, and refugees to be discussed later, but not later than the beginning the third year of the process.

The conference itself was to offer an elaborate setting for launching the process. While Presidents Bush and Gorbachev were the conveners, the participants were represented at the foreign minister level. Shamir, however, had chosen to lead the Israeli delegation, prompting his Foreign Minister, David Levy, not to attend. Each of the participants would make opening statements on the first day of the conference and brief follow-up statements on the second day. There would be a break on Saturday for the Jewish Sabbath, and on the fourth day there would be the initial bilateral meetings at the level of negotiators, not ministers. While we did not have high expectations for what would be produced at the conference itself, we hoped that each side might take the high road in terms of declaring its determination to make peace and avoiding attacks on their negotiating partner. We also hoped the initiation of the bilateral talks would not only come off without a hitch but also set a tone and an agenda for the subsequent talks. We were bound to be disappointed.

No one from the region took the high road. It was as if, with the whole world watching, neither the Arab foreign ministers nor Shamir wanted to look like they were surrendering their claims or were going to be soft on their adversaries. To be sure, the worst was Farouk Shara, the Syrian Foreign Minister. He portrayed Yitzhak Shamir as a terrorist, displaying a "wanted" picture of him that the British mandatory authorities in Palestine had issued in the 1940s. Shamir was little better, documenting the history of Arab rejection of Israel and questioning the basic Arab desire for peace. Amre

Moussa, the new Foreign Minister of Egypt—the only Arab state at peace with Israel—was so negative on day one, offering only an indictment of Israel, that we threatened not to let him speak on the second day. Ironically, Haidar Abdel Shafi, speaking for the Palestinians, gave one of the better speeches—focusing more on Palestinian hopes than on his criticism of Israel.

Until Haidar spoke, however, I was uneasy. We had insisted that the Palestinians show us their speech beforehand, particularly because we did not want Haidar to say something that would provoke Shamir to walk out. Hanan Ashrawi, no doubt trying to limit our ability to make changes, came to me very late with the speech. As a result, we were fine-tuning a few of the lines just minutes before Haidar was to go to the podium. I was not trying to censure anything about Palestinian aspirations, provided those did not rule out Israel's existence and provided Abdel Shafi was not about to declare that his speech was written by Yasir Arafat. Given the way everything had gone, I could not breathe easy until Haider finished his speech—parts of which approached the edge but all of which even the Israeli delegation admitted was better than had been expected.

If the speeches were generally a disappointment, the Israeli-Syrian bilateral talks remained in doubt until they were convened. King Hussein had assured us that he would bring the joint Jordanian-Palestinian delegation to meet with the Israelis. But after President Bush's speech to the conference in which he spoke of the need for "territorial compromise"—something the Syrians interpreted to mean that we might support partial, not total, Israeli withdrawals—Farouk Shara told us that the ground rules for the conference had been changed and that unless the President's statement was corrected he could not sit with the Israelis. Using Prince Bandar—who was with us in Madrid—and President Mubarak from Cairo to pressure President Asad, we finally received assurance that the Syrians would sit with the Israelis bilaterally. Just to make sure, we did not have Baker's plane depart Madrid until we knew the bilateral meeting had commenced. Nothing, it seemed, was ever certain in this process until it had taken place.

Here again, it is important to put Madrid and its aftermath in perspective. Madrid was designed to launch a process, not conclude it. It succeeded in getting negotiations under way, but it accomplished little else. The negotiations stalled quickly. The substantive gaps were enormous. On the Syrian track, since the Shamir government would not agree that UNSC resolution 242 even applied to the Golan Heights, negotiations over the Golan became little more than disquisitions over what 242 required and who was betraying the Madrid principles. With the Palestinians, Shamir's desire to empower Palestinians from the territories was undone by his need to respond to his settler base. Confiscation of land and new settlement activity responded to the pressures he was under politically, but totally undercut the Palestinian delegation to the negotiations.

Thus, Shamir's desire to circumvent and weaken the PLO in Tunis was defeated by his inability to hold the line against the Israeli right. Had he permitted the Palestinians in the negotiations to demonstrate that they were producing increasing Palestinian independence, had he stopped the Israeli actions that most outraged Palestinians—land confiscation, continued settlement activity, daily humiliations at checkpoints—he might have truly empowered the Palestinians from the territories and made it possible for the "internal PLO" to become an alternative to Yasir Arafat's PLO in Tunis. But he did not. His insensitivity to Palestinian needs and concerns mirrored Arafat's insensitivity and indifference to Israeli needs a decade later. In no small part there emerged an increasingly credible peace camp in Israel because Shamir was not willing to give up the right-wing agenda, and the Israeli public saw the cost of this, in terms of both Israel's relationship with the United States and the possibility of peace.

| LOAN GUARANTEES AND THE DEFEAT OF YITZHAK SHAMIR |

Nowhere was the right-wing agenda more costly than on the determination to spread Israeli settlements throughout the West Bank and Gaza. Not only did it outrage the Palestinians—absorbing land they considered to be theirs—but President Bush believed that the settlement activity was simply inconsistent with peacemaking. Bush's opposition came back to haunt Shamir on the issue of U.S. loan guarantees to Israel.

With Gorbachev finally opening the gates to Jewish emigration, Israel suddenly faced a need to absorb what in all likelihood would be a million Soviet immigrants. The very reason that the state of Israel existed—to be a safe haven for Jews everywhere—now confronted Israel with an awesome challenge: it had to be able to absorb the equivalent of 20 percent of its entire population within a few years.

To do so, Shamir sought loan guarantees from the United States. The guarantees would allow Israel to borrow substantial sums of money at much lower interest rates. Initially, before knowing the size of Israel's needs, Shamir requested a relatively small package of $400 million in guarantees. In 1990, I persuaded Baker and the President to accept such a package for Israel.

This was not an easy sell on our side, for President Bush feared the money would be used to promote Israeli settlement activity in the territories—the very activity he strongly opposed. But I was able to persuade him by going over the assurances that we had received from the Israeli Foreign Minister, David Levy, in the form of a negotiated letter; the Levy assurances would enable us to see the level of Israeli expenditures on settlements and determine if these increased after the provision of the loan guarantees. I told President Bush that the $400 million package would be only a small down payment on what Israel would need for absorption, stating "Shamir would be a fool to jeopardize that by violating the terms of the Levy letter."

As it turned out, however, I was wrong. I failed to appreciate that for political and ideological reasons Shamir would never permit the provision of the information promised in the Levy letter. Politically, he could not afford for the Israeli public to see how much money was going to settlements and by comparison how little was going to development towns in Israel. Ideologically, he could not accept that there was a difference between Israel within the "green line" and Israel beyond it in the territories. Revealing the monies spent on settlements beyond the green line would indicate that these areas were somehow different from the rest of Israel, and he wanted to resist any such imagery.

Basically, Shamir's approach became one of stringing us along. He would delay providing information, and when pressed, would only provide incomplete information on settlement expenditures. His behavior convinced the President that he had been right and I had been wrong. When Shamir, believing the Gulf War and Israel's willingness not to retaliate for the Scud missile attacks put Israel in a good position, requested $10 billion in loan guarantees, President Bush was not about to listen to my arguments on how to deal with this request. He was determined to reject the request unless Shamir would accept a freeze on settlement activity.

All this was about to come to a head in September of 1991, as Shamir made clear he wanted to inform Congress of Israel's request. We were in the final stages of resolving the issues for getting to Madrid. While I could not persuade the President, Baker—hardly a slouch on the settlement issue—understood that the strategic issue at this point was launching negotiations. He agreed with me that we needed to delay the loan guarantee issue, in order to avoid having a battle with the Israelis over settlements at the very moment we were trying to persuade the Shamir government to concede on the procedural points necessary to get to the conference. Moreover, Baker also agreed that by emphasizing the issue now, we would leave the Arabs no choice but to make a settlement freeze a condition for talking to Israel. We wanted the Arabs to understand that if they wanted to affect Israeli behavior they had to talk to Israel.

In the end, the Secretary was able to persuade the President that our interest was in postponing congressional discussion of loan guarantees until January 1992, two months after Madrid and the initiation of bilateral talks. But delaying congressional consideration of the loan guarantees did something else as well: it thrust this issue directly into the Israeli elections set for June 1992. Baker was determined not to do anything that might help Shamir. Providing the loan guarantees would show that he could have settlement activity and still get our support. There would be no cost to him and he could use that in the election.

I was mindful of that, and certainly did not want to help Shamir in the election. But I was ambivalent. Israel had needs with the Soviet immigrants. My thought was to give Israel only one year's worth of loan guarantees—$2 billion—and tie that to implementation of the Levy promises. No delivery on those promises, no further loan guarantees. Israel could get needed help, but the Israeli public would be reminded that its government had not kept promises and might not get all that was available if the behavior did not change.

In discussions with Zalman Shoval, the Israeli ambassador to the United States, it became clear that such an approach could work. Baker had authorized me to conduct these discussions, but when I offered a possible one-year $2 billion loan guarantee, Baker rejected it.

Instead, Baker fashioned with Senator Patrick Leahy—a strong supporter of Israel, but highly troubled by Israeli settlement activity—a full $10 billion loan guarantee package but with a dollar-for-dollar reduction from the loan guarantees for every dollar spent on settlement activity. Senator Leahy was ready to sponsor legislation to that effect.

Shamir rejected that. There was no deal and clearly no prospect of loan guarantees as long as Shamir was Prime Minister. Was this decisive in defeating him? It certainly was a factor. The Russians who had already immigrated to Israel voted overwhelmingly against Likud and its leader Yitzhak Shamir.

In the election, that vote was sufficient for Labor, and its leader Yitzhak Rabin, to be elected. Elections were for parties, not individual leaders. Had elections at that time been held between two individuals for Prime Minister, I believe Rabin would have won easily, since voting for parties had more to do with one's identity. In Israel at this point, before the election reform act that divided voting into a vote for the prime minister and a vote for parties, party identity tended to be paramount. Thus, a switch from a Likud-dominated government to a Labor-dominated one represented a big change.

In Israel, it was as if a great weight had been lifted off the body politic. Hope was alive again. Expectations soared about peace being possible.

It was not just the loan guarantees that had done Shamir in. It was also that Shamir made a basic miscalculation: when the Israeli public believes they have a partner for peace, they want a government that is capable of negotiating peace. By the same token, if the public feels there is no partner, if the public feels security is the paramount issue, if anger and fear are the dominant concerns, the Israelis vote for those who will show the Arabs the consequences of not being a partner—and will vote against those they deem too "soft" toward Israel's neighbors.

In 1992, the Israeli public, post-Madrid, believed that there was an opportunity for peace and they wanted a government capable of pursuing it. A Rabin-led government certainly seemed to promise this.

It was June 23, 1992. As the initial election returns were coming in, I told Aaron Miller (who worked for me on the Policy Planning Staff): "There is good news and bad news. The good news is that we now have an Israeli government that can make peace. The bad news is that we won't be here to be able to help them do it."

| AMERICAN POLITICS AND ONE LAST GAMBIT |

At this point, Baker was hoping that he would not have to go to the White House as the Chief of Staff to take over President Bush's re-election campaign. It was an open secret that President Bush would turn to Baker, given plummeting polls, the disarray in his campaign, and the emergence of Bill Clinton as a charismatic and adroit national Democratic candidate.

It was not that Baker was disloyal, far from it. It was that he had unparalleled standing as Secretary of State. If there was a new world order, Baker was seen internationally as its architect. He was seen around the world as having managed the effective end of the Cold War, midwifing the unification of Germany in NATO, negotiating landmark strategic and conventional arms reduction treaties (START 1 and CFE), and molding, shaping, and sustaining the Gulf War coalition against Iraq. To be sure, he was also credited with breaking the taboo on talks between Arabs and Israelis and having launched the negotiating process.

On our trips—regardless of where we were—Baker was accorded the stature of a world leader. Now he would have to return to the White House and, in his words, decide "whether we would have balloons or ducks at a campaign rally." That was very hard for him to contemplate. He knew the President was in trouble politically. He doubted he could save him in the election, believing that the public wanted a change. He wanted to help his friend of thirty-five years; he wanted him to remain as President. But he did not see his going to the White House as the solution.

Shortly after Rabin's election, he asked whether it would be possible for us to go on an extended Middle Eastern trip and broker a major breakthrough. In such circumstances, the President would not ask him to leave State and manage the campaign from the White House. While telling him we should go to the Middle East once Rabin formed his government, I also said it would take some time before Rabin was ready or able to think in terms of deals. He would have to satisfy himself on whether his Arab partners were real—or simply seeking us to deliver concessions from Israel. A short

Middle East trip would be necessary soon; a Middle East shuttle to broker deals would not be possible before the end of the year—much too late for Baker to avoid going to the White House.

But I did have one idea for transforming our political realities and obviating the need for Baker to move: have the President announce that he was going to ask General Colin Powell to replace Vice President Quayle as his running mate. Have the President explain that Powell would be put in charge of developing and carrying out the domestic agenda in the second term. This would be seen as a revolutionary move. It would capture the imagination of the media, shifting attention away from Clinton and breaking his momentum, and show that the President could bring to the domestic arena the kind of decisive leadership he had demonstrated internationally.*

Baker had his doubts, but he passed on the suggestion—as my suggestion—to Bob Teeter, who loved the idea, imagining that the three former Republican Presidents (Nixon, Ford, and Reagan) would go to Quayle to ask him to step down for the good of the country. But the President simply rejected the idea. The Vice President had served him loyally; he would not oust him. Doing so would violate his personal code. If loyalty cost him the election, so be it.

By early July, Rabin had formed his government and Baker was still at the State Department. We went to the Middle East to set the stage for new diplomacy, not to launch a shuttle. Baker had told me that he expected Bush to ask him to move to the White House during the Democratic Party convention, which would take place shortly after our return from the Middle East. Baker still hoped to avoid leaving the State Department, and I came up with one last "Hail Mary."

Madrid had made it possible for direct talks to take place at the negotiator level between Israel and its neighbors. If we could bring the leaders together in Washington for a summit, it would be a breathtaking event: Asad, Fahd, Hussein, and Mubarak sitting with Rabin and the President. It would create a totally different climate; it would signal we were in a very different Middle East, in which Arabs had accepted Israel. It would have a dramatic effect in Israel, and give Rabin an incentive to move much more quickly. Even if it risked compounding the President's political problem—of appearing to be focused on foreign, not domestic, policy—it would dominate the news for a few days and have a lasting legacy in the Middle East. And, needless to say, it would require Baker's full attention in August and September.

---

*Two years later when this story came out, President Clinton told me, "Damn good thing they didn't listen to you." And Vice President Gore joked with me, "Dennis, if you get any ideas about Vice President in this administration, keep them to yourself."

Baker thought it was worth a try, but wondered if it would be possible. I told him Asad was the key. If Asad went for it, the others would do it. But, I continued, "it goes against everything Asad believes." It would mean giving the Israelis a huge concession for nothing in return. It would mean he would have to meet an Israeli leader without having gotten his land back. It would mean giving the Israelis the symbols they crave with no assurance of getting the substance he wants.

But, I went on, if you tie it to our politics and Bush's reelection, there is "a very, very, very slight possibility" he might go for it. You have to go over it with Asad alone. You have to make it clear that we need something dramatic to turn the election around. You have to make it clear that you have high confidence in Rabin, that you believe a deal is now possible between Israel and Syria, and that such an event will give us and Rabin leverage to do what is necessary.

Baker, feeling we had little to lose, decided to see if he could sell Asad on the idea. We saw Asad shortly after his mother had died. He was more emotional than I had ever seen him, speaking fatalistically about life and the importance of faith at times like these.

Following our larger meeting, Baker saw Asad alone, with only his interpreter, not ours. Later he told me he had made an impassioned argument for the idea of the summit, telling Asad that we would hold it in Washington in the first week of September, and that it would be extraordinarily significant for us domestically, for our relationship with Syria, and for the prospects for peace.

Asad, he reported, listened carefully. He wanted to know about Bush's prospects. Would this really help him? It was not easy for him even to consider it, but he respected the President and Baker very much and said he would consider it and get a message back to Baker on his answer.

Both Baker and I took this to mean there was a shot. About three weeks later, shortly after the announcement that Baker would be leaving the State Department and becoming the White House Chief of Staff, we got a message from Asad saying he could not accept the idea Baker had raised in their private discussion. There were no more gambits to be played.

<{ 3 }>

Rabin, Presidential Transition,
the Syrian Pocket, and Oslo

TODAY, YITZHAK RABIN IS seen in Israel and throughout the Middle East as a hero. Nearly all Israelis believe his assassination marked one of the darkest moments in Israeli history. In July 1992 when he became Prime Minister, he was not a hero, just a leader who was seen as ushering in an era of possibility. For us, he offered a welcome relief from the frustrations of dealing with Yitzhak Shamir.

Secretary Baker traveled to the Middle East to meet with Rabin on July19, shortly after the new Prime Minister had established a government. The Rabin government was a center-left government, consisting of the Labor Party, the leftist-dovish Meretz party, and also a religious party, Shas, made up of Jews who had come from Morocco and the Arab world. The Shas leadership was more preoccupied with its religious schools and social services than with the peace process per se. But in representing those who had grown up in the Arab world and who were generally less trustful of the Arabs and less willing to make concessions to them, Shas took a harder line on questions related to peace. Notwithstanding Shas' position, it became clear very quickly in our meetings that we were dealing with a very different Israeli government and with a very different leader. Unlike Shamir, Rabin was not interested in expanding Israel's hold on the West Bank and Gaza, and he was interested in seeing if a deal was possible with Syria. Emotionally, he was not ready to deal with the PLO and Arafat, but he signaled that Israel's approach to the Palestinians had to change.

Rabin was not ready to get into specifics with Baker. It was simply too early, particularly as he was still expanding his governing coalition and he had not yet had time to formulate his plans. But he was eager to resolve the loan guarantee issue. In his initial meeting with Baker, he made clear that he was determined to shift priorities away from building settlements in the territories; to that end he was going to cancel seven thousand contracts on settlement housing units, and also end the Likud policy of providing monetary incentives to those who would move into the territories. Baker's reaction initially was to get into a negotiation and insist on more from Rabin for the loan guarantees. After that first meeting, Rabin, who had not yet moved into the Prime Minister's residence and was staying, as we were, at the King David Hotel, got onto an elevator that I had been riding alone. In his deep, somber voice he said, "Dennis, tell the Secretary that he is dealing with a different Yitzhak now."

I told Baker of the encounter, observing that he "feels you are treating him as if he is Yitzhak Shamir, not Yitzhak Rabin." Baker got the message, and though we did not resolve the loan guarantee issue, we set the stage for doing so during Rabin's planned visit to the Bush summer home in Kennebunkport in August.

Instead of returning home with Baker at the conclusion of the trip, I returned to Israel from Saudi Arabia to give a speech at Tel Aviv University. Rabin asked to see me privately, and I went to see him at the Defense Ministry, which, unlike other key ministries, is located in Tel Aviv, not Jerusalem. He was both Prime Minister and Defense Minister. It was Friday afternoon, nearly Shabbat, and we sat alone for over an hour drinking a couple of beers.

Rabin was relaxed and unusually expansive. In response to my questions about his priorities on peace, he became both strategic about the imperative of succeeding and steely in his determination (even chilling in terms of what it would take) to overcome inevitable internal opposition.

The strategic imperative: Israel would never be in a stronger position than it was today; militarily it was more powerful than ever and the United States had transformed the region. But within a decade, if Israel did not capitalize on the current favorable conditions, it could face grave dangers from Iran or possibly a resurgent Iraq—each of which might acquire unconventional military capabilities. It was necessary to transform the Middle East before that could happen.

The steely determination: he said he was prepared to do what was necessary, even though he anticipated violent opposition from the Israeli settlers. While he was not speaking of total withdrawal from the West Bank, he clearly was contemplating significant withdrawal from territory and settlements. His determination to proceed was driven by his conviction that his generation—the fighters for the creation of Israel—

had an obligation to pass on to the next generation the possibility of living in peace. His confidence that he could overcome the internal opposition, violent as it might turn out to be, stemmed from the IDF's support for his actions.

He told me that the entire leadership of the IDF was made up of his "boys." They had been with him throughout their careers, he had promoted them, they were the best the military could produce, and "they are completely loyal to me." I asked, "It sounds like you are talking about civil war—do you really believe that you will face something that extreme from the settlers and others?" He was unequivocal in his response: "Yes, and that is why it is so important that I have people I can count on" in the IDF. He took a long swallow of beer and concluded with, "It will get ugly." Ironically, three years later when it was very ugly, he failed to take the threats against him seriously.

| WHO WAS YITZHAK RABIN? |

In describing Yitzhak Rabin in his memoirs, Henry Kissinger wrote, "Taciturn, shy, reflective, almost resentful of small talk, Rabin possessed few of the attributes commonly associated with diplomacy," adding, "I grew extremely fond of him though he did little to encourage affection."

Few who knew Rabin would disagree with Kissinger's observation. Yet I would often see a softer side of Rabin. To be sure, it was never directed at me. Rather, I would see it directed at his wife, Leah, or their family. On Shabbat afternoons, he would often invite me to his home in Tel Aviv—a two-story apartment with a garden on the roof of the building. While with me he was all business, he would relax when his family was present. He would reveal his softer side when Leah might knock on the door of his study to see whether we wanted anything. No matter what we were discussing at the time, his look would change; with his glance at her, his demeanor, even his tone, would soften. It was the same with his children, and especially his grandchildren.

His demeanor otherwise was straightforward, even gruff and blunt. He had no time for and little interest in small talk.

His was a first-class mind. More than any leader I have dealt with, Rabin was an analyst. His thinking was structured and highly organized. He would summarize in a staccato fashion what were the regional developments as he saw them. He might offer four or five points to capture the strategic reality, always presenting them in sequence and literally saying first, second, third, fourth, and fifth.

He respected leaders who were tough and straightforward. Even before we began the negotiations with the Syrians, he had a great deal of respect for Hafez al-Asad, whom he found tough but true to his word. He drew much from the experience of negotiating the 1974 disengagement agreement with Syria through Henry Kissinger's shuttle. Rabin believed that reaching any agreement with Asad would be extraordinarily difficult, but if reached, Asad would live up to it, just as he had with the 1974 agreement. Rabin often reminded me that Asad never allowed a single terrorist act to be launched against Israel from the Golan Heights and that Asad also observed limits in Lebanon, "Israel's redlines," about where Syrian forces could and could not be located.

He saw Yasir Arafat very differently. He held Arafat responsible for countless acts of terror, the most egregious in his eyes being the grisly attack in 1974 on Ma'alot in which twenty-six people were killed, nearly all of them children. Terror made Arafat an implacable foe for Rabin. Arafat's equivocation and lying—as Rabin saw them—rendered him someone unworthy of respect.

And yet by the summer of 1995 Rabin was to compare Asad unfavorably to Arafat, telling me, "At least Arafat is prepared to do things that are difficult for him. Asad wants everything handed to him and he wants to do nothing for it." For Rabin, the measure of leadership was a readiness to make difficult decisions. It was also the measure of seriousness about peace. He had to take steps that were very hard for him, practically and emotionally. He wanted to know that those he was negotiating with were prepared to do likewise. Rabin was not one to rush to decisions. But he was also not one who would avoid them. He simply knew the consequences of rash behaviors, and so would never be pushed into doing something before he was ready.

Growing up, he had not envisioned a life as a warrior. He studied water engineering, and one time at his home he took great pride in describing to Secretary Christopher, me, and others the automated watering system he had designed for his roof garden. But security and Israel's War of Independence transformed his life. He joined the elite commandos of the Palmach at the age of nineteen in 1941, and became its deputy commander under Yigal Allon in 1947. He commanded the Harel Brigade during the War of Independence and fought in the defense of Jerusalem, keeping the road open to break the siege of the city and helping preserve at least the western part of Jerusalem under the new state of Israel's control.

I never met a more secular Israeli. But for Rabin Jerusalem remained the soul of Israel. One time with me he was indignant over right-wing critics accusing him of being soft on Jerusalem because he was resisting pressures to increase the Jewish Israeli presence in the Arab neighborhoods of East Jerusalem: "No one can preach to me about Jerusalem," he said. "I fought for it, I made sure we liberated it, and I will not surrender it."

While there was no ambiguity about his position on Jerusalem, he often saw the world in shades of gray. It was not just that he could come up with artful compromises like, for example, the "dual addressees," which suggested that Rabin knew that compromises on Jerusalem itself might be necessary. It was also that he would adjust to realities no matter how painful they might be.

There is no better example of that than his readiness to deal with the PLO. To do that, he had to overcome his own deep misgivings. But Rabin was a practical man, and his public explanations reflected that. "What can we do? Peace you don't make with friends, but with very unsympathetic enemies. I won't try to make the PLO look good. It was an enemy, it remains an enemy, but negotiations must be with enemies."

His practicality was always informed by his power of analysis. His analysis might well run ahead of his politics; indeed, he would not allow his analysis to be distorted by political considerations even though he might not act on his analysis because of political considerations. Again, his approach to the PLO is a good example. In March of 1993, he held an "analytical" breakfast with the new Clinton administration's Middle East specialists to go over regional developments and prospects. Over the meal, he gave a compelling explanation of why no Palestinian leader from the territories would ever have the authority to make commitments or deliver on them, and why Israel would have to deal with those who had such authority, wherever they were based.

Several of us asked the obvious question: Aren't you saying that you will have no choice but to deal with the PLO? Rabin demurred; though his analysis logically led to this conclusion, he was not ready to embrace it. The politics of Israel at that juncture ruled it out, and Rabin the cautious pragmatist was not ready to break the taboo on direct talks with the PLO. Rather, he still hoped to avoid this by, in effect, breaking another taboo and having Faisal Husseini, a Jerusalemite, become the head of the Palestinian delegation to talks with the Israelis—but he wanted us to propose this idea.

If Faisal were the head of the delegation, Jerusalem would be on the agenda. There was no ambiguity here; Faisal was a Jerusalemite, who had a political preoccupation with preserving East Jerusalem for the Palestinians. Rabin the pragmatist could deal with this if it was an American idea and it allowed him to see if there was an alternative to the PLO.

Following that breakfast, knowing Rabin as I did, I knew it was only a matter of time before Israel would begin to negotiate with the PLO. Two months later, when it became clear that even someone of Faisal's stature did not have the authority to negotiate, Rabin authorized negotiations with the PLO through a back channel. With Rabin, one always needed to pay attention to his analysis. Sooner or later his behavior would reflect it.

Rabin trusted his own assessments more than those of others. He drew information from others, and it was possible to influence him if you could do so before he had thought an issue through. Once he had made his analysis, though, you would not move him; only events would. For example, Rabin's analysis told him that it was both possible and desirable to do a deal with Asad before doing one with Arafat. When it became clear that this was not the case, Rabin turned to Arafat; he did not give up on a deal with Asad, but he altered his assessment accordingly.

Rabin was very much an intellectual loner. He compartmentalized information, sharing it sparingly; he never shared the private commitment he had made to us on withdrawal from the Golan Heights with anyone on his side except Itamar Rabinovich, his negotiator and ambassador to the United States, so that when Shimon Peres became Prime Minister, he was surprised by it and Ehud Barak still questioned it even years later, telling us that he did not believe Rabin would ever have kept something so vital from him.

He trusted few people completely, but if he trusted you he would take you into his confidence on what he believed you needed to know. Over the years, he shared highly sensitive views with me—in part because I never betrayed a confidence, in part because I would ask him searching questions and would not simply accept his assessments without offering my own—and no doubt in part because he saw me as instrumental to the process.

His basic trust in himself, in his judgment, provided him with an inner calm in the midst of the storms raging around him. While his political enemies would from time to time whisper scurrilously about his "nervous collapse" of May 23, 1967, the scuttlebutt never had resonance or credibility in Israel because he resumed command prior to the Six-Day War in June and was its unquestioned architect.* Maybe his inner confidence stemmed from his life's experience. He had faced all the trauma of war; he had helped forge Israel's defenses and masterminded its successes in battle; he had buried his close friends and borne the tragic news to their families; he had transformed the Israeli military and the country; he had been Prime Minister before and dealt with the world's leaders from the 1970s onward. There was little he had not seen, and his logical mind told him to maintain perspective and a clear mind in a crisis.

On more than one occasion, I went to see him in the Prime Minister's office in the immediate aftermath of a suicide bombing in Israel. The outer office would be in turmoil, with the press hounding his assistants for answers, his military secretary scurrying around to get updates, and cabinet ministers gathering to meet him and settle on a response. But in his office it would be quiet and he would exude calm. He might be angry, but rarely showed it. He might be uncertain as to his course of action, but never conveyed any doubt.

---

*Rabin collapsed on May 23 from exhaustion, pressure, and, as he later suggested, from too much nicotine and too little food.

In January 1995, for example, after a double suicide bombing killed twenty Israeli soldiers and a civilian at a bus stop at Beit Lid, Rabin was steady as could be. The country was traumatized; the soldiers (all aged eighteen to twenty-one) had been returning from leave and pictures of them led the news broadcasts. Amid the uproar, Rabin calmly asked me to convey a specific set of security demands to Arafat, and a very clear message: If you don't deal with those responsible, we will. He made it clear he would not conduct any further negotiations with Arafat until Arafat assumed his responsibilities on security, and then said to me, "Peace will not be possible until Arafat has his own *Altalena*."

In 1948, during the first UN truce adopted to try to stop the fighting between the newly declared state of Israel and all of its neighbors, a ship, the *Altalena*, departed southern France transporting a large number of volunteers for the Irgun and 5,000 rifles and 270 light machine guns. Prime Minister David Ben-Gurion wanted the arms and the volunteers to be integrated into the new unified Israel Defense Forces. Menachem Begin, hoping to preserve the Irgun as a fighting force separate from the Israeli army, rejected this. For Ben-Gurion, there could be only one authority: "Jewish independence will not endure if every individual group is free to establish its own military force and to determine political facts affecting the future of the State." Ben-Gurion ordered the Irgun to hand the ship over to the Israeli army. When they refused, he ordered Israeli forces to take the ship; in the ensuing firefight, the ship was sunk, and more than thirty members of the Irgun were killed. The commander of the Israeli forces was Yitzhak Rabin.

He was no stranger to tough decisions, no pushover in political infighting. If he gave you his word, he would keep it, even if the circumstances changed and it was very difficult for him to do so. Later, as we will see, he felt he had made a mistake in what he committed to us on the Golan Heights, but he would not retreat from his commitment.

His word defined him. He would not lie. He might tell what I coined the "technical truth"—something that was technically true but actually misleading—to preserve secrecy on sensitive issues, but even here the right question would elicit the truth.

Yitzhak Rabin was for me the embodiment of the Israeli experience. He was close to the land, blunt in his demeanor, personally fearless—a warrior by necessity but desirous of a different life for his children and their generation. He was a man preoccupied with history, always thinking about the possibilities of change for both better and worse. His last words to me were strangely prophetic: "Dennis," he said, "expect anything."

| THE TRANSITION FROM BUSH TO CLINTON |

When President Bush asked Secretary Baker to go to the White House, Baker insisted that I go as well. I was not enthusiastic, feeling the main issues in the campaign would be domestic and that my own philosophy put me far closer to the themes Clinton would be emphasizing than to the traditional Republican themes certain to guide the Bush efforts.

Baker, however, wanted his team around him. I did not feel I could say no to him. I felt I owed both the Secretary and the President a great deal. They had invested in me, giving me extraordinary responsibilities for shaping our policies on the Soviet Union and toward the Arab-Israeli conflict. And I also had enormous respect for President Bush, believing that he had guided the country and the world through tumultuous times—the end of the Cold War, the demise of the Soviet Union, and the undoing of the Iraqi absorption of Kuwait—with skill, insight, and great personal strength. So there could be no question of my saying no to Baker's request to go to the White House with him for the campaign.

I asked only that I be allowed to return to the State Department following the election, regardless of its outcome, believing I could have a greater effect on the transition that way. After Bill Clinton defeated George Bush in November 1992, I returned to State. I did not expect to be asked to stay. Working with the new Secretary, Larry Eagleburger, to whom I had become close over the years, I set about shaping the briefings that would be given to the new team. As it turned out, I was able not only to do that but also to work closely with him on the final stages of the START 2 negotiations as well.

The Clinton transition team did ask me to give them briefings, and then in early January Brian Atwood (the head of the State Department transition team) and Peter Tarnoff (who would become the Undersecretary for Political Affairs) asked if I would be willing to stay for a three-to-six-month transition period to help the new administration. They were not precise either about what I would be asked to do or about the position from which I would be doing it.

I knew that my friend Martin Indyk, who was involved in the transition and would become the senior Middle East advisor on the National Security Council staff, was also pushing to have me stay. He was keeping me informed of appointments to senior positions as well.

Sandy Berger was shaping the NSC staff at the White House. While I had known Sandy from our days working in the McGovern presidential campaign, I knew there was considerable opposition to my being asked to stay. After all, I had gone to the White House with Baker. My purpose there was to defeat Clinton. The Democrats had been out of power for twelve years; I had been with the Republicans; it was time to reward the faithful, not to keep representatives of the other side.

In Washington such arguments are rarely made in private. Journalist friends of mine would tell me what they were hearing. My reaction: I don't expect to stay; if I am asked, I will consider it. In fact, I had resolved that if asked, I would stay. My reasoning was that I had done so much to produce negotiations between Arabs and Israelis that I did not want the transition to a new administration to risk those negotiations. And beginning in December, there was a troublesome break in the negotiations.

In response to several acts of terror, Yitzhak Rabin ordered the deportation of four hundred Hamas activists across the border into Lebanon. While this deportation was not to be permanent, Rabin (strongly supported by his military Chief of Staff, Ehud Barak) believed that such deportations could be an effective deterrent to terror. Palestinians did not want to be uprooted from their land and villages, and if they persisted in violence they would be. If they "behaved themselves," they would be permitted to return in a year or two.

I told them it was a dubious proposition. But ultimately it was not the plan that failed Rabin and Barak; it was the failure to anticipate that the Lebanese would not simply absorb the deportees. On the contrary, the Lebanese government announced that they were an Israeli responsibility and would not let them move from the area in which they had been deposited, just across the Israeli border in southern Lebanon. There, in a no-man's-land, the four hundred deportees were stuck. Televised around the world, their plight became a new grievance against Israel, and Palestinians declared a suspension of the negotiations until the deportees were allowed to return home.

The new Clinton administration would have to contend with this in its first days. I felt a need to help. In the week prior to the inauguration, Peter Tarnoff approached me again and said that the new Secretary of State, Warren Christopher, would like me to stay on as a "Special Advisor" for six months, to give him advice principally on the Middle East. I would stay in my office down the inner corridor from the Secretary's, send my memos directly to Secretary Christopher, and see him if I felt it necessary. I would also be included in all Middle East policy discussions.

Over the course of the first few months of the Clinton administration, then, I offered advice, was among those who briefed the President before his March meeting with Rabin, and accompanied Secretary Christopher on his first trip to the Middle East. But I underestimated what it would be like to be a kibitzer after having been in the center of the action, as one of the most trusted advisors of the Secretary and the key point of contact for leaders and advisors from other countries. Now others had the responsibility to carry out the policies—even though I might be able to affect those policies with my ideas. But this too was not satisfying as often those ideas were distorted in their implementation.

Inescapably, I was on the periphery because I had come from the other camp. It is human nature to trust those who have labored with you in life's battles. Political campaigns are crucibles of group definition. The choices are clear; the battle lines are drawn; winning and losing have a consequence; passion and exhausting effort forge a common sense of mission and extraordinary personal bonds.

After four months in the Christopher State Department, while feeling I had been treated very fairly, I also felt isolated. Though I had come to respect Secretary Christopher and had developed a close relationship with his Chief of Staff, Tom Donilon, I decided it made sense to leave. I told the Secretary I would like to leave by May 1; feeling that we were still in a difficult period, he asked if I would remain until June 15, and I reluctantly agreed to do so.

Tom Donilon had other ideas. Tom was the person closest to Warren Christopher. He'd come from the Secretary's law firm, O'Melvany and Meyers, had been intimately involved in the Clinton campaign, and was respected by all the key White House advisors. Although he belittled his own foreign policy expertise, he was very smart, an unusually quick study, and a voracious reader. Moreover, he quickly demonstrated both intuition and good judgment—attributes that are typically more important than narrow expertise. Given what I had done in the Bush administration, Tom was always keen to talk to me about broad lessons learned in dealing with the Russians, security issues in Europe, the imbroglio in the former Yugoslavia, as well as the Middle East.

Convinced I should not leave, Tom explored ways to have me stay, including the creation for me of a new Undersecretary of State position on regional conflicts. I was flattered, but not interested. Every time he would bring up my staying, I would change the subject. Finally he asked me, "What is the one position you could not say no to?"

I told him I could not say no to being the chief U.S. negotiator on Arab-Israeli peace. "But forget it," I said, because "to satisfy me you would have to upset the whole bureaucratic structure. The Near Eastern Affairs Bureau (NEA) has the lead now, and Ed Djerejian and his team will not want to accept a situation where I run things. The Secretary does not need the trouble." I thought that would end the story, but I underestimated Tom and Secretary Christopher.

It is not often that one is called away from one's going-away party to be asked to stay. But that is what happened. I was scheduled to leave on June 15. In the midst of a party thrown for me by my former staff from the Policy Planning Staff, I was called down to see Peter Tarnoff, who informed me that the Secretary, then away in Europe, had asked me to become our negotiator for the Arab-Israeli conflict. I would have my own office, report only to him, and use NEA for support whenever and for whatever I felt necessary.

Does NEA know this? I asked. Knowing about bureaucratic instincts, I fully expected NEA to resist the Secretary's decision. (I would have, if I had been in Ed's position.) I wanted to be sure that the Secretary would stick with his decision in the face of that resistance. The last thing I needed was to make the decision to stay and then find that because of bureaucratic angst the ground rules would be modified to accommodate the NEA concerns—and I told Peter this. Peter told me Ed had not yet been informed, but if he was not comfortable with the new arrangement, he would be offered the ambassadorship in Israel.

Peter assured me this was a final decision: the Secretary wanted me to be his negotiator for the Middle East. There would be no question about my authority either within the State Department or outside it. The Secretary had obtained the President's approval.

I agreed, and shortly received a call from Secretary Christopher telling me he was "thrilled" I was staying, and was confident that in my new position I would make a difference on the Middle East.

To say I was surprised would be an understatement. True, I had told Tom Donilon what it would take for me to stay, but I never expected this. Suddenly I was no longer a kibitzer. I now had the responsibility to make something of the peace process once again.

| THE CLINTON ADMINISTRATION'S MIND-SET ON THE MIDDLE EAST |

The Clinton administration did not come to the Middle East generally or the Arab-Israeli conflict specifically with a strong orientation. Initially, Warren Christopher, like James Baker before him, saw dangers in getting bogged down in endless and nonproductive Middle East talks, and told Lawrence Eagleburger that he would not fall into that trap.

He was also sensitive to the political minefields of Arab-Israeli diplomacy. He got wind of unease about him in the Jewish community, where it was felt that Christopher, having been the Deputy Secretary of State during the Carter administration, shared Jimmy Carter's approach—that he would be too quick to criticize Israel, too inclined to be responsive to the Arabs, and too open to the PLO and Yasir Arafat. Senator Joseph Lieberman hosted a meeting for Secretary-designate Christopher with Jewish leaders in which Christopher made clear his commitment to a strong Israel and to an open-door policy with Jewish leaders. If there were openings for Arab-Israeli peace, he would be ready to pursue them. But he was not going to be active in trying to create openings if they were not there.

The new National Security Advisor, Anthony Lake, had not been a particularly close observer of the Middle East. He saw little need for presidential activism there, and he felt the Middle East should be the Secretary of State's preserve.

Tony appointed Martin Indyk his lead specialist on the Middle East on the National Security Council staff. Tony and his deputy, Sandy Berger, had arranged for Martin to brief candidate Clinton, then President-elect Clinton, on the Middle East. Martin, highly thoughtful and articulate, was a devotee of a "Syria-first" strategy, believing that Syria would affect the regional dynamics, and that the Palestinians, especially the Palestinians in the territories, would not.

The Palestinians could make life uncomfortable for Israelis, but not threaten their existence. Syria, with its conventional and unconventional forces, could. Settling the conflict with the Syrians would give Israel a "circle of peace." Jordan, not feeling threatened by Syria or its rejectionist clients, would follow Syria's lead, Lebanon too, and suddenly Israel would be at peace with all of its neighboring states. This would influence the Saudis and the Gulf states, insulate Israel from more distant threats from Iraq and Iran, and provide great leverage over the Palestinians. Knowing the other Arab states had a stake in peace with Israel, the Palestinians would find little support for hard-line positions, making an agreement more likely even on the most existential questions—or so the logic of the Syria-first approach went.

Of course, while the Syria-first approach reflected Rabin's preferred strategy—and certainly influenced the Clinton administration's orientation at its inception—reality does not always conform to preferred strategies. And that was certainly the case in the early days of the Clinton administration.

In its first week, it was not Syria that preoccupied the administration, but the issue of the Hamas deportations that had been raised at the UN Security Council. Suddenly Secretary Christopher had to contend with a number of questions: How to avoid problems at the UN, particularly in the Security Council? How to get the negotiations resumed again? How not to get off to a rocky start either substantively or politically on Arab-Israeli issues?

To overcome the deportation issue, Christopher took a trip to the region from February 18–25, far earlier than he might have, and reached an understanding with Rabin that permitted some of the deportees to return immediately and the rest to return over the period of a year. That paved the way for a resumption of negotiations in Washington on all the tracks.

Several weeks later, Rabin came to Washington, hoping to focus on the Syrian track. But a series of terrorist stabbings in Jerusalem prompted him to cut his trip short.

It was on this trip that Rabin suggested including Faisal Husseini on the Palestinian team as a way of breathing life into those negotiations. On the Syrian track, little progress proved possible as the Syrians in Washington insisted that Israel must first commit to full withdrawal from the Golan before Syria could make any comments about peace with Israel.*

---

*As a compromise between the Israelis, who wanted the talks in the Middle East, and the Arabs, who wanted them to remain in Spain, we proposed that the bilateral talks initiated in Madrid would continue in Washington.

Shortly after Rabin had become Prime Minister, he had reversed Shamir's policy that resolution 242 did not apply to the Golan Heights. This meant that in theory Israel was willing to withdraw from the Golan, but Rabin felt the scope of that withdrawal must be a major topic for the negotiations. For their part, the Syrians responded to the Israeli change on 242 by being willing to engage in discussions of a framework agreement, but they would not begin to give it content or speak about peace unless the Israelis committed to full withdrawal.

During this time, prior to my becoming the negotiator, Ed Djerejian was managing our effort in the Washington talks, and given his background as former ambassador to Syria, he spent most of his time on this track. To break the stalemate, he tried to see if the Syrians would engage on the basis of hypotheticals—e.g., assume you get full withdrawal, how would you respond on peace and security—but this effort too was unavailing. The Syrian negotiators would not budge.

Similarly, no headway was being made in the Palestinian negotiations. Even after Faisal Husseini was made the head of the delegation, Arafat imposed his authority by having Husseini spend his time in Tunis rather than in Washington with the delegation. The signal to the Israelis was clear. You can talk with those in Washington, but you will get nothing done unless you deal with us here—meaning the PLO.

Rabin, at least as far as I was aware, had not yet made the decision to deal with the PLO. At this point, we had no dialogue with the PLO either, having suspended it back in June 1990 over an act of terror.* We could hardly reengage with the PLO and we were thus left with little room to maneuver. In my initial move as negotiator, I tried to give this track a push by having the Israelis agree to the concept of "early empowerment." In particular, I wanted the Israelis to agree to turn over functional power to the Palestinians in the areas of education, health, welfare, tourism, and taxation, feeling that it might demonstrate to Palestinians that change was possible. But neither side showed much enthusiasm for this idea—with the Palestinians feeling it did not address what they wanted, namely, jurisdiction over the land, and the Israelis not wanting to cede any powers unless the Palestinians gave up the idea of having jurisdiction.

So as I entered the process as our negotiator, the situation, even with a Labor government, looked similar to the way it had during Shamir's time. But there was one very important piece of the situation that I did not fully grasp—and that was Oslo.

---

*At that time, Abul Abbas, a member of the Executive Committee of the PLO, had been responsible for an attempted act of terror in Tel Aviv. Arafat had not been willing either to condemn the act or to expel Abbas from the Executive Committee, our two conditions for not suspending the U.S.-PLO dialogue.

| THE OSLO PROCESS |

Even before the Israeli elections in 1992, the Norwegians had sought to establish a back channel between Israelis and the PLO. Because of the Israeli law forbidding Israeli officials from contacting official members of the PLO, meetings in academic settings or conferences were acceptable; more formal meetings were not. Terje Larsen headed the Oslo-based Institute for Applied Social Science (its Norwegian acronym was FAFO). Terje and others, like Marianne Heiberg, wife of the Norwegian Foreign Minister, Johan Jørgen Holst, had done studies for FAFO on life in the West Bank. Their work had brought them in contact with many Palestinians and Israelis and built a strong commitment to trying to promote peace.

Terje was a great believer in creating informal channels of communication, and in 1992 his preoccupation was setting up a back channel between Yossi Beilin, a leading dove in the Labor Party who was a close disciple of Shimon Peres, and Faisal Husseini, who (unbeknownst to Terje) had been meeting discreetly already.

In early December of 1992, Ahmed Qurei of the PLO (better known by his Palestinian patronym of Abu Ala), was in London to informally coordinate Palestinian participation in the multilateral negotiations launched the previous January. Yair Hirschfeld, an Israeli academician, had close ties to Palestinians in the territories and had been urged to meet with Abu Ala in London. Hirschfeld asked Larsen if he would arrange a meeting and Hirschfeld and Abu Ala met twice in London.

Yossi Beilin, who had been appointed as Deputy Foreign Minister under Shimon Peres, was also in London, leading the Israeli delegation to the multilaterals. Hirschfeld, without revealing that he had already met with Abu Ala, asked Yossi for permission to meet Abu Ala in Norway. Yossi approved the idea, and beginning in January of 1993 the Oslo channel was born.

For Yossi, this was a perfect opportunity to retain deniability, but also to test what PLO thinking might be. He had low expectations that these talks would lead anywhere, believing at most that they could generate ideas that might prove useful for breaking impasses in the Washington talks.

Hirschfeld brought fellow academic Ron Pundak to the talks. Abu Ala brought Maher el-Kurd, a longtime associate of his and a member of Arafat's office, as well as Hassan Asfour, a former Communist and close collaborator of Mahmoud Abbas—better known by his patronym Abu Mazen.

Abu Mazen, one of Arafat's earliest colleagues in Fatah, was a leading dove in the PLO, arguing for coexistence with Israel and the negotiation of a peace settlement. Though Abu Mazen would never directly take part in the Oslo discussions, Hassan Asfour was his eyes and ears in the discussions with Hirschfeld and Pundak.

In the first round of talks Hirschfeld and Abu Ala agreed on three ideas: Israeli withdrawal from Gaza; economic cooperation between the Palestinians and Israelis; and an international Marshall Plan for the "nascent Palestinian entity in Gaza."

In Israeli eyes, this was a promising beginning. The Israelis wanted out of Gaza— an impoverished area with over a million Palestinians crammed into 360 square kilometers. (By comparison, the West Bank had double the population but in 5,860 square kilometers.)

Beilin briefed Peres, who briefed Rabin, who approved more talks. Still, Yossi Beilin believed that the talks could only yield real promise and real insight into PLO thinking if the two sides began to draft a declaration of principles (DOP) for the interim period. Abu Ala agreed to this.

The Israeli approach continued to be shaped by the Camp David agreement, calling for an interim period in which there would be autonomy for the Palestinians, followed by negotiations on the permanent status issues of Jerusalem, refugees, and borders. We, too, had embraced the logic of such an approach, actually embedding it in the invitation letter to Madrid. For their part, the Palestinians preferred going directly to permanent status, but adjusted to this basic approach—with the provisos of gaining real independence from the Israelis early and with statehood understood as the objective of the process.

In two rounds in February and March, Hirschfeld and Pundak and Abu Ala and Hassan Asfour came to an understanding on a six-page document. In it both sides made important moves. Israel would agree to withdraw completely from Gaza in two years (with a UN trusteeship to replace Israel); to negotiate the permanent status of Jerusalem; to permit the Palestinians of East Jerusalem to take part in the elections for self-rule throughout the territories; and to accept binding arbitration of disputes. The Palestinians revealed their flexibility more by what they did not say than by what they did. For the first time, they were ready to accept a document that did not provide explicit jurisdiction and control over the land; did not ensure that East Jerusalem would be part of the area of self-rule; and did not have guarantees on statehood.

In reality, this document seemed to contradict everything we knew about both sides' positions; and at the end of March, when the Norwegians shared the DOP drafted by Hirschfeld and Abu Ala with us, I found it hard to believe, especially on the Israeli side.

I knew that Rabin wanted out of Gaza, but doubted he would agree to dismantle settlements or include East Jerusalem in the self-rule areas at this stage. And there was no way that Rabin, of all people, would accept that disagreements with the Palestinians could be subject to outside and binding arbitration; he would not put Israel's fate in someone else's hands.

Naturally, the paper led us to doubt the seriousness and meaning of the channel. Sure enough, by May, when official Israelis became involved in the Oslo channel, they insisted that the passages about binding arbitration, the complete withdrawal from Gaza, and Palestinians running for and voting in elections in East Jerusalem all had to be changed.

Why did Rabin make the Oslo channel an official one? To begin with, he saw the Washington talks going nowhere, with Faisal in Tunis and the negotiators in Washington demanding that self-rule must provide not only for jurisdiction over the land but also for authority over the Israeli settlements in the West Bank and Gaza. Worse, they would not accept exclusion of East Jerusalem from the self-rule arrangements and insisted on statehood being the acknowledged outcome of the negotiations.

Rabin believed his domestic realities required that he be able to say that he had preserved Israel's options for the future. He saw the interim period as one in which Palestinian intentions would be tested and both sides would learn to live together. That would make tackling the existential issues of the conflict possible over time.

With this in mind, he decided to test the Oslo channel, and, in effect, to test Arafat, by saying he would discontinue the channel unless Faisal Husseini took part so as to keep public attention on the Washington talks.

No doubt sensing that Rabin was undecided on the utility of the channel, Arafat responded to these Israeli demands and Abu Ala even went so far as to tell Hirschfeld in the fourth round of talks in April that East Jerusalem would be excluded from the area of self-rule. By May, however, having acceded to Israeli demands and seen very little in response, the Palestinians felt it was their turn to impose a demand. Abu Ala told Hirschfeld that either the Israelis upgrade the channel—to include official participation—or the Palestinians would no longer take part in it.

Now Rabin had to decide the future of this channel. He decided that Peres could send Uri Savir, the Director General of the Foreign Ministry, to participate in the talks. A major threshold was being crossed: Israel was officially dealing with the PLO, albeit in secret. There would be no more deniability.

Though Uri was to retreat from many of the positions Hirschfeld had taken and Abu Ala was to harden the Palestinian positions, these two would forge a bond that would ensure eventual agreement at Oslo. As I was to see later, Uri and Abu Ala each understood the other's fundamental commitment to peaceful coexistence. Whatever the difficulties they would face, whatever manipulations they would engage in for the sake of achieving their ends in negotiations—and no two negotiators have ever been better manipulators—they forged a bond of trust.

Abu Ala saw in Uri an Israeli who grasped Palestinian needs in human and political terms, who believed occupation was wrong, and who understood that Israel needed to accept Palestinian national aspirations—provided the aspirations were not defined in a way that threatened Israel's existence. Uri saw in Abu Ala a Palestinian who was a leading PLO official and close to Arafat, who was committed to peaceful coexistence with Israel, and who believed that the well-being of the Palestinians depended on it. The two struck an implicit bargain: "statehood for security." Uri acknowledged that Palestinian national aspirations would need to be recognized ultimately; Abu Ala understood that Palestinian national needs could only be accepted if Israeli security needs were satisfied. Everything else could be worked out.

That is not to say the process of negotiating the Declaration of Principles was easy or without crisis and brinkmanship. Indeed, the norm in these and the negotiations that would follow over the next seven years was crisis and brinkmanship. The crisis in Oslo would come at the end of July when Abu Ala would provide twenty-six reservations—reservations that walked back Palestinian flexibility on nearly all the issues.

With the talks on the brink of collapse, Uri offered a basic trade-off: to get Abu Ala to give up the points Israel could not accept, Uri offered to push for formal and mutual recognition. Abu Ala knew that for Arafat mutual recognition would be the big achievement. His readiness to accept an interim period and a gradual process was probably always tied in his mind to the political gain of recognition and recognition inevitably meant acceptance of the PLO raison d'être of independent statehood.

While Rabin was not keen to give this away, Uri understood it was necessary to play the recognition card if the Palestinians were to accept all of Israel's security needs, including Israeli jurisdiction over all Israelis in the West Bank and Gaza—and also agree to drop their demands on holding East Jerusalem elections, binding arbitration, total withdrawal from Gaza, and creating a Palestinian corridor between Gaza and Jericho.

Uri's offer to push for mutual recognition broke the crisis and put them on a pathway to agreeing on the Declaration of Principles. I was to learn all of this in great detail later from Uri and Abu Ala—each of whom I became very close to. But as I readied myself for my first trip to the region as our envoy in the middle of July, I was unaware of how much they had discussed or that their talks were in crisis at this time.

However, I was aware that there were multiple contacts between Israelis and Palestinians who were either PLO representatives or had close ties to PLO leaders. Once the Knesset had lifted the ban on meetings between private Israeli citizens and members of the PLO, the channels proliferated: Shlomo Gazit, a former head of Israeli military intelligence, led a group who met with Palestinian academics to discuss security issues; Ephraim Sneh, formerly the Israeli administrator of the West Bank and Gaza, was apparently meeting with Nabil Sha'ath of the PLO. And, of course, there was the Oslo channel.

I felt my initial trip should be used to see if there was a way to foster movement on both negotiating tracks. I would see what Rabin would tell me about contacts with the Palestinians, probe on any possible flexibility on the jurisdiction question, and use resistance on it to push early empowerment to create a new dynamic on the Palestinian track. On Syria, I would suggest Rabin let me convey a different type of message to Asad to see if that might allow us to generate a different Syrian response on the content of peace. Secretary Christopher approved my plan.

Martin Indyk, Aaron Miller, and Gamal Helal would accompany me on this and many subsequent trips. They became known as members of the peace team.

Martin Indyk, originally an academic from Australia, was the first executive director of the Washington Institution for Near East Policy. I met him before leaving to go to Berkeley and we became close friends. Martin is smart, eloquent, and passionate about America's role in the Middle East. Our views on the Middle East tended to mesh closely. We were both strong believers in the strategic importance of the U.S.-Israeli relationship, convinced that Israeli deterrence and the possibility of peace depended on never allowing a wedge to be driven between America and Israel, and certain that the risks of pursuing peace were less than the risks of not pursuing it. We would work closely together in each of his positions in the Clinton Administration, first as special assistant to the President on the NSC staff, then as Ambassador to Israel, then as Assistant Secretary of State for the Near Eastern Affairs Bureau, and finally as Ambassador to Israel a second time. It was not unusual for Martin and me to speak four or five times daily, no matter where either of us was in the world. And, when I was in Israel, I would spend time with him before and after meetings, chewing over what was happening and what to do.

Aaron Miller would be my deputy. I had known him since the mid-1980s, and he had been on my staff in Policy Planning at the State Department. Aaron was a historian by training, and the author of several books, including one on Saudi Arabia. He brought great passion to the pursuit of Arab-Israeli peace. Like Martin and me, he was Jewish and in no small part that helped to shape his personal commitment to peace. He deeply believed in Israel's moral legitimacy, while also understanding the profound sense of grievance that Palestinians felt. Perhaps, because of his training as a historian, Aaron always tried to evaluate what was going on in terms of basic trends. He would often say that this conflict evolved in stages and would only be settled in stages. He tended to be more risk averse than I, always seeing the value in the process, and fearing its alternative. He was also guided by his own sense of fairness, believing instinctively that the Palestinians should not be treated differently from any other Arab party. Aaron's analysis was thoughtful, logical, and honest. One thing I knew for sure: With Aaron, I would have a deputy who would never shy away from expressing the truth as he understood it, no matter the audience.

Gamal Helal was born in Egypt and came to study in America when he was twenty. He had stayed, become an American citizen, and joined the State Department as an interpreter. We met for the first time the night before Secretary Baker's January 9, 1991 meeting in Geneva with Iraqi Foreign Minister Tariq Aziz; Gamal would be the interpreter in the meeting that was the last-gasp effort to produce Iraqi withdrawal from Kuwait and avert war. Gamal knew the stakes for the meeting and, anxious to be precise, asked if I could show him the "talking points" Baker would use. Even though we were still working on them, I let him review them, and jokingly told him, "Hey, there's no pressure on you. You are a rookie and just treat this as the Super Bowl and World Series rolled into one. Don't worry, you will do fine." And, in fact, he did. From that time onward, he became the Secretary's and the President's lead Arabic interpreter in the Bush and Clinton Administrations. I came to appreciate Gamal's extraordinary talents and insights on the region and made him one of my senior advisors.

Over the course of the next several years others became members of the team: Mark Parris, when he took Martin's place at the NSC; Jonathan Schwartz, the deputy legal advisor in the State Department; Bruce Riedel, who replaced Mark Parris at the NSC; David Satterfield, when he served with Martin at the NSC and later in the Near Eastern Affairs Bureau; and, finally, Robert Malley, who worked with Bruce and had a particularly strong commitment to Israeli-Palestinian peace.

Three others bear special mention: Toni Verstandig, Nick Rasmussen, and Henrietta Mickens. Toni was a deputy assistant secretary in NEA. She had spent nearly two decades as a lead congressional staffer. She was savvy, energetic, and determined to get things done. She had an intuitive feel for economic development and played the leading role in our efforts to provide assistance to the Palestinians. Nick was my special assistant. He had a general background on security issues. He had worked for Bob Gallucci on the negotiations with North Korea, and when Gallucci was leaving the government, he called to tell me he was going to do me a great favor by suggesting I hire his aide, Nick Rasmussen. Bob was right—Nick was indispensable. From logistics to substance to highly sensitive assignments, Nick could do it all—tirelessly and with great skill. Finally, Henrietta ran my office. She did it with great professionalism and enormous dedication. Without Henrietta, I could not have done my job

With this group of people in support of my efforts, I was now the point person for the Clinton administration on the Arab-Israeli peace process.* I was given a wide man-

---

*Secretary Christopher effectively deputized a number of individuals to be responsible for particular policy areas: Strobe Talbott was responsible for Russia and the newly independent states, later Richard Holbrooke became responsible for Bosnia, and I was responsible for the Arab-Israeli issues.

date by the Secretary and the President, and I could call on any part of the State, Defense, or CIA bureaucracies to support our approach to diplomacy. To manage our policy on a day-to-day basis, I would have a meeting at 10 a.m. every day in my office at the State Department. I did this not only to hash out what we should be doing but also to deal with any issue that needed to be addressed that day: guidance for the White House and State Department spokespersons; responses to congressional inquiries; finalizing talking points for presidential phone calls; conveying messages to our ambassadors in the field; reacting, as necessary, to overnight developments.

The meetings helped ensure bureaucratic cohesion and minimized my being blindsided by actions that one part of the bureaucracy might be taking in the region that could cut across the diplomacy I was responsible for conducting. At different times, depending on the needs of the negotiations, I would bring senior military officers representing the Chairman of the Joint Chiefs of Staff to these meetings and on my trips. In 1995 and 1996 Lt. General Dan Christman played this role in the Syrian negotiations. Later, Lt. General "Doc" Foglesong assisted me in this manner on both tracks. Both men played an enormously helpful role in the diplomacy when called upon to do so. And the 10 a.m. meetings, always held when I was not in the region, became a focal point for responding to tactical needs and a continuing forum for intense discussion on what was happening in the region and whether it was validating our assumptions.

| JULY TRIP: EARLY RABIN SIGNALS |

Knowing Rabin, I had little expectation that he would reveal anything new in the larger group meeting with our respective delegations. That would have to wait for our private meeting.

In the larger meeting, the Prime Minister greeted me warmly and then proceeded to take a tough line, opposing any softening on the jurisdiction question. On Syria, he said there was nothing more he could do. He felt he had done his part and taken a risky step by announcing several months earlier that "the depth of withdrawal will reflect the depth of peace." He was being critized in Israel for having signaled that he would be prepared for significant withdrawal without there being any change in Syria's negotiating posture. For Rabin, the ball was in Asad's court.

Our private meeting proved to be far more interesting. Once we had gone into his

---

Each of those so "deputized" had enormous independence and authority in their areas. When Madeleine became Secretary, she operated differently in general but not toward me.

inner office, just the two of us, I opened with Syria: What did he want me to convey to Asad? He thought a moment and asked, did I have anything in mind? I did. Why not let me say that "Prime Minister Rabin understands your needs. He knows if they aren't met, if you aren't satisfied on withdrawal, there will be no deal. He wants a deal, but he does not believe that you understand his needs. And just as your needs must be met, so must his be met if there is to be an agreement. How do you understand his needs and what would you like me to say about those needs in response to the Prime Minister?"

In a noncommitting and indirect fashion, I would be signaling on Rabin's behalf that he knew there would be no deal without full withdrawal, and that he wanted a deal. At the same time, I was putting Asad in a position in which he would need to respond with a signal akin to the one Rabin was sending through me.

I did not need to spell this out for Rabin. He got it. He thought for a minute and then said, "It is okay for you to say that," revealing no emotion or concern, even though I would be implying Israeli readiness for full withdrawal under certain circumstances.

Relaxed now, Rabin told me he wanted to show me something. He went over to his desk and returned with a handwritten letter, which he handed to me, saying I must tell no one but the President and the Secretary about it. The letter was from Arafat. He had fundamental doubts about Arafat, wondering whether he would ever really deliver. But in this letter (conveyed by the Egyptians from the PLO ambassador in Cairo), Arafat made clear he would defer all the sensitive issues, especially Jerusalem and jurisdiction, in order to reach an interim agreement.

If this was true, it signaled the possibility of progress with the PLO. Rabin said he would respond to the letter and test Arafat's reaction to his answer.

When I asked about other discreet channels giving similar signals, he dismissed them. This, not the Oslo channel, seemed to be the one he took seriously.

As I left the office and headed to Syria, I realized that Rabin was testing on both tracks. Who would respond first, Asad or Arafat?

MEETING WITH ASAD · I met Asad not in Damascus but in his summer house along the Mediterranean Sea in Latakia. The climate was pleasant and the setting was beautiful. Somehow I could not envision Asad rollicking in the sea or taking hikes in the mountains above his sprawling house. But he must have relished the escape from the capital.

Asad, like Rabin, welcomed me. He had liked Baker, and admired his readiness to be tough on the Israelis. Having me as the envoy signaled the kind of continuity that Asad liked—links to those he took seriously and to those responsible for Madrid.

Our meeting was long and cordial. Knowing that Asad always wanted to settle into a meeting, I did not rush to the Rabin message. I set the stage for it, explaining why the President and the Secretary had made me the envoy and how they saw my role. I also wanted to wait until after Asad brought up the subject of Bush and Baker—something I knew he would do to remind me of his confidence in them and of the Madrid commitments.

I had to choreograph the meeting this way because I knew that if I raised the Rabin message prematurely or made too much of it, Asad would belittle it. Instead, I eased into it by talking about how both sides had needs, and no agreement could be reached unless the needs of both sides were satisfied—and the public opinion of both sides was addressed.*

Asad nodded, saying, "This is correct." Then I told him I had a message from the Prime Minister, which I then summarized. Asad listened carefully, then declared the message "useful."

When I asked him to describe how he understood Rabin's needs, he replied: "Rabin needs peace." When I pressed him on what that meant in practical terms, he said, he needs "full peace; peace between neighbors." He resisted being more precise. But he offered a formula, "full peace for full withdrawal"—his answer to Rabin's "the depth of withdrawal will reflect the depth of peace."†

Back in Jerusalem, I briefed Rabin, who saw little for Israel in the formula but found Asad's response interesting enough to suggest that I return for another round of exchanging messages between himself and Asad in a couple of weeks.

I returned to Washington believing that on the Syrian track I was now involved in a diplomatic minuet that might offer a new direction to Israeli-Syrian negotiations. I had not made any real headway on the Palestinian track, but I believed the next step there should be Rabin's response to the Arafat letter.

| LEBANON INTERVENES |

At the end of July, there was an eruption of violence in southern Lebanon between the Israeli military (IDF) and Hizbollah. Hizbollah killed a number of Israeli soldiers in Israel's security zone in southern Lebanon; Israel retaliated against villages that Hizbollah operated from; and Hizbollah fired Katyusha rockets into northern Israel. With the Israelis living in shelters in the north, Rabin and his military Chief of

---

*Asad was forever lecturing Westerners who he felt discounted Arab public opinion.

†Shara had raised this formula once in public previously, but it had not been repeated.

Staff, Ehud Barak, were determined to deal a more decisive blow against Hizbollah's capability to disrupt life in northern Israel. To that end, Israel launched "Operation Accountability," a plan devised by Barak and approved by Rabin. If Israeli citizens in the north would have no peace from Hizbollah rockets, the thinking went, then Lebanese living in southern Lebanon would also know no peace. Except that in the Lebanese case, residents would be forced to leave their homes, triggering a mass exodus of Lebanese villagers from the south that would force the Lebanese government inevitably to plead with Asad to stop this kind of Hizbollah behavior—or so the plan presumed.

Logical, perhaps, but as I told Rabin in our first conversations as the fighting escalated, the Israeli campaign was based on a flawed assumption. Asad did not care if the Lebanese were suffering; moreover, he was surely pleased by a situation that put the onus on Israel internationally. With 250,000 Lebanese streaming toward Beirut in a human caravan, Asad saw only gains, not losses, in such a situation; and militarily the Israelis could not stop the Katyusha rockets without occupying all of southern Lebanon.*

At the time, I was in Washington and Secretary Christopher was in Asia taking part in the annual ASEAN meetings. Though we were half a world apart, we spoke frequently and I was cabling the points to be used in the phone calls he was making to Rabin and Syrian Foreign Minister Shara.

Over the course of several days, we forged a set of verbal understandings that civilians on each side of the border would not be targeted. Once agreed, there would be a cease-fire. The main sticking point was that Syria would not commit to stopping Hizbollah attacks against Israeli forces in Israel's self-declared security zone in southern Lebanon. As Shara told the Secretary, Hizbollah had the right to resist the Israeli occupation in its country. The line was being drawn only on attacks against civilians by each side.

Rabin was initially reluctant to accept these ground rules for a cease-fire; but ever the realist, he knew he was not going to do better. He called me to say he would accept the terms but wanted to be clear on one point and certain that Syria accepted it: if Hizbollah would still be free to attack the IDF in Lebanon, Israeli forces would return fire against any source, even if the fire was coming from within villages, and such an action would not constitute a violation of the cease-fire. When Shara told us that President Asad accepted this point, we had a cease-fire agreement.

---

*Rabin, as Defense Minister in 1985, had presided over the Israeli withdrawal from most of Lebanon and was not going to reenter now.

| RABIN'S SECRET COMMITMENT ON THE GOLAN HEIGHTS |

In the first week of August, Secretary Christopher traveled to the region, mainly intending to see each leader and have them reaffirm the cease-fire terms face-to-face with him.

The Secretary and I were in for a surprise. In a private meeting—involving only Rabin, Itamar, the Secretary, and me—Rabin quickly moved beyond Lebanon and suggested that the cease-fire agreement might mean that Asad was ready for something larger and more strategic. Sometimes opportunities came out of crises. We should find out if there was an opportunity with Syria now.

He proposed to have us convey the following: He would be prepared to commit to the United States that Israel would withdraw fully from the Golan Heights provided Israel's needs were met and provided Syria's agreement was not contingent on any other agreement—such as an agreement between the Palestinians and Israelis. He went on to explain Israel's needs: (1) There must be normalization of relations, with full diplomatic relations and an exchange of ambassadors after the first phase of withdrawal. Withdrawal should be spread out over five years; (2) Full normalization required trade and tourism; (3) There must be satisfactory security arrangements, with the United States manning the early-warning sites in the Golan; (4) Israel's water needs must be safeguarded.

Rabin said that Asad should understand that what we were conveying had to remain absolutely confidential. If it leaked, he would deny it and withdraw it altogether.

If Asad could accept this, Rabin wanted to move quickly to agreement. Christopher asked if Rabin expected anything to happen with the Palestinians. Rabin was skeptical, making a cryptic reference to secret talks with the Palestinians but doubting they would lead anywhere. His focus was clearly on Syria, not the Palestinians.

In retrospect, I believe that Rabin still doubted that Arafat would deliver in the end through the Oslo channel. But before finding out, Rabin wanted to know whether a breakthrough with Asad was possible. In his mind, he could not do both; the public could not absorb two such shocks—a commitment to withdraw fully from the Golan and a deal with the PLO—at the same time.

SEEING ASAD IN DAMASCUS · Given the sensitivity of the Rabin message, we arranged a private meeting with Asad, with only the Secretary and myself on our side and Asad's Foreign Minister, Farouk al-Shara, and his new interpreter, Butheina Sha'-aban, joining Asad.

When we conveyed the Rabin message, Asad made no effort to belittle it. "Very important," he said, clearly aware that he was hearing an explicit commitment to full withdrawal for the first time. He then offered a qualified response: he did not like the term "normalization" (he preferred "normal peaceful relations"); he could not mandate trade or tourism, but he would not block them either. He accepted that satisfactory security arrangements would be required, but said this was a mutual interest. Water was also important for both sides, not only one.

Finally, he accepted that a Syrian agreement would not be dependent on a final deal with the Palestinians—but stressed his expectation that Rabin would seek at least a partial deal. I explained that that was what the Israelis and Palestinians were currently trying to negotiate, and he nodded approvingly.

When the Secretary repeated that Rabin had to know that Asad would not condition an agreement with Israel on any other agreement, Asad said Syria would proceed to reach agreement with Israel but he did require an Israeli-Lebanese agreement at the same time. In a classic bit of understatement, he said he did not foresee any difficulties in reaching an agreement between the Lebanese and the Israelis if a deal with Syria had been concluded. Rabin, he said, understood Syria's special relations with Lebanon, so here again he anticipated no problems with the Israelis on his tying his agreement to the Lebanese.

It is noteworthy that later, after the Oslo agreement was disclosed, Asad justified making his own deal with the Israelis on the grounds that the Palestinians had left him. But, in fact, he was ready to make his own deal from the beginning. He was willing to leave the Palestinians out in the cold, but not the Lebanese.

Now Asad raised a problem. In 1974, in the Disengagement Agreement, it had taken the Israelis twenty-two days to withdraw, so why, he asked, did Rabin now say five years was necessary for withdrawal? Though the Secretary and I pointed out that the two agreements were different—one interim and limited, one final and total—the Secretary said we would ask for an explanation.

But Asad could not bring himself to say more. I believe he foresaw tough negotiating ahead, and he saw little reason to give Rabin leverage in the negotiation. Asad, much like us, did not appreciate that the Israelis and PLO were on the brink of a breakthrough. Even had he known, I doubt he would have changed his posture.

Asad was never one to move in leaps. His response was not historic in nature. But it would have been out of character for him to respond differently.

Rabin was hoping for more. In his eyes, Asad's response did not signal a readiness to move quickly to a peace agreement. Rabin found the Asad response minimal and said so. He did not seem troubled by Asad's qualifiers; he even answered Asad's question on the timetable for withdrawal, contending it would take four to five years to build new housing in Israel for the Israelis forced to leave the Golan Heights. Smiling, he said, "I could do it in less time if he is willing to allow Israelis living there to remain under Syrian sovereignty."

For all that, he was prepared to start a private negotiation with the Syrians, provided it involved only one Syrian with Itamar. Even then, the Syrian representative would not hear from Itamar what was given to us. But the process of negotiating an agreement could begin.

So Warren Christopher and I returned to Damascus and summarized Rabin's response to Asad. It was Asad's turn to smile; sardonically, he replied, "First you want me to let the Jews leave and now you want them to remain."*

Asad listened carefully as we described Rabin's unwillingness to convey what he had put in our pocket directly to the Syrians at this stage. From this time onward, Rabin's conditional offer on full withdrawal became referred to as the "pocket."

Asad raised no objections, except that he preferred to have two negotiators on his side and wanted to be sure that I would host the negotiations. This, I noted, would make Rabin nervous about a possible disclosure of the "pocket."

Asad's response was both chilling and convincing: Anyone who would leak the pocket would hurt Syria's national interest, and all Syrians knew what the consequences were for "hurting" Syria's national interest.

Clearly, Asad wanted more than one person on his side. The reason, I assumed, was to keep his negotiator honest and to ensure that he was informed of everything that was discussed. While we told Asad we would have to get Rabin's approval before committing to the arrangement he wanted for the negotiations, Asad confidently asserted that Rabin would agree.

We were getting ready to leave when Asad said, "You may think this a strange question, but does Israel have any claim on the territory?" Secretary Christopher said, "No, the Prime Minister spoke only of full withdrawal."

Not wanting any possible misunderstanding, I asked, "When you refer to claims are you referring to claims anywhere? The Israelis do make claims in the West Bank." Asad quickly responded, saying he was only asking about "claims on Syrian territory or on the Syrian front."

I shook my head no, saying, "There are no claims that we are aware of." I added "that we *are* aware of" to protect us in case Rabin did, in fact, have some claims he had not mentioned.

With that very much in mind, I drew special attention to our exchange on this point when I subsequently briefed Itamar back in Washington on the meeting. He lis-

---

*During the Bush administration, we had worked hard to get Asad to allow the small Jewish community in Syria to leave; after much prodding, he permitted them to do so. With only Secretary Christopher and me sitting there, it was pretty clear the "you" in this conversation was directed at me.

tened and did not correct our responses to Asad. I was able to tell Christopher after this briefing that Itamar had raised no objections to what we had told Asad and that it was safe to assume now that there were, in fact, no Israeli claims. Unfortunately, as we were to find out later, there might not have been claims, but there were different definitions of what full withdrawal meant.

At this stage, however, none of that was clear. Asad in all of our private conversations and in his public posture spoke only of "full withdrawal" from the Golan Heights. Rabin promised "full withdrawal, provided Israel's needs are met."

For now, we did not know there was a dispute over the meaning of full withdrawal. That would come the following year, tying our diplomacy in knots for over two months.

Asad, as we were to find out in nine months, viewed all the territory that was in Syrian control on June 4, 1967, as Syrian. Rabin felt any territory beyond the putative international border—the one affixed as part of the British and French mandates in 1923—should be Israeli. The difference in territory between these two lines was not significant, but for Asad every inch of the territory that he considered Syrian was "sacred." And for Rabin, the difference had meaning for Israeli control of water, specifically their need to preserve the Jordan and Hasbani Rivers on the Israeli side of the border.

For now, we thought we had a historic breakthrough between Israelis and Syrians. The Syrians would get the Golan Heights back if they could offer peace and security for the Israelis. I, for one, thought the negotiations with Asad would be excruciating, but that we would produce a deal in time. On our return, in mid-August, we expected to start the negotiations in Washington the first week of September.

Then "Oslo" intervened.

| THE SECRET OSLO CHANNEL PRODUCES |

Both Secretary Christopher and I left for vacation to California shortly after our return from the Middle East. I had briefed Itamar on the second meeting with Asad and he seemed quite upbeat after that report. As we left for California, both the Secretary and I had high hopes on the Syrian track, and a view that with the Palestinians nothing would turn around quickly.

Here again we were in for a surprise. On August 25, Rabin called Secretary Christopher and asked if Foreign Minister Johan Holst of Norway and Shimon Peres could visit him secretly in California to brief him on an agreement that had been reached in Oslo, one involving Israel and the PLO.* He would also send Itamar to join

---

*Holst had become foreign minister after earlier serving as the defense minister.

the meeting. Christopher told Rabin this was fine (he would arrange for a military base in California to host the meeting) and that I would join him. Was there anything else? he asked. "No," Rabin replied, but "I would appreciate it, Mr. Secretary, if you could call me back with your reaction after you have seen Holst and Peres."

Christopher had alerted me in advance of the call so I could listen in; after the call, Christopher phoned me and asked, "What do you make of that?" I told him the secret channel Rabin always dismissed had now produced something significant or he would not be asking you to see Holst and Peres secretly and urgently. But he was still reserving judgment. Is it because he is uneasy about the content? Or about our reaction to their having done this without our knowing? "I suspect a little of both." The Secretary thought that made sense. The meeting would take place at Point Mugu, a naval base a half hour from Santa Barbara. He asked me to come meet him at his beach house in Carpentaria, ten miles south of Santa Barbara.

I was staying in Burbank with Debbie's family. We were due to return to Washington the next morning, and I took Debbie and the kids to the airport and proceeded to Carpentaria. As Secretary Christopher and I rode to Point Mugu, I observed that we might be on the verge of having breakthroughs on both Syrian and Palestinian tracks. I wondered if that was another reason for Rabin's unease—that he was worried about how much change his public would absorb?

Both of us felt great anticipation over the prospect of an agreement between Israel and the PLO. It was not just the history of terror, violence, hostility, and mutual rejection. An agreement would indicate mutual recognition and all that it entailed. For Israel, mutual recognition would mean an acceptance of the PLO agenda, including statehood. For the Palestinians, it meant unequivocal acceptance of Israel and its right to exist. That meant a complete redefinition of the PLO and an acknowledgment of Israel's needs. In effect, it would transform an existential conflict into a political conflict. In the Middle East, nothing could be more revolutionary.

When we arrived at the base it became clear that Secretary Christopher and I were not the only ones wondering about this meeting. Holst and Peres wondered about how we were going to respond.

Holst began by telling us the secret channel in Oslo had now produced an agreement on a Declaration of Principles, a very important agreement, a historic agreement. To gain the full support of the international community and the other Arabs—which was critical for Arafat—he proposed that the signing take place in Washington. Massive amounts of assistance would also be necessary to get the Palestinian economy up and running so the Palestinians could feel the benefits of peace.

He turned to Shimon Peres, who explained there were two ways to confront a conflict: "With the power of power or with the power of wisdom." His government, in his view, had chosen the latter, and agreed with the PLO on a Declaration of Principles. The DOP created a process in which Israel would gradually get out of the business of running Palestinians' lives; there was a timetable and targets for creating a Palestinian Authority first in Gaza and Jericho; Israel would withdraw from most of Gaza, leaving its settlements there in the interim period; the Palestinian Authority would govern the Palestinians, ending the military government. A second or "interim" agreement would expand the Authority through the West Bank, through "redeployment" of Israeli forces to specified military areas. Permanent status negotiations would begin after two years and would need to be resolved by the end of the five-year interim period. Jerusalem, refugees, borders, security arrangements, and relations and cooperation with neighboring states would be negotiated in permanent status.

The two peoples, Israelis and Palestinians, would learn to live together. The Declaration of Principles emphasized cooperation in economic and security spheres. The logic, Peres stressed, was to build a network of cooperation so that the harder issues would become resolvable in a very different climate. Israel's interest dictated finding a way to live with the Palestinians, ending occupation, and developing a mutual, not a unilateral, approach to security; helping the Palestinians prosper was good for peace and good for Israel.

This Israeli government had made a choice to try to settle the conflict with the Palestinians, and to recognize that peace with the Palestinians would offer the best guarantee of security. The DOP offered the pathway for doing so. While Israel could content itself with filling in that pathway, he and the Prime Minister had made the decision not to take a partial step now. If you face "a gorge, you must leap it in one move." That is why they would also move to recognize the PLO, even though recognition was not necessary.

Peres asserted that the DOP stood on its own; it was an agreement and did not require Israel to recognize the PLO or vice versa. But since you could not walk across a gorge, but must leap across it, he and the Prime Minister were prepared to take the leap.

The question was how to proceed now. "Our Norwegian friends have been very helpful." However, Peres continued, "They know that only the United States can sell this agreement to the world and mobilize the resources necessary to meet the economic needs of the Palestinians." Holst nodded in agreement.

In light of that, Peres suggested that we announce the agreement as one the United States had brokered with the two parties and hold a signing ceremony at the White House. What did the Secretary think?

Warren Christopher asked to have a few minutes alone with me to go over their document and give a more considered response. But he said outright that he did not feel that we could claim it as our own.

I could tell that both Peres and Holst were uneasy as we broke. They feared we might not support it because it was done without us. Would we resist it on those grounds?

Secretary Christopher had been right to say we could not declare that we had brokered this agreement, and when we were alone I told him I agreed with him. Inevitably, both sides—Israeli and Palestinian—would reveal how the agreement was produced.

Peres's aide, Yoel Singer, had given the document to me while Holst was speaking, and now Christopher asked me what I thought of it. I told Christopher it was indeed historic—a comprehensive statement of aims on the interim period and permanent status. The interim period was linked to the process as a whole with timetables and targets laid out for the creation of an interim self-governing authority in Gaza and Jericho, elections for a council, the expansion of the authority to the remainder of the West Bank, the beginning of permanent status negotiations, and much else. The issues for permanent status were identified and the eventual agreement on this would lead, in the words of the document, to the "implementation of Security Council resolutions 242 and 338." In sum, I said it was a document of mutual accommodation and designed to produce mutual reconciliation. We had to support it enthusiastically.

We needed, however, to recognize two things. First, the hard work would now have to be done, translating the principles into a new reality on the ground, and it was clear even from a cursory reading that there were a lot of holes in it—not to mention that all the hard decisions were deferred. Second, I did disagree with Peres's insistence that Israel could sign this document without recognizing the PLO. I told Christopher that made no sense. Without mutual recognition, who would be making the agreement? Who would implement it? Who would be held responsible if it was not implemented?

The Secretary agreed it was historic and deserved enthusiastic support, but thought I should press Peres on the mutual recognition issue. Then he asked, "Dennis, do you think we should host the signing ceremony at the White House?"

There was no choice. A historic threshold was being crossed. We needed to promote it, elevate it, and generate momentum behind it. Nothing could more effectively do that internationally than having the President host the signing agreement at the White House. But I wanted to press both parties in some areas of our needs before we gave that away. The Secretary wanted those around him to call him "Chris," and at this moment I said, "Chris, if you would permit me, I would like to push Peres on the recognition issue and make it clear that we, for our own reasons, need a clear renunciation of terror and violence from Arafat and a readiness on his part to act against those who might engage in it. Our own dialogue with the PLO has been suspended since 1990. We cannot resume a dialogue, much less have the PLO in Washington for a signing ceremony at the White House, without such commitments on his part."

The Secretary agreed, and we rejoined Peres and Holst, who relaxed visibly when

Secretary Christopher told them we would do all we could to support the agreement. In response to my comments, Peres asked me to dictate the language we would need the PLO to accept, and I did so.*

Then Christopher invited Peres and Holst and those who had come with them to have some refreshments. Wine and cheese were served and the Secretary, a man of civility and grace, offered a toast to "your extraordinary effort, your dedication to peace, and to continued success in the hard work of diplomacy that lies ahead."

Peres came over to me and asked, "Dennis, what do you think?" "Mr. Minister," I replied, "Ben-Gurion would be proud."

Shimon, whose anxiety had given way to relief, was now very touched. His eyes watered and he offered me a simple "thank you."

| NOTHING IS EVER EASY |

We had all agreed in parting that we would wait a few days before announcing anything so the Secretary could begin calling other Arab leaders to gain their support for the agreement. But not surprisingly, news of the Peres trip to California leaked out the next day in Israel, and with it the story of a possible breakthrough with the PLO. Over the coming two weeks, I was on the phone day and night as the Israelis and Palestinians tried to work out the document on mutual recognition. Arafat was resisting being held responsible for those who were opposed to the agreement and the violent acts they might commit, and wanted certain assurances on Jerusalem. Because we were not prepared to resume our contact with the PLO until the mutual recognition agreement was completed, I could not deal directly with anyone from the PLO at this point. So I worked through Terje Larsen, with whom I would soon develop a lasting friendship.

After much give-and-take, the issues related to mutual recognition were embodied in a public exchange of letters between Arafat and Rabin on September 9, 1993. In his letter, Arafat committed the PLO to resolving all outstanding issues of permanent status through negotiations, renounced terror and other acts of violence, and assumed "responsibility over all PLO elements and personnel in order to assure their compliance, prevent violations and discipline violators." Rabin's reply confirmed to Arafat that, "in light of the PLO commitments included in your letter, the Government of Is-

---

*Yoel Singer also showed me language they had already drafted on renunciation of violence. I suggested an insert on the Palestinian responsibility to prevent violence as well as to act against those who would carry out acts of terror or violence.

rael has decided to recognize the PLO as the representative of the Palestinian people and commence negotiations with the PLO within the Middle East peace process."

This exchange was made possible in no small part by our insisting we would not announce a signing ceremony until the letters were signed, and by Terje Larsen's and Johan Holst's pressure on Arafat to conclude lest he lose this historic opportunity. As would be the case in every subsequent agreement, the existence of a deadline was the only way to produce an outcome.

There was one other complicating factor: Who would sign the agreement? Peres believed it was too much for Rabin and the Israeli public to have an event with Arafat, and so proposed himself and Abu Mazen, the putative number two in the PLO.

Rabin agreed; Israelis were not ready to see Arafat celebrated at the White House. But so long as Arafat thought Abu Mazen would be feted at the White House and not him, he had little stake in finalizing the agreement—or so Terje was telling me.

While I understood this, I thought it wrong to go against Rabin. President Clinton, however, had different ideas. When we were finally in a position to announce the event at the White House, the President made clear that he felt Arafat would have much more of a stake in the DOP if he was at the signing. He then asked Martin and me what he should say if asked about Arafat attending, and we suggested that he simply say the two sides had made the decision on representation and they preferred, at this stage, to be represented at the senior level by Peres and Abu Mazen. Not surprisingly, the President did not look convinced.

When he met the press to announce the event and was asked whether Arafat would be welcome if he wanted to come, the President simply answered "yes." Martin and I looked at each other and in unison said, "Arafat is coming." We also knew that now Rabin too would feel he had no choice but to come.

The ceremony was set for September 13. We had problems up to the last moment. I was up the whole night prior to the event. First, the Palestinians objected to the absence of any reference to the PLO in the DOP. Then Rabin declared that he would not show if Arafat was in military dress. We employed Prince Bandar bin Sultan, the Saudi Ambassador, to persuade Arafat: no guns and no uniforms.

Suddenly both sides were threatening not to come: the Palestinians if the PLO was not mentioned in the text; Rabin if Arafat was in uniform. I did not take the threats seriously. Was Arafat, who was desperate for the international stature and recognition that would come with the event at the White House, ready to turn around and not see the President? And would Rabin, having made the hard decision to do a deal with the PLO, now say forget it? I doubted it, and while bringing the Secretary up to date on our problems in the morning, I told him we should insist each side come and tell them they would pay the price if they did not.

I used these very words with Hanan Ashrawi, who had come as part of Arafat's delegation and called while I was riding with Secretary Christopher to the White House. She was pleading for the inclusion of the words "the PLO" in the document. I told her we could not do that, only the Israelis could, and that the Chairman needed to come now to the White House or lose everything.

As we arrived outside the Oval Office, the President's secretary, Betty Currie, informed me that I had a call waiting for me. Across from her desk was a credenza with phones on each end. Martin was on the phone on one end, obviously exasperated with Eitan Haber (Rabin's senior aide) over Rabin's resistance on Arafat's dress. I picked up the phone and Hanan asked me to speak to Nabil Sha'ath—one of Arafat's closest aides. Soon both Martin and I were screaming into our respective phones.

I could not hear everything Martin was yelling, only that he was yelling. For my part, I yelled at Nabil that the Chairman was about to make the biggest mistake of his life. Before the world he would be seen as unable to conclude what had been negotiated. He would embarrass the President of the United States and he would never again be welcome in America. We would have nothing to do with the PLO. Finally, Nabil wearily asked was there anything we could do, and I said, Nabil, nothing is possible if you do not show up. Expectantly, he asked could something be done if they did? "Nabil," I said, "all I can tell you is that nothing is possible if you don't. And if you don't, the consequences will be disastrous for you."

After a short pause—probably to tell Arafat—he said with a note of resignation, "Okay, we are coming." In the meantime, Martin had persuaded Haber and Rabin would be coming—all this barely fifteen minutes prior to the start of the scheduled ceremony.

When Nabil arrived with Arafat, who wore his customary olive drab uniform, he went over to Peres and said it would be a disaster for them if the PLO was not in the text. After all this, Peres agreed to write in the PLO both in the first line of the document and in the signature block at the bottom. Because we had prepared the documents for signature and there was no time to retype them, the words "PLO team" and "For the PLO" were inserted in handwritten letters.

The only thing that remained was the ceremony and the "handshake." Prior to the ceremony former Presidents Carter and Bush were in the Oval Office; while Martin and I were screaming at the two sides, Jimmy Carter was urging President Clinton to bring Rabin and Arafat together and have them talk to each other. I believe that it was Carter's urging, together with the President's own instincts, that led him to nudge Rabin and Arafat to a public handshake.

Rabin's personal difficulty in shaking Arafat's hand was there for the world to see. Clinton's literal embrace of the two, seemingly moving Rabin to shake Arafat's hand, became the symbol of the ceremony. It was certainly one of Clinton's proudest moments.

September 13, 1993, was a day of extraordinary hope. The handshake between Rabin and Arafat symbolized a new beginning. Rabin's speech spoke to the emotional trauma many Israelis felt in embracing Arafat and the PLO, given their history of terror against Israelis. He identified with the grief of those whose families had been the victims of terror. But for the sake of all Israelis, he concluded it was time to take a chance on peace, time to end a hundred years' struggle, and time to reach out to each other and say, "Enough of blood and tears." Little did we know how hard that would be.

⟨ 4 ⟩

From Oslo to the Palestinian Authority

LEAVING THE WHITE HOUSE on September 13, no one—not among the Israelis, the Palestinians, or ourselves—believed we would fail to meet the first important milestone of the Declaration of Principles: the establishment of the Palestinian Authority (PA) in Gaza and Jericho on December 13. As it turned out, however, this agreement producing the PA would not be reached until the following May.

To understand why it took so long and what happened along the way, it is best to divide the period after the signing at the White House into three phases: first, the efforts to negotiate from September 1993 to February 25, 1994; second, the intensive, at times desperate, effort—from February 25 to April—to save the process after an Israeli settler went into the Ibrahimi Mosque in Hebron and murdered twenty-nine Palestinians as they were praying; and, finally, the renewed effort that culminated in the May 4, 1994, agreement.

| PHASE ONE: RECONCILING DIFFERENT
MIND-SETS, SEPTEMBER TO FEBRUARY |

In the weeks following the signing, the Israelis and Palestinians began to try to translate the DOP's general principles into specifics: What powers would the Palestinian Authority have? What would its relationship to Israel be? The Oslo agreement had been reached bilaterally, essentially without us, and we were content to support the parties' efforts but not to intervene in them. Instead we sought to reinforce the DOP, believing we could best do so by organizing an international donor effort to show that peace would pay real economic dividends for the Palestinian people. A State Department event on October 1 generated pledges of nearly $2.4 billion in assistance to the Palestinians—to be provided once they developed institutions for the Palestinian Authority.

However, because Yasir Arafat was loath to surrender any control, a problem emerged on the donor effort and with the Israelis. Arafat resisted efforts to delegate authority or to create transparent mechanisms for the flow of the assistance. It was "his money" and he wanted to use it the way he always had: to buy loyalty, curry favor, sow rivalries, and be the sole problem-solver. The international community wanted to build institutions; he wanted everything to run through him, the "fixer."

At the same time, however, he wanted the attributes of a state-in-waiting, even though such a state belied the purpose of the phased approach to negotiations embodied in the DOP.

Did he not understand the DOP? Did his negotiators sell him a bill of goods? Was it one thing for him to sign an agreement, and quite another to create a credible Palestinian Authority? Or was he simply negotiating to see what he could get?

Whatever the reasons, the Israelis and Palestinians soon had two different ideas of what the first implementing agreement should be. The Israelis envisioned a Palestinian Authority profoundly limited not only in its geography but in its powers, one in which, from security to economics, little could happen if the Israelis did not want it to happen. It was one thing for the Israelis to theoretically accept autonomy as a necessary stage in a gradual transition to statehood; it was another to actually begin to surrender control.

The Palestinians envisioned the authority having symbols of independence, and so expected minimal Israeli presence in its operations and little Israeli interference in the lives of Palestinians. This would make the Palestinian Authority credible and demonstrate that the occupation was ending.

The gap was easy to see, but I was looking at it from a distance. Though both sides were keeping the United States informed, Yitzhak Rabin did not want us involved in the negotiations except to keep the Palestinians from changing the ground rules. The Palestinians, naturally, wanted us to lean on the Israelis to grant the Palestinians genuine autonomy.

During this phase, I would speak on the phone nearly every day with the negotiators and several times a week with Arafat. In these calls, Israeli complaints were consistent: The Palestinians are demanding concessions without assuming responsibilities—wanting no Israeli presence at the border, no control on their trade, their own passport and currency—while being reluctant to do what was necessary on security.

Palestinian complaints were similarly consistent: The Israelis should be looking to relinquish controls, not cement them. The negotiations were about ending occupation, not legalizing it. The more the PA could show it was running things and the Israelis were not, the more the rejectionists would be discredited and lose any following.

As would be the case so often in the succeeding seven years, each side had a point. Palestinians needed to demonstrate that it was a new day; however, Israelis needed to know that Palestinian control would be mirrored by Palestinian responsibility that would not be abused.

If they differed on what the initial agreement should reflect about the powers of the Palestinian Authority, they also differed on how they thought about the significance of the December 13 target date. Rabin declared that there were no sacred dates. For Arafat, to miss the date was to violate the agreement; and yet he offered few concessions as the date approached.

I began hearing from both negotiators, Uri Savir and Abu Ala, that our presence would help create pressures on both sides to be more flexible and find solutions. I decided that the Secretary should make a trip the week prior to December 13.

The Israelis were certain they understood Arafat and they were convinced that he was engaging in his typical game of brinkmanship in which he would create a crisis and then agree at one minute to midnight, as he had on the DOP. I was not convinced; even though Arafat was treating December 13 as a deadline, he knew he could not return to Gaza before there was an agreement establishing the Palestinian Authority, and I doubted that he would return to Gaza before he was satisfied that the agreement was the best he could get. Once he was convinced, he would agree and package the agreement to meet his public needs. In my eyes, that meant the date was not magical but his return to Gaza was.

As a result, I saw the Secretary's trip as one that might either facilitate an agreement or manage the situation if no agreement was reached by the thirteenth. The parties saw the trip according to their conflicting mind-sets. The Israelis saw the Secretary pressuring Arafat to concede and act consistently with the spirit of the DOP. The Palestinians saw the Secretary as the equalizer, leveling the playing field with the Israelis, who had all the power.

The trip was noteworthy not because it produced agreement but because it shaped Secretary Christopher's view of Arafat. Arafat was still operating in the realm of the national liberation movement leader: creating a mystique, putting on a show, shocking his guests so they would feel a need to find ways to accommodate him.

With Christopher in Amman, in what was his first substantive meeting, Arafat made up stories about Israeli atrocities; he spoke about Israeli violation of sacred commitments; he said he would not be humiliated by Israeli demands; he warned of a looming disaster in the whole region if there was no agreement on December 13 "as required in the agreement President Clinton witnessed and sponsored." He was rising out of his chair, literally screaming.

I had tried at several junctures to get Arafat to focus on the essential problems, and what might be done about them. But I had not succeeded, as clearly he'd decided that he could frighten Christopher into pushing the Israelis to accommodate him.

If Arafat thought this would affect Christopher, he badly miscalculated. No leader I have ever known is more polite and proper than Warren Christopher. As Secretary, he understood that not all problems lent themselves to rational solutions, but he would not give into irrational or brutish behaviors. He would assess what was possible and make every effort to find ways to bridge differences. If he thought there was little to be done, he saw no point in making much effort. In Rabin, he saw a tough-minded leader who was not always easy to deal with, but who was predictable and true to his word. In Asad, he saw a leader who could move only in small steps, riveted on not appearing weak, and bound and determined to make every issue a subject of negotiation—but he read him as someone who, in the end, could make a deal with the Israelis and stick to it.

Arafat was another story. Rather than persuading the Secretary that American pressure on Rabin was necessary to prevent a major crisis in the region, Arafat convinced Christopher that he, Arafat, was irrational and that dealing with him might be necessary but unpleasant.

At the tail end of our trip we went to Tunisia, where, after seeing Tunisian President Ben Ali, we would see Arafat again. I asked to see him alone. I told him that his meeting in Amman had been a disaster, and that if the meeting later in the day was a repeat performance, I doubted Christopher would see him again. I told him, "Be practical, don't shout, and don't just spend your time complaining."

Arafat nodded his head. He said nothing but the point registered, and Arafat was on his best behavior in the meeting, promising Christopher that he would work to manage the problems with the Israelis, would meet with Rabin the next day (December 13), and that there would be no crisis—even if an agreement was not reached.

In this case, he was true to his word. December 13 passed; there was no agreement and no crisis. Over the next several weeks I worked daily on the phones with both sides, on the issue of the crossing points—the places near the borders of Jordan leading to Jericho, and Egypt leading into Gaza—from which Palestinians or Arabs from the region entered or departed from the territories. The Palestinians wanted no visible Israeli presence. The Israelis wanted to be sure terrorists were not infiltrating the territories. The solution was the use of opaque glass behind which the Israelis could screen those who were entering without being visible. Naturally, the visibility of Israelis was only one problem. The Israelis wanted to be able to question those who gave them concern, the Palestinians did not—or at the very least did not want Palestinians to see any such questioning.

Over the course of the next two months, differences were gradually narrowed, albeit, very slowly. As the end of February approached, I foresaw another trip for us to the area to help them close the deal.

But an American émigré to Israel, Dr. Baruch Goldstein, was about to intervene and shake this fledgling process to its core.

| FEBRUARY 25: TERROR IN HEBRON AND MY TRIPS TO TUNIS |

Dr. Goldstein, a settler from Kiryat Arba, just outside of Hebron, saw the peace process with the PLO as a historic mistake, and the prospective turning over of land to the Arabs as sacrilege. On the morning of February 25, 1994, in the city of Hebron, he entered the Tomb of Abraham in an army uniform, walked into the adjacent Ibrahimi Mosque, and gunned down twenty-nine Arabs while they prayed—an act of murder designed also to kill the Oslo process.*

Bob Pelletreau, the Assistant Secretary for the Near Eastern Affairs Bureau, called me a little after 3 a.m. to tell me about the catastrophe; nothing could be worse or more incendiary in the Arab and Islamic world than an attack on a mosque and the worshippers there. Instead of peace, we would hear calls for a holy war, and Arafat would be under pressure not to negotiate with those whose purpose was to attack Islam.

And so it was. Notwithstanding our best efforts and strong Israeli condemnations of what had happened, Palestinians began rioting in the streets of Hebron and the Israelis imposed a curfew on the city—making Palestinians even angrier. As Saeb Erekat, one of the Palestinian negotiators, called me to say: First they kill us, and now we are the ones who can't go out of the city.

A process in which Israelis and Palestinians were beginning to work together was now replaced with outrage on the Palestinian side and guilt on the Israeli side. Rabin was under pressure from many in his cabinet to remove the settlers in Hebron. Totaling nearly four hundred, they were among the most zealous, extreme, and messianic of all Israeli settlers—and they required a large Israeli military presence to protect them.

Given the Palestinian rioting, Rabin did not want to pull the settlers out under pressure from the Palestinian street, especially when intelligence indicated that settlers from all over the West Bank were prepared to go to Hebron and violently resist any expulsion.

---

*Abraham, the father of Jacob and Ismail, is revered by Jews and Muslims alike, and his burial site in Hebron is sacred to both the Jewish and Islamic faiths.

Rabin had made a promise publicly at the time of agreement on the DOP: no settlements would be removed in the interim period, only in the context of an agreement on permanent status. Moreover, he believed that the time and circumstances were wrong for such a confrontation with his right wing. Others in the cabinet disagreed: What better moment to do so than now, when there was a reason to give the Palestinians something and settler resistance would only discredit them further with the Israeli public?

He decided to let the settlers stay. Eighteen months later, when Rabin was being vilified by the settlers for concluding the Interim Agreement—bringing the Palestinians into control of all the cities in West Bank except Hebron—he wondered with me whether he had made the right decision. He made the decision he did in part because he saw Arafat trying to exploit the situation to get things he had always sought. Arafat wanted internationalization. He called for UN intervention to send international troops to the territories and protect the Palestinians.

From before Oslo, Arafat's agenda had been to mobilize the international community to get for him what he could not get for himself. Rabin recognized the real anger on the Palestinian street, but felt any Israeli withdrawal must come from a negotiated understanding with the Palestinians, not from an outside intervention, which would permit the Palestinians to avoid any painful compromises. In his eyes, internationalization would inevitably develop a life of its own, preempting negotiations and building Arafat's expectation that he could be spared the need to make the hard choices.

On Saturday, the day after the Goldstein killing spree, my day started with a phone call just before 6 a.m. from Terje Larsen. For the next fourteen hours I was literally never off the phone trying to see what combination of steps might defuse the situation—every call generated a need to go back to check the reactions of those I had been speaking to. I asked the State Department operations center to create conference calls, sometimes joining me, Terje Larsen, Uri Savir, and Abu Ala. At several points, Secretary Christopher called but I concluded the other calls before taking his.

In fourteen hours I never moved from our bedroom, where I had taken the first call. (Debbie took pity on me, bringing me food; my kids, thinking it strange that I sat on the floor leaning against our bed, unshaven, unkempt, dressed in the first item of clothing I could find, my gym shorts, somehow read this as important and did their best to be quiet.)

I felt at the end of the day that we had made progress on several items: the content of a possible Security Council resolution condemning the killing but calling for a rededication to peace; additional declarations the Israelis might make about restricting settler provocations; and meetings between Israelis and Palestinians to discuss possible steps to reassure Palestinians before formally resuming the negotiations. But in a pattern that would often be repeated in the coming years, the next day there were new demands from the Palestinians and the Israelis were then reluctant to do all we had discussed the previous day.

Early on Monday, I got an irate call at my home from Yitzhak Rabin. He had heard I had agreed with Uri Savir on the terms for a meeting with the Palestinians in Tunis that would require additional public statements, and he refused to make such statements. Uri could not speak for him, and I must check every commitment with him personally.

It was my turn to be angry. I had not only spoken with Uri but also checked the very point he was raising with his military secretary, Dani Yatom, and Jacques Neriah, his policy advisor. How was I to do business if the only one who could speak for Israel on every issue, no matter how small, was the Prime Minister? "If I screwed up and committed Israel to things it could not do, you would be right to be angry, but I did not do that and I resent this call," I told him.

Uncharacteristically, he apologized, asking me to use my judgment about things that were sensitive and to check those with him personally. I promised to do so, and I never again received such a call.*

We still had to defuse a crisis and resume negotiations. With Arafat upping the ante daily, I felt it necessary to stop doing business over the phone and sit with him. But I also wanted to bring the Israelis as well. Let them forge their understandings with him personally. In a phone call with Arafat, I suggested that I come to Tunis to see him, provided a small Israeli team would come at the same time. He agreed.

Having the Israelis come as well was my way of resuming direct contact between the two sides. But there was one problem: the Israelis had no diplomatic relations with Tunisia and could not simply fly into Tunis. The Palestinians assured us they would take care of the arrangements for the Israelis.

| THE MARCH 7 ADVENTURE |

I took an Air Force Gulfstream, part of the USAF's fleet of executive jets, to Tunis. With me were Martin, Dan Kurtzer, the Deputy Assistant Secretary for the Near Eastern Affairs Bureau, and Aaron Miller. We had a full communications package on the plane, meaning I could make secure or nonsecure phone calls around the world. That turned out to be essential.

---

*The call was a reminder that Uri was Shimon Peres's man, not Rabin's. Oslo had always been more their process than his. They would agree to positions with the Palestinians that he would instinctively reject. However, so long as "his guys"—typically Dani or Uzi Dayan, both military men—agreed, it was okay.

Two and a half hours before we were to land, I received an urgent message from our deputy chief of mission in Israel, Jim Larocco, that the Israeli team was flying over the Mediterranean and had no clearance to land in Tunis—and because they were on a small plane would have to divert soon given fuel problems.

I called our ambassador in Tunis, John McCarthy, to ask him urgently to contact the Tunisian government and get clearance for the Israelis. Within fifteen minutes he called back to tell me there was a real problem: the Palestinians had simply assumed they could arrange this and had not informed the Tunisian government. The Tunisians did not like being taken for granted; no one on the Tunisian side who had the authority to make the decision was available. McCarthy had been told that today was a national holiday and that the President, Foreign Minister, and Defense Minister were all out of town and not reachable—and no one below their level could make the decision.

Often, to be heard on airplane phones, one had to shout. Now I was shouting both to be heard and to make a point: "John, the Israelis are flying in circles over the Mediterranean. They will have to divert shortly and I won't stay in Tunis if the Israelis are not there. If you can't reach the Tunisians, Arafat can; call him and get him to fix this."

I had visions of a looming disaster. I was making a high-profile trip into Tunis in an environment of great tension in the region. I had made the Israeli presence a condition for my going, and I could not back off now and be taken seriously in the future. Was I being tested or was this just a colossal screwup?

Needing a fallback plan, I asked one of our pilots if it was possible for the Israelis to land at a nearby U.S. base and have us pick them up and bring them to Tunis. He checked the map and suggested our base at Siganella at the tip of Sicily, an hour's flight time from Tunis.

Unfortunately, we did not have enough space in the plane to pick up five Israelis. The only alternative was to have the plane drop us off in Tunis and then fly the plane to Siganella to retrieve the Israelis. But to do this, our pilots would exceed the number of hours permitted by the Air Force to fly without a break.

I called Lieutenant General Dan Christman in the Pentagon, asking him to intercede with Air Force operations to cut the orders for our pilots. He promised to do his best and get back to me immediately.

I called John McCarthy again to see if there was any chance of getting clearance from the Tunisians. The Palestinians had no more luck than he had. The only way the Israelis were getting into Tunis was if we flew them in.

Now I had to reach the Israelis. Since it took too much time to go through Larocco, I asked if we could communicate directly with the Israeli plane. They had no phone, only the pilot's radio. But they were in contact with Rafi Barak, Uri Savir's assistant in the Foreign Ministry. Through the Pentagon's operations center, we were able to keep several lines open: one to Rafi Barak, one to Dan Christman, and one to our embassy in Tunis.

I told Rafi to have his plane divert to Siganella Air Force Base. When we were about a half hour outside of Tunis, our pilots got the approval from Air Force operations to fly to Siganella and retrieve the Israelis. I finally began to breathe easier. Now I joked we only have the "small problem" of producing in these meetings in Tunis.

I had breathed too early. Shortly before we were to land, there was a call from Rafi, and Dan Kurtzer took it as I was trying to nap for a few minutes before arrival. Suddenly I heard Dan shouting. I opened my eyes and Dan said, "You won't believe it. Rafi thought Siganella was the name for the Rome airport, so that is where he told them to fly. Dan then explained to Rafi that the Israelis must fly to our air force base in Sicily and asked the Israeli pilot to confirm the location of the base.

My plane landed in Tunis just before 6 a.m.; Martin Indyk and I deplaned. And our pilots then took off again. I asked Dan and Aaron Miller to stay with the pilots and fly to Siganella to pick up the Israelis. At eight-thirty in the morning, the Israelis arrived in Tunis. It was quite a delegation that arrived at the Tunis Hilton: Amnon Shahak, the Deputy Chief of Staff of the IDF, Uri Savir, the Director General of the Foreign Ministry, and Jacques Neriah, Rabin's foreign policy advisor. They were exhausted by their misadventures. Of course, now the real work would begin.

I asked Amnon and Uri, both of whom I had known for some time, how they wanted to proceed. They wanted private meetings with the Palestinians. I suggested they meet with the Palestinians first, and afterward we would meet with them. Then I would decide whether a three-way meeting made any sense.

They went off to get cleaned up and see Arafat. I took a shower and met with Terje Larsen, who had spent the last few days in Tunis. He had seen Arafat several times. Terje felt that Arafat was under genuine pressure from the Palestinian street, and advised me to present a package to Arafat now for resuming the negotiations. I disagreed, observing that "anything we present now, he will treat as a going-in position and demand more." Moreover, I argued, "We don't know what the Israelis are prepared to accept." I suggested to Terje that I probe Arafat on his reaction to his meeting with the Israelis and emphasize that he was not going to achieve anything without the negotiations. Terje was persuaded, but worried about the situation taking on a life of its own and it becoming harder, not easier, to get back to negotiations. I took the point.

| MEETINGS WITH ARAFAT |

The meeting with Arafat was memorable. Upon arriving at his house for the meeting, we—Martin, Dan, Aaron, Ambassador McCarthy, and me—were ushered into a room with a long table. There were large posters on the wall. One was of Jerusalem and centered on the Dome of the Rock; several were of a younger Arafat, dressed in fatigues, gun in hand, and with Abu Iyad and Abu Jihad, the founders, along with Arafat, of Fatah. (The former was killed by the Abu Nidal group, the latter by the Israelis in a raid in Tunis.) The posters made the room feel like a revolutionary headquarters, which in a sense it was.

But there were several incongruities. Our Palestinian hosts had entered middle age and did not look revolutionary now. And what revolutionaries, I wondered, watched *The Golden Girls*, the show that was playing on the television in the adjoining sitting room? The irony made me laugh; here I was in Yasir Arafat's house, and there were the Golden Girls, rich in Jewish humor, on the tube.

Arafat himself arrived late and was apologetic. As I was to see over the years, hospitality, a valued aspect of Palestinian culture, was uniquely important to Arafat. Before meeting, he insisted on serving lunch, cutting up the pieces of chicken and serving each of us himself. The hospitality was genuine but also part of an effort to forge a relationship with the United States. American power was a source of both envy and jealousy in the Middle East; it attracted and repelled. For Arafat it could be a source of status with his people. At this stage, he saw little cost and much gain in associating with us. America was not blamed for the Ibrahimi massacre; Israelis were. America could right the wrongs—this was the not so subtle message Arafat was promoting in public.

With me, he said, as I would hear so often in the coming years, "we are in need of your help." And my response also became part of my refrain in the coming years: "If you want us to help, work directly with the Israelis. Our help will always be most effective when you are trying to work things out directly—we cannot and will not take the Israeli place, nor will we simply deliver the Israelis."

This day, he was eager to tell me about his meeting with the Israelis—perhaps to show he was working with them. But I sensed something more; when Arafat and I were alone, he told me how Amnon Shahak had brought him an apology from Rabin—a statement of regret and acknowledgment that an Israeli reservist had committed a grave wrong, bringing dishonor on all Israelis in uniform. With great emotion, he said to me, "Imagine Rabin and Shahak conveying this message. This is very important." As I was to see, Arafat always took the "generals" especially seriously, either because he saw them as the real Israel or because he wanted to be seen as equal by them. In this case, he felt a need to respond, and did so by agreeing to have the two sides meet quietly in Israel in the coming days and again in Tunis in a week's time.

This time the Tunisians facilitated the Israeli entry, though the Israeli team did fly out on our plane. In the intervening week two issues had come to the fore. One was a UN Security Council resolution that would condemn the terrorist act at the Ibrahimi

Mosque, and the other was the question of some form of international "protection" for the Palestinians in Hebron.

Arafat wanted a strong UNSC resolution condemning the act and Israeli settler provocations as well as criticizing Israeli practices and calling for corrective actions by Israel. Together with at least symbolic international protection, he would have his "explanation" for why he was resuming negotiations.

For his part, Rabin, while understanding Arafat's predicament, remained dead set against any outside presence being introduced into Hebron. At the same time, he saw the Security Council resolution as giving Arafat an explanation as well as providing an alternative to the calls for an international presence. His problem: he could not have it appear as if he was supporting a resolution condemning Israel.

The administration was under pressure from some Jewish community leaders to veto any Security Council resolution that condemned Israel in any way. Yet the Israelis in Tunis were imploring me to avoid an American veto of the resolution, feeling that Arafat had to have something and that the emerging resolution was tolerable.

I found little sympathy for this position in the administration. Tom Donilon told me that if the Israelis see the resolution as an explanation for Arafat and an alternative to an international presence, it was up to them to call off the leaders in the Jewish community. "Then we can avoid a veto." I knew this was not going to happen. Rabin wanted to have it both ways. So did we. We wanted to find a way back to negotiations, we wanted to help give Arafat an explanation, and we wanted to avoid any controversy in providing that explanation.

In the meantime, I was on the front lines in Tunis. I was being told to pressure Arafat not to push for a resolution, and to oppose any international presence. Instead, I tried out another idea to meet Arafat's need. In response to his pressing for some international protection in Hebron that he could show he had produced, I asked whether it might be possible for the Red Cross or a similar kind of international organization to play such a role. If a credible organization could establish a presence, it certainly could report on conditions in Hebron, and this might have a calming affect.

Yasser Abed Rabbo—a member of Arafat's delegation—erupted in response. This was a joke! Would the Red Cross frighten Israeli settlers? Would it stop even one act of provocation? This wasn't serious. It would be better to go back to struggle than to submit to such ideas.

Arafat cut him off. "No," he said, "we won't go back to struggle. We have made our choice. There is no going back." It was a particularly poignant moment. No one on his side of the table said a word. He, in effect, had spoken, and it impressed me.

In the coming years, he would never be so unambiguous in public or private. He would send conflicting signals, but at this point he was very clear. I knew that whatever difficulties we might face, he would find a way to resume the negotiations.

And, in fact, he did. The UNSC resolution passed, in no small part because, as I explained to the Secretary, it would enable Arafat to justify negotiations to his people. And the Israelis and Palestinians developed a creative idea for an international presence— the Temporary International Presence in Hebron (TIPH). The TIPH was a small observer presence, with distinctive uniforms and made up largely of Norwegians. They had no enforcement powers and could only file reports, but they gave Arafat something to point to and the Israelis something they could say established no precedent for international protection.

Before the Israelis and Palestinians reached agreement on the TIPH, I decided that in addition to giving Arafat cover for resuming the negotiations, we should also give him a need to do so. All the negotiations—both bilateral and multilateral—had been suspended at the time of the Ibrahimi Mosque massacre. With this in mind, I thought if we could get Asad to announce he would resume Syria's negotiations with Israel by the end of April, it would also force Arafat to make the decision. His temptation to try to get more would be great unless there was a point by which he knew he had to decide. A resumption of the Syrian talks would mean that the Arabs would not wait for him. I tried this idea out on the Syrian Ambassador to the United States, Walid al-Moualem, and Itamar Rabinovich, and both liked it, with Walid suggesting that if President Clinton were to call Asad and ask it as a favor, he believed Asad would agree. In fact, after considering it overnight, Asad did agree, and a short time later Arafat agreed to resume negotiations.

| CONCLUDING THE MAY 4 AGREEMENT AND ARAFAT'S SHOW |

One general rule about high-stakes negotiations: when one has cracked the hardest issues, then the remaining issues become hard; or when reaching agreement represents the crossing of a threshold, any remaining issue is suddenly transformed into a deal-breaker.

The May 4 agreement, as it came to be called, proved the rule. This agreement would create the Palestinian Authority and bring Arafat from Tunis to Gaza and Jericho. Each side got cold feet as they approached the finish line. What was Arafat's title to be, President or Chairman? Could the Palestinian Authority have its own stamps? What kind of travel documents could Palestinians use? Could the Palestinians station a single policeman at the Allenby Bridge across the Jordan River? How far along the beach road would the "yellow Israeli security zone" extend in Gaza?

Most of these issues dealt with the Palestinian desire for the symbols of independence; in the endgame of producing the agreement, each side began to treat them as if they were mandated in the Torah and the Koran.

At the end of April, with the negotiations bogging down, Secretary Christopher and I went to the area. I felt our presence could be a catalyst for helping to put together a package of trade-offs on these final issues. Moreover, I felt that the only way the two sides would actually decide at this point was if there was a deadline—and I felt the Secretary's presence and readiness to leave by a date certain was the most likely way of producing that.

The Egyptians invited the Israeli and Palestinian negotiators to Cairo for a joint meeting, after which I put together a short paper that summarized the remaining issues and the possible solutions to each. (As one example, to overcome their differences on whether Arafat should be referred to in the agreement as "Chairman" or "President," I proposed using the Arabic word *Ra'aes*, which could be translated either way.)

Following a day in Israel,* the Secretary and I returned to Cairo on May 3 and suggested to President Mubarak that he bring Rabin and Arafat together with their negotiators to try to wrap up an agreement. To be sure there was a deadline, we also agreed that Mubarak would announce a signing ceremony on the morning of the fourth.

Mubarak brought the leaders together with us in his office in Cairo and we went over the scenario, the need to resolve everything this evening, and the U.S. readiness to help if there were any problems. Then he asked Rabin and Arafat to join their negotiators in the adjacent conference room while Secretary Christopher and I remained with him and Foreign Minister Amre Moussa and presidential aide Osama al-Baz.

Over the next several hours, Moussa or Osama or I would go next door every so often to see how they were doing. Rabin and Arafat directed the negotiators to resolve the remaining issues and rejoined us in Mubarak's office. As the evening wore on, Mubarak brought in *fool*—pronounced "phul"—sandwiches made largely of beans. Like a watchful parent, he insisted that everyone eat.

Around 2 a.m., we brought everyone together in a four-way meeting in the conference room to try to resolve the remaining differences. Mubarak asked Rabin to give us a status report. He reported that there were three open issues: the size of the Jericho district, the issue of a single Palestinian policeman on the Allenby Bridge, and the exact location of the joint patrols in the "yellow zone" in Gaza. Osama asked if it was possible to keep these issues open and continue discussions but conclude the agreement

---

*Dan Kurtzer had remained in Cairo to work on resolving the differences summarized in our paper.

anyway. Rabin felt only the yellow zone issue needed to be resolved now; the others could continue to be discussed. Arafat said nothing. Moussa asked Arafat, "What do you need on the yellow zone?" Arafat wanted joint patrols throughout the yellow zone to show a Palestinian presence there. Christopher asked if such patrols could be phased in, and he agreed. Then I asked if it was possible to phase in the patrols and postpone the issue of the policeman and the size of the Jericho district for discussion over the next few months.

Arafat said yes, over the next three months. Mubarak said, "So we have agreement." Rabin said yes. Mubarak then declared that the signing ceremony would be held at 11 a.m.

Everything seemed done; then suddenly, as if we had not just had this discussion, Arafat asked, "What about the Jericho district, the policeman, and the joint patrols?"

Amnon Shahak could not contain himself and began to laugh. Arafat said across the table, "You think I am a joke? You think I am a joke?" To which Rabin responded in his low, deep voice, "No, we take you very seriously. Let us go over it again." He did and Arafat agreed on the compromise we had just gone over. Ending, I thought, the endgame.

But I was wrong. Arafat reserved the real melodrama for the next day. On live TV, in front of the world, with Mubarak, Christopher, Russian Foreign Minister Andrei Kozyrev, Rabin, and Shimon Peres all onstage, Arafat would not sign the maps attached to the agreement. As Rabin's face turned progressively redder and Mubarak, Moussa, and Peres took turns trying to persuade him to sign, Arafat was unyielding. His behavior was a complete surprise to his colleagues. Nabil Sha'ath, the Palestinian who had negotiated the final text, did not know what the problem was. Nor did Yasser Abed Rabbo. As I went around the hall, no Palestinian official—or for that matter Egyptian official—could explain what was happening.

After about twenty minutes of stalemate on the stage, Tom Donilon came up to me and said, "You have to do something. This is a disaster." Lacking any explanation for Arafat's behavior, I had been reluctant to go up on the stage to try to fix things. But Tom was right, and I went up on the stage and conferred with Secretary Christopher. Together we went over to Mubarak, and at our urging he called a brief recess so we could try to resolve the problem offstage.

Once off, Rabin turned to Arafat and bluntly asked, "What is your problem?" Arafat said, "Will you agree to discuss the size of the Jericho district and the policeman on the bridge over the next three months?" Rabin said, "I agreed last night to that." Arafat then asked if Rabin would put it in writing, to which Rabin answered: "If I said it last night, I will put it in writing." Arafat said okay, "I am ready to sign the maps."

We were off the stage for four minutes. Unbeknownst to either Rabin or Arafat, after we had reached agreement at two-thirty in the morning, I had asked Jon Schwartz, our main drafter from the department's legal office, to put that agreement in writing. He had done so, and Rabin and Arafat had signed all the documents at the outset of the ceremony, stopping only when Arafat refused to sign the maps. So what Arafat wanted in writing, he and Rabin had already signed.

Why had Arafat balked? Obviously not for the reasons he indicated to us. No, here Arafat, on a world stage, was demonstrating to his public that he would stand up for their rights. If it meant embarrassing Hosni Mubarak, who was hosting the event, no matter. If it meant upsetting the American Secretary of State and the Russian Foreign Minister, no matter. If the Israeli Prime Minister did not like it, no matter. On the eve of his return to Gaza, he would insist on Palestinian rights in a way that would add to his charismatic appeal and weaken whatever hold fundamentalists like Hamas might have, especially in Gaza.

His behavior in Cairo had one longer-term consequence. Mubarak would, from this time on, be reluctant to play a guiding or forward-leaning role in a negotiation. While he might send envoys, meet the leaders separately, or help on security and terror questions (as he did in 1996, 2000, and 2003), he would never again play peacemaker—and risk having Arafat burn him again.

<⟨ 5 ⟩>

The Evolution of the Syrian Talks

AFTER THE OSLO ACCORD, Yitzhak Rabin made it clear to us that the Israeli public would require time to absorb the agreement with the PLO. Given his politics and the psychology of his public, Rabin likewise needed time before moving ahead in the negotiations with the Syrians. While these concerns were undoubtedly true, they led Rabin to a practice of playing the two tracks against each other. If he made headway on one, he would go slowly on the other. But the obverse was also true: if progress was not being made on one, he would try to energize the other.*

In September 1993—following the conclusion of the DOP at the White House—it was time to go slowly on the Syrian track. Dealing with the PLO was explosive in Israel. But I also suspected that Rabin felt Asad should have been more responsive to what he had put in the American pocket: full Israeli withdrawal from the Golan Heights in return for meeting Israel's needs on peace and security. In Rabin's eyes, this was a historic move, and he wanted Asad to see there was a price for not being sufficiently responsive.

In August, when we had conveyed the "pocket," we had also come to an understanding that I would host negotiations between the Israelis and Syrians beginning in late

---

*There was, of course, another track of negotiations involving the Israelis and Jordanians. They did not involve any great controversy, but even here, Rabin was in no hurry to appear to be making concessions after the DOP with the Palestinians. The story of the Jordanian negotiations appears in the next chapter.

August. Rabin had accepted that Syria would send two negotiators to meet with his ambassador in Washington, Itamar Rabinovich. While several meetings were held between
Itamar and his two Syrian counterparts, Walid al-Moualem and Muafak Allaf, Itamar was
soon to inform them that Rabin needed time to digest the agreement with the Palestinians and would not be able to pursue the talks with Syria for the time being. Needless to
say, they were disappointed. In true Syrian fashion, however, they did not want to signal
that they needed negotiations more than the Israelis. So their position was, "Let us know
when you are ready."

In this period, I began a pattern that would last as long as Walid was the Syrian Ambassador to the United States. I would see him often in Washington, typically going to his
house for lunch or dinner or late afternoon snacks; Walid always insisted on feeding me.

Walid al-Moualem is a man of intellect and humor. His colleague Muafak Allaf reminded me of dissembling Soviet-era diplomats; he would never grant the Israelis the
slightest consideration, or acknowledge their concerns. Walid was different. He would
acknowledge Israeli concerns while noting that they could be addressed in a context of
ending Israeli occupation of Syrian land. He would work with me to find creative
solutions—often raising ideas that he would ask me to present. He was genuinely committed to achieving peace, not as a favor to Israel but out of the conviction that peace
would serve Syria's interest, particularly in modernization. Once he told me that his
fondest hope was that his son would not know war. His personal commitment to
peace, he would tell me, was a sign of Asad's intentions.

Even so, Walid could be as suspicious or unyielding as any Syrian. Following
Itamar's declaration that Rabin needed time to absorb the DOP with the PLO, Walid
let me know that Asad was now extremely dubious about Rabin's intentions. Maybe
the "pocket" was a trick, Rabin's way of quieting potential Syrian opposition to the Israeli deal with Arafat, figuring that Asad would mute his opposition lest he jeopardize
the prospect of getting his land back.

I tried to allay these suspicions, pointing out "the obvious opposition Rabin faced
in Israel" over dealing with the PLO. However, when I saw Rabin in Israel in October,
his posture made me think that the Syrian suspicions might have a basis. After discussing the Palestinian track, I told Rabin I would see Asad the next day and asked,
"What am I to say when he inevitably asks me if you are still standing by the pocket?"
Rabin's answer: "Tell him you did not ask me."

I could not do that, I explained. "Asad would never believe I hadn't raised this with
you." Rabin basically told me that that was my problem. Even though I pressed him,
he was not prepared to budge. He did say, however, that he wanted to visit Washington to discuss the pocket with President Clinton. That gave me something, and I told
Rabin I would tell Asad "the Prime Minister had conveyed a request to me to see the

President to discuss this issue. As a result, we did not discuss it." I did not expect this to satisfy Asad but it gave me something.

Naturally, Asad immediately asked about the pocket, and interpreted Rabin's request as a retreat and the pocket itself as "a trick." I replied, "Do you think given his relationship with the United States he would trick us? If he were tricking us, why would he ask to see the President now to discuss this issue?" Asad told me I had a point.

To show Asad that we remained serious about working the Syrian track, I suggested to him that we take the unusual step of inviting the Syrian Foreign Minister, Farouk Shara, to Washington to see President Clinton while Shara was in the United States for the United Nations General Assembly meetings in New York. This was agreed. Before seeing Shara later in October, the President phoned Rabin; while Rabin did not back away from the pocket, he did ask for four months before reengaging with the Syrians. With Shara, though, President Clinton played up his belief in Rabin, his seriousness, and the President's conviction that it was possible to reach agreement between Syria and Israel. I had raised the idea of a delay with Walid, who suggested that if Asad could see President Clinton he would accept the delay because Clinton would "make him feel at peace, and quiet his suspicions."

This led to the decision to have President Clinton meet with Asad in Geneva on January 16, 1994, and to the Syrian decision to accept a four-month delay in negotiations with Israel.

| THE JANUARY MEETING AND ITS AFTERMATH |

In preparing for the January meeting, I talked with Walid and Itamar. I had known Itamar Rabinovich since 1975. Itamar was a scholar and one of Israel's leading experts on Syria. When Rabin had won and made Itamar Israel's ambassador to the United States and his lead negotiator with the Syrians, Walid was pleased, referring to Itamar as moderate and knowledgeable. He was both, but he was more. A man of civility and charm, he understood the workings of Washington, establishing excellent relations and access both in the White House and in the Congress. Given his closeness to Rabin—and Rabin's ground rules for who could know about the pocket—Itamar also had access to Secretary Christopher whenever he wanted it, a privilege he did not abuse. When we were both in Washington, it was not unusual on a given day for me to speak to Itamar three or four times, and I probably saw him at least two or three times a week.

Itamar saw the Geneva meeting as an opportunity for the United States to get Asad to cross a public threshold on peace, committing in writing to "normal peaceful relations with Israel." Working with Walid in advance of the meeting, Martin and I succeeded in producing a draft that not only included these words but also emphasized that Syria had adopted the strategic option of peace. At the meeting, Asad, taken with Clinton's personal style and command of the issues, approved the joint statement. When Clinton was asked in their joint press conference how Syria defined peace with Israel, he replied that Asad accepted full diplomatic relations, with embassies, trade, and tourism. I feared that Asad would contradict him, and that this would of course be the "story" reported by the media out of the summit. But Asad said nothing.

At the end of the meeting, Asad came over to me and, holding my arm as he shook my hand to convey greater warmth and appreciation, stated: "You know I liked President Bush. But President Clinton is a real person. He speaks to you with awareness and understanding. He knows our problems better and he is committed to solving them. I haven't felt this from an American president before." For someone who had previously met with Presidents Nixon, Carter, and Bush, this was a remarkable statement. Why was Asad so impressed? Clinton had listened to him and explained how he was determined to reconcile both sides' needs and how he understood the importance of the land to Asad, and of security to Rabin—and how he was convinced he could foster an agreement between two leaders who could make decisions. It was his style as much as the substance of his remarks that had such impact.

President Clinton was also elated with the meeting. He felt he had gotten through to Asad, and he believed I had good news to bring Rabin. But in Israel the next day, Rabin immediately belittled what Asad had given us. Notwithstanding that we produced exactly what Itamar had suggested—"normal peaceful relations" in writing—Rabin said it meant little because it was Clinton, not Asad, who defined peace at the press conference. When I argued that Clinton's statement in Asad's presence meant it represented Asad's position, Rabin suggested I go make the case on Israeli TV. I did so, whereupon Rabin surprised me by announcing that there would be a referendum in Israel should an agreement with Syria be reached. While I did not see how this was particularly helpful, Rabin told me it gave him the flexibility he needed to resume negotiations now.

Naturally, Walid, echoing Asad, saw the referendum as wholly illegitimate. How could Israel hold a referendum about Syrian land—it was not their land to vote on! And if Syria made concessions the Israeli public might still ask for more! Anticipating these objections, I had elicited a promise from Rabin that he would fight to win the referendum and not accept additional conditions. In any case, after the Geneva meeting, the negotiations resumed—only to be interrupted by Dr. Goldstein's February 25 killing spree in the Ibrahimi Mosque and all that followed.

Following Asad's acceptance of President Clinton's request in March to resume the negotiations, I went to see Asad in Damascus, meeting him at 8:30 a.m. Asad never met foreign visitors early in the day, but on this particular day he would be visiting the grave site of his son Basil, who had been killed in an auto accident on January 21. He was in a somber mood, thinking about the son he had groomed to succeed him.

| WHO WAS HAFEZ AL-ASAD? |

An incident that offers great insight into Hafez al-Asad occurred at the time of Basil's death. Basil was Asad's favorite. But in a one-man-rule system like Asad's Syria, who tells the father that his favorite son has died? In this case, the duty fell to the chief of staff of the military, Hikmat Shihabi, and the head of the Presidential Guard, Adnan Makhluf. Both had served Asad loyally for many years. When they arrived to give Asad the terrible news, their faces obviously revealed that something awful had happened. Asad, so the story goes, looked at them and asked, "What is it, a coup?"

At this point, Hafez al-Asad had been ruling Syria for twenty-four years. And yet Asad's first instinct, notwithstanding having presided over Syria since 1970, was to ask if it was a coup. This was not a man who felt secure. This was not a man immune to a sense of conspiracy. Of course, he sought to convey an image of strength, not weakness. In Arabic, Asad means "lion," and he certainly wanted to create the impression that there was a lion in Damascus. But the question—is it a coup?—speaks volumes about Asad's own sense that his hold on power could be tenuous.

Asad was always looking over his shoulder. A leader who grew up hatching conspiracies and plots was bound to feel that he could also be the victim of such plots. Asad was born in the village of Qurdaha. His was a mountain village above the Syrian coast. The city of Latakia, along the Mediterranean, was not far away. His village was poor and primarily Alawite—an ethnic minority consisting of slightly more than 10 percent of the population of Syria. While they see themselves as Muslim, they are considered heretics by many Sunni Muslims. Like many Alawis of his generation, Asad chose the military as a path toward upward mobility.

He was attracted to the Arab nationalist politics of the Ba'ath party. The Ba'athis represented an amalgam of secular, Pan-Arab, and so-called Arab socialist principles. In the aftermath of the defeat in the 1948 war, Asad (like many of those drawn to the military at this time) embraced what was perceived as an ideology that would foster Arab unity and restore Arab strength. For an Alawi, the secular nature of the military and the Ba'ath also made them perfect vehicles for submerging one's minority status in the service of the larger Arab cause. He became an air force officer with very limited exposure to the outside world.

Though he felt that Egypt trampled on Syrian national pride, he opposed Syria's secession from the United Arab Republic in 1961. The Arab nationalist in Asad did not want to admit that a larger Arab entity could not be sustained. His opposition to secession actually led to a brief period in which he was forced out of the Syrian military. Again to promote his objectives in Syria, he had to go underground and plot with members of the military. His underground military committee helped to lead a coup that succeeded in toppling the Syrian government and replacing it with a Ba'athist-led leadership in 1963; in 1966, he was the guiding force behind another coup in which he became the defense minister. He was defense minister in 1967 when Syria lost the Golan Heights. Interestingly, though provocations from Syria set in motion events that helped lead to the Six-Day War, Asad did not launch a major invasion of Israel. When the Israelis attacked the Heights and fought their way up them, the fighting was tenacious. But Asad was not going to see Syria's army destroyed and ordered a retreat even before the Israelis had completed their conquest of the Heights.

Throughout this period, one could see the trademarks of the Asad character that I would see much in evidence in all our meetings. He was cautious, leery of taking risks toward either war or peace. He was suspicious, certain that we were conspiring with the Israelis and that, in Rabin's case, the Israeli Prime Minister was trying to gain advantage over him. He was mindful as the last true Arab nationalist that his deal—if there was to be one—had to reflect that Syria was not defeated. Syria must recover all its land. Having held out, he wanted to get what Egypt got—full withdrawal—and wanted to give less. He wanted to show that he could do better than Egypt. Moreover, Israel must neither gain nor be seen as gaining from the agreement—other than Asad's offering them an end to the conflict.

Asad seemed particularly incapable of understanding that outreach to the Israeli public would make it easier for Israeli leaders to do what he wanted. But a zero-sum view of the world was deeply ingrained in Asad, hardly surprising given that he saw conspiracies everywhere. Moreover, because Asad genuinely worried about how he was perceived, he worried that any gestures toward Israel might be perceived as personal weakness in a way that could be exploited by potential rivals; he was dead set against giving anything away. Everything must be part of a deal.

With Asad, until the end, when he was obviously no longer well, no detail in our discussion could ever be too small. He saw discussions as a kind of sport. Negotiations were an exercise in attrition. He could always hold out longer. He was never in a hurry. He was content to live without an agreement, especially if the agreement would not meet his standards of dignity and honor. He would never let anyone get the best of him in any way.

Once when I saw him in Latakia during the summer he did something very unusual: He stood up after having met with me for nearly five hours and left the room.

When he returned, he said, "You remember the time Baker had to wave his handkerchief? I did not have to do that." In one meeting that had run for seven and a half hours, Baker took out his handkerchief, waved it, and admitted he needed a bathroom break. Even in this instance, to indicate there was no personal weakness on his part, Asad felt obliged to explain he had left the room for a different reason. Not to be outdone, I said, "Mr. President, have you ever noticed in all our meetings, regardless of how long they run, that I have never gotten up and had to leave the room? It is not because I have never had to go to the bathroom, it is just that I have an iron will." He nodded approvingly.

My relationship with him was unusual. At one level, he respected my knowledge and attention to detail. He was always asking me about the black binder I would carry into our meetings, into which I seemed to write everything that was said. He would say, "That has all your secrets," and I would say, "Absolutely." At times he would try to test us to see what he could get away with, modifying what we had discussed or agreed to and seeing whether we would react. Lesson number one in any negotiation is to never allow a test of this sort—no matter how small the issue—to go unchallenged. Asad soon found that I would correct him, and, because he prided himself on his word, he would typically agree that my understanding was right.

At one point, acknowledging that I was correct, he declared, "You never forget a thing." To which I replied, "With you, it is important to remember everything with great precision." But he was not content to let me have the last word, so he repeated with emphasis, "*No*, you never forget a thing." This time I said, "I learned that from you, Mr. President." Not good enough; he did not want me to say it was because of him, and he again repeated, "No, you never forget a thing." I learned my lesson and said, "You are right, Mr. President, I never forget a thing." Now he was satisfied; I had acknowledged that I never forgot anything, at least from our meetings, and I knew there was also a message there: Never forget anything from our meetings. Every detail was important, and one never knew when the detail would be essential.

Asad also liked our "off the record" discussions at the ends of meetings. Whether I was visiting on my own or with the Secretary of State, at the end of a meeting we would stand, and this became the cue for him to say something special, to level about something important, or to receive a private message from the Israeli prime minister. Our "standup tradition" began in 1994, when Yitzak Rabin asked me to find a way to convey separately that he appreciated that Asad would resume negotiations after the Ibrahimi Mosque massacre and that he understood this had not been simple for Asad. If there was ever something that President Asad felt he should know, or if he sought a particular step from Rabin, Asad could use this channel. At the time, Asad listened, commenting only that it had been a difficult decision for him and that he would like me to convey that to Rabin. Following this initial exchange, if I was traveling on my own, every meeting would end with our standing for what might be ten minutes or longer.

It was not all sweetness and light between us. I knew that Asad also was suspicious of me. Here, I am convinced, my being Jewish was a factor. In his eyes, that necessarily made me close to the Israelis. My arguments that he needed to reach out to the Israeli public no doubt further confirmed this view of me. It mattered little that I was telling him that he could create pressure within Israel to respond to his needs by convincing the Israeli public that it was a new day and he was truly willing to end the hostility toward them. He saw this as meeting Rabin's needs, not his; he saw this as putting pressure on him, without offering an immediate tangible return that he could point to. He saw this as somehow belittling his own domestic needs as he defined them. And for Asad, showing that he did not have to do what Sadat had done or Hussein had done or even what Arafat had done in reaching out to or meeting with Israelis would demonstrate that he was superior to them. His Arab credentials were paramount. He would not play the game the way they did, and yet he would gain something from the Israelis.

From his standpoint, however, I was always pushing him to take steps what would indicate he was not different from the others. I was pushing him to pay a price, as he defined it. And he was convinced, rightly, that I pressed the President and the Secretary to lean on him to reach out to the Israeli public. Moreover, while he would often probe me about Israeli politics, I have little doubt that he viewed what I told him with at least some skepticism. Surely he knew there might be nuggets of information, but he undoubtedly believed I was also trying to manipulate him.

He was certainly not subtle about his likes and dislikes. He passionately disliked Arafat. He found Arafat untrustworthy. He spoke with pride about having put Arafat in jail, and was wistful in explaining that he came under pressure to release him and had done so.

Asad was rarely emotional. The only time I saw him genuinely sad was after his mother died and Basil had been killed. In our first meeting after Basil's death, the day Asad would be visiting his grave, he was soft spoken, fatalistic, and clearly touched when I expressed my sorrow for his loss and the difficulty of this time for him personally. This was not a day in which he would argue a point. It was as if his heart was simply not in it.

Was Asad truly ready for peace with Israel? He wanted his land back. He lost it as defense minister, and he wanted as one of his legacies to get it back. He would do the minimum to get it back; he understood that that required a peace agreement with Israel. When I would ask him what kind of relationship he envisioned with Israel after an agreement, he would be vague, saying, "one of peace." When I probed deeper and tried to understand which relationship with a neighbor the relationship he sought with Israel might be most like, his answer was "Turkey." That was not exactly a warm relationship, and one characterized by hostility and rivalry at different times. Asad would make peace with Israel, meaning the end of war, but the truly open relationships would have to come after him—that is undoubtedly the way he saw it.

The last Arab nationalist might get his land back and do the minimum on peace to get it. But no one would make him a warm partner with the Israelis. That could wait for the next generation.

| A NEW STALEMATE EMERGES |

Before my early morning meeting with Asad, I had seen Rabin. He suggested that the way to make progress was for Israel to offer a formal, comprehensive proposal (one without the "pocket"), believing Syria's response would create a new dynamic for the negotiations when they resumed.

Asad was agreeable, and we decided to come with the Israeli proposal by the beginning of May. But everything was to change when we presented the proposal and he responded.

The Israeli proposal was comprehensive, with a heavy focus on security shaped by the IDF and its leader, Ehud Barak. It divided Syria into four different security zones, put limits on the whole range of Syrian armaments, and where Syrian forces could be stationed; it proposed constraints on how the Golan could be developed (so as not to adversely affect the water feeding the Sea of Galilee); and it linked Israeli withdrawal from the Golan to a timetable of normal relations, beginning with the first Israeli withdrawal. The whole proposal relied on the concept of "interphasing," meaning that peaceful relations, security arrangements, and withdrawal would be tied together in a sequence of steps. The Israelis were adhering to their understanding of negotiations: start with maximal positions because the other side will try to erode everything you ask for.

In truth, I don't think that Asad was surprised by the maximal nature of the Israeli proposal. He offered a counterproposal. The Syrians used many of the same categories in the Israeli proposal—security arrangements, phases for implementation, normal peaceful relations. But there was an enormous gap in the content. The security zones would be small, constraints on Syrian forces would be minimal; the phases would be marked by "the end of the state of war" once an agreement was signed, but full diplomatic ties would be announced only when Israel had completely withdrawn from the Golan Heights, which was expected in six months, not five years. Moreover, in a retreat from his commitment to us, such ties would come only after Israel reached peace agreements with Jordan and Lebanon. Finally, all of this was conditioned on "full withdrawal," meaning withdrawal, to the June 4, 1967 lines. Without this, Asad was very clear: there was no Syrian proposal. This was a first. Asad throughout all of our conversations had only spoken of full withdrawal from the Golan Heights. Now he was defining full withdrawal and making it the precondition for an agreement.

Upon our hearing Asad's counterproposal, Rabin exploded. He rejected it, telling us full withdrawal in his eyes had always meant to the international border, not the June 4, 1967 lines.

What was the difference? The international border, which appeared on most maps, was really the mandate border affixed by the British and the French in 1923 after World War I and the advent of the League of Nations. There was no map of the June 4 lines; it represented the positions of the two sides on the eve of the 1967 war. Roughly speaking, there were three basic differences between the 1923 border and the putative 1967 border. In the 1948 war, Syrian forces succeeded in seizing territory to the west of the 1923 line in three areas. As part of the armistice agreement, the Syrians withdrew from these areas and returned to the international border, making these areas demilitarized zones. The Israelis after the 1948 war would cultivate in the DMZs, arguing that this was their territory. Syrians would fire on the Israelis in the zones, claiming that the final disposition of these territories was to be determined by final peace settlements, not by creating facts on the ground. By 1967, the Israelis had seized about two-thirds of the DMZ areas, with the Syrians taking the remaining territory, including an area in the south called Hama.

Even though the actual difference between the two lines totaled only about sixty-six square kilometers, there were vital implications for water, both with regard to the Banias springs and shoreline of the Sea of Galilee—and Rabin no doubt feared that an actual presence on the lake would give the Syrians a share of Israel's only natural freshwater reservoir.*

When we returned to Damascus, Asad was as adamant as Rabin; he withdrew the Syrian proposal. Though I was to argue long and hard with him, he said if he did not know what the land was, there was no point in negotiating. He described this as a "stone in the road," and said that until it was removed nothing was possible. No agreement on June 4 as the lines of withdrawal, and no negotiations.

---

*I did not know how real Rabin's fear on the Sea of Galilee was; after all, the international border was only ten meters off the shoreline, and Rabin was prepared to accept that line, even though it should have raised the same doubts about water.

Initially, Rabin was no more willing to concede than Asad. With Rabin having just concluded the Gaza-Jericho agreement, he was in no hurry to resolve the issue.

Meanwhile, both leaders agreed to let their ambassadors—al-Moualem and Rabinovich—work with me (but not directly with each other) to try to break the stalemate. By the end of May, I had language that committed Israel to full withdrawal to the June 4 lines, provided all Israel's needs were met, including its needs on water. But what were Israel's needs and how did they affect the definition of the June 4 lines? We went back and forth for nearly two months, with my drafting countless formulas with increasingly arcane language. Finally, in the middle of July at a lunch with the Secretary and me, Itamar made a suggestion: "They get their one sentence, we get our two pages." In other words, Syria should get a simple statement that the border would be June 4 while Israel should get the qualifiers on this that meant the border would not be a threat to either its security or its water requirements.

I liked Itamar's idea, and also saw it as a clear indication that Rabin wanted to break the stalemate. We saw Rabin on July 18. Since Rabin later suggested that Christopher had conveyed more than he was supposed to convey to Asad—and Barak, among others, took this as an article of faith—it is important here to recount the exact exchange that Secretary Christopher had first with Prime Minister Rabin and then with President Asad—meetings in which I was the only one accompanying the Secretary and kept the record of the conversations:

CHRISTOPHER: I talked about this with Itamar at lunch. He said they want their one sentence of clarity. They get it, but then we get our two pages. That's fine. But it is essential to give him the one sentence of clarity that he expects at the end of the line, assuming you reach agreement on all other subjects; it's not a commitment, this is the nature of withdrawal if all other things are met.

RABIN: You can say you have all the reasons to believe this is the result, but Israel will not spell this out before knowing that our needs will be fulfilled.

CHRISTOPHER: That's all I need.

RABIN: You can tell him you understand this, and that he will not get the commitment without fulfilling our needs.

CHRISTOPHER: It is not on the table, it is in my pocket. It will take some time.

Though each spoke in a kind of shorthand, there was a very clear understanding of what was meant—namely, that Asad would hear that withdrawal would be to the June 4 lines, provided Israel's needs were met. The next day we saw Asad. With Asad, who had not been a party to the Rabinovich idea, everything was explicit:

CHRISTOPHER: I have just come from Israel and I can tell you that at the end of the day and as part of a package in which Israel's needs would have to be met, the United States understands that your needs would be met, and that therefore the meaning of full withdrawal, in these circumstances, would be to June 4, 1967. This only has meaning if you come to an agreement on everything. If you don't come to an agreement on everything, it has no meaning. In any case, this is in our pocket, not yours. It is our understanding, and you will not hear it from them until their needs have been met.

ASAD: This is clear.

Was there room for misunderstanding in this exchange? Perhaps. Does this exchange demonstrate the risks of having third parties convey highly sensitive messages? Perhaps. While Christopher conveyed what he was authorized to convey, there was ambiguity built in. In this case, Rabin felt—I believe—that in the Syrian satisfaction of Israeli needs, the June 4 line itself would be defined. Asad, for his part, had a fixed definition of the 1967 lines and expected that Israeli needs on security and water would be satisfied through assurances and not through territorial adjustment.

Even as they swapped "one sentence for two pages," they were, in effect, postponing the hard negotiations on the exact meaning of June 4—while they each sought to gain advantage in terms of determining that meaning.

Regardless, Rabin had moved and Asad had accepted the move. In their meeting, Secretary Christopher reminded Asad of his promise: Solve this issue, and Syria would be flexible and everything would become possible. Asad responded to the formula by resuming negotiations and agreeing that for the first time they could take place outside the State Department and would involve only Walid al-Moualem on his side. He also agreed to increase from six months to one year the timetable for Israeli withdrawal from the Golan. Once again, Rabin was not particularly impressed, but he went along with this new arrangement for talks—believing that the more informal the talks, the more one could explore creative ways to bridge differences.

| A PERIOD OF QUIET TALKS |

Having broken the stalemate, we resumed the talks in an entirely new format. Itamar, Walid, and I would meet informally at my house in Maryland, mostly during the daytime but sometimes at night. With negotiations outside the State Department, Walid became more open. Being alone, without Allaf, no doubt contributed to his greater candor. But there may have been another reason. According to Walid, Asad had given him increased authority.

In the initial meeting, Walid described going to the top of a mountaintop to see what was possible over time between Syria and Israel—an image certainly unprecedented for a Syrian negotiator with Israel. Still, there was a basic gap between the parties. For the Syrians, there was an interesting paradox. Since Syria was offering Israel peace, the Israelis did not need extensive security arrangements. But because Syria could not immediately embrace a peace of reconciliation and warmth—given the legacy—Israel would not receive much of what it wanted in terms of the web of relations that could signal to the Israeli public that the enmity of the past no longer existed. The contrasting Israeli view was, if you cannot reassure us on the nature of peace now, we need the insurance of extensive security arrangements to guard against the breakdown of the agreement—and indeed, to reduce the incentives of the Syrians to break the agreement. The more Itamar would emphasize this, the more Walid would resist, arguing that Syria could be trusted to keep its agreements and that the Syrians could not make an agreement in which Israeli security arrangements appeared to infringe on Syrian sovereignty.

I knew we could not crack this basic divide if the discussions remained largely philosophical. So to become more practical, I suggested that we build a scenario in which we could link what the Israelis wanted—peace—with what the Syrians wanted—withdrawal. Over the next few months we developed a framework for what would happen in phase one—which involved a partial withdrawal from the Golan and a number of steps by the Syrians that would create openings on academic and media exchanges and third-country tourists being able to move directly between Israel and Syria for the first time. We did the same for phase two, expanding the scope of the Israeli withdrawal and widening the signs of more normal relations—including official Syrians and Israelis meeting together in their respective countries, commercial groups being permitted to meet, and Israeli tourist groups—not individuals—being allowed to visit Syria. Our effort was to fill in the frameworks with as much detail as possible.

While useful, the discussions reached a dead end on two points. Walid could not accept more formal ties as long as the Israelis occupied any Syrian territory: "There was no way to have an Israeli flag flying in Damascus while Israel still occupied the Golan."

Yet it was this kind of normalization that Rabin sought before withdrawal was complete; Egypt had been willing to do it as part of its peace deal with Israel and he could not accept less from Syria. Similarly, there was an impasse on time. Both could agree that the first phase might take place in six or nine months. But when would the second phase take place, and would it be the final phase or would there be a third phase? The real problem was not the number of phases but the difference on the time frame for the agreement: Walid's suggestion was one year and Itamar's was four to five years.

By October, we had taken this effort as far as we could without involving the leaders. With President Clinton traveling to the area for the signing ceremony of the Israeli-Jordanian peace treaty and visiting regional leaders, we had an opportunity for him to see both Asad and Rabin. Although his domestic political advisors were concerned about Syria's being on the list of terrorist states and saw only risks in the President going to Damascus, Martin and I knew we needed a substantive step from Asad if Rabin was to consider compromising on the timetable for withdrawal and normalization. Clinton's visit was the way to move Asad.

Both Martin and I knew that Asad would not want to be the only major Arab leader whom Clinton failed to visit, and that gave us leverage to produce a move both in private and in public. Eight days before the trip, a suicide bomber had struck an Israeli bus in Tel Aviv, killing twenty-one Israelis and a Dutch citizen. We made clear to Walid that there was no way that Clinton could stand with Asad one week after such a bombing and not have Asad condemn terror. The public payoff for Clinton going to Damascus would be Asad condemning for the first time terrorist acts against Israelis. Walid understood and we worked out an agreed script in which Asad would say he "condemn[ed] the killing of civilians whether in Beirut, Ramallah, or Tel Aviv."

My game plan was to arrive in Israel with an air of change in the Arab world—a celebratory peace treaty signing in Jordan, Asad crossing a public threshold on terror, and Asad making a private move to push the negotiations. In such circumstances, Rabin would find it easier to respond, both practically and psychologically.

Unfortunately, what once again seemed logical in theory did not play out the way I had hoped or expected. Asad did make a move in private with President Clinton. He agreed to lengthen the timetable for the agreement from twelve to sixteen months and to permit an Israeli diplomatic presence although not an embassy—four months prior to the completion of Israeli withdrawal. Characteristically, he also linked the two— Rabin had to accept both together or he would not alter his position on either. While his concessions were certainly limited, Asad nonetheless had altered one of his principles: namely, that there could be no Israeli diplomatic or official presence in Syria so long as Syrian territory was still occupied. Alas, at the press conference, Asad, rather than condemning terror, actually said Israel—given its policies—was to blame for it.

This was a disaster. Here was the President of the United States standing next to the President of Syria one week after a suicide bombing in Tel Aviv, and Asad was blaming Israel for acts of terror. There wasn't a new day, just a repetition of Arab hostility toward Israel. I felt responsible for putting the President in this position.

What happened to our carefully worded script? Asad did not follow it. When he got the question on terrorism, posed by Rita Braver of CBS News, he saw her as accusing him of being a terrorist, and responded accordingly.

I was livid—and so was Secretary Christopher. What was the point of having an agreement, I asked Farouk Shara, if President Asad was free to ignore it? Shara's answer was that the questioner had been rude to President Asad. Christopher urged Asad to make amends to President Clinton, but there was little prospect of that.

Understandably, Rabin belittled what Asad had agreed to in private with the President, but he did publicly thank the President for his efforts to try to promote peace between Israel and Syria—something the President appreciated after the debacle in Damascus.

| AN APPARENT BREAKTHROUGH LEADS ONLY TO A NEW STALEMATE |

Shortly after the President's trip, Rabin suggested a way to move the negotiations. Saying a breakthrough was possible only if Israel knew its security needs would be satisfied, he proposed that senior military officers on each side meet. This would be a first; it would tell him that Asad was serious about dealing with the security issues and would signal that he was ready to move toward an agreement.

I took the proposal to Asad, reminding him that the people in the IDF were the closest to Rabin; your readiness to deal with them, I said, will be taken very seriously by the Prime Minister and is the best way to produce a breakthrough. Later I wondered if I oversold the military meetings, leading Asad to feel that if he made procedural moves the Israelis would reward him with substantive concessions. In any case, Asad was persuaded—no doubt at least in part because he felt a need to respond to us after embarrassing the President in Damascus.

Whatever his real reason, he agreed to a sequence of steps that included senior military officers meeting for the first time. The first step of this sequence was a senior military man on the Israeli side meeting with Walid al-Moualem. Rabin sent his most senior military officer, IDF Chief of Staff Ehud Barak. We held the meeting at Blair House—the President's guesthouse across the street from the White House. In the formal meeting, there was no new ground broken. But when we went into the garden at Blair House, Barak began to talk about creative ways to meet the concerns of both sides, implying Israel understood the importance of the land and of preserving Syrian dignity in any deal. Walid was clearly impressed. The second step in the sequence was for a senior Syrian military officer to meet Itamar. But Asad surprised us by saying he would send his most senior military officer, Hikmat Shihabi, to meet with his Israeli counterpart right away.

This was the most serious step Asad had taken in the negotiations, for Shihabi was a well-known and ranking figure in the regime. He was the Chief of Staff of the Syrian military, a known problem-solver, and someone the Israelis felt they knew—even if only indirectly. Rabin all along had sought a channel to Asad that was discreet and authoritative. Now he had it.

I chaired the meetings at Blair House, which were held secretly and lasted two days during the last week of December. Rabin and Asad had completely different expectations for these talks. Rabin saw them as the opening of a private, high-level channel, one in which he would ease into making serious moves on the substance. Conversely, Asad felt that for sending his military Chief of Staff and for showing a qualitatively new Syrian engagement with Israel, he was owed a comparable move on the substance.

Meanwhile, Ehud Barak, not knowing about the pocket, came with a largely theoretical presentation on the need for confidence-building measures and security arrangements that would limit the location of Syrian forces. He was not prepared to talk about the border—the issue Shihabi most wanted to address. How, Shihabi asked, could Syria talk about security arrangements if it did not know the border? Confidence-building measures would be possible once Syria knew that an agreement was possible.

Without denying the obvious gap in mind-sets, I began to outline areas of convergence that I believed could serve as building blocks for the security arrangements. For example, both sides would want to guard against surprise attack, minimize friction along the border, and reduce the danger of a war breaking out. Why not explore how different security arrangements could promote these objectives? While Shihabi was disappointed that he could not pin down Barak on anything but abstractions in the meeting, he was willing to explore my suggestion.

But time was not on our side. Shihabi was going to stay in the country for two weeks, visiting his son—an M.D. specializing in nuclear medicine in Newport Beach. While he was still in the country, I pushed to get Rabin to authorize a follow-on meeting with either Barak or Amnon Shahak, Barak's replacement as military Chief of Staff, beginning on January 1. Without such a meeting, I feared Asad would not authorize additional Chiefs of Staff talks, believing that nothing had been accomplished. We needed, I believed, to get something done before Shihabi returned to Syria.

Rabin, however, felt it inappropriate to have Barak continue the channel, and did not want Shahak to leave the country immediately after he assumed command of the military.

Unfortunately, my fears materialized. Asad read the minutes of the Blair House meetings (kept religiously by Walid) and saw not an Israeli response to Syria but expansive demands pertaining to Israeli security needs, involving elements that, Asad later said to me, "would leave me worse off than I am today."

As with the border in May, Asad now said there could be no further meetings between military officers until there was agreement on certain core principles on security arrangements.

To make his point clear, Asad even kept Walid in Damascus for six weeks. We were stuck again.

| THE "AIMS AND PRINCIPLES" NONPAPER |

Walid returned to Washington in the middle of February 1995. The only way to break the new stalemate was to see if we could hammer out a general framework on security arrangements. This set in motion a four-month negotiation, principally between Itamar, Walid, and me, over principles rather than the specifics of security. Our purpose was to reach an understanding on these principles and codify them in a "nonpaper."*

The negotiations proved tedious, to put it mildly. The Syrians wanted to emphasize mutuality and equality in the security arrangements—meaning limitations on forces would be applied to both sides equally. The Israelis, for their part, wanted the security arrangements to take account of the geographic asymmetry of the two sides: Syria had large territory with great depth; Israel had neither large territory nor strategic depth; its cities were extremely close to its borders, and its forces had to be constantly on alert because there was little margin for error in mobilizing against possible threats. Given the difference in size, Israel could accept that all security arrangements would apply to both sides, but not equally. Demilitarized areas or areas where only limited forces could be deployed had to be different.

With much effort, we began to develop language designed to try to reconcile the conflicting approaches to security. Relatively early in the process, Rabin agreed that the security arrangements—where the restrictions on forces and weapons would apply on both sides—could be limited rather than extending throughout Syria, as Barak

---

*Nonpapers diplomatically made understandings informal, not legally binding, but still concrete.

had suggested to Shihabi. Of course, his definition and Asad's of these "relevant areas" still differed, and the difference went to the heart of the problem we had to overcome: how to handle the asymmetry in geographic scope of the security arrangements.*

In trying to come up with a formula at one point for the nonpaper, I proposed what I considered to be innocuous language: "The relevant areas would be on both sides of the border." This triggered a debate over the relevant areas and their size having to be linked to a definition of the border. Walid insisted on explicit reference to the border; Itamar rejected that. Now we had a new stone in the road. To overcome it, I suggested a U.S. note to Asad explaining that, assuming Israel's needs were met, the United States understood the relevant areas would be drawn from a border based on the June 4 lines. Walid was fine with this and Itamar did not object, saying this was an American undertaking. Both President Clinton and Secretary Christopher liked this approach.

But belatedly, only after I had gone to the region to see the two leaders, did I discover that Rabin had a major problem with such an American note to Asad. He wanted nothing in writing on the pocket. It did not matter how conditional we made the reference to the June 4 lines, nor that we referred to this only as an American, not Israeli, understanding. As far as he was concerned, we were taking his "commitment out of [our] pocket and giving it to Asad" before Asad had met Israel's needs.

When I reported Rabin's opposition, the Secretary was concerned that Asad would freeze the negotiations again, and wanted me to take one more run at Rabin. Normally, I would have simply accepted the Secretary's request, but in this case I knew I was not going to persuade Rabin, and I was now convinced it was a mistake to proceed over his opposition—after all, it was Israel's informal commitment to us that we were, in effect, formalizing. Rabin was right that we would create a new baseline, written and therefore less deniable, at a point when Asad had given little.

I was angry at myself for not thinking through the idea I had proposed. I had fallen victim to thinking only of how to solve one particular problem in the negotiation and had lost sight of the larger issues at stake in the process. But now there was a problem. Walid had informed Asad of what he would be receiving from us, and I was now on my way to Damascus to tell him there would be no note.

LEVELING WITH ASAD AND RABIN'S SECOND THOUGHTS · There were
many times throughout my tenure when I dreaded going into a meeting, knowing

---

*Rabin's definition of the "relevant areas" was from Safed in Israel to Damascus in Syria; Asad's was from Safad in Israel to Quneitra in Syria—Quneitra being the Syrian capital of the Golan Heights.

what was in store, knowing how difficult and unpleasant the meeting was going to be. This comes with the territory of being a negotiator, and I began to treat such difficult meetings as a challenge.

In this particular case, I had someone other than myself to worry about—Walid. He had told Asad I was bringing a letter, and I feared Asad would blame Walid for having failed. I had to make sure that Asad held me responsible, not Walid. And I had to show Asad that we were not questioning the "pocket," we were still trying to find the right way to break through so it would become tangible—and to that end I would propose to raise the level of our efforts to produce the nonpaper in a way that would demonstrate our stakes in the process.

First things first, however. Walid would greet me at the airport for our short ride to the meeting in Asad's summer residence in Latakia. I felt I must tell him upon my arrival that I did not have the letter and, given Rabin's opposition, would not be producing one. As soon as I told him, his whole demeanor changed. There was no doubt in my mind that he was reading this in personal terms—understandable in a regime like Asad's where the wrath of the leader could mean far more than only losing one's job.

We did not have a lot of time to discuss this in the car, and in any event, knowing that Walid would tell Asad whatever I told him at this stage, especially to protect himself, I did not want to reveal to him that I had some ideas. Anything new I might raise had to emerge in the meeting lest it be devalued.

I did not have to wait long to see Asad. He revealed nothing as the meeting began, but Walid looked ill; his visage was literally gray. I explained at the outset that it had been my idea to have a U.S. letter to Syria, but Rabin opposed it at this stage, because a letter meant taking the Israeli commitment to us out of our pocket and formalizing it before Rabin knew whether Israel's needs would be met. Perhaps, I explained, I should have thought of this earlier; but, I continued, we would treat a private commitment from Asad the same way we were treating a private commitment from Rabin. "Logic and fairness required that."

Asad's expression had not changed. He simply listened. I went on to explain possible suggestions on language for the nonpaper. Asad still said nothing, but Allaf was in the meeting and he objected. At first, I was patient in response. But when Allaf suggested that I had betrayed the Syrians by withdrawing the letter, and how could they trust any language I might now suggest, I blew up. The letter, I said, was ours to give or not give. We had not given it to them yet, and we had not taken something away from the Syrians that they already had. Had we given it to them and then retreated from it, it would be right to charge us with bad faith—but not yet. If Syria felt the way Allaf did, perhaps it was best for us to stop making any efforts and Syria could work with someone else.

Now Asad intervened. Of course, Syria was disappointed that there would be no letter, but the United States would decide when it would send letters. For its part, Syria could accept only one border: June 4, 1967. The security arrangements would be on both sides of that border or there would be no agreement and no security arrangements.

I acknowledged that we understood that was the Syrian position, and that my suggestions were geared toward getting at the heart of the problem between the two sides—which was not the border but taking account of the geographic asymmetries between the two sides. Even if the Syrian position in the talks was to insist on absolute equality, I said to President Asad, you at least implicitly recognized the geographic differences when you suggested that the relevant areas be from Safad to Quneitra—meaning that the area on your side of the border would be larger than that on Israel's side. "You and Rabin may still disagree on what the size of the relevant areas should be, but my suggestion on language is designed to say that there will be equality on security arrangements with the exception of geography."

Asad acknowledged my point but feared that the Israelis would abuse the exception on geography. Obviously, I said, this was something the two sides would have to negotiate in practice; we were now trying to establish *the* principles because Asad wanted them, and they could not exclude the difference on geography or they would defy logic and common sense.

Asad, ever the stickler for what was "logical," did not dispute this. I now raised the idea of having Shara come to Washington after Rabin's upcoming visit to see if we could reach agreement on the "aims and principles" nonpaper.

While Asad said he wanted to think about this suggestion, it was clear to me that he liked it. If nothing else, it tended to further highlight the U.S.-Syrian relations and readiness to work together. Our meeting ended around 6 p.m., having started shortly after noon. As he was saying good-bye, Asad turned to Shara and asked him to take me out to "lunch." Over lunch, Shara said, "If the Israelis will accept the principles, we can be flexible on the details." I told him that the principles were largely agreed but the Israelis feared that "you will treat them as a straitjacket and the principles have little meaning without practical application." Shara, echoing what would so often be part of the Syrian and Palestinian mantra in negotiations, repeated, "We can be flexible on the details if we have the principle."

At the conclusion of the day, the happiest man was Walid. As we rode to the airport he was relieved and, in his words, "amazed." When he told Asad there would be no letter, Asad said simply, "This is how your friends treat you"—a chilling response which explained why Walid had looked stricken. He assumed that Asad would end the meeting after I explained there would be no letter. But Walid continued, "You persuaded him with your explanation and with your suggestion on Shara." Walid had gone from complete despair now to near euphoria—"We could finish the paper when Rabin and Shara come."

I, too, was relieved as I headed back to Israel. Upon my return, Rabin wanted to see me alone, and we left Itamar, Dani Yatom, Martin, and Mark Parris in his living room as we went alone into his study. He was curious about Asad's response.

I told Rabin that it had not been an easy meeting, and I proceeded to describe it. Without painting too upbeat an outcome—particularly because I wanted Rabin to feel we had protected his interests at some price—I said Asad would think about my suggestion to have Shara come to try to resolve the nonpaper. Rabin thanked me for what I had done in Damascus, but he then wondered whether the President and the Secretary understood sufficiently the risks he was running and the best way to deal with Asad. Asad was "a tough cookie," and one had to be tough with him. They needed to push Asad, and not just be pushed by him. Did the President and the Secretary understand that?

I replied that Rabin saw what I had just done in Damascus, and the Secretary knew exactly what I was going to do. That should answer your question. His look suggested it had not. So I changed my tack and said, "You are the one who launched us on this path with Asad, and Secretary Christopher has been meticulous in acting on the basis of your guidance. Both the Secretary and the President are committed to you and would never harm Israel."

Rabin had listened. I did not know if I had reassured him. Shortly after my return, I found I had not done so. Martin called me on the secure line and told me Rabin was clearly having second thoughts on the Syrian track and the "pocket," believing that Secretary Christopher had gone too far with Asad.

Martin felt that Rabin himself was now feeling that he had gone too far with Asad and wanted to walk back the pocket. That, I said, was his prerogative—only he could decide what Israel could afford to concede. However, we would have to remind him of exactly what he had authorized so he saw clearly the consequences of walking back now.

Was Rabin trying to get us to turn the tables on Asad? Was this a tactic on his part or was it a strategic turn? I was not sure. I knew, however, that I must put together the file of each of Rabin's statements to us, going back to August 1993, and that Secretary Christopher should go over this file alone with Rabin so as to resolve their problem.

Secretary Christopher and I discussed Rabin's motives before their meeting. I was not sure whether we were seeing a Rabin desire to slow down the Syrian track in light of quiet progress that was now being made with the Palestinians or whether he genuinely felt that he had made a mistake on Syria. The Secretary felt Rabin was thinking that it was simply too hard to do what he had originally thought he might be able to do on withdrawal from the Golan Heights.

We were both anxious for the meeting. But it turned out to be uneventful. The Secretary met alone with Rabin for less than ten minutes. He showed Rabin the file, and Rabin had taken only a quick glance, acknowledging that we had only done what he had asked us to do. Now, however, he wanted us to push harder on Asad so that Asad understood that he would have to give—the giving could not come only from Rabin.

Later I asked Itamar what was going on. His explanation: Rabin felt he was always expected to deliver, not Asad. That was all. Were there no second thoughts about the decision on the pocket? I asked. There probably were, but Rabin would never retreat once he had given his word.

| FINISHING THE NONPAPER AND THE CHIEFS OF STAFF MEET AGAIN |

Prior to Rabin's arrival in Washington, I decided to prepare the ground to try to finish the nonpaper. On the key sticking point of handling the geographic asymmetry, I had offered Itamar and Walid three different proposals on modifying the meaning of equality in security arrangements. The eventual formula was exceedingly complicated, with equality qualified in a long convoluted set of clauses: "If in the course of the negotiation, it transpires that the implementation of equality, from the standpoint of the geographic dimension, proves impossible with regard to specific arrangements, then experts from both sides will discuss the problematic aspects of the specific arrangement and solve them—whether through modification (including additions or subtractions) or through some other agreed-upon and acceptable solution."

Rabin had accepted a formula close to this before Shara's arrival, and Secretary Christopher came up with the parenthesis to assuage a Shara concern on the word "modification" being misused. With help from Shimon Peres, Rabin accepted this change and we had an agreement.

The agreement on the "aims and principles" nonpaper was the high point in the Syrian track during Rabin's tenure as Prime Minister. Without referring specifically to the nonpaper, Rabin declared that there had been a procedural breakthrough on security arrangements with Syria. Asad then echoed him, using the words "procedural breakthrough" as well, to explain that the two military Chiefs of Staff would meet. We no longer had to try to hide the meeting; we were announcing it.

Having learned from the past, however, I did not want to go directly to the Chiefs of Staff meeting. I wanted to prepare it, and have both leaders bless the sequence. First, I would meet with the two military chiefs in the region to prepare the agenda for the talks; second, they would meet in Washington. Third, senior military experts—major generals on each side—would hold follow-up meetings. Both Rabin and Asad accepted the sequence, and Secretary Christopher announced it.

Initially, everything went better than at any time in the negotiations. In my premeetings in the region, I was able to come to a quick agreement on the agenda and even found for the first time a Syrian willingness to discuss military confidence-building measures now—not only after peace was achieved.

But the basic conceptual gap between the two sides on the early-warning issue quickly reemerged once we assembled for our two and a half days of talks at National Defense University in Washington. For the Israelis, the great security danger in getting off the Golan Heights was the loss of early warning of attacks. The Golan, particularly with the Israeli ground early-warning facilities sitting on top of it, gave the Israelis the ability to look not only into Damascus but far beyond it to Syria's eastern border with Iraq. From this vantage point, Israel could see any changes in the status of Syrian forces—the kinds of changes in location, disposition, or readiness that could signal a possible threat of attack. For Syria, the Israeli ground stations in the Golan Heights represented one symbol of occupation; having Israel withdraw from the Golan but preserve the ground stations meant the occupation continued.

We spent a considerable part of the initial discussions going over what was required for early warning to be effective. Shahak's argument was that the most reliable form of early warning came from ground stations—they were more reliable than aircraft or satellites for giving a continuous picture of what was happening with forces on the ground. Shihabi countered that Israel could get all the early warning it needed from satellites and aircraft or even tethered balloons.

Dan Christman, a lieutenant general in the U.S. Army, joined us for the talks. He traveled with Secretary Christopher representing the Chairman of the Joint Chiefs of Staff, and he became a member of the peace team in 1995, accompanying me on my many visits to the area. (I asked Dan to give his assessment of the challenges involved in early warning without taking sides in the discussion.) While discussing what air- and space-based early warning could and could not do, Dan observed that nothing was as reliable as ground-based early-warning stations. He noted there were ways to compensate for ground stations if alternatives were needed, but the compensation would inevitably be tied closely to the disposition of the forces on the ground. If, for example, the forces being monitored were to be deployed farther from the possible fronts, if those forces were to be in a lower state of readiness, and if some of the critical items necessary for launching attacks (ammunition, engineering equipment) were not colocated with the troops, the requirements of early warning would be greatly reduced.

Dan basically highlighted the interrelationship between early-warning needs and the location of the forces. Amnon Shahak picked up this very point in an exchange that went to the crux of the differences between the two sides. As the two were going back and forth on what was sufficient for early warning, General Shihabi accused Shahak of "exaggerating what you need for security arrangements. You will be in a state of peace, not a state of war." Amnon answered him, saying, "You are right. We probably do exaggerate what we need. If you will deploy your forces like you are in a state of peace, not a state of war—not with 80 percent of your forces opposite Israel, your smallest border—we will scale back what we ask for on the security arrangements." Amnon was signaling that there might be alternatives to ground early-warning stations, but Syria had to redeploy or demobilize its forces. Shihabi was not prepared to answer this point, other than to say that only the Syrian leadership could make such decisions.

Since it was clear to me we could not resolve the early-warning ground station here, I suggested that I would take up this issue with the leaders the next time I was in the area. In the meantime, we would record each side's position on this issue and explore all the other aspects of the security arrangements—demilitarized zones, zones of limited arms, transparency measures, third-country monitors and forces, etc.

Over the course of the meetings, we were able to cover more of the security agenda than at any previous point. Shihabi did not present a revolution in Syrian thinking, but he did offer a number of new positions for the Syrians, offering a ratio (10 to 6) to describe the difference in size of relevant areas for the two sides; suggesting that Syrian armor forces would not be positioned closer to Israel after Israeli withdrawal; and accepting a number of confidence-building or transparency measures.*

At the end of the meetings, I offered a summary in which I outlined fifteen points of agreement on which the senior military experts should follow up in their meeting. I also noted again that I would discuss the issue of ground stations with both leaders—wanting to put on the record that there was no agreement on this issue. (This would prove to be important later.)

Generals Shahak and Shihabi bid good-bye to each other, and I saw each of them separately before they returned to the region. Both were encouraged, though Amnon was more reserved: "Shihabi was professional and ready to tackle problems and that was important. But we can not wish away the gaps, they will have to be addressed and both Rabin and Asad will have to make hard decisions."

For his part, General Shihabi was quite upbeat. He described Amnon Shahak as "a man I can do business with." Having heard Amnon's cautionary comments about hard decisions, I decided to do some conditioning in this meeting. Shihabi was joined only by Walid, and I had brought Gamal Helal to interpret. I observed that I did not expect

---

*The 10-to-6 ratio meant that for every ten kilometers on the Syrian side of the border of force limitations, there would be six on the Israeli side. The transparency measures that were accepted included prenotification of exercises below the division level and provision of information on mobilization or buildup of forces.

to be able to resolve the ground stations now. They would be resolved only when we put together a package on all the elements of the security arrangements or alternatively only at the end of the whole process when each side would decide what essential trade-offs they could accept. Perhaps, I said, the Israelis would give up the ground stations if there were a redeployment of Syrian forces, with far-reaching transparency measures and earlier manifestations of normalization like tourism and an embassy. Or perhaps Syria would accept a ground station if it was manned by Israelis and the United States and the Israelis were prepared to accept a shorter period for implementation and with-drawal. I did not know what the package would be, but in all likelihood the ground station issue would be bound up in larger trade-offs.

Both Shihabi and Walid listened, never disputing and at times acknowledging that this might be right. We were all in for a surprise.

| ASAD'S SURPRISE—RABIN HAS HAD ENOUGH |

As I arrived in Israel following the Chiefs of Staff meeting, a Damascus Radio commentary suggested that Syria might accept a third-party presence in the ground early-warning stations. Both Rabin and Itamar were very intrigued, believing that Asad might now be prepared to move more quickly than we had thought. Nothing happened by accident in the Syrian media. Could it be that Asad was already signaling a concession on the ground stations? It seemed out of character, but I had no other explanation.

When I arrived in Damascus the next day, Walid greeted me full of good cheer and good news. Everything had gone well on Shihabi's return from Washington, and he was encouraged about moving on to the next stage.

There was no hint of trouble to come when I opened the meeting. I briefed on the COS discussions, the fifteen points of convergence that had come out of the meeting, and our desire to press ahead quickly with the experts to try to tie different issues down. Asad had not said a word—his back was bothering him—but both Shara and Walid were nodding as I went through my presentation.

When I finished, Asad transformed the mood immediately. He said nothing had been accomplished. There was no point in having military experts meet until the Is-raelis dropped the issue of the ground station. I looked at Shara and Walid; both had blank expressions on their face. Neither knew that Asad was going to do this. What was supposed to be a short meeting turned into a four-and-a-half-hour argument.

You are retreating from a commitment you made to Secretary Christopher, I told Asad. I reminded him that this had been agreed with Secretary Christopher and the Secretary had announced the sequence of steps from Damascus. Did his commitment to Christopher mean nothing? We could not work in a way in which the Secretary of

State makes an announcement in light of an agreement and Syria decides unilaterally to abrogate it.

Asad was unmoved. The Israelis, in his eyes, had violated the agreement by retreating from their pledge to give up the ground stations. I protested that there had been no such agreement and Asad said that is what he had understood from Shihabi. Neither Shara nor Walid were saying a word; there was no way that Shihabi could have reported this to Asad.

Asad suddenly changed course. He began telling me he was losing and Rabin was winning in the process; Israel was gaining by meetings that showed Syrian acceptance of Israel. What was he gaining? "Nothing," he answered.

I challenged him. You are gaining the chance to get your land back. You are gaining a relationship with the United States. Does that mean nothing to you? Do you think there will be no consequence if you violate your commitment to the Secretary?

Now his only answer was that he was not stopping negotiations, only not agreeing to allow senior military officers to get together until the Israelis conceded on the ground stations. He would not budge. He suggested that I sit with Shara to discuss a formula for proceeding. I told him I doubted that Secretary Christopher would accept any formula except the one that he had announced. Before I left Damascus, I said I wanted to see General Shihabi, and he agreed.

It took eight hours to arrange the meeting, suggesting that the Syrian side was scrambling. Asad had surprised everyone. What was going on? Was the Damascus Radio commentary a mistake? Were events moving too quickly for Asad, and he feared them getting out of control? Had he learned something about Rabin? There had been recent stories in the Israeli press quoting those close to Rabin as saying he would not move on Syria until after the next Israeli elections.

During the eight hours my team waited in Damascus for the meeting with Shihabi, we discussed all these possible explanations. No one had an answer. In this regime, there was one decision-maker; he could switch course with no notice. When I finally saw Shihabi later that night, he presented the new party line with no emotion. When I recounted the actual facts—not the fiction of the day—he made no effort to argue or contradict me. He had too much self-respect. Instead, he hoped we would be able to meet again soon and continue the work for a peace agreement.

For unknown reasons Asad retreated. Maybe Asad had not authorized the Damascus Radio commentary and this alarmed him, especially as it suggested he was too anxious for an agreement. Maybe he saw the third party in the ground station as his eleventh-hour concession in return for something of significance to him. Regardless, he was back to the strategy of insisting on his substance in return for a procedural move on his part. Only in this case he was selling the same procedural move twice. And Rabin was not buying. When I saw Rabin the next day he asked me to see if I could persuade Asad on the agreed sequence before leaving the region. The most Asad would accept was an Israeli military man joining Walid and Itamar and then a Syrian officer joining after that. Rabin said "no way" and pulled the plug.

Enough was enough. Asad had to learn that the process would stop—no negotiations, not with the ambassadors or anyone else until Asad abided by the sequence he had accepted.

In July, then, the Syrian track was put on hold. But, of course, there was another track, and at this moment the Israeli-Palestinian negotiations on the Interim Agreement—one that would be highly controversial in Israel as it would install the Palestinian Authority throughout the West Bank—appeared to be in their final stages. Perhaps Asad's retreat gave Rabin—who knew of the expected imminence of the Interim Agreement—a reason to prove that Israel had options with others if Asad chose to hold back or once again sought to dictate how the process would operate.

Of course, Rabin already had the peace treaty with Jordan—and Israeli participation in an international economic summit in Amman with heavy representation of Arab businessmen—to prove that even in the Arab world others were not prepared to wait for Asad. Seemingly out of character, King Hussein had not waited for Asad. To understand why, we will turn next to a discussion of how the Israeli-Jordanian peace treaty emerged.

⟨ 6 ⟩

King Hussein Fulfills His Grandfather's Legacy

ON AUGUST 5, 1994, I walked with the deputy chief of Mossad, Ephraim Halevy, to one of King Hussein's yachts in Aqaba. We had just witnessed the opening of the Israeli-Jordanian border. Moved by the occasion, I said, "Ephraim, we have just watched a field of mines transformed into a field of dreams." Only days before this ceremony, this area, known as the Wadi Arava, had indeed been a no-man's-land of mines and barbed wire, a testament to the state of war that existed between Jordan and Israel. Now the state of war had ended and the border, in an elaborate and affecting ceremony, had been opened. Along with teams of Israeli media, Ephraim and I and other members of Prime Minister Rabin's and Secretary of State Christopher's delegations walked together around the grounds of the King's palace in Aqaba. Before us was an extraordinary scene. Israelis and Jordanians were commingled in public at the King's palace. As we climbed onto the yacht to tour the respective harbors of the Jordanian city of Aqaba and the Israeli city of Eilat, we watched an armada of private boats filled with Israelis and Jordanians approach us sounding horns and carrying makeshift placards proclaiming peace, some written in Hebrew, some in Arabic, and some in English. We felt like they were literally cheering us, even though we knew their plaudits were directed at the King and the Prime Minister. We knew we had played a special role in getting to this day, and amid our joy we each became reflective.

I told Ephraim of my trip to Aqaba with then Vice President Bush in late July 1986 in an effort to draft for the first time a statement of common principles between Israel, Jordan, and Egypt. During the negotiations, I had gone to the beach in Aqaba

at sundown and looked over at the Israeli city of Eilat and pledged to myself that some-
day, somehow, I would do something to remove the barriers that made these cities,
which nearly touched each other physically, light-years apart in political distance.

For his part, Ephraim told me of all the secret meetings he had held here with the
King over the last decade. "Now," he said, "I no longer have to do business under the
cover of darkness and in the dead of night."

How had this moment come about? The history of Israeli-Jordanian relations had
been one of covert cooperation even during a period of overt denial and rejection. King
Hussein's grandfather, King Abdullah, had held many secret meetings with the Jewish
leaders of Palestine before the emergence of the state of Israel. He had sought to avert
a war in 1948, offering the Jews of Palestine autonomy in an enlarged Transjordanian
kingdom that would encompass all of Palestine. This was unacceptable to the leaders
of the Yishuv, but for Abdullah, recognizing the Jewish state was more than the traffic
could bear. Instead, his army, the Arab Legion, financed by the British and led by sec-
onded British officers, succeeded in capturing East Jerusalem and the area west of the
Jordan River known as the West Bank. Controlling both the East and West Banks of
the Jordan River, the state of Jordan was proclaimed in 1949, replacing Transjordan.
While the international community did not recognize the annexation of the West
Bank by King Abdullah—an area the UN partition plan had designated to be part of
the Arab state of Palestine—the name of Jordan stuck.

Following the armistice agreement in 1949, King Abdullah entered into secret negotiations with the Israelis to replace the armistice agreement with a peace agreement.
Abdullah was bitterly denounced for his "secret dealings with the Jews." King Abdullah paid the price; he was assassinated by a Palestinian Arab just outside the Al-Aqsa
Mosque in the Old City of Jerusalem. His grandson Hussein bin Talal was with him at
the time of the assassination.

Because of his father's mental incapacity, Hussein became King in 1952 at the age
of seventeen. Having witnessed his grandfather's assassination while accompanying
him to the Al-Aqsa Mosque in Jerusalem, he understood the necessity of being cautious. Jordan was weak and very poor; Palestinians outnumbered the Bedouin tribes
that made up the Jordanian population of the East Bank; Syria, a radical state, constantly posed overt and covert threats; Egypt, under Nasser, sought to foment unrest
against the King; support from the Saudis was inconsistent, reflecting a broader reality
that the King could count on no Arab support; relations with the United Kingdom and
the United States became a mainstay of his rule.

While his weakness militated against carving out a path separate from the Arab
world vis-à-vis Israel, he could ill afford to absorb Israeli reprisals against Jordan for attacks by Palestinian fedayeen (literally, self-sacrificers) against Israeli villages. He em-

ployed his army to stop such attacks from Jordanian territory, and over time he began meeting secretly with Israeli officials, including Israeli prime ministers. That did not prevent his going to war with Israel in June 1967, although the Israelis, especially after Egypt closed the Straits of Tiran on May 23, urged Hussein to stay out of the conflict. He did not; not because he sought war, but because he was, in his eyes, in a lose-lose situation. Nasser had succeeded in mobilizing the Arab world into a frenzied expectation of Israel's imminent destruction. If Hussein stayed out of the war and the Israelis defeated Nasser, Hussein knew he would be accused of colluding with the Israelis to defeat Egypt and the Arab cause. Alternatively, if he joined the war, he ran the risk of losing East Jerusalem and the West Bank to the Israelis. In the end, he opted for joining the war, believing that he could retain his throne this way even if he lost part of his kingdom—something that did, in fact, transpire.

The June 1967 war may have cost the King the West Bank, but that did not prevent him from resuming his contacts and covert cooperation with the Israelis. In 1970, during Black September,* the Israeli stake in Jordan and that cooperation saved Hussein. Israel's mobilization deterred a Syrian intervention to save the PLO in the battle that led to the Jordanian army's ouster of the PLO from the kingdom. The King stayed out of the 1973 war, believing that another defeat might bring his demise.

Over time, Jordanian-Israeli covert cooperation expanded into areas beyond security to include agriculture, irrigation, and even spraying to guard against threats to crops and health. But the King saw himself as far too weak to make peace with Israel. While he supported peace initiatives, he could not go it alone. In 1987, he met then Foreign Minister Peres secretly in London and the two agreed on the terms for an international conference that would provide an international umbrella for negotiations. However, Prime Minister Shamir vetoed the agreement and the conference became a dead letter until Madrid in 1991.

Hussein wanted peace—indeed yearned to fulfill his grandfather's legacy—but always felt his peace efforts must be wrapped in a multilateral context. He would not separate himself from the Arabs. He would not "pull a Sadat" and make his own peace, even after Sadat had done so with Israel. His was a kingdom in which his Bedouin base was a minority. Palestinians were a majority, and he could not act before the Palestinians did so with Israel.

Oslo, however, created an opening for the King, but he chose to move with char-

---

*Black September refers to the campaign that the Jordanian military launched in response to the growing strength of Palestinian militants in the country. The threat of an impending coup attempt against the Hashemites and the embarrassment of having three hijacked international airplanes landed in Jordan by Palestinian radicals provided the impetus for the crackdown.

acteristic caution. The day after the Declaration of Principles (DOP) between the Israelis and Palestinians was signed at the White House in September 1993, Jordan and Israel concluded an agreed agenda. In addition to detailing the issues that the two sides would seek to resolve, the agenda declared that a peace treaty was their mutual objective.

While we expected rapid movement from them toward an Israeli-Jordanian peace agreement, the King's initial steps were limited, as he sought to use the process to create economic benefits for Jordan. In October 1993, Shimon Peres, seeking in his words to produce peace with Jordan by "storming ahead," proposed that Jerusalem and Amman jointly host an international conference of several thousand CEOs who would be ferried back and forth between the two cities. The purpose would be to capture international imagination and demonstrate that the Middle East was now open for business. Though not leaping to the conference, the King agreed to the formation of a trilateral group of Americans, Jordanians, and Israelis to consider how developmental projects could be put together and funded. I headed this group, which met in Washington every two or three months; my guidance to the group was that every time we met we had to create a new baseline. Even if the movement was not great, I said, each meeting had to advance us from where we had been.*

In November 1993, Shimon Peres, meeting secretly with the King in Amman, reached what Peres believed was the outline of a peace agreement. But Peres, though discreet, could not contain his enthusiasm; when he returned to Israel it leaked that he had been in Jordan, whereupon he proclaimed that November 3 would be a day to remember.

The King was not ready to move so fast. He retreated, loath to rush ahead of the Palestinians at a time when the first milestone of the DOP had yet to be achieved.

His reluctance became even more clear several months later when Secretary Christopher and I met the King in London. It was a disappointing meeting; it was clear he had no plans to move toward a formal agreement anytime soon. This changed in May.

On May 4, 1994, the Gaza-Jericho agreement between Rabin and Arafat was concluded, establishing the Palestinian Authority headed by Yasir Arafat. Suddenly Jordanian interests were involved. With Arafat basing himself at least part-time in Jericho, a city next to the Jordan River, Arafat would now be in a position to affect Jordanian interests. The King now knew it was only a matter of time before Arafat's writ would extend throughout the West Bank and possibly also East Jerusalem. Jordan had its own claims to the Old City of Jerusalem and the holy sites there, and Hussein (who personally paid for the ren-

---

*In the post-DOP world, I was convinced that progress was possible between the Israelis and Jordanians and that the best way we could push it was by pressing for progress in each meeting.

ovation of the Dome of the Rock) could trace his family lineage back to the Prophet. He could not sit aside and watch Arafat preempt his interests in Jerusalem, or stake out positions on refugees that could affect the very stability of Jordan, the only Arab country to grant Palestinians citizenship and also the home to over one million Palestinian refugees.

After May 4, the King had the cover to pursue an agreement with the Israelis and the need to do so—or at least that is what we were soon to find out.

| LEARNING ABOUT THE MAY ISRAELI-JORDANIAN BREAKTHROUGH |

In the middle of May, the King suggested to Rabin that they hold a secret meeting in London. The King made it clear to Rabin he was ready to move rapidly to a formal peace agreement. To do so, he would need Israel to address the territorial questions—questions that involved Israeli absorption of lands that were Jordanian according to borders outlined in the 1949 armistice agreement. Rabin had resisted this previously but now agreed to resolve these issues. He saw the King's readiness to conclude a formal peace agreement as a strategic transformation of the Middle East map, potentially putting Israel formally at peace with two of its neighbors.

Hussein was motivated to act partly for the reasons noted above, and partly for other very practical and psychological considerations. First, subsumed within the Gaza-Jericho agreement was an economic protocol that mandated categories of goods that could be traded into and out of the West Bank and Gaza and directly affected what Jordan could export to the territories. These territories constituted a natural market for Jordanian goods and Jordan could not afford in the long term to have no say in the character of economic relations that were going to develop between Israel, the emerging Palestinian entity, and Jordan. This represented a very practical concern. The King also had a psychological problem. After the January meeting, we saw little point in focusing our efforts on Jordan. I would continue to host the trilateral meetings at the negotiator level. But in the trip to the region that culminated in the conclusion of the Gaza-Jericho agreement—a trip that lasted over a week—the Secretary did not stop in Jordan. That sent an unmistakable signal that the Secretary of State believed we had little peace process business to do with Jordan. Hussein was on his own.

When Secretary Christopher and I returned to the Middle East in late May, Rabin informed us of the secret meeting in London almost in passing, indicating that he did not want to go into it now. Nothing in his demeanor suggested there had been a breakthrough.

I was to be briefed on Jordan by Ephraim Halevy and Eli Rubinstein at the King David Hotel later that evening. I was in for a surprise. Ephraim pulled out a paper that summarized the understandings that had emerged from the secret meeting in London. In essence, the King had agreed to begin drafting the elements of a peace treaty. The

King also agreed to have trilateral meetings—the United States, Jordan, and Israel—in the region. The latter meant that Israelis and Jordanians would meet openly for the first time in Jordan and Israel, crossing a major psychological barrier. In return, Rabin agreed to discuss border demarcation and water allocation—the King's two key issues— despite his misgivings.

In presenting the paper Halevy said he could not say with certainty that the Jordanians would live up to it. Knowing that I would be hosting a trilateral meeting in Washington in a week's time, he asked me to see if the Jordanians present would either confirm the commitments or accept their reality by starting work on the elements of a peace treaty and agreeing to a trilateral meeting in the region. I was intrigued, and ready to see if the London meeting had produced a breakthrough.

Back in Washington, I called the Jordanian ambassador, Fayez Tarawneh, who told me, "Dennis, I have instructions to begin accelerating the negotiating process of drafting elements of a peace treaty," but he said nothing about trilateral meetings in the region.

The next morning when Eli, Fayez, and I met privately, I raised the idea of follow-on trilateral meetings in the region, and Fayez was quick to agree. He was not prepared at that point to say when they would take place.*

The meetings with our three delegations also made headway on very practical matters: tourism, Jordan Rift Valley Development, a transnational theme park in the Dead Sea, civil aviation, and the development of "the Camp David road" that would connect Egypt, Israel, and Jordan. I saw clear signs of change in the scope of what the Jordanians were now willing to accept in practical terms. Much to my surprise, Fayez suggested we present our results at a three-way press conference; this would be a first, a sign of practical cooperation with the Israelis.

I was eager for such a public demonstration, but fearful that in public Fayez would feel constrained and might even retreat from some of our understandings. I asked him to clear it with Amman, and Fayez's answer was quick in coming: the King wanted him to do the press conference.

Still, I wanted no surprises, so I asked for both Fayez and Eli to meet in my office first to go over our answers to all possible questions, especially those about the next trilateral meeting because the communiqué we were issuing declared it would take place in the region. We will be asked, "Where will you be meeting? And the answer has to be either Israel or Jordan, anything else won't be seen as a major step forward." I looked expectantly at Fayez. Without hesitation he volunteered, "We will meet in either Jordan or Israel." I now knew something had changed.

---

*Without prompting, Fayez came back to me within a day to say the King would accept a regional trilateral in July.

At the time, Secretary Christopher was in Brussels attending the June meetings of NATO foreign ministers, and it was essential that he not meet the press in Brussels and be unaware of the progress that was being made between Israel and Jordan. Given the time differences and his schedule, I called Tom Donilon, not the Secretary, the night before our press conference. Part of Tom's job was to protect the Secretary and also make him look good. Even with my caution about our press conference in the morning, he would have liked the Secretary to get some credit for the developments. Could we, he wondered, delay the press conference until the Secretary got back to Washington? Tom, I replied, if the Jordanians are ready to do this, I don't want Fayez to report to the King that we have asked to delay the press conference a day, and give the King time to reconsider. Tom understood.

Secretary Christopher called me after the press conference to tell me how pleased he was with this development. I had gone from being cautious to wanting to set our sights higher. Soon we would be able to do so.

| STORMING THE JORDAN |

Within days of our press conference, the King informed us that he would be coming to Washington. With several of his children in school in the States, and with a beautiful estate overlooking the Potomac River—forty minutes from downtown Washington—he never found it difficult to contrive a visit.

We each had an agenda for meeting now. The King wanted to know what he could get materially for accelerating progress with the Israelis—no doubt to enable him to explain to his public what Jordan would gain for doing so. We wanted to pin down where and when the trilateral meeting would actually take place.

The Israelis were not indifferent observers in this process. They had an enormous stake in making the leap to peace with Jordan, and had learned that the more they could be seen as improving relations with the United States for others (such as the newly free countries of Eastern Europe), the more their own relations with others would improve.* Small wonder, then, that when King Hussein arrived in Washington for his June visit, Ephraim Halevy arrived as well.

On June 18, 1994, Bob Pelletreau, the Assistant Secretary for the Near Eastern Affairs Bureau, Martin Indyk, the special assistant to the President at the National Security Council staff, Pete Martinez, the director of the Jordanian desk at the State Department,

---

*Many developing countries began to believe that they could use the Israelis to help them create stronger ties with the United States.

and I went to greet King Hussein at the Four Seasons Hotel at the outset of his visit. I recall sinking into the large soft sofa and listening to the King speak. He declared that the Jordanian people needed to see the concrete benefits of peace, not just the sacrifices.

He called our attention to Jordan's economic needs, its very heavy debt burden, and the importance of modernizing its military even while reducing its size. He was determined to accelerate his own effort to reach agreement with Israel, but as he explained, "I must know that I am not alone."

On our side, Bob, Martin, and I spoke in general terms of trying to meet Jordan's needs, but given the budgetary difficulties and residual congressional reluctance to increase foreign assistance to Jordan, we would need to be creative in trying to do so. Then Bob, trying to be encouraging, suggested that we would be willing to take a look at the modernization needs of Jordan's air force and consider how the F-16 fighter might relate to these. This made me uncomfortable: I was certain the King would interpret what he heard as an indication that we would sell F-16s to Jordan, which I knew was out of the question, at least for now. So I quickly added that we had our own constraints politically and that both countries needed to be realistic, especially in the absence of an actual peace treaty between Jordan and Israel.

Having hinted that what we could do for Jordan depended on its making peace with Israel, I turned to the question of the trilateral meeting and suggested that we might meet in both Jordan and Israel; given the proximity of Israeli and Jordanian hotels on the Dead Sea or in Eilat and Aqaba, I raised the possibility of meeting in alternating sites. This, I suggested, would demonstrate that it was truly a new day and the path to peace was accelerating. The King said he would consider my suggestion and we concluded the meeting.

Later that day, Itamar Rabinovich called me from Israel, where he was celebrating his daughter's wedding; Rabin, he said, wanted me to see Ephraim Halevy, who was now in Washington. So began a dual Israeli strategy: Rabin would push to be sure Israeli needs were being met by Jordan, while Ephraim would push us to be sure we were responding to the King. The next morning, we met with the Jordanian delegation, led by Prime Minister Abdul Salam Majali. Majali opened the meeting by saying, "You know I am not a diplomat. Let me be clear: the Jordanian people have seen no benefits from the peace process, they see only a harder life." His colleagues Marwan Qassem, head of the royal court, and Michel Marto, the Deputy Governor of the Central Bank of Jordan, echoed his sentiments.

On behalf of my colleagues, I told them I appreciated their candor, and I felt the need to be equally candid in response. First, I said we were working actively to get other key creditors to reschedule Jordan's debts, but I did not want to mislead them. We could make some headway here, but there were obviously limits as to how much effect we would have on Japan and France in particular. Second, we were clearly limited in how much money we could provide directly to Jordan given our budgetary squeeze and the reality that many in Congress had not forgiven the King for his support of Saddam Hussein during the Gulf War. Notwithstanding our constraints, we were prepared to be creative in terms of putting together a package of items that could help Jordan economically: we could restructure Jordanian debt; provide PL 480 agricultural assistance, principally wheat;* and offer EXIM bank credits and loan guarantees from the Overseas Private Investment Corporation (OPIC), each of which could be used to attract foreign investment to Jordan. In addition, on security, I noted we would look at whether we could provide some excess military equipment.

Frankly, I concluded, to do more, we would require much greater drama in Jordan's peacemaking with Israel. Only that would make it possible to persuade the Congress to increase aid to Jordan significantly. Martin reinforced this point, saying Jordan needed to make a visible move toward peace with Israel. Wes Egan, our ambassador to Jordan, observed that to get debt restructuring, Jordan would also have to demonstrate that it was putting its economic house in order.

Prime Minister Majali was unhappy. Jordan did not need debt restructuring, which would only defer debt; it needed debt forgiveness. I shook my head, noting that given our laws we could not forgive their debt without an allocation from Congress of an amount equal to their debt to us (e.g., $700 million). Again, I said that's just not in the cards if we don't have a demonstrable Jordanian move in peacemaking that we can use with the Congress.

Seeing their expressions, I felt the need to offer more of an explanation. We were not just being difficult. There was a history here beyond the legacy of the King's position during the Gulf War. They were also now the victims of the Bush administration's decision to cancel Egypt's debt during the Gulf War—a decision that proved to be very controversial, particularly because American farmers who had a mountain of debt asked why their debt could not also be canceled. Apart from the controversy, the laws had since been changed to require a dollar-for-dollar allocation for whatever debt would not be repaid to the U.S. Treasury. The combination of new money required and the political price made it essential for us to have a compelling case to make on the urgency of debt cancellation for the sake of peace. Absent the drama, the best we would be able to do would be something like the package I had described.

The next morning, Ephraim called requesting an urgent meeting. He reported that the King's mood had soured after the reports of our meeting with Majali and com-

---

*Public law 480 permitted the U.S. government to provide agricultural commodities to poor countries in need of assistance.

pany. He quoted Zaid bin Shaker, the King's cousin and a central figure in ensuring critical support in the military for Hussein, as saying this was the King's worst visit to Washington in twenty years.

"Ephraim," I said, "that's ridiculous and Zaid knows it." I continued, saying we would do what we could. We were counting on the Jordanians to make a good case to our Treasury Department so we could do more with Paris Club debt rescheduling for them. I mentioned the other ideas we were exploring in both the economic and security areas. But I added, "Ephraim, I know what is going on here: the Jordanians are using you to convince us that we must do more for them. At one level, that's great. It is wonderful that they see the value of using you with us; that certainly indicates that they have a high stake in good relations with you. On the other hand, it makes me wonder who is manipulating whom." Don't misunderstand me, I told him, we are prepared to help the Jordanians, but there are profound limits as to what we can do at this time.

While acknowledging my point, Ephraim said that the King felt he needed real help from us economically and militarily if he was to move further on peace, and the King was now concerned he would not get it.

I repeated we would do what we could, but absent something dramatic we were clearly limited: "If the King makes a move toward you on peace we might be able to do more on debt relief. For debt forgiveness, he has to pull a Sadat." Ephraim's expression mirrored what I had seen from Majali, and so I asked him do you want us to give them F-16s? If so, it will take more than the drama of something even like a public meeting between the King with Rabin. It will take a peace treaty, and even then I doubt F-16s make sense given Jordan's more practical needs.

Ephraim, a little embarrassed, responded by saying that he was certainly not suggesting in any way that we should provide them with F-16s. I told him he should tell the King and his aides that we were taking his needs very seriously and doing the very best we could. If he sought much more from us, we needed more from him. Ephraim said he would convey this to the King.

Following the meeting, I called Fayez and told him we were doing our best to come up with creative ways to meet Jordanian needs. The King, I said, needed to be very specific with the President about his most important needs. In addition, it would certainly help engage President Clinton and give us something to use with the Congress "if His Majesty would tell the President that Jordanian and Israeli officials would meet soon in Jordan and Israel."

Fayez understood, telling me that the King was considering this very issue, and would also send a letter to the President that evening that would outline his most important needs and areas where we could be helpful. Fayez promised to get me a copy of the letter as soon as it was drafted.

The King's letter summarized his economic and security needs and promised the President he would move toward peace, provided we would respond to his needs—in effect asking President Clinton to demonstrate his readiness to stand by him. Attached to his letter was an annex containing ten different proposals designed to deal with improving Jordan's economic and security circumstances. Martin prepared the briefing memo for the President and attached the King's letter and annex to it.

When we went into the Oval Office to brief the President prior to his meeting with King Hussein, he had read the letter and annex. He wanted to be responsive to the King and wondered on which proposals he could provide some positive answers. In one way or the other most of the items I had suggested for a package for the Jordanians figured in the King's requests: PL 480 agricultural assistance, OPIC guarantees, our readiness to press our allies on debt relief, and provision of ammunition and excess military equipment.* To be sure, the King sought much more military and economic assistance over time, but this was what he sought now.

Psychologically, I told the President, significant debt relief would have a huge impact on the King. But both Martin and I emphasized that the King needed to know that without his taking politically significant moves toward Israel, we would have no chance of moving the Congress on debt. While pointing out that the King's willingness to meet Rabin openly would be a huge step, I said I did not expect it now, and at this point it was important to get the King to agree to meetings between Israeli and Jordanian negotiators in both countries.

The President understood the point, but still preferred to press for a meeting with Rabin. Clinton's style and command of detail typically had an effect on those with whom he was meeting. Nowhere was that more evident than in this meeting. He conducted the meeting without any notes. His ability to go over all the points in the King's letter and annex without the use of any notes wowed the King and his key aides. Indeed, by going over arcane issues of assistance to Jordan and pointing out what we could do and what we could not do, he persuaded the King that he had personally delved deeply into all of Jordan's needs and was personally looking for ways to respond.

For King Hussein, a leader who always placed great stock in personal relations and commitment, the President's mastery of the detail convinced the King that the President placed a high priority on Jordan and the King. After going over each of Jordan's ten requests in the annex, President Clinton focused the bulk of his time on his desire

---

*Legislation permitted us to provide excess military equipment to countries we specified as equivalent in our relations to NATO.

to do something that would greatly ease Jordan's debt burden. He said he knew this was the most important of all of Jordan's economic requests, and he understood that we must get the other major creditors to respond on debt as well. But to be effective with others, we had to lead by example. To do otherwise—to simply exhort others to recognize Jordan's needs—would be unlikely to work. Instead, the President wanted to be able to show that we were actually forgiving Jordan's debt. This would make his appeals to others, especially our allies who were the main creditors, far more compelling.

At this point, he turned to our political realities, saying the Congress would reject debt forgiveness unless he had a powerful argument to use on Jordan's behalf: "A public meeting with Rabin will give me that argument." If it would make it easier, Clinton said, he would be very glad to host such a meeting anytime it was convenient for the King and Rabin.

Clinton asked the King to think about it, and the King said he would. The meeting ended, and in the postmortem in the Oval Office, the President asked whether we thought the King would be willing to come to such a meeting anytime soon. Both Martin and I felt that the King might do it, but not immediately. Knowing that the King would not want to be unresponsive to the President, yet was probably still unwilling to go to a meeting with Rabin as the first step, I suggested we now seek to raise the trilateral in Jordan to the ministerial level. We would bring together political figures, the Secretary of State could go to the meeting, and we would make this much more of a political milestone in the region. "Good," the President said, "but if we can get more, I am ready to host a meeting of the two leaders." (Much like with Rabin and Arafat in September 1993, the President was thinking in more ambitious terms than I was.)

I had my marching orders. As soon as I left the Oval Office, I called Fayez. The key was playing up what the King had gotten out of the meeting—namely, the President's personal engagement. Here I was pushing on an open door. Fayez was still gushing over the meeting, saying the King had never had such a meeting with any president since Eisenhower. "Fayez," I replied, "we need to build on the President's interest now. Let's not lose the moment." The President is looking forward to the King's response on the meeting with Rabin. "Let's do something quickly, maybe something that can set the stage for that. We should do the trilateral at the Dead Sea and do it at the ministerial level, unless of course the King is ready for a meeting with Rabin and the President now." Echoing the King, Fayez said he would check and come back to me. While this was certainly not a yes, Fayez was not acting like this suggestion was out of the question.

Ephraim also confirmed the impact of the meeting on the King. He reported that the King had been "amazed" by the President and was "thrilled" with his visit to Washington. I explained what the President had done with the King, and then emphasized that while I did not expect the King to leap to a meeting with Rabin now, we needed to nail down the trilateral in Jordan and raise it to the ministerial level. Halevy said he would see the King in London and let me know where things stood soon, probably in the coming week.

Over the course of the next two weeks I heard little more. Halevy did not see the King in London as the King had become ill. Fayez also said no decisions had been made, though the ardor after the meeting had cooled and he felt the King and the Crown Prince probably preferred to have the first meetings with the Israelis at the border and below the ministerial level.

Now I feared a retreat, and I pressed Fayez to recognize that there would be a cost to pursuing business as usual. Fayez knew the political realities on Capitol Hill. He understood why I was pressing, but he was unable to get answers from Amman. That changed on July 4.

| THE KING'S JULY 4 MESSAGE |

Debbie and I had been playing tennis, and as I walked in the house my son Gabe bellowed that the State Department was on the phone with the Jordanian ambassador. Fayez told me he had a message from the King that had to be delivered today. Fayez, I asked, is it really important? I am planning to spend the holiday with my family. Can't it wait until tomorrow? His reply was blunt: "Dennis, it cannot wait." I thought the Jordanians must be willing to meet with Peres and the Secretary in Jordan. As I stood dripping sweat onto our kitchen floor, I was learning that another threshold in Middle East peacemaking was about to be crossed.

Now Fayez and I had to work out the mundane details of getting together on a holiday. He said his driver had the day off. I said I would be taking my kids to the State Department later to watch the fireworks from the roof. Could he leave the sealed message with the operations center and I would pick it up from there? That was fine with him, and I left instructions for him to be met at the entrance of the department and for his envelope not to be opened or given to anyone but me.

The State Department is located in an area called Foggy Bottom—close to the Potomac River, figuratively in the shadow of the Lincoln Memorial, near soccer and softball fields, and in an area devoid of good restaurants. When we arrived at the department early that evening, I told my kids I had to stop for a minute at the operations center before we could go to the roof. That produced a collective groan as they were convinced this would be a "Dennis minute"—meaning anywhere from fifteen to thirty minutes of work. I said no, this would be really a minute, as I was simply picking something up. While doubting me, they trudged along and were surprised when I picked up the envelope and we went to the roof.

Once there, I opened the heavily sealed envelopes and read and reread the message. It was clear and unambiguous: the King was ready to have Secretary Christopher come to the region within two weeks to take part in a trilateral meeting at the Dead Sea with a Jordanian delegation led by his Prime Minister and with an Israeli delegation led by a minister designated by Prime Minister Rabin. He asked that a bilateral meeting of Israeli and Jordanian negotiators at the border precede the ministerial meeting. He also asked us to get Israeli approval for this sequence of steps, and he pledged himself to work for peace in the spirit of his meeting with President Clinton.

I was thrilled. I read the King's desire for sequence as his way of conditioning his public. He would use bilateral negotiations between Jordan and Israel on the border to get the Jordanian public accustomed to negotiations in the area, and use Secretary Christopher's presence to provide cover within Jordan itself. It made sense and it would permit us to bring together an Israeli delegation, probably led by Shimon Peres, the Israeli Foreign Minister, with his Jordanian counterpart for a historic first: a public meeting of Israelis and Jordanians in Jordan.

When I informed the Secretary of the message, he, too, was pleased, congratulating me on producing it. "Chris," I said, "this was the President far more than me."

Then I called Fayez, asking him to convey to the King that the President and the Secretary were extremely pleased with his message. We accepted his proposed sequence and would contact the Israelis to gain their agreement to it.

I conveyed the essence of the King's message to Itamar, and Itamar let me know a few hours later that the Prime Minister accepted the sequence proposed by the King. Although nothing had been announced, everything was falling into place, with plans for the border meeting during the week of July 11, and the trilateral timed for a week later. And then we had a new development—one that was both extraordinary and complicating.

| THE KING "PULLS A SADAT" |

On July 9, King Hussein, in a speech to the Jordanian parliament, declared that if it would help to meet Jordan's needs in the peace process, he would meet with Prime Minister Rabin. His speech took place on a Saturday; the *Washington Post* ran a small wire story, and the *New York Times* did not report it.

I, too, paid it little attention. On Monday morning, July 11, Martin Indyk called me and asked what I thought of Hussein's speech. Being riveted on the trilateral meeting, I said it was probably designed to condition the Jordanian public: by making it clear that he would be willing to see the Israeli Prime Minister, he made our meeting seem modest in comparison.

Martin thought that was probably right. But wasn't it possible, he asked, that it was a Sadat-like speech—the one he made to the Egyptian parliament in 1977 in which he declared he would even go to the Israeli Knesset in Jerusalem if it would help to make peace. Wasn't it possible that the King, much like Sadat, was actually now signaling a much more ambitious agenda than we were developing? Wasn't it possible that, much like the Carter administration, we might be underestimating what was being publicly signaled?

I had to admit that Martin might be right. Like the Carter administration, which had been riveted on its plans for an international conference in Geneva,* I was probably too focused on a sequence of steps that fit my view of what was possible, rather than what the parties desired. Maybe I said, Hussein is testing the waters to see the reaction— our reaction as well as his public's.

In response, Martin suggested we send the king a private message from President Clinton applauding his speech and proposing that the meeting with Rabin should take place soon. I was reluctant to seem to be pushing him when he was moving on his own. Instead, I suggested we ask our ambassador in Amman, Wes Egan, to probe whether the King was, in fact, ready for such a meeting now.

But events were now moving very quickly. Before I could check with Wes, he conveyed a letter from the King to the President, in which Hussein proposed a meeting with Rabin in a week's time, to be followed three or four days later by a meeting of the two of them in Washington with the President. Having crossed the Rubicon on public meetings in Jordan, Hussein now saw himself ready for more historic steps of his own.

I did not want us to seem hesitant in response, but I wanted us to be able to take maximum advantage of his steps—in the region and with the Congress. I felt the first meeting between the two leaders must be in Washington with the President. I suggested we go back to the King enthusiastically, but argue that if the Rabin-Hussein meeting took place on the border first, it would rob the Washington event of its drama—and drama with the Congress was a must.

---

*Carter entered office determined to pursue Middle East peace as one of his administration's top foreign policy priorities. His initial effort focused on a plan for achieving comprehensive regional peace by bringing all the relevant parties together for an international conference in Geneva. It was not until these diplomatic efforts broke down and Sadat made his dramatic trip to Jerusalem on November 19, 1977, that the Carter administration began working to facilitate a bilateral Egyptian-Israeli peace treaty.

Ideally, I told the Secretary, the best way to set up the meeting—and also prepare it—would be for him to meet in Jordan with the Crown Prince or the Jordanian Prime Minister and Peres, and emerge from the meeting announcing that the King, Prime Minister Rabin, and President Clinton would meet in several days in Washington. The Secretary agreed. I briefed Itamar, asked him to treat this very discreetly; he said he would talk only to the Prime Minister and get back to me.

That afternoon, I went to watch my daughter, Rachel, perform in a play. But Itamar had the operations center page me, and I left the play to take his call. With a bad connection on a cell phone, I found myself outside the Whittier Woods School in Bethesda yelling to be heard, even while emphasizing the importance of preserving discretion. In any case, Itamar reported that Rabin was very pleased by the news and thought our preferred scenario made sense.

I reported this back to the Secretary and we got to work on a formal letter from the President to the King.

Now, unfortunately, life became much more complicated. The Israelis did not wait for us to respond to the King. Before we could go back formally with the President's response, we heard from Wes that the Jordanians and Israelis had agreed that Rabin and Hussein should meet on July 19 at the border and only then come to Washington.

We were livid. It looked like we had received a private communication from the King, shared it with the Israelis, and they had used it against us. I called Itamar and asked for an explanation. Martin called Eitan Haber, Rabin's chief of staff and principal political advisor, and told him that they had better treat us as something more than the "kosher caterer."

The initial reaction from the Israelis was that they were not arguing for the meeting on the nineteenth on the border; the King wanted it. The Secretary called the King to explain directly how we saw things—and that our ability to deliver on the debt forgiveness depended on our being able to sway Congress in Washington. The Secretary proposed a sequence of steps starting with the negotiators meeting on the border on the nineteenth, holding the trilateral the next day in Jordan, and the summit in Washington by early August—a sequence that allowed him to make a once-postponed trip to Asia.

In response, the King saw the argument for having a summit meeting in Washington, but was loath to wait too long. He had made a decision and wanted to act on it.

I went back to the Secretary and urged him to change his plans—either to skip ASEAN or to hold the summit earlier and go late to ASEAN. The King was right to want to do the summit quickly; there was, after all, always the risk of an act of terror or an event in the Arab world that would make it impossible to convene the summit.

Christopher agreed. I went back to Itamar and did not mince my words. Since Israel is counting on us to pick up the cost of debt forgiveness, among other things, "the

PM had better accept that we need the initial summit meeting to be here and we need to ensure that it is filled with a sense of drama and fanfare."

Of course, there were still two problems. We had neither a date on the President's calendar nor any plan for the summit itself. What would be its results? I had not yet given up on a trilateral meeting prior to the summit. But now I was thinking less of its symbolism and more of its substantive role: to announce specific understandings between Israel and Jordan. Christopher said he would get a date from the President for the summit, and I should work on the Israelis to accept the ministerial meeting in the region prior to the summit.

Rabin, however, was now not in favor of the ministerial meeting, preferring an early summit. Once again, we were facing resistance on a procedural issue—one we now considered essential to having a successful summit. Martin and I went to see Itamar and I started our meeting by saying that this had not been a good week for U.S.-Israeli coordination. From the President and Secretary on down, we felt used by the Israelis. Apart from violating a confidence, they were giving us short shrift, even though we were the ones expected to deliver for the Jordanians.

Before Itamar could respond, I received a call from the Secretary. He told me the only date open for the summit in Washington was Monday, July 25. I told Itamar that the scenario that made sense was the following: the negotiators meet on Monday, July 18 (four days hence), the ministerial meeting in Jordan takes place on the twentieth, and the summit on the twenty-fifth. Itamar undertook to persuade Rabin to accept this sequence and did—informing me of this the following morning with one proviso: all three parties should announce this sequence by noon Washington time.

This made for a mad scramble in the morning, getting the White House on board, producing the announcement, and making sure the Jordanians accepted this. Martin was in charge of producing the announcement and the Secretary and I got in touch with the King. As the Secretary was speaking to King Hussein, it became clear he was principally concerned about making sure that the announcement made certain points important to Jordan. Perhaps because his characteristic humility made it unseemly for him to be asking for what amounted to praise, he asked to put Crown Prince Hassan on the line with me to discuss Jordan's needs in the announcement. Hassan asked that we make three points:

—The meetings and summit were not an end in themselves but would be helpful in moving to a comprehensive peace settlement in the region;
—They grew out of the King's statement to the Jordanian parliament;
—And President Clinton appreciated "His Majesty's leadership role in the pursuit of peace."

I wish I could say that we always orchestrated everything in a neat fashion. Obviously, we did not. But we did this time, with Martin faxing me the draft announcement while I was still on the phone with the Crown Prince; I adjusted it to accommodate the points Hassan asked for and faxed it immediately to him. The Jordanians were now on board. On the Israeli side, however, there was a new request.

Eitan Haber had called Martin with a new idea: after Rabin and Hussein came to see the President in Washington, President Clinton should fly to the region and address first the Israeli Knesset and then the Jordanian parliament. While this move would be highly symbolic and bound to create an aura of excitement, I was against it. We needed to save this for when the two sides concluded their peace treaty. If we did this now, what would the President do then? We nixed the idea.

THE WASHINGTON DECLARATION

All our energy had gone into producing a sequence of events. But the events needed to have content. There was not much time to plan, but there was a need to produce. Our objective should be the issuance of a statement—one we would call the "Washington Declaration"—with it becoming one of the milestones on the road to Middle East peace. I suggested that it have three basic elements: it should end the state of belligerency between Israel and Jordan; it should outline immediate and concrete steps of cooperation between the two countries; and it should set a timetable for the achievement of an actual peace treaty. I told the Secretary we should prepare a draft Washington Declaration and present it to the leaders and refine it in the trilateral in Jordan.

Secretary Christopher agreed. As we soon discovered, Prime Minister Rabin had a similar goal, but a very different idea about how to produce it. At his office on the following Monday, he became increasingly uncomfortable as I began to outline key elements for the declaration, like, for example, an end to the state of belligerency.

I was puzzled. As usual, to avoid surprising Rabin, I had previewed with Itamar what we would cover in the Rabin meeting. I knew the ideas could not be the problem. Rather, it was my raising these ideas in front of too many people on his side and ours. It was a large meeting, and it quickly became apparent that Rabin's great fear was that our plans would be leaked, expectations would be raised, and he wanted to avoid any danger of falling short of them.

This was understandable and sensible. But his approach was basically to cut us out and do all the work on a statement directly and secretly with the Jordanians.

When we got to Amman, the King listened to the Secretary but said little and showed no particular interest in seeing our declaration—a sign that the Jordanians were secretly working with the Israelis. I told the Secretary that we could hardly complain about them working together as this is precisely what we had always sought. That said, to avoid any surprise and protect our interests, we decided to have Martin Indyk stay in Amman and go over our draft with the Crown Prince while we went to the trilateral at the Dead Sea.

The meeting at the Dead Sea Hotel, the first public meeting ever held in Jordan with senior Israeli officials, was remarkable for its symbolism and the eloquence of the statements made by Shimon Peres and Prime Minister Majali. Peres spoke of representing the hopes and dreams of Israelis and Majali spoke of writing a new chapter between two peoples and of creating peace as a state of mind. After the speeches, we went upstairs to a meeting room for our actual trilateral. Peres emphasized the importance of being able to announce in Washington agreement on economic projects, including specifically agreement on the concept for development of the Jordan Rift Valley—the area from the Dead Sea south to the Red Sea. He spoke of developing the energy, water, mineral, and tourist possibilities in the Jordan Rift Valley; of announcing a free-trade area in the Eilat-Aqaba area; of developing a common port in this area and a common international airport. He urged that some combination of these projects be announced in the statement that the President, the Prime Minister, and the King would make in Washington on the following Monday.

Majali was more restrained. He agreed we should seek to finalize an understanding on the Jordan Rift Valley concept. But he preferred to give prominence to the other issues—cooperation in tourism and the completion of a road linking Jordan, Israel, and Egypt—delaying more ambitious schemes until after the issues of borders and water had been resolved.

This discussion and the disagreement it embodied were also played out as I sought to finalize our communiqué for the trilateral meeting. Finally, I simply proposed the final text and the Secretary and I appealed to Prime Minister Majali to accept it, and he did.

Once the text was completed, the ministers went to hold a joint press conference downstairs. The air-conditioning was not working and the room was stifling, but the Israeli press and Israeli delegation could not contain their excitement. They were in Jordan, and they could not believe it. My friend Ehud Kofman, now the director of external relations for the Israeli Finance Ministry and my friend for over twenty years from our days as students at UCLA, hugged me; Israeli reporters and Foreign Ministry people alike were calling Israel from their cell phones just to say they were in Jordan.

I explained to Secretary Christopher that this was a moment of extraordinary psychological meaning for the Israelis. For their whole lives they had looked across the Dead Sea and seen Jordan. The inability to go to Jordan, despite its closeness, despite the fact that Jordan quietly cooperated with Israel in many ways along its border, reminded Israelis of their isolation and rejection in the area. To be able to come to

Jordan—officially, openly, and with a sense of friendship and possibility—provided both a psychic release and sheer exhilaration.

There, of course, was one other factor affecting Israeli emotions on this day. While Israelis had forever dreamed of peace and considered it in theoretical terms, most had a hard time really believing it would come. But here in Jordan, the theoretical was no longer removed from reality. And as one Israeli after another came up to the Secretary and expressed thanks, Warren Christopher's taciturn nature melted and he, too, became emotional.

Following a trip to see the extraordinary sight of Petra—ruins from the very advanced fourth-century Nabatean civilization—we returned to Amman. It had been a stunning and emotional day. Martin, unfortunately, had not been able to share in it. While I practically floated into my room, Martin brought me back to earth, telling me that he had seen the Crown Prince and it was clear that the Jordanians and Israelis were working their draft declaration in private.

After leaving the Crown Prince, Martin called Eitan Haber, telling him that if we were expected to host the event on Monday and invest heavily in it, it was unacceptable to keep us in the dark. Eitan told him he would check with Rabin and call back; when he did, he told Martin that they were crafting a virtual peace treaty, and put Rabin on the phone. The Prime Minister told Martin that only the President and the Secretary must know what was going on, that only one other person besides Eitan in Israel knew, and that Eitan would share with him the elements of their draft.

Not surprisingly, the essential points were not very different from what we had drafted. They spoke of an end to the state of belligerency or war, border openings, limited tourism, telephone service, joining electricity grids, establishing an air corridor, and moving expeditiously toward a peace treaty.

However, there was one surprising item: a reference to Jordan's special role in the managing of the holy shrines of Jerusalem and the Israeli acknowledgment that when permanent status negotiations between Israel and the PLO took place, Israel would give "high priority to the Jordanian historic role in these shrines." Nothing could have more clearly indicated how important it was to King Hussein to be a part of any discussion on the ultimate disposition of Jerusalem. Yet it did not make what they were working on a virtual treaty of peace.

Next we went to Israel where Christopher sat alone with Rabin, who showed him the draft declaration. He emphasized with Christopher (as he had on the phone) that only two other people in Israel knew about the negotiations—he concluded by saying he would keep us informed of the status of the discussions, but he clearly did not want us involved in these talks.

Christopher was content with this arrangement, provided the declaration was shared with us by Sunday evening, the night before the summit. Rabin agreed.

We returned to Washington on Saturday, trailed by Rabin and Peres, and had a bizarre meeting with them in Rabin's hotel room Sunday evening. Before the meeting, Christopher asked me if I thought Rabin had informed Peres of the declaration. Given their personal history, I said it would not surprise me if Peres was still in the dark. That turned out to be prophetic.

In the meeting, it quickly became apparent that Peres was not "the one other person" and that he was unaware of what would happen the next day. Not for the first or only time in the process, we were put in the awkward position of taking cues from Rabin as to what we should be saying to Peres.*

That night Martin and I went over the draft. It had not changed dramatically in substance from what Christopher had seen in Israel. It was more polished; it gave greater emphasis to President Clinton's role in making this possible. While it settled none of the outstanding issues between the two countries, it was significant as a political declaration, and heralded a new day in relations between the two countries.

Still, Rabin hoped that the declaration would explicitly state an end to the state of war, not just the state of belligerency, as it did now. By midnight it was clear the Jordanians were not prepared to say that in the declaration. Because Rabin had asked us to stay out of the discussions, we were not in a position to press the Jordanians. Indeed, the phrase "end the state of belligerency" is one I had put in our draft, believing it was an important legal statement to make.

Hussein obviously understood that using these words "an end to the state of war" was important to Rabin. Had this been a legal document, ending the state of belligerency would probably have been more appropriate. But Hussein understood this was a moment of high politics and symbolism. And he acted in accordance with the moment.

When it was his turn to speak at the White House ceremony on Monday morning, he referred to ending the state of belligerency and, pausing for dramatic effect, said everyone knew that in any language this meant ending the state of war with Israel. I watched as the key Israeli negotiator, Eli Rubinstein, visibly lifted up out of his seat. Rabin, too, brightened. The words had instinctively struck a chord even among an audience largely unaware of the private effort to produce them.

The remainder of Monday and Tuesday were largely devoted to celebrating this political milestone in Middle East peacemaking. But there were practical issues to attend to as well. First, we had to fulfill our side of the bargain with King Hussein, namely, act with the Congress to provide debt relief to Jordan. On Tuesday, before Ra-

---

*At this stage, Rabin still tended to view Peres more as a rival than a partner.

bin and Hussein addressed a joint session of the Congress, Wendy Sherman, the assistant secretary responsible for congressional affairs in the State Department, took me around the floor of the House of Representatives to speak briefly to Speaker Newt Gingrich and Senate Majority Leader Robert Dole on the importance of our now responding to the King at a moment when he was taking a real risk for peace.* Second, we had to plan the follow-up to the specifics outlined in the Washington Declaration. To get the ball rolling, I organized a trilateral with the Israelis and Jordanians for Wednesday morning.

I started the meeting by saying we were now in a new era. What was unthinkable before—or at least premature—was now the order of the day. We should be ambitious. We should recognize that Secretary Christopher's visit to the region in ten days gave us a need and an opportunity to act on at least two issues—the border opening and the initiation of phone and postal service between Israel and Jordan—in order to show that the Washington Declaration was not just words but a blueprint for tangible change.

Though there were different views between the two delegations on how quickly broader ties and ambitious economic projects could be pursued, especially prior to concluding a peace treaty, there was no disagreement on my suggestion. Within two days I heard from each side that they agreed to try to open the border and initiate phone and postal service by the time of Christopher's visit.

The hardest part was clearing the area where the border was to be opened of mines and barbed wire. A road then had to be built on each side of the border crossing. Procedures for handling those wishing to cross the border had to be established. The practical problems were immense, and yet only eight days later we found ourselves traveling by bus from the Jordanian airport above Aqaba to the border crossing point that would be opened. Suddenly I was moved by the most mundane of road signs: there, in Arabic and English, was a new sign giving both the direction and distance to Eilat, a town that had never been acknowledged before in Jordan, even though it was unmistakably visible from the Jordanian city of Aqaba.

The world had changed in Jordan. I marveled at the sign, calling everyone's attention to it. I marveled at the newly constructed road, and as we traveled down it to the site of the ceremony marking the opening of the border, I knew my dream of drawing Aqaba and Eilat together—something I would soon talk about with Ephraim Halevy—had moved from dream to reality.

---

*I was subsequently to meet with the Democratic caucus on the House side to explain at some length why it was critical for us to provide debt relief and forgiveness to Jordan.

| THE ISRAELI-JORDANIAN PEACE TREATY |

The Washington Declaration and the opening of the border at Wadi Arava ten days later marked an emotional high. The mundane work of actually negotiating a peace treaty brought everyone back to earth. On the Jordanian side, there were two fundamental preoccupations: land and water. If Israel would meet them on the land and water issues, Jordan would meet Israeli concerns on security and normalization. A seemingly neat trade-off, but one that was not so simple to produce, especially in three months' time.

Since 1948, Israel had come to occupy 340 square kilometers—nearly the size of Gaza—that had belonged to Jordan at the time of the 1949 armistice agreement. Both in the Wadi Arava, where a number of Israeli kibbutzim had their agricultural fields on the Jordanian side of the armistice lines, and far to the north in the area where the Yarmuk and Jordan Rivers came together, Israel had come to occupy territory that should have been Jordanian according to the armistice lines.

The King was not prepared to surrender Jordanian territory. But he was willing to be flexible in accommodating Israeli needs, including with regard to the land. Rabin, for his part, was willing to resolve the territorial dispute, but felt the need to maintain the areas that Israel was actually using.

Water was another problem. Jordan was facing dire water shortages. Moreover, because underground aquifers had been overused, existing water resources were becoming increasingly brackish. Jordan felt Israel, since its settlers had contributed to Jordan's water problems, needed to provide water to Jordan. Through August and September, the land and water differences between the two sides remained stuck. In late September, I went to New York to see Crown Prince Hassan, and he pleaded for help with the Israelis on each issue. I probed Jordan's flexibility on the land issue—would, I asked, King Hussein be open to land swaps, to leases of territory, to the disputed areas having a special status? His answer was interesting: Jordan could be flexible, but its flexibility on land depended also on Israeli provision of certain levels of water. In other words, the trade-offs with Israel were not simply Israel getting security and normalization in return for Jordan getting the land and water; the trade-offs must also be within the two issues of land and water with Jordan's ability to be flexible on land depending on Israel finding ways to meet Jordanian water needs.

I promised Hassan I would see what I could do with the Israelis, and I did so. I produced no answers, but a short time later, Rabin suggested that he and the King meet. At that meeting, they agreed on the basic trade-offs: their treaty would be one of peace and cooperation, with extensive provisions for relations in security, economic and financial fields, tourism, agriculture, health, environmental management, and other endeavors. Jordan would either have its sovereignty restored to territories that had been Jordanian or there would be land swaps to ensure that there was no net loss of area to Jordan. To meet Israeli needs, Jordanian land would be leased to Israel and the land would be given a special status. Israel would commit to providing Jordan 50 million cubic meters of water per year and to help ensure international funding for a dam that would provide Jordan with another 50 million cubic meters of water per year.

Eli Rubinstein and Fayez Tarawneh, the two negotiators, translated the conceptual understandings of the two leaders into practical arrangements and treaty language. The peace treaty was signed on October 26, 1994, in the Wadi Arava. President Clinton attended, and subsequently addressed the Knesset and Jordanian parliament, much as Eitan Haber had proposed prior to the Washington Declaration.

Rubinstein and Tarawneh created a model negotiation, with each of them often developing creative solutions once given their guidelines by their respective leaders. They worked out provisions in which Israel would swap 11.5 miles of territory, Jordan would grant areas under their sovereignty a special status to permit Israelis unimpeded access, and land would be leased for twenty-five years to Israel.

Their creative concepts not only made sense for Israel and Jordan but could also have made sense in terms of resolving the territorial questions in the other negotiations between Israel and Syria and Israelis and the Palestinians. At different points in the future, I would raise these concepts with mixed results. I still believe they provide a good basis to reconcile the symbolic needs on the Arab side and the practical needs of the Israelis. As we will see later, Yasir Arafat was not prepared to countenance such means on the permanent status issues of borders and Jerusalem, but his negotiators were prepared to be ingenious in resolving the interim issues that would make a Palestinian Authority throughout the West Bank possible. Ingenuity is certainly what the Israelis and Jordanians demonstrated in producing a peace agreement that may yet prove not only its value as a symbolic precursor to Middle East peace but a practical one as well.

⬦ 7 ⬦

The Interim Agreement

THE GAZA-JERICHO AGREEMENT meant that there would be a Palestinian Authority. It meant that the DOP was being translated into a pathway for reconciling two competing national movements. For that, Yitzhak Rabin, Shimon Peres, and Yasir Arafat would all receive Nobel Peace Prizes seven months later. But the difficulty of crafting the Gaza-Jericho agreement paled in comparison to what would be involved in bringing the PA to all the Palestinian cities, towns, and villages of the West Bank. This was the next negotiating task after completing the Gaza-Jericho agreement, but for understandable reasons neither the Israelis nor the Palestinians were immediately focused on it. Rather, the first task was implementing what had been agreed, and this was no small task. A Palestinian Authority needed to be established, with institutions that needed to be set up, services that needed to be provided, security responsibilities that needed to be assumed—and according to the agreement, Israel would have to vet all those who would serve in the Palestinian police forces, whether they came from within or from outside the territories.

The Palestinian Authority, as a functional government, would have expenses and so would need a tax collection mechanism. Meanwhile, it would depend on the Israelis to provide electricity, telephone service, and significant health care. Cooperation with Israel would be essential, and at one level was designed to create a web of relations that would make living together a hallmark of coexistence.

In economic relations, too, cooperation was essential, as Israel would still control what could flow into and out of the territories. Categories of goods from Jordan and the Arab world were permitted to be traded to the PA but under tight controls—both to limit the effect on the Israeli market and to ensure adequate health safeguards, especially as related to agricultural produce and livestock. (With no real barriers between Israel and the West Bank and Gaza, goods flowing into the territories could easily find their way into Israel.) Israeli controls on imports were understandable; their controls on Palestinian exports—such as cut flowers—were harder to rationalize but became an important part of our ongoing efforts to create greater manifestations of Palestinian independence and economic vitality. For the United States' part, we focused initially on helping finance Palestinian institutions, especially the police. The Holst Fund, named for the late Norwegian Foreign Minister, was established and managed by the World Bank to meet the recurring costs for the PA in its first year of existence.

On top of the practical issues, there was the issue of Arafat's departure from Tunis and his arrival in Gaza and Jericho. Who could he bring with him, and on what terms? Should he be inspected like any other arrival (lest he smuggle in people and arms)? And who should have pride of place in the PA—insiders or outsiders? From the beginning, Arafat gave the outsiders pride of place, much to the resentment and anger of the insiders, who saw the corruption from the outside increasingly transplanted to the territories.*

The DOP's nine-month timetable for extending the Palestinian Authority throughout the West Bank was probably never realistic. The Interim Agreement (IA) was far more complicated than the initial agreement involving Gaza and Jericho, given the number of Palestinian cities involved, the large number of Israeli settlements and settlers that could be affected, and the vastly larger territories that had to be considered. The West Bank totals 5,860 square kilometers; Gaza and Jericho, 360 and 62 square kilometers, respectively.

Exploratory work on the next agreement did not even begin until the fall of 1994. Even then, the work was shaped initially by a number of terrorist acts carried out and trumpeted by Hamas and Islamic Jihad—the fundamentalist religious groups opposed to peace with Israel: a shooting attack in the heart of Jerusalem that left four Israelis dead; the kidnapping, heart-wrenching videos, and subsequent death of a dual U.S.-Israeli citizen, Corporal Nachshon Wachsman; and a bus bombing in the center of Tel Aviv that killed twenty-two people and wounded fifty-six. Israel was preoccupied with security and Rabin not only insisted that Arafat fulfill his responsibilities but also wanted negotiations initially to focus on security arrangements for the West Bank before anything else. Palestinians wanted to see a complete devolution of authority from Israel to the PA, including security responsibilities throughout the West Bank; this

---

*Neither we nor the Israelis questioned what Arafat was doing internally. At this point, we both felt he was the only one who could manage the Palestinians. As we would hear often from Rabin, we shouldn't be pressing Arafat on human rights or even corruption.

step, which Israelis would have found difficult in any circumstances, became unthink-able given the spate of violence and what they saw as Arafat's permissive approach to security. Arafat would blame terror acts on Israeli agents, even as Hamas and Islamic Ji-had were taking responsibility for particular attacks.

Then as later, Arafat seemed unwilling or incapable of controlling the extremists who were determined to wage terror against the Israelis. When I would confront him with the need for him to take action, he sought instead to have it both ways, promis-ing to co-opt or divide the groups rather than confront them directly. He would whis-per that he was succeeding in splitting these groups, but there was no sign of their loss of power. During the fall of 1994, I took a tougher line with him, making it clear that we could not support the PA if it would not fight terror.

In part, I was simply telling him the U.S. position. In part, I was informing him of the effect of terror in Israel: the violence was unraveling Oslo. Rabin's peacemaking stance was weakening. Pessimism was growing and the mood was souring. And as a re-sult, Palestinians, too, were souring on the process. For the Israeli response to acts of ter-ror was to impose closures on the territories. Palestinian workers were blocked from coming to Israel to work, compounding economic hardships. The behavior of Israeli soldiers and border police at checkpoints became more intrusive and arbitrary. Palestin-ian negotiators with VIP cards would be subjected to long, often humiliating checks, frequently making them late to meetings with their Israeli counterparts or with me.

By the late fall of 1994, two negative realities were taking hold. Israelis saw the Palestinians not fulfilling their side of the bargain—security. Palestinians saw the Is-raelis maintaining pressure on them and not fulfilling their promises to cede control over daily life. Israeli permits were still required for nearly every facet of Palestinian life—whether one wanted to build, start a business, travel, import or export—the Israelis had to okay it. Oslo seemed more than ever to be a dead letter.

I talked to Uri Savir and Abu Ala daily, seeing what we could do to reverse deep-ening frustration on both sides. Into this mix came a new idea.

In early December, in separate meetings with Rabin and Peres, they reported that Arafat, in a discreet channel, had raised the idea of an Israeli redeployment out of one or at most two cities on the West Bank, with the redeployment from the remaining cities occurring only later. This constituted a reversal of the process laid out in the DOP, in which the IDF would withdraw from the cities first so that the PA could hold elections for a Palestinian council. Peres told me he would meet Arafat in Oslo on De-cember 9—where Rabin, Peres, and Arafat were to be given the Nobel Peace Prize—and try to finalize an understanding on this approach.

Later, Uri Savir would write that this was, in fact, Peres's idea, not Arafat's. At the time, however, Arafat mentioned the idea to me favorably and did not attribute it to

Peres; and when I asked if there was anything we could do to help, he uncharacteristically said (and he never would again) that he was "satisfied with [the] private discussions with Rabin and Peres."

While Arafat might have been satisfied, both negotiators—Uri Savir and Abu Ala—were dead set against the idea. They believed that changing the DOP to make Israeli redeployment in the West Bank incremental, not comprehensive would guarantee further delay that would be counterproductive over time.

Abu Ala argued that Hamas and Islamic Jihad were growing in strength because the everyday lives of Palestinians were not improving as Oslo promised they would. The stronger the Islamic opponents of Oslo grew—the less occupation seemed to be ending—the less willing and able Arafat was to confront them, or so Abu Ala believed. Uri accepted this and was firmly convinced that further delay would only exacerbate the problem.

Typically, I was sympathetic to Uri. He was passionate about peace. He was empathetic to the Palestinians, and at the same time he saw the continuing occupation as corroding Israel and its values. He saw from the demographic trends that it was only a matter of time before there would be more Arabs than Jews between the Mediterranean Sea and the Jordan River—something that for Uri meant that Israel could not retain the territories and be both Jewish and democratic. He understood the emerging forces of globalization and believed Israel could prosper in an era that removed borders as the impediment to the movement of capital, ideas, and communication. But to do so it needed to free itself from a conflict that would scare international investors away.

Uri was also a highly talented negotiator. He used his empathy and humor—he is an extraordinary mimic—to build relationships with his negotiating partners, then persuaded them through his instinctive ability to marry tactics and strategy. Most negotiators are consumed by tactics; Uri always had his eye on the bigger objective. Where did he want to end up? How did today's maneuver affect what he was trying to accomplish over time? How could he bring his negotiating partner to a point of seeing that Uri's strategic objective could also serve the other side's interest?

Uri's strategic intuition told him that if the Palestinians now acquiesced in the procedural switch that Peres sought, they would demand more on the substance of their position—especially with regard to broader Palestinian control—as part of the Interim Agreement that would be negotiated. Though Uri usually could persuade Peres, this was one case where he could not.

Rabin, for his part, liked the idea, especially because it promised to postpone what would be very contentious in Israel—the redeployment from cities like Hebron, Nablus, and even Bethlehem, places of great meaning to the Jewish people.* It was not

---

*Abraham's, Joseph's, and Rachel's tombs are located in each of these towns, respectively.

just that redeployment would make the likelihood of full withdrawal from the West Bank palpable; it would awaken religious and nationalist forces over what they considered a retreat from the heartland of Eretz Yisrael.*

I faced a dilemma. Instinctively, I agreed with Uri: Why rewrite the agreement? Once you do that, there is no telling where it will stop. But both Rabin and Peres wanted to proceed on this course, and Arafat certainly seemed to agree. Was it my role to oppose something that the leaders on each side favored? When I informed Secretary Christopher of my discussions, he, too, saw merit in this idea and felt I should not raise questions about it.

Regardless of whether it was Peres's or Arafat's idea, it died after the Nobel ceremony in Oslo. I suspected that Abu Ala talked Arafat out of it, portraying it as an Israeli trap—never a difficult thing to do.

Nevertheless, a new discreet or back channel was now established. On December 21, Peres and Arafat, meeting alone in Gaza, agreed to have an open negotiating channel in Cairo, focused on Palestinian elections. This channel would be a cover for a back channel which would negotiate the Interim Agreement; Uri and Abu Ala would lead it. Uzi Dayan, General Gadi Zohar and then his successor General Oren Shahor (the heads of the Israeli civil administration in the territories), and Yoel Singer would join Uri. General Abdel Razak Yehya, Hassan Asfour, and Hassan Abu Libdeh would join Abu Ala. Yehya had been a leader of the Palestine Liberation Army (PLA), living all around the Arab world until he returned with Arafat in 1994; Hassan Asfour had been Abu Ala's partner in Oslo; and Hassan Abu Libdeh headed the Palestine Office of Statistics—I knew him to be an economist by training and a problem-solver in practice. I was to meet secretly with Uri, Uzi, Abu Ala, and General Yehya once a month. They would report to me on their approach, what divided them, where they could see progress being made—and listen to my reactions and suggestions.

Initially, there was a broad conceptual divide. The Israelis insisted on preserving Israeli security responsibility throughout the West Bank lest Israeli cities be subjected to far more terror (especially in the aftermath of an Israeli withdrawal). Gaza had a fence around it, but the cities of the West Bank did not. A pullout in Ramallah, in the words of Uzi Dayan, would put terrorists only minutes away from Jerusalem. In such circumstances, Israeli security was paramount.

The Palestinians naturally resisted, believing that Israeli responsibility for security

---

*Eretz Yisrael (literally, the Land of Israel) is the biblical name for the land given to the Israelites by God. While the phrase in modern Hebrew does not necessarily have a political connotation, the religious and nationalist bloc in Israel see it including all of the West Bank, what they call Judea and Samaria.

would establish a new kind of occupation. They argued for Palestinian jurisdiction, Israeli withdrawal, and in the meantime greater cooperation between Palestinian and Israeli security forces. Otherwise, they declared they would lack the legitimacy to do what Israel wanted on security.

At one point in January of 1995, Uri and Abu Ala met secretly in Washington, and I met with each of them separately. I pushed Abu Ala on security, but was also taken with his emphasis on a security partnership with the Israelis. With Uri, I emphasized Abu Ala's focus on cooperation as a possible answer to Israeli security needs. Truth be told, I was pushing on an open door in each case. Abu Ala was trying to get Arafat to do what was necessary on security even while he sought to get the Israelis to truly commit to withdrawal. Uri understood that Palestinians had to see that peace would bring independence, not occupation under a different guise, and that cooperation was the right means as long as the Palestinians delivered on security.

| TERROR STRIKES AT BEIT LIT |

On January 22, a suicide bomber struck at a bus stop in the Israeli town of Beit Lit. Twenty soldiers returning to duty after Shabbat, as well as one civilian, were killed in the attack for which Islamic Jihad claimed responsibility. The next morning pictures of each of the dead dominated both the print and electronic media. One headline in an Israeli newspaper captured the public mood: "The Children Who Will Not Return Home."

Immediately, Israeli President Ezer Weizman called for a suspension of the negotiations with the Palestinians. By contrast, Yitzhak Rabin vowed to fight terror as if there were no peace process and to pursue peace as if there were no terror. Yet he felt more than ever that Arafat had to change. While he would not close the back channel, Rabin was adamant: he would not countenance any real movement in the negotiations until Arafat arrested those responsible—not just large numbers of irrelevant followers of Hamas or Islamic Jihad—and imposed real sentences on them. We reinforced the message, and Arafat did arrest a number of operatives from the Hamas military wing and created "security courts" to try them. Satisfied, Rabin urged us not to pressure Arafat on the human rights questions raised by these courts, hardly paragons of due process.

In February, Rabin told me that Arafat was finally acting on security. The Israeli security organs likewise believed that Arafat had shown Hamas and Islamic Jihad that he meant business. Against this backdrop the private negotiations began to make headway. However, I felt a need to find public expressions of the progress being made in private—signs that the region was changing and that peace was a possibility. With this in mind, I tried out an idea of having President Mubarak, King Hussein, and Chairman Arafat visit Rabin and declare a common commitment not just to peace but also to confronting the enemies of peace. I saw this as demonstrating to Israelis that peace would produce Arab partners for combating terror and to Palestinians that they would have Arab support as they did so.

Unfortunately, President Mubarak, who had never been to Israel, rejected the idea in private correspondence with President Clinton. I was hoping that the threat to the peace process—as well as his need to rebut criticism over his hosting of a summit where Hafez al-Asad and Saudi King Fahd had been seen as calling for a slowdown of normalization with Israel—would make him willing to take a step he had always resisted.* But Mubarak once again proved more concerned about preventing his potential opponents (latter-day Nasserists and Islamists) from uniting than with taking a dramatic step toward Israel. At the same time, loath to turn us down flatly, he offered to host Rabin in Cairo. Unfortunately, it was not new for Mubarak to host an Israeli prime minister. It would seem like business as usual. We needed drama to capture attention. We needed it for Palestinians as much as for Israelis.

I tried a new idea. The United States would host a meeting of ministers at Blair House to include Israelis, Palestinians, Egyptians, Jordanians, and Saudis—at which the presence of a Saudi would show that a widening circle of Arabs was now dealing openly with Israel. When King Fahd agreed to send his Foreign Minister to Washington, the idea seemed promising. A day later, Fahd reversed himself, having his Foreign Minister inform us that he would come to Washington but only *after* the meeting.†

We decided to hold the Blair House meetings without the Saudis. The Israelis, Jordanians, and Palestinians worked together to produce a forward-leaning communiqué, only to see the Egyptians obstruct the efforts. At one point, Shimon Peres and Amre Moussa engaged in a shouting match, with Moussa saying that Israel needed to fit into the region and refrain from trying to dominate it, and Peres replying: "Why would we want to dominate your poverty?"

In March 1995, Secretary Christopher made a trip to the region. While his purpose was to try to break the stalemate that had emerged on the Syrian track, I also used the trip to meet with the back channel negotiators.

At this point, there was a broad concept emerging: the Palestinians would implement a comprehensive security and antiterror policy, there would be cooperation in all spheres—security and civil—between Israelis and Palestinians, and talks to conclude

---

*Mubarak strongly denied that the summit held in Alexandria, Egypt, on December 27–29, 1994, was designed to slow the pace on peace, but Arab commentary and different Arab foreign ministers from Tunisia to Jordan and Qatar told us otherwise.

†Bandar was in Sibley hospital at the time, recovering from back surgery; though sympathetic, he was unable to deliver.

an Interim Agreement would be accelerated, with July 1 the target date for completion. More importantly from a Palestinian point of view, Uri acted to make clear that Israel was serious about turning control over to the Palestinians over time, proposing that Israel's redeployment from all the cities in the West Bank, with special arrangements for Hebron, would be the first stage of transferring the area to Palestinian control. "Thereafter, a 'further redeployment' from unpopulated areas, to be effected in stages over two years . . . would be tailored to Israel's security needs."

Uri and I agreed that we would produce a statement after Peres and Arafat met on March 9, and Secretary Christopher would endorse this statement, giving it enhanced standing and a sense of mutual obligation.

What emerged from the meeting was not exactly what I had envisioned. It was more parallel announcements than one integrated statement. Arafat announced a comprehensive security policy stipulating that the Palestinian police was the only security organization permitted to operate on the ground, that the PA would thwart terrorism and violence, that only those licensed by the PA could carry arms, and that the PA would intensify security cooperation with Israel. Peres for his part announced the acceleration of the negotiations and declared that every effort would be made to reach the Interim Agreement by July 1. Now there was a clear date for completing the Interim Agreement and the United States had endorsed it.

Yet Israeli settlement activity was expanding, not contracting, in the West Bank and Gaza, threatening to undermine our efforts. The Palestinians saw the new settlements as a sign that the negotiations would not stop Israel from taking land Palestinians considered to be theirs—grist for extremists, which inevitably weakened the PA and Arafat. Arafat himself would rarely raise the settlement issue, leaving it to his deputies. It was as if he felt he had an implicit deal with Rabin: "You don't push me beyond where I can go with my opponents and I won't push you beyond where you can go with your settler constituency." It was a rare instance of diplomatic subtlety.*

REACHING A CONCEPTUAL BREAKTHROUGH

As part of the process of phasing in the Interim Agreement, Israel outlined three zones in which it intended to retain security control even after the transfer of internal security powers to the Palestinians. The Palestinians proposed instead dividing the

---

*While tactically useful, this complicit bargain was strategically damaging. Israeli settlement activity convinced Palestinians over time that the process was a sham, and gave Arafat, at least in his mind, an excuse not to fulfill his responsibilities on security.

West Bank into three areas: one to be under Palestinian control; one to be under Israeli control; and one to be under joint control.

In response, the Israelis developed the "A," "B," and "C" zones, referred to by colors on their maps: the brown (or A) areas would be where the Palestinians would have civil and military control; the yellow (or B) areas would be where the Palestinians had civil control but Israel retained military control; and the white (or C) areas would be under exclusive Israeli control.

On the surface, there appeared to be much agreement between the approaches. But beneath the surface, there were two profound gaps: one was on the size of the respective areas and the other was on the meaning of joint control. On the former, the Israelis envisioned the brown or A areas to be very small at least initially, and the Palestinians saw them as being large, encompassing all Palestinians cities, towns, and villages—all the populated areas. On the latter, the Palestinians envisioned joint control to be just that—joint; the Israelis saw it as a strict division of responsibilities: Israel would control security; the Palestinians would control their civil powers or functions of government.

Both Uri and Abu Ala understood the gaps but believed they had the basis on which to negotiate. Abu Ala could yield on security, but not at the expense of the land. He could be more flexible if he could point to joint control on security in territory in which Palestinians gained authority. Uri saw joint control—real shared responsibilities on security—and a gradual transfer of additional territory to the Palestinians as the essential bridges to overcome the divide I saw. The two negotiators were more optimistic than I was—and would remain this way through the succeeding months.

They had growing trust in each other. I had come to admire the creativity of each and their unmistakable determination. Each also used me with the other and with their respective leaders. After every meeting—whether separate or together—I would ask what they needed from me. Typically, it was help with their leaders—either on a particular issue in which they wanted the flexibility to move or to have me explain why their opposite number had a problem. Frequently Abu Ala wanted me to help convince Arafat of something—why the three zones were necessary, why the joint zone was important, or, more generally, why I believed progress was being made. Uri was much the same—though at times his attention was more on his own side than on the Palestinians. He saw value in my explaining to Rabin the limits of what the Palestinians could swallow.

Uri, for tactical reasons, had held back on going over the size of the A, B, and C areas—believing it was critical first to get agreement on the specifics of security arrangements and the broad concepts for each area. However, on June 23, with the July target date for agreement approaching, he presented the Israeli views on the size of the areas. (This was a time when I was preoccupied with the Syrian track and the preparations for the Chiefs of Staff meetings.) While Abu Ala understood the gaps conceptually, I don't think he had anticipated how little territory the Israelis envisioned turning over in the initial redeployment, how many Palestinian villages would not be included, and how large the area under exclusive Israeli control would be. Accordingly, he rejected the Israeli concept, saying that Israel wanted 90 percent of the territory and nearly 100 percent of the security responsibility. In a call to me, he reported that the negotiations were in crisis, and that Israel was using "security" to redefine the DOP and legitimize Israeli control all over again. He could accept Israeli responsibility for Israelis in the B areas, but not for Palestinians. This was the only opening I heard in the conversation. I promised to see what I could do.

When I called Uri, he was not surprised. He had expected that there would be a blowup over what Israel was asking, but still saw the gradual transfer of additional territory to the Palestinians as the way to offset the initially small redeployment Israel envisioned. When I floated the opening, saying it suggested a way to give the Palestinians some symbolic security responsibility in an area in which there would be a large number of Palestinians, Uri said nothing. I read his silence as a sign of his belief that he and Abu Ala needed to find a way to overcome this mini-crisis on their own. It was not simply a case of the stronger power not wanting a third party to level the playing field for the weaker power. Rather, it was part of the deeper Israeli conviction that the proof of Palestinian commitment to peace with Israel lay in its willingness to persevere in the face of difficulty—its willingness to overcome differences without resort to an outside party.

There was the expectation that Peres and Arafat would meet on July 1, so the target date would not pass without some development. Abu Ala met Uri on June 28 with an amended security proposal: in area B the Palestinians would assume responsibility for public order and the Israelis would retain responsibility for countering terror and for Israelis who might be in the zone. Uri could accept Palestinian responsibility for public order, but only with the understanding that Israel must have "overriding responsibility" for security in area B. Abu Ala was not prepared to agree to this terminology, leaving the issue and the impasse for Peres and Arafat to overcome.

Their July 1 meeting, however, resolved little. Peres remained adamant that final "overriding responsibility" for security in area B must be Israel's—lest there be confusion—whereupon Arafat asked to adjourn the meeting.

Peres and Arafat met again on July 4, with the two sides telling me they would resolve the key conceptual gap on their own. And they did. Abu Ala gave the Israelis "overriding responsibility" on area B, but in return he sought and received two important trade-offs: Palestinians would have responsibility for public order in area B, with Palestinian police stations and presence permitted; and the Israelis would complete the remaining transfer of land (the further redeployments) to Palestinians by mid-1997, two years before the five-year interim period would end—and two years before the permanent status issues of borders, Jerusalem, and refugees had to be resolved. In effect, Abu Ala made promises on security in exchange for promises on territory and the date by which it would be transferred.

Responsibility for security throughout the West Bank was now agreed. The Palestinian Authority would have full security and civil powers in area A, principally the Palestinian cities. In area B, primarily made up of approximately 470 Palestinian villages, Israel would have the "*overriding* [author's emphasis] responsibility for security for the purpose of protecting Israelis and confronting the threat of terrorism." The Palestinian Authority would have civilian powers and the Palestinian police would be responsible "for public order." In area C, the largest and generally unpopulated territory, Israel would have full security and civil powers. What I always considered the toughest nut to crack on the way to the Interim Agreement was now resolved.

Rabin had gone to Martin's residence for our Independence Day Celebration, and he called Secretary Christopher from there to tell him about the breakthrough. Already he was rehearsing a new public line: The further redeployment would "stop if the Palestinians two months after the elections of their Council do not change the Palestinian Covenant—as they are obligated to do."* Finally, Rabin reported that July 25 was now the new target date for completing the agreement.

While there was indeed a conceptual breakthrough, we would not come close to making the July 25 date. It would take another two months of difficult, painstaking, and at times very emotional negotiations before the interim agreement would be completed.

| THE BACK CHANNEL BECOMES THE FRONT CHANNEL |

After the July 4 breakthrough, both sides agreed that now intensive work in all areas should commence in order to reach the agreement. Working groups were set up on all conceivable issues—transfer of powers, security, civil, financial, legal, elections, water, religious sites, energy, electricity, etc. What had been a private, informal negotiation—what I referred to as a boutique negotiation—now became a bureaucratic one held at Zichron Ya'akov, a small coastal town not far from Haifa. At one level, the transformation was useful as it brought nearly one hundred people from each side into the negotiations—drawing from the whole spectrum of society and exposing Israelis and

---

*The Covenant, or Charter, contained many provisions that denied the existence of Israel, and as part of the Oslo process Arafat had agreed to change it; the Palestinians would, in fact, revoke the Charter in language worked out with the Israeli government in the spring of 1996, two months after the convening of the Council. The leader of Likud, Binyamin Netanyahu, did not accept the Palestinian language as sufficient and made the repeal of the Charter a continuing issue.

Palestinians to each other's arguments for the first time. I doubted that bringing together two hundred participants for negotiations could be workable, and initially my concerns seemed to be borne out; to make matters worse, right-wing Israeli demonstrators and hecklers sought to disrupt the negotiations, making it difficult to get to the site and keeping up a constant din. In order to be far less accessible to demonstrators, the negotiations moved to the Patio hotel in Eilat, at the southern tip of the Negev Desert, a four-hour drive from Jerusalem. But the absence of demonstrators did not make the negotiations any easier. Abu Ala was determined to try to get something more on further redeployments. He was holding back on permitting any real movement on all other issues pending an Israeli commitment to spell out what amounts of territory they would turn over to the Palestinians. Uri resisted this, believing that Israel could not now commit to what it would turn over before seeing how the Palestinians would actually perform on security.

I understood what both Uri and Abu Ala were doing. I was a big believer in not rushing to agreements and not signaling desperation—lest one side or the other believe it could simply wait for concessions to be made. But I was becoming increasingly uneasy about the political environment in which the talks were taking place. In Israel, while the demonstrations at the site of the negotiations stopped, they picked up everywhere else. Settler groups were seizing hilltops. A right-wing group, Zo Artzeinu (This Is Our Country), began organizing to block traffic throughout the country. Members of the Likud Party were declaring that Rabin did not have the right to concede parts of Eretz Yisrael to the Palestinians without submitting any agreement to a referendum of the Israeli public. Rabin's government was looking less and less secure in the Knesset and in Israel generally.

The mood among the Palestinians and the Arab world was also deteriorating. First, the July 25 target date was missed; then Israeli settlers seized hilltops and attacked some Palestinian villages, triggering commentaries about how the Israelis had no intention of living up to their obligations to turn over the land or responsibilities to the Palestinians. They were deliberately going slow, governed, in the words of one Saudi commentator, by the Israeli "logic of refusal." Palestinians increasingly complained that Israeli demands for "security, open borders, normalization, and water and other rights [were] for it alone" asking, "What about our security, as the settlers wreak havoc in the West Bank and Jerusalem and the Israeli government is unable or unwilling to curb them?"

Both Uri and Abu Ala were aware of the mood and uneasy about it, but neither felt he could make a move until he saw more from his counterpart. Though I was now phoning each of them daily—and usually talking to Arafat as well—I felt that we needed to pick up the pace by bringing Peres and Arafat together again.

At one level I knew that Uri agreed with me. He had confided in one phone call that he could do nothing so long as Abu Ala insisted on knowing the specifics of territory. This, Uri said, was simply "an impossibility."

I placed phone calls to Peres and Arafat, and both agreed to the meeting. Prior to it, I suggested to both that they bundle the issues into a package: To Peres I said: You are asking Arafat to give up knowing what further redeployments the Palestinians will actually get and to phase in the actual withdrawal from the Palestinian cities; in return you need to give him something on Hebron, prisoners, and the timing of the subsequent redeployments. To Arafat I said: It is not realistic to get the Israelis to commit to the size of any withdrawal now, but it is legitimate to ask when it will take place and to ask for something on prisoners and Hebron. Peres agreed; Arafat listened.

The setting for the meeting would be a dinner that Terje Larsen, now the UN Special Coordinator, would host at his residence in Gaza. By the night of the dinner, Abu Ala and Uri were angry at me, feeling that I was trying to go over the heads of the negotiating teams. On this at least they agreed. To Uri, I said, "I don't get it. You know you are stuck. I am trying to get you unstuck. What gives?"

In reply, Uri told me something revealing about most successful negotiations: his relationship with his negotiating partner had to take precedence over everything else. If Abu Ala felt a third party was undercutting him, then, in Uri's words, "solidarity with Abu Ala" was more important. Ultimately, that would be "the key to negotiating the deal."

In this case, I disagreed with him. Abu Ala, as important as he was, was not the decision-maker. Arafat was. While Uri believed that Abu Ala could bring Arafat around, I saw how Arafat manipulated all those around him, including Abu Ala.

In many ways, Abu Ala and Uri were similar. They had come from different worlds, but had in common the insecurity that comes with nonrecognition. Abu Ala was from Abu Dis, a West Bank village just outside of Jerusalem. Born before Israel's birth and the Palestinian dispersal or exile, he was older than Uri. Like so many Palestinians throughout different parts of the Arab world, he had been forced to move, never knowing if he would be able to return.

Below the surface with Abu Ala was the enduring sense of grievance that nearly all Palestinians share. However, also embedded in his psyche was a profound pragmatism. He wanted a different future for his people. He wanted it on their own soil. He understood this could only happen in peace with the Israelis. He found in Uri and Shimon Peres Israelis who recognized that they would not have peace without coexistence with Palestinians. He knew well the limits of his leader, Yasir Arafat, but also intrinsically believed that only Arafat could make peace with the Israelis and deliver it.

He had been with Arafat since the late 1960s, and he knew well Arafat's manipulations, maneuvering, and pattern of deception. Like many around him, however, he saw this behavior as a function of the Palestinian condition and weakness. Arafat had to maneuver and manipulate to advance the cause. The "proof" that Arafat was right to do so was his having won acceptance for the Palestinians on the world stage. No other Palestinian leader had done this. Factions seemed endemic to the Palestinian movement, but Arafat had succeeded in becoming their one unifying symbol.

Abu Ala could be scathing about Arafat in private—much like every other Palestinian I dealt with—but he also revered him. He understood that Arafat made the decisions. It would never be easy to produce them, but through guile and maneuvering and flattery and alliances with those like Abu Mazen, he would bring Arafat around.

To be sure, Abu Ala always had to satisfy himself that he had produced both what Palestinians needed and what could be sold as defensible to Palestinians. He sought to hook the Israelis by showing his understanding of their needs. But then he would focus on getting the Israelis to accept his principles. Several years later, after the Wye agreement, when Abu Ala and Ariel Sharon (then Foreign Minister) met to discuss how to approach permanent status issues, Abu Ala told Sharon, "I don't mind if you are on my roof as long as I own my house." That is, I am prepared to cooperate with you in finding ways to meet your security needs as long as I have sovereignty—"as long as I own my house."

To the task of negotiations, Abu Ala also brought not only shrewdness and intelligence but humor, with which he could defuse tense situations. When we ate together—which was often—we would spend as much time laughing as talking.

I came to appreciate Abu Ala for his talents, his warmth, his insights, and his commitment to peace. But like Abu Ala, I never lost sight that it was Arafat who had to be moved—and notwithstanding Abu Ala's resistance to the Peres-Arafat meeting at this juncture, I believed that it was necessary now.

In fact, the Peres-Arafat meeting turned out to be more than just a dinner. The two met for several days and produced another set of understandings, encapsulated in a joint statement initialed on August 11. Much to Abu Ala's unhappiness, Arafat conceded that the Israelis should not have to commit to a figure on the size of the land they would turn over to the Palestinians as a result of the redeployment process. In return, Peres agreed to carry out three further redeployments (FRDs), one every six months over an eighteen-month period beginning after the inauguration of the Palestinian Council. In addition, Peres conceded more on release of Palestinian prisoners, agreeing to release 5,000 prisoners, not 1,500, in three stages: the first upon the signing of the Interim Agreement, the second before the Palestinian elections, and a third at a later time. Together Peres and Arafat agreed on the ticklish issue of Palestinian police in area B settling on the number of police stations in area B, and the ground rules of their movement on roads.

There was one other development. During the course of the Peres-Arafat talks, I remained in constant phone contact with Uri and Abu Ala as well as both Peres and Arafat. To facilitate progress on the vexing water issue, I proposed (and Arafat and Peres agreed) that we would establish a trilateral—U.S., Israeli, and Palestinian—committee as a way to focus on the allocation of water, rather than the control of the aquifers; in so doing I was sure we could expand both the quantity and quality of water to the Palestinians while postponing the question of the status of the aquifer itself.

The committee had another purpose: to signal to Arafat that there would be a more intrusive U.S. role from here on. I knew that he would see a committee with U.S. participation as a new lever to get the Israelis to fulfill their promises on FRDs and other issues, and that Peres and Uri would see it as an additional lever to ensure that Arafat lived up to his commitments.

I considered it a way to facilitate agreement, not as a fundamental transformation of our role. We could not take the place of the two sides as they negotiated.

In reaching agreement on water, the Peres-Arafat meeting created a breakthrough of sorts, overcoming what appeared to be the hardest issue after the decision on security and the zones that would divide the West Bank. But as my experiences with high-stakes negotiation so often revealed, resolving a tough issue often raises the importance of the issues that remain.

| GETTING TO THE ENDGAME |

I went to Israel a week after the Peres-Arafat meeting for a family vacation. Debbie and I wanted our three children to visit the area where I was laboring so hard to bring peace. Naturally, both Uri and Abu Ala—and Rabin and Arafat—assumed I would also see them. While Secretary Christopher thought I was crazy to take a "busman's holiday," it was beneficial to everyone. For two weeks my family and I would tour during the day—and I made calls and attended meetings during downtime and at night. I saw each leader and went over with them what I saw as the main sticking points. When we were in Eilat, I joined the negotiators at the Patio hotel from 10 p.m. until to 3 a.m. It may not have been a restful vacation but it was useful.

With the leaders, I had focused on how to close—emphasizing with Rabin that we should have a White House ceremony that was a Middle Eastern event, bringing Mubarak and Hussein as well as the Russians, Europeans, and Norwegians to join in the signing ceremony. This would not only demonstrate our stake in the agreement, but would also demonstrate that Mubarak and Hussein were a part of it as well. It would show both the Israeli public and the larger Arab public that a new stage in peacemaking was being established. Rabin saw the political benefits in Israel of such an event, particularly at a time when he would need to sell a controversial agreement. Of course, I knew such grand international attention would also appeal to Arafat, and I described this setting and ceremony with him as well. I talked with both leaders about the size and powers of the Council, something the Palestinians wanted to be a parliament. Rabin, fearing it would look as if he had already accepted Palestinian statehood, opposed the Council taking on the trappings of a legislative body. We discussed possible compromises on the numbers of Palestinian representatives and how to use the Council's rule-making powers to ascribe to it "legislative and executive powers." We also talked about Hebron. While countless technical issues still had to be resolved, it was increasingly clear that both sides were digging in on Hebron.

With Rabin and Arafat at this stage, I focused on what the other side needed: Arafat had to show that Hebron would ultimately be treated like other Palestinian cities in the West Bank, even if it meant there had to be special arrangements; Rabin had to be able to demonstrate that the Israeli settlers living in Hebron would be able to remain, fully protected by the IDF, and living their lives in a city of great historic meaning to religious Jews. Neither leader rejected what I had to say, but both emphasized the special difficulties of Hebron given the zealotry of those on both sides. The Israeli settlers were among the most politically extreme in Israel, and Arafat, without acknowledging that Hebron was a Hamas stronghold, referred to the Hebronites as his "Scots"—saying they were particularly hardheaded. I heard laments from both leaders, but not much responsiveness as I probed for solutions.

When I saw Uri and Abu Ala, they too spent their time in our separate meetings trying to convince me of what the other must do. But Uri also sought to use my presence to affect his own delegation. He asked me to meet with a number of his colleagues, Uzi, in particular, with whom he wanted me to work on Hebron. I did, but could not tell if I was having any effect.

Though the negotiations were obviously difficult, I could not help being encouraged by the setting itself: the entire Patio hotel. The negotiating teams were broken down into teams of three or four to deal with every conceivable issue. Each team had its own room and was so labeled: there was the water-team room; the electricity-team room, energy-team room, the archaeological team, the elections team, and so on. Each team literally spent all its time together—not just negotiating but eating together and walking around together. It was a peacemaking laboratory—and I could only hope that the effort could be transferable to the Israeli and Palestinian publics.

Before I left, I told Uri, "Be careful not to make being here too appealing; you will never leave."

| THE TWENTY-FOUR-HOUR ENDGAME
THAT TAKES TEN TWENTY-FOUR-HOUR DAYS |

In September, the pressure began to build on both sides, especially as the domestic climate in Israel worsened. But even as our three-way phone conversations became more extended and intensive, I found Uri and Abu Ala trying increasingly to get me to produce from the other what they could not produce on their own. With September 13, the second anniversary of the signing of the DOP at the White House, a logical deadline or pretext for finishing, each held back, waiting for the other to concede. At one juncture, I asked each to tell me where he could be flexible, and I would then explore how to put together respective packages. Unfortunately, each assumed the other would hold back, and therefore neither gave me very much to use.

Finally, on September 10, I said I would no longer work with either unless they would simultaneously present their respective packages. Over the next few days both Uri and Abu Ala—probably because they knew they had played out the string—proceeded to wrap up nearly all the issues they could.

I also introduced one new factor into the equation. If we did not complete the agreement before the end of the month, Congress would not extend the waiver that permitted us to maintain an office for the PLO in Washington, which operated as a quasi-embassy.* With the mood souring in Israel and with members of Likud lobbying the Congress to let the waiver lapse, I told Abu Ala that if we did not have the new agreement to point to, I doubted we could persuade the Congress to renew the waiver. Abu Ala took this seriously and asked me to tell Arafat. I did.

Was I manipulating the waiver issue to try to create a deadline? Yes, but I would never have been able to do so successfully if there hadn't been a genuine problem on the Hill, and if Arafat had not seen the symbolism of having his office in Washington closed as an unacceptable cost.

It was now nearly the middle of September, with the Jewish High Holidays beginning on September 25, creating a point at which the Israelis would necessarily have to put the negotiations on hold until well into October. The clock was ticking. Uri and Abu Ala had called me and said they had set September 22 as the deadline for an agreement. Shimon Peres, however, was not ready to move to the endgame with Yasir Arafat and his team without knowing that there was a basic agreement on Hebron. He asked if I could find out Arafat's essential needs.

I called Arafat, who was clear: he needed the Israelis out of most of Hebron; the Palestinians must be able to put their police in the current IDF headquarters, with the Israelis controlling the Jewish Quarter and immediately adjacent areas for the remainder of the interim period. When I asked whether this included the "Tomb of Abraham"—what the Israelis referred to as the Tomb or Cave of the Patriarchs and the Palestinians as the Ibrahimi Mosque—he said special arrangements would need to be worked out. While noting this

---

*At the time of the signing of the DOP, given the new relationship between Israel and the PLO and the PLO's renunciation of violence, Congress passed a waiver on existing legislation that pre-

was very sensitive, I agreed that special arrangements would be necessary. I then slowly repeated each of his points, and asked, "If the Israelis accept each of these points, would that provide the basis for resolving Hebron in the Interim Agreement?" His answer was "yes."

I called Peres, who in turn promised to work to get his side—especially the IDF—to accept these points. He succeeded in convincing first the army and then Rabin, and the negotiations were set to begin on September 17 at Taba, a beach resort just across the Israeli-Egyptian border from Eilat. The Palestinians could feel that they were in Egyptian territory; the Israelis were five minutes away from Eilat.

Once at the Taba Hilton, Shimon Peres and Yasir Arafat and relatively small teams led by Uri and Abu Ala worked literally around the clock. I was in Washington, with what amounted to an open line to them; except for the last night of the talks, I did not have to remain up through the night. This negotiation was their negotiation. Early on in the Taba talks, Peres told me that Arafat was now asking for more on Hebron; although Peres said he had held firm, he expected Arafat again to seek help from me. Perhaps Peres was testing my reaction; in any case, I told him I would not budge, having told Arafat that "I would only seek to get Israel to agree to his needs if what he was asking for was the extent of his needs. He was clear and so was I."

Arafat did, in fact, come back to me and I was very blunt: "You told me what your needs were and I pressed the Israelis to meet those needs. I will do nothing more for you on this issue, and if the Israelis ask me to support their position I will." Arafat asked for nothing more on Hebron.

But that did not mean we were out of the woods. When the Israelis presented the maps of the areas A, B, and C, it was apparent how small the A+B areas would be—about 3 percent (the immediate vicinity of each Palestinian city in the West Bank) and 19 percent, respectively—totaling together 22 percent of the West Bank. Seeing this, Arafat flew into a rage and walked out, claiming the Israelis were humiliating him. First, Avi Gil—Peres's Chief of Staff—called, telling me that Arafat was threatening to leave and I had better call him. Then, literally within a minute, Nabil Abu Rudeina—Arafat's Chief of Staff—called to say the same thing. He put Arafat on the phone, and the Chairman ranted for several minutes more, calling the areas nothing but "cantons," all isolated and separated from one another. He had no choice but to leave.

Mr. Chairman, I said, "if you leave, nothing can be fixed and we cannot help you. My advice to you is to find ways of creating connections that address your concern about the appearance of isolated islands that are cut off from each other." Eventually he calmed

cluded an American relationship with the PLO. The waiver was not permanent and had to be renewed. In this case, it was scheduled to lapse at the end of September.

down, and I called Avi Gil and said there has to be a way to improve some of the connections between Palestinian areas. In fact, after some give-and-take, the Israelis increased the B areas by 5 percent, raising the total of A+B from 22 to 27 percent of the West Bank.

They were now nearing the finish line, and I was pressing hard for them to conclude the negotiations before Shabbat on September 24. I did not want to run out of time, with Rosh Hashanah (the Jewish New Year) commencing at sundown on the twenty-fifth. I spent most of the day on the twenty-third on the phone pressing on the issues related to security arrangements for Rachel's Tomb in Bethlehem. At one point, I had an open line into the suite with Peres and Arafat—and they would switch the phone back and forth to me. During one pause in the conversation someone else in the adjoining room got on the line to order room service. I told them I would like to help, but room service was beyond my capacity.

Press as we might, there was no way to conclude before Shabbat. Ironically, it was Arafat who was most determined to break for Shabbat, literally apologizing to me for not finishing but insisting that Peres must stop since "we don't want to create problems for our partners with the religious."

But his sensitivity on Shabbat did not rule out one last crisis. Around 8:30 p.m. Washington time on Saturday evening September 24, Peres and Arafat called me to report that everything was falling into place and they expected to be done within an hour or two. They wanted to place a joint call to Secretary Christopher to inform him once agreement had been reached—but not if it was too late for us. I laughed, knowing it was now three-thirty in the morning in Egypt, where they were. I suggested that they call me first when they finished, and I would check to see if the Secretary was still awake. They agreed, with Arafat apologizing and saying, "You are missing enough sleep because of us. We must thank you."

No call came, and I knew that meant there was a problem. In this case, I knew they would call when they were either ready or in need of my help. When the phone rang finally, at 2:30 a.m. Washington time, it was Uri, who sounded completely dispirited. Arafat had blown up over the issue of the police movement between areas A and B. The Israelis had insisted all along that Palestinian police only move with Israeli approval lest something unforeseen happen between the police and the IDF or Israeli settlers. Now Uri reported that Arafat had blown up over the word "approval," proclaiming that he would not accept the humiliation of his security people, and he was not "your slave." He had walked out, perhaps for good.

Was there anything I could do? I responded by asking whether Uri could play with the word "approval." Could he "come up with a synonym for approval—acceptance, confirmation, acknowledgment?" Exhausted, he was not sure, and reluctant to water down the substance of the Israeli position. I understood, and told him I would call Arafat.

I called Nabil Abu Rudeina, who, interestingly, suggested that I get Shimon or Uri to speak to the Chairman first, once again signaling that the two parties wished for this to be their negotiation. When I tried to reach Uri, he was unavailable; he was in with the Chairman.

Shortly past 6 a.m. on September 25, Uri called and said they were done. After a rather soulful discussion, he had offered to find a softer formulation and Arafat had relented. "Approval" became "confirmation," with the understanding that the Israelis would require only "notification." In return, Arafat had accepted an IDF presence and security arrangements around the religious site of Rachel's Tomb in Bethlehem. The deal was done; sunset and the Jewish High Holy Days began.

| THE POSTSCRIPT |

With Arafat coming to Washington for the signing ceremony on September 28, the one eventuality that I wanted to avoid at all costs was a replay of Arafat's performance in Cairo when, with the whole world watching, he refused to sign the maps of the Gaza-Jericho agreement. In the days after the agreement and prior to his arrival in Washington, I informed every Palestinian around Arafat that he would lose his relationship with President Clinton if he caused a scene at the signing. Abu Mazen and Abu Ala both said I must sit with Arafat myself and communicate this before the signing ceremony. So I did so, going to see him the night before the event at the house of a Palestinian-American, Hani al-Masri. Sitting alone with him in Hani's house, I was blunt: "Mr. Chairman, there better not be any surprises tomorrow. No holdups, no questions, no reluctance to sign. Any of that takes place and you lose President Clinton. Understood?" He nodded; this was an important event and he wanted nothing to spoil it.

In fact, that is the way he behaved, even though an issue did emerge at the White House the next morning. As the President was hosting Rabin, Peres, Mubarak, Hussein, and Arafat in the Oval Office—and I was sitting with them—I was given a message that I needed to come out and see Uzi Dayan and Abu Ala in the Cabinet Room. There, they told me of one problem that had to be corrected before the agreement could be signed: the timing of when the Palestinian police station could be manned in Halhul, a Palestinian village close to Hebron. Nothing on redeployment was set to happen in Hebron until after a bypass road for settlers was completed. Would the police station be manned before (as Abu Ala insisted) or after the Hebron bypass road was completed (as Uzi argued)? "Why," I asked, "can't the two of you resolve this?" Abu Ala was unwilling to, angry at being excluded from the leaders' meeting and being relegated to a secondary role at the White House by Arafat. "Let the leaders decide this," he said.

I returned to the Oval Office and interrupted the meeting, asking to see the Prime

Minister and the Chairman for a few minutes. It was clear that neither Arafat nor Rabin had the slightest idea of what was going on, and Peres joked that the negotiators
were always good at creating problems but not always at solving them. I took Rabin and
Arafat into the President's private kitchen (just down a small inner hallway from the
Oval Office) and explained the issue. For once, Arafat had taken my warning to heart,
and said, "Whatever the Prime Minister decides is acceptable to me." Rabin decided
that the Palestinians could man the police station before the bypass road was completed,
and we all returned to the Oval Office. There would be no hitches at the ceremony.

If there was a high point between the Israelis and Palestinians in the Oslo process, this
was it. Rabin had come to appreciate Arafat, believing that he was taking steps that were
hard for him. The Palestinians had made genuine commitments on security, which we
could later urge them to reaffirm and fulfill. People-to-people programs were being touted.
The Amman economic summit—scheduled for the month after the signing—would
bring large numbers of Arabs and Israelis together to discuss economic cooperation and
development. Yossi Beilin and Abu Mazen would complete a secret effort on permanent
status issues one month later—on October 31—which showed that even the most existential issues could be resolved.* And, finally, an extraordinary document—the Interim
Agreement—had been negotiated and concluded by the two sides largely on their own.

Soon enough, however, a terrorist struck right at the heart of the process.

---

*Starting in October 1994, Yossi Beilin and Abu Mazen led small teams of negotiators for a pe-
riod of nearly eighteen months in a secret discussion of permanent status issues. They came to an
agreement on October 31, 1995. Beilin was not able to brief Yitzhak Rabin prior to the assassination,
and neither Shimon Peres nor Yasir Arafat embraced the Beilin-Abu Mazen agreement. Arafat went so
far as to say that the understandings were not authorized, producing deep resentment from Abu
Mazen. The Beilin-Abu Mazen understandings were never published formally, but certain elements
were leaked to the Israeli press. Most notable was the idea on Jerusalem: The municipal boundaries of
the city would be expanded to include Abu Dis as a way of providing for two capitals—Israeli and
Palestinian—in the greater municipality of Jerusalem. To be sure, the understandings went well beyond the Abu Dis idea. On Jerusalem, a borough system would be established, with questions of sovereignty on the Temple Mount/Haram al Sharif deferred; on security, the Israelis would retain a
presence of several battalions in the West Bank for twelve years; on territory, there would be adjustment of the 1967 borders to accomodate Israeli settlement blocs, but there would be territorial compensation on nearly a one-for-one basis. And, finally, on refugees, each side would state their respective
positions, but then address the question using practical guidelines.

The Rabin Assassination:
Would Tragedy Produce Opportunity?

ON OCTOBER 31, 1995, I met with Yitzhak Rabin in Jerusalem. We discussed two issues. One was Arafat's need to crack down on Hamas; Rabin asked me to press Arafat,
but when I asked for specifics Rabin reconsidered and said his security people would
deal with Arafat directly. The other issue was Syria. Rabin was ready for me to shuttle
between the two military Chiefs of Staff—Israeli and Syrian—in order to see if I could
break the stalemate. Before I did so, he wanted to have a more extended meeting with
me on the security issues; since he would be coming to the States in November, we discussed whether I could see him in New York. His parting words that night turned out
to be strangely prophetic: "Dennis, expect anything."

I never got the chance to see Yitzhak Rabin again. On Saturday, November 4, the
unthinkable happened. Rabin was murdered—shot in the back by an Israeli as he left
a massive peace rally in Tel Aviv.

I was paged in my car as I was returning from taking my son Gabe to his ortho-
dontist. I was en route home, hadn't taken my cell phone with me, and felt no particular need to rush to answer the page. I would be home in fifteen minutes and would
call the operations center then.

As I walked into the house fifteen minutes later, I was met by Rachel and Ilana
yelling, "Rabin has been shot." I said what are you saying? What are you talking about?
Debbie was on the phone with Jim Mann of the *Los Angeles Times* and she passed the
receiver to me. He asked for my reaction, but I was not prepared to comment without

knowing the facts. I called the op center and they told me Martin had called, Rabin was in surgery and had been hit by two or three bullets.

I could not imagine it happening to Yitzhak Rabin of all people. He had devoted his life to Israel. Literally as a youngster, he had been a leader of the Palmach,* and had fought for Israel's emergence and survival. He was the architect of its greatest military victory, the Six-Day War, in June 1967. He had faced death countless times on the battlefield confronting Israel's enemies. Notwithstanding the increasingly ugly climate in Israel and ultranationalists calling him a traitor, I could not conceive that an Israeli Jew would assassinate Rabin. But I was so wrong.

I called Tom Donilon, and the State Department press spokesman Nick Burns to say we had to hold the line on all press inquiries and make sure "no one but the President or the Secretary should be out saying anything publicly until the situation clarifies."

While awaiting a call from the Secretary, I decided to write a statement the Secretary could issue. The phone rang incessantly and Debbie told the callers that I was not available. She looked at me sitting at the kitchen table trying to write and asked if I was okay. I was not; I was devastated and started to cry.

Even in this initial statement, I wanted to say that Rabin was one of the "towering figures" of this century, and when Christopher's call came, I read aloud what I had written. Christopher did not want the statement to sound like a eulogy.

I said, "Look, Chris, we need to make the point that Rabin is a historic figure. Apart from the importance of you speaking about him in a way that shows your personal respect for him, it is essential to help shape Israeli attitudes about what is being threatened by this unthinkable act of violence."

Christopher, Tom Donilon, and I were on the phone together when we heard the announcement that Rabin had died. Immediately we were confronted with the matter of the U.S. response. To the Secretary, I said, "You need to call the President and tell him he needs to go to this funeral." Israel would be in a state of shock, and the public would need to know that Israel was not alone; that we would stand by it in this hour of great trauma. The President's presence would also remind the world of our collective responsibility to fulfill Rabin's legacy and work for peace.

Christopher agreed, called the President, and a short time later President Clinton announced that he would attend the funeral.

In the interim, I finished the statement Christopher would issue. As I read it over the phone, my voice began to break when I said, "Israel has lost one of its greatest sons, the world has lost one of the greatest leaders of this century, and the United States has lost one

---

*Formed in 1941, the Palmach was the elite strike unit of the Haganah, the Yishuv's defense force and the precursor to the IDF.

of its greatest friends." Tom volunteered to have his aides clean up the statement, but Secretary Christopher replied, "It does not need to be cleaned up; go ahead and release it."

We spent the next hours contacting regional leaders to see who would attend the funeral. We wanted as many Arab officials as possible to attend to demonstrate that Rabin had changed the Middle East. Before Christopher was able to reach him, King Hussein announced he was coming. Because President Mubarak had never visited Israel, even though Egypt was at peace with Israel, we assumed it would take President Clinton to persuade him—in fact, it did. King Hassan of Morocco would have come were he not suffering from pneumonia; he sent his Prime Minister. We knew Asad would not come, but we still sought some expression of personal condolence to Leah Rabin; that proved too much for Asad, but he told Christopher that, contrary to what some might think, "there will be no rejoicing in Syria."

Of course, there was another basic question: Who would accompany the President? Christopher suggested all the ex-Presidents and Secretaries of State. After a discussion with Tony Lake, we settled on asking Cyrus Vance, George Shultz, James Baker, Henry Kissinger, and Lawrence Eagleburger—all those who either had worked actively on the peace process or had had a real relationship with Rabin. Not all could attend—Kissinger was in Hong Kong, Baker had recently had back surgery—but the makeup of the delegation became an extraordinary demonstration of bipartisan support for Israel, especially as the leaders from both houses of Congress and from both parties joined the delegation.

The themes of our pilgrimage to the funeral became standing shoulder-to-shoulder with Israel in its crushing hour of need and working together to fulfill Rabin's legacy—a legacy of defending Israel and pursuing peace. Indeed, less than an hour into our flight on Air Force One, I was asked to brief the delegation on developments in Israel, including the formation of a new government likely to be led by Shimon Peres.

As I rose to speak, I marveled at the presence of three Presidents (Clinton, Bush, and Carter); three Secretaries of State (Christopher, Shultz, and Vance); the leaders of the Senate and House (Dole, Daschle, Gingrich, Gephardt); the Secretary of Defense and the Chairman of the Joint Chiefs of Staff (Bill Perry and John Shalikashvili); our ambassador to the United Nations (Madeleine Albright); and a Nobel laureate (Elie Wiesel). It was a remarkable assemblage, and I wanted to use it to underscore the point that the pursuit of peace would not be stopped by a murderer.

With that in mind, I reminded the delegation that we were going to visit a country in shock; the Prime Minister's murder was totally alien to Israel's tradition and its sense of itself; Israelis needed reassurance, needed to see that America would be with Israel and that we and the international community were coming to Israel in an unprecedented way as a testimonial to Yitzhak Rabin and his pathway.

Shortly afterward, we went to the President's cabin and both the President and the First Lady were there. I started by reminding the President what we had in our pocket from Rabin—a conditioned commitment on full Israeli withdrawal from the Golan Heights—then explained that as far as we knew the commitment and its refinement involving the June 4, 1967 lines were unknown to Peres. The President would need to tell him of this. I said Peres's own position had been that full withdrawal should be to the international border, not to the June 4 lines, going over the crucial differences between the two: namely, the three demilitarized areas to the west of the international border and water rights.*

The President asked, "What should I do?" I said that although Peres might explain why he couldn't accept the June 4 lines, my guess was that he would stand by Rabin's commitment. In any case, this was a time primarily to inform him of the commitment, not to press him on anything, especially given Peres's own sense that no one could fill the void left by Rabin. "Peres needs to be bucked up," I said with tears in my eyes, "particularly because he feels and is saying that it should have been he."

Clinton's speech at the funeral, which he improved on the plane by adding the thought that if we give in to the hatred of our enemies we will sow hatred among ourselves, struck an emotional chord in Israel. Many Israelis contrasted President Weizman's remarks unfavorably with President Clinton's. More than this, the genuine sense of friendship and commitment, the unprecedented magnitude of the delegation, and the literal embrace of Peres all had a profound impact.

After the funeral, the President met alone with Peres for forty-five minutes and discussed Rabin's commitment on the Golan Heights. As expected, Peres, though expressing surprise and saying he would not have committed to the June 4 lines, promised to live up to any commitment "Yitzhak has made." He also told the President he would try to broaden the coalition by bringing in the religious parties; in his words, they didn't care about the peace process, they cared about their religious issues, so he would "try to give them money for their needs and get them into the coalition." Having a broader coalition would make it easier to pursue a deal with Syria.

At the time they were meeting privately, Uri and I were meeting in my room across the hall on the fifth floor of the King David Hotel. The room was small and had not been made up when we arrived. No matter, I pulled up the sheets of the bed and sat on it and Uri sat in a chair, and shortly thereafter Martin and Mark Parris joined us.

---

*Only in the summer of 2001 did I find out that Peres had known about the "pocket"; Amnon Shahak had guessed what Rabin had done and confronted him—only to be asked by Rabin to explain it to Shimon. Itamar Rabinovich, who had traveled with our delegation from the United States, later told me he had briefed Peres upon arriving in Israel after the assassination.

Before they joined us, Uri said the shock was overwhelming in Israel, but no one could tell how long it would last. For now the right in Israel was on the defensive.

Uri said that he believed we must try to move quickly on Syria; that track, not a permanent status deal with the Palestinians, must be the priority now. In his eyes, the key to a peace deal with Syria was transforming the Golan Heights from a strategic plateau into a mountain—meaning it must lose its security significance and become like any other topographical feature.

I took out a two-page paper that encapsulated the outcomes of the discussions between Itamar and Walid at my home. Uri read it and was clearly surprised at how much we had accomplished, saying that a more developed version of my paper could provide the backbone of a framework agreement.

I told him I agreed. He asked, "Does Asad want it?" I replied that the question was not whether he wanted it—he thought he did—but was he up to it? Could he make peace with Israel even if it came at a real cost to him?

At this point, we received word that the President and Peres were ready to go downstairs to the meeting room and join their respective delegations. The meeting was noteworthy for its symbolism, not its substance. At the conclusion of the meeting, Shimon Peres came over to shake the President's hand and instead got a hug from Bill Clinton. He did not expect it, but I could see the embrace seemingly lifted Peres, convincing him he was not alone.

Next were meetings with Mubarak and then King Hussein. Before the Mubarak meeting, the President asked, "What do you want me to do with him?" I said, "Mubarak is going to be interested in what we will do now on the Israeli-Syrian track of the negotiations and he will emphasize working closely with us. There is little they can do because Asad wants a relationship with us and will not work through the Egyptians. But Mubarak can be helpful in terms of conditioning Asad on our expectations. You should tell him that we would not understand if Peres moves in a big way and Asad reacts in his typically minimalist fashion. If Asad does that, we can't help him. Mubarak can certainly communicate that to Asad." As always, President Clinton said, "I got it," and he did get it and communicated it.

At one point in the meeting, Amre Moussa sought, I felt inappropriately, to get into the specifics of the security issues, raising the question of the Israeli ground stations and whether Israel could give them up. I responded by saying that one could not look at early warning in isolation: if the Syrians were prepared to move their forces farther from Israel and allow inspections of their forces on a regular basis, Israeli early-warning needs would change. But I then turned to Mubarak and said, "Understand, Mr. President, Peres might want to move much more ambitiously, addressing all issues and not only security issues." That, I said, was why President Clinton's point was important. We simply could not have Peres make a big move (and I gestured with my hands wide apart) and Asad offer a minuscule response (and here I held my fingers an inch apart).

Mubarak told the President that he understood and said he would send Moussa immediately to tell Asad what we needed. He made a plea that we coordinate closely and keep each other informed of where we were with the Syrians, and the President, closing the meeting, told him we would stay in close touch.

Next came the meeting with King Hussein. Just before the King came in, Mark Parris briefed the President, reminding him to bring up the Secretary of Defense's trip to Jordan the following month, the point at which we would be able to decide on whether to provide F-16s to Jordan. The President then turned to me and asked, "Is that it?" In reply, I urged the President to applaud the King's speech: "It was extraordinary, eloquent, emotional, and tinged with history. In contrast to Mubarak's, Hussein's showed what peace is supposed to be about in terms of empathy and connecting as people." The King, I went on, will have some concern about Shimon Peres, fearing that Shimon is too sensitive to Arafat. He needs to hear from you that you understand that Jordan's interests will be heavily affected by the permanent status talks, that we will coordinate closely with the Jordanians as these progress, perhaps even suggesting four-way talks between the Israelis, Palestinians, Jordanians, and ourselves.

The President started the meeting by telling the King that his speech had deeply touched the Israelis and the Americans who were there. The King responded by saying he had hoped to find the right words and was not sure he was up to the task. The President said no one could have been more up to the task. He then told him that he had heard the King had taken his delegation onto the terrace of the King David Hotel to look over at the Old City. The King replied this was the first time he had seen Jerusalem since 1967 and it was a memorable and wonderful sight.

When the President made the point on the permanent status talks and the importance of our consultation, the King said they would do that "with pleasure, sir . . . we will work closely with you." Hussein then raised Syria, saying he could not figure out why Asad was not moving on peace. Was it because Asad hoped to create a coalition with Iran and Iraq? He was not certain. He kept asking himself why Asad was not moving, why did he keep holding back?

The President said, I think he wants to do it but finds it difficult to act, then turned to me and said, Dennis thinks he has a number of psychological barriers he must overcome and we must push him to overcome them. I explained: "He sees himself as the last Arab nationalist and he wants a process of reaching an agreement that sets him apart from all others. Similarly, he also wants the substance of his agreement to set him apart. We don't yet know if he is up to doing an agreement, but he tells us he wants an agreement. Time will tell whether this is the case."

The King emphasized that movement from Asad would benefit everyone in the region, were he prepared to move, but Jordan would press on regardless. The President said we would support Jordan in every way we could, including the F-16s. We were having a problem finding the way to pay for them, but expected Defense Secretary Perry to resolve this issue soon.

After the King departed, we had one last meeting with the Likud opposition leader, Bibi Netanyahu, and several of his colleagues, including my friend Dan Meridor. Bibi was on the defensive, blamed by many in Israel for creating the ugly climate that incited radical fringe elements toward assassination. Earlier in the day at the Knesset, Dan had expressed his deep concern about the existence of Jewish fundamentalists, and had persuaded Bibi and the other key members of Likud that there could be no change in government as a result of the assassination, prompting Bibi to announce publicly that he would support Shimon Peres's new government. Shimon would now have the Rabin shield on which to pursue his chosen path, while Bibi had to keep a low profile because he was now too associated with the radical fringe.

With the President, Bibi himself had two basic themes. First, it was necessary to root out any elements in Israel that did not respect the rule of law. Second, Likud was a party of peace, and its policy of peace was bound to be much more successful than Labor's. Likud had been responsible for the treaty with Egypt and Likud had gone to Madrid. He said the Arabs would come around when they realized that Israel would not accept certain things. If they did, peace would be durable; if they did not, the peace would be illusory.

The President listened. Once the Likud group had left, he turned to me and said it took "all the self-control I had not to respond and not to look at you since I was sure you would say, yeah, you are the party we had to drag kicking and screaming to Madrid." I smiled for the only time that day, saying, "The thought crossed my mind."

A long, exhausting, and emotionally wrenching day was over. On the plane trip home I began to think about the next steps. I felt ambivalent. On the one hand, I knew there was now an opportunity. Terrible as it was, the assassination had changed the circumstances, creating, in Dan Meridor's words, a shield behind which Shimon Peres could pursue the Rabin legacy, giving him the credibility in Israel that he had always lacked.

The thought made me uneasy. How could Yitzhak Rabin's murder lead to something good? How could I think in those terms? As I wrestled with these thoughts, I began to think that Uri was right: we had a moment and we had to move quickly. I felt a profound sense of loss, but also felt a sense of possibility—assuming Asad was up to it.

Was Asad Up to It?

AS WE TRIED TO seize the moment after the assassination, Syria would now have priority. The Interim Agreement had been concluded six weeks before the Rabin assassination. Implementing it would take time. The logic of Oslo would be tested on the West Bank where Israelis and Palestinians lived in close proximity; here a web of cooperation had to lay the basis for changing attitudes and making the existential issues easier to resolve. But Syria figured here as well. A deal done with Syria would make it easier for the Palestinians to conclude their own permanent peace deal at a later stage. If nothing else, Syria, rather than being a source of opposition to Palestinian concessions—as the declared embodiment of Arab nationalism—would now be a supporter of a Palestinian peace deal. But, of course, Uri and others saw increased leverage for Israel in dealing with the Palestinians if all of Israel's other neighbors had already concluded their own peace agreements, and had no interest in continuing conflict. So Syria was the focus.

Knowing Peres's penchant for bold, ambitious moves, I felt the key unknown was Asad's capacity to move. I assumed that Asad would be uneasy after the assassination. For all his suspicions of Rabin, Asad saw Rabin as a pillar of predictability. Suddenly uncertainty was introduced into his world, and at such a moment I felt it important to affect his calculus.

Upon my return to Washington from the funeral, I called Walid in Damascus and told him that Peres, with Clinton's support, was determined to press forward on peace.

Walid said that President Clinton's comments at the funeral had been very well received in Damascus. He asked if the President had been satisfied with what we heard from Peres, and I replied very much so, especially under the circumstances. Frankly, I added, neither the President nor the Secretary had understood why President Asad had been unwilling to allow us to convey condolences to Leah Rabin, a basic human response. Walid replied that Asad had done as much as he believed his public opinion would allow. He would explain more when he saw me, but he would see what else he could do. He said he would be in Washington in a few days and we could begin to work at that time. But he was very hopeful in light of my call, and he would be passing on to others what I had conveyed. He thanked me for calling, saying, "Your call has come at the right time."

| THE SAUDIS ENTER THE PICTURE |

Walid returned the evening of November 9. The next day was Veterans' Day, and I went to play golf with my friend Alan Mintz at a new course in Lake Manassas, Virginia. Alan was used to my being interrupted during a round and today was no exception. I received a page that Prince Bandar was trying to reach me, that he was only in town for the day and urgently needed to see me.

I arrived at Bandar's house around nine in the evening and was ushered into the library by his security. The library was a picture of serenity, with elegant decor, and photographs of Bandar with the American Presidents he had known. It was two stories and filled with books, with a movable ladder to access books on the upper floor. Two couches faced each other, separated by a wooden table with a glass surface, topped by a deep bowl filled with cashews. The manager of the house greeted me in the library and asked what I would like to drink; as always, I asked for orange juice, and as always, it was fresh-squeezed.

From long experience with Bandar, I knew that no matter the urgency of the meeting, we would never get down to business immediately. But tonight Bandar, having just finished a phone conversation with Colin Powell (who had explained why he would not run for president), came right to the point: he had just come all the way from Saudi Arabia to convey King Fahd's belief that there was a moment of opportunity between the Syrians and Israelis. He quoted the King as saying, "If we miss this moment, it may not come again for a very long time." Bandar explained that the King had sent him to find out what we planned to do. Were we prepared to make a big push? If so, they would do their utmost to support us with the Syrians.

In response, I told him before deciding to make a "big push," we needed answers to several questions. First, could and would Peres move now? Second, if he did, was Asad up to moving too? Third, what could the Saudis do to be helpful?

My question for Bandar was this: Could the Saudis affect Asad so he would actually move, and move in a way that fit the moment? I recounted the President's conversation with Mubarak in Jerusalem, emphasizing his point that if Peres was ready to move ambitiously, Asad must meet him in kind. Perhaps King Fahd could reiterate this message to Asad. Perhaps he could condition Asad on what would constitute a serious response and what would not. "Bandar," I went on, "the real pressure on Asad would come if he came to believe that Saudi Arabia would not stick with him if he turned down a reasonable offer from Israel." Bandar replied by suggesting that we coordinate on what his response to the Israelis should be—"We will go work on him."

It sounded good, but I was not persuaded the Saudis would really lean on Asad. "Are you really prepared to create a moment of truth with Asad?" I asked. Were they prepared to criticize Asad for forgoing an opportunity? That would imply a readiness to take the Israeli side—a true revolution in Middle East politics. Maybe that was too much to expect. But if we were going to make a big push, we had to have something meaningful from the Saudis. Indeed, if Bandar wanted us to take the Saudis seriously, we needed, at a minimum, to be able to communicate to Peres and Asad that Saudi Arabia was prepared to establish full diplomatic relations with Israel.

Bandar nodded, but insisted that any such commitment would have to be tied to a deal between Israel and Syria. That, I noted, would continue to make Asad the arbiter of what Saudi Arabia could do. True, Bandar replied, "but it does send a signal to Asad and to Peres. It tells Asad he has Arab support for his move and it tells Peres when he makes peace with Syria, he is really making it with the Arab world."

I had not expected more from the Saudis. But if the Saudis wanted us to take their entreaties seriously—entreaties that I knew were more about their encouraging our actions than theirs—I wanted at least to get a commitment from Saudi Arabia that it would establish full diplomatic relations with Israel if we produced a breakthrough between Israel and Syria. Bandar also read me well, and he concluded our evening telling me he was authorized to say: "Saudi Arabia will make such a commitment. King Fahd is ready to make peace with the Israelis" once the Syrians do so. Once again, the issue was Asad—what was Asad prepared to do.*

---

*Crown Prince Abdullah's commitment in 2002 to normalize relations with Israel was the first time a Saudi leader publicly stated what Bandar was committing on behalf of King Fahd in 1995. Throughout the process launched in Madrid, the Saudis felt comfortable operating behind the scenes, not in the open or in taking the lead.

| AN OPENING IN DAMASCUS? |

I saw Walid the next afternoon. He told me my call had made a difference. As a result, the public commentary in the Syrian media after Rabin's assassination had suddenly referred to the hope that something "good might come from something bad," a phrase, Walid reported, that had been dictated by Asad.

I told him the tonal change in the Syrian media had been noticed in Israel, but it did not undo the damage of not being willing to pass condolences even privately. Walid said Asad's problem was twofold. First, in the two weeks prior to the assassination, Rabin had used his toughest language on Asad and Syria, saying Damascus was the center of terrorism. Asad felt he could not just turn around after that. Second, he had sent his security people into the Palestinian camps in Damascus to ensure there would be no celebrating after the assassination. The Syrians had clamped down hard, and that was as much as Asad felt he could do in the circumstances, particularly given what Rabin had been saying.

Notwithstanding the explanation, I told Walid, the lack of explicit condolences was not understood here or in Israel because offering condolences the way Rabin and Peres had when Asad's son Basil had died reflected a basic humanity.

Walid shrugged at this point, as much as telling me there was nothing more he could do. Walid then told me he had had a private four-hour discussion with Asad. This was unprecedented and by itself made clear that Asad was invested in peace again and that Walid was in charge of pursuing it.

Asad had made a number of points. First, "Peres wants peace." Second, perhaps because of this, peace was now his [Asad's] priority. Third, the assassination of Rabin meant he could not take developments in Israel for granted and he was "ready to move." Fourth, Asad understood that Peres would need some time now to form his government and Syria would be patient and respond when Peres was ready to act. Finally, Asad preferred to move according to the last scenario we had agreed on—namely, my going between the two military Chiefs of Staff and getting agreement on an agenda or nonpaper to guide the military officer discussions. This could in turn lead to a comprehensive nonpaper on security arrangements.

Peres, I told Walid, had previously been skeptical of such an approach, believing that the military tended to be stubborn when it came to their security needs. Yet Peres had indicated after the funeral that he might broaden the approach and make it much more ambitious. If Asad was serious about moving rapidly, he should be willing to broaden the approach as well.

Walid did not resist this conclusion. But he said the first item of business for Asad was Peres's reaffirmation of Rabin's commitment to the pocket. Believing that this should not be given away for nothing, I told him we first had to bring Peres up to speed, and I would be going to Israel next week to do so.

Once again, Walid agreed, and we ended our meeting. As I walked to the door, Walid said, "Dennis, I am optimistic again." "Walid," I laughed, "that's always been the key to our success."

| FIFTY-FIVE HOURS IN ISRAEL |

As I left for Israel ten days later, before Peres had presented a government, Secretary Christopher was caught up in the Dayton talks that would settle the conflict in Bosnia, and knew only the general outlines of how I intended to brief Peres and the options I would present for next steps: negotiate a more comprehensive nonpaper on security arrangements; seek a new Israeli proposal on process and substance; or offer the more ambitious suggestion that we present a broad proposal on the four big issues of peace, withdrawal, security, and timetable—which would bring everything from all the previous discussions and include a package of trade-offs for at least conceptually resolving the key differences. In the aftermath of the assassination, I felt this last option was far too ambitious; nonetheless, I believed that I also needed to crystallize all the choices for Peres so that he could then make his own judgment of how best to continue the negotiating process with the Syrians.

To prepare for this trip, I went back through the notes of all the key meetings: most importantly, the August 1993 meetings in which Rabin had initially conveyed his commitment to a full withdrawal; the May–July 1994 period in which Asad had frozen the process until we resolved the basic definition of full withdrawal; the nonpaper exercise on aims and principles of security arrangements, and the reasons we pulled back on a letter to Asad that would have explicitly referred to the June 4 lines in the nonpaper. I also revived the formulations Rabin had approved when we were trying to resolve the meaning of full withdrawal in the May–July 1994 period. The formulations gave more insight into how Rabin qualified his commitment on the June 4 lines—with unquestioned Israeli control over the Sea of Galilee being his main preoccupation. I packed a map that showed the international border and a possible June 4, 1967 line. Finally, I shared with Itamar the various papers I was bringing—my purpose was not to surprise but to educate.

We left Friday evening, scheduled to arrive in Israel at 3 p.m. on Saturday. Because we planned the trip at the last minute, and I flew in coach class, sleep was a casualty.*

---

*I typically flew on a U.S. Air Force executive jet when I might be shuttling between Israel and Syria. But in this case I would be only in Israel and the commercial option was simple and cheap.

Uri had told Martin he wanted to see me alone and hear the entire record. Martin felt it best to do this at his residence. The ambassador's residence was in Herzliya, twenty minutes from downtown Tel Aviv; situated above the beach with a spectacular view of the Mediterranean, the house had guest bedrooms and a comfortable sitting area on the first floor behind the study. We would meet here, in complete privacy—the perfect setting for many such meetings over the years to come.

Fortunately, the plane arrived a half hour early which gave me time for a shower, if not a nap. Then Uri, Martin, and I reviewed the evolution of the Syrian track: the initial move by Rabin, and Asad's response in August 1993; Rabin's desire to go slow after the Oslo agreement, and his subsequent reluctance to reaffirm his commitment to us on full withdrawal which led Asad to suspect that Rabin was using him to provide cover for the Palestinian track. While not wanting to excuse Asad's rebuff of Rabin, I felt it important that Peres be shown why Asad might be suspicious:

—Rabin's effort to put the Syrian track on hold for three or four months after Oslo;
—Rabin's initial reluctance to reaffirm his pocket commitment to us;
—Rabin's devaluing of Asad's January 1994 public declaration of "normal peaceful relations" with Israel, a declaration we told Asad would make a difference;
—Rabin's effort in May 1994 to resist the meaning of full withdrawal when Asad defined it for the first time as withdrawal to the June 4, 1967 lines;
—Rabin's unwillingness to permit us to send a letter to Asad saying that if all Israeli needs were met, the security arrangements would be on both sides of the June 4 lines, a letter the Israeli negotiator had not objected to in the spring of 1995.

In every case, Rabin had good reasons for his posture, especially given Asad's non-responsiveness to Israel's substantive needs. But Asad interpreted each of these moves as evidence that Rabin was trying to trap him, trying to get everything else in the region resolved and leaving Syria for last. Asad, I observed, lived in a world of leverage; you either had it or you did not. He saw Rabin as trying to deny him leverage, and one thing was certain about Asad: he was not prone to self-criticism. I told Uri, "He does not believe he bears any responsibility for these 'retreats' by Rabin; on the contrary, Asad believes Rabin showed bad faith, and that he is the aggrieved party."

Uri had arranged a trilateral meeting with Abu Ala to discuss the Palestinian track, and as we now rode to Tel Aviv where we would hold it, he told me he had learned a lot from the briefing. Sounding like Bandar, he said Israel had a moment now in which to move to reach agreement with Syria, but no one could say how long this moment would last. The night before he had asked the Prime Minister whether he was ready to move and Peres had responded: "I'm going to go for it."

But was Asad ready for it? I was not sure. It was still very difficult to determine if his approach was simply tactical, designed to get the best possible deal, or was psychological. If we were to produce a deal, I said, we would need to convince Asad how much he had to lose if a good deal was available and he turned it down.

At the trilateral meeting with Abu Ala, we discussed issues such as the problems involving water projects and the very slow development of the industrial zones to be set up on the borders separating the Palestinian Authority from Israel. But it was our discussion of how to change the perceptions of the publics on each side that made the meeting noteworthy. The Interim Agreement had a "people-to-people" annex; during this evening, the two sides agreed to build broad people-to-people contacts in cultural and professional areas, to create events for children, and to foster joint programming in the media. This was the stuff of peace. It was both promising and necessary. Promising, because it would transform the Israeli-Palestinian relationship, making stereotyping and demonizing far more difficult. Necessary, because it would allow us to begin to condition attitudes that would have to be transformed if the existential issues of Jerusalem, borders, and refugees were to be resolved.*

The contrast with the Syrian track could not have been more pronounced. Asad would not engage in even the simplest outreach to the Israeli public, and saw principally the dangers of any change in the balance of power in the region. Following the trilateral, I used this as my point of departure for sharing my impressions of Asad with Uri: "Asad is a leader who sees dangers and conspiracies, not surprising given how he rose to power and has maintained it." He is, I said, very smart and immediately cuts to the core in any discussion of what is important. But he is narrow, excessively tactical, and appears capable of only small incremental moves. He is extremely cautious. He never initiates, he only responds. He feels he should be paid for any steps he takes, and tends not to see how his own passivity actually increases what is required from him. Rather than seeing the commitment in our pocket as being unprecedented and his own actions having been paltry in comparison, he saw only risk for himself. Rabin, he believed, could walk away from this commitment at any time, and we would not hold him to it. But in his eyes, he had exposed himself to criticism by sending his military Chief of Staff to meet with his Israeli counterpart—thereby giving other Arabs cover to deal with Israel—and yet he had received little for this.

---

*Unfortunately, over time these programs materialized only in very limited terms. Arafat was far more comfortable promoting hostility as a lever against Israelis and as an outlet for anger that might otherwise be directed against him.

My general conclusion: he wants an agreement; he wants a relationship with the U.S.; he does not want to be lumped with the pariah states in the region; but he seeks an agreement in content and process that sets him apart. In light of his desire for a relationship with us, we have leverage but the leverage should not be exaggerated. If we create a test of wills, he will go to great lengths to prove that will never work with him. Nonetheless, he must believe that we will walk away and blame him if he fails to respond to what is a serious offer.

As for what to do now, I told Uri that it was the wrong time psychologically for us to come with an ambitious proposal, particularly because we did not know if either side was up to it. By the same token, the nonpaper route was probably a prescription for losing the moment, not capitalizing on it. That only left one option: a new Israeli proposal on substance and procedure. On balance, I preferred it. It seemed to split the difference between the nonpaper route and an ambitious U.S. proposal. It would put us in a position in which we could demand a Syrian response, though it did run the risk of convincing Asad that Peres was too anxious.

Uri agreed, but was not sure how Peres would respond, and we concluded so I could get some much-needed sleep.

| THE MOOD IN ISRAEL: COULD WE PUSH PEACE NOW? |

I was set to meet Peres Sunday evening. I spent Sunday morning in preparatory meetings with Itamar and Uri focused on the question of whether I should carry a message from Peres to Asad. I was willing to do so, but not in the way Uri suggested, by going to Damascus the next day. I said that would raise expectations too high, and it was inconsistent with our position that we could not be in negotiations before Peres had a chance to form his government. Uri acquiesced, but emphasized that we must show that it is not business as usual and that there have been some dramatic changes. I was all for that.

In the afternoon, I got together with four people I knew well: Amnon Shahak, the Chief of Staff of the IDF, Uzi Dayan, the head of planning, Boogie Ya'alon, the head of military intelligence, and Dani Yatom, who remained as the military secretary for the Prime Minister. In my discussions, I found both commonality and divergent views. The pervading sense of depression was palpable. The military leaders seemed to take the assassination the hardest—their commander had been murdered and the effect was searing. Perhaps because of that, they seemed the least willing to think about next steps, especially with Syria. Amnon was very clear in this respect; though he and Uri had become close personally as a result of the Oslo negotiations, they now had very different perspectives. Amnon could not imagine pushing for anything with Syria now, while Uri feared losing the moment.

Before leaving Tel Aviv to see Peres in Jerusalem, I went to see Leah Rabin. En route, I asked to be taken to the square where Rabin had made his speech and then been shot. It was an extraordinary sight. A makeshift shrine marked the spot of the assassination. The ground literally was raised at the site because there was a thick layer of wax from all the candles lit to honor Rabin's memory. In addition, the walls of the building that was under the area where Rabin had spoken were filled with written homages, highly personal statements identifying Yitzhak Rabin as the hero of Israel, the flower of Israel's hopes, the leader who was better than the people he led.

Leah took comfort from the emotional outpouring of Israel's youth. She spoke the entire time about her commitment to peace and "Yitzhak's legacy," which would now give meaning to her life. With great passion she urged me to carry on, especially with Asad.

As I left her apartment and got into Uri's waiting car for the ride to Jerusalem, he said, "Pretty tough, huh?" "Yes," I answered, "but uplifting too."

In Jerusalem, Uri showed that he was not nearly as confident about Shimon's determination to "go for it" as he had been the previous evening. He asked me to see Peres alone and tell him that I would need to report to President Clinton on whether he was, in fact, ready to try to reach an agreement with Syria in 1996.

I was prepared to do that, but wanted to start the meeting by letting Shimon know of the President's personal support for him. Only then would I tell him of Clinton's readiness to push for a deal with Syria, particularly because it would transform the region.

Before going to see Peres, I raised one other delicate issue: How should I deal with the fact that it was not only Rabin who kept Peres out of the picture but the United States as well? Uri advised me not to belabor the point, simply to make it and say, "It created some awkward moments." Ruefully, I said, "Uri, it is still creating an awkward moment."

| SHIMON'S VIEWS |

As I entered the Prime Minister's office, my first impulse was to look for Rabin. Instead, I saw Shimon Peres, who looked tired and still bore an expression of deep sadness. One change was immediately present. In meetings with Rabin, I had always sat on a couch with its back to the window, facing the Prime Minister.

Now Peres motioned me to sit in a chair opposite the couch. One reason for that was Amnon and Dani Yatom were sitting on the couch, joining Itamar, who sat in a chair at the end of it. Clearly, our meetings, always held so tightly, were going to expand.

After a brief exchange about Leah, Peres asked, "Well, what do you think about our Syrian friends?"

As Uri had suggested, I started by saying that the way we had been asked to deal with the Syrian track had obviously made things awkward for us. Peres nodded his understanding, indicating that the matter need not be further discussed. I then spoke of the President's determination to push ahead with him, the messages we had received from Asad, and my conversation with Bandar. Peres listened, and responded positively to my request to go over a map of different borders before proceeding to explore the options before us.

As I gave him two panels of maps—one showing the international border and one possible June 4 line—I noted that we believed that the Syrians would not claim the demilitarized areas with the exception of the area of Al-Hama. Shara had told us this area was very important to Syria, and that Syria could be flexible on the remaining demilitarized zones. Peres opened a book he held, and compared the maps in it to the side-by-side maps I showed him.

Peres's main concern was that the Syrians not be on the shoreline of the Kinneret— the Hebrew name for the Sea of Galilee. Hama was not on the shoreline, but I reminded him that the international border was only ten meters off the waterline.

He did not comment further on the maps, and I then went through the options I thought he had now: go back to producing a more detailed nonpaper on security; try for a nonpaper on all issues, security and nonsecurity, building on the summary of the Itamar-Walid talks; have us present a bridging proposal on the big issues; or have Israel make a move on substance and procedure. When I finished, Peres said he was prepared to lose "the Golan or the elections, but not both," so he needed to know whether Asad was ready to do his part. It would be very difficult to sell a withdrawal to the June 4 lines to the Israeli public. Why, they would ask, should Asad get more than the others?

At this point, he invited me to move to the next room to continue over dinner. For the next three hours we had an open-ended discussion. Peres asked if I thought a partial agreement was possible. I answered that Asad would go along with a phased implementation but not a partial agreement. Peres asked if Asad would go along with implementation after "our elections"; could Israel avoid any withdrawal until after its elections, scheduled for the latter part of 1996?

I said yes, since the first phase could be implemented over a six-to-nine month period. He asked what would Israel get from this, and I said Israel would get diplomatic relations with the Saudis and others at the time of the signing. That would demonstrate a dramatically changed Middle East. I went on to summarize the various Syrian positions. Peres then said he would not make any decisions that night but considered all the options I had presented acceptable except the first, which would simply pick things up where we had left off. He repeated his concerns about putting all the focus on the military and the security arrangements. We needed to create more drama and we needed to create more urgency. He preferred to launch everything with a meeting with Asad. He knew Asad would not be likely to come to Israel, but why not have Peres fly with President Clinton to Damascus, or if not there, Riyadh?

Here was Shimon thinking big, trying to change the landscape with a dramatic move. As much as I liked the drama, I knew that Asad would never go for it. Peres asked, "What's he afraid of? If the meeting does not solve everything, we shall have another."

"That," I answered, "is what he is afraid of." Asad, I explained, would not want to make meetings with the Israeli leader routine, fearing Israel would get what it wanted—namely, normalization—without Syria getting what it needed—"the land." I continued, explaining that I had always felt "the basic trade-off is one between his responding to your tangible needs on security and normalization and your responding to his on a more rapid timetable on getting the land. In other words, if he meets you on the peace and security, you could agree to a shorter timeline for withdrawing from the land."

Itamar said that, given the way Asad negotiates, if you make a proposal you'd better pad it well. True, I said, but you need to strike a balance between preserving your bottom lines for later and having enough new that you can give us leverage to produce a meaningful response to your needs. How, I asked, do you define them now?

Peres responded with what he regarded as important. First, there was comprehensiveness. The deal with Syria could only be sold if it really ended the Arab-Israeli conflict. He must be able to show the Israeli public that a deal with Syria—one that required giving up the Golan—was in fact a deal with the region. Then he said there must be an end to terror. Dani Yatom added there must be acceptable security arrangements, and Peres nodded.

Again, Peres proposed an early meeting with Asad, really an idea the late French socialist Pierre Mendès-France had suggested to him: Why not just announce he was going to Syria to talk peace with Asad? He asked me, "Why not, Dennis?"

At first, I joked that it might not be so safe. He said what are they going to do, "shoot me down?" With dark humor and the assassination weighing heavily on him, he said, "I don't mind the risk, I may be safer there than here."

"Prime Minister," I replied, "we need you. In any case, Asad will see this as a stunt, not as a serious move. Why don't we launch an effort based on one of the options I have outlined and test Asad that way." I could see everyone on his side of the table was relieved that I dissuaded him on this point.

He then went back to the question of the border. The June 4 lines would not be acceptable in Israel. Maybe he could offer a permanent peace border based on 242 and 338.

I asked Peres if this was a question of public description or the substance that could be put in an agreement. He said both. Referring to Asad, Peres questioned, "Why does he get more than the international border? What has he done to deserve it?"

Our discussion then turned to whether I should carry a letter from Peres to Asad when I returned in a week's time. Peres liked the idea, saying, "I want to begin to engage him directly," and he asked me to suggest what he might say.

Now I closed our discussion by stressing that we must not send mixed messages to Asad, given his suspicious nature. I made clear that Secretary Christopher was concerned about sowing confusion with multiple channels. So long as private channels were consistent with the messages we both felt should be sent, we would not have a problem.

Peres reassured me that he would only work through us. I knew this was unlikely, given his inclination to work with anyone who promised access to Arab leaders. I was not particularly troubled by this, believing that good could come out of such private channels—but also knowing that because Asad wanted a relationship with us, he was unlikely to do much without us.

I also knew there was an interesting channel emerging involving Uri and Osmane Aidi, a Syrian businessman who owned the Shams hotels in Syria and also the Royal Monceau in Paris; they had begun meeting to focus on economic issues, not politics, after Aidi had approached Lester Pollack, a prominent American businessman and leader in the Jewish community, and asked for his help in introducing him to Uri. Uri got Rabin's go-ahead to meet only after getting my approval. As it turned out, Uri could not meet him until after he finished the Interim Agreement negotiations, so their first meeting was not until October. I thought this channel was interesting for reinforcing the negotiations, not conducting them.

Before departing Israel on the red-eye that evening, I visited Rabin's grave on Mount Herzl. It was dark and the simplicity of the grave site and its place of honor on the mountain seemed to fit Rabin the man. It also added a sense of finality to my dealings with Rabin. As I looked at the grave, I wondered what he would think of what we were now trying to do with Syria. Would he approve? Would he agree there was a moment now? What would he want to see from Asad at this time? What would convince him that Asad was up to doing what was necessary? Indeed, what would convince me?

| HOW TO AFFECT ASAD? |

Upon my return to Washington, Mark Parris joined me for a meeting at Walid's house where I summarized my meeting with Peres.

I told him that Peres had been surprised that Rabin had committed conditionally to the June 4, 1967 lines, for this would be very hard to sell in Israel. Peres had also stressed that Israel's needs must be met if he was going to be able to convince a skeptical public about peace with Syria: comprehensiveness, regional development and economic cooperation, ending terror, credible security arrangements, and process. On the question of process, I described Peres's views on the importance of holding an early meeting between leaders to dramatically demonstrate the commitment to peace. But I emphasized that above all else Peres wanted to reach agreement quickly and would work to create a public climate of support for a deal—something Asad had always said Rabin had not done.

In response, Walid worried that Syria was being asked "to pay the price for the assassination."

"Come on, Walid," I said, "Peres is looking to see if he has a partner who will engage him seriously and meet Israel's needs the way you expect to have Syria's needs met. What did you hear that is so difficult or unexpected? It cannot be comprehensiveness, or an end to terror or acceptable security arrangements. So what about the regional development and the process?"

Walid became more serious; while saying that some of what Peres sought was premature, we soon were focused on how best to approach Asad initially. Walid was giving advice: You will have to raise the idea of the summit with Asad, but prepare the way for this. Similarly, do not push for too much on economic issues too quickly—let Asad feel this is reflecting Syrian interests, not Israeli conditions. Talk about turning the Golan into "a zone of prosperity," with investment in its development. Let that be a bridge to future cooperation. Of course, Walid also said, the only possibility of Asad responding is if he knows Peres is prepared to address his needs as well—let him know that Peres will address the "pocket" when he sees President Clinton in a few weeks.

In the following days, as I thought about how best to influence Asad's thinking, I also stayed in daily contact with Uri in order to influence Israeli thinking. I kept reminding Uri that it was not enough to have new ideas—which Asad would see as new requirements—but at a minimum, he also had to hint at how Israel would respond to Asad's interests on the main items. If Uri and Shimon wanted to move quickly on the Syrian track, they too had to understand what might be required. Uri understood, but like any good negotiator, he was reluctant to offer more to the other side.

Prior to my departure for the region in early December, Uri went to meet Aidi in

Paris on November 29. He told me beforehand that he would be going and only Peres would know about it. Around midnight on November 29, just after I had gone to bed, Uri called saying he had just returned from Paris, where Itee had indicated much greater awareness of the issues of negotiations than before. Itee suggested bringing Asad around by presenting ideas not as conditions for Israel's withdrawal but as a natural outgrowth of a state of peace. Echoing what I had often heard from Walid, Itee suggested that giving Asad something on principle—namely, the land and rapid withdrawal—would facilitate flexibility on his part. For his part, Aidi gave Uri a brochure on tourism in Syria and seemed very open to how tourism might be developed in a way that created connections. (I could not help thinking that Walid and Aidi were coordinating closely.)

Before we hung up, I asked Uri about an incident in Jenin, a city in the West Bank, where two Israeli border policemen had been kidnapped and subsequently released by the Palestinians. What had happened? Having been off in Paris, Uri told me he did not have the full picture. In any case, the good news was that the two sides had coordinated and cooperated quickly and effectively, and the incident did not delay the redeployment of the IDF from the six major Palestinian cities in the West Bank, which proceeded smoothly.

Even though my first formal stop would be in Damascus, I left Sunday evening, December 3, on a flight to Israel. On this particular trip, I was picking up a U.S. Air Force plane in Israel and flying to Damascus. Since what was known as "in-theater travel" was far less costly than flying on an Air Force plane from Washington to the Middle East, this arrangement allowed us to save a substantial amount of money. I had told Uri I would stop in Israel for about two or three hours to pick up the letter from Peres to Asad. Ehud Barak, the new Israeli Foreign Minister in Peres's government, also asked me to dinner at the LaRomme hotel in Jerusalem. Itamar joined Uri and Barak for the dinner and Barak started off by asking my impressions of Asad. Thus began a brainstorming process with the Israelis that would continue through Peres's trip to Washington in mid-December.

From our conversation over dinner, I could see there was not yet a consensus among them on how to proceed. Both Barak and Uri, for example, did not want me to emphasize an early meeting between Peres and Asad lest it appear that Peres was desperate for a meeting.

Uri accompanied Martin and me as we drove from Jerusalem to Ben-Gurion, and he said that what I brought back from Damascus would have an important effect on Peres's thinking and on their approach. He added that it would be very difficult to be seen as giving any more away at the very beginning of the negotiating process.

As I got on the plane, I knew that if I wanted Peres to move toward Asad, I would have to produce something new from the Syrian President in Damascus. Perhaps the letter I was carrying from Peres would do the trick. The tone of the letter was very good and even referred cleverly to Rabin's "commitment" to reach a comprehensive peace with Syria that Peres would stand by. I was not in a position to say that Peres would stand by the pocket, but the letter was suggestive. I recommended only one change in it, to a line where Peres said that Asad could become a leader of the Arab world with a peace agreement, because Asad already thought of himself as a leader in the Arab world and would read this as patronizing.

| A NEW ERA IN DAMASCUS? |

Walid greeted me at the airport in Damascus late that evening. He told me Asad was in a very hopeful mood. I told him I had a letter from Peres for Asad and asked if he wanted to see it. He did not. He said it would be best for Asad to be surprised by it, but I suspected he did not know how Asad would respond to such a letter and even feared that Asad, not wanting it known that he was receiving correspondence from the Israeli Prime Minister, would be unwilling to receive it at all. I decided then I must simply give the letter to Asad at the outset of the meeting.

We did not arrive at the Damascus Sheraton until after midnight. I gave the Peres letter to our Ambassador to Syria, Chris Ross, to translate it from the English to Arabic and went to sleep, knowing we would get a call from the palace in the morning for the meeting.

The call came shortly before noon, and upon my arrival Asad explained that he had a cold. As usual, we got into our conversation slowly, discussing the good omen of the rain that had accompanied my visit. When he signaled it was time to get down to business, I outlined the areas I would cover and then said, "But first, reflecting Peres's desire to begin to do business differently," the new prime minister had asked me to deliver a letter. I handed him the original, signed by Peres, along with the Arabic translation. Asad read the letter very carefully, then said the letter reaffirmed his positive impression of Peres. It had good ideas. Naturally, they were general, but one would not expect specific ideas to be spelled out in a letter. Such specific ideas must be discussed directly.

This was already noteworthy. Apart from applauding the Israeli Prime Minister—unusual, to say the least, for him—Asad seemed to be showing an openness to direct meetings. I did not want to jump to a conclusion, but I knew that Peres would see it positively. I told Asad that I would convey his reaction to Peres and then began my presentation, conveying Peres's surprise over Rabin's commitment to the pocket, his desire to discuss it with President Clinton in Washington soon, and his list of Israel's needs, which fell into five broad categories.

First, the peace deal with Syria must produce comprehensiveness; concessions made toward Syria must be seen as producing peace not only with Syria but with the Arab world. Second, it must isolate and discredit those who would use violence and terror against Israel. Third, it must have credible security arrangements; the Israeli public must see an agreement that makes Israel more, not less, secure. Fourth, there must be a clear investment in peace, such as a regional investment fund or an umbrella for development; the Golan, for example, should become a regional zone of joint development, thus demonstrating an unmistakable intention to pursue peace and not war, while also responding to Syria's need to reabsorb the Syrian returnees to the Golan. Fifth, the process was important; Peres's view was that we must produce a serious and practical mechanism for peacemaking, which clearly required doing business differently.

To Asad, I deliberately stressed the fourth point on joint investments, noting that this point was new and obviously critical to Peres. I concluded my presentation with some thoughts on the changes in the political landscape in Israel: the opposition was on the defensive, the religious parties were engaging in very serious soul-searching, and Peres was exploring ways to broaden the base of support for his coalition. I also said he was working to prepare the Israeli public for peace, as was Leah Rabin, who had great moral authority. All this created a moment of opportunity that could be seized or lost.

Asad thanked me for my comments, and started by saying he agreed that there was a moment and it could be lost if not seized. He said Leah Rabin's support for Peres was very important, and he felt she offered this because it was in support of her husband's efforts. He then said he saw Peres as "a leader with vision, imagination, and creativity."

It was unprecedented for him to say anything this positive about an Israeli leader, even in private, and I immediately thought he, too, felt that the atmosphere was more hopeful in the region and that he would do nothing to spoil it. His subsequent presentation confirmed this to be his intention.

Four years of discussions had passed, he said, and if we had not signed anything, we now agreed on the four elements of peace—withdrawal, normal peaceful relations, security arrangements, and the phases or time for implementation—stressing that he understood the value of not addressing a single element in the abstract but in relation to all others.

He said he felt that agreement was possible quickly on the security arrangements, but that Rabin had been hesitant, noting this was so "probably because he was afraid of the extremists"—a deliberate effort not to be critical of Rabin himself.

He then reiterated the point that he was not against any idea that would push the process forward rapidly—clearly trying to show he was open to Peres's ideas. He even seized on a Peres idea that he liked—namely, that peace itself provides security—and so Peres's interest in regional investment was a means to peace and security: "Peres sees investment in the region as a security arrangement itself. I do not mean to suggest that Peres does not pay attention to the mechanisms of security arrangements, but he seeks to solve security issues with nonsecurity issues. This reflects not only his intent but his view of the whole landscape."

This too was an extraordinary statement for Asad to make, even if it was tactically useful as a way of downplaying zones of separation, early-warning facilities, limited-deployment areas, and the like. Whether or not it was designed as a tactic, Asad was making positive statements about an Israeli leader and the way he approached peace-making. Gone was the grudging quality of his normal comments on the Israelis and peace. In its place was an unprecedented openness as to how to proceed.

In his closing comments, Asad said, "We are at a turning point, and there is a new government, with new ideas." He was eager to hear what Peres would convey to President Clinton, expecting Secretary Christopher or me then to come to Damascus. At the time of that trip, he expected that people would see "a new launching of the peace process and that would create a better situation in the region."

As we stood up to conclude the meeting, I decided to push for an even more meaningful signal. I said it was clear we were now going to be entering into an intensive phase of negotiations. And it was also clear that acts of terror in Israel or an escalation in southern Lebanon would tie Peres's hands. Asad nodded, saying, "That is correct." If that is so, I continued, why not, for the duration of this intensive phase, which we hope will conclude in a peace agreement, do all we can to ease the situation in southern Lebanon? Wouldn't any violence counter our objectives? Again he answered, "That is correct."

While I doubted Hizbollah had an interest in peace, I went on—but Asad interrupted me to say, "No, they don't just lack an interest in peace, they oppose it." All the more reason, I replied, that they should not be allowed to ruin the opportunity that now exists. Again he nodded, and I said, "I have not raised this with Peres, but what if there were simply an informal understanding that every effort would be made to stop the violence in southern Lebanon for the duration of the negotiations? It would not be announced, it would simply be a tacit understanding that the violence would stop or be controlled to the extent possible."

Asad recounted Syria's history with Hizbollah, noting how Hizbollah had emerged during the war in Lebanon, and that at the time of the Hizbollah hijacking of a TWA plane, Syria had helped to end the hostage crisis. Syria did not control Hizbollah, but could exercise influence. Now I interrupted: Could he use his influence to try to stop or control the violence in southern Lebanon? Asad said, "Yes, we will exert efforts. But Israel must also exert efforts, and they have a disciplined army so it is easier for them to do so. If we exert efforts and they don't stop shooting, then the resistance will turn their guns on us."

I then asked if I could tell Peres what Asad had told me, namely, that Syria would exert efforts to try to stop the violence and calm the situation in southern Lebanon, but that Israel must do likewise. There would be no formal understanding, merely a de facto situation as the negotiations moved into an intensive phase. Asad replied that, "yes, you can convey that to him."

As I left Damascus to return to Israel, Asad's willingness to restrain Hizbollah was, I believed, genuinely significant. His remarks on everything else had been positive, with a new, unprecedented tone. But little of difficulty was required of him. Lebanon was a different story. He would have to impose his will on Hizbollah, and it could cost him. Perhaps he, and we, really were at a turning point.

| "HOW IS THE GENTLEMAN IN DAMASCUS?" |

As I arrived at the Prime Minister's office, Shimon Peres and his staff were just returning from a memorial service marking the end of "shloshim," the initial thirty-day period of mourning for Rabin.

Peres told me the service had been very moving. He then asked, "So how is the gentleman in Damascus?"

I told him we had had our best meeting ever. Asad liked Peres's letter. He had been positive, determined to avoid criticism, and had favorable comments to make about Peres—"not exactly the norm in Damascus."

Peres listened intently, nodding as I went through these points. In such meetings, I felt it essential to look right at the leader, not to read anything. As I summarized the meeting's main points, I sought through eye contact to build Peres's sense of trust not only in Asad but in my judgment as well.

Peres liked what he heard—the tone of the meeting, the openness to ideas, the readiness to deal with all the issues at the same time, not to concentrate only on security, and the making of the Golan into a zone of investment. Upon telling him in private my suggestion about a tacit cease-fire in southern Lebanon and Asad's response, he replied, maybe "our Syrian friends are ready for change." I hoped neither of us was reading more into the meeting than was warranted.

| PERES REAFFIRMS THE RABIN POCKET |

When Peres arrived in Washington a week later for his meeting with President Clinton, it was a forgone conclusion that he would reaffirm the Rabin pocket on withdrawal to the June 4 lines. In return for standing by Rabin's contingent offer, Peres wanted Asad to make a deal. Repeating what he had said to me—he was prepared to lose either the Golan or the election, but not both—he wanted us to push Asad to create a different negotiating process. I am ready, he told President Clinton, to "fly high and fast, or low and slow, to an agreement. It depends what Asad wants."

President Clinton wanted high and fast as well—also believing that the politics in Israel created openings that would not last. For Peres, the measure of flying high and fast was an early summit. But heeding the advice of Uri, Peres was careful not to seem desperate for a summit. If Asad wanted one, we could move quickly. If not, Israel was willing to wait.

Still, neither President Clinton nor Prime Minister Peres wanted business as usual. In Peres's case, this also extended to the U.S.-Israeli relationship and the American role in the region.

Peres asked us: What would change in the U.S. relationship with Israel if there were a peace deal with Syria? In his eyes, it was time for a formal U.S.-Israeli alliance, treaty-bound guarantees that would enhance Israeli security and deterrence and compensate in part for the dangers of getting off the Golan Heights. There was no great surprise in this request, a common one from Israeli prime ministers.[*]

What set Peres apart, however, was his vision of an America immersed in the region, shaping a new strategic reality by promoting economic reform, massive new investments and assistance, new initiatives on education and computerization, and a new emphasis on building trade and financial cooperation throughout the area. In his view, peace would be a function of shared interests and stakes, not a tactical accommodation to the balance of forces.[†] We were sympathetic to his vision, but not yet able to think in such grandiose terms—especially on the eve of a U.S. election, when talk of massive new amounts of foreign aid was unlikely to be welcome.

But Shimon Peres rarely thought "small." Why? What shaped him? Where did he come from?

---

[*]Subsequently, both Netanyahu and Barak, when contemplating full withdrawal from the Golan Heights, sought similar commitments from us.

[†]Peres spells out this vision of a modernized, economically developed Middle East creating the foundations for a comprehensive regional peace in his book *The New Middle East*, New York: Henry Holt, 1993.

| WHO IS SHIMON PERES? |

Peres was born in Poland, and made aliyah with his family to Israel in 1934. He grew up on a kibbutz, and at a young age became an aide to David Ben-Gurion, who made him the first Director General of the Israeli Ministry of Defense. The ministry had to be established; the army after the War of Independence was in desperate need of equipping and reorganizing, and Israel's basic national security doctrines needed to be forged. That task fell to Shimon Peres, at the age of twenty-nine. It is one of the ironies of Israeli history that Peres, who was responsible for building the Israeli defense establishment, later was seen as soft on security because he had never served in the Israeli military. For Israelis of his generation, this was unthinkable, and his lack of military service was used unfairly against him throughout his political career.

There was another damaging perception of Peres: he was seen to be a schemer, an image that Yitzhak Rabin had done much to shape. The two had been rivals in the Labor Party, vying for leadership. When Rabin succeeded Golda Meir as head of the Labor Party (and then as Prime Minister) after the devastating 1973 war, Peres became his Defense Minister. When Rabin resigned as Prime Minister because of a financial scandal involving Leah, Peres led the Labor Party to its first electoral defeat in its history. Rabin subsequently published a book in which he accused Peres of subverting his government so as to replace him. The image of a schemer and an opportunist dogged Peres even as he remained the leader of the Labor Party. But his electoral fortunes continued to suffer. He again led Labor to defeat in 1981. And in 1984, when the disaster of the Lebanon war, Begin's resignation, and an economic crisis made Labor's victory over Likud a foregone conclusion, he could only manage a dead heat with Yitzhak Shamir. In 1992, Rabin defeated Peres as the head of the party and subsequently won the election to become Prime Minister for the second time.

Rabin remained concerned that Peres would try to undermine him. It was Peres who went to Rabin and said I know I will not be Prime Minister; this is our last hurrah, and we have an obligation to make peace for the next generation, so let's work together. It was not, however, until the negotiations on the Interim Agreement that Rabin saw Peres as his full partner.

Over fifty years of rivalry, Rabin, however, had always taken Peres's views seriously. He recognized that Peres had built the defense establishment—and saw Peres's capacity to think in visionary terms as a natural complement to his own more cautious instincts. Likewise Peres was emboldened to think big by the knowledge that Rabin would limit those actions that were too risky to pursue.

Unlike the loner Rabin, Peres always surrounded himself with bright younger assistants. Yossi Beilin, Uri Savir, and Avi Gil were smart, not afraid to challenge Peres, and identified with—and often led—those in Israel who felt Israel must do more to promote peace.

Ben-Gurion was more than his model; he was his idol. I heard Peres speak emotionally about Ben-Gurion more than once, emphasizing his vision for Israel, his readiness to lead, make historic decisions, and preserve Israel's Jewish character and unique moral standing. The Ben-Gurion legacy and the corrosive effects of occupation led at least in part to a transformation in Peres's attitude toward the Palestinians.

Throughout the 1970s and into the 1980s, Peres clearly hoped that the "Jordan option" would resolve the Palestinian issue. Like most in the Labor Party, he looked to King Hussein as the partner for a territorial compromise on the West Bank—with Palestinians becoming part of the Hashemite Kingdom of Jordan. But by the end of the 1980s, and certainly with the advent of the first Intifada, it was clear that King Hussein could not represent the Palestinians. Increasingly, Peres came to share the assumption of his closest assistants: there would be no peace without dealing directly with the Palestinians and no dealing with the Palestinians without talking to Yasir Arafat and the PLO.

But his transformation also embodied a much broader assessment of international relations. Peres saw the global economy becoming increasingly interconnected, with fewer borders and barriers to information, investment, and economic growth. He believed globalization could be a powerful force for peace in the Middle East, whose people could achieve neither security nor economic progress if they remained consumed by conflict. He envisioned a "new Middle East" and grew obsessed with convincing Israel's neighbors—including the Palestinians—of the economic benefits of peace. At times between 1993 and 1995 Rabin would disparage Peres's vision with me, but Peres was undeterred, asking, "Why do we need to set our sights low? If we don't try, we surely won't succeed."

This grand vision informed Peres's readiness to move quickly toward peace after the Rabin assassination. For the first time in his political career, he wore the mantle of "statesman." He was Rabin's obvious successor, his partner in the historic leap with the Palestinians. Those around him in the Labor Party saw an aura of invincibility and began to press him to call early elections. He was torn between his belief that he should work for an early agreement with Syria or focus instead on being elected with an unmistakable mandate which could then be used to tackle peace with Syria and eventually with the Palestinians.

His ambivalence about pursuing peace before elections hung over the negotiations that would resume with the Syrians. After Peres's visit to Washington, Secretary Christopher and I went to see Asad in Damascus. We did not press him for a summit.

Instead, we suggested a radically new format for negotiations: to have each side bring a small team to an isolated location to permit us to work intensively together for a week at a time on all the issues. Never before in these talks did we have anything resembling real teams for negotiations. Now we would have military people to deal with the security issues; a legal expert to draft; and the political negotiators to lead the negotiations. Asad was open to this approach, provided the negotiations were trilateral, held in the United States, and publicly announced (so as to avoid any comparisons with Oslo). After each round we would return to the region in order to brief the leaders on the progress—or lack of it.

Secretary Christopher and I picked the Aspen Institute's Wye River Plantation as the site for the talks. The Wye River Plantation was a retreat for conferences and was spread out over several miles. It was on the eastern shore of the Chesapeake Bay in Maryland, about seventy-five minutes by car from Washington. Two houses—River House and Houghton House—were several hundred yards apart, but the conference center and the cabins near it were four miles away from these houses, across rolling fields and wooded parkland. Though we would be meeting in December, the image of the proverbial walk in the woods where ideas could be discussed off the record was very much in my mind.

All together, we would have about fifteen people staying at River House; we would meet together and eat together and spend our days and nights in one place. This was also a first.

The Syrians had never agreed to eat with the Israelis, resisting even this minimal sign of civility and acceptance. Eating together suggested socializing together; socializing together suggested that there were normal relations; and for Asad, normal relations were impossible as long as Syrian territory was occupied.

So something as routine as dining together had been previously excluded—notwithstanding my arguments that the Syrians could hardly expect the Israeli public to take the Syrian commitment to peace seriously if even basic human gestures could not be made to Israelis. Now, however, not only would the Syrians be eating with the Israelis (and, of course, their American hosts), but they would also be sleeping under the same roof for several days at a time.*

---

*On the eve of our departure to Wye, Dr. Jeffrey Jay, a friend and neighbor, dropped off a bag of snacks for me to take along, hoping they would contribute to a relaxed atmosphere. It was not uncommon for friends and acquaintances to offer encouragement, both orally and in kind, and I appreciated their concern and thoughtfulness.

| THE ISRAELI-SYRIAN NEGOTIATIONS AT WYE RIVER |

The Israeli-Syrian talks at Wye stretched from the end of December 1995 until the end of February 1996. There were two and a half rounds. We would meet Monday through Thursday and then break for the weekend, with all sides returning to Washington for the Muslim Sabbath on Friday, the Jewish Sabbath on Saturday, and the Christian Sabbath on Sunday.

We would meet for two weeks at a time. Over the weekends, I would bring Uri and Walid to my house for private discussions. After a round was over, the two sides would return to Jerusalem and Damascus. Following the first round, I went to the region as well to meet Peres and Asad in their respective capitals, mainly to get Asad's blessing for a proposal on future economic cooperation. Following the second round, Secretary Christopher traveled to the region with a very different purpose: to persuade Asad to allow negotiations to continue even though Shimon Peres would soon call for early elections in Israel—an unmistakable sign that there would be few Israeli concessions and certainly no agreement before the elections.

What transpired in these negotiations? Why did Peres call for early elections?

| ROUND ONE AT WYE |

In negotiations, I am a firm believer in focusing first on developing relationships between the two key protagonists. Every negotiation is about manipulation, with each side trying to convince the other that its redlines are truly red while the other's are simply pink. But every negotiation comes to a critical point, and when one side tells the other that he/she is capable of doing X and not Y, the counterpart has to believe that this is for real and not another manipulation. Many factors go into making yourself believable in a negotiation—taking steps that are hard for you and delivering; always delivering what you promise and never promising what you cannot deliver; showing awareness of your counterpart's needs and demonstrating in tangible ways your understanding that your negotiating partner also has to have an explanation for what is to be agreed.

In these negotiations, I wanted to take advantage of the creativity of both Uri and Walid. The first day at Wye, then, I had Uri and Walid sit together just to talk about their objectives, their leaders' views and expectations, their relationship with their leaders, their perspectives on the future, and what they envisioned the day after peace to be like. While Walid had worked with Itamar and respected him, he did not know Uri. Now Uri, given his closeness to Peres, would be in charge of the negotiations in a completely different setting—a setting that I believed meant Walid would have a little more latitude to negotiate and a setting that played to Uri's informal, instinctual style of negotiating. The first item of business was to get these two to talk about themselves and their purposes. Knowing them, I felt certain that each would impress the other and that a foundation of trust could be laid from day one.

The two spent nearly four hours together that day, at least half of which was spent alone when I left them to have a "four-eyes" discussion.

We had established a premise for the Wye talks. Based on the Rabin commitment—which was in our pocket, not the Syrian pocket—the Syrians would assume that full withdrawal from the Golan would take place once Israeli needs had been addressed. The Israelis would not discuss this issue, but also not openly contradict it. This way the two sides could focus on the preconditions for withdrawal—peace, security, and the timeline for any agreement—rather than the territorial issue itself.

The first negotiating round turned out to be productive. Basic concepts were agreed: a "timeline," "comprehensiveness," and developing the content of "normal peaceful relations."

The "timeline" was designed to allow us to deal with the Israeli concern that while withdrawal was very tangible and concrete, Syrian responses to Israeli requirements needed not only to be measurable but also to be tied to specific junctures in the process. We began to identify milestones for concrete Syrian steps on both security and normalization. We focused on the period prior to an agreement; the time at which agreement would be reached; the time the first Israeli withdrawal would take place; the point at which the Israeli withdrawals would be completed; and the period afterward. In this way, we began to create Syrian obligations toward Israel both before and after an agreement had been reached.

"Comprehensiveness" meant that the agreement between Israel and Syria should not be limited only to them but should be the key to broader peace between Israel and the region. Walid accepted that Syria had an obligation to make the peace one that would change the region, and we recorded an agreement on this point.

Similarly, we agreed that "normal peaceful relations" meant full diplomatic relations with embassies, trade, and tourism. Israel wanted to take these categories and fit the infrastructure of broad normalization into it. Israel's lawyer Yoel Singer had eighteen categories of normalization that would make possible all sorts of ties, from banking, to aviation, to postal, to customs, to agriculture, to health, to environmental, etc. Walid had agreed to have Singer work with Riad Daoudi, the Syrian lawyer, on fitting these categories into the three headings of diplomatic relations, trade, and tourism.

Finally, there was an informal understanding on how to build economic cooperation. When and how would joint projects become feasible? Walid said only Asad could decide this, but suggested that I raise with the Syrian President the idea of trilateral projects organized by us in which Israeli companies could take part along with their American and Syrian counterparts. When I raised this idea privately with Asad in Damascus, he agreed, provided American, not Israeli, companies took the lead.

| ROUND TWO AT WYE |

In round one, military officers had not taken part. They did in round two, without any hesitancy on Asad's part. General Ibrahim Omar and General Hassan Khalil represented the Syrians. General Omar was expressive, revealing his emotions in every discussion. His colleague from Syrian intelligence rarely changed expression, and my conclusion was that he was there more as a watchdog than as a negotiator. Major General Uzi Dayan took the lead on the Israeli side. At lunch and dinner, Uzi and Brigadier General Shlomo Brom would engage Omar and Khalil on all kinds of questions, ranging from military questions on the relative advantages of large standing armies versus reserve armies to the differing concepts of God in the Jewish and Islamic faiths. Gamal Helal, who was serving as interpreter, would laughingly tell me that the Syrian President might have an aneurysm if he knew what was really being discussed at Wye.

In our discussions, Walid took the lead on security for the Syrians, Uzi for the Israelis. The "aims and principles" nonpaper served as our framework for the negotiations, meaning there were still plenty of differences to overcome between the two. For the Israelis, the main issue was the location of the Syrian forces. The farther removed Syrian forces were from the Golan, the less the Israelis needed ground early-warning stations in the Golan after withdrawal. Conversely, the closer the forces to the Golan, the more they would need the early-warning stations, particularly to gain enough time to mobilize their forces to contend with a possible attack.

For the Syrians, the main issue was the proximity of Damascus, the Syrian capital, to the border with Israel. Damascus was roughly seventy kilometers from the June 4 border. Syria needed forces to be able to defend the capital, and this, much like the principle of June 4 as the border, was nonnegotiable.

The sensitivity over Damascus produced a memorable, highly emotional performance by Walid at one point. We had spread a map over the round table at which we were holding our discussion. Describing the area that Israel needed to be free of Syrian tank or mechanized divisions, Uzi put his hand over it and his reach in this case extended beyond Damascus. Walid asked, "Is your hand covering Damascus?"

Uzi looked at his hand, raised his fingers, and nonchalantly said "yes," whereupon Walid exploded. "You want to control Damascus. You are going to tell us that we cannot defend ourselves, that you will determine what can be done in our capital. You don't want peace, you want to occupy the area. No Syrian would allow you to tell us whether we can defend ourselves." And he was just getting warmed up; as he went on to rant and rave, my colleagues Aaron Miller and Toni Verstandig leaned over and asked, "Aren't you going to stop this?" I shook my head no, understanding that Walid was performing for his team (and for Asad, who would be briefed on the episode). He had to explode; he had to prove to Asad how tough he was on this point. Finally, I called for a break, asking Uri and Walid to join me privately. Walid walked into the back room still betraying great agitation. As soon as we closed the door, I said, "Uri, Uzi stepped over the line by putting his hand over Damascus. But Walid, all your yelling is not dealing with the Israeli concern that you have large, highly mobile armored forces that with no notice could be at the border within hours. That issue will have to be addressed."

There were no winks, no knowing glances, only Walid's cryptic comment that he was obligated to respond to what Uzi had done. For his part, Uzi later that evening sought to explain to me that there was a substantive reality that the Syrians would have to respond to if there were to be a deal. But he acknowledged that there were probably better ways for him to have presented his fundamental point.

At my house that weekend, as it turned out, Walid made a significant move on the security arrangements. Uri and Walid each brought one person with them to the house for an off-the-record discussion on security issues. Uri brought Uzi and Walid brought Michael Wahbe, his successor as the Chief of Staff of the Foreign Minister's office, a Christian who Walid had told me was committed to peace. Bringing Michael signaled that Walid was going to try out an idea and he wanted Michael to be a part of it.

We met in our dining room over coffee, cake, and fruit. Debbie always made whoever came to the house for discussions feel comfortable, welcome, and certain never to leave hungry. To resolve security, I explained, we had to find a way to overcome the early warning/force deployment and location issue. I could see a way to overcome every one of the core issues except this one. Uri quietly explained that, notwithstanding Peres's vision of making the Golan an economic zone of prosperity, neither he nor Peres would ever be able to sell an agreement in Israel if there was not a credible basis for security arrangements.

Walid was now all business. "Let's discuss what really matters to you. It is not the six divisions that Uzi raised, it is the three armored and mechanized divisions that are west of Damascus on which you need assurance." Walid took out a map and pointed to three divisions deployed outside Damascus, to the west and south of the Syrian capital. He continued, noting that he did not think it was feasible to move the divisions, but that the divisions could be made into "shells," reserve rather than active ones. When Uzi asked if the Syrians could move the ammunition and engineering equipment to other areas—far from these bases—Walid replied, "Now you are thinking." It was clear that we had the basis of a conceptual breakthrough on the core security problem.

Uzi, who had triggered Walid's explosion, was in fact much appreciated by Walid and his military colleagues, and Uri's announcement that Uzi would be leaving the delegation to assume one of the IDF's major commands brought Wye's most poignant moment. Uzi stood and asked to say a few words to his Syrian colleagues. With great emotion, he said it had been one of his proudest moments to represent his country in these negotiations with them. He had devoted his whole adult life to the defense of his country. He had been wounded three times in war. He had never known his father, who was killed during Israel's War of Independence. His uncle—Moshe Dayan—had known the pain of war wounds his entire life. He had three children, who he hoped would never know war the way he had. So it was a privilege to negotiate for peace with Syria. Peace would serve both sides. Neither would sacrifice what they considered essential for their security, but Uzi concluded, "I am confident that, [working together as we are doing now,] we will overcome all differences and a peace of dignity and mutual respect will be possible." That was his hope, and he looked forward to the day when they might meet again.

In a spontaneous response, both Syrian generals, including General Khalil, a man who had revealed no emotion throughout the two rounds, rose from the table and embraced Uzi. Stunned by the image of two Syrian generals hugging an Israeli general, I turned to Uri, who had tears in his eyes, and said, "You know, we might just make it."

While we had made real headway on security in the off-the-record discussion at my house, the second round of formal talks had been affected throughout by all the speculation in the Israeli media of pressures on Peres to call new elections. Not only was this distracting, but Foreign Minister Ehud Barak began making, in Walid's eyes, provocative statements that seemed to contradict the Rabin pocket: that Israel would never withdraw to the June 4 lines, that the Syrians would never be allowed to dip their toes in the waters of the Kinneret, that it would take a long time to negotiate a final deal with Syria—all seemed at odds with what Uri had been saying about Peres's intentions.

In private discussions with Uri and me, Walid asked whether Peres had decided not to go for an agreement now? Uri assured Walid that Peres remained committed to reaching an agreement, but that he was under a great deal of pressure to go for early elections.

In planning for his trip to the region after the second round, Secretary Christopher and I felt it best to explain to Peres the effect the speculation was having on the negotiations. When President Clinton asked me if I thought Peres should go for early elections, I was categorical in response: "It is a big mistake. Today, Peres is seen in Israel as a statesman. As soon as he declares for early elections, he will once again look like the politician seeking an advantage. What's worse, what happens if there are two terrorist bombs? He won't recover."

The President told me I was probably right, but said it was very hard to tell Peres that he should not call for early elections, especially when the polls showed him with over a twenty-point lead and the prospect of gaining a mandate. Secretary Christopher agreed. The decision on early elections was Peres's to make. We should focus on the Syrian negotiations while making clear that once the elections were called, little would be possible until they occurred. (If the Syrians thought no deal was possible until later, they would not make any moves now.)

In Jerusalem, Peres was blunt. He would forgo early elections only if Asad was prepared to meet him and to push for an agreement. If that were the case, Asad would be signaling his readiness to move quickly; if not, Peres would pursue the "low, slow preference of Asad," but would then go for elections while the discussions at Wye continued. Peres felt it was important for political reasons that the Wye talks continue lest it look like his call for early elections stopped an ongoing negotiation.

The Secretary's task in Damascus was thus to see if a summit was possible, and if not, to get Asad to agree that negotiations would continue. In truth, I did not believe this to be particularly difficult. I reasoned that if Asad turned down the summit, he would want to show that his opposition was to a high-level meeting at this point, not to negotiations. And that is precisely what he did. When the Secretary raised with him Peres's proposal, Asad countered that we were not at a stage where he could make a summit understandable to his own public. While he inevitably questioned the use of negotiations during an election campaign in Israel, he agreed that the Wye talks could continue—as if to make us feel he had done us a favor by agreeing to the talks.

| THE LAST ROUND |

The last round at Wye turned out to be a half round, ended by suicide bombings in Israel. We did not advance much on the security issues, in part because I put the emphasis on filling in the other issues, saving security for the latter meetings of the round which never took place.

There did emerge, however, a very interesting development that I kept in the back of my mind for the future. In private discussions, Uri told me, Walid had asked for the formation of a number of working groups, including one on demarcation of the border. Uri told Walid he would check with Peres, stressing that if Peres approved, "you understand we will have some real battles in it." Uri was thus putting Walid on notice: the principle of June 4 was vague and its application would require hard bargaining over what Israel could live with and what Syria wanted. Uri told me that Walid acknowledged the bargaining over the location of the border would be difficult.

But we would not get to a demarcation group at this time. We would not be able to take advantage of the progress made at Wye—the sixty items of convergence that I summarized as we broke for what turned out to be our last time.

The first of four suicide bombings in Israel had taken place on Sunday, February 25, with large numbers of casualties; the second took place on the same bus route in Israel on the next Sunday, again with terrible carnage. After the first bombing, Walid had expressed his private condolences. Uri had said it could make a difference if he could express such condolences in public. That did not happen.

Instead of resuming negotiations the next Monday, Uri requested we resume only on Tuesday, as it was not appropriate to be negotiating as Israel was burying its dead. I called Walid, who agreed, and again asked me to convey condolences to Uri. Like Uri, I now suggested this was the right time for public words of condolence. "Walid," I said, "if there was ever a time to reach out to the Israeli public as people, this is it." He said he would check with Asad.

Unfortunately, there was a third suicide bombing in Tel Aviv the next day; it claimed the lives of Israeli children dressed in their costumes for the Purim holiday, igniting shock and anger in Israel. The people were reeling; the country was in crisis; the Peres government was under siege, urged to form a national unity government with Likud. With Islamic Jihad, headquartered in Damascus, taking credit for the bombing in Tel Aviv, Uri told me he would be asked to have the negotiators return to Israel.

I called Walid and said it was now or never: Syria must condemn these bombings now and no longer permit Islamic Jihad to operate out of Damascus.

Again, he said he would see what he could do. When I called him later, he told me that there would be no statement; when he tried to explain, I cut him off: "This is bullshit. How do you expect the Israeli public to believe they have partners for peace when something as human as expressing outrage or even sadness over the killing of innocents is not possible?"

To be sure, a statement by the Syrians at this point might not have made any difference. In its absence, however, Uri told me "everything we have worked for is now in doubt." Without a serious crackdown by Arafat on Hamas and Islamic Jihad, there would be no peace process and no Peres government.

And so it was. I am convinced that had Peres been elected in 1996, we would have been able to conclude a Syrian deal within a year's time. Instead, four suicide bombings in Israel in nine days had killed fifty-nine Israelis and shaken the faith of the Israeli public in the possibility of peace. Once again terrorist violence precluded agreements, foreclosed options, and dominated the political landscape. That was bad enough. But

I was also troubled by the Syrian response: their unwillingness to condemn those who would terrorize Israelis, their intimation that they deserved something other than condemnation, and their reluctance to reach out to Israelis. All of this combined to make me wonder how real any peace with Syria or the Arab world would be.

If we were to have a peace process worth saving, we would need to produce a dramatic event at which the Arab leaders would condemn the terror and agree to take steps to combat it. The Summit of the Peacemakers was born from this concept.

{10}

Could the Peace Process Be Saved?

W ITH URI'S WARNING RINGING in my ears, I told Secretary Christopher that we were in danger of seeing the Peres government and the peace process collapse. The only way to reverse the damage, I said, was to get Arab and world leaders, with President Clinton in the lead, to meet with Peres, condemn the bombings, and develop an action plan for combating the terrorists. That would demonstrate to the Israeli public that pursuing peace was transforming the region and that Israel was not alone in fighting the terrorists.

The Secretary agreed with the concept of such a summit, and arranged for the two of us to go see President Clinton. When we entered the Oval Office, Christopher explained that he felt we were at "a unique moment of danger" in the Middle East, and he let me run through what I had in mind.

George Stephanopoulos, one of the President's top political advisors, was against his going to and leading such a summit. George asked the legitimate question: What happens if you go to the region and there is a bombing when you are there or just after you leave? You won't have stopped this; the collapse might happen anyway. It looks like a big risk with little chance of success.

President Clinton looked at me and asked very simply, "Dennis, do I need to do this?" "Yes," I answered. "You may not save the process if you go, but if you don't go, I think we are going to lose it."

Clinton then declared, "We are going."

Now we had to actually pull it off. Who would host it? Where would it be? Who would attend? How could we guarantee that there would be follow-up actions to counter terror? All these questions required immediate answers because we needed a dramatic intervention now.

The most obvious choice of host was President Mubarak of Egypt. Once we had this settled, we could then start inviting participants and drafting the declaration we would convey to other participants even prior to convening. President Clinton called President Mubarak and he agreed immediately, suggesting Sharm al-Sheikh, a beach resort on the Red Sea and lately a popular tourist destination. New hotels with conference facilities had recently been completed; the isolated location at the tip of the Sinai Peninsula offered security for the world's leaders, and there was an airport there that could accommodate Boeing 747s.

Mubarak's readiness to host the summit reflected an interesting reality about the Egyptian President. Hosni Mubarak was not a risk-taker or a reformer. He would brutally crack down on Islamic fundamentalists who used terror and violence against the regime, but he also appeased Islamists who assaulted liberal thought and civil society using subtler means. He believed this dual approach would forestall any real Islamic threat to his regime.

Mubarak's posture toward Israel reflected a similar duality. On the one hand, he permitted only a "cold peace," doing nothing to foster a climate of openness and at least implicitly encouraging the extremely anti-Israeli—even anti-Semitic—bias of the state-run Egyptian media. Yet whenever he felt the peace process was entering a danger zone, he always tried to defuse the dangers and preserve the process. Egypt and Sadat had led the way on peace, and a collapse would call into question the wisdom of Egypt's course.

Mubarak also seemed to understand the limits on our side. If he were too hostile toward Israel, he could lose U.S. assistance to Egypt, totaling $2 billion annually. The aid was obviously valuable, but it was also a symbol of Egypt's importance in the region and made Egypt a bridge to the American superpower.

Still, Mubarak wanted to keep his opposition—the Islamists and the Nasserists—from uniting against him, and the easiest way to do this was to preserve his distance from the Israelis and demonstrate his clear independence from us from time to time. Distancing was legitimate; going beyond the breaking point was not.

The balancing act he struck reflected his judgment on how to manage his society and the forces in the Middle East. Whenever we would push for him to reach out to the Israelis or get the Saudis, say, to do so, he would say in his distinctive voice, "Believe me, I can't do more. You will be creating a hell of a problem."

He would imply that we were crazy to press too hard on the Arabs, and not nearly insistent enough on the Israelis. Was Mubarak's caution a function of having watched

Anwar Sadat get gunned down? Did his longevity in office convince him that risk aversion was the way to preserve his power? Was he simply cautious by nature? Probably a combination of these three factors, but the longer he served as President, the more set in his ways he became. Just now he understood that he must help preserve the process, and naturally he liked the idea that the world's leaders would convene in Egypt. But he doubted that we could get the Saudis to come. Without the Saudis, I believed that the impact of the summit in Israel would be limited, for it would tell the Israelis that not much had truly changed in the region.

So I called Bandar and told him "peace is at stake" and we needed the Saudis to send their foreign minister at the least. He called back within a day. He told me it had not been easy, but that he and Foreign Minister Saud would attend, would join the general meetings with Peres, and would support the creation of working groups on countering terror that would include Israelis.

In the end, twenty-nine world leaders came to Sharm, including representatives of fourteen Arab states. Unfortunately, neither the Syrians nor the Lebanese attended. We had invited Syria along with every other regional actor except Iraq, Libya, and Iran, but Asad understood that the focus would be terror and our call for action would inevitably lead to pressure to crack down on Hamas and Islamic Jihad, the groups responsible for the bombings in Israel—the very groups he permitted to operate out of Damascus. Asad, not surprisingly, saw the summit as a trap to promote the Israeli agenda and pressure him, and he refused to attend or send a lower-level representative.

But that, of course, left Syria excluded from the international summit, leaving it grouped with the other pariahs. And, as it happened, no sooner had the summit ended than Hizbollah escalated its attacks against the IDF in southern Lebanon, and Israel responded, whereupon Hizbollah fired Katyusha rockets into northern Israel. It was as if Asad was showing us the consequences of acting without him.

I certainly considered how Asad might respond to such a summit, including the possibility of an escalation in Lebanon. I understood that his exclusion would make it look like major events could happen in the Middle East without him, without Syria, and that he would probably react in some way. That is why we tried to include Syria. But the reality was that terror was the issue and it was threatening to undo everything. It could not be appeased. Asad needed to understand that terror threatened to destroy the process, and his chance to recover the Golan Heights. Now the focus had to be on dealing with the trauma in Israel as a result of four suicide bombings in nine days.

The Summit of the Peacemakers, held on March 13, 1996, did that, bringing the Israelis together with the regional and international community to condemn terror and act against it. The summit's declaration strongly condemned "all acts of terror in all its abhorrent forms . . . including recent terrorist attacks in Israel." In addition, it emphasized cooperation and "coordination of efforts to stop acts of terror . . . ensuring that instigators of such acts are brought to justice; supporting efforts by all parties to prevent their territories from being used for terrorist purposes; and preventing terrorist organizations from engaging in recruitment, supplying arms, or fund raising." Finally, it created a working group to implement these decisions and report back to the summit's participants within thirty days on the steps being taken.

On every measure of combating terror—counterterror training, sharing intelligence, law enforcement, cutting off finances—there was general agreement. In fact, if the working groups that we set up had functioned the way they were conceived at the Summit of the Peacemakers, Al-Qaeda might never have been able to destroy the World Trade Center five years later. But the working groups did not function the way we had hoped. In relatively short order the Arab participants limited their involvement on the grounds that peace with Israel had to come first.

Nonetheless, the summit served its purpose in Israel. As Shimon Peres stood before the cameras of the world media with Arab leaders, the Israeli public saw a regional transformation, and President Clinton's visit to Israel immediately following the summit was a source of comfort and reassurance. At a time of shock, here was an American president who understood their reality and their desires. In his speeches—especially one he gave to three thousand children in Tel Aviv—he once again met their anger and fear with empathy, support, and hope. Martin and I had drafted the speech, and as I stood on the stage behind the curtain while Clinton spoke, I saw the audience spellbound, as if the President were a preacher restoring their lost faith.

Afterward, when several Israelis and members of the President's traveling party congratulated me on the speech, I demurred, telling them that President Clinton had ad-libbed two-thirds of it, adjusting the text to fit what he believed the Israeli public needed to hear. He left Israel with a bond with the Israeli people stronger than any other American had ever had, or may ever have again. The newspapers ran banner headlines with the words "*Shalom Haver.*" *Shalom*, which means peace, is also used to greet or bid farewell to someone; *haver* means friend. Clinton had used these words to bid good-bye to Rabin after the assassination. Now Israelis conveyed the same emotional farewell to him.

The President's visit had uplifted the spirit of the Israeli public. As Uri Savir saw him off at the airport, Clinton said, "I hope my visit helped." Uri could only say, "More than you will ever know."

| OPERATION GRAPES OF WRATH |

Later in March, Hizbollah intensified its attacks on Israeli soldiers in the Israeli security zone in southern Lebanon. The verbal understandings that had halted the fighting in August 1993 protected the Israeli and Lebanese civilian populations, not soldiers.

Hizbollah, however, was now operating as if there were no 1993 understandings. In escalating its attacks (including suicide bombings) it showed far less concern than previously about shooting from Lebanese civilian areas. If Israel retaliated against those sites—as the 1993 understandings permitted—and there were any Lebanese casualties, Hizbollah would fire Katyusha rockets, in violation of the understandings, into Israeli civilian areas on the border—effectively driving the Israeli population into shelters. Facing an election in two months' time, Shimon Peres could ill afford to appear soft on security. He appealed to us to get the Syrians to stop Hizbollah's escalation, making clear that if they did not, Israel would strike back decisively.

After Katyushas hit northern Israel in late March, Israel did not retaliate and Syrian Foreign Minister Shara assured us that Hizbollah would halt such attacks. But the calm was short-lived. On March 31, Hizbollah fired rockets into northern Israel, claiming this was retaliation for an Israeli helicopter attack that had killed two Lebanese civilians the previous day. Peres continued to urge us to produce a diplomatic solution, while noting that the pressure on him to respond decisively with force was mounting by the hour.

Once again we intervened with Syria, cooling the situation temporarily. But on April 9, Hizbollah fired Katyushas again. Typically Katyushas caused little damage or injury, but this time thirty Israelis were wounded. Hizbollah justified its action with the specious claim that a Lebanese teenager had been killed by a mine which Israel must have planted.

Israeli patience had run out. Anger in northern Israel, combined with Peres's political need to show force, produced a major Israeli military operation in Lebanon— one the Israelis called "Operation Grapes of Wrath." Several precision attacks against Hizbollah offices in Beirut sent the message that Israel would go after the Hizbollah leadership and infrastructure. Lebanese power plants were also targeted, apparently to convince the Lebanese government that they had a stake in stopping Hizbollah. While not targeting Lebanese villages initially, continued Katyusha attacks into northern Israel soon led the IDF to pound the villages throughout southern Lebanon from which they thought Hizbollah was operating. Now Israel too was targeting civilian areas, and by April 15 an estimated 400,000 Lebanese had fled southern Lebanon. Still the Katyusha rocket attacks continued.

As in 1993, Secretary Christopher and I were in different locales during the crisis. He was with the President in the Far East. I was in Washington, trying over the phone to forge a reaffirmation of the 1993 understandings between Israel and Syria (in which Syria had produced the Hizbollah commitments). The Lebanese Prime Minister, Rafiq

Hariri, was desperate to stop the fighting; he traveled to France to try to enlist the help of President Jacques Chirac, who was publicly calling for Israel and Hizbollah to revert to the 1993 agreement that required each to avoid hitting civilian targets.

By April 16, I could report that in conversations with Shimon Peres and Farouk Shara I had made some headway. There was one basic gap at this point. Peres did not want the understanding to be verbal; he wanted Syria to assume responsibility for it. Shara was willing to accept a written document, provided the Lebanese government would also be a party to the agreement, and provided Syria and Lebanon did not have to agree in writing that Israel would be permitted to fire on Lebanese villages from which Hizbollah fire had originated. That right, of course, had been essential to the informal understanding of 1993.

While I saw ways to finesse this difference, the situation changed altogether on April 16, when Israel shelled a UN camp at Cana in southern Lebanon. Lebanese civilians had taken refuge at the camp. The IDF spotted Katyushas being launched from the camp and fired five 155-millimeter howitzer shells at the suspected site. Instead of hitting Hizbollah gunners, they hit a building housing several hundred Lebanese. Initial reports put the number killed at close to one hundred Lebanese civilians.

This was a human tragedy and a diplomatic disaster. With the Israeli election looming, we muted our criticism of the Israeli action, striving instead more visibly to produce a cease-fire. The President announced the Secretary would go to the Middle East within a few days and that I would be there overnight.

It turned out we would not be alone. The French Foreign Minister was on his way to see Asad before going to Lebanon and then Israel. The Russians announced that their Foreign Minister, Yevgeny Primakov, would be going as well.

Asad found these circumstances to his liking. Whereas the world had gone to Sharm al-Sheikh and he had not, now it seemed that the world was coming to him.

| SHUTTLING FOR A CEASE-FIRE |

Arriving in Tel Aviv on April 19, I met with the entire Israeli leadership, starting with the Foreign Minister Ehud Barak. The problem, I suggested to him, was that neither Hizbollah nor Asad saw themselves losing in the current situation, only the Lebanese did. Barak likewise was in no hurry to have the fighting come to an end; when I asked how he was going to stop the Katyushas, he had no answer but said Israel's enemies would have to pay more. What, I asked, would change the current reality? His answer was that Israel should offer to withdraw from Lebanon, provided there was calm. Hizbollah would lose its rationale for resistance and what would Syria do, argue that Israel should not withdraw? If so, that would reveal Syria's real agenda of preserving its control of Lebanon and its ability to use Lebanese-based attacks as a lever on Israel.

Much as he was to do three years later, Barak saw an offer to withdraw as a kind of trump card to play against the Syrians. While I was sympathetic, I pointed out that once Israel made the offer, the Syrians and Hizbollah might call for Israel to withdraw without delay or preconditions, citing UNSC resolution 425. Barak at this point was not prepared to do that, only to wait for calm before withdrawing.

I soon found that Prime Minister Peres also believed that Israel should withdraw after a period of calm. His argument was that a new cease-fire, even if based now on written understandings, was still likely to be temporary. Why not go to the source of the problem?

Here again I was sympathetic, but felt obliged—as I did so often—to explain the world as Asad saw it. Asad would not let Israel live easily in Lebanon so long as the Golan Heights remained occupied. This was his pressure point on Israel. "So let's remove it," Shimon responded.

I understood that the real point here was the Israeli government seeking leverage in the current situation. The Israeli leadership wanted Asad to know it had options, and that if he did not go along with a cease-fire Israel could accept, Israel might choose to withdraw—or at least publicly offer this as a way of putting pressure on him.

I did not mind pressuring Asad, but I thought this would reveal Israeli weakness more than strength. In such circumstances, I did not think it would impress Asad. Rather than produce a cease-fire, I thought it would delay it. After seeing Peres, I told Uri that. Privately, Uri agreed; however, he said, in the immediate aftermath of Cana there is no great desire to look like we can be pressured into a cease-fire now.

This was the setting in which Secretary Christopher arrived. I could see a way to forge the basic terms on the cease-fire. But I was afraid we were in for an extended shuttle. Neither the Israelis nor the Syrians was in a hurry.

When I informed Secretary Christopher of this, he wanted to know how could we build pressure on both sides at once. With the Israelis, it was our threatening to leave; for all the bravado, especially of Barak, the Israelis did not have an answer to the Katyushas. As for the Syrians, they did not want us to tell the world that the Israelis will get out if there is calm, but that the Syrians are blocking that to preserve their control of Lebanon.

The Secretary liked the idea of putting pressure on both while also getting to work on "our draft." Over the next seven days we shuttled back and forth between Asad, Peres, and the Lebanese, principally Prime Minister Hariri. The principal issues were how to describe Hizbollah and the SLA—the Southern Lebanese Army that Israel supported, armed, and financed in the security zone; how to preclude Hizbollah from using civilian areas as a base for staging attacks; and how to preserve an Israeli right of self-defense in the context of the cease-fire.

One way or another, I had dealt with each issue in the draft before we arrived. But with Asad going over the draft word by word in our meetings, it took a week to resolve every issue.

Hizbollah's use of civilian areas as a base for attacks was the most difficult one to resolve. If Hizbollah was going to use civilian areas as staging grounds for attacks, we told Asad, we could not prevent the Israelis from striking there; the 1993 understanding provided for the right to return fire—even if the source was from a village. If Asad could not accept a reference to that in the written agreement, then he must make it a violation of the agreement for Hizbollah to use civilian areas as staging grounds for attacks.

We went around and around on this one. I had proposed "staging grounds" as a term the Israelis could accept. Assuming the language had come from the Israelis, Asad made a point of not accepting it. But he did accept our logic on the point—with Secretary Christopher saying, "You are a logical man, if you want to say there can be no attacks on civilian areas, how can you deny the logic of Hizbollah not using civilian areas for launching attacks?"

Asad eventually suggested the phrase "launching grounds for attacks," but I feared that he did so to give Hizbollah more latitude, not less. "Staging" in our parlance referred to the preparation of attacks, not just their execution. Secretary Christopher and I illustrated our concern: If you plan the attack, prepare the materials for it, organize it in the village, move five hundred yards away from the village to fire the weapon and then move back, you are using the village as a launching ground. Understood?

Asad accepted the point, saying that launching grounds meant not using the villages as "staging grounds"! He then said that if "fighters on each side wanted to kill each other, that was okay," but they should not be killing or threatening civilians. That was the essential point.

True to every Middle Eastern negotiation, there was a last-minute problem. On April 26, after we had worked out all the language, Asad raised an issue he'd never mentioned before: the Israeli naval blockade of Lebanon. Unless this was lifted, he said, he would not accept the agreement.

Christopher had had enough. He had already been embarrassed three days earlier, when he arrived in Damascus and Asad had been "unable" to see him. What played around the world—and especially in the States—was the imagery of the Syrian dictator refusing to see the U.S. Secretary of State. American pundits were asking: How could we put up with this? And for some, this episode became an enduring image of Warren Christopher's term as Secretary of State. That is unfair, because the real story was that we had not gone to Damascus to see Asad but to stage a surprise, unannounced helicopter flight to Beirut as part of our shuttle diplomacy. Since Baker's time, all trips into Lebanon had been by daytime motorcades from Damascus. For security reasons, we needed to keep our plans unknown until the last minute. With our delegation assembling and the press contingent ready to leave the hotel, we learned that the U.S. commander in Europe had turned down approval of the helicopter flights, citing unspecified security reasons.

We were stuck in Damascus. It was too late to organize a motorcade to go to Beirut. At this point, we sought a meeting with Asad, and he proved to be "too busy." There is no question that Asad liked the suggestion that he would see the Secretary of State only on his terms. Secretary Christopher had every right to walk away at that point. He could have postured and made himself look good. However, this would have jeopardized the cease-fire and we would have ultimately had to go back to Asad to produce one. Meanwhile, we'd have to live with a situation in which half a million Lebanese refugees were forced out of southern Lebanon, but Israelis remained in shelters in the north. That situation would lead the Israelis back into Lebanon north of the security zone and subject them to a continuing guerrilla war. In these circumstances, Warren Christopher chose not to take the easy way out.*

But Christopher was also not prepared to take any further humiliation. When Asad raised the naval blockade, Christopher simply stood up, buttoned his coat and retrieved his briefcase, and said, "Mr. President, there is nothing more to talk about. I am leaving." Asad asked, "What is he doing, what is the problem?"—so surprised was he by Christopher's break with his normal methodical approach to negotiations.

I stood with Christopher and asked him what he wanted to do. He was clear: "Dennis, I am leaving. This is outrageous; after all this he raises a new condition. I will go out and explain publicly that he is not serious." Can I have a word with him first? I asked. Christopher nodded and I went around the table and stood with Asad. He acted genuinely perplexed. What was the big deal? I explained that the Secretary was not playing games. Either we finished now or he was leaving and would tell the world why. Asad relented, asking only would the Secretary or I raise the question of the naval blockade once the cease-fire was accepted. The Secretary was prepared for that. Asad had followed his pattern of testing to be sure he had gotten what he could, and we had an agreement.

Following his pattern, Binyamin Netanyahu, the leader of the opposition and can-

---

*When we arrived back in Israel late that night, I met an Israeli group led by Barak and he said the Secretary of State should not put up with such treatment. I snapped, "You are right. Are you prepared to have us leave the area? That's the right response. And, believe me, I am ready to have the Secretary go." Neither Barak nor Shahak nor Yatom nor Uri said a word.

didate for prime minister, criticized the agreement. Because (like the 1993 under-standing) it did not rule out Hizbollah attacks against the IDF in the security zone, Bibi claimed that the agreement legitimized Hizbollah's war against the IDF in Lebanon. It surely did. It did not solve the problem of Lebanon. It simply stopped the escalation of conflict and provided greater protection to civilians on each side of the border. The proof that Bibi did not have a better alternative is that once he was elected Prime Minister, he not only accepted the agreement but approved the negotiations on the terms for the monitoring group of the agreement. The monitoring group, consist-ing of the United States, France, Israel, Syria, and Lebanon, was essential for imple-menting the agreement—and the terms for it were finalized only after Netanyahu became Prime Minister.

11

Bibi Wins: Will Peace Lose?

As a candidate for prime minister, Shimon Peres won every poll and lost every election. This history combined with the residual effect of the four bombings in nine days made me uneasy in the two-month run-up to the May 29 election, in spite of Peres's consistent four-to-seven point lead in the polls. But there were other reasons for my concerns. On the eve of the mandated thirty-day campaign period, Peres visited Washington and we all but endorsed him, with the President lavishing praise on him and pledging additional American assistance. Clinton, a hero in Israel since the Rabin funeral, sought to transfer his own credibility to Peres, and in so doing "save" Labor and the peace process. Yet there was no boost for Peres when he returned to Israel; the polling numbers held steady, with Peres up by at most five points.

On top of this, Peres's campaign made no sense to me. Having lost so often, he distrusted his own instincts and shied away from drawing distinctions between himself and Binyamin Netanyahu. Additionally, to reassure the Israeli public on security, he could have made use of Ehud Barak, the ex-Chief of Staff of the military, but Barak was given almost no role in the campaign. Meanwhile, Netanyahu effectively ran away from his weaknesses. Whereas the Israeli public was willing to compromise in the pursuit of peace, Netanyahu's platform ruled out any compromise with the Palestinians, even as Netanyahu pledged to pursue peace effectively. How would he do so? Instead of challenging him on this question, Labor ran a campaign assuming victory was theirs provided they made no mistakes; Netanyahu ran a campaign by stoking the public's fears about security, stressing the need for a leader who could protect them.

President Clinton instinctively knew Peres was politically vulnerable. In their first meeting in March 1993, Clinton had told Rabin that if the Prime Minister ran risks for peace, the United States would act to minimize those risks. Now Rabin was dead, and the President felt a responsibility to his legacy and his successor. He saw Netanyahu as an unmistakable threat to that legacy and he would not sit idly by.

Interestingly enough, there was one issue on which Peres sought our help. During the campaign Netanyahu had been charging that Peres would divide Jerusalem. Through Uri, in mid-May Peres asked us if we could announce that we intended to move the U.S. embassy from Tel Aviv to Jerusalem. Uri felt this would have a dramatic effect in Israel, strengthening the confidence in what Peres was able to deliver and taking the steam out of Bibi's claims. Secretary Christopher was willing to support this if it was truly necessary for Peres to win, but Sandy Berger was not willing even to raise it with the President unless it would save Peres from certain defeat. Martin and I could not say that. Nonetheless, I argued for it on the grounds that it would put Peres over the top, and the Palestinians—given their fears of Bibi's election—would do little to oppose it. I am sure President Clinton would have done this if we had raised it with him, but we did not.*

Still, he tried to help in other ways. On the eve of the election, the President was preparing to give a speech and asked for an insert he could use on the Israeli elections. Mark Parris and I agreed that he could hint about the stakes of the election by saying that Israelis would be making fateful decisions when they voted—but no more. Both Mark and I underestimated President Clinton's determination to be explicit about the stakes, leading him essentially to say that Peres must be elected for the peace process to survive.

It is certainly what we collectively believed. But we were not voting, Israelis were. Israelis might read this as an illegitimate intrusion into their election, and recoil against being told whom to vote for. Moreover, if Bibi won, the last thing we wanted to do was create a self-fulfilling prophecy. I felt the President had crossed the line, but Uri called me to say it would help and Peres was very grateful.

Martin predicted in his final cable before the election that Peres would win 51 to 49. I worried that this was more wishful thinking than hard logic, but was relieved when he called me, shortly before the polls were to close in Israel, with good news: the

---

*Had Secretary Christopher felt strongly about this issue, he would have raised it with the President. Berger was the Deputy National Advisor at this time and accepted that Christopher had the lead on Middle East issues. In this instance, Berger did not want the President to look like he had backtracked on Jerusalem. We had resisted congressional efforts to move our Israeli embassy to Jerusalem. Sandy feared the imagery of "another Clinton reversal."

projections from the exit polls that would be announced in about fifteen minutes would be for a narrow Peres victory. There was a collective sigh of relief in both the White House and the State Department.

But it proved to be premature. With nearly half the votes actually counted, the Israeli television networks suddenly reversed themselves and now projected correctly that when all the votes were counted, Netanyahu would win by a razor-thin margin.

Our collective relief now became a collective dread. Shimon would be out. Bibi, who had opposed Oslo, would be in. While I suspected that he would hint at putting together a national unity government, it would merely be a tactic to get his own party and the other center-right parties to meet him on his terms as he worked to form a government.

The United States has a special relationship with Israel, enduring regardless of who was in office. We had some immediate work to do. We had to get the Arab world to hold their horses and not rush to judgment. We had to reassure but also remind Arafat that there were agreements and they would have to be honored by both sides. We would need to have a strategic discussion with Bibi about the peace process.

All these thoughts ran through my mind as I turned the television off, not wanting to watch the commentary. When Debbie came into the living room, she was amazed that I was not watching. My reaction: I know the outcome. I know I am going to have to deal with it. I will do so tomorrow. For now I am going to read a book. I was reading the David Herbert Donald biography of Abraham Lincoln and was in the middle of the chapter dealing with his depression. On a night when I believed the prospects for peace had been dealt a serious setback, this seemed especially appropriate.

| INITIAL PROBLEMS WITH BIBI AND REASSURING ARAFAT |

Whatever I was feeling, it was nowhere near what Martin was feeling. This was not going to be an easy time to serve as U.S. ambassador to Israel. Martin would go from enjoying an intimate relationship with Rabin and Peres to enduring a distant relationship with the new Prime Minister. Worse, the shared assumptions that had guided U.S. and Israeli policy would no longer exist—Martin on a daily basis would now be dealing with people who did not see the Palestinians as partners and who still could not publicly accept the principle of land for peace.

Martin suggested I call Bibi and congratulate him, and I did, telling him that I looked forward to engaging in an early strategic discussion on realities in the region, where he wanted to take Israel, and how America and Israel could best work together. Bibi was cool, and clearly in no hurry to have us work together. In the days ahead, he or those around him leaked that he was in no rush to see me because he associated me (correctly) with Oslo and Rabin and Peres.

The next day I called Arafat. I knew he was reeling. He had placed his bets on Oslo. Now, in his eyes, the process would stall or be reversed altogether. He spoke in a voice that was barely audible. I told him that we were not going to walk away from peace, and neither could any Israeli government. Netanyahu had inherited not only agreements but also relationships of one sort or another with eight Arab countries. He would not want to undo what he had inherited. That would be his failure and he could not afford to let that happen. Preserving what was clearly in Israel's interest would shape his behavior even as security would inevitably be his priority. Don't forget, I reminded Arafat, that Netanyahu had been elected because of four suicide bombings in nine days. We would have to ensure that he could not use security as an excuse not to pursue peace. That meant there must be no violence and the Palestinians must maintain their security cooperation with the Israelis. This is the way "you can prove to Netanyahu that you are a partner and he has a stake in the relationship."

By the end of my peroration, Arafat's voice was at least audible. He would do what I said.

| FIRST ENCOUNTERS WITH BIBI |

Netanyahu would take several weeks to form his government, and we scheduled his first visit to Washington for early July. I had hoped to see him beforehand, but he wanted no advance preparation; he and no one else was going to set the agenda for his initial meeting with President Clinton.

If I could not shape his approach to the President, I still hoped to affect the thinking of those around him on dealing with the Palestinians. So in mid-June I called Dore Gold, one of Bibi's advisors, and offered some thoughts on the Palestinians. Dore was originally from Connecticut and had made aliyah to Israel in 1975. An academic by training and experience, he had always been very reasonable in our previous discussions. This was no exception. Dore, I said, your boss is going to need to create a private channel to Arafat that is taken seriously and is trusted. You won't do this as a favor to Arafat; you will do this to have a private way to solve problems or preempt them. At some point, you may be able to use it to advance real understandings between you and the Palestinians. "Sooner or later," I concluded, "you will need this channel. If you don't set it up now, you won't have it when you need it."

Dore listened to me, and said he would pass it on to Bibi, but it would not be appropriate to set up such a channel until Bibi was installed as Prime Minister at the end of the month. Fine, I replied, but have someone you know communicate to Arafat now that Bibi will create such a channel—that alone will build Arafat's stake in good behavior. Dore took the advice seriously, but Netanyahu did not.

Bibi was overcome by hubris. He had surprised us all by winning: the Americans, the Israeli media, and even his own party leaders. Now he would prove to the world that he knew best how to deal with the Arabs and Palestinians.

Binyamin Netanyahu was no stranger to America. Benzion Netanyahu, his father, a historian and onetime political secretary to Vladimir Jabotinsky—the leader of the Revisionist movement in Israel—chose to come to the States in 1962 and taught at Dropsie College of Hebrew and Cognate Learning in Philadelphia. Bibi, a teenager at the time, went to high school in a Philadelphia suburb. He returned to Israel to do his compulsory army service in 1967 and subsequently joined the elite commando unit Sayeret Matkal, a unit his older brother Yonatan (Yoni) would later command. But Bibi, having been Americanized, returned to attend MIT, and some believe he considered staying in the States. His brother Yoni was the commander of the daring Israeli raid at Entebbe in 1976. An Israeli airliner was hijacked and flown to Entebbe, Uganda, with over a hundred Israelis held hostage. Their rescue was a stunning achievement and restored the spirit of the country—a spirit that had been largely sapped by the 1973 war. Yoni was the only member of the Israeli forces killed in the raid.

Bibi became committed to preserving Yoni's memory. Yoni had been destined in Bibi's eyes—and in the eyes of many in Israel—to be a leader of the country. I always suspected that Bibi felt he had a responsibility to fulfill his brother's legacy—though once when we were chatting privately in his office late one night he disparaged the "psychobabble" about how he was trying to measure up to his brother.

His own political rise came about in no small part as a result of his eloquent public defenses of Israel first at the United Nations in the mid-1980s where Israel was constantly under assault; then at the Madrid conference, where Bibi was the Israeli face seen by the world, effectively parrying the Palestinian spokeswoman, Hanan Ashrawi. Moshe Arens, the Israeli Foreign Minister in the Shamir government, made Bibi the Deputy Foreign Minister, giving him a base in the government. But all along he was assiduously working to develop his support in the key bastions of the Likud Party. With the defeat of Yitzhak Shamir, Bibi seized on the need for new blood to run the party and defeated all his rivals in becoming the Likud Party leader in March of 1993—just a few months before the conclusion of the Oslo DOP, which he bitterly opposed.

Now, however, he was coming to Washington not as the leader of the opposition but as the Prime Minister of Israel—and he would teach us the realities of the Middle East, or at least that is what he thought. In the meeting with President Clinton, Netanyahu was nearly insufferable, lecturing and telling us how to deal with the Arabs. He would respect the Oslo agreement because a democratically elected government in Israel had adopted it, but there would have to be adjustments and new negotiations over part of it. Hebron, the only city in the West Bank from which there had been no Israeli redeployment following the Interim Agreement, was an example of where the terms would have to be modified.

After Netanyahu was gone, President Clinton observed: "He thinks he is the superpower and we are here to do whatever he requires." No one on our side disagreed with that assessment.

Following this visit and discussions between Secretary Christopher and Netanyahu, I traveled to the region to brief Arab leaders—Mubarak, Asad, and Arafat. As I set out, I had two real purposes with Asad and Arafat: First, I needed to persuade Asad to continue negotiations with Israel. He would have one question. Will Netanyahu reaffirm "the Rabin pocket"? If yes, he would proceed. If not, he would be unwilling to proceed for fear he would never get it again. Netanyahu had written a letter to President Clinton saying he would not reaffirm the Rabin pocket commitment "at this time." We seized on the subtle qualifier "at this time" to keep open the possibility that he might reaffirm at a later point.

Second, I hoped to urge Arafat to continue to perform on security. In the period following the four bombings in nine days, Arafat had directed the most severe crackdown on Hamas and Islamic Jihad since the advent of Oslo. He had replaced many of the imams in mosques and arrested many of the leaders even of the military wing of Hamas. He had permitted real security cooperation with the Shin Bet to continue. As I had asked, he was not giving Bibi an excuse on security.

My visits with both Asad and Arafat were successful, but Netanyahu—believing that his policy of talking tough but not doing anything was working—squandered what I delivered.

I was able to use Asad's desire to develop the U.S.-Syrian relationship—and our ability to point to ongoing peace negotiations as a means to blunt congressional efforts to impede it—to secure a pledge to "resume talks before the [U.S.] election in Maryland [meaning at Wye] on the Syrian track with the participation of the United States and with acceptance of what has been achieved on the Syrian track." This formula did not necessarily include the Rabin pocket commitment, which had been given to us, not to him.

When I described the formula Asad had accepted to Bibi—and then made a case for accepting it on the grounds that it was hardly demanding given Asad's history—Bibi demurred. He read Asad's willingness to be flexible on the formula as an indication that he (Netanyahu) could negotiate this further.

Prime Minister, I replied, "there is an opening with Asad, but it will close. Don't expect that he will be interested in negotiating the terms of the resumption of negotiations. If we don't come back immediately with a yes, you will lose the opportunity to resume the negotiations without signing up to [the] Rabin [pocket]."

Bibi said he would think about it and come back to me. It took several weeks for him to do so, and then it was with a modified formula that Asad predictably rejected. The moment between the Israelis and Syrians was lost, but, ironically, something else was gained.

Bibi and his colleagues became convinced that I was a very effective negotiator with the Arabs, and suddenly there were stories in the press about Bibi's capacity to work effectively with me. Some of my hard-line critics in America heard that Bibi had confidence in my ability to conduct diplomacy.

In the zero-sum world of Arab-Israeli diplomacy, what I gained in Israel, I would lose among the Arabs. One could not make both sides happy at the same time. For me that was never the issue; the issue was delivering, and I could see it would now be increasingly difficult to do so on the Syrian track.

With Arafat, I had some leverage, but I could see it was diminishing, as he grew loath to make arrests and cooperate with Israeli security forces in an atmosphere in which there was no prospect of political movement and there were unilateral Israeli steps—announcements about new settlement activity, demolitions of Palestinian houses, new pressure against Palestinians in Jerusalem—that embarrassed him before his public.

I mentioned this to Netanyahu, stressing the consequences for security. "You have to begin to talk to them," I said, "even if in private, about how you will proceed: what you can do soon, what you can't, what you need from them, what you can do that will make a difference for them, and what you can each do to make life easier, not harder, for the other." At this point, he agreed to create a private channel between Dore Gold and Abu Mazen.* Initially, it gave rise to an effort to produce a nonpaper about the resumption of negotiations. Over the last week of August and the first week of September 1996, the effort became intense, with me working through the night of September 3 on the phone with Arafat trying to work out the text, which became the basis for Arafat and Netanyahu's first meeting on September 4. The content was scaled back—giving up the effort to address Hebron, economic issues, and the resumption of the permanent status talks—and settling instead for establishing a steering committee to handle talks on all the issues that grew out of the Interim Agreement (security cooperation, the Gaza airport, safe passage between the West Bank and Gaza, etc.).

---

*Terje Larsen was instrumental in facilitating and hosting their meetings.

Having moved toward an understanding, Netanyahu then drew back, prompted no doubt by his need to placate his right-wing base. This was a consistent pattern in his tenure as Prime Minister. Whenever he sought to reach out to the Palestinians, he would seek to offset his action with steps that would appease his right-wing constituency. Yet it was precisely those steps that would inflame Palestinian opinion.

In this case, the situation became more explosive because of conciliatory steps the Palestinians had taken as a result of the Abu Mazen–Dore Gold talks. Proving that direct talks don't always yield greater understanding, the Palestinians agreed to close down two offices in East Jerusalem. Gold had explained that this was very important to Netanyahu; in return for closing the offices, Abu Mazen understood that the Israelis would move on Hebron, lift the limitations on Palestinian workers coming into Israel, and resume the negotiations on permanent status. But what Gold meant by moving on these issues was not to act immediately on them, but rather to be open to discussing them. Unfortunately, as I soon found out, Abu Mazen had sold closing the offices— which appeared as a symbolic retreat on East Jerusalem—to Arafat on the basis of settling Hebron, permitting Palestinian workers into Israel, and launching permanent status talks. Adding insult to injury for Abu Mazen were two Israeli steps that came almost immediately after the closing of the offices: the Israelis demolished a Palestinian community center in East Jerusalem and announced the building of fifteen hundred new settlement units in the West Bank.

It was not enough for Bibi to have the trophy of the offices in East Jerusalem. As he prepared for negotiations—and indeed was naming a team for them—he would cover himself further with the right. But this came at a time when nothing had been delivered to the Palestinians. Dore was caught unawares, but Abu Mazen was embarrassed and, in his words, "burned"; not surprisingly, he hardened his position, losing interest in trying to develop a broader understanding at this point. For his part, Arafat "supported" the calling of a strike in East Jerusalem to protest the Israeli actions. At this point, Mohammad Dahlan, the Palestinian security chief in Gaza, told our security liaison to him that the mood on the streets was very bad, and would spin out of control unless the Palestinians had something positive to point to soon. Instead of something positive, however, they got the opening of the Hasmonean Tunnel in Jerusalem in late September.

| THE HASMONEAN TUNNEL IS OPENED, VIOLENCE ERUPTS, AND A SUMMIT IN WASHINGTON |

After the 1967 war, Israel began extensive excavations in the Old City of Jerusalem. For a people steeped in biblical history, archaeological digs were a means of uncovering the past and confirming it, or at least describing it more accurately. Excavations around the Wailing Wall—a retaining wall from the era of the Second Jewish Temple—revealed life in the period of Roman rule of Jerusalem. Underground, one could literally go back in time, seeing the remnants of houses, storage areas, baths, and wells.

While not excavating under the Haram al-Sharif—known to the Islamic world as the Noble Sanctuary, the third-holiest shrine to Muslims—an underground walkway was dug along the Western Wall, and became known as the Western Wall tunnel. It could be entered from the plaza created in front of the Wailing Wall, the visible part of the Western Wall, and extends nearly four times as long (about 480 meters) and runs under the Muslim Quarter of the Old City. The Western Wall tunnel, really a pedestrian walkway, is narrow and controlled by Israel, which permitted entry only in guided tours. Apart from getting a better visual picture of life in ancient Jerusalem and a better understanding of where the Temple was, there is one point along the walkway identified as the location closest to the holy of holies, where the Ark of the Covenant—the Ten Commandments—was kept.

A different tunnel, the Hasmonean Tunnel, is about 80 meters long and lies outside the perimeter of the Haram al-Sharif, what the Jews call the Temple Mount (Har Ha Bayit). It served as an aqueduct in the Hasmonean period of Jerusalem. Excavated by the Israeli Religious Affairs Ministry in 1987 and then connected to the Western Wall tunnel, Israel's Religious Affairs Ministry sought to make it possible to enter the Western Wall tunnel, walk through the Hasmonean Tunnel, and exit in the Muslim Quarter of the Old City. But the Waqf—the Muslim Religious Authority—opposed all such plans, for creating an exit would require the tearing down of a wall under the Monastery of the Sisters of Zion, blocking access to an underground pool known as the Starothyon Pool. For nine years beginning in 1987, every time the Religious Affairs Ministry argued for breaking down the wall, the Waqf—seeing this move as establishing a precedent for further Israeli actions to alter the character of the Muslim Quarter—would set off disturbances until Israeli governments heeded the advice of their security officials not to "open" the tunnel.

But in the middle of the night on September 24, 1996, that advice was no longer heeded. The Israelis unsealed the walled gate. The next morning as Palestinians erupted in protest, Bibi claimed that the mayor of Jerusalem, Ehud Olmert, had had it done. He claimed it was a nonevent. If that was so, I asked him, why was it done in the dead of night by a contingent of IDF soldiers?

The reason was self-evident. Jewish activity in the area around the Haram al-Sharif was enormously sensitive, conjuring up Palestinian fears of a perceived Jewish desire to rebuild the Temple. Historically, these fears had been repeatedly exploited and manipulated. In 1928, Arabs rioted when Jews created a screen in front of the Wailing

Wall that was portrayed as the beginning of a synagogue—something that might, it was claimed, lead to the effort to resurrect the Temple in place of the Al-Aqsa Mosque and the Dome of the Rock. In 1929, the riots that escalated and led to the massacre in Hebron were sparked by continuing tensions between Muslims and Jews over access to the holy sites.

Predictably, the "opening" of the tunnel was again manipulated. Though the unsealed gate was not near the foundations of either mosque—and disconnected from any load-bearing structures—it was quickly portrayed as an action that would endanger the mosques on the surface. History repeated itself, word spread that the mosques were at risk, and riots began and spread throughout the West Bank. Ever prone to create and spread new mythologies, Arafat added fuel to the fire, talking of the grave threat to the Haram.

Was he trying to exploit an obvious misstep by Bibi to get the international community on his side? Was he tired of being taken for granted by Bibi and determined to demonstrate that he could create real trouble for this Prime Minister? Was he trying to ride a wave of Palestinian anger? Was he genuinely angered and fearful that the move revealed a new Bibi effort to transform the Muslim Quarter? Whatever the reason, Arafat's remarks fueled the violence, and he then disclaimed any responsibility for stopping it on the grounds that he was not permitted by the Israelis to do anything in Jerusalem.

Netanyahu, meanwhile, was traveling to Europe and rushed back to Israel to face a public relations disaster. The Palestinian rioting got worse; Israel responded with force, leaving scores of Palestinians dead and hundreds wounded. Israel, too, suffered casualties. However, when rioting Palestinians engulfed an Israeli platoon at Joseph's Tomb in Nablus, Netanyahu threatened a massive Israeli military reprisal, and Palestinian security officials managed to ease the situation, but not before fifteen Israeli soldiers were killed, with Palestinian police siding with the rioters, some firing at Israeli soldiers.

Nothing like this had happened since the beginning of the Oslo process. Both Secretary Christopher and I had been talking daily with Arafat and Netanyahu, trying in vain to get the situation under control. But the violence seemed to have a life of its own, with Arafat and those around him claiming that it was likely to be stopped only with the closing of the tunnel. Netanyahu, however, would not close the tunnel lest he look like he was backing down in the face of violence on Jerusalem, implying that Israel must consult with the Palestinians before it could act in Jerusalem. This would be an admission from a man who won office by accusing his opponent of being ready to divide Jerusalem, that Israel was not sovereign in the city.

Netanyahu was now caught in a trap of his own making. Arafat saw the trap as an opening to gain something on Jerusalem, arguing he needed an Israeli concession if there was any hope of restoring order.

After a week of escalating violence, we needed to provide each side with an out. I believed that only a dramatic step would suffice. I urged the Secretary to call the leaders to Washington for a summit with President Clinton.

Once again, the Secretary felt we must make the case directly to the President, and again his staff was reluctant to go along with what we were proposing. With five weeks to go before the presidential election, and President Clinton up by a comfortable margin in the polls over Senator Dole, why risk a giant failure now?

In the end, we made the case to the President; once again, he asked me: Was it necessary to intervene now and in this way? Was there really no alternative? And once again, I told him there was no other way. My fear was that Netanyahu would come under increasing pressure to put down the riots with overwhelming military force—and as he did so the risk of suicide bombings would increase and the ability to pursue peace would be fundamentally shaken. The President was convinced, and he agreed to call the leaders to Washington.

| THE WASHINGTON SUMMIT: SEPTEMBER 30–OCTOBER 2, 1996 |

The summit itself posed two problems. One was easy, and involved inviting the key players to come. I did not anticipate any difficulty with either Arafat or Netanyahu coming. I felt we should also invite King Hussein and President Mubarak in order to symbolize that the peace process was a regional effort. While the King was prepared to come, Mubarak was only prepared to send his foreign minister, explaining that he was concerned about what would come out of such a meeting.

So was I. That was my second problem. What did we hope to produce? I knew that Arafat would want something he could point to, preferably on Jerusalem. I knew that Netanyahu would need to show he had not rewarded the violence. These were seemingly irreconcilable desires. Was there a way to square the circle?

I thought there might be. Outside of his right-wing base, Netanyahu was receiving scathing criticism as the rest of the country saw the move on the Hasmonean Tunnel as irresponsible. Though loath to cave in to our pressure, he would want to show the mainstream of Israel that he had not destroyed Oslo. With that in mind, I thought that he would be open to several proposals or outcomes:

—resumption of intensive negotiations on Hebron;
—designation of a target date for the redeployment in Hebron;

—permission for the Waqf to excavate in what the Israelis referred to as the Solomon Stables area adjacent to the Al-Aqsa Mosque (an idea he had raised with me earlier in the week).

Taken together, these three items certainly gave Arafat concessions to show his public, while Bibi would not have to close the tunnel. I was convinced this would get us beyond the crisis. However, in forty hours of negotiation and meetings, we were able to produce only one of the three outcomes: the resumption of intensive, continuous negotiations on Hebron.

What went wrong? To put it simply, Netanyahu was not willing to concede anything. Although he was freshly elected and re-election was far into the future, he was riveted on his political base rather than on the needs of the process. He might traffic in the symbols of change, meeting privately with Arafat twice and agreeing to continuous negotiations. But he would not accept anything on the tunnel, though King Hussein had come up with a "face-saver"—suspending the opening of the tunnel until archaeologists could prove it posed no danger to the structural integrity of the mosques. He would not accept any new oversight for the Waqf in the Solomon Stables area, although he had proposed it before coming to Washington. He would not go along with a target date on Hebron redeployment, although he pledged to resolve the issue quickly. His stubbornness incurred Clinton's anger, triggering a private tirade he could obviously hear from the adjacent room; nevertheless, Bibi would publicly come to the President's defense in response to the charge that Clinton was conducting a "photo op" foreign policy: "I would ask you, what did you want him to do? We had a major rupture. He was in contact with both me and with Arafat. He offered his good offices and we both agreed that he could perform an important service by giving us a venue, a locale, and by facilitating the talks between us. He did exactly that."

It was vintage Bibi Netanyahu. He would try to have it both ways. He would be stung (over lunch the last day of the summit) by an eloquent, emotional, and personal attack from King Hussein, who accused him of threatening the hopes for peace of Arabs and Israelis alike with his immaturity and poor judgment. He would respond by promising to resolve Hebron through negotiations now, moving to a couch with Arafat and telling the Chairman "we can surprise the world, we can reach agreement quickly."

Bibi needed to return to Israel with evidence that the summit was a success—no concessions made but the peace process saved nonetheless. Having stood up to the pressures in Washington, he would then be able to compromise. There was only one problem with this strategy: Arafat now knew that Bibi was the desperate one. If they were to "surprise the world," it would be Bibi who would make the concessions, not him.

All this would become clear to me only belatedly as I set out three days after the summit to help with the negotiations over Hebron. Little did I know that the U.S. role in the Israeli-Palestinian negotiations was about to be transformed. Rabin had wanted us in the background, helping but not negotiating for the parties. With Netanyahu in the Prime Minister's office, I was to become a full-time mediator. No longer would we be in the business of helping the parties, easing their efforts, reassuring them at critical moments, bringing them together at times, and pressuring when necessary to get them to cross thresholds and make decisions. I was about to become a broker, negotiating with each side, finding out what they could do, drafting for them, and brokering the compromises.

12

The Endless Hebron Shuttle

Why had Hebron become the focal point for resolving the violence triggered by the opening of the Hasmonean Tunnel? Hebron was the only city in the West Bank from which the Israelis had not redeployed. From the outset, Netanyahu expressed reluctance about proceeding with the Hebron redeployment, and it was clear that his colleagues in the government opposed doing so. Hebron was a test case: Arafat wanted to know that Netanyahu would not walk away from Oslo, and many in Bibi's right-wing base wanted to see that he would. To be sure, redeployment from Hebron was not a simple matter, even if it was required by the Interim Agreement. In fact, had Hebron been like all other West Bank cities, Peres's government would have carried out the redeployment. But it did not.

Hebron, with 400 Israeli settlers living in the heart of the city, presented unique problems. No other Palestinian city in the West Bank or Gaza had an Israeli community living within it. The Interim Agreement acknowledged this by dividing Hebron—a city of roughly 140,000 people—into two sectors: H-1 and H-2, the latter including the small Jewish community. H-1 would constitute about 80 percent of the city's territory; H-2 would have a population of approximately 20,000 Palestinians. Redeployment meant that the Israeli military would move out of H-1; however, because of the Israelis living in H-2, there would be no departure from H-2, at least during the interim period.

The loss of fifteen soldiers at Joseph's Tomb in Nablus as well as the anger over the violence triggered by the opening of the Hasmonean Tunnel—including the role Palestinian policemen played in the violence—put a premium on instituting special security arrangements for Hebron. When I arrived in Israel three days after the summit for initial meetings with Netanyahu and Arafat, it was easy to see two conflicting approaches to the impending negotiations. From Netanyahu, I heard that the IDF would need freedom of action or the right of reentry into H-1 after redeployment; buffer zones would be needed between H-1 and H-2, manned by Palestinian police armed with pistols, not rifles; joint patrols must operate in H-1, the Palestinian zone, but not in H-2, the Israeli zone—there only the IDF would be present. Other limitations would be imposed on the Palestinians in both security and civil matters to ease the lives of those Israelis living in H-2.

Not surprisingly, Arafat and the Palestinians thought this Israeli redeployment should be no different from any other. In their view, Palestinian rights in H-1 should be as unfettered as in any other city—or A area—in the West Bank, and that H-2 should be like any other B area, meaning that Palestinians would have responsibility for civil affairs and public order while Israel would retain overriding responsibility for security. The Palestinians pointed to the general guidelines for negotiations on Hebron in the Interim Agreement, and Arafat, Abu Mazen, and Saeb Erekat all insisted that Israel could not now modify the terms: special security provisions were acceptable, provided they did not alter the character of the agreement.

From these meetings, then, I could see that the challenge was to construct special security provisions that could satisfy the two parties and honor the Interim Agreement. This would not be a simple task, and it was made all the harder by the two sides' different views on what the Interim Agreement did and did not require.

But the substance was not my only concern. The process and structure of the negotiations as planned by each side was also unwieldy. Our opening session at Erez* placed two large delegations on each side, giving speeches, with me heading a small American team at one end of the table. English was the language of the talks. But the leader of the Israeli delegation, Dan Shomron, a retired general, spoke little English or Arabic. Saeb Erekat, the leader of the Palestinian delegation, was a fluent English speaker but knew little Hebrew. This produced an ironic scene: Dan Shomron would speak in Hebrew; Jibril Rajoub, the head of the Palestinian Security Organization (PSO) in the West Bank, having learned Hebrew during his eighteen years in Israeli jails, translated Shomron's Hebrew to Arabic, and Gamal translated Rajoub's Arabic to English. Clearly, we would have to create a different format for talks to make real progress.

---

*Erez was at the border separating Israel from Gaza.

Without that, we would have drawn-out negotiations with no results—a prescription for a resumption of the violence. Adding to my sense of urgency was Bibi's desire to get this done fast—in fact, to surprise the world. Because the Prime Minister's residence was undergoing renovation, the two of us met alone in his Jerusalem apartment shortly after the first round of the negotiations. I explained that the current negotiating setup would guarantee a long negotiation, and Bibi's response was, "Let's finish by this weekend. We can have a secret meeting with Arafat at Martin's residence and then a public meeting to seal the deal."

Netanyahu, too, was anxious for rapid movement to prove he could achieve something and not just produce a mess. But he had not thought through how to meet his needs and those of the Palestinians at the same time. Absent that, I was against a Netanyahu-Arafat meeting now, believing also that Arafat would see Netanyahu's eagerness and almost certainly reject ideas that might work at the right moment—and I wanted to be sure we reserved those ideas for later.

Bibi took the point, but basically looked to me to figure out how to square the circle. I decided that now was the time to create a back channel, especially to explore confidentially possible ways to meet both sides' concerns. My candidates for this channel were Amnon Shahak and Abu Mazen. I had several reasons for this pairing: Amnon, the Chief of Staff of the military, was known to the Palestinians, respected as a problem-solver, and willing to level with me on what he could and could not do. For his part, Abu Mazen, the putative number two in the PLO, was perceived as serious and moderate by the Israelis, even by Netanyahu, who generally trusted no one from Arafat on down.

I knew that if I raised Amnon with Bibi first, he would probably suggest someone closer to him. However, were I to get Arafat's okay for a Shahak–Abu Mazen channel first and call Bibi from Arafat's office with his agreement, I reasoned that Bibi would say yes and I would have a channel.

Of course, I had to do this without giving away the existence of the back channel. Moreover, I wanted to be a part of the back channel, even while the "front channel" of public negotiations was ongoing. Everyone expected me to take part in those and obviously I could not be in two places at the same time. My solution was to take part in the public negotiations, but leave "to brief the leaders" every few days—in truth, to work with Amnon and Abu Mazen. I hoped to have conceptual understandings emerge from the back channel, get the leaders to endorse them, and give guidance accordingly to the front channel.

At this stage, naturally, this was all theory. I had no back channel, and I could not simply go through the motions in the front channel. The front channel was to meet for its second round in Taba, Egypt, and I told both sides I would stay for twenty-four hours and then leave to brief the leaders. I did work through the night in Taba, taking part in private meetings with Shomron and Erekat, private meetings between the two security people—General Shaul Mofaz* and Jibril Rajoub—and the plenary session with the delegations. Rather than focusing on their differences, I chose to summarize what I thought were six possible points of understanding that could create a baseline for the ongoing talks:

—Solutions must remain within the confines of the Hebron guidelines in the Interim Agreement;
—Hebron is a special case;
—Special support systems of cooperation, like, for example, Saeb Erekat's idea of a twenty-four-hour-a-day joint operations center to deal with any security threat, would be necessary;
—Special security provisions would probably be necessary for the Israeli citizens in H-2;
—Any such special provisions should be temporary;
—And if the Palestinians did not act against a security threat coming from H-1 into H-2, the Israelis would.

I knew the last point was controversial, but Rajoub, the head of the Palestinian Security Organization (PSO) in the West Bank, had acknowledged it in the discussions with Mofaz, and my purpose was to highlight areas of convergence. Saeb liked the summary, but wanted no intimation that the last point indicated Palestinian acceptance of an Israeli right to reenter H-1. This, of course, was the key point for the Israelis and the nub of the problem as the negotiations began. Before leaving, Saeb ironically told me that we needed a different format for more informal and intensive discussions. I agreed without revealing that I was about to go see his boss and suggest a back channel.

| THE GOOD NEWS, AND BAD NEWS ON A BACK CHANNEL |

While I had not previewed my idea of the Shahak–Abu Mazen back channel with Bibi, I had mentioned that Amnon had a lot of credibility with Arafat—not because he

---

*Shaul Mofaz at this time was a Major General in the IDF in charge of planning. Whoever headed the planning branch assumed a leading role in the negotiations with Israel's neighbors. Uzi Dayan had this position before Mofaz, and Shlomo Yanai had it afterward.

was soft, but because he was straight. Now, with Arafat, I explained that the initial discussions in Taba promised no swift breakthrough, and that the only way to make progress was through a back channel, suggesting that General Amnon Shahak meet with Abu Mazen. "You know Amnon and trust him," and Arafat nodded, saying, "Amnon does not exaggerate." (By this he meant that if Amnon said Israel needed something for security reasons, it was because he believed it, not because he was seeking to gain advantage over the Palestinians.*)

Arafat said he would support this channel and any discussion in it. I suggested that I call Bibi and tell him that you agree to such a channel and see if he would as well. Arafat agreed, and I got Bibi on the phone, telling him I was with Arafat and had suggested a back channel starting today involving Amnon Shahak and Abu Mazen. Arafat had agreed, would he? Bibi's answer was "absolutely," and he asked if I could put Arafat on the phone.

Bibi proceeded to tell Arafat that the two should work to conclude an agreement quickly and that it was possible to do so. Arafat replied, "We hope so"—a standard response which committed him to nothing. However, his pleasure over Bibi's quick agreement was unmistakable. He was plainly ready to negotiate.

But that didn't mean he was ready to make a deal. No sooner had he agreed to a meeting in three hours' time than he told me that he would like Abu Mazen to be joined by Yasser Abed Rabbo, a supporter of Oslo but one known for lambasting the Israelis in public on a regular basis. Though I had my doubts that Abed Rabbo would be constructive in a back channel, I was loath to reject him lest Arafat grow suspicious of my motives for the channel. The most I was willing to do was put Arafat on notice that Abed Rabbo had to be constructive or it would be clear who was responsible for the failure of such a channel. Arafat told me I need not worry about Abed Rabbo, and that proved to be the case throughout the Hebron negotiations.

The meeting held at Martin's residence in Herzliya (Martin, of course, was in Taba with the rest of our delegation) was very much what I had expected it to be. Shahak and Abu Mazen arrived within minutes of each other and greeted each other warmly. To signal that this was their channel, I suggested at the outset that they meet without me and ask me to join them when they had something to report. Meanwhile, I called Secretary Christopher at the State Department and briefed him on the new back channel for the first time.

After meeting for just over an hour, Abed Rabbo asked me to join them, and Am-

---

*Arafat had been impressed with Amnon from their first meeting in Tunis after the killings in the Ibrahimi Mosque.

non summarized their discussion. Amnon explained that they had dealt principally with the issue of Israeli reentry into H-1 in the case of violence, an issue both sides called "hot pursuit." Despite Palestinian fears, he went on, Israel was not looking to go back into H-1, and Abu Mazen nodded, saying that Amnon had "reassured us that this is not Israel's intent." Amnon then pointed out Israel's fears: Palestinians in H-1 would shoot at Israelis in H-2, or carry out attacks from H-1 into H-2, and the Palestinian police would be unable to prevent this. If so, did the Palestinians accept that the IDF would enter H-1? Amnon said Abu Mazen had "reassured me about this," and Abu Mazen said, "We understand if there is a threat and we cannot handle it, they will."

Both were pleased with the discussion, and I told them it had served the purpose I had hoped it would: namely, to provide a conceptual understanding on how to solve the issue of hot pursuit. At this point, Amnon had to leave, but Abu Mazen, Abed Rabbo, and I spoke for a while longer, focusing on how to translate this conceptual understanding on hot pursuit into a formal agreement. I pointed out that there were several provisions in the Interim Agreement that allowed the Israelis to respond to threats of the sort that might come out of H-1. Both Abu Mazen and Abed Rabbo suggested that we simply refer to those provisions, rather than make explicit reference to Israeli reentry. I told them I would draft several formulations; the right of reentry would not be explicitly mentioned, but the articles in the Interim Agreement that justified Israeli responses to threats in Hebron would be specifically enumerated.

Abu Mazen and Abed Rabbo agreed with this approach—as did Bibi when I mentioned it to him later that day—and that same day I did draft four different formulas. These should have resolved the issue, but, as a harbinger of things to come, our conceptual understanding fell apart as it was taken back to the leaders. Abu Mazen could not persuade Arafat over Saeb Erekat's opposition: Saeb wanted all provisions for responses to threats to be mutual, not limited only to Israel. For his part, Bibi now insisted that Israel's right to respond be mentioned specifically—referring to articles in the Interim Agreement was insufficient because the right would only be implicit and he wanted it spelled out explicitly.

I had hoped that once we broke through on the "hot pursuit," everything else would fall into place. But I was wrong. We were only in the early stages of a negotiation. One lesson here is that conceptual understandings may be important but their translation into textual agreement is rarely automatic or immediate. But, in truth, at this stage neither side had a great incentive to reach agreement on the hot pursuit issue when they might yet want to trade off the language addressing it for something else later on the security or civil issues.

Ironically, the relative success of the back channel meeting prompted both leaders to bring the two participants into the front channel. Rather than seeing value in preserving a quiet channel, they both argued that the presence of Shahak and Abu Mazen would make the front channel negotiations successful.

Their presence did not have that effect. On the contrary, they too got bogged down in discussions on the security and civil issues. Over the following week, we met and worked through the nights, debating endlessly over what Israel could and could not do in terms of protecting Israelis; whether the Palestinian police would have to notify the Israelis of their activities, at least in the area between H-1 and H-2; whether the two sides would carry equal weaponry in the joint mobile units (JMUs) or joint patrols, as the Palestinians wanted, or unequal, as the Israelis wanted; whether the Palestinian police could carry rifles in H-1—the ostensible area of their control, and so forth.

Typically, Saeb Erekat would argue that the Israelis were trying to transform Hebron into two different cities, which was unacceptable. Yitzik Molho, Bibi's lawyer and confidant, would challenge him. Amnon would try for practical "fixes"; Saeb would resist; Yitzik would resist Saeb; and Abu Mazen would opt out. When I tried to separate out the security people because they seemed more inclined to work out practical solutions, Saeb blocked this as well.

At one point, Jibril Rajoub growled that they could deal with the security issues, including the joint patrols and the arming in them, if only "our American" would just leave the room; their American was Saeb.

Who was Saeb Erekat? A professor at Bir Zeit University in the West Bank, he had done his undergraduate work at San Francisco State University and had spent a great deal of time in America. He spoke colloquial English, complete with American slang, and had extended family in the United States (hence the jibe about "our American"). He lived in Jericho but had family in Abu Dis, just outside of Jerusalem. He was articulate and prone to speechifying, whether on TV or in negotiations. As part of the Palestinian delegation that met with Secretary Baker after the Gulf War in 1991, for example, Saeb made speeches about Palestinian suffering, Israeli abuses, "President Arafat's" needs, and American responsibilities, prompting Secretary Baker to judge him a "blowhard." His reputation was cemented in Baker's mind when, at the opening of the Madrid conference, he arrived with a black-and-white checkered kaffiyeh, an Arab headdress, draped around his shoulders—no doubt seeking to symbolize the absent Chairman's presence.

Among Israelis and even some of his Palestinian colleagues, he earned the moniker

"Mr. CNN." He was effective on television, and seemed to relish the role of being the Palestinian spokesman.

While Abu Ala negotiated the Interim Agreement, Saeb had been responsible for drafting it with Yoel Singer, and from then on could cite it chapter and verse. He was adept at showing Arafat how to use the agreement to highlight Israeli "violations." Naturally, he did not point out the Palestinian failings.

Saeb had no political base outside of Arafat, but that was more than enough. Belatedly, I came to realize that he could talk Arafat out of any understanding negotiated by other Palestinians—at least before Arafat was ready to do a deal.

That is what happened in the early stages of the Hebron negotiations. Saeb thwarted my attempt to finalize the Shahak–Abu Mazen conceptual understanding on hot pursuit, and blocked an understanding that would have resolved many of the key security issues.

After two weeks of seeing progress undone, I decided it was time for me to leave the area lest my presence be taken for granted. At an afternoon press conference on October 21, I announced I would be returning to Washington.

Both sides were put on the defensive by my announcement. They each sought to blame the other for the lack of progress. In answer to questions, I said I was not in the business of "fixing blame, my focus was on fixing problems." My plane did not leave until midnight and shortly after my announcement I agreed to host a meeting on the civil issues with Abu Mazen, Yasser Abed Rabbo, and Jamil Tarifi on the Palestinian side and on the Israeli side Major General Oren Shahor, the Israeli responsible for the civil administration of the territories.

We met at six-thirty in my room at the Tel Aviv Holiday Inn. I suggested we all try a different approach: Start by trying to draft understandings on each issue, rather than discussing all the problems involved with the transfer of civil responsibilities. Take, I suggested, the issue of town planning. The Palestinians wanted to exercise authority in all of Hebron, including H-2, without the Israelis being able to veto Palestinian plans or building; Israel wanted to know that Palestinians would not build in ways that would invite friction or dwarf the Jewish neighborhood. Abed Rabbo suggested that we agree in writing that the historic character of neighborhoods could not be altered. Such a formula would protect both sides: the Israelis who lived in the Old City of Hebron, and the Palestinians who feared Israeli expansion. Shahor approved and I asked Jon Schwartz, the deputy legal advisor in the State Department and the only one who had accompanied me to the meeting, to craft language reflecting this point.

Jon was a wonder. No one I ever worked with had a better disposition for negotiations. He is brilliant, untiring, self-effacing, patient, and capable of mastering any issue, no matter how obscure or abstruse. Both sides came to see him as fair and his legal analysis compelling, and each was tempted to ask him for legal help.

In this case, Jon quickly drafted a formula in which both sides were "equally committed to preserve and protect the historic character of the city in a way which does not harm or change that character in any part of the city." Abu Mazen and Shahor each accepted this formula, and I suggested that we turn to specific Palestinian powers on planning and zoning. Within an hour we had a formula on coordination of construction of residential and nonresidential buildings, and a list of sensitive sites where limitations on height and size might apply.

We began to work through every civil affairs issue, with Jon drafting formulas as we finished our discussion on each question, and by 10 p.m. we had resolved 90 percent of the civil arrangements that would be part of the Hebron redeployment. As I rose to go pack my bags, first Abed Rabbo and then Oren Shahor said, "You cannot leave." I told them I was going to leave but they should wrap up the document without me. Now Oren Shahor came into my bedroom and said, "Dennis, I know you. You are committed to helping us. You will help us finish. You cannot leave now."

"Oren," I said, "I announced I was leaving, and I am going to do so. Keep up this pace, and I will come back in a few days and help you complete the whole deal." He shook his head, saying, "When you go, the work will stop."

I bid them good-bye at about 10:45 p.m. As I rode to the airport, I began to doubt my decision to leave. In one night we had gone from having no understandings on the civil side to being on the verge of an ad referendum agreement. My announcement to leave had shaken both sides up, and perhaps because of that I had finally hit on an approach that worked: draft formulas at the outset with a very small group. Why not take the same approach on security? Leaving went against a basic principle of mine in negotiations: when you have momentum, don't stop; build on it, and work around the clock. Why shouldn't I call Netanyahu and tell him I had finally found what I believed was an authoritative way to forge written understandings, that I wanted to apply the same mechanism to the security issues, and that if it worked we could resolve Hebron within a few days?

I called Martin, who liked my line of thinking. I then reached Netanyahu from the access road to Ben-Gurion Airport. He was enthusiastic, exclaiming: "Let's go for it."

Gamal was in a car behind mine, and I asked him to call Arafat. But Gamal—who could always get through immediately—was told that Arafat was not available; he was meeting with several hundred Hebronites. Instead, Saeb came on the line, telling Gamal that he was authorized to receive any message for "the President." Gamal told him I was on another phone and would call back when I had a chance. I knew that

Saeb would not be enthusiastic about a model relying on Abu Mazen and Abed Rabbo rather than himself, yet I did not want to stay unless I had Arafat's backing for the approach I had in mind. This was not the time to talk to Saeb. No doubt that added to Saeb's interest.

I continued into the airport and went to the VIP lounge. I got a distress call from Abu Mazen at the Holiday Inn, who was about to leave, feeling that the Israelis were backtracking on what had been agreed. Yitzik Molho had joined Shahor in the meeting, and had begun to raise some questions. I asked Abu Mazen to put Yitzik on and I explained to him how Abu Mazen was interpreting his questions. Yitzik had no desire to undo what had been agreed, but he needed reassurance on some minor issues. I listened to him and told him Jon would call him on a separate phone while I calmed Abu Mazen down. In turn, Jon was able to assuage Yitzik's concerns and Abu Mazen agreed to stay.

This episode further convinced me that I could not leave; leaving would undo the understanding on civil affairs. But I had a dilemma. I had not been able to reach Arafat. What if he did not buy either the substance or the mechanism from tonight? How would I explain my decision not to leave—having publicly announced I would be leaving only that afternoon?

My midnight TWA flight was fully loaded and getting ready to depart. But I was not yet ready to make the decision to stay. At this point, I took advantage of being very well known in Israel—with the peace process always leading the news—and asked to see the airport manager, to whom I explained that I needed a little more time to finish some discussions I was having. Without my saying more, he said he could hold the plane without explaining why for about fifteen minutes; it would be difficult to hold it any longer, but if necessary he would figure something out.

I thanked him and said I would resolve what I was doing within ten minutes. I called Secretary Christopher in Washington and explained my dilemma, telling him I was reluctant to leave now but also fearful that Arafat would not back what Abu Mazen had done this evening and my scenario for resolving the security issues might be based on an illusion. Still, my instinct was to stay. If it did not work out, I told the Secretary, I would simply announce I was working on some additional ideas before leaving and had postponed my departure temporarily. Secretary Christopher left it to me to decide, saying he would back my decision. That settled it; I would remain. I called Bibi and asked him to say nothing about my staying; if I reached Arafat and got his support, I would put out a statement to the press explaining that we had made progress during the night. I did not want Arafat to contradict me and say that no progress had been made. If Arafat was not ready to back Abu Mazen, I would leave tomorrow, simply saying I had done some additional work before departing.

Bibi agreed with the entire scenario. I returned to the Holiday Inn, and was greeted by the negotiators like a long-lost hero. Working together until 3 a.m., we completed a document on all the civil issues that was now ready for presentation to the leaders.

After Yitzik Molho and Oren Shahor left, Abu Mazen and Abed Rabbo explained that they would go to see Arafat now and meet him alone in order to sell him the civil affairs agreement. They would call me once they had his agreement.

That was their intent when they left for Ramallah, at least an hour's ride from Tel Aviv. But by the time they got to Ramallah, Arafat had gone to sleep, having had a stormy meeting with the Hebronites. Discretion being the better part of valor, they decided to wait until he was awake to present the draft agreement to him.

I had gone to sleep around four-thirty, and asked to be awakened at eight-thirty, expecting to have received a message that Arafat had approved the draft text and I could issue my statement to the press. But there was no message, and the word from Ramallah was that everyone was asleep on the Palestinian side. I was in an exposed position; it would become known shortly that I had not left as I had announced. Speculation would be rampant that something was up.

At noon, I learned that Abu Mazen, Abed Rabbo, and Jamil Tarifi had yet to sit with Arafat. I suspected that Abu Mazen and Abed Rabbo had already faced opposition from Saeb and perhaps others on the draft agreement—otherwise I would have heard something already. As if to confirm this, Abu Mazen, when I reached him by phone, asked me to give him one more hour (until 1 p.m.) before issuing any statement. One p.m. became 2 p.m. and then 2:30, and finally 4 p.m.—or nine in the morning Washington time. At this point, I told Abu Mazen that we both knew it would now be nap time for Arafat and only God knew when they would have their discussion. But I was out of time; the press spokesman for the State Department would need an answer on what was happening to my mission. Already there were competing rumors that I had left but turned around and returned to Israel before getting home; that I was actually back in Washington; and that I had not left, notwithstanding my announcement. Abu Mazen told me to issue my statement, and that he would publicly endorse it if there were any problems with Arafat.

I issued the statement, and at six-thirty Arafat and I spoke. He was pleased that I had stayed, agreed that progress had been made, and approved taking a similar approach to the security issues, beginning that evening. I was now very hopeful that we would be able to wrap everything up quickly. Once again, that hope proved to be wrong.

| BACK TO THE TEDIUM |

Unfortunately, neither side stuck with the approach that had worked overnight at the Holiday Inn. Instead, delegations of at least ten from each side appeared at my suite.

Rather than working with an informal but authoritative mechanism, I was once again confronted by the same unmanageable group that had led to my decision to leave.

I tried to re-create the informal, efficient approach of the previous evening by asking only Abu Mazen and Jibril Rajoub on the Palestinian side and Amnon Shahak and Yitzik Molho on the Israeli side to join me in my suite. Immediately I was faced with an embarrassing situation. David Agmon (the Chief of Staff of the Prime Minister's office) and Dan Shomron (the putative head negotiator) insisted on joining the group. I took Yitzik Molho aside and told him that it would have to be two from each side. Yitzik was understanding, but felt powerless to ask them to leave since he had no formal position in the government. Embarrassment aside, I was not powerless to ask them to leave, and I did so, explaining that the understanding with each leader was for there to be two on a side—and I understood the Prime Minister wanted Shahak and Molho to represent him. They left very reluctantly.

Now we were two on a side again, but the magic of the previous evening was gone. This was no longer a discreet discussion, insulated from the rivalries and second-guessing of larger delegations on both sides. It was a semi-public negotiation, with the two delegations literally waiting outside my suite to see what would emerge.

It was my imminent departure that had put pressure on both sides. Now that I had reversed myself and stayed, the pressure was off, and they could revert to the usual process. What better indication of their reverting to an unmanageable process than both leaders sending large delegations to convene on an evening when the understanding had been only two on a side?

I called each leader and expressed my displeasure at the circuslike atmosphere of that evening. Now I proposed we have two-on-two marathon meetings at the U.S. ambassador's residence. Arafat, however, sought three on a side, and Netanyahu agreed. I knew that, given the security questions to be resolved, it meant adding Saeb to Abu Mazen and either Abed Rabbo or Rajoub.

I had finally learned my lesson: it was fruitless to try to exclude Saeb from the negotiations. Now we would embark on a marathon round of negotiations to try to reach agreement on Hebron.

| WOULD I EVER SLEEP AGAIN? |

Our first session began with dinner at Martin's residence. It was not unusual in this negotiation to wait for the Israelis to appear.* On this night, we were informed af-

---

*When we had gone to Taba for the second round of talks on Hebron, the Israeli side was five

ter the Palestinians had left Gaza that Amnon Shahak had been delayed at the Lebanese border because of the security situation in the north, and that the Israeli team would not arrive until 11 p.m. This left our team of Martin, Aaron, Jon, Gamal, Nick Rasmussen—my all-purpose assistant—and me to have dinner with the Palestinian team of Abu Mazen, Abed Rabbo, and Saeb Erekat. Over the meal, Saeb was in a good mood, but was also blunt: "You have done a great job getting us reengaged with the Israelis, but now it is best for us to deal with them on our own without you." Philosophically, I agreed with him, but I knew that at this time such an approach meant a long negotiation. Fearing fresh violence, I thought we needed to conclude a deal more quickly. And I thought it was possible. I did not believe the differences were great.

In retrospect, I believe Saeb saw the situation more clearly than I did. I failed to recognize that Arafat was in no hurry, believing that the pressures would build on Bibi to make concessions to the Palestinians. Bibi, an opponent of the Oslo process, had had the perfect opportunity to end it when, in the aftermath of the Hasmonean Tunnel opening, Palestinian policemen shot and killed Israeli soldiers in the city of Nablus. But Bibi had not declared the end of Oslo; on the contrary, he had declared himself ready to launch negotiations on Israeli redeployment from Hebron—one of the Interim Agreement requirements most opposed by his Likud Party base.

Nothing could have more clearly demonstrated that Bibi understood he did not have an alternative to Oslo, and that he needed an agreement—that he needed Arafat, in other words. Seeing this, Arafat felt he was in the driver's seat, and able to get better terms on Hebron and reassurances about the future as well. Moreover, his constituency—the Palestinian "street"—was in no rush for an agreement. They were still taking pride in their police for having stood with the demonstrators against the Israelis in September. No agreement would be good enough for his "street." So he needed to show he was resisting and holding out, and by holding out he would increase the pressure and get a better deal over time.

As for myself, I took Netanyahu too literally about the dangers of not reaching an agreement immediately. Bibi was constantly harping on intelligence information about an imminent terrorist threat that would thwart the whole process, and emphasizing his political difficulties if an agreement was not achieved soon. I became too convinced of the dangers he constantly emphasized—believing that an outbreak of violence would put us out of business on peace for a long time to come.

In truth, the threat to the process lay less with the violence on the Palestinian street

---

hours late—prompting an angry call from me to Bibi: "You want to keep the Palestinians waiting, that's a mistake, but it is your business; you want to keep the American team waiting, that is a sign of disrespect, and I won't put up with it." He was apologetic.

than with the violence aided and abetted, albeit passively, by Arafat himself. But I did not fully appreciate this at the time. On the contrary, I shared the view of the Israeli security establishment and Palestinians like Abu Mazen that there was genuine anger on the street and that there were limits to Arafat's ability to control events if there was not some clear promise of political change over time. But how much change was enough in Arafat's eyes, and were there any time pressures on him? No one knew. Small wonder, then, that we all had trouble reading Arafat's clock and figuring out when he was ready to close a deal.

At dinner with Uri Savir on Shabbat evening after I had reversed my decision on leaving, we discussed Arafat's sense of timing. Uri was convinced that Arafat would do the deal before the 1996 presidential election: "He wants credit from Clinton." While hoping he was right, I was not sure. As I said to Uri, "The problem is that the clock is in Arafat's head and no one knows what is there. Sometimes I wonder if he does."

The meetings at Martin's house took on a tortuous character. We would meet each evening and work until 6 or 7 a.m. Painfully, we made progress on each security issue— the number and location of the Joint Mobile Units (JMUs), the location of Palestinian checkpoints between H-1 and H-2, resolving the issue of Palestinian police having rifles in H-1, and the schedule of opening Shuhada Street (the main road though H-2) and the adjoining Hasbahe market. The last two issues were particularly tricky. On the one hand, they went to the heart of whether Palestinians living in H-2 would have a normal life; on the other, the normal operation of Shuhuda Street and the Hasbahe market could increase the opportunity for attacks against the Israeli settlers in H-2, especially given their immediate proximity to the Israeli settler presence—hence the Israeli wish to limit their operations.

Usually Yitzik and Saeb would debate a point to death, then Amnon would come up with a practical suggestion and I would summarize and encapsulate what appeared to be agreed. Yitzik, in particular, seemed to have no space even to try out ideas, so paralyzed was he by his fear that the Palestinians would pocket anything new that he would present.

I saw a contradiction between Bibi's haste and his negotiator's temporizing. The Prime Minister was asking me daily to push Arafat to finish, clearly hoping to minimize his own concessions and getting me to deliver Arafat. I made it clear to him I would try to do so, but as I told Bibi, "I need something from you if I am to produce."

The one area in which we had made no headway was on "hot pursuit." My earlier efforts at translating the understanding between Amnon and Abu Mazen into a formula had not yielded anything. I decided to try to sell Netanyahu on a formula which I could then try to sell to the Palestinians. I had two formulations. The premise was the same in each, but one offered explicit reference to Israeli responses and was in the active voice, and so would be easier for the Israelis to accept:

—In the event of a threat or a danger to Israelis in the city of Hebron, Israel will act in accordance with the following provisions of the Interim Agreement (IA), including article XII of the agreement and articles II, VII, and XI of annex 1 of the IA.

The other formula was implicit with regard to Israeli actions and was in the passive voice, and so would be easier for the Palestinians to accept:

—In the event of a threat or a danger to Israelis in the city of Hebron, actions will be taken in accordance with the following provisions of the Interim Agreement, including article XII of the agreement and articles II, VII, and XI of annex 1 of the IA.

Jon was not convinced that the Palestinians would accept even the passive-voice formula as written. Based on what Saeb was saying, Jon felt we needed to introduce greater mutuality into the formula; he suggested that the introductory clause read: "In the event of a threat or danger to either the Israelis or Palestinians . . ." I knew Bibi would not accept this, but I decided to present it to him as a third formula, hoping to steer him to the passive-voice formula that I was convinced Arafat could ultimately accept.

Sure enough, Bibi pounced on Jon's formula, determined to talk me out of it. Referring to this as the mutuality formula, I told him that this gave us the greatest chance of producing an agreement soon. The active-voice formula offered us the worst chance. Would he let me split the difference and try the passive-voice formula? As I'd hoped, he said yes.

The next day, however, he called me and said he needed the active-voice formula to do the deal. "Then there probably won't be a deal," I responded. Bibi countered, "See what you can do." I took this to mean that, depending on other possible trade-offs, I could play with the formula—that in other words I was free to begin to shape the final package myself. That was the good news. The bad news was that I was basically going without sleep.

For the next week I presided over all-night sessions. I would return to my hotel in Jerusalem between 7 and 8 a.m.; nap for one hour, take a shower, and then sit with Bibi and go over the results of the previous evening. During the day I would meet with the negotiators on each side separately, trying to narrow the differences further and plan for the evening session; then, typically, I would helicopter down to Gaza to brief Arafat; finally I would return to the ambassador's residence to convene the evening negotiations. The picture of an agreement was gradually emerging, but I needed to find a way to close.

In any negotiation, the hardest thing to do is conclude. In a high-stakes political negotiation in which each side is making concessions and knows it will be criticized for them, it is always easier to keep talking and defer the moment of truth. No political

leader I have ever dealt with or observed relishes taking a difficult, potentially costly decision if he or she can avoid it or delay it. Even assuming both sides share an interest in
closing—and I was not certain that was the case here—they are unlikely to do so unless there is a deadline or some event that forces them to act.

My team could not keep up a round-the-clock pace forever and I thought Arafat's
upcoming departure for a European trip could provide a deadline of sorts. All along I
had conditioned Arafat to know that I could not become part of the landscape in the
region—"the furniture," as I put it to him—where my presence was routine and without impact. Consequently, when he reported to me that he had invitations to go to
Norway and Italy and would be leaving at the end of the month, I told him I would
leave the region then as well. This, I hoped, would be the deadline we all needed.

Of course, a deadline without a proposal cannot get each side to decide. It is the
combination of the deadline and proposal—typically a package proposal with built-in
trade-offs—that produces a deal. I could see an obvious swap necessary for closing.
Basic outlines of written understandings existed on everything but "hot pursuit" and
"Shuhada Street," but the gap on these two remained wide.

Saeb and Abed Rabbo had told me that if we could meet the Palestinian needs on
Shuhada Street, everything else would fall into place. With this in mind, and with
Arafat due to depart in twenty-four hours, I decided I would go to Bibi and propose a
swap deal: Shuhada Street for hot pursuit.

The Israelis would get a formula they could live with on hot pursuit or reentry and
the Palestinians would get one they could live with on the opening of Shuhada. I went
by helicopter to the northern Israeli port city of Haifa to meet Bibi, who was set to arrive in the office of the commander of the Israeli navy. The office had portholes for
windows, and on this pristine day with a bright blue sky, I found myself looking out at
the Mediterranean and wishing I were out sailing, not inside trying to close a deal.

After about fifteen minutes Netanyahu arrived and asked where I thought things
stood. I told him I would be leaving the area when Arafat left the next day; that I
thought this gave us some chance to press for an agreement; that I felt the two issues
blocking an agreement at this point were reentry and Shuhada Street. Then I proposed
a swap deal.

Bibi immediately said: "Agreed, let's do it." I told him I would go see Arafat. Since
Arafat's nephew had died and the funeral was that day, I did not know how soon I
would actually see him.

The Israeli press was milling around the helipad as I left Bibi to make my way in
a van to the helicopter. I decided to up the ante a little more by announcing to the press
that I would, in fact, be leaving tomorrow. Before doing so, however, I needed to let
Secretary Christopher know what I was doing. Unfortunately, we could not make the

phone connection immediately. As I waited, the press came around the van taking pictures of me; once on the line, Christopher agreed with my strategy, and ironically, the pictures of me talking on the phone from the van lent a sense of urgency to the process.

I was trying hard to shape a climate in which Arafat would feel the need to conclude. Because of the funeral in Gaza, I guessed I would not see him until seven-thirty that evening. That gave me time to arrange for President Clinton to call Arafat in my presence, and to emphasize the need to close a deal tonight—and to imply that if he did close, Arafat would get the credit from Clinton he so craved. In the meantime, I needed to nail down the precise language of the swap deal. I met Yitzik, General Shaul Mofaz, and Daniel Reisner—the Israeli legal advisor from the Defense Ministry—and went over a proposed formula. After some resistance, they agreed to it, and we had lunch all feeling hopeful that we might be on the verge of an agreement.

| BREAKTHROUGH IN GAZA? |

I headed down to Gaza and entered a scene unlike any I had seen before. Yasir Arafat was in Fatah headquarters in Gaza receiving condolences for the loss of his nephew like a sitting monarch. Hundreds of people were crowded outside the hall waiting to get inside. I was ushered by security through a tiny entryway. Here people stood in a line approaching Arafat, who sat at the front of the hall surrounded by the Fatah hierarchy: Abu Mazen, Hani al-Hassan, Abu Ala, Mohammad Dahlan, and others. The building had a musty, austere, earthy quality to it.

I walked up to Arafat and whispered my sorrow for his loss, and my regret at having to see him in these circumstances. He explained (as Ed Abington—the U.S. Consul General in Jerusalem—had told me earlier) that he had raised his nephew, who had been like a son to him. Eventually, he suggested we go upstairs to a separate room. When I repeated my regret to have to talk business at a time like this, Arafat answered in English, "There is no time-out for leaders. We must continue."

I told him President Clinton would be calling very shortly, and the call, put on a speakerphone, came exactly at the appointed time of 7:40 p.m. The President had been campaigning in Virginia, and he explained he was taking time out of his day to express his condolences to the Chairman. Arafat was very appreciative. But when the President then called on him to complete the Hebron agreement before the Chairman left for Europe, Arafat fell back on his standard line of passivity—"We hope so." President Clinton wanted more than that; he warned Arafat about the danger of drift. Then, with a bluntness I had not expected, he said that if the agreement was not completed by the time Arafat departed, it would not be completed prior to our election—and the President feared there might be a long delay with all the attendant risks and dangers.

He added that I had some ideas that I would share with the Chairman that ought to make it possible to conclude the deal tonight; in any case, that was his hope and he looked forward to hearing from me later.

Arafat told the President that I was sitting with him in the room and he promised to do his best to finish the agreement. He said he was in need of our help, that he could not do this on his own; he repeated his promise to do his part and wished the President good luck in the election. The President thanked him and concluded by saying "I am counting on you."

I thought Arafat's "We are in need of your help" and "We cannot do this on our own" were his standard lines, his way of avoiding responsibility for a quick conclusion to Hebron. But his promise to Clinton to do his best and to do his part to finish were lines I thought I could use, and so once he and the President had said their good-byes, I turned to him and said, "That was an extraordinary call. It is remarkable that the President took time out from campaigning to call you. It says a great deal about his commitment to you and to this process. I don't know that another American President would have made such a call in these circumstances. He is clearly counting on you to finish the agreement before you depart for Europe, and I know he will take your promise seriously. And I also believe that the ideas I will present to you tonight should make it possible for us to break through and conclude a deal before you leave tomorrow."

Arafat replied by saying how much he appreciated the President's call, and knew its significance. He dearly hoped the President would be successful in his election.

Then, as we stood there talking, Nabil Abu Rudeina, who had left the room and now reappeared, reported that he had just received a message from Saeb about the security negotiations: the Israelis were now insisting on twice as many joint mobile units (JMUs) in the Palestinian sector of H-1 as in H-2—trying, in Saeb's words, to humiliate the Palestinians. Arafat, his mood suddenly darkening, wondered aloud how we could conclude the agreement when the Israelis were giving nothing and squeezing him. He started to work himself into a near frenzy, claiming the Israelis had put 250 tanks into Gaza. "Imagine 250 tanks, more than they had when they seized Gaza in the 1967 war. What are they trying to do? Humiliate me, squeeze me. They won't succeed. They did much more against me in Lebanon and they could not succeed."

He was on a tangent, and a quixotic one at that—I knew the charge of 250 tanks was ridiculous. But I knew him well enough to know there was method in his madness. He was trying to undo the deal and put the onus on the Israelis to explain that he was in no position to conclude when he was under such pressure from the Israelis. I told him I would call Prime Minister Netanyahu on the tank question, and did so. Bibi was incredulous at the charge but I insisted that he check and call back with an explanation. (He would call back shortly to explain that three armored personnel carriers had moved into Gaza.)

Having defused this, I then asked Arafat for a private meeting and (once all his aides had left) began patiently to remind him that, in fact, the Israelis were making concessions in the negotiations. But he refused to listen, instead insisting that he was being squeezed and we were in a "stalemate." I told him I had worked my butt off to produce those Israeli concessions. He would have none of it; saying he was being squeezed and everything was stuck.

I put the cap on my pen, closed my notebook, and said, "Fine. There is nothing left for me to do. You promised the President you would do your best but all you want to do is complain. That is not doing your best and there is no point in my presenting the ideas the President referred to. . . ." I was all set to tell him I had had it when Gamal, who was interpreting, suddenly switched from translating and pressed in closer to Arafat's chair, half standing, half leaning into Arafat's face, and shrieked, "You can't do this to this man! Do you know how hard he has worked? Do you see how he is moving the Prime Minister? He has gone without sleep the last twelve days. He is working tirelessly for you. Who else is going to help you? Don't let him go like this. . . ."

I put my hand on Gamal's shoulder and asked him to sit down, saying I would speak for myself. I told Arafat, "If you think someone else can produce for you, fine. If you think you can do better if I leave now, fine. If you want to stretch this process out with all the risks that runs, fine. But you need to know that I will leave tomorrow and don't expect me to come back anytime soon. It is a pity, because I had come with a swap to close the deal. But what is the point now?"

Suddenly Arafat's tone and demeanor changed again. "We still have twelve hours," he said. "We can still finish. Don't give up now."

I asked, "Are you ready to do your part?" He said yes. I asked, "Are you ready to go over our ideas on a swap deal?" Again, his answer was yes. Sitting next to him, I went line by line over the language on Shuhada Street and "hot pursuit." On Shuhada Street, I pointed out that the language was essentially what his people had proposed. The only difference was that they had proposed the street opening in three months; I was proposing six months. He immediately said, "How about four months?" (I had already pushed four months on Bibi and he had been willing to accept it.)

Next, I went to the language on "hot pursuit"—which was the language of the Palestinian proposal, plus the active-verb formula I had sold to Bibi: "In the event of a threat to Israelis in the city of Hebron, Israel will act in accordance with the following provisions of the Interim Agreement. . . ."

Together Arafat and I studied the language closely: I flagged the active-verb sentence, and explained that while it gave the Israelis what they wanted, it did not talk about Israeli rights of "hot pursuit" or reentry and made clear that any Israeli action must be in accordance with the Interim Agreement—thus giving Arafat an explanation to take to his people.

He studied the paragraphs on the road and reentry for another five minutes, comparing what I gave him to the language he had gotten in English from Saeb. Again, I pointed out that he was getting what he wanted on the road and the Israelis were getting something on "hot pursuit," but that the formula was much less explicit than they had wanted and gave him cover. With agreement on this language, we could conclude tonight. Was he, I asked, prepared to accept the swap deal?

Arafat said yes, but he might have a small change to suggest on "hot pursuit"; if so, Abu Mazen would let me know. I said okay, provided it was very minor. Anything more and there would be no deal.

I told him I would now need to deal with Netanyahu, who had approved the concept of a swap but not the language. To do that, I needed Arafat's final approval; I wanted to be able to present it to the Prime Minister as a formula the Chairman had accepted. So I said to Arafat, "I really want your final okay before dealing with him."

Arafat said he understood and would have me called within an hour. We said good-bye, both expressing our feeling that we could complete our work tonight.

When Gamal and I climbed into our Suburban, he started to laugh: "We got it," he said exultantly. "We did it." I felt very hopeful but said to him, "It ain't over yet."

As we flew by helicopter back to Tel Aviv, I wondered whether we might actually finish tonight. Gamal said again, "We got him." I replied, "I'm not sure, let's see what changes they want; I'm not so sure they will be minor."

We reached the ambassador's residence at about 10:45 p.m., and I regaled Martin and the rest of the team with the dramatic points of the meeting with Arafat, declaring that Gamal "deserves the best supporting actor award for his performance." Not long afterward, Abed Rabbo called from Gaza to report that the Chairman wanted two points incorporated in the language: first, rather than using the word "threat," which was too broad, he wanted to say "threatening actions" in the "hot pursuit" formula; second, replace the "six months" with "four months" for the opening of Shuhada Street. Telling Abed Rabbo these amendments were acceptable to me and that I now considered this final, I said that I would present the swap deal shortly to the Prime Minister and hoped to have an answer before Abed Rabbo and his colleagues arrived for the three-on-three meeting at Martin's.

Arafat's reaction suggested that we were, in fact, on the brink of a deal. I called Netanyahu and reported that Arafat had accepted the swap deal and had only minor changes in language. In reply, Bibi pointed out that he had just seen the language for the first time and felt the formula on Shuhada Street lacked sufficient qualifying language on security. I told him I had gone over this language with his representatives before taking it to Arafat—as he had asked me to do—and they had okayed it; now I had Arafat's approval, and "it would be a big mistake to go back to Arafat with new language on the road now. The deal will unravel."

While not happy, Netanyahu said the mistake had been his people's, not mine, and therefore he would accept the deal provided Arafat didn't seek further change. Everything looked promising.

Then Saeb Erekat arrived at Martin's by himself, not with Abu Mazen or Abed Rabbo as expected. Immediately he asked to see the language I had presented to the Chairman. I told him Arafat had accepted a swap deal on the road and reentry. Then, playing coy, I said we could go over the language on both the road and reentry when Abu Mazen and Yasir arrived, couldn't we? He insisted, saying he needed to see it, especially because Arafat said he had some reservations. I told him Abed Rabbo had called me with Arafat's reservation and it was very minor; why not wait for his colleagues to arrive?

Saeb said, "Please, Dennis, I need to take a look at the language, the President has asked me to look at it. Please let me see it." Fearing that I would make a bigger issue of this if I refused, and knowing Abu Mazen and Abed Rabbo were due any minute, I decided to give Saeb the language. He read the formula for the deal and said the language on the road was fine but the one sentence on reentry would have to be dropped.

I said, "Saeb, this is a package deal. You don't get to take what you want and drop what the other side wants. You drop the one sentence, you lose the language on the road."

He replied, "Arafat has reservations and his main reservation is that sentence. He agrees to the deal without that sentence." I said, "That is not what the Chairman told me and it is not what Yasser [Abed Rabbo] told me." I proceeded to tell him exactly what Yasser had asked for—on the reentry (threatening actions in place of threats) and on the road (four months rather than six months for reopening). Based on getting this from the Chairman I had then presented this to Netanyahu, and "the PM had wanted to toughen the language on the road, but I rejected that on the grounds that further changes would destroy the logic of the swap deal." The Prime Minister had acquiesced. So "if you want to undercut the deal and betray what the Chairman had told me and Yasser confirmed, go right ahead."

Saeb said he would have to call President Arafat, and he went into the next room and placed a call. Meanwhile, Abu Mazen and Yasser arrived, and I asked what was going on? They told me Saeb was causing problems but they would try to manage them.

That proved difficult. Saeb returned and began raising questions on everything, and introducing totally new and impractical demands such as the joint patrols in H-2 must be restricted only to the Old City of Hebron, where the Jewish presence was. It was clear his purpose was to prevent an agreement this evening. I asked Abu Mazen to go outside with me.

It was now well after midnight. We walked out into the garden overlooking the Mediterranean, and again I asked, "What is going on?" He replied that while I had genuinely persuaded Arafat on the swap deal, once I was gone and he and Abed Rabbo had left to come here, Saeb had gone to work on Arafat, who now was reluctant again.

I asked, "How are we to do business if agreements we reach can be undone afterward?" I went on to say that it would not be good if I left under these circumstances, but I clearly could not stay and would leave once Arafat departed for Europe—and unfortunately my report to the President would not be good. Surely he could imagine the impact it would have on his willingness to be involved and have me return. "The Chairman needs to understand this as he weighs the advice of Saeb and his allies," I concluded. Abu Mazen said he understood and would talk to Arafat.

Back inside, Abu Mazen went into Martin's study and was on the phone with Arafat for at least a half hour. When he returned, he gave me a wan smile and said he had tried. He felt the only chance now was for me to call Arafat myself. I was willing to do so, but suggested to Abu Mazen that the two of us discuss the real options first. One was to make a deal as planned. The problem was Arafat was due to leave in three hours, and it was hard to see how we could finish in time. Could Arafat delay his departure to Norway until early afternoon? If he could, I would see it as a sign that he was ready to conclude. Abu Mazen replied, "You are the only one who can convince him of this."

I was not so sure of that, and I said so, adding, "Perhaps if he understands the alternatives, he will become convinced." That led me to a second option: I return home, with no promise of returning. That will signal we are giving up the effort. The problem with this one is it may create a sense of despair, and we could be facing the dangers of September all over again. So I proposed a variant of this option: for me to return home and make clear at least that I would not return to the area to resume my shuttle until there was a firm commitment to conclude the agreement. While wanting me to try one more time with Arafat, Abu Mazen doubted we could finish in time, so he opted for the idea that I would only return when there were ironclad assurances on finishing. Indeed, when I said to him, "Realistically, I cannot come back unless I know for sure that Arafat is ready to close, particularly given the impact on my credibility." He replied, "I will promise you before you return that he is ready."

At around 4 a.m. I called Arafat. I told him that his negotiators had not accepted the swap deal he and I agreed to, and that they were opening issues that I thought had been closed. As a result, we would not finish before he left for Europe. I said the President would be disappointed. I asked him if he could postpone his departure a few hours so that we could finish. He replied that he could not postpone his trip; he was expected in Norway. He asked whether I could stay after he left, since he would only be gone for three days, and I said no, "it does not make sense for me to be here when you are outside the region." Almost pleading now, he asked, "Could you say you are leaving but will return next week?" I replied that the talks could go on without me. I would return if there was a reason for me to do so, but certainly not before our election—nearly two weeks away. He said he understood, but that we would not be able to conclude an agreement unless I was there to work with both parties. I closed the conversation by saying I would stay in touch, but noting again that the President would be disappointed and that it was hard to see how we could do much together if understandings we reached were undone after the fact. "How would you react," I said in closing, "if I walked away from understandings you and I reached?" He did not reply.

When I rang off, Abu Mazen told me it was a pity we could not finish tonight and repeated his promise to me that he would let me know when we were truly on the verge of finishing. I asked him what's the problem—after all, we both knew that Saeb would not be able to prevent an agreement if Arafat wanted it. He replied that the Chairman did not trust Prime Minister Netanyahu and was not convinced that he would proceed on all the other issues after Hebron. He also feared that Netanyahu would trumpet "hot pursuit" in a way designed to embarrass Arafat. If this was so, I asked, why had Arafat left me with the impression that he was ready to close the swap deal? Abu Mazen shrugged his shoulders and said, "He was persuaded sitting with you, but then all those around him played on his fears and suspicions."

The two of us returned to the table where Saeb and Yitzik were battling over the issue of rifles all over again. At 6:30 a.m., I called a halt to it. Announcing that I would be leaving later that day, I expressed my hope that as the talks continued, both sides would find ways to resolve the remaining problems together.

My deputy, Aaron Miller, drafted a statement saying that we had made progress but had not overcome the differences, and that I would return when appropriate to work with the parties. I then called Netanyahu and explained that the swap deal had not been agreed upon, we were in for a prolonged period of negotiation—and if Arafat was in no hurry, neither should we be.

Bibi agreed, and asked when I was leaving. When I told him late that evening, he invited me to dinner. We ate in a quiet corner of the downstairs restaurant in the King David Hotel. Bibi was in a relaxed, philosophical mood. He spoke of how he would surprise everyone with his reforms of the Israeli economy, which would produce real privatization and streamline the banking system.

Then he raised Syria and asked questions designed to pique my interest: How was Israel to know that the United States did not intend to treat Syria the way it had treated Egypt after Camp David? Israel could not afford to have us arm Syria as we had Egypt—

"You don't have such an intention, do you?" The issue, I replied, would only come up if you were prepared to do a deal with Syria like the one with Egypt—where you withdraw fully from the Golan in return for a peace treaty. Do you intend to do that? I asked. Bibi smiled and said, "This is something I want to talk to the President about."

Netanyahu's wife, Sarah, joined us at this point, with Bibi noting it was her birthday. After a few minutes of small talk, she asked me if I really understood the meaning of Hebron to the Jewish people. This was obviously not an idle question; in effect, she was asking how I could ask the Israelis to redeploy from Hebron. I wasn't in the mood for a debate about Hebron; nonetheless, I answered, saying I was very familiar with the historical ties of the Jewish people to Hebron, but the decision to redeploy from 80 percent of Hebron was the Israeli government's, not mine (though I agreed with it). Moreover, I asked her how she felt about the 140,000 Palestinians who lived in Hebron: did they have no rights? Should the 400 Israelis who lived there have precedence over the 140,000? Palestinians asked me this question frequently; how would she answer it?

Sarah acknowledged that it was difficult and had wished only to stress that I keep history in mind as we negotiated on Hebron. Bibi said nothing during this exchange; for him this was to be a night of congeniality, not contention.

Myself, I was exhausted by the histories of Hebron, Israeli and Palestinian alike. After twenty-three days of nonstop shuttling between the leaders and negotiators, I was returning home empty-handed. For the first time in eight years, I did not expect to return anytime soon.

One Last Push to Settle Hebron

IN NOVEMBER 1996, BILL Clinton was reelected President by a wide margin. Warren Christopher had told me confidentially in late September that he would not stay for a second term as Secretary of State, but he knew the President thought highly of me; he would want me to stay on as the Middle East negotiator, or else move to another higher-ranking position. I had no interest in moving. My passion was Arab-Israeli peace. I told Secretary Christopher that I would stay as negotiator, but that if it became clear that little could be achieved, I would leave the government sometime in the second term.

In the region, meanwhile, the parties (not surprisingly) made little headway in their joint discussions. Upon my return to Washington, I had announced that I would return to Israel and the territories when I felt my presence could make a difference in the negotiations. While I envisioned no early return to Israel, I knew there would be an opportunity to try to move Arafat during the Cairo Economic Conference (November 12–14). It was the third regional economic conference sponsored by the World Economic Forum. The first had been in Casablanca in 1994, and the second one had taken place in Amman in 1995. The economic conferences had, in fact, been the brainchild of Shimon Peres, who believed opening the Middle East for business might catalyze far-reaching reforms and build a stronger stake in peace in the Arab world.

Yasir Arafat would attend the conference, as would several Israeli cabinet ministers; so would Secretary Christopher. I thought this confluence of actors—and the international attention—might create an opening with Arafat. Maybe he was waiting for a grander international stage to conclude the Hebron deal to attract greater support.

Maybe not, but with the Secretary going to Cairo, I felt the need to see what was possible. I decided to probe Arafat on his thinking. My daughter Ilana gave me a pretext. The Israeli and Palestinian press had reported that I would not be coming back to the region because my daughter had had minor eye surgery. After the operation, Arafat's Chief of Staff, Nabil Abu Rudeina, called Ilana at our home to ask how she was feeling; then Nabil gave the phone to Arafat, who invited her to come see him in Gaza. My daughter the diplomat naturally agreed. Then she handed the phone to me. After thanking him for his concern about Ilana, I asked, "What would it take for you to do the deal on Hebron?" He was explicit, telling me that he did not trust that Netanyahu would continue the process once a Hebron deal was done. What if we offered the same basic swap deal as before but tied it to assurances on other issues? I asked.

I had in mind offering assurances that the further redeployments, safe passage between Gaza and the West Bank, and the development of the Gaza airport and seaport would be addressed. In suggesting this, I was hoping either to make it easier for Arafat to conclude a deal or to deny him the pretext for not making one.

Arafat was enthusiastic, it turned out, and I told him the Secretary would explore a package deal with him in Cairo. To be sure, Secretary Christopher had a special interest in closing a deal in Cairo if at all possible. Several days after the election, he announced that he would not serve a second term as Secretary of State. He and his wife, Marie, wanted to return home to California. After making nearly thirty trips to the Middle East, he did not want to end his tenure with a stalemate between the Israelis and Palestinians.

| AVOIDING A TRAP IN CAIRO |

I had warned the Secretary that my offer to seek assurances might itself be turned into a prolonged negotiation by Arafat, but Secretary Christopher felt that as long as he was going to Cairo anyway, it was worth probing on a package deal. Sure enough, whatever enthusiasm Arafat had for a package deal earlier was not in evidence in his late-night November 11 meeting with the Secretary. Instead, he resisted every effort to speak about assurances, preferring to recite his litany of complaints against Netanyahu. Why he would waste what was likely to be his last meeting with Christopher was a mystery to me. But as we were saying good-bye at the end of the meeting, Abu Rudeina whispered to Gamal that I should meet Arafat for breakfast early the next morning. We had flown overnight, I had not yet slept, and the breakfast meeting would take place only six hours from now. What was the point, I wondered, especially after Arafat's performance with the Secretary? Gamal's answer was that Arafat had not taken the evening meeting seriously, perhaps because it had been held in the Egyptian Foreign Minister's

(Amre Moussa's) office. Over breakfast, in his "own villa" in Cairo, Gamal felt Arafat would do business. I wasn't persuaded, but reluctantly agreed to go.

Gamal and I arrived at Arafat's villa at 8 a.m., and no one was up. After a few minutes, Nabil, looking sleepy, appeared and apologized that the Chairman was not yet awake. I groaned inwardly. But not more than two minutes later the Chairman appeared and we sat down to breakfast, joined by Abu Mazen and Saeb Erekat. After the Chairman made sure I tasted every dish on the table, including *foul*, the Egyptian beans, a tapioca-type dish, hard-boiled eggs, and a variety of pitas with jam and honey, I explained why, given the nature of the transition from one U.S. administration to another, it would be in Palestinian interests to conclude a deal. "Secretary Christopher has already announced he will be leaving as Secretary of State," I went on, and no one could "guarantee that his successor will have the same commitment to the Middle East."

Arafat said yes, but "you will stay and we all know how important you are." While not minimizing my role, I told him that a different Secretary might have different priorities and might also want different people. Even though I expected to stay and even though the President was committed to Middle East peace, Arafat should not assume that the Middle East would command the same level of attention that it had in President Clinton's first term, particularly if it looked like little could be achieved. Reaching an agreement soon might help sustain the level of commitment. Failing to do so might undercut it.

He had listened very carefully and said he understood and was prepared to come to an agreement now, but he could not be cornered in front of his people. Osama al-Baz—the Egyptian presidential advisor—had now joined us and said, "Dennis is right. You need to reach agreement quickly." Osama then asked me whether Netanyahu could give anything more on Hebron. I replied that I thought Bibi had only limited flexibility on Hebron—but could offer meaningful assurances on non-Hebron issues and the process as a whole.

Osama then asked Arafat: Could he accept where we were on the Hebron issues? It would be difficult, Arafat said. He asked me: Could we move any further with the formulas on "hot pursuit"? I said I was willing to try but there was not much room to maneuver. Osama offered to work with me, and Arafat said that was good, and we should come back to him with our suggestions.

Once Osama was gone, I asked Arafat for a few minutes in private, and when we were alone (with Gamal), I told him I could try to fine-tune the "hot pursuit" formula but that I was not going to take a run at moving Netanyahu unless I knew we were really in the endgame—until I knew what he really needed.

Uncharacteristically, Arafat responded clearly, saying he was in the corner in front of his people on two issues: first, the Israeli right to reenter H-1 was too explicit, and second, the Palestinian police were forbidden from carrying rifles there. Deal with these issues and provide assurances that there will be serious negotiations on the non-Hebron issues, he said, and that would meet his needs. I said, "No promises, but I will see what I can do."

Osama had signaled that Egypt would play a role, and Arafat's whole demeanor had indicated that he needed perhaps only a fig leaf to conclude a deal. I called Bibi to brief him on my conversation with Arafat. Once again Bibi was anxious, asking me if we move on these issues—H-1, the rifles, and assurances on the non-Hebron issues—"will there be a deal?" Honestly, I replied, I was not sure, but Arafat was about as straight as he had ever been in my meeting with him. Why not have a quiet meeting of your senior representatives and his and test whether they reflect what Arafat said to me?

Bibi agreed, saying that if it were possible to conclude an agreement now he would cancel his scheduled trip to Seattle the next day to speak to the General Assembly of the Jewish Federations of America.

I advised him not to cancel anything yet lest Arafat think that Bibi was desperate for a deal. Shortly afterward, Martin reported that the Israeli press was now calling a deal imminent. I told him that was news to me, and briefed him on my conversations with Arafat and Bibi. In all likelihood (Martin surmised) Bibi had put out word of a deal in the offing so as to cancel his trip. Coming to the States and not seeing the President or other senior officials was an embarrassment sure to produce many stories in the Israeli press that Bibi had major problems with the administration.

Martin told me that the press was also saying that I was on my way back to Israel. I told him I was "determined not to go back unless we were in the endgame; otherwise I would take all the pressure off of Bibi and Arafat to make a deal and I would be trapped there."

This determination was soon to be put to the test. Within an hour of my conversation with Martin, Dore Gold phoned me in Cairo, telling me, "This is hush-hush, but the Prime Minister is going to cancel his visit to the States." I told him I hoped he was not canceling because he thought a deal was in the offing, it wasn't; in fact, I was leaving Cairo that very evening to return home.

That was true up to a point. All flights out of Cairo were booked, and the only way I could return anytime soon was to fly on our Defense Attaché's aircraft from Cairo to Ben-Gurion Airport and take the TWA flight from there.

I then called Martin, who told me that Yitzik Molho and Saeb would be meeting to follow up on my suggestion to Bibi to test what was possible. This was bad news.

This was not a channel that would probe anything. In this setting, Saeb would have every incentive to negotiate, not conclude. Martin recommended that so long as I was going to have to fly to Israel I should see the Prime Minister when I arrived and consider staying to try to conclude the deal.

No way, I said, this is not the endgame. If you tell me the outcome of the Molho-Erekat meeting is different than I expect, I will consider staying. But, I said, I don't want to see Bibi unless I am staying, and right now "I ain't staying."

My effort to avoid staying soon became more difficult. Secretary Christopher was in Europe, and when CNN ran as its lead story that Bibi was canceling his trip to America because a deal was imminent, I got a call from the Secretary's Chief of Staff, Tom Donilon, who asked, "What is going on?" I explained that CNN was overreporting the possibility of a breakthrough, but Tom was worried that an agreement might take place without us, and I was unable to convince him that was not going to happen. Unbeknownst to me, Tom had arranged for the Secretary to call Martin, who felt I should stay, though Martin acknowledged that I thought it was a mistake to do so.

As a result, shortly after I arrived at Ben-Gurion that evening, Secretary Christopher reached me and urged me to stay. When I stressed that my credibility with Arafat—and our leverage—would be undone if I stayed prematurely, Chris uneasily said, "You are on the scene and I won't second-guess your judgment."

The reports from the Erekat-Molho meeting confirmed my judgment and I returned that night to America, preserving my posture that I would not return to the Middle East until Arafat demonstrated he was ready to conclude. It was a posture I would not be able to sustain much longer.

| BIBI MOVES, ARAFAT POCKETS, AND VICE PRESIDENT GORE WEIGHS IN |

The ongoing Erekat-Molho discussions produced little. The two sides were again mired in the minutiae. Bibi's urgency diminished, and Arafat remained in no hurry. But Bibi grew impatient. Over Thanksgiving weekend, he called me at home to say he was now ready to move on the two Hebron security questions of "hot pursuit" and the rifles. To guard against Arafat pocketing his move, he wanted me to talk to Arafat first. I told him it would be smarter to present everything as part of a package; I feared that if he did not at least convey a commitment for dealing with each of the Interim Agreement issues—and a timeline for doing so—he would give Arafat an excuse for holding out, notwithstanding his moves on Hebron.

Understandably, Bibi wanted to get Arafat to move in response to the moves he was making on Hebron. I was sympathetic but did not think it would work. Bibi was convinced that I could persuade Arafat, and suggested that I remind Arafat of the pressure the Prime Minister was under from his cabinet, when Arafat asked for more than Bibi had offered.

I refused to do this. As I would tell Bibi more than once, it was important for Arafat to see that "you act out of conviction, not from weakness or political pressures." Bibi would often protest that Arafat should be made to understand the constraints upon an elected prime minister. I agreed, and worked hard to convince Arafat, Asad, and other Arab leaders of the need to reach out to and condition the Israeli public. But Bibi's cabinet did not reflect the public per se; it was much more the captive of the far right and thus less representative of the country as a whole. It surely could not be ignored, but if Arafat saw Bibi yielding to pressure from within the cabinet, he would see the value of pressuring him as well.

Instead, then, I would raise with Arafat the importance of his reciprocating what would be important moves toward the very concerns on Hebron that Arafat had raised with me in Cairo. Still at home over the Thanksgiving weekend, I called Arafat and told him that Israel was now going to make meaningful moves "toward you on 'hot pursuit' and rifles," as per our discussion in Cairo. I had made a major effort to produce these moves, and argued that "you have to respond or it makes little sense for me to continue to push them to be responsive to you. Whatever you do, don't pick on the details, but respond in kind. If you do that, if you show you are ready to close, I will be prepared to return to the area to help put together the final package."

Arafat told me this was good news and he would respond seriously. In fact, the Palestinians did the opposite. Saeb, when he saw Molho, debated the details of the Israeli proposal, trying to get more, and offered nothing in return.

We were now stuck again. It mattered little that Bibi had not followed my advice of putting together a package. His worst fear had materialized: "When I make a move, Arafat simply pockets it and asks for more."

Angry now, I called Arafat: "You ask for my help, I give it, and you do the opposite of what you tell me you will do. I cannot do more for you now."

When Arafat claimed that the Israelis had not offered much, I grew angrier: "They moved on the principle of what you wanted on each issue, and your response is 'not good enough.' Why should they do more? Why didn't you counter with your own proposal? You aren't negotiating, and I won't help you."

Within a few days I got a message that Mohammad Rashid would be coming to Washington carrying an important message to me from Arafat and Abu Mazen. Rashid was known as Arafat's moneyman; he managed all the slush funds, all the authority's monopolies on cement and oil—that Arafat reportedly skimmed off the top to fill his private accounts. While I had not dealt with him much, I knew he was close to Abu

Mazen, Mohammad Dahlan, and a number of Israelis, including Yossi Ginossar, the man who had been Rabin's private channel to Arafat.*

I was not sure how to read the message. Was it for real? Should I take him seriously? Could this be a response from Arafat to our last conversation? There was no point in prejudging what he would convey; I would wait and see.

As it turned out, Rashid brought a counterproposal in the form of a nonpaper. It was comprehensive; it suggested language on "hot pursuit," on arming the police, on the JMUs, on Shuhada Street, on the Hasbahe market, as well as on the civil and non-Hebron issues. On the non-Hebron issues, the nonpaper took a simple approach, calling for negotiations as soon as there was an agreement on Hebron redeployment, and offering an assurance that all of the Palestinian obligations (especially on security) stemming from the Interim Agreement would be fulfilled—an important priority for Bibi if he was to move on other issues.

If I had been looking for a sign that the Palestinians were ready to close, this was it. It was their first comprehensive proposal for a package deal. Surely Bibi would not like everything here, but it was serious and every issue was in the ballpark.

The question was, how to proceed? Rashid wanted me to accept everything here and make it an American proposal to the two sides. I was uneasy about this for two reasons. First, we had commitments going back to the Ford administration that we could not present a proposal in peace negotiations without first consulting with the Israelis.†
Second, what if it was not authorized by Arafat? What if I sold this to the Israelis and then Arafat said no?

I did not want to insult Rashid, but I needed to know this was authoritative. He suggested I call Arafat, and also had Osama al-Baz call me to vouch for what he had brought me. Osama, I asked, do you think this "represents Arafat or Rashid and Abu Mazen"? Osama's answer gave me pause: he was not sure. He, too, suggested I call Arafat.

So I called Arafat, with the recollection of the swap deal debacle making me doubt that anyone but Saeb was speaking for him now. Alas, my misgivings turned out to be right. Arafat was positive about the nonpaper, but vague when I tried to pin him down.

Clearly, there was a Palestinian constituency led by Abu Mazen that was trying to

---

*Yossi Ginossar spent his career in the Shin Bet. In the 1980s, representing the Shin Bet, he opened contact with the PLO. After the Declaration of Principles, Rabin realized that he needed a confidential way to communicate with Arafat. He chose Yossi to play this role.

†In a letter to the Israeli Prime Minister Yitzhak Rabin dated September 1, 1975, President Ford recognized "the special relationship" between the United States and Israel, and committed the U.S. to coordinate any proposals for peace originating with Israel. Ford sent the letter as part of American efforts to broker a second disengagement agreement—known as Sinai II—between Egypt and Israel.

finalize the deal, but they could not deliver. Before he left Washington in early December, I told Rashid that the nonpaper was "probably in the ballpark," but that I would neither act on it nor return to the region until I knew it was authoritative. He said he would get back to me, but I heard nothing after his return to Gaza.

Meanwhile, President Clinton called a meeting in the second week of December to discuss where we stood. Vice President Gore, Secretary Christopher, Tony Lake, and Sandy Berger attended, along with Madeleine Albright who would become my new boss. The President had recently appointed her the next Secretary of State.

I first came to know Madeleine during the 1988 presidential campaign. She was Governor Dukakis's chief advisor on national security. I was Vice President Bush's foreign policy advisor. We debated each other frequently, and cordially, and though we were obviously competitive in those circumstances, I found it hard not to like her. In truth, our instincts on most foreign policy issues were not very different. Moreover, I felt she was thoroughly decent, both thoughtful and knowledgeable, and we had enjoyed a good working relationship while she was the U.S. ambassador to the UN.

The President's meeting was more than a simple transition briefing of a new team. At this time, there were reports warning of the possibility of terrorist violence in Israel to coincide with the upcoming anniversaries of the Israeli killing of Fathi Shikaki, the former head of Islamic Jihad, in 1995, and Yahya Ayyash, the "engineer" of Hamas, in 1996. What was more, Israel had just announced new settlement activity. With the negotiations bogged down, the White House (and Al Gore in particular) worried that a terror attack now would unravel the negotiations and the peace process as a whole. In these circumstances, the Vice President asked, wouldn't it be good for me to return to the area and push to reach agreement now—or at least nail down everything that had been agreed to in order to preserve a framework for later?

President Clinton was sympathetic to this argument. He knew I did not want to return until we had a clearer sign that Arafat was ready to close, and he accepted the logic of my position. But he now believed there was a real danger that everything could blow up and we could be out of business on peace. If so, the risk of my going back now was real but acceptable given the alternative.

I told him I accepted his analysis but felt the current talks were finally beginning to make a little progress and I preferred to give them another week before returning lest the two sides conclude that the pressure was off.

President Clinton seemed convinced, but not Vice President Gore. He suggested that I go as soon as possible; to deal with my concerns about not easing the pressure on each side, he suggested the President send a letter to each leader telling them they had to change their behavior on my return to the region: Bibi on settlements, Arafat on security and a general reluctance to make a deal. That was agreed, along with the public description of my trip—to prepare a "report to the President" to be delivered by Christmas. (This added to my leverage both in terms of being able to say who was responding and who was not as well as giving me a deadline I could use.)

Before the meeting adjourned, I reminded President Clinton that if there was one reality about negotiating with Arafat, it was that he would never agree before he thought he had to. The greatest leverage we had was walking away, telling him we had done all we could, this was the best he was going to get, and that holding out for more would cost him dearly. I made this argument not only because I believed it, but also because I was still trying to convince the President that I need not go to the region immediately.

But I failed to convince him. President Clinton called the Secretary later that day and asked him to have me leave for the area without delay.

| INITIAL HEADWAY |

The President's letters arrived before I did, and once in Israel I found Netanyahu to be on the defensive. Given his low political standing, he did not need what his political enemies would portray as criticism from President Clinton. As a result, he was most agreeable in our meeting—and for the rest of my stay, which, with a three-day break to return to Washington, would last for over three weeks.

Arafat was a different story. I still did not know his clock or his calculus. But I was certain I could affect him by playing on his desire for America's intensive engagement. In our private meeting, then, I focused on President Clinton. Making a virtue of necessity, I told him I had not been in favor of coming out right now, but had come at the President's initiative, for he was banking on the Chairman now to do a deal.

"My advice to you," I told the Chairman, "is don't let Clinton down. If I go back empty-handed in a few days, the President will know that his assessment of you was wrong and that his initiative failed. With a new Secretary of State who has little background in the Middle East, I suspect the priorities of the administration in the second term will change. In any case, these priorities are being shaped now. So don't let President Clinton think he misjudged you. Put me in a position where I can say you responded."

In closing, I suggested that he and Bibi meet—and I would join them—to try to resolve the main issues separating them. Arafat demurred, saying he feared that such a meeting would make everything worse if we failed to make clear progress. I told him I did not want to limit the meetings to the negotiators; they simply went in circles, with neither negotiator capable of making decisions.

As a fallback, though, I suggested and he accepted that the negotiators on each side meet with each leader first. He agreed; Abu Mazen and Jibril Rajoub went to see Bibi, and the meeting actually produced some progress. The Palestinians agreed to the need for Palestinian checkpoints to keep Palestinians away from Israeli military positions; Bibi agreed to scale back the Israeli desire for a buffer zone between H-1 and H-2—something the Palestinians opposed lest it appear the city was being divided forever. Yitzik Molho's meeting with Arafat, though good atmospherically, was not productive. None of the core issues was resolved, and the issue of releasing women prisoners was now coming up in every meeting. There were twenty-nine women prisoners held by the Israelis; releasing them was important to the Palestinians, and Israeli President Ezer Weizman was prepared to pardon them. But Bibi had to request the pardon and he was reluctant to do so because the women had "blood on their hands."

On meeting Arafat again, I told him that at the moment it looked like I would be going back to President Clinton empty-handed. So I wanted the two leaders to meet, and I wanted a "result" to take back to Washington. "Will you come to such a meeting?" He nodded. "All right," I said, "but Mr. Chairman, don't just come to the meeting, make sure you give me a gift from that meeting that I can take to President Clinton." He promised he would.

We scheduled the meeting for December 24. By the night of the twenty-third, both Saeb Erekat and Yitzik Molho were bemoaning the meeting, fearing it would fail and create a crisis. In their own painstaking way, they felt they were making incremental progress. I was struck by the irony of the negotiators being against the leaders meeting, much the way Abu Ala and Uri Savir had opposed the meeting I had pushed in the summer of 1995 between Arafat and Peres. Negotiators often develop a stake in a particular kind of process, one in which they define its rhythm, its timing, and the pace of movement. They feel they know best when to take on certain issues and when to make concessions. They develop a proprietary feeling and resist intrusions from the outside.

If I had not had the experience of 1995, I might have been far more worried about their opposition to the meeting. But I was convinced that I had moved Arafat and that we would produce something from this meeting. And, rightly or wrongly, I was also convinced, much as I had been in 1995, that we could not move at a negotiator's pace—that the process might be overwhelmed by an external event if we did not accelerate progress within it.

Prior to the meeting on the twenty-fourth, I went to Bibi. Sitting alone with him, I said, "You know how to make this meeting a success? You do something up front and don't ask anything for it."

Bibi wanted to know what I had in mind. "Look," I said, "ask to see him alone, without me, for the first fifteen minutes. Make sure Gamal is there to translate. Tell him you are going to do something very hard for you. You are going to agree to release the women prisoners. You do not want this to be part of the formal agreement. You want it as a private understanding between the two of you since you know it is important to him."

Bibi asked if I really thought this would have a big effect and I nodded, saying that Arafat would see this as a personal gesture and feel the need to be responsive in some way. Bibi said he would think about it.

As I was en route to the meeting in Erez, Bibi called me and said he would do what I had suggested. He asked one thing of me. The Israeli press had raised expectations sky-high: we would not produce an agreement today. Could I speak to the press when I got there and lower their expectations and then speak to the press on behalf of both sides afterward? I agreed, provided Arafat also agreed, which he gladly did.

| THE EREZ SUMMIT PRODUCES A BREAKTHROUGH—OR SO I BELIEVE |

True to his word, Bibi asked to begin the meeting privately with Arafat and offered to release the women prisoners during the upcoming holy month of Ramadan. Arafat was pleased and thanked him for this gesture.

When I joined the meeting the mood was good, and so I said, We are going to produce results today. Before we have the negotiators join us, let's agree that today we will resolve "reentry" and the issue of weaponry in the joint mobile units. Both agreed. I asked Bibi what he needed on reentry, and his answer was that he could agree to a formula that did not refer to Israel or threats to it, but instead referred to "the applicability of the provisions in the Interim Agreement for dealing with threats to security." I wrote this out, showed it to Arafat, and asked can you accept this? "Okay," was his reply, and I asked him what he needed on the arms in the joint mobile units. His answer was acceptance of "equivalent weapons" for the IDF and the Palestinian police. I asked Arafat what "equivalent weapons" meant, and he explained that the weapons did not have to be the same, just similar. Bibi said how about "you get Mini-Ingrams and we will accept short M-16s." "Okay?" I asked Arafat, and he nodded, saying "okay."

At this point, I wondered whether we could resolve the other security issues—the circumstances under which Palestinian police would have rifles in H-1, the checkpoints (for reducing points of friction) on the maps, and the routes for the joint mobile units. Arafat suggested that the two leaders give instructions to their security people to resolve these issues in a separate meeting. "Agreed," was Bibi's staccato reply.

Bibi raised the non-Hebron issues and suggested that I set up a meeting to try to final-ize agreement on all the relevant issues and obligations. Earlier I had suggested that we not make understandings on these issues part of the Hebron accord but formalize them instead in a "Note for the Record" that I would sign along with the negotiators.

It was Arafat's turn to agree. Bibi then suggested that we all work toward one more summit meeting. Arafat agreed with this, but also asked for Israel to consider granting Palestinians a role in the administration of the Ibrahimi Mosque in Hebron—a review of the Palestinian status at the mosque had been promised as part of the Interim Agree-ment but nothing had been done. Bibi offered a short-term fix: What if during Ra-madan a Turkish representative could sit outside the mosque? Arafat consented but he still wanted a more visible Palestinian presence as well. I raised the idea of the Waqf having a more visible presence there, and both leaders said they would think about it.

All in all, the meeting had been very good. We had agreement on two big issues and goodwill on the others, even the extremely sensitive matter of the Ibrahimi Mosque.

The mosque produced the only drama in the meeting. When the delegations from the two sides joined us, the leaders asked me to brief them on our discussions. When I described that we had discussed a possible Palestinian presence or role at the mosque, General Mofaz, from the Israeli side, said bluntly, "The Palestinians have no role there." Arafat bridled: "We have no role there?" Mofaz replied, "You have no role there." Arafat stood up, buttoned his jacket deliberately, muttered that he was leaving, and as he walked around the table both Mohammad Dahlan and Gamal literally put their hands on his chest, keeping him from doing so.

Rather than injecting myself into this issue, I asked Bibi if there was anything he wanted to say, hoping he would raise his idea of a Turkish presence. Cautiously he ac-knowledged that he was prepared to consider such a possibility, whereupon Arafat—having made his point that he had needs on the mosque—returned to the table. Soon we were joking, and I went out to brief the press, telling them that I would return to Washington with the news that we had made progress in a good meeting.

I was hopeful now. Arafat looked to be ready to solve problems, not perpetuate them. Bibi was obviously eager, and the positive atmosphere and goodwill carried over to the meetings we scheduled between the negotiators on Christmas Day.

Before returning to Washington on the red-eye flight Christmas night, I saw Arafat privately in Ramallah. He was completely relaxed, and suggested he had done what I asked—given me a gift to take back to Clinton.

I told him I would brief the President and return to the area by December 29, ex-pecting all the security issues to be finalized in my absence. He nodded approvingly and walked me out to the car, suddenly whispering in my ear that it would help him to conclude the agreement if Osama al-Baz could come to join me on my return. Could I ask Mubarak to send him?

Wouldn't Mubarak be more likely to respond to a request from you, not us? I asked. It would help, he said, if we would ask also.

I interpreted his mood and his request as indications that he had made up his mind to close and was now thinking about the trappings—Egyptian involvement—and the packaging of the deal. Once again, however, my judgment turned out to be wrong, or at least premature.

| THE ENDGAME THAT WASN'T |

I gave the President an encouraging report, but observed that Arafat usually created a crisis before finally closing just to test whether he had gotten all he could. On my return to the area, however, I discovered two problems. First, Mubarak had not sent Osama, but a lawyer from the Egyptian Foreign Ministry—someone more likely to nitpick issues than give Arafat cover for a deal. Second, with the pressure off, the two sides had failed to resolve all the security issues, and were haggling again.

I let both leaders know that neither side had fulfilled what each had promised. Naturally, both blamed the other side's negotiators. I resolved to sit with the security officials. A new issue had emerged: the Israelis, citing the potential for friction between settlers and armed Palestinian police, did not want a Joint Mobile Unit to patrol Route 35—a route used by settlers. After Jibril Rajoub pointed out that a bypass road existed for the settlers to use, the Israelis yielded. In turn, Rajoub accepted the locale for the JMU in H-2 and the Israeli proposal to permit four Palestinian rapid-response teams in H-1 to be armed with rifles. With the exception of Shuhada Street and the market, all the security issues were now resolved—or so I thought. To settle the market issue, we arranged for the local Israeli and Palestinian commanders to get together and work out how to reopen it—perhaps closing some stalls and creating a wall to insulate the Israeli settlers from potential trouble. To resolve the road issue, I proposed that we survey it and construct security barriers to guard against possible shooting from Palestinian vehicles that otherwise would pass in front of the yeshiva and Jewish community center—and this was accepted.

Now, when I thought we were out of the woods, Saeb asked for a "favor." He wanted to change just one word in the reentry formula. Instead of both sides "recognizing" the applicability of the specified provisions of the Interim Agreement, both sides would "honor" these provisions. One word—but he was suggesting a change on the most sensitive issue of all, making the language that bound the two sides abstract rather than precise. Bibi would inevitably demand a change of language on "equivalent weapons" in return. I suggested to Saeb that this was the wrong time to raise this; I would hold this until such time as Bibi asked for something new—almost a certainty—and try to trade it at that time.

Saeb said, "Dennis, we need this." To which I replied that his boss had accepted one formulation and now was changing it, even though it had been part of a deal. I would do my best for them, but he had to trust my instincts on how to try to do it. He accepted that, and later I was able to make the change he sought.

We were done on the security issues. Next I turned my attention to the civil issues and the Note for the Record, suspecting as always that as we truly got into the endgame each side would make the remaining issues more important than they had been. Sure enough, on December 31 Bibi told me that the Note for the Record could not refer to more than one further redeployment (FRD). I pointed out that the whole reason for the Note for the Record was that the Palestinians did not trust Bibi to carry out his obligations on the Interim Agreement, which required three FRDs. The Palestinians wanted a very specific timeline for when the FRDs would be completed; I was resisting that, but I needed a reference to Israel completing all of the further redeployments. I could not sell them anything less. I reminded Bibi that he had promised me the FRDs would not be a problem.

Bibi said, "Dennis, the cabinet will not accept anything more than a reference to the first FRD." The more I pressed him, the more he dug in.

It was New Year's Eve day, I would be seeing Arafat that evening, and the deal was threatening to unravel again. Arafat was expecting a discussion on the further redeployment. I decided to tell Arafat that the most I could get him on the FRD issue was a reference to doing all of them. This, of course, contradicted what I had just heard from Bibi. But I knew that if I went to Arafat now and told him there could be a reference to only one FRD, he would insist that the Palestinians had to know chapter and verse of every Israeli FRD—and I had to preempt that possibility from becoming the new Palestinian baseline or there would be no deal.

To be sure, I was also convinced that Bibi's position on the FRD was ultimately a tactic, and that at the end of the day he would concede the point if it meant the difference between a deal and no deal. So in my New Year's Eve meeting I told Arafat that the most we could get on the further redeployment issue was a commitment to doing all of them; if he pressed for more, he would lose everything—no Hebron deal, no commitment on all the Interim Agreement issues. Arafat said he understood. I left believing I had moved him, but doubting whether I could move Bibi anytime soon. On this score, I was in for a surprise.

| BIBI TURNS FLEXIBLE, ARAFAT HARDENS HIS POSITION |

On January 1, I was eating breakfast before my meeting with Bibi when I learned that an Israeli soldier, unprovoked, had opened fire on a crowd of Palestinians in Hebron, leaving many dead or wounded.

My heart sank. It looked like a replay of the Ibrahimi Mosque massacre. How many were dead? Who were among them? Would we have to put the negotiations on hold? Would Arafat reopen all the security issues, insisting that Palestinians, not Israelis needed security? How would Bibi respond?

By the time I arrived at Bibi's office, there was news that while more than twenty Palestinians were wounded, none had died, at least not yet.

This act of Israeli terrorism had made Bibi more open to the Palestinian positions. Suddenly he volunteered that the "Note" could have a reference to Israel carrying out all three further redeployments. In my presence, he called Arafat, expressing his sorrow for what had happened, offering condolences and medical assistance for the wounded, and explaining that the IDF reservist (Noam Friedman) who had committed the crime had a history of mental problems. It was especially important for the security officials on both sides to cooperate closely now, he said, and Arafat promised such cooperation.

I was not sure what I would find in Gaza when I met Arafat. Would he rant and rave? Would he demand new protections for Palestinians from the Israelis in Hebron? Would he insist on an international presence in Hebron and elsewhere to provide for Palestinian security? Would he stake out a new position on reentry?

To my surprise, I found him relaxed and at ease, even in good humor. It occurred to me later that whenever I saw him after Israeli violence against Palestinians, he was relaxed. On these days, he knew I would not be coming to pressure him. On these days, the onus was certain to be on the other side. This particular day Arafat surprised me by not demanding more on security. Instead, he demanded more on the further redeployments.

What he had acknowledged the previous evening was now gone. Knowing the onus was on the Israelis, he upped the ante, seeking a deadline for the completion of the FRD or withdrawal. As he put it, he needed to know whether the FRDs would be completed "in 1997 or 2097."

I was not ready to tell Arafat that Bibi had moved on this issue, knowing that at this point what Bibi was ready to do still fell far short of what Arafat was seeking. To get him to do more would be an enormous challenge. For now, I decided to play it straight with Bibi and simply report what Arafat sought—namely, to know, in his words, whether the last FRD would be in 1997 or 2097. But the Prime Minister was not buying. He was at the limit of what his cabinet could accept. Would the Palestinians fulfill their obligations? Were they accepting what Israel needed in the Note for the Record?

His response convinced me that he would give something on the FRD issue, but not in this way and not now. We had agreed that the two leaders—Netanyahu and Arafat—would meet when we were in a position to close. Now, however, it occurred to me that perhaps another unannounced summit meeting could be used to try to forge an understanding on the FRD issue. My deputy, Aaron Miller, had been meeting with Dore Gold and Yasser Abed Rabbo on the Note for the Record, and it was clear to me that the gap—at least on the FRD issue—would not be bridged by them. Dore, even after Bibi had given me the *s* on the word redeployment, was still balking at referring to the "phases of further redeployment." Instead, he was only willing to refer to the "process" of further redeployment. Yasser insisted on having a specific reference to the six-month interval on each phase of the FRDs that was mandated in the Interim Agreement. Aaron had offered a formula designed to give the Palestinians what they wanted, and to give the Israelis cover: "The FRDs will be completed as specified in the Interim Agreement." However, Bibi would not accept that. It left him no flexibility, and precious little ambiguity. Perhaps, sitting with Arafat, he would budge.

I proposed a secret meeting, and Bibi agreed, suggesting it be held at a Mossad safe house. Arafat was leery, doubting it would remain secret. I agreed, but told him that an unannounced meeting would neither raise expectations nor create a letdown. Arafat relented, provided the meeting was at Erez. Bibi agreed and elaborate steps were taken to keep the meeting secret; I told only my security detail and Gamal, who would interpret for the two leaders.

Bibi arrived early, traveling not in his normal car, an armored Cadillac, but in an unmarked ambulance. Two hours later—at 2 a.m.—Arafat arrived. Perhaps because he was not keen on this meeting, Arafat was testy from the outset. Immediately he raised two issues: the end point for the FRD and the Ibrahimi Mosque. On the first, Arafat repeated the question, when would the last FRD take place, was it 1997 or 2097? On the mosque, when would the Turkish official arrive to assume responsibilities? Bibi gave negative answers to both and then sought to make them acceptable. On the FRD, he said the cabinet would not accept a specific end date, but he personally promised to complete all three redeployments prior to the end of the interim period, May 1999. On the mosque, Bibi now rejected the Turkish officer's presence altogether, saying it was too difficult for him, but he would try to work something out for Ramadan.

Arafat blew up. "You raised the Turks coming; I did not—now you back away from your own proposal." On the FRD, Bibi was suggesting that Israel would hold re-deployment until the last possible moment, whereas the Palestinians wanted the FRDs—in keeping with the Interim Agreement—completed well before the end of the interim period lest the Israelis hold land as a card in the permanent status negotiations, using it to get more favorable terms on Jerusalem or refugees.

Perhaps Arafat was genuinely angry, perhaps tactically so. Whatever the reason, I suggested we take a break and that I hold discussions with each of them separately.

I sat first with Bibi. He was defensive, and looking for a way out, with us and with his cabinet. I raised two possibilities.

On redeployments, perhaps we (the United States) could write a letter to Arafat stating our view of the end point; that would provide Arafat with an assurance "without necessarily requiring you to state a position that gets you in hot water with the cabinet." On the mosque, I asked whether a Turkish observer could be added to the TIPH—the group of international observers in Hebron established after Dr. Goldstein's killing rampage in the Ibrahimi Mosque: "TIPH," I said, "is already in Hebron, and can move around the mosque. From your standpoint you are not really breaking new ground, but Arafat gets his symbol."

Bibi was enthusiastic about the idea of an American letter on the FRD end point, and promised to consult with his security people about the mosque.

While I worked with Bibi, Abu Mazen—who accompanied Arafat to the meeting—had been working on the Chairman for a possible compromise on the mosque; unbeknownst to me, he was pushing an idea close to my own—namely, giving the Turks a low-key role in the TIPH and letting them patrol around the mosque. Now I went to see Arafat and began to outline my discussions with Bibi, starting with the mosque. Quickly Arafat interrupted to say that Abu Mazen had suggested a similar compromise and suddenly we were joking about how great minds think alike.

Next I explained my idea for a letter from us "to you that spells out our view on the general timing for concluding the FRD process." Arafat responded with "Yes, why not?"

I suggested we get back together with the Prime Minister so I could summarize where we stood. We did so, and both Bibi and Arafat agreed that the American letter was a good way to overcome the difference on the FRDs. It was nearly 6 a.m., and for secrecy's sake Bibi would have to leave soon, before Israelis began arriving for work at the military facility in Erez. But before letting him go, I suggested that since we were now making headway on the non-Hebron issues, why not tie down the agreement on the Hebron protocol that evening?

Both the Prime Minister and the Chairman accepted this suggestion. Bibi joked that he needed to get back in his ambulance if news of the meeting were not to be broadcast all over Israel.

After Bibi left, Arafat invited me to come over to his side of the Erez crossing for breakfast, and I did so. I was ready to eat and to cement Arafat's understanding of the importance of getting an American letter—to build up what I was offering him while conditioning him not to expect too much.

As I pointed out to him, he could use the letter to put the onus on the Israelis internationally if they did not fulfill their responsibilities. I told Arafat that I had not run this idea by the President or the Secretary of State, and could not be sure they would accept it. I would push hard for them to be prepared to send the letter to him. But the letter was unprecedented—we had not written a letter offering our interpretation of any part of the Interim Agreement—and he should not push the President on its content. "Do that," I warned him, "and you will lose the letter."

Arafat now sought to reassure me: he understood the importance of the letter and would respect what we could and could not do; he was eager to try to finish the agreement soon. Could the letter finally give him his rationale to close? We would soon find out.

| STRUGGLING TO CLOSE |

In proposing the letter to get around the problem of the redeployments in the Note for the Record, I knew I had created yet another object of negotiation. What had begun as a negotiation on Hebron redeployment would end with us negotiating a protocol on Hebron, a Note for the Record, and what became known as the Christopher letter, making Hebron far more complex than anyone had anticipated in the always complex peace process.

And, of course, what we thought had been concluded with Hebron was not quite done. Shuhada Street continued to be a sticking point. Having promised that the United States would survey the road and reconstruct it as necessary, I had an American civil engineer produce a drawing of the reconstructed road, the safety barriers that would be filled with shrubbery and flowers, necessary improvements of utilities, installation of lampposts, and construction of concrete median strips and sidewalks. We now recorded all this in an "Agreed Minute" attached to the Hebron protocol and the issue was finally settled.*

Five nights earlier we had concluded a one-page text summarizing agreements on modified language on the civil arrangements and also on the outstanding security questions, but that did not mean that recognition of the agreement was a given. Our evening session on the night of January 2 stretched into the next morning of January 3; at around 4 a.m., Martin suggested we record what had been understood, and I dictated the precise terms of agreement and then proposed that each side initial it so as to "acknowledge the understanding we have reached." As Yitzhak Mordechai was about

---

*I got Arafat to sign the engineer's schematic and recorded an agreement for the reconstruction of Shuhada Street on January 7, 1997.

to initial, Yitzik Molho told him that as the Defense Minister he had no such authority. Abu Mazen then said if Mordechai would not initial, then neither would he.

Incensed, and fearing everything would be reopened the next day if there was no initialing, I shouted, "Give it to me, I will initial it." Everyone watched quietly; we made copies for each side and we were on the way to finalizing agreement on the Hebron redeployment. After both sides left, I asked Jon Schwartz, "Do my initials have any legal standing?" He laughed, saying it was hard to see how my initials could bind anyone but me.

That left us the Note for the Record and the Christopher letter. Over the next days, I found myself going around and around with the negotiators on each side. For example, Abu Mazen still wanted the Note to include some reference to the phases of redeployment called for in the Interim Agreement. I said I could not get that, but would work to persuade Bibi to accept the word "phases," and a general reference to the responsibilities that would be carried out by each side in accordance with the Interim Agreement. That "ought to meet your needs," I said, and Abu Mazen and Abed Rabbo went into Martin's study to call Arafat. Gamal had placed the call for them from another room and stayed on the line.

Gamal returned to the living room alone, clearly agitated. "The Egyptians just screwed us," he told me. Abu Mazen had explained to Arafat what I was offering, and Arafat said that sounded "pretty good." But then he asked Abu Mazen to explain it to "our Egyptian lawyer," who deemed it much too soft, instead giving him a formula requiring a specific date for each FRD—essentially undoing a week of painstaking Palestinian movement.

Abu Mazen and Abed Rabbo were visibly sheepish as they walked back into the living room, and they were even more embarrassed as they presented what they were being asked to produce on this issue.

It was now my turn to blow a fuse. After listening to the formula, I started yelling that this was ridiculous. Why should we produce a letter to the Chairman if they were going to come back to us with a formula that had been so drastically altered and was obviously unacceptable? Why should I even continue this process? As Martin tried to explain politely to them it was a mistake even to present this formula, I yelled at him to "shut up. I don't want to explain that this is wrong. I am not negotiating like this any longer." I proceeded to walk out of the room and retreated to the den in the guest rooms' side of the residence. I had not meant to yell at Martin, but I was mad and I wanted Abu Mazen and Abed Rabbo to know I was out of patience. I also wanted Arafat to know that if he listened to this kind of advice from his Egyptian advisors, he would lose us.

Before they returned to Gaza, Abu Mazen and Abed Rabbo came apologetically to see me in the den. They said they would do their best to produce the formula I had told them I could accept. I told them I was not angry at them personally, but I would not do business this way, and if it kept up, there would be no agreement and no American envoy out here. This would not be my last explosion.

| MY CONFRONTATION WITH ARAFAT |

Two nights later I went to see Arafat at the Greek Patriarch's house in Bethlehem. We had dinner as a large group together, and then he and I adjourned to sit privately. No doubt he knew about my explosion from the other evening.

Little had changed since then and I saw the pattern of the negotiations on the Hebron protocol being repeated on the Note for the Record and the Christopher letter. I was not prepared, I told Arafat bluntly, to go through that again. I would simply not stay in the region to debate the same issues over and over again. The Hebron protocol was done. If he was ready to do a deal, he should tell me exactly what it was he needed to close; if it was within the parameters of what I thought was possible I would try to get it for him.

To my surprise, he responded clearly, specifically, outlining what he needed on six issues to close: (1) the letter from Christopher; (2) the TIPH arrangement on the mosque; (3) a commitment from Bibi not to build unduly in the Old City of Hebron; (4) Shuhada Street to be reopened incrementally over four months, and made secure without inconvenience to Palestinians and disruption to their shops; (5) the first FRD to take place in less than twelve weeks; (6) a fair and clear end point for the FRDs.

Never had Arafat been as clear and precise with me. Never had he been so systematic. He had used no notes. He seemed to know what he wanted.

I took it all down and then asked him a question: Are you telling me that if I can produce these six points, we have a deal? "Yes," was his direct reply. I told him I would go to work on it.

It was now close to midnight. I called Bibi from my Chevy Suburban as we were leaving Bethlehem and briefed him on the meeting, telling him I thought we should work tonight on coming up with responses on all six points. He agreed and I went directly to see him.

We worked together, thrashing out answers. The only real sticking point was on the specific end point for the FRDs. He wanted a time frame, not a specific date, and he wanted it to be as late as possible, preferably the end of 1998. We discussed this at some length; I told him the end of 1998 would not fly; he suggested by the last quarter of 1998; I countered with by the beginning of the last quarter of 1998. He said he would accept this only if it "seals the deal."

It was dawn when we concluded our discussion. Did I think this would do it, he asked? I was hopeful, but not certain. It would be evening before I saw Arafat in Gaza, who was busy that day with ceremonies in Bethlehem and would be returning to Gaza late in the afternoon. But I assured him that when I saw Arafat I would test the ground before giving anything away lest Arafat pocket it and ask for more.

On the ride down to Gaza, I knew I had to see if what Arafat had said last night in Bethlehem was real. If it was, we could conclude very quickly; if it was not, I needed to keep in reserve what Bibi had given me.

As usual in our Gaza meetings, the Chairman, Gamal, and I met in the Chairman's meeting room. The room had two sliding doors that separated us from what served as his cabinet room and the formal dining room. Members of both teams were in the outer room behind the sliding doors. The Chairman and I sat in chairs that were next to each other but separated by a small table on which Arafat had a phone. The chairs, with their backs to the wall in the front of the room, did not face each other; we would turn in these big chairs so our bodies would face each other. Gamal took a small upholstered footstool and sat on it directly in front of the Chairman. In this way, he was sometimes literally "in his face."

Gamal was exceptional. He was not just an interpreter of language but also an interpreter of people and culture. He had become indispensable to me during the Hebron shuttle. He had developed a relationship of trust with Abu Mazen, Mohammad Dahlan, and Jibril Rajoub and they would confide in him. I understood that they knew this was a deniable way to communicate with me, and I took it for what it was. I did not take everything at face value, knowing this was also a way to try to influence me. Nonetheless, the communication would often provide insight into the competition on the Palestinian side and what might or might not work. Gamal's instinctive reaction to certain arguments or points often mirrored what I would later get from the Palestinians, and he became a sounding board I would use to test different ways of proceeding. In addition, his instincts for what to do in the negotiations from a tactical point of view were very similar to mine. At times he would predict to other members of the team how I would likely respond to one approach or another—and he was usually right.

What made Gamal such an extraordinary interpreter was his talent not only for mastering the subject he was interpreting but also for capturing the mood and the emotion of every point. He never gave a technical interpretation unless it was called for. But if a point needed to be made with great emotion, he made it. At times in meetings with Arafat, he asked me if he could try another way to make the point I would be trying to convey, and almost always I approved his doing so. Arafat's English is pretty good, but I did not want him to use language as a pretext for claiming a misunderstanding—and I did not mind if he heard something twice.

On this night, I told Gamal, I would protect what I had from Bibi by testing Arafat's initial reaction on the least sensitive of the six points. If Arafat was ready to close, I would proceed quickly with what I had produced; if not, I would explode. Gamal understood and was ready to convey my mood.

As the Chairman and I began our meeting, I told him I had gone directly from Bethelem to Jerusalem and had spent most of the night with the Prime Minister. I now believed I had very serious responses on the six points the Chairman had said he needed in order to do the deal. I started with the Christopher letter, its main points and our willingness to say in it that the agreement was based on the Interim Agreement. I paused, wanting to see Arafat's reaction. It was not promising. He was dismissive, saying that gave him very little, effectively ignoring what he had asked for the previous night. But I was still only testing him, so I tried another item from his list of six: Shuhada Street. I explained that we had sent Aaron Miller down to Hebron with an engineer, who had developed plans for Shuhada Street designed to ensure that Palestinians would not be inconvenienced by the security configuration—and Bibi was prepared to accept whatever plans the engineer proposed. Arafat said he was glad we had sent the engineer down and he looked forward to seeing the plans but Bibi's acceptance of them meant little. He could have no say in the plans.

The whole negotiation had been about reconciling Israeli security concerns with Palestinian needs in H-2. How could Bibi have no say in the plans?

At this point, I stopped. Mr. Chairman, I said, last night I asked you what it would take for you to close the deal. You identified six items. I did what was required of us and produced what was necessary from Prime Minister Netanyahu. I have mentioned two items on your list; the list was yours, not mine. Now when I start to tell you what I have done, you dismiss what I say and tell me it is unimportant. What is going on here?

Arafat's reply was to deny that he had asked for what I was now describing. Incredulous, I asked did you not give me six items to produce for you to make a deal possible last night? Yes, he allowed, he had asked for a number of things, but not those I was now presenting, which "are unimportant."

I told him that while these were not the full list, they were certainly part of it; I had now produced on them and I saw little point in continuing if he was going to deny that he had asked for them. How did I know he would not continue to deny the other items on the list?

He shot back, "Are you calling me a liar?" Coldly, I said, I am simply telling you what you told me last night. "You are calling me a liar," he blurted out. "Look," I said, "you ask me to produce for you. I work almost all night to do so, and now you dismiss what I describe and deny you asked for it. What is the point of my asking you about what is important, and of working to produce it, if I am then going to be confronted with you denying the whole effort? I cannot do business this way and I won't."

He responded in English now in singsong fashion: "You are always right and I am always wrong. You are always right and I am always wrong." I said, "I did not say that. But I am right this time." Again, he posed the question in English, "Are you calling me a liar?" At this point, I said, "If the shoe fits." I then stood up and walked to the double sliding doors, opened them, and to the astonishment of both teams standing out there, I flung my black binder a good fifteen feet to the table where we normally ate and watched as it knocked over a pitcher of grapefruit juice.

Obviously, I was furious and I wanted everyone to know it. I had not intended to hit the pitcher of juice; I had not even seen it as I flung the binder. But it certainly demonstrated that there was a major problem. My team rushed to me and Arafat's rushed to him. Everyone on my side wanted to know what had happened, and I said he'd denied he asked me to produce what I had produced. We were not going to do business this way, and Arafat must understand that.

Everyone on my side simply listened. Ed Abington asked if he should go talk to Abu Mazen and then maybe to Arafat. I told him no, not yet. They must see that they had a big problem; it was their problem, not ours. I wanted them to take the first step to correct it.

In the meantime, I would add to the pressure on them. I asked for a cell phone and called the White House, reporting what had happened to Mark Parris in a voice loud enough for them to hear it in the next room even behind the sliding doors.

After about thirty minutes, Saeb came out and approached me. He told me this was all a big misunderstanding; the Chairman greatly appreciated everything I was doing, he had enormous respect for me, and he knew we would only reach agreement with my efforts. "Saeb," I said, "that's all fine and good, but he asked for several things last night, and I have produced what he asked and now he denies this is what he asked for. Why should I work through the night to produce from Netanyahu if this is what I get when I do so?"

Again, he repeated this was all a big misunderstanding. I should go sit with the Chairman again and we would iron all this out. Saeb, I said, if he denies what he asked, we are nowhere. There was no misunderstanding on my part.

Saeb asked me to give him a few minutes. This time he returned with Abu Mazen. They said the Chairman wanted to apologize to me. Fine, I will accept it, but I have to know whether he stood by what he told me last night? The answer was ambiguous; he was interested in hearing what more I had to say. "Not a chance," I told them, "unless he accepts what I have said so far." Their expressions told me that this was not going to happen that night.

Abu Mazen asked if I could just sit with him; he wanted to apologize. Okay, I said, but I will not go through what else I had produced, and I will tell him I did not intend to ask anything more from Bibi until there was an acknowledgment of what he asked me to do.

When I returned to see him, Arafat was contrite personally, but not on the substance of our discussion. "Mr. Chairman," I said, "I am not going to rehash our discussion. But understand that I will not go back to Netanyahu for anything more." He said he understood.

As we were driving back to Jerusalem from Gaza, I asked Gamal what he thought had happened. He did not know, but would ask Abu Mazen and Dahlan. The next evening I heard that Arafat had gone over the six points with the Egyptians and they told him it would be a big mistake to settle for so little.

The following day Saeb came to me and suggested that if we could agree on the specific date for the last redeployment, the Chairman would stand by our earlier discussion and everything would fall into place on the Note for the Record. He said Arafat had wanted it by the end of 1997, but after last night, as a show of good faith, he was prepared to accept February 1998 or "the first quarter of 1998." I told him Bibi was at the end of 1998, and we would probably need to find a formula somewhere in between. Saeb's response seemed like a non sequitur: Maybe you should go talk to Mubarak. When I asked him if the Egyptians were prepared to help or hinder, he answered, "If you go there, they will probably help."

I took this to mean that they weren't helping now but if I were to go to Cairo—demonstrating publicly that I needed and valued the Egyptian role—the Egyptians would lend a hand. I was uneasy, feeling that by going I was rewarding their obstructionist behavior. But if they required a visible acknowledgment of their importance, it made sense to go—and when I called Secretary Christopher to talk it over, he encouraged me to do so.

It was late Thursday night and I made a plan to go to Cairo on Saturday. On Friday, as we negotiated over the language of the Christopher letter—something I was doing with both sides—Saeb suggested that he would recommend to Arafat a May 1998 end date for the FRDs. I told him I doubted we would produce that, but I acknowledged that this was an important move on their part.

In Cairo, my first meeting was with President Mubarak. Prior to my arrival, Bibi had called Mubarak to ask for his help, which irked me for it implied that I was there to do Bibi's bidding.

I had sought such a call to Mubarak from President Clinton, but the best I could get was an oral message "from the White House" which I drafted myself and conveyed.

In any case, Mubarak showed scant interest in the oral message or the details of the

Hebron protocol, the Note for the Record, or the specific gains the Palestinians had made. The only issue that mattered to him was when the Israeli redeployments would be completed throughout the West Bank. If that end point were satisfactorily resolved, he would tell Arafat he should settle.

I had in my pocket Bibi's suggestion of the beginning of the last quarter of 1998, but I hoped not to use it. Instead, I told Mubarak I had an idea. What if we said that the last FRD would be completed within twelve months of, but no later than eighteen months of, the beginning of the first FRD. It was now January 1997, so if the first FRD took place this spring, the last one would end as early as the spring of 1998, but not later than September or October 1998. Mubarak suggested that I work on this formula with Moussa, and we adjourned to do so.

When we arrived at Moussa's office, Saeb Erekat and Yasser Abed Rabbo were already there. Moussa launched immediately into the details, not just those on the FRD, as if to negotiate issues that I felt were basically closed. The last thing I wanted was to add an Egyptian participant to the negotiations.

When Moussa asked me to brief Saeb and Yasser on the "not later than eighteen months end point" idea I had raised with Mubarak, I told him I had not cleared this in Washington and I needed to do so, leaving to go to our embassy to phone Secretary Christopher. My real reason for breaking the meeting was that I was not willing to negotiate every point with the Egyptians.

When I returned, Moussa said he had a suggestion: How about May 1998 as the end date? Egypt would support that, but not a later date or my twelve-to-eighteen month proposal.

I had no doubt that Saeb had put him up to this. But I was not going to be in a position in which I tried out a new idea and then had him trying to negotiate it down. In response, I said, I was in no position to accept his suggestion. The end date would go in a letter from the U.S. Secretary of State. What I had presented to President Mubarak was a suggestion—and a stretch on my part. Since it was not accepted, I would now withdraw it, and maybe, I said, it was a mistake to try to produce a precise date.

"Fine," Amre Moussa said with his usual self-assurance, but he claimed it was doubtful that a deal would be possible without the Palestinians getting May 1998.

At this point I did not know what was going on with Egypt. Was it possible that Mubarak, feeling he had called on the Arab world early in Bibi's tenure to give him a chance, believed he had been burned by Netanyahu and wanted nothing to do with him now? Going back to the Bush administration, there had been a constant, if quiet, Egyptian effort to work with the Israeli Labor Party whenever Likud was either in power or leading a national unity government. Were Mubarak and Moussa banking on the idea that if there were no agreement, this would undercut Bibi and hasten Labor's return to power? As I flew back to Israel, I wondered whether Arafat would allow the Egyptians to frustrate an agreement if he really wanted one.

As I got off the plane from Cairo, there was a message from Prime Minister Netanyahu asking me to call as soon as possible. I did, and he had interesting news: King Hussein of Jordan had requested overflight clearance for a trip to Gaza tomorrow. Did I think this was a good sign? I told him I was not sure but it might be. Hussein would never go to Gaza unless Arafat had invited him. Perhaps Arafat, feeling thwarted by the Egyptians, was seeking help from another Arab country, either to play the two off against each other or to teach Egypt a lesson.

Shortly after, King Hussein called me, and (sure enough) Arafat had asked him to come to Gaza. He was determined to be helpful, but he needed to know the state of play. Could I brief him? I spent close to an hour doing so, stressing the need to reconcile an end point of the FRD process between the spring of 1998 (as the Palestinians sought) or the fall of 1998 (as the Israelis sought). Clearly, I observed, there was room for a compromise, but it would not work unless it sealed the overall deal once and for all.

The King thanked me for the thorough briefing, and told me he would call after he finished with Arafat. Then Saeb came with another offer—July 1998—which I read as indicating that Arafat wanted the King to provide him cover for doing the deal.

I told Saeb I could work with this, but that I had promised King Hussein I would wait until after his meeting with Arafat before taking my next step. A short time later the King called from his meeting with Arafat in Gaza, telling me Arafat would accept "summer 1998" if this would settle the issue and offering to come to Israel that night if I thought it would help. I was sure it would, provided Bibi accepted the compromise. I had one suggestion on the compromise: Could Arafat accept the slightly vaguer language "mid-1998" rather than "summer of 1998"? The King asked Arafat and he had no problem. Now I asked the King to wait with Arafat until I was sure Bibi would accept the compromise.

I called Bibi, explaining "mid-1998" not only as a tactical move on the date but as a strategic opening in which Jordan—clearly more constructive than Egypt—intervened and succeeded. I told him, "Arafat is permitting it and you have a stake in promoting it. The King is willing to come here to see you tonight, provided you accept the compromise on mid-1998. You have to accept this."

Bibi quickly understood what was at stake, but he said he needed a little time. I did not want to keep the King and Arafat sitting for long—long enough to concoct some other demand. So I called Secretary Christopher and asked him to call back and speak to the King and the Chairman together and hold them to "mid-1998." He did so.

I was patched into the call so I could hear the conversation, and the moment it ended Bibi called and said that if we could give him an assurance that mid-1998 could mean as late as August, he would accept the deal. I told him we would do so, and actually put Gamal on the line to explain that mid-1998 in the Arabic world could actually be from June to September.

With the compromise agreed, King Hussein of Jordan came to Israel for an 11 p.m. meeting in Tel Aviv. Saeb Erekat represented the Palestinians as Bibi, the King, and I sat in a large meeting room in the Defense Ministry compound. The only discordant note came from Saeb, who said it might take more than twenty-four hours to finalize the language in the Note for the Record. Saeb again turned out to be a better predictor than anyone else.

| ONE LAST THREAT TO LEAVE |

The next morning I assembled the negotiating teams on the balcony of my suite at the LaRomme hotel in Jerusalem to go over the Note for the Record. We identified twelve disagreements in the text; some were minor and easily fixed, like the precise titles of the two leaders. Others masked deeper concerns. The Israelis wanted to qualify their obligations on Palestinian performance, seeking to condition their actions on "reciprocity." The Palestinians, too, had their demands, seeking to make all their obligations clearly tied to provisions of the Interim Agreement, not Israeli demands. Both tried to impose standards of measurement on the other side—with the Israelis demanding "adequate and effective" punishment of terrorists by the Palestinians, and the Palestinians insisting on "adequate" Israeli prisoner releases and FRDs.

All day I took turns putting pressure on one side and then the other to accept the text as it was or with my minor adjustments to accommodate each side's concerns. Finally, after working hard on Saeb alone, I persuaded him to drop eight of the Palestinian points on language in response to my suggestions—suggestions Yitzik told me he could accept.

That left us with four issues, involving the two sides' different views of how to describe commitments on Israeli prisoner releases, Palestinian punishment of terrorists, Palestinian transfer of suspects, and the location of Palestinian offices—an issue designed by the Israelis to rule out any Palestinian Authority presence in Jerusalem. Before bringing Yitzik and Saeb together to resolve the remaining issues, I talked to Yitzik and said, "I got them to move toward you on the other eight issues; we can finish this now if you will be flexible on what remains." He promised me he would be. But after nearly an hour of discussion, I saw no give, and told Yitzik I was not happy and would now go see Bibi. Yitzik asked me to wait about fifteen minutes before coming to see the PM. I said I would be there in fifteen minutes and my purpose was to close this tonight.

Yitzik must have told Bibi I was coming and was I loaded for bear. As soon as I walked in, he said, "Let's finish this tonight." "For real?" I asked, and he said, "Absolutely." In response, I said, I am going to suggest something that goes against my own beliefs. Normally I believe it is essential for you and the Palestinians to deal with each other directly. But I am now convinced that the negotiators on both sides have reached the limit of their capacity to overcome differences. The gaps need to be resolved tonight lest we see new issues emerge. You want to finish tonight, "let me negotiate the remaining issues with the Palestinians."

Bibi did not hesitate: "Go do it," he said. I left and asked Saeb and Abu Mazen to meet me at Ed Abington's residence, and by midnight we hammered out compromises on the last four issues. I told them I would sell these compromises to Bibi if they would sell them to Arafat. The deal was done as far as I was concerned. Abu Mazen and Saeb agreed.

But, of course, after such a tortuous negotiation it was unrealistic of me to expect that the conclusion of the agreement would come easily. At three-thirty in the morning, Saeb called to say they had a few minor suggestions. I replied, "Not with me you don't; I am going to sleep."

At 9 a.m., Saeb called and I refused to take the call, instructing my team that I would not take any calls from the Palestinians, and would leave at midnight, having done all I could—unless they accepted all the compromises, in which case there would be a summit tonight with the leaders. Apart from Gamal, no one on my team was comfortable with this strategy. They were not alone.

The calls started coming in: the Egyptian ambassador to Israel, Mohammad Bassiouny; then Osama al-Baz; and finally, King Hussein. Even Sandy Berger—about to become the new National Security Advisor—questioned whether I was sure I was doing the right thing. In all cases, I was adamant. I explained what I had done last night. That was it. They would accept what we had done or I would leave tonight; it would be unfortunate, even tragic for them, but enough was enough.

Why was I so determined? I knew it was all about closing now. If I agreed to see the Palestinians at this point new issues would be raised, and it would indicate that I was still willing to negotiate. It was hard for each to decide to close when they were sure to face criticism, and they still wondered if they might yet improve language in one way or another. In the back of my mind, I also suspected that Arafat at the very last minute might yet ask for something more and I wanted Bibi to see that I had played hardball and stuck to my guns.

Would I have acted this way if I was not satisfied that the key to closing was to play hardball and create a deadline? Not a chance. As a negotiator one cannot do this at any other point in a negotiation. One can do it only when one knows both sides' essential needs have been met and one's own posture—and unwillingness to back down—is unmistakable.

It did not hurt that in the last days I had become very testy. Anger was not a part of my normal posture in negotiations. I was the reasonable one, always trying to find the bridge between the two sides, calming them down, or defusing their crises. My explosions, out of character as they were, showed that I had hit the wall.

At two-thirty in the afternoon, the Palestinians relented, saying there would be a summit that evening to conclude the agreement. (I insisted that they announce the summit publicly before I would talk to anyone on their side.) As it turned out, Arafat was ready to close at last, but did want two private notes from me reaffirming the understandings reached on the Ibrahimi Mosque and the women prisoners as well as a small change on the prisoner reference in the Note for the Record.*

I promised the Palestinians I would consider these changes only, but I did go to Bibi and explain we now had a deal, with these last adjustments. "For real?" he asked— and I said, "For real."

Naturally, given my experience with Arafat, even as we drove down to Gaza, I wondered whether there would be one last surprise. Would I have to threaten to leave one more time?

---

*On the provision of requests for transfers of suspects, the Palestinians wanted the interim agreement provision to be "article II (7)(f) of annex IV," not "article II (7) of annex IV." Paragraph 7 of article II had many subparts. The Palestinians wanted to narrow this to the particular provision that made it clear that Palestinians would only have to transfer suspects to the Israelis in the circumstance where the suspects were not now in Palestinian jails. This made it easier for the Palestinians to explain to their public that as long as such suspects were in Palestinian jails there would be no transfers to the Israelis. Bibi and I had often discussed the issue of transfers and he knew that nothing was more neuralgic to the Palestinians. He understood that this provision in the Interim Agreement was designed to ensure that those who committed terrorist acts against Israelis would be imprisoned—not that they would be transferred to Israel. He accepted the reference to the narrower provision.

Not this time—there never was an easier meeting. Within fifteen minutes of our arrival at Erez, we had signed everything. The Hebron deal was done.*

---

*Two conversations the day after the agreement revealed much about what we would have to contend with substantively and procedurally in the future. Bibi moved to pass the agreement in his cabinet the day after the agreement, January 16, 1997. At one point during their debate, Bibi froze the discussion because there was a report that an unnamed American official in Washington had stated that the further redeployments had to be negotiated with the Palestinians. Dani Naveh called to tell me the Prime Minister could not pass the agreement unless we repudiated this report and issued a statement declaring that the Israelis did not have to negotiate the FRDs.

Dani, I said, this is ridiculous; you have the Christopher letter and it makes it clear this is an Israeli responsibility to carry out. The PM simply needs to point to that; the letter is authoritative, an unnamed official by definition cannot be. Dani's response was simple: The Prime Minister had done this and the cabinet does not believe him.

I was not in the business of lending credence to every report, and I was not going to start now. I told Dani I would spend all my time having to repudiate rumors in the Israeli press if I had to make a statement on this one. I was prepared to have a statement issued in Martin's name stating clearly the FRDs were an Israeli responsibility, not something that required negotiation. The PM could use that but it was the most I would do.

Bibi's lack of credibility and his reluctance to confront those who opposed him were in full view in this episode. In what became a pattern for the future, he needed our word because his colleagues did not take him seriously.

The second conversation was with Saeb. After fending off Bibi's problem, I went down to have dinner with the Chairman. I brought him the signed version of the Christopher letter. He was in a wonderful mood. We talked about the future, but tonight was not for substantive discussion. Before the dinner, I sat alone with Saeb to give him the letter and the unilateral notes. Saeb was very friendly but blunt. It was not good that I had to do this deal. They must work on their own. "Dennis, they have the tanks, we have only our brains. I will use all my talents to get us what we deserve. You may find it more difficult to deal with me than others on our side. But I will watch out for our interests and that is why the President depends on me."

I appreciated his candor. I agreed it was best for them to negotiate directly and I would say so publicly on my return to Washington, emphasizing that I felt it best for us not to take over the negotiations, as I had done in this case. We had a role to play and would maintain it. Saeb's claims of his primacy in the negotiations were exaggerated, and more indicative of his ongoing efforts to be the preeminent Palestinian negotiator. He had been prominent during Hebron, but his comment reflected his desire to convince me of something that was more fiction than reality. One thing was for sure: the dysfunctional side of intra-Palestinian competition would plague us throughout the negotiating process until the very end of the Clinton administration.

From Breakthrough to Stalemate

DURING THE TIME BETWEEN the two shuttles on Hebron, I had seen Mort Zuckerman in Washington. Mort was a major real estate developer, publisher of *U.S. News & World Report* and the New York *Daily News*, a leader in the Jewish community, a friend of Bill Clinton's, and a confidant of Binyamin Netanyahu. I had told Mort we could get Hebron done, but that Bibi should avoid the impulse to compensate his right-wing constituency, lest he put us back in a period of crisis. Knowing Bibi, Mort said he agreed and would work on the PM.

In the closing days of the Hebron negotiations, I also made this point to Bibi directly, and he told me he would do Hebron "clean" without "immediate" compensation.

"Immediate" was of course the operative word here. He would compensate his base at some point, and I understood that, telling him that when he did he should "wrap it" in other moves toward the Palestinians. He nodded agreement.

True to his word, Bibi did not take any immediate steps to compensate his right wing. Rather, he redeployed the IDF in Hebron, fulfilled his promise to release the women prisoners by the end of Ramadan, and even authorized his Finance Minister, Dan Meridor, to resolve the Palestinian grievance over value-added taxes, an irritant since 1994 over essentially double taxation of goods going into the Palestinian territories.

Having done this—and the Hebron deal too—Bibi came to Washington with credit in the bank for the first time. As I briefed the President and the new Secretary of State, Madeleine Albright, I emphasized that Bibi had taken difficult steps and deserved increased support from us. As we looked ahead to his upcoming obligation to carry out the first phase of the further redeployments (FRDs) from the rest of the West Bank, I suggested we embrace Bibi even as we "encouraged" him to make the first FRD credible. Otherwise, we would surely be mired in a new diplomatic stalemate.

The beginning of the FRD process in the remainder of the West Bank would reveal the true intentions of the Netanyahu government in the eyes of Palestinians. Hebron and women prisoners were all inherited obligations. So, too, was the FRD process, but the FRDs had not been defined. And now we would be dealing with the heart of the matter: land. Arafat, at this stage, was living up to his side of the bargain, so conditioning Bibi on what would be needed for the first FRD was a critical objective for his visit.

I did not expect it to be easy to persuade Bibi to do so. Just as the land was critical to the Palestinians, so, too, was it the main battleground for Bibi's constituency. Without getting into a fight with him, I would have to make clear to him what it would take for us to support his initial further redeployment or transfer of additional land and authority to the Palestinian Authority. The Palestinians had at least partial control over nearly 27 percent of the territory of the West Bank at this time—2.9 percent in the A category and 24 percent in the B category. Raising their partial control up to 37 percent, with a 10 percent FRD met, I believed, the symbolic test of credibility. Even if the Palestinians would complain about it, which they surely would since they wanted the FRD process to provide nearly all the West Bank, we could defend it.

Yet I knew that Bibi had an entirely different agenda for his trip. He wanted to talk strategy with the President, going over his constraints on both the Palestinian and Syrian tracks with an eye toward gaining our understanding on what he could and could not do when it came to withdrawal on the West Bank and the Golan Heights. This was entirely legitimate, even necessary, provided he did not leave feeling we had simply accepted these limits. Necessarily Bibi would outline maximal limitations, anticipating that we would seek to get him to go much further once the negotiations were underway and at a meaningful stage. For his sake and for the sake of any possible agreement, it was important for us to be sensitive to his real limits without tying our hands by committing to positions that would make any agreement impossible.

Thus, on the eve of Bibi's arrival, I was focused on getting him to do what was necessary on the first FRD due in three weeks (prior to March 10) and on ensuring that we did not box ourselves in on final status negotiations by accepting his permanent status "limits." These issues, not compensations for his right-wing base, dominated my thinking—erroneously, as it turned out.

| COMPENSATING THE RIGHT GETS LOST IN THE SHUFFLE |

Dore Gold arrived in town the day before Bibi to help prepare for the meeting with the President, and I told him it was essential that they carry out a credible FRD. When he asked, "What's a credible first phase?" I told him, "You have to reach the 10 percent figure." While Dore's demeanor was always low-key, he was not much of a poker player. In this case, he literally gulped, observing that 10 percent would be "very, very difficult." This conversation reinforced my concern about Bibi's plans; I knew if we did not take advantage of his Washington visit to persuade him to do a serious initial FRD, we would lose the opportunity to do so.

The Prime Minister and I met at 11 p.m. the next night at Blair House. Martin had accompanied me, but Bibi asked for a few minutes alone and then quickly declared he had been surprised by my conversation with Dore and that "10 percent is out of the question." His government could never accept it because he had been "paying out, and getting very little from the Palestinians or the Arabs."

I told him if he did less than 10 percent we would be back in the soup, and he insisted, "Trust me on this, I cannot get it through the government. I cannot push something I know will be rejected. That won't help either of us."

I told him we couldn't back a token FRD, and he replied that our lack of support "will create a crisis and maybe even violence from the Palestinians." All the same, I said, we can't back a token. Obviously troubled, Bibi asked, "How do we get out of this?"

"Why can't we be creative?" I asked. "Why not look at the FRD as having two parts? There is the FRD that involves additional territory going to the Palestinian Authority, and there is the area where they already have some authority, but not all authority." In other words, since we have three zones—A, B, and C—let's think about how all three come into play. Presently, Zone C is Israeli and involves 73 percent of the West Bank. The Palestinians want to know that your exclusive zone of 73 percent is going to shrink. Zone A is where they have both civil and security responsibility but it is only 2.9 percent. Maybe if Zone A can grow from being only 2.9 percent—meaning the area where Palestinians have virtual sovereignty—they will have something to show their own public and may not need to have the area of their partial control—Zone B—expand so much. Bibi asked what I had in mind, and I said the FRD could involve both redeployment from Zone C to B, which actually involves turning additional territory over to the Palestinians, as well as from B to A, which involves turning over additional authority (security on top of civil) to Palestinians. In this way, I said, you could reach 10 percent without actually transferring that amount of the West Bank to the Palestinians.

He doubted this would work. I repeated we would have a real problem if it did not, and we concluded the meeting.

In briefing the President and the Secretary the next morning, I urged the President to make the general point about a credible redeployment while the Secretary should show her immersion in the details by pushing the 10 percent figure.* By no means, I argued, should we let him off the hook—"He must leave here believing that he has to find a way to get to the 10 percent threshold." (I chose not to tell the President about my creative approach on dividing the authority and the land to be transferred because I wanted Bibi to realize he had a problem and needed to find a way to solve it; at the right moment, my solution could be his lifeline.)

The sequence for meetings with Bibi involved first a lunch and then a private meeting between the President and Bibi with note-takers. As it turned out, the discussion over lunch was more interesting than I had anticipated. Given the numbers on each side (six on six), I assumed the discussion would be very general in order to minimize leaks. Yet there turned out to be a remarkable give-and-take over how to move forward in the process. When Bibi suggested that a token first FRD would actually make it easier for the Palestinians because it would clearly not be an indication of the future, the President responded: "I think you are going about it the wrong way." Then he put his comment in context, suggesting with rare candor that Bibi had given so much on Hebron because he had lost the moral high ground; he had been cornered internationally, and the President did not want to see him put in that position again. A token step would simply put him back in the corner. "Everyone will come down on you all over again, and we'll both have difficulty." The President continued, "Frankly, in my mind the first step may be more important than the subsequent steps because you will affect the climate of the whole process."

It was a clever way to make the point that Bibi's own interest dictated more than a token first FRD. And Bibi, in response, agreed: "What you say makes a lot of sense."

---

*Madeleine was entering a process in which everyone involved knew the issues very well. This applied to President Clinton and his new national security advisor, Sandy Berger. Berger, unlike his predecessor Tony Lake, felt he needed to be more involved on the Middle East, perhaps because there was a new secretary not particularly familiar with these issues. Perhaps also because he knew the President was comfortable dealing directly with me, and often eager to play a more active role. While the President had great respect for Madeleine, she quickly understood that her role on Middle East peace issues would have to be defined. In truth, she never had the prominence in peace process diplomacy that she had on other issues like Kosovo. Nonetheless, she worked to understand the complexity of the issues, the personalities involved, and the nuances of the diplomacy. And she was always ready to travel, make a call, convey a message, or raise questions about whether our approach was working.

Then, almost parenthetically, he said, I will have to satisfy my constituency on Jerusalem by doing roads and maybe some other things, but "this should not be a problem." The President did not respond. Before the lunch broke up, Martin sent a note to Sandy asking the President to "put down a marker on Jerusalem," and Sandy had given the note to President Clinton. When the President continued to ignore Bibi's parenthetical comment even as the lunch concluded, Martin and I asked Sandy to speak to the President before he was alone with Bibi to make sure that Bibi understood we considered building anything in Jerusalem to be a real problem. I, too, wanted to up the ante now because of Bibi's reference to building roads and "maybe some other things." Given the increasing congestion, roads around Jerusalem were needed for both sides. I believed any such road-building could be managed if we had a credible FRD, and I accepted that Bibi would find it difficult to sell a credible first phase without pointing to something for his constituency. But I was worried by the reference to "other things."

While the private meeting was to include only Bibi, the President and a note-taker, I had suggested to Sandy that Madeleine sit in as well. She needed to be taken seriously by Bibi and he needed a sign of her closeness to the President. Sandy agreed and Madeleine joined the President and Mark Parris, the note-taker. After the meeting, the Secretary and Mark briefed Martin and me. Bibi had two military officers give briefings on Israel's strategic needs as they related to the West Bank and the Golan Heights. The purpose of the briefings, he suggested, was not to ask for U.S. support, but rather to seek American understanding of the security constraints and realities facing Israel. With regard to the West Bank, the focus was on preserving some strategic depth for Israel and the Jordan River as Israel's security border.* On the Golan, Israel needed the early-warning presence in the Golan to ensure that Israel would have the time to mobilize its forces in the face of a surprise attack.

When his military officers left the room, he said he had to retain early-warning stations on the ground and with that could withdraw to the ridgeline in the Golan Heights but could not get off them. He asked for our help in pushing Asad to get back to the table. While saying we would make an effort on the negotiations, the President did not respond to Bibi's position on his "bottom lines" on the Golan Heights. At the same time, the President again pushed on the importance of Bibi not giving up the moral high ground on the initial FRD. But once again he did not respond to Bibi when he repeated his comments on taking some compensating steps on Jerusalem—steps I interpreted as his way of signaling to his constituency that whatever concessions

---

*Bibi argued for thickening the area of the green line, the line that existed on June 4, 1967, the eve of the 1967 war. He also explained the importance of a presence in and guaranteed access to the Jordan Valley for the IDF.

he was making would be more than offset by his assertion of Israeli sovereignty on the ground in what the Arabs saw as their part of Jerusalem.

The Secretary reported that she had given the President a few notes to say something about this approach to Jerusalem, but he had not responded and obviously did not want to be pushed further. I suspected that the President probably felt he was making headway on the FRD, and he did not want to dilute his impact on that issue.

Hearing the briefing, I became concerned that Bibi might leave with misimpressions on two issues: Syria and compensating steps on Jerusalem. With regard to Syria, it was fully legitimate for Bibi to decide he could not withdraw from the Golan Heights, but he had to know from us that, after spending four years on this in very tough negotiations, we knew that without full withdrawal a deal was impossible. There was no point in our investing our credibility in something we knew stood no chance of success.

With regard to Jerusalem, he must not leave Washington believing that he could take whatever steps he wanted in order to compensate his constituency.

The following morning we talked with Sandy about how best to communicate these two messages, and concluded that Madeleine should see Bibi and be blunt on both. However, Sandy was far more concerned with Syria than with the Jerusalem side of my concerns. He had good reason. Bibi, following the meeting with the President, had announced to the Israeli press that we would be making a renewed effort to resume negotiations with Syria. Sandy wanted Bibi to understand it was pointless for us to make a major effort on Syria if we knew it was headed nowhere. Unfortunately, once again, that meant that Bibi's Jerusalem comments ended up getting short shrift.

At the conclusion of a dinner at the Israeli embassy on Thursday evening, Madeleine saw Bibi alone in the ambassador's office. She focused on Syria, and never discussed his Jerusalem comments. Bibi did not resist her main point on Syria. Instead, while noting that he thought it unlikely that we could compensate Israel enough to make up for what it would be surrendering militarily by getting off the Heights, he suggested two steps that Madeleine accepted: the United States would discreetly explore with the Israelis the security needs related to withdrawal, and I would craft a formula for how to resume the negotiations. Bibi asked that I work with him on the formula before he returned to Israel, and it was agreed that I would go see him in New York City on Saturday night.

| SATURDAY NIGHT IN MANHATTAN |

Bibi was staying at the Essex House on Central Park South. For our post-Shabbat meeting at 6:30 p.m., I had taken the 4:30 p.m. shuttle from Washington; having arrived early on an unseasonably pleasant evening in New York, I walked for about forty-five minutes, browsing Doubleday's at Fifty-fourth Street before making my way to the hotel.

While I enjoyed a walk in a beautiful atmosphere at dusk, Bibi had not had such a good day. He had been cooped up all day inside his suite, and he complained that when he had wanted to take his two little boys for a walk in Central Park—directly across from his hotel—he was told that security and the NYPD would have to close down the park for everyone else. He laughed, saying that would probably not be a good idea for U.S.-Israeli relations. He had David Bar-Ilan—his chief advisor on the media and probably his most right-wing aide—and Eli Ben-Elissar, his ambassador to Washington, in the room with him as we began our meeting. He started not on Syria but on Jerusalem and his problems at home. He asked whether our embassy was reporting what was happening, saying he hoped it was, because he faced a major problem now. There was, he noted, an unholy alliance emerging that involved the right and center in his cabinet as well as some members of the Labor Party. They were demanding that he build in Jerusalem now, and he would have no choice but to do so.

Was he speaking about the roads? I asked. "Yes," he answered, "and Har Homa as well." Har Homa was an area in the southeastern part of Jerusalem; it was a hilltop overlooking Bethlehem; it sat between Bethlehem and the Arab neighborhoods in Jerusalem. Should the Israelis now develop this hilltop with major settlement construction, the Palestinians would inevitably—and not incorrectly—see this as an effort to cut off Bethlehem from the Arab neighborhoods in and around Jerusalem.

Seeing the look on my face, he quickly added, "I have no choice, but I figured out how to do this. We will build for the Arabs at the same time, and there won't be a problem."

"Prime Minister," I said, "you will have to do what you have to do, but there will be a problem and you should not kid yourself." I went on to say that Har Homa will create a major problem for Arafat, and he will need to respond. Moreover, it will also unite the Arab world against you because it looks like you are deliberately acting to cut Arabs off from Jerusalem and preempting the negotiations on permanent status with new facts on the ground. With David Bar-Ilan and Eli Ben-Elissar sitting there, I did not want to turn this into a battle over Jerusalem, something over which all Israelis would man the barricades. Consequently, I said I know you are not asking for our approval on an issue like this, but by the same token don't expect American sanction for what you do.

He listened but then repeated that he had no choice. He, not Arafat, was being put in the corner. Again, I repeated that he should have no illusions: There would be a very real problem if he proceeded with this.

Bibi chose not to argue the issue further in front of his colleagues. Instead he launched into a general discussion on how to get at the existential issues of permanent status—final borders, refugees, and the resolution of Jerusalem and settlements. Here, I suggested a discreet conceptual discussion without any effort to negotiate at first, explaining that each side must feel free enough to explore ideas and possible points of convergence without the constraints of feeling that whatever was said was binding on them. The Prime Minister agreed with this but wondered who were the right ones to do this on each side. Just as he raised this question, Dore Gold joined us, and he said, "Maybe Dore." I said maybe, but why don't we discuss this later. Bibi said, "Agreed," and asked David, Eli, and Dore to excuse us. Dore lingered for a moment, believing we would be discussing Syria and that he might be asked to remain. But Bibi said he needed some time alone with me.

When Dore left, Bibi asked me what I thought. I said I think we are facing a very grim scenario. You may feel you have no choice, but this is the situation you are going to create: You will have a crisis with the Palestinians over Har Homa, and probably no negotiations; you will have the Arab world against you, and probably have relations frozen; and you will have no negotiations with the Syrians or Lebanese, meaning that you will have a total stalemate.

He listened and said, "Well, we have to avoid that, but I am telling you I don't have a choice on Har Homa. If I don't do it, I will be in real trouble. I will build for the Arabs, and after I have done Har Homa I won't need to do anything for a long time. So what can we do on Syria?"

While saying I had an idea I would present to him on Syria, I asked whether there was a way for him to delay on Har Homa. He said there might be, and he had an idea how to do so. In any case, he would try to defer it for a while.

On Syria, I said he should be under no illusions. Asad would never agree to a deal in which he did not get back all the Golan. He would prefer no deal to something less than full withdrawal. Additionally, our problem was that Asad would be very unlikely to go back to the table without the conditional offer on withdrawal that had been in our pocket from Rabin and Peres.

The Prime Minister cut in and said he could not give him that just to get him to the table. "Where are you on this at the end of the day?" I asked. At this point he said nothing about the ridgeline; he simply said we have to have the early-warning ground stations. I then pointed out that neither Rabin nor Peres had ever agreed to give those up, "so embracing their conditional offer does not require you to do so." This appeared to be news to him, but he said he was not willing to go as far as embracing what had been in our pocket.

I told him I had come up with a formula that did not go that far. I said Asad would see that and not like it, but it would be a credible formula that we could argue was reasonable. He asked to see it and I gave him the following:

—Israel is serious about pursuing peace with Syria, and is not interested in returning to square one in the negotiations;

—Israel has its needs, which must be satisfied to reach a peace agreement. And it recognizes that Syria has its needs, which must be satisfied if there is to be an agreement;

—Israel is under no illusions. It understands that it is the Syrian view that there must be full withdrawal from the Golan Heights;

—While seeking a peace that will make Israel and Syria good neighbors, Israel's first priority in the negotiations will be to ensure its security and water resources;

—Withdrawal must not leave Israel vulnerable to surprise attack or endanger its only freshwater reservoir, the Sea of Galilee;

—Israel looks to the United States to help restart the negotiations and to work with the parties to help reconcile their respective needs.

I told Bibi I had used lots of "code words and phrases" that would be meaningful to Asad, but "without ever committing you to full withdrawal." The formula is suggestive but vague, and while Asad won't like that, it offers a reasonable basis on which to resume negotiations.

Bibi listened to me and read over the formula, and then said: I know you don't think you can do less than this, but I can't go this far—I can't sell the word "withdrawal" to the coalition. Let me think about this and come back to you. I said okay, but you have to give us something to work with if you want us to be able to help you—and, I added, not only on this issue.

The New York discussion represented both the worst and the best of Bibi. Too often he would make his decisions based on strictly political calculations such as his fear that his cabinet would "fry" him if the word "withdrawal" appeared in even a discreet formula. And yet when apprised of the real problems he would be creating, Bibi almost always would look for practical ways to overcome them. He might put us in an impossible position, but would always look to us—usually me—to figure out a way to rescue him.

I suspected I could rescue him in this situation as well. But that, too, proved overly optimistic.

| HAR HOMA GAINS STEAM |

My New York conversation with Bibi convinced me that he would soon succumb to the pressures he was under to take action on Jerusalem, and speculation in the Israeli press seemed to confirm this. My strategy now was to steer Bibi onto a path that would either produce the least destructive decision or at least offer a way to manage whatever he chose to do.

Dore Gold had remained in Washington to meet Sandy Berger and me. It was the Presidents' Day holiday weekend, and Dore came to my house accompanied by Ambassador Ben-Elissar.

I drew a distinction between roads and building a major new Israeli neighborhood in East Jerusalem. I told them we could defend the roads; we could not and would not defend Har Homa. In any event, I argued, the Prime Minister should not put us in a position where we had to distance ourselves—or even criticize him—immediately after a trip here. "His claims to your press of a very successful meeting with President Clinton will be exposed as hollow." In such circumstances, all the political gains from the trip would be lost quickly.

I realized that Bibi might read my words as a reason to defer Har Homa but still build there after a decent interval from the trip. With that in mind, I told Dore that "whatever you do, you have to go quietly to Arafat as soon as possible to explain your difficulties and why you may have to go ahead with a step on Jerusalem—to show you realize this could create a real problem for him, and to ask him how best to minimize the difficulties for both of you."

Dore said he would go over all this with the Prime Minister, who was stopping in Europe on his way back to Israel. Upon his return, Bibi found Likud Party Knesset member Benny Begin sponsoring an item for debate in the parliament entitled "Netanyahu's division of Jerusalem," an obvious attempt to hoist the Prime Minister with the same petard that Bibi had used successfully against Peres in the campaign. Others on the right wing were putting pressure on Netanyahu at the same time, even maneuvering to bring him down if he refused to go ahead with building in Jerusalem.

Under the pressure, Bibi announced the plan to build new roads in Jerusalem. Oddly, it drew almost no response from the Palestinians, who had now also become riveted on Har Homa—what they called Jebel Abu Ghneim—and appeared relieved that roads rather than a major new Israeli neighborhood were going to be built on land they believed was theirs or should be theirs.

What was good for the Palestinians was not good for Bibi's right-wing base. They wanted Har Homa developed; they wanted Bibi to announce, at a minimum, a plan to build thousands of apartments there. Such a decision would not be long in coming. Unfortunately, in the interval between his Washington trip and this decision—a period of two weeks—he had not followed my advice of apprising Arafat of his predicament and trying to work something out. Not until the plan on Har Homa was leaked by his office two days before the official announcement did he seek to have Yitzik Molho go to Gaza; not surprisingly, Arafat and Abu Mazen saw this Israeli attempt to talk as a ploy to make them complicit in the decision, and so refused to meet.

Bibi's reluctance to hold the meeting earlier reflected his own fears that his enemies could exploit the imagery of his going to Arafat, making it look as if he were giving Arafat a veto on Israeli action in Jerusalem. What was needed here was a channel both sides believed would remain completely secret; yet while Yitzik Molho was completely trustworthy, neither Netanyahu nor Arafat felt this channel—at least at this point—would be free of leaks. As a result, the ability to manage both sides' needs on Har Homa was lost.

| COMPOUNDING THE HAR HOMA DECISION |

To make matters worse, the Israeli decision on the first phase of FRD compounded Bibi's announcement on Har Homa. Notwithstanding Bibi's professed understanding with President Clinton that he recognized the importance of maintaining the moral high ground and agreed with the logic of doing something credible on the first phase, he ended up falling short on this as well.

In our eyes, Bibi's announcement that Israel would build on Har Homa made it imperative that he reclaim the high ground by undertaking a credible first FRD—a point Madeleine Albright was now making in almost daily phone conversations with Bibi.

But Bibi always dealt with the pressure of the moment, and now treated the Har Homa announcement as if it carried no weight with the settlers and religious nationalists, for the FRD is "what they really care about."*

The person responsible for recommending the size and location of the FRD was Yitzhak Mordechai, the Defense Minister, who surprisingly had heard nothing from Bibi concerning what we were asking. Once Martin told him that we were pressing the PM for a credible first redeployment, he came back to us—without going through Bibi—with three options: 4 percent, 6 percent, and 8 percent.

In response, I called him and said, in light of Har Homa, it would be a disaster if the FRD did not reach 10 percent. In turn, Yitzhak asked me if it was possible to do the very thing I had earlier suggested to Bibi, namely, to reach 10 percent by combining the transfer of land (from C to B) with the transfer of authority (from B to A). I told Yitzhak this was a good way to go and suggested he produce something like 5 percent C to B and 5 percent B to A. He said that he would do his best.

At this point, the 10 percent figure was now out in the Israeli press, and drawing

---

*At one point, I asked him how it was possible that the Har Homa announcement bought him nothing with his base? His earlier comments to me on Har Homa were now a distant memory, and he answered, "Because I haven't done it [built anything] yet."

strong criticism from the rightist members of the cabinet. Perhaps Netanyahu found it convenient to hide behind his opposition; perhaps he really believed he had no choice but to low-ball the first phase. In any case, when Martin went back to him after our respective conversations with Mordechai, Bibi told him he could possibly get to 8 percent overall, provided we endorsed it, but no higher, and certainly not to 10 percent because that figure had already drawn fire in public. When Martin asked for guidance, I told him no endorsement without 10 percent. And I added, "He leaks the figure and then uses that as an excuse for why they cannot go to 10 percent. Tell him if the 10 percent figure has been compromised because it is public, we suggest he do 11 percent." Bibi was not amused, but we maintained our posture.

As the Israeli cabinet deliberated on March 7, Dan Meridor called Martin and floated a 9 percent FRD consisting of 2 percent from C to B and 7 percent from B to A. While this put the Israelis close to our target, there was a problem: the Israelis would only be turning over 2 percent more territory to the Palestinians. My idea of dividing the FRD between turning over additional land and turning over additional authority had been designed to help the Israelis manage the difficulty of transferring additional land. Its purpose was not to allow them to reduce to a minimum the land to be transferred. The Israeli 9 percent was made up mostly of increasing Palestinian authority where they already had it in part. Even this, Dan told Martin, would not be possible unless we endorsed it. Absent our endorsement, they might as well go with a lower figure.

I was not inclined to endorse their move, but first I wanted to know what effect it might actually have on the ground. What, I asked Martin, would be the practical consequence for Palestinians of increasing the A area from 2.9 percent to 9.9 percent of the West Bank? The IDF's answer was that fifty villages and nearly 200,000 Palestinians would come under exclusive Palestinian control. Upon learning this, I devised a formula for our response to the Meridor proposal. If Israel announced this step, we would say it was "a serious move, but on the second and third phases of FRD we expected more." That was the best we could do.

Martin passed the word to the Israelis, but uncharacteristically put the emphasis on the "serious move" part of the formula, not the implicit criticism of our expecting more in the future. That became clearer later that evening.

The cabinet session in Israel went through the night. I went to play basketball with my synagogue team at the Jewish Day School in Rockville, arriving at about 8 p.m. As soon as I arrived at the gym, I was paged—it was the State Department telling me that Martin was trying to arrange a conference call with the Secretary, Mark Parris, and me. My cell phone did not work well from the gym, so I dropped out of the call and phoned back in from a pay phone. Martin, having heard from Netanyahu that he needed us to say something quickly endorsing the cabinet's decision, was discussing with the Secretary and Mark what our public statement should be.

When I rejoined the call I reiterated that it was fine to say we regarded this as a serious move, but we also had to say we hoped to see more in the second and third phases of the FRD. Martin initially said they might regard that as bad faith since he had only told them we would say that in answer to questions. I replied that they had not gone to the 10 percent; we were nonetheless saying this was a serious move, the Palestinians would find the 2 percent from Zone C "outrageous," and we had to retain our credibility.

Martin again said to expect a complaint from Israel, as he had misunderstood what I had wanted. "We should probably be prepared for some bounce back," he said. I laughed, and said no problem, "we'll just blame it on you. That's what ambassadors are for."

As it turned out, no one much noticed our qualified support. Instead, it was the Palestinian response that drew all the attention. Ignoring the 7 percent, and focusing only on the 2 percent, the Palestinians rejected the Israeli proposal, arguing that on top of Har Homa this Israeli unilateral move demonstrated that the Netanyahu government had no intention of pursuing the process seriously.

The world press seized upon the situation, and for reasons of both genuine anger and tactical benefit, the Palestinians decided to milk the attention for all it was worth. The daily drumbeat out of Arafat's headquarters was that Bibi was killing the peace process.

With progress now seemingly impossible, pressure started to build on Bibi to find a way out of the apparent dead end he had created. Knowing that starting the bulldozers now at Har Homa could make the situation explosive, we again pressed Bibi to delay the work on the ground.

The night of March 12, Martin called to tell me that he had learned the Prime Minister's office had commissioned a poll to test the public reaction to a delay on Har Homa. On top of that, it was now being reported that because of lawsuits, breaking ground at Har Homa would be delayed for several weeks, maybe longer.

Even before knowing this, I had been looking for ways to defuse the impact of building in Har Homa, and I believed it was important to use any delay to put together a package of positive Israeli gestures to the Palestinians: permitting the Gaza airport to be completed and put into operation; stopping Israeli demolitions of Palestinian houses; opening one route of the safe passage between Gaza and the West Bank; and removing the continuing impediments to building hundreds of housing units for

Palestinians in the East Jerusalem area around Har Homa—something Bibi had said he was committed to doing but had done nothing to make a reality. Such a package could demonstrate to the Palestinians that the process was practically producing for them.

I had raised the package with Bibi and he agreed. Now, with the likelihood of delay on Har Homa, I was convinced we had a pathway out of the deepening stalemate. Unfortunately, as would happen so often, an unforeseen act of violence was about to dash my hopes and plans.

| KING HUSSEIN DEMONSTRATES HIS HUMANITY WHILE BIBI EXPLOITS A TRAGEDY |

On the morning of March 13, a mentally deranged Jordanian soldier shot and killed seven Israeli teenage girls on a field trip along the Israeli-Jordanian border, stunning Israel. For King Hussein, the killings were an abomination, and his shame and discomfort were compounded by the charge that a stinging letter of criticism he had written to Netanyahu earlier that week (and which had been made public) had fomented the violence. Whatever his disappointment with Bibi, the King put it all aside. It was not enough to condemn this unspeakable act; the King felt he must go to Israel immediately to atone for it.

Prior to the King's arrival in Israel, Bibi called Martin in and told him "the game is rigged, whatever I do is criticized, so the bulldozers will start at Har Homa the beginning of next week." When Martin raised the package for the Palestinians, Bibi's response: Maybe later, but we are going ahead on Har Homa now.

I was angry, but not surprised. Bibi saw the killings as a political opening—who could criticize this move at a time of national tragedy in Israel?

Even when King Hussein arrived in Israel, met each grieving family, and on bended knee expressed his shame and asked forgiveness, touching the heart of Israel, Bibi did not back off. When asked a question about Har Homa at a press conference—a question whose answer was bound to embarrass the King—he announced that the building would begin in the next few days.

At the same time, Bibi tried to soften the blow by offering the King two ideas to put the peace process back on track. He proposed an acceleration of the final status negotiations, with a resolution at Camp David if the negotiations were inconclusive after six months, as a way of showing the Palestinians that the process would not be preempted by Israeli unilateral acts; he also offered again to build for the Palestinians.

The problem here was that the Palestinians were naturally suspicious, assuming he was proposing to move to permanent status negotiations now to avoid his remaining obligations under the Interim Agreement—on the airport and seaport in Gaza, the safe passage between the West Bank and Gaza, and especially on the three phases of further redeployment in the West Bank. From the Palestinian perspective, they were being asked to give up tangibles for intangibles.*

If Bibi's idea was to be attractive to the Palestinians, it had to be presented carefully and privately. It had to address inevitable Palestinian suspicions by making clear the Interim Agreement process would go on and be accompanied by a discreet channel on permanent status, which could build the Palestinian confidence that Bibi was ready to make a fair deal—assuming, of course, the Palestinians were also ready.

Unfortunately, Bibi rarely seemed to know how to act on his ideas—how to present them, to whom, and even when to do so. Translating an idea into action seemed beyond his grasp. It was not a lack of intelligence; few are more intelligent than Bibi Netanyahu. It was an impulsive lack of judgment, and a lack of a feel for the Arabs generally. But there was something more: often he would come up with ideas simply to get himself out of a jam.

That is what he sought to do with the King: Float the final status idea in order to give the King something he could use with Arafat. But King Hussein could not be the one to sell an approach on final status to Arafat, given Arafat's suspicions that the Hashemite Kingdom too still coveted the West Bank and retained an obvious interest in Jerusalem.

When King Hussein presented Bibi's idea to Arafat, the Palestinians were cool to it, expressing serious doubts about Netanyahu's motivations. Because I felt Bibi's idea had merit and because the Palestinian criticism was more about Bibi than the idea, I thought we might be able to overcome their doubts, but again my hopes were to be undone by events.

| BIBI'S BULLDOZERS AND THE APROPOS CAFÉ BOMBING |

On Monday, March 18, Netanyahu ordered the bulldozers to begin clearing ground for new building on Har Homa. At the same time, he launched a public relations campaign designed to deter the very acts of terror his own intelligence agencies predicted would be the result, claiming that Arafat was giving a "green light" to terror acts. Bibi undoubtedly hoped that such charges would leave Arafat with no choice but to do everything he could to prevent any acts of terror.

Under the circumstances, Arafat had no interest in appearing to be Israel's police-

---

*Ironically, for many Israelis, it is precisely the logic of Israel having to give up the tangible of land for the intangible of promises of peace that they find unsettling about the peace process.

man. At one level that might be understandable, but it was typically shortsighted at another. Arafat could not afford to lose the Israeli public, whose desire for peace created the greatest pressure on Bibi to show he could deliver peace.

But Arafat's preoccupation would always be with how he looked to his public. Given a choice between his standing with his public needs and his ability to affect the Israeli public, it was no contest. His needs always dominated. Even more than Bibi, he was all tactics and no strategy. In his eyes, it was essential to demonstrate that he could make life difficult for an Israeli prime minister who acted unilaterally—even if doing so cost him practical advantages or harmed the process. Defiance, being so much a part of Arafat's appeal to Palestinians, always took precedence over accommodation, particularly if he judged the mood to be negative on his street.

So it was that Arafat, after having kept the pressure on Hamas and Islamic Jihad for a year, now actually began to reach out to them. He held a "national reconciliation" meeting with them; he released prisoners, including a leading Hamas activist, Ibrahim Makadmeh and, while I doubted that Arafat had given an explicit green light to terror, it was easy to see that these gestures and his silence about attacks against Israel could signal these groups that they were free to act.

When we challenged Arafat on these moves and their potential danger, he argued that Bibi had cornered him before his own people and he had to defuse opposition.

Three days after Bibi sent in the bulldozers, there was a terrorist bombing at the Apropos Café in Tel Aviv, killing three women. Bibi blamed Arafat directly. After calling Bibi to express condolences and promising to cooperate on security again, Arafat left for a trip to South Asia. Running away from responsibility had been another constant of Arafat's existence. As Arafat traveled to India, Pakistan, and Bangladesh and sought to build pressure on Israel over Har Homa, Bibi was acting to discredit him in Israel, emphasizing persuasively that there could be no movement on political issues— no negotiations—until Arafat acted definitively against terror.

| GENESIS OF A NEW AMERICAN APPROACH |

With the peace process now in a free fall, Madeleine and Sandy Berger became increasingly concerned. Even prior to the bombing, I had been focused on a package of steps the Israelis would take. Now there would need to be steps taken by Israelis and Palestinians alike, and we intensified our discussions on our options.

Sandy's main concern was about Bibi: Could anything be done with him? Madeleine, joined by Mark Parris, doubted it, even raising the possibility of announcing that we could not work with him.

I had a different position. I had no illusions about Bibi, but also believed we could not wish Bibi away. He was Israel's Prime Minister, he would remain so for at least the next two years, and we could not shun him unless we were prepared to do so indefinitely, no matter the consequences in the United States or Israel.

It was important, I argued, not to lose sight of who Bibi was and what he wanted. He saw himself in historic, grandiose terms. He knew that he had to deliver on peace because that would be his political salvation. For all the difficulties he presented, his desire for success—and our importance to his achieving it—gave us a basis to get him where he needed to go. It was clear that Bibi was constantly giving in to pressures from within. We needed to apply our own pressures. If we could demonstrate that we were making every effort to work with him, we would have a basis for taking him on later if he did not deliver. Better to let him fail than to cut him off—allowing him to say that we were unfairly pressuring Israel, and making failure a self-fulfilling prophecy.

Both Madeleine and Sandy had doubts. They feared that Bibi was deliberately trying to destroy the Oslo process; if that were the case, we needed to resist him now and confront him as necessary.

In reply, I said that all of his behavior to date represented an ad hoc response to the pressures of the moment. Our biggest problem was not that Bibi had a design, but that he didn't. I quoted the line that the British ambassador to Israel had used with Martin, likening Bibi to "a drunk who lurches from lamppost to lamppost."

His impulsiveness made it clear that we could not continue with the step-by-step approach that had been the hallmark of the Oslo process. We would not and could not walk away from Oslo, but it was being overwhelmed by actions that were destroying confidence step by step. So we should try for an accelerated approach to permanent status.

Both Madeleine and Sandy liked this idea, and we discussed it quietly among ourselves in the winter of 1997, prior to Bibi's raising it with King Hussein. But given Madeleine's travel schedule and the administration's focus on NATO expansion, we did not have the opportunity to shape and present it before the events of late March.

Madeleine was initially drawn to the idea of our presenting a plan for permanent status, outlining a position favoring a Palestinian state, providing a rough sense of its dimensions, and a solution to Jerusalem and refugees. I considered it unthinkable to present a final status plan before the two sides had begun talking to each other and to us about the substance of their positions on these issues. (If nothing else, we had to begin to get a feel for where there might be flexibility and for what was truly beyond the pale.)

Sandy was leery of anything that smacked of an "American plan," and would only accept American ideas offered as "suggestions for a pathway or approach." In the end, we gravitated back to a quasi-Oslo posture—one that combined mutual and reciprocal steps on the ground in order to create an environment in which progress would be possible and a basis could be laid for pursuing accelerated permanent status negotiations. It was an illusion to think that the two sides could move quickly to resolve the existential issues of permanent status—Jerusalem, refugees, and borders—in an atmosphere of stalemate and mistrust. With President Clinton's approval, I prepared a package of steps both sides would take even as we sought to launch intensive negotiations on permanent status.

| ONCE AGAIN INTO THE BREACH |

The March 21 bombing in Tel Aviv sharpened our awareness of the dangers. But by taking all the pressure off Bibi to move on political issues, it also reduced our leverage. Nonetheless, we had to intervene quickly to prevent a further deterioration. The President and the Secretary decided that I should meet Arafat before he returned to Gaza to elicit promises from him on security, setting the stage for our then being able to present a package of steps each side would take. In a call from the Secretary to Arafat, the Chairman agreed to meet me in Morocco, where a meeting of the Organization of the Islamic Conference (OIC) would take place.

I arrived in Rabat the evening of March 26 and immediately went to see King Hassan, who had received a letter from President Clinton urging him to use his influence both on Arafat (to act on security) and on the OIC (to avoid inflammatory anti-Israeli resolutions). I was carrying a letter from President Clinton to Arafat declaring that he was committed to reviving the peace process, and, assuming Arafat took meaningful steps on security, was ready to launch an initiative to achieve that objective.

In receiving me, King Hassan made it clear he had great faith in President Clinton, but none in Prime Minister Netanyahu. He complained that Bibi's action on Jerusalem was like that of "a child who gives no thought to any of his actions," and he called him "a man who threatens the hopes of the Arab people and Israeli people alike."

I used his belief in President Clinton to say we needed his help. I told the King we needed to calm the atmosphere, not worsen it, especially with OIC resolutions that might escalate the rhetoric on Jerusalem. In reply, he said he could calm his Arab allies if he could show them Clinton's letter promising an initiative. Not having shared with Bibi that we would be prepared to launch an initiative—provided Arafat acted on security—I asked the King to keep the letter to himself until I got to Israel the next evening.*

---

*He protected the letter, assured no leaks, and also held the line on the resolutions at the OIC meeting.

The next morning, Arafat and I met over breakfast—only he was not eating because he had picked up a bug in South Asia—and I gave him the President's letter.

When he had finished reading it, I leaned over to him and stressed the letter's importance. President Clinton was prepared to assume the "risk and responsibility" of launching an American initiative to save the peace process. These words, I said, should convey great meaning to you; they indicate the President is prepared to take criticism and pay a political price to see this through. That kind of presidential commitment is, I emphasized, what you know is going to be needed if we are to reach agreement in the end.

He responded immediately by saying, "You are right, this is very important." I nodded, but then said to him, President Clinton will not proceed—indeed cannot proceed—if he does not have an assurance from you that you will in fact do all you can to fight terror and leave no doubt in anyone's mind that you will not tolerate it.

Arafat was matter-of-fact in response, saying, "I don't tolerate it. It's a disaster for us." You are right, I replied, but when you release a Hamas activist like Ibrahim Makadmeh you send a signal that you are tolerating it, especially when he calls for terror right after you release him.

Arafat frowned: "Makadmeh has never acted against Israelis, only against those in the Palestinian Authority." Then he added, "Makadmeh has betrayed his promises to me, and he will pay for it."

Mr. Chairman, I said, we need some very specific actions now if President Clinton is to see you are doing what he asked, thereby enabling him to launch an initiative. Arafat nodded and asked what we wanted him to do. I went over my list:

—condemn terrorism publicly and emphasize that the Palestinian Authority will not tolerate it or the groups that carry it out;
—resume serious, meaningful, and continuous security cooperation with the Israelis;
—arrest those who commit acts of terror or plan them; I said we had the names of three people in Hebron who we believed may have been involved in the Tel Aviv bombing and five members of the Islamic Jihad who were planning acts of terror;
—work with the Israelis to resolve the issue of questionable Palestinian releases of prisoners.

Arafat agreed on all of these. He said, "Even if other contacts are cut, the security contacts must not be stopped." He promised to act immediately on the three in Hebron once we gave him the names, and he told me that he had already had four members of the Islamic Jihad arrested and they might be the ones we were talking about. Finally, on his release of Palestinians from prisons, if his side and the Israelis disagreed on who was safe to release, the United States could resolve the difference.

He could not have been more responsive. I now had assurances to present to Bibi, but I wondered about how well they would hold up once Arafat sensed the mood on his return to Gaza.

In Israel, I saw Bibi with his Foreign and Defense Ministers, David Levy and Yitzhak Mordechai. They focused entirely on security. When I reported my conversation with Arafat, Bibi said, "Let's wait and see."

Once I was alone with him, I asked him what his game plan was. He replied that he wanted a gap of two to three weeks to show he was not rushing back to business as usual and to be able to point to specific steps Arafat was taking. He also said he wanted some assurances that Arafat would not simply take a few steps and then stop them. I told him that was legitimate. Assuming we worked along these lines, I again asked, what then? And Bibi emphasized that it was time to go to accelerated permanent status, raising once more the idea he had first broached with King Hussein.

Now I told him we were prepared to launch an initiative with accelerated permanent status talks as the centerpiece. But the initiative would be dead on arrival if we did not also address Palestinian concerns; the whole Arab world would see accelerated permanent status as a trick. To prove otherwise, and to give accelerated permanent status talks a chance, we would propose that several elements be part of our initiative:

—The interim negotiations must proceed in parallel with the accelerated permanent status talks;
—There must be no "new Israeli facts on the ground" for the period of the accelerated permanent status talks. (I reminded Bibi that Prime Minister Begin had pledged a settlement freeze for the three months he thought it would take to transform the Camp David accords into an agreement—and that he himself had told me he did not need to do anything for a while once he did Har Homa);
—The items for Palestinians in Jerusalem (build housing, end demolitions of houses, and stop confiscating identity cards and land) must be implemented;
—Finally, neither Arabs nor Israelis would move into housing in the Har Homa area until all housing had been completed for both.

Bibi felt that in one way or another, these were doable. As usual, however, as we went into the details he began to water down what he would be able to do. He said, for example, that his government could not handle a freeze, but he would think about how to use the Begin precedent. Similarly, he said he could not openly agree to anything on Jerusalem, but could take some steps and would build for Palestinians. But he demurred on not having either side move in until all housing was finished for both, even though no housing would be completed until after the six-month timetable he'd proposed for conclusion of the accelerated permanent status negotiations. (What are you giving up by agreeing to this if your own idea of six months is serious? I asked. He did not respond.)

Nonetheless, he was generally ready to work along these lines after a decent interval of two to three weeks, assuming Arafat did what was necessary on security. He added, "You know it is popular for me to do nothing now; the attack in Tel Aviv did not exactly come in an area where I am politically strong, and even there when I went to the hospital, people said to me, 'No more concessions.'" I replied that I understood, but even so at some point "people here will want to know what you are doing to achieve peace, and doing nothing won't cut it." He nodded his agreement.

I returned to Washington with the understanding that I would come back to the region in two weeks. That turned out to be a mistake. My concerns about Arafat were justified. Once he returned to Gaza and heard complaints from those around him, he was no longer prepared to have the security meetings if there were not parallel political negotiations at the same time. Bibi, for his part, would not authorize negotiations until there were tangible signs of cooperation on security.

Arafat maintained that he was doing what was necessary on security, but this was clearly not the case. There were no arrests, no condemnations of terror, no suggestions that it was intolerable to the Palestinian Authority, and no security cooperation with the Israelis. I called Arafat, but the telephone rarely worked with him—and my calls were in vain. Perhaps had I stayed, I could have held his feet to the fire through daily meetings. In any case, Arafat did not perform, and the process was frozen.

| THAWING THE FREEZE AND RESUMING SECURITY CONTACTS |

Our initiative could not be launched until Arafat met his commitments to us. On my return to the region seeking to reestablish security cooperation, I told Netanyahu and Arafat that I wanted a trilateral meeting on security: with me, the Israeli heads of the military and Shin Bet (Amnon Shahak and Ami Ayalon, respectively) and Arafat and his security chiefs. Both agreed.

We met at Arafat's office in Gaza at 10:30 p.m. There were no cameras out in front, signaling that there would be no media covering this meeting. In addition, Arafat was at the curb waiting to greet Amnon. This was not only a sign of respect but also an indication of his pleasure at seeing Amnon again.

Inside, Arafat thanked me for organizing such a meeting. He said it meant a great deal to see Amnon and Ami again, emphasized how well they had worked together in the past, and declared that they must work together in the future. He pointed out the presence of all his leading security officials in the room, made clear that cooperation was important to him, and then turned to me to start the meeting.

I wanted to limit my participation and have them air their problems and ideas for overcoming them. As a result, I limited my remarks to explaining that this meeting was not a social gathering but should be a problem-solving meeting. Our task tonight was to clear the air and resume security cooperation in a way that respected both sides' needs and the threats to their common interests.

The Chairman nodded approvingly, and we turned to Amnon. His approach was a reminder of why Palestinians held him in such high esteem. He was straightforward, respectful, self-assured, and yet pulled no punches. He stressed that the Israelis and Palestinians should not need anyone to set up meetings between them. They must be able to meet together, talk together, and cooperate together on their own if peace between them was going to work. Many doubted that it could. He believed they should be proven wrong. It would not be easy, but he believed the vast majority of Israelis and Palestinians wanted peace. Those who were enemies of the peace were common enemies. His Palestinian colleagues should know that he had a responsibility for Israeli security and he would fulfill it. Having said that, he wanted them to know that from his personal perspective, his greatest concern about the current situation was not the terrorist bombs but the growing violent demonstrations that pitted Palestinian kids against Israeli soldiers. "We must educate our publics in peace and we must educate our young people in peace."

After a brief response, the Chairman asked his key officers to comment. Each emphasized their commitment to cooperation; while Arafat took the high road, and refrained from using political difficulties to justify a cutoff of bilateral security contacts, each of his security officers made a reference to the difficult environment created by Israel's settlement activity. Still, the atmosphere of the meeting remained extremely warm and positive until Jibril Rajoub spoke.

Rajoub, the head of preventive security in the West Bank, said he was pleased to see such friends as Amnon and Ami, but he felt he must tell them the truth. He would, of course, follow the instructions of the Chairman, but his Israeli friends should understand that it was very difficult to cooperate on security when Palestinians saw bulldozers at Jebel Abu Ghneim (what Palestinians called Har Homa); when they saw an insulting approach to further redeployment; when Palestinian security officers were not treated with any respect and attacked in the Israeli press. He himself had been the target of such attacks, and he was hardly eager to work with those who attacked him.

Ami asked if he could speak and he said there was no place for such attacks on Rajoub or other Palestinian security officials in the Israeli press. He, too, understood that

Palestinians had grievances, and they would need to be addressed. Neither he nor Amnon could address the political issues this evening. They were there to emphasize that Israelis and Palestinians must collectively face those who were opposed to peace. If they worked together, they could be successful. If they did not, the enemies of peace would gain. He and Amnon had come in a spirit of respect and partnership, and they hoped this spirit would be reciprocated.

Arafat responded by saying it would be, and invited everyone into the next room for dinner. We sat around a large table. Amnon sat next to the Chairman, I sat across from him, with Abu Mazen on my side. Down one side of the table, Ami and his deputy Yuval Diskin sat next to Rajoub. Everything seemed to be going fine, and Abu Mazen, who was fervently committed to security cooperation, told me Amnon's presence made a big difference.

At the end of the dinner, our security liaison to the Israelis and Palestinians came up to me and told me that Ami, after speaking to Rajoub, was now convinced this was all a show and nothing would change. I went over to Ami and asked him what the problem was. Ami told me that Rajoub had made it clear that he did not intend to cooperate, and had no instructions to do so. "Ami," I said, "let me see what I can do about it."

I took Abu Mazen aside and told him of Ami's conversation with Rajoub, and also told him I had no interest in being part of a charade. Was this for real or not? He said the Chairman was serious, and that I should suggest that Amnon go and speak to the Chairman now. He did, followed by Rajoub. They all sat together for half an hour, concluding with Rajoub saying he had instructions to cooperate and with an understanding that Stan would host a meeting in the morning with the security chiefs to go over practical steps. We broke at 2 a.m. feeling that we had made headway.

I felt both hopeful and uneasy at the same time. Hopeful, because we had made progress in getting the security contacts resumed. But uneasy, because I wouldn't always be in Israel and Amnon could not always go to Gaza and see Arafat. Clearly, in the absence of a political pathway, we would find it difficult to sustain meaningful security cooperation.

The next morning, when I reported to Bibi about the meeting, I was cautious about what had been achieved, stressing that we needed to get the political process going again if we really wanted to make security work over time. Bibi was encouraged, and ready to talk.

I told him the longer he deferred moving on the political side, the less likely it was that he would get what he wanted in the security area—and the greater the price he would have to pay to move the Palestinians to resume the permanent status negotiations later. Bibi listened and said, "All right, let's see how the next few days go." I was

not asking for more than that, and now believed Bibi would be ready to resume the political contacts shortly and work on the terms of our initiative. But once again a new
event put everything on hold.

| "AN EARTHQUAKE IS ABOUT TO HIT ISRAEL" |

As I was riding to Gaza to see Arafat that evening, Martin called me: "An earth-
quake is about to hit Israel." Martin had just learned that the eight o'clock news (to air
in ten minutes) would report that the Israeli police were recommending that the Prime
Minister be indicted over the Bar-On affair.* Everything we were doing was about to
be overwhelmed, and it was not certain that Bibi would survive.

We arrived in Gaza and Arafat and I began our private meeting, but within a few
minutes one of his aides kept coming into the room with news flashes about the indictment, calls for Bibi's resignation, and questions about his future.

I told Arafat that while I did not believe in leaping to snap judgments, clearly it
would be hard for us to get anything done until the situation in Israel clarified, and it
made sense for me to return to the States in the meantime. He agreed, and added that
he thought Netanyahu would survive because it took two-thirds of the Knesset (81
votes out of the 120) to bring him down.

Notwithstanding his comments, it was clear that he and all those around him were
hoping the indictment would be the end of Bibi, and almost gleeful in their anticipation. My team was likewise smitten. I had spoken to Martin in the car out of Gaza and
he explained that the police recommendation would now go to the Attorney General,
who would decide whether to indict. All the pundits were predicting Bibi would not
survive. Aaron was waxing philosophically about how we would now be rescued not by
a Bibi mistake on the peace process but by this scandal. Who would have thought this
was the way we would get rid of Bibi?

I was much more reserved. I said I was not convinced. Maybe I thought it unlikely
that Eli Rubinstein, given what I knew about him, would be the first Attorney General
to indict a sitting prime minister. Or maybe I did not want to give in to wishful thinking. In any case, I told our group what I had said to Arafat—namely, that we should
not leap to conclusions.

Aaron then asked, "You don't really think he could survive this, do you?" Perhaps
because I was leery of our team speaking too loosely and having their speculation on

---

*Netanyahu was accused of improprieties in offering Roni Bar-On the position of Attorney
General.

Bibi's demise showing up in the Israeli press, I replied, "Yes, I do think he can survive." That seemed to sober everyone.

The next morning, Friday, I attended the state funeral for the former President of Israel, Chaim Herzog, then saw Bibi afterward so it would not look like I was running away from him. I told him I would leave for home that evening. While he was trying to put on a show of great confidence, he was clearly agitated: speaking a mile a minute and eating cookies on the table in front of him as if there were no tomorrow. He suggested I should go and see the switchboard, which was inundated with supportive phone calls; he explained that this would all be over soon, already practicing his public line—that he had done nothing wrong and the indictment was an attempt by his elite opponents to deny his voters their vote.

I was thinking about Chaim Herzog, and was struck by the contrast between him and Netanyahu. Herzog was one of the founding fathers of Israel. He had fought for the state at its infancy when its survival was truly in doubt. He was a man of great military accomplishment, having helped to establish Israel's military intelligence arm. He had a yeshiva education, making him a unique bridge between the secular and religious in Israel—his father having been the Chief Rabbi of Israel. He had been a leading lawyer in Israel, and written several insightful books on Israel's wars. Finally, he had held the honorific post of President of Israel. He was a man of great integrity, character, courage, and vision.

As I thought of Herzog and Israel's need for a leader like that now, I listened to Bibi intone about the switchboard, and couldn't help noticing that his fly was unzipped.

| BIBI SURVIVES |

By the time I left Israel that evening, however, I was convinced that Bibi would survive. I had seen my friend Natan Sharansky for Shabbat—it was nearly a ritual for me to have Shabbat dinner with Natan and his family. Natan held the key to Bibi's future. If he opposed Bibi, then Avigdor Kahalani, the Minister of Public Security and the head of the Third Way Party, would do so as well. Bibi, he told me, was calling him every hour on the hour, promising he would change the way he made decisions. Natan told me that if there was no indictment he would support Bibi, provided business would be done differently in the future. I could not help asking Natan if he felt he could trust Bibi's promises. Natan said he could. He was no fool. He knew Bibi was desperate but felt that he could hold him to his words.

On Sunday, as I expected, Attorney General Eli Rubinstein announced that while there was questionable behavior by the Prime Minister there was insufficient evidence to indict. Bibi went on the offensive immediately, repeating the populist line he had practiced with me.

At a minimum, I knew that this mini-drama would take several more weeks to play out. The Labor Party and several citizen groups announced that they would challenge the Attorney General's decision in the Supreme Court. I called Arafat after Rubinstein's announcement and said we would have to wait for the legal process to play out, and again he agreed.

We could not expect any conciliatory moves toward the Palestinians soon. In briefing the Secretary and the President after the trip, I cautioned them not to have any illusions: the legal process would not bring Bibi down. Our main hope in the near term, I said, was that Bibi would now see the need to show he could do something—indeed accomplish something—other than avoiding indictment. As I made this case, I wondered whether I, who was telling them not to engage in wishful thinking, was engaging in some wishful thinking of my own.

15

The 13 Percent Solution

BINYAMIN NETANYAHU SURVIVED THE indictment threat, and while he was quick to agree on the importance of making some tangible and visible progress with the Palestinians, getting him to accept the steps he would have to take to reach out to them proved difficult. Compounding that difficulty was the newfound Palestinian belief that doing business with Bibi would serve his interests, not theirs. Like their partners in the left wing of the Labor Party, the Palestinians believed that Bibi's game plan was to fool the Israeli public by creating the illusion of progress while actually trying to reverse the Oslo process.

During the remainder of May and June 1997, I sought to identify the core elements of an agreed package that could end the stalemate in the peace process and restart negotiations. Building for the Palestinians, taking the pressure off them in Jerusalem, resolving some of the interim issues like the Gaza airport, slowing the pace of building in Har Homa, and producing tangible Palestinian security measures all were part of the prospective package. While security talks resumed after the Arafat-Shahak meeting, the Palestinians would attend only trilateral discussions with the United States as host. They were not going to have bilateral security meetings if there were no political meetings. This was their way of demonstrating that they were cooperating with us—not necessarily the Israelis—on security at a time when the Israelis had stopped the political process. Yet they showed little interest in progress without something on Har Homa. Bibi, for his part, made no effort to fulfill even his promise to build for Palestinians in and around Har Homa. Bibi was content to go slow, satisfy his cabinet, and show that he did not have to make concession after concession—indeed, any concessions at all.

I reminded Bibi of what his Finance Minister, Dan Meridor, had told me shortly after Bibi's election: The peace process was like being on a bicycle; one must keep peddling lest you crash and fall off. Bibi knew better, but he was not willing to take a step that would cost him politically and he resented what he saw as the effort of some Israelis to encourage Palestinians not to work with him.

While I understood his resentment, I was frustrated by his unwillingness to take any steps that could give Palestinians an explanation for their cooperation with him. But my frustration was nothing compared to Madeleine's, Sandy's, and President Clinton's. In their eyes, he had started Har Homa. He had offered an insulting first FRD. He had put Arafat in the corner. Now they saw him using the bombing at the Apropos Café in Tel Aviv as an excuse to avoid negotiations on implementing the interim issues. All felt that our regional interests were being damaged as Arab leaders and Europeans alike complained that Bibi was killing any prospect of peace.

The fear of the deepening stalemate—a fear I shared—led me to propose a way to put the process back on track. Madeleine felt we should put Bibi to the test and establish distance between us if he failed the test—her version of Baker's dead cat on Bibi's doorstep. I did not mind testing Bibi at this point, but my proposal was designed to put both sides to the test. Palestinians would have to produce on security, make real arrests, take a public posture making terror and violence intolerable, and accept accelerated permanent status negotiations. Israelis would have to produce on building housing for Palestinians in East Jerusalem, end the confiscation of identity cards that forced Palestinians out of Jerusalem, stop the demolition of Palestinian homes built without permits, negotiate the terms for allowing the construction of the airport and seaport in Gaza, and suspend settlement expansion for the period of the accelerated permanent status talks. On top of this, I also said Israel would have to carry out the FRD scheduled for September.*

Our "no surprises" commitment with Israel referred only to not presenting a proposal without first consulting them. It did not mean we could not surprise Israel in private with a proposal. And, in effect, that is what we did, when President Clinton called Bibi in early July, and told him over a secure line that he wanted me to come to Israel secretly and reveal our thinking on the steps we felt must be taken—and soon— to break the stalemate.

---

*Since the Israeli FRD offer of March had been rejected by the Palestinians, the Netanyahu government had not implemented it. September was the due date for the next FRD, and as a result Israel would need to carry out both the first and the second FRDs.

| A SECRET TRIP TO ISRAEL: MEETING
BIBI AT THE MOSSAD SAFE HOUSE |

Why the secret trip? There were two reasons: one, we would get Bibi's attention, and he would know we were dead serious; two, no proposal would survive if the Palestinians believed it had been precooked with the Israelis.

To support me on this secret mission, I brought along Bruce Riedel, who had taken over for Mark Parris on the NSC staff, and my deputy, Aaron Miller. The CIA handled our travel, producing an aircraft and a fueling stop en route in which our passports would not be checked. I traveled under the name of Harvey T. Long and carried a white three-by-five card with that name and associated passport number on it. The officials at the airport where we stopped for refueling were accustomed to dealing with passengers being ferried by the Agency under assumed names. However, I was not used to traveling in this fashion. When a local official came aboard our aircraft and asked for my name, I hesitated as if I did not know what to say and then just gave him my three-by-five card. I could tell he was surprised, but he nodded and then departed. I turned to Bruce, saying, "I handled that well. Real pro, wouldn't you say?"

Our arrival in Israel was similarly handled in cloak-and-dagger fashion. We were picked up in a remote part of the airport and conveyed to a waiting van with curtains which took us to a Mossad safe house where the meeting with the Prime Minister would take place.

We were taken to a conference room to wait for the PM. Bibi was obviously nervous as he entered the meeting room. After initial pleasantries, he asked to see me alone, and we went to a guest room next door. Bibi immediately asked, "Is the President trying to jam me? You wouldn't have come this way unless the President was planning something that I will find difficult to swallow."

In any negotiation, there is always a need to reassure without giving up leverage that produces responsiveness. Bibi's nervousness confirmed our leverage, and I did not want to surrender it. But I also did not want him so uneasy that he would become too defensive. So, within limits, I sought to put him at ease. "Prime Minister," I said, "if President Clinton were trying to jam you, he knows how to do it. He would do it in public. I am here not to jam you but to underline the President's seriousness. He believes there is a big problem that will become worse unless we can put the process back on track. The status quo creates the illusion of stability and when it breaks we are going to face a far worse situation. I have a package of mutual actions that requires you and the Palestinians to take meaningful steps. They may not be easy for either of you but are important for both. President Clinton plans to announce these as a package, but wanted this private consultation first."

Bibi calmed down and asked to see the package. As he read over the paper that listed what each side should do, he began to comment on each item. Not surprisingly, he liked what he saw on Palestinian steps, but was far more reserved on his side of the ledger. The two FRDs in September, for example, might be doable, but would take very careful study, and he could not freeze the settlement activity but could consider some limits on it.

Looking intently at me to judge my reaction, he asked: How soon do we have to take these steps? "Soon," I answered.

We then joined the others and discussed the elements of the package through the night. Bibi made some suggestions on Palestinian steps, all of which I felt were appropriate. But most of his comments were designed to give himself wiggle room on the Israeli steps, and I was not buying. After working until the early hours of the morning, I told him I could not remain in Israel for meetings that night lest it become known I was there.

Bibi offered to convey additional comments. I told him I would stay at Martin's residence until the next evening and would be happy to receive Yitzik Molho. Bibi was playing for time and hoped to be able to take the next several days. I told him I would brief President Clinton, who would decide how soon to act. This made Bibi fearful that Clinton would commit him to steps he could not take. Now I chose to play on his fears: "Prime Minister, the President wants to act soon. I would focus on the points that are essential to you."

Yitzik Molho came to the ambassador's residence that evening. He was Bibi's private attorney. More importantly, he was his lifelong friend. His father had been an economic advisor, serving as the equivalent of a dollar-a-year man. Like his father, Yitzik Molho devoted himself to public service without ever joining the government. As the only person Bibi trusted completely, he had become Bibi's negotiator. Not a Likudnik—his own political instincts were center-left—he was probably the only one around Bibi who could tell him what he did not want to hear. However, like any good lawyer, he was an excellent advocate for his client, fully capable of engaging in attrition-type tactics as necessary.

In our discussions, Yitzik always referred to the Prime Minister as "BN." Now he told us he was not sure how quickly "BN can move on the ID question or building for the Palestinians, but it will take time." Moreover, the room for maneuvering was very slim on settlements. As I returned to the States that evening, I knew that unless there was a deadline for actions on both sides, Bibi would try to erode his steps until they were meaningless.

Back in Washington, Madeleine was eager to announce the initiative—thereby putting pressure on both sides—but the President and Sandy Berger felt I should continue to try to work something out with Bibi. They did not want to let him off the hook. Still, President Clinton believed I had made headway. Following several secure-line phone calls with Bibi, I decided to let him know he would have to decide soon since we would present the proposal to the Palestinians privately by the beginning of August. He assumed, as I did, that even if the Palestinians did not leak what we were asking of them, they would leak what we were asking of the Israelis. There would be no playing for time after that. He would either have to respond to us, enraging the Israeli right, or he could try to resist our proposal, enraging the mainstream in Israel. Either way, he was going to have to make some tough decisions soon.

| A TERRORIST BOMB LETS BIBI OFF THE HOOK |

On July 28, Bibi gave an interview on Israel TV's Channel 1 on the anniversary of his first year as Prime Minister. In it, he boasted about the distinction between his government and his predecessor's on security. He was tough on terror and as a result, he declared, the Palestinians understood "very well that the game of tipping the wink to Hamas and to Islamic Jihad and telling them that they may go ahead and blow up buses in Israeli cities [is over and they] will not get off scot-free. That is why the Palestinians have taken measures to restrain them. . . ."

We will never know if the interview gave Hamas an incentive to demonstrate the hollowness of Bibi's words, but two days later, on July 30, 1997, Hamas carried out a twin suicide bombing in the Jerusalem market Mahane Yehuda. Sixteen Israelis were killed; 178 were wounded.

Bibi now went from claiming that the Palestinians (at his instigation) were taking measures to restrain terrorists to charging Arafat and the PA with having "encouraged the violence."

If Bibi felt exposed after the bombing, he also saw its political value for him. In President Clinton's condolence call, Bibi listened to the President's outrage over the bombing and his first words in response were, "Of course, you cannot go ahead with your proposal now." The President's words of concern for the victims mattered little to Bibi; this was his moment to preempt a U.S. proposal that would require steps his hard-core constituency would reject. Though President Clinton was surprised by the PM's preoccupation, he agreed we could not be exerting pressure on Netanyahu now and we put our initiative on hold.

Yet doing nothing was also a prescription for further deterioration, particularly at a time when Bibi—and we—understandably would increase the demands on the Palestinians to make arrests, stop releasing Hamas prisoners from Palestinian jails, seize illegal weapons, destroy the terrorist infrastructure, and end incitement to violence. All these demands were legitimate and necessary. But would any of it happen if the Palestinians believed Bibi, hamstrung by his right, would never respond to any of their needs? This was the question we asked ourselves.

Feeling that we must try to preempt an even more explosive situation, and believing we must set the stage for our proposal even if we were unable to present it now, we chose this moment to have Secretary Albright give her initial speech on the Middle East. We hoped the speech could fill the vacuum, possibly even giving each side a reason to pause and respond to what the United States was calling for. If nothing else, it was important in these circumstances to set a tone and a direction for the peace process during the Secretary's tenure.

| MADELEINE'S MAIDEN VOYAGE IN THE MIDDLE EAST: STRONG WORDS ARE NO MATCH FOR TERROR |

In discussing the themes of Secretary Albright's speech in advance, I suggested that we needed to come down hard on terror: "The Rabin notion that we will pursue peace as if there is no terror and fight terror as if there is no peace is not going to work with this Israeli government and in light of the mood in Israel." But Netanyahu must know—and the Israeli public must see—that "there must also be a serious approach to peace if the Palestinians act against terror." Bibi wanted accelerated permanent status talks but did not want to alter any Israeli behaviors, including unilateral Israeli steps on settlements and confiscations. He cannot, I said, have it both ways. Madeleine agreed, and with Aaron taking the lead in drafting, the thrust of her speech embodied these twin elements: the Palestinians must stop the terror in word and deed; Israel must avoid the unilateral steps that poison the environment and appear designed to prejudge what the negotiations are supposed to be about—namely, resolving the status of the land. She was not saying these were the same; simply that peacemaking could only succeed in a transformed environment. "Let me be clear," she said. "There is no moral equivalency between suicide bombers and bulldozers, between killing innocent people and building houses. It is simply not possible to address political issues seriously in a climate of intimidation and terror."

She revealed that prior to the Jerusalem bombing she and the President were about to send me out to the area to present U.S. ideas, and announced I would go to the area now in order to set the stage for work on the broader political problems. If we made headway on the security issues now, she would travel to the region in late August, early September—her first trip to the region as Secretary of State—in order to "consult closely with the leaders . . . to improve the climate for negotiations, and to discuss the procedural and substantive aspects of the permanent status issues."

This would signal Arafat and the Arab world that we would address the political issues (even discussing the permanent status questions of Jerusalem, borders, and refugees) provided there were tangible steps taken on security. My job was to produce those tangible steps.

When I arrived in Israel, Bibi was relaxed: the onus was on Arafat. Security definitely came first, but I warned against any unilateral Israeli acts that would enflame Palestinian or Arab opinion. And assuming the Palestinians did begin to perform on security, the Secretary would prepare for an accelerated approach to permanent status—and Israel would have to take the steps we had previously discussed to transform the environment. Bibi nodded, but was rarely prone to worry about something that was not imminent.

Arafat was similar in this respect. He may have welcomed the Albright speech, focusing on the call for Israel to stop unilateral actions and ignoring the language that suggested that he winked at terror instead of fighting it. Even so, he knew that my arrival signaled he now had to act decisively on security.

As I arrived, my game plan was to call him to account for the Mahane Yehuda bombing and play on his desire to have the Secretary visit the region and see him. Arafat always believed that such high-level visits lent him and the Palestinian cause stature. I wanted him to understand that if this was important to him, he would have to give me something to get it—and that something was security cooperation that was continuous, with sharing of information and action taken against all those who were a threat. I would attend a trilateral meeting the next evening where the Palestinians had better be serious, using the forum not to lodge complaints but to discuss information that the Israelis had about threats and to work out a joint response. If we judged that the Palestinian security people were not doing what was agreed, the Secretary would not come to the region.

Arafat listened and agreed to everything I asked. Over the next two weeks security cooperation resumed. It was not perfect—the sharing of information was limited, the Palestinians were reluctant to arrest all those on the Israeli lists of Palestinians who needed to be arrested, there were few meaningful steps against the infrastructure of Hamas and Islamic Jihad—but Shin Bet said the Palestinian security organizations were now making an effort. They wanted to encourage it, not dismiss it.

Meanwhile, I met with both Netanyahu and Arafat, as well as their security people, to keep the pressure up, and by the end of the month I reported to the Secretary that the standard she had set for coming to the region had been met. Again, we were poised to begin a more serious effort on negotiations. Again, we were thwarted by another terror act.

On September 4, suicide bombers struck in downtown Jerusalem, killing 5 and wounding 181 on the Ben-Yehuda pedestrian mall. Madeleine had already announced she would be arriving in Israel the next week. To cancel the trip now would send a signal to terrorists that they could stop our efforts. In condemning the terror, she called on Arafat to do more while also declaring that "we cannot give in to terror, and it is with this in mind that I plan to travel to the Middle East as scheduled."

But, in reality, there was little we could accomplish on this trip. Bibi was clear and on strong footing: he would not make concessions in the face of terror; indeed, even if he wanted to, it was politically impossible.

The Secretary spent a week in the Middle East traveling throughout the region; everywhere she went, she heard the same refrain: the U.S. must do more. Her answer was there was little we could do if the suicide bombings continued. She could, and to some extent did, speak about Israeli actions that also must stop, with Arafat complaining publicly about Israeli violations of their commitments under Oslo. But the Ben-Yehuda bombing guaranteed that this trip would be about security and Arafat seemed to understand that the bombing had damaged him at precisely the wrong time.

When I spoke to Arafat and Abu Mazen at the conclusion of the Secretary's trip, I said it had been a lost opportunity. Abu Mazen acknowledged that I was right: the Palestinian Authority had no choice now but to act against Hamas. Arafat listened, offering no comments. I looked at him, and asked whether he would act against Hamas. He said he would. In fact, he did. The arrests, at least initially, were—as Bibi might have put it—of "the sharks, not the sardines" of Hamas and Islamic Jihad. While there was no dismantling of the Hamas infrastructure, there appeared to be a new message: You carry out suicide bombings, we come down on you like a ton of bricks.

There was not to be another suicide attack for more than a year as Arafat sought to turn the tables on Netanyahu. He wanted the onus to be on Bibi, not him. For his part, Bibi's own missteps would continue unabated, including one that was about to threaten Israel's relationship with Jordan.

| SAVING THE ISRAELI-JORDANIAN RELATIONSHIP |

Shortly before 7 a.m. on Saturday morning, September 27, I got a call at home telling me that Prime Minister Netanyahu would be calling me shortly on my secure telephone line. It was unusual for Bibi to call on Saturday, the day Bibi typically slept into the afternoon. Something was up.

The call was put through, and Bibi launched right in, telling me that there was a big problem and King Hussein was threatening to cut off relations with Israel by midnight. I must call him or get President Clinton to call him and prevent what would be a catastrophe. Bibi was a very worried man.

"Prime Minister," I said, "you have to tell me what is going on. What has happened?"

I had seen reports that a leader of Hamas, Khaled Meshaal, had been attacked in

Amman but I had not thought much about it. Now Bibi explained that the attack was an Israeli Mossad operation gone bad. Several Israeli agents, traveling on Canadian passports, had attacked him by injecting him with poison and two had been arrested by Jordanian police as they botched their getaway. Meshaal was in the hospital and would die without the antidote. The Jordanians were demanding the formula for the antidote from Israel without promising to release the Mossad agents. And now the King had given an ultimatum, threatening to sever relations by midnight.

Though mindful that I was on the line with the Prime Minister of Israel, I could not help myself, and blurted out, "What were you thinking?" When Bibi said the attack was a response to the Mahane Yehuda and Ben-Yehuda bombings, I asked, "Why didn't you go to the Jordanians and see whether they would arrest Meshaal and quietly turn him over to you?" Bibi's only answer was Mossad had been certain they could get Meshaal. "Didn't it occur to you that something could go wrong?" I asked. I was dumbfounded when Bibi replied, "No."

At this juncture, I realized that it was pointless to berate Bibi further. His irresponsibility might have created the crisis, but we had a huge stake in avoiding Jordan's breaking off relations with Israel, which, once done, would not be so easy to undo and might prompt Egypt to do likewise.

I told Bibi he would have to get the antidote over to Jordan immediately. He was reluctant to do so if the Israeli agents were not going to be released. "Prime Minister," I said, "you have embarrassed the King, you have taken advantage of your special relationship in security, and you are going to have to make amends. Start with the antidote, make an apology, and promise you won't do anything like this again and these agents will never again set foot in Jordan. You can always tell him if there is ever a threat within Jordan you will come to him and explain the threat." Bibi said he was ready to send Dani Yatom, now the head of Mossad, to Jordan immediately with the antidote, but he feared the King might not see him. I promised I would get the President to call King Hussein, but he must get moving immediately so we could show he was acting to correct his mistake.

I called Sandy Berger and explained the situation. The President needed to call the King, placate him, and suggest that the King quietly release the two Israeli agents with the understanding they would never again return to Jordan.

President Clinton made the call and, having let a livid King Hussein vent, persuaded him not to break off relations and to quietly release the two Israelis. That should have been the end of the story. But it was not.

The King told the President that he sought the antidote, an apology, and a promise that nothing like this would happen again. But Bibi feared that the King might hold the two Israelis for a while and not resume security cooperation—something essential to Israeli security given Jordan's long border with Israel.

So Bibi threw in a sweetener for the King. He would permit Sheikh Yassin, the blind and paraplegic spiritual head of Hamas, to return to Gaza from Jordan—a privilege the King had sought but not made a condition for settling this crisis. What started as an operation to demonstrate the costs to the Hamas leadership outside the territories ended with Israel permitting the spiritual leader of Hamas to return to Gaza as a hero. An operation ill conceived from the beginning ended with yet another blunder, strengthening Hamas in the process.*

| LAUNCHING ONE MORE EFFORT TO BREAK THE STALEMATE |

After the Meshaal affair, Bibi needed more than ever to demonstrate that he could do something right. Internationally, his standing was low, with the respected British journal the *Economist*, in its October 11 edition, featuring Bibi on its cover with the caption "Serial Bungler." Polls in Israel indicated that the public was increasingly dubious about his competence and neither felt secure nor had much hope that he could make any progress on peace. Bibi, as Abu Mazen had pointed out, had missed another milestone called for in Oslo—the September 1997 date for the completion of the second of the three further redeployments. The Palestinians were sure to insist that the first two further redeployments be implemented as part of any package of steps designed to end the stalemate. Progress on peace—or at least the appearance of it—was now in Bibi's interest. Since, needless to say, Bibi was grateful for our stealthy intervention on Jordan, I thought we might use this to relaunch our efforts to find a way to resume peace negotiations.

The next week, in early October 1997, I traveled to the area and brought Bibi and Arafat together for the first time in eight months. The meeting was a very good one, but I knew we needed something fundamental to sustain the security efforts and to restore a political process. With that in mind, I developed an approach on the substance that was similar to what we had been doing previously, but with two twists: first, we would now need not only to call for a credible FRD but actually to propose the size of the first and second FRDs; second, we needed to be able to transform the climate by having each explicitly stop those behaviors that created a problem for the other.

Proposing the actual size of two further redeployments was difficult for us to do. We did not know the terrain, how each percentage of land might affect particular settlements or roads, the priorities the Israelis had from a security standpoint, or the pri-

---

*Knowing Arafat's conspiratorial mind, I also understood that the Chairman would see Yassin's return to Gaza as part of an Israeli plot to work with Hamas to undermine him.

orities the Palestinians had from a political standpoint with respect to different parts of the West Bank they wanted turned over to them. But we certainly did know what the Interim Agreement required: when all three FRDs had been carried out, Palestinians would control all the territory of the West Bank that was not explicitly related to Jerusalem, settlements, and specified military locations or areas that might affect security. No matter how you sliced it, our interpretation (shared by the Israelis who had negotiated the Interim Agreement) was that by the end of the FRD process, therefore, a majority of the West Bank should be under at least partial Palestinian authority.

Even assuming we could work out two FRDs, we had to change the climate for further negotiations. That argued for a "time-out"—a concept Martin had suggested during the summer. Effectively, each side would take a time-out from bad behaviors: the Israelis from settlement activity, demolition of houses, and confiscation of territory or Jerusalem IDs; the Palestinians from incitement, blaming Israel for all ills, and trying to delegitimize Israel in all international organizations.

In place of the bad behaviors would be an integrated package of "good behaviors" or mutual responsibilities in which the Palestinians would perform up front on an explicit timeline and the Israelis would perform later on. (Here Bibi was right on the question of sequence: How could Israel be expected to turn over land and work out the terms for the airport, the seaport, and safe passage if the Palestinians were not performing on security?)

Once again, I felt I needed to condition Bibi on what was coming. While that ran the risk that he would try to water down whatever we presented, it also avoided a confrontation, which I knew President Clinton was far less willing to have than either Madeleine or Sandy. But how should we go about launching such an effort?

A secret trip would not impress Bibi the second time around, so I recommended that I first see discreetly his trusted confidant Yitzik Molho in New York, where he came often on business, and then the Secretary could openly see the two leaders separately in Europe. I did not want the Secretary to go back to the region yet; in some ways, I had contributed to a weakening of Secretary Christopher's authority by encouraging too many trips when the results were likely to be incremental at best and hard to measure.

Madeleine, by definition and desire, was a more public Secretary of State than Chris. She could articulate a public message with clarity and authority. That was her great strength. I did not want to see it weaken—hence the European setting. We could lower her personal stakes in the meetings by tying them to trips she was already scheduled to make. Yet for Netanyahu and Arafat, the meetings would be high-profile and certain to build expectations about what they would have to do.

Madeleine accepted the strategy I had in mind, and I saw Molho in late October.

We would arrange for what would be the first of three meetings the Secretary would have with each leader starting in the middle of November.

In our private meeting in New York, Yitzik Molho sought to convince me that Bibi could be much more responsive to President Clinton if only the President and the Secretary would show him a "warm shoulder." He had real political constraints from the "right," and when we confronted him, Yitzik argued, "BN" was forced to "stand up to you." We must help him, not confront him.

I had my own message to convey: that no matter how understanding I might be of Bibi's constraints, neither President Clinton nor Secretary Albright believed that Bibi had any real interest in pursuing peace. Because of that, even when Bibi would raise legitimate problems, they tended to discount them, believing Bibi was simply seeking excuses to avoid his own responsibilities. If Bibi wanted a warm shoulder, he would need to show one to the Palestinians, focusing on their needs, not only his own.

Yitzik was a problem-solver. He wanted to know, How could we fix the relationship? I outlined the package of steps that we were contemplating, making clear what we expected for the two further redeployments—at least 20 percent of the West Bank ceded to partial Palestinian authority. He made no effort to suggest it would be easy, but he undertook to "pass everything on to BN."

Predictably, Yitzik focused on what the Palestinians would have to do to prove they were finally serious about security. There was no disagreement between us on this, but, I emphasized, Bibi did have to deliver on his end; so long as the President and the Secretary doubted his real intent, the more slack they tended to cut Arafat, who argued that it was difficult to be Israel's policeman when there was no prospect of Palestinian political needs and aspirations being addressed.

I said to Yitzik, "Help me to help you." He took the point and told me he would do what he could.

Secretary Albright saw Bibi on November 14 in London, then Arafat the next day in Bern, Switzerland. Bibi was quick to agree with the four parts of our framework for discussion: further redeployments, a mutual time-out, security, and initiation of the permanent status negotiations. Arafat, too, was agreeable, but asked us to include the outstanding interim issues in our framework—not just in a package of steps we would produce to foster a new environment for negotiations. Both leaders sought to portray themselves as responding to us.

At least at the outset, the meetings had the desired effect, and given the initially promising responses from each, we planned follow-up meetings. Bibi promised to come with an approach to the FRDs. Arafat promised to return with an explanation of all the steps the Palestinians were taking—and would take—on security. While being open to permanent status talks starting, he continued to hold out for a completion of all the outstanding interim issues before moving on to the final status negotiations.

| ROUND TWO IN EUROPE |

The Secretary met again with Bibi in Paris on December 5, 1997, and with Arafat in Geneva on December 6. Round two proved to be less promising than round one. Bibi's approach to the FRDs was to bring a military man—General Shlomo Yanai, the head of planning in the IDF—and have him explain on a map all the limitations Israel faced in carrying out redeployments in the West Bank. He explained the difficulties in providing security for settlements, major roads, and Ben-Gurion Airport. How much territory, I asked him, did the IDF believe was a "doable" FRD? He demurred, saying those were "political decisions." After he left the room, Bibi put a figure on the maximum that was possible for the Israeli withdrawal given the security constraints: "Thirteen percent." Prime Minister, I asked, you mean to say that "the maximum you can do even for permanent status is 13 percent? At the end of the day, the 27 percent that the Palestinians partially control today can be expanded only to 40 percent of the West Bank? And Israel must retain control of 60 percent the territory? Bibi's answer: "That is what the security requires."

If that is the case, I replied, we don't need to worry about pressing for permanent status talks to begin because there will be no deal. "No Palestinian alive will accept that as the outcome of the conflict." Bibi said, Give us a chance to negotiate—implying that this was an initial negotiating position for permanent status.

But at this stage we were talking about the further redeployments. And Bibi was saying that 13 percent is what he was willing to do for all three FRDs. Here again I came back and said, "Prime Minister, there is no way to read the Interim Agreement and conclude that you will hold a majority of the territory when the FRD process is completed."

Interestingly, Bibi did not argue the point, and when Madeleine interjected that he would still need to do a credible first and second FRD, Bibi did not dispute it. Instead, he asked if we accepted the first FRD he had offered in March but not implemented. Both Madeleine and I nodded that we did. Prime Minister, I said, we are focused on what you can do in the second FRD to make the first two together credible. It was his turn to nod, and he did.

As we returned to our hotel, I was not sure how much we had accomplished, but I observed to Madeleine that there had been at least one interesting development: Bibi focused the whole time on the further redeployment. We heard about Israel's constraints instead of getting a new list of demands for what the Palestinians must do. Bibi was addressing our agenda now, not simply trying to avoid it.

Madeleine thought that Bibi was actually working hard now to come up with a further redeployment. Did I think, she asked, he would actually deliver? I was not sure, but told her that the key would be getting Arafat to produce; that would put pressure on Bibi by making the Israeli public Arafat's ally.

The next day the Secretary pushed Arafat on the specifics of what he must do on security. He, of course, had other ideas. He wanted the onus to remain on Bibi, and employed the old strategy that the best defense is a good offense. Every time Madeleine would press, he would speak about his political difficulties. He was "in the corner" before his own people, he said, reciting the litany of everything Netanyahu had done—Har Homa, seizing IDs and forcing Palestinians out of Jerusalem, preventing Palestinians from working in Israel through closures, demolishing homes, reneging on his obligations on FRDs, the Gaza airport, and safe passage, permitting settlers to "terrorize" Palestinians, and so on. He was only asking for "the accurate implementation of the agreements"—agreements we had either witnessed or negotiated.

I intervened, observing that some of the steps he most objected to, like closures, came after the bombings in Israel. If he wanted us to help reverse these steps, we needed the systematic approach to security that the Secretary had been asking him for. He was on the verge of erupting in anger when he controlled himself.

Neither Gamal nor I had ever seen him about to erupt and not do so. What had stopped him now? Had he recalled the lesson of how not to deal with Christopher? Or was it because he, the product of a traditional society, thought it inappropriate to begin ranting and raving at a woman—even if the woman was the U.S. Secretary of State?

Or was it just another tactic? After all, Madeleine steered the discussion away from what we were asking of him and onto his demands, as he wanted. What he had to say on the FRD, however, only highlighted the profound gaps between the two parties on the issue.

Arafat stated without qualification that he was entitled to 30 percent. (He never drew a distinction between himself and his cause, so his exact words—"The Israelis owe me 30 percent"—came as no surprise.) Why 30 percent? Again, in what would be a mantra he would repeat endlessly, he said he was entitled to 30 percent in each of the FRDs because, according to the Interim Agreement, the only issues not to be included in the further redeployments were Jerusalem, settlements, and specified military locations. These were reserved for permanent status negotiations. By his calculation, Jerusalem, settlements, and specified military locations amounted to no more than 9 or 10 percent of the West Bank. Therefore, according to his calculation, when the FRD process was completed the Palestinians should have 91 percent of the territory. Interestingly, he suggested the settlements only amounted to about 3 percent of the West Bank and he defined the specified military locations as also not being more than 3 to 4 percent of the territory. (Here there was a big gap even with the Laborites in Israel, who defined specified military locations as well as areas important to security as being excluded from the further redeployment process and involving substantially larger territories.) The bottom line for Arafat: If he was entitled to 91 percent once the three FRDs were completed, he should get 30 percent each time.

Madeleine was uncertain how to respond. For my part, I did something out of character. I chose not to tell him at this point that he was neither entitled to nor did he have any chance of getting anything like 30 percent in the second FRD, let alone 60 percent for the first two together. This violated a fundamental tenet of my approach to negotiations: it is better to leave a meeting with unhappiness than to create a misimpression or misunderstanding. The former is unpleasant, but the latter fosters greater problems down the road.

Why did I limit my response? No doubt I was not interested in having Arafat explode in anger. But that was not my real problem: I had not prepared the Secretary adequately for Arafat's response, which should have come as no surprise to me. Since she and I could not have a discussion now on how to respond, I put only a mild marker down on this issue: "There is a big gap between your view of what the Interim Agreement requires on the FRD process and the Israeli view." Arafat did not respond, and Madeleine, reading the intent of my "marker," said we would need to discuss this some more. She then broached the idea of meeting again, and Arafat agreed. When she urged him to come with something concrete on security, he suddenly turned agreeable. (In fact, as we were walking out, he suggested to me that I should organize a trilateral security meeting for that purpose.)

Later that evening, I briefed her in detail on how to understand what Arafat was doing on the FRD issue. I also reminded her of what the Interim Agreement actually specified, and how Uri Savir and the other Israeli negotiators of the Interim Agreement would not accept Arafat's interpretation—nor for that matter Bibi's, which would leave Israel retaining a majority of the West Bank.* We would surely have leverage with Bibi

---

*Uri's view was that the Interim Agreement required the Israelis to turn over a minimum of 51 percent of the West Bank by the time the FRD process was completed.

on the size of the further redeployments if Arafat moved on security, but there was no way we could come close to what Arafat was talking about, and we would, I told her, have to condition Arafat to what was possible. What, Madeleine asked, was the maximum we could press for? Given the Yanai presentation, I said 15 percent was probably the outer limit; this would leave little doubt that the Palestinians would have more than half of the territory by the final FRD. But don't kid yourself, I added, getting this from Bibi will be very difficult. Our only chance is if the Palestinians produce on security in a dramatic way.

Ironically, the Palestinians did sign up to an ambitious security plan the night before our meeting with Arafat in London on December 18. In our meeting the previous day in Paris with Bibi, he had returned to the need for the Palestinians to agree to a serious security plan. When we pressed him for what was possible on the FRD, he asked for some time, emphasizing that he was in the middle of trying to get a budget done before the end of the year. The budget was politically charged; by law, if he did not have it accepted by the end of December, his government could fall, and the mixing of the FRD and budget issues was creating strange political bedfellows quite ready to embarrass him.

I gave Bibi a way out. Even prior to the meeting, I had suggested to the Secretary that at the conclusion of these meetings, with an inevitable break now for the Christmas holidays, we needed to show that we had set the stage for decisions. Three meetings with both leaders over the last month required something: if not a breakthrough, at least the preparation for a meaningful next step. Since we were not at the point where we could produce that, my alternative was to tell each leader that the Secretary was going to recommend that each leader come to see President Clinton, provided they were prepared to make decisions when they came. The Secretary would have me go to the region to prepare the meetings beforehand, but the objective would be to have the President see them in the second half of January.

Bibi jumped on the opportunity to delay; Arafat leaped at the idea of coming to see the President, which he continued to believe was hugely symbolic for the Palestinian cause. But now he also believed he would be in a strong position when he saw the President. The night before the London meeting, our security liaison to the Israelis and Palestinians had hosted a trilateral security meeting that went on for six hours. On an ad referendum basis, the Israeli and Palestinian security officials agreed to a sixteen-point memorandum of understanding (MOU).

On its face, it seemed to respond to everything that Bibi had sought and we had been asking for. Palestinians pledged to:

—cooperate fully with the Israelis in responding "immediately and effectively in the event of a terrorist incident or plans for terrorist activity . . . [and] take all the steps necessary to prevent such events";

—confiscate illegal weapons and take all necessary steps, "in coordination and collaboration with Israel—to prevent the infiltration of illegal weapons into the PNA [Palestinian National Authority]";

—pursue illegal militias and "outlaw militias of opposition parties and organizations";

—step up "the efforts to arrest people involved in terrorist activities" and bring them "to court";

—publicize their "categorical objection to any act of terrorism or violence against Israel, as well as against the PNA";

—increase efforts to "sever communication channels and the transfer of funds to suspected terrorist cells";

—place under surveillance the civilian infrastructure of "those who exploit religion for terrorist purposes";

—take "all the security steps necessary to infiltrate the terrorist organizations and put them under close surveillance with the aim of weakening them and destroying them from within."

As I showed the memorandum to Madeleine, I said with amazement that it covered every base. It dealt with fighting the terrorist infrastructure, including the civilian infrastructure of those who exploit religion for terrorist purposes—meaning Hamas. It reflected a commitment to activism and preemption that had been one of the most important Israeli demands and one of our greatest concerns. It specified commitments on arrests of terrorists, confiscation of illegal weapons, cutting off the monies of terror groups, the public repudiation of terror and violence, full security cooperation with the Israelis, and even had in it a supervisory mechanism to oversee the implementation of the agreement.

"Madeleine," I said, "Arafat can now tell us he has produced a systematic agreement with the Israelis on security with provisions for its implementation, and it is something we can hold him to because it was also done in our presence." Madeleine was very pleased, and our meeting with Arafat went well. He was in a good mood, knowing that we would not put pressure on him in this meeting, and while we did not do so, we did begin to condition him on the FRD, with the Secretary telling him we did not think that 30 percent was in the ballpark.

When he repeated his mantra on his being entitled to 91 percent after the three

FRDs, I told him that there were different interpretations of what the Interim Agreement required on FRD. We had never taken a position on what was required at the end of the FRD process, but instead had looked at what was possible at each phase. Now we would push for a credible FRD, and we believed that had to be a double-digit number, but not 30 percent.

Abu Mazen was present and he asked, "What does double-digit mean?" That, he said, could be "10 percent." I said we had not made any final judgments yet, but by the end of the day the number would be closer to 10 percent than 30 percent. This time Arafat chose not to get angry, simply repeating 30 percent whereupon Madeleine suggested that we come to a decision on this when I went out to prepare the Chairman's meeting with the President in January—and Arafat agreed.

Meanwhile, the security agreement was creating problems for Bibi with his right wing. To get the Palestinians to agree, the Israeli security team had accepted some provisions that required Israel to act against Israelis who might commit acts of violence against Palestinians. One provision called on both sides to "act to ensure that violence or terrorism, whether committed by Israelis or by Palestinians, is dealt with immediately and effectively." Similarly, while Palestinians pledged to confiscate illegal weapons, Israel, too, promised to "confiscate weapons from Israeli citizens who plan, overtly support, or are involved in terrorist activity." Most problematically for Bibi, the provision on nonrelease of prisoners stated that "neither side will release suspected terrorists from prison without giving the other side the opportunity to provide information to reconsider the release."

This was not the "reciprocity" that Bibi had envisioned. He wanted a one-way set of promises on security from the Palestinian side, and in response Israel could then turn over land and authority to Palestinians. True, the law already required the Israeli government to crack down on settler violence against Palestinians, but this proved difficult to do in Israeli courts since often the evidence against violent settlers came from Palestinians and was too often dismissed for lack of corroboration. The net effect: Israeli settlers who committed acts of violence against Palestinians rarely served much, if any, time in jail.

The MOU was an effort to answer this; it gave the Palestinian security forces cover to take difficult steps against Palestinians planning acts of violence. For Prime Minister Netanyahu, however, it created a political problem with the settler community, which was literally up in arms over the implication of moral equivalency between them and Palestinian terrorists. Bibi's reaction to the MOU was to say that it required revision and renegotiation.

Arafat, and the Palestinian security officials who had negotiated it, suddenly treated the MOU as if it were the Koran—it was a standard and could not be touched or improved upon. Since Stan had coordinated the meeting, the Palestinians also declared that this was a three-way agreement and we were also responsible for it.

In truth, Bibi's position lent credence to the view that every position he took was governed by political considerations—even those related to Israel's security requirements. Because it embarrassed him before his constituency, Bibi would not accept a document that mandated very important steps by the Palestinians on fighting terror and its supporting political, religious, and civilian infrastructure.

That was not Bibi's only problem. If the Palestinians would agree to rigorous security steps—and fulfill them—he would no longer have an excuse to delay the FRD, which, more than any other issue, challenged the heart and soul of his constituency. Further redeployment meant giving up the land. It meant surrendering the West Bank—or Judea and Samaria, the biblical names that Israelis used to refer to the area. The further redeployments in the Oslo process essentially meant land for peace in the West Bank. The Likud Party had never accepted this principle as it applied to Eretz Yisrael—the land of Israel. The West Bank was not the Sinai Desert. Israel's biblical history was connected to towns like Hebron, where Abraham was buried, or Nablus, where Joseph's Tomb was located, or Bethlehem, where Rachel's Tomb marked a place of tears for those in the Diaspora.

Finding the going very rough within his cabinet in early January, Bibi began to present not a proposed FRD, but possibilities for further redeployment. Even this produced intense resistance. Bibi's style was of course always to have it both ways. With the cabinet, he announced that there would have to be extensive study on what the right level of FRD might be; to the Palestinians he declared that there would have to be a prolonged interval of five months of Palestinian performance on security before Israel would carry out the FRD, whatever it was. Bibi's posture unfortunately satisfied no one. On the right, they saw him as still prepared to go ahead with a further redeployment. Conversely, the Palestinians saw his calls for five months as a trick, and were convinced that no matter how they performed, he would find an excuse not to follow through.

From our standpoint, whatever credit he got for working the FRD issue, he lost by complicating it in the region. As if to prove that point, when I saw him in January to prepare for the President's meeting, he began to raise other issues. He began to push for a convening of the Palestinian National Council (PNC) to revoke the Palestinian charter; he needed assurances that we would not press him later on the third phase of FRD; he needed guarantees from us on both the substance and procedure of the permanent status negotiations. And, of course, he tried to suggest that the Palestinians must still revise their approach on security. I told him that he discredited his legitimate points when he raised those that had no merit. Like it or not, the MOU was serious and he needed to find a way to explain why it was not acceptable. He hadn't.

When we turned to specifics on the FRD, I suggested to Bibi that he try for "low teens"—he did not ask for greater specificity and I did not offer him a number. With Arafat when we met in Gaza, I again talked about a double-digit FRD closer to 10 percent than 30 percent. Later, when Abu Mazen joined us, Abu Mazen pressed me, and I said "probably low teens." Abu Mazen smiled and said, "High teens would be better." Perhaps, I replied, but it is likely to be low teens.

I raised one other issue: I told Arafat and Abu Mazen that Bibi had made the PLO charter into an issue, seeking to have another Palestine National Council meeting to revoke it. In May 1996, before the Israeli election, Arafat had convened the PNC and its nearly six hundred members to annul the articles in the charter that rejected Israel, adopting a resolution whose words had been negotiated with the Peres government. Bibi wanted something more explicit, but since we had recognized the 1996 action we could now hardly say it meant nothing. Thus, I suggested that Arafat bring a letter to Washington from him to President Clinton reaffirming the 1996 PNC decision and his 1993 pledge to live in peace with Israel. Abu Mazen asked whether we wanted the numbers of the articles in the charter that had been annulled in the letter, and I nodded. Abu Mazen said "okay," and Arafat nodded his approval as well.

Arafat remained relaxed. The image of American pressure and unhappiness with Bibi was consuming the Israeli press, and divisions within his government (Foreign Minister Levy had resigned on the eve of my arrival) were again raising questions about whether Bibi's coalition could survive. In this zero-sum world, Arafat felt he was winning and was arriving in Washington confident of his standing with Clinton. That would change during the course of his visit to Washington.

| PRESIDENT CLINTON OFFERS END-OF-CONFLICT PROMISES TO NETANYAHU AND ARAFAT |

The meeting with Bibi was slated for January 20, with Arafat for January 22. Bibi arrived in town bringing with him members of families who had been the victims of terror. Together they would tour the Congress. In addition, Bibi arranged to see Jerry Falwell and Pat Robertson, two evangelicals who were strong supporters of Israel and very pronounced opponents of President Clinton. The message was clear: Don't press Bibi too hard or he could make life difficult politically for the President.

We had long, intense meetings with Bibi throughout the day on January 20. In Israel, the cabinet had not authorized a number on the FRD—something Bibi told us gave him flexibility. He claimed that he was prepared to stretch to the limit on the FRD if he could return to tell his cabinet there would be no third FRD no matter what the Interim Agreement mandated.

His argument might have been more compelling if he had been ready to stretch far on the FRD, but he was not, telling us the most that was possible was less than 10 percent—and even that depended on our relieving him of the need to do a third FRD, producing a PNC meeting on the charter, and delivering an extended period of performance first from the Palestinians on their obligations.

After his initial meeting with the President, Madeleine, Sandy, and I met with Bibi and pressed him on the FRD. He did not budge, convincing me that he had promised Ariel Sharon and other ministers who were pressing him that he would not agree to anything on the FRD while in Washington.

Instead, he kept coming back to the third FRD, telling us that his flexibility on the size of the second FRD was dependent on doing away with the last of the further redeployments. What flexibility? I asked. You are offering 9 percent for the whole FRD process. Palestinians would partially control 36 percent of the West Bank and the FRD process would be over. "Prime Minister," I said, "that won't fly."

Bibi went back to see the President in the evening. I did not join the meeting, but briefed the President in advance, telling him Bibi wanted to return with a trophy—namely, the dropping of the third FRD—which he would then use to move the right-wing members of his cabinet. I envisioned Bibi going back and saying, "Look what I produced. I got us out from under the Rabin commitment on having three FRDs, so give me something to keep the Americans satisfied."

When he saw Bibi, the President offered a trade-off: Get to the low teens in return for dropping the third FRD. Bibi still did not budge. So President Clinton offered one additional incentive: should Bibi go to the low teens, the President, unprompted, proposed to have the United States offer Israel a formal defense treaty. I had always envisioned such a pact as part of a permanent status deal—and at different points had suggested as much to the President, observing that our commitments to Israel had always been verbal, but not enshrined in a formal treaty. Psychologically, the difference was important for Israelis. I thought I was conditioning the President for what would be needed later. But he now chose to play the defense treaty card to try to get a credible FRD.

Bibi was taken with the offer; while not agreeing to raise what he could do on the FRD, he promised the President he would consider this offer carefully. (No doubt his promise to the cabinet on not agreeing to a number precluded accepting even this offer, but the imagery that he would produce what no other prime minister of Israel had produced was bound to appeal to him.)

The President's meeting with Bibi went on until after midnight. I had been at the White House while the President was conducting the meeting in the residence upstairs. Because of the hour, the President preferred not to do a postmeeting debrief but rather to get together the next day to go over where we stood in advance of the Arafat meeting.

While we would hold the meeting the next day, it was clear the President's mind was elsewhere.

| MONICA LEWINSKY CASTS A SHADOW OVER THE ARAFAT VISIT |

The Monica Lewinsky story broke on January 21 between the Netanyahu and Arafat meetings. Suddenly there was a media frenzy over whether the President had had a sexual relationship with the former White House intern and whether he or his friend and advisor Vernon Jordan had counseled her not to tell the truth about their relationship if Ken Starr, the independent counsel, called her before the grand jury.

President Clinton was known for his capacity to compartmentalize. But on this day he was being put to the test. He would appear on the *NewsHour with Jim Lehrer* that evening and deny an "improper relationship" or any suggestion that he had ever asked anyone not to tell the truth. He would use the occasion of the interview to say he was working hard on the nation's business and national security in particular—noting that he had been meeting with Prime Minister Netanyahu until past midnight and would be meeting Chairman Arafat the next day, trying hard to put the peace process back on track.

While he sought to stay focused, it was difficult for others to do so. Bibi called the President from Andrews Air Force Base as he was about to depart for Israel and told him to "hang in there, these things have a way of blowing over." Clearly Bibi knew the pressure was on the President and off him.

Arafat arrived that same evening. President Clinton had asked me if there was any way to get Arafat to drop the third FRD; I felt there was very little chance that he would—he was, after all, entitled to it according to the Interim Agreement.

"What can we give him?" President Clinton asked. I suggested one symbolic act we could promise. "Mr. President," I said, "you could tell him that you know it is difficult for him to give up the third FRD, but you are convinced that moving to permanent status now is the best way to achieve Palestinian aspirations, and that if the Chairman agrees to forgo the third phase, you will commit to him to support Palestinian statehood in the permanent status discussions."

This is a leap for us, I continued, since we have not taken a position on statehood during the Oslo process, though we did oppose it previously. President Clinton immediately liked it, saying, "Yeah, that might just work." Having raised it, I became a little uneasy. Mr. President, I said, you have to qualify this. You aren't committing to a state with particular powers or borders, and your offer is conditioned on no third FRD. The President said, "I got it." I hoped so.

President Clinton did not raise the idea of statehood until his evening meeting with Arafat. First, in the photo opportunity with the President, Arafat sat expressionless as the President was asked about Monica Lewinsky.

The meeting in the Oval Office that followed was largely ritualistic. Arafat offered a litany of complaints about Netanyahu even while lauding the President's involvement in trying to promote peace. The President thanked him for his letter reaffirming the 1996 decision on the charter, and pressed him on developing a timeline for the steps that the Palestinians would take on security, suggesting the phased "parallel obligations" approach I had devised: assuming the Palestinians performed immediately on their initial obligations on arrests and confiscation of weapons, the Israelis would be obligated to carry out a partial FRD in the first two weeks of the timeline and the rest by the end of three months, not five.

This was not prolonged Palestinian performance before any Israeli obligations were assumed. Arafat was pleased, but when the President suggested dropping the third FRD, Arafat was not buying, even when Clinton argued the merits of moving to permanent status rather than sweating out the final FRD—which he argued would rob Netanyahu of the political capital he would need for conceding on the permanent borders. But Arafat doubted Netanyahu would ever do a permanent status deal and he was not going to surrender what was rightfully his. Israel must fulfill its obligations, especially on the land.

Since the President had also met Bibi in the evening in the East Wing of the White House—the residential part of the White House—he would do likewise with Arafat. (This, too, represented a potentially significant departure: now Arafat would be given similar treatment to the Israeli Prime Minister. This was as much a statement of unhappiness with Bibi as it was an effort to use symbolism to try to move Arafat on the substance.)

In the meeting that night in the residence, the President decided to play the statehood card. If Arafat would accept a move to the permanent status negotiations, the President would support an independent Palestinian state in the negotiations. This, the President suggested, was a historic move by an American president. But he was willing to do it only if the Chairman would give up the third FRD and move rapidly to permanent status talks.

Arafat was unmoved. Abu Mazen was present, and when he suggested the Palestinians could accept what the President was proposing and the negotiations should now commence, Arafat declared, "Fine, I will resign and you will go back to Gaza and run everything." Abu Mazen went silent at this point. Arafat would not give up the third FRD, and he began reminding the President that all he was asking for was what the agreements required.

The President had gotten nowhere, even though he had now played the statehood card. Against my better judgment, I had stayed out of the meeting in the hopes that Arafat would understand it was time to make decisions, not negotiate. Now I kicked myself for raising the statehood idea with the President. He had played the idea, Arafat now saw it as something he could get later on, and he was not going to pay for it up front.

I went to see Arafat the next day at his hotel. Mohammad Rashid called to tell me that Arafat needed some reassurance. He had come to town very hopeful, but now he was concerned. The President had been ready to walk away from the third phase, even though this was part of the Interim Agreement. The larger question, however, was about the President's political health. The perceived walkaway was related in Palestinian eyes to the Lewinsky scandal. They felt the President was weak, and so would not press Bibi to meet his obligations. He might even be forced out of office. What then? Arafat was anxious.

This created an opportunity for me to send Arafat a message. Believing the President's denials and doubting that he had done anything that might force him from office, I assured the Chairman that Clinton was not going anywhere.

I then told him that while he was within his rights to insist on the third redeployment, the President had offered our support of statehood—a historic move, something unprecedented for the United States—and "your response convinced him that it was probably a mistake to do so." So that idea was now off the table. What was on the table? My guess, I told the Chairman, was that we would probably present a package proposal soon, including Israeli obligations on the FRDs, Palestinian obligations on security performance, a time-out on bad behavior, and a timeline on the respective obligations with milestones for completing the interim issues and beginning the permanent status talks.

We had been meeting alone (with only Gamal present), and Arafat sat impassively throughout; only when I explained that President Clinton would survive as President did Arafat show any emotion—obvious relief. Otherwise he was expressionless. I often thought that of all those with whom I negotiated, the one person I would never want to play poker against was Arafat.

Yet I knew he had heard me. I had no illusions on the statehood issue. My purpose had been different. I wanted him to understand that he had disappointed President Clinton—making the President less likely to stick his neck out for Arafat now and making him realize that when he received our upcoming proposal, which would contain some items difficult for him to swallow, he might realize there were costs for him in disappointing Clinton again in his response.

We had played out the string on having meetings. It was time to make our proposal. I recommended that we now present it secretly, giving the two sides a choice: Negotiate something on your own or have us go public with the proposal. Since each was likely to have problems with our proposal, they might just have an incentive to do something on their own.

| MAKING THE PROPOSAL EVEN AS A CRISIS WITH IRAQ INTERVENES |

Even as Netanyahu and Arafat were visiting Washington, a crisis was burgeoning with Iraq. By the end of January, matters came to a head when Saddam Hussein blocked UN weapons inspectors from access to possible weapons facilities and development sites. President Clinton had made it clear we would not tolerate Saddam's prevention of the UNSCOM mission and there would be a military response if Iraq continued to block the inspectors. UN Secretary-General Kofi Annan was trying to find a diplomatic way out of the impasse, but increasingly the world's attention became riveted on the prospect of a fresh military conflict with Iraq.

This was especially true in Israel. When Saddam had launched thirty-nine Scud missiles against Israel in 1991, hoping to transform a conflict that had pitted the world against Iraq into an Arab-Israeli war, Israel had not retaliated. But those Scud missiles were loaded only with conventional warheads. Now it was said that Saddam had Scuds topped with chemical warheads, and that if the United States attacked Iraq, he might employ them against Israel. Israelis were understandably nervous, but unlike in 1991, when Palestinians had cheered Scud attacks on Israel, Palestinians now shared Israeli disquiet.

The threat of chemically armed missiles hitting Israel inspired fear among Israelis and Palestinians alike. Given the proximity of the West Bank, the Palestinian Health Minister now appealed to the Israeli government to make gas masks available also to Palestinians and to provide emergency assistance if necessary. Paradoxically, Saddam Hussein was showing how intertwined Israeli and Palestinian destinies were. Yet in such an environment, the crisis over Iraq made our diplomacy between the Israelis and Palestinians a sideshow—at least for the time being.

I did not know how long we would be riveted on Iraq, but I reasoned that even before a military showdown we should present our proposal quietly to both sides. This would avoid putting pressure on either side while also providing them with an agenda for their own discreet negotiations. With world attention—and ours—diverted elsewhere, they could try to produce their own understandings, being aware, of course, that if they did not succeed in doing so, we would go public with our ideas at some point. That might spur their talks, and in any case, once the showdown with Iraq was over and the Egyptians, Saudis, and others looked to us to do something more on the Palestinian issue, we would have a proposal already on the table and ready to announce.

The President, Madeleine, and Sandy all agreed with this approach. The Secretary called Netanyahu and Arafat and asked each to send one person to meet me in London secretly.

| SECRET MEETINGS IN LONDON |

Bibi sent Yitzik Molho and Arafat sent Saeb Erekat. I met each separately and secretly in London on January 31, 1998, and outlined our proposal to them.

For the first time, I offered a definition of low teens—13 percent for the new territory to come under at least partial Palestinian control. I offered a sequence in which the Palestinians would have to perform immediately on arrests, confront Hamas infrastructure, begin to confiscate illegal weapons, and resume bilateral security cooperation with Israel, while Israelis would have to carry out the first FRD, the one they had offered the previous March, by the end of the first two weeks. That consisted of transferring 2 percent from Zone C to Zone B. (It also involved increasing Palestinian authority in areas of existing responsibility by moving 7.1 percent from Zone B to A status—and this, too, would be done by the end of the first two weeks.) By week six of the timeline—or halfway through the three-month period for implementation—the Israelis would carry out an additional redeployment, now increasing Zone B by an additional 5 percent. That meant that of the 13 percent, 7 percent would be transferred by week six and the remaining 6 percent of the FRD would take place at the end of the twelve-week period. The logic was to satisfy the Israeli need to know that Palestinians were meeting their security obligations first while also satisfying the Palestinian need to show they were getting something as they fulfilled their obligations.*

To be sure, Palestinian obligations were ongoing, but some responsibilities—like reducing the numbers of Palestinian police—were also phased in on the twelve-week timeline. Similarly, by the end of the three-month period for implementation, the Gaza airport, the seaport, the industrial zone, and safe passage had to be resolved. In other words, with the exception of the third FRD and the completion of the further redeployment process—which we did not address in this proposal—all the obligations of the interim period were to be fulfilled.

The time-out on Israeli settlement activity and on Palestinian incitement would not be a part of our formal proposal. However, we expected informal understandings on each side in order to create a climate in which permanent status negotiations would have a chance to succeed.

---

*We also proposed a second 7.1 percent B-to-A transfer of authority at the end of the three-month timeline.

Yitzik took every word down carefully. He had two concerns. He did not think Bibi could go to 13 percent, and felt there needed to be more time for Palestinian performance before Israel should have to carry out any of the FRD. He asked if I could delay my presentation to the Palestinians, and I said no, pointing out that we had structured the proposal in a way that created a sequence of Palestinian performance first and Israeli delivery only second. "I can assure you," I said, "that Saeb will complain about precisely this point when I see him. The Palestinians want either strict parallelism in obligations or at least delivery of what matters to them very early in the process."

My prediction turned out to be correct. Saeb argued that the Palestinian obligations were "front-loaded" while they received meaningful land only later in the process. This, he argued, would "not fly." In reply, I pointed out that we were not doing what the Israelis wanted. They want a prolonged period of your performance before having to redeploy from any land. We have divided up the 13 percent FRD so you get something by two weeks, by the middle of the process, and by the end—and the whole period is only three months long. Saeb, I argued, we have had a stalemate for the last year. You don't have to wait that long to get tangible achievements—not only in terms of the FRDs but also on the other interim issues like the airport and safe passage.

Like Yitzik, Saeb did not resist, saying only that he doubted that Arafat would accept this. I answered that we were not going to do better.

I asked both Yitzik and Saeb to have their leaders come back to us with their reactions, and they both said they would report the ideas fully.

| BOTH SIDES RESTRAIN THEIR ENTHUSIASM |

For once, neither side leaked either the fact of the proposal or its content in the days after the meeting. Perhaps each side saw the benefit of keeping this secret while international attention was riveted on Iraq. Perhaps each saw that our ideas drove them together in their opposition to what we had presented—believing that we would announce a proposal they each disliked if they failed to come to agreement themselves.

Whatever the reason, both sides informed us that they would now try to produce an understanding on the interim issues and the resumption of the permanent status negotiations on their own. If we would give them some time, the two sides would work together through their own secret channels.

That was fine with me. I had often joked with my colleagues that my main objective was to drive the parties together either in support of what I was doing or in opposition. If they had a stake in working together, that represented progress.

But ultimately such progress required actually reaching agreements. Here, the substance still divided them. Bibi was willing only to do token FRDs; instead, he was trying to persuade the Palestinians to settle for getting the airport and an industrial zone in Gaza, forgoing the rest of the interim issues, and moving immediately to the permanent status talks. But the Palestinians wanted the land, weren't persuaded by Bibi's argument (in private meetings with Abu Mazen and Abu Ala) that he could do more in permanent status if he did not have to do much on the FRDs, and in any case weren't willing to pay the price of confronting Hamas and Islamic Jihad if they were going to have little to show for what they were getting in return.

Their discussions remained secret for several weeks. So long as they remained secret, I knew the two sides were serious. I remained in close touch with both sides during this period. But once the existence of their talks leaked, I knew the prospect of their reaching agreement was nil. So even before the end of March and the end of the Iraqi crisis—with Saddam backing off and saying UNSCOM could do its work unimpeded—I knew that we would have to intervene. Having put both sides on notice with our proposal, we now faced the question of whether to go ahead with it. Would we go public?

| BIBI SEEKS TO HEAD OFF OUR PROPOSAL |

With the Iraqi crisis over, with Monica Lewinsky and her mother's appearances before the grand jury generating a great deal of attention and sympathy—and increasing questions about Ken Starr and what all this had to do with his Whitewater investigation—and with the atmosphere with the Palestinians souring again, Bibi now feared we would make our proposal public. He took several steps to make it more difficult for us to do so. First, he began to publicly attack Arafat, emphasizing that the chairman was not fulfilling any of his obligations under Oslo. Second, he sent a small team, headed by David Bar-Ilan, his person in charge of public communications, to reiterate the attacks in visits to key members of the U.S. Congress. Third, he spoke with leaders in the Jewish community (such as President Clinton's friend Mort Zuckerman), emphasizing that doing more than a 10 precent FRD would be a mortal threat to Israel.*

The Palestinians saw Bibi's offensive and worried that it might deter us. So they now leaked the 13 percent figure on the FRD, hoping to make it difficult for us to walk away from it. They also sought to answer Bibi's charges with charges of their own: Israel's unilateral steps continued unabated—increased settlement activity, confiscations

---

*After his calls with Bibi, Mort would convey Bibi's comments to both the President and me. Mort said Bibi was categorical, saying that he might be able to stretch to 11 percent for the FRD but that was the absolute limit. Anything more, and Israel's security would be seriously threatened. While Bibi could move on the quality of the land for the FRD, he could not move on the quantity. He told

of Palestinian property and Jerusalem identity cards, forcing Palestinian families out of their homes in Jerusalem, demolition of Palestinian houses, and other "violations" of the Oslo process. Each side sought to make the other side look worse.

While there were no new terrorist acts, there were increasing reports of terrorist threats. (After one leading Hamas figure high on Israel's wanted list died in a mysterious explosion in Ramallah, Bibi was quick to publicly deny responsibility—no doubt fearing Hamas retribution, despite his earlier boast that Israel would go anywhere, anytime, to stop those who were threatening Israelis.)

Madeleine and Sandy were furious at Bibi for his lobbying here, and felt we should put him on the spot by making our proposal public. The President, however, remained uneasy, fearing that if we announced our proposal now, we would get two "no's" and then be much worse off.

I shared his doubts. Only a "yes" from the Palestinians would put Bibi on the spot, for the Israeli public would put pressure on any leader if there were a perception that the Arab partner was ready to take steps for peace and the Israeli government was not. Meanwhile, Bibi could hide behind the lack of a Palestinian "yes"; indeed, he could say "no" without creating a political problem.

My instincts did not square with either Sandy's or Madeleine's—or the instincts of most of those on my team or in the Near Eastern Affairs Bureau at the State Department. But I also read the President's reluctance to confront Bibi as an indication that we would not sustain a tough position we might stake out. And sure enough, when I told the President that I preferred to go to the area and try to produce a "yes" from Arafat first before pressing Bibi, he was visibly relieved and Sandy and Madeleine soon embraced this approach.

I set out for the region on March 25, 1998, bearing a letter from President Clinton saying: "Mr. Chairman, I would like to move forward with our ideas. But to do so I need to know that you are going to accept them. Frankly, I do not see the value in presenting our ideas if you're not going to accept them. . . . Mr. Chairman, I am ready to make my decision and looking forward to Dennis's return with a 'yes' response from you."

Embedded in the Clinton letter was a presumption that we were the key to mov-

---

Mort that we had also surprised him with the 13 percent figure. I asked Mort how could we surprise him with the 13 percent when we had told him repeatedly that we would come with a figure in the low teens? "Mort," I said, "we came with the lowest teen there is." Mort said Bibi thought the lowest teen meant 11 percent. Given Bibi's well-known and highly touted command of Americanized English, I could not resist the sarcastic jibe that I had forgotten that Bibi's English was so poor; "that must explain the misunderstanding."

ing the Israelis, the key to leveling the playing field, but Arafat had to give us the means to do so. Oddly, Bibi's reluctance to do a 13 percent FRD had made this low figure more acceptable to the Palestinians. I read it this way, and though few of my colleagues agreed, I thought I could produce a Palestinian "yes." That did not mean that I expected Arafat to make my mission easy or comfortable. I knew I would have to work for it, that I would not get a "yes" in one meeting, and that Arafat would want me to understand how difficult this was for him. In this respect, he did not disappoint me.

| PRODUCING A "YES" FROM ARAFAT |

I arrived at Arafat's headquarters in Gaza on the evening of March 26, having seen Bibi first and having briefed him on what I would be trying to accomplish with Arafat. Having me bang heads with Arafat never bothered him, and he was very relaxed—after all, there was no pressure on him at the moment. With Arafat, it was a different story. I began the meeting by explaining that my purpose was to go through the whole proposal and that a partial, ambiguous "yes" in response would not be acceptable.

I started by presenting President Clinton's letter, telling the Chairman that without a yes, I did not believe the President would proceed, much less stay engaged. He was asking for "a yes from you not because we know we can produce a yes from Netanyahu, but because we know we cannot produce it without your yes."

I was trying to anticipate Arafat's arguments, and so I said you are going to ask me what is the point of my saying yes if Netanyahu will say no? My answer to you: We will pull back without a yes from you. With a yes, if we don't succeed with Bibi, the onus will be on him and not you. He nodded his agreement on this point. This was the easy part.

When I went to the proposal—essentially the same one presented on January 31 to Saeb—I started with the FRDs, their phasing, and both the areas from C that would become Palestinian in whole or in part and the areas from B that would become A areas. I told Arafat the area of your civil control in the West Bank will grow from 27 percent of the territory to 40 percent. And with the B-to-A transfer of authorities, the area in which you exercise virtually total control—civil and security—will grow from only 2.9 percent to over 18 percent of the West Bank.

I pointed out as well that the airport—something that would give Palestinians far greater freedom of movement—safe passage between Gaza and the West Bank, and the industrial zone were all to be agreed upon and implemented during the twelve-week timeline of mutual obligations. (The seaport would be agreed upon, but would take several years to construct.)

These were items that he gained with this agreement. But I pointed out that he also had obligations—obligations for full, unqualified, and continuous security cooperation with the Israelis; for developing and acting on a work plan to arrest those carrying out or planning terror and dismantling the infrastructure that supports them; for preventing incitement to violence; for confiscating illegal weapons; and for acting in two areas where the Palestinians were in breach of their Interim Agreement responsibilities: the numbers of police exceeded what they were permitted to have, and they had not acted against Palestinians who had killed Israelis and were at large in the Palestinian areas. Finally, with regard to the PLO charter, I said: the letter to President Clinton had been very helpful, but we wanted to give to it greater institutional weight by having the Executive Committee of the PLO reaffirm it.

I emphasized that these were an integral part of the package and required early action on the timeline, which I now showed to Arafat, pointing out what should be done by each side and when.

Next we went through the time-out on bad behavior: Palestinians must stop challenging Israeli credentials in international organizations while trying to upgrade their own status in them; stop building without permits in the C area; and agree not to take unilateral steps—e.g., declare statehood—recognizing that only negotiations can resolve the conflict. Israelis must stop demolishing Palestinian houses built without permits, confiscating Jerusalem IDs, building bypass roads without consulting Palestinians, and expanding settlements beyond the "immediate, contiguous periphery of existing settlements."

Summing up, I said, Mr. Chairman, I have no doubt that you feel there are difficult demands on you. But the fact is that you will be gaining very tangible assets in the form of land and the conclusion of most of the interim issues. Moreover, the time-out on the Israeli side will change the climate dramatically for your people. This is not the end of the road, but it is a road that won't be traveled unless I can return to President Clinton with your "yes."

Arafat had listened while I spoke for nearly an hour. He had not been impassive this time. He clearly did not like many of the demands, but I had persisted even as he showed signs of unhappiness. Now he offered some comments. He started on incitement. He accepted the need to end incitement but it should be a mutual obligation—the Israelis must stop as well. Where, he asked, was the third FRD? I had not mentioned it. How could he reduce his police force if he was to fulfill all the security obligations? What about the content of the 13 percent of the territory? Netanyahu often spoke of "quality" land. Would the land be contiguous? On the time-out, he suggested that the Palestinians would not change the status of the land prior to May 4, 1999, the date the interim period ended. (I understood this to be his way of preserving his right to declare a state unilaterally at that time if there were no agreement.) Finally, there was something else missing in our proposal. If he would be required to make arrests, Israel must also release prisoners in accord with the requirements of the Interim Agreement.

I addressed each of his points—some sympathetically, some negatively. On the third FRD and the incitement, I suggested that these were areas in which we would form committees. On the land and contiguity, our reading of the Interim Agreement did not require the Israelis to negotiate the territory but to coordinate with Palestinians prior to implementing a handover of territory or authority. In those coordinating sessions, the issue of contiguity could be raised, and we would also encourage the Israelis in this regard. On the time-out, he should be under no illusions: while we wanted the permanent status talks to get under way and succeed well before May 4, 1999, we would oppose all unilateral steps. Only a negotiated outcome would be stable and enduring. On the police, the Palestinians had an obligation according to the Interim Agreement and they were not living up to it. He could hardly call for the "accurate implementation" of agreements if his side was not doing so. Finally, on the prisoners, I took the point and agreed that we would introduce the Palestinian prisoners held in Israeli jails into our consideration.

Arafat thanked me for my comment on the prisoners. He said he could not decide anything tonight. We were asking much of the Palestinians and offering far less than they were entitled to. Unlike a normal visit to Gaza for a late-night meeting, where I would usually leave immediately after our discussion, I met next with Abu Mazen, and reinforced my central message: Without a yes from Arafat, we were out of business. He told me he would work hard to produce it.

The next night when I saw Arafat, Abu Mazen joined him again. Arafat began by reciting a long list of complaints about Netanyahu and his immaturity as a leader. Israel was not meeting its obligations, how could he meet all of his? How could he know that if he said yes and Netanyahu said yes that Bibi would not insist on Palestinian performance but then find an excuse to avoid his own responsibilities?

He looked at me as if he had trumped anything I could say. "Mr. Chairman," I responded, "I negotiated the Hebron deal and Netanyahu pulled out of Hebron. I have no guarantees for you, except that we will monitor both sides' obligations, and the risk you take by saying yes is far less than the risk you take by having me return to see President Clinton with a "no" or a "maybe" from you. What do you want me to tell him?"

In Arabic, he said tell him "with God's blessing." Abu Mazen smiled for the first time in the meeting. (Later he would tell me he had been uncertain what Arafat would do, but he said "with God's blessing" meant that Arafat was saying yes in an unqualified way, whereas "God willing" was a way of avoiding responsibility and leaving everything to fate.) Arafat then said in English, tell "President Clinton I have said yes, in principle." He explained that it was yes in principle because he had not yet seen the proposal in written form, only heard it presented orally.

I nodded and then asked him to keep this confidential for the time being. I wanted the President to hear the yes from me and not read about it in the papers. Moreover, President Clinton could make better use of the Palestinian yes—could better persuade Netanyahu—if we could be the ones to announce it. Arafat nodded agreement, but I knew this would only buy us a few days before the Palestinian "yes" became public.

Before returning to Washington, I met Bibi and told him Arafat had said yes, in principle. I went through the details of the proposal again with him to underscore what it was the yes meant on all the issues he had always referred to as the reciprocity issues: security, arrests of suspects, confiscation of illegal weapons, confronting the terrorist infrastructure, reducing the size of the police, reaffirming the action on the charter, smuggling, and incitement. I wanted Bibi to know that a yes in principle meant yes on his agenda as well as an acceptance of FRDs far smaller than the Palestinians had been demanding.

He listened, realizing the pendulum would now swing and the pressure would be on him. He said he could have told me that Arafat would say yes. Why, I asked, didn't you? Why, if that were true, did your military assistant tell me your intelligence was certain he would say no? Bibi had no answer, perhaps because he was already thinking about the fix he was about to find himself in.

| DESPERATION BREEDS A BRIDGING IDEA |

The Palestinian "yes" on undisclosed American ideas did not leak for a week's time, permitting me to return to Washington and brief the President without any public awareness of a potentially important development. But Bibi had a problem. Arafat had said yes to the proposal—a proposal that imposed security obligations on the Palestinians but also called for a 13 percent further redeployment by Israel, an action opposed by the Israeli right wing. Bibi's initial reaction was to emphasize that he could not do 13 percent, but that, in any case, he wanted us to nail down what the Palestinian commitments would actually mean—and in a way that was favorable to Israel.

At the President's behest I returned to the area to see if there was a way to get Bibi to buy the proposal now. Our first few meetings did not go well. He kept pressing for me to produce more from the Palestinians and I kept answering that I had something from them but I had nothing from him, and I was in no position to go back to them asking for something more. His initial solution to this was that I should work with him, Yitzik, and Dani Naveh to understand what they needed from the Palestinians to carry out the FRD. This did not mean he was committing to 13 percent—he could not do that—but that we should reach some understandings about what Israel required on the "reciprocity issues."

Thus began a tedious discussion of what had to happen on each issue, ranging from who needed to be arrested to confronting the terrorist infrastructure. While I could see the need for clarity, we would never achieve it if we could not produce the Israeli FRD of 13 percent. Bibi now said that we had cornered him. He could never do the 13 percent, particularly now that Arafat had accepted it. "You should never have gone public with this figure." We waited, I told him, over two months to do so, and he knew as well as I did that whatever figure was out there, he would try to accept less simply to placate his right wing.

"Your mistake," I said, "was to talk of the quality of territory for two months without ever defining it with us or with the Palestinians." Why, after January 31, didn't you use your private channel to tell the Palestinians? Look, we can go to 11 percent of territory that will matter to you or you can accept 13 percent from the Americans that will be mostly desert and that they will never be able to produce? Why not explain your difficulties and offer them an option that might have been attractive to them? Bibi had no answer. He had played for time; now there was no time left.

When I briefed the Secretary and Sandy on where we stood with Bibi, they were even more eager to confront him now, especially with Arafat's yes in hand. But the President still appeared eager to avoid a confrontation.

Consequently, in my last meeting with Bibi before returning home in the middle of April, I decided on my own to try out an idea. I did not clear it with the Secretary or Sandy. I met Bibi alone and told him I had been racking my brain to see if there was a way out of the impasse on the FRD. While the President did not want a confrontation with the Prime Minister, he would prefer confrontation to a retreat and a loss of our credibility. So something had to give, and I had an idea that I had tried on no one. I had no way of knowing at this point if the President would even support it, but I would try it on the Prime Minister if he would promise that it would stay just between the two of us.

Bibi was now sitting on the edge of his seat, leaning toward me and blurting out, "What do you have in mind?" If eagerness is a sign that someone will be open to an idea, I was never going to have a better moment to present a bridging idea—or so I thought.

"Mr. Prime Minister," I said, "the 13 percent is now a symbol for you, for Arafat, and for the President. You cannot accept it, and neither Clinton nor Arafat can accept something less than 13 percent. What if we come up with a formula that allows you to say you gave up 11 percent of the territory and yet permits Arafat to say that he got 13 percent for the Palestinians?" You could do it by designating 11 percent of the territory for the FRD and designating 2 percent for Palestinian roads, or for a Palestinian special economic development area, or for Palestinian nature reserves. Or you could take the "yellow area" in Gaza and transfer all or part of it to total Palestinian control.

Bibi's response was immediate: "I like it." He asked for maps to be brought into his office, and we began to see how it might be done. It quickly became apparent that the yellow area in Gaza—given the small size of Gaza, only 380 square kilometers in toto—could not come near to closing the gap between 11 percent and 13 percent of the West Bank, in which 2 percent would equal 118 square kilometers. But the idea on roads or a special zone for economic development or for nature reserves—something provided for in the Interim Agreement—was a distinct possibility. Bibi said he would have to work on it. I reminded him that he must explore this secretly lest I find it far more difficult to sell the idea to the President and the Secretary.

Bibi laughed, saying, "Dennis, you can sell it to them." Unfortunately, his enthusiasm for the idea suddenly made me nervous that I had gone too far.

| PRESIDENT CLINTON BUYS, BIBI RETREATS, AND MADELEINE'S "ULTIMATUM" |

En route to Washington, I called Madeleine to tell her what I had done. She was more supportive than I expected, telling me it was a brilliant solution and probably one "the boss will like."

She was a good predictor of President Clinton's reaction. On my return, we met in the President's study in the residence, and when I explained what I had proposed, President Clinton exclaimed, "That is just the sort of idea that would appeal to Bibi. It lets him off the hook and he can claim he held out and he shows his constituency that he gave up less than anyone else would have."

Of course, we were not home free. Bibi still hadn't figured out where the 2 percent would come from; it would have to be seamless enough to make the Palestinians feel the total constituted a 13 percent transfer of territory.

Bibi requested my return to talk about the idea—an idea that had not leaked—and within three days I boarded a plane again for Ben-Gurion. Unfortunately, he now took the idea and downgraded it, claiming there was not enough land available to create a bridge between what he could do and the 13 percent. Again, he was back to the 9 percent for the FRD, with my bridging idea to be added to that. Now I felt that he had used my idea to reduce what he was willing to do on the FRD.

I was livid; I told him I had sold my bridging idea to the President and now I looked like a fool. I would not have gone to the President with this idea if I had known "you were going to redefine what you could do on the FRD." Perhaps I should now withdraw the idea. Bibi said he could get to 12 but he could not do 13 percent—and I asked what had changed between when I presented the idea and today. His answer was that there was simply not sufficient land to provide a credible bridge. (Obviously untrue if he was prepared to go to 12 percent from a base of 9 percent.)

Maybe I had been naïve to think that the bridging idea would work for both sides. Even if I had not been, I was convinced that I had violated one of my rules in negotiations: Don't try a bridging idea until it is clear that both sides are desperate for it and are looking for a way out. I had played the idea too soon. Bibi clearly felt he had time to negotiate and was doing so.

But I refused to negotiate. I would not consider anything less than 13 percent. He could use the bridge to get there, but by the end of the day it would add up to 13 percent or there was no deal. His response: Since we could not solve that today, why not solve everything else? Why not work out understandings on the assurances he would need on the third FRD and permanent status to do a deal? He was implying that he would go to 13 percent, but I did not trust him—believing this was another delaying tactic. I told him I would need approval from Washington for any such discussions.

Madeleine was also suspicious but felt I should proceed with the discussions, provided we also moved to force some decisions. What did I think, she asked, about having her meet with the two leaders again in London? Feeling that we did need to create a deadline for Bibi if he was to make a decision, I agreed that this made sense. She subsequently proposed a May 4 meeting in London, and the two leaders agreed to it. I would remain in the area until then. Vice President Gore would be arriving for celebrations related to the fiftieth anniversary of Israel's declaration of statehood. I would use the Vice President's presence to see if we could push Bibi to the 13 percent figure even while I negotiated assurances that would be contingent on concluding a deal. I would also use his presence to keep Arafat on board—noting with Arafat that it was important to build his relationship with Gore since he could well be the next U.S. president.

Arafat was on his best behavior with Gore, committing to a determined effort against terror and a readiness to move ahead to permanent status talks once Netanyahu agreed to the American proposal. Bibi held out on the FRD percentage, focusing on the assurances he needed and the demands of Israeli security. By the time we flew to London, I had in my pocket assurance language on the third FRD, opposition to any unilateral steps including a declaration of Palestinian statehood, and a reaffirmation of a no-surprises policy in the permanent status negotiations. I did not feel we should finalize these unless we had an agreement with Bibi on the 13 percent.

Beyond this, I was convinced that the only way to get Bibi to agree was for him to understand that at the end of the London meetings either we would announce we now had two yes's in principle or we would announce that the Prime Minister was not able to accept the President's ideas and there was little more we could do at this point. This was music to Madeleine's ears. She felt we had been too soft on Bibi. We had made every effort to accommodate him, especially with my bridging idea; it was time for him to put up or shut up—and face the consequences before the Israeli public.

No matter how determined she might be going into a meeting with Bibi, she often found him hard to pin down in their direct discussions. He seemed responsive, was rarely confrontational, offered reasonable observations—and Madeleine afterward would often say to me, "How did he avoid what we were trying to do with him?" The initial meeting with him in London proved no exception. Madeleine gave him her ultimatum; Bibi, seemingly unrattled, parried it by saying there were really three elements that would go into a package for any announcement: Palestinian compliance with the Interim Agreement and Hebron accords on security, incitement, illegal weapons, and the like; understandings between the United States and Israel on the third FRD and permanent status; and a resolution of the impasse over the 13 percent. Then, inevitably, Bibi suggested that we keep the 13 percent for last, finalizing the first two elements of the package beforehand and allowing him to sell them to his cabinet by next week. Madeleine asked him why he could not simply bring whomever he needed from his cabinet to London to finalize the issue. He was willing to consider this, but then said, "I will stretch on the FRD, but can't do 13 percent. You, perhaps with Tony Blair, can go to Arafat and tell him you got me to 12 percent, and if he will meet you there we will have a deal. We know the Egyptians believe that Arafat will accept 12 percent."

Madeleine looked at me and I said, "We have heard nothing like that from the Egyptians." She was prepared to work with Bibi on the first two items of the package, but she was not prepared to have us ask Arafat to accept less than 13 percent. Bibi suggested that Yitzik Molho and Dani Naveh work with me on the first two items of the package and he would think of ways to finesse the 13 percent.

Yitzik came to me a short while later with proposals on the assurances Bibi would need from us on the third FRD and on permanent status. The third FRD assurance was more or less as expected, but the assurance Bibi sought on permanent status went well beyond what I had drafted, for it suggested that we could not present any idea on permanent status—even informal ideas—to the Palestinians without prior Israeli approval. This went way too far. I was prepared to offer a strong assurance on not surprising Israel and taking Israeli concerns into account before presenting anything. But if Israel could veto even the discussion of an idea, our hands would be tied.

At one level, I told Yitzik, this discussion was probably moot: given the continuing gap on the 13 percent, there would not be any permanent status discussions. But when Yitzik said assurances on permanent status might help Bibi to overcome the impasse on the FRD, I said I was willing to try, but explained that the assurances he sought could never be accepted by any American administration. Yitzik was willing to modify the language and we made progress on addressing our differences.

Later that afternoon Bibi and I talked about the incitement committee and the other issues of Palestinian obligation. Again, I told him, "We aren't going anywhere if we don't have an agreement on the 13 percent." He told me "his guys" had an idea and he wanted Dani to come and talk to me about it. Within the hour Dani arrived at my hotel room. Their idea for the Israelis was to come close to 13 percent now and agree that the gap between their number and 13 percent—"call it X"—would be carried out by Israel after the three-month implementation period. He said the Palestinians would know they would get a 13 percent FRD, only later than called for in the twelve-week timeline.

I asked Dani whether Bibi really gained much by such an approach. He felt the PM did with the Israeli right. But I had two problems. First, I was concerned that Bibi would simply declare later that the 1 percent gap—which is what I suspected they were considering—would be his third FRD.* Second, I worried that stretching the timeline beyond twelve weeks was bound to trigger new Palestinian demands, at a minimum a request to change the timing for performing their obligations. We concluded our meeting without agreement.

Our meeting with Arafat earlier in the day had been noncontentious. Madeleine told him she was still shooting to have two yes's, and if she failed to get them she would declare that Arafat had said "yes, in principle" and Prime Minister Netanyahu had not. Arafat was delighted.

Now we were at a crunch point. Could we accept Bibi's new effort to finesse the 13 percent? Madeleine was intrigued by Dani's proposal but very uneasy because of my concerns. She decided to call Bibi and tell him we wanted to consider their idea overnight.

At dinner late that evening, I persuaded Madeleine that the most we could accept was the original bridging idea I had offered Bibi—one that was still known only to very few Americans and Israelis. If Bibi sought more, he could always go directly to Arafat with this suggestion and throw in a "sweetener" like, for example, prisoner releases.

---

*Indeed, when I asked Dani how they would distinguish this additional transfer from the third FRD, he said it might be part of it; however, Bibi had already told me the third FRD would be very small, and he wanted an assurance from us that we would not make an issue of it.

Traveling with then Vice President Bush to Jordan in 1986 (*above*), and saying farewell after his failed presidential reelection bid in 1992 (*below*) (OFFICIAL WHITE HOUSE PHOTOGRAPHS)

As Secretary of State, James Baker was careful not to be drawn into "endless shuttling" around the Middle East. Even so, he traveled constantly, and we invariably spent our time together trying to "noodle" this or that problem of U.S. diplomacy. (PHOTOGRAPH COURTESY OF THE AUTHOR)

With Secretary of State Warren Christopher in the West Wing (*above*), and meeting with Prime Minister Yitzhak Rabin and his ambassador to the United States, Itamar Rabinovich (*below*)

My first meeting with Yasir Arafat, Tunis, 1994. This was soon after a Jewish zealot had attacked worshipers at the Ibrahimi Mosque in Jerusalem, and Arafat greeted me warmly in what was a difficult time. (PHOTOGRAPH COURTESY OF THE AUTHOR)

Advising President Clinton on what to do next at Wye, October 1998. Moments earlier
the President had lashed out at Bibi for raising new demands on Arafat.

Binyamin Netanyahu and I worked best one-on-one. Here, Bibi and I were meeting in the Prime Minister's office a month before the Wye summit.

As Prime Minister, Ehud Barak was eager to press ahead to a peace agreement. Here, he and I discuss Syrian President Asad's readiness to resume political negotiations in 2000 after resisting such talks since the Madrid Conference in 1991. (OFFICE OF PUBLIC AFFAIRS, U.S. EMBASSY, TEL AVIV, PHOTOGRAPH BY MATTY STERN)

On the last day of the 2000 summit at Shepherdstown, West Virginia, Secretary Albright invited Barak to lunch at her farmhouse nearby. He brought his wife, Nava, and Amnon Shahak, his successor as head of the IDF. (OFFICIAL WHITE HOUSE PHOTOGRAPH)

On the last day of the Camp David summit, President Clinton and I prepare for a meeting with the negotiators at his cabin; at the time we were hopeful, believing we had made progress on the security issues and could overcome differences on refugees and the borders using the same model.

We had breakfast the next morning with Bibi and told him we could not accept his 13-X idea. I raised the idea of his going to Arafat with it along with other sweeteners, but he felt that Arafat would only respond to us, not him. He suggested that for today the Secretary could say we were close to agreement, and because of that, the Secretary was inviting the two leaders to Washington for continued discussion next week. Madeleine was uncomfortable with that, and felt that we needed wording that made such a Washington meeting less certain and more conditional. I suggested we announce that progress had been made and that if the remaining issues could be resolved, President Clinton would invite the parties to Washington on May 11 to begin permanent status negotiations. Madeleine liked this, and so did Bibi. He then left to return to Israel, no doubt believing that, at least for the moment, he had dodged another bullet.

Arafat also liked this public formulation, but asked one thing of the Secretary: in any statement she would make, she would say that he had accepted our ideas in principle. "This was only fair." She agreed that she would, keeping in mind that she had assured Bibi that she would publicly say that he was making a constructive effort.

She was true to her word. But three points combined to create a problem for Bibi after he left London. First, Madeleine stated that Arafat had accepted our ideas in principle—and though Bibi was making constructive efforts, there was no mistaking that he had not. Second, that the President's invitation was conditional on acceptance of our ideas. And third, in answer to questions, Madeleine, though trying to be careful, said the ideas would not be watered down, and when asked if the eleventh was a deadline, she said, "If you want to say it is a deadline, the deadline is such that there is no point in talking about permanent status . . . if we have not agreed on these other issues."

We had not planned to use the word "deadline," much less to build a story around it, but a story was built nonetheless. Bibi had left before the press conference, believing he had no problem. When he arrived in Israel, he faced headlines proclaiming that the United States was presenting him with an ultimatum.

He called me to complain that Madeleine had put him in the corner. She must walk back the words that made this seem to be an ultimatum. I told him we could say that there was no ultimatum, but she would stand by the point that there would be no meeting next week to launch permanent status talks with the leaders if there was still no agreement.

Bibi said, "I have a long-scheduled trip to the States next week. I will be in Washington anyway. We can find a way to work this out, just get Madeleine to soften the words."

Madeleine had traveled home shortly after the press conference while I remained overnight in London to brief the Europeans. As I traveled to Washington the next day, Bibi responded to the pressure by publicly calling for me to come to Israel to keep negotiating. Having been out of touch on the commercial flight across the Atlantic, I was completely unaware of this, and I arrived at Dulles Airport expecting to go home. Instead, I was given a message that I needed to see the Secretary of State urgently. A car whisked me to the department and Madeleine told me what Bibi had done, and apologetically said she saw no alternative but for me to travel to Israel the next day. "Bibi wants you there, and I think it is a good sign. But even if it isn't, we cannot permit him to say he was willing to work to overcome the gaps and we prevented it." I reluctantly agreed, explaining to Debbie that even though I had been gone for two weeks, I would have to leave again in the morning. She did not much like it, but she understood.

If I had known what was going to happen once I got to Israel, I would never have gone. To this day, I don't know if I was deliberately set up or if a new, unexpected development led Bibi to put on a show for his cabinet with me as the prop.

The new development was this: First Lady Hillary Clinton, in a videoconference with Israeli and Palestinian teenagers taking part in a Seeds of Peace* convention in Rome, answered a question by speaking about Palestinian statehood. Bibi's right wing seized on this statement, pressing him not to give in to American pressure, lest first it would be the 13 percent FRD, and next it would be Palestinian statehood.

The First Lady's statement appeared innocent enough to me. Bibi, however, was over the top about it—or at least wanted his cabinet and me to believe so.

Upon arriving, I went directly from the airport to the Prime Minister's office. I knew I was in trouble immediately. Bibi had a large number of ministers waiting in the cabinet room—only he was not there. I suspected he would make a grand entrance, sit down with an air of great authority, and launch into a diatribe—one that was not difficult to imagine: The United States, Israel's friend, had issued an ultimatum, and implied that the Palestinians agreed on a reasonable course when Israel did not; the First Lady of the United States (and everyone would assume she was speaking for the President) had now endorsed statehood and Israel had to accept conditions it could not accept or be labeled an enemy of peace. This was a betrayal of commitments to Israel and raised grave doubts in Israel about the good faith of the United States.

Sure enough, Bibi arrived grandly and said precisely that. It was as if I had read his script—reflecting both the content and the style of his presentation. As I sat there listening, I decided simply to say "you are wrong" and asked him one question: "Why did you want me to turn around and fly here?"

To this, he had no real answer, and Natan Sharansky looked embarrassed. Yitzik

---

*Seeds of Peace is an organization that brings together Israeli, Palestinian, and Arab youngsters with the purpose of permitting them to see each other as real people with real hopes, fears, needs, and grievances.

Mordechai, almost apologetically, said it would be helpful if we could make a stronger denunciation of the First Lady's comments. I replied that the First Lady's comments did not reflect our policy (the White House had said that publicly) and the President was not going to rebuke his wife—any more than Israeli prime ministers rebuked their wives for any comments they made that might not reflect official policy. (I made this point looking at Bibi, knowing Sarah had made statements on policy from time to time that were embarrassing for him.) But I was not going to engage him on his assertions, and instead chose to keep the focus on why the Prime Minister had asked me to return. Bibi, having performed in front of a large group—ensuring that his points would now be fully reported in the press—and having no good answer for why it had been urgent for me to return to Israel, was ready to adjourn the meeting.

In private, he said, "You put a gun at my head," what do you expect from me? I told him I had come very close to walking out of the meeting. It had been insulting, and I had not flown halfway around the world to be insulted. We were his only friends; we had tried to meet his needs; we had moved the Palestinians, and on my own, I had offered him a bridging proposal that the Palestinians could easily say was a retreat from what we had proposed and they had accepted.

At this point, Bibi became conciliatory. We had to work together. It was possible to put the process back on track, he wanted that and I should "trust that he wanted that." But "I have a real problem"—namely, it was even harder for him to do the 13 percent now. He needed a breathing space; why not have him use his upcoming visit to Washington to try to finalize the non-FRD issues and I could come back to the region to work with him alone on the territory question?

As I listened to him, I became convinced that he was under a great deal of pressure (not necessarily a bad thing). I also became more certain that we should *not* finalize the non-FRD issues. The fact that he wanted them badly gave us leverage and I wanted to use that to get him to concede on the 13 percent first. I was ready to try to relieve the image of an ultimatum, provided he would commit at least privately to me now to resolve the FRD issue by the end of May. Once we met with him in Washington and demonstrated that there was no ultimatum, I knew the pressure would be off—so I wanted to get a commitment from him here and now.

Maybe he was persuaded by what I said and agreed. Maybe he understood that he had stretched this game for as long as he could and he would have to decide by the end of May. Whatever the reason, he was ready to agree to our issuing a statement that read, "U.S. and Israeli negotiators will meet in Washington beginning the week of May 11. Our common objective is to reach an agreement and be able to convene a U.S.-Israeli-Palestinian summit in Washington by May 28 to launch permanent status negotiations."

| BIBI RELENTS ON THE 13 PERCENT FORMULA. COULD I PERSUADE THE PALESTINIANS? |

The meetings in Washington were predictable. There was no crisis. And we did not close on anything. Afterward Bibi wanted me to go back to Jerusalem, probably to create the illusion of progress, but I was not willing to travel again, and said there was no reason we could not work this over the secure phone line.

Little changed before the last week of May. Bibi tried several times to get me to accept that the FRD could be very close to 13 percent—asking at one point whether or not I could accept 12½ percent. I was not buying. The number, I said, is symbolic for everyone. If you can do 12½, then you can surely do 13 percent—"the closer you get, the more you make it clear this is not about security." Why not focus harder on my bridging proposal?

In our secure call the next day, Bibi raised my original bridging idea—not so much the notion of 11+2 as his being able to say he had done something less than 13, and Arafat and Clinton being able to say it was a 13 percent transfer of territory. But now Bibi said he did not know how to actually do this. There needed to be an area of special status that would make up the difference between what he was doing for the further redeployment and the total we were asking for. I saw an opening here and probed: Is the problem that roads or an economic zone can't cover sufficient territory to reach the 13 percent given the size of the FRD you can do? Yes, was the answer, and he could simply not increase the size of the B area—an area where Israelis retained the security responsibility but the Palestinians had the civil responsibility. Previously, I had raised the idea of creating what might be termed a "B-" area—an area that gave the Palestinians more authority than in the C areas, but less than a full-fledged B area. Bibi had explored it, but also said it was not doable. I revisited this idea now but with a slightly different twist. What if we created an area that you could say was a "C" and they would be able to say was a "B"?

Bibi's reaction was, "Great idea, but it is not possible." But it was. I reminded him that the H-2 area in Hebron could be a model. Ostensibly, the Palestinians had responsibility for civil relations and public order just like in any B area, but in fact they couldn't build there without coordination with Israel. "If we use the H-2 model, you can say it's a C area, and they can say it's a B area." Bibi replied, "I like it, but I have to check it."

Since Bibi was going to China, I knew I would not hear anything for a few days. On his return the next Friday, he called and said, I have a proposal but you have to take all of it: You get Arafat to convene the PNC again and have it explicitly annul the charter; you give me greater assurance that you will adopt no position on the third FRD;

and you accept 9+4 approach on the FRD, with my doing a 9 percent FRD and an additional 4 percent being like H-2 with a special status. "It lets me cover my bases here and you are able to say you got 13 percent."

I doubted I could sell it here. We had to produce something that we were dubious about—namely, the PNC meeting—and 4 percent for a special-status area like H-2 would be hard to rationalize. It would look like he was doing less than a double-digit FRD. Bibi said it allowed him to do a deal and reach 13 percent; it allowed him domestically to draw a line in the sand and yet Arafat would know he would get the full 13 percent. Moreover, "once it is an H-2, the Palestinians know it will be theirs. It will certainly never be ours again." He closed, telling me this was the best he could do and he was finally at 13 percent, we simply had to respond.

I told him I would talk to Madeleine and Sandy—and he, being dead tired from his trip, asked if he could call me tomorrow during Shabbat.

Madeleine and Sandy were uneasy with the package, but also realized that we had finally gotten Bibi to 13 percent. At Sandy's suggestion, I called Bibi and told him we could discuss the package, but only if the numbers were the original 11+2, not the 9+4. Uncharacteristically, Bibi blew a fuse. He was literally screaming, "We may as well stop now. . . . This borders on the absurd. . . . You will break my coalition. . . . You cooked a deal with them. . . . Screw up your courage. . . . I am supposed to sell this to my coalition. . . . Act like a superpower and tell them this is it."

I could not get a word in edgewise. Finally, he paused as if to take a breath, and I joked that I would not put him down as undecided on this. He was not laughing. So I said, I heard you, but if you tell me we have to accept your package and it is 9+4, I will agree with you, "we might as well stop here." There was silence on the line, telling me he did not want to stop here. I was not going to break the silence; this was his problem and he had to offer a way to solve it. Finally, he quietly said, "Dennis, I cannot do 11+2; there is no way. I am stretching to my limit. You have to help me." Prime Minister, I replied, I cannot go back to Madeleine, Sandy, and the President with 9+4—either give on that or give on the rest of the package. He was not willing to give on the rest of the package, but he said, Look, I am going to "have the battle of my life," but let us settle on 10+3.

I believed we were now at his limit and told him I would try to sell the 10+3. "Dennis, don't call me back if the President won't accept the 10+3." I called Madeleine and Sandy and described the conversation, and we subsequently talked to the President.

No one needed persuading. As far as the President was concerned, we had succeeded in bringing Bibi around. Madeleine was also pleased, but asked what the next step was. Knowing that this was going to be a tough sell with the Palestinians and I would need the best possible context for doing so, I suggested that the Secretary call the Chairman, tell him we believed we could now move Prime Minister Netanyahu, and ask him to send Abu Mazen and Abu Ala to see me secretly in London so I could brief them on what we had in mind. He agreed, and in early June, with only Gamal accompanying me, we met secretly at our deputy chief of mission's house in London.

I had picked this house because I knew Bob Bradke well. He had been Secretary Christopher's special assistant and had handled many sensitive assignments over the years. The house was beautiful and in a neighborhood that made discreet meetings possible.

I had always gotten along well with both Abu Mazen and Abu Ala; no two Palestinians were more committed to the Oslo process and peace with Israel. Neither was prepared to surrender what they considered critical to the Palestinian cause, but they both believed that living in peace with Israel was a necessity for Palestinians and Israelis alike. They wanted to get on to the permanent status discussions and do so in an improved atmosphere. They each worried about a failure to create any hope of progress, fearing that the potential for renewed violence was very high.

Knowing that, I presented the 10+3 proposal, saying it was what we could persuade Bibi to buy. I did not want to say we had already produced this for two reasons. First and foremost, Bibi had asked me not to. Second, they would be loath to accept anything they perceived as "Bibi's proposal."

I began my pitch by saying this was obviously an unusual meeting, but the President and Secretary felt it was an essential one because we had to find a way to break the stalemate. We were not prepared to accept anything less than the 13 percent FRD over the twelve-week period. However, we had also reached the conclusion that we would not be able to produce the 13 percent without some creativity and a package of steps which the President was prepared to press the Prime Minister hard to accept.

I proceeded to describe the idea of an area of special status, like H-2, in which Palestinians basically had the same rights as in any other B area but had to coordinate with the Israelis. I also explained the idea of convening the PNC once more on the charter. Not surprisingly, this triggered a long discussion on both the H-2 idea and the convening of the PNC. On H-2, they wanted to know where it would be and how they would explain it; in Hebron, there was a special explanation given the presence of Israelis living in a part of the city. Also, in answer to my saying that it did not really matter where it was because they would assume the basic responsibilities of a B area, Abu Ala said, "Yes, but in H-2 we have to coordinate on building. If we don't have assurances the Israelis will go along with building, no one will believe we will be able to build."

Each made a suggestion on how to make it work: Abu Mazen suggested that we select a nature reserves area to be the 3 percent because no building was allowed in them anyway and there would be no question of having to coordinate with the Israelis.* Abu Ala suggested that if Bibi wanted to make it look like less than a B area, why not simply exclude the Palestinian responsibility for public order? It was a police function, and since the Israelis retained responsibility for security it was not very important, whereas building and planning and zoning went to the heart of controlling the land. They also opposed the idea of convening a PNC meeting again on the charter.

While friendly, the discussion was not always easy. After three hours, we took a break and then went out to dinner. Abu Mazen and I walked together while Abu Ala and Gamal walked ahead of us. Abu Mazen confided that Bibi was not easy to deal with, even though he liked him personally. The problem was that he never seemed to know what he wanted. The task wouldn't get easier with permanent status, but there was no choice and it was time to work out all the interim issues and move ahead. Abu Ala, he went on, was the best negotiator on the Palestinian side. He was a true negotiator, and he could work with the Israelis—even these Israelis. Abu Mazen said his role was to help make it possible for Abu Ala to negotiate.

I said, "Abu Mazen, I know what I am presenting is not easy, but it is the best we are going to do. You cannot imagine how difficult it has been even to put something like this together. You have to find a way to accept it. Don't try to look for every reason not to do it." He said he would do his best. Later that night, alone with Abu Ala, I made the same point. "Dennis," he said, "we will need planning and zoning—without coordination with the Israelis—in the 3 percent; otherwise it will not look like a B area." It was clear to me that nature reserves were the answer and I joked with him that since I came from California, it was only natural for me to look at nature reserves as the way to solve problems. "Yes," he laughed, " we must protect the rabbits."

| TRANSFORMING THE PROPOSAL INTO A WRITTEN AGREEMENT |

In any negotiation, as I had seen especially with Oslo, it is one thing to have a conceptual understanding; it is another to turn it into a written agreement. Once in black and white, once fixed in writing, what was initially understood becomes much harder to accept.

After my return from London, I knew we had to start a drafting exercise, and soon found that Bibi did not want to put the 10+3 in writing until after we—the United States and Israel—agreed in writing on all the "reciprocity" issues—all the issues that

---

*In fact, knowing that 5 percent of the West Bank had been set aside for nature reserves, I had pushed this with Bibi and he had rejected it.

mattered so much to him. To that end, he wanted Yitzik Molho and Daniel Reisner—
the leading lawyer in the IDF—to come and meet me privately in New York.

I feared this would be a long and tedious effort, but Bibi was adamant. This, too,
was part of Bibi's transformation of the negotiating process. Bibi wanted to put us in
the middle. He wanted to negotiate with us and then have us sell it to—or more likely
impose it on—the Palestinians, letting us do the dirty work and keeping a safe distance
for himself.

Eager to make a deal, the President and the Secretary urged me to go ahead. I
agreed, but sought to create a limit of two days for our discussions in New York. While
I succeeded in imposing the limit, I did not succeed in short-circuiting this process.
Phone calls between Bibi and me, and Bibi and the Secretary, dragged into early July as
we had to balance what he wanted from the Palestinians with what the Palestinians
could, and legitimately should, do.

We produced a six-page document that spelled out the Palestinian requirements
on security and reciprocity, with subheadings on: apprehension, prosecution, and punishment of security suspects; combating terrorist organizations; prohibiting illegal weapons;
preventing incitement; cooperating with the Israelis; the Palestinian police forces; requests for arrest and transfer of suspects and defendants; and the PLO charter/covenant.

We ended up debating where on the timeline the Palestinian obligations should be
met. This became a real battle, with Bibi insisting that we must have basic agreement on
all this before we could present the details of the document to the Palestinians. We drew
the line in a series of calls that culminated in joint secure calls the Secretary and I made
to Bibi from her home on July 4 and 5. We simply were not prepared to be bound in
discussions on both the text and the timeline that we now had to initiate with the Palestinians. In fact, we refused to agree on the timeline, and told Bibi so. Though not happy,
he did drop his objections, and we began to discuss the document with the Palestinians.

| THE PALESTINIANS SEE THEIR REQUIREMENTS
IN BLACK AND WHITE—AND THEY OBJECT |

Arafat sent Saeb Erekat, who always presented himself to Arafat as the one negotiator who protected his interest, to the meeting in Washington on July 8. The more I
had sought to cut Saeb out in the past, the more I realized that doing so built his credibility with Arafat. I had stopped trying to do that during Hebron. I knew I would
never have the relationship with Saeb that I had with Abu Mazen and Abu Ala; however, with Saeb, if we each knew the ground rules—he was not going to fool me, I was
not going to fool him—we could work effectively together.

Saeb came to see me in my office and I told him we had developed a text on the security issues based on the proposal that the Chairman had accepted in principle. It was now time to work out the details, resolve all outstanding interim issues, and get the permanent status talks under way. Saeb went over the document and offered comments—there needed to be more mutuality built into the security provisions, there needed to be less detail and specificity on apprehension of suspects, there needed to be more ambiguity on the issue of talking to us before the Palestinians could release prisoners, etc. Then Saeb promised he would try to sell the document with amendments reflecting our discussion.

I left the meeting thinking we were in better shape than we'd expected. But things got complicated after Saeb returned to the region. I had no doubt that Saeb would sell the document as promised. But several days after his return he informed John Herbst—now our consul general in Jerusalem—that when he'd sought to go over the draft with the "Palestinian security guys," they were not prepared even to discuss it. It was "an Israeli document" and they would not deal with it. They would only discuss the security memorandum of understanding (MOU) from last December 17.

I called Abu Mazen and Saeb and said, "It is most definitely not an Israeli document," and when "we give you something we expect a response." Both said they would see what they could do, but their efforts were to no avail. The "Palestinian security guys"—led, I knew, by Mohammad Dahlan—had blocked the proposal. Now we were stuck again, and we had no understanding on the words for the 10+3 formula.

| ACTIVATING A NEW BACK CHANNEL, WITH SOME UNUSUAL PARTICIPANTS |

I had been keeping Bibi and Yitzik Molho informed of what was happening with the Palestinians. Several weeks passed, with seemingly no way to break the impasse. Yitzik called me and raised an idea. What if he and Abu Ala worked the issues discreetly as a back channel? Would it work?

My answer: It was the only pathway likely to work now. But we both agreed Arafat was unlikely to accept it unless I proposed it. I did, and he agreed enthusiastically.

Meanwhile, the Israelis most responsible for Oslo and most determined not to let it collapse—Shimon Peres, Uri Savir, and Yossi Ginossar (who had served as Rabin and Peres's private channel to Arafat)—had now quietly entered the picture. Uri had remained close to Abu Ala and they talked frequently. Yitzik had begun to consult with Uri. Shimon was always willing to be helpful to Bibi, and Bibi trusted Shimon more than any of his own ministers. In Bibi's eyes, Shimon had no agenda to hurt him and focused only on getting something done. And Yossi remained in almost constant contact with Arafat and Abu Mazen.

Their contacts may have been the reason for Arafat's enthusiasm about starting an Abu Ala–Yitzik Molho back channel. So began multiple conversations on a daily, nearly nonstop basis. I would go over formulas separately with Yitzik and Abu Ala, focusing on three issues. How to describe what this agreement was—meaning was it only an implementation of the Interim Agreement, as the Palestinians wanted, or was it an implementation of the Hebron accord, which the Israelis wanted, since they were trying to indicate it superseded the Interim Agreement? How to present the number for the FRD—meaning was it 13 percent, as the Palestinians wanted, or was it 10 percent and an additional 3 percent of a different character, as the Israelis wanted? How to portray the 3 percent of territory—as under Palestinian control or as an area in which Palestinians faced limits on building and having police present?

Within a few days there was a conceptual breakthrough on each issue. This agreement would implement both the interim and Hebron accords. Israel conceded that the FRD would be described as totaling 13 percent, in return for the Palestinians accepting that the 3 percent would be portrayed as a "green area" in which there would be no construction.

We still had to put this conceptual trade-off in language, and after another ten days of intense discussions we had a formula in which Bibi moved far to respond to the Palestinian needs as Abu Ala had described them. However, when Abu Ala took it to Arafat for decision, the Chairman, instead of approving it, referred it to a review committee of Saeb, Yasser Abed Rabbo, and a number of others. They, of course, wanted to reopen what had been agreed. While Arafat had operated this way during the Hebron process, he had never done this to Abu Ala before.

Abu Ala responded by withdrawing from the negotiations; Bibi and Molho refused to discuss anything except the formula that had been worked with Abu Ala and me. At this point, Uri, Shimon, and Yossi became involved with Saeb and Abu Mazen in trying to rescue what had been agreed.

Meanwhile, Abu Ala suggested that I come to the area to try to work out the formula directly with Arafat. Molho and Bibi suggested the same.

Since I had been invited to Oslo for the fifth anniversary of the Oslo agreement on August 25 and since Shimon Peres and the Chairman were going to be there, I preferred to try to work the issue there. Shimon and I made separate runs at Arafat, with Shimon saying to him in my presence, "You will make a big mistake if you can get up to 40 percent of the territory now and you pass it up. You won't do better now, so use this to give yourself a better base." Arafat demurred, raising the prisoner issue and emphasizing that he must see the whole deal before concluding a part of it.

He told me he was "ready," but needed me to come to the area and work intensively on all the issues. I told him I would come if he would accept the Abu Ala–Yitzik

Molho formula. He would not give me an unambiguous answer. Absent that, I was not inclined to go, but after Shimon and Uri pleaded with me, I agreed I would go to the area after Labor Day, ten days hence.

In the preceding year and a half, I had been trying to break a stalemate that had completely soured the climate between Israelis and Palestinians and between most of the Arab world and Israel. I had started by trying to put together a package to provide the Palestinians with something to offset the consequences of Bibi's decision to build a new Jewish neighborhood in East Jerusalem—the neighborhood of Har Homa. The killing by a Jordanian soldier of seven Israeli teenage girls had cost us one opportunity to delay Har Homa, instead leading to the decision to press ahead with it. The suicide bombings in the summer of 1997 had cost us the ability to move Bibi on a ten-point package that would have affected the climate but not dealt with the further redeployment issue. The period since the previous September had produced an approach to further redeployment that was close to agreement. Bibi wanted to know that the formula would fly; it was clear to me that most of the rest of the package of interim issues and security was also basically resolved in concept, if not in detail. It was time to find a way to put all this together. I knew at some point we would probably need an intensive summit to force the decisions necessary to translate concepts into agreed details. However, I also knew that with President Clinton's admission of an "inappropriate relationship" with Monica Lewinsky—an admission that had taken place while I was working the Abu Ala–Yitzik Molho formula—it would be very difficult to hold such a summit soon.

It was in this context that I headed to the region in early September—having in fact set the stage for what would need to be done, but knowing there was a great deal of difficult work yet to do.

Prelude to Wye

It could not have been a more surreal time to begin intensive negotiations in the Middle East. With CNN's wall-to-wall coverage of President Clinton's admission of an "inappropriate relationship" with Monica Lewinsky and the soon-to-be-released Starr Report, I could hardly insulate my efforts from the drama being played out in Washington. Anyone listening to the news reporting—and the punditry in Washington—could see that President Clinton's ability to survive in office was in doubt, with ill effects for the peace process. While I was in Norway to mark the fifth anniversary of the Oslo agreement, the President had written Chairman Arafat telling him that we must work to finalize the security part of our initiative. Now I was going to take a run at it, and my efforts, and the pressures I was under from Washington, would lead by the middle of October to a summit held at the Wye River Plantation.

Upon my arrival the day after Labor Day, I went to see Arafat. Though the Starr Report had not yet gone to Capitol Hill, Arafat was naturally wondering what was going to happen to the President.

Though I obviously had no special knowledge, I told the Chairman that I believed that the President would survive; that he had the support of the American people, who felt his actions did not rise to the standard of impeachable offenses; that the public did not want the President forced out of office, and that those in the Congress who were supporting Starr were out of step with the country. Arafat, who saw the President as his equalizer against Bibi, took my word as if it were the gospel and was greatly relieved.

I told Bibi something very similar, but I could see he had his doubts and tended to rely on his own reading of the American political scene. As I watched the reporting frenzy, I wondered if Bibi were not more right than I, and the President's remorseful prayer breakfast added to my sense of uncertainty.

As if the events in Washington were not enough of a distraction, I began to come under what can only be described as a daily "assault" from Sandy and Madeleine to wrap things up or bring the leaders to Washington. During the first few days of the trip, I spoke on a secure phone to Sandy and Madeleine from my balcony at the King David Hotel. I described what I was doing, and what was possible. They were invariably dissatisfied, declaring, "Nothing is changed," "You won't get there," "We need to shake everything up" and, in Sandy's words, even jump into the "abyss." I wondered if they weren't already in the abyss in Washington.

I had come to try to wrap up the formula on the 13 percent for the FRD and get the Palestinians to move on our security text, but first I sought to resolve other interim issues that could produce a visible sign of progress: the Gaza airport and the Gaza industrial zone. The airport was a symbol of independence, and being able to complete it would give the Palestinians a new sense of freedom. Similarly, making it possible to establish the Gaza industrial zone would create several thousand jobs for Palestinians.

Unfortunately, neither side had much interest in resolving either issue at this moment. The Palestinians were focused on the land, and feared that the Israelis would try to buy them off with moves on these issues. The Israelis were focused on security. For Bibi, the deal really was land for security, not land for peace. So I began to concentrate on how to resolve the 13 percent FRD and security.

On the eve of my arrival, the Israelis had put out the word that I was coming only to work on security, putting the Palestinians on the defensive. I knew they would not respond on the security issues unless I was dealing with their agenda as well. Prolonged negotiations on their agenda were not really possible at this point, especially given Madeleine and Sandy's eagerness to make a deal ASAP. But I could not ignore their agenda and so I adopted a strategy designed to show the Palestinians I would work on the whole package (all interim issues, including prisoners), not just security. After explaining that to Arafat, he wanted me to see every one of his ministers or representatives who dealt with each issue. I also agreed to go to Gaza and spend a day meeting people at the behest of Mohammad Dahlan, the key to moving on security.

A meeting with the families of Palestinian prisoners held by the Israelis proved extremely emotional: a little girl the same age as my daughter Ilana cried to see her daddy; a seventy-two-year-old man described the indignities of trying to visit his son in prison. I was determined not to give these people false hopes (and I said so), yet I was also determined to do something on the prisoner issue.

The prisoner issue was extraordinarily sensitive on each side. To the Israelis, the

Palestinian prisoners (because many had been responsible for killing Israelis in acts of terror) were both a neuralgic issue and a card to be withheld or traded for Palestinian concessions, even though Israel was required by the Interim Agreement to consider release of prisoners according to several criteria. The Palestinians saw the Israelis as not fulfilling their obligations on one of the few issues where the Palestinian Authority could visibly deliver for its public. Apart from these tactical considerations, the two sides had a very real difference in their view of the prisoners. The Palestinians believed that all prisoners who had carried out acts of violence prior to the Declaration of Principles (probably a quarter of the several thousand prisoners held) should be released, on the logic that these acts were part of an armed struggle undertaken on the orders of those—like Arafat, Amin al-Hindi, and Abu Mazen—who were now negotiating with the Israelis. Abu Mazen repeatedly asked, "Does it make sense to keep in prison those who carried out the orders of those that you meet with?"

Dahlan took a much more instrumental view, saying there was no way he could make the arrests required in any security work plan unless Israel released those seen by Palestinians as political prisoners. But every time I raised the issue with Bibi, he would say there were only a handful of prisoners who did not have blood on their hands and therefore only fifteen to twenty might be releasable.

I knew I could not solve the prisoner issue now, but I also knew I had to demonstrate to the Palestinians that we would develop a serious approach to it. I had to do so in a way that did not mislead them. I suggested both sides share their data on who was being held, what their affiliations were (Fatah, PFLP, Hamas, Islamic Jihad), when they were arrested, why they were arrested, and why each saw them as either fitting or not fitting the criteria on prisoner release already sanctioned in the Interim Agreement. I did not know where this would lead us, but the Palestinians took this seriously and Bibi accepted it as a way to proceed.

This enabled us to make some headway on the security issues. In a meeting with me, Dahlan and Amin al-Hindi—the head of Palestinian intelligence, the Mukhabarat— agreed to all the security principles embodied in our initiative, but emphasized that there must be reciprocal Israeli responsibilities, especially the sharing of information and acting against Israeli settlers who harmed Palestinians.*

While I worked with the Palestinians, I also pushed Bibi to finish on the 13 per-

*Dahlan was focused in particular on a recent case in which a settler was accused of killing a ten-year-old Palestinian boy. While the settler denied killing the boy, Palestinian witnesses claimed he accused the boy of throwing rocks at him, caught the boy, and kicked in his skull. The settler was held for a short time and then released, enflaming Palestinian opinion.

cent formula. He agreed to work with me, and we slowly began to make headway. I was now making measured progress on both the FRD and security, but we were still far from the circumstances that would justify a summit in Washington.

The pace of progress was not good enough for the President, Sandy, or Madeleine. There was no doubt in my mind that under the pressure of the Starr Report, there was a strong desire to show that the President was doing his job, was not distracted, and was visibly dealing with highly sensitive, serious issues such as Middle East peace. Progress on the 13 percent formula and security issues was not dramatic enough to meet the President's needs. Thus, Sandy and Madeleine kept pressing me to bring the leaders to Washington to produce an agreement.

I argued we weren't at the point where we could produce an agreement, whether we were in Washington or in the region. If they pressed now, we would produce a failure for the President. Apart from the fact that we were not yet close enough on the issues, I told them both sides were watching the drama in Washington and had their doubts as to the President's staying power. I added bluntly: "The President doesn't have the authority or clout with them now that he had previously—and they won't make concessions just because he needs them to do a deal."

Neither Madeleine nor Sandy was happy to hear this line of argument, but they listened. Initially, they were not persuaded. The pressure from them reached an absurd point, with Madeleine calling me and actually interrupting a meeting with Arafat with the admonition: "Tell Arafat and Bibi this is going nowhere, it is time to do the deal, this is it, we can't do anymore, and they need to know we may have to say this publicly."

But I couldn't say such a thing to either Arafat or Bibi unless we were actually prepared to walk away. And we weren't in fact threatening that. Quite the opposite; I was under pressure not to walk away, but to bring them to Washington.

I was sure the call was not Madeleine's idea, and when Arafat returned—he had left me alone in his office—I simply said the Secretary was deeply concerned that we were running out of time, and that the process could collapse if we could not make progress more quickly. As I expected, Arafat took this in without being particularly impressed.

On the way back from Gaza in our armored Chevy Tahoe, Rob Malley (who had assumed responsibilities on Arab-Israeli issues at the NSC), Gamal, Jon, Aaron, and I tried to figure out what the call was all about. Gamal asked, "Are they smoking dope in Washington?" I said it is either desperation with the situation in Washington over the Lewinsky scandal or a need for cover for an expected action against Iraq—in which a new crisis was brewing over Saddam once again impeding UNSCOM inspectors. Rob thought it was the latter.

Back in Jerusalem I learned from Martin—who was now based in Washington again, having been appointed by Madeleine to be the Assistant Secretary of State for the Near Eastern Affairs Bureau—that the President had pounded the table in a meeting with Sandy and Madeleine demanding that we bring Bibi and Arafat to the United States now in order to wrap things up. Martin went on to say that I could not just continue to argue against bringing the leaders to Washington at this time. I had to lay out an approach that showed how we could bring things to a conclusion. If we had a plan, Madeleine and Sandy could persuade the President to hold off for the moment.

After discussing various options with Rob, Aaron, and Gamal, I proposed the following sequence: first, I would either close on the 13 percent formula or know that I was unable to do so on this trip; second, we would take advantage of Bibi's and Arafat's presence in New York for the opening of the UN General Assembly the following week to have the Secretary meet the two of them, and also have them come see the President in Washington, possibly to announce understandings on at least part of the further redeployment and security package; third, the Secretary would go to the region in early October after Yom Kippur to build on the progress made; and last, we would bring the leaders back to Washington or Wye or Camp David for an intensive summit with the President to close on the whole package by the middle of October.

Gamal argued against this, doubting we could move the Palestinians that fast. I told him we didn't have a choice. Washington had made clear that we had to have a plan and this plan was the most realistic I could come up with. Moreover, at our current pace we would need three months to finish everything, and "God knows what could intervene in that time to undo everything."

Sandy and Madeleine accepted my plan. Whatever their motives, they were right about our need to change the dynamic. Even though I now believed that the incremental progress we were making signaled that both Netanyahu and Arafat would do a deal at some point, it was clear they would not change the pace of the effort unless we forced it. Here the President, Sandy, and Madeleine read the situation correctly. Where they were wrong was in pushing prematurely and in a way that signaled desperation on our part.

As it turned out, when I met Bibi alone in the courtyard of the PM's residence on Shabbat, my last day in Israel, it became clear that he now wanted to close on the 13 percent formula. He responded to my suggestions on what it would take, which came out of a meeting I'd had the previous evening with Abu Ala and Molho: namely, that in the 3 percent set aside for the nature reserves, improvements in the land, and movement of Bedouins or Palestinian police within it would be permitted.

I always preferred to meet Bibi alone, and especially at home. On Shabbats at his house, he would be in a jogging suit, and our discussions tended to be more expansive and open. If, as was the case now, we were trying to resolve a problem, it would always be easier. On this day, he was in a problem-solving mood, and he was giving me what I needed to get Arafat to go along.

What also became clear was the reason he was being so forthcoming. He wanted to arrive in the States with the onus entirely on Arafat, being able to say: "I did the territory, Arafat must do the security." A successful trip to the States would also give him a much-needed boost with his public.

After seeing Bibi, I went to see Arafat in Gaza with language on the two remaining problems: construction and Palestinian police movement in the 3 percent nature reserves. I solved the construction issue and made a suggestion on the police that I persuaded Arafat to accept, knowing that Bibi would buy this suggestion. Yet I chose not to close on the formula that night, even though it violated one of my rules of negotiation: When you can close on an issue, do so.

I chose to violate my own approach because doing so would take the pressure off Bibi to make any additional moves. With the onus on Arafat, Bibi would feel no pressure to do a larger deal, and we would wind up with an agreed formula for the 13 percent FRD but nothing else.

There was another reason not to close on the formula. At his home earlier that day, Ehud Barak, now the leader of the opposition, urged me to be very careful of leaving "land mines" out there that would detonate only after agreement. He was very fearful that some of Bibi's requirements for security went beyond what the Palestinians would be able to accept. In this case, Bibi would still look like a peacemaker when in fact he had no intention of carrying out the agreement. He would meet his political needs in Israel but actually explode the peace process and I should not help him do so.

While I believed we could structure the agreement in a way that prevented Bibi from escaping his responsibilities, Barak's point left me uneasy—and further convinced me that Bibi must not be let off the hook before we had clear understandings on the most sensitive issues.

After seeing Arafat, I was determined to leave that night and return home in time for Rosh Hashana, the Jewish New Year. But Bibi had asked me to see his kitchen cabinet—Mordechai, Sharon, and Sharansky—before my departure for home. I agreed, though I suspected he would try to talk me into staying until he left for the States in three days' time.

When I arrived, I asked to sit with him before joining Sharon, Mordechai, and Sharansky. He immediately made a pitch for me to remain. But I was adamant that I would celebrate Rosh Hashana with my family. As a result, I had to be out of his house and onto the helicopter that would take me to the airport by 11:20 p.m.—and that gave us about forty-five minutes.

To my surprise, he had not briefed anyone on the compromises he had made with me on the 13 percent formula, including even Molho. Instead, he wanted me to brief the others. I agreed to do so, but I wanted him to understand that the Palestinians would only close on the formula for the 13 percent if they had assurances on the transfer from B to A as well. Though previously the Palestinians had ignored or played down the 7.1 percent transfer of authority from Zone B to Zone A called for in the original March 1997 Israeli offer, now they were very keen to have it and the additional 7.1 percent that we suggested at the end of the three-month implementation process. In other words, they were not prepared to say this phase of the further redeployments was done until the B-to-A part of the American initiative—the 14.2 percent transfer of additional authority—was also agreed.

Predictably, Bibi said he had never raised this with the cabinet. He asked me if we would accept anything less than the 14.2 percent and I said no. "You have known about it from the beginning and never objected to it." We would not revise our initiative now, but I told him I would tell the Palestinians that while they could make their acceptance of the 13 percent formula contingent on also getting the B-to-A transfer, we were only trying to finalize the 13 percent formula at this time. Bibi liked this, and told me he understood that we would insist on the 14.2 percent B-to-A transfer as well (While he was certain to resist later on, this told me he would eventually go along with the 14.2 percent.)

| THE MEETINGS IN NEW YORK AND WASHINGTON |

I made it home in time to celebrate Rosh Hashanah with my family, grateful for the chance to dip apple in honey at dinner to symbolize our hopes for a sweet year and to enjoy some respite the next day in synagogue. I needed it, for there would be little rest for me before having to quickly choreograph our meetings in New York with Netanyahu and Arafat.

I knew we had to use these meetings to set the stage for a summit. With Bibi, I wanted to condition him on how we would have to structure the text if there was to be agreement. With Arafat, I wanted to produce the Palestinian work plan on security so we could credibly say to Bibi we now had a Palestinian approach on security that was responsive to Israeli needs.

When I had seen Dahlan in Gaza, he had assured me there would be a work plan, but he said the presentation in the text must allow the Palestinian Authority to appear to be making its own decisions based on its own interests, not simply arresting whomever Israel demanded. He also urged me to have our text of the agreement begin with the FRD—with the land first, and then security.

Dahlan's argument was that the Palestinians could accept difficult substantive requirements if they were presented in a way that took account of their sensitivities. I found him persuasive, and asked my team—Aaron, Gamal, Jon Schwartz, and Rob—to, at a minimum, change the structure of the text, putting the further redeployment section first and the security second.

While this might seem simple, it was not. Since July, the Israelis had assumed that security would come first. The only reason to reverse the order was to take account of Palestinian needs, and if we did so, I could expect Yitzik Molho to argue that Israel had needs too.

Rather than fight this battle with Yitzik, I tried to persuade Bibi directly: he would still get his substance, I told him, just in a different sequence and with some limited modifications in language. Bibi was in an agreeable mood, and he accepted my argument—as long as I would go over all changes with Yitzik. Predictably, Yitzik was uneasy with the changes. However, Daniel Reisner worked with Jonathan and eased Yitzik's concerns.

Meanwhile, I worked with Arafat and Dahlan, who had shown up in New York without the promised work plan. When I pressed him, he resisted the very idea, saying we cannot do what the Israelis want: "Their idea of a security work plan is we should kill half the Palestinians and arrest the other half." I told him, Mohammad, that is not our concept, and it is certainly not the concept of the serious Israelis that you have worked with. If there is to be a deal, the Israelis have a right to know what you are going to do about those who represent a threat to them. And if you want a relationship with us, we need to know too.

He nodded, saying that was fair, and proceeded to outline for the next three hours how the security organs would do their work; who they would act against; how they would do it; how cooperation should work with the Shin Bet and the IDF; and what we could do to help them trace monies going to extremist groups in the territories.

It was a comprehensive description of the security steps they were either taking or would be prepared to take. I asked if he could go over this with the Israelis, and he said he would prefer to do it with George Tenet, the U.S. director of Central Intelligence first. After that he would go over it with the Israelis, but only with the director or deputy director of the Shin Bet, Ami Ayalon or Israel Hasson—"The rest will try to screw me."

I agreed that the Israelis should not decide what the Palestinians would and would not do, but stressed that they needed to see that the Palestinians were serious and had a credible plan. We would not ask for more than that, but we could not accept less. Dahlan said he understood.

At this point, my game plan for New York was generally working. Bibi had bought the idea of a restructured text. Arafat was allowing Dahlan to give us more detail on security. Now there was the question of formalizing some understandings on the FRD and security in meetings with the Secretary.

I had raised with Arafat the idea of meeting with Bibi and the Secretary in New York, meeting with Bibi and the President in Washington the following day, and meeting the President bilaterally the day after that. Knowing he would also see the President separately, he was agreeable. Bibi was as well. But whereas Bibi was anxious for an announcement limited to the 13 percent FRD before he arrived in the United States, now he wanted to have such an announcement only if he could tie it to the creation of an anti-incitement committee and resumption of security cooperation between the two sides. When I told him I doubted we could get that except as part of an overall deal, and asked why he was seeking to announce more than he had been pressing me for only a few days ago, his answer was that politically he would have a hard time if he did not show that he was getting a lot for agreeing to the 13 percent.

As a fallback option, I asked, "What if we announce after the three-way meeting with the President that the Secretary will go to the region next week, and that by the middle of October the two leaders will bring their teams to Washington to meet with the President and resolve the outstanding issues on security and the further redeployment?" Though it would be an announcement solely on procedure, it would send a signal of heightened activity and would make news with the announcement of a summit within about three weeks' time.

It was also a way to test Bibi's interest in bringing everything to a conclusion. If it was a test, he passed; he liked the idea. Now it was worth testing what Arafat might agree to. We arranged for a three-way meeting not in the Secretary's suite, but in the suite of the U.S. ambassador to the UN.

For Secretary Albright, this was a homecoming. The magnificent suite in the Waldorf Towers had been her home for the first term of the Clinton administration. While we waited for Bibi and Arafat to arrive, she proudly showed me around, joking that she'd lived a lot better as our ambassador to the UN than she did as Secretary of State. "The Foreign Service knows how to live," she said, to which I replied, "You got that right."

After the tour, she turned to me and said, "So, Dennis, what are we doing in this meeting?" I told her we were testing to see if we could get close on the 13 percent, the security principles, and now, also, on the anti-incitement committee—a committee, I reminded her, that Bibi hoped could be used to stop the incitement in Palestinian media and schools. Given the venom against Israelis in Palestinian newspapers, TV, and textbooks, this was an important objective—and would be an achievement for Bibi. I had already briefed her on the fallback idea of an announcement tomorrow with the President and she was comfortable with it.

Bibi arrived first and told us he wanted to see Arafat alone and try to sell him on a partial package to be announced with the President. Arafat arrived, and after initial pleasantries he and Bibi met alone for almost two hours. Gamal (who was interpreting) reported after the meeting that Bibi had pushed hard for a partial deal, but Arafat was not buying. The meeting convinced Bibi that we should only go for the procedural announcement after the President's meeting.

When we met at the White House the next day, the roles reversed. In our prebrief with the President, I told him that he still ought to take a run at Arafat on the partial package announcement. Here in the Oval Office, Arafat was ready to agree. But now Bibi, the author of the idea, had changed his mind, preferring the announcement of steps leading to a summit since it showed his public something was happening but did not require any concessions that might anger his right wing.

Following the three-way meeting with the President and Arafat, Bibi met the President bilaterally and then returned to Israel. The next time he returned, it would be for the Wye summit.

| PREPARING THE SUMMIT |

Arafat stayed in Washington another day so he, too, could meet the President. Seeing the President on his own—in effect, having the same standing as the Israeli Prime Minister—was a big deal for Arafat. It played to his hunger for stature and also to his own sense that he was producing a relationship with the United States—the country the whole Arab world believed was the key to an agreement. In this case, I used his desire to be sure he would agree to the three-way meetings with Bibi.

I also saw his stay as an opportunity to begin to condition the Palestinians— namely, Arafat and Abu Mazen—on what they would have to accept in an agreement. They would not be able to hide from their responsibilities on security or disguise them. There would be language that would be difficult for them, I stressed to Abu Mazen, and they should have no illusions in this regard.

When I briefed the President before his meeting with Arafat, I told him of my warning to Abu Mazen and my warning that the text would contain tough language but both sides had to swallow tough positions in an agreement that was effectively land for security. "Arafat must hear this from you as well," I continued, so that when we get to the summit what we "present does not come as a shock."

Unfortunately, in the meeting the President did not do this. He went "soft," emphasizing his commitment to reaching agreement and his readiness to do the summit. It was all give on our part and nothing was required of Arafat.

I was unhappy, feeling we had missed an opportunity to affect Arafat's thinking and believing that my efforts with Abu Mazen had been wasted. What had happened? With the Secretary afterward, I surmised that the President was distracted by the Lewinsky scandal and the prospect of impeachment. That would have to change, for we could not go to a summit unless the President was "on his game."

Interestingly, Gamal did not share my unhappiness. He told me Arafat had been thrilled with his meeting with the President, amazed that the President would put himself on the line with a summit at a point when he was under such pressure at home. If anything, this had built Arafat's trust in and admiration of President Clinton. I was not convinced, but said, "Gamal, let's hope we can trade on that later."

We departed for the region a few days later. Madeleine would stay for two days— to try to fix the date for the summit and the nature of the final package—and I would remain afterward to nail down as many details as possible. After Madeleine's first day, I sat late into the night with the negotiators on both sides, but while I helped them close the gaps, neither side was empowered to reach agreement on any of the issues. It was clear that both would hold back for the summit, believing that they might be able to trade concessions on some of these issues for something else of greater value to them in a final package agreement.

Apart from setting the date of October 15 for the summit, giving us one more week of preparation, the only noteworthy development of the day was that for the first time an Israeli prime minister crossed a couple hundred yards into Gaza. The rule of thumb had been that Israeli foreign ministers would go to the Palestinian side of the Gaza border for meetings with Arafat, and Arafat would come to the Israeli side for meetings with the Prime Minister. That pattern was repeated on this day. But at the end of the meeting, Arafat invited Secretary Albright and Prime Minister Netanyahu to lunch at his compound just beyond the no-man's-area separating their respective border checkpoints. Bibi agreed, and we adjourned to the visitors' compound that the Palestinians had built to receive guests who did not journey all the way into Gaza.

Everyone was in very good humor, but I knew the mood was unlikely to last after the Secretary left the region and I had to confront the Palestinians alone on two hard issues. One was a set of side understandings on avoidance of unilateral actions by both sides that would fall well short of what the Palestinians wanted on Israeli settlement activity. The other was on security arrangements and what the Palestinians would have to swallow if there was to be an agreement.

I would deal with both the next day in Gaza. I had asked both Abu Mazen and Arafat whom I should sit with on their side to discuss the informal understandings on unilateral actions (such as settlements) and they both named Nabil Sha'ath, Minister of Development in the Palestinian Authority, who was often used by Arafat as a negotiator with us, the Israelis, and the Europeans. I visited him at his home in Gaza.

Nabil had an apartment in Gaza, nicely appointed but not extravagant. He had recently been remarried, to a younger woman who was both charming and highly intelligent. Healthwise, he now seemed to be doing well. Nabil was diabetic and had to watch his diet. A year earlier, not feeling well and having gained weight, he had gone to see a doctor friend of mine, David Jacobs, who bluntly told Nabil that if he did not change his diet and start to get exercise, he would not see him again. Nabil knew David was a friend of mine, and he would typically begin most of our conversations by talking about him. Today was no exception, and only after he finished telling me about his exercise program—no doubt hoping I would report all this to David—did we get down to business. I told Nabil we would have only a general reference in the text of the agreement to unilateral acts and that what I was about to tell him would be private understandings between us and each side separately.

I suggested that we could get the Israelis to commit to us, not to the Palestinians, that there would be no confiscation of private property; demolition of houses, including all houses built without permits, would cease provided the Palestinians stopped building new illegal dwellings; and settlement activity would be clearly limited. There would be no new settlements and expansion would only take place on "the immediate contiguous periphery of existing settlements." I drew a diagram in which I illustrated that new building in settlements could only take place next to existing buildings; the Israelis could no longer build out a kilometer or two from the last row of buildings and then fill in the gap, calling this natural growth.

Nabil probed to see if it was possible to get an unannounced moratorium on any new building. I was sympathetic, but did not want to mislead him; I doubted it. On your side, I told him, we need commitments covering two basic areas. Incitement to violence and hostility must stop internally, and the effort to campaign against the Israelis in the UN—and related international institutions—must also cease.

Nabil said the proposed anti-incitement committee should obviate the need for a separate understanding on incitement. As for Palestinian behavior at the UN, he argued that this was a rare outlet for Palestinian frustration. Better to take grievances to the UN than the street, no? Nabil, I replied, we are trying to create an environment in which each of you stops creating problems for the other. We are trying to create a climate in which the Palestinians don't need an outlet and can break the habit of always feeling the need to put the Israelis in the docket.

Nabil responded that if the Israelis were not taking the steps that put us in the corner, we would not need to be putting them in the docket. I noted that was the aim of these parallel understandings with us, and we concluded with Nabil telling me he would do what he could to be supportive.

As we parted, he asked where was I headed. I told him I was going to see Dahlan to have a similarly confidential and honest meeting on the security issues and what would be necessary once we were at the summit. I did not expect this to be an easy meeting, but it was necessary. Nabil thought this a good idea and said he might join us later in the afternoon.

| DAHLAN AND THE MEETING AT THE BEACH HOTEL |

Dahlan, knowing why I was coming to see him, ordered lunch for us first and we had a feast at the beach. As we sat under umbrellas on a perfect day—sunny, light breeze, and comfortable temperature—I, too, preferred just to talk and eat the mounds of grilled fish, chicken, and meat that we were being served.

Finally, I said, Mohammad, we have to go over the security issues and what will have to appear in our text. I told him I did not want him surprised when he came to the summit. I was going to do something the President and Secretary did not know about: I was going to read him part of the text we planned to go with at the summit, focusing not on the parts that would be easy for the Palestinians but rather on those parts that would be most difficult for them. I said I took no pleasure in making such a presentation, but I did not want either him or his colleagues arriving at the summit with false expectations. Some of what I would outline reflected the reality that the Palestinians had not performed in a number of areas. For President Clinton to vouch for the Palestinians—something Arafat clearly wanted—he had to know that they knew what would be required of them. I would not pull any punches in this regard.

Notwithstanding my prefatory remarks, Dahlan blew up when he heard the text. He shouted that it was better not to have an agreement than for it to look like the Palestinians were being told what to do by the Israelis or by the United States. He was very emotional, and Nabil, who had joined us, suggested that the two of them go for a walk, and they did. Then Gamal took a turn for about five minutes. At that point, having regained his composure, he came back. We sat quietly for a few moments. I finally said, "Look, Mohammad, I can try to meet you on form, but I cannot change the substance. Tell me what your problem is." He cited two issues. First, we could not publicly say that we would vet all their prisoner releases. If he lost the wherewithal to make such decisions, his own men would never respect him again. Second, the Palestinians could not have the United States sending in "forces" to take control of weapons collected in the Palestinian Authority. Again, it would make him and his men look like lackeys.

I told him I understood the need not to undercut him. But on the vetting issue, I said we would not be raising it if the Palestinians had not released people who we both knew should not have been released. There had been a "revolving door" on arrests and releases and we had to know this would stop. True, Bibi had made it a big issue, but he did not invent it—and releases sent a message of tolerance for terror.

On this and collection of illegal weapons, it was, I said, the reality that we cared about. If you have a better way of formulating language on these issues, give me your suggestions.

He agreed to do so. There was one other sensitive issue we had to find a way to address: the arrest of those now in the Palestinian security forces who had committed acts of terror against Israelis since the beginning of the Oslo process. Ghazi Jabali, the head of the police in Gaza, was a special case; Arafat denied that there was any evidence that proved he had given orders to three of his officers to attack Israeli settlers. The Israelis felt they had evidence proving he had; they had shared it with us, and our people felt it was suggestive if ambiguous.

I was not focused on Jabali, I was focused on the other twenty-nine names the Israelis had shared with us. This was one of those land mines Barak had talked about; however, it was important to Bibi, and not only for reasons of political symbolism. I had asked Bibi to give me not only the names but also the crimes or acts of terror that each of "the thirty" was accused of having committed. Many were accused of having committed murder. The symbolism on Bibi's part is that he wanted these thirty transferred to Israel. He knew he would never get that. According to the Interim Agreement, transfers were required only if those charged with such acts by the Israelis were not imprisoned by the Palestinian Authority. This was done to finesse the issue, as the Palestinians believed their own public would not accept both the imagery and the reality of turning over Palestinians to the Israeli security forces. Since these thirty were not imprisoned now, Bibi had a right to ask for transfer, but this was just a tactic.

Of the "thirty murderers," approximately thirteen were in or had an affiliation with the Palestinian security forces. When I discussed this with Dahlan, he said there were, in fact, a few who were still in the security forces and had become instrumental in handling Hamas. I suggested that he discuss with Ami Ayalon the status of the handful that had become instrumental, with the understanding that the rest would be arrested. I also told him I would talk to Bibi about how to handle this. He noted this was delicate for him but he would talk to Ami.

It had not been an easy day, but I felt that it was productive. Before returning to Washington that night, I arranged to see Bibi alone one more time. I raised the issue of "the thirty," describing my conversation with Dahlan only in general terms and suggesting a Dahlan–Ami Ayalon channel for dealing with the list of thirty. Bibi agreed to the channel, and then returned to the third FRD issue, arguing that to manage the price he would pay for doing the 13 percent, he had to show that he would not need to do much more; the proof of that would be that the United States would accept a third FRD of 1 percent. I told Bibi "no way. We would lose all credibility if we endorsed a 1 percent third FRD." But, I said, you can tell the cabinet that we will neither make the third FRD an issue nor support the Palestinians doing so; instead, we will insist that the focus must be on permanent status negotiations and not on a new battle on the third FRD. That, I told him, means no comment on the size and should be good enough for you. But it was not. Bibi persisted, saying, at a minimum, he must have an understanding with us on the language in the text on the third FRD. We went over different formulations, and though he was willing to accept one, I sought to preserve some wiggle room, telling him the President and the Secretary had not seen it. Bibi said, "Dennis, if you sell it, they will buy it." "Prime Minister," I replied, "believe it or not, it does not always work that way."

Next we moved to the issue of the Palestinian security work plan. The Palestinians had shared their thinking with us, but it certainly fell short of being a work plan at this stage. On this, Bibi came on like gangbusters. "I am not coming to the summit if there is no work plan." We can only fail in such a circumstance, "why would you want to put the President in that position?"

I knew we needed a work plan, but I was convinced we would only be able to put that together at the summit, and I suspected that Bibi was getting cold feet as the reality of the summit approached. I argued he would have the high ground if there was a summit and it failed because Arafat would not do what was necessary on security, whereas he would be in trouble if there was no summit because he refused to come. And the truth was that he could get what he needed on security only by going to the summit, where I suggested the President could use his leverage to tell Arafat there must be a credible Palestinian plan on security or there would be no deal, no more meetings with him, and no more leveling the playing field for the Palestinians by us.

That, of course, did not mean that nothing more should be done prior to the summit. The parties should discuss the gaps in what the Palestinians had developed—with not only Ami meeting with Dahlan but the Prime Minister doing so as well. Now Bibi calmed down and agreed that this all made sense.

Just prior to my departing for the airport later that evening, Martin gave me an article from *Ha'aretz* that purported to summarize the private understandings we had with Bibi—e.g., that we would not oppose a 1 percent third FRD; that we would insist on the arrests of the "thirty murderers"; that we would demand that there was a work plan with lists of those the Israelis wanted arrested and a timeline for their arrests; that we would also insist on guarantees on ending the "revolving door," etc. This was terrible, for it looked like we had simply agreed to impose Israel's conditions on the Palestinians. I was livid, knowing the instinctive Palestinian reaction and knowing that our task would now be far more difficult. Paradoxically, I thought, Bibi's effort to sell the agreement before we had it would probably jeopardize the very things he most wanted in it.

| MY FEARS ON THE EVE OF WYE |

Even before I read the article on the plane, I had begun to worry not only that the President did not understand the issues but also that neither Bibi nor Arafat had the same need for success that we had. Bibi's need to "get something right" gave us some leverage if we were prepared to apply it. But Arafat was under little pressure to produce a deal, and might see greater value in demonstrating his capacity to say "no" to the President in front of his street, particularly if he felt he was not getting enough or being asked to give too much. There was no way to be sure.

Since the President, Madeleine, and Sandy were all looking to me to tell them how to make the summit work, my unease grew as I returned to Washington over the weekend and saw Thursday, October 15, approaching. But as the week unfolded, my confidence about Bibi began to rise. He made two threats not to come—one about the work plan and one about the formula on the third FRD—and backed off of each. Clearly, we had more leverage on Bibi than I had first believed. Arafat was still an unknown, and I was still wrestling with the question of how to launch the summit, shape it, and tie everything together in a final package deal.

As Thursday approached, and as I talked with Gamal, Martin, Aaron, Rob Malley, and Bruce Riedel, I became more and more focused on a building-block approach. At the outset of Wye, we needed to produce for each side. Bibi wanted the security work plan, Arafat knew he had the 13 percent, but had never heard anything on the 14.2 percent of B to A. We would focus initially on Bibi getting his security plan and Arafat his 14.2; it was a "security for land" trade-off. We would use this as our foundation, building other issues onto it and ideally winding up with a package deal which Clinton could justly take credit for putting together.

In truth, knowing that negotiations have their own dynamic in a summit, I doubted things would work exactly this way. But for preparing the President, particularly given the fact that he had not been immersed in the issues or our diplomacy, the building-block approach was a good heuristic device: it provided an initial focus for our actions; created a context for the issues; portrayed what was important to each side; and introduced the possibility of key trade-offs.

In my mind, our strategy depended on getting the Palestinians to deliver on all the elements of security in the plan and in the text. With that, Bibi would have little choice but to respond to Palestinian needs. In our last briefing in the Oval Office just prior to the arrival of the two leaders, I put special emphasis on this point, noting for the President, "Now you are going to have to use the relationship you have developed with Arafat to get what is needed on security." The President said, "I got it." We would see if he did.

The Wye Summit

THE WYE SUMMIT WOULD begin on October 15. The midterm elections were only two and a half weeks away. How would the Democrats be affected by the Lewinsky scandal? How soon could the President get out on the campaign trail and help state and local candidates? The White House operatives were eager to have the President campaigning, in no small part because many Democratic candidates wanted his presence and were not running away from him. I would hear frequently in the coming days that we had to wrap up the summit to permit the President to hit the campaign hustings.

| DAY 1 |

The President was scheduled to meet both leaders at the White House before heading to the Wye River Plantation on the Eastern Shore of the Chesapeake Bay. The purpose of the initial meeting was to go over the ground rules for the summit: We would impose a news blackout; the U.S. press spokesmen alone would issue daily statements, to be coordinated with the two sides; nothing would be agreed until everything was agreed; and we would present our text at the moment we felt we had done the best we could to meet each side's essential needs. This meeting added to the sense of drama, and certainly gave the Palestinians a feeling of having "arrived," of coming to the Oval Office with the same standing as the Israelis, something they'd sought, something they'd asserted, but something they had long doubted they would actually achieve.

I wanted to play up this drama with Yasir Arafat, especially since I saw this as being the most likely way to move him on the substance. The psychology of being treated equally applied on the security issues. Reciprocity had been Bibi's term, but Arafat wanted it to apply on security as well. He wanted, as Dahlan had repeatedly pointed out, for Israel to act against settlers who took the law into their own hands against Palestinians and were rarely punished. If Palestinians would be arresting Palestinians, would the Israelis act against "rogue" settlers? Knowing this was in Arafat's mind, I asked Gamal to see Arafat before the meeting at the White House and convey a suggestion from me. My suggestion: Arafat should raise the issue of settler violence with Bibi at dinner that evening in front of the President. In this private and relaxed setting, he should tell Bibi, "It is only fair and right that as the Prime Minister of Israel you should know the specifics of the Palestinian plans for fighting terrorists since the lives of Israeli citizens are at stake. We will provide this because it is right. But just as you have to answer to your people, I have to answer to mine when a settler kicks in the skull of a ten-year-old or shoots a sixteen-year-old; it is right and fair for me to know from you how you plan to protect my people."

With this idea, I hoped to show Arafat we were sensitive to his concerns, and thinking about how to address them, while also subtly reminding him of his responsibilities toward the Israelis. Whether he "received" everything I intended, he clearly appreciated the message. Just before entering the Oval Office he came over to me in the Cabinet Room, put his arm around me, and thanked me for sending Gamal with my suggestion. To take advantage of the moment and stress the importance of responding to the President, I said, "Mr. Chairman, this is the third president I have worked for; no one cares about this issue the way Bill Clinton does; his political advisors all told him don't do this until after the congressional elections on November 3. But the President listened to us, not to his political advisors. Don't let him down." Arafat listened, grabbed my arm, and nodded. The body language was good, but we were about to see if the message got through.

Shortly after the Oval Office meeting, we headed to Wye in our respective helicopters. For our 1996 talks at Wye, the American, Israeli, and Syrian teams were housed in one residence—River House; now we were using all of the Wye River Plantation. There were good reasons for the difference. In 1996, we had small teams headed by the negotiators; now we had large delegations, and with the presence of the Prime Minister, the Chairman, and the President, a huge number of security personnel were required as well. The plantation is quite large, and the U.S. delegation was housed at the Wye Center, four miles away from River House and Houghton House, two houses only about five hundred yards apart, where the Israelis and Palestinians, respectively, were staying. Our distance from the two parties would be a constant source of worry for Madeleine and Sandy when I went off to work with one side, the other, or both in their residences while they remained behind; cell phones did not work well on the plantation, so once I was off working, it was hard for them to know what I was doing.

Once at Wye, we launched the discussions in an opening plenary session in the conference center. The mood was upbeat, with Arafat walking over to the Israeli side and shaking hands with each member of the delegation. Bibi shook hands with some Palestinians and nodded to the others, and in their brief opening statements Bibi and Arafat echoed each other: They were here not to delay but to finish and reach an agreement.

It was time to go to work. Having seen Bibi first at the White House in the morning, we decided to reverse the order and have the President see Arafat first at Wye. While the President was meeting Arafat, Madeleine and I sat with Bibi.

With Arafat, the President stuck largely to the initial game plan. He pushed Arafat to finish the security work plan; with this in hand, we could lean on the Israelis to respond to Palestinian needs. Without it we would have no leverage with the Israelis. George Tenet had joined the meeting, and Arafat told the President, "We are working with George Tenet and will do what is necessary." So far so good.

With Bibi, meanwhile, Madeleine and I had pushed him to put the 14.2 percent B to A transfer in the President's pocket and to discuss the third FRD informally with Abu Mazen and Abu Ala—the former so the President would have something to offer Arafat at a point when inducements, not just pressure, might be called for; the latter to keep differences on the third FRD from disrupting the permanent status negotiations. But Bibi did not respond on the 14.2 percent, and he refused to discuss the third FRD with Abu Ala and Abu Mazen for fear that he would get into a negotiation on it. However, he said he would be willing to talk about it informally with Arafat at dinner later that evening.

It was now time for the President to see Bibi, and Madeleine and I went to see Arafat. Abu Mazen joined him. In our meeting with Arafat, I raised the value of reaching an understanding that the third FRD would not be allowed to disrupt the permanent status negotiations. Arafat merely listened, without offering a response. When I told him I knew he was cooperating with George Tenet on the work plan, he nodded approvingly. As critical as that was, we did need his people to respond to our text on security, and I had yet to hear from Dahlan on suggestions he was supposed to give me.

Here I made a mistake. It was quickly apparent that Dahlan had not briefed Arafat on our beach conversation. In response to my cryptic references to vetting and arms collection, Arafat claimed that Israelis had a revolving-door policy on releases, and that Israelis were responsible for the illegal arms in the territories. Abu Mazen, knowing I would have to respond to such ridiculous comments from Arafat, quickly interjected that the Palestinians would get their suggestions to us. "That's fine," I said, "but they will have to be realistic or we won't be able to use them." I could not let Arafat's comments stand completely unchallenged. Abu Mazen understood and Arafat said nothing.

We concluded our meeting but found that the President was still closeted with Bibi. When he reappeared he briefed us on the meeting. Though we had emphasized before his meeting that he should push to get the 14.2 percent from Bibi, the President, while raising it, pursued a different tack, pushing Bibi to accept the idea that it was in his interest to have Arafat emerge stronger rather than weaker from this summit. If Arafat was weaker, he could not deliver on Bibi's needs, but would feel pressured to go for a unilateral declaration of statehood on May 4, 1999, the end of the five-year interim period called for in the declaration of principles. Coming out of what had been a philosophical discussion, the President described Bibi as being responsive.

Though I felt that what the President had done with Bibi was useful, I would have preferred that he push harder on getting the 14.2 percent FRD. However, whereas I was focused on the building blocks, the President was trying to affect the PM's psychology rather than pushing him on specifics up front.

We turned our attention to the upcoming private dinner with only the President, Bibi, and Arafat attending. The President asked me what he should cover. I felt there were two useful topics. One was the third FRD—reaching an informal understanding so as not to let this become a disruptive issue later on. The other was the Palestinian concern about settler violence—their "reciprocity issue." I told the President about my suggestion to Arafat, and why the dinner was the right place to have this discussion, and he agreed. He also agreed when I suggested that I see Bibi and "soften him up" on this before the dinner.

The dinner was at the Stewart House, a posh but small and remote residence often used for special guests or for special dinners. The President's dinner with the two leaders would be in the dining room. In a larger adjoining room, Madeleine, Sandy and I would join a number of others in a parallel dinner.

Bibi arrived before Arafat, and I asked if I might see him privately for a few minutes. He was clearly in a relaxed mood, a good indication that the President had put him at ease. I told him of Arafat's concern on "reciprocity"—especially as it related to settler violence—and suggested that he make it clear that such violence was neither accepted nor condoned by the Israeli government. "Let him know that you are determined to deal with it and won't shy away from saying that publicly." Bibi said "okay." He then raised the issue of the thirty who had committed acts of violence against Israelis—thirteen of whom were part of the Palestinian security apparatus—saying this was a tough one. Had Ami Ayalon and Mohammad Dahlan discussed this? I asked. Bibi said they had not. I now explained that Dahlan was willing to arrest all those whom he was not using actively against Hamas now. Their number was small, but, according to Dahlan, they were quite effective in combating Hamas. Bibi wanted to claim that all thirty had been arrested. But he also wanted to ensure that Hamas was controlled. He rubbed his forehead, obviously troubled, saying he did not know how to explain this. "How many are there? Couldn't he just let these guys leave?" I told him I did not know, but I would explore the options quietly with Dahlan and come back to him. Bibi agreed with this approach, emphasizing that he wanted me to talk to no one else on his side about it.

At the leaders' dinner, the discussion was blunt. According to the President's description, he initiated the discussion by asking Arafat to describe his security concerns. Arafat, notwithstanding my advice, did not acknowledge Israel's concerns but frontally challenged Bibi, charging that "[you] release people who commit violence against Palestinians." Bibi responded by saying Israel had a judicial system and Israelis were put in prison for crimes committed against Palestinians. Arafat countered that he had lists of all the Israelis who had killed or wounded Palestinians who were not in prison, and when Bibi did not ask for the lists, Arafat dropped this issue and went on to raise his other security concern: the threats from extremist Islamic forces throughout the region—a concern that he and Bibi could agree on.

It was late and there had not yet been a discussion on the third FRD. So the President suggested a private lunch the next day and he gave Bibi and Arafat a homework assignment: he asked them to work on a third FRD understanding, and also to think about the steps they each believed, politically, they might need to take after reaching agreement that might create problems for the other side—and how to alleviate them. They agreed to the lunch, which Madeleine and I would join after about an hour of private discussion.

The President was upbeat, believing rightly that his "homework assignment" addressed one of the fundamental problems with the Oslo process to date: neither side ever seemed to think about the daily needs of the other. Even so, I did not believe either would start thinking of the other side's needs until we were closer to reaching agreement.

As the meetings concluded, I observed this first day had been about psychology, about making each leader feel comfortable. That might be necessary, but I tended to believe that agreements emerged from high-stakes settings where each side felt uncomfortable. No one made hard decisions unless they had to.

There was one strange development after the dinner. As President Clinton was briefing us on the dinner, he had his arm around Martin Indyk, who had been at our dinner. After the President left, I asked, "What was that about?" Martin explained that out of the blue the President had raised Jonathan Pollard with him—the American who had spied for Israel and had been imprisoned since 1985.* I suspected that Bibi must have raised Pollard's release in the private meeting. Martin had reminded the President that even though Rabin had asked for Pollard's release, he had not given him to Rabin. The President's response was that we needed to think not in terms of what was fair, but what would help us to do a deal. Martin interpreted the arm around him as the President's way of softening the impact of what he had said.

This was not the last we would hear of Jonathan Pollard in the Wye summit.

| DAY 2 |

The President was not staying at Wye, but planned to come daily or as necessary. Secretary Albright wanted to push the summit along, believing we needed a breakthrough within three days. Day 2 was Friday, and she was convinced we would not have beyond Sunday given the pressures on the President to get out on the campaign trail. Starting this morning at breakfast and continuing each day thereafter, the Secretary asked me to give my impressions of where we were and what we needed to try to get done during the day. I told her I felt the first day demonstrated that the President could do critical conditioning of each leader and possibly change the nature of their relationship with each other. But based on day 1, the building-block approach was unlikely to work since it did not fit the President's style. He sought to embrace and educate the two on what was needed, rather than force decisions to establish the first basic trade-off from which we would build.

Yet because of the timetable the Secretary had in mind, we needed each leader to feel that he must now make decisions, and this would not happen until they were put in a position where they would have to respond to something—indeed, "until there is an air of urgency created by crisis." The President wouldn't want to create crisis in his meetings. But "we should create the crisis, not wait for one of them to create one." How? By laying the text of an agreement on the table. Since we had a commitment to

---

*Pollard, while working as a civilian intelligence analyst for the U.S. Navy, had spied for Israel, sharing highly classified materials. He was sentenced to life imprisonment, had been held in solitary confinement for seven years, and many in Israel felt he had been abandoned. Some in the organized American Jewish community felt great ambivalence. On the one hand, he was a spy and should be treated as such, particularly because he raised the ugly specter of "dual loyalty." On the other hand, he had spied for Israel, a friendly country, yet he had been treated as if he were a mortal enemy of the United States. Would he, they asked, have received such a harsh sentence if he had been caught spying for a NATO ally? They tended to doubt it, and believed that there was not-so-subtle anti-Semitism at work in singling him out for especially harsh treatment. The complete story of Jonathan Pollard's case is reported in Wolf Blitzer's *Territory of Lies*, New York: Harper and Row, 1989.

share everything first with the Israelis, we would have a crisis with them as soon as we got ready to put the text out and they saw us softening the language to get the Palestinians to produce on the substance. If we hoped to have a breakthrough by Sunday, I told her, "we need to shoot to create this first crisis with the Israelis before sundown today—or at the latest tomorrow after Shabbat ends." But, I continued, we should not go this route unless we have the two essentials from the Palestinians: a credible work plan on security and suggestions on textual language from the Palestinians so that we can tell Bibi that Israel's security needs are being met.* In other words, we were once again hoping that Palestinians would produce real substance on security, enabling us to pressure Bibi. I turned to George Tenet, who was sitting with us, and said "George, you have to be able to say their guys have put together a very serious and very concrete approach on security."

George was feeling good about what we already had from the Palestinians: "a real security plan of action," with detailed information from them on the steps they would take in all categories now—both military and civilian. He said he was satisfied, and he reported that Ami Ayalon said that he was also satisfied with what he had received from the Palestinians.

Though Madeleine felt the plan to proceed this way made sense, she asked how it fit with the homework the President had given to the two leaders for their lunch meeting, now two hours away. I doubted they would do the homework and doubted their meeting would produce anything. But I said if I am wrong and it does, forget my plan, and stick with what they are doing and build on it. Madeleine agreed, and we waited to join the private Netanyahu-Arafat lunch.

It was a beautiful Friday and Bibi and Arafat were sitting alone, with Gamal serving as their interpreter, under an umbrella on the deck behind River House, the Israeli residence. When Madeleine and I arrived, Bibi summarized their discussion. He told us that rather than doing what the President had asked—which meant focusing on what might be done after an agreement—he had felt it most important to focus on what it would take to get to an agreement. So he had chosen to raise the issue of the PNC meeting and the "transfer" of the thirteen policemen on the list of thirty who had killed Israelis. Arafat's face reflected his unhappiness, and when it was his turn to speak he ignored the PNC issue and addressed instead the question of "transfer."

He was blunt. He did not trust lists provided by the Israelis. He believed "they are all made up, based on the words of those who are paid as informers."

At that moment the Secretary was called away to take a phone call, and in her absence Bibi turned to me and asked if, after what I had heard, I had a suggestion. Given

---

*Notwithstanding Abu Mazen's assurance, we still had no response from Dahlan on the comments he had promised at the beach in Gaza the previous Friday.

our discussion the previous night, I was surprised that he had raised the issue of the thirteen police at all. But now, looking at the two of them, I asked what if the Israelis gave this list to us and we examined it to see if it was credible? To signal to Arafat that we would not just be a rubber stamp for the Israelis and their lists, I added that we did not share Israel's view of what should be done to people on whom there was credible evidence, since "we read the Interim Agreement differently than the Israelis on requiring the jailing of such suspects by Palestinian security services, not transferring them to Israeli authorities."

Bibi asked Arafat if he had any response to my suggestion and Arafat said he had no comment. The Secretary returned; I explained what we had done in her absence, and Bibi now said he, too, would have no comment on my suggestion. He then turned to the issue of convening the PNC. His idea was to persuade the PNC to ratify the agreement reached here and to deal with the charter. "That way you don't look like you are convening the PNC on the charter." Arafat was still not responding; in answer to a question from the Secretary on what might be done now, he said all the committees covering all the issues should meet. We concluded the lunch with an agreement that the committee heads should brief the two leaders and the Secretary on their discussions later that day. Bibi said good-bye to Arafat, but did not see him to the door of River House—in Arafat's eyes an indignity that grated on him.

The meeting had revealed Bibi's agenda. He wanted the thirty suspects jailed or transferred and he wanted a PNC meeting on the charter as trophies. He hoped to be able to persuade Arafat on these issues, but had gotten nowhere. Their meeting had predictably produced no responses on the President's homework assignment and there was no sign that either had any interest in dealing with it. After lunch on this, the second day, there was little sign that anything would move quickly.

My game plan for the morning was the only way to get things moving. Unfortunately, we still had not gotten the Palestinian security suggestions we needed, and when I sought out Abu Mazen, I discovered he had gone shopping at an outlet mall not far from Wye. When I was finally able to reach him, he promised to get to work, but once again we were the only ones with a sense of urgency.

Late that afternoon the committees met, and shortly before Shabbat the committee heads briefed the leaders and the Secretary in Houghton House, the Palestinian residence. The focus was almost entirely on economic issues and safe passage between Gaza and the West Bank, issues that, while not central to an agreement, greatly affected the daily lives of Palestinians. Arafat said little throughout the meeting, other than to ask Bibi to "please" consider responding on each issue.

Though two safe passage routes between Gaza and the West Bank had been mandated by the Interim Agreement, the two sides had never been able to negotiate the terms for their implementation. The security restrictions Israel sought to impose on these routes, which had to run through Israel, made travel, in Palestinian words, "neither safe nor free." Since the Hebron agreement I had explored ways to overcome the differences on safe passage. Progress had been made, but the Israeli insistence that Israel be able to exercise its sovereignty in an area that was part of Israel rankled the Palestinians, who feared the Israelis would abuse this right. They did not want Israeli sovereignty to be mentioned in the text (lest it render safe passage meaningless), but the Israelis refused to sign an agreement without it. Bibi had no answer for overcoming this difference, but said he would think about the problem.

On the economic front, the Palestinians raised the issue of the constraints Israel imposed on trade between Jordan and the Palestinian territories. Trade between the two was limited to certain categories of goods that benefited the Israeli economy, but imposed hardships on two economies that were a fraction of Israel's. Bibi agreed to consider relaxing the limitations that had been imposed as a result of the 1994 economic protocol between Israel and the Palestinian Authority. Lastly, Bibi heard an impassioned plea from Mohammad Rashid on the illogic of the purchase tax—a tax paid on top of a value-added tax by Palestinian importers for goods that Israel required to go through Israel before going to Gaza or the West Bank. If this tax, which raised the cost for Palestinian businessmen, was to be imposed, at least it should go to the Palestinian treasury, not to Israel's. Bibi was prepared to study this issue for six weeks and try to come up with a solution.

As it was nearly sundown and the onset of Shabbat, we had to conclude the meeting. I walked back to River House with Bibi and tried out an idea for resolving safe passage: The agreement would say that Israeli law applies in the area (thus obviating the need to refer to your "sovereignty"); you will give them and us an assurance that Israel will not use this as a trap for arresting Palestinians; and we will assure that any arrests will only occur in extremely rare circumstances. Bibi, thinking practically, clearly liked the idea. But when he turned to Dani Naveh and asked him what he thought, Dani told the Prime Minister there was no need for Israel to give any more to the Palestinians at this stage. Bibi suddenly changed his posture: "We don't offer any more to them until I see them respond to us."

I felt like saying "Sorry I asked." Instead, I said, We are working on your concerns. The issue is principally not the substance of your concerns but the presentation. I left it at that, and got a car to return to my room back at the Wye Center. The minute I walked in the door of my room, the phone was ringing. It was Bibi; Dani had clearly worked him up. Bibi now wanted no more committee meetings until it was clear the

Palestinians were responding to the Israeli needs. Fortunately, the connection was bad, and I told him we would have to discuss this tomorrow. For now, I bid him Shabbat Shalom.

The Israelis held a Shabbat dinner for their delegation only. So the Secretary hosted a dinner for Arafat and his top aides, who were clearly eager to have our full attention. I was seated next to Arafat and quietly asked him, "What do you think?" His response was surprising: "I have to be patient with Netanyahu"—implying that he was the more mature political leader and Netanyahu could be brought around. He was in good humor; when I proposed that if we succeeded here we should consider organizing a retreat for Abu Mazen and Abu Ala to meet secretly with Ariel Sharon (now the Israeli Foreign Minister) to explore permanent status, he turned to me and said, "Magnificent idea." And when the Secretary toasted him as a special friend, he responded that she had touched his heart and the hearts of all Palestinians.

I had no problem with building his confidence in us, but I also wanted him to produce. I leaned over to Abu Mazen, who was sitting on my other side, and whispered, "I still have no response from you. The 'old man' may be a special friend, but you may not like what we will present. If you don't get comments to me tonight, consider that I have given you fair warning." He told me I would get them, but I should get them from Saeb. Saeb would see me tonight.

Shortly before midnight, Saeb came to see me, pleading for some additional time—he would come in the morning. "For real, Saeb?" I asked, and he said, "For real, Dennis."

| DAY 3 |

I knew the Israelis would not get up early on Shabbat morning. I had told Natan and Yitzhik Molho I would come over and go for a walk with them at around eleven. Instead, I waited for Saeb, sending word that I would see them in the afternoon. But that proved impossible as I was needed to brief the President, who was returning from the White House. As a result, I never got over to see any of the Israelis prior to the President's meeting with Bibi at 4 p.m., leaving them alone to wonder what we were cooking up with the Palestinians—not a brilliant move on my part. But I was getting what we needed from the Palestinians.

Saeb came alone to my cabin at 11 a.m. I had only Aaron and Gamal with me. He said, "Guys, I am not here to negotiate or play games with words. Do the Israelis want advertisements or substance? If it is the latter, they will get it; the former we can only do at the expense of the latter. I will be straight with you and tell you what we can do with the security part of the text you presented to Dahlan. We can accept nearly all of it."

I focused on the "nearly," not the "all," and waited for the other shoe to drop. It did, but in a milder form than I had anticipated. He cited four points that had to be changed, saying they would do what we wanted on each point but needed new language: "Make no mention of a *specific list* of suspects to be apprehended; make no mention of the vetting mechanism for prisoner releases; make no mention of the U.S. removal of illegally confiscated weapons; and make no mention of the Palestinians providing a list of where the surplus police would be going."

Saeb had repeated the two areas that Dahlan had so vehemently objected to, and added two additional problems, but unlike Dahlan, he was explicitly saying they would accept the rest of the security text.

While this was very useful, I could not let him think we could accept removal of all reference to these four points. "Saeb," I said, "I have heard you and I understand your position very well. I am prepared to consider what you are asking, but I cannot promise you we will be able to accommodate you. On the Israeli side, they will say there is no ambiguity on their obligations; the land gets turned over to you and the text is clear. At a minimum, we will have to have something in the text that gives us a handle on each of these issues."

We discussed each of the four issues—a list of suspects, vetting prisoner releases, U.S. collection of illegal weapons, and what happens to the surplus policemen—and Saeb proposed vague formulations on each, saying this was the limit of what was possible.

He asked for a word alone with me, and we walked outside where he showed me the draft of the negative comments. He said Abu Mazen had rejected what the others wanted to say, knowing that "you would tell us 'to go fuck ourselves.'" (He was right.) "Abu Mazen told me go get this done," he went on. "I have convinced Dahlan and he can live with what I have described to you. We will do the substance, but don't put us in the corner. Don't take away our self-respect. I am not negotiating now, I am trying to get this done in a way that they can live with and we can live with."

I told Saeb I knew he was making a genuine effort. I appreciated that. I could not make any promises, but I would see what I could do. Saeb said, "Try, Dennis, really try."

After Saeb left, I went to see Madeleine and told her I've got good news and bad news: The Palestinian response on security was actually much better than I had expected, with critical sections such as going after the terror groups and their infrastructure left completely intact. But four key specifics are removed from the text, and I don't believe the Palestinians will be more explicit in public. Bibi will say, "You are cutting the substance, not the style." He will argue that we are "gutting what Israel is supposed to get from the Palestinians."

From the standpoint of Bibi's politics, I told the Secretary, he would be right. Our argument with him would be that we were producing the substance of what he needed, and that ultimately that had to count more than symbols.

I continued to believe that Bibi would go along with an agreement if we had solid commitments from the Palestinians on what they would do practically on all the security questions. I knew he wanted to sell an agreement in which he was withdrawing from territory in the West Bank—ideological heresy to his own base—by showing that he was producing more from the Palestinians than people thought possible and certainly more than Labor ever produced. That was why he needed some "trophies." I was now more sympathetic to his desire for trophies—particularly because we were going to have to weaken the appearance of what he was getting on security.

But, I emphasized to Madeleine, our first priority has to be to get the reality, in a credible work plan, of the arrest or apprehension list, the vetting mechanism, action against the civilian infrastructure supporting terror, and confiscation of illegal weapons. Palestinians must actually do these things, even if they would not publicly describe their obligations so explicitly. We must have these commitments in hand before we press Bibi to accept softer language than we had worked out with him on all the security questions.

Madeleine agreed this was the right strategy to pursue, but wanted to know what the President should do with Bibi and Arafat when he returned to see them this afternoon.

With Bibi, I said, we will need George to say in front of the President that the Palestinians have now produced a plan that is credible; it covers all categories—military and civilian—and gives a clear picture of what the Palestinians will be doing.

Then I felt the President could ask Bibi to give him the 14.2 percent in his pocket and to give us more leeway on the third FRD committee language. If President Clinton could get these, we would be in a position to go back to Arafat and get more, including the private understandings on security that would be so necessary for us to have.

Madeleine agreed, but wanted me to go over all of this with Sandy when he arrived.

Next to Houghton House there was a guesthouse with a beautiful garden, and Madeleine and I met Sandy and George Tenet there. Aaron, Rob, Bruce, Martin, and Gamal joined us for the briefing. It was a brilliant fall day, sunny and warm with a crystal-clear blue sky, and I found myself thinking that I'd rather be playing golf or taking a hike or doing anything other than talking about how we are going to get Bibi to put something in our pocket so we can move Arafat and be in a position to put our text on the table.

Sandy either read my mind or was having similar feelings; as I was about to begin, he joked, "Shouldn't we be out playing golf on a day like this instead of trying to figure out how we are going to move these guys?" "Yeah," I said, "but here we are." I proceeded to outline a general approach, and while Sandy accepted it, he preferred a blunter line with Bibi: We've produced on security and you have given nothing in two days; put something in our pocket or we aren't going to get this done.

I told him that so frontal a challenge would make Bibi lash back, claiming he was giving on the airport, on fiscal issues, on safe passage—and he was getting only promises in return. What about the thirty killers? What about the PNC? What about his needs on reciprocity?

Sandy asked how we should respond to that and I said the answer to Bibi is that we are working *your* agenda: arrests, work plan, monitoring of Palestinian steps, unconditional security cooperation, weapons confiscation, dealing with the thirty "killers," anti-incitement, and the charter.

Sandy and Madeleine thought that was great, with Madeleine asking me if I could give her a card that listed everything we were trying to get done for Israel on security. Sandy suggested that the President would not be able to counter Bibi's charges unless I was there. I noted that we needed George to be there to make the case on security; perhaps we could make it three on a side. This was agreed, along with the basic approach to Bibi.

We went inside to brief the President. Rahm Emanuel, perhaps the President's most important advisor on domestic issues, had accompanied the President to Wye, and he asked me to state what the President should say: "Mr. President," I said, "simply say I have produced a real security plan; now, Bibi, you must put a few things in my pocket."

The President said he "got it," but then asked wouldn't it be better for him to do this in a small group rather than a one-on-one meeting? We all nodded, and he then asked, Okay, but then what do I do with him alone? I suggested that we could take a brief break between the two meetings to discuss what else might be usefully done then. The President agreed, and we walked the five hundred yards to River House looking a lot like an army with hordes of security people and our whole team traipsing along with us. Feeling ridiculous with such a spectacle, the President turned to George and said, "You think we have enough people with us?"

Unfortunately, when we arrived there, our well-conceived plan went out the window. Bibi greeted the President, and when the President suggested a small group meeting first, Bibi replied "good" and proceeded to bring eight people out to the deck. Because they had not met with any American all day, the Israelis were nervous, hence the expanded delegation. I held back so as to make our group smaller, and from where I stood I could see George, Sandy, and Madeleine on our side and twice as many people on Bibi's side. After a few minutes, Sandy motioned for me to join them. I squeezed in on a chair that Bibi's military aide brought for me and realized that the meeting was already going Bibi's way—not our way. I had made a big mistake in not getting over to

River House earlier in the day at least to hold Israeli hands, allay suspicions, and explain what we were doing.

As I sat down, Bibi, speaking as much to his side as ours, was emphatic that he had not yet heard anything on his needs. Instead of responding directly, the President asked George to explain what was being done on Israeli security needs and where things stood on the work plan. That might have worked had Bibi not insisted that the Israelis hear it directly, not secondhand. "As much as we trust you," Bibi said, "it is our security, and our people must hear the Palestinian plans from the Palestinians."

Though George had been confident that we now had a work plan from the Palestinians, he became uneasy claiming there was a work plan that met Israel's security needs when the Prime Minister of Israel was saying this was news to him. At a minimum, the Israelis must see it and also accept that it was credible—and as a result George chose not to counter Bibi's argument. The premise for this meeting, and what we would do in it, had just been undone. Rather than allowing Bibi to put us totally on the defensive, I chose to leap in: "Look, Mr. Prime Minister, what your security guys have heard from the Palestinians at this point covers both military and civilian categories and goes way beyond the comprehensive plan of 1996, which you have always held up as the model. And your people are saying this plan is serious."

Bibi countered, calling the plan promising but incomplete, and now George, when confronted with Bibi's argument, said at the end of the day, "it is your security and we will work to get the Palestinians to present a real plan"—acknowledging that we needed to produce more from the Palestinians for there to be a real plan.

Here the President stepped in, asking Bibi to go over his needs. Around and around we went, with Bibi reciting his needs again, until finally the President looked at me. Before I could respond, Sandy said: "Mr. Prime Minister, we are only working on your agenda and you are putting nothing in our pocket. You need to put something in our pocket if you want us to get what you need." Bibi parried, saying, "We have given what there is to give."

I leaned over to Sandy and said, "This is a terrible setting; Bibi will give nothing in front of all his guys. Let the President see him alone, and get the 14.2 percent in his pocket. Just give me a minute with the President before he sees Bibi alone." Sandy agreed and suggested to the group that maybe it would be useful for the leaders to meet alone at this point.

The President came over to see me and said, "I couldn't jam him in front of all those people. What do you want me to do with him now?" I said, "Tell him George will work the security and there will be a credible plan; we need to know that we have the 14.2 percent in our pocket. Just tell him you have to have that." President Clinton said, "Got it." And he did get it.

But in their private meeting Bibi raised a new proposal. Why not go for a partial deal? That would produce progress without forcing him or Arafat to do what they could not do at this juncture. Since Arafat could apparently neither meet Bibi on the thirty killers now nor organize a PNC meeting on the charter, Bibi could do the 13 percent but needed these two steps from Arafat to do the 14.2 percent B-to-A transfer of authority. If what Bibi needed was too hard for Arafat now, why not make progress but with a lesser package agreement?

Now the President was due to see Arafat alone. Without asking us, the President said he did not think he should go over any of this with Arafat at this point, so what should he do? I said we are nowhere without the security work plan. You just have to repeat once again we have to have a credible work plan or we cannot produce for him. George must be in the meeting with you and Arafat must give instructions to his security people to give George what he needs. The President nodded his understanding, and Arafat said he would do what the President asked. In private, the President also told Arafat he had the 14.2 percent in his pocket, clearly reflecting the President's judgment that he needed to give Arafat something. As we closed day 3, I wondered if Arafat was really prepared to give us what we needed.

| DAY 4 |

I knew the discussion on a partial deal would reemerge today. Sandy and Madeleine were dead set against it, seeing it as another Bibi trick to avoid doing what was necessary while creating the illusion of making progress. I did not totally rule it out, only because I thought Arafat should know what his choices were. He might yet find that a partial deal was more attractive than no deal, or that a deal at this point was too hard for him to do. Nevertheless, knowing Bibi, I knew that tactically to produce a partial deal that was credible, we would need now to press him for a complete deal. I explained this to Sandy and Madeleine, but they were not persuaded. They believed a partial deal of any sort would be a disaster for Arafat, and did not want the President thinking in those terms.

We all knew very little was possible as long as the security card remained in Bibi's pocket, not ours. With this in mind, George Tenet began the day working with the Palestinian security people. Notwithstanding Arafat's assurance to the President on security, George ran into a problem—Mohammad Dahlan felt the goalposts were constantly being moved. We had seemed satisfied, now we were not; regardless of what he told us, the Israelis would keep requiring more and we would simply go along with them. In his eyes, he was being bled dry of his positions and in a way that would expose him in Gaza. He wanted to know that we would stop at some point and that would be it—no more questions, and no more demands on what he must provide. As a result, he resisted what George was asking, especially on the civilian infrastructure to be combatted as part of the struggle against terror. This was the challenge we would have to overcome.

It was Sunday; the President would arrive at around eleven in the morning and Vice President Gore would join him. We had programmed about an hour of discussion with the President so that he would be ready for a planned lunch with Bibi and his ministers—Foreign Minister Sharon and Defense Minister Mordechai, who had arrived that morning. To meet and prepare for the lunch and the day, we went to yet another private house on the compound—the Tennis House, situated along the Wye River and about a five-minute walk from the Wye Center.

The house looked like a Swiss chalet, with a tennis court next to it, and we met in the upstairs sitting room. While the house's setting gave it an air of privacy, there was little privacy in the house itself. This was a problem, given the large contingent of security and nonsecurity people who traveled with the President—and the smaller but still significant group that accompanied the Vice President.

During his long discussions at Wye, Clinton would often get up and walk around the room as he either listened or made a point; but at the Tennis House there was no space—figuratively or literally. I could see he was feeling claustrophobic as we described where we now stood.

We used our briefing time to reiterate what we needed from Bibi if there were to be any hope of reaching agreement. Sandy and Madeleine argued strongly against doing a partial deal on the grounds that it would weaken Arafat. The President agreed. Both Sandy and Madeleine wanted the President to present an overall package to Bibi and say this is what we can do; if you can't go for it, let's admit we simply cannot do this.

Taking this course was a gamble, but I said there was value in acting now to smoke Bibi out. Sandy thought Bibi might back down. Madeleine thought it was time to make Bibi put up or shut up. (She thought the latter more likely.)

The President and Vice President had listened to them, and to my discussion of what would be included in the package. The President then asked me what I thought we should do. I offered my assessment of Bibi: he could not leave here without a deal of some sort, even a partial deal, which would offer progress but not force him to break with his right. The center in Israel had come to doubt that Bibi was capable of doing any deal, even if it was demonstrably good for Israeli security. While Bibi did not want to lose the right by giving away too much, he could not afford to lose the center—and that would happen if we declared our effort over. That gave us leverage, and we should not shy away from using it.

In light of that, I suggested the President make clear that he could not continue simply having discussions. He should present the overall package to Bibi, telling him this is what we are prepared to push with Arafat and we need to know whether we should go ahead or not.

The President asked Vice President Gore for his thoughts. The Vice President responded that he thought there was no more than a 10 percent likelihood of getting a deal. He doubted Bibi was really up to it. But he thought the approach I outlined was the right course to follow. In order to move Bibi, Gore argued that we must show the great lengths we had gone to and how much Bibi would give up by forgoing what we had achieved for Israel on security. He thought it best for the President to make this pitch in front of the other ministers over lunch. While agreeing with the thrust of the Vice President's comments—and my assessment—President Clinton disagreed with the Vice President's suggestion that he make this pitch to Bibi and his ministers together. The President argued that the best chance to get Bibi to go along was by doing this privately. He believed he had to give Bibi a chance to bring the others along in his own way, and not look like he was giving in to the President.

The lunch at the Wye Center began with the President noting that it was the twenty-fifth anniversary of Ariel Sharon's crossing of the Suez Canal in the 1973 war— a rather "auspicious day for us to be meeting to talk about peace." The President's comment triggered a series of reminiscences from Sharon, which Bibi then chose to use to explain why it was difficult for Israel to make concessions on land, but why it was willing to do so with the FRDs under discussion. What did he need to make such concessions? Ironically, he answered his own question not by focusing on security but by emphasizing the importance of convening the PNC to revoke the Palestinian charter, which, in his words, "would show the Israeli public that Israel was getting, not just giving, at Wye." Speaking with an air of great authority, he said this was not difficult for Arafat because he commanded five hundred votes in the PNC. The Vice President took issue with him, not on the value of the PNC but on the relative ease of Arafat pulling it off given the presence of rejectionist groups in the Palestinian National Council.

As the lunch broke up, the President and Bibi went off alone and met on a deck overlooking the river, where they became locked in a conversation that lasted for nearly an hour. Bibi had a yellow pad and was showing it to the President. Finally, they finished; when the President walked behind Bibi and looked over at me, his glance signaled exasperation. Bibi, he told us as we reassembled over at the Tennis House, had proposed a partial deal again, arguing that it was impossible to go for the full package.

In Bibi's partial deal, Arafat would get the 13 percent, the airport, and easing of trade restrictions with Jordan. (He would not get the 14.2 percent, safe passage, prisoner releases, the purchase tax, or the Gaza industrial zone.) Bibi would get security cooperation, the security work plan, confiscation of illegal weapons, and the anti-incitement decree. Everything else—the third phase, the PNC, the thirty killers, safe passage, the other economic issues, and the 14.2 percent would be left for thirty days from now.

The President asked us what we thought. Sandy and Madeleine were vehemently against it: Arafat was getting too little to justify what he would have to do. Without expressing a position, the President nonetheless said he felt he should share it with Arafat because Arafat should know his choices. I agreed, saying let's not prejudge Arafat's attitudes. If his choice is a partial deal or no deal, let's not be so sure he will choose no deal. I made two additional points. First, the President must not look like he was trying to sell Bibi's deal; he was simply reporting it because he owed it to Arafat to do so. Second, Bibi would have to offer more to Arafat to make a partial deal attractive. But we should leave that up to Arafat; if he was interested he would tell us what else he needed. If not, we would lose nothing by presenting it this way. Moreover, Arafat should see us leveling with him and should consequently be uncertain as to whether we could get Bibi to go for the whole package.

Sandy was uneasy, fearing it would look like we were trying to sell Arafat a partial deal. The President, seeing Gamal sitting in the corner of the room, asked him what he thought Arafat's reaction would be. Gamal said he did not know, but that Arafat would probably appreciate it "if the President laid it out the way Dennis has suggested. You won't be selling him anything. You thought he should know it. You don't know if you will be able to produce the whole deal, but you are prepared to try, and you wanted Arafat to hear what Bibi suggested and get his reaction."

The President nodded, saying, I'll emphasize that I want him to emerge stronger from here, not weaker, and he must tell me what he wants me to do—and "whether a partial deal does him any good or not."

Before asking Gamal to summon Arafat to the Tennis House, I raised the security issue again. I told the President that George does not have now what he feels he needs from the Palestinians, especially in the aftermath of the meeting with Bibi yesterday. We have to have that. Repeating what had by now become my recurring theme, I said, "Bibi cannot afford to be in a position in which we can show that he walked away from here for the sake of scoring political points after turning down a deal that offered Israel what it needed from the Palestinians on security. That's our best bet of getting a deal, and making Bibi pay the price should we fail to do so. Arafat must understand that and also understand that without what we need on security, the failure will be his."

Gamal called to arrange the Arafat meeting, and about forty-five minutes later, Arafat arrived with Abu Mazen, Abu Ala, and Nabil Abu Rudeina. Sandy, Madeleine, and I joined the President for the meeting.

The President described his conversation with Bibi and what Bibi had offered, and suggested that Arafat might want to confer with his colleagues and consider the Bibi partial deal with a return in thirty days before giving us a reaction.

Before doing so, however, he wanted Arafat to hear from me on the security issue. The President had not told me he would turn to me in the meeting to make this pitch. But it struck me that he was trying to avoid being an advocate at this moment.

The sitting room was not large. I was sitting across from Arafat, about six feet away. In private meetings with him, when I wanted to make a very important point, I would lean closer to him—and now I leaned so far forward on my chair that I was actually crouching. "Mr. Chairman," I said, "you will make your own decision about whether to go for the full deal now or a partial one; regardless of which way you decide, the President does not want you to lose coming out of here. If we can't get a deal, we need to show that you did all you could to produce one and the failure was not yours. If we can say that you did everything asked of you on security—and there was clearly a very credible plan, an unprecedented security plan—you can't lose and the pressure and onus shifts to the other side. That is also our best guarantee of a deal, but in any case you don't lose. For us to be in that position, indeed for you to be in that position, we must get from your side everything that George is asking for on security and he does not have it yet."

Arafat looked right at me the whole time I spoke. When I finished, he nodded, and then said he would like to confer with his colleagues. The President asked if he would like to do it here, and Arafat said no, they would return to their residence and call the President when they were ready to continue the discussion.

We reassembled two hours later at the guesthouse next to Houghton House, with George joining us. Arafat told the President that he did not want to accept a partial deal. He was prepared to stay several more days if that is what it took to reach agreement. If it was not possible to get everything done in the time the President had available at this point—and it created difficulties for the President to stay longer now—he would be willing to stop now or tomorrow, say we had made progress, and return in a week to ten days' time. He felt it was too long to wait a month.

The President told him that he, too, felt it best to do the whole deal, and if it meant staying a few extra days, he was willing to try to make it work. The President then raised the security issue, pointing to George, who explained that the one area that was lacking in the plan was on the "civilian categories" of fighting terror—going after the social and religious infrastructure that was used by Hamas in particular to recruit, finance, organize, and promote terror.

Arafat resisted at first, saying, "Dennis Ross knows that no one else in the Arab world has been willing to act against the mosques the way I have." While acknowledging that, the President said we have to take the security card out of Bibi's hands. If we cannot do that, we will have no leverage on him and the blame will be far more on you than on him for a failure of the summit.

The Chairman relented and told George he would give instructions to include the steps that would be taken against the civilian infrastructure in the work plan. Then, after a brief discussion of Palestinian economic needs, Arafat asked to meet the President alone. In the private meeting, Arafat said he could not organize a PNC meeting. He could, however, have the Central Committee of the PLO meet and endorse his letter to the President that had described the actions taken to revoke articles in the PLO charter. He suggested that this was a good compromise because the Central Council was a formal body that met in place of the PNC. The President told him he would think about this.

Though it was late, the President (acting on Bibi's request) wanted to see Ariel Sharon alone. Sharon arrived at midnight, and they met until close to 1:30 a.m., whereupon the President asked Sandy, Madeleine, and me to join him. He was feeling down and regretted seeing Sharon, who had been "hard over on everything," insisting on the partial deal approach and even lecturing the President on Jonathan Pollard. Clearly, the President concluded, Sharon would not help Bibi reach an agreement at Wye.

| DAY 5 |

After going to sleep at 2:30 a.m., I was awakened at 3:15 by Sandy: there had been a terrorist act in Israel, and he wondered what I thought the impact would be. That, I said, depended on the circumstances—where the attack was, how many victims there were—but in all likelihood Bibi would relax and Arafat would grow defensive. We could at least take advantage of that with Arafat.

I sagged as I went back to bed, feeling depressed and fearing again that terror might trump whatever we were doing. Four hours later I found out what had actually happened: a grenade attack in Beersheva at a bus stop had wounded sixty-seven people, including more than twenty soldiers, but had killed no one. The attacker had been captured. Things seemed to be under control in Israel. Israeli President Ezer Weizman had said that the attack made it more important for the negotiations to succeed, and Bibi had not threatened to leave—not surprising, I told the Secretary, for Bibi could not leave with nothing lest he appear unable to provide either peace or security.

While I expected Bibi to go on the offensive this morning, I suggested that Madeleine see him, offer condolences on the attack, hold her ground, and emphasize that we must keep working toward the full deal.

Madeleine agreed; she wanted to press ahead and, in her words, to stop having all "these nice discussions and tell them we have to get something done or this is over." The Secretary and I went and saw Bibi on the deck outside River House. Predictably, he told us this attack proved the Palestinians had to produce on security or there would be no agreement. Thus provoked, Madeleine turned combative, telling Bibi: "If you keep going the way you are, you will have no peace and no security, is that what you want? You treat the Palestinians with no respect and no dignity; you just always make demands. And we are not going to continue this way. We may just have to admit it is over."

Bibi angrily denied he disrespected the Palestinians, prompting me to say, "Well, what about this morning? Arafat tried to call you this morning to express condolences and you would not take his call; a small example, perhaps, but you should not underestimate the impact on the other side of such slights." He said he would take the call, and when I suggested he call back now, he did so, and while making the point that Palestinians must do more to stop such attacks, he did thank Arafat for his concern.

By the time he finished the call, Bibi was all business. He quickly approved a draft statement we would issue on behalf of both sides condemning the attack. Then he asked to go over the elements of the partial deal, arguing that "we must leave here with something."

The discussion, however, broke no new ground, but shortly after Madeleine and I left, I got a message that Bibi wanted to see me. I returned to River House and Bibi sat alone with me. He showed me his yellow pad with some revisions on what could go into a partial deal; he was willing to include the Gaza industrial zone and possibly one of the safe passage routes in it. But he remained convinced we could not go for the full deal. I disagreed, telling him, "You need to resolve the thirty, the approach on the third FRD, and the PNC to go for the full deal, right?" He nodded. I told him I did not have an answer on the PNC, but I had some ideas on the thirty and the third FRD. Bibi was all ears.

On the thirty, I said, what if of the thirteen police, only two or three are special cases? What if you know twenty-seven or twenty-eight are definitely going to be arrested and two or three, no more, are dealt with in a private understanding between Ami Ayalon and Mohammad Dahlan. To be sure, Ami has to be satisfied that these two or three are legitimately important for the security effort. If he is, they are not arrested; if he is not, they are. If the Wye agreement is ultimately about security, let's have security considerations govern the outcome of this issue. Bibi was not ready to commit to this, but I could tell he liked it.

Next, I turned to the third FRD. The issue, I said, is how we talk about a third FRD committee; the Palestinians want to be able to say the third FRD will be discussed, while you want to be able to avoid any appearance that you have to negotiate the third FRD, particularly because it raises fears that you will inevitably be forced to do another major redeployment. "Let's," I suggested, "bring the Christopher letter into play. It makes clear that the FRD is an issue for you to decide not to negotiate, but it also makes clear that the FRD must be completed. What if we say that the FRD will be addressed consistent with the Christopher letter and in relationship to the permanent status negotiations? The former protects you, since Christopher says this is an issue you decide; the latter protects them because it makes it clear there will be a discussion—and it will be related to permanent status. Again, he was noncommittal, but clearly interested.*

We concluded the meeting, with Bibi telling me he wanted to think about the ideas I had raised and come back to me. Knowing Bibi as I did, I knew we now had a shot at both "the thirty" and the third FRD. I knew something else as well: Bibi was not leaving Wye without an agreement. His readiness to sweeten the partial deal was one indication of that. His openness to my ideas was another.

I told this to the Secretary, who was hopeful but asked what we needed to get done before President Clinton returned the next day.

I said that George and I must work in parallel. He needs to finish the work plan; I should finalize our language on the security part of the text—letting the Palestinians know that while we would soften the formulations on the four issues of special concern to them, our language (which would be part of the public agreement) would be more explicit than they would like.

Madeleine liked this approach. Naturally, since nothing ever went according to plan or schedule, George and I worked not only the rest of that day but into Tuesday as well as we both faced resistance from the Palestinians, who knew we were pressing them and not the Israelis.

| DAY 6 |

By Tuesday afternoon, our sixth day at Wye, we still did not have agreement between George, the Palestinians, and the Israelis on the work plan. But we had not yet gone over the formal language of the security section of the agreement with Bibi and we could not delay doing so any longer. When we did discuss it, he resisted initially, saying, "You are softening what I most need." After some predictable give-and-take, he then said the only way he could accept such language was if he had secret "side understandings" with us on each of the issues, which he could use to placate his cabinet. Both Madeleine and I

---

*I was not just trying to overcome a problem on the third FRD formula solely for the purposes of Wye; I also wanted a formula that allowed us to keep the focus where it should be once we had an agreement here: on permanent status and not on the last FRD.

told him we would provide side understandings on each issue, but knowing the cabinet members would leak them, we said these would not be as explicit as he might like. He said he could not make his decision on the text until he saw these side assurances.

That is where we chose to leave it until the President arrived early in the evening. I felt we had used days 5 and 6 to condition both sides on what was coming. That did not mean they would like the text or not resist it, but they would not be surprised by it. In negotiating, surprise always stretches the time needed to overcome problems, if for no other reason than that one side will feel the need to respond to the surprise by making a point—and when one is at the "point-making" stage, one is not at the problem-solving stage.

Conditioning both parties to avoid surprise is necessary to take the emotion and sometimes very genuine anger out of the negotiation. If one is in the position of being the "presenter," it is important to be able to go through a text to show how you have made an effort to respond to every concern that has been raised. At this stage, I felt we were in as good a position as possible to do that. But I still felt that we should get Bibi's agreement to the security work plan before presenting the actual text. That was the point of our maximum leverage.

For now, the President wanted to know how best to use his presence that evening. I suggested that he bring the leaders plus two on each side to a meeting and go over the status of each issue. "Your objective," I said, "ought to be to build the base of understanding on all the issues and isolate those issues on which the leaders will have to make decisions."

We gathered in front of the blazing fireplace in the Wye Center.* The President eased into the meeting, saying this was the right group to get together to move us toward a resolution on all the issues. He said he wanted to proceed issue by issue, see where we stood, what we could agree on now, and what issues we would hold only for the leaders.

We met for nearly three and a half hours, with the President alternately summarizing on a yellow pad where we were in virtual agreement (as on most of the economic issues) and where further discussions between the two sides were appropriate. The issue of prisoners came up with Abu Mazen making an impassioned plea for significant prisoner releases and the President giving a poignant response on the sensitivity of the issue—a sensitivity he knew firsthand from his experience as governor of Arkansas where a prisoner he had pardoned committed a murder soon afterward. He knew the families of prisoners had endured a great deal, but one had to take account of the feel-

---

*Arafat came with Abu Mazen and Abu Ala. Netanyahu brought Molho and Sharansky. And Madeleine, Sandy, and I joined the President.

ings of the victims' families. He talked about possibly creating different categories of prisoners, whereupon Bibi said there was one category of prisoners that he could not release: those with blood on their hands. Abu Mazen said he understood the Prime Minister's problem, but emphasized that the Chairman had a problem as well, particularly because many of those who sat in jails were there even though it was a different era. He pleaded for a way to release prisoners and Natan Sharansky agreed to sit with him to see what could be done.

By the end of the evening, the President had concluded that the negotiators could resolve all issues except the PNC, "the thirty," and the third FRD. He was feeling hopeful, believing we had made some progress. Sandy and Madeleine agreed, but felt we needed to push harder. It was Tuesday night; the President would be available only until Thursday. It was time to present the text to Bibi.

The President said nothing, waiting to see what I would say. We were not in the position I had hoped to be in vis-à-vis Bibi, but I said, If we are talking about wrapping up by Thursday, we need to give it to Bibi tonight. It will create a crisis with him, but I suspect it will be more for show than for real. The President listened and said, "Go do it."

It was now a little after midnight. I called Yitzik Molho and told him our plan, explaining that we needed their response by morning because we wanted to present the text to the Palestinians later that day. Molho said, "I will tell BN. When will we get it?" I said, In half an hour. "And Yitzik," I said, "you know the ground rules, handle this discreetly, the Palestinians don't get this until tomorrow."

Just after 1 a.m. I went to report to the President. The President was in the Wye Center with Sandy and Madeleine chatting about the congressional elections. When the President saw me, he shifted gears; did the Israelis have the text, he asked, and when I reported they did, he asked Sandy and Madeleine to leave so he could discuss a few things with me.

I assumed that he wanted to talk about where my private discussions stood with Bibi and Dahlan on "the thirty." But I was wrong; he did not want to talk about the thirty, he wanted to talk about releasing Jonathan Pollard. "Is it a big political issue in Israel? Will it help Bibi?" "Yes," I replied, because he is considered a soldier for Israel and "there is an ethos in Israel that you never leave a soldier behind in the field." But if you want my advice, I continued, I would not release him now. "It would be a huge payoff for Bibi; you don't have many like this in your pocket. I would save it for permanent status. You will need it later, don't use it now."*

---

*I also said I was in favor of his release, believing that he had received a harsher sentence than others who had committed comparable crimes. I preferred not tying his release to any agreement, but if that was what we were going to do, then I favored saving it for permanent status.

The President had a different view. You know, he said, "I usually agree with you, but this stalemate has lasted so long that it has created a kind of constipation. Release it and a lot becomes possible. I don't think we can afford to wait, and if Pollard is the key to getting it done now, we should do it."

Madeleine walked back into the room at the tail end of the conversation and later asked me about it. I told her, repeating my view that it was a mistake to release Pollard for this deal, but making clear that the President was seriously thinking about doing so.

| DAY 7 |

Wednesday produced the "crisis" I had anticipated. As expected, once the Israelis had the actual text, they had a big problem with it—so big a problem that they threatened to leave Wye.

Madeleine and I were having breakfast at the Wye Center. We had been trying to arrange a meeting between Madeleine and Bibi when Pat Kennedy—who was in charge of the logistics of the summit for all parties—reported that the Israelis had approached him asking for help to go to Andrews in the next few hours. Madeleine looked at me and asked what we should do. How do we respond?

I said we expected a crisis with them once they saw the softened language in black and white; they were not going to get everything they wanted. Moreover, they are probably playing up their anger in order to convince us things are so bad we must give them explicit side assurances. "The most important thing we can do," I said, "is to make clear we are not rattled by their little show. Let's tell them if they want to leave, we are quite willing to help them to do so." I concluded by telling Madeleine that this is "a no-lose approach for us. Either we call Bibi's bluff or if it proves not to be a bluff—which I very much doubt—and Bibi has left the peace talks, then he has to explain why he is walking away from the peace process."

When his team put their bags outside River House a short while later, we knew it was a bluff. If you are leaving, you leave. You arrange a time for your plane's departure, you call for the vans, and you load your bags in the vans. There was no suspense in their putting their bags outside, only false drama.

The Palestinians, of course, also saw the Israeli show. Naturally, they assumed the Israelis were having a problem with us. I used this to build the credibility of our efforts. I could not give the Palestinians the entire text yet because we did not have any comments from the Israelis—and we might yet make some changes in this revised text to make it more palatable to them. But I did meet with Saeb and another Palestinian negotiator, Hassan Asfour, and explained that we were going over the security formulations with the Israelis, that we had tried to take account of the Palestinian concerns, and that the Israelis did not like this. But don't kid yourselves, I said, we could "only go along with the softening in the text if we have clear assurances from you on the apprehension of suspects, vetting of releases, the police, and confiscation of illegal weapons."

While the Israeli bags remained outside for most of the day, we ignored them and worked with both sides on the assurances. With the Palestinians, we focused on producing a letter to the Secretary from Arafat that proceeded issue by issue, assuring us the Palestinians would fulfill their responsibilities, especially that there would be "no revolving door" on prisoner releases. We needed this language to use with Bibi.

Our meeting with Bibi and his ministers—Sharon, Mordechai, and Sharansky— was noteworthy for two reasons. First, the Secretary agreed to Bibi's request for a letter confirming that Palestinian performance on all their responsibilities must be carried out before we could move from one phase of the timeline to the next. Second, in response to the Secretary's statement that the Palestinians had a right to expect performance from the Israelis as well, Sharon took umbrage and referred to the Palestinians as "a gang of thugs."

Following the meeting with Bibi, I finalized our side understandings alone with Yitzik Molho. This did not mean we were out of the woods. It simply meant that the Israelis would now give us their comments on the whole text for our response. I expected that the discussion with Yitzik, Dani Naveh, and Daniel Reisner to be a nitpicking one, with them trying to go word by word through the text to see what more they might produce.

I had Martin, Aaron, and Jon Schwartz join me for the discussion. The discussion was taking the course I expected when my assistant, Nick Rasmussen, brought in a Reuters wire report quoting Aviv Bushinsky, Israeli press spokesman, "threatening" to leave Wye if the Israelis were not satisfied with the results of the review they were currently conducting with us of our proposed text. The "threat" was unacceptable posturing, but posturing nonetheless. More importantly, the reference to the fact that we were currently reviewing the proposed text with the Israelis violated our understanding that sharing the text with them in advance of presenting it to the Palestinians was based on complete confidentiality. Violating that rule, as we had maintained all along, would mean that we would no longer be bound by any understandings reached between us, and I told them so. We would need to consult with the Secretary on what should be done at this point.*

---

*Martin, with great emotion, had reacted to the Bushinsky quote by declaring to the group that we could not negotiate under public ultimatum.

The Israelis knew they had a problem. Shortly after we broke off our discussion, Dani Naveh and Zalman Shoval called and asked if they could come see the Secretary. They told her that Bibi had not known about the press release; the Secretary countered that was "hard to believe." Dani and Zalman suggested that the Secretary should go and talk to the Prime Minister alone and clear the air. She agreed.

As she was getting ready to go to River House, George came in and announced, "We got it"—a "deal on security," done between Mordechai and Dahlan. They have "agreed to my summary of their understanding," and the Palestinians will have one week to finish the thirty-day work plan.

With Mordechai's agreement in hand, I told Madeleine, You have a lot of leverage with Bibi. We don't have to chase after him or work according to his schedule. We can work according to ours, which at this point was being determined by the political side of the White House. With the midterm election only six days away, they insisted that the President be on the road campaigning and that tomorrow—Thursday—would be the last day of the President's availability at Wye.

Madeleine went to see Bibi and returned reporting that Bibi was ready to proceed with the text and to try to finish everything tomorrow.

I got together with Yitzik and Dani and told them "the PM had agreed to have us give both sides the text now." They seemed surprised, saying their understanding was we were to finish going over the text before the Palestinians got it, but they would go "check with the PM."

My instructions were to give the text to the Palestinians now, and I was not about to lose time while they went to see Bibi. I told them so, but said I would give them the next half hour to finish going through their comments. They thanked me, but their pleasure soon turned to real pain. Before concluding, I told them we would provide neither a letter on moving from one phase to the next only after completion of responsibilities, nor a timeline in which all Palestinian responsibilities came prior to Israeli obligations. Notwithstanding the Secretary's earlier promise and our desire to be responsive to the Israelis, the leak had undercut us with the Palestinians—and "we meant what we said about our understandings not holding if they did not respect the principle of confidentiality." While both Yitzik and Dani looked as if they had been punched in the solar plexus, they quickly acquiesced. Nothing could have signaled more clearly that they were desperate to conclude a deal.

Madeleine was anxious to get going, and at her urging I asked Aaron to present the text—with a few modifications to take account of what we had heard from the Israelis—to the Palestinians within the hour. He did so and reported that they had listened to his description of each section and asked a few questions. But, Aaron said, "they were in an acquiescent mood." Why not? I thought. They saw us doing battle with the Israelis all day, not exactly what they had expected.

It was now about two-thirty in the morning. I went back to my cabin. The President would arrive at nine. How should he be briefed? I told Rob Malley, who would write briefing points, that the President must operate with a mind-set that "this is it"; he must communicate his urgency to both Bibi and Arafat, and they must see from his demeanor and actions that we were going to finish today—"one way or the other."

I then went over the status of each issue, concluding with the ones reserved for the leaders. With regard to the third FRD, Bibi had now accepted language I thought we could sell the Palestinians: "A committee would be established to address the third phase and its relationship to the permanent status." While Bibi would say this meant the third FRD was subordinated to the permanent status negotiations, the Palestinians could say that this language meant the third phase had to be discussed on its own merits—the key for them. With regard to the thirty, I thought I could resolve it with Dahlan.

The issue of the PNC meeting was more complicated. I had one idea that involved combining the Palestinian Legislative Council and the Palestinian Central Committee and having enough PNC members participate in this joint session to call it a PNC meeting. Alternatively, Gamal had an idea that was a real wild card—the President would go to Gaza if Arafat convened a PNC meeting to receive him and endorse the Arafat letter to him on the charter. My guess was that Arafat, seeing this as a colossal act of recognition, would accept such an idea.

I told Rob, "Obviously, the President's going to this sort of PNC meeting is a high-risk proposition, so we ought to think of this as the last-gasp idea—one to keep up our sleeve to play only if everything else fails."

Summing up, I said our strategy in the morning should be to solve the issues we can solve—the airport, numbers of police, weapons confiscation—and in so doing create enough momentum to be able to close on the last big issues: the third FRD, the thirty, the PNC—and probably also the prisoners.

By the time Rob and I had finished, it was after four in the morning. Rob asked if I wanted him to come back and show me his write-up. I said yes, but first I was going to sleep.

| DAY 8 |

Rob's one-page summary was well done. I reviewed it with Madeleine at breakfast, and she presented it to the President when he arrived. He agreed with the thrust of the strategy, and we were set to start at 10 a.m.

Around nine-thirty, Sandy arranged for him, George Tenet, and me to sit with the

President, and Sandy began explaining that the President was considering releasing Pollard. In the President's presence, he explained, that this is what it might take to do the deal and he wanted to be able to take this step if necessary. George blew up. "Mr. President, you can't do this," explaining that the release would signal that spying could take place with impunity and further that it would greatly damage the morale of the intelligence community that he had worked so hard to restore. At least, he concluded, if you are considering a release, have a procedure in which all agencies can express their view—"otherwise you will be savagely criticized."

The President remained largely impassive. With George still sputtering, he and I went out to the boardwalk. He told me that if the President released Pollard, he would have no choice but to resign from the CIA; having spent the week at Wye, he would be seen in the intelligence community as having been a part of the deal. He would lose all credibility and effectiveness.

I relayed this to Sandy, who asked George to see the President alone.

With that as prologue, we began the fateful last day at Wye; the entire day's negotiations were carried out in the Wye dining room complex overlooking the river. It was a day without end, one that began in brilliant sunlight at 10:00 a.m. and concluded in the clear and bright sun of the following afternoon. It was a day of poignancy and pique. It was a day with fateful consequences for peace and Binyamin Netanyahu's future.

The President began the day by meeting with Bibi, who arrived shortly before Arafat. After Arafat arrived, the Secretary sat with him and discussed the number of Palestinian police.* She tried to see if he would accept the 28,000 figure on police, a number I had raised with Bibi the previous day—not the 30,000 the Palestinians sought, but not the 24,000 the Israelis sought, either.

I was wrong in believing that Arafat would see the 28,000 as a move toward him. I joined the Secretary after about ten minutes, and it was clear that Arafat was not going to go below 30,000. I sensed that on every issue Arafat would adopt an unyielding posture if the discussions were trilateral or with anyone other than the President.

Madeleine and I then went to see the President, who told us he'd told Bibi he had a speech prepared that would say we had done the best we could and we could not do this; it would break his heart to have to give it, but he would if we did not make it today. Bibi had said, "Let's go for it today."

---

*According to the Interim Agreement, the Palestinians could have 30,000 police, but only after the FRD process was completed. Since they were permitted 24,000 now and we were talking about implementing two of the three further redeployments, I thought we should allow the Palestinians 28,000 police, or two-thirds of the additional 6,000.

With Arafat clearly in a wait-and-see posture, I suggested we alter our game plan. I said it made no sense now to bring the leaders together; Arafat's stubbornness would make Bibi dig in—and rightly so. Instead, I told the President, given Bibi's response to you, why not go back to him and ask for his bottom lines? Tell him you need them to know what you need to get Arafat to do.

The President agreed, saying "You come with me," and "you and I will work Bibi and then you and I will go work Arafat." Accordingly, we went through each issue with Bibi and he offered the following:

—On weapons confiscation, he only needed some "show" collection and destruction of weapons; the weapons to be destroyed would be any that the Palestinians brought us for destruction. (The Palestinians had objected to small weapons being destroyed, and this was Bibi's suggestion for getting around that objection);

—On the airport, he would accept a required inspection of Arafat's plane only when he was flying a plane loaned to him, and he was willing to go along with an intrusive camera system or American inspections;

—On police, he would accept 28,000 as the total permitted;

—On the third FRD, he thought my "committee" formulation was "clever" and he could accept it;

—On the PNC, he would need to have it, and on the thirty "killers," all would be arrested with the understanding that he would look quietly at a very small number of cases for special handling.

The President and I then met with Arafat, who wasn't prepared to agree to any of these positions, though we had gone through each of them, laying out what we thought to be possible. On the airport, he wouldn't accept any inspections by the Israelis or by us of the planes loaned to him. When I suggested the possibility of a camera system as a form of insurance to be used for surveilling all aircraft, including those on loan to him, he said he would think about it. On police, he would not budge on the total; on the third FRD, he listened to my formulation and how it responded to his needs and he asked me to go over this with Abu Ala. I asked him if I had his proxy, and he responded, "Always." On the PNC and the charter, he still thought of bringing the Central Committee and Legislative Council together, and he did not answer us on the thirty, referring the issue to his security people.

By the time we finished with Arafat, it was lunchtime. The President asked me what we should do now. I replied that Arafat was clearly still negotiating, and to help him focus, you need to go back to him alone and repeat the point you made to Bibi:

Today is the day, either we reach agreement or we announce that we can't. The President did so and Arafat said he understood.

Meanwhile, Yitzik Molho had suggested to Gamal that the two sides have a meeting alone—without any Americans, so that even Gamal would not stay to interpret. Following the President's private chat with Arafat, I asked Gamal to convey Molho's request to Arafat, who agreed to the private meeting.

Bibi with Sharansky, Sharon, and Mordechai assembled in the large all-purpose room overlooking the river along with Arafat, Abu Mazen, Abu Ala, and Nabil Abu Rudeina (who would act as the interpreter). The American team adjourned to a small side room for lunch. After eating, I asked to see Saeb because I wanted to try to sell him my formulation on the third FRD. I asked Aaron to bring him upstairs to the only other room in this part of the building.

The room was austere, containing only a table and folding chairs. It was also full of cobwebs. I could not tell whether they were real or were the kind one buys to decorate for Halloween. I suspected the latter—and hoped that was true.

When Saeb arrived, I told him we would dub this the cobweb room, but we would use it to be creative. I went over the formulation I had presented to Arafat on the third FRD and explained why it responded to Palestinian concerns. I also told him we were not going to do better.

Saeb said, "Let me be honest with you. I think it is good language but Abu Ala is dead set against it and has persuaded Arafat. I can't sell it now. I can't sell the language that has the word 'relationship' in it." Abu Ala believes that by using the word "relationship" to tie the discussions on the third FRD to permanent status we are making an unacceptable concession—but "don't ask me to explain why." I believed Saeb and asked, "What if I come up with a synonym for the word 'relationship'?" He said, "Come up with something and give it to me to sell." I told him I would try to craft something without the word "relationship," but might in the end have to go back to the language I'd shown Arafat.

Martin had joined us at this point, and Saeb asked if we could go through the text and get it ready for completion. I told him to start that with Martin while I tried to find a way to keep the substance of my language on the third FRD but without the word "relationship." Nabil Sha'ath now joined us and he began to work with me on several formulations in which a committee would be established to discuss the last FRD and permanent status but without using the offending word.

This took about an hour. I then left the two of them with Martin and went downstairs. The meeting between Bibi and Arafat and their colleagues was still in progress; the President had decided to take a catnap and now Sandy and Madeleine were anxious about the day slipping away. Should I join the meeting? Madeleine asked. I told her, "No. Bibi wants the deal; Arafat now knows today is it, but wants to see directly from Bibi what he can get. Let them play it out."

Their discussion continued for another hour; as it was breaking up, Abu Mazen and Abu Ala told Gamal that Mordechai and Bibi had come up with ideas to solve the PNC problem: an expanded meeting in Gaza that brought together PNC members and the members of other organizations, with President Clinton present—this was Bibi's idea—to ask for a demonstration of support for Arafat's letter on the charter. Clearly, the President had raised the wild card idea of his going to Gaza in his meeting with Bibi that morning—and Abu Mazen and Abu Ala felt it would work.

Very quickly, however, we had a problem: the wild card idea had been in the written briefing points, but I had not raised it verbally during our meeting with the President early in the morning. Sandy had not been aware of it, and he was very resistant when Natan walked over to him and explained, in new terms, that there was now a solution to the PNC problem and it involved the President going to Gaza to appear before the PNC and asking the members to vote on annulling the charter. Fearing a possible embarrassment for the President, he told Natan, "You cannot put the President in that position," and went to talk to Clinton.

We had moved to a tent attached to the Wye Center and Sandy, the President, and Madeleine were huddled in a part of it. Natan Sharansky and I were in another part and Bibi joined us, saying to me, "Dennis, this will work, don't let Sandy talk the President out of it. All you need is for the President to ask the group the question and they can applaud or raise their hands." I said you can't ask the President to be the ringleader; let him be on the stage with Arafat and have Arafat ask those assembled to reaffirm his letter to the President on the charter. Bibi, clearly relieved that I was backing the basic idea, responded enthusiastically, saying, "Yeah, sure, let them raise their hands, stamp their feet."

The President joined us and asked me what I thought. I said if it was acceptable to the two sides we should help make it happen, not make it harder. Confident that he had raised the idea with Bibi, I was not surprised when he agreed. "Look, I know how to work a crowd; I can get them to respond." Sandy was still worried, but I assured him, saying, "Arafat is not going to put himself in a position where he gets rejected in front of the President."

At this point we certainly felt the back of the PNC issue had finally been broken. The other issue on which there appeared to be a breakthrough was that of "the thirty": Arafat agreed that all thirty would be arrested. For his part, Bibi agreed to 30,000 police for the Palestinians.

Suddenly it appeared that everything was falling into place. Natan Sharansky approached to tell me he was leaving now to be home in time for his daughter's bat mitzvah. I wished him mazel tov, but thought to myself that I hoped we would not need his presence as we entered the home stretch.

It was now about 5 p.m., and the President suggested we gather as a group and resolve each remaining issue, and as we did, "Dennis will put it in language to be sure it is agreed." So we gathered around a large elongated table: the President, Madeleine, Sandy, and me on our side; Bibi, Sharon, Mordechai, Dani, and Yitzik on the Israeli side; Arafat, Abu Mazen, Abu Ala, and Nabil Abu Rudeina on the Palestinian side.

As he began the meeting, the President asked me if the airport and policemen issues had been solved—and I said yes, essentially—and we turned to put the PNC issue in agreed language. The critical point here was to ensure that enough members of the PNC would attend to legitimize the decision to endorse the Arafat letter. Abu Ala suggested that a general invitation could be issued to all PNC members—as well as to the others who would be invited—and it could be issued in the name of the chair of the PNC, the Speaker of the Legislative Council, and Arafat. The President said that seemed reasonable, and Abu Ala's suggestion was agreed. I went off to draft a paragraph describing both what had been agreed and the purpose of the PNC meeting: "to support the peace process and the aforementioned decisions" on nullifying the charter embodied in the Arafat letter and subsequently reaffirmed by the Executive and Central Committees of the PLO. Everyone accepted my draft.

Next we went over the issue of the thirty and I produced general language on that for the text. It was agreed. Next the Palestinians raised the issue of prisoners. This had been discussed multiple times, starting in earnest after our Tuesday night meeting when Sharansky and Mordechai met with Abu Mazen. Bibi said he understood the importance of the issue to the Palestinians and was willing to release as many as he could, provided they weren't Hamas and had no blood on their hands. He said the problem was that there weren't large numbers of Fatah prisoners who did not have blood on their hands, and Israel had never drawn a distinction between those with Israeli blood on their hands and those with Arab blood on their hands. He thought there were only a hundred or so who fit the category. Abu Mazen said the most important thing was to create a mechanism, based on the criteria from the Interim Agreement, for trying to release more over time. The President asked, "Is there no way to release a larger number?"

Bibi said he could release those who were in for non-security-related offenses—those who had been working without permits, those who were in for criminal offenses. In this way, he could free up to several hundred. Madeleine turned to me and whispered, "Should we push for releasing those with Arab, not Israeli blood on their hands as a way to increase the number?" I told her it was worth a try, but should probably come from the Palestinians, not us. I suggested she go over to Abu Ala and see if he would raise it. She did, Abu Ala raised it, and Bibi said he would consider it.

We moved on to the remaining issues: safe passage, the seaport, and the third FRD. On safe passage—on which, according to the Interim Agreement, there should be two routes between Gaza and the West Bank—Nabil Sha'ath was asked to join us and brief us on where the issues stood; he explained that nothing blocked agreement now as he had conceded on the remaining points, including the critical one of the Israeli right to arrest during the safe passage. He said it was now possible to conclude the safe passage issue. Dani Naveh said much progress had been made but more work needed to be done—and Bibi agreed that the southern route of safe passage would be concluded within one week of the Wye agreement's entry into force, and the northern route as soon as possible thereafter. Arafat agreed to this.

On the seaport, with Sharon taking the lead, it was quickly agreed that the protocol would be finished within sixty days. The construction of the port could begin at that point.

The President asked me to draft the language that would be recorded in the agreement. As I was about to leave to get these drafted, typed, and copied, word came that King Hussein would be joining us soon. The King's lymphoma was advanced and he was highly susceptible to infection; the Secretary announced to all of us that we needed to rub a special disinfectant soap on our hands shortly before greeting him. The State Department's Chief of Protocol walked around the table squeezing the soap from a bottle onto the hands of President Clinton, Arafat, Netanyahu, and the rest of us. This act and the gravity of the King's physical appearance—bald, gaunt, and gray—made the moment extremely poignant.

After the King greeted everyone, the President summarized where we were, going over each of the issues and referring to my drafting each item as we did so. When the President finished, the King spoke movingly of his being with us, the importance of the progress that was now being made, his expectation that we would finish this evening, and the need to put the remaining differences in perspective: "These differences pale in comparison to what is at stake. After agreement both sides will look back and not even recall these issues. It is now time to finish, bearing in mind the responsibility that both leaders have to their people and especially the children."

When he concluded, he again walked slowly around the table shaking hands. Arafat refrained from giving him his customary kiss, on both cheeks instead kissing his shoulder in order to avoid making contact with his skin.

The King's appearance and words moved us all. A pall hung over the table, and for ten minutes or so Bibi and Arafat spoke about the King's humanity and dedication and commitment to peace. I stepped out to get the typed language on safe passage and the seaport. When I returned, the discussion was again focused on the prisoner issue. Arafat was emphasizing the importance of the prisoners to his public, and the President was asking what he needed on this issue. Arafat said he needed 1,000. Bibi responded by saying he would be willing to go up to 500 over the three phases of the twelve-week period of implementation.

At this point, Bibi asked to see the President and Arafat alone. The three of them, with Gamal interpreting, sat for about ten minutes; then suddenly Arafat got up and stalked back to the table, clearly angry. As I rose to see what had happened, the President erupted, shouting, "This is outrageous, this is despicable. This is just chickenshit, I am not going to put up with this kind of bullshit." He got up and stalked away, leaving Bibi sitting alone.

Everyone in the room was stunned. Gamal approached us and told Sandy, Madeleine, and me that Bibi had said he could do 500 prisoners only if Arafat made sure that Ghazi Jabali—head of police in Gaza and a man the Israelis accused of having given orders to attack Israeli settlers at one point—was "taken care of" and the thirteen police who were on the list of thirty were arrested in the first two weeks of the timeline. Arafat responded by saying, What am I supposed to do with Jabali, execute him? According to Gamal, Bibi responded flippantly, saying, "I won't ask, you won't tell." At this point, Arafat said there was nothing more to discuss and stood up and walked back to the table. The President then exploded.

The President had returned to the back room, and Sandy and Madeleine left to join him at this point. Molho asked me to talk to Bibi. He was sitting alone, obviously stunned, and feeling he was the victim, asking me, "Why is Israel treated this way, why am I treated this way? What have I done to deserve this?" (I was struck by his belief that he and Israel were one and the same, and that he was the innocent victim of mistreatment.)

I responded by saying what do you expect? "You commit to one thing on Ghazi Jabali as part of the deal on the thirty (effectively excluding him from arrest) and then you choose to add conditions later—after you have already elicited commitments from them. You never, in all the time we have been here, said the thirteen police on the list of thirty had to be arrested within the first two weeks; on the contrary, you have insisted that there needed to be a one-third, one-third, one-third breakdown of arrests on the list to coincide with each phase on the timeline. So when you finally respond to something you know is of great importance to them, you condition your commitment after having already given it."

Bibi was now feeling defensive, and he asked, "What should we do?" I told him I would see the President but I felt "only a private meeting between you and the President can fix things."

When I saw Clinton, he was irate, pacing back and forth and saying, "That SOB doesn't want a deal. He is trying to humiliate Arafat and me in the process. What the hell does he expect Arafat to do in that situation?" He paused and looked at me, and I told him about my conversation with Bibi. At first, the President was incredulous—wondering how Bibi could feel he was the victim. As I began to speak, saying, "Look, you have him on the defensive," Sandy grabbed my arm and whispered to me, "Don't calm him down, let him see Bibi feeling this way." As the President looked at me waiting for me to continue, the deputy chief of staff, Maria Echaveste, came in and told the President that "the Prime Minister wants to see you alone."

Sandy literally pushed all of us out of the room, telling me again as we left, I don't want his anger to dissipate.

They met alone behind closed doors for forty-five minutes, with us hearing the President's raised voice in the early part of the meeting. While we waited, I wandered out into the outer room and saw a large number of the Palestinian delegation sitting around Arafat. Dahlan and Mohammad Rashid had joined them. I motioned for Abu Rudeina to join me, and I told him I hope you know what it means for the President to do what he did. He said they were talking about precisely that and how they were amazed by the President's willingness to get so angry at Bibi in front of everyone in the room. While I did not know what would emerge from the President's meeting with Bibi, I wanted the Palestinians to feel they owed the President something.

Before Bibi walked in to see the President, Madeleine had suggested to the President that he press Bibi for a release of 750 prisoners, the midpoint between Bibi's 500 and Arafat's 1,000. When the President emerged from the private meeting, he said Bibi had agreed to 750; that he would go along with those with non-Israeli blood on their hands, meaning that around 340 of the security prisoners would be released and the remainder would be common criminals; that he would not insist that Jabali be included among those who had to be arrested. The President said that's the good news: the bad was that he would need to do Har Homa "tenders" and he would need to get the Egyptians to free Azzam Azzam.*

---

*Har Homa "tenders" meant the actual construction of the housing units would begin on the site now that the clearing of the land was completed. Azzam Azzam had been arrested by the Egyptians of spying for Israel. He was an Israeli Druze; Druze are an ethnic group, existing largely in Lebanon, Israel, and Syria, that religiously are an offshoot of Islam. In Israel, they are seen as loyal citizens, and, unlike most of the Israeli Arabs, serve in the IDF.

The President saw my facial reaction on Har Homa, and quickly added, "I did not agree to that, and we can still discuss it with him. I also did not promise I could get Mubarak to free Azzam Azzam, but I said I would call Mubarak to try to get it done."

The President then said, "I think I should see Arafat now and tell him what I have gotten from Bibi." We asked Arafat to come in, and the President briefed him exactly as he had briefed us. He discussed the prisoners, including the 750 total and the categories of security prisoners that could be included in that total; he told him about Jabali, and to my surprise he told him not only about Azzam Azzam but also about Har Homa. Arafat went back and briefed his team about what he had heard. Abu Ala came over to me afterward and said, "How can he insist on doing Har Homa?" And I replied, "Talk directly to Bibi about it."

Interestingly enough, my first instinct would have been to try to talk Bibi out of it. Declaring the intent to create this Jewish neighborhood in East Jerusalem, effectively cutting off Bethlehem from the Arab neighborhoods of Jerusalem, had created the stalemate that had now dragged on eighteen months. We were trying to break the stalemate and I would have said no to Bibi on Har Homa and not mentioned it to the Palestinians at this stage. But as I thought about what the President had done at least with regard to telling Arafat about Har Homa, it occurred to me that his instincts were right and mine were wrong. The President rightly understood the importance of effectively conditioning Arafat to what he had to expect. This way there would be no surprise later. In addition, he was giving Arafat an opportunity to make clear what he could and could not accept. Had Arafat exploded over Har Homa and said it would make a deal impossible, we could have relayed that to Bibi. Perhaps Bibi would have offered certain sweeteners to Arafat to make it palatable to him; or, alternatively, he might have identified something else that mattered for his domestic purposes and sought Arafat's acquiescence.

The President's instinct to tell Arafat more rather than less also helped to build Arafat's confidence in the President. He came to feel that nothing was being hidden from him. Again, that was the good news; the bad in this situation was that when Arafat was alone in these meetings he did not always pay close attention to details. This became a problem later regarding the prisoner issue. Har Homa was one thing, but the details on the prisoners became something very different.

However, at this stage we seemed to be very close to an overall deal. We still had the issue of the language for the third FRD committee to resolve. Before tackling it, however, Bibi wanted to sit with the President and see how the discussion with Arafat had gone. The President asked me to join him, and he and I met with Bibi. The President told him that Arafat seemed to accept the arrangement on prisoners. In addition, he told Bibi that Arafat said he would see if he could help with Mubarak on Azzam Azzam. Bibi was very struck by this, and said he would tell Arafat how much he would appreciate anything the Chairman might be able to do.

The President skirted the issue of Har Homa, avoiding comment on Arafat and asking me what I thought about the tenders. (This was a clever move on his part; he could stay above the fray and yet allow me to argue against it with Bibi—and he certainly knew I would.) I turned to Bibi, saying, "Prime Minister, this is what got us stuck in the first place, and I fear that you are once again greatly underestimating the impact of taking this step."

Bibi responded by saying that he would not initiate this, he wouldn't rush to do it, but he would have to do it: "Politically, I have no choice." The President nodded, and looked at me, seemingly waiting for my response. I repeated that I thought it was a big mistake, but then asked if he could wait until May. (I thought that would give us eight months of permanent status negotiations; either we would have made progress making this possible or Bibi would have to decide if he wanted to take such a step and possibly trigger a Palestinian declaration of statehood in response.*)

Bibi said he would delay as long as he could, but he suspected "my hand will be forced by Olmert."† He would do his "best to do it after the first redeployment," but that was the limit of what he could do. The President listened, effectively sending the message that he understood Bibi's political needs and wouldn't fight him on Har Homa if done this way.

The Prime Minister asked the President when he would call Mubarak about Azzam Azzam and the President said he would do it immediately. Bibi then asked me if I could get the Palestinians to accept the language we had discussed on the third phase committee. I told him I had tried and that Abu Ala was fighting it. I showed him what Nabil and Saeb would accept, and noted they were trying to help. But he could not accept their language so I suggested I bring Nabil with me to see Bibi to try to work the language together. Bibi agreed.

We broke for the President to call Mubarak who flatly rejected the appeal on Azzam Azzam. Arafat made his own call to Mubarak with the same result. Before resolving the third FRD committee language—something that required first my working with Nabil and Bibi, then Nabil and I trying to sell our language to Arafat and the Palestin-

---

*A unilateral Palestinian declaration of statehood was a big deal. Where would the borders be? Would other states recognize the Palestinian state in its claimed borders? Wouldn't Israel feel the need to respond by annexing certain territories it valued? We opposed any such unilateral steps, emphasizing that statehood could emerge only through negotiations.

†He was referring to Ehud Olmert, the Likud mayor of Jerusalem.

ian delegation, and finally going back to Bibi with Nabil with one last suggestion—we tried one last gambit with Mubarak to get Azzam Azzam. We tried a trade: Bibi determined that Israel was holding an Egyptian prisoner for spying and would be prepared to trade him for Azzam Azzam. While we thought this would have some promise because it would provide Mubarak with an explanation for the release, we were all disappointed when the President called Mubarak back and Mubarak declared that he had no interest in this prisoner and any such swap.

Bibi was disappointed, but felt that the President and Arafat had done what they could; indeed, Bibi took Arafat aside and thanked him for his effort with Mubarak. At this point, the only thing to be done was to finalize the text.

Martin was working with Jon and Saeb and Daniel Reisner to go through everything on both the text and the timeline for carrying out the responsibilities spelled out in the text. This took about two hours, until around 5:30 a.m., when Martin came back with the news that there remained a few sticking points on the text and timeline.

Martin explained that the problem areas were that the Israelis wanted three collection stages for arms confiscation and the arrests of the thirty to be clearly represented on the timeline. Conversely, the Palestinians did not want collection stages or the issue of the thirty mentioned explicitly on the timeline. We brought Bibi and Arafat and their key people back together into the President's side room.

Initially, things went badly. Bibi was pushing on the arrests of the thirty, insisting they be arrested on a one-third, one-third, one-third basis according to the timeline of two weeks, six weeks, and twelve weeks.

Dahlan responded by saying he might not arrest them all. Bibi asked, "Is this still an open question?" The President suddenly became alarmed, turned to me and said, "Dennis, he [Dahlan] is opening up the issue and everything will come apart." As the discussion had been unfolding the President had continued to look to me to intervene, but I had actually put my hand up toward him to indicate not yet. However, at this moment I did intervene, saying definitively: "No, Mohammad knows that the Chairman made a commitment on the thirty and he will act on it." Dahlan replied, "Okay, but I have to know which list I am supposed to act on, and the Israelis are always changing the lists." He then pulled out the list I had given him and said he would act on this list if I would sign it. I said I would and told Bibi that this was the list his people had given me, and with everyone watching and no objection from the Israelis, I proceeded to sign it.*

---

*After all the Israelis' insistence at the number thirty, and after I had made many requests to be given the names with the acts of terror each had committed, the list the Israelis finally provided had only twenty-eight, not thirty, names on it.

The issues of weapons confiscation, and "the thirty," and whether they would be explicitly in the text, and/or also on the timeline remained to be solved. The essence of the debate was not on the substance of whether the Palestinians would take these steps but whether they would be advertised in some fashion. As had been the case throughout Wye, the Palestinians wanted no exposure on these steps and the Israelis wanted maximum exposure, meaning explicitly in the text and on the timeline.

So now I stood up and said, "Look, there are effectively three issues." Turning to Bibi, I said, "You want the weapons confiscation in the text and the timeline; you want a reference to the arrest of the thirty and the timing of arrests in the text; and you also want the breakdown of the arrests one-third, one-third, one-third reflected in the timeline on weeks two, six, and twelve. The Chairman wants the opposite. I propose a Middle Eastern compromise where we divide these three questions down the middle and give each of you one and one-half."

As everyone looked at me quizzically, I went on and said: "Prime Minister, you get the weapons confiscation in the text and the timeline, that's one for you; Mr. Chairman, you get to keep the arrest of the thirty and the one-third, one-third, one-third timing on arrests outside the text and the timeline (in a side assurance of the work plan) so it is not public, that's one for you. We will say in the text that all arrests of suspects will be completed over the twelve-week period, giving each of you a half: Prime Minister, you get the reference to the time frame for arrests in the text; Mr. Chairman, you get only an indirect reference to the thirty that is tied to the whole implementation period. That's a fair deal. Agreed?"

I had made this up on the spur of the moment, but Arafat stood up and saluted me and said "agreed." Bibi said "okay." I did not know if everyone understood what I had done, but it sounded fair and we had a deal. Everyone started shaking hands and coming over and congratulating me. Dahlan, in what was a portent of things to come, was pleased, but offered a warning: "I will make these arrests, provided the Palestinian prisoners are real. Make sure all 750 prisoners are political; don't let them be criminals. This is what makes it possible to do all these arrests."

Everyone was euphoric, and no one, least of all me, wanted to negotiate further. But I knew that Dahlan was putting down a marker that I could not let go unanswered. So I said to him, "We will do our best on the prisoners, but they won't all be security or political prisoners." He again said they can't be criminals, and I repeated we would do our best but we won't produce the 750 without criminals. He didn't prolong the discussion because Arafat was getting ready to leave after shaking hands with the President and Bibi.

It was now about 6:30 a.m. We walked out into the all-purpose room and Bibi had gone over to the couch and was sitting by himself. The President went over to join him. I could see Bibi's whole visage change. Everyone on the U.S. and Israeli delegations was talking and laughing; it wasn't just euphoria that an agreement had been reached, it was relief that we had come through this ordeal and had succeeded.

But in this atmosphere of joy there was an incongruity and I could see it. The President and Bibi were sitting alone; no smiles, only stern looks. They were barely talking and Bibi looked positively stricken. At this moment, Jamie Rubin and Joe Lockhart—the State Department and White House press spokesmen—came over to me and asked if they could announce agreement. They were each stunned when I said "not yet." Why they asked in unison, "The Palestinians are putting it out, we think the Israelis are as well. You finished, right?"

I asked them not to do it yet; we weren't ready yet. Joe walked away. Jamie asked why are you hesitating, and I answered, "Jamie, I don't know, but something is wrong, look at Bibi and the President. Something is wrong."

The President left Bibi and walked over to me and asked me to go with him. We walked past Madeleine and Sandy and into the bathroom. He sat up on the counter, and told me Bibi wasn't going to sign the deal unless he released Pollard. He told him he couldn't do that and Bibi said he couldn't do the deal without it. He said he'd made concessions on the prisoners based on the assumption that he would have Pollard and on that basis could sell the prisoners, indeed, could sell the whole deal. He couldn't sell the agreement otherwise and he had been counting on Pollard and that's why he'd agreed to the things he'd agreed to.

The President then asked what he should do. I asked him, "Did you make a commitment to release Pollard? If you did, you have to release him." The President swore he had made no promises; he'd said he would see what he could do, but he had made no promises. I then said, If you did not make a promise to him, you should not give in to this. "This is Bibi's problem and it is not tenable. Is he going to forgo a deal that enhances Israel's security, breaks the stalemate on peace, and gives the process a major push so he can have Pollard? That is not sustainable in Israel. He can't do it, and you can't give in to this kind of bullshit."

The President listened but did not respond. So I continued and said, "Look, I know Bibi wants this and probably believes he needs this, but he can't forgo the deal over Pollard. This is a bluff and you have to call it."

The President nodded and said he would not release Pollard. When we left the bathroom, the President gathered Sandy and Madeleine and told them what was going on. They both were equally adamant about not giving in to this. The President returned across the room to talk to Bibi. Bibi still sat with a deep scowl on his face. He had spoken to Dani Naveh and Aviv Bushinsky. As the President sat down with him, Bibi's demeanor remained unchanged.

After about twenty minutes, the President came over to us and said Bibi hadn't budged, even though he had pushed him hard to conclude. The President had also told him that while he could not release Pollard now, he would institute a review of the Pollard case within the next two weeks. That was as much as he could do at this point.

Bibi had said he needed the release to be able to sell the deal. He would need to talk to his colleagues in the cabinet before making any final decisions. The President told us he believed that Bibi had a real problem; while he had not made Bibi any promises on releasing Pollard, Bibi had acted on the assumption he would be released and this had colored Bibi's concessions. So the President concluded that Bibi was really in a bind.

Sandy said, If so, it is a bind of his own making and it is not up to us to rescue him. Madeleine was furious at Bibi for what she saw as a simple case of blackmail. She knew George Tenet's position, and agreed that under no circumstances should we accommodate Bibi.

Bibi was still sulking on the couch, and Madeleine decided to walk over to him to urge him to do the deal and accept the President's offer of the review. He would not get anything more and he should not jeopardize an agreement that was so clearly in Israel's interest. When Bibi told her that he could not do the deal without Pollard, Madeleine warned, "You are making a fatal mistake."

Sharon, who had returned to River House prior to concluding the deal, now returned. As he walked in to see Bibi, he acknowledged that there was a real problem and that he would talk to the Prime Minister about it. He talked for a short while to Bibi and Bibi then decided to leave the Wye Center and return to River House. We walked down the boardwalk back to the main Wye Center building and the President's holding room where the President, Sandy, Madeleine, and I congregated. The President was adamant that he had never promised to release Pollard. Joe Lockhart came in and told us the Israelis were putting out that the deal was being held up over Pollard—and some were being quoted as saying the President had reneged on a promise to release him, while others were saying Pollard would be released imminently.

Lockhart said we had to say something. We agreed to keep our statement minimal, without addressing the Pollard issue. The President spoke to Bibi on the phone and Bibi told him he was going to take a nap and decide what to do after that. Madeleine spoke to Mordechai who said he would come by in about an hour to help fix the problem.

I chose to go to River House, hoping to see Bibi but willing to talk to his people if he really was asleep. I walked into River House and it became apparent to me that Bibi was meeting with Sharon, Mordechai, and others in the study. When the door was open, I could hear Bibi's voice. He clearly was not sleeping. Dani Naveh and then

Yitzik Molho came over to talk to me. I decided to make my pitch to each of them, knowing they would report to Bibi.

I said, it is clear to me there is a misunderstanding: the President is adamant that he made no promise to release Pollard; it is clear that Bibi believes he had such an assurance. We can't settle that, but let's be honest with ourselves about what you are going to face. Whatever the immediate political gains of holding out for Pollard now, where will Bibi be next week when it is clear he has sacrificed an agreement that served Israel's security interests; that he can now go only backward with the Palestinians; and that he will have destroyed his relationship with the President? How popular will his stand on Pollard be then?

Dani did not try to argue the case, saying simply that Pollard was a very important issue and he felt it personally, having visited Pollard in jail. He did not suggest there would not be a big price to pay if everything agreed was sacrificed for Pollard now. But he asked if we could put ourselves in Bibi's shoes: he had made difficult concessions and they had been based on the assumption of getting Pollard. Couldn't we give Bibi a commitment that Pollard would be released by a date certain? Impossible, I told him. Any chance in this regard, which I considered to be very slim in any case, was destroyed by all their leaks now on Pollard to the Israeli press. Nonetheless, the President had made clear that Pollard's case would be reviewed. That was something; they would not be able to get more at this point—and if it was not good enough, they would have no agreement, a very sour situation with us, and no review of Pollard.

Yitzik Molho joined us but said very little until Dani left. He said it was very complicated for Bibi now. I repeated that their leaks made any finessing now impossible. I then said, "Yitzik, the President won't budge now. Tell Bibi he will lose everything if this collapses over Pollard. You can evaluate the damage to him in Israel, but I can tell you he will kill himself here." Yitzik shrugged a sigh of despair, but I read him as understanding very well what was at stake and I knew he would talk to Bibi.

I returned to the Wye Center and walked into the President's room. He had spoken to the Vice President and to Rahm Emanuel, and while being uneasy, he understood he had to hold firm. What clearly helped with the politics on our side was Sandy's conversation with Speaker of the House Newt Gingrich. Gingrich was outraged that Pollard would even be discussed as part of the agreement. He made it clear he was absolutely opposed to Pollard's release.

Mordechai was about to arrive. He met initially with Madeleine, Martin, and me. He was anxious to find a way out. But his only suggestion was that Bibi and the President meet again. He said he would help to "fix everything," but Bibi needed to sit with the President once more. He met privately with the President for a few minutes and repeated the same points, and the President agreed to see Bibi. It was now about 1 p.m. and we needed to resolve things one way or the other. We were already running out of time if we were to have a White House signing ceremony. It was Friday, and with the onset of Shabbat, the ceremony would have to end before sundown.

Bibi arrived a little before 2 p.m. He saw the President alone and left. When the President came out to brief us, he was clearly relieved. Bibi would conclude the deal. He had thought about reducing the prisoners from 750 to 500, but felt that Arafat should not have to pay because of a problem between the two of us. According to the President, Bibi would, however, change the mix in the third tranche of prisoner releases so that there would be many more criminals and far fewer security prisoners released. And Bibi wanted us to inform Arafat of that.

The President asked whether that would be okay with Arafat. I said yes, provided we make it clear that we will work hard between now and then to try to ensure the original mix. The President had no problem with that. Sandy and the President said I should see Arafat to tell him this before we announced the deal and went to the White House for the ceremony. I was not inclined to go, fearing that if I went now with this kind of message Arafat would see it as part of the negotiation and might ask for something in return. I wanted to preempt that possibility. If we felt we needed to inform Arafat of this, I argued that it should be the Secretary who goes, emphasizing that Arafat will see the Secretary coming not to negotiate, merely to inform. There would, I concluded, clearly be less risk if the Secretary went. Madeleine agreed with this and I accompanied her.

Madeleine told Arafat what had occurred with Bibi. She told him in the end Bibi was willing to accept the deal without an assurance on Pollard, just the President's willingness to review the case. Bibi would change the mix in the third tranche of prisoner releases but we would work hard to get back to where we were. Was Arafat ready to go to the White House for the signing? He beamed and said yes.

In retrospect, I probably made a mistake. I should have pressed harder on what the President understood Bibi to mean by changing the mix on the third tranche of prisoner releases. As I was to find out later, that meant no release of prisoners with blood on their hands, period. Had I understood that—and I should have thought harder about it at the time—I would have understood that would get us back to fewer than 200 prisoners instead of nearly 350 with a broader opening over time to do more. Arafat, Abu Mazen, Abu Ala, and Saeb, who were sitting in the last meeting, needed to know that. But in our haste to close the deal after nine grueling days and a last sleepless night, we saw the finish line and did not desire any complications.

That was a very human response. But it clouded my thinking. I took as a given that we could work on Bibi in the context of implementation taking place, especially if the

Palestinians were fulfilling their obligations, and would fix the prisoner problem over time. That made sense. But I was not thinking about how Bibi might be changing the rules of the game on the prisoner issue and how that might create problems in the interim. Had I pressed the President, I might have heard that Bibi had rescinded his offer on releasing Palestinians with non-Israeli blood on their hands. The President did not say that, he said merely that the mix in the third tranche would be changed. Maybe Bibi was not so clear. Maybe he presented it to the President that way. But by not pressing, and not really asking myself what that meant in practical terms, I allowed the ambiguity to continue. In so doing, I violated one of my cardinal rules in negotiations: It is better to leave a meeting with ill feeling than to leave with a misunderstanding.

This, of course, was not just a meeting but also the "reclosing" of the deal, under the time pressure of an event that had to be held at the White House before sundown on this Friday afternoon. With the congressional elections approaching, the President needed to get out on the road, and there was a question about when the signing ceremony could take place if not on this Friday afternoon.

And we needed the event. We needed it not because the President deserved to have such an event and it would be helpful to him politically, but rather, because reaching such an agreement needs to be celebrated and recognized. Agreements like these will always be controversial; they will always engender opposition. Public support needs to be mobilized quickly. Momentum needs to be generated immediately. We needed the White House event to give the agreement the springboard it would require as it faced what I knew would be determined opposition from those who either fear progress or hate it.

As we were riding in the car back from Arafat's cabin on the way to the helicopter, Jamie Rubin congratulated me and saw hesitancy in my face. He asked what was wrong. I replied, "Bibi has already robbed us of the joy of reaching agreement." Little did I know how true this observation would become.

18

Bibi Surrenders to the Right
and Loses the Israeli Public

TO SAY I WAS exhausted after Wye would be an understatement. I had gotten no more than three hours' sleep any of the eight nights we had been there, and the last night I did not sleep at all. This, of course, had followed a period when I had also been doing without much sleep, so by the time I got home after the Friday afternoon White House ceremony, the adrenaline that had kept me going had shut off—and I was in a deep sleep by 8:30 p.m. When President Clinton called at about nine-thirty, to thank me for all I had done, Debbie had to wake me. While I typically could operate immediately when awakened in the middle of the night—something that happened all too often—I was in a daze as I talked to the President. As I told the Secretary the next day, I know the President asked me a few questions, and I hope they weren't policy-related, because I don't have a clue as to what I told him.

I was hoping for some rest, if for no other reason than to recuperate and regenerate. I was also hoping to derive some pleasure from the success of Wye—a success that was being internationally applauded and seemed quite real, with both Netanyahu and Arafat taking the high road in the White House ceremony, emphasizing the significance of the agreement and their hopes for the future. But I was to get neither rest nor enjoyment.*

---

*The White House Ceremony had been uplifting and moving. Bibi was magnanimous in his praise of the U.S. efforts, while also speaking of Israel's hopes for living in peace with its Palestinian

| THE RENEGOTIATING BEGINS |

On Saturday, Natan called after Shabbat ended in Israel to complain about stories in the Israeli press quoting unnamed American officials saying that Bibi had raised the issue of Pollard's release at the very last minute and tried to blackmail the President with the issue, and that this had deeply soured relations between the President and Bibi. I told Natan that President Clinton had been effusive in his praise of Bibi at the ceremony and that Madeleine and I had already explained on the record that Bibi had raised Pollard early during the Wye summit, not just at the last minute, and that the President understood and appreciated the difficult decision the Prime Minister had made. The off-the-record quotes were inevitable reactions to the claims of Bibi's people that Bill Clinton had reneged on a promise.

Natan asked if we could do more with Israeli journalists to beat back the story, and I told him "no problem." That was the easy part. At 2:30 p.m., the hard part began. Yitzik Molho called me to say he needed to discuss the assurances with me, because Bibi was facing real problems domestically and would need more from us to sell the agreement. Already—he was still in Washington—Bibi was signaling that he would not go on the offensive and sell the agreement, but rather would be on the defensive.

This was a strategic mistake which ultimately cost him his job. Bibi was in a very powerful position with the agreement. Initially, 80 percent of the Israeli public supported it. With Wye in hand, Bibi could move to the center and have the commanding position in Israeli politics; he could call for a national unity government to deal with the existential issues of the permanent status, and Ehud Barak, the leader of the Labor Party, could not have rejected this call. But he did not move to the center, he began to backtrack, fearing his right-wing base.

Bibi chose to see Wye as a problem, not as an asset. As usual, he looked to us to fix his problems. I told Yitzik I would, of course, discuss anything he wanted to raise, but there should be no illusions: we could not renegotiate the assurances on the third FRD, unilateral actions, the approach to permanent status, monitoring of the agreement, or anything else.

For now, Yitzik wanted to get our general letter of assurances about the agreement and the future so Bibi could present it to the cabinet on his return to Israel. He would

---

partners. Arafat, for perhaps the only time, reached out to the Israeli public, speaking of the Israeli need for security and reassuring Israeli mothers. President Clinton orchestrated the event with humor and eloquence, at one point joking that I had a head full of black hair when they began and it had turned gray. King Hussein made light of his appearance, joking that my hair might have turned gray, but his was all gone. Everyone left the ceremony believing we had turned a new page.

be most appreciative if I could bring that to the hotel, and we could discuss the other assurances when I came.

The general assurance letter was not a problem; in fact, it was done, just not yet signed by the Secretary. I went to the Secretary's house, she signed it, and I took it to Yitzik. But when Yitzik raised the other assurances, I saw major problems looming. On the third FRD language, he wanted a new introduction in which we would effectively endorse an Israeli 1 percent redeployment—something that had previously been raised and rejected by us. I rejected it again. I responded similarly to his request for us to be more explicit in singling out only Palestinian unilateral steps such as a declaration of statehood. In each case, our assurances left little to the imagination as written: we were making clear that we would not take a position on the third FRD; that Israel had the right to determine what it could do on it, and that the third FRD must not be allowed to distract from the necessity of negotiating permanent status now. On the permanent status issues, we stated explicitly the United States would only support negotiations, not unilateral actions, in resolving all the issues and we had singled out Palestinian statehood in this regard. I explained to Yitzik we would stick by what we had agreed, but would not go beyond it.

Yitzik, whom I always found to be honest, was very clear in telling me why he was seeking these additions: "BN is going to face a firestorm when he returns to Israel, and he must get some more help from you." I told him we would do what we could, but neither he nor his boss should assume there was much more we could do.

Sure enough, when Bibi returned to Israel he did face a great deal of criticism from the right. But, in my judgment, he played into their hands by acting defensive. Worse, he hesitated; rather than going immediately to the cabinet to get the agreement approved, he chose to wait. He had all the momentum when he returned to Israel, but by hesitating, he created an opening for the right and left alike to go after him.

The "right" did so for reasons of ideology and a sense of betrayal—after all, Bibi was giving away part of Eretz Yisrael—the land of Israel. The "left" did so simply because they hated Bibi and just could not bear to give him any credit, especially because he was wont to claim that he'd done "better than Labor would have done."

It was an unholy alliance, but one that Bibi could have preempted if he had acted decisively. Instead, Bibi was under siege within a week. The more he conveyed a sense of vulnerability, the more he was attacked, and the more he sought from us. Yitzik and Dani asked for us to make each assurance a separate letter so they could demonstrate six or seven separate assurances. However, by highlighting each of these assurances—rather than lumping them together—we would begin to strip away the cover the Palestinians felt they needed to take difficult steps, and indeed make them feel we (in cahoots with the Israelis) were now going beyond what was in the agreement.

To try to meet Yitzik's request for separate letters, I devised the following approach: our press spokesman would offer the assurances we had agreed in answer to questions on issues like the third FRD and unilateral actions, and our ambassador would then forward those statements to the PM's office with a note saying they represented U.S. policy and would remain U.S. policy. Bibi would have his separate assurances; the Palestinians would retain their cover.

It was the best we could do, and Yitzik accepted it. But every day brought a new request, or more accurately, an urgent plea. At the same time, if a Palestinian made an unhelpful statement, we were expected to respond immediately—or else it would be "a disaster for BN."

On November 5, nearly two weeks after Wye, with Bibi still not taking the agreement to the cabinet, Yitzik called to say that Bibi needed us to publicly state that "the thirty" would be arrested. I told him we could not; that would violate the understanding we had used to conclude the Wye agreement. He persisted and said Bibi was being attacked for having nothing explicit on the issue of these specific arrests—and he needed us to say something.

I told him the most we could say in answer to a question about the thirty was that we were confident that all those subject to Israeli requests on transfer would be dealt with in a timely fashion and in a way that would meet the legal obligations of the agreement. Yitzik told me he thought that would do it, and I breathed a sigh of relief.

I relaxed too soon. Yitzik called later on Sunday and told me that "BN" found that too vague. He needed us to be explicit. I told him we could not do that, and Yitzik asked me to "talk to BN." I called Bibi and told him that we could not be put in a position in which we violated the understanding that had been worked out on the thirty. He said no one "believes me" and he needed something less vague from us, and, in any case, the Palestinians were violating the understanding by not having a side assurance in the security work plan on this point. Here he was right, and I told him we would make sure the side assurance was done and inserted in the work plan. Bibi was blunt: This was not good enough and he would not take the agreement to the cabinet for a vote without something more specific from us.

This was ridiculous and I said so, but he did not back down. When I reported this conversation to Madeleine, she was livid, seeing Bibi as retreating from commitments and changing the rules whenever it suited his needs. She asked whether she should call him, and I said it couldn't hurt but she shouldn't expect much. To be fair to him, I added, "He has a real problem, he is not making it up, but unfortunately he helped to create it."

Madeleine called Bibi, and predictably got nowhere. Meanwhile, working with Mohammad Dahlan, I had reached agreement on what the side assurance for the work plan would say: all thirty would be arrested, one-third at a time, with a very small number of special cases to be discussed and resolved mutually, not unilaterally by the Palestinians.

In the meantime, however, the Israelis put out all thirty names in public in a government press release, and Natan (who had left Wye before we reached the compromise on the thirty) announced that the thirty were to be arrested one-third, one-third, one-third, according to the two-, six-, and twelve-week periods of the Wye agreement. This was correct, but violated the understanding that this would remain secret, embodied only in the secret minute.

Dahlan was furious and so was I. Dahlan made it clear that he would not agree to anything in writing because nothing would remain secret. When I spoke to Bibi, he claimed to know nothing about the press release or Natan's statement, arguing we could not hold this against him because he had not done it. (I asked sarcastically, "So you will be all right with our holding Arafat to that same standard?")

Recognizing there was a problem for Dahlan, however, he did back off his demand for the secret minute to be written into the work plan now, accepting instead a private assurance from us on the thirty. However, Bibi remained adamant that he could not take the agreement to the cabinet without us publicly saying all thirty would be arrested.

I saw only one way to fix this problem. Bibi wanted President Clinton to speak on Israeli TV to bolster the case for the agreement. We would have the President appear and answer a question on the thirty—saying that he was assured that action would be taken against all those in question in a way that was consistent with the requirements of the Interim Agreement and in a way that would satisfy the Israeli concerns. I told Bibi that was the best we could do, and it should meet his public needs because it came from the President. After initial hesitation, Bibi accepted this solution.

Once again, I thought this would be sufficient and Bibi would now take the agreement to the cabinet. But his vulnerability and needs knew no bounds. When his friend and supporter Natan Sharansky wanted assurance that we would regard the release of any of the thirty from jail as a violation of the agreement, Bibi called, telling me this was his last request. I reminded Bibi that he might not want to go down this road; if we started talking about violations, we would have to be very clear on what constituted Israeli violations—especially of the side understandings. Bibi was unmoved by my argument. He would deal with his problem of the moment, not a hypothetical problem he might face in time. I came up with a way for Jamie Rubin to answer a specific question the Israelis would plant at his daily briefing on the issue of arrests, saying unauthorized releases would constitute a violation of the agreement but we would not make it a practice to recite what was and was not a violation of Wye.* That was good enough for Bibi—since all he wanted was to hold up a U.S. transcript that seemed to confirm what he claimed before his cabinet.

Bibi's "last request" highlighted the basic problem: no one believed him. He needed us to say things or reinforce his arguments because he lacked credibility even with his own cabinet. Not surprisingly, the "last request" did not end the ordeal of getting cabinet acceptance. Barely three hours after Yitzik had called me saying that Jamie's answer had solved the problem, I got a call from Ariel Sharon, the Foreign Minister, complaining that Abu Ala had given an interview and in it he'd said there would be no vote at the PNC meeting. Since Abu Ala was a significant figure, unless he retracted his statement, the Israeli cabinet would not vote for the Wye agreement. Sharon asked me to convince Abu Ala to do so, since he understood Abu Ala would find it difficult to back down in the face of an Israeli demand.

I told Sharon he should call Abu Ala and quietly figure out a way to resolve the issue; "you are right not to make it a big public thing." Sharon was willing but thought I should talk to Abu Ala first. I did so, and it quickly became apparent that Abu Ala would not back off. For one thing, it was correct that Arafat had never agreed to a vote. And like Dahlan, he was livid at everything the Israelis had said publicly—making the point that they were destroying the Palestinian position on the street and in the Arab world.

I called Yitzik back and explained that there was no way Abu Ala would retract the statement. Dani Naveh got on the phone and said, If he can't, can you come out and say publicly there will be a vote?

No, I replied, our only chance of producing the vote depended on working quietly with the Palestinians. If we went public, there would be no vote—and the agreement did not require them to have one. This was yet another Israeli demand after the fact, which we were willing to help produce, but only if we could do so discreetly. While understanding my point, Dani said that without this the agreement was unlikely to pass in the cabinet. I told Dani we would all have to deal with that reality.

I called the Secretary back and said, "Enough is enough." I didn't believe they

---

*Whenever I asked Jamie to find a way to answer a query without calling undue attention to it, he did it with polish and finesse. Jamie was not only the State Department's spokesman. He was probably Madeleine's closest advisor. He would learn a lot about all issues to know not only what to say in public, but also what not to say. That gave him a strategic feel for the full array of challenges in foreign policy. He saw his role as giving Madeleine strategic advice on priorities and she understandably appreciated his good judgment and guidance.

would let everything fail on this basis, and it was time for us to draw the line. I would not call Yitzik or Dani back—they had heard our last word. A few hours later I heard from Ned Walker, our new ambassador to Israel, that Bibi was ready to fold and take the Wye agreement to the cabinet. I was relieved, but once again, I relaxed too soon.

At about 5 a.m. the following morning—noon in Israel, Richard Roth, the deputy chief of mission in our embassy, called to tell me that there had been a bombing in Jerusalem. It looked like two were dead and many wounded but none seriously. My heart sank. I could see everything being put on hold. Sure enough, Richard informed me that the cabinet meeting had been suspended and there were now new demands on the Palestinians.

Shortly before 6 a.m., Ned called to tell me that the two dead were the bombers. Miraculously, no Israelis had been killed. Then Bibi called to tell me he had saved the process by suspending the cabinet meeting. He would have lost the vote and that would have been the end of Wye. Then he said we should not press him to move quickly on getting cabinet approval, and under no circumstances indicate that we thought he was somehow trying to find a way to avoid ratifying Wye: "That would be a big mistake and tie my hands."

While I had expected that Bibi would be emboldened by the bombing, feeling that all the pressure was off, the phone call struck me as indicating that Bibi was feeling the opposite; he was feeling defensive. The timing of a 6 a.m. call suggested nervousness. Then his request that we should not suggest that he might be seizing excuses to avoid carrying out Wye was nothing short of bizarre; Bibi must have felt it might look this way, and he was afraid of our saying so.

Ironically, he emboldened me. I said I could understand his need for time after the bombing, but how did he expect us to push the Palestinians to take decisive action on security if it was an open question whether the cabinet would ever vote on the agreement? We could neither push the Palestinians in these circumstances nor defend his government. He said he would go ahead with the vote in the cabinet (though he would not say when), but, he said, after the bombing he needed some demonstrative and visible action on arrests by the Palestinians before going back to the cabinet. On this, I was in complete agreement, and said we would press Arafat accordingly.

In fact, the Palestinians were to take extensive action in response to this bombing, particularly in Bethlehem, where it was determined the two bombers had been part of a Hamas cell. But for once Bibi acted first. Three days after the bombing, Bibi declared his readiness to go to the cabinet if he could speak to President Clinton first. The President was, of course, willing to receive the call.

The unexpected gains for the Democrats in the midterm elections publicly vindicated the President and the conventional wisdom now in Washington was that the

Lewinsky scandal would produce a resolution of censure in the House of Representatives, but not a vote for impeachment. The public did not want it, and moderate Republicans would join with Democrats in the House of Representatives to oppose it and fashion a face-saving compromise—or so the thinking went.

The President's mind was not on his troubles but on building the peace process, in which, especially after Wye, he felt he was now playing a much more central role. The call to Bibi was arranged, and Sandy, Madeleine, Bruce, Rob, and I were all sitting around the speakerphone in the Oval Office with the President, to whom we had emphasized that there was nothing more we could give Bibi.

True to form, Bibi pressed the President with one last request. He needed to issue the tenders now for construction of the housing units in Har Homa. Once more Bibi was looking for a pretext to move ahead on Har Homa—first it was the decision to make it a Jewish neighborhood, then to start the bulldozers to clear the area, now to put out the bids to the contractors to build the housing. We all leaped up to get the President's attention, saying no, we had given Bibi enough, he did not need this too just to bring Wye to the cabinet.

But the President did not see it that way. In his mind, he had already acquiesced in this at Wye, and had informed Arafat of it at that time without it getting even a rise out of him. So his initial response to Bibi was in the form of a question: "Is this really necessary to get cabinet approval?"

Bibi's answer was predictable: "Yes." Madeleine and I were standing by the President's desk furiously scribbling notes to him to say we couldn't support this and it was a mistake. But the President was not prepared to press Bibi that way—and Bibi was audibly relieved.

Sensing that we might get something from Bibi—given his relief—I scribbled the President a note suggesting he press Bibi to release prisoners who would matter to Arafat, open the airport in Gaza, and maybe also safe passage—and "don't announce the Har Homa tenders as part of the cabinet decision." Bibi agreed to everything except the safe passage, and said he would begin taking these steps next week and inform Arafat immediately. When the call was completed, the President said, "We weren't going to stop him on Har Homa now, so I thought we should get what we could for it."*

---

*Yitzik Molho did speak to Arafat, explaining the PM would release prisoners and open the airport in the coming week but would also be announcing tenders for Har Homa soon. Arafat did not respond, largely because I expected he did not want to jeopardize the Israeli cabinet's approval in the beginning of Israeli implementation. Besides, as Yitzik was to explain to Arafat, putting out the tenders was itself a process, with actual building unlikely to begin for several months.

The President was right, and at long last, the way was cleared for the cabinet to go ahead. Once again, we were in for a few unpleasant surprises.

On Wednesday, November 11, the Secretary was in New York. It was a spectacular day in Washington, and my friend Alan Mintz had asked if I could join him for a round of golf at a course in Virginia, about an hour outside of Washington. Once I knew the Israeli cabinet was going to vote on Wye, I agreed to do so.

I knew I would receive a number of calls once the vote was taken, and sure enough the State Department's operations center did call me to report that the cabinet had just approved Wye by a vote of 8 in favor, 4 opposed, and 5 abstentions.

I was surprised by the vote. I knew Bibi had wanted not just to win the vote but to get an absolute majority in the cabinet. He had failed to do so. Har Homa tenders had seemingly made no difference. Moreover, the numbers signaled the abstentions of all the Likud ministers who had not been at Wye. I began to wonder how sustainable Bibi's coalition was if, after all this effort and his attempts to appease his right, he could still not get the support of his own Likud ministers.

As I was returning home, I learned that the vote was more complex than the numbers indicated. Even to get this vote, he had promised—at Sharon's insistence—that he would return to the cabinet before each phase was implemented to get their approval again. This made no sense. It effectively meant that the cabinet had approved the Wye agreement but there would be no Israeli implementation of it without another vote at each stage—before which they would go over every aspect of Palestinian performance with a fine-tooth comb.

At Wye we had talked with the Palestinians about my traveling to the region to help with implementation once the agreement had entered into force. I had envisioned going ten days after the signing, but the process in Israel had made that impossible; now it was time to go, but not only to put Wye into action. The United States would soon launch an intensive bombing campaign against Iraq, and Sandy and Madeleine wanted me to be in Israel to hold Bibi's hand.

| IRAQ INTERVENES |

The Iraqis had been blocking UNSCOM from doing its inspection work since August, and on October 31 declared they would not cooperate any further. Rather than launching a highly public buildup of forces, as we had done the previous January, with very public threats, we were quietly lining up support from Gulf states for intensive air strikes and working in the Security Council to remove the possibility of lifting sanctions as long as the Iraqis refused to permit inspections in Iraq. The Russians and French were put on notice that the only way to prevent military strikes against Saddam was for them to succeed in getting him to let UNSCOM resume its work unconditionally. As it happened, Saddam rejected all their compromise approaches. Thus, they felt no particular need to defend him or block us.

Suddenly we had a very different environment for striking militarily against Iraq—one that had ironically been enhanced by Wye; after all, now it appeared that progress was being made for the Palestinians. And that further altered the mood in the Arab world.

The only problem was that Bibi's focus on the prospect of an Iraqi strike on Israel either distracted him from implementing Wye or gave him a pretext for not doing so. At the same time, our strikes against Iraq would increase the Palestinian need to show the Arab world that they were, in fact, getting something out of the U.S.-brokered agreement.

With all these balls in play, I felt I had to give Bibi and Arafat as much notice as possible on the prospective air strikes. Here, I was limited by requirements of operational secrecy. The Iraqis clearly did not believe we were about to strike, and we had to be careful not to give them reason to believe otherwise. If we told Bibi, all Israel might be put on alert; if we told Arafat, we ran the risk that he might let Saddam know.

But Israel was our ally and we had an obligation to inform the PM, not least because we deemed there was a high probability that Iraq would hit Israel with missile attacks as it had done in the Gulf War in 1991. I arrived in Israel Friday afternoon, November 13. Just prior to my arrival, Bibi had received a letter from the President telling him he should assume that we could strike Iraq at any time. I had been instructed to tell Bibi when I first saw him that he should consider this his advance warning, and that I did not know when the strike would come. In truth, I did not know, but I was also told that after seeing Arafat on Saturday morning, I needed to see Bibi again Saturday afternoon. I took that to mean that the strikes would begin sometime Saturday evening.

I saw Bibi at his residence after sundown, after Shabbat had begun. We went to his study, leaving our ambassador Ned Walker and Yitzik Molho in the living room.* As we sat down, he smugly asked, "Are you here to babysit me, like Eagleburger did Shamir?"† When I replied "yes," he seemed startled, even taken aback. He immediately became more aggressive, saying, almost in a rote fashion, if "we are hit, we will hit back.

---

*Ned Walker had replaced Martin as Ambassador to Israel when Martin had become the Assistant Secretary for NEA.

†As part of the effort to show support and also restrain Israel from retaliating during the 1991 Gulf War, Deputy Secretary of State Eagleburger was sent to Israel.

We have to. If we get hit again with missiles and don't respond, we will lose our deterrent."

He paused, as if the cassette had hit the end of side one, and I responded by saying, "You will do what you have to do. I am not going to tell you what you must do for Israel's security. But I would ask you to consider the following. First, your deterrent doesn't suffer if it is not your conflict. Iraq would hit you because of us, not because of you. You are under our umbrella because we are hitting them, not because you are weak. Second, we can understand if you are hit with unconventional weapons that there would be no restraint on your side. But if you get hit with a conventional missile and it causes few, if any, casualties, why would you hit back then? You will gain nothing, but you might succeed in letting Saddam off the hook at a time when we have him isolated. Third, at a minimum, if you are hit, we would ask you at least to come to us before taking any action."

He listened and then chose his words carefully, saying that if they were hit and there were few, if any, casualties, they would not necessarily have to respond—though that was not a "commitment" not to respond. And they would come to us before doing anything. "Fair enough," I said.

He then asked me when would we strike. I told him I did not know and he scrutinized me, trying to determine if I really did not know or if I just would not tell him. He then told me he figured we would be hitting Saddam that night. Again, I told him I did not know, but I assumed the President would call him just before the strikes began.

Bibi then began to focus on which targets the U.S. should hit as the best way of getting Saddam, trying to think through with me those that would have the maximum effect on the Iraqi leader.

I told him we had in mind very intensive air strikes that, unlike in the Gulf War, would not go on for forty days before the ground war, but would last a few days and would involve targets that would weaken Saddam's ability to use weapons of mass destruction as well as the underpinnings of his regime.

At this point, he asked me whether we needed to cover anything else. I said I do want to get into Wye implementation. He spent a few minutes telling me that he was ready to implement Wye but would have to go back to the cabinet. He acknowledged that the Palestinians seemed to be acting on security, but he would have to show that the Palestinians had fulfilled each of their obligations. My sense was that he was now preoccupied with Iraq and not Wye. I told him I would see Arafat tomorrow and would come see him after that, and we called it a night.

From our consul general's residence in Jerusalem, I called Martin in Washington on the secure line, and reported the conversation, and Martin informed me the strike would be at 6 p.m. my time on Saturday. Having described Bibi's interest in the nature of the strike, I asked if I could bring Doc Foglesong—a three-star Air Force general who had been sent as liaison to the IDF—with me to brief Bibi on what we would be doing. Martin said he didn't see a problem, but would check.

I also asked about how far I could go with Arafat. Martin said no one wanted me to go very far with Arafat. I said I would simply tell him what was now in the news: namely, that our embassy dependents were being withdrawn in Israel and Kuwait and UNSCOM personnel were being pulled out of Iraq, and that none of this would be happening if we weren't at a very serious point. I would add that he could draw his own conclusions but in the absence of Saddam's backing down it was hard for me to see how strikes against Iraq could be avoided. Martin thought that was fine, but made clear that I was to tell no one else—not even our ambassador, who would accompany me and Doc to the meeting with Bibi.

This meant I could not tell my team—Aaron, Jon, Nick, or Gamal—which placed me in a difficult position. Everyone in Israel was worried about possible Iraqi missile strikes with chemical or biological weapons, and we would be at risk of such attacks if the United States struck at Iraq. Here I knew we actually were about to strike and I could not tell the people closest to me that we could be facing this risk—and I felt a responsibility for their safety. No one in this group would complain, but didn't they have a right to know? While I had to live with guilt in this regard, I chose to confide in Gamal alone for the reason that he would accompany me to see Arafat. I wanted my comments to Arafat to stay within the bounds of my instructions but not put me in a position where later Arafat could claim that I had lied to him. Gamal would be interpreting, and together we would strike the necessary balance. (Another one of my rules for negotiations: Never lie in a negotiation. You don't have to tell the whole truth, you can certainly manipulate, but you should never lie. It will come back to haunt you.)

I proceeded to tell Gamal about my instructions, what I planned to say to Arafat, and, finally, that the strike would be the next evening. Gamal knew all about the strike, its details and duration—indeed, here he knew more than I, since he had been with Secretary of Defense William Cohen in the Gulf interpreting for him as he told the Gulf leaders of our plans. But he did not know it was scheduled for the next evening, he thought it was planned for this evening, and had anguished over not being able to tell me!

He told me his big fear: that this would be the end of implementation. He saw Bibi seizing this as an excuse, saying he could not implement in these circumstances, and Arafat would have no choice but to stop implementing. I said, "Look, we are going ahead with the strikes, we just have to manage the best we can. The fact that the strikes will only be for a few days should make it easier. Think about it: if Bibi holds off, what will be his excuse after we have acted? And for our part we will be in a stronger position to insist that he must carry out his obligations."

Gamal said, "We'll see, Dennis, we'll see."

The next morning we went to see Arafat in Ramallah. He was clearly uneasy when I described the situation with Iraq. Almost plaintively, he hoped we could find a peaceful way out, but I got the sense that while he saw this as a big problem for him, it was secondary to his preoccupation with implementation of Wye—the exact opposite of Bibi.

Accordingly, I told him I would work with Saeb on the details of implementation on his side to ensure the Israelis had no pretext for not carrying out their obligations. He agreed, and we had lunch with the group—his colleagues and mine.

We left Ramallah a little later than planned, and I separated from my team and headed to the consul general's residence where I had asked Doc and Ned to meet me in the secure conference room—a sealed area where conversations could be conducted with defense against electronic eavesdropping.

It was 3:45 p.m. when I arrived and joined my colleagues in the conference room. We were to see Bibi at 4 p.m. and I now informed Ned of what I was instructed to tell Bibi. I asked Doc if he had heard anything that changed the plan to attack as of 6 p.m. He said no. I asked if he had heard anything suggesting he should or should not brief Bibi. He said no. I told him I had not heard back from Martin but Martin had assumed there was no problem with Doc doing such a briefing for Bibi. It was about 3:52 and time for us to go, but I said I was uneasy about having Doc brief without hearing explicitly that it was okay for him to do so. Doc was pretty relaxed; as far as he was concerned, this was my show, and if I thought it made sense for him to brief Bibi, fine, if not, that was fine too.

Ned, noting the time, asked if I really felt it was necessary to call Martin again. I said, "It's Shabbat, Bibi can wait a few minutes, and I would just feel better knowing this had actually been approved in Washington." I called Martin, and he was on the phone with Walt Slocombe, the Undersecretary of Defense. He came on the line and asked if I could hold, and I told him it was a problem because I was supposed to see Bibi in five minutes. He said just hold for a second, "let me finish with Walt, it bears on whether you should be saying anything to Bibi right now."

I looked at Doc and Ned and said, "What the hell?" The only reason I was calling was to see if having Doc brief was, in fact, okay. Now, when I should have been out the door and would have been had I not called, there seemed to be a question as to whether I could say anything to Bibi. Martin came back on the line and informed me that Kofi Annan had sent a letter to Saddam spelling out what was required of him to avert a crisis and he had now received a reply that Kofi felt was serious. As a result, while nothing had changed at this point, it might change—and the United States might not strike—and I should simply tell Bibi about my meeting with Arafat and not discuss Iraq. "It is a damn good thing I called," I told Martin. "I was about to go and tell Bibi when the strike would be."

Just as I pulled up to the Prime Minister's residence, Martin called and told me Kofi had gone public saying that the Iraqi response was serious and he would report that to the Security Council—though the view in Washington was that the Iraqi response was insufficient and we might still go ahead in twenty-four hours. I told him I had to go in and see Bibi, but he was kidding himself if he thought we would go ahead with the planned attack in the current circumstances.

I had hardly entered the PM's residence when Bibi jumped all over me. He had been told he would receive a call from the President in an hour. Is the President going to call me with the missiles in the air? Is that considered fair warning? I told him I did not know, and then I reported the news about Kofi Annan. Bibi's response was the same as mine: That means it won't happen now. He was clearly relieved that he would not imminently face Iraqi missiles hitting Israel. But he also lamented the loss of an opportunity to go after Saddam and bring him down. Indeed, he was already giving me advice for next time, declaring that the regime must be brought down and "you have to be bold."

I suggested we be bold about getting implementation done. He said he would go to the Knesset on Tuesday and back to the cabinet by Wednesday or Thursday so he could begin the first phase—pending, of course, the Palestinians have done everything required of them. I raised my concern that he was postponing what he had conveyed to Arafat about the timing of the airport and the prisoners. Bibi said he simply could not move more quickly.

That might well have been true, but here was Bibi holding the Palestinians to every single item on timing—no matter how small—while viewing his own obligations and promises as conveniences to be carried out when circumstances permitted. In other words, the timeline of Wye applied to Arafat, but not to him.

I closed our meeting by saying I would review all the Palestinian obligations with them but he was also going to have to deliver. He said he would on the basis he had described.

Later, back at the consul general's residence, Martin told me that, in the eyes of the White House, the Iraqi response was not, in fact, serious, and the plan was only "on hold" for one day. I asked him if he really believed that, and he said that was the general conviction. I said you are all talking to each other too much. There's no way we will go ahead now if Kofi Annan is saying this is a serious response. He said don't be so sure.

But I had no doubts. As it turned out, we would strike militarily, but not for another month—only after Saddam once again had broken his promises of cooperation
with the inspectors.

As I'd promised Arafat, I got in touch with Saeb to keep Palestinian implementation on track. We met alone on my balcony at the Hilton Hotel in downtown Jerusalem. "Saeb," I said, "we are here on the no-bullshit balcony, are you really serious?"
He said, "Dennis, we are. We know Bibi's government can't survive. It is being kept
afloat by the Labor Party. We would like to see Wye implemented before the government falls. Tell us what we need to do and we will find ways to do it."

I was pushing on an open door. He was totally determined to do what was necessary, and was asking for our help in identifying potential problems. This surprised me.
Obviously, Bibi was vulnerable, but I did not see his government on the brink of collapse. I asked Saeb why he thought this, and his response was that on every single issue
coming up in the Knesset, no matter how trivial, Bibi was losing the vote except when
Labor saved him. Labor was prepared to save Bibi on implementation, but would eventually have the votes to bring down his government, and Palestinians would shed no
tears over it: Bibi would never be able to negotiate seriously on permanent status and
he would always approach the Palestinians as an enemy, not a partner. But implementing Wye—an agreement he had done—would build a strong majority in Israel for
peace and this was in Palestinian interests. It was also necessary for the Palestinian
street to see that land would be turned back and that the process could work. The
Palestinian Authority needed this to compete with Hamas.

This was a remarkable discussion. I was sobered by Saeb's analysis of the prospects
for Bibi's government. I was heartened by the implications for implementation, provided we could get it through Bibi's cabinet. I told him we may need him to have a
quiet channel with the Israelis to sort out any problems. He said he preferred to handle all this through the United States to protect himself. I said we will take a look at
what he produced on the anti-incitement decree and the legal statement on confiscating illegal weapons—the two areas in which the Palestinians had to publicly state what
they would do immediately—but "don't you rule out seeing them quietly to resolve
any possible differences." Saeb agreed.

When I saw Dani Naveh, I suggested the same thing. His response was the same
as Saeb's: You do it. In fact, the private channel proved necessary. Saeb made a good-
faith effort in each area, but I knew his drafts would be too general for the Israelis. I

told Dani that what Saeb had done was reasonable and that if it was not good enough for the cabinet, he and Saeb needed to work this out discreetly. I decided to call both Netanyahu and Arafat to make the same point.

Just as I was about to call Bibi, he called me in a panic. Nearly shouting into the phone, he asked if I had heard what Arafat had said? I told him I had not. He told me Arafat had been speaking to a group of Fatah and had said Jerusalem was their capital and they would use arms to get their rights there. I told Bibi I had a hard time believing Arafat had said that. Bibi told me to check for myself, but he could not go forward unless this was corrected.

Molho called me shortly afterward and read me the exact quote. While not as direct or as alarming as Bibi described, it certainly left an impression that Arafat was calling for "the raising of arms" if anyone thought Palestinians could be denied their "rights to pray in Holy Jerusalem." Molho listed what Arafat would have to say in retraction in order for Bibi to relent: that there was no call for the use of arms, there was no place for threats, and all differences needed to be settled at the negotiating table.

Once again, however, Molho wanted my intervention. I told him he had a private channel; he should use it. I argued that my mediation on this was not beneficial to them; neither the Israelis nor the Palestinians needed to have it appear that Arafat had recanted only because of pressure from me.

Molho agreed, went to work, and ninety minutes later produced a statement acceptable to both sides. Meanwhile, I was set to see Arafat at his residence in Ramallah. When I arrived, Saeb greeted me and told me that Arafat had just appeared on Israel TV and recanted the statement. Because of that, other than making the point that he must not make statements that could so easily be interpreted as inciting violence, I chose to focus the meeting on the prisoner issue, reminding Arafat that not all those Bibi would release would be security prisoners and that we would continue to work the issue.* As it turned out, Arafat's recantation was not as direct or as clear as Saeb had indicated to me. Indeed, as I was returning from my meeting with Arafat, Molho called to explain why this was so, and I had to agree. I told Molho I would see Abu Ala shortly and ask him to make sure Arafat made the right statement in the morning. Abu Ala took care of it, and Bibi and Molho were satisfied.

One more obstacle to implementation had been removed. The last obstacles were removed when Dani and Saeb worked out understandings on the anti-incitement decree and the legal framework on weapons confiscation.

---

*My purpose was to condition Arafat on what was coming; recalling Dahlan's warning at Wye, I feared this issue could easily become a problem—a fear that turned out to be prophetic.

I was ready to return to the States. I left Aaron Miller behind to help Dani and Saeb as necessary. Neither Molho nor Bibi was comfortable with my going, but I told them they didn't need me there to get the implementation under way. And they did not. Aaron, who had been convinced that there would be a crisis and they would not be able to implement, was surprised at how smoothly everything went over the next three days: Saeb and Dani cooperated, acting to solve any problem that cropped up; senior officers of the IDF went and briefed Arafat on the exact locations of the initial 2 percent redeployment from Zone C and the additional 7.1 percent redeployment from Zone B; and when a last-minute problem cropped up with the IDF in response to settler complaints, changing the plans already briefed to Arafat, these problems were resolved by security officers from both sides working together. In fact, Aaron's reports were marked by great enthusiasm, noting that this was the way the process was supposed to work.

| THE PRISONER ISSUE ERUPTS AND BIBI'S CALCULUS CHANGES |

Unfortunately, the prisoner issue soon became explosive. Before leaving, I tried to create a channel in which the two sides could discuss who was important to the Palestinians to release and how far the Israelis could go in accommodating the Palestinian priorities. I brought Abu Mazen and Dahlan together with Avigdor Kahalani, the Israeli Minister of Internal Security. Before doing so, I spoke to each, arguing that the issue was not the 750 releases promised at Wye, but rather how to deal with the differing definitions of prisoners with "blood on their hands." Absent that, Israel would never release those who were important to the Palestinians.

The Palestinians saw the "blood on their hands" category as applying only to a limited number of prisoners who had committed truly heinous crimes. The Israelis saw it as applying to anyone who was even indirectly involved in an attack on an Israeli. There was no clear way to bridge this divide, and as a result I suggested to both sides that they review the list of prisoners name by name. I suspected, as I told Kahalani, that the Israelis had lumped prisoners of very different character, crime, and threat together under the "blood on their hands" rubric. Evaluate the prisoners one by one and let the Palestinians make a case for each one to be released. Not all prisoners were of equal concern— and a name-by-name approach might make the issue far more manageable. Abu Mazen, Dahlan, and Kahalani all agreed with this approach prior to their meeting together.

When they got together, however they focused more on numbers than on process. Both Abu Mazen and Kahalani were well intentioned but (as I subsequently discovered) talked past each other: Abu Mazen believed that Kahalani would increase the numbers of the security prisoners initially and Kahalani promised to try but felt he could be more responsive over time. Dahlan told me it was better to postpone Israeli releases than have a misunderstanding on the issue. But neither Bibi nor Arafat wanted such a postponement.

In retrospect, I should have tried harder to forge an understanding on who was to be released and when in each of the three phases of prisoner releases. Two factors complicated reaching an understanding. First, the Palestinians oversold the prisoner release issue. Seeing how popular this part of the Wye agreement was with the Palestinian public, Arafat claimed that all 750 prisoners to be released were security/political prisoners. This was patently untrue. Second, Arafat underestimated his ability to manage the issue. When I saw him on this trip and explained to him that we could not get Bibi to release 250 political prisoners in phase one, that the key was to break the back of the "blood on their hands" issue, and that we would continue to work the issue, he was agreeable. He wasn't looking to create problems, and, in fact, was pleased with the unfolding of the agreement.

In truth, Arafat was not looking to create problems, period. He saw implementation as a good thing, but he also had his eye on a larger prize. He understood that a presidential visit to Gaza was an extraordinary boon for the Palestinians, symbolizing their advance toward statehood. This was due at week 6 of the timeline, and he was not going to do anything that would jeopardize the President's visit.

While Arafat underestimated the potential explosiveness of the prisoner issue, Dahlan did not. He saw this as affecting his own base on the street. He feared that Hamas could seize the issue and weaken him. He preferred delay to a release that would open him up to criticism. But I took my cue from Arafat's response and did not heed Dahlan's warning signs.

For what was probably the first time, Bibi wasn't interested in delay. He wanted to show that he would be in compliance with Wye. But that did not mean he was open to altering the mix of prisoners, particularly after having received only very narrow cabinet support to go ahead with the first phase of implementation. (Bibi won the vote for implementing phase one with 7 for, 5 against, 3 abstentions, and 2 absent—with Natan Sharansky abstaining because of unease over the lack of a clear understanding on the prisoner issue.)

Unfortunately, when the Israelis released the 250 prisoners required in phase one, 100 were security or political prisoners and 150 were criminals; there was an uproar from the remaining security prisoners' families, who had looked forward to seeing their loved ones ever since the summit at Wye. Some went on hunger strikes. Others began to demonstrate. Fatah quickly took over these demonstrations, with Dahlan in Gaza and Rajoub in the West Bank leading the way to preempt the possibility that Hamas could make this issue their own. Soon there were daily demonstrations in the territories that involved rock-throwing at IDF outposts and retaliatory tear gas firings by the IDF. The mood was souring on both sides, with Arafat on the defensive and Bibi's cabinet seizing on the demonstrations as a violation of Wye.

| BIBI SUSPENDS IMPLEMENTATION OF WYE |

On December 2, an ugly incident occurred outside of Ramallah. A settler and a young Israeli soldier drove too close to an ongoing demonstration over the prisoner releases and their car was set upon by a number of the demonstrators. The car was stoned and the two beaten. Each escaped, although the soldier had his gun taken away. (Palestinian police subsequently returned the rifle to the Israelis.) All this took place in front of cameras and the footage played on Israeli TV and CNN. I had not seen any of this when Dani called me and described the incident and the Israeli inner cabinet's decision.

Bibi's inner cabinet, in response, declared that Israel was suspending further implementation of Wye until it was satisfied on a number of conditions. The most important of these conditions was that the Palestinian Authority must renounce its intention to declare statehood; it must agree to the prisoner releases according to the terms the Israelis had announced, meaning there would be none with "blood on their hands"; and the Palestinians must cease all demonstrations over the prisoner issue.

Certainly, part of the Israeli response was appropriate. But what did this ugly event outside of Ramallah have to do with statehood?

It was hard to escape the conclusion that Bibi—facing real difficulties with his cabinet, reflected in the narrow approval on the first phase of Wye implementation—was seizing on this incident to avoid further implementation. This was unfortunate, because the Palestinians were working diligently to carry out most of their commitments under Wye, particularly in the area of making arrests and fighting terror. Yet they clearly were instigating the demonstrations. Was that a technical violation of their Wye obligations? This was debatable. But there could be no debate on whether it was inconsistent with the spirit of the Wye agreement. It was. In the same way, Bibi's suspension violated the spirit of the agreement, and seemed to change the terms of the agreement to fit the needs of his government.

The President was due to go to Israel and to Gaza for the PNC meeting eleven days later, on December 13. Now the question was raised at least internally about whether the President should still go. When Sandy asked me, I told him we had no choice. It was the President's trip that was preserving the Palestinian stake in implementing at a time when Bibi had suspended Israel's implementation. It was the President's trip that was necessary to get the PNC meeting and the charter definitively revoked (something that would inevitably put the onus on Bibi to take steps on his end). Moreover, the President's trip had been part of the timeline; if we reneged on our obligation, both sides would have an excuse to avoid their obligations, and the Wye agreement would unravel.

My arguments were accepted, and I doubt the issue of canceling the trip was ever raised with the President. I also doubt that he would ever have considered canceling the trip or postponing it. But at the time, I realized there might be other considerations to delay the President's travel. Notwithstanding the conventional wisdom in November that a face-saver would be found to halt the impeachment process, the opposite was happening. In the first week of December, the moderate Republicans in the House of Representatives, rather than supporting a censure resolution as expected, suddenly began to come out in favor of impeachment.

In this environment, I went to the Middle East on December 7 to prepare for the President's trip. My main objective at this point was to try to get the Palestinians to stop demonstrations over the prisoner issue, which were producing daily violence. They gave Bibi a legitimate excuse to say the Palestinians were not living up to Wye, so how could he?

At Wye, Bibi had been very enthusiastic about the President's trip; he had envisioned exploiting it to show he was capable of producing a PNC meeting that no one in Israel thought possible, and claiming a great victory. But now it was producing the opposite. From right to left, everyone in Israel attacked him for doing what even Labor had never done: producing a statelike visit of the President of the United States to Gaza, lending enormous legitimacy to the movement for Palestinian statehood.

From the beginning, Arafat had seen the President's visit to Gaza as a giant step toward statehood and recognition. What was more, holding the PNC charter meeting with the President would symbolize that he was taking all necessary steps to meet his obligations under Wye. This turn of events made Bibi suddenly wish the meeting weren't taking place—for if the PNC effectively canceled the charter, Bibi would have to respond with steps of his own.*

With Bibi, then, I resolved to see if I could work something out on the prisoners as a way of defusing the issue that had soured the environment—and as a way of testing Bibi's willingness to implement the Wye agreement. He clearly read my mind. The first thing he said to me was, "I am glad you have come, it gives us a chance to save Wye." Bibi then proceeded to lay out an argument that was convincing. The Palestinians must stop taking their grievances to the street. He had carried out his commitments. They did not like the prisoner releases, but he had done what he was obligated

---

*What looked like such a winner for Bibi at Wye was producing a classic set of unintended consequences a month later.

to do. Unless they changed their behavior, Wye could not be implemented. His conditions for resumption of Wye implementation were designed to save Wye, not end it.

I felt he was correct about the need for the Palestinians to stop the daily demonstrations. But I told Bibi that his demand that the Palestinians rescind their intention ever to declare statehood had nothing to do with Wye and his insistence that they must publicly agree to his approach to the prisoner issue was an impossibility for them and he knew that. If he was serious about implementing Wye, our focus should be on defusing the prisoner issue in a low-key way and on making sure that the PNC did what it was obligated to do.

Bibi replied that little could be done on the prisoner issue. On the last day of Wye, he went on, he had told the President that since we would not release Pollard he was rescinding the offer to release Palestinians who had "Palestinian" blood on their hands—and he had asked the President to convey that to Arafat. Hearing this gave me a sinking feeling in my stomach; we had not told Arafat any such thing. We had simply said that the mix of the last tranche of prisoner releases would be different than had been discussed but we would work to get it back to the numbers the President had spoken about with Arafat. This is what the President had told us.

This was the first I had heard of Bibi rescinding his offer to differentiate between those who had Israeli and Palestinian blood on their hands. I did not feel I could reveal that, instead telling him there was apparently a misunderstanding, but that did not change our need to defuse the prisoner issue. My idea was to formalize the process I had always had in mind—Palestinians could go name by name through a list and justify to the Israelis why they thought a release was in order. In return for this process, they would put an end to the demonstrations.

I also told Bibi that I had looked closely at the prisoner issue and it was clear to me that many more prisoners could be released if there was this kind of a painstaking review. He was doubtful but open to my suggestion.

Going into the meeting, I had what I thought was an ace up my sleeve. I had seen the head of Shin Bet, Ami Ayalon, in the Bethesda Hyatt Hotel the night before coming to Israel. He felt more could and should be done on the prisoner issue, particularly considering what Dahlan and Rajoub were now doing to combat Hamas and Islamic Jihad. I asked him to get me the data on the actual numbers of prisoners who fell into different categories: who had killed Israelis; who had wounded Israelis; who had killed Palestinians; who had wounded Palestinians.

Bibi always emphasized in public that he would not release murderers. So I began to think about those being held who might have blood on their hands but had not, in fact, killed either Israelis or Palestinians. If the point was to find a way to release Palestinians whom Palestinians would see as being political prisoners—not common criminals—these prisoners might fit the bill. Ami estimated that the numbers would probably be several hundred—a number that would certainly help solve the Wye problem and give the Palestinians something to point to. This was, of course, a card I could not yet play.

When I saw Arafat, I outlined my suggestion for a case-by-case review and an end to the demonstrations, adding that the demonstrations that frequently escalated into violence put the President's trip in jeopardy, especially because the Secret Service might simply decide that the area was too dangerous for the President to visit. Arafat desperately needed the President to come, and he responded by saying he would do all he could to stop any violence and would also consider my suggestion on the prisoner issue. He asked me to follow up with Jibril Rajoub on the prisoners. I did, and over the course of several meetings Rajoub bought my approach on the case-by-case process, committed to stopping the demonstrations—which he succeeded in doing—and even agreed that certain prisoners with blood on their hands should not be released because of what they had done.

I was determined not to raise my more far-reaching idea on prisoners until the President's trip, believing this was a proposal I needed to spring on Bibi at a point when he might be looking for a way to show he was open to making progress (assuming he was). I doubted he would be as open with anyone but the President. If he was truly interested in making progress, his biggest payoff would come in doing something positive with the President. But this depended on whether Bibi was willing to do anything. Was he paralyzed now by fear of his right-wing base? Would he pay lip service to making progress, but only as a way to avoid being charged with responsibility for scuttling Wye? Did he now expect there to be elections and was he simply positioning himself for those, and if so, where did Wye and the President's visit fit into his calculus? Could the President alter Bibi's calculations, given the President's extraordinary popularity in Israel?

My doubts about Bibi grew when I informed him that Rajoub accepted my suggestion of a case-by-case review of the prisoners. His response: This was fine but there weren't really any prisoners who could be released. When I pointed out that this was a big retreat from his previous position, he replied that his people had done their own case-by-case review of the prisoners and that the numbers that could be released—using his criteria—were far smaller than he had given us at Wye. This contradicted what Ami Ayalon had told me. My conclusion: Bibi could make no move that looked like a concession to the Palestinians lest his government fall.

In light of this, the President had to focus on making the Palestinian side of his trip a success, forcing Bibi to respond if he wanted to avoid holding the right but losing the rest of the Israeli public.

Sandy and Madeleine felt I needed to come back to Washington to brief the President before the trip. So I left Israel at three in the afternoon on Thursday, December 10, arriving home at 2 a.m. Friday morning. I would depart with the President from Andrews on Air Force One the next morning at 6 a.m.

As I flew home, I believed the President's visit would produce one of two outcomes: either we would produce implementation of Wye or we would produce elections in Israel—meaning the end of this Israeli government. Bibi's government was in a state of paralysis. Even Foreign Minister Sharon had told me that things could not go on as they were: "Every issue can't be a crisis for the government." We could not let the peace process become paralyzed because of Bibi's incapacitation. So as I arrived back in Washington for twenty-seven hours, my purpose was to explain to President Clinton, Madeleine, and Sandy, the realities in Israel and the necessity for Arafat not to let the President down.

I had left Gamal and Aaron behind to continue to work the PNC issue. When I left, Saeb and Abu Mazen told me they would have at least 400 members of the PNC present at the PNC meeting on Gaza. They told me it would take a monumental effort to get to that number, but they would do so. I had told them the minimal number was 450—though I knew we could accept the 400 number. In addition, they were suddenly questioning whether there would actually be hands raised or just applause in response to the call for a reaffirmation of the Executive Committee decision on the charter. We had made the decision that a vote needed to be taken even if we had not publicly demanded this. Here again, I left no doubt that if they wanted a successful presidential visit, the raising of hands was an absolute must: anything less, and the President would suffer a great embarrassment. I said, "the Chairman could not do this to his guest." I felt the Palestinians would respond on both but would probably make us sweat until the last minute. Indeed, I assumed that the President would have to ask Arafat directly for the hands to be raised to ensure this actually would take place.

As it turned out, I did not brief the President on Friday; he was busy all day, trying hard to head off the building momentum in the House of Representatives for a favorable vote on articles of impeachment. Instead, I briefed him aboard Air Force One Saturday morning, stressing the value of the visit to the Palestinians and the strain it placed on Bibi's already precarious government.

I told him Bibi probably felt an election was now inevitable, and would want to use the President's trip to give him a boost with the political center of the country while also using it to avoid Wye implementation so as to minimize losses to his right-wing base. The best way to keep him from setting the agenda was for the President to be able to say the Palestinians were complying. I told the President, "Bibi knows how popular you are in Israel; he wants some of your popularity to rub off on him, and he must see he won't get any of it if he does not produce on implementation." My parting words were, "Don't let him set the agenda either in public or in private."

The President understood this and probably also knew it would be no easy task. Bibi was a master in public, and we did not have to wait long to see him try to shape the visit. His welcoming remarks at the airport were, in effect, the first salvo of his re-election campaign, not the welcome to Israel of its best—often only—friend in the world. He spoke less about the enduring friendship of our two peoples and more about how the Palestinians were not implementing Wye; he laid down a challenge to Arafat, not a welcome to President Clinton. As we listened to Bibi, I leaned over and said to Martin, "Well, at least there is no doubt about what he is going to try to do for the next two days." Our challenge was clear: Don't back down, but make damn sure to produce on the Palestinian side.

| THREE DAYS IN ISRAEL, THE PNC, AND THE SHADOW OF IMPEACHMENT |

As it happened, Bibi got to control the agenda far less than he would have liked. American and Israeli journalists alike were riveted on the prospect of Clinton's impeachment, especially now that most Republican moderates in the House had declared their support for one or two of the four articles of impeachment voted on by the Judiciary Committee. At their joint press conference on Sunday, December 13, the first full day of the visit, the press focused on how the specter of impeachment was affecting the President's trip: Could he really get anything done now? Bibi tried to put the best face on this, saying it did not figure in any discussions. And President Clinton said he would keep doing his job—and here in the Middle East that meant trying to ensure that the implementation of the Wye agreement unfolded as called for.

Clinton's troubles aside, it was hard for Bibi to compete with the President when it came to shaping the public message of peace. When the two spoke to several thousand Israeli youth, Bibi tried to focus on the difference between the Israeli and Palestinian approaches to peace, claiming that Palestinians felt comfortable coming into Israel, but Israelis feared going to Gaza. He received a very tepid response. Then the President focused on what united both sides—their common desire for peace, an end to violence, a different future, a hopeful future. One could see him striking an emotional chord, and the response was boisterous.

While I spent the day in Israel with the President, I had Aaron and Gamal working with the Palestinians in Gaza. They were facing rough sledding. Palestinians were trying to produce countless symbols of statehood and I had given instructions that we could not accept thousands of Palestinian flags at the airport or have the President speaking from a lectern bearing the insignia of the PLO. Moreover, we could not be in a position where Arafat gave a speech in front of the President that had objectionable statements in it—we had to know what he was going to say and it had to be acceptable. Finally, we had to know that at the PNC there would be a show of hands in answer to Arafat's call to have the members reaffirm his letter on the charter. In the end, I was prepared to concede some of the symbols, but not the language in the speech or the need for a very clear assurance on the raising of hands in the PNC meeting. I asked Aaron to convey that to Saeb, along with the message that we would react publicly and immediately to any embarrassment on either one of these issues.

Saeb told Aaron the President would (as I expected) have to talk to Arafat about the issue of raising hands, but he promised to show us the final version of Arafat's speech in the morning to ensure there would be no surprises or embarrassments. On this, Saeb was true to his word, and not only were there no embarrassments, but the discussion on peace with Israel and with the Israeli people was also responsive to what we had hoped to see. In addition, the speech explicitly called on those in the hall to affirm the Executive Committee and the Central Committee decisions endorsing the Chairman's letter to President Clinton on the charter.

This did not mean we were home free. After the ceremony officially opening the Gaza airport, the President and his delegation arrived to meet Arafat and his delegation in Arafat's office compound. This very crowded meeting was quickly transformed into a much smaller meeting, with the President, Madeleine, Sandy, and me on our side and the Chairman, Abu Mazen, Yasser Abed Rabbo, and Saeb on their side. As always, Gamal interpreted for both the President and the Chairman.

Arafat was in a buoyant mood. The President's visit was everything he had hoped for. Arafat began by telling the President that Palestinians would never forget this day and he could never forget what the President was doing for the Palestinians and for peace. Everything was fine until the President raised what was necessary for him to raise: namely, we needed a clear demonstration of the reaffirmation of his letter on the charter from the PNC. Arafat said that would be no problem; they would "applaud and maybe stand" to signal their positive response. While I shook my head very negatively and almost came out of my seat, Sandy and Madeleine looked at me nervously, and Saeb signaled to me that everything would be all right. Almost simultaneously, the President, who had been looking at Arafat and had his back to us, said, "That should be okay." In response, I blurted out, "No it won't."

The President, suddenly realizing that was not sufficient, said, "Dennis, what do we need?" And in stereo, Madeleine and I responded, "We need the hands to be raised." Saeb and Abu Mazen both quickly said it would be done, it was all worked out, and Saeb again signaled to me to cool it. Notwithstanding our discussion from the previous evening, this now indicated they had worked it out but did not want to discuss it further with Arafat. I quickly said, Okay, it will be done as needed, and we did not discuss it further in the group. But as we broke, I went up to Saeb and said, "The hands go up, right?!" And he said, "Don't worry." But I would worry until the hands went up.

As we were breaking for lunch, where the President was to make some remarks, Saeb brought in a few of the children whom I had met whose fathers were in Israeli jails. One, the same little girl I had met earlier in the year, began to cry for her daddy as she described to the President of the United States what it was like not to have her father at home. The moment was so powerful that Gamal lost his composure, leaving it to Saeb to translate what she was saying. The President was also moved, and later mentioned the encounter in his speech to the PNC.

The lunch turned out to be noteworthy for two reasons. First, in the middle of it I received an urgent message to call Natan Sharansky: he had seen a draft of what Arafat was going to say and nowhere in it was there any mention of peace with Israel. Natan said this would be a disaster, especially if we then said that the Palestinians had fulfilled their obligation on the charter. I told him I had gone over the final draft. There were very clear statements about peace with Israel in Arafat's speech, and that put his mind at ease.

When I returned to the luncheon, my mind was suddenly not at ease. As the President gave his remarks, he said words that I had changed in the earlier draft version of the speech: "The Palestinians now have the opportunity to determine their own destiny on their own land." I recalled changing that language to "The Palestinians now have the opportunity to shape their own future on their own land." My change reflected my judgment that the word "determine" went too close to the language of "self-determination," the code word for statehood. As it turned out, I had changed the language, but the new language got incorporated into the President's speech to the PNC, not into his luncheon remarks. For now, I was concerned that we had the President almost embracing self-determination without even having the PNC issue settled. What if the members of the PNC did not raise their hands? After the lunch, the President went to a villa to rest while the PNC assembled. I asked John Herbst, our consul general, and Aaron to go to the meeting site and grab each of the key Palestinians we knew and tell them they could not let the President down now. As we sat at the villa, Madeleine and Sandy asked me whether everything would be all right, and I answered that, to make sure, the President needed to tell Arafat before they went up on the stage that he had to have the hands raised; anything less, and he would damage the President. I said if the President says that, Arafat will know that means the end of the relationship.

Sandy said the President "is napping and I suggest you ride with him to the site and tell him what he must do." I did so. Whether he actually told Arafat, I do not know. But Arafat did exactly what we asked and produced a stunning response from the hall; as I sat watching nervously, he called for the PNC to reaffirm his letter and about three-quarters of the over 500 present raised their hands. With their hands still raised—just to leave no doubt—they rose as one, stood, leaving around a quarter of those in attendance sitting. Sitting on the side with Martin next to me and Aaron behind me, I turned toward them and said, "We did it."

The President followed Arafat with an extraordinary speech—one I believe only he was capable of delivering. He took his prepared text and wove a new theme into it, acting as much as preacher and teacher as world leader. He asked this, the most nationalist of all Palestinian bodies, to understand not only their needs and fears but also Israeli needs and fears. He spoke about suffering that had been mutual, not unilateral, noting in particular how the children of both sides were innocent and felt the pain of their fathers' death or imprisonment. He called on the Palestinians to truly commit themselves to peace, emphasizing that it was not acceptable to talk of peace and at the same time to have a media or an educational system or a religious leadership that continued to spawn hostility toward Israelis. He told this group that they had a responsibility to reach out to Israelis as people, even if they disagreed with the actions of an Israeli government.

I thought it was the best speech ever given on peace, particularly given its setting and circumstances, and the Palestinians in the hall were visibly moved. I saw the First Lady after the speech to tell her so, but was so moved myself I couldn't speak. She nodded and gave me a hug.

Bibi was, of course, already reacting. On the one hand, he quickly said the PNC obligation on the charter had been met. On the other, he said this just showed that if we stick to our guns and insist on performance, the Palestinians will do what is necessary—and there are many other steps that are necessary. We had been thinking of having a trilateral meeting with the President, Bibi, and Arafat after the PNC meeting, but Bibi did not want to commit to it until he saw the results from the PNC meeting—and even then he was clearly leery of having pressure put on him now to implement. As we left Gaza, Dani Naveh reached me to say that the Prime Minister had not yet made up his mind on such a meeting, and would be discussing it with his inner cabinet in the next hour.

When I reported this to the President, Madeleine, and Sandy, I also suggested we go back to Jerusalem and discuss whether it made sense to have such a meeting in the morning. That was agreed. This gave me a chance to see if we could actually get something done in the meeting.

At this point, I was dubious about having a meeting. Bibi would posture in it, and that would be the final image of the trip. Rob Malley and some of the White House staff felt that it should be held lest it look like the President failed to produce such a meeting. I understood this rationale, but felt the President had just produced an extraordinary moment of Palestinian affirmation of Israel's existence, hadn't he? Let that be the enduring image of the trip.

Madeleine and Sandy asked what the rationale was for the meeting. The only rationale that made sense to me was to elicit a move from Bibi in the aftermath of the PNC that we could use to reestablish talks between the two sides on implementing the Wye agreement. The move, I argued, had to be on prisoner release—with that we could press the Palestinians to establish committees on each issue of implementation.

Madeleine and Sandy agreed, and I set about testing Bibi's readiness to act. Deciding that now was the time to try out my idea on the release of those who had wounded but not killed Israelis, I called Defense Minister Mordechai and floated the idea. I said this would allow Bibi to say he was not releasing murderers. Could he persuade Bibi? He told me he would try, but Bibi was listening to Sharon, and according to Mordechai, Sharon was seeking to block any moves toward the Palestinians now.

Before I heard back from Mordechai, I heard from Yitzik Molho, who told me that Bibi did not want to have a meeting in which there was a substantive outcome; he would accept a meeting that focused on process—anything more would mean trouble with his right wing. I told him that we needed to do something on the prisoners; I had an idea, Mordechai liked it, and if it was possible to act on it, the process of implementation could be put back on track. Molho did not try to talk me out of this; instead he told me to give Bibi a call and suggest this to him.

I did so. Bibi agreed the President should not leave without having held a three-way meeting, but he bluntly said he couldn't do anything now on prisoners—his coalition simply could not handle it. I told him I did not know if it made sense to have a meeting under such circumstances. He argued that at the least it would allow the President to show he had brought the other two leaders together.

I described the situation to Sandy and Madeleine. Ironically, when I finished, Sandy and I said in unison, "We need a new government." My own instinct was now reinforced; there was no point in having the meeting. But Sandy had talked to the President and Clinton wanted to have the meeting, feeling that it still looked better to have Arafat and Bibi brought back together than not to have a meeting at all.

It had taken a long time to get together with Sandy and Madeleine because they had been on a lengthy secure conference call with Secretary Cohen and others about Iraq. While I had not been a part of the call, I had a pretty good idea of what was going on. Saddam was not living up to the promises he had made to Kofi Annan in November, and we were on the verge of launching military strikes.

This, of course, was not the only factor that might be influencing the President's desire to show his trip was producing on the peace process. The news on impeachment became progressively worse for the President each day. He needed to show he was doing his job, and if he could not bring Arafat and Bibi together, it would look like the Lewinsky scandal had limited his ability to conduct diplomacy. So the decision was made to have the three-way meeting.

The next morning, December 15, Madeleine, Sandy, and I joined the President on Marine One helicopter—which had been transported to the Middle East—to fly down to Gaza. The President said he had not been able to sleep—a sign, no doubt, of what he was going through. As I briefed him, he listened but uncharacteristically asked few questions and made few comments. I told him, "You should try to manage the meeting in a way that gets Bibi to commit, especially in light of the PNC show of hands, to working out the differences on implementation in a structured way." I thought Arafat might be open to this, particularly in the afterglow of the events of the previous day. But I told him we should also have no illusions: I doubted at this point that Bibi would be willing to do anything other than engage in process.

The real issue here, I went on, was finishing his trip on a positive note, recognizing he had accomplished what he had come to do—namely, produce the PNC's action on the charter. In all likelihood we were headed for either elections in Israel or a national unity government. Today's three-way meeting should be another device to get Bibi either to produce or to expose that he was incapable of doing so with the present government.

The meeting took place at the Israeli military facility at Erez on the border with Gaza, a place I knew only too well from all of our meetings during the Hebron negotiations. Each party had its own side room, and the Israelis had laid out fresh fruit and pastries and juices in each room. As planned, Arafat was the last to arrive, and immediately things did not go well.

When he and his colleagues walked into the main meeting room, they began to shake hands with Bibi and his colleagues—Sharon, Mordechai, Sharansky, Molho, and Naveh. Gamal, seeing Sharon, positioned himself between Sharon and Arafat, hoping to avert embarrassment much the way we had at Wye when Sharon made it clear he would not shake Arafat's hand. Unfortunately, Sharon decided to move past Gamal and toward Arafat. Arafat, seeing this, extended his hand, and Sharon left it out there, leaving Gamal to grasp Arafat's waiting hand. Everyone in the room saw this little drama, and it immediately soured the mood on the Palestinian side.

Bibi did little to set things right. He acknowledged that action had now been taken on the charter. But he immediately read a laundry list of Palestinian failings, including the alleged stockpiling of illegal weapons, including heavy weapons—prompting Arafat sarcastically to say, "You left out the nuclear weapons, why haven't you mentioned those?"

Now Saeb in turn began to recite all the Israeli wrongs. The President was quiet, and he was writing on his yellow pad of paper, "Focus on your job, focus on your job, focus on your job." Mordechai's whole demeanor indicated that he was completely disgusted. Finally, Mordechai and Sharansky intervened, with Mordechai saying let's address problems practically together, and Sharansky telling Arafat that he and the Israelis appreciated very much what he'd done at the PNC. But the meeting was going nowhere, and I gave the President a note suggesting that he propose that committees be set up to deal with each of the problems on implementation. He made the proposal and it was accepted. It provided an outcome to the meeting and got us through the visit, but not beyond.

The President was going off to Bethlehem with Arafat before returning to Ben-Gurion Airport to see Ehud Barak and then fly home. I was not joining him for the trip to Bethlehem, which was primarily a chance for the President to tour the city and its religious sites. As we left Erez, Mordechai asked to see me later in Tel Aviv. He and Molho wanted to move on the prisoners, but felt the only way to do so was for me to stay behind and work the issue. I asked what they meant by my working the issue, and they said go back and forth between the Palestinians and us. I told them I would do so only if I had something new I could tell the Palestinians about what Israel would do. It was fruitless for me to stay without that, and they ruefully acknowledged that they had nothing new to offer.

That did not mean I was free to return to Washington, however. U.S. air strikes would be launched against Iraq within thirty-six hours of the President's departure, and Sandy Berger wanted me to babysit Bibi. Having already had a dry run with Bibi the previous month, I saw little point in staying behind. If anything, I feared my presence might actually prompt Bibi to retaliate if Saddam Hussein struck Israel—to show, especially in the current political circumstances, that he would not allow anyone to determine what Israel must do for its security. I explained this to Madeleine, and she convinced Sandy that we should leave Bibi alone.*

---

*My additional reason for not wanting to stay was my certainty that if anything could be done on the prisoners by Mordechai, it would not happen if I remained. My presence would lead the two Yitziks back to me to try to work on Bibi. And I was convinced that would not work.

So I was to return to Washington after all. As I waited at the airport for the President and Ehud Barak to arrive, I read the digest of the Israeli press coverage of the previous day's events in Gaza. Rather than the political trophy that Bibi had originally envisioned, the President's visit and the PNC had been a disaster for him. Across the political spectrum, everyone agreed that Bibi had driven the United States and the Palestinians together, had advanced the cause of Palestinian statehood with an American emblem of support for the first time, and had gotten nothing of value in return. The right was, if anything, more hostile than the left. Clearly, Bibi's days as Prime Minister were numbered.

Barak said as much to me and Madeleine when he arrived, emphasizing that he knew I was concerned that fresh elections would put the peace process on hold for many months. In his view, it was better for peace to have elections and a new government. As the President arrived, Barak concluded with, "Don't worry, Dennis, we'll win and it will be good for peace." Though I did not say this to Barak, I hoped he turned out to be right.

| BIBI'S GOVERNMENT FALLS, NEW ELECTIONS, AND MANAGING THE INTERREGNUM |

The President's trip did not prevent impeachment at home, nor Bibi's fall in Israel. The difference was that the Republicans could only impeach in the House, not convict in the Senate.

Within two weeks of the President's trip, meanwhile, the left and the right in Israel came together and produced an overwhelming majority in the Knesset to bring the Netanyahu government down with elections for a new government set for May 17, five and a half months away. Bibi would represent Likud, and Ehud Barak, Labor.

We would have much preferred a far shorter election period; the thought that the peace process would simply be frozen for the six to seven months it would take to hold the Israeli elections, have a possible runoff, and then form a government, was a daunting one—and for the Palestinians, possibly a provocation. Would the Palestinians accept a situation in which they must continue to fulfill their obligations, knowing they would get nothing in return for such an extended period? Would they be willing to forgo the end of the five-year transition period called for in Oslo and not declare statehood on May 4, scarcely two weeks before the election? Could we count on the Palestinian Authority's ability to prevent terrorist bombings throughout this extended period leading to the elections? Did Arafat understand his stakes in preventing terror? What might Bibi do during this period? Would he provoke crises, trying to polarize the environment? How should we behave toward Bibi's caretaker government? We did not want to help him, but we did not want to look like we were intervening against him lest that produce a political backlash in Israel.

Over the coming months all of these questions would be answered. I would make one more trip to Israel in January to the Peres Peace Center's annual event—an event that gave me, an American dipomat, a justification to be in Israel during the election period. I would meet with Bibi, Arafat, and all the Palestinian security officials.

Two basic realities emerged during this visit—and subsequent meetings I would have in Europe with Chairman Arafat and his security officials Mohammad Dahlan and Jibril Rajoub in the months before the elections. First, Bibi wanted no trouble with us or with the Palestinians. Though, as he told me, he could respond to a Palestinian declaration of statehood on May 4 by annexing areas in the West Bank, that would, in his words, "create a real mess." Second, the Palestinians knew their stakes in the Israeli election and they would do what it took to stop terrorist acts.

The end of the interim period and the desire for statehood was more complicated. Arafat and his colleagues understood that a unilateral declaration of statehood thirteen days before Israelis went to the polls could undermine Barak and serve Bibi's interests. But they also did not want the Oslo five-year period to end without a consequence. As far as they were concerned, they were entitled to declare a state at that point whether it was convenient in Israel or not. They expected something from the international community that acknowledged the passing of the Oslo period and that indicated they were entitled to a state by a date certain—or at least that is what Arafat's colleagues argued.

Arafat himself was coy in these months, letting Nabil Sha'ath and Saeb make the argument for what the Palestinians needed in May to forgo a declaration. While they sought to lobby the Europeans to get at least a statement of the Palestinian right to declare a state or get recognition of statehood in the coming year, I worked with the Europeans to make sure they did not endorse a unilateral move on statehood. Negotiations, not unilateral acts, must remain the hallmark of peacemaking. In the end, while the Europeans would make a more forthcoming statement of support for Palestinian statehood than I might have liked, they did emphasize that it must come through negotiations.

For our part, we would engage Arafat during this period through meetings, two in Washington and one in Madrid, each designed to reinforce his stake in preserving calm and not making a declaration of statehood. While Arafat's colleagues sought to get us to break new ground on Palestinian rights to statehood, we would not do so. Instead, we issued a statement on April 26 that, while not referring to statehood, used the President's more forward-leaning language from Gaza about the Palestinians determining their destiny on their own land. Even here, however, we said they would only be able to realize this destiny through negotiations—not unilateral steps.

In retrospect, I am not sure we needed to be so worried about what the Palestinians would do on May 4. Arafat was not going to do anything that might jeopardize Barak's victory and Netanyahu's defeat. When I saw Dahlan discreetly in Rome one week before the election, I was struck by how carefully the Palestinians watched the Israeli elections. He had poll results that we did not have, all indicating a Barak victory. They were intricate, with far more penetrating questions and different measures that indicated much deeper dissatisfaction with Netanyahu than I had seen previously. Dahlan was clear: the Palestinians wanted an agreement with Israel, and that could come with Labor, not Likud; they would not let other Palestinians spoil this prospect.

On the Israeli election day, May 17, Abu Mazen was in Washington and staying at the Ritz-Carlton in Pentagon City, and we agreed to watch the returns together. When I arrived, he said, "Either we toast the outcome or we jump out the window together." Neither of us was prepared for Barak to win in a landslide. When less than 5 percent of the votes had been counted, Bibi conceded and announced he would give up leadership of his party. It was stunning. As Bibi was on the screen conceding his defeat, Abu Mazen, echoing what I had heard from Dahlan the previous week, said, "We can now make peace. These are our natural partners."

He asked me if I thought this was the end of Bibi, and I said, "In Israeli politics, never say never. Bibi has lost credibility and trust with the Israeli public, but if there is a catastrophe he can come back."

Both of us became reflective at this point. Neither of us disliked Bibi Netanyahu. Abu Mazen felt that Netanyahu wanted "to do the right thing, but will always be limited by his base." In this, he captured the essence of Bibi's dilemma. Netanyahu had great ambition, once telling me he would be like Ben-Gurion. When I corrected him, saying you mean Begin, he said, "No, Begin had it easy, I will make the hard decisions like Ben-Gurion." This was striking because Ben-Gurion, being willing to settle for a state of Israel without the biblical areas of the West Bank, was the scourge of the Revisionist movement in Israel of which Bibi's father was a leading intellectual. Yet that did not make Ben-Gurion an unacceptable model for Bibi. Ben-Gurion was the father of the state of Israel, and Bibi—and Barak subsequently—would relate their decisions to his.

One night when we were speaking alone in his office, Bibi confided to me his view that a leader can never afford to give up "his tribe"—those who are fiercely loyal to him, who identify with him because of shared roots, long-standing ties, and emotional connections. Bibi never figured out how to reconcile his ambition to be a historic peacemaker with the reality of his political tribe, which did not believe peace with the

Palestinians was possible, and they were certainly not prepared to pay the price that a test of peace might entail. That is why I often referred to Netanyahu as a leader who had two legs walking in different directions. That is why every move toward peace then required compensation of the base. He hoped he could lower Palestinian expectations. He hoped he could move very slowly and through attrition give up less than the Labor Party—demonstrating that he was superior to others because in the end he could manage peace but at a lower price.

While his vacillations might be maddening—and moves like Har Homa were driven by his perception of what he needed to preserve his base—he was, for the most part, neither reckless nor anxious to use force. He was very sensitive to avoiding explosions. He feared steps that could produce escalatory cycles that spun out of control. After the opening of the Hasmonean Tunnel, he did not react when fifteen members of the IDF were killed—though he easily could have done so to break Oslo and the Palestinian Authority. In the summer of 1996, when Asad moved special forces from Lebanon to the Golan, Bibi requested our intervention with Syria to ensure that Asad knew that Israel had no hostile intentions; in the spring of 1998, he quickly denied that Israel had any role in the death of one of the leading Hamas bomb-makers, Muhi al-Din al-Sharif, even though he was among the most wanted Hamas underground militants and the normal Israeli practice was to say nothing. Bibi did not want bombs going off in Israel in response.

Was it because Bibi feared confrontation or feared Hamas? I don't think so. But he clearly did fear the political consequences of violence that would be ongoing, and that would show he had produced neither peace with Israel's neighbors nor security in the everyday lives of Israelis.

In a sense his ambition was tempered by his politics and by his desire to be accepted as serious by the Israeli security establishment, which he held in reverent esteem. His reverence for the military and the security forces may have been driven by the memory of his older brother Yonatan—the hero of Entebbe. Bibi's own service in the Israeli elite commando force Sayeret Matkal no doubt reflected a desire to follow in Yoni's footsteps. As Prime Minister, he would not play politics with appointments in the military or the intelligence services lest he undermine those responsible for Israeli security.

Bibi had a well-developed belief system, clearly articulated in books and articles. But his ideology limited him less than his reading of his own situation from day to day. Had he been willing to forswear his right-wing base after the Wye agreement, he might have redefined the center in Israeli politics. He might have had an unassailable position politically.

But on the night of May 17, 1999, the Israeli public rejected his effort to fuse his ambition and his political base. No one in Israel—not the elite, not the public—

trusted Binyamin Netanyahu any longer. Instead, they voted for Ehud Barak, a Labor general who ran in the image of Yitzhak Rabin, proclaiming that he would fulfill Rabin's legacy on peace. Bibi was out, Barak was in, and overnight expectations in Israel, among the Palestinians, and within our administration were sky-high about the prospects for peace. We were back in business.

Great Expectations for Barak

BARAK'S ELECTION GAVE ME and everyone else a renewed sense of hope, but I worried about assumptions that the task would now be easy. It would not be, not only because the permanent status issues—the toughest, most existential—had to be faced but also because Ehud Barak was an unknown quantity as a negotiator and a peacemaker. He was very smart; he was a strategic thinker; he prided himself on living up to his word; he was methodical and cautious, a centrist, not a leftist; he did not play games or tricks; he did not fear peace but saw it as a strategic imperative; he would try to solve problems, not simply score points. He was, we believed, everything Bibi was not. However, we did not yet know his priorities or have a sense of his strategy or positions on the issues.

While I was eager to hold discreet in-depth discussions, the new Prime Minister insisted on having no direct contact with us during the period he was putting his government together in order to avoid even a hint that we were influencing his decisions on coalition-building. For the same reason, he refrained from having contact with Arafat. Through others we heard he might want to make the Syrian track a priority, since he had made a campaign promise to withdraw Israeli troops from Lebanon within a year. Similarly, we heard that he wanted to defer the implementation of Wye in favor of working more rapidly toward a permanent status agreement—a posture similar to the one Bibi had once advocated.

Neither of these views inspired confidence about Barak's possible first steps, but his initial moves after establishing his government restored our hopes for him. In his first speech to the Knesset as Prime Minister, he made clear that peace was his priority and that he saw his neighbors as partners, not competitors. In addition his visits to Mubarak, Arafat, and Abdullah before visiting Washington were all designed to rebuild relationships and trust with his neighbors first. But none of this told us what his priorities were.

This, he suggested through trusted friends like Itamar Rabinovich, would be revealed only in his first private meeting with President Clinton after formation of his government. He wanted no meetings below the presidential level—not with me, not the Secretary of State, not with the National Security Advisor—before his discussion with President Clinton.

No doubt he wanted to demonstrate very dramatically that it was a new day: business would be done differently—principally with the President—and his relationship with the President would be better than Bibi's. He would, I surmised, also seek to show that the special nature of the U.S.-Israeli relationship had been reestablished at a time when existential questions would be confronted—questions he believed could only be resolved by leaders.

The Secretary was uneasy, but Wendy Sherman—the department's counselor—and I convinced her that we should not push to alter the one-on-one format for the initial meetings. However, I did worry that without a note-taker, the two leaders might have very different impressions of what had been agreed, particularly because the President's agreeable style might be mistaken for agreement on specific issues. This concern eased somewhat when we were told prior to the meetings that Barak was interested in discussing broad approaches, not specific understandings.

In preparing for the meetings, I tried to focus the President and the Secretary on who Barak was: his attitude, his bearing, his supreme self-confidence, his belief that we had to break the mold in the peace process and move away from incrementalism and toward comprehensiveness. "Breaking the mold," I said, was good, and in a new setting we, too, had to stretch our thinking. But breaking the mold did not mean we could avoid practical steps for achieving peace. I expected Barak to lay out ambitious goals; I wanted to be sure the "how" of getting there was not neglected.

To connect the general to the particular, I wanted the President to offer Barak his own ideas on how best to initially proceed with the Palestinians and with the Syrians, and how to think about our role. With regard to the Palestinians, I again emphasized that Barak needed to establish a private channel to Arafat for solving problems and also open a separate back channel for quietly exploring permanent status issues. He would need to reverse Bibi's provocative steps on settlement activity. He should know that if he wanted to modify Wye he would not have our help; for that, he must persuade Arafat directly, and to do so would probably require some inducements. With regard to Syria, I felt he should understand that if he wanted to move quickly on resumption, he would need to reaffirm what Rabin had put in our pocket on full withdrawal from the Golan Heights.

Finally, concerning our role, it was important for Barak to understand that we did not want to be negotiating for the parties as we had during Bibi's time. This was their responsibility. But if Barak wanted to pursue comprehensive peace agreements, he would need to involve us, and would also need us to retain our independence from Israeli positions. We would stand by Israel, but to be most helpful to Israel we had to maintain our ability to influence Israel's negotiating partners; we had to be seen as fair and not simply as parroting or presenting Israeli positions.

Sandy, Madeleine, and I made all these points as we briefed the President. We also emphasized that if Barak wanted to talk about permanent status issues in detail, it was important that the President not make commitments that had not been thought through on the percentage of land to be turned back to the Palestinians on the West Bank; on not promising to sell Asad on something other than the Rabin pocket, at least at this stage; on not accepting any suggestion on Jerusalem at this time; and on any large financial package of assistance as part of a final deal.

As President, Clinton would make his own decisions, but Madeleine, Sandy, and I wanted him to be sensitive to certain areas where exercising caution now would preserve our options later.

| THE FIRST MEETINGS WITH BARAK |

Thursday, July 15, 1999, became the Clintons' day with the Baraks. After a three-hour private meeting betweeen the leaders in the Oval Office, the two couples would go to Camp David to have dinner and spend the night. The President and the PM would have hours upon hours of discussion together. No one knew how detailed our briefing by the President would be.

Following their initial meeting and just prior to leaving for Camp David, the President described their first discussion as a mix of good and bad news. The good news was that Barak wanted to reach a permanent status agreement with the Palestinians much sooner than anyone suspected, by April 2000, he said—but to do so he wanted to defer his obligations under the Wye agreement as long as he could because the final Wye redeployments raised security questions for a number of Israeli settlements at a time when no one had any idea what permanent status might look like. The President reported that he told Barak that Arafat would be reluctant to change Wye without something new from Barak, and that Barak understood this.

I asked the President what's the bad news? He said, "On Syria, Barak won't do the [Rabin] pocket. He says he cannot give up the waterline, and he won't mislead Asad." The President said they talked about Asad and Barak was very interested in the President's impressions. Clinton then described Asad as being very smart but very constricted. In turn, Barak said, "Asad wants everything, but won't do what is necessary to change everything."

Barak had also asked the President about longer-term threats, and when the President had spoken about the nexus of criminals, terrorists, and weapons of mass destruction, Barak used this to explain why he was in a hurry to do a permanent status deal. He feared that once Iran or Iraq had nuclear weapons, Israelis would go into a shell out of fear, and his capacity to make concessions to Israel's neighbors would disappear. Barak believed he did not have more than a year or two to transform the region—which suited the President, whose term had seventeen months remaining.

The President had to leave for Camp David. The next morning Madeleine and I were scheduled to have breakfast with Barak at her home in Georgetown; in preparation Madeleine called the President to hear what had transpired over dinner and afterward. The President was sleepy; he and Barak had spoken until about two in the morning, and he felt Barak was very serious about getting things done with the Palestinians.

Barak arrived at Madeleine's house as she was concluding her talk with the President. One central point came through very clearly over the Secretary's breakfast table: Barak wanted to keep the mainstream of Israel with him on peace. To do that, he needed to act from a position of strength in negotiating. With both the Palestinians and the Syrians, then, that meant that his initial moves must not appear to be preemptive concessions.

There was logic in his approach. But we also knew what the Palestinians and Syrians expected, and Barak's approach, rather than restoring hope in the peace process and a sense of renewal, could easily lead back into stalemate.

The challenge, we explained to Barak, was to find a way to do what he wanted without alienating the Palestinians and Syrians in the process. To keep the Palestinians on board, he had to show Arafat that he was serious about permanent status. To that end, I recommended that he set up a private negotiating channel with Arafat immediately. This would allow Arafat to see that Barak truly wanted to get down to business—and that his wish to stretch Wye was not a Bibi-style trick. Barak agreed.

On Syria, we said Asad will insist on a reaffirmation of the pocket in order to resume talks. Barak repeated he could not do that—if he did, it would look like he had conceded everything up front without having gotten anything for it. Contrary to what he had told the President, this implied that it was not so much the content of the pocket that was the problem for him as the timing of when to play it. For now, he asked us to work on a formula for resumption.

Yet, as our discussion continued, he made clear he had basic questions about the Rabin pocket, even implying that Rabin would never have wanted to go as far as the "pocket." At one point, he said that he doubted Rabin had done so. When I explained exactly what Rabin had said, he responded: "Well, I can't ask Rabin now—maybe in thirty years. . . ."

No doubt Barak had a hard time accepting that Rabin would have kept this from him. With that in mind, the next morning when again he implied that we had gone further than Rabin had authorized us to go, Martin explained to Barak that Rabin "was protecting you"—that he had made a point of telling us that only Itamar Rabinovich would know, and that he would not tell others (such as Barak) because he did not want to put them in a position where they might have to lie when questioned in the Knesset. While this seemed to persuade Barak, he remained unwilling to embrace the Rabin pocket, telling us now that Israel could not afford to jeopardize its control of the water of the Kinneret—the Sea of Galilee. When I pointed out that Rabin had qualified his commitment to ensure that Israel's water needs must be met—indeed, that the "pocket" could not put Syria in a position to jeopardize Israel's control of the Kinneret—Barak sought to change the subject.

Later, Bruce Riedel of the NSC, having been debriefed by President Clinton at Camp David, briefed Sandy, Madeleine, and me on the President's chief impressions from his evening's discussions with Barak. On Syria, the only new element was Barak's belief that Israel's early-warning needs that would result from its withdrawal from the Golan would be shaped more by monitoring arrangements than by where Syrian troops were deployed—a shift from the 1996 position. On the Palestinians, he wanted to double the length of the Wye redeployment process from twelve to twenty-four weeks and would look for some "sweeteners" to give Arafat in compensation. On permanent status, Barak saw no problem with statehood. As for Jerusalem and refugees, his position was that Jerusalem would have to remain undivided, but that there could be some cosmetic moves and the Muslims could govern the holy places. On refugees, there could not be a right of return to Israel, but once the Palestinians had their state, they would decide who would return to it, not Israel. In addition, there would have to be a compensation fund for the refugees who chose to live elsewhere.

If there was a surprise with Barak, it had less to do with the substance and more with the timing and the financial cost of peace in the region. He told the President we must work together to wrap everything up by the spring of 2000 and not to wait until near the end of the year and the President's term.* He believed there was an opportunity; he did not think it would last; he recognized a strategic imperative to seize it while Arafat and Asad were alive, and before Iraq or Iran acquired weapons of mass destruction and the capacity to deliver them, which he emphasized again would freeze peacemaking in Israel.

In addition, he felt the price tag for peace would be substantial. He said that Israel alone, given the steps it would take, would need $23 billion to meet security and resettlement needs. To this amount he added $10 billion in loan guarantees. He saw the Palestinians needing $5 billion; he said the Syrians would also need a substantial amount and he felt that it was actually in Israel's interest to see Syria reorient itself militarily toward the United States.

For us, the price tag seemed completely unrealistic and should have drawn at least some questioning from the President. It had not. Instead, the President told us that it was very possible to provide these monies—if peace was in the offing. He saw neither Gore nor George W. Bush (the President's guess as to who would win the Republican nomination) opposing peace if we produced it, and they could not oppose the funding it would require.

As a result of his discussions, the President was enthusiastic. His only disappointment was with Barak's approach to Syria. A Syria-Israeli deal was one Clinton could envision. It was not complicated. It was state-to-state, it would essentially be full withdrawal for full peace and security. But Barak's reluctance to embrace the Rabin pocket meant it would take some time to try to move Asad. And here, the President knew even a creative formula on the pocket was not going to work.

Following his initial meeting with Barak, I gave him a formula I thought addressed Barak's concern on the water but allowed us to reaffirm the pocket: "Prime Minister Barak stands by what Prime Minister Rabin deposited with President Clinton. But he will never mislead President Asad, and he wants President Asad to know that he has a serious concern about control of water. This concern will need to be taken into account as the parties work out and demarcate the border."

President Clinton liked it, believing it might work with Barak because it gave him the ability to say he had not agreed to any specific border with Asad, and that when he did, it would protect Israel's water needs. But Barak felt the formula went too far. He

---

*Barak told my wife, Debbie, when he greeted her at the formal state dinner at the White House on July 18 that, "I need your husband for a year. If you loan him to me for one year, then we can make peace."

was not ready to explicitly reaffirm the Rabin deposit. Was it because he was simply not prepared to go that far or was it because he felt it was a tactical mistake to be that forthcoming now?

Whatever the answer, Barak, after his last private meeting with the President, told me, "You have a feel for what Asad might accept; work with Dani [Yatom] and try to come up with something that we can both live with." As Barak and I were talking, the President came up to us and put his arm around me and said, "The Prime Minister wants you to try to come up with something; can you go ahead?" I said I would try. Dani Yatom had been Rabin's military assistant, the head of Mossad later, and now was Barak's Chief of Staff. He and I met at Blair House—and then again secretly in Europe—ostensibly to try to fashion a formula on Syria that Secretary Albright would convey to President Asad when she visited the Middle East. The plan had been for her to visit the region two weeks later, at the end of July, but as it turned out, Barak told the Secretary that he needed some time to work with the Palestinians on his proposed modification of Wye. So she agreed to postpone her visit until the middle of August.

Already Barak's eagerness to do a deal quickly was yielding to the practical requirements of diplomacy.

| FIRST MOVES: ARAFAT IS SUSPICIOUS |

Barak had told the President that he would see Arafat immediately on his return to Israel to get things rolling on his ideas on Wye. They agreed to see each other later that week on Saturday night. Unfortunately, King Hassan of Morocco died on Friday, and they postponed their meeting until after the funeral.

For our part, the President agreed that he should go to the King's funeral scheduled for Sunday. We left Saturday night hoping the funeral would give us a chance to talk to Arafat in advance of his meeting with Barak, and believing that Asad might come to the funeral, giving us a chance possibly even to have a Barak-Asad meeting. In death, we saw King Hassan continuing to play the role of a leader who would bring Israelis and key Arab parties together.

While Barak brought an impressive Israeli delegation, President Asad, ever the one to miss opportunities, decided on the day of the funeral not to attend. There were two theories as to why Asad chose at the last minute not to attend—either health reasons or fear he would have no excuse for not meeting Barak. President Clinton's reaction was, "No matter what the explanation, it isn't a good sign." Even so, the funeral allowed us to promote the new spirit of peace in the aftermath of the Barak election. Almost all Arab delegations at the funeral were eager to talk to the Israelis, and Barak met and spoke in front of Israeli TV to President Abdelaziz Bouteflika of Algeria—a remarkable development, given Algeria's traditional rejectionist posture toward Israel.

Although it had been a long and tiring day, particularly because the President had felt that as a sign of respect he should walk the entire three-mile length of the funeral procession in the searing heat, he met Arafat afterward.* If the President was tired, you would not have known it. He told Arafat that he had spent hours with Barak, and Barak was sincere; that the new PM would treat Arafat as a real partner, but that he had some concerns about Wye and some ideas that he felt could work to the benefit of both sides. The President said, "You don't have to accept Barak's ideas, but I would ask you to give him a fair hearing." He added, I know you endured a lot with Bibi and have needs now for your people. But give Barak a chance, he is very serious about wanting to work with you and reach agreement and he has already begun to think about how to solve the permanent status issues. The President concluded with two points. First, Barak has real credibility in Israel and internationally. If he says you are doing what is necessary on security, everyone will believe him. But Barak won't lie; if he thinks you are not doing what is necessary, he will say so and everyone will believe that. Don't put yourself in that position. Second, he, the President, would be there for Arafat throughout the process—probably the point Arafat most wanted to hear.

Arafat responded in kind: he would not let the President down on security and he would listen carefully to Barak's ideas and consider them.

We left Morocco drained but uplifted. On the flight back to Washington, the President came to the back of the plane and told me, "This was a good day." I was feeling especially good about the Arafat meeting. But I was assuming that Barak—given our discussions in Washington—would not just make his suggestions to Arafat but would combine them with some "sweeteners." This assumption turned out to be wrong. In his meeting with Arafat two days later, Barak offered no sweeteners in return for stretching the timetable for Wye, and worse from a Palestinian perspective, he did not want to say publicly in the joint statement they would release after the meeting that he would implement Wye. This raised Palestinian suspicions, and made them less receptive to Barak's desire to delay the Wye redeployments by three or four months.

The Secretary was mystified by Barak's behavior. Either Barak was convinced he could persuade Arafat through logic alone, or he feared that if he offered such "sweeteners" at this stage, Arafat would simply pocket them and demand more. Given Arafat's approach to negotiations, this latter fear was very legitimate. But there were ways to signal a move on such sweeteners without exposing himself to this problem: for

---

*While our entire delegation walked the length of the funeral procession, most of the Arab leaders, including Arafat, did not.

example, to ask Arafat what steps by Israel might help him to explain to his constituency a delay in the Wye timetable—rather than offering to make them.

I told the Secretary, "We have to recognize there is a learning curve here," and, unfortunately, given his supreme self-confidence, Barak would need to see for himself that his approach truly would not work.

Sure enough, Barak called the President and admitted that he had been unable to persuade Arafat—indeed that the level of suspicion on Arafat's side surprised him. The President gently reminded him that the Bibi legacy could not be wished away, and urged him to offer Arafat some sweeteners if he expected Arafat to agree to modify a signed agreement. Barak said, "We will do so."

Discussions between the Israeli and Palestinian negotiators began a week later, and after the second meeting an angry Saeb called me, dismissing the Israeli sweeteners as Bibi leftovers (e.g., shuttle buses between the West Bank and Gaza as opposed to genuine safe passage) and little more. I was worried that if Saeb did not hear something concrete that was of value to the Palestinians, he would soon advise Arafat to demand implementation of Wye as written. The United States, as brokers of the Wye agreement, could hardly oppose this.

How could we get Barak to offer real sweeteners now? Even a phone call from the President had not worked. So I hoped my secret meeting with Dani Yatom in Zurich—supposedly devoted to the Syrian track—was the place to push the Israelis and get the Palestinian track started again.

| A SECRET MEETING IN ZURICH |

Dani and I had arranged to meet at the Zurich Marriott on the morning of August 8; he would come with Zvi Stauber—Barak's assistant on national security policy—and Martin and Aaron were to accompany me. Rob Malley, who was vacationing near Geneva, joined us too. Dani and Zvi had been with Barak in Moscow and had not yet had a chance to sleep, so we agreed to meet at 5 p.m. after they had rested and work as long as necessary. In the meantime, Bruce Riedel informed us that Barak had called the President and informed him of a private channel to Asad. He was able to convey little about the content, and I knew that we would have to know about this channel and the messages being passed in it prior to the Secretary's trip.

But for now, I wanted to start our conversation on the Palestinian, not Syrian, track. I reasoned that we would have discussions that evening and again in the morning, and that Dani would speak to the Prime Minister between our two rounds. I wanted Barak to hear of our concern on the Palestinian track first.

When we began our meetings, Dani first went over Barak's discussions in Moscow. I thanked him for the briefing and moved us into our discussion on the Palestinians, stressing that "there is a fundamental problem: you are asking them to change an agreement that your predecessors signed, and in return for that you are offering them less than the agreement itself." I said, "If Arafat is to buy what you want in terms of three or four months' delay, you have to offer him Wye plus, not Wye minus."

Dani said, "Wye minus?" I said, "Yes, Wye minus,"and I explained, You have dropped the third FRD committee, which is part of the Wye agreement and a symbol of the Israeli commitment to withdrawal; you have not offered safe passage, which is also a part of both the Interim Agreement and Wye, but shuttle buses, which were previously offered and rejected by them. What is in it for them? How is Arafat to explain that he accepted less than he was entitled to according to the agreement and got nothing in return for this? If the tables were turned, how would you react?

Dani answered that Israel was only asking to delay the last part of the FRD, and asking the Palestinians to consider the benefit to both sides of working out a framework agreement on permanent status in this three-to-four month period of delay. Both sides would then know where everything was headed, and it would make it possible to improve the quality of the land the Palestinians would get. If a framework agreement did not prove possible in this time, the last FRDs would be implemented as required by Wye by February. Maybe, he said, we are being too ambitious in terms of thinking we can do a framework agreement in this time, but we are willing to try. "What do the Palestinians lose? If they don't like our suggestion, we will go and do Wye as written. There is no risk for them."

Martin responded that the Israeli press had quoted those close to the Prime Minister as threatening consequences to the Palestinians if they did not accept the Prime Minister's suggestions. This was hardly the way to get Arafat to respond, particularly when the intent seemed so different. Dani said they would work to correct this impression.

Aaron sent me a note asking whether we shouldn't get a clearer sense from Dani of what "sweeteners" the Israelis would offer, and when they might do so. I nodded, but approached this issue indirectly, saying, "The sooner you go with a package, the sooner you will know whether a deal is possible. Do you plan to offer a package soon?"

Dani answered that they were thinking about what could be offered to the Palestinians, principally focusing on the timing of the FRD, economic steps, and prisoner releases. They were looking at what was possible on the prisoners, but he was not certain there would be a very large number that could be released. I told him of my discussions with Ami and Mordechai the previous December in which it seemed as if it might be possible to release a few hundred, particularly if you drew a distinction between those who murdered and those who wounded Israelis or Palestinians. He agreed to check this.

Again, in different ways, Aaron, Martin, and I all tried to make clear that the Israelis had to offer Wye plus, not Wye minus, even suggesting opening safe passage sooner, or increasing the land to be turned over to the Palestinians by a token of 1 or 2 percent. Dani was noncommittal on all our suggestions.

We had made our point on the Palestinians. Dani had heard it, and clearly was not going to tell us any more. It was time to turn to Syria.

We probed how close we could come to talking about the Rabin deposit or full withdrawal but without reference to the June 4 lines, noting, in particular, Asad's fear that he not give up the deposit lest he never get it back. Given that, I explained that we were looking for leverage in our conversation with Asad. We wanted a formula that would allow us to tell Asad that what we were conveying should be sufficient to reassure him about his needs and the content of the deposit. If Asad held out for more in such circumstances, we could tell him that his position was not reasonable and that he was blocking the resumption of negotiations.

To have such leverage, we needed—because of the history—to be able to refer to the Rabin deposit or full withdrawal in some way. Dani made clear this was not possible for the Prime Minister.

Zvi said there were indications that Asad might be more anxious to move, and that we should see if he would accept something less than withdrawal to the June 4 lines. "Zvi," I replied, "if there are such indicators, I would love to know what they are." This drew no response, so I said, "We are not going to push you to do something you cannot do. It will be your call. But we owe you our best judgment of what is likely to work with Asad and what is not likely to work with Asad. Our judgment is that lesser, vague formulas that don't refer to the deposit stand no chance of working with Asad."

Dani, legitimately, asked, "What about our needs? We should know whether our needs are going to be met." That gave me an idea and I suggested the following formula, to be conveyed to Asad:

"Based on our discussions with Barak, it is clear to us that the differences with regard to meeting Syria's needs on territory are small, but that, in Barak's eyes, the differences on meeting Israel's needs are still significant."

Dani liked this. It gave Asad a reason to feel confident that his needs on the territory would be met, and was honest in that Israel was, in fact, uncertain whether its needs would be satisfied. But I added that I did not think this would work with Asad. The absence of even an indirect reference to June 4 ensured, in my view, that he would reject it. This did not deter either Dani or Zvi, who wanted to see if Barak would accept this formula. Clearly, Barak and his close colleagues believed that Asad was prepared to resume negotiations on a basis far more vague than we believed.

I told them they might be right, and in any case if this was the way they wanted to proceed with Asad, we would respect their wish. However, I told them I was concerned about where we were likely to be on both tracks at the time of the Secretary's visit; given their preferences on how to proceed, it now looked to me that, at the end of her trip, we would likely see a stalemate with both the Palestinians and the Syrians. If that were the case, there would be a big letdown, and all the hopes associated with the Prime Minister's election would dissipate in the region. Indeed, if there was a stalemate after the Secretary's visit, I was afraid that the impression in the region would be that Barak was, in fact, no different from Bibi.

In making this point to Dani, I was hoping to convince him that their approach on at least one of the tracks would have to change. Instead, it led him to suggest that the Secretary delay her trip another two weeks—until the end of August—so that the Israeli and Palestinian negotiators would have more time to see if a package understanding on delaying Wye could be worked out or if Wye would be implemented as written.

"Will anything really be different at the end of August?" I asked. The Secretary is not going to postpone a second time, particularly if there is no reason to believe anything will have changed. Dani assured me there would be a change. Will you have started implementing your obligations under Wye even if the Palestinians have decided they are not prepared to accept your delaying the FRDs? He nodded, then hesitated, feeling that he needed to check with the PM for a more formal answer.

Since it was midnight, we decided to break and reconvene in the morning. When we did, Dani began by saying he had spoken to the Prime Minister, who promised to implement Wye by the time of the Secretary's visit, even if the Palestinians had not accepted a new approach. But the PM definitely wanted the Secretary to postpone her trip until the end of the month.

Having spoken to the Secretary, I knew she was unhappy about postponing her trip a second time, so I told Dani, We will need two assurances from you. You must offer something tangible to the Palestinians between now and the end of August on prisoner releases or the FRD to show you are not simply trying to postpone your obligations on Wye. And you must also announce that you requested the Secretary to delay her visit a few weeks to give you and the Palestinians a chance to negotiate a new package on Wye and the approach to permanent status negotiations. Dani agreed.

| WORKING WITH THE ISRAELI AND PALESTINIAN NEGOTIATORS AND THE SHARM AGREEMENT |

The Zurich meetings prompted new developments on both tracks. Regarding the Syrians, we now learned of the private channel—involving an American citizen,

Ronald Lauder—and what had transpired in it.* As for the Palestinians, negotiations now began in earnest, and brought me into daily contact with Saeb Erekat and Gilad Sher. Sher was Barak's negotiator; like Yitzik Molho and Bibi, he was a lawyer with a long personal relationship with the Israeli Prime Minister. These two were designated by Arafat and Barak to put together a package of understandings, and initially both were enthusiastic—Gilad told me of Saeb's seriousness and Saeb told me it was clearly a new day with the Israelis. Before long, each was calling with complaints. Saeb sought to get the Israelis to do more of the further redeployments earlier in the timeline without any link to achieving a framework agreement on permanent status; he sought stronger commitments on safe passage and the seaport, and most important he wanted a large prisoner release and a continuing mechanism to ensure ongoing releases. Gilad wanted a clear reaffirmation of Palestinian commitments on security and an indication that the Palestinians would work seriously to produce a framework agreement on permanent status. The more they did so, the more Israel could accelerate some of the FRD phases and improve the quality of the land they were turning over to Palestinian control.

Several times during the last two weeks of August, I got plaintive calls from one or the other, suggesting their partner was making it difficult to proceed. From time to time, they would call jointly to brief me, and I enjoyed these calls—they would be cooperative and in good humor. Their negotiations were serious, but I could see a conceptual divide: the Palestinians wanted to see the Israelis deliver on their Wye commitments before addressing the permanent status issues; Barak wanted to see if he really had a partner—and Palestinian engagement on the permanent status issues was his measure of this.

Truth be told, however, Barak's real interest was on the Syrian track, and I, too, would shortly be preoccupied with it. Still, after the daily conversations with the negotiators—and Barak and Arafat—I became confident that Gilad and Saeb would reach agreement, especially because their bosses each had a stake in doing so. Barak wanted to show that he was managing the Palestinians; and Arafat wanted to show us that he was cooperating with the new Israeli Prime Minister, even while he gained concessions on prisoners and other interim issues in return for accepting a longer timetable for the Wye further redeployments.

Their efforts, with some fits and starts, culminated in the Sharm al-Sheikh agreement on September 3, 1999. At one point, Gilad called fearing the agreement was

---

*Chapter 20 covers the details of this private channel between the Israelis and the Syrians.

falling apart because Saeb was retreating from understandings already reached on the timing of the framework agreement and the number of prisoner releases. With the help of Abu Mazen and Osama al-Baz, we overcame the last-minute crises, and the Secretary's visit provided an opportunity for us to receive assurances that made the final deal possible.*

The Sharm agreement marked a new beginning for the Israelis and Palestinians. It put an end to the Netanyahu interregnum. It established the timetable for resuming permanent status negotiations, beginning September 13, 1999. It established September 13, 2000 as the end date for reaching agreement. It provided a milestone along the way of reaching a conceptual framework for permanent status—a framework agreement on the core issues of permanent status targeted for the end of January. And, of course, it resolved to implement on the basis of the Wye agreement, a specific new timeline including all the outstanding issues from the Interim Agreement. Specifically, between September and the end of January, the Wye FRDs were to be implemented in phases and 350 Palestinian prisoners were to be released by Israel.

With the Sharm agreement, Barak felt he had managed the Palestinians—putting his own stamp on the process—and now could return to his preoccupation: Syria.

---

*The Palestinians assured us that they would negotiate seriously to reach a framework agreement on permanent status (FAPS); and the Israelis promised us they would implement the last 6.1 percent B-to-A transfer of authority by January 31, regardless of whether a FAPS had been achieved.

⟨20⟩

"Syria's My Priority"

CANDIDATE EHUD BARAK HAD made a promise: he would get Israel out of Lebanon within one year. Barak knew that if he reached a peace agreement with Syria, Israel would—given Syrian control of Lebanon—be able to withdraw from Lebanon peacefully as well. However, without an agreement with Syria, there was the unmistakable risk that attacks from Lebanon would continue even after the withdrawal, especially because Syria always used Lebanon as a pressure point against Israel; it was safer than permitting attacks out of Syria, which would inevitably produce direct Israeli retaliation.

So Barak's commitment on Lebanon inevitably meant a Syria-first approach to peace. But that was not the only reason for his focus on Syria. Barak saw Syria (unlike the Palestinians) as a strategic threat to Israel's very existence. Sure, Palestinian violence made life difficult for Israelis, but Barak, like many Israelis at the time, did not believe the Palestinians could wage a war against them. Syria, however, could.

Barak was also far more attracted to dealing with Hafez al-Asad than to dealing with Yasir Arafat. In his eyes, Asad was everything Arafat wasn't. He commanded a real state, with a real army, with thousands of tanks and hundreds of missiles; he was a tough enemy, but one who kept his word and was respected and feared by other leaders in the region.

Finally, Barak, like Yitzhak Rabin, saw a peace agreement with Syria as the best hedge against the threats coming down the road from Iran and Iraq. Insulating Israel from these countries, building a common regional coalition against them, isolating them in the area, all depended on finding common cause with Syria.

Barak clearly knew that there would be no peace with Syria unless the Golan Heights was returned to Asad. His view of Asad convinced him that a deal was possible. As head of Israeli military intelligence he had followed Asad closely, and as head of the IDF he routinely sought my impression of Asad—seeking to absorb every morsel of information.

Barak's discussion with Patrick Seale, a British journalist and Asad's sympathetic biographer, reinforced his belief that he could reach an agreement with Asad. Shortly after the election, Seale (who had great access to Asad) told Barak that Asad was serious about doing a deal, but that it would take President Clinton's personal intervention, nothing less. As if to prove his credibility, Seale then helped orchestrate an unprecedented exchange of positive statements between Barak and Asad shortly after Barak's victory. He got Barak to refer to Asad's legacy as "a strong, independent, self-confident Syria . . . Syria is extremely important for stability in the Middle East." Then Seale prompted Asad to be, for the first time ever, publicly complimentary about an Israeli leader, calling Barak "a strong and sincere man." Even if indirect, this public exchange was extraordinary.

Barak's belief that a breakthrough with Asad might be possible with American intervention made him more eager to move toward us and actually more reluctant to move toward Asad lest Asad pocket any Israeli concessions in anticipation of a U.S.-brokered peace treaty. But even this tactical reserve couldn't explain his unwillingness to embrace the Rabin pocket. What did? From Blair House to our Zurich discussions, it became obvious to me that Barak and his colleagues had received a piece of information that convinced them Asad would be willing to live with something less than an Israeli commitment to withdraw to the June 4, 1967 lines. I was dubious and cautioned Dani and Zvi to take any such information with a grain of salt, but they seemed convinced.

Immediately after Zurich, I learned what—or, rather, who—had convinced them. It was Ronald Lauder, the American businessman and friend of Bibi Netanyahu. Bibi had used Lauder as a go-between to President Asad beginning in the summer of 1998, going to Damascus with messages from Netanyahu. When the Secretary asked me about this, I told her we had no problem with their coming up with something on their own—if they could.

Though Bibi was now out, Lauder was still in. Upon my return from Zurich, I learned that Barak had called President Clinton and told him he was talking to Lauder about his meetings with Asad and they appeared to be very interesting. In a second call, Barak went much further, declaring that Lauder had a paper consisting of ten points that Lauder claimed was largely agreed with Asad. If it was, Barak felt it would be possible to move quickly to agreement with Syria. Was Asad prepared to "validate" it? Only President Clinton would be able to find out, and so Barak believed it essential for Clinton to see Lauder and determine for himself if this was a promising track to pursue. If it was, it would have the added benefit of political cover, for it would enable Barak to say to the Israeli right that he was only agreeing to what had been accepted by Netanyahu.

THE LAUDER TEN POINTS: UNDOING A MISIMPRESSION

Sandy and Madeleine were cautious, and not prepared to accept Barak's suggestion that, "given the sensitivity," the President see Lauder alone. They wanted me to sit in on the meeting with the President and "tell us if this is for real or not." Lauder came alone and spent twenty minutes explaining the genesis of his channel to Asad. In the summer of 1998, he had met Walid al-Moualem in Washington and told him that Bibi was serious about trying to do a deal and wanted to open a secret, private channel to Asad. Walid had arranged for an initial meeting with Asad, and over the course of five weeks Lauder was able to go back and forth between the two leaders repeatedly. Over this period, he spent countless hours with Asad.

Asad had told him he believed that agreement was only possible through this kind of mechanism, and that he felt the past negotiations had been too complicated, with too much paper; instead, a simple document of a page or two should spell out the agreement on the key issues. Lauder said they had basically reached agreement on all issues—the border, security arrangements, peace, and Lebanon—and had boiled them down to ten points which they would have finalized except for Asad's insistence on reviewing maps on the border and the security arrangements and Bibi's refusal lest he lose all deniability. Then came Wye and the agreement with the Palestinians, Lauder explained, and Bibi did not have the political cover to pursue the effort further.

Lauder said he had a ten-point paper with him, but because he had assured Barak he would share it only with the President, he apologized for asking me to leave the Oval Office. Before stepping out, I posed a number of questions. First, where had Asad shown flexibility? Lauder said on the border, on security arrangements, and on an early-warning monitoring station. I pulled out a map and asked him to show me the flexibility on the border, and he pointed out that Asad was prepared to draw the border off the Sea of Galilee and off the Jordan River. Second, I asked what did "basically reached agreement" mean? His answer was that what he would show the President was 99 percent agreed. Did the 1 percent represent disagreement on any of the core issues—meaning the definition of the border, the concept of security arrangements (including early warning), the content of peace, and the timing for carrying everything out? Lauder believed there was no disagreement here. For him, the main open questions concerned clarification and application to maps more than to negotiation.

After Lauder departed, the President called me back into the Oval Office, and Sandy and Madeleine soon joined us. The President handed me the paper with ten points on it. It was entitled "Treaty of Peace Between Israel and Syria." There was a short preamble stating that Israel and Syria had decided to establish peace between them and that the peace would be based on the principles of security, equality, and respect for the sovereignty, territorial integrity, and political independence of both.

The "parties" agreed to ten provisions: (1) They would terminate the state of war between them upon signing the treaty; (2) Israel would withdraw from the "Syrian lands taken in 1967" to "a commonly agreed border based on the international line of 1923"; (3) The withdrawal would be in three stages but the period of time was left blank (in the margin, the President had written that the Syrian position was eighteen months for withdrawal and the Israeli position was thirty); (4) Simultaneously with the Israel-Syria deal, Lebanon would sign an agreement with Israel, and the Syrians would make every effort to ensure that no futher paramilitary or hostile activities would be launched against Israel from Lebanon; (5) This point was in brackets; it was language on security arrangements borrowed from the "aims and principles" nonpaper, and the President's notation said "language to be worked out"; (6) There would be three zones that limited the deployment of forces—a demilitarized zone, a zone of limited arms, and a zone free of offensive weapons (the President's note defined the location of each zone on the Syrian side of the border: the Golan would be demilitarized, the limited-armament zone would extend halfway to Damascus from the Golan, and the nonoffensive weapons zone would extend to the highway before Damascus); (7) The existing early-warning and monitoring stations could remain in the Golan Heights but be run by a multinational presence of American, French, and Syrian personnel (in brackets, there was a reference to an Israeli presence in the multinational monitoring center); (8) Full normalization of relations would be established, consistent with the laws of each country; (9) Water needs and rights would be addressed in accordance with international norms; (10) Syria would seek to make the peace with Israel comprehensive in the region.

Once I had looked this over, the President asked me what I thought. I told him it was "too good to be true." But now I understood why Barak and his colleagues believed they did not need to commit to the Rabin pocket and the June 4 lines.

Now Sandy and Madeleine joined us, and the President told them I was skeptical about the content of the paper. But did I think Lauder was lying? I said, "No, he is sincere and I believe he believes much of what he is saying. But I am afraid he is not precise and what he considers minor differences are not so minor. Moreover, I think there is some real wishful thinking here." Where did I have the greatest doubts? I knew that the 1923 line was a complete nonstarter with Asad; in Asad's eyes, those were the colonial borders, and he would never accept them in a document. I was also highly dubious that Asad would ever acknowledge, much less accept, an Israeli presence in the early-warning stations on the Golan Heights after Israeli withdrawal. But Lauder's description of Asad's not wanting a complicated document rang true, as did several of the ten points.

"We must check this with Asad somehow," the President said; he clearly thought there was something to Lauder's paper, and he was eager to proceed. But how? Should we have Lauder go see Asad? Both Sandy and Madeleine were uneasy about this, whereupon the President decided to call Asad. But, uncharacteristically, we were told Asad would not be able to take the call for several hours—leading me to conclude that he was ill.*

I suggested that Madeleine and I see Lauder in order to probe him on the areas in which I had grave doubts, and to tell him that we planned to send the document to Asad with the message that if he found it basically acceptable, the President believed it would be possible to move very rapidly to a final agreement between Syria and Israel. President Clinton liked this approach, and told us to go ahead.

Lauder came to Madeleine's office to meet us. I described what we planned to do; he agreed this made sense, and then I asked him what questions he thought Asad might pose about the paper. He said Asad would have a problem with the bracketed language on the Israeli presence in the early-warning station—and that was all. What about the 1923 lines, not the June 4, 1967 lines? To my surprise, he insisted that Asad had agreed to this—and when Asad received the paper, we would see it was not a problem.

Back at the White House, the President called Asad again. This time Asad took the call. Clinton told him of his meeting with Lauder and the ten-point paper. Did President Asad, in fact, agree on the ten points?

Asad's response tended to reinforce my doubts. "This was really a bit strange," he said. He acknowledged having seen Lauder a number of times, but professed to know nothing about ten points. He said the effort with him had not succeeded and it had ended. He did not want to embarrass anyone and preferred not to have Lauder come to Damascus—something Clinton now suggested. Instead, he asked the President to send him the paper Lauder had provided and he would respond to it.

After the call, the President asked me to get the paper ready with a cover note explaining the areas that Lauder said required clarification. Based on his conversation with Lauder and ours, he suggested we soften the wording on the monitoring center to

*We were receiving an increasing number of reports about Asad's deteriorating health and mental acuity.

exclude the reference to the Israeli presence. Sandy correctly objected, saying we could not have one version that Barak had seen and another one for Asad. Only if Barak accepted such a change should we make it—and when we checked with him, he wanted no changes in the paper: "This was the paper that Asad had supposedly accepted, and we should test his response." Barak was anxious to see how Asad would respond.

"How are you going to get this to Asad?" Clinton asked—and I told him that I would secure-fax the paper to our ambassador in Damascus with strict instructions that only he could receive it from the fax machine and he must seal it in an envelope and take it directly to the presidential palace and offer no comments on it. "Fine," the President replied. Two days later, Asad responded, calling the President to say that Syria had not accepted this paper, and would not now. The effort with Lauder had ended; Asad preferred to work from the Rabin commitment—the "pocket"—and have us make suggestions to the two sides.

What I had suspected all along was now clear to everyone: Barak's initial approach to the Syrians had been based on a faulty premise: that he did not have to reaffirm Rabin's "conditioned" commitment to withdraw to the June 4 lines.

The President called and told him so, but Barak was not entirely convinced. Maybe Asad was simply negotiating; maybe the paper with a few changes might still provide the basis for an agreement. Maybe what was needed was a direct secret channel with the Syrians that the United States could host. Barak would send a confidant of his, Asad should do likewise, and we should try to move quickly to develop an agreed framework. If Asad knew President Clinton would be personally and intensively engaged in this effort, he might respond.

The President, having had his hopes raised with Lauder, was encouraged by Barak's enthusiasm and agreed to try to persuade Asad to accept a secret channel. Before he called Damascus, though, I told him that Asad as a rule resisted the idea of secret diplomacy with the Israelis because it was the way everyone else had done business—Sadat, King Hussein, even the Palestinians. Asad had to show that he did business his own way. (The Lauder channel had been secret but not direct.) To get Asad to work in a secret channel, the key was to make it clear this was a trilateral, not a bilateral, channel. That would allow Asad to show he was different, not pursuing secret diplomacy with the Israelis but working with the American cosponsor on his terms.

To sell the secret channel, the President decided to embellish what we had in mind. He told Asad he had been talking with Barak and Barak was anxious to move quickly to an agreement. He, the President, thought that this was certainly possible, but it could not be business as usual. We would need to accelerate the process by having a secret trilateral meeting of negotiators who would have an open line to the leaders—Asad, Barak, and the President—to ensure that impediments could be overcome.

Asad was interested, but wanted to know whom Barak would send to the meeting. Uri Saguy was the answer, and I knew that would please Asad. Saguy, a retired general and a former head of Israeli military intelligence, had publicly acknowledged that Asad was prepared for peace with Israel if Israel would withdraw from the Golan Heights, and was a well-known supporter of doing such a deal. He was also the link between Barak and Patrick Seale, Asad's biographer.

Sure enough, Asad was enthusiastic about Saguy, who he said had a good reputation with the Syrian side. He said he would send Riad Daoudi—the Syrian lawyer who had been at the Israeli-Syrian 1996 talks at Wye.

Whom would we send? Asad asked. The President told him he would send me. Asad said, "Mr. Ross has not always been positive with us." The President's response: Dennis can go secretly; I cannot send the Secretary of State and he knows the details and history in a way that no one else does. To which Asad replied, "That's true, but we hope he will be a little more positive."

Later, the President asked me, "What was that about?" I told the President there were probably several reasons for the comment. First, I had come to represent the peace process in the region only during Bibi's time, during which we had focused almost exclusively on the Palestinian track. I had not been to Damascus since 1996, and Asad doubtless felt ignored. Second, I had been tough on him on terror in our last meeting, which took place shortly after the explosion of TWA flight 800, telling him that if the explosion turned out to be an act of terror and any of the rejectionist groups based in Syria proved to be involved, we would hold him accountable. Third, Asad was trying to put the President and me on the defensive so we would be more responsive to him.

Now I had to figure out where to hold the secret meeting. I brought Pat Kennedy, the Assistant Secretary for Administration, into my confidence, and asked him to find the perfect place for a discreet meeting for three people that might last several days and would support our every need so we would not have to venture out from our compound. Pat had orchestrated the logistics for the Dayton conference and the Wye River summit and was a wizard at such things. He decided on Switzerland, where we were between ambassadors, and the ambassador's residence in Bern was vacant but fully staffed. So I set out for Switzerland, hoping that this secret channel would prove more productive than the one Bibi and Ronald Lauder had left behind.

| THREE DAYS IN BERN |

I was met in Zurich by Carey Cavanaugh, our deputy chief of mission, who had been brokering efforts to settle the conflict between Armenia and Azerbaijan—a conflict with some similarities to the Israeli-Palestinian conflict. I had brought only Nick

Rasmussen from my office with me. I did not tell Aaron, Gamal, or even Henrietta—my executive assistant—about the trip. Other than Nick and the Secretary, no one in the State Department was aware of it.

We reached Bern by car at midday on August 26, 1999. The site was perfect: no one was around, the weather was beautiful, and the residence allowed us to meet either in the house or outside on the grounds. That afternoon I worked on my balcony in glorious weather with a pristine blue sky and majestic mountains providing my vista—not exactly a hardship assignment.

I approached the meeting with great anticipation; it was a first, and I wanted to take maximum advantage of it, knowing that Asad might retreat if we did not produce enough. That had been his previous pattern: Make a move on procedure, and expect big returns on substance. And this time why shouldn't he, I thought, given that we had raised the stakes simply by arranging such a meeting?

With that in mind, I began to consider what he might expect to get. Though he had rejected the Lauder paper, I suspected there were parts of it he would accept. In light of that, I thought I would take the four topics he had always accepted—withdrawal, peace, security, and the timetable—and see if it was possible to subsume many of the Lauder points under them. If it was possible, we could build the structure of an agreement and incorporate into it a core set of understandings.

When Uri arrived, I described what I had in mind. He was generally agreeable, but concerned about stretching beyond Barak's limits at this stage. "Let's not push too quickly," he urged me.

I was not trying to push too quickly, but I told Uri he needed to think about how Asad would approach the meeting and what he would expect from it. Uri understood that but said that Barak had not given him an unlimited mandate. Well, I asked, what did Barak want him to do? Uri replied, To have open-ended discussions in which Barak's seriousness about reaching an agreement could be emphasized, Israeli needs would be outlined, and of course Syrian needs would be discussed.

All understandable, I said, "but Uri, you have to think about what Asad will expect from this meeting, and make Barak understand that." Uri nodded, and told me not to worry; but he also warned that Barak faced real political constraints. Now I began to worry because this sounded like Bibi all over again, only this Prime Minister was pushing to raise expectations he would then fail to meet.

"Don't get me wrong," I said. "I am not interested in pushing you beyond where you can go. But Barak has to understand that he raises expectations when he pushes for these kinds of meetings with this kind of urgency. Asad has a favorable image of you, but he will be looking for some concrete advances from this meeting, and they all start with June 4, 1967."

Uri promised to show an understanding of Asad's needs but said he had to approach the meeting a certain way. He must explain who Barak was, what he was generally ready to do, and the constraints he faced.

Riad arrived late in the evening, and our initial discussion confirmed what I feared. His mandate from Asad was to reach an agreed formula for resumption of formal negotiations—that formula must acknowledge the Rabin commitment to withdraw to the June 4, 1967 lines. Having approved an unprecedented secret meeting, Asad expected to get a direct Israeli confirmation of the Rabin pocket in return—something that Rabin had declared could not happen until Israeli needs had been met.

I informed Uri of the conversation, and suggested we start the direct discussions in the morning after breakfast, where I hoped some informal conversation among the three of us might convince each of them of the goodwill and commitment of the other. Over breakfast, Uri and Riad seemed to connect immediately. Uri spoke of his background in the military, his experience with the pain and suffering of war, and his belief that the only answer for Israel was peace. He and Barak were both realists; they knew that what mattered to the Syrians was the land, and that what most mattered to Israelis was security and water. Now he had retired from the military and was a farmer who produced olive oil; his fondest hope was that he could one day bring a bottle of olive oil and give it to President Asad—a leader he and Prime Minister Barak respected.

Riad was similarly eloquent. He had been trained as a lawyer and had lived abroad before returning to Syria and joining both the Syrian Foreign Ministry and the law faculty of Damascus University. Having taken part in the Wye discussions, he had been impressed with the Israelis he had met there. He, too, was a believer that both parties—Syrians and Israelis alike—needed peace. War had produced great suffering for both sides. Both sides needed a different future, and he believed it was possible to produce it. He felt honored to be sent to meet Saguy, known to Syrians as a man of peace. Of course, for the Syrians, "as General Saguy has said, the land is what matters." The Syrians must know they would get it back. Everything flowed from there.

After a break to consult with each of them on how best to proceed, we began an interesting discussion that continued over lunch and into the afternoon, with each outlining what they expected from an agreement. At one point, Daoudi asked Saguy a direct question: "You say you understand our needs on full withdrawal. Do you accept the principle of withdrawal to the June 4 lines?" Until this point, Uri had been finessing the issue. Now he declared: "We accept the principle of withdrawal to the June 4 lines." He then sought to qualify his answer in the following way: There are "information gaps" between the two sides on the border; there may also be "technical questions about the location of the border"; and there are some areas where Israel has some specific concerns, especially about "water and its relationship to the border," that the two sides would have to resolve.

When Daoudi suggested that they put this in writing, Uri declined, saying that more understanding must be achieved between the two sides first—whereupon Daoudi told him that he had to return to Damascus with a clear formula on the June 4 lines in writing. In reply, Uri explicitly said he could not put anything in writing now. Both acknowledged they had a problem.

I suggested that I try my hand at "an American formula." Riad, I said, would be able to point to something new from us, and Uri could say that this was an American formula, and obviously not binding on Israel. Both men liked this approach; we took a break and I went off to write the formula.

I wanted to craft something that would clearly be new from the Syrian standpoint but would not be explicit from the Israeli point of view. With that in mind, I drafted language to the effect that the Rabin deposit given to President Clinton on full withdrawal stands, should not be withdrawn and should guide the outcome of negotiations if there is to be an agreement. While I was not spelling out the Rabin deposit specifically in terms of June 4, I was implicitly referring to it and adding the important provisos that it "should guide" the final outcome and "should not" be withdrawn. I went over this formula with Sandy and Madeleine, and Sandy urged me to confirm this with Barak, especially because the United States would now not simply be holding the Rabin deposit but be saying it should guide the outcome.

I checked with Uri and understandably he wanted to be sure that Barak was comfortable with this formula before I gave it to Daoudi. I warned Uri that I could not wait for long lest Daoudi believe I was simply cooking this with the Israelis—making the formula dead on arrival. Uri understood and succeeded almost immediately in obtaining Barak's approval, provided "I not go further." This ignored the reality that there would have to be some give-and-take on the formula. I pointed out to Uri that I had deliberately used "should" rather than "would" or "will." Uri, I said, I might have to give him a "would" or a "will"—especially because he will almost certainly press for June 4 to be mentioned explicitly and I won't give him that.

Uri understood this and, interestingly enough wanted me to be as forthcoming as possible, even though he felt my formula was at the outer limits of what Barak would go along with. He saw in Daoudi someone he could negotiate with and he wanted to bolster him with Asad.

When I showed the formula to Riad, sure enough, he wanted the "shoulds" to be changed to "woulds" or "wills," and he wanted June 4 lines mentioned explicitly. I told him I had leaned far forward in drafting this formula; the United States was going from being the passive holder of a deposit from Rabin to adopting an active posture that it guide the final deal. That gave the Syrians an assurance about the deposit they had never had. Questions were already being raised in Washington about our taking on a new responsibility, and I told Riad I doubted I could lean any further forward: "Riad, you have something significant from us; grab it."

He acknowledged that the formula was an important step forward, but he worried that it would not be enough in Damascus. I decided to try a different tack. I pulled the Lauder paper out and showed it to him with the President's notations. I told him the President had gotten very enthusiastic when he saw the ten points, and I reminded him about the value of having enthusiastic presidential involvement. The key for us was to take some of these points and build a structure around the traditional headings of withdrawal, peace, security, and the timetable. We should use the formula I crafted as a way to get beyond the threshold issue of resumption of negotiations. After all, as I argued, "we are negotiating now and you have already heard things from Uri that have never been said directly before to your side."

Daoudi looked over the Lauder points, clearly impressed with the President's notes in the margin. But he said, "Dennis, I have seen these points; we spent thirteen hours going over them and drafting comments, and they don't reflect any of our comments. This is the first draft given to us, not the final version"—in which he knew they had insisted on the June 4 lines replacing the 1923 lines.

That, I responded, was very important for us to know. Still, I added, there were legitimate points in the Lauder paper. We had a channel now, and we should build on it.

He told me he would see what he could do. It was by now late evening. We had a social dinner, where we each inquired about the other's respective families. Both Uri and Riad were clearly preoccupied and left as soon as the meal was over to communicate with their capitals.

Shortly after Uri departed, Prime Minister Barak called me. He had spoken to Uri but he also wanted my impressions of the talks. I told him that Daoudi was remarkably open and trying hard to find ways to be responsive, but Asad was riveted on a formula, and I feared that instead of getting into the real give-and-take of diplomacy, we would get bogged down in fighting over how to resume formal talks. I had tried to leap over that prospect both with the formula I had drafted and by going over the Lauder points with Daoudi. It didn't help, I told him, that the draft of the Lauder points lacked any of the Syrian comments—a very troubling discovery.

Barak was equally troubled by the Daoudi revelation, but then observed that even if the Lauder points were not accurate, Asad had accepted negotiating over them. Daoudi was admitting as much. Barak wanted to be able to have such a negotiation with the Syrians without having to pay the price of conceding anything beyond the formula I now crafted. That was his limit, and he bluntly said: "I will tell the President I oppose an American formula that goes beyond what you have drafted."

The next morning Daoudi asked to see me alone. He said he had spoken to Syrian

Foreign Minister Shara, and the Lauder points were off the table. Syria required a formula that was explicit on June 4 and on the "aims and principles" nonpaper as well. This was the starting point for a formal resumption of negotiations; nothing less was acceptable.

I suspected we had now reached the limit of what we could do here in Bern. I told Riad I could not improve on the formula I had given him and he was now unable to accept it.

But I suggested we not despair. Riad had heard the acceptance of the principle of June 4 from Uri and he could report that to President Asad. He could also report a more forward-leaning position from us. The Secretary of State would be traveling to the region in a few days and I promised to think about how best to take advantage of her upcoming meetings with Asad and Barak. Interestingly, Uri felt the meetings had been a spectacular success; he was more convinced than ever that Asad wanted a deal. We just had to find the right way to turn "the key in the door to unlock the progress available."

I rolled Uri's point over in my mind. I also kept coming back to Barak's observation that the Lauder effort had produced a serious give-and-take on a paper. As I was being driven back to Zurich to catch a plane to Cairo, I came up with an idea. Why not recreate an indirect negotiation on a paper like the Lauder points. We could bring both sides to a secret location; we could talk intensively to both sides separately; in light of those conversations we could then craft a document; and then the two sides could negotiate that document. This way, the give-and-take would not be on a general formula for resuming negotiations but on the substance of each of the issues that had to be resolved.

I reasoned that neither Asad nor Barak should have a problem with this approach: Asad, because he would initially be working with us, not the Israelis, and would not need a public explanation for why negotiations had resumed; Barak, because he was not being asked to concede on a formula before getting into the nitty-gritty of the issues. I outlined all of this to Barak in a phone conversation during the car ride and he immediately agreed. "Yes, this is a good way to go." The President and the Secretary, too, agreed, and the Secretary presented the idea to Asad on her trip the following week.

Asad agreed at once. Clearly, he had heard enough from Daoudi to convince him that these kinds of talks might actually produce. In any case, they were no-lose for him. He did not have to acknowledge a formal resumption of negotiations, yet there was promise that he might get his land back through this process.

| PRELUDE TO THE SECRET TALKS |

During the Secretary's trip to the region, it was agreed that we would conduct these secret proximity talks in the Washington area beginning in the middle of September—

in two weeks' time. I was due to return to Israel and preside over the formal resumption of permanent status talks between the Israelis and Palestinians, scheduled for September 13. Barak was eager to see me before the proximity talks with the Syrians began, and my presence in Israel for the beginning of the permanent status talks provided a good cover for us to meet. That he would want to meet before the secret talks with Syria came as no surprise. Barak was a micromanager who doubted anyone could explain his point of view and his arguments as well as he could. In anticipation of the talks, I had drafted a three-page outline of the essential elements of a peace agreement between Israel and Syria; I gave the draft to Barak, but he showed no interest in it; instead he wanted to know if it was possible to move to an agreement very quickly—indeed, he was ready, he said, to conclude an agreement by the middle of October at the latest! To do so, he needed to know only if the Syrians would accept a border that touched neither the northeast quarter of the Sea of Galilee nor the Jordan River north of it.

Was that all he needed to be satisfied that an agreement was possible that quickly? What, I asked, about the content of peace and security arrangements, including early-warning stations? Again Barak surprised me. "Yes, those are important," he said, almost as an afterthought, but the key was knowing whether the Syrians would accept a border that did not touch the water.

At this point, I took a map out of my folder and asked him to show me what he meant. He drew a line on my map that was just to the east of the Jordan River, and south of it he drew a line off the Sea of Galilee—the latter, he said, would be "a few hundred meters off the lake." He was prepared to compensate for moving the border in the north slightly to the east; to demonstrate, he drew a line that, in effect, moved the border opposite the southern part of the lake slightly to the west. (See the map of Syria on the following page.) If he knew that Asad could accept the line he drew, Barak told me, "everything will sort itself out."

If there was one trait that characterized Barak as Prime Minister, it was his instinct for the ambitious or grandiose move. He always wanted to know whether such moves were possible, whether a grand leap forward could be made. In theory, seeking clarification of a grand aim is desirable. But his constant search for clarity—when he was not always prepared to live with the wrong answers—created a certain urgent, even manic, quality to his policy, hardly the way to build one's leverage in a negotiation.

He was driven by a heroic instinct: He would conclude historic peace agreements whatever the political risk. He would focus on what he needed to do to sell hard decisions. As he negotiated with Syria, he needed to show his public that Israel would retain control of essential water resources. What he wanted from me was to know if the Syrians were prepared for this outcome. It mattered little to him that he had agreed to

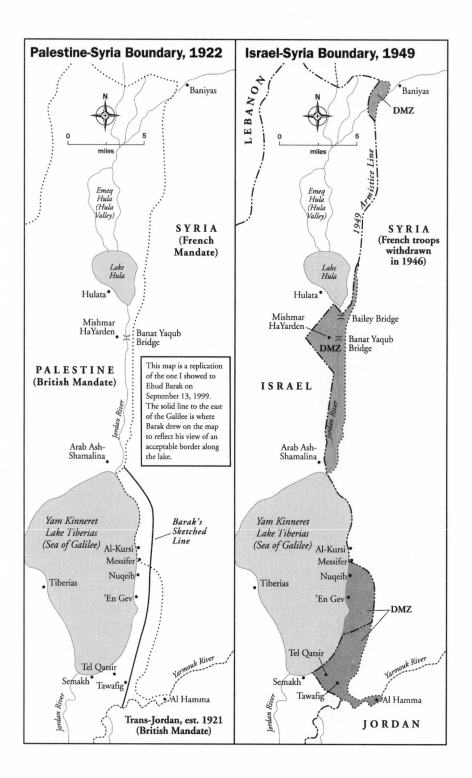

Palestine-Syria Boundary, 1922

N

0   5
miles

Baniyas•

Emeq Hula (Hula Valley)

SYRIA (French Mandate)

Lake Hula

Hulata•

Mishmar HaYarden•   Banat Yaqub Bridge

PALESTINE (British Mandate)

Jordan River

Arab Ash-Shamalina•

This map is a replication of the one I showed to Ehud Barak on September 13, 1999. The solid line to the east of the Galilee is where Barak drew on the map to reflect his view of an acceptable border along the lake.

Yam Kinneret Lake Tiberias (Sea of Galilee)

Barak's Sketched Line

Al-Kursi•
Messifer•
Nuqeib•

•Tiberias

'En Gev•

Tel Qatsir•
Semakh• Tawafig•

Yarmouk River

•Al Hamma

Jordan River

Trans-Jordan, est. 1921 (British Mandate)

Israel-Syria Boundary, 1949

LEBANON

N

0   5
miles

Baniyas•
DMZ

1949 Armistice Line

Emeq Hula (Hula Valley)

SYRIA (French troops withdrawn in 1946)

Lake Hula

Hulata•

Mishmar HaYarden•   Bailey Bridge
DMZ   Banat Yaqub Bridge

ISRAEL

Jordan River

Arab Ash-Shamalina•

Yam Kinneret Lake Tiberias (Sea of Galilee)

Al-Kursi•
Messifer•
Nuqeib•

•Tiberias

'En Gev•

DMZ

Tel Qatsir•

Semakh•
Tawafig•

Yarmouk River

•Al Hamma

Jordan River

JORDAN

the proximity talks with the aim of producing a genuine give-and-take on the core issues. He was not rejecting that effort, but he wanted to leapfrog over it and make a deal rapidly on these terms.

Providing an answer to his question was easier said than done. For one thing, only Asad could say for sure. For another, pressing Asad for an answer like this might actually mislead the Syrians into thinking that nothing else was important—and that Israel would forgo its other needs (such as early warning in the Golan). Lastly, Asad did not like to rush under any circumstances; it was not his style. He was never in a hurry lest it appear that he needed an agreement more than the other side. And that, of course, was the very message Barak would be sending—he was anxious, and if so, why would Asad concede anything?

We had come to create a genuine—if indirect—negotiation, and only that was likely to give me a good answer to Barak's question. I decided to stick with the idea of working the draft document.

| SECRET MEETINGS AT THE BETHESDA HYATT |

My negotiating partners from Bern would now join me in Bethesda, Maryland. They would not meet directly, but both would stay at the Hyatt hotel. Riad Daoudi arrived with General Ibrahim Omar—the military official who had also negotiated at Wye in 1996—on September 24.* But before I could meet with him, I was in for a surprise. To preserve secrecy, neither the Israeli nor Syrian embassies in Washington were informed of these meetings. We reserved three suites for the three parties on three separate floors. The hotel was ten minutes from my house, and Nick Rasmussen would stay in the hotel to deal with any needs that either side had.

Dani Yatom had called me to say that the Mossad would handle all of Saguy's travel arrangements. But Dani did not mention that anyone would be joining Uri. Shortly after Uri called to tell me he would be delayed, I left our suite and Yoel Singer—Uri Savir's partner in the past negotiations with the Palestinians and Syrians— appeared in the hall. I was surprised, not knowing if he was there by coincidence. My first instinct was to protect the secrecy of the talks. I greeted him warmly, giving away nothing as to why I was there. It turned out Yoel was not sure why he was there either; he told me Barak had asked him to meet Uri Saguy here. Did I know why?

I was in an awkward position, knowing Yoel well from all the negotiations during the Rabin and Peres period. A brilliant lawyer, he was probably the shrewdest drafter on the Israeli side. He was a master at getting his Arab interlocutors to accept his

---

*Uri's arrival was delayed by a storm that swept up the eastern seaboard.

frameworks and to draft language accordingly. He was probably more familiar than any other Israeli with every peace agreement Israel had ever negotiated with an Arab partner. It seemed obvious that Yoel had been sent to help Uri negotiate, and his presence suggested that Barak was ready to work with a document.

But he seemed to have little or no idea why he was here—or at least he wanted me to think that. I decided to fill him in at least in part, telling him of the genesis of these meetings and what the ground rules would be.

Naturally, Yoel (who had not negotiated since 1996) wanted to know where things stood on the substance. He had once told me the Rabin deposit was "a big mistake." Now he wondered where Barak was on it. I was reluctant to tell him and suggested that he let Uri brief him. "I can only offer you my impressions." He nodded, noting a little ruefully, yes, but "your impressions are good."

Instead, I told him my game plan: I would try to draw out the two sides on the four issues of withdrawal, peace, security arrangements, and the timetable for implementation, reminding them I wanted to put a draft on the table and that I needed their help to do so. I needed them not to present maximal positions but realistic ones.

Hearing this, Yoel wished me luck. I laughed, telling him he might need it as well.

In the initial meeting with Daoudi and General Omar, I proceeded in the way I'd told Yoel I would. To make clear that real give-and-take was expected, I told them that if neither side was prepared to give, we might go to the leaders on each side and tell them that their representatives were not living up to the ground rules that had been agreed.

As usual, the best-conceived plans had to be modified on the run. First Daoudi and then General Omar gave me a detailed but maximalist presentation on each issue, which together represented a retreat from the positions taken in the 1996 talks. This mechanism, I said, was supposed to move us forward, not backward. In particular, I asked them to reconsider the positions on the border—where Daoudi suddenly spoke of the border extending 200 meters into the Sea of Galilee—and security arrangements, where he now demanded that the security zones must be exactly equivalent on each side of the border.

I asked Daoudi to come with me to my room after the meeting. When we were alone, I told him I was deeply disappointed by the presentation I had just heard. President Clinton would wonder what was going on, and what was I supposed to tell him? Daoudi asked for my understanding; he had instructions, he had to open this way, but he could adjust Syria's positions. Riad, I said, I will not even attempt to begin to draft a document until we have moved forward from 1996.

As it turned out, Uri had no interest in developing a draft document. Similarly, he showed very little interest in my description of Daoudi's presentation, except to say that the claim of 200 meters into the lake was outrageous. Instead, Uri was quick to say that the best way to proceed now was to go over maps, but he had not brought his maps—he would bring his maps next time. Yoel, who was sitting in, was clearly uncomfortable with this approach.

So was I. Maps meant dealing with June 4 and the border up front. Was this what the Israelis really wanted to do? Did they really want to start with the Syrian, not Israeli, agenda, knowing this would inevitably raise Syrian expectations?

Uri did. He wanted to talk about the disposition of Syrian forces on June 4, 1967. For Uri, if Asad's definition of the border was based on where the forces were on June 4, "we may be able to move quickly."

Though I still had my own doubts, I now understood why Uri wanted to proceed with a discussion over maps. As remarkable as it may seem, the June 4 border had nowhere been depicted. It existed on no map. It was simply Asad's concept of the situation on the ground prior to the 1967 war. Indeed, this was the answer Asad had given me in 1994 when the issue of the June 4 line first arose, and I had asked him how he defined this line. Specifically, he had said, "it is where the forces were on June 4, 1967"; at the time, I had briefed Barak on this exchange. Clearly, Barak and Uri had studied this and felt that the Israeli position, especially as it related to the Sea of Galilee and the Jordan River, could be protected with such an interpretation of June 4. Certainly, a discussion of where the forces were on June 4, 1967, was possible. But it could not be done indirectly through us. It would have to be direct. We weren't the keepers of this information. I would have to ask Daoudi if he was willing to change the ground rules. I never felt my role was to tell the parties to slow down when they wanted to go faster. I might caution them on how particular moves might be read, and in this case I did that with Uri. But he and Barak felt they knew better—and maybe they did.

Not surprisingly, Daoudi welcomed the Israeli willingness to go over maps, and quickly got approval to meet Uri directly. We held the meeting in our suite. General Omar brought a large map and spread it out over the table, explaining that it was a UN map of the 1948 armistice lines between Israel and Syria. Uri looked at it, noting this map had been used during the Mixed Armistice Commission meetings that Israeli and Syrian military officers held most frequently between 1949 and 1955.

Going over every inch of the map, north to south, Uri and Omar got into a detailed discussion of the border, with Uri suggesting that the disposition of the forces on June 4, 1967, should provide the basis for it. Soon the two of them were disputing exactly where the forces were actually deployed on June 4, 1967. Uri pointed out that there were no Syrian forces on the Jordan River north of the lake (the Sea of Galilee). Omar disagreed, pointing to a bridge where the Syrians had been. Likewise, Uri said that Syrian forces had left their positions on the northernmost part of the lake in the weeks prior to June 4. Again, General Omar disagreed—and so it went for nearly two hours. This was not a trivial debate; on the contrary both sides saw its outcome as shaping the eventual border.

Finally, Uri decided that he could not convince Omar of the locations at this stage. Perhaps that could come later over more detailed maps. For now, he wanted to shift gears and describe Israeli needs using the map. Daoudi again asked whether Uri accepted the principle of withdrawal to the June 4, 1967 lines? Uri again said yes, but the Israelis needed areas to the east of the Jordan River and to the east of the northernmost part of the lake—an agricultural area, which was clearly east of the 1923 line.

At this point, General Omar got visibly upset, saying in Arabic, "You want Syrian land," and Daoudi rose and asked to adjourn the meeting. I saw little point in trying to keep them in the room, and agreed.

I gave Daoudi a few minutes and then went to see him alone. He was very composed, apologizing for having to walk out but saying he could not let claims to the area east of the 1923 line stand without a clear response. Riad, I said, yesterday you claimed 200 meters into the lake; I am sure that was just as shocking for Uri as his claims today were for you.

Daoudi noted that he had done that with me, not directly with Uri. Would you not have done it with Uri as well? I asked. His silence implied "point taken." He then leaned over and said that around the northeastern part of the lake the June 4 and 1923 lines are the same. We can accept that as the border. Gone was any claim on the lake. Gone was a border that touched the lake.

Riad, I asked, what if they need only a very small space off the lake? He noted that the 1923 line was 10 meters off the lake, and the Syrians would accept that. At this point, I pulled out the map on which Barak had drawn what would be acceptable bor- derlines for him and showed it to Daoudi. Without saying that this was Barak's map, I asked, what if you could get this? Would you really say no if you knew you could get the whole Golan Heights? If you knew you got the Israelis to withdraw from the Heights except for this narrow strip of land off the lake?

Obviously believing that the map had some standing, Daoudi studied it intently. While carefully observing that the Syrian government had made no decisions, he said it might be possible to accept something like 50 meters off the lake. The 50 meters was certainly less than the area Uri had suggested Israel would need; nonetheless, it indi- cated some flexibility. But Daoudi then said that Uri's raising of the agricultural valley was a particular problem because it was a very fertile area and Syrian farmers would want to have access to it again. He was certain that when he reported this to Damas- cus, he would be told to cease direct meetings with Saguy, only the indirect discussions that had been the ground rules for these meetings could be held.

After seeing Daoudi, I described our conversation to Uri, noting in particular his reaction to the map I had shown him. Martin was there, and he cautioned Uri: "Asad will need nominal sovereignty over the area around the lake that you want."

For Uri, this was not a problem. He suggested a "peace park," with normal access to the area for Israelis and nominal sovereignty for Syria. Uri was now very optimistic. But when I asked him how he wanted to proceed, once again he had no interest in my draft, preferring instead to break off the talks and return to Israel to discuss the next steps with Barak. Should they raise the idea of the peace park? Should they focus on getting certain Syrian assurances on Israeli needs before addressing the peace park idea? Agreement was definitely possible but it was essential now to take each tactical step very carefully.

I could not help thinking that this discussion should have taken place before Uri had come to Bethesda, and I told him so. It hardly mattered, though. Just as Daoudi would now say he could not meet directly with Saguy, so Saguy would report that to Barak and be forbidden to continue indirect discussions for now—in no small part because the Israeli focus was not on producing a document now.

One point was crystal-clear: Daoudi could not move further on the border, and I doubted he would be able to do much with me that was useful. I told him that because his boss, Foreign Minister Shara, was about to arrive in New York for the United Nations General Assembly meeting, I now preferred to have the Secretary and then the President meet Shara to discuss how to proceed. Not surprisingly, Daoudi was agreeable.

Once again, promising secret talks were being abandoned. In this case, I was not happy with Barak. As he had done before, while formally accepting one approach, he impulsively opted for another. This was his M.O. He believed that he knew best and did not feel particularly bound by our ideas—even if he had initially agreed to them. He would have been more responsive to our desires only if he had thought we might walk away. That, however, was not likely. Not only was President Clinton enthusiastic about trying to reach Arab-Israeli peace, but in Barak he saw a leader who was prepared to break the taboos and make courageous decisions for its sake. Understandably, he felt he had to cut Barak some slack, particularly because, in the end, it was Barak—far more than we—who would be running the risks.

| SHARA AND PRESIDENT CLINTON BREAK NEW GROUND |

Foreign Minister Shara arrived in New York the third week of September. Shortly beforehand, Ronald Lauder appeared briefly on our horizon again. Lauder, still professing his desire to be helpful, sent a letter to President Clinton enclosing an eight-point paper which he claimed included the final points that had been agreed by both sides in 1998. Gone was the reference to the 1923 borderline, replaced by withdrawal to a commonly agreed border based on the June 4, 1967 lines. Gone was the Syrian assumption of responsibility for stopping all attacks against Israel from Lebanon, replaced by a simple reference to a peace treaty between Lebanon and Israel. Gone was the reference to the different zones of armaments on the Syrian side of the border, replaced only by generalities on security arrangements. Gone was any reference, even bracketed, to an Israeli presence in an early-warning station, with nothing in its place. Syrian concerns were clearly addressed, but this was a very different paper from the ten points we had been shown.

Why hadn't we—American and Israelis alike—been shown this paper? Why had we seen only the first Israeli draft instead? My guess was that Bibi didn't want to give up deniability and so asked his friend to reveal only the ten-point version—not this later version reflecting Syrian comments. Whatever the motivation of the Lauder effort—or the reason for presenting a preliminary paper as a final version—it had certainly sown confusion. Now Lauder's "clarifying" letter to President Clinton indicated that Bibi Netanyahu had committed to withdrawal to the June 4 lines—which meant that Barak's position on peace with Syria was less forthcoming than Netanyahu's, at least insofar as it was revealed by Lauder's eight-point paper.

Interestingly, I showed Foreign Minister Shara the eight-point paper in New York and he confirmed that this had been acceptable to Syria. But it was not acceptable to Barak. The points he had seen as so advantageous to Israel were gone. Yet Barak was still eager to move quickly. He hoped that we might use the meetings with Shara, particularly the President's at the White House, to press the Syrians to accept Barak's need not to have the borderline touch the water.

I knew we must set the stage for Shara's visit to the White House, conditioning Shara, and through him Asad, to the idea that Israel needed to retain a small piece of the land area off the lake to show its public that its control of the water was not in jeopardy. We also needed to press Shara to produce something new for President Clinton, making Asad understand that he might not have the President's involvement in the future if his Foreign Minister did not give the President something to work with.

In the meeting Madeleine and I held with Shara prior to his going to the White House, I began by explaining that Barak felt the need to demonstrate to his public that the lake was truly Israel's. A Syrian presence on the lake would raise doubts about that both psychologically and legally. Shara was adamant that the Syrians required sovereignty to the June 4 lines, but Syria could address Israel's concerns about the water. What then, Madeleine asked, could Syria do to reassure Israelis that they would have access around the lake, that Israeli control of the lake was not in question? He did not respond.

I then raised the issue of early-warning stations in the Golan, telling Shara that water and security were obviously the key considerations for the Israelis. Syria's negotiator had now heard Barak's negotiator say that Israel was prepared to accept the principle of withdrawal to the June 4 lines; maybe Barak sought to define June 4 a little differently, providing Israel with a presence and access around the lake. But Barak also needed to know that Israel's security needs were going to be satisfied. What could Syria agree to when it came to early warning in the Golan?

Shara resisted making any moves in his meeting with Madeleine and me. Likewise, with President Clinton, he initially simply restated Syria's positions. But the President pushed him on both issues. On the early-warning stations, Shara—for the first time directly with us—said that as long as the Israelis did not remain, there could be an early-warning station manned by Americans, ideally under a UN flag. On the lake, the President tried hard to convince Shara that only a small surrounding area was needed and that it was the key to moving quickly to agreement. Shara said Syria would consider some kind of cooperative arrangement.

I had made the mistake of telling the President about Uri's idea of a peace park or a tourist area, and he raised it with Shara. This was a mistake because I did not know if Barak would accept a peace park. I knew that the President tended to play creative ideas too early, and I knew that one had to save such ideas until a time when the parties were looking for a way out. But the President played it now and Shara, loath to say no to the President, said he was willing to consider the peace park idea, with free access for Israelis, provided there was no question about Syrian sovereignty over the land in question.

Shara seemed to be embracing the very idea Uri Saguy had conveyed to us. Unfortunately, Barak did not accept the peace park idea. Quite the opposite, Barak said, "I need the reverse of what he is offering. We must have the sovereignty and we will give them access to the lake for tourism, for water for their farmers, and for their fishermen." He acknowledged the Syrian move on early-warning stations, but said that Israel required a limited presence in at least one of the stations even after withdrawal.

While Barak might belittle what we were reporting from Shara, he remained riveted on doing a deal quickly. Then, as so often in the peace process, an extraneous event intervened and froze our efforts.

| SHARA NEARLY DIES; EVERYTHING IS ON HOLD |

Shortly after returning home, Shara, who had become the central player for Asad, suffered an aortic aneurysm. At this point, both the Israelis and we were picking up increasing signs of Asad's deteriorating health. On the peace issues, he was showing increasing signs of dependency on Shara. But now Shara was gravely ill. We did not know if he would survive. He was in a Lebanese hospital and would likely be out of commission for two months even in the best of circumstances.

This, however, did not slow Barak down. Indeed, Shara's illness made Barak more aware of Asad's frailty and more concerned that the opportunity might slip away with Asad's passing. He wanted us to bring everything to a head with Asad, and urged the President to deal with Asad directly.

While we too did not want to miss the opportunity, I was certain that chasing after Asad was the wrong way to proceed. It would simply highlight our desperation and Barak's.

Instead, I proposed that the President send a letter to Asad in which he would explain that, given the secret discussions in Bern and Bethesda, we now knew that the differences on the issues were small but clear: it was time to decide on the definition of the border, the relationship of the border to control of water, and early warning. Technical experts could not resolve these questions; only the leaders could make such decisions. The President was convinced that Barak was prepared to respond to Syria's needs if President Asad was prepared to reciprocate. If that was so—the last bit was Barak's idea—the United States would be able to develop bilateral relations with Syria, making a strategic turn in the region.

Before sending the letter, the President had asked me to clear with Barak the passages related to Israel's positions. I read the letter on a secure phone to Dani Yatom, who reported back that Barak approved it. The letter was sent on October 12. But we heard nothing back from Asad. Indeed, Shara's illness ruled out a response. In retrospect, how was Asad supposed to respond? We had said that we were past the point of having technical-level officials meet, but Asad was ill and so was Shara. Who was he to send? Once again we were driven by Barak's timetable, and the timing of the letter made no sense and sending it in these circumstances made us appear desperate.

| ASAD'S ANSWER AND BARAK SUGGESTS "SHOCK TREATMENT" |

I was in Israel when, a month later, Asad replied at last. Our ambassador in Damascus, Ryan Crocker, secure-faxed me the letter in Jerusalem. Like Daoudi's opening presentation in Bethesda, it retreated on every issue. It took the position that Israel must accept Syria's definition of the border before there could be any more talks; it walked away from Shara's position on early-warning stations, saying there was no need for any; and it took a legalistic position on water, suggesting that Syria had claims of its own to Sea of Galilee water.

The only good thing about Asad's response was that it was so bad that even Barak could see there was no point in chasing after Asad. For nearly five weeks Barak had been relentless in pressing the President to take another step toward Asad. He went so far as to ask the President to take advantage of a trip to Istanbul at the OSCE (Organization for Security and Cooperation in Europe) summit meeting to "drop by" Damascus, which was "right next door."

Sandy, Madeleine, and I were dead set against his suggestion. For one thing, the President of the United States does not simply "drop by" anywhere. For another, Asad had not yet responded to the President's letter. If a nonresponse would produce a visit to Damascus—something Asad always desired as a way of demonstrating Syrian centrality—Asad would never feel he had to produce on anything in order to have his needs met.

Asad's letter, I explained to Barak, made clear that under no circumstances could the President see Asad now: "You don't reward a retreat on issues by having a meeting." Rather, the proper response to such a letter was a nonresponse—one that made Asad think that he now had a problem with us.

Barak agreed, but argued that since the Secretary had a scheduled trip to the region in two weeks, we should consider how to act toward Asad at that time. I saw two possibilities. First, even though Uri Saguy had in my judgment gone beyond the Rabin deposit, we had never conveyed to Asad that Barak—not his representative—had adopted it. Asad's suspicious mind would want to know that there was, in fact, a Barak deposit; with that, we could exact something from Asad. Alternatively, we could present a bridging proposal on the border, its relationship to the water, and security arrangements. We had never made such a proposal, and it would signal we were now in the endgame and Asad had to respond.

Barak did not like the bridging idea, saying he would end up compromising twice: first with our bridging ideas and second when Asad, treating our ideas as a point of departure, insisted on additional modifications. To assuage that concern, I said we could condition the bridging idea as a onetime offer which, if not accepted, would be withdrawn, but Barak wanted nothing of it.

He was less opposed to the first idea, but still did not want to fully embrace the Rabin deposit. This prompted me to address his approach to the negotiations head-on. The problem, I told him, is that you use every mechanism you can to send messages to Asad—the Jordanians, the Europeans, and us—to suggest you're serious. That convinces him you are eager for a deal, but not the one he wants to cut. That's okay, but you are constantly pressing us to move Asad and we can't move him unless you or we have something new to offer. My advice, I concluded, is to stop chasing him. But if you are not willing to do that, I only see the two options I have presented to you.

Barak had listened, appearing deep in thought as I spoke. Finally, he said, Try some new formula on the Rabin deposit. "I don't want to embrace it without any qualification, but give me a few formulas I can think about." I did that overnight, and they ranged from being most forthcoming and positive on Rabin to an essentially negative reaffirmation, declaring that Barak would not ask us to withdraw the Rabin deposit.

Barak was open to accepting one of these formulas, telling me that if one of them produced negotiations with Asad, he was convinced that "there is a 95 percent chance of success." I wondered about his confidence. If there was a 95 percent chance of success, why should he fear the bridging proposal idea? Though Barak had a very logical mind, when he became convinced of his own ideas, there was no moving him. I was to discover this again, soon.

Barak was also invited to Istanbul for the OSCE meeting—a summit bringing all the leaders of Europe together with a few outside guests to discuss security issues—and in a short meeting with President Clinton, he again said we would need a bold, dramatic move if there was to be a deal with Syria. His proposal was not long in coming. On December 3, he telephoned President Clinton and proposed that the President go to Damascus with no preparation or warning to "shock" Asad and make him see it was now or never. The President would tell Asad that he would press Barak for his commitment to the Rabin deposit—using one of "Dennis's formulas on Rabin"—if Asad resumed negotiations. Asad should understand that he would receive "carrots if he says yes, and that there will be nothing more that we can do if he says no."

I was in the Oval Office for the call and afterward the President asked me what I thought. I could see the President liked Barak's idea. I told him it was a high-risk, potentially high-gain approach. But there might be an alternative that would expose the President less. Since the Secretary was going to the region, why not have the Secretary ask Asad what it would take to resume the negotiations? While Asad might press for more, she could make it clear that the most that we would try to produce was a reaffirmation of the Rabin pocket by Barak. If Asad would buy this, we might not need a Presidential trip, and if the President did make such a trip anyhow, it would not be taking "a leap into the unknown."

President Clinton nodded his assent to my suggestion, but he was quick to tell me he did not mind taking a risk if a deal was possible. He felt the bigger risk would be to lose any chance of doing an Israeli-Syrian agreement—and he left no doubt that he liked Barak's idea.

I told the President I would be meeting Secretary Albright in the area, and would make the case for the approach to Barak before Madeleine arrived in Israel.

However, Barak chose not to wait for our meeting. As I was en route to his home, he called the President and declared that the key to moving Asad now was the shock of a presidential visit out of nowhere. If the Secretary or anyone else but the President raised the possibility of Barak's reaffirming Rabin, Barak argued, there would be no shock effect. Consequently, he did not want the Secretary to do anything with Asad.

I arrived at Barak's house at midnight, knowing nothing of this call, and right away I received a message that I had an urgent call from Secretary Albright. At the Secretary's insistence, I left the meeting with Barak, which had just begun—though it was highly unusual for me to ask a sitting prime minister to wait while I took a call.

Madeleine was livid over Barak's call to the President; what Barak was doing was making her irrelevant—"I'm not chopped liver"—and was risking the credibility of the President of the United States while protecting the credibility of the Prime Minister of Israel. I had to talk Barak out of this idea.

Madeleine, I said, I agree with you, but "I will be a hell of a lot more convincing if the President poured cold water on Barak's idea. Did he?"

Madeleine, who was also traveling, had not heard the call, and all Sandy could say was that the President also understood this was not a good idea. That did not inspire me with confidence. In effect, I was being asked to talk Barak out of an idea that the President had either vaguely encouraged or actively accepted. I told Madeleine I would do my best.

Martin had come with me to Barak's house. We rejoined Barak, then all moved into Barak's study. For the next three hours, while the PM smoked a cigar and drank cognac, I tried, with Martin's help, to convince him that it made no sense for the President to go to Damascus in these circumstances. I tried every argument I could think of:

—Barak was exposing the President to a great risk for too limited an objective. For the President to go with such a dramatic gesture, it should be to produce an agreement, not simply the resumption of negotiations. Unfortunately, Barak's counter was that resumption would almost guarantee an agreement. On this we disagreed.
—The President was being asked to take all the risks up front. Why not find a way to test whether his going would produce resumption of the negotiations? Why not have the Secretary meet Asad and tell him that President Clinton will come to Damascus if he will accept a resumption of negotiations based on a reaffirmation of Rabin? Barak's response: "No way. It will destroy the shock effect." Alternatively, I said the President could call Asad and say he will press Barak to affirm the Rabin deposit if he knows Asad will agree to resume the negotiations. Barak countered again that the President would not have an effect unless it was face-to-face.

The more I argued, the more resistant Barak became. I was not convincing him, I was succeeding only in getting him even more dug-in. When Martin tried to reinforce my points Barak got increasingly angry—turning red and saying it was ridiculous not to take this bold step if it could produce Israeli peace with Syria. That angered me:

"We'll take bold steps to produce peace. But we are not talking about producing peace. You want us to take a blind leap to resume negotiations, and I know how Asad negotiates, you don't."

Barak was not persuaded. The risk to us was manageable, in his view, largely because he was convinced we would succeed. He had thought it through, he understood, we did not. Nothing short of the "shock effect" would work. Because my suggestions lacked a shock effect, my approach, not his, would encourage Asad to hold out for more than the reaffirmation of the Rabin pocket—or so Barak argued.

Why, I asked, won't the President's going to Damascus send him that very same signal? "You overlook the fact that the President's trip will raise expectations sky-high and the President won't want to leave there empty-handed. Asad will know that. Asad will know that he has the leverage. He will press for more. You will produce the very thing you fear."

Barak paused, and for a moment I thought I had finally found a way to persuade him. I was wrong. He paused to think and then simply said the President would have to be tough. "A shock will work, nothing else will."

We concluded the meeting with my telling him I did not know what the President would decide. Barak made it clear that he would call the President again. Meanwhile, Barak said the Secretary could not speak on his behalf, and therefore could not use any of the formulas I had developed. She must approach the meeting with Asad as if she did not know that Barak had told the President he would reaffirm the Rabin deposit if Asad resumed negotiations.

I returned to the hotel at nearly 4 a.m. Madeleine was in Europe and I was not going to wake her. So I called Sandy Berger in Washington, particularly because I fully expected that Barak would call the President soon.

Sandy was even angrier than Madeleine, and urged me to tell Barak his "shock" idea was unacceptable. Sandy, I said, I spent three hours arguing with him, and "I succeeded only in getting him to dig in even more. If you want to turn this off, have the President say no when Barak calls."

We hung up, and I went to bed in hopes of getting a few hours of sleep before an early morning meeting I had scheduled with the Israeli and Palestinian negotiators. No such luck. Sandy called me at 5 a.m. and rather sheepishly told me that the President was not against the Barak idea and would not say no if Barak called. He felt that both Madeleine and I needed to know that before we went to Damascus.

Sleep now took a back seat to figuring out what we would be doing with Asad in Damascus. After thinking about it, I decided on an approach that Barak could not complain about and just might work. I knew from Prime Minister Tony Blair's personal envoy to the Middle East, Lord Levy, that Asad had asked Levy to convey to Blair that he was "not raising obstacles to peace."* With this in mind, I felt that the Secretary could test Asad by saying that his letter had retreated on every issue; he did indeed seem to be raising barriers to negotiations, if we were in fact reading his letter correctly. If he wanted an out, a chance to show he was not raising "obstacles to peace," we would provide it by giving him a chance to say that we had misunderstood his letter. But we would expect him to then change his posture accordingly.

I convinced myself that this might be a useful way to move Asad without mentioning the Rabin pocket. The Secretary grudgingly accepted that this was the best we could do, though she had no expectations that it would produce anything. She was angry with Barak, feeling he was marginalizing her and ready to sacrifice the President's currency in the process. But both of us were in for a surprise.

---

*While the British did not have a major role to play on Arab-Israeli issues, Prime Minister Blair was deeply interested in doing whatever he could to resolve the conflict. He had a close relationship with Barak and he used Lord Levy as an envoy to convey messages and be supportive in the process.

Asad's Surprise

WE MET ASAD IN Damascus on December 7, 1999, and it was very quickly clear that something had changed. Shara, apparently healthy again, also attended the meeting. But the change wasn't in Shara; it was in Asad. When the Secretary told him that we read his letter as a retreat, indeed a bar to negotiations, Asad insisted otherwise. The letter, he said, only raised Syrian ideas which needed to be negotiated with the Israelis and was never meant to suggest that these ideas were preconditions for negotiations. He was "not imposing any conditions for negotiations."

This was a remarkable formulation—one that created an obvious opening—and I asked the Secretary to request a brief time-out. She did, and Asad said we could go to another room if we wished, but we simply went to the rear of the large meeting room. Had I really heard something new? Madeleine asked. I said yes. She was not sure but was willing to press it, and I suggested she ask him explicitly now what would it take to resume negotiations.

This Madeleine did, and Asad replied: "They never truly stopped." Shara at this point did leap in and try to walk Asad back, saying that we would need to come up with a public formula to explain their resumption. Such a formula would create a problem; it would inevitably force us to address publicly the question of an Israeli commitment to June 4 or to the Rabin deposit. So I said, "President Asad clearly does not want to complicate the matter; why don't we limit what we say in public?" Madeleine added that in this case "less is more." Let's say very little.

Asad suggested a simple and clever formula: Say that the negotiations would resume "where they had left off." This effectively allowed each side to offer their own explanation of where the talks had left off.

I had not seen Asad in such an agreeable mood since his meeting with Baker in July 1991; he seemed as eager as Barak, and I decided to see if, after eight years, we could also change the level of negotiations as well. "Mr. President," I asked, "are you ready to have the negotiations take place at a political level?" That, I now argued, is the key to moving rapidly to an agreement. Asad did not hesitate: he was ready, and asked whom I wanted from his side. "Why not your Foreign Minister?" I asked. "You mean Shara?" I nodded, and he looked at Shara for a moment, and then said, "Yes, why not."

For eight years Asad had resisted anything like this. Yes, at one point he had raised the level of the negotiations by allowing the military Chiefs of Staff to meet, first in secret, and later only in private with no media present. He had rejected meetings of political-level officials, as if that represented a level of recognition that he was not prepared to grant Israel. Now suddenly he was prepared to do so. I wanted to know why.

As we rose to depart, I took advantage of our past practice to ask a typically informal or off-the-record question reserved for our stand-up discussions. "Mr. President," I asked, "you obviously believe that something is different now. What is different now?" His answer was simple: "Barak is serious; he wants to reach agreement quickly and so do I."

I believed him. In any negotiating process, when a decision-maker acts in a way that is totally out of character, it is a good indicator of intent. It may be good news or bad news, but for sure, *it is news*. Asad was acting out of character. He was never in a hurry; he never gave something away for nothing. Yet here he was resuming negotiations without conditions, and raising the negotiations to a political level. And he was saying it was time to move quickly. I suspected this was about his health and paving the way for his son to succeed him—he would take the difficult step to make peace with Israel and relieve his son of the need to do it. For the second time in this process on the Syrian track, I now believed we would reach agreement.

| WOW! |

As we were leaving the palace, Shara said to the Secretary that his counterpart in the negotiations must not be Israeli Foreign Minister David Levy. The Europeans all told him that Levy was not a decision-maker and did not have much influence. The counterpart had to be Barak himself.

Madeleine's first step was to return to our embassy in Damascus to call the President on a secure line and report that we had achieved an extraordinary move without having to give much away. We could not reveal this publicly before knowing that Barak would accept the formula of announcing that negotiations would resume where they had left off. After the call, we would fly to Israel. It would be four or five hours before we could see Barak.

I did not expect that to be a problem. Barak was getting negotiations at the foreign minister level for the first time in this process, something no Israeli leader had been able to produce with the Syrians, and he would be getting this without having committed to anything new or old. Should he resist, we could easily argue that we had produced more for him at a far lower price than he had been prepared to pay.

Knowing Barak, I told the Secretary that he would want to lead the delegation in any case, and he would have to manage David Levy's sensitivities. But the immediate problem was that Levy would be present at the initial meeting—and we could not convey Shara's message in his presence. I told her I would call Dani Yatom and explain that due to something extremely sensitive, the Secretary would need to see the Prime Minister alone upon arrival.

Not surprisingly, my message to Dani piqued his interest, and he asked if we could meet immediately upon our arrival. I said we would call upon landing.

In the meantime, the Secretary had spoken to the President and he was thrilled. The Secretary suggested to him that he announce the resumption of the talks once we knew that Barak was on board. The President could be the first to talk about the resumption and the President could finesse the meaning of resuming talks at the point where they had left off, and both sides could then hide behind his public explanation.

When we arrived in Israel, Madeleine called Barak and explained what we had. "Wow!" was his one-word response. He said he needed to think about this and how he would have to handle Levy, but he asked the Secretary to make no mention of this request when we met the next morning at Barak's house with Levy in attendance.

| BARAK GOES FROM HOT TO COLD |

We had breakfast with Barak and Levy at the Prime Minister's residence. To say that Barak was eager would be an understatement. "From my military experience," he said, "I know that when you have the initiative you must capitalize on it or lose the momentum and the opportunity." Given the importance of the moment, he declared that he and his Foreign Minister, David Levy, should lead their delegation. (This was obviously the way he would handle Levy's involvement.) He proposed that we initiate intensive talks within a week, and not break off these discussions until we had agreement.

We were ready to organize the talks very quickly, but were hesitant to commit to discussions involving Barak and Shara in Washington that would last until agreement was reached. None of us had any idea how long it would take. As Prime Minister, could Barak really be away from his country for an open-ended period?

Barak, ever confident of his own judgment, was convinced that in such circumstances it would be possible to reach agreement very quickly, but I worried that politically it was a mistake for him to look like he was rushing to give up the Golan Heights. Later that day I asked him if he didn't have need, for political reasons, to demonstrate that in an extremely tough process he had managed to produce peace with Syria on the best possible terms?

He acknowledged this was important, but he also felt that his personal credibility with the Israeli public was high. He seemed to be saying that if he said something was a good deal, his public would support him; they were eager for peace, and he did not want to lose the moment.

To respond to his understandable desire to get things moving quickly, we organized an initial set of meetings at Blair House on December 15–16, 1999. Barak asked that this be followed by a five-day break and then, with President Clinton's participation, an uninterrupted round that would continue until agreement was reached. I explained that we could not run this negotiation through the Christmas holidays, especially because of the millennial celebrations that required presidential participation (and the threat, then looming, of Y2K disasters). Barak wasn't happy but Sandy told him the best we could do was to resume at the beginning of January 2000.

At this point, Barak's initial enthusiasm began to wane as domestic opposition to a Syrian deal began to mount. First, the Knesset endorsed the negotiations with Syria by a vote of only 47 to 31, with many of Barak's putative supporters absenting themselves. At a time when he was cruising along with very high public approval ratings, this was a dash of very cold water.

Then, on the day before his arrival in Washington, he called to say that the two days at Blair House should be primarily concerned with process, not substance, and that he could not agree to any one-on-one meetings with Shara. I was incredulous. Prime Minister, I said, you are the one who insisted that we must move quickly. We must not lose the moment. We have high-level discussions for the first time and you don't want to discuss substance or meet privately with Shara?

Barak as much as told me it was my fault for insisting on a break for the holidays, saying, "I cannot afford to discuss the substance. The risk of leaks is too great. If our positions are exposed in the break period, I may be undercut politically and rendered incapable of making the decisions necessary for agreement."

He had a point, but nothing prevented him from meeting privately with Shara. "He is not going to leak something you say to him in a one-on-one conversation." Barak's answer told me he was retreating: "He will expect me to say that I confirm June

4 in a one-on-one meeting and I don't want to do that now." Prime Minister, I responded, you were prepared two weeks ago to have the President of the United States fly to Damascus to say that and "now you won't say it when you have the first-ever meeting between an Israeli prime minister and Syrian foreign minister?"

Barak knew he was on weaker footing here, but refused to budge, claiming he did not trust Shara not to leak their conversation. This was hardly credible; I asked him, "Would Shara risk something highly valued by Asad, guaranteeing our wrath and your denial?" But Barak held fast to his position, prompting me to tell him that no one on our side would understand his reluctance to meet Shara privately. I could try to convince the President and the Secretary that we needed to focus the first round on process, not substance. But he would have to convince the President himself that he could not meet with Shara alone if Shara wanted it.

As we found out shortly, Shara wanted it. The Secretary and I went to Dulles Airport to greet Shara on his arrival the evening of December 14. He met the press briefly and spoke positively about the talks, Syria's hope for peace, and his readiness to meet Prime Minister Barak. In the car, he was explicit with us: he needed to return to Damascus from these two days with a clear Israeli commitment on June 4. He could meet Barak alone if this would make it easier for the Prime Minister.

We had a problem. We could try to convince Shara that Barak had to be careful now so he could deliver in two weeks. Still, I believed that Asad would insist on some results from the initial two days.

To make matters worse, the beginning of these meetings was anything but auspicious. Before going to Blair House on the morning of December 15, Barak and Shara were to meet together with the President and appear before the press, but only the President would make a statement. (I had insisted on this, fearing that Shara, much like he had on Israeli TV in 1994, would fall back on a traditional, old-think formula if he was standing next to Ehud Barak. That was not the way to get off on the right foot.)

Unfortunately, Barak had other ideas. In the Oval Office just prior to the event in the Rose Garden, Barak suggested that each of them, not only the President, make a short positive statement to the press, doubtless wanting a sound bite for the evening news in Israel. He was to get exactly the opposite of what he needed. The President agreed to Barak's request, and Barak made a short positive statement; then Shara, with all the cameras rolling, read from a long statement highly critical of Israel. I was angry with the President for changing our plans. I was angry with Barak for once again thinking he knew best. And, of course, I was angry at Shara.

When I walked back into the Oval Office, the President was pacing and muttering that Shara had "screwed us." He stood right here and agreed to make a short positive statement. Then Barak came in and said he could not trust the man, and, "for sure,

I can't trust him to keep a confidence." The President said he had whispered to Shara, "You are destroying everything with what you have just done," souring the first political-level meetings between Israel and Syria before they even begin.

Barak now had his argument for why he could not meet privately with Shara, and the President was now sympathetic to him. The only silver lining I could see was that Shara knew the President was angry, and that would give us leverage with him.

With that in mind, Madeleine and I went to sit with Shara to make him realize he now owed us something. He had embarrassed the President, and was now in a precarious position; unless he was responsive to us, the President might choose to walk away from this initiative.

Shara had to be uneasy, particularly knowing how much Asad valued Clinton. When we confronted him along these lines, he tried to shift the responsibility onto me. "It had been agreed only the President would speak, and I asked you to ensure there would be no surprises." Madeleine at this point became angry, reminding him that "you agreed with the President to make a short positive statement." Shara then tried to argue that he had been positive, prompting Madeleine to reply, "Farouk, don't insult my intelligence. You blew it and we have a big problem."

I then told him we had to find a way to rescue the situation. And, revealing his genuine unease, he asked me what I had in mind. I was not about to let him off the hook, so I told him I would have to think about it. For now, I said, You have a problem with the President and you have created a problem for Barak, making him look weak and naïve before his own public. Look, I said, I know what you want out of these talks. Frankly, it is not unreasonable. But you have just made things a lot harder for Barak. He was already fearful of appearing as if he was giving you what you needed but not getting anything meaningful in return. His great fear is that he will have to commit now to something that explodes in his face in Israel in the interval between these two days and the beginning of an intensive round. He wants to know that you will go for an intensive round and not put him in a position in which he cannot deliver later on.

Shara said that neither he nor President Asad had any interest in weakening Barak. But they were here in Washington and what was the basis of these negotiations? In reply, Madeleine and I emphasized that we should use these two days to create an agreed structure for the intensive round that we proposed to start on January 3. Shara was open to this, but not ready to give up on getting something from Barak now. I told him not to build up his hopes. I could see that Shara was backing off, less insistent on what he would need and probing to see what he could get. Nevertheless, I was fairly certain he would still press for something new from Barak, even if he knew it was a mistake to do so.

Before the talks began, I briefed Barak on what we had done with Shara. He was pleased. His hope was to actually reach agreement in the intensive round and then re-turn to Israel with a whole package he could sell his public.

Once again, however, Shara surprised us. Though we had told him to be careful about what he pressed to have Barak confirm, Shara, in front of both delegations, re-cited the history of negotiations with Rabin—the Rabin deposit, Asad's question to Christopher on whether there were any Israeli claims to territory, my response, the stalemate of 1994, and Rabin's acceptance of the June 4 lines, provided Israel's needs were met.

Madeleine asked me if she should intervene, fearing Barak's reaction. I was watch-ing Barak very carefully. He was impassive. So was his team. I whispered, "Let's see how Barak responds." I sensed Barak had thought about how to handle this. I chose to rely on one of my rules of negotiations when you are the third party: Be careful about in-tervening in a way that preempts discussion, even if the discussion may be uncomfort-able. In most such circumstances, these are discussions that need to take place. They cannot be avoided; preempt them and you delay the inevitable.

In this case, my instinct turned out to be right. Barak's response was brilliant: "While my government has made no commitment on territory," he said, "we don't erase history"—repeating the last phrase for emphasis. With that simple phrase Barak gave Shara something to take back to Asad, while avoiding a new commitment.

I could tell that Shara was impressed, and when the session was over I went and sat with him, hoping to cement the favorable impression before it was undone by his team. We did not go to the Syrian quarters; instead we sat and had tea in the sit-ting area adjacent to the conference room. I started by congratulating him: "You put everything on the record, and Barak not only did not contradict it, he effectively ac-knowledged it and he did so before his whole delegation. This is a big deal, and you produced it."

Shara was appreciative and felt the discussion was very good, but he still felt he needed to tell Asad something more. I told him not to press for more than the traffic could bear, saying it would be better to "focus on preparing the process for when we go to the intensive round."

In response, Shara said that it would be reassuring to Asad if there could be agree-ment on a border demarcation group for the intensive round. Would I ask Barak if he would accept that? I agreed I would explore the possibility with Barak. But I needed something from Shara as well. The end of Ramadan came on January 7, 2000, four days after the intensive round would commence. I told him that Barak did not believe he could launch an intensive round and then have it break after only a few days; he would not make the basic concessions without getting something to show for them. Was it possible, I asked, for the Syrians to come on the third and remain through the

Eid, the feast celebrating the end of Ramadan? After some back-and-forth, he said not only that the Syrians would be prepared to stay through the Eid, but that "peace makes it important to work through the Eid." We would have our intensive, unbroken round.

Barak was pleased when I told him about this, and he initially agreed to Shara's request for a border demarcation group. But a short time later, Eli Rubinstein told me that the Prime Minister would accept a border "delineation," not "demarcation," group. Demarcation suggested that the border was already agreed, while delineation suggested that it had yet to be worked out. I knew this was not a nitpick, and that Eli had probably pointed out the difference to Barak. Knowing that the name of the group could easily become a problem, I decided that we would simply give each group a simple name: the security group, the peace group, the water group, and the border group.

Sure enough, when we assembled the delegations again, Shara came on too strong on the need for the border demarcation group, and Barak predictably turned more cautious, clearly thinking that people in Israel should see that Israel's needs—security and peace—were being addressed first, and the border later.

For someone bent on insulating this round from any public exposure, Barak was unusually sensitive to appearances—fearing that even the order of the groups would suggest he was making concessions. Shara was eager to get the border group started from the beginning and made one point on which we would have occasion to quote him subsequently: in arguing for the immediate advent of the group, he acknowledged that you "cannot find the June 4 line in any map in any book." There were, of course, plenty of maps that showed the 1923 line and the armistice lines of 1948. But there were no maps in "the library that showed the June 4 line."

It was an interesting argument and could easily have been a source of reassurance to Barak. If there were no maps of June 4, there could be different interpretations of what the line might be. But Barak was now riveted on imagery. Because he did not want to concede on the sequence of the working groups, he failed to seize on Shara's argument.

As we listened to the exchange over when each group should be formed, I suggested that the United States, as the convener of the talks, would make a decision on the timing and sequence of the groups. Looking at Barak and then Shara, I asked if they were willing to let President Clinton decide this. Both said "yes." And that is effectively where we concluded the discussion, with both sides looking to the intensive round to begin on January 3, 2000.

| BARAK'S ANXIETY LEVEL GROWS |

Though I expected that the two weeks before January 3 would not be restful or relaxed, Barak was as anxious as I had ever seen him. In retrospect, I should not have been surprised. For all his determination to make historic decisions, it was one thing to theorize about them and another to execute them. Giving up the Golan Heights was a historic act, and he could not be indifferent to its political costs. He had to focus on what he needed to sell it. As he confronted what was necessary, he inevitably wavered.

On December 18, he called full of worry about leaks, not by the Syrians but by his side. His side might leak any detailed discussions on the border and he could not afford that if we did not finish in one round. Of course, he realized that not talking about the border now would lead either to disappointment or even to a crisis on the Syrian side. On top of this, he now also raised a concern about the asymmetry in representation: he was the leader and decision-maker and Shara was not. He would make a commitment that he had to keep, and Shara would have an out. What did I think about the dilemma, and what should be done in light of it?

I found myself wondering why Barak had not considered these questions from the beginning. There was, I told him, no way to avoid dealing with the border early on. The Syrians see themselves as having crossed the threshold to political-level engagement, and are willing even to stay and work through the Eid; now if you refuse to talk about the border, "the issue that matters most to them, they will interpret this at best as a trick and at worst as a trap. They will no longer believe that you are serious."

Barak answered that "you could reassure them." How, I asked, unless we can tell them what they want to hear on the border? At a minimum, I said we must be able to say that the Rabin deposit is now a Barak deposit. Bear in mind, I continued, that you were willing to have the President go to Damascus to say that just to resume the negotiations.

There was silence on the phone for at least a minute, so I decided to add one other possibility. "You know," I said, "we could keep the negotiations going by offering a draft agreement with brackets on the areas of disagreement. That would protect you, but I think it would probably have to be accompanied by a reaffirmation of Rabin. If the draft leaked, you would be protected, but the reaffirmation would protect them as well."

"Let's think about this," Barak replied. But he began to shift gears, thinking about what he would need to be able to sell an agreement. He gave me a laundry list of Israel desiderata: the Lebanon track needs to be resumed; at least one Arab state in the Gulf or North Africa needed to upgrade their relations with us; we need an announcement of a free-trade zone in the Golan; and we need clear security benefits from you to show that we will be stronger, not weaker, as a result of this agreement.

It was my turn to listen and be sparing in my comments. The last thing I needed to do with Barak, who was suddenly focused on how he could sell an agreement, was to cool his ardor.

| TRYING TO CHANGE THE CLIMATE IN ISRAEL: ASAD AND THE ISRAELI MISSING IN ACTION |

In briefing first Madeleine and Sandy and then the President, I supported acting on all of Barak's requests, but I argued for something more. "We need," I said, "to get Asad to make an unexpected move toward the Israeli public—a step that will resonate with Israelis; that will show him reaching out to them as people. That could build support for what Barak is doing."

I suggested several possibilities, including having Asad invite a Knesset delegation led by the spiritual leader of the Shas Party, Ovadia Yosef, to Damascus; psychologically, however, I felt we could have even more of a dramatic effect if Asad would help on three Israeli MIAs from the Lebanon war—Zecharya Baumal, Zvi Feldman, and Yehuda Katz. Their families had waged an international campaign to get them back, believing they might still be alive but at least seeking the recovery of their bodies if they were not.* On occasion we had brought letters from the families to President Asad, and his unwillingness to help, in Israeli eyes, cemented the impression that he was implacably hostile to Israel. I told the President that now was the time for him to ask Asad to let us go quietly to the cemetery in Damascus where the Israelis were certain we would find the remains. If their information was right and we were able to recover the remains, Asad would be seen as making an unusual human gesture to all of Israel.

Historically, Asad had rejected any steps designed to reach out to the Israeli public lest he give away something for nothing. But it was a measure of Asad's readiness to reach an agreement that this time he was prepared to respond at least to this request. On December 19, President Clinton made a secure call to Asad in which he made two requests. The first was to have the Lebanon track resume simultaneously with the Syrian negotiations, (in which Asad promised to consult with the Lebanese), and the second was to permit us to retrieve the remains of Israeli MIAs in Syria. Clinton told Asad we now had what we believed was rock-solid information on the location in a Damascus cemetery of the remains of three Israeli MIAs. Would President Asad allow us to discreetly send a specialized team to extract the remains? We understood that digging up remains in Muslim cemeteries was very sensitive, and we would do this in a way that conformed with Islamic traditions, under close Syrian supervision.

---

*Recovery of the remains was especially sensitive in Israel given the Israeli tradition of never leaving a soldier in the field and the Jewish law holding that a spouse may not remarry without a definitive finding of death.

Asad thought for a moment and then agreed, saying he hoped our team could act quickly and quietly and successfully.

The President assured him we would, telling him that the recovery of the remains could have a major effect in Israel and in America if successful. "We hope so," was Asad's reply.

Arranging for a forensic team that included a rabbi and could go to Syria secretly and quickly to extract and identify the remains of the three Israeli MIAs was no simple task. Yet Frank Kramer, Assistant Secretary of International Security Affairs and the MIA office in the Pentagon, managed to get a team to Damascus before the end of December. True to Asad's word, the Syrians cooperated completely in the effort. Unfortunately, the Israeli information led the team to the wrong remains.

| DEALING WITH BARAK'S REQUIREMENTS |

Asad, now feeling he had done enough, called the President and told him that the Lebanese leaders in his consultations preferred to resume the talks only after some headway had been made between the Syrians and Israelis. (Asad may have wanted a deal, but he was not going to give away his leverage.)

Barak, for his part, was now riveted on two interrelated points: how to create the political climate that would make a deal acceptable in Israel, and how to produce the terms in an agreement that he could more easily sell to his country. In a phone conversation with me on December 23, he outlined in great detail the timing of what he needed and the importance of his knowing it would all be done before he came to the States: the Lebanon negotiations must resume by January 10; Tunisia should upgrade its relations with Israel by January 12; on January 13, we should announce the formation of a free-trade zone in the Golan Heights, with two or three multilateral business leaders declaring their readiness to invest in the FTZ. In addition, he would need to know that the military equipment, technology, and new assurances that Israel required, given the risks it would be running in getting off the Golan Heights, would be forthcoming.

I told him we were prepared to work with great urgency on each issue but could not guarantee that we could get everything done in advance of the intensive round.

Whenever Barak was trying to convince me of something he would lower his voice and speak very, very slowly. Now he did the same, saying, "Look, it is very, very important to get all this done and for me to know it will get done before the round begins." Then, without skipping a beat—or letting me respond—he raised the asymmetry issue again, insisting that we would not be able to close on the border until the endgame with Asad—trying to justify avoiding the subject.

This was a mistake, but there was no convincing Barak of that in this call. Instead,

I tried a different tack: "Prime Minister," I said, "Asad won't come to a meeting with you unless he knows it is a done deal in advance. He will cross this last threshold only to finalize an understanding that he believes already exists."

Barak again insisted that we must convince Asad the deal was available. As I would hear him say many times in the coming two months, "it would be ridiculous not to reach agreement" when Israel's needs were so modest—only a narrow strip off the lake and the Jordan River, only a small presence in the Mount Hermon early-warning station, and only the exchange of embassies in the first phase of implementation.

Barak was spelling out his side of the bargain. Not surprisingly, his bottom lines of September had expanded. From his standpoint, Asad would get all the territory, save a narrow strip off the lake; in return, Israel would get a small presence in the main early-warning station at Mount Hermon and an early demonstration for the benefit of the Israeli public that Syria would recognize its existence—diplomatically—even before the withdrawal was carried out. Interestingly, he added that he would need two years to withdraw the settlers from the Golan Heights—since Israel could not confront settlers from both the Golan Heights and the West Bank simultaneously.

This was actually the first time I became convinced that Ehud Barak also intended to do a final deal with the Palestinians. He had delayed naming a negotiator for nearly two months after the ostensible beginning of the permanent status negotiations. He had agreed to a secret channel with Arafat on permanent status, but refused to let the secret channel get under way. He had refused to enter into a substantive discussion with us on what he might be able to do with the Palestinians until he knew whether he would have a deal with Syria. And yet here he was telling me that his timing on Syria and the settlers in the Golan was influenced by what he would need to do later with the Palestinians and the settlers on the West Bank.

That part of the call was encouraging. The rest was not. I remained concerned he would try to avoid talks on the border when he called the President in the next few days. I wanted the President to reassure him on his requests, but also to be firm on the issue of the border as well as the issues of concern to Israel: security, peace, and water. I knew instinctively that getting Shara to be responsive on these issues depended on our being able to address the border issue with him.

The President was well primed for the call, and Barak, true to form, generally repeated the points he'd made with me. However, he did raise one additional point. He told President Clinton that Clinton's pollster, Stan Greenberg, had also done a poll for Barak on what he would need in order to sell the agreement on the Golan Heights, and Barak wanted the President to see the findings. Not surprisingly, they confirmed the importance of what he was asking for: dealing with Lebanon, ensuring water rights, and demonstrating it was a new day with Syria and in the region.

I was present for the call, and I had no doubt about the enormity of the task before Barak. Nor did I question what he needed. My concern related to how we could produce what he needed, particularly if he was going to pull back again on the border.

The President did not share my concerns. On the contrary, he was encouraged by the call. In his view, Barak's emphasis on what he needed proved he was ready to do the deal in one round. Moreover, the President was convinced we could achieve everything Barak was asking for.

After reading the Greenberg polling data, the President was even more eager to try to meet Barak's needs. We were working on every front. We had sent high-level messages to Tunisia, Morocco, Qatar, and Oman to try to get an immediate upgrading in relations with Israel. We pressed them hard, making it clear that we needed them to do their part as we were working for a breakthrough between Syria and Israel. They could help us if they would now raise the level of their relations with Israel, something that would assure Israelis that it was a new day in the region. The responses, while supportive, were noncommittal and vague. We pressed them again, getting each to say they would take a step, but all stopped short of anything dramatic like the establishment of formal diplomatic relations.

On the FTZ, we began working with Jim Wolfensohn of the World Bank. In addition, Sandy and I met with Mort Zuckerman and Felix Rohatyn, our ambassador to France and formerly a leading financier, to see which firms might be ready to invest in such a zone. Though neither man felt that an investment in the FTZ made sense economically in the near term, they were committed to helping put it together. In every area in which Barak sought tangible accomplishment, there was promise but little likelihood of imminent results. Barak himself was still not yet ready to send his military people to Washington to present a package on Israel's security needs if there was a deal with Syria.

In any case, we had nothing concrete on what he wanted. The President wanted to call Asad again on Lebanon. I was uneasy. I knew what Barak wanted, but I feared the more we pressed on the resumption of the Lebanon talks, the more we would transform the resumption of talks into a strong bargaining chip for Asad. In a phone call, Asad would try to bargain with the President on what he might get for resuming the Lebanon negotiations. Better to see what could be done in the intensive round of negotiations.

We would not have the substance of what Barak wanted to set the stage for the endgame. We would, however, have the process: an intensive round of political-level negotiations in an isolated setting—Shepherdstown, West Virginia.

⟨22⟩

The Rise and Fall of the Israeli-Syrian Deal

SHEPHERDSTOWN, WEST VIRGINIA, IS about seventy-five minutes from Washington, D.C., by car. It is a small town in a rural setting. Just off interstate highway 81, the area is beset with rolling hills and farms dotting the landscape. During the summer, its craft fairs and theaters attract tourists. Other tourists pass through on their way to the Civil War battlefield of Antietam. Shepherdstown is old, quiet, and sleepy. How did we end up there for eight days of intensive talks involving a top-heavy Israeli delegation led by the Prime Minister, a smaller Syrian delegation led by the Foreign Minister, and a large U.S. delegation led by the Secretary of State but with daily visits by the President of the United States?

Once again Ehud Barak was the reason. He insisted that he could only go into an intensive round of negotiations if he could be assured there would be no leaks that might expose him politically. That required an isolated environment. That required our being colocated without any press access to where we were staying. And, finally, for Barak, it required blocking the use of all cell phones to restrict who could be calling in or out from our location.

Barak wanted the three delegations to live in a virtual cocoon. We ruled out Wye River and Camp David mostly because the Syrians would not want to be in either place. They would never want to look like they were following in the footsteps of Arafat. He had been at Wye, and that, in Shara's words, made it unacceptable. Camp David, of course, was where Sadat and Begin had been. The Syrians had opposed the Camp David agreements, and specifically requested we not go there.

Once again I called on Pat Kennedy to find us the place that met the Barak demands. Shepherdstown was his choice. There was a large hotel just outside the center of town that we could take over. It was easily cut off from the surrounding areas, with only one road into it and well removed from the highway. It was easy to secure and no one from the press would or could gain access to it. In addition, about ten minutes from the hotel was a beautiful retreat owned by the U.S. Fish and Wildlife Service which was used for training and conferences. It did not have enough rooms for the three delegations, but we could use it for more intimate discussions. It was surrounded by trees, had rustic rooms, and a grand conference facility made entirely of wood, boasting high ceilings, large fireplaces, and an imposing chandelier.

One other virtue of Shepherdstown was its close proximity to the White House. We wanted to be in a place that the President could reach by helicopter in about twenty to thirty minutes. The place fit all the criteria. Would the negotiations fit the place? Would Barak be ready to work toward an agreement in one round? If not, would we be able to sustain the negotiations?

My unease with the answers to these questions was magnified by my last phone call with Barak before he left Israel. He called me the night of January 1. Debbie and I had been invited to watch the Rose Bowl game and have dinner at the home of our good friends Gary Marx and Julie Rabinowitz. Dani Yatom had called shortly before we were to leave for their house to tell me the Prime Minister wanted to speak on a secure phone with me before he left Israel. I brought my bulky secure phone with me to Julie and Gary's house, plugged it in and disappeared downstairs for over an hour when Barak called.

The call was a repeat of Barak's last two conversations with me and with the President. Except now Barak was on the offensive: we had not produced what he said we must; as a result, he would have to be very careful with what he said. It was our job to reassure the Syrians and avoid a problem. It was our responsibility to convince the Syrians that he, Barak, would meet their needs, provided he heard more about how his needs would be addressed. My arguments—some hard, some soft—had no impact.

Barak, the man who so often spoke of paradoxes, was presenting us with one. He had come into office determined to get us out of the middle of negotiations. He had criticized Netanyahu for putting us in the middle—for putting us in a position where we had to negotiate with the other side, inevitably becoming sensitive to what Israel's Arab negotiating partner needed and ineluctably looking for ways to respond to what either Syria or the Palestinians wanted. Barak wanted us to be focused on his needs, not trying to find ways to accommodate the concerns of the Arab party to the negotiations. Yet here he was putting us in the middle. What added to the irony was his desire to put us in the middle at the very moment the Syrians were signaling a greater seriousness about coming to a conclusion with the Israelis. Once again, it was Barak who was opposed to tête-à-tête meetings with Shara, fearing that they would put him on the spot and force him to avoid a response. So once again, he wanted us to be Israel's surrogate.

I was very uneasy about playing this role at this stage and in this setting. However, if we were left with no choice and had to do it, we would need to be able to say something new to Shara, and Barak was not yet ready for that.

| SQUARING THE CIRCLE AT SHEPHERDSTOWN |

I had become increasingly convinced that the only way to reconcile Barak's approach with Shara's needs was for us to present a draft agreement while also reaffirming the Rabin pocket.

But Barak was resisting a reaffirmation, knowing how much the Syrians wanted it and trying to get something for it. This was understandable, but unlikely to work given his timing and how he had raised their expectations and ours.

In his briefing before the President's initial meetings with Barak and Shara at Shepherdstown, Sandy Berger focused exclusively on the issue of reaffirming the Rabin pocket. He told the President we could look at what was possible "BP" (before pocket) and "AP" (after pocket). His conclusion: nothing was possible "BP," progress was possible only "AP."

The President looked at me and I nodded in agreement. There was, I told him, one other possibility if Barak would simply not reaffirm the Rabin pocket: We could tell Shara that the U.S. position was that the June 4, 1967 lines should be the basis of the negotiations on the border. This way Barak would not have to reaffirm; instead, Syria would be getting something new from the United States. Let Barak choose which he prefers, his reaffirmation or our affirmation.

President Clinton liked that approach, but Barak did not. In Clinton's first meeting with him at Shepherdstown, Barak would accept neither option, offering only to permit the President to say that "the endgame would be determined by the pocket," and even then only if Shara first agreed to the resumption of Israeli-Lebanese negotiations. Madeleine and I met Shara while the President was meeting Barak, and Shara was as unyielding as Barak. He insisted that he must have June 4 directly from Barak and that the border demarcation group must begin immediately. When I reminded him that he had agreed that the President would determine how best to proceed with the groups, he waved that off, saying that nothing could happen on any other issue until the border demarcation group met. Madeleine pressed him very hard on this, but he would not budge. Yet when he met with the President, he backed off this position, telling President Clinton he would be flexible on the procedural issues and could agree to the security and peace groups meeting first. On Lebanon, he said that *once* there was some progress here in Shepherdstown, it would be possible to resume those negotiations. So began a pattern at Shepherdstown in which Shara would generally, though not always, assume a very hard-line position with the Secretary and me and then be much more conciliatory with the President. (I remarked to the Secretary that Asad must have told Shara to stay on Clinton's good side. "Great," she said, "that means we will get all of Shara's crap.")

With the President leaving and not returning until the following evening, Shara quickly resumed his harder-line posture, insisting that the border demarcation group must begin simultaneously with the other groups and retreating on the Lebanon negotiations.

Throughout the next day, we were stuck in a tug-of-war on the procedural issue of the groups starting. Barak insisted that the peace and security groups must meet for several days before the water and border groups could meet. Shara would not budge from the position that they all start together or not at all. Finally, I suggested a compromise: two groups, security and peace would start that evening in a U.S.-Israeli-Syrian format; the two remaining groups, border and water, would begin with indirect meetings that evening. Each party would meet with us, not with the other; we would speak to each side and learn more from them on what they needed in order to make the direct discussions more productive. Shara accepted this, and once Barak knew that Shara accepted he too agreed.

While this overcame the procedural hurdle, little substantive work took place. In the formal trilateral meetings in which there were direct discussions, each side simply repeated its previous positions. Our efforts to produce new ideas, either in these or in our bilateral meetings, elicited nothing from either side. Shara would not authorize anything absent the border demarcation group meeting; Barak would not authorize anything absent the resumption of the Lebanon negotiations. Nothing, even informally, was going on.

To create a new dynamic, I suggested that we inform both sides that we would shortly table a draft with our understanding of each side's position on all issues. We would push the envelope by providing our understandings of what we believed to be the real, not formal, positions of each side; obviously, each side would be free to correct our understandings if they felt we were inaccurately portraying their positions. We would put in brackets the differing positions of the two sides where there was no convergence. But there would be no brackets in those areas in which we assessed there was basic agreement.

Given our commitment to Barak that we would not surprise him, we promised to go over the draft prior to presenting it. But I told the Prime Minister that "this has to be our draft, not yours. We are *not* going to negotiate it with you in advance lest it lose its American character and therefore its credibility." He agreed with this, asking only that we not have something in it that Israel could not live with. That was not a problem.

Without necessarily showing the Syrians the draft, I felt the need also to ensure that the Syrians would not be surprised by the content or structure of the draft. I asked Shara to authorize someone on his delegation to have discussions with me so I could describe the basic approach we would follow in the draft and go over a number of our understandings of Syrian positions to ensure we did not misrepresent the Syrian side in the text we would present. Shara sent Daoudi to see me. But in response to my general comments and questions about some of their positions, Daoudi was unusually laconic, saying he would have to check "with the minister" before responding. I never heard back from him, leading me to conclude that the Syrians wanted to keep their distance from the draft until they saw it. They did not want to have any responsibility for it, giving them maximum maneuvering room to engage it or reject it.

In parallel with the effort of developing the draft, I met with Barak alone and also subsequently with Dani. In each conversation, I heard that it was critical to determine if Shara had any authority to negotiate. Barak would not expose himself unless he knew that Shara was truly empowered to negotiate. Dani asked for at least a sign that Shara could be flexible. "What," I asked, "would be a convincing sign to you?" "See," Dani replied, "if he has the capacity to tell us that they will give us the sovereignty over the water." While he said it would not give Israel what it wanted in terms of "a strip off the lake, it would be a step."

With this in mind, I decided it might be useful for Madeleine and me to sit with Shara. I had several purposes in mind. First, we could show him that the real gaps between the parties were less than appeared from the initial discussions. Second, in an informal setting we could get him to confirm what I believed to be the actual, not formal, Syrian positions. Third, if I was right, I would be able to come back to Barak and Dani and respond to what they had asked—showing there was flexibility on Shara's side so that real negotiations were, in fact, possible here.

Before going to Shepherdstown, I had prepared for the President a breakdown of the gaps on each issue based on what I thought the actual positions were. This is what I would present to Shara. Shara brought Butheina Sha'aban to the meeting with Madeleine and me.

Our meeting room had a white board opposite the table. Using a marker I drew two columns on the board: on one side I listed the Israeli positions, on the other the Syrian positions:

On the border, the Israeli position was full withdrawal from the Golan save for a narrow strip along the northeast part of the lake, and a similar narrow strip along an area of the Jordan river above the lake; the Syrian position was full withdrawal to the June 4 lines, which in the northeast part of the lake were defined by putting the border 10 meters off the shoreline.

On security arrangements, the Israeli position was a limited presence in the Mount Hermon early-warning site for a period even after Israeli withdrawal from the Golan Heights. In addition, the Israelis sought three zones of demilitarized or limited-deployment areas for Syrian forces extending at least to the Damascus area; it would accept limited deployment, though not demilitarized zones on its side of the border. For their part, the Syrians wanted no presence at the Mount Hermon early-warning site after Israeli withdrawal. It wanted demilitarization on both sides of the border, and it would not accept the limited deployment zones extending to Damascus.

On the content of peace, the Israelis wanted the establishment of full diplomatic relations, to be implemented in the first phase of withdrawal, meaning embassies would be established after a partial Israeli withdrawal from the Golan. In addition, the Israelis wanted the peace treaty to incorporate into it an infrastructure making full economic, tourist, commercial, banking, communications, aviation, postal, and other relations possible. The Syrians wanted embassies to be exchanged only after Israeli withdrawal was completed. But the Syrians would accept a limited, preparatory Israeli diplomatic presence four to six months before completion of withdrawal. They also sought a much simpler agreement stating only that diplomatic, trade, and tourist relations would be established with Israel.

On the timing of implementation, the Israelis wanted three years for withdrawal; the Syrians wanted eighteen months. And on water, the Israelis wanted a control mechanism to oversee the flow of water through the Golan Heights to ensure that the quality and the quantity of water feeding the Sea of Galilee would not be altered. The Syrians were prepared to offer verbal assurances to that effect, but also wanted us to produce comparable assurances from Turkey on water flows into Syria.

Shara sat in rapt attention as I wrote everything on the board. When I finished, he asked questions and corrected me in one place to the benefit of the Israelis. Initially, he asked how much of a strip the Israelis were talking about. Here he meant both the length of the area along the northeast part of the lake where the Israelis would need the strip and the width of the strip itself. His question on whether the strip had to extend down to Ein Gev seemed to imply that if the length of the strip were small enough, something might be worked out.

On the question of whose sovereignty applied where, he was straightforward and unequivocal: *The Israelis would have sovereignty over the lake; the Syrians would have sovereignty over the land, at least all the land to the east of the 10 meters off the shoreline.*

On early warning, he actually pointed out a mistake I had made in describing the Syrian position. Inadvertently I had written that the Syrians wanted no presence at Mount Hermon; Shara corrected me, saying Syria wanted no "Israeli" presence at

Mount Hermon. That is what I had intended to write. Shara volunteered that the Syrians would accept an American presence at the Mount Hermon early-warning station for five years after the Israeli withdrawal.

Shara indicated more flexibility than I had expected. For the first time with Madeleine and me, Shara looked to be trying to find ways to overcome the differences between the two sides. He confirmed the very thing Dani said would demonstrate that Shara had sufficient flexibility to negotiate—namely, that Israel would have sovereignty over the lake. He also confirmed that the Syrians accepted an American presence at Mount Hermon—something that addressed, at least in part, Barak's concerns about early warning.

It may not have been revolutionary, but Shara not only looked to be responsive but open to creative solutions. When Madeleine and I informed Barak of our discussion, he acknowledged that Shara had some authority to negotiate but not enough to make a difference. He had to have Lebanon resumption or there was no way to do anything in this round. "Well," I replied, "Mr. Prime Minister, you may not have another round." He was unmoved, convinced that, in Dani's words, "he must have more to overcome his domestic opposition."

I drew the conclusion that Barak intended to leave after a week with the objective of being able to show his public that he had made no concessions at Shepherdstown, even while he gleaned that Shara had sufficient flexibility to negotiate and, perhaps, revealed to his public that he had succeeded in gaining concessions from the Syrians. In this way Barak would, in his view, cement the political basis on which he could move to a conclusion. That worked for him, but obviously not for Shara.

The meeting with Shara had lifted our hopes of being able to make real progress now. The Barak response had deflated us. It also added to our worry of how we would manage Shara for the rest of the time at Shepherdstown. Madeleine had the idea of talking "privately" to Butheina, believing that this might offer another way to reassure Shara and convey positions "off the record."

| THE "CHICK CHANNEL" |

Butheina was surely an unusual Syrian woman. She had written books on the role of women in Islamic societies. She was highly critical of Islamic regimes that repressed women. She was an academic by training and had secured a postdoctoral fellowship to a small university in Michigan for the spring. Since she had become Asad's interpreter she appeared increasingly confident in his presence. According to Gamal, she was an expert interpreter, but took liberties in her translating. While being precise with Asad's words she offered editorial commentary in her translations of what we said to him. If she had any uncertainty about her position, she would not dare to take such liberties. In addition, as Asad's health declined, she would fill out Asad's thoughts when he had difficulty expressing himself in phone calls with the President. In a sense, I believed she had become an additional pair of eyes and ears for Asad.

I liked Butheina and had side conversations with her. She was very intelligent, easy to converse with, and always professed her commitment and desire for peace. But I also had no illusions about her: her loyalties were to her regime and its leader. She would not reveal anything her President did not want revealed. She would not, in my judgment, suggest any areas of flexibility or openings as a way to push the negotiations unless she was authorized to do so. The "chick channel," as Madeleine dubbed it, would not be a vehicle for us to influence the Syrian position; instead I believed it would be a channel for the Syrians to influence us.

I did not believe this would necessarily harm us, but I also saw limited benefit in it. True to my expectations, Butheina used the channel to tell Madeleine that Shara was under a great deal of pressure, was not sleeping, and needed us to give him something on June 4. She asked Madeleine whether we could put in writing what the President had told Shara about Barak not withdrawing the Rabin deposit from the President's pocket.

It was not an unreasonable request, but I did not want to rush to do something about it. If this was something that Shara would value, I wanted to hold it until such time as we truly needed it. However, Madeleine, Sandy, and the President were feeling defensive in light of Barak's behavior. Butheina's conversation reinforced their sense that Barak was creating a problem for Shara. In light of that, they felt the need to present the letter that Butheina asked for. Martin and I drafted it.

The President liked it. Since he would be conveying Barak's position, he understandably felt the need to review the letter first with Barak before sharing it with Shara. When we met with Barak, President Clinton summarized Madeleine's conversation with Butheina; Barak was intrigued with the channel and agreed that presenting the letter to Shara was a good idea. Upon seeing it, he softened it by replacing "Barak has told me that he will not withdraw the Rabin deposit" with "[it was the President's] understanding that Barak did not intend to withdraw the Rabin deposit." The change might not have been dramatic, but again it reflected Barak's mind-set of qualifying everything that would be said to Shara about what Barak would do. Nonetheless, he, too, was in favor of giving the letter to Shara now, especially because it fit his belief that our reassurance would substitute for any steps he should take.

I continued to be against giving the letter to the Syrians at this moment. I told the President and Barak that we did not know how Shara would react to an American draft peace treaty. That Daoudi had not responded indicated they would reserve judgment.

We were banking on the draft providing the basis for continuing the negotiations. Why not, I argued, wait until after we had given both sides the draft. If we had a problem with Shara at that point, we could then use the letter. In this way, Shara would be able to show Asad he had produced something new from President Clinton to give added reassurance about the border, especially because the language on the border would be bracketed in the draft text.

Barak and Madeleine were agnostic. The President and Sandy were not. They felt it would make it easier for Shara to accept the draft as the basis for further negotiations if the President was also giving him something that would be reassuring. I disagreed but the President was going to see Shara that night, and I was guilty of ignoring a basic reality in a situation like this: the President of the United States is never going to want to go into a critical meeting with nothing in hand. The letter would give him something—almost certainly bound to make Shara responsive at least for the moment—and I was leaving him empty-handed.

Instinctively, I knew we were making a mistake by putting the President in a position where he felt he must deliver "something." We were overusing the President at Shepherdstown and creating a situation in which the President would feel the need to present new elements in every meeting. Barak helped to create the situation by insisting on a setting with continual presidential involvement, and by never offering anything new on his end. Shara quickly realized that appearing responsive to the President would yield dividends, and Barak used the President to keep the Syrians on board while he held out.

It was fruitless to try to get the President to hold off on the letter until after we had presented the draft. He had the letter to present; next he could present the draft.

I, too, tried to take advantage of the President's presence to give added weight to the draft. Having him present it, and having him emphasize that this reflected his best judgment, was bound to make Shara take it more seriously. So even if I was worrying about devaluing the President's currency, I was still in the forefront of contributing to the overuse of President Clinton.

Whatever my misgivings about presenting the letter Thursday night before knowing the Syrian reaction to the draft, the President's instinct seemed more correct than mine. I watched the President sell the letter to Shara as a step he felt he must take to reassure the Syrians. Shara read the letter very carefully and then stated it was a very good and important letter. Shara also responded favorably to another suggestion. Because I was still searching for a mechanism for discussion that would make progress possible once we delivered the draft on Friday, I asked the President to propose to each side the creation of an informal discussion channel. It would be a one-on-one meeting on each issue, with a single American joining an Israeli and a Syrian. The President sold this as giving us a chance to help narrow the gaps that would be reflected in the draft text.

He turned to me to explain what I expected from each side in the meeting, and I emphasized that this had to be a forum for new ideas. They need not be committing, but they had to reflect a serious effort among the three of us to generate new ways to overcome the differences that the bracketed language in the draft would identify.

Here, too, Shara was agreeable. The stage was set for the President to present the draft on Friday morning. He would do so in a three-way meeting with Barak and Shara and members of both delegations. We would give each side Friday and Saturday to develop responses to the draft, and on Saturday night and Sunday morning, the one-on-one meetings could commence.

| PRESIDENT CLINTON PRESENTS OUR DRAFT PEACE TREATY BETWEEN ISRAEL AND SYRIA |

Friday morning, on a frosty day in Shepherdstown, the President arrived and with a fire blazing in the fireplace behind him, presented our draft peace treaty. I wanted him to sell this as something he had personally invested in; something he had studied carefully. He must present the draft as a distillation of our judgment of what was already agreed, and what remained to be resolved. He must also present it as an extraordinary development, marking the first time an Amercian draft peace treaty between Israel and Syria was being put on the table.

No one was better at convincing others of the significance of a step than Bill Clinton. He asked both sides to study our draft carefully. He asked them not to nitpick over the draft but to focus on ways to overcome the gaps we identified with the bracketed language—language that reflected the differences in how the two sides would resolve the issue in question. He told them he was optimistic we could now reach agreement, but we all had to work hard to do it. He looked forward to their comments to us, but again with an eye toward overcoming the remaining problems, not trying to "score points or improve language for yourself while making it impossible for your negotiating partner."

Barak's response was very good, emphasizing his respect for Asad, his belief that an agreement could be reached soon, and the importance of each side taking into account the sensitivities of the other. Shara, too, was on his best behavior, generally agreeing with Barak.

I was suddenly more hopeful, though I was anxious to see how the Syrians would respond to the draft. I knew we had taken a leap in the draft because the issue that mattered most to the Israelis—the principles of peace—had no brackets, and the issue that mattered most to the Syrians—the border—was bracketed. Our text accurately reflected the reality of the Syrians agreeing on the principles of peace and the Israelis not accepting June 4 as the border. But it was one thing to say that to each side and something else to put it in black and white in a text, even a text labeled a draft and described as reflecting American understandings of the two positions. The President had just said our draft peace treaty represented a major step, and yet on the core issue for the Syrians there was clearly no agreement on June 4. There were certainly plenty of brackets on issues of importance to the Israelis, like security, water, and the extent of normalization, but I wondered about the Syrian response to seeing what they might consider a fundamental asymmetry in the draft.*

After giving both sides the draft in the morning, we heard nothing from the Syrians through Friday afternoon. I reminded Madeleine that Daoudi had told me in Bern that the Syrians took thirteen hours to go over the Lauder ten points. If that took thirteen hours, then this comprehensive text of roughly eight pages would take far longer. With that in mind and believing there would be nothing more we could do before getting a Syrian response, I asked Madeleine if I could go home for Friday night and return late Saturday afternoon before the end of Shabbat. Playing on her maternal instincts did not hurt; my son, home from college, was returning to UCLA in the morning, and this would give me a chance to see him before he departed. Madeleine, always sympathetic to my family requests, told me to go ahead.

It was great to leave Shepherdstown, even if for less than a day. I was looking forward to having a nice evening with the family and getting some sleep.

|BACK TO SHEPHERDSTOWN AND REALITY |

I returned to Shepherdstown late the next afternoon. The Syrians had still offered no reaction to the draft. By Saturday night, we heard that the Syrians had comments but had not yet shared them with Shara.

Recognizing that the Syrian position might be to hold off on a response pending Israeli reactions or even until after they were able to share the draft with Asad, we decided to push to convene the one-on-one meetings that Shara had already accepted. Shara seemed almost relieved to convene such meetings, perhaps seeing it as a way to avoid having to comment on the draft at this time.

---

*On the border, the Syrian bracketed language was clear, leaving no doubt that the border was based on "withdrawal to the June 4 line." The Israeli bracket made no reference to the scope of withdrawal, reading simply, "the border to be mutually agreed." The Israeli formulation did not necessarily contradict the Syrian position, but did not indicate agreement either.

Shara designated General Omar the representative for the border and the security meetings, Daoudi for the water meeting, and Walid for the meeting on implementing normal relations. I was pleased to see Walid assume an important position again. With Daoudi's emergence in Bern and Bethesda, Walid appeared to have been eclipsed, with his role redefined. I suspected that he was paying a price because of the Lauder episode. Though Asad had met with Lauder repeatedly—which was obviously his decision—someone had to pay a price for what was subsequently considered a mistake, and it had apparently been Walid. That he seemed to have a role again was also a good sign about Asad's intent. No one on the Syrian side could be more creative in reconciling Syria's considerations with Israeli needs on normalizing relations.

General Omar's partner for the security meeting would be Shlomo Yanai, chief of planning in the IDF. Uri Saguy would be Omar's counterpart on the border. I decided to join these meetings, believing that movement on security and the border could make Shepherdstown a success and greatly increase the likelihood of an agreement.

To my surprise, General Omar was forthcoming in both meetings. He made significant moves on both security and the border. On security, he proposed security zones—areas in which forces would be separated and with their arms limited—closer in size to what the Israelis had in mind.* In addition, he accepted General Yanai's proposal for extensive active and passive monitoring of Syrian and Israeli ground forces, weapons depots, and logistic support units. (Barak had repeatedly emphasized that extensive inspections, together with passive monitoring using cameras at different bases, provided greater warning indicators for preventing surprise attack than being able to get the Syrians to redeploy their forces somewhat farther from the Israeli border.)†

General Omar tied his moves on security to Israel accepting June 4 as the basis for border demarcation. Yanai could not reply on the border, but was keen to develop what he, too, saw were Syrian moves on security, especially as they related to early warning.

In the border meeting, General Omar also demonstrated unexpected flexibility. Taking topographical features into account—principally, the hills above the Jordan River—he suggested that the border could be adjusted as much as 50 meters to meet mutual needs and concerns. He implied that this principle could apply throughout the

---

*He proposed changing the Shihabi ratio from 10:6 now to 10:5 for the relevant areas—meaning that the zones on the Syrian side would be twice the size of those on the Israeli side.

†Knowing that Damascus was only 60 kilometers from where the June 4 border might be, Barak understood that the defense of the Syrian capital precluded any significant movement of Syrian forces far away from the Israeli border.

were born. As usual Debbie would fill in while I was away, being strong for them despite her own loss. My place was not here at Shepherdstown. It was with my family.

When I told Madeleine, she was not just sympathetic, she was almost insistent that I should leave at any point I felt I must. Debbie was concerned that I shouldn't leave Shepherdstown if I could still do something today; the funeral would take place on Tuesday. I was torn, but I decided that it made sense for me to stay for the day to try to salvage the end of Shepherdstown in a way that might yet preserve the negotiations, and leave to join the family the next day. It was already clear that Barak intended to leave then, and once he left Shara would leave as well.

Madeleine had invited Barak to her farm for lunch. I viewed this as an opportunity to see if we could move him either to do something directly with Shara or to give us something beyond what the President had written to Shara.

What complicated the effort to do this was a story in the Arab media that had the earmarks of a Syrian leak. While no details of the talks were, in fact, revealed, the issues discussed, including the border, were outlined in a way that reflected Syria's priorities. The Israelis cried foul, claiming a violation of the ground rules. A close examination of the article showed it could have been written before Shepherdstown, but Barak saw it as further evidence of the danger of saying anything new on the border.

Barak brought Nava, his wife, and Amnon Shahak to the lunch. I joined Madeleine. Initially, the lunch revolved around pleasantries, talk about the farm, the countryside, and the like. Then, whether to make conversation or because he genuinely wanted to know what I thought would happen now, Barak asked for my assessment. It was a good opening and I bluntly told him that he might feel the Syrians had not done enough, but they knew they had moved on every issue. They knew, as well, that Barak had not. Believe it or not, I said, because you have raised their expectations, they will feel betrayed in these circumstances and Shara, to protect himself, will surely exaggerate that sense with Asad. I said I was not sure how we would salvage this, and I asked what it would take now for him to signal something new.

If I hoped my argument would move Barak, I was wrong. His answer remained unchanged: "Resume the Lebanon negotiations." Although I argued that what was going to matter to your public was that you concluded Lebanon, not that you were able to talk about it, Barak was not convinced.

Unfortunately, Shara was convinced. In our meeting with him later in the day he was clear: Shepherdstown was a disaster; Syria had been flexible and exposed concessions and gotten nothing in return. Barak was not serious and he would have to report to his President that he had failed. That would be very hard to do, but he could not lie to President Asad.

Some of this was surely for our benefit. But Shara was also genuinely angry, and perhaps a little fearful of the personal consequences of returning home empty-handed.

When the President arrived for what would be a final dinner with both Barak and Shara, I focused on what he needed to do with the Prime Minister. I doubted President Clinton could get anything more from Barak at this time. Barak had made his decision and was not going to be moved. The challenge now was for the President to get something from Barak that he could use with Asad immediately *after* the close of Shepherdstown. That might give us a peg on which to sustain the negotiations.

I focused on a Clinton call to Asad in which he could convey what we had not been able to convey to Shara—namely, that the Rabin deposit was now a Barak deposit. The President could explain that Barak, believing that his political base needed to be shored up first, felt comfortable having us convey this only after Shepherdstown. As I explained to President Clinton upon his arrival, this was "pretty thin gruel," but it was new for Asad. While Asad would be skeptical, we were unlikely to have anything else to salvage the process, and even this would require him to press Barak hard.

Though President Clinton had exhibited much sympathy for Barak's position throughout Shepherdstown, now, as he was staring a breakdown in the face, he was angry. Why had Barak put us in this position? Didn't he know everything could fall apart, that Asad would feel betrayed and tell the world, especially the Arab world, that?

I did not much feel like defending Barak, and I knew that this was the President's way of rehearsing how he would approach Barak. He asked how bad Shara's mood was, and Madeleine said, "It is very bad. He is going to tell Asad this has failed."

The President understood what was at stake. He would see Barak before the dinner and get him to be more forthcoming now, but failing that, he would try to get him to allow a call to Asad with "a Barak reaffirmation of Rabin."

Knowing the President, I knew he would push Barak to make a move at the dinner with Shara. He did, emphasizing Shara's mood. But Barak stood firm, no doubt believing that Shara was manipulating us. Barak said he could not afford to reaffirm Rabin or deal with the border until he knew he was in the decisive round. It was an old argument, and not persuasive since his behavior at Shepherdstown had made it impossible for this to be a decisive round.

When the President asked what would convince him that he was entering a decisive round, his answer was the resumption of Lebanon. To me it was a strange measure. It did not reflect any flexibility on Syria's part. A deal on Lebanon with the Lebanese would not be possible until the Syrians sanctioned it. However, Barak had convinced himself that the moment Asad stopped withholding negotiations on Lebanon, Barak would have the sign that he was no longer manipulating the Lebanon card.

Ironically, Barak had turned it into more of a card by insisting on resumption.

Now he told President Clinton that he would reaffirm Rabin once the Lebanon negotiations resumed or were about to resume; once Shepherdstown was over, he had no problem with the President conveying that to Asad. That was as much as the President could get from Barak prior to the dinner.

| THE LAST SUPPER |

Given everything, it probably would have been advisable to cancel the dinner. Barak repeated his admiration and respect for Asad, but Shara had heard all this before. He was not going to be satisfied with Barak's platitudes. He asked Barak directly if he would reaffirm the Rabin commitment. With the President looking on, Barak's only response was a smile. Knowing Asad's suspicion and propensity for seeing conspiracies everywhere, Shara was bound to interpret Barak's silence in the worst possible light.

The notion that Barak might need to show his public in Israel that he had not conceded anything during this round was never going to be accepted by the Syrians. In any case, Shara was focused on his needs, not Barak's. He knew his boss needed to hear something on the deposit and would not have sent Shara if nothing was going to be forthcoming in this round. The Syrians had been led to believe by Barak and by us that this would be a decisive round—that was the reason for staying through the Eid.

Following the dinner, the President sat alone with Shara and worked on him. He told him he did have something new and meaningful from Barak, but Barak had not been prepared to reveal it at the dinner. He had, however, authorized the President to convey it to Asad, and he set a time with Shara for the call to Asad. Shara asked the President not to call Asad before his return to Damascus. He suggested that the President call Asad in three days—on Thursday. In turn, the President asked Shara not to be negative in public in his comments or to be negative when briefing Asad. The President also wanted us to formulate a public statement announcing the conclusion of this round of talks and the resumption of talks within ten days. Shara was agreeable, but I was dubious. My doubts were soon borne out.

| THE LEAK AND TRYING TO PRESERVE THE SYRIAN TRACK |

I flew to California Monday evening. I was available by phone off and on before the President's planned phone call. Rob Malley was responsible for writing the President's points for the call, and we talked about how to make the pitch to Asad.

However, a new factor was introduced even before the call. While both sides assured us that they would protect the bracketed draft of the text, it leaked in Israel. Upon his return Barak had been greeted with a large demonstration against giving up the Golan Heights. Perhaps someone in the government chose to leak the draft to show what Barak had gained at Shepherdstown and that he had not given away the border.*

We had tried to lessen the damage of a possible leak by putting a disclaimer at the top of each page of the draft, making clear that the positions in the text reflected the U.S. understanding of these positions and was not binding on either side. But when the text was leaked the disclaimer had disappeared.

It might not have mattered, but at least the disclaimer would have given the Syrians some cover. As it was, it appeared that the Syrians had conceded the principles of peace to Israel without any qualifiers and had not gotten Israeli acceptance of the border in return. I had thought about adding a note in the text to make it clear that the Syrian position on peace was contingent on the June 4, 1967 border, but I did not do so, assuming that the Syrians would add that. Why, I thought, water down the formulation if the Syrians were likely to water down any formulation they got. Unfortunately for Shara, he had chosen not to comment on the text and now he was exposed in Damascus.

In fact, Shara told Madeleine in a protesting phone call that he was under severe attack. For once, he was not exaggerating. In an unprecedented move, Shara was criticized by the Syrian Writers Union for conceding but not achieving. This was bound to have an effect on Asad.

Nothing happens by accident in an authoritarian state like Syria. The Writers Union did not just decide to criticize Shara. Someone in a position of power had used the Writers Union to criticize the negotiations. Asad's health situation made him less capable of maintaining total control, and he was bound to read the criticism as a warning shot over concessions that Syria was making. Quite apart from that, I knew that Asad, even weakened by deteriorating health, would not tolerate a situation in which he appeared to be losing. If such a scenario was unacceptable before, it might be even worse now with succession on his mind. He would want nothing to happen that might jeopardize his son succeeding him. Criticism of Shara in these circumstances was bound to set off alarm bells for Asad and trigger some reaction to demonstrate that Syria was not losing.

It was in this environment that the President placed his call to Asad. I was not able to listen in, but I had told Rob the President would have to use all his persuasive pow-

---

*In 2002, Martin Indyk told me he had learned that Nimrod Novik was responsible for the leak. Nimrod was not part of the government but remained close to Yossi Beilin, who was the Minister of Justice in the Barak government. Supposedly, Yossi and the people around him were troubled by Barak's focus on Syria, believing the priority should be on the Palestinians. The question remains whether Beilin and his staff ever obtained an actual copy of the draft treaty.

ers given Asad's likely perceptions and the negative briefings Shara had already given him. When Rob called to brief me on the call, he started by telling me that the President had gone overboard. No doubt fearing that everything was at stake in this call, the President had promised that if the Lebanon talks resumed, Barak would not only reaffirm Rabin but also agree to demarcate the border based on the Rabin deposit.

To be sure, if we had another round, which was supposed to be decisive, Barak would have to go along with this. But logic was one thing; promises were another. The President did not have this in his pocket from Barak. Sandy and Madeleine felt that I needed to call Barak and convince him to accept these positions without revealing what the President had done.

I spoke to Barak on Saturday and used his own logic against him. I told him that if we got Lebanon talks resumed that would mean, according to Barak, that Asad was signaling his readiness for the decisive round. Necessarily that required from Barak not only the reaffirmation he had already promised but also his readiness to demarcate the border based on the deposit. Barak agreed, qualifying this only by saying that we could demarcate under the implicit title of June 4, but that Israel would initially only listen to the Syrian presentation of the border and then explain what Israel would need to agree to a border that would replace the 1923 international line. While knowing the demarcation process would be hard, I felt relieved that I had gotten Barak to agree to what the President had promised Asad. Knowing Asad was likely to retrench because of the leak, I was nonetheless hopeful that we might be able to proceed on the basis of what the President had told Asad.

But that was not to be. The Syrians now upped their demands. In his call to the Secretary on the following Monday Shara told her that the Lebanon negotiations could only resume after the demarcation of the border was complete. This was a total dead end. Syria was now no longer looking for reaffirmation of Rabin or the launching of a demarcation committee; it was looking to finalize the border as the price of resuming Lebanon talks.

Why would the Syrians up the ante in this way? Partly because they were angry with Barak, feeling they had been had, and now he would have to pay. Partly because Barak had made the mere existence of Lebanon talks so important. And partly because the President's phone call committed to the demarcation committee based on the deposit. At a minimum, the Syrians wanted to see what they could get. Beyond this, Asad was probably in no hurry to go back to the talks. He felt burned and he would not rush back into a situation whose outcome was now uncertain and potentially costly to him in the succession sweepstakes.

Knowing we were dead in the water with Shara's position, we decided to have the President call Asad to tell him what we could and could not do. Asad was clearly not in good shape during this call. He found it difficult to express his thoughts; voices in the background prompted nearly all his answers. Asad simply repeated what Shara had told Madeleine.

As the President pressed Asad, telling him that he was asking for too much to resume Lebanon talks, Asad made one comment on his own. He did not know what the Israeli requirements were; they always seemed to grow. Nothing could be decided unless the Israeli needs were clear once and for all.

Following the call, I suggested to the President that we could either spin our wheels trying to get back to negotiations or we could try to cut to the quick. Asad would not now ease his position on Lebanon, and lacking that, Barak would not reaffirm Rabin or demarcate the border. We were stuck. Asad did provide one opening, however. He had asked what Israel required. In light of that, I saw our only possibility was to get from Barak his near-bottom-line requirements. We could then present these to Asad and see if we could broker an endgame.

The President agreed. Into this mix came Prince Bandar again. He asked to see the President, telling him he was prepared to go see Asad if it would help. The President leaped on this. In light of his conversation with Asad, he explained what we would now do with Barak. He asked Bandar to reassure Asad that a deal was possible and that he would want to see Asad when we had what we needed from Barak. Bandar understood the President to be telling him that he knew what Asad needed and that he would not meet with Asad until he had that from Barak.

This created a misunderstanding insofar as Bandar believed we would only go to Asad when we had what we knew he demanded, and that is what he conveyed to Asad. What we intended to convey was that we would go to Asad with Barak's requirements so Asad could then decide whether he was ready to do a deal on that basis. For now, Bandar went to Damascus and saw Asad. Following the meeting, he sent me a message through his deputy Rihab Massoud, asking me to meet him secretly in Geneva.

Bandar suggested Geneva because he knew I would be going with the Secretary to the World Economic Forum in Davos, Switzerland. It had the benefit of being near the Middle East, and if there was a need for him to return to see Asad, he could do so quickly.

| ANOTHER SECRET MEETING IN SWITZERLAND |

Our meeting was set for January 28 in Geneva. Bandar greeted me warmly, and uncharacteristically launched very quickly into the reason for the meeting. He had spent three and a half hours with Asad. Bandar had many impressions, but unlike in any meeting I had ever had with him, Bandar pulled out a piece of paper, making clear that this was a report that the Syrians wanted conveyed to the United States. The points were clear and blunt: Asad was determined to do a deal, and had thought he had a partner in Barak for that purpose. Now he was not sure. Barak, he felt, had played a game in Shepherdstown. Asad was not Arafat; he could not be treated this way. The two sides should take their bitter pill together and not stretch things out. He could not afford to have his people coming and going in multiple rounds. They should get together in one round and stay until they finished. The border could be demarcated in secret and not revealed until the deal was done. But it must be demarcated. The Israelis did not want him to negotiate over their security requirements; they could not expect him to bargain over June 4.

When Bandar finished reading from this paper, he added a number of impressions: Asad was surprisingly fit in the meeting and was focused for the full three and a half hours. But this was not the Asad he had known in the past. Asad had always been one to play for time; not now. Asad had referred to the issue of succession and his health, acknowledging that he wanted to get the deal done now, not play games. Asad was clearly disappointed with Barak and wondered whether he had misjudged him.

Bandar concluded that if the demarcation of the border occurred he believed everything would fall into place quickly. There was an opportunity and it should not be lost.

I outlined what I thought had happened and how we might overcome the problems we now faced. Barak, I said, had raised expectations and Shara had probably exaggerated what he had heard from Barak at Blair House. The two sides had, I believed, very different expectations of what would be done at Shepherdstown. For this I said Barak was more at fault than the Syrians. He was the one who had insisted that he could not go to multiple rounds; indeed, he was the one whom Asad now sounded like. But the blame could not be laid exclusively at his doorstep. He was looking for more from the Syrians about Lebanon, the content of peace, security arrangements, and the border. Barak, like Asad, did not want to make concessions that might expose him politically if the deal was not about to be done.

From all this, I drew one basic conclusion: we could not go back to the next round of negotiations unless we prepared the ground. Next time both sides had to know what was expected of them and what each could do. I concluded by asking Bandar about the meaning of Asad's point that he could not be expected to bargain over June 4. Did he mean the principle of June 4 must be accepted, but the line itself could still be negotiated and worked out; or was he telling us that the line was not subject to negotiation? If the former, we were in business; if the latter, he was walking back the Shara statement at Blair House and General Omar's moves at Shepherdstown.

Bandar was not sure. But he reported that he had told Asad that he believed each side—the Syrians, Israelis, and Americans—probably each had their own definition and their own maps of what the June 4 line should be. (I smiled as Bandar recounted this, knowing that I had told Bandar this as a way of conditioning him to the old Peres idea that June 4 was more of a concept than a border.) According to Bandar, Asad agreed with this point—something that implied Asad was prepared to be flexible on the line, just not on the principle.

As our next step, we agreed that I would brief the President and the Israelis, and we would then collectively decide if there was any message we wanted Bandar to take back to Asad.

Amnon Shahak, then the Minister of Tourism, was in Geneva at the time. Following my meeting with Bandar, I met with Amnon and we decided to go to dinner. Gamal, who had accompanied me to Geneva but not to the Bandar meeting, joined us. We walked to the old part of Geneva to find a restaurant. Tucked away in the corner of a lively Italian restaurant teeming with young people, we ate pizzas and chewed over the meaning of Bandar's report.

We doubted that Asad was physically fit, alert, and capable of sitting through a three-and-a-half hour meeting. But clearly the Syrians wanted us to think that, and Bandar, in this respect, was doing their bidding. Nonetheless, we both still saw value in Bandar's report, particularly because it probably did offer a picture of Asad's thinking. Amnon also saw value in Bandar seeing Asad again, if for no other reason than to have someone other than Shara reporting to Asad on Israeli and even U.S. positions.

We then discussed whether a deal was possible. Gamal didn't think so, noting it did not seem like there was anything new. Yes, Asad was in a hurry, but only if the deal was on his terms. Amnon did not challenge that, but was less certain than Gamal that there was no flexibility on Asad's part. I was also not sure. But I was uneasy about Bandar's depiction of Asad's views on June 4. I had a feeling that Bandar told me what I wanted to hear on the issue of flexibility on the line versus flexibility on the principle. Somehow I felt the meeting had been a Syrian idea to make us sympathetic to Asad and his "needs" and to make Barak feel defensive—and of course to produce Saudi understanding of the position in which Barak was putting Asad.

Amnon did not argue about whether there was a deal there with Asad now. But he felt we had to find out. Barak would not move on the Palestinians without knowing where he stood on Syria, and this meeting added to our collective need to determine if a deal was possible. Amnon was now convinced that communicating Barak's bottom lines to Asad was, in fact, the best way to proceed. He saw no other way to determine if Asad was prepared to conclude a deal at this stage, and he would tell Barak that on his return.

| DETERMINING BARAK'S BOTTOM LINES |

It would be several days before I would go to Israel. I would be at Davos for two days and then spend another two days in Moscow for the resumption of the Middle Eastern multilateral negotiations—negotiations that had been suspended during Netanyahu's tenure. Amnon had time to brief Barak and condition him to the idea of our drawing out his essential requirements for presentation to Asad.

Through Martin, Amnon communicated with me before I arrived in Israel. Barak was impressed with Bandar's report. He agreed with the approach of presenting his bottom-line requirements to Asad, but felt that only the President could do that with Asad. If he was presenting bottom lines or near bottom lines, this had to be done with drama and a sense of finality to determine if Asad was ready for a deal—or just trying to "pocket" what he could. No surprise here. Martin conveyed one other message prior to my arrival: Barak was completely out of step with the country's mood on Syria. No one was keen to do a deal with the Syrians.

On my arrival on February 2, I found that, if anything, Martin's message was understated. Barak was completely isolated in his own cabinet on Syria. Even Amnon, who felt we had to determine if a Syrian deal was possible, believed that it was a major mistake not to be engaging the Palestinians on the permanent status issues. A consensus in the country favored resolving the conflict with the Palestinians. There was no such consensus on Syria. The author, Amos Oz, a leading peace advocate, expressed the country's skeptical mood in his now-famous line that the Syrians "think that we will give them the Golan and they will send us a receipt by fax." The grudging nature of the Syrian approach to peace, the absence of a public handshake with Barak at Blair House or Shepherdstown, Shara's statement at the White House, Israeli soldiers being killed in Lebanon, editorials in the Syrian press emphasizing Holocaust denial, all tended to convince the Israeli public that Syria was not ready for peace—and therefore a deal should not be pursued now.

This was extraordinarily ironic. The issues involving the Syrians were straightforward and not complicated. True, the Golan Heights would have to be given up, but that could not compare to the existential nature of the issues involving the Palestinians. Yet the Israeli public believed the Palestinians were ready for peace and thus preferred to deal with the emotional and highly complex questions involving the Palestinians.

But Barak was not on that page. He had committed during his campaign to getting out of Lebanon and he would do so. He understood that a unilateral withdrawal might not bring quiet along Israel's border. Instead, in a circumstance in which there was no deal with Syria, President Asad might have a stake in keeping the Lebanese-Israeli border boiling as a way of ensuring that Israel would know that it could not have peace without giving up the Golan Heights. If so, Syria would prevent the Lebanese army from establishing control in the south after an Israeli withdrawal. And that might mean that Hizbollah or radical Palestinians would continue attacks, only now into northern Israel. Israel, having withdrawn and now having its citizens, not its soldiers, as the target, would hit back hard at the source of the attacks—even if that meant going after Syria.

In an hour-long car ride from Jerusalem to his home in Kochav Yair just before sundown and the onset of Shabbat on February 4, Barak explained all this to me, emphasizing, "There could be a major escalation after we get out of Lebanon. I owe it to my people to have exhausted every opportunity to do a deal with Syria before getting out. Maybe it won't be possible, but at least I will know and our people will know there was no other way."

To find out definitively if there was no other way, we had to be able to present what Barak could do to meet Asad's fundamental need on withdrawal and what he required from Asad on peace, security, and water to be able to do that. If this was acceptable to Asad, we would proceed; if not, we would be unable to continue.

Barak accepted the logic of this in the abstract. As I explained to him, our message to Asad must be stark. We must show that we had cut to the heart of the matter in terms of what we were bringing from Barak, and it was time to determine whether a deal was possible. We would be preparing the ground for the endgame of negotiations in the only way we could. We would be engaging Asad directly both to do away with the asymmetry between Barak and Shara and to deny Asad the excuse that he did not know Israel's true requirements. We could not expect Asad to respond with his essential requirements unless we were in "a make-or-break setting with the President."

Barak agreed with this strategy; indeed, he basically insisted on it. It played to his instinct of clarifying the situation. It reflected his judgment that hard decisions were only made in make-or-break settings. It built pressure on Asad to decide, even as we put pressure on Barak to decide. And it involved the President with Asad directly, face-to-face, something that Barak—perhaps because of Patrick Seale—believed was the key to a deal.

All this was great in theory. But in practice, Barak had to decide on his bottom lines—or at least what he was prepared to have us convey as his essential requirements. He wanted to think about this. As was often the case with Barak, he was anxious to move, but as soon as you pressed him for answers, he needed time. Hurry up and wait, was the motto I ascribed to his approach to the process.

To be fair to him, he had big decisions to make. For our part, we were also not in a rush. We wanted to know but we did not want to have a crisis on both the Syrian and Palestinian tracks. We knew we might fail with Asad. If we did, we did not want to be dead in the water with both the Syrians and Palestinians. That gave us leverage with Barak, particularly as he was anxious for the President to see Asad and test him. That was high-stakes for us and we let Barak know that we needed to be sure that the Palestinian negotiations were on a solid footing, not in crisis, before we would set up the Asad meeting.

Chapter 23 discusses the details of the package we put together to break the stalemate with the Palestinians at this time. Suffice it to say that every meeting with Barak at this point had to deal with the Syrians and also with my effort to get him to respond to Palestinian concerns. Palestinians were feeling resentful, believing that Barak treated them as if they were derivative of the Syrians. (They began referring to the Syrian track as "the other woman.") I was trying to get a package for them, and Barak was reluctantly responding because of his desire to have President Clinton meet with Asad.

He was preoccupied with Syria. Now, as he dealt with us to fashion a package for the Palestinians, he also had to decide what he would allow us to present to Asad. That was easier said than done, as Barak clearly preferred to describe his needs in general terms. On the border, he told me he needed a few hundred meters off the lake, and several dozen meters off the Jordan River; on early warning, he needed to have a small number of Israelis remain on Mount Hermon for a number of years; on security arrangements, he did not need expansive security zones if he had the kind of monitoring and verification regime that would show changes in military installations and arms depots beyond Damascus; on normalization, he needed to have ambassadors and embassies exchanged during the first phase of implementation.

All this remained too imprecise. I told him that the President could not have "a make-or-break meeting" with Asad with only vague descriptions of Barak's core needs—he had to be able to "spell them out with specificity and precision." And, I added, these core needs have to be very close to "your real bottom lines. President Clinton cannot go to Asad saying that this is the best that Barak can do, this is what he must absolutely have, and then find out later that you are prepared to live with much less." The Prime Minister agreed. But he said he needed two weeks to develop these positions. "Fine," I said, "I will return in two weeks and we can resolve everything then."

In the interim, we agreed that Martin would work with Dani on Barak's bottom lines and what President Clinton could say to describe Barak's needs; when I returned I would go over everything with the Prime Minister to be sure what we had represented was the best Barak could do. Finally, we agreed that I would bring a map depicting our understanding of the borderline Barak could accept. Barak preferred an American map; that would avoid leaks from within his own government that he had drawn up a map of full withdrawal.

In preparation for my return to Israel on February 22, I had the CIA mapmakers develop multiple maps with different withdrawal lines—ranging from 200 to 600 meters off the northeastern shoreline of the Sea of Galilee. I also had the CIA provide maps depicting the Sea of Galilee and its shoreline based on May 1967 and August 1999 photographs. Because of drought conditions in the 1990s, the waterline had receded significantly from where it was in 1967.

From the time of Shepherdstown when I had a discussion with Barak on the shifting shoreline along the northeastern edge of the lake, I saw a possibility for providing both sides with what they demanded on June 4 and the shoreline. Asad insisted that the border must be where it was geographically on June 4, 1967, and Barak insisted that he must have a strip of land off the lake that would prove to Israelis that the water was theirs. Because the water had receded in the thirty-three years since the June war, a line drawn exactly where it existed on June 4, 1967, would be several hundred meters off the waterline in the northeast corner of the lake. Asad would have his June 4 line; Barak would have his strip of land. The borderline had not changed, but the waterline had moved westward.

I could not play games with Barak on this issue. As a result, I asked for withdrawal lines on both the 1967 and 1999 photomaps of the lake and the area off of it. Since September, Barak had consistently said that he needed a few hundred meters off the lake and several dozen meters off the Jordan River. We assumed that meant 300 meters off the lake and 50 to 100 meters off the river. Much like with Bibi saying "low teens" was "eleven," not thirteen, in the run-up to Wye, I should have expected that a few hundred was not a few hundred. Indeed, shortly before my arrival back in Israel, Dani told Martin that Barak's few hundred meters actually meant 600 meters. I suspected this was just the initial jockeying before deciding what the line would be.

But it was not just jockeying that I now faced. Barak, the man in a hurry, now did not have time to go over the Syrian positions until the weekend. I was to spend five days in Israel before having our discussion on Syria. It was not as if he was responding on the Palestinian package I had suggested in the meantime. He was not. It was that he was not ready.

Rarely had I ever been in a position where I was marking time on a trip. But now I was. I met with Arafat and the Palestinians and told them I could not break the current stalemate on their track if they insisted on getting a third further redeployment from Israel before making an effort to achieve a framework agreement. When I saw Barak, I told him that if he continued to weaken Arafat by not responding on any of his requirements, he would not have a partner when he needed him. Barak acknowledged that but was in no hurry to develop the package of steps I was seeking. After five days of largely fruitless efforts on the Palestinian track, I finally sat down with Barak at his home late Saturday night, February 26, to learn what his essential requirements were for a deal with Asad.

We started with the maps I had brought. Barak immediately rejected my use of the 1999 photomap. He wanted us to use only the 1967 photomap of the lake and the shoreline. You realize, I told him, that your demand for 500 meters off the waterline of 1967 will mean that in some places you are actually asking for a border that is 1,000 meters from the waterline of today. He nodded, even as I said that would never fly with Asad.

I suspected that Barak was seeking to get the principle of a certain distance off the lake accepted and only later would he then accede to using the current, not the 1967, shoreline. In his mind, this could be a last-minute concession to let Asad feel as if he had won what he had been demanding. Barak did not want to give this away except as part of an endgame package in which he got what he wanted at the same time.

Knowing he would not reveal this to me now, I chose not to press him on this point. But I did ask about the minimum distance he felt he must have off the lake under Israeli sovereignty. "Five hundred meters," he answered. Was that his bottom line? I asked, and he replied he could go to 400 meters but that was the limit.

We moved on to the issue of the early warning and Barak said he needed approximately ten Israelis in the Mount Hermon early-warning station for seven or eight years. Why? He explained that until intelligence alternatives became available, Israel needed a limited presence in Mount Hermon to have an insurance policy against surprise. Could we, I asked, substitute for that presence given the Syrian willingness to have us manage the ground station? Barak said there were certain intelligence items the Israelis had to know for themselves. When I asked if ten was a magic number, he signaled it could be less.

He was more forthcoming on the security zones, saying he was adopting a position that went against the IDF's posture. He said he did not need limited-deployment zones that extended beyond Damascus, provided he had a monitoring and verification system that did. He said he would overrule his military and not require the moving of Syrian forces north, south, and east of Damascus, but he did need monitoring by installations of cameras beyond the "relevant areas." If the cameras were turned off, that would be a violation and justify Israeli mobilization.

On normalization, he said he needed a clear signal that it was a new day. That required open borders and embassies in the first phase of implementation at three or four months. If he had what he called "SOGIs"—signals of good intentions—he could be more relaxed on the timing of normalization. Here he sought the return of Eli Cohen's remains, a resolution of Ron Arad's fate, and the exhuming of the other possible grave sites for the Sultan Yaqub MIAs (Baumal, Feldman, and Katz).*

It was now nearly one in the morning. Yossi Ginnosar was waiting to see him; Barak told me he needed to see Yossi to go over what he wanted Yossi to convey to Arafat. I wanted him to do that, but our not finishing that night meant that I would be unable to leave as I had planned on Sunday.

Based on our discussion, I did not have enough to go back to Washington and brief on what Barak was prepared to have the President say to Asad. True, I had heard his positions. But I certainly had not had a chance to question him closely on all or nearly all of them. I wanted to know more about possible trade-offs. What did it mean that if he got certain SOGIs that he could be less demanding on when he needed embassies to be opened? Did that mean with certain signals of good Syrian intent, he could wait a year to have embassies exchanged in Israel and Syria? Similarly, if it was make-or-break decision time, I needed to know what size security zones he would be willing to accept if he got a passive monitoring system for the area beyond Damascus. Would, for example, he accept the Syrian ratio on the zones presented at Shepherdstown? Hadn't General Omar agreed to the passive monitoring system? More precision was required before I could go back to Washington, and yet I was being pressured by both Madeleine and Sandy to get back, particularly because they felt we were losing the window for a meeting with Asad. The President was scheduled to leave for India within a few weeks, and that trip would not be postponed.

Necessarily, I had to be focused on getting specific answers on Syria, but no one knew this publicly. The public image of the trip was that I was trying to forge new understandings between Barak and Arafat given a new stalemate on that track. Unfortunately, staying an extra day or two to see Barak sent a misleading message to Arafat. He interpreted my delayed departure as indicating that I would offer some new ideas of my own. I had been pushing Barak to present a package of steps to Arafat and he had finally done so through Yossi Ginnosar. Arafat's response was maximal, indicating he saw this as the opening of a negotiation on the proposed Israeli steps.

I could read Arafat's intent. He now wanted me to broker a deal between what Barak had offered through Yossi and what he had countered with. I might be able to do that once I had what I needed from Barak for the meeting with Asad. Once I had that, I could tell Barak, "No meeting with Asad until we have a deal on the package to

---

*Eli Cohen was an Israeli spy who penetrated Syrian political circles in the 1960s before being discovered and executed in a public hanging. Ron Arad was an Israeli pilot who had been downed over Lebanon and captured in 1986; there were rumors about sightings, and Hizbollah or Iranian Revolutionary Guards holding him, but nothing definitive was known about his status.

resume the negotiations with the Palestinians." Then I would have more leverage; now I did not want to dilute the leverage I needed on the discussions I was having with Barak on Syria.

Under these circumstances, I did not want to see Arafat again. However, I was trying to keep my Syrian agenda secret and I needed the visibility of my meetings with Arafat to keep the Israeli media from sniffing that something might be up on Syria. There was no synergy here, only complications. I managed to convince Arafat that I was pushing Barak, and that had led to the new ideas Yossi presented. If he wanted me to help him, he had to help me by making a real effort now to work with Yossi on a package. I would return in a few days and would be far more able to finalize a package if he made a good-faith effort that I could use with Barak.

I was in a strange position. For different reasons, neither Arafat nor Barak wanted me to leave the area. Arafat still hoped I would broker the differences, believing I would produce more for him than his people working with Yossi would. Barak, who had delayed our discussion on Syria and then had not allowed me the time to explore everything with him, suddenly decided it was time to go for broke.

Perhaps because I was going to be leaving, he made a decision that amounted to jumping out of a plane without pulling the rip cord. In our meeting on Saturday night he had asked me, in passing, if I thought he ought to go to his cabinet and tell them that each of his predecessors had committed conditionally to the June 4 lines. My reaction was that he ought to prepare the ground for this, but, obviously, it could give him enormous cover at the right moment. Indeed, while he could not say Shamir had committed to June 4, he could say that Rabin, Peres, and, most importantly, Netanyahu, had done so. Clearly, in Bibi's case, Barak would be positioned to say, "How could I offer less to Asad if even the Likud Prime Minister had committed to this?"

Barak nodded approvingly. I was not telling him anything he had not already thought of. What surprised me, however, was that Barak did this the next day with his cabinet before we met again. What was not surprising was that such a revelation would signal that he was going to concede on the principle of withdrawal to the June 4 lines. Inevitably that would raise enormous expectations and signal that a deal was imminent. Inevitably that would also mobilize the opposition to a deal with Syria. Those opposed to getting off the Golan Heights knew the Israeli public would be unlikely to reject a deal with an Arab neighbor once completed. Their moment to block Barak was now.

Having raised expectations, Barak was the one who needed to move quickly. Now he was the one anxious for further discussions to work out the precise timing of the Asad meeting. However, he was still not keen on giving me more on the details of his positions. I told him that I had to return to Washington to brief the President on Barak's positions—"There is no substitute for my doing this face-to-face." I also reminded Barak that the President would probably not schedule the meeting with Asad before being assured that the stalemate on the Palestinian track had been overcome.

Here there was an irony. Barak's signal on June 4 also convinced the Palestinians that a Syrian deal was imminent. Suddenly they wanted to work out something lest they be left behind as an afterthought. They assumed that "Asad will screw us, and the Arabs will ignore us." Their newfound interest and Barak's need to satisfy the President combined to make it possible to produce an understanding. Of course, nothing ever came easily or without some painful meetings and discussions. Barak did not like our withholding a commitment on setting a time for the meeting with Asad. I was withholding such a commitment initially because I wanted to be sure he would make a good-faith effort to work out something with Arafat. While he resented that, he authorized Yossi to present yet another new package. (Paradoxically, as described in the next chapter, it went beyond what I felt was necessary to offer.)

I could not delay my departure any longer, particularly because Sandy and Madeleine wanted me back to join them and the President in a discussion of when the President should see Asad in Geneva, whether it should be before or after the South Asia trip, whether we had enough for such a meeting, what more we might ask of Barak, and what we should require on the Israeli-Palestinian track before seeing Asad.

I was home for three days, and arrived back in Israel on the afternoon of March 5. The night I returned, Barak and Arafat met and finalized a package deal. The next day I announced the resumption of negotiations in the context of a public three-way meeting in Ramallah that I attended along with Barak and Arafat.

Over lunch, I mentioned to Arafat that I expected the President to meet Asad in the near future. He was not surprised; he fully expected a deal.

I did not share his view. I felt that Asad would not accept what we were bringing from Barak. Barak continued to hold back, belying the idea that this would be a make-or-break meeting. He was anxious to move, but clearly felt the real endgame would need to involve his direct discussions with Asad, and he wanted to save concessions for that endgame. When I told him we might not get to such an endgame without a little more from him, he was not persuaded. But that was not the biggest problem I faced with Barak at this point.

From his standpoint, the only way to do the deal was for the President to commit to see Asad and spend enough time to make the endgame with Barak possible. Given the President's planned trip to India, that was unlikely to work the way he envisioned it. Not surprisingly, Barak was livid when I told him this.

| "GROSS UNPROFESSIONALISM" |

I returned and informed Barak that the President could only spend a few days in Geneva before heading to India. Barak, having publicly signaled his intent to do a deal based on the June 4 lines, now felt exposed. He was realistic enough to know that Asad would not simply accept what the President would be presenting. For all his talk of "make or break," he was anticipating a tough negotiation. In his mind, the President had to commit to staying in Geneva to finish the job. As was often the case with Barak, he assumed that the President would simply accommodate his schedule to fit the timetable the Prime Minister deemed appropriate. That the President of the United States might have other obligations—like, for example, going to India and Pakistan—was immaterial and could be adjusted. President Clinton, having always been available for any call or discussion with the Prime Minister, no doubt fortified Barak's view that we would drop everything whenever Barak decided it was time to act.

When I informed him now that the President would not be available for the scenario he had envisioned, he blew up. This was "ridiculous." There was a "historic deal," a historic opportunity; it was "ridiculous" to let the schedule determine whether it could be realized. When it came out that we had lost the historic chance to change the strategic landscape of the Middle East because of scheduling considerations, there would be "no way to understand it."

He went so far as to accuse me of "gross unprofessionalism" for not making sure that we had the time needed now to complete the deal.

For him the answer was simple: the President should reschedule his South Asia trip, and he would call him to get him to do so. Anticipating this reaction, I had asked Sandy if there was any chance of rescheduling the trip or of the President agreeing with Barak to do so. Sandy was adamant. The trip had been rescheduled once; it would not be for a second time. That would be devastating to our interests in South Asia.

I told him he could call the President but he would be making a big mistake. The only thing that would be ridiculous and irresponsible would be for the President to forgo a trip to the one region of the world where there could actually be a nuclear war. No one could explain that, particularly if the reason was a meeting with Asad that I thought was at best a long shot to producing an agreement. Barak might not be able to do more, but what he was permitting us to bring to Asad was not going to produce a deal or even an endgame negotiation. How could we justify pushing the President to such a meeting, recognizing the very real nuclear dangers in South Asia? What would be ridiculous would be the President rescheduling his trip.

My response seemed to sober Barak. He was quiet, rubbing his forehead. Knowing that he was searching for a possible way to resolve this problem, I now offered the solution. Let the President start with Asad in Geneva. He could be there for several days if the meeting warranted it. Secretary Albright and I could stay behind when the President left for South Asia. If we were making enough headway, Barak would come to Geneva for proximity discussions, with the Secretary shuttling between the two sides. Provided a deal appeared possible, the President would return at the end of the South Asia trip to finalize an agreement. Though I remained skeptical that we were on the verge of a deal, if Barak was right and I wasn't, we could use the prospect of the President returning to create a deadline; either Asad and Barak produce enough to justify the President's return, or if they fail to do so they run the risk that they may never again have this kind of Presidential intervention available. No endgame ever worked without a deadline; so I argued we should make a virtue of necessity and use the President's return or nonreturn as leverage to forge a deal if it was possible.

While it may not have been his preferred path, Barak accepted it. When I reported the outcome of my meeting there was relief at the White House. My trip was seen, in Rob Malley's words, as having "moved two mountains": the stalemate between Israelis and Palestinians was broken and we now had an agreed timeline with Barak on the meeting with Asad.

There was only one problem. We had not yet called Asad to schedule the meeting.

| ASAD IS ABLE TO RESTRAIN HIS ENTHUSIASM |

It never occurred to us that Asad might not be eager to see President Clinton—he had always been eager before. Having confirmed the understanding with Barak on March 8, the President was anxious to proceed. He wanted to maximize the time with Asad in Geneva, believing that he personally could do the deal. As a result, he called Asad even before I left Israel, offering to meet him almost immediately in Geneva on either the ninth, tenth, eleventh, or twelfth of March. He told Asad that he would be leaving for South Asia on March 18—timing that explained why the President wanted to get together right away. Naturally, he told Asad that we had produced with Barak and he needed to go over what was a very important message that could make a deal possible.

Asad's response was tepid; he was hesitant, saying he would have to check but perhaps the thirteenth or fourteenth might work and that the two should speak again in the next day or so. President Clinton called the next day, planning to tell Asad that we would meet the thirteenth. But the presidential palace informed us that Asad could not take President Clinton's call. He was in the midst of deliberating on a new cabinet and would not be available all day.

This was a first during President Clinton's tenure. While Sandy and Secretary Albright thought there must be a health reason to explain Asad's unavailability, I felt there might be a more worrisome explanation: either Asad saw us as being desperate and understood he could make this work for him, or, more pessimistically, he was losing interest in doing a deal, believing that an agreement no longer served his interests.

As if to confirm that the Syrians had no interest in moving quickly, Shara called the Secretary the next day to tell her that President Asad would accept the President's proposal to meet on March 18! Neither Madeleine's anger at his selecting the date the Syrians knew the President would be leaving for India nor her efforts to pick an earlier date for the meeting had any effect on Shara. An earlier date would not work, he said, because of the demands of forming a new cabinet.

Had a new government of reformers emerged, as was rumored, this might have had some credibility. But after much anticipation, the cabinet Asad appointed was characterized by old thinkers and continuity, not change. Perhaps that too should have been another tip-off that Asad was not about to move on anything. Managing succession was his priority; doing a deal with Israel no longer fit into his plan.

But we were not reading the tea leaves accurately. We did not back off the idea of meeting with Asad. Even though Barak was disappointed by Asad's unwillingness to meet anytime soon, he accepted that we could not meet until after the President's trip to South Asia. That meant seeing Asad in Geneva on the way back from South Asia. March 26 was the date agreed and Barak remained anxious to press for a deal—or at least to determine that one was not possible now.

| GENEVA: LAST PHONE CALLS WITH BARAK |

I arrived in Geneva the evening of the twenty-fifth. Shortly after I arrived, I learned that Barak wanted to speak to me on a secure line.

To do a secure call in most embassies meant going into a small, nearly airtight booth. In Geneva, the booth was not only small, but I could barely breathe in it. I proceeded to speak to Barak for ninety minutes. Nick had come to the embassy with me, and he watched as every few minutes I would open the door to the booth to get air.

Barak, ever the micromanager, wanted to be sure that the President would approach the meeting the "right" way. Meeting Asad was about determining if there was a deal, not whether negotiations could be resumed. Barak's understandable fear was that Asad would pocket everything the President conveyed—and agree to nothing other than a resumption of negotiations. Asad would reveal nothing but he would have these new baselines—new points of departure—from the President and Barak.

I reassured Barak that the President would make clear to Asad that it was time to cut to the heart of the matter, saying: "Here is what Barak can do to meet your core needs and this is what it takes for him to do so. Are you ready to meet what he needs? If so, we will move to frame the agreement; if not, I know I cannot help you produce an agreement."

Barak liked this approach. But he had another agenda. He wanted to come to Geneva now. He wanted to arrive in the morning. He might not want us to acquiesce in Asad's possible strategy of simply resuming negotiations. But he fully expected that a negotiating process would be necessary in Geneva. He needed to be there to permit the President to shuttle between the two leaders and then in the endgame bring them together.

That, I acknowledged, would be necessary. However, at this stage it would be premature for him to come. If nothing else, his arrival would dramatically raise expectations before we knew if there was a deal. That had to be our first priority. We had to find out if there was even a chance for a deal. I told Barak I was highly skeptical now. I felt Asad's calculus might have changed, reducing his interest in a deal. Moreover, I doubted that Asad would accept what Barak was offering and requiring, especially on the border and on an Israeli presence in the Mount Hermon early-warning station.

I sounded deliberately negative, indeed overly so. My reason was both to deter Barak from coming and to put pressure on him to give us his real bottom lines. His desire to come immediately to Geneva confirmed my suspicion that he was holding his real positions in reserve for the endgame he still expected. He would not come to Geneva unless he could convey something new to Asad. I wanted him to understand he would not get to Geneva unless we had enough to move Asad and that there was a real risk that, based on what he was giving us to convey, that would not happen. If nothing else, I wanted him to reveal more to the President and understand that what he had given us at this point was not sufficient.

On that, I failed to move him. But at least he did concede that he would not come to Geneva before learning the outcome of the President's initial meeting with Asad.

I knew this gave me what I needed. If the meeting with Asad did not go well, Barak's coming would be moot; if it did go well, we would want him to come.

Having moved him enough on Geneva, I tried once more to convince him that he should let us use the 1999 photomap to depict the line of withdrawal the Israelis would accept, arguing that was more practical, and that Asad would be very suspicious if we were to switch the maps and their bases later on.

Barak was not buying. He argued that an end to the drought would re-create the former shoreline. He insisted that we use the 1967 photomap, arguing that was the only shoreline he could operate with—even though, as I protested, it did not exist today. This further convinced me that Barak was holding back and would simply not give us his real or proximate bottom lines on withdrawal. Telling him that if he did not give us more on at least some of the issues, he would convince Asad that this was a negotiating session—not a make-or-break meeting—Barak finally agreed to be more flexible with the President on Mount Hermon and on the timetable for Israeli withdrawal.*

Barak's call with the President offered no surprises. His "bottom lines" showed some improvement over what he'd told me: The border had to be 400 meters off the shoreline of the 1967 photomap; the Israeli presence on Mount Hermon need not be nine Israelis for seven years, but could be seven Israelis for five years; and full Israeli withdrawal from the Golan Heights could be over two and a half years instead of three.

President Clinton felt this was reasonable to take to Asad. Even if Asad was not prepared to accept it, the Barak positions were far-reaching and by any measure justified an Asad response that we could then work with. I shared this view, but also told the President that I thought the most we would get out of Asad with this presentation was a "no, but" answer—meaning he would reject it but be prepared to talk without offering much of anything in return. We were all in for a surprise.

| GENEVA: ASAD'S NOT INTERESTED |

While I had warned Barak that Asad would not accept these "bottom lines," even I was not prepared for Asad's response. He was simply not interested.

In all my experience with Asad he always showed an interest in, at a minimum, having a discussion. Asad had always enjoyed the sport of debate. Not today, and his lack of interest was evident within the first five minutes of the meeting.

Only Madeleine and I accompanied the President, and Asad had only Shara and Butheina with him. After initial pleasantries, the President told Asad he was going to read his points to ensure precision and understanding. It was uncharacteristic for him to do so, but this meeting was so important and had so much promise for reaching agreement between Syria and Israel that he felt he must present the points with great care.

The very first point was designed to hook Asad and get him to consider what Barak was asking. With great drama the President read that Barak, based on "a commonly agreed border," was prepared to withdraw to the June 4 line as part of a peace agreement.

Asad immediately said that is "a problem." We all looked incredulously at him. The President had just informed him that Barak would withdraw to the June 4 line,

---

*It was not only intuition that told me that Barak was holding back on the borderline he would accept. Amnon had told Martin on the eve of my departure for Geneva that Israel could live with a buffer off the lake of 100 meters and even then the Israelis could dredge around the perimeter of the lake to build a strip off the waterline.

and he was raising an objection. June 4 was his mantra, this is what he had repeatedly sought, and yet now he was objecting. What was his objection? That the border had to be "commonly agreed." This was exactly the language that Shara said Syria had accepted in the eight-point Lauder paper. (In fact, I had simply taken the language from that paper for the President's point here.) As I looked at Shara, I saw the same expression I had seen in July 1995; while he would not admit it, he was surprised.

President Clinton explained that this was Barak's commitment to withdraw to June 4 and of course any agreement would have to be based on a commonly accepted border. How could there be an agreement otherwise?

Asad did not comment further, but simply said it was a problem. The President then asked if he could go through all the points, and Asad nodded. I leaned over to Madeleine and whispered, "We are in trouble. This guy ain't interested."

We did not need to wait long to have that view confirmed. The President's next point was that June 4 was acceptable to Barak, but he needed to make sure that Israel retained sovereignty over the water of the Sea of Galilee and the Jordan River and therefore the borderline should not touch either one.

Asad's reply: "Then they don't want peace." Full stop. He was ready to have no further discussion. Again, we were incredulous. As if to ask, "How can you say that?" the President challenged Asad by saying, "Your Foreign Minister at Shepherdstown told us the water was theirs, provided the land was yours." In Arabic, Asad turned to Shara and asked bluntly, "Is that what you told them?"

Shara skillfully shifted the focus from the sovereignty question over the lake to the sovereignty issue over the land, saying he had made it clear that Israel could not have sovereignty over any of the land. At this point, the President said that they were only talking about a narrow strip of land around one part of the lake, and he asked me to show Asad a map that portrayed the withdrawal line.

Though Asad's body language indicated it was pointless to continue, I spread a large map about two feet wide and four feet long on the table in front of him. The map was based on the 1967 photomap of the whole Golan Heights; it portrayed more than two thousand square kilometers, covering the area from just west of Damascus, stretching down to the lake, and extending in the area north of the Sea of Galilee into Lebanon and the Mount Hermon area. Three different borderlines off the Golan Heights were depicted. Unlike the maps I had initially shown Barak, these did not show how many meters off the lake each line was. Instead, with Barak's approval, we had portrayed three different lines to give Asad a means of comparison. One line was the 1923 international boundary line; a second line was one expert's interpretation of what the June 4 line might be, a line we described as the Hof line; and the last one we described as "the line to be demarcated according to June 4, 1967." (When I had shown the map to our ambassador to Syria, Ryan Crocker, prior to going to Geneva, he was impressed and had been convinced that Asad would accept "the line to be demarcated according to June 4.")

This last line was the Barak line. It provided for a narrow strip off the lake; Shara, obviously in a mood to protect himself, immediately pointed out that the narrow strip off the lake was to the east of the 1923 line.*

In explaining the map, I noted the obvious: it was true that at that point the line was marginally to the east of the 1923 line. But I then showed how it was well to the west of the 1923 and the Hof lines opposite the southern part of the lake. It also provided that Syria would get Hama—an area not easy for Barak to concede and an area that both Shara and Walid had told us in 1994 was the main distinguishing feature between the 1923 and June 4 lines. Finally, I observed that the Barak line returned more land to Syria than even that called for in the Hof line's interpretation of June 4. In effect, I said, you are getting more than 100 percent of the Golan Heights.

Asad was dismissive, and for the first time in the history of this process, he suddenly claimed—contrary to Shara and his own previous discussions with us—that "the lake has always been our lake; it was never theirs . . . There were no Jews to the east of the lake." He could not last in power for a day if he were to agree to what Barak was asking.

He saw no point in continuing. The President several times asked for him to listen to the whole presentation so he could see everything Barak was prepared to do. Here we were less than ten minutes into the presentation and Asad wanted to hear no more. Was he simply posturing? Was he trying to get a better deal?

It was hard to conclude that. He did not want to talk about anything. President Clinton was pressing him, literally asking for the courtesy of being heard.

For my part, I was ready to have us walk away; Asad's behavior, I felt, was a sign of complete disrespect for the President. Again, I leaned over to Madeleine and said, Let's not beg him to hear our presentation. Why should the President have to ask him to stay to hear us out? Here we were offering him nearly everything he wanted. The President had traveled to see him. It appeared as if Asad was doing us a favor by seeing us. Most amazingly, Asad did not even ask a question about how far off the lake the line would be—indeed, given the scale of the map, it was impossible to tell if the line was 40 meters or 400 meters off the lake.

Yet Asad did not want to go on. When Madeleine whispered to the President that maybe we should not stay and continue the meeting, Shara convinced Asad that he

---

*The 1923 line was only 10 meters off the waterline in the northeast sector of the lake.

should, as a courtesy, hear what the President had to say. Asad reluctantly agreed—again, as if he was doing us a favor.

But every point of presentation—even Barak's readiness to accept the Syrian proposal on the size of the security zones, provided there was a passive monitoring system—brought the same response from Asad: "Why do we need that?" President Clinton, with his face getting red as he got angry, was clearly unhappy. Shara suggested that maybe it would be best if we took a break and the Secretary and I would brief on the whole package.

Following a brief break, we provided Shara with an overview of the remainder of the Barak positions. Shara asked if the President's presentation to Asad could be given to the Syrians in writing. I was against doing so. Barak had made important concessions on which he could be exposed. Even if they were not his real bottom lines, they deserved better than total rejection. Asad had not even been willing to listen to the presentation, and now the Syrians wanted it in writing. We had gone through the points slowly enough for Butheina to record everything. They did not need to have a paper from us that formalized the Barak positions. Madeleine agreed and rejected Shara's request.

Before getting together again with Asad, the President asked me what else we could do. "Very little," I said. "He is not interested. If this is posturing, we still have one last chance when you meet him again. But you have to tell him that you brought something from Barak. You consider it quite significant, even historic. You do not understand why President Asad dismissed what you brought, but one thing is clear: you cannot be in a position in which you bring something significant from Barak, get nothing from Asad, and in effect are told not good enough, go back and bring something more from Barak."

When we got together again with Asad, the President paraphrased what I had suggested, emphasizing that he could not be in a position where he now went back to Barak and asked for more. Asad must give him something. Asad was pleasant but unyielding, offering only to consider what the President said. Nothing was going to happen here. Nothing was going to happen now.

The President softened at the end of the meeting, telling Asad he was not giving up and hoped Asad would not either. Asad said he was not giving up and remained committed to the path of peace, but "this is not the right path."

Asad was not going to close doors; he was not looking for a confrontation; and he, of course, as a principle always wanted the onus to be on the other side, not on him. So he did not want the meeting to end in bitterness; fearing that I would be the one to go out and blame the Syrians for the failure of the meeting, he came over to me after bidding good-bye to the President and the Secretary, and said: "We have always had friendly relations." I acknowledged that, and said we would continue to have them. For different reasons, I, too, did not want to close all doors. I knew now that Barak would unilaterally withdraw from Lebanon, and I wanted Asad to have a stake in preserving calm, not an interest in having the earth burn beneath the Israelis as they withdrew. We had to admit we had not achieved anything here in Geneva, but we should not declare this track dead.

I had been struck by one thing when Asad came over to me. He had grasped me by my upper arm and I had done the same in turn to him. Though he did not seem weak, I noticed that when I clasped his upper arm, there was nothing there—no muscle, no fat, no tissue, just bone. It struck me that the reports about his declining health must be right, and in this small but noticeable way I could see that he was deteriorating physically—and probably did not have too much time left.

| THE AFTERMATH |

No president likes to have a high-profile meeting fail. As President Clinton would often say to us, "The people don't pay us to fail." It was his way of saying that failure might be unavoidable and we might not be at fault—and the public might even understand we were not at fault—but in the cold light of day it was still a failure. The American public wanted their leaders to succeed, and that was the basis on which they judged them.

The meeting in Geneva had been a high-visibility failure. Whatever other considerations he might have, the President was likely to seize on anything that would soften the imagery of a failure. Not surprisingly, when he called to brief Barak right after the meeting and Barak, though obviously disappointed that his strategy had not worked, requested that I be sent immediately to Israel to go through the details with him, the President was quick to agree to this request. If nothing else, it signaled that everything was not dead and we were still working on the problem.

Of course, there were others who were concerned about the failure. When I got back to my room in the hotel, I received two calls. The first was from Prime Minister Hariri of Lebanon, the second from Prince Bandar. Each wanted to know what had happened. With each, I was very candid. Both were stumped. Each had expected a breakthrough. Each desperately wanted a breakthrough.

In Hariri's case, an Israeli-Syrian deal was the key to a different future for Lebanon. In the near term, a deal would ensure a peaceful Israeli withdrawal from Lebanon, and one in which Hizbollah would be unable to claim credit for driving Israel out. This would make Hizbollah less of a force in Lebanon. Over time, peace between Syria and Israel, and Lebanon and Israel would make it harder to justify Syria's continued presence in Lebanon. Even if that might take longer to produce, the end of the conflict would make it possible for Lebanon to take advantage of its natural potential to be a financial center again in the Middle East.

Bandar did not even bother to say hello. Instead, as I picked up the phone, all I heard was, "What happened?" After describing the meeting, Bandar pleaded that we not give up on the Syrian track. My answer: Produce something from Asad that we can work with. "The ball is in his court."

When I met with Barak the next day, my point was to be clear about Asad so Barak would not keep chasing him and ignoring the Palestinians. Of course, I wanted him also to see the value of not killing the Syrian track entirely. It was not only Lebanon that I had in mind. I knew the possibility of a Syrian deal would always create leverage on Arafat and I did not want him to think he was the only game in town. Barak, while disappointed, began to look forward.

Would anything have made a difference at Geneva? Bandar would say yes; I say no. Bandar believed that a misunderstanding produced Geneva. Asad expected to have his needs met as he defined them, and Bandar believes that Asad simply shut down when he saw that the President had not brought what he expected from Barak.

While I don't doubt there was a misunderstanding (at least with Bandar), this cannot account for Asad's behavior in Geneva. It cannot explain Asad's objection to the President's first point. How could "a commonly agreed border" based on withdrawal to the June 4 line be a problem? Why did Asad never even ask about the width of the strip off the lake? What if it had been only 40 meters or 75 meters wide? Asad was not the type to assume that everything he wanted would simply be given to him without further discussion. Barak was right to assume that there would be an endgame of bargaining in Geneva; certainly, everything about Asad's experience and mind-set would have made him believe that and act on that as well.

No, Asad had made up his mind before coming to Geneva that now was not the time to do a deal. Even if Barak got out of Lebanon unilaterally, Israel would not lose interest in having a deal with Syria at some point. That could wait. For Asad, he had something more fundamental to deal with. He was preoccupied with succession. He was not healthy enough now to deal with more than one big issue. Managing succession would be demanding enough. And what he saw as Barak's "betrayal" at Shepherdstown had raised the cost of doing an agreement. The unprecedented criticism of Shara by the writers union after the Shepherdstown draft leaked in Israel told Asad that an agreement with Israel was too risky now.

Though he was in no rush to go to Geneva, a high-profile meeting with the President could also be useful on the succession question. It would signal those who had been responsible for criticizing Shara that Asad was prepared to stand up to the President of the United States and not compromise vital Syrian interests. He would not do a deal just to avoid his son having to do that later. I suspect that Asad saw the criticism of Shara coming from powerful elements of his sect—the Alawis—elements that were important for succession.

The moment for a deal was in December and January, when Asad wanted to move. At that point, he was ready; his own suspicions, fears, and even weakness brought on by deteriorating health emerged later and doomed the deal. Amnon Shahak was to tell me in the summer of 2002 that the Middle East changed the day in Shepherdstown when, unbeknownst to us, Barak received the results of a poll that made doing the deal with Syria more problematic than he had thought. It was at that time that Barak decided to hold fast in Shepherdstown regardless of the Syrian moves. It was then that a deal was probably lost—and with it a chance for Israel to withdraw from Lebanon as part of a deal, not as if under the pressure and threats of Hizbollah.

Good fortune and luck have never been a part of peacemaking in the Middle East. Between Arabs and Israelis the worst always seems to happen. Even when the circumstances seem propitious for deal-making, it does not take much to intervene and frustrate the best-laid plans and strategies. Would events have transpired differently if Barak had not believed in his first two months in office that he need not accept even the principle of withdrawal to the June 4 lines? Would an agreement have been possible if Shara had not fallen ill and been out of commission for two months in the fall of 1999? Would Barak have behaved differently if he knew how small the window of opportunity with Asad might be?

Unfortunately, the history of peacemaking, especially between Israel and Syria, suggests that opportunities are fleeting and fragile. They are easily lost. After the Rabin assassination, there was a moment. Asad was not up to moving quickly, but the original talks at the Wye River Plantation showed great promise. If not for the four Hamas bombings in Israel in nine days in 1996, there might well have been an agreement in that election year. If not for Barak's cold feet, there might have been a deal in January of 2000. If not for Asad's shifting view of the requirements of succession, there might have been an agreement in March or April of that same year.

Why, one might ask, is it so easy to undo opportunities and so difficult to exploit them? Maybe it is because the fundamentals of peacemaking continue to be lacking. For Arab leaders—and no one more clearly epitomized this attitude than Asad—peace with Israel is a favor, not a necessity; peace is the absence of war, not reconciliation with a former enemy. Having never made any effort to prepare their publics for a peace that requires genuine acceptance of Israel, much less compromise, Arab leaders are easily put on the defensive by charges that they have surrendered their rights when compromising with Israel. Somehow compromise that entails giving up any of their demands guarantees charges of betrayal. For leaders who are themselves insecure, who is going to risk that?

Israeli leaders do not lack legitimacy. But they, too, have found it easier not to level with their publics about what it will take to make deals with their putative Arab partners. Barak, to his credit, did more to condition his public than any of his predecessors. As with them, however, fear of losing necessary support, giving away his "cards" in the negotiations, and making concessions that did not produce irrevocable steps in return led him to hold back.

Even if both sides want peace, those who oppose it can create circumstances in which the politics of peacemaking become untenable. Acts of terror, which highlight rejection of Israel's very existence, undercut the political strength of any Israeli government to make concessions. On the Arab side, either the absence of unmistakable Israeli concessions—indeed those publicly wrenching in Israel—or the existence of tough Israeli responses to acts of terror and violence gives Arab leaders reasons to shy away from the steps necessary. Absent heroic leaders on the Arab side, it is hard to cross the threshold and far easier to hold out. In the end, Asad passed. Was Arafat likely to be different?

From Stalemate to Camp David

BARAK'S PREOCCUPATION WITH REACHING agreement with Syria made him unwilling to expose himself with the Palestinians at the same time. He did not know how much the Israeli public could absorb, and he was reluctant to commit to anything with the Palestinians that might undo his political base for doing a deal with Syria. He deliberately chose to go slowly with the Palestinians; took nearly two months after the Sharm agreement even to appoint a negotiator, my friend Oded Eran; and resisted my efforts to get him to approve a back channel to the Palestinians to explore possible openings on permanent status. While he might proclaim his intent to achieve a framework agreement on permanent status (FAPS) with the Palestinians, he would not grant anyone on his side the mandate to offer serious ideas for shaping such a deal.

To be fair, Israel could not negotiate with itself. The Palestinians might complain about Barak not negotiating, but the Palestinians were hardly adopting anything but the most maximal positions in even the quiet discussions that Oded was conducting with Yasser Abed Rabbo, his counterpart. Nonetheless, largely by dint of Oded's efforts, negotiations on permanent status were at least under way by January of 2000. However, they were in a preliminary, inchoate stage, and it was abundantly clear there would be no FAPS by the target date of January 31.

Unfortunately, in January Barak was suddenly coy about whether or when the last of the Wye further redeployments (FRDs) would be implemented—even though he had committed to carrying out the last phase of these FRDs by February 15, regardless of whether a framework agreement had been achieved. The last FRD of Wye involved transferring an additional 6.1 percent to area A from area B. With this 6.1 percent being added to the A area, 18.2 percent of the West Bank would come under virtually complete Palestinian control. Knowing of our unhappiness with his reluctance to do much on the Palestinian track—especially after his performance at Shepherdstown—Barak decided to hold a private meetings with Arafat. He was not ready to make commitments on permanent status issues, but then again neither was Arafat. Instead, Barak, knowing the last target dates of the Sharm agreement were coming up, saw value in letting Arafat know he would do the 6.1 percent.

Arafat also wanted such a meeting. After Blair House and Shepherdstown, the Palestinians were being treated as a sideshow. Arafat sought a new symbol to show what the Palestinians were gaining—or at least what he was gaining for them. In the meeting he made a personal request that Barak include three villages on the periphery of Jerusalem in the 6.1 percent that would become A areas. The villages—Abu Dis, Eizariya, and Ram—bordered the municipal boundaries of East Jerusalem, and were B areas. From Abu Dis, one could see the golden Dome of the Rock in the Old City of Jerusalem. Arafat explained that this was personally important to him, and while Barak was careful not to promise to do it, he did say he understood this mattered to the Chairman.

Arafat probably did not expect to get all three villages, but given the way he had made the request and Barak's response, he certainly expected to get at least one of these "near Jerusalem" villages. Conversely, Barak, knowing that he had made no commitment, decided it was simply too explosive politically to turn over these villages. (He feared, not unreasonably, that he would be accused of being prepared to divide Jerusalem—after all, if he was ready to let villages that touched Jerusalem become A areas now, he would have nothing else to give in a permanent status deal except Arab East Jerusalem.)

Had Barak informed Arafat privately as to why he could not accede to his request at this time, Arafat probably would have reluctantly accepted the explanation—and sought to gain something else in return. But Arafat only learned of Barak's decision through the Israeli media. Now Arafat was embarrassed. He had not raised his request for the villages publicly, and he took this as a slap in the face, designed to make him look bad for Barak's benefit.

Now positions hardened on each side. Barak would not transfer the three villages. But Arafat insisted on them, making clear he would not accept a 6.1 percent FRD that excluded the villages.

This was not necessarily a case of Arafat playing games. He genuinely believed that Barak, concerned only with Syria, was taking him for granted. So Arafat would prove he could not be ignored. With the passing of the Sharm dates, he suspended negotiations with the Israelis.

In Israel, this put pressure on Barak. Pursuing Syria was not popular. Most of those in Barak's coalition believed it was important to deal with the Palestinians first—a theme that their Palestinian contacts constantly emphasized. Suspending the negotiations was bound to create a problem for Barak.

At this time, Shaul Mofaz and Ami Ayalon, the Chief of Staff of the IDF and the head of Shin Bet, respectively, separately sought to persuade me to drop the efforts on Syria and put all our emphasis on reaching an agreement with the Palestinians—and to convince Barak of the importance of this.

Both argued there was no support for a deal with Syria. Each believed that the Israeli public saw the Palestinians as partners and would support far-reaching concessions toward them. Both feared that at some point Palestinian frustrations, especially on the street over corruption in the Palestinian Authority and the failure of Oslo to end Israeli occupation, would boil over and there would be an eruption of violence. Once that happened, the support within the Israeli public for a deal with the Palestinians would disappear.

Hearing this from Ami came as no surprise; he had been bemoaning Barak's focus on the Syrians at the expense of the Palestinians for the last few months. But Mofaz was a major surprise. Two months earlier, when he was visiting Washington in late December, we had lunch together and he had made an impassioned plea to do the deal with Syria immediately. Now he was convinced that a Syrian deal would tear the country apart. And "dealing with Jerusalem and borders and refugees won't?" I asked. Mofaz was adamant: Israelis have come to believe the Palestinians want to live in peace and are ready to end the conflict. But if prolonged violence erupts with the Palestinians—and it will if there is no deal soon—"we will lose the ability to do the deal with the Palestinians and a historic opportunity will be lost."* Since I was hearing the same message from those most responsible for Israeli security, I wondered why they thought I would succeed with Barak where they had failed. Both men simply said, He might listen to you; he is not listening to us.

I was no more successful with Barak than they had been. He was riveted on the dangers of withdrawing from Lebanon without a deal with Syria, and determined to see if such a deal was possible before doing anything else.

In late Februrary, after spending nine days in the region and making it clear that President Clinton would not meet with Asad if things were stuck with the Palestinians, I still had to reconcile certain realities. Barak would not transfer the villages as part of

---

*In retrospect, both Ayalon and Mofaz effectively predicted the second Intifada and its consequences; interestingly, at this time, they both thought Arafat would do the deal.

the 6.1 percent. Yet Arafat needed to show he could get the villages at least in part. (For Arafat, the need to prove that he was not, in his words, "Barak's slave" and did not have to submit to Barak's diktat was now his overriding imperative.) With that in mind, I proposed a twofold solution to Barak. First, offer to do one of the three "Jerusalem" villages by a *date certain* as a down payment on the third further redeployment, not as a part of the last Wye FRD. Second, present to the Palestinians areas totaling 10 percent and let them select the 6.1 percent they preferred for the Wye redeployment.

Perhaps because this was our final meeting before my return to Washington and he needed me to report that he was doing his part to overcome the stalemate, Barak responded favorably to both ideas. At this point, I already had reason to believe the Palestinians would accept the down payment idea.

Earlier in the day, I had met over lunch with Mohammad Dahlan, Mohammad Rashid, Saeb Erekat, and Yasser Abed Rabbo. Like Arafat, they felt that Barak must know that the Palestinians could not be ignored. At the same time, they feared the consequences of continued stalemate on their track. They were convinced that Asad would do a deal with the Israelis, and once that happened, Barak would claim that he could not act on the Palestinians as well. As Saeb Erekat said, "You will buy his argument that the Israeli public cannot absorb existential concessions with the Palestinians after giving up the Golan Heights. We need to break the stalemate and reach agreement soon." Clearly, here too, I had some leverage, and I used it, saying, "Barak is not going to put a village in the 6.1 percent, so don't ask me to get you that. But if you want choice in determining the 6.1 percent, if you want to be creative in dealing with the villages later on, if you want a firm date for the third FRD, and if you want movement on other issues like money and safe passage, give me something to work with."

Mohammad Rashid did. With Dahlan, he took me aside and suggested "an advance" on the third FRD. That would show the third phase would be carried out— something Arafat needed to know and to be able to sell. And, Rashid argued, Barak won't have to return the villages as part of the 6.1. I liked the idea, and said that I would see if I could sell it to Barak.

I asked Gamal to stay behind and work with the Palestinians on a package that could be agreed. Before leaving I called Dahlan, telling him I would push Barak, but he had to do his part too if he wanted me to help close the deal. He agreed.

I also called Yossi Ginossar to inform him that Barak had accepted my twofold proposal. Yossi and I had been working closely together on the idea of a package. We were working in parallel with Dahlan and Rashid and also briefing each other on our respective meetings with Arafat and Barak. Yossi would pass Barak's messages to Arafat. But he was not someone who would only pass messages. He also tried to get Barak to understand

Arafat's needs, and Arafat to understand Barak's problems. He was not happy with Barak's treatment of Arafat and told him so. But he also worried that Arafat would overplay his hand, and told him that. Most importantly, he felt it was critical to repair the relationship between Arafat and Barak. Without that, nothing would be possible, and he felt the starting point was working out something on the villages and the 6.1 percent.

Not surprisingly, Yossi was pleased to hear that Barak accepted the twofold idea: "Dennis, I will go to work now and put together a package of understandings so we can put this mess behind us." I asked him to stay in touch with Gamal, and told him I would return soon.

I did not speak to Yossi for thirty-six hours. In that time, he produced an approach that was more ambitious than I had in mind—perhaps taking advantage of Barak's desire to demonstrate everything was fine with the Palestinians so that we would no longer hold back on a Clinton-Asad meeting. Whatever the reason, Barak was now willing, according to Yossi, to do a full package that included all three villages: two villages would be transferred on April 23 and the last one on May 23. May 23 would also be the new target date for a framework agreement (FAPS). June 23 would be the new date for carrying out the third FRD, and it would be implemented even if a FAPS had not been achieved by May 23. The 6.1 percent would be selected out of an area of 13 percent, not the 10 percent I had suggested. And understandings on safe passage, prisoners, and the purchase tax would be worked out.

But there was one catch: the understandings on the villages must remain secret. Should they leak, Barak would not go ahead with them.

The package was great, but the secrecy on the villages made no sense to me. How could Arafat keep this secret? The villages were the reason for the current stalemate. Why, I asked, isn't it better to do one village and do it publicly? Then, I pointed out, Arafat could explain why he was resuming the negotiations. "Dennis," Yossi replied, "this is agreed by the two leaders. They are comfortable with this, and Arafat will protect it." He explained that only Dahlan and Rashid knew about it on the Palestinian side and they had been instrumental in persuading Arafat to accept it. "Believe me," Yossi went on to say, "Arafat won't tell anyone else on his side, not Saeb, not Yasser, not anyone else. The 'old man'* is okay with it and Ehud wants it this way."

I still had my doubts, but Gamal confirmed Yossi's account, especially about the role Dahlan and Rashid had played in the understandings. But he also reported that Dahlan raised two requests. First, could I see Arafat and offer an American assurance

---

*Yossi often referred to Arafat as the "old man" in our conversations.

that Barak would live up to all the elements of the package? Second, could I move Barak to do the first village sooner than April 23?

Gamal had told Dahlan that he had to check with me on the first, and that he was crazy to ask for the second. Yossi had been clear that this was the best that could be done. For my part, I was not ready to offer an assurance without knowing directly from Barak that he would carry out all of these steps and without his knowing that Arafat was seeking our assurance that he would do so. As for the second, I would ask Barak. When I spoke to Barak, he said he would do what was called for in this package and he did not mind if the President assured Arafat of that. On the dates, he was adamant. This was the best he could do. He could not go earlier than April 23 because it would be Passover, members of the religious parties would be in Jerusalem for the holiday, and turning over one of the villages while they were there would be a major political problem. "No way to do it." I let Dahlan know, and he thanked me for trying.

I returned to Israel on the afternoon of March 7. Barak wanted to have a private meeting with Arafat to finalize the package of understandings directly. Arafat wanted me to be there, no doubt seeking a witness on the package and hoping I would announce that the negotiations would be resumed. Through Yossi, Gamal, and Dahlan, we worked out that Barak and Arafat would meet privately that night, the President would call Arafat to assure him that he would have Barak's commitment on the specifics of the package when I returned to Washington, and we would have a three-way meeting the next day in Ramallah in which I would announce the resumption of the talks.

While Barak and Arafat met, Gamal and I had dinner in East Jerusalem with Mohammad Dahlan and Mohammad Rashid. We were in a self-congratulatory mood. With Yossi, we had worked as a team, and overcome a serious stumbling block. They saw this as a model for dealing with the inevitable crises in the permanent status talks. I was still troubled, however, by the secrecy on the villages. How would they deal with Saeb, Yasser, and the others around Arafat? They were not worried; Arafat would simply tell them he was satisfied with the understanding—and it would be against Palestinian interests to say more. Knowing Saeb, I was not convinced. (And, indeed, when I saw Saeb alone the next night, he tried the classic journalist trick with me, saying he knew that one village would be transferred on May 23—and waiting to see if I would confirm it. "Saeb," I replied, "I am not going to lie to you, so I will not comment." "Fair enough," Saeb said, and he did not raise it with me again.)

The next day's meeting would be a first. Never before had there been an open, announced meeting between an Israeli prime minister and Arafat in the West Bank. For Arafat this was a chance to recapture public attention. But it was much more. It was a moment of pride and recognition. The Israeli Prime Minister was coming to see him in a Palestinian city, on his turf. Not under the cover of darkness, not shrouded in secrecy, not at a security facility, but in the open. The meeting was at the Grand Park Hotel, in Ramallah. Naturally, it did not come off without a hitch.

I was sitting with Barak at his home in Jerusalem just before leaving for the meeting when Dani Yatom burst into the room saying the route to the hotel and the hotel itself were bedecked with Palestinian flags. "So," I asked, "what did you expect them to do? This is a big deal for them."

That was the wrong thing to say. The zero-sum nature of the reality was still a part of Barak's instinct. If it was a big deal for them, it was not a good deal for him.

"There will be no flags or I will not go. I will not look like I am going to a Palestinian state for a celebration." Knowing Barak's personality, I knew if I fought this now, he would simply dig in. Instead, I got Gamal, who was waiting for me outside Barak's study, and said, Get Dahlan or Abu Rudeina on the phone and tell them the flags have to come down. Gamal called them, and they reluctantly agreed—feeling, in Dahlan's words, that this was "bullshit."

To confirm that the flags had been taken down, Dani placed his own call and reported that there was still a flag in the hotel lobby. Gamal called Dahlan back, who screamed that the only flag left was a two-inch flag behind the check-in counter and that was not being removed. "Fuck the Israelis if they don't want to come."

Enough was enough. I told Barak the flags had come down, the only one left was a two-inch flag on a stick, and he would look ridiculous if this was the reason he was not going to go. I was leaving to go to the meeting, and expected to see him there. Our mini-crisis was over, and Barak arrived in Ramallah before I did.

Arafat, having already greeted Barak, came out to receive me. He was beaming; nothing was going to ruin his mood today. As we walked through the lobby of the hotel, I spied the little flag—the kind a child might wave. I started to laugh, and Arafat, reacting to my laugh, smiled and took my hand, saying, "It is a good day."

Everything went smoothly in the meeting. Afterward Arafat hosted our three delegations for lunch. I was sitting between Arafat and Barak, and at one point confided to Arafat that I expected the President would meet with Asad soon. I did not want Arafat to learn about this from a public announcement after I left the area. I wanted him to know that I took him into our confidence, and, of course, expected him to keep such confidences. I let him know that I had my doubts about what would emerge from the meeting, noting I was not optimistic. Arafat disagreed, saying, "Asad is not a fool, there will be an agreement." "You may know Asad better than I," I countered, "but I don't think he is capable of compromising on the remaining difference, even though it is very narrow." Arafat was not persuaded. "There will be an agreement."

Was this his worst case and he was preparing for it? Was he trying to show me that nothing shook him? Was he now seeing a Syrian deal as having some benefit: making it easier for him to justify that his borders must also be based on June 4, 1967? Or was he convinced we would not go to such a meeting unless we knew it would succeed? Maybe some combination of all these considerations figured in his thinking.

| BARAK GETS SERIOUS ABOUT THE PALESTINIANS |

Upon my return to Washington, I briefed the President while he was watching a first-round NCAA tournament game involving his favorite team, the University of Arkansas Razorbacks. I told him his call did not require give-and-take with Arafat; he was simply going to read him the elements of the package and say we had Barak's assurance that he would do all of it.

That was fine with the President, but he asked again if Barak knew he was going to assure Arafat. "Yes," I said, "Barak knows you are going to say you have his assurance and he is fine with your saying that." There was a subtle distinction I was drawing here between our having Barak's assurance and our giving Arafat our assurance. Saying we had Barak's assurance meant we would hold Barak accountable. Saying Arafat had our assurance meant we had to deliver or we were breaking a commitment. But I did not mention the distinction to the President. I should have.

With the television still tuned to the game, the President called Arafat and read from the points, emphasizing at the end not that we had Barak's assurance that all the elements of the package would be done, but that Arafat had his assurance they would be done. It was a Clintonesque touch, but one we would later regret. Perhaps if I had been paying more attention to the call and less to the game, I would have given him a note and had him correct the impression. But, truthfully, I did not expect there to be a problem; I thought that Barak would carry out his commitment, particularly since he had endorsed the President's call to Arafat before we decided to make it. With us, Barak liked to pattern himself after Rabin, emphasizing that, like Rabin, he kept his commitments—so I asked myself, why worry?

At this moment, everything seemed to be on track. The Israelis had carried out the 6.1 percent redeployment, and had coordinated with the Palestinians on the territory that became part of the A zone. Though there had been some speculation in the press about the villages, including some from unnamed Palestinians, the deal on the villages had not become public. Arafat was in a good mood, and Barak was riveted on Syria.

The Geneva meeting with Asad took place on March 26. In my meeting in Israel with Barak the next day, the main focus was on how to deal with the Syrian issue publicly. I was cautioning him not to go to battle stations both to manage his withdrawal from Lebanon and to make sure Arafat did not think he was the only game in town. Barak did not need persuading. He had no interest in giving Asad a reason to make life difficult for him in Lebanon as Israel withdrew, and he understood that Arafat would only harden his position if he thought there was no longer any possibility of a Syrian deal. But Barak also recognized that he could no longer defer dealing with the Palestinians on permanent status.

When I probed his thinking on the core issues with the Palestinians, I found his mind was still elsewhere. That would soon change.

|"I MUST SEE THE PRESIDENT"|

Barak, ever the man on a mission, called me on April 6, insisting "I must see the President by early next week to go over my thinking" on the permanent status. He was determined to press decisively for a permanent status agreement, but he would need certain understandings with the President first. With Barak finally ready to get down to business, Sandy persuaded the schedulers to work out time for Barak as soon as possible. That turned out to be April 11.

In typical Barak fashion, he wanted to see me, Secretary Albright, and Sandy separately before seeing the President. Barak believed that no one could express his ideas as well as he could—so he wanted each of us to hear his presentation and not rely on one of us briefing the others. Sandy and Madeleine agreed that this was crazy, they would see him together, and I should see him first.

I went to Blair House to meet him. The scene in his room conjured up my image of Einstein at work. Clothes and papers were strewn everywhere. Pages from a yellow pad were on the desk, full of handwritten notes. He told me he had not slept, and his appearance left little doubt that this was true.

He had a full agenda for his meeting with the President; he would go over his plans for withdrawal from Lebanon over the next six to eight weeks, and he would need assistance from us politically and economically to get this done. With the Palestinians, he was ready to stretch very far. He knew that he needed to make the bulk of the concessions, but he must see some demonstration from Arafat that he was serious. Israel could not do all the giving. He could do some things up front, but he needed some concessions from Arafat in order to show Israel's ultimate flexibility. His moves would be based on an end-of-conflict deal—with no more claims. This is how he would justify to the Israeli public the concessions that would be required. He had given this a lot of thought, and while he had not yet finally decided, he did not see how a deal could be done on Jerusalem now. Perhaps it could be left open in a way that would allow both sides to preserve their claims. He was still thinking about this, but he did not see his public or theirs capable of a compromise at this stage on Jerusalem. On territory, he had a 66-22-12 formula in mind: The Palestinians would get 66 percent of the territory quickly; 22 percent would be gray areas involving important security areas, but nearly all of the 22 percent would become Palestinian over a five-to-ten-year period; and Israel would annex the 12 percent to meet their needs for settlement blocs. He felt this was eminently fair and met the needs of both sides.

I was not interested in dampening his enthusiasm. In his very first move, he was signaling that he would withdraw from 88 percent of the land. But there was a logical inconsistency in his approach. He wanted to justify his concessions on ending the conflict, but he did not want to touch Jerusalem. How, I asked, could you do both? Wouldn't Jerusalem, the most evocative of all issues, become the focal point of conflict? How could he proclaim that all claims and grievances were resolved when differences would all be riveted on Jerusalem? Wouldn't he run the risk of turning this national conflict into a religious one?

Barak had no answer to these questions, but that did not prevent him from making the same presentation to Sandy, Madeleine, and President Clinton. He acknowledged he would have to think more about how to handle Jerusalem given his desire to present a package deal that would declare that the conflict was over and these were Israel's final concessions.*

I had the President raise one other point with Barak. Martin had alerted me that he was getting hints from Barak that he might have to delay the timing on the three villages. He had not mentioned this to me, but I wanted the President to preempt on this point, making it clear that there could be no delay on the villages unless Arafat was agreeable to it. The President did raise this, reminding Barak he had assured Arafat only after getting Barak's okay to do so.

DOMESTIC REALITIES INTERVENE

Shortly after the Barak meeting I flew to California for Passover. This would be our first Passover without Debbie's dad and it was bound to be a sad time—one I hoped to spend with family and friends. But Barak called me to say that he had sent Yossi to see Arafat to explain that, given the politics of his coalition, he would need to delay transferring the two villages scheduled for April 23 for eight or nine days. Arafat had agreed, and Barak wanted me to communicate that to the President before his upcoming meeting with Arafat on April 20. I told him I would do so, and asked about his strategy for transferring the villages.

---

*With the President, Barak also raised Syria, his idea of using a canal to fashion the strip off the lake, and the security-related costs Israel would have to absorb as it withdrew from Lebanon.

He told me he was laying the groundwork now and would be able to act by May 1. During his meeting with the President, it had been agreed that I would go out to the area to give the permanent status talks a push. Barak now asked if I would delay a day so he could transfer the villages prior to my arrival; he did not want it to look like he had been pressured into doing this.

Unfortunately, Barak's coalition was beginning to fray, making the decisions regarding the villages far more difficult than he had expected. The Sephardic religious party—Shas—had seventeen seats in the coalition. Barak had chosen them over Likud in forming the government because he believed they would acquiesce in his peace process agenda. Now, however, Shas was chafing in the coalition because Minister of Education Yossi Sarid was blocking its efforts to run its religious schools. Sarid, leader of the decidedly secular and dovish Meretz Party, would not give in, believing that to do so would mean diverting money to schools that did not prepare young Israelis for the modern world.

Eli Yishai, Shas' political leader, realized that the issue of the villages gave him leverage to get what he wanted on education. Once Barak announced his intention to turn Abu Dis into an A area—which he had done in the middle of April—opposition immediately crystallized. In the Beilin–Abu Mazen plan of 1995, Abu Dis had been mentioned as the capital of the Palestinian state in an enlarged Jerusalem municipality. Though Beilin–Abu Mazen had never materialized as a basis for the permanent status negotiations, its major elements had leaked and Abu Dis became a symbol of Palestinian entrée into Jerusalem—a symbol that several religious parties rejected. With Yitzhak Levy of the National Religious Party (NRP) declaring that the NRP would leave the coalition if Barak turned over Abu Dis, keeping Shas "happy" became critical to the survival of the coalition and to the pursuit of peace.

Thus, the villages became the catalyst for settling with Shas. Shas would not support the villages unless its concerns had been addressed. And for Shas that meant money. No money for their educational system, no support for the villages and no support for the Barak government. In all likelihood, that would put Barak in a position where he would probably be driven either to a national unity government with Likud or to early elections. Either outcome would spell the end of the process for the Clinton presidency, and probably mean that the historic moment would be missed. This was a recurring fear for us, and it affected our decision-making for the remainder of the year.

So the key to any forward motion was to hold Barak's coalition together, which now became a constant juggling act. As if Barak's coalition politics were not difficult enough, Eli Rubinstein, the Attorney General, now entered the fray. Eli offered his unsolicited written opinion—which was naturally leaked—that if Barak wanted to transfer the villages to A status, he needed Knesset approval. Even though the villages had already been transferred to Palestinian civil authority as part of the Interim Agreement—an agreement already ratified by the Knesset—and even though the Interim Agreement mandated that all B areas should become A areas by the end of the further redeployment process unless they affected Israeli security, Eli's legal opinion was that the government needed Knesset approval of transfers of land that might be controversial.

Were it only a matter of the cabinet approving the villages, Barak would have the votes. But in the Knesset it was a different story. The stakes were higher, and there was limited room for maneuvering. And Shas, ever a party to raise the stakes in pursuit of its interests, did precisely that by announcing that it could only vote for the villages if another religious party joined in the vote.

Barak's predicament now became acute. With the Shas declaration and the NRP threat, his commitment to do Abu Dis became a threat to his government's survival. Yet having promised Arafat—and having agreed that President Clinton could reassure Arafat that Barak would deliver on the package—Barak could not easily walk away from the commitment he had made. But he once again was forced to delay moving on the villages until the Knesset was back in session after the Passover recess on May 15.

Among Palestinians, the political firestorm that had emerged over Barak's intention to transfer the villages began to raise questions about his ability to deliver, with many asking, "If he has this much difficulty doing Abu Dis, how in the world can he possibly do all the permanent status issues?"

Ironically, rather than seeing that he was making a heroic effort to condition the Israeli public to accept the transfer of Abu Dis, Palestinians gave him little credit, preferring to focus on his weakness and the possibility that they might be asked to pay for his weakness with concessions. It was in this setting that I arrived in Israel to join the permanent status talks, knowing that the original April 23 date had been postponed by agreement and the May 1 date postponed by political necessity, but I did not know that Barak had not gone back to Arafat to explain that politically—and legally, according to Eli Rubinstein—he had to wait to present the villages to the Knesset. I made the mistake of assuming that Barak would use Yossi Ginossar again to explain the new situation. He had not.

Once again, feelings were turning raw: Barak, because he thought it ridiculous that he should risk his government over the villages and still be expected to "explain" this to Arafat; and Arafat, because he had a commitment and his conspiratorial mind told him this was all a game that Barak was playing to avoid implementing it.

I confronted a range of emotions in my initial meetings with each of them. Barak was harried. He told me he was not sleeping as he was working around the clock to fix his coalition problems. He resented the fact that the "villages" had created this mess. What had Arafat done to deserve such an effort by him? Why should he be expected to deliver now on the villages when it might bring down the very government that could go so far to respond to the Palestinians? Why should he have to explain anything to Arafat? He used the word "ridiculous" five times.

I couldn't help think that it was he, not Arafat, who had created this mess by making every step he took on the Palestinian track derivative of those he took on Syria. He did not have a strategy toward the Palestinians; he had one toward Syria and it did not work. But he had fallen into transferring the villages as a way of satisfying us and avoiding a problem with the Palestinians at a time when he desperately wanted a Clinton-Asad meeting. Paradoxically, I had not pushed for the three villages because I knew that Abu Dis, in particular, would be a lightning rod. But Barak had promised the three villages, and from this point on Barak's political fortunes began to progressively unravel.

| OTHER BATTLES: THE BACK CHANNEL VS. THE FRONT CHANNEL |

The political battles in Israel took center stage. But there was another battle going on that might not have been as visible but ultimately may have done more to destroy the ability to reach agreement on permanent status. That battle, the one between the back channel and the front, or public, negotiating channel on the Palestinian side, undercut the one negotiating forum that offered the best chance for success.

All along I had known that the most sensitive issues could only be dealt with out of the limelight in a discreet channel. Concessions exposed prematurely on Jerusalem, borders, or refugees could kill the few ideas that might work or, alternatively, create such an outcry that one or both sides might have their hands completely tied. Yet the most existential questions needed to be discussed in an environment of complete confidentiality and trust—where brainstorming could take place; where ideas could be tried out without fear of leaks or concern that everything raised was somehow a commitment; where each side could explore what the real, not artificial, limits were for the other side. In such an environment, each side could become more sensitive to the needs of the other. Each side would work harder to find an explanation for the other on the most sensitive issues. And the kinds of bonds that deepen mutual stakes and forge incentives to find creative solutions would be more likely to emerge.

I had repeatedly sought to get such a back channel launched. While Arafat had been willing, Barak had not. Now, in April, one was finally established. On the Israeli side would be Gilad Sher and Shlomo Ben-Ami, the Minister of Internal Security.

On the Palestinian side, two veterans of the original Oslo negotiations, Abu Ala and Hassan Asfour were the representatives. The four began to have secret meetings; I joined them in the Israeli Arab town of Abu Ghosh for a discussion. The chemistry was very good among them. While at this stage the talks were still very general, both sides in conversations with me felt they could accelerate progress if they could leave the country for several days of secret, intensive talks. But both sides also had concerns.

Shlomo saw great potential in their talks, but fretted over Abu Ala's reluctance to reveal much. To move Abu Ala, he felt that he needed to be able to present a forward-leaning package on all the issues, including Jerusalem. This could transform the negotiations, and lay the basis for the central trade-off between the issues: the more the Israelis could give on Jerusalem and territory, the more the Palestinians should give on refugees and security. But Shlomo was not yet at a point where he could say this to Abu Ala, since Barak was not yet prepared to have him say anything on Jerusalem. Here he needed my help with Barak.

For his part, Abu Ala felt he should not be expected to yield on his principles; he needed a picture of what was possible on all the issues before he could focus on the practical ways he could respond to Israeli needs. But he, too, had his own concerns about his boss, and they were more profound than Shlomo's concerns. While he did not admit this to me, it was clear that Abu Ala was not sure whether Arafat truly was supporting him. Why else would he ask me to speak to Arafat about the back channel and my conviction that it was the only one likely to work? Abu Ala knew that Arafat had not backed him (prior to Wye) in his last back channel effort with Yitzik Molho. Now the stakes were vastly higher. This was not an interim agreement where if the Palestinians did not get everything they needed, they could get it in the next agreement. This was it. The infighting among the Palestinians would be worse than ever before. Would Arafat stand by Abu Ala?

Abu Ala told me "[his] man" was ready for a permanent status deal, and Arafat would back what he was doing, but I sensed from his demeanor more doubt than confidence. And while Abu Ala would not admit this, Arafat was not choosing between the back channel and the front channel at this time.

Yasser Abed Rabbo and Saeb Erekat were the front channel in negotiations with Oded Eran. They had been talking with Oded for several months. They did not want to be a sideshow. They were convinced that they could negotiate a deal—or at least protect Palestinian interests better than anyone else. For months they had fought any other channel. For months they complained to me that Oded was "a good guy but not authorized." Of course, when I asked them what ideas they had put on the table, the answer was always, "Oded must move first."

Now there were rumors in the Israeli press of a back channel. Oded's instructions on what issues he was permitted to cover convinced them the rumors were true. While Barak trusted Oded, he did not trust Saeb or Yasser. He was certain they would leak any sensitive discussion, and that would devastate him politically. He would allow the back channel to deal with borders, refugees, and security arrangements—reserving Jerusalem only for the endgame of a summit. He would allow the front channel to deal with all the functional issues—water, economic relations, border regime, day-to-day security coordination, legal questions, environment, religious sites, etc. This was a practical division of labor, and with me and with Barak, Arafat accepted it—provided the back channel also dealt with Jerusalem.

Unfortunately, Arafat never imposed such a division on his negotiators. Yasser and Saeb were never given instructions to focus only on functional issues. He did not tell them about a back channel, but he did not have to. Oded's mission told them. Oded would not lie to Yasser, with whom he developed a good relationship. He could only deal with the functional questions, and when Yasser asked about the core issues, Oded said others would deal with them.

Neither front channel was happy about such an arrangement. Oded had put together a strong team that had done their homework on all issues. They had spent the last few months engaged in conceptual discussions with Yasser and Saeb. Oded felt he was conditioning them to certain realities. He knew the issues in all their complexity better than anyone on his side. But he was under orders from his boss, and he would follow them. His counterparts had no such orders, and the more Oded would seek to focus on the functional issues, the more they would insist on dealing with the core questions. This might not have mattered except that Yasser and Saeb began to be very negative in their public statements that the negotiations were a sham. Nothing serious was being done. They would not make concessions on core principles, no Palestinian should do that—a not-so-subtle threat to the back channel.

I faced the problem of the front and back channels directly when I joined the front channel negotiators on April 30. To make it possible for the front channel to work more intensively in a more isolated environment, we had decided to spend a week together—the Israeli, Palestinian, and American teams—in Eilat. My plan was to leave Aaron, Jon, and Rob Malley in Eilat for the entire week and use my need to brief the leaders as an excuse to be away from time to time; my real purpose was to join the back channel both to facilitate its work and to discuss problems and possibilities in it with Barak and Arafat. However complicated I thought this might be, it is fair to say I underestimated the difficulties.

When I got to Eilat, I found Yasser and Saeb completely dispirited. They were not interested in discussing anything. What was the point? What was their role? This was all a charade.

When I asked, Why not start by tackling a very practical problem, like water, to see if headway here could create a stronger basis on which to get at the core issues, they resisted, saying they could not explain to others that they were dealing with functional issues, not the political issues. When I protested that water was certainly a profoundly political issue, they weren't buying. They were dug in; I would not persuade them.

I turned to Mohammad Dahlan for help. He had joined Saeb and Yasser in Eilat. He was a supporter of the back channel, believing it was the only way to make real progress. While he was not close to Abu Ala, he respected him, and his close friend and collaborator Hassan Asfour was part of that effort. Dahlan had thought his presence would lighten the mood of Yasser and Saeb—after all, if Dahlan was there, the effort must be serious. But he acknowledged his presence had not changed their attitude. "So," I asked, "what do we do? There is real work that needs to be done, and there will be a price if Yasser and Saeb keep souring the environment and convincing your public there is no negotiation going on." Dahlan wasn't sure, and he gave me no reason to believe that Arafat would impose any discipline.

Why wouldn't Arafat impose any discipline? Why wouldn't Arafat impose a division of labor? There were probably two reasons, one which reflected a practical concern for Arafat and the other which reflected his operating style. The practical concern was that alienating Yasser Abed Rabbo could create a problem. Abed Rabbo was not a member of Fatah; he headed a small party called FIDA, and had originally been a member of the Democratic Front for the Liberation of Palestine. FIDA was a very small party, but for Arafat, Abed Rabbo's lead in the negotiations portrayed an image of different parties and factions supporting Arafat's approach to permanent status. What he certainly did not want or need was his lead negotiator publicly opposing his approach. Thus, he had a practical interest in keeping Yasser happy.

But that is only part of the story. Arafat's operating style has always been to foster competition among those around him. That ensured him that no one ever became too powerful or too much of a threat. On negotiations with the Israelis, competition kept everyone honest, looking over their shoulder and fearful they would be charged with giving too much away. This was an unquestioned, if frustrating, reality that I had to confront in negotiating the Hebron and Wye agreements. In doing the original DOP and the Interim Agreement, Arafat used back channels to make progress when he felt this was necessary. With Hebron and Wye, he promoted internal competition, shutting the competition down only at the very end.

It was clear to me at this point that the Abu Ala channel was not being given pride of place, and that in such circumstances, given the issues and stakes involved, it took considerable courage for Abu Ala to take on the task of back channel negotiations. He ran the considerable risk of being accused by his detractors of selling out fundamental Palestinian rights. Without unmistakable cover from Arafat, without Arafat's readiness to assume responsibility for any concessions that might be negotiated, Abu Ala would be under personal threat. However, as long as the back channel was only rumored and resented, but not publicly exposed, Abu Ala could stick with it.

In light of that, I became convinced that it was essential for the front channel to be credible. If it was, it would absorb attention, thus insulating the back channel; moreover, Yasser and Saeb would be focused on their own effort, rather than the need to subvert their putative competitors.

Barak had informed Oded about the back channel. Barak promised him that he would be briefed on developments in it, but that his work, for the time being, would be separate. Given my view that we needed to make the front channel credible, I asked Oded for his thoughts on how to do so. He felt I should convince Barak that the two channels should be merged. He could contribute more to the Israeli side, and Yasser and Saeb would be part of an effort, not excluded from it. This was logical, but probably not workable: Barak was never going to trust Yasser or Saeb, and I did not see Abu Ala ever wanting to work with them. As an alternative, I asked whether it was possible to create more of a parallel effort; "why can't you also work on some of the core issues?" If Yasser and Saeb felt these issues were not off-limits, but they and Oded could deal with issues like borders and security first and Jerusalem and refugees later, they would no longer feel they were being excluded from the real work.

Oded had no problem with this. He had already made a case to Barak that for reasons of dignity, if nothing else, it was a mistake to make Yasser and Saeb feel they would deal only with nonpolitical issues. Barak had authorized him to present a schematic map on the territory as a result, and he planned to do that here in Eilat.

I thought this created a way to deal with the Yasser and Saeb concerns. Unfortunately, I was wrong. Perhaps I should have asked Oded to make the presentation to me first, but I did not. Instead, I informed Yasser and Saeb that Oded would make a presentation on territory. They were pleased until they saw the presentation. Oded presented a blank map, but then drew in areas of Israeli security and settlement bloc needs. The implication of the needs was that the Palestinians would get something close to 60 percent of the territory of the West Bank and over time this could grow to 80 percent. The Palestinians would not have a border with Jordan, and the settlement blocs would separate parts of the territory, leaving narrow strips to connect different parts of the Palestinian areas.

Oded thought that as a first cut, an initial offering, this was reasonable, and after all, this was a negotiation that was just beginning, with real bargaining to follow. In any case, he was not authorized to present more than this. None of the Palestinians liked this presentation, and Dahlan vented his anger and walked out. Yasser explained that what was presented would guarantee no state, but rather a collection of separated cantons. Palestinians would be surrounded by Israel, and separated by Israelis. Who would look at this as a state? He could not continue discussions on such a basis—and then he, too, walked out.

Oded and his colleagues were shocked by the walkout. I was angry. To deal with Yasser's concerns about being a sideshow, I had pushed to be sure the territorial issue would be addressed. And they reacted in this way. I told Oded I would take care of it.

I went to see Yasser, Saeb, and Dahlan. They were fuming, saying this was an outrage. The Israelis did not want a deal, they wanted to occupy the Palestinians forever. I listened for a few minutes and then exploded: "You don't like what they presented, tell them so. But don't walk out. I am insulted. You did not walk out on them, you walked out on me. I did not come here so you could walk out on me. If this is the way you are going to behave, it is bullshit, and I am going to leave."

For the moment, I got them off their preoccupation with being a sideshow and got them focused on their need to keep me in Eilat. They did not mean to insult me. They respected me, they needed my role, what could they do now? I suggested some options: Come with their own schematic map, or have them explain their needs; if disaggregated, they may be easier to deal with or there may be alternative ways, not involving territory, to respond to them.

We had a short break and the Palestinians offered to explain their problems with the Israeli schematic, and after doing so to engage in a discussion of security. I thought we might be getting somewhere, and by the evening the Israelis agreed to give a presentation on their security needs.

The discussion on security was interesting, but highlighted the enormous conceptual gap between the two sides. The Israelis felt they needed to be responsible for their own security and believed their capabilities and security arrangements must be measured against an eastern front threat spearheaded by Iraq. The Palestinians doubted such a threat existed, felt that the Israeli security needs were exaggerated and could, in any case, be largely addressed by U.S. security guarantees and an international presence. To see if there was a way to reduce what Israel might require on the ground, I raised a number of cooperative measures, including "early-warning" arrangements with Jordan. Oded and the senior military man on his team, Mike Herzog, were open to creative options, but made it clear there were certain irreducible minimums for Israel when it came to early warning, guaranteed access routes through the West Bank, and zones of Israeli security responsibilities.

Dahlan, who had the responsibility for dealing with the security arrangements, was in favor of continuing our discussion on security the next day. But Saeb in particular settled back into a funk, arguing that Oded's presentation proved that these negotiations were only for show. The evidence: in the Israeli media there were reports that the Israelis were talking about withdrawing from 90 percent of the territory. Yet here was Oded talking about 60 percent, growing eventually to 80 percent, but with cantons. Either Oded was out of the loop or he was not authorized. "Either way we are wasting our time."

"Saeb," I said, "I don't know the Israeli bottom lines, maybe Oded doesn't either, but you are being unfair. You know the Israeli press is notoriously unreliable. What did you expect the first time he laid a schematic map on the table? You have to give this a chance." He and Yasser said they would, but they only went through the motions.

Yasser had truly turned sour. At one point, Oded, who was doing his best, suggested as a heading for discussion, "state-to-state relations." Yasser refused to enter into the discussion. I saw Yasser separately and expressed astonishment: Oded is conceding statehood as a principle by offering this heading. Statehood is not going to be used as a card, and rather than grabbing it, "you won't even discuss it. Why?" His reply, "Statehood means nothing without borders."*

Oded had tried a schematic on territory, and it angered Yasser and Saeb; he tried the principle of statehood, and they would not engage. Dahlan had made an effort to respond both on security and on borders, proposing at one point that Israel get 4 percent of the West Bank for its settlement blocs provided Israel swapped an equal amount of territory elsewhere.

It was Oded's turn to reject a Palestinian idea, but at least he acknowledged it was a Palestinian idea. It was clear that Yasser and Saeb were not going to do anything now except complain publicly that these were not real negotiations. We returned to Jerusalem. I tried one other idea to keep them engaged and to create a public focal point away from the back channel: for the next several days they would not meet directly, but I would meet with each of them daily and pose certain questions to each. Yasser was not enthusiastic, but Saeb saw merit in this approach. Saeb liked it because he saw the possibility of getting us involved with opening the political issues he believed were off-limits to Oded. Saeb became more convinced when I posed questions like, Could the Palestinians envision zones of special cooperation to accommodate Israeli security needs? Could they envision Palestinian sovereignty with an Israeli presence in some areas?

My questions signaled interest in maximizing the area of Palestinian sovereignty if Israeli security needs could be addressed. Saeb was interested in engaging and said he would respond.

At least I had created a focal point other than the back channel. The back channel had met a few times, but was on hold for the moment as Shlomo had business out of

---

*In 2002, Palestinians, including Yasser, were prepared to accept an even murkier concept—a state with provisional borders. This concept of recognizing a state first and negotiating the borders was embraced in the road map to peace. See the Epilogue.

the country. It was important for him to maintain a normal schedule to divert attention from his secret diplomacy. With Shlomo traveling and with my own uncertainty about whether the back channel would operate the way I hoped it would, I felt the need to develop more of a game plan for moving ahead. After consulting with Yossi Ginossar, I suggested we convene what I called our troubleshooting group: Yossi, Mohammad Dahlan and Mohammad Rashid, Gamal, and me. We met at the American Colony Hotel in East Jerusalem.

I started the meeting asking whether everyone in this group believed that a permanent status deal was possible; and assuming it was, what kind of scenario would move us from where we were to agreement? Rashid and Yossi did most of the talking in response. Both felt there was a deal, and that the gaps were definitely bridgeable. When I asked what the territorial deal looked like and how to solve Jerusalem, they each said that the percent of the West Bank the Palestinians would need would depend on whether there would be a swap of territory. With a swap, it could be in the low 90s; without it would be mid-90s. With regard to Jerusalem, both said it would be tough to resolve, but Rashid raised a possible idea: perhaps the Old City could become "a kind of B area, at least for a transition period."

This was certainly a creative idea designed to defuse the sovereignty issue in its most sensitive place. Would the back channel be the forum for raising similar types of ideas and moving us to agreement? Again, there was consensus that it would be, but that the back channel now needed to produce quickly and the only way for it to do so would be for Shlomo to present a package on all issues, including Jerusalem. "Yossi," I said, "I see two problems. Barak fears early exposure on Jerusalem and is resisting any discussion of it now. And he is also convinced that if you present a forward-leaning package now, the Palestinians will simply pocket it and not respond. I sure as hell don't want to push him to okay a serious package proposal and then find out the Palestinian response doesn't move off of the initial, going-in positions."

Yossi acknowledged that Jerusalem was a problem and that he and I and Shlomo would all need to push Barak; if we succeeded and there was a serious package presented, he would "personally guarantee that the Palestinians will respond."

We were all agreed that we needed to start with a package that Israel would present and to which the Palestinian side must seriously respond. In the aftermath of an Israeli package and a counterpackage proposal from the Palestinians, the United States could offer a way to bridge the differences. Rashid promised to work hard toward a meaningful Palestinian response, saying he would work quietly with Abu Ala and Hassan Asfour. As we left to go to lunch, Dahlan sounded the only discordant note. The scenario we discussed was fine, but we should not be counting on either him or Rashid to be able to deliver anything at this point. Both he and Rashid had been burned by

Arafat. They were the ones who talked him into accepting the understandings on the villages, and until the villages were delivered, neither he nor Rashid would have any credibility with him. Worse, given Arafat's anger, a serious deterioration was possible. Yossi got the point, responding that the Prime Minister was working on it, notwithstanding the opposition he was facing.

I decided to return to Washington, but before doing so I met separately with Abu Ala, Barak, and Shlomo. With Abu Ala, my purpose was to probe his strategy, and implicitly his level of confidence. He was in an upbeat mood. He had met alone with Shlomo just before Shlomo's trip. "He is a good man, and he is determined to do a deal. I can work with him" (words that made me think that Abu Ala was increasingly seeing Shlomo the way he had seen Uri Savir). "Were the gaps bridgeable?" I asked; with a straight face, he said it will be difficult and the Israelis will have to move much more, but "I think we can do it." I laughed, saying he did not need to negotiate with me, we both knew the Israelis were not the only ones who had to move. He laughed too and then, reading my mind, turned serious: I am working hard on my man and Abu Mazen. It makes Abu Ammar* feel easier if he sees "me and Abu Mazen" working together. I am thinking of "including one of his people—either Hussein Agha or Ahmed Khalidi—when we leave the country" for intensive talks.[†]

I was encouraged by this and told Abu Ala so. It was not just that both Agha and Khalidi were creative and committed to a deal, but also this would give Abu Mazen a stake in the channel. I liked Hassan Asfour, and knew that he gave Abu Ala cover with Dahlan; however, because of Abu Mazen's deep personal animus toward both Dahlan and Asfour, I worried that Abu Mazen might oppose the channel. Including one of his "academics" alleviated that concern.

After the meeting with Abu Ala, I was more hopeful the back channel could succeed, and even more convinced that the key to its success would be Shlomo's ability to present a comprehensive proposal. That is the case I made when I saw Barak. He was uneasy. He feared the Palestinians would not respond. Then what? Where would we be then? I was not about to quote Yossi's words, but I did say we would insist on a response—and if they want our help down the road, "they will know we will do nothing more for them without a meaningful response."

Barak would pledge only to think about my argument. I reported this to Shlomo,

---

*Arafat's nom de guerre.

[†]Hussein Agha and Ahmed Khalidi were two academics based in the United Kingdom. Both had been drawn in by Abu Mazen to develop ideas and creative options. Khalidi was part of a well-known Palestinian family, many of whom had been leading intellectuals.

advising him not to go out of the country for an intensive session without a package proposal: "When you leave the country, the message is it is time for business. The expectation will be high that you will produce. You won't without a package that includes Jerusalem." Shlomo was in agreement, and he was going to press Barak to give him enough to work with.

Within a few days Martin called to say the back channel had met, had additional discussions, and felt it was now appropriate to have a three-day session outside the country. They were going to go to Sweden and wanted me to join them for the last day. I would hear from the Swedes on the arrangements. "Shlomo feels he has enough to go?" I asked. Martin replied, "Yes, but he still does not have authorization to do Jerusalem." I wondered if it made any sense to argue this further, and Martin doubted it.

Shortly after Martin's call, I received a call from Par Nuder, the Chief of Staff of the Swedish Prime Minister. He told me "the parties are coming tomorrow night. We will be putting them up at the Prime Minister's official country residence about ninety minutes outside of Stockholm. Secrecy will be preserved." He told me they would make arrangements to whisk me into the country once I let them know when I would be arriving.

A SECRET MEETING IN SWEDEN: THE RISE
AND FALL OF THE BACK CHANNEL

To preserve secrecy, I knew I could not fly commercially. I also knew that once we put in the request for a military aircraft, a large number of people in the Pentagon and the White House would know I was going to Sweden. That would make a leak of my trip far too likely. So I called George Tenet and explained the problem. He took care of it by having his deputy, John Gordon, arrange for a private plane.

Par called me several times before I left to give me an update on the mood. He reported initially that the chemistry was very good and everything seemed promising. Later he called with a report that the mood had worsened, especially on the Israeli side, because they were hearing nothing new from Abu Ala. I then spoke separately to Gilad and Shlomo on the one side and Abu Ala on the other. Shlomo and Gilad focused on the importance of my getting there as soon as possible to change the dynamic and push Abu Ala. I asked if they had presented a package, and the answer was "a partial package." I knew what that meant. When I spoke to Abu Ala, he reported that the conversations were difficult, but he expected that things would improve once I arrived. "Abu Ala," I replied, "it had better or there is no point in my coming."

I had seen and lived this movie before. Both sides knew they had to produce now, but the hard part was always making the first serious move. My role now would be to push each to be responsive to the other. I decided I would sit with each side separately when I arrived before bringing everyone together in a three-way meeting.

I brought Aaron, Jon, and Gamal with me, and we landed at a small military airport in Stockholm at 11 a.m. The Swedish secret service met us with a van at the foot of the plane, and we were en route within minutes of landing. This was the way to slip into a country unnoticed.

The ride to the residence was scenic; this was my first time seeing the Swedish countryside, and I was surprised by how lush it was. Everywhere I looked I saw open green fields, full of wild flowers with intermittent lines of pine trees. Farms occasionally dotted the landscape, doing little to detract from the beauty of the scene before me.

I was struck by the similarity in appearance to some of the meadows I had seen as a boy in the High Sierras of my native California. It was hard not to be in a good mood as I arrived at the residence. The residence itself, while spacious with large grounds, sat, surprisingly, immediately adjacent to the road.

My mood shifted rather quickly when Par greeted me and told me that the talks had leaked. "What exactly has come out, and where has it come out?" I asked, hoping that it might still be fuzzy enough to protect the Palestinian side of this. Par told me that there had been an AP story from Palestinian sources saying there were secret negotiations going on in a European capital, followed in close succession by other stories coming out of Israel identifying Stockholm as the site. Now he also feared that the participants had been identified. Par sought my guidance on what they should say publicly in response to questions: "We have not said anything yet." "Par," I replied, "keep it simple, don't confirm anything but don't lie. Say something like the Prime Minister is willing to help promote peace any way he can, is in touch with the parties, but there are no talks in Stockholm at this time." (Technically true, the talks were in Sweden but not in Stockholm. Telling the technical truth is something I had learned from Rabin. He would never lie, but also not reveal.)

Handling the press was the least of our problems. If the channel was exposed, I feared that Abu Ala and Hassan Asfour would shut down. My worries deepened when Par told me who was present on the Palestinian side. Neither Hussein Agha nor Ahmed Khalidi were there. That told me Abu Ala would be unlikely to have Abu Mazen's help in protecting what he was doing—or at least in pressuring Arafat to protect whatever might emerge from these discussions.*

That was the bad news. But there was good news. Par told me the mood had

---

*I subsequently learned that Mohammad Rashid had opposed the presence of Agha or Khalidi and persuaded Arafat not to send them.

changed after my phone calls with the two sides. They had worked through the night and had been drafting. (This was prior to the press leaks—leaks the two sides were only finding out about now as they were just getting up.)

Though I had slept only about an hour on the plane coming over, I wanted only a shower before going to work. In a situation like this, adrenaline takes over. I was keyed up and ready to find out where we stood not in mood, but in content. (While Shlomo and Abu Ala were talking to Par, they were not revealing the substance of their discussions.)

I sat with both sides over lunch, and agreed to a sequence of seeing Shlomo, then Abu Ala, and then bringing us together in a three-way meeting. With Shlomo and Gilad, I heard a muddled message: There had been a session deep into the night in which they had drafted, and were "pretty close" to crystallizing the decisions the leaders would have to make to resolve the refugee issues. To give things a push, they had played a partial package offering 87 percent on territory, including gray areas that would largely become Palestinian; Shlomo, anticipating my question, said he offered some general thoughts on Jerusalem, emphasizing the need for a special regime to take account of both sides' interests.

They had been disappointed with Abu Ala's initial responses. The discussion improved during the evening session, and I asked how. Shlomo explained that Abu Ala and Hassan Asfour had made two moves. They acknowledged that settlement areas like Gush Etzion, Ramot, and Gilo could become part of Israel given either their contiguity or their significance in terms of historical Jewish presence. In addition, they would consider "an area" of the Jordan Valley for Israeli security presence, not "areas" for such a presence. Shlomo said it was his impression from the talks that the Palestinians have "a single digit in mind" for Israeli annexation of territory.

While Shlomo and Gilad were hopeful about the direction of the talks, they still wanted me to push Abu Ala to give a percentage of the territory the Palestinians had in mind for settlement blocs. This, I felt, was a mistake: "He's signaling you that there are openings on both settlement blocs and security presence. These conceptual openings are more important than pressing for numbers or percentages now. You are getting principles from him; if you press for numbers, you will get a disappointingly low one. Try to build on the principle at this stage."

Ironically, this is what Abu Ala had argued with them. He resisted seeing their map at this point, saying he preferred to build the map from concepts rather than to build the concepts from the map. Of course, this was Abu Ala's way of getting them to be more responsive to his concepts. Nonetheless, I thought he was right; he had conceded two key principles for the Israelis on settlement blocs and on security presence.

Now they needed to focus on the essence of Israeli needs in each case. That would give the Israelis their best shot at meeting their real requirements.

Shlomo and Gilad were sympathetic to my arguments, but also thinking about what they would be able to report to Barak when they returned. Generalities would not work when they had put 87 percent on the table. There might be openings from Abu Ala, but they were limited and unlikely to impress Barak. With the exception of Gush Etzion—the Etzion bloc south of Jerusalem—Gilo and Ramot were neighborhoods in Jerusalem, not settlement blocs. They had nothing specific on security, just a concept for an area in the Jordan Valley. "Dennis, you said you would push hard for a counter-package if we presented one."

"I will," I said, "when you present one." I observed that they were thinking about what they would report back to Barak, but what did Abu Ala have to say to Arafat? You have offered generalities on Jerusalem that he won't understand and will read as the perpetuation of Israeli control under a different name. On territories, you say you will go to 87 percent over a period of many years, but the figure he will see up front is 77 percent. "Certainly an improvement over what Oded presented, but still you talk about gray areas, saying that the Palestinians will get most of them. The Palestinian experience with ambiguity in the agreements so far is that you exploit them and they never get what they think they are entitled to."

My point was not to belittle their partial package, but to say that from a Palestinian perspective it did not look so generous. From my vantage point, both sides had made moves. The question was how to build on them.

Not surprisingly, my conversation with Abu Ala and Hassan was the mirror image of the one I had with Shlomo and Gilad. Abu Ala felt he had made all the significant moves—didn't they realize how significant it was for him and Hassan to give "examples of neighborhoods [across the green line] that would become part of Israel?" He had responded on security too. I needed to push Shlomo to give him more.

I laughed, saying, That's what Shlomo asked me to do with you. "The truth is," I continued, "you have offered them some very important openings. But you know that he is basically telling you that you will get 87 percent of the West Bank, and that Jerusalem is going to have to be governed by a special regime that responds to both sides' needs. That by itself may offer room for a creative outcome and, in any case, is way beyond anything you have heard from the Israelis. You know it is way beyond where Rabin was prepared to go, and you are just beginning to do business." (I threw in the reference to Rabin, who after the assassination had become an icon to Palestinians, to build up what Shlomo was presenting.)

I repeated these basic points when I brought Shlomo, Gilad, Abu Ala, and Hassan together with me. In response to my suggestion, they agreed to continue their drafting exercise to try to create clearer baselines on what they could agree on and on what was more difficult. When I asked if they would like me to join them for that, they preferred to do drafting on their own. Before they left to go to work, I asked to see Shlomo and Abu Ala both separately and alone.

My purpose now was to focus on where they really needed my help. Shlomo said we need a fat framework agreement—a fat, not a thin, FAPS. "I agree with you that Abu Ala has given us serious openings which we must develop. But the Palestinians seem to be thinking in terms of an agreement that leaves issues and claims open. We need a framework agreement that is not very different from a final agreement. If we are going to make far-reaching concessions, our people must see that we are ending the conflict."

Similarly, Abu Ala acknowledged that Shlomo was serious and determined. There was a lot of work to do and the gaps were still significant, but, he said, "You have to convince them to get rid of the gray areas." We cannot do a deal with gray areas. Everything "must be clear. No ambiguity. The timeline must be clear." I asked him if there was a way to treat areas that might be more sensitive for the Israelis differently in terms of the timing of withdrawal. He got my drift: "As long as they will withdraw and the time is clear for when they will do so, it does not matter if some areas would be withdrawn from early and others later on."

While his timeline would inevitably be shorter than the one I had in mind, the principle of withdrawing from some areas early, some on an intermediate time frame, and some only much later could be used to remove the Israeli need for gray areas. These were areas that were sensitive for either security or political reasons. For example, the Jordan Valley was an area that the Israelis felt they either could not give up or could give up only in part. The concept of a gray area gave the Israelis flexibility to decide later on what they would give up and to preserve some ambiguity with their own public about just what areas would actually become Palestinian. We could not preserve the ambiguity and respond to the Palestinians. But the longer the timeline for some areas, the more the Israeli public could be made to feel that Palestinian performance would have to precede Israeli withdrawal in particularly sensitive areas. No fulfillment on the Palestinian side, no need for the Israelis to withdraw.

They worked for several hours on drafting, but Abu Ala and Hassan became more passive. They decided not to have a mutual draft. Rather, it was a paper that Gilad drafted based on the discussions and the comments from both sides. In other words, he was describing the positions of each side as he understood them. The Palestinians did not necessarily confirm or deny what he wrote.

I suspected that Abu Ala and Hassan might be more cautious now because the channel had leaked. There had been two other developments in the meantime. First, Dani Yatom had called to tell me of very firm information that the Palestinians were planning massive and violent demonstrations for the next day, the anniversary of the Nakba—"the catastrophe" that befell the Palestinian people as a result of the creation of the State of Israel. He hoped we would intercede with Arafat and persuade him to prevent violent outbursts. This was especially important because the Knesset was reconvening and the Prime Minister would present the three villages for a vote tomorrow. Second, because the Prime Minister was now proceeding with the villages and fighting to win their approval in the Knesset, Shlomo was caught up in the effort to hold the government together. He was working the phones, doing all he could to keep Shas in the coalition.

Yatom's information was disturbing. If correct and there was an explosion of violence tomorrow, it would undercut Barak politically, making him look like a fool to be arguing for the village transfer on the day of Palestinian violence. It also would affect the credibility of the back channel; how could there be an explosion of violence at the very moment we were finally seeing serious negotiations on the most sensitive issues? Was Arafat double-dealing? Was this channel not really authoritative? Was Arafat going to use violence as a lever on negotiations?

Hoping that we might affect Arafat's calculus, I called the Secretary. I reported on what was developing here, with its inherent promise, but also explained my fears based on Dani's call. We needed the President to call on Arafat to prevent the violence. Madeleine agreed and suggested a short, blunt oral message from the President that could be delivered to Arafat within the next few hours.

John Herbst was now our consul general in Jerusalem. He would deliver the message and I called him to emphasize the urgency of the message; I wanted him both to insist on an immediate appointment with Arafat and to be very blunt with Arafat about the President's concerns and the meaning of this message.

Arafat's response to the President's message was not reassuring. While he received it right away, he told John that he would do what he could, but could "not guarantee anything." In "Arafatspeak," I took that to mean he would not take any serious steps to stop the violence. Again it made me wonder what Arafat was up to. While Barak had not delivered the promise on the villages, he was now struggling politically to do so. As I was to find out when I arrived in Israel the next night, Barak had sent Yossi to see Arafat four days earlier to inform him he was going to the Knesset to do the villages, and, in light of that, to impress on him the importance of preserving quiet on Nakba day. But Arafat did not listen to the Israelis or to us.

In retrospect, I believe that Arafat felt violence at this point served several useful purposes. It was a safety valve for releasing the anger that Ami Ayalon kept telling us was building up on the Palestinian street. It highlighted the consequences of not satisfying the Palestinians. And, in his eyes, it put pressure on the Israelis to be more forthcoming.

While Nakba day created an emotional context for the violence—and therefore was a convenient opportunity for Arafat to "let" the violence happen—it was also clear that the impact on Barak was not his concern. Partly this resulted from his anger at Barak. Partly this reflected his judgment of how to affect Israelis. And partly this was driven by his focus on his own needs, always paramount in his thinking, and his fundamental disregard for Israel's—something we would see demonstrated repeatedly over the coming months.

I did not see all of this at the time. But I was very concerned that Arafat, at a minimum, was demonstrating with his tolerance of violence a lack of interest in the work of the back channel—or any negotiations. I was not about to share this impression with Abu Ala at this point, but I did want to get a feel for his thinking.

I went to see Abu Ala late in the evening in his cabin. Behind the main residence were cottages that extended down to a pond. I knocked on Abu Ala's door and Hassan Asfour answered, joking that Abu Ala's accommodations were for royalty while he was being put up in a small "birdhouse." In Arabic, Asfour means "bird," so I joked in turn that Abu Ala's place seemed to fit him, while what was wrong with a birdhouse for "the bird"? Both laughed, and seemed upbeat. Both felt they could work with Shlomo and Gilad, though they felt that Gilad was on a tighter "leash" and more tentative. They were confident they could make the channel work.

But when alone with Abu Ala, I saw less confidence. He was anxious for me to meet with Arafat and make the case for what was produced here. He wanted me to tell Arafat that I had pushed both sides to start drafting with an eye toward identifying what they could agree on and what would be more difficult and reserved for the leaders. Finally, he wanted me to emphasize that I had pushed Shlomo to give up the "gray areas"—something I had, in fact, already done.

"Okay," I said, "I'll do it. But I am also going to tell him they need a 'fat FAPS,' and that it makes sense for both sides to produce a framework agreement that is as close as possible to a final agreement. I will also say that if there is violence, it will destroy our ability to play any role. And he will discredit those Israelis who want to do a deal."

"Good," Abu Ala replied, telling me that Shlomo had asked him to call Arafat and request that Arafat do all in his power to limit the disturbances the next day, particularly given what he and Barak were now trying to do. Abu Ala had done so and he was hopeful things would not get out of hand. I told him we had also done so, but I was worried that Arafat was not taking any of us seriously. Abu Ala doubted that, but I sensed that despite his words of hope about Arafat and what was now possible, he was uncertain about where Arafat was going. Unless addressed, that very uncertainty would force Abu Ala to draw back in the negotiations.

I left Abu Ala after midnight. Hassan joined me as I was walking back to the main house. Earlier in the evening he had been telling me that I needed to listen to the Palestinians more in general and him in particular. "You don't listen to us. You listen to Abu Mazen. You think Abu Mazen wants peace. He does not. Where is he now? Do you think he is doing anything? He is not."

I knew there was bad blood between the two, but I did not think that perpetuating a feud would serve the cause of negotiating peace with the Israelis at this point. With Abu Mazen out, would Arafat really be prepared to go forward? I doubted it, and told Hassan that. He was not buying, saying they would make progress in this channel and Abu Mazen would not matter. I did not buy this.

Ironically, I felt internal divisions on each side were coming to the fore at precisely the wrong moment. They would pull the rug out from Abu Ala and Hassan Asfour, notwithstanding Hassan's conviction. And Barak could only be weakened by the struggle with his coalition.

In the morning, Shlomo described "Barak's struggle" as he and I sat on the back porch. The NRP would pull out of the coalition over the villages. He did not know about Sharansky, but he felt Barak had made the decision to keep Shas in, regardless of the price with Meretz. He felt this was wise. They were a powerful social force in Israel that needed to be recognized. There would inevitably be a new alignment, but even if it reflected a smaller majority, it could be stable. But Barak would have to work at it, and catering to others and being attentive to their needs was not exactly his strong suit.

When he asked me what I thought we needed for the next step in this channel, I focused on substance, not procedure. For the first time I said, Both of you have taken a meaningful step toward the other on permanent status issues. To take it to the next level, you need to drop the idea of the gray areas and replace it with a timeline that allows you to withdraw from different areas at different times. They will not accept ambiguity on the territory. You also need to be able to say something more specific on Jerusalem. You want them to broaden what they will accept on settlement blocs, accept a fat FAPS and effectively the end of conflict. Your only chance of getting them to move in this direction is to bring Jerusalem into it. If you hold out on discussions on Jerusalem, Abu Ala won't move beyond what you heard here.

Shlomo agreed that the gray areas were not going to work. He was willing to try to discuss Jerusalem in the next round, but he said, "Dennis, I cannot get out front of Barak on Jerusalem." He would do what he could, joking, "if we still have a government when I get home."

That brought me back to reality. Shlomo and Abu Ala and their colleagues were

ready to leave and the Swedes were taking them back to the military airport we had arrived at twenty-four hours earlier. While the back channel had leaked, my participation
in it had not. Along with the actual location of the talks, I hoped to preserve that bit
of secrecy about the back channel. Thus, I wanted to arrive in Israel a few hours after
Shlomo and Abu Ala.

At this point, however, I knew that a discreet channel would no longer exist.
Shlomo and Abu Ala might well be the right negotiators, but their subsequent discussions would not be out of the limelight. The hope of reaching basic conceptual understandings in a protected back channel was not going to be realized. Maybe, given the
competition and the stakes, especially on the Palestinian side, this had always been an
illusion. Maybe it was not even the right approach for getting publics ready for the kind
of compromises necessary. Maybe, Abu Ala—the most creative negotiator on the Palestinian side—would not need a discreet channel in which to try out ideas if he knew he
had Arafat's backing and cover. Already he had taken a conceptual leap while being
here. Or maybe, as I sat next to the pond on a glorious day in a placid and nearly silent
Swedish countryside, I was rationalizing. Negotiators often do that. When the situation is not what one wanted or planned, one makes do and figures out how to make
the best of the circumstances. I would have to do that as I headed to Israel.

| VIOLENCE AND BARAK'S NEW PLAN |

I left a serene setting and flew into a war zone. We had heard nothing en route
from Stockholm on the events of the day, but as I deplaned my diplomatic security
(DS) agents met me with the news that there had been at least three Palestinians killed
with hundreds wounded in clashes with the IDF that day. Shooting between the Palestinian security forces and the IDF had continued throughout the day. Looking less
than enthusiastic, they wanted to know if I wanted to see Arafat tonight in Ramallah
because it might be a little "iffy."

I was stunned. Violent demonstrations were one thing, but these kinds of clashes
another. This looked like the events after the opening of the tunnel in September 1996.
Yet there had been no Israeli provocation. The "provocation," or more appropriately
the pretext, was Nakba day. Palestinian rage was being demonstrated; Arafat had done
nothing to prevent it, and Palestinians were the ones dying and suffering as a result.
And this rage, these clashes, were appearing on Israeli TV at the very moment Barak
was fighting in the Knesset to win approval for transferring the villages. While I had
feared the impact of violence at the moment Barak was in the Knesset, I had no idea
the clashes would be so bloody.

Martin was not at the airport but up in Jerusalem, trying to stay informed about

Israeli actions. He called me as I was contemplating whether to see Arafat. His advice was not to do so. He informed me that Yossi and Ami Ayalon, who had just retired as head of Shin Bet, had been working intensively with Arafat and the Israelis knew that Arafat had now given clear orders to prevent the demonstrators from getting close to the Israeli positions. They were hopeful tomorrow would be calm.

I had also asked Gamal to call Nabil Abu Rudeina to see what he was saying before I made a decision on seeing Arafat that evening. While I was on the phone with Martin, Gamal, riding in the same van with me, was speaking to Nabil. Nabil reported that everything was now under control. I knew Arafat would want to see me, but I wanted him to ensure calm so I asked Gamal to "call Nabil back and tell him, assuming it is quiet, I will come to see Arafat tomorrow."

It was quiet in the morning and I saw Arafat for lunch. He was now acting to keep demonstrators away from Israeli positions and the situation was calm. We talked a little about that, and he emphasized all he was doing to control the situation. In front of his colleagues, I told him that was important, but it was strange, indeed, to see Barak fighting in the Knesset to transfer the villages and simultaneously to see pitched battles in the streets of the West Bank. President Clinton had sent an oral message because it was important to prevent the violence, not simply to respond to it after the fact. Arafat listened without comment.

When we were alone I said the violence was a disaster and would prevent the very thing he wanted: the transfer of the villages. He offered no comment. I continued to emphasize the need for calm, particularly given the first truly substantive talks on the core issues. "In Sweden," I said, "real business was done." To follow up, I told him I had asked Shlomo to drop the gray areas; Abu Ala to focus on producing an end-of-conflict framework agreement; and both sides to draft their points of agreement and identify the key differences on which only the leaders could decide.

I went on to tell him that time was now of the essence. The next step should be Abu Ala and Shlomo meeting for five or six days, and following that the Secretary should come out to meet with you and Barak and focus on bridging some of the key differences reserved for the two of you. "My worry," I said, is that Israel will withdraw from Lebanon soon, and "we don't know what is going to happen when it does. We need to make progress before events in Lebanon intervene."

I did not know whether Hizbollah and Syria would try to make it appear that Israel was fleeing when it left Lebanon, possibly triggering a major Israeli response. I knew a major escalation at the time of withdrawal could divert attention away from the Palestinians and also discredit what Barak had done, inevitably making him more cautious on the Palestinians. Whatever the possibility, I told Arafat, you would be far better off reaching some new threshold with Barak before the withdrawal from Lebanon.

He listened intently, but said nothing. I asked if he was worried about the Israeli withdrawal from Lebanon, and he replied that he still doubted it would happen without an agreement. He continued to assume that the Syrians and Israelis would cut a deal at the last minute. "Don't bank on that," I said. But even if I was wrong and he was right, it was still in his "interest to get something done with the Israelis now."

His passivity bothered me. He let the violence happen. He was content to wait for the Israeli withdrawal, or an agreement between the Israelis and Syrians. He was not reacting to anything I said about the back channel other than to say "we hope so."

It was not enough for him to hope so. He needed to act to get things done, prompting me to say to him, "You have a moment now. I don't know how long it will last. If Barak's political position weakens too much it could lead to a national unity government, and if it does there will be no final status deal for the foreseeable future. You will never have a better Israeli government to work with. You will never have a better chance to do a final peace agreement than you have now with this Israeli government and with this President."

He reacted only to my reference to Clinton, saying, "No one was like Clinton." I could tell I had not moved him. He was anxious for me to go out and publicly say that both sides were working to calm the situation and we would continue to work on the negotiations. I did so, but I was not optimistic that Abu Ala was going to get the support he would need to move the negotiations ahead quickly. On the contrary, I now believed that Arafat was in no hurry.

Barak, however, was a man in a hurry. While the violence may have been politically damaging and embarrassing, particularly given its coincidence with Barak's call in the Knesset to transfer the "Jerusalem" villages, Barak nonetheless was ready to switch into high gear.

When I saw Barak that evening, he was preoccupied with his coalition problems. Rather than making him hesitate, however, these problems propelled him toward the fast track. While this logic was counterintuitive, Barak felt that if it looked like Israel was on the brink of a historic breakthrough to peace, it would be harder for those in the coalition to play petty politics. In such circumstances he would gain the upper hand in holding the coalition together and be less subject to the parochial demands of one party or another. But, of course, for this to happen, historic decisions had to be at hand. His surprising conclusion: we must move to an endgame in two weeks.

He had it all programmed. I would join the next round of talks within the week. The Secretary would come out by next week, and we would move to an endgame summit in two weeks.

While I had tried to convince Arafat that time was of the essence, this made no sense. We had just begun a serious negotiation that was still, at best, conceptual, not yet practical and concrete. The issues were too hard, we did not have time to prepare the ground, he himself was still sputtering over the Palestinian police firing at the IDF and how this undercut the ability to portray them as partners, and yet here he was with a two-week timetable for an endgame summit. It was astonishingly unrealistic. Yes, as I now said to him, we have to move, but we would never be able to move as quickly as he wanted—and there was a problem with trying to do so. Having seen Arafat, I told him it was clear that Arafat was in no hurry. "You must not appear desperate to him or he will lose all incentive to compromise."

His approach made me retreat from what I had told Arafat about the Secretary coming next week. Now I knew it was a mistake for her to come unless the next round created more of a basis for us to bridge differences at the leader level. While Barak agreed with this, he was not giving up on the idea of a very fast track to a summit. I wondered to myself if I may have been inadvertently responsible for this with my pushing Shlomo to discuss Jerusalem in something other than generalities. Barak had always resisted such a discussion, fearing it was too politically explosive in any environment except that of an endgame.

If that was the case, we were caught in a classic catch-22. The Palestinians would never contemplate an endgame, much less major concessions to the Israelis, without knowing what was possible for them on Jerusalem. With their own public, the explanation for any concessions would be largely, "Look what we got on Jerusalem." Shlomo understood this very well, having told Abu Ala in my presence, "You can justify giving up some territory if it is the price for gaining a position in Jerusalem that the Muslim world has not had for fifteen hundred years."

Was Barak riveted on a fast track to an endgame because of his recognition that there was no escaping discussion of Jerusalem now? Was he pressing it because he feared the unknowns of the Lebanon withdrawal and wanted to resolve things with the Palestinians prior to that? Was he being driven by coalition politics and his natural predisposition toward "moments of truth"—although in this case, was the moment of truth required in order to determine just how far his own coalition could go in a permanent status deal with the Palestinians?

I suspected all three factors might be at play. However, the coalition remained uppermost, and Barak asked me to see various members of his cabinet in order to explain that we were making real progress now.

With the situation on the ground now calm, I saw value in returning home. But I agreed to stay one more day to see members of the cabinet. And since I was, in effect, working the internal politics on the Israeli side, I thought it useful to do likewise with the Palestinians.

On the Palestinian side, it was essential to see Abu Mazen. Abu Mazen is a very proud man. When slighted by Arafat, he would withdraw and remove himself from any activity involving Arafat or the diplomacy. When insulted by others, he got angry and often got even. I did not know how he felt about Abu Ala at this time, but I wanted him to feel neither slighted nor ignored by us. I also wanted him to know that peace was possible but we were not going to get there without his help.

While very pleasant as always in our meeting, Abu Mazen was uncharacteristically unyielding on the substance, saying the Palestinians had made their concessions. They could only accept the full implementation of the UN resolutions now—on both territory and refugees.

When I asked what Oslo was about if the Palestinians had made their concessions before entering into it he answered, "Learning to live together." When I asked what Beilin–Abu Mazen was about other than compromising on the key issues, especially on Jerusalem and refugees, he said, "It was never accepted." When I said you have an Israeli government prepared to do what none of its predecessors could or would do, but they could not give 100 percent of the territory or accept the "right of return" with its implications, his response was that it would take time.

This was not the posture of a negotiator trying tactically to gain advantage. This was the posture of someone who did not want anything to happen soon—no doubt given his continuing anger at Dahlan and his unwillingness to be out front of Arafat.

The two sides were out of sync again. Coalition politics made Barak want to hurry. Internal competition, which Arafat was manipulating, led Palestinian negotiators to go slow.

When I saw my friend Natan Sharansky, it was clear to me that Barak's pushing for the moment of truth would drive Sharansky out of the coalition. He was not comfortable with the kinds of concessions Barak had in mind, at least as reported in the Israeli press. The media were reporting that Barak was prepared to give up to 95 percent of the territory and to divide Jerusalem. Maybe that was where Barak was headed, but I said, "Natan, this has to be the strangest negotiation I have ever been a part of. Usually, the most forthcoming ideas are mentioned in private, but here it is just the opposite. The public positions are way beyond anything that your side is conveying in private. I don't know what is real, but I do know what is being said in private and it is not close to what you are afraid of."

I proceeded to tick off the red lines that had governed the Israeli approach in the negotiations. On the borders, modify them to allow 80 percent of the settlers to be incorporated into three blocs. "Do you have a problem with that?" I asked. "No," he answered. On security, ensure that the security arrangements meet Israeli needs in the Jordan Valley and on early warning. "Do you have a problem with that?" "No," was again his reply. On refugees, make certain there is no right of return to Israel. "Do you have a problem with that?" "No," Natan answered. As for Jerusalem, I told him Barak had not authorized the negotiators even to talk about it so I could not tell him what the position was. "So, Natan, what is your problem?" He replied succinctly, "Dennis, my problem is you are telling me this, Barak is not."

I called Barak after the meeting, recounted the conversation, and suggested he give Sharansky a call—"he is not necessarily a lost cause but you have to talk to him."

Barak was pleased to hear this, but quickly asked me if I had seen Yossi Sarid yet. I had not, but was seeing him next. "Very important. Let him know we are on the threshold of making the most historic decisions since the founding of the state." That was Barak's job, not mine—especially at a point when the Palestinians were not positioning themselves for historic moves.*

I felt uneasy as I boarded my TWA flight home a little after midnight on Wednesday, May 17. The situation was calm in the territories. But there was great turmoil on each side. Had I known the violence would erupt again on the morning after my departure, I might not have left. While the demonstrations (ostensibly organized to protest the prisoners held by the Israelis) turned violent and involved exchanges of gunfire between Palestinian security forces and the IDF, they did not produce any fatalities. Nonetheless, they did plenty of damage on the Israeli side, at least as far as Barak was concerned.

According to Barak, "even traditional peaceniks" were now pressing for a suspension of talks. The image of armed Palestinians—armed under the terms of Oslo—firing on Israeli soldiers was completely unacceptable to Barak. The belief that the Palestinians would resort to violence whenever they were unhappy fed the view of many that no deal with the Palestinians would hold. Under such circumstances, Barak decided not to deliver the villages that he had succeeded in getting the Knesset to approve. Nor did he go ahead with his promise to provide at least a down payment on the purchase tax monies. And, worst of all from the perspective of the Palestinian street, there would be no prisoner releases, the very issue that triggered the second eruption of the riots.

Perhaps this was a logical response to the situation on the ground. But was it consistent with Barak's continuing desire to press ahead quickly on permanent status? Moreover, he drew back on promises he had made even after Arafat took clear steps to calm the situation. Barak held to the paradoxical position of not delivering on prom-

---

*I saw Sarid and emphasized the stakes, reminding him that his entire career had been devoted to peace, and his problems with Shas should not be permitted to undermine that goal. He remained a terribly conflicted man.

ises reaffirmed by the President while continuing to press for rapid movement to the endgame.

Lebanon was about to be introduced into this mix in a way that convinced Barak of the urgency of going for agreement, and Arafat of the need to demonstrate that he was not weak and not making concessions to the Israelis.

| LEBANON AND UNINTENDED CONSEQUENCES |

Through April and May—following the failed Geneva meeting with Asad—Barak orchestrated a series of coordinated moves with us and UN Secretary-General Kofi Annan to make sure the UN would confirm that Israel's withdrawal from Lebanon complied with UN Security Council resolution 425. Even though this required a withdrawal line different from the one the IDF wanted, and necessitated considerable expense to rebuild new military positions along the border, Barak wanted the international community to recognize and support Israel's withdrawal. This would deny Hizbollah any excuse for continuing attacks, legitimize strong Israeli retaliation in the event of attacks after withdrawal, and promote a strong deterrent to such attacks.

Understandably, Barak sought to make withdrawal look like Israel's decision, made out of strength and conviction. But Hizbollah had other ideas.

As Israel began to dismantle some of its outposts and turn over others to its proxy army, the Southern Lebanese Army (SLA), Hizbollah went on the offensive. Initially, Hizbollah was simply attacking the SLA, not the Israelis. Then, in a masterstroke of public relations, they organized a march on the remaining Israeli positions. Here was a mass of humanity seeking to force the Israelis out—in effect, the Lebanese people pushing Israel out of Lebanon. The IDF sought to hold their ground, initially firing over the heads of the crowd. That did not work. When they fired into the crowd, they killed several people. The march stopped, but Barak saw a disaster in the making. Quietly, he informed us that Israel would be out of Lebanon in twenty hours—a deadline the IDF actually beat.

As a logistical feat, it was another source of pride for the Israeli military. But in the region, particularly given the collapse of the SLA, the withdrawal looked like a defeat.

Suddenly there was a new model for dealing with Israel: the Hizbollah model. Don't make concessions. Don't negotiate. Use violence. And the Israelis will grow weary and withdraw.

It mattered little that Barak had announced his intentions a year in advance, or that Israel had no claims, no historical attachment, and, most importantly, no Israeli settler presence in southern Lebanon, as it did in the West Bank and Gaza. In a textbook case of unintended consequences, the Israeli withdrawal from Lebanon fostered

an environment supporting increased radicalism, not moderation. Hizbollah was celebrated for forcing the Israelis out. Resentment toward the Israelis, the West, the
"haves," spilled out and expressed itself. The latent desire to humiliate those who humiliated the Arabs was once again apparent.

The pullout also made Arafat look bad. He was vilified in the Arab media as a
weakling. He was portrayed as someone who negotiated with the Israelis and got nothing but crumbs while his people suffered under occupation. Thus characterized, Arafat
once again saw himself as the victim. In a profanity-laced monologue he had with
Gamal, Arafat complained, "Barak is screwing me." He fulfills his commitments on
Lebanon, but "not with me."

When I saw Arafat a short time later, he felt beleaguered and blamed Barak. He
had no interest in permanent status. If Barak wanted to move on that, let him fulfill his
promises first. Do the villages. Provide the purchase tax. Complete the northern safe
passage. Release prisoners. Carry out the third FRD on June 23. Arafat's position
would then improve and then we could talk about permanent status.

Needless to say, Barak's view of Lebanon was far different from Arafat's. After the
initial shock of the Israeli withdrawal, most of the Israeli public—and the Israeli media—were giving Barak enormous credit for having the courage to break the inertia of
the past and pull the Israeli troops out.

Barak saw great benefit in bold, decisive action, and felt it needed to be applied
now to the Palestinians. Obviously, political factors affected his sense of timing. But so
did several other factors. First, as only Barak could do, he had convinced himself that
Clinton's clout with the Congress would exhaust itself by the end of June. His "lame
duck" status would diminish his ability to get a large assistance package through the
Congress for Israel and the Palestinians—something critical to finalizing a deal and
also "selling" the Israeli public.

Second, Barak's ability to conclude a deal with the Palestinians depended on calm
in Lebanon—which he feared could vanish at any moment.

Finally, Barak was worried about the third further redeployment, set to take place
by June 23. Every FRD to date had created a crisis. This one was bound to be the worst
because it was the last. Arafat had developed a mythology on the third FRD, saying
that the Palestinians should have 91 percent of the territory after it was implemented.
The Israeli view was completely different, seeing at most 50 percent of the territory in
Palestinian hands after the third FRD. Barak knew there was no way he could satisfy
what Arafat wanted. Moreover, he knew that even doing a 10 percent FRD would
make it appear that he was giving away more land to the Palestinians and getting nothing in return—thereby costing him the political capital he would need to make far-
reaching concessions on borders and Jerusalem. Barak thus convinced himself that the

permanent status deal had to take place before the June 23 deadline. In the meantime, to ensure that he did not squander any political capital, he refused to transfer the villages near Jerusalem.

| HOLDING OFF BARAK ON THE SUMMIT |

We faced two conflicting mind-sets. One wanted to make history, by taking a big leap and ignoring the short-term effects of his failure to fulfill his promises. The other wanted to deal only with the interim issues, fearing what it would take to make history and believing in any case that he was entitled because of the promises made to him. While I might not have agreed with their perspectives, I understood why each leader felt the way he did. For Barak, if the interim issues would be subsumed in the permanent status agreement, why focus on them now and politically undo his capacity to reach such an agreement? For Arafat, why should he have to confront the bigger issues with a leader he did not trust, and without first restoring his own political capital?

Barak now sought to accelerate the process by seeing President Clinton. He had been scheduled to visit Washington May 22–24, but had canceled the trip because of the events in Lebanon. With the withdrawal completed and with everything calm in the north, he was now anxious to see the President. The President was in Lisbon for a U.S.–European Union summit, and agreed to see Barak there for a few hours on the morning of June 1. I flew there overnight to brief the President and the Secretary. Martin had flown on Barak's plane to Lisbon and he reported that Barak planned to tell the President we should simply go to a Camp David summit to see if an agreement was possible. Only in a summit, he would argue, would Arafat have to face up to the moment of truth, and then we would know if he was a partner for settling the conflict.

Knowing Barak, I realized we were unlikely to change his mind. But we did have leverage. He wanted a summit, and we did not have to convene or host one unless we were convinced it made sense to do so. I suggested, therefore, that the President make clear he was ready to go to a summit provided (1) we knew enough about each side's position to know if a deal was possible, and (2) Arafat's grievances in terms of the villages, the money, and some prisoners were addressed so as to position him better to make big moves—and also deny him excuses for not doing so.

In the meeting, the President followed this script, but Barak resisted. He dismissed the notion that Arafat had any legitimate grievances, acknowledging that promises had been made on the villages but that Arafat, by permitting the violence, had made it impossible for Barak to turn them over. In any case, Barak argued this was a side issue. Arafat would use everything as an excuse to run away from facing the big decisions.

Was Arafat ready to make peace? Or would he always avoid facing the moment of truth? We would, he argued, never know unless we went to a summit and put him to the test—and we needed to do that now.

The President resisted, emphasizing that he would go to a summit, but not if we did not have more of a basis or a document to work from. Barak felt it was pointless to work on a document at this time. Neither side could put on paper their concessions on the core issues like Jerusalem, borders, and refugees. The document could leak and paralyze him and Arafat. The negotiators could not do more; during Carter's time they had done more at "Camp David in eleven days than they had done in eleven months." A summit was the only answer for dealing with the core issues.

The President did not relent. At a minimum, we needed to satisfy ourselves that a deal was possible before taking the leap to a summit. Barak reluctantly agreed that the Secretary should come to the region, preceded by a day or two by me. After that, we might have the negotiators come to Washington for an intensive round and have Arafat see the President. By the middle of June, we would make a judgment on whether it made sense to go to a summit.

With this in mind, we set three objectives for Secretary Albright's trip: get Barak to move on the villages, the money, and at least a serious review process for releasing prisoners; get Barak to accept another round with the negotiators in which they would either work on a joint draft or, barring that, work with us so that we might prepare a draft that could be tabled at the summit; get Arafat to drop his focus on the interim issues, including the third FRD, and commit instead to a concentrated effort to produce a framework deal now.

Each would get something. Barak would get the shot at determining if a framework deal could be done at a summit soon, and without having the third FRD looming. Arafat would get the villages, the money, and something on prisoners, but would then have to be prepared to face the big issues—with a guarantee of President Clinton's help to do the big deal, but also with the certainty that if he insisted on only doing the interim issues he would lose the President's involvement.

When we arrived in the region, Barak was locked in a new political crisis with Shas. In response to a Shas threat to support a bill for early elections if their demands on education were not met, Barak suspended the negotiations that had been designed to meet their needs. Barak's brinkmanship did not pay off. Shas proceeded to vote for the early elections bill.

In these circumstances, getting Barak's full attention was difficult. But the Secretary and I pressed Barak hard on the villages, the money, and prisoners, urging him to move on each prior to Arafat's upcoming trip to Washington on June 15. With these moves, we told Barak we could put the onus on Arafat to respond. Without them, we would be on the defensive, and Arafat would say we had made commitments to him about Barak and failed to deliver.

Barak was not convinced, no doubt believing that if we just pushed Arafat hard enough, he would have no choice but to respond to us. Nonetheless, he agreed to provide at least a down payment on the purchase tax monies by June 15, and to consider some prisoner releases as well. But he remained noncommittal on the villages. As for sending his negotiators to Washington, he was not enthusiastic, but would do so for four days: "I am not sending them for an extended negotiation."

Given his concern about the third FRD, I asked, "If we could ensure that Arafat would not make the third FRD a crisis, would you still be so concerned about the June 23 date? Isn't that the issue that concerns you? If we resolve that, then presumably, we would not have to rush to a summit without knowing whether or not it could succeed."

Barak's answer surprised both Madeleine and me. He agreed with the basic point, but then offered a completely new explanation for why June 23 was a critical date with the Palestinians. Syria was again influencing his thinking. There was a Ba'ath Party congress, the first in fifteen years, on the twenty-second and Barak felt that Asad would want to preserve stability until then. Maybe he would be less interested in keeping the border quiet after that. That would be dangerous. But he added there might be a very different possibility. Maybe once the party congress blessed Asad's son, Bashar, President Asad might no longer be concerned about succession and be able to shift gears again toward Israel. Barak, the man of paradoxes, was now arguing that because of possible changes in Syria—good or bad—June 23 was the critical date. Don't move by then on permanent status and the world changes.

I did not see it that way. Asad gave the impression of a leader totally consumed with succession, and until everything was settled he did not need trouble. His behavior at the time of the Israeli withdrawal indicated that. Syria had done nothing. And Arafat was doing nothing now. If we could persuade Arafat not to make the third FRD a crisis, then the twenty-third would not be an issue.

But our meetings with Arafat made clear he would not let either Barak or us off the hook so easily. Arafat would only agree with us on having the negotiators come to Washington. He would not give up his focus on the third FRD, calling it "the crux of the matter" and the "litmus test." When I challenged him that borders, refugees, and Jerusalem were the crux of the matter, he asked, If Barak could not do the little issues, how could he do the big ones? Secretary Albright answered that it was easier for Barak to wrap everything in a package for the Israeli public than expose himself continually to "piecemeal" steps with uncertain returns.

Arafat would not budge. He had been promised the villages, he was promised a timeline, he was entitled to a third FRD, and he would insist on these. He would hold Barak and the President to their promises, while allowing his negotiators to go to Washington.

There was one potentially hopeful development on this trip. I had dinner alone with Saeb at the Jerusalem YMCA one night. He knew that "the stuff of peace," the stuff of relations, was what happened between Israelis and Palestinians on a daily basis. It was necessary to solve the core questions or questions of principle, but solving them would mean little if there was no Palestinian economy, or if the Palestinians had basic water problems, or if fundamental issues of trade and commerce with Israel were unresolved. People had to live, and he would take it on himself to work these practical issues with Oded. Ironically, the division of the issues—Abu Ala working the core issues, Saeb working the functional issues—was something Saeb was now prepared to pursue.

Saeb was very earnest, and I hoped this was a sign that on the Palestinian side they knew we were heading for an endgame. Of course the larger question was, particularly given Arafat's attitudes, whether Abu Ala would be forthcoming on the core issues at this stage. I was dubious, but determined to try to find the way for us to draw more out of each side.

It would not be easy. The negotiators were coming to Washington but, given the different mind-sets of their leaders, would be increasingly inclined to talk past each other. Moreover, with a summit being talked about publicly, I was afraid each side would hold back all flexibility for the endgame. Indeed, this was the essence of Barak's argument: negotiations outside a summit can only produce bitterness, not results.

Knowing this, I focused on working with the two sides separately, assuming they might find it easier to reveal their real thinking to me than to each other. I also began to think about how we would use the President's meeting with Arafat to move toward the endgame.

| ASAD DIES AND ARAFAT COMES TO WASHINGTON |

In the midst of all this, on June 10 Asad died. The funeral would be two days later, on Monday, and Bashar was in charge. The clearest sign of that: Toni Verstandig reported to me that our embassy in Damascus was informed that Rifaat—Bashar's uncle—would be arrested if he tried to come back to Syria.*

Asad was a thirty-year fixture in the region, and now he was gone. We could not now know how the landscape would change, only that it would. I felt we should not

---

*Rifaat Asad had been forced into exile after launching what amounted to a coup against his brother in 1984—a time when Hafez al-Asad was recovering from a serious heart attack.

wait to see how the land would resettle. Israel was out of Lebanon; now Asad was dead. Both were potentially transforming events. Asad's death would mean that Arafat would have far less to fear from Palestinian rejectionist groups based and supported in Damascus. It meant that if Arafat made historic concessions, he would not have to fear Asad's charges of a sellout—charges that would make the Gulf states hesitate in their support for Arafat's moves. Arafat now would also have to consider the Asad model of holding out for everything and getting nothing. If Arafat had a chance for a fair deal, he might find it easier to grab it now—or so I hoped.

Unfortunately, Arafat arrived in Washington feeling not only aggrieved but very angry. On the eve of his trip, Barak in effect broke his promises to us. He did not move on the villages, explaining to the President that his coalition problems ruled that out. He effectively did not move on prisoners, announcing that only three would be released, without any process for subsequent releases. While Barak did move on the money, Arafat understandably felt he was being embarrassed on the symbolic issues.

What was he to say to his public—that he was grateful for three prisoners? Rather than help us move Arafat off the third FRD, Barak's announcement on the three prisoners persuaded Arafat to insist on its implementation in his meeting with the President.

Given Arafat's mood, I suggested that the President initially meet him alone and Madeleine, Sandy, and I could join them later along with Abu Mazen and Abu Ala. As we entered the Oval Office following the two leaders' private meeting, Gamal gave us a thumbs-down sign. He shook his head and mouthed the words, "We are nowhere."

The President summarized the discussion he had had with Arafat, pointing out his desire for a few weeks to work toward a summit and a FAPS and Arafat's insistence that he get a third FRD on June 23. At that point, Arafat launched into a litany of reasons why he was entitled to the third FRD, adding falsely how all Israeli prime ministers had accepted his right to get 91 percent of the territory at the end of the FRD process.

When it was clear that nothing was changing, the President looked expectantly at me and asked, "Dennis, do you have any thoughts?" My unspoken thought at the moment was to tell Arafat that he had no right to 91 percent as part of the further redeployment process—but that would have only sidetracked us into a long theological discussion which the President was obviously not interested in having. Instead, I initially began to try to separate the two issues—FAPS and the third phase of redeployment—when Arafat interrupted me, saying, "You will just take his [Barak's] side."

Angrily, I challenged him, "Is that what you think?" There was silence in the Oval Office. Arafat did not respond, and no one said anything. My gaze did not leave Arafat, and I let the silence linger for a minute before asking him the following question: If you knew you would get a third redeployment if there was a good-faith effort by you,

Barak, and us to achieve a FAPS and it did not succeed, would you be willing to give us a few weeks to work with both sides on such a good-faith effort?

Arafat did not say yes or no, clearly reluctant to commit himself. But Abu Ala leaped in, repeating my formulation and saying it was acceptable. Arafat seemed relieved. So did the President, unfortunately adding that he would not blame Arafat if a summit failed and would support a substantial FRD if we could not produce a FAPS.

The mood was transformed. No doubt the President felt that Arafat had given on what we were asking him to do—defer the third FRD—and wanted to offer him some reassurance. Fearing the unqualified nature of the assurance yet not wanting to contradict the President, I added with the President's nodding approval that, of course, everything depended on both sides making a good-faith effort on the FAPS, with special emphasis on the "good faith."

We had planned for a lunch at the Secretary's house in Georgetown. Arafat came with Abu Mazen and Abu Ala and I joined the Secretary. We agreed we would talk about how we would proceed over the next few weeks.

Before starting the lunch, the Secretary wanted to meet for a few minutes privately with Arafat. She made two points. First, the meeting in the Oval Office had made her sad because Arafat was not giving his friends—the best he could hope to have in an administration—the chance to work toward an agreement on everything. Second, he should not have attacked me. That was not the way to behave toward us.

Whether because of the Secretary's "motherly" admonition to him or because he had vented with the President or some combination of the two, Arafat was agreeable throughout the lunch. He apologized almost immediately to me. Moreover, when I described that our effort would be focused on distilling the points of agreement and disagreement on the three issues of territory, refugees, and Jerusalem, he asked almost plaintively if I would add the fourth issue of the third FRD to this in our work over the next two weeks. He added that it was essential for all of us to say that work was continuing on the third FRD, not that it was postponed or ignored.

| DRAWING THE NEGOTIATORS OUT ON WHAT MIGHT BE POSSIBLE IN THE ENDGAME |

When the Secretary called Barak to brief him on the outcome of the meeting with Arafat, he was unimpressed. Nothing had changed for him. Arafat's acquiescence to a few additional weeks meant nothing. Additional preparation for a summit promised only problems, no benefit. He had reluctantly agreed to send his negotiators to Washington (they were now meeting in relative isolation at Andrews Air Force Base), but he argued it was all "downside"—"you will learn nothing more from the Palestinians; you will only be pressing to learn more from us." Without him saying it, I understood that Barak did not want to reveal more to us prior to the summit lest it affect his room for maneuvering at the summit.

But as I explained to his negotiators—Shlomo Ben-Ami and Gilad Sher—President Clinton would not go to a summit unless we had reason to believe it could succeed. Maybe, I said, if we learned more from each side separately, we could see where the possible bridges were.

After trying with minimal success to draw each side out I asked Shlomo and Abu Ala to tell me what they thought the other needed and could do. In effect, I was challenging them to prove that they not only were thinking about their own needs but understood the other side well enough to explain credibly what was possible for them.

Initially, I said to Shlomo, "You want them to move, tell me, at the end of the day, what do you think is possible for them as they see it?" I could tell he, Gilad, and Gidi Grinstein (the young, highly committed, and very smart lawyer on their team) were intrigued by this question. Here was a way for them to say something new without having to say anything explicit about their own positions. Yet they understood immediately that by indicating what they thought the other side could do, they would be sending a signal about what they thought was possible. Abu Ala understood as well, but was more cautious.

Shlomo and Gilad took the logic of this approach and extended it. They produced a paper of sixteen "assumptions" or "essential bridges" between the two sides' positions. These were not Israeli positions, but what they described as American bridging ideas— ideas that represented what they believed would be our views of what each side could live with at the end of the day. Disclaimers aside, they obviously would not outline positions to us that were completely unacceptable to them.

The sixteen "assumptions" constituted an extraordinary signal of what they could accept in an endgame. (For example, the green line, or June 4 line, would be the basis for the border and the Palestinians would have sovereignty in the Jordan Valley, provided there were modifications of the border to account for three Israeli settlement blocs and Israeli security needs were addressed.) That they had gone too far for Barak at this stage was indicated a short while later, when Gilad called after speaking to the Prime Minister. Clearly nervous, he asked me not to "breathe a word about the assumptions paper; it does not exist."

While Abu Ala and Shlomo had been insulated at Andrews Air Force Base, we had put Oded and Saeb at Bolling Air Force Base. Only a few miles apart, they nonetheless stayed away from their colleagues working ostensibly on the more functional issues.

Since I had been working primarily with Shlomo and Abu Ala, I invited Saeb and

Oded to our house for dinner. Oded drove the two to our house, but had called me in advance to suggest that at a certain point that evening he would speak with Debbie and allow Saeb and me to speak privately. Early in the evening Saeb, in Oded's presence, pushed for holding two summits on the grounds that not everything could be solved in one. Later, when he and I adjourned outside to our deck on what was an unusually pleasant mid-June night, I said, "Saeb, there won't be even one summit if we don't see the makings of a deal. Today, I can't tell the President in good conscience that I see one," even though we have an opportunity that we may miss "with an Israeli government that you know is prepared to take unprecedented steps."

In response, Saeb was eloquent and to the point: "Dennis, it is possible. And we cannot miss the opportunity. We will never have an Israeli government like this one. If we cannot do it with an Israeli government that includes Yossi Beilin, Yossi Sarid, Amnon Shahak, Shlomo Ben-Ami, and Haim Ramon, we will never do it." So, I asked, tell me what the deal looks like. Again, he was to the point: on the land, 92 percent of the West Bank to the Palestinian state, with the Israelis swapping an equivalent amount of land next to Gaza—more than doubling the size of Gaza; on refugees, "let them deposit a number" they can admit to Israel and "give us the principle of [UN General Assembly resolution] 194 or right of return"; on Jerusalem, the Israelis have eight large neighborhoods, counting Ma'ale Adumim, Givat Ze'ev, Pisgat Ze'ev, and Gilo in East Jerusalem; "those become part of Israel. The Arab neighborhoods become part of Palestine, and one municipality will deal with transportation, water, electricity, and sewage."

On each of Saeb's points, I had outlined likely Israeli reservations, noting that as a whole I was not sure Barak could go as far as he was suggesting. As Oded and Debbie joined us for dessert, Saeb said, "Dennis, we can do this."

For the first time, I was beginning to agree. Taken together, what I had heard from Saeb and seen in the "sixteen assumptions" paper made me hopeful. I decided to probe more. The next morning, Saturday morning, June 17, I went to visit Abu Ala and Shlomo at Andrews. They were returning home that night. I saw Abu Ala first. With Abu Ala, there was still very little give on any substance. I said, "I know you feel you have very few cards to play, and I am not going to ask you to tell me what you feel you cannot reveal. But we have a small window for a summit. The President will ask me for my recommendation, based on whether we can succeed, and when he does, I have to give him an honest answer. At the right moment, I will give you my sense of what is possible on the issues, and you have to level with me: "Can we do it on that basis or not. If you tell me not, I will tell the President we probably cannot do it. Once I tell him that, there will be no summit. You know, no summit, no deal. And it probably means the end of this Israeli government. So no deal now means no deal for some time to come, especially given the political change here as well."

Abu Ala said, "I understand. I know no deal now means no deal for the next four or five years. I want it for us and for you personally. You deserve it. You deserve to close the file. I will tell you honestly when you come to me [and tell me it is time to decide]." My only hope to learn more from Abu Ala was at that moment of decision on going or not going to a summit. He would not reveal more now.

My farewell meeting with Shlomo proved more revealing. We sat alone, and I told him I was going to be brutally candid with him. Barak, I told him, would not persuade the President to go to a summit by the force of argument. Barak had two strikes against him on this count. First, we had gone to Geneva with Asad because Barak had insisted this was the way it had to be done. Barak might rationalize now that it was a success, but the President saw it as a failure that was costly to the United States. Second, Barak had broken his promise on the villages and the timing of the third FRD. Thus, Barak's arguments would have no impact; to go to a summit, we had to know that we had a basis for success.

Shlomo listened very carefully, and his response was designed to lay that basis, especially on the issue of the border: He said what mattered to Israel was the Palestinian western border with Israel, not what could be the Palestinian border with Jordan. Even the IDF acknowledged that the eastern border in the Jordan Valley and along the river was less significant than historically thought. Modifying the green line to take account of the big settlement blocs would mark the end of the conflict. It responded to Israel's needs, it would mark the critical border with the Palestinians and give Israel recognized borders for the first time in its existence.

Shlomo went on to say that he agreed with Barak that Israel should not give on the eastern border now, saving that concession for the summit where they could trade that for what Israel wanted on modifications on the western border. "Does that mean that Barak accepts what you are saying about the eastern border?" I asked. Shlomo replied, "He is very close to this if he gets a defense treaty with you."

I turned the conversation to Jerusalem, and at least indirectly tried to test Saeb's idea. Shlomo, I asked, why couldn't you accept an approach that unites Jewish Jerusalem east and west? Why do you want to rule 200,000 Arabs? If all the Jewish neighborhoods in East Jerusalem become part of your Jerusalem, you will have a united Jerusalem, few Arabs to govern, and Jerusalem will be demographically stronger than ever. Why isn't this a good solution for you? Shlomo answered, "It is, but it is difficult politically and Barak is definitely not there." He drew a map that showed the Arab neighborhoods and observed that it made no sense for Israel to control Arab neighborhoods like Shua'fat. But he said, "Work on Barak."

Shlomo had gone beyond the "assumptions" paper both in terms of explicitly spelling out Israeli positions and with regard to Jerusalem. After these discussions, I could see the outlines of a deal on the core issues. The question was how to authenticate what I had heard. Shlomo and Saeb were signaling this could be done, but did they really speak for Barak and Arafat and could we use my upcoming trip and then the Secretary's on June 27–28 to get authentication?

| COUNTDOWN TO THE SUMMIT |

To put in perspective where we stood, I wrote a paper that compared the positions that each side had formally presented with the positions that had been informally presented to me. In a meeting in Madeleine's office with Sandy, Rob, Gamal, and Aaron, I presented what I had heard and my judgment of where we were on the eve of my departure on June 23. Sandy was riveted on the authenticity of what I had heard. "How do we know what you heard represents either Barak or Arafat?" If we don't know that, he insisted, we cannot go to a summit. To get the authentication, he wanted us to pose very discrete questions to both leaders on each of the core issues. He put special emphasis on Jerusalem, saying that this was the one issue he felt could not be bridged, and without hearing from the leaders that it could be, he would advise the President there should be no summit.

While sharing his concern, I felt he was establishing an impossible standard and told him so: "Leaders don't give away their bottom lines—indeed, might not even know their bottom lines before being in a summit-type situation. And to insist that they must give us their definitive positions on Jerusalem or else there is no summit is to guarantee no summit."

Sandy was not persuaded. Madeleine agreed with him, even though she shared my concern that we must not be so fearful of the risks of a summit that we miss the historic moment to see if an agreement was possible—particularly with an Israeli government that might be willing to take unprecedented steps toward the Palestinians.

I was certainly mindful of the need to minimize the risks of going, and also determined to ensure that we did not fail if we did. But I also did not want us to be paralyzed by our fears. Still, I decided that I could use Sandy's hesitancy, especially with Barak, to try to elicit answers that addressed Sandy's fears.

There was, however, one other concern that I decided to raise at this time. I wanted us to go to a summit, but not on Barak's timetable. I knew it was too early for Arafat; he never made a decision one minute before he had to, and in all likelihood he probably viewed September 13—the target date in the Sharm agreement for the permanent status deal—as the point when he would be forced to make a decision. July would never be credible to him as his moment of truth—"decide now or lose the chance." I therefore recommended, even knowing Barak would hate it that we not to go to a summit until the end of August.

Sandy's response was preemptory: Then there will be no summit. The President will not go to a summit once the Republican and Democratic conventions are under way. He will not want to look like he is competing with the conventions or trying "to suck all the air out of the campaigns" with a dramatic event.

So now the reality was clear. We could go to a summit, but only before it made sense to do so. Yet if I could not authenticate what I was hearing from the negotiators, we would not go at all. Despite my misgivings, if presented with the choice between a summit held prematurely or none at all, I was in favor of going lest we face the inevitable explosion that Ami Ayalon and Shaul Mofaz foresaw without ever knowing whether a deal had been possible.

I was struck by the irony. Bill Clinton's critics always accused him of thinking only in self-serving political terms—and acting accordingly. Here, the fear of looking like he was grandstanding and detracting from others would preclude our going to a summit to try to end the conflict in the Middle East.

| ONE LAST EFFORT TO DRAW OUT BARAK AND ARAFAT AND BUILD A BASIS FOR THE SUMMIT |

Though I arrived on Friday and saw Barak briefly, we agreed to get together on Shabbat for a more relaxed discussion. Our meeting would take place at Kochav Yair, a neighborhood in which Barak, Dani Yatom, and many other current and former leading figures of the Israeli security establishment resided. It was a neighborhood filled with single-family dwellings that looked much like a typical suburban America neighborhood. Only this well-manicured neighborhood sat adjacent to the West Bank Palestinian city of Qalqilya. Kochav Yair was on the green line, and from Barak's backyard it was only about 800 meters to Qalqilya. Imagine the distance from the back of the White House to the Washington Monument—something that appears almost as if it is a part of the White House grounds—and this was the distance from the Israeli Prime Minister's private home to a large Palestinian city. If nothing else, this was certainly a vivid reminder that the lives of Israelis and Palestinians were intertwined and unlikely to ever be disentangled.

Barak preferred to meet at Dani's home, and because it was Shabbat he walked from his house to Dani's. In Israel, governments could fall if they did not respect the religious strictures of Shabbat; so meetings on Shabbat were always handled discreetly—and the Prime Minister showed respect for Shabbat by walking, not driving. (Driving required the operation of a machine, and to the orthodox Jews who would stone cars driven on Shabbat, it was not only a violation of Shabbat but also a symbol of disrespect.)

Wanting this to be a conceptual, not practical, discussion, I had Martin, Aaron, Gamal, and Jon join me. I would have other opportunities to see Barak privately and I wanted to ease into efforts to draw him out. We sat in Dani's garden as we waited for Barak, and his wife brought us lemonade and popcorn. We would go through several more bowls of popcorn after Barak arrived.

Once we began our discussion, I posed questions to him, designed to see if he would be open to the use of certain tools to help us overcome the differences:

—Could he accept a trade-off between sovereignty and time? In other words, if the withdrawal period was stretched out for particular regions, could he accept eventual Palestinian sovereignty in those areas? (This was a device to obviate the need for gray areas.)
—Could he accept Palestinian sovereignty in the Jordan Valley if Israel had security arrangements that addressed Israel's core security needs there?
—Could he accept the principle of territorial swaps, even symbolically as a way to provide the Palestinians with an explanation for the modification of borders? (This would allow the Palestinians to say that the borders were modified to meet the needs of both sides, not only Israel's.)
—Could he apply his concept of separation (a concept based on separating Israelis and Palestinians if a permanent agreement could not be negotiated) to Jerusalem? After all, as I said to him, Jewish neighborhoods in East Jerusalem would be his, Arab neighborhoods would be Palestinian—wasn't that the essence of separation? Wasn't separation designed to end Israeli rule over the Palestinians? Wouldn't it be better for Israel to unite Jewish Jerusalem, east and west, to have a demographically secure Jerusalem?

His answers were a disappointment. Barak was buttoned down tight as a drum. On the gray area question, he could not accept the sovereignty versus time trade-off; "I don't know which areas we might need." On the Jordan Valley, his negative answer was so convoluted as to be unintelligible. On swaps, he could not even consider giving up any part of pre-1967 Israel. On Jerusalem, he declared, "I don't want to discuss Jerusalem now." It was hard not to conclude that he was holding everything for the summit.

Sunday evening I asked to see him alone, and tried a different tack. "Mr. Prime

Minister," I said, "I am not going to ask you to commit to anything now. But I need to know if the hints I am hearing from your side represent your position. You always say that there is an asymmetry between your negotiators and Arafat's, with yours being authoritative and his not. Well, I have indications from your guys on what you can do, and if they are authoritative I can much more confidently tell the President and the Secretary we can get there."

Looking very intently at me, he asked, "What did they tell you?" I summarized what I had heard: Israel can cross the 90 percent threshold and give the Palestinians sovereignty in the Jordan Valley if its security needs are met. (I chose not to say anything on Jerusalem for fear I would scare him off.)

Barak sat silently, simply rubbing his face, clearly unsure how to respond. The more he rubbed, the more he seemed to be trying literally to massage an acceptable answer. Finally, he slowly said that the hints I had heard went too far, but he might be able to do one more percent of the territory by including part of the Dead Sea in what was given to the Palestinians. That was interesting, but if added to the 87 percent in phases, meant we were talking about 88 percent (or possibly 89 percent based on his April presentation) of the West Bank.

I could not let the meeting end this way: if I did not get more from him now, I would never learn more before we needed to decide on the summit. So I tried chiding him: "Mr. Prime Minister, you always say that the Palestinians never tell us anything about what they might be able to do, always waiting for us to deliver more from your side. But, in fact, I have heard from some Palestinian negotiators a great deal about what might be possible. Would you like me to tell you what I have heard?" He nodded, and without referring to him by name, I summarized everything I had heard from Saeb: "Okay," I said, "I have been told that the following might be possible." On borders, "92 percent plus an equivalent territorial swap." On refugees, "an agreed number plus a formula on right of return." On Jerusalem, "you get the Jewish neighborhoods, they get the Arab neighborhoods, and there will be a common municipality for services and infrastructure."

I asked for his reaction, stressing that I could not say this represented Arafat. Very deliberately, he responded, "Overall, this is too much. But if it comes down to a deal or no deal, I will be able to do one of these." He then got nervous, telling me he simply could not say more lest he reveal something he did not want to reveal to his government at this juncture. Instead, at this point he asked if I might meet with his faction heads to summarize the negotiations.

I was uneasy about this request, but loath to say no to him now. I knew he had just revealed something very significant: that if it came to the crunch point, he was prepared to meet terms I had heard from Saeb on either borders, refugees, or Jerusalem.

In any meeting with faction heads, I told him, he should be present and he, not I, should speak about the Israeli positions—and no one should expect that I would reveal my views of Palestinian bottom lines or near bottom lines since everything I said in the room would leak. He accepted this and said he would arrange the meeting for the next day.

The meeting took place in the cabinet room, a room furnished with a large mahogany table and comfortable leather chairs and with a large-screen television built into the wall in one corner. The cabinet room adjoined the Prime Minister's office—permitting the Prime Minister to enter it from his side door. Barak and I met first in his office while the faction heads were arriving; he explained that every leader of the coalition would be there. At this point, no faction had pulled out of the government, so Yitzhak Levy of the National Religious Party, Natan Sharansky, representing Yisrael Ba'aliya, David Levy of One Israel, Amnon Shahak of the Center Party, Eli Yishai of Shas, and Yossi Sarid of Meretz would all be there.

Barak was finally facing up to the need to condition the members of his government on what he was prepared to do. There was a twofold problem. First, the Israeli media was full of stories that described Barak's readiness to give up between 90 and 95 percent of the territories, but his coalition partners had heard nothing from him except denials. Second, this was the first time he was briefing them on his positions, but he was doing so in my presence.

That certainly provided a procedural reason to take issue with Barak, and Natan Sharansky did, complaining that Barak was outlining his positions on borders and security for the first time—something that should have taken place sooner and not with outsiders present: "Nothing against Dennis, but we should not be hearing positions for the first time in front of him."

While Natan had a legitimate gripe, truth be told, procedure was less of a problem for him than substance. He simply was not prepared to go as far as Barak. Even now, Barak was holding back, speaking of less than 80 percent of the territory going to the Palestinians, and Natan—and Yitzhak Levy, as indicated by his body language—felt this went too far. Natan believed this should represent the outer edge of the endgame position, not what would inevitably be treated as an opening posture.

I knew that Barak's full coalition was very unlikely to survive the compromises that would be necessary for a permanent status agreement. Because of my friendship with Natan and my belief that he could help sell any agreement in Israel, I had hoped he could stay in the coalition, but that was probably unrealistic. His views of what Israel could withdraw from were likely to be too limited for even the most forthcoming Palestinians.

While Natan had pressed Barak, the others questioned me. In one way or the other, nearly every question was geared to trying to understand what the Palestinians could either live with or wanted. I responded, explaining that the Palestinians had their own doubts about Israeli intentions, and that given their disappointments with Oslo—a process long on promise and short on delivery in their eyes—they, too, wanted no more interim agreements. They wanted to settle the conflict now.

This surprised nearly everyone there. Those who were right of center in the cabinet had assumed that the Palestinians wanted to keep "slicing the salami"—e.g., getting Israel incrementally to surrender more land without having to give anything meaningful in return. Not having been exposed to the Palestinian point of view, they had not realized that the Palestinians might have their own reasons for opposing more limited deals now.

Only Eli Yishai of Shas did not ask a question. He preferred to make a point. He accepted my observation that both sides seemed to favor a comprehensive, not limited, agreement at this time. In light of that, he argued against rushing to a summit. The stakes were too high, we should know more about what was possible before going, and at this stage it might be better for President Clinton to meet with the leaders in Washington separately.

I sneaked a glance at Barak while Yishai was speaking. He was impassive. Indeed, in speaking to him later that day, it was clear that the meeting had not altered his views or sense of urgency one iota.

I had been pushing Barak to engage Arafat directly, believing this might help us learn more about the real positions on each side. Though he was not ready to have a substantive discussion himself—for fear this would be too committing and Arafat would pocket whatever he heard—Barak decided to send Shlomo and Gilad to Ramallah to see the Chairman.

Yossi, who arranged the late-night meeting and also took part in it, called the next day while I was en route to see Arafat. He was elated with the meeting, feeling that Shlomo had been very effective not only in summarizing what he had presented in Sweden on territory, security, borders, and Jerusalem but also in eloquently explaining that this Israeli government understood it was time to end the conflict; had the courage to take the most profound decisions since the founding of the state of Israel; appreciated that the Palestinians had real needs on statehood that must be addressed in a credible way; saw Arafat as their partner; and, with Clinton as President, now had the historic moment to act. "Yossi," I replied, "that's all very interesting on Shlomo's side. But what did Arafat say? Did Shlomo elicit anything new from him? Yossi admitted that there was nothing new, but he felt Arafat's thinking would be affected in time.

If so, I saw no evidence of that. Arafat described Shlomo as a very good man, pointing to his heart to tell me "he believes in peace in here." But when I asked if he felt they were closer on the substance after the meeting, Arafat said "no." He went on to say that he could not sleep after the meeting because Shlomo had spoken of a special regime for Jerusalem but not explained it. "Imagine," Arafat repeated, "I could not sleep because of it."

Further probing of his concerns yielded nothing except his regard for Shlomo. I was not only unable to move Arafat, I now found that Abu Ala was in full-scale retreat. He would not address anything unless the Israelis first conceded the eastern border—ensuring that Israel would have no presence between the putative Palestinian state and Jordan. No matter how I tried to probe, he was not going to reveal more. (Indeed, unbeknownst to me, Shlomo and I both asked him hypothetically, "Assume you get the border you feel you must have, how do you deal with Israel's security concerns?" And neither of us got anywhere.) In all my discussions with Abu Ala at this point, I heard only maximal positions, whether it was on Jerusalem, refugees, or borders. The openings from Sweden were a distant memory.

I concluded that Arafat and his colleagues saw Barak pushing for the summit. If he wanted it so badly, their thinking seemed to be, either he should pay for it by conceding more to them up front or there was reason for them to be suspicious of it—it was a trap and he would create a gang-up with Clinton.

This was the environment in which Secretary Albright now arrived in the area. It was an environment in which there was great speculation about her arriving to announce a summit; an environment in which I had gotten as much from Barak as he was willing to give at this stage; and one in which I could see possible bridges even on the hardest issues, but in which the Secretary was unlikely to hear anything from either side that would allay her concerns. In fact, she did not.

Barak, obviously feeling he had gone further with me than he had wanted to, pulled an Abu Ala. Not only was he not willing to reveal any more on the substance of his possible positions, but he was also not forthcoming on any of the measures on the ground that we felt could create a more favorable climate for the summit.

Madeleine was stymied with Barak and similarly unable to move Arafat on the substance. In private, however, Madeleine effectively argued to Arafat that he had three options: (1) no summit, lower-level negotiations, and basic paralysis; (2) a summit that created the chance for an agreement; (3) the traditional Palestinian approach of seeking a Pyrrhic victory of getting a limited third FRD, declaring a state in September and producing a harsh Israeli reaction. In her judgment, that left only option two, taking the calculated risk of going for a summit.

In response, Arafat expressed his fear that if he went to a summit and it failed, all hope would be lost, and "the people must not lose hope." But he also said he would go to a summit if there were two more weeks of preparation. He did not make the results of that preparation a condition for going. Rather, he said if the President decided to go at that point, he would come.

This was certainly an advance in his position on the summit. But either he did not empower his negotiators or he did so in a way that left them feeling exposed. The net effect: they would not move. Not with the Israelis, unless the Israelis conceded more, and not with us. (In this environment, I knew Abu Ala would not give me a straight answer on what might or might not work—and as a result I never tested his promise.)

By not permitting any real preparation to take place, Arafat denied us leverage with Barak. When the Secretary reported Arafat's readiness to go to the summit provided there were two weeks of preparation, Barak adamantly rejected it. "We will be negotiating with ourselves. We propose, they reject and tell us to give more. I won't do more or let my people do more except at a summit."

Secretary Albright found it hard to argue with him. If anything, the Palestinian posture in the talks at this point fortified his argument, and undercut Arafat's for preparation.

As we left the region, we did not know enough to meet Sandy's standard for going to a summit. What should our recommendation to the President be? I slept very little during the plane ride. Instead, I was either talking with Gamal, Aaron, and Rob or going over the options with the Secretary. There were two basic alternatives, I told her. First, since it is a huge decision to go to the summit, the President should simply tell Barak he needs more from him or we won't go. Specifically, unless Barak acts to improve the climate for a summit—by finally doing the villages and releasing prisoners—and also accepts the principle of a territorial swap and/or Palestinian sovereignty for at least some East Jerusalem neighborhoods, we simply do not have what it takes to succeed at a summit. Or, second, we could develop a basis for the summit, setting the parameters on each of the issues and then bringing each leader to see the President separately. If those discussions went well, we could move immediately to a summit. This had the advantage of testing whether Barak and Arafat, separately, were prepared to accept the parameters on borders, security, Jerusalem, and refugees that we thought provided the boundaries of an agreement.

Madeleine and I spoke with Sandy from the plane. He preferred option one to option two. He liked insisting on more from Barak in private, but did not like the idea of bringing Barak and Arafat to Washington for what amounted to a high-profile test; ironically, Sandy did not mind being tough with Barak in private, but worried about the effect of posing a public test in which Barak failed.

We saw President Clinton in the morning, but given Sandy's opposition, we decided to present only the first option to the President. Perhaps because I brought him up to date on all the conversations first, he was less inclined to push Barak hard. He was very impressed—even noticeably buoyed—by my private conversation with Barak, and Barak's reaction to the 92 percent plus swap, the agreed numbers on refugees, and the Jerusalem idea. He felt if we pushed Barak hard, notwithstanding his hints, we would force him to harden positions he might otherwise be open to in the "cauldron" of the summit. President Clinton was very clear: "I don't want him to dig in now, and make it harder for him to be flexible later." He also was operating on a different standard from Sandy. In his words, "the cost of going to a summit is far less" than the cost of not trying and seeing a collapse of the process. The President ended the meeting, telling us he was ready to call Barak but did not want to press him on territorial swaps or East Jerusalem. He asked that we get together the next morning to see what he might say in a call to Barak.

After leaving the White House, I was closer to the President than to Sandy on the terms for going to the summit. But I did want the President to push Barak at least on the issue of the villages and the prisoners. If we went to a summit, I did not want Arafat to have a grievance he could hold over us.

With that in mind, I suggested a softer formulation of our option one: Why not push for the villages and prisoners, and at the same time have the President tell Barak a deal without a territorial swap and sovereignty for some of the East Jerusalem neighborhoods was improbable? This was not a condition for going to the summit, just the President's judgment of what it would take to succeed. The President liked this approach; it was now Saturday morning, July 1, and the President was ready to call Barak.

But I made one mistake in writing this up for the President. I reversed the order, putting the President's judgment on the swaps and East Jerusalem first and the villages and the prisoners second. This was a mistake because the President got into a discussion with Barak on the swaps and East Jerusalem, and devoted only a limited time to the villages and prisoners.

Barak, using his customary convoluted style when responding on a sensitive point, launched into a desultory description of what might be possible. This was Barak's way of trying to respond without ever saying anything that might be quotable.

Listening to the conversation on the speakerphone in the Oval Office, Sandy did not like Barak's fuzzy response. He slipped the President a note that reverted to trying to get more out of Barak on swaps and East Jerusalem; surprisingly, the President, given his views of the previous evening, simply read Sandy's note asking whether Barak would exclude these if at the end of the day they meant the difference between a deal and no deal. Barak said if it was the difference between an agreement and losing one, "we can contemplate it together."

The President was pleased with that answer. In a more cursory way, he then raised the prisoners and the villages. Barak's answer: he could do something on the prisoners only at the beginning of the summit, and he demurred on the villages. I frowned and shook my head, prompting the President to ask him to think about this and they would talk again in two days. That struck me as a good response. It told Barak, who was in a hurry, that the President could wait and needed an answer before deciding.

While I would have liked the President to have pushed Barak harder on the villages and prisoners, I told him that he had at least gotten confirmation from Barak that he would not exclude swaps and something on East Jerusalem neighborhoods as part of the endgame. Sandy disagreed, saying Barak had "stiffed" the President.

I responded to Sandy, saying, "You don't understand how this guy's mind works." He fears we will pocket whatever we get from him, and press him for more; he obsesses on preserving his room for maneuvering so he can be flexible when the moment of truth comes. He signals ambiguously so he can never be accused of lying to his colleagues, while hoping we will pick up on the subtle message. Turning to the President, I said, There is a danger that we will misread him, but if you wanted to know if you will "have swaps and some of the East Jerusalem neighborhoods in your kit bag for the endgame," the answer is yes.

Sandy had not heard that at all, and wanted to call Barak and press him himself. The President said, "Go ahead," he was going to play golf. Sandy did call Barak. When he told Barak that he had to confide in the President so he will know he has the tools necessary for success in the endgame, Barak responded by telling Sandy to study carefully what he had told the President; "there is a lot of flexibility there." It was classic Barak, but Sandy felt more comfortable now.

Of course, we were still nowhere on the villages and the prisoners. I asked Martin to see Barak and tell him he owed the President something on these issues—now, before Clinton made his decision on the summit. The result: Barak would not do the villages, but would release thirty prisoners once the summit convened. We were not going to get more. It was time for us to decide.

Calls were arranged for the President to make to Barak and Arafat from Camp David on July 4. Madeleine, Sandy, and I went to Camp David to meet with the President. Madeleine and I rode together. Sandy went separately. Madeleine was convinced that we had taken this as far as we could and it was time to go to the summit. She had spoken to Sandy, and he now agreed. We had seen where the President was, so it was time to nail this down.

We ate lunch while we waited for the President, and I described how to orchestrate the beginnings of the summit. The keys, I said, were creating the basis on which we would lay a paper on the table that both sides would negotiate, and finding a way to meaningfully engage Arafat. The former required us to outline parameters from the outset for each core issue—borders, security, Jerusalem, and refugees; have the two sides negotiate with each other and us on that basis for the first two days; and in light of those discussions have us then put a paper on the table. I knew we had to have the two sides negotiating on a paper as soon as possible given the difficulty of translating concepts into text. This would shrink the gaps from the outset and create a textual framework for the discussions.

I knew as well that we stood little chance of getting to that point rapidly if we did not succeed in involving Arafat. I feared he would sit passively, divorced from the discussions and surrounded by those ready to play on his suspicions of what was going on in the negotiations. We needed him to feel ownership of what was transpiring. To do that, we needed him engaged with the Israelis whom he respected and whose respect he often sought. That did not mean Barak, whom he continued to distrust, but rather Amnon Shahak and Shlomo Ben-Ami. For the sake of parallelism, we would need to have Abu Ala and Abu Mazen sit with Barak.

Both Madeleine and Sandy agreed with this approach and wanted me to go over it with the President when he joined us. I was struck by how both Sandy and Madeleine felt it was time to convene a summit. Both had come to believe that if we did not act now, we would lose the chance ever to do so. Whether it was because Barak had convinced them that politically his government would not hold—something that was made more credible by the threats from the NRP and Sharansky—or because of the imminent end of Clinton's term, it was now or never.

I still felt the need to talk to John Podesta, the Chief of Staff at the White House, about my concerns on timing. John was very smart and very straight. One always knew where he stood on an issue and where the President was as well. I needed to know if the timing issue was only Sandy's concern or if it was John's and the President's as well. John's answer was just as stark as Sandy's: there would be no summit once the Republican and Democratic conventions were held.

I was convinced that it would be irresponsible to forgo the opportunity to try to settle the conflict, believing that the alternative to breakthrough now would not be a peaceful status quo, but a descent into violence. It was not just that the violence of May was a harbinger of things to come; it was that Arafat, having forgone the May 4, 1999, date to declare a state, was unlikely to do so again.

But if Sandy, Madeleine, and I believed that it was "now or never," the President's demeanor on the summit had changed. We met in Laurel, the large cabin where the President met guests and hosted visitors. We had moved from the dining room to his study—a room that was full of his memorabilia, campaign pins, posters, bumper stickers, and the like. The President's entire political career was encapsulated in this room. As we sat down, he became wistful, wondering how he was going to move everything in the room. Somehow the reality of leaving this, of his own political career ending, of having a responsibility to Al Gore, began to give him pause. He was a political animal after all, and he worried about the political consequences of a failure on the eve of the Republican convention. He felt we needed an "exit strategy" if the summit failed.

Neither Sandy nor Madeleine made any attempt to counter the political argument. Now Sandy took on the President directly, focusing on the stakes in the Middle East if we did not try and everything collapsed. Madeleine went further, arguing that we would be judged poorly by history if we let our fears prevent us from trying to go the last mile.

For my part, I explained how we could orchestrate the summit, lay down a paper, and engage the two leaders. I did so pointing out the importance of an American paper becoming the basis of the negotiations, of the President presenting parameters initially to justify the paper we would subsequently present, and the necessity of engaging Arafat in particular.

The President began to come around, being taken with the arguments and the approach. We were in the midst of discussing ways to make the summit work when we were interrupted by a message that Barak was facing a vote of no confidence and had to leave within ten minutes to go to the Knesset—he was ready for Clinton's call. Suddenly the President seemed back where he had been in the Oval Office. It was time to go for the summit, but he would not let Barak know that until he had pushed him again on the villages and the prisoners.

We moved from the study to the formal meeting room in Laurel. Here there was a large rectangular table that could probably seat twenty to twenty-five. The White House communications people had set up four phones, one for each of us: the President, Sandy, Madeleine, and me. It was a secure call, but the connection was very good.

Barak was pushing on an open door, but did not know it. He did not wait for the President to say anything, he simply launched in. There were thirty-two prisoners he could release once the summit began. And, the President must keep this to himself, and not use it, but if at the end of the day these were the keys to an agreement, he could contemplate limited symbolic moves on both territorial swaps and the East Jerusalem neighborhoods.

Finally he had become explicit. The President was pleased and promised to protect the information. Having received more than he expected from Barak, President Clinton asked for nothing more on either the prisoners or the villages. And he told Barak he would now call Arafat and propose July 9 as the starting date for a summit at

Camp David. Clinton asked Barak not to tell anyone; he did not want Arafat hearing this on the news or from anyone other than the President.

Meanwhile, a secure call with Arafat had already been arranged. We anticipated that Arafat would argue against doing the summit without more preparation and wrote the President's points accordingly. Surprisingly, Arafat did not resist the summit. But he did make two points. First, he could not get to the summit before July 11 because he had an African summit to attend and he wanted the negotiators to come right away, getting to Washington July 5. The President pushed back, arguing that he had to leave for the G-8 summit by July 19, and Arafat must give us sufficient time to reach agreement because Clinton wanted to present the deal to our G-8 partners to generate international money, enthusiasm, and momentum in its support. Arafat finally said he would do his best to get to Camp David by the night of the tenth—the Camp David summit was set.

Of course, we still had to work out the details of the announcement and hold it for the next day. July 4 was not the day to make such an announcement. But the deed was done.

Madeleine read the President's mood. He was ready, but understandably uneasy. She said to him, "We have to do this." As we walked out the door, he looked at me and said, "This is the right thing to do, isn't it?" Nodding, I simply said "yes." He walked over to a golf cart and rode off alone.

His being alone seemed to be a metaphor for the moment. We might all bear the responsibility for putting him in this position, but history would judge him for this summit. All those who saw Bill Clinton as trying to redeem his presidency with a Middle East peace deal misread him profoundly. Sure, he understood the value of Middle East peace for his legacy. But, ultimately, he acted on the summit because he believed it was the right thing to do.

Knowing it was the right thing to do did not ease my own feeling of dread. I knew how hard, indeed painful, this would be. I knew both sides needed to struggle in fact and in appearance—for no concession could look like it had been made too easily. I knew we would be on the brink of failure before we ever even saw the possibility of success, and I was by no means confident of success. The summit would be an endurance test as much as a negotiation, with sleep a luxury I would do without. Lastly, I knew that Yasir Arafat was coming with a profound sense of gloom and suspicion. It would be the President's great challenge to convince Arafat that this was not a trap Barak was setting to corner him, but an opportunity the President was creating to fulfill Palestinian aspirations.

◆24◆

The Camp David Summit

EVEN IF ONE CAN intellectually anticipate the intensity and drama of a high-stakes summit to end a historic conflict—where the hopes, fears, and collective histories of two peoples weigh heavily on the shoulders of the participants—it is something else to actually live it. For me, the summit did not get off to an auspicious beginning: the van taking our team to Camp David on the evening of July 10 got lost. Driving in western Maryland in the Catoctin Mountains at night, with few signs and no streetlights, is a challenge. As we stopped at an information station in Catoctin Mountain Park—naturally, unmanned at 9:30 p.m.—I could not help joking that "here is the peace team, lost on the way to Camp David, and praying we are not going to be lost once we get there."

If this was an omen, it was not a good one. But there were others. Barak had to delay his departure for the summit because of a vote of no confidence. While he won the vote, he came to Camp David as the head of a government that represented a minority of the Knesset as the NRP, Sharansky's party, and Shas—in a last-minute surprise—withdrew from the government. Were we to reach agreement at the summit, Barak would have to appeal over the heads of the Knesset to the Israeli public for approval.*

Similarly, if body language sends a message, Arafat's spoke volumes. Unlike when I spoke to him on his arrival for the Wye summit—when his whole demeanor sug-

---

*Later both Amnon Shahak and Martin were to tell me that Eli Yishai of Shas had asked Barak to share with him his bottom lines for the summit; Yishai pledged to share these only with the spiritual head of Shas, Rabbi Ovadia Yosef. With that private knowledge, Shas would stay in the government; without it, it would withdraw. Barak would not reveal his positions.

gested we would succeed—now as I greeted him he was completely impassive, as much as shrugging his shoulders in response to my saying that we had now all arrived at a historic moment.

This did not come as a surprise to me. Arafat wanted us to be the ones to deliver to him at this summit. I had anticipated Arafat's approach in the considerable preparation time that had filled our days with President Clinton after the July 4 phone calls.

In the extensive briefings with the President, we went through the likely strategies of each side; the issues on which they would be likely to hold out; what would trigger crises, and where the trade-offs were both within and between issues. We discussed the dynamics of each negotiating team, including the likely turmoil within the Palestinian team given the rivalries that Arafat would exploit to limit the impulse to make concessions—all the more reason, I reminded the President, to engage Arafat and ensure he could not stand aloof from the negotiating process. Finally, we went through the possible fallbacks in the event that an end-of-conflict deal was not possible; President Clinton was especially interested in a partial deal involving statehood for the Palestinians on borders that would not be permanent but involve Israeli withdrawal from roughly 75 percent of the West Bank.

President Clinton was like a sponge absorbing information. Whatever the issue, he wanted to delve deeply into it. At one point, we spread highly detailed maps of Jerusalem over the table to go through the different Arab neighborhoods of East Jerusalem—distinguishing between those that might be more or less sensitive to both sides. President Clinton's great strength as a negotiator was his extraordinary capacity to marry the detail on issues with his great empathy for those with whom he was dealing. That empathy would be critical because the President, in asking for a concession, had to demonstrate that he understood unmistakably why it was so difficult to concede, and why he must produce something of even greater value in return. Sensitizing him to the critical trade-offs was important, but also a matter of timing. As I had seen at Wye, his weakness as a negotiator emerged: if I briefed him on the key trade-offs too early, he tended to play the ideas prematurely.

As for the strategy and tactics of managing the summit, I proposed and the President accepted that we would need to present a paper on all the core issues to the two sides early on during the course of the summit. It was no small move to table an American paper on the permanent status issues. Never in the history of the conflict had the United States adopted positions on what the border should be, on how to handle the refugee question, on defining Israeli security needs, or on detailing how to resolve the question of Jerusalem. But that is what we might be doing if we presented a paper. The more ambitious the paper, the more formal U.S. positions would now be on the most existential issues of this conflict.

Though I outlined the pros and cons of presenting less ambitious papers—namely, ones that either summarized the formal positions on every issue of each side or presented our understandings of their informal positions—we settled on the idea of offering our judgments of what they might be able to accept. This, I argued, would be far more feasible if we reduced the scope of their differences by first establishing parameters on each issue that the two sides could discuss with each other or with us. Following a two-day discussion on our parameters, we would, I suggested, have a much better insight into what might actually fly with each side. Fundamentally, the idea was to use the "pressure cooker" environment of the summit immediately—with the President in his first meetings with Barak and Arafat shrinking the scope for negotiations on each issue by presenting parameters within which they should seek to resolve their differences.

President Clinton liked this approach and was poised to present the parameters once the summit began.*

| ARRIVING AT CAMP DAVID |

With Barak unable to arrive before noon on July 11, the President decided not to come until the morning. Having been rescued, we arrived two hours before Arafat, and after greeting him and getting him situated, I set about finding my cabin. The Secretary, Sandy, and I had our own cabins, and the rest of our delegation shared rooms in different cabins.

My cabin was nestled in a wooded area. It had a large screened front porch with two rocking chairs, a large sitting area next to the double bed, a fireplace, a television with a full array of cable channels, a fully stocked fridge, plenty of towels in a well-appointed modern bathroom complete with shampoo made especially for Camp David, and a bathrobe in the closet with the Camp David logo on it. I laughed as I explored the cabin with Nick Rasmussen, saying, "Nick, too bad I can't bring Debbie here for R & R, we could have a good time."†

---

*Given the limitation of space at Camp David and to guard against leaks, we established the following ground rules for the summit: each side could have twelve individuals at Camp David; support personnel could stay outside of Camp David, and would be admitted if we were informed in advance with an explanation for the visit; no one staying at Camp David could depart without our permission; there would be one outside phone line each reserved for Barak and for Arafat.

†At Camp David, there is plenty of opportunity for recreation and relaxation; there are tennis courts, a golf driving range, a two-lane bowling alley, basketball courts, plenty of hiking trails, a movie theater, a billiard table in a large game room filled with video games, and a horseshoe pit. If I'd had time, I could have enjoyed it.

My cabin would become the meeting place for our team, and a place where I would hold discreet discussions with Israelis and Palestinians. When I would meet with the President, Madeleine, Sandy, and John Podesta, other members of the team like Martin, Aaron, John Herbst (our consul general in Jerusalem), Jon Schwartz, and Nick would often wait there for me to return and brief them on where we were and what needed to be done now. One night I returned a little after 4 a.m. to find Martin and Jon Schwartz asleep on my bed and Aaron and Nick asleep in the chairs next to the bed.

I had a golf cart assigned to me but preferred to walk. From Aspen, the President's cabin, to my cabin was about a ten-minute walk. Laurel, where we would all eat, was also about a ten-minute walk to the President's cabin and five to mine. The cabins where Barak and Arafat would stay were situated close to Aspen, literally across the roadway. It would take a day or so to get my bearings, but after two weeks of being at Camp David, I could navigate the narrow paths to my cabin, and to the Secretary's even in the dead of night and with no lights.

| DAY 1 |

Our first decision at Camp David was to see Arafat before seeing Barak. We decided to have no meetings until late morning, but recognized that Barak would sleep for a few hours after arriving and it was best to engage Arafat sooner rather than later. This initial meeting was to be about mood, not about our substantive plans.

In briefing the President, I reminded him that we would go nowhere if he could not succeed in getting Arafat focused on a deal, not transfixed on his grievances. That required lifting Arafat up and showing him what he had to gain, emphasizing that he now had a chance to transform the movement he had launched—the Palestinian national liberation movement—and realize his dream. He could do for the Palestinians what no other Palestinian or Arab leader had been able to do for them.

Elevating horizons and fulfilling dreams was a Clinton specialty. Not surprisingly, the meeting went well. As only he could do, the President played to Arafat's sense of history, speaking of his fervent hope to be there with Arafat when the flag was raised on the new state of Palestine. Arafat was seemingly thrilled at that prospect and, at least for the moment, chose to forgo any discussion of grievances.

Before the President's first substantive meetings of the day with Barak and Arafat, I rehearsed for him again the key to our strategy—e.g., getting the two leaders to accept the President's parameters for the core issues, and setting up small teams to discuss security, borders, and refugees on the basis of those parameters. The purpose of the parameters was to shrink the gaps and guide, shape, and manage the discussions on these core issues. On Jerusalem, given the sensitivity, especially Barak's, I reminded the President that he would discuss this only with the leaders for the first few days, and I gave him an eleven-point paper I had written on Jerusalem.

My thinking was that Jerusalem was too sensitive to dive into with the negotiators, but I knew that Arafat would need to see that we were not avoiding Jerusalem lest he not permit engagement on any other issue. What better way to show him we were taking Jerusalem very seriously than to have the President say he would reserve these discussions for himself with the leaders?*

Once again, all this was good in theory, but we were not able to carry it off in practice. The President met Barak with only a note-taker, Bruce Riedel.† Barak, as usual, had his own sense of timing and his own game plan. It was not ours. Barak wanted to have nothing happen the first two days; only after two days of struggle should we put down some ideas. He told the President that the crisis—and key point of decision—should only come Sunday night, July 16—five days after the start of the summit.

It was completely artificial. Our purpose was to get both sides focused on a very concrete set of parameters for each of the core issues; as the President explained to Barak, this would crystallize the essential differences and create a basis for us to present a paper that outlined the bridges for overcoming those gaps. That required real discussions, not artificial battles that simply rehashed old arguments.

The President proceeded to outline to Barak the parameters we had developed:

1. On territory, we segmented the borders of what would be the new Palestinian state into the western border with Israel and the eastern border with Jordan. The western border would be based on the 1967 lines, but would be modified as necessary. The Palestinians needed the 1967 line to be the basis; the Israelis needed modifications in the line to meet their settlement bloc requirements (e.g., absorbing 75 to 80 percent of the settlers on the West Bank). We would simply note that the Palestinians believed in compensation for modifications made to accommodate Israeli needs. But we would not introduce the concept of a swap at this stage.

---

*It would also be a way to engage Arafat in addition to having Amnon and Shlomo meet with him.

†Unlike at Wye, where I would typically go with the President to his private meetings with Netanyahu or with Arafat, here it was decided—no doubt reflecting the President's own confidence and desire to see the leaders alone without negotiators with them—he would go alone but with a note-taker. Of course, with Arafat, Gamal would be there to interpret. The note-takers would be from the NSC; that meant Bruce was the note-taker for the Barak meetings, and Rob was the note-taker for Arafat.

On the eastern border, the principle was the Palestinians get sovereignty, the Israelis security. This formula was designed to meet Palestinian symbolic needs while also responding to very real and legitimate Israeli concerns about security.

2. On refugees, we had a concept for an international mechanism and fund that would finance the rehabilitation, resettlement, and repatriation of Palestinians to Palestine, to third countries, or in limited circumstances to Israel. Beyond this, we sought to reconcile Palestinian symbolic needs with Israel's practical needs. The Palestinians wanted the right of return; this was fine for Palestine but not for Israel. If there was to be a "right," it had to be carried out in a way that was very clearly limited. So our parameter acknowledged that the Palestinians needed the right, but that Israel must have the sovereign right to determine who could be admitted to Israel.

3. On Jerusalem, we took a more conceptual tack. Jerusalem would be described as being three cities in one. It was a practical city that had to be governed and managed on a day-to-day basis; it was a holy city, holy to the world, holy to the three monotheistic religions, home to more than fifty-seven holy sites in the Old City alone; and it was a political city.

We had eleven points that formed a basis for discussion and were tied to each of the three cities; many of the points—e.g., having one undivided city for municipal services, free, unimpeded access to religious sites—were not contentious and represented building blocks for agreement. The most sensitive points were on political control, not functional responsibility. Here, initially, questions would be posed rather than solutions suggested. The logic was to forge understandings on practical and functional ways to manage the city before tackling the harder questions.

Barak listened to the President's presentation and was willing to accept the parameters, provided they were modified. He ran through the parameters he wanted. On borders, the Palestinians believe the western border must be based on the 1967 lines, Israel wants modifications to accommodate 80 percent of the settlers; on the eastern border, the Palestinians believe there must be no limitation on their border with Jordan, Israel believes its security needs must be met and that it should retain a narrow strip of land along the entire length of the Jordan River (meaning Israel would interpose itself between the new state of Palestine and Jordan). He went over the other issues, seeking, in effect, to transform the parameter exercise into the equivalent of an "I" and "P" ("Israeli" and "Palestinian") presentation on the parameters. The President should lay out how he saw each side's position on each issue, not the American view of the parameters. Barak might say he was accepting our parameter approach, but he was in reality sticking to his game plan of struggle for the first two days on old positions. (Similarly, he demurred on the idea that Amnon and Shlomo should engage with Arafat, and subsequently rejected it.)

When the President briefed us on the meeting, he made it clear he had acceded to Barak's wish on how to handle the parameter exercise. He did not want to "jam him" at the start of the summit. Naturally, this meant that we had to redo the approach for the President's meeting with Arafat. Already we were altering our strategy for the summit. We were not bounding the discussions and crystallizing them; as a result we were not taking control of the summit at the outset.

Maybe the President was more realistic than I was. Maybe it was an illusion to believe we could impose the parameter exercise the way I'd envisioned. But we were at a summit; the stakes were very high and our actions had to reflect that. Imposing the parameters was one way to do that. Moreover, I was riveted on how to create a justification for something far more controversial than our parameters—namely, our paper.

The President, though having agreed to my strategy, altered it as he faced opposition from Barak. At the same time, however, with both Barak and Arafat he said we would table a paper in two days. Having softened what we would present to each side on the parameters, he sought to put pressure on them by saying we would put a paper down by Thursday night.

Barak was in favor of this, but also told the President his people would present us with their version of such a paper. The President made clear we would only lay down something that was credible and was perceived to be making a genuine attempt to bridge differences. Again, Barak accepted this, provided there were no surprises and he had a chance to see what we would present first. Arafat simply accepted that we would present a paper.

| DAY 2 |

The discussions between the two sides began but quickly became a repetition of old arguments and positions. Moreover, because we had told both sides we would put a paper on the table in two days no matter what, neither side had a stake in moving. Each preferred to wait and see what we would present. The American paper became not a spur to action but a reason to sit tight. I had envisioned our parameters making their initial discussion concrete and signaling to them our seriousness and the direction of our thinking, giving each an incentive to tell us as much as possible lest they find their interests not well reflected in our paper.

Thus stymied, we devoted ourselves to developing the paper. But what was the paper to be? Was it supposed to outline the essential principles for guiding the solution on each of the core issues? Or should we be presenting a draft framework agreement?

I had always felt we needed to know more from each side before presenting definitive U.S. positions on each of the issues, especially Jerusalem. But that is not where
Sandy and Madeleine were. Shortly after sitting with Jon Schwartz, our drafter, I was
called down to see the President with Sandy and Madeleine. It was a glorious sunny
day and we sat outside on the back deck of Aspen. The setting is picturesque, with a
valley on the horizon, the mountain's forests leading down to the valley, and President
Eisenhower's legacy to Camp David serving as Aspen's backyard—one golf hole, with
a large green for putting and different tee boxes from which to pitch short-iron shots
to the green. I felt more like hitting golf balls than engaging in this discussion, but
Madeleine and Sandy launched into their argument very quickly.

The clock was ticking. Nothing meaningful was going on now. The President
would leave in seven days for the G-8 Summit in Okinawa. We needed to put a draft
agreement on the table. If we did it by the next evening, there would only be five days
left to negotiate an agreement. I listened, saying nothing. The President turned to me
and asked what I thought. I told him I was ambivalent. I was not sure we were ready
to put a full-fledged draft agreement on the table. I worried about how we would handle Jerusalem. While we had our own ideas about what might work on Jerusalem, we
had not yet engaged enough with either side to know whether we were in the ballpark.
I suggested we put together both a "principles" paper and a draft agreement. We would
try to have both ready before the President left to go to Baltimore the next morning.*
He could read them before his return and decide which he felt we should present by
the evening. The President liked this approach.

Jon drafted both, and Aaron, Gamal, Martin, John Herbst, Bruce, Rob, and I
went over the drafts together. During this process, we heard that the Israelis had their
draft ready. We got it and Jon went to see Gidi Grinstein at midnight to hear his explanation of what it contained. But the paper had many points that had never been
raised with either the Palestinians or us. For us to incorporate them would signal to the
Palestinians that this was not our paper, but an Israeli paper. Jon was able to take a few
of the Israeli comments, and I decided to have him produce only one draft, not two.

Notwithstanding my reservations, I decided we would proceed with the draft
agreement, not the principles paper. Looking at both, it seemed as if the draft agreement, even with the limitations on Jerusalem, would advance us more than the principles paper. Additionally, what we had received from the Israelis made it clear that at
this point they were thinking in terms of an actual agreement, not generalities. Of
course, it was one thing to think it and another to confront it—especially in a paper

---

*The President would be speaking to the NAACP annual convention.

that was clearly not theirs. As I went to bed a little after 4 a.m., I thought, "Well, the rubber is going to meet the road tomorrow."

| DAY 3 |

Once one begins to deal with paper in a high-stakes negotiation, everything becomes more serious. One leaves the world of abstractions and begins to think about how an agreement might actually look in black and white—and maybe more importantly what one is going to have to live with and explain. My overarching strategy for the summit was to produce a paper that would be the basis for the negotiations. This is when the hard work would begin and the hard choices would be made. Over breakfast, I warned Eli Rubinstein that we had spent the night working and not sleeping. Tonight, it would be their turn. But once again events did not go as I had forecast.

The day started out well enough, with both Sandy and Madeleine pleased that I had decided in favor of a draft framework agreement and also pleased with what had been drafted. They were both anxious for me to go through it with the Israelis and also curious about how I intended to proceed with the Palestinians. My response: I would meet shortly with Shlomo and Gilad, and after that I suggested that Madeleine and I meet with Abu Ala and Hassan Asfour and go through the structure and main points of the draft. This was agreed and I went to work.

We used Holly cabin as our meeting place and Shlomo came with Gilad, Amnon, and Gidi. Shortly after the meeting began, Eli joined them. In keeping with our commitment to Barak not to surprise the Israelis, I decided to do a mix of summarizing the points but also reading those parts I considered most sensitive.

They did not like the way we had done the borders. They objected to our writing that the western border would be based on the 1967 lines with modifications taking account of demographics and strategic needs. This was surprising because this language not only met their needs by tying modifications to demographics and strategic needs but also was literally taken from the language Shlomo and Gilad had put in their nonpaper drafted in Sweden with Abu Ala and Hassan Asfour. I could not say so, however, because Eli had joined our discussion and I did not know if he knew about the secret nonpaper.

But here we were in a position of preparing to put down an American paper and they wanted this language—their language—either dropped or put in brackets. I told them if it went in brackets it would defeat the purpose of the paper, which was not supposed to be an "I" and "P" paper. They still insisted, and said they would report this to Barak. This was only the beginning of their objections: They did not like the refugee section, objecting to language that suggested that Israel—along with others—had a responsibility to help resolve this question once and for all. (We were not suggesting that Israel was responsible for the problem—which is what the Palestinians wanted; instead we had introduced a concept of responsibility that was collective and included Israel.) Every section except the Jerusalem section, which was kept very general at this stage, drew objections from the Israeli team.

In the next meeting, Abu Ala came with Mohammad Dahlan, Hassan, and Saeb. Without going through the details of the draft, I went over the categories and structure of what we were planning to present. I did not want them to feel they had no input into what we were doing; I also wanted to avoid a feeling of total surprise when they saw the draft. They mostly listened, but Abu Ala kept returning to whether we were being specific, especially on Jerusalem. I told him we were inclined to be more general on Jerusalem at this stage. Abu Ala insisted that we must not go "light" on Jerusalem. (Dahlan, like Amnon Shahak, had privately advised me that we should start only with a general outline on Jerusalem in any paper we initially offered. But he was now silent as Abu Ala argued for greater specificity on Jerusalem in the paper.)

After his speech to the NAACP in Baltimore, the President returned to Camp David a little after 5 p.m. We met at around five-thirty at Aspen in what had become the core group: Sandy, Madeleine, John Podesta, Bruce, Rob, and me. I brought the President up to date, noting what the Israeli reaction had been. I mentioned that Barak had asked to see me now and I had no doubt it was to complain about the draft and try to get modifications in it. While the President had read the draft and thought it was good, he felt it was still premature to force something down Barak's throat. Instead, he suggested why not do an "I" and "P" draft but then suggest several possible solutions as well. He felt by doing so that we would be pointing the way toward the solutions rather than forcing either side to accept a position at this stage on one of the sensitive issues.

The President asked me what I thought, and I said my preference was to stick with our original draft. I told him there was a cost in backing off from what we had told both sides, and I did not take the Israeli reaction too seriously, believing they were simply trying to deter us from going beyond the positions in the paper. The President was not persuaded. He preferred his alternative approach and asked me if I could put it together quickly. I told him it would take several hours because we had not done an "I" and "P" draft and I also needed to come up with a range of possible solutions on each issue. Notwithstanding the time it would take, the President asked me to prepare the new draft.

I went to work with Jon Schwartz and the others to do so, and the Secretary went in my place to see Barak. She called me after seeing him and said he had been in a dark mood, saying we could not put the points on the border in the papers.

I was still not particularly worried about Barak—he was now manipulating us, seeking to preserve his room for maneuvering for later. But I was worried about taking too long to present the paper, knowing that the Palestinians would interpret the delay as meaning that we were seeking to get Israeli clearance first. And I knew the Palestinians would either reject the paper or insist on putting their imprint on it.

But there were no shortcuts to producing a new paper, and it took us several hours to draft it. When the President asked to see me at ten-thirty, we had finished all the substantive work on the paper but Jon was still integrating its different parts: the "I" and "P" positions and the possible solutions for bridging the gaps. Consequently, when I went to see the President, Madeleine, and Sandy, I did not have the paper with me, and naturally I had not had a chance to proofread it. This turned out to be a big mistake.

The President was anxious to present the paper. He had promised Barak that he would see it before we presented it to the two sides, so he wanted to "get going." I described what was in the paper, giving examples of how we had handled possible solutions on the western and eastern borders. (I had actually come up with five possible solutions on the eastern border, ranging from one possibility that the Israelis would have liked to one the Palestinians would have preferred with several options in between.)

The President said it sounded good. Sandy reported his conversation with Barak, who approved going ahead with the paper as long as it reflected their comments. The President asked me how I thought we should proceed, and I repeated what I had said earlier, namely, that if I had my way, I would present our original draft with only minor changes on the grounds that this is what both sides expected. Both Sandy and John Podesta said it was too late to do that.

During the course of our meeting, Rob brought the paper and the President went off with it to see Barak. The President went over it with Barak but did not allow him to read it, saying we had changed our whole approach to accommodate Barak's concerns, and he needed now to present it to Arafat. Barak did not resist. When he finished with Barak, he asked to see Arafat. During the course of the meeting at Aspen, Dani came down and grabbed Bruce and me as we stood outside the cabin. He was agitated, saying there was one real problem with the draft paper. He said that the last point in the paper on Jerusalem was not in brackets and it implied that there could be two capitals in the existing municipality of Jerusalem. That would mean the division of existing Jerusalem and Barak could not accept that, "no way."

I did not know what he was talking about; we had decided to do only "I" and "P" positions on Jerusalem, with a few points on which there was no disagreement. On such a point, there was obviously disagreement.

But sure enough, the last point said there would be two capitals in the municipality of Jerusalem. Dani said that we could not give the paper to Arafat with the point written that way. I wrote in the word "expanded" to modify "municipality," and while Dani was uneasy he accepted it. I told him, "Don't worry; the Palestinians will see this handwritten word and their attention will be drawn to this and they won't like it." (For the Palestinians, the word "expanded" might imply the Belin–Abu Mazen concept of enlarging the municipality in a way that made Abu Dis a part of Jerusalem so that it could constitute the Palestinian capital.) Bruce got Doug Lane, the President's executive assistant, to substitute this copy for the version President Clinton was about to hand over to Arafat.

Rob had been the note-taker in the President's private meeting with Arafat, and when he came out of the meeting I confronted him, asking how the last point on Jerusalem got put in the paper. He said he and Jon had added it, but had neglected to tell me they had done so. I was angry, telling him, "No way that should have happened and now we are going to have a problem."

Rob was very contrite, but said he doubted there would be a problem: "Arafat was pleased to receive the paper from the President." I went into Aspen, and the President was in a good mood. He asked me why we had substituted the paper and I explained what happened. Sandy then began to emphasize that it was now early Friday morning, maybe the two sides would give us comments before the end of the day, but with Shabbat tomorrow they would not engage seriously until Saturday night. We needed to push them hard to accelerate, and we should lay down a full-fledged draft framework agreement by Saturday night. The President wondered whether it was possible to get them to move on a faster timetable. He asked me what I thought, and I said I agreed we had to push them, and be prepared to present the full draft agreement by Saturday night. But I added that we should be under no illusions. They both will wait until closer to the last minute and "not really start to cook until Sunday night—even if we push very hard." Unbeknownst to me at the time, this had made Sandy very angry; he feared the President would not force them to confront the key decisions in time to reach agreement before the President left for Okinawa, and he was certain everything would unravel if the President had to leave and there was no agreement.

Sandy grabbed Madeleine as we were leaving to tell her he was very upset with what I had said. (He was to tell me directly the next morning.) But when Madeleine told me about Sandy's reaction, I told her, "Look, I am not going to lie to the President. Moreover, Sandy is kidding himself if he thinks there will be an agreement before the

President has to go. The President will leave and we will stay behind and the President will return—only then will we have a chance for an agreement."

We were in mid-discussion at the Secretary's cabin when Gamal walked in and said he had gone to deliver additional copies of the paper to Arafat and had walked into a buzz saw. He said Arafat was upset with the paper and Saeb was very destructive. He is stoking Arafat up; misleading him about the paper; claiming it is Barak's, with the inserted word on Jerusalem proving that, and telling him he must not accept the paper. Madeleine had never seen Gamal appear shaken but I said Arafat throwing a tantrum was par for the course.

A few minutes later we got a call that Abu Ala and Saeb wanted to come see the Secretary. They arrived about 2:20 a.m. They started to complain about the paper, saying, Why do we need an "I" and "P" paper? It was not what they expected and it was not fair. The Secretary read them the disclaimer at the top of the page, saying this is the way we understood each side's position but they were not bound by our interpretations. That did not satisfy them. I said, "The purpose of the paper is to concentrate and accelerate your discussions with the Israelis; if it does not do that, then either do better on your own or use the possible solutions we outlined and make some headway."

Saeb immediately leaped on what I said, observing to Abu Ala that I made clear they did not have to use the paper as a "basis." I said that's right provided you are prepared to do better on your own. Saeb and Abu Ala were satisfied and left. It was now two-thirty in the morning and I said to the Secretary, "That was all for show. They came to the conclusion that we had rewritten our paper after Israeli resistance—why else had it taken us so long to produce the paper. Now they would show they, too, could reject our paper."

As I returned to my cabin, I knew we'd had a bad day. We had backed off when the Israelis had complained and rewritten what we had in mind, and now with what I had said to Saeb, we had done the same with the Palestinians. I was not happy with myself. I knew better. I should have more strongly resisted the President's instinct to write a different paper. I knew the Israelis were mainly posturing, and there was no need to back off. I should not have backed off with Saeb; my challenge to them to do better on their own at least gave us a good justification to come up with a real draft and present it. I resolved to give them a chance to work on Friday while we readied a real paper designed to overcome the gaps. The question I had in my mind as I tried to get a few hours of sleep was whether we would stick with anything we laid down.

| DAY 4 |

Over breakfast, Shlomo and Gilad separately told me that we should have gone with our original paper, not the "I" and "P" approach. Perhaps, I told them, "you should posture less." But I knew that they were posturing so that we would not take their concessions for granted. This just reinforced my view that we had to stop backing off at the first sign of resistance.

With that very much in mind, I gave Jon instructions to go ahead and redraft our original prospective framework agreement; only now I decided to go ahead on Jerusalem with a bridging idea—sovereignty in a few of the outer neighborhoods, Palestinian autonomy for the remaining Arab neighborhoods with responsibility for planning and zoning, and Palestinian control (not sovereignty) of the Haram al-Sharif with a flag and their own police.

We were going to give the negotiators until Friday afternoon to work and they would report to the President on the status of their work. I would join the President, Madeleine, and Sandy as the negotiators briefed them on the results of their discussions before Shabbat. I anticipated being able to take Jon's draft and work on it during the day on Saturday.

Before the President's meetings with the negotiators, I briefed him at Aspen and emphasized that he should keep in mind the general trade-offs on the issues as he listened to the negotiators' reports. He should try to steer them to the trade-offs either in order for them to make headway or to condition them for what would be in our draft. I reminded him of the basic trade-offs on land and refugees: on the western border, the Palestinians get the 1967 lines, but with modifications to take account of the Israeli settlement blocs; on the eastern border, it's sovereignty for the Palestinians, with Israel's security needs met; on refugees, it's the general principle for the Palestinians in terms of reference to UN General Assembly resolution 194 (not the "right of return") and it's practical limitations for the Israelis. Since Jerusalem would be discussed in the last meeting, I decided to wait to go over how to handle it until just before the President saw the Jerusalem negotiators.

In the first meeting on territory and borders, Abu Ala tried a new tack. Whereas previously he would not discuss security until the Israelis accepted the Palestinian concept of their eastern border, now he added the condition that he would not discuss possible modifications to meet Israeli needs on the western border unless he knew that the total size of the Palestinian territory would remain unchanged. As he put it, so long as the Palestinian state would comprise the 6,500 square kilometers that currently made up the West Bank, Gaza, and East Jerusalem, he could consider modifications to meet

Israeli needs; if not, he could not. This was Abu Ala's way of trying to get the Israelis to concede both the eastern border and equal swaps of territory as conditions for considering Israeli needs.

This was, of course, a prescription for going nowhere. We might be at a summit, and he might be briefing the President of the United States, but for Abu Ala, the tactics of negotiation would not change. Shlomo was thoughtful, not provocative, in response: "I cannot agree to that, but why don't you [Palestinians] assume the basis you want and then explore how to respond to our [Israeli] needs; otherwise there can be no discussion and no progress."

The President listened, then said to Abu Ala, "You lose nothing if you assume the 1967 line; they will need to get modifications, but if you are not satisfied on the swaps, you know there will be no deal. You have to talk, you cannot hold back, otherwise we know there cannot be a deal." Hassan told the President that this is very sensitive for us, "we cannot be asked to give up the settlement blocs and have this in their press."

The President was sympathetic to this fear. But he noted both sides had reason to fear being exposed on the concessions they might make. He offered that "we are here and can protect much more against this, and we can also make clear that nothing is agreed until everything is agreed." I then suggested that each side could also pull whatever it said off the table and "we can assume the responsibility for ideas or concessions that are leaked, either saying they were ideas we raised or even denying that any such sensitive proposal had been made by one of the sides."

Hassan did not look persuaded, but the President seized on this point, saying, "It protects you." Poignantly, he went on to say, "You know I want an agreement. That's why we are here, that's why I am taking a considerable risk in doing this. It is important enough to me to take the risk. I want to reach agreement, but we owe it to ourselves to know that if we cannot reach agreement, it is because it is impossible. I don't want any of us to leave here thinking it could have been done in the aftermath of having failed. If we can't do it, let's be sure it was because it was impossible. Let's not live with a regret that we could have done it if we had just tried a little harder or if we had just tried a different approach to the discussions." He looked at Abu Ala and asked, "Will you try my way?" Clearly moved, Abu Ala said, I will ask Abu Ammar if it is okay.

I thought the President had been brilliant. But he got better in each of the next two meetings. With the negotiators on refugees—Eli Rubinstein and Oded Eran for the Israelis and Abu Mazen and Nabil Sha'ath for the Palestinians—he got into the details of the international mechanism for financing resettlement and rehabilitation. When Abu Mazen switched the focus to the Palestinian need for acceptance of the principle of "right of return," the President responded that the Israelis could not be expected to give a blank check on return if they did not have guarantees in very concrete terms on how this would be limited. He used the example of a bungee jumper being told to accept the principle that he could leap without knowing whether the gorge he was leaping into was deeper than the length of the bungee cord. You cannot ask the Israelis to accept a principle that they see as threatening their existence without offering very specific guarantees on the limitations to ensure it is not a threat. The President concluded the meeting by asking both sides to do their homework on the international mechanism and for the Palestinians to present practical ideas on limiting the application of the principle they sought.

By now it was 8:30 p.m., well past sundown and the start of Shabbat. The Israelis had invited the U.S. and Palestinian teams to attend a Shabbat dinner, and we needed to get going. But we had not yet met with the Jerusalem group. Saeb and Yasser and Gilad were waiting and anxious to meet with the President. We decided to meet but had no time to talk among ourselves before the meeting. I had no chance to suggest to the President what he might say; no matter, he did better on his own than I might have advised. Each side reported briefly and the President said to each, "Do me a favor. Each of you assume that you get the sovereignty outcome you want. Go over what life looks like in Jerusalem. How do things function, what is life like, how will things actually work? You know we cannot solve the question of sovereignty right now, but you also know there are powers and functions in the city. Develop such a list and go over it together without reference to sovereignty—assuming you have it." Both agreed. It was as good as, if not better than, I could have done.

Following the Shabbat dinner, the President saw Arafat and the Chairman agreed that Abu Ala could proceed the way the President proposed, that is, to assume the Palestinian basis on the border and address seriously the Israeli needs. All in all, I was beginning to feel things were going better. After the President's meetings, there was the possibility that the formal meetings might make some headway. But there was also a new and important development.

Mohammad Dahlan had begun to meet quietly with Shlomo, Amnon, and Yossi Ginossar to discuss all the issues, including Jerusalem. They had started to meet in Amnon's cabin in the early-morning hours. Here was a real back channel operating which was discreet and informal; here ideas could be tried and explored. After being briefed by them, I informed the President, Sandy, and Madeleine. In our concluding session with the President well after midnight, I said we have three levels at which we must now work: (1) prepare our proposal to put on the table; (2) work quietly with the back channel to help ensure that what we put on the table succeeds; and (3) let the formal negotiating teams see what they can develop, incorporating that into our proposal.

This made sense to them, and we all went to bed feeling we were finally on the right track.

| DAY 5 |

This was to be a day of real developments. It started with a meeting I had with Barak in the morning. Though I was more hopeful, there was still a problem. Over breakfast, Shlomo and Yossi informed me that Barak did not want anyone on his side to raise anything new.

So when Barak asked to see me, I resolved to press him. To start our meeting, I asked him, "Why are we here?" We are in the fifth day of the summit you insisted on having, and we have not heard anything new from you or your side. What's worse, when we wanted to present a paper, "you resisted our quoting language your own guys had written, not just said, to Abu Ala in Sweden." So "for the life of me I cannot figure out why you wanted this summit, and why I pushed it, particularly because we could be having these discussions anywhere and without the same exposure or stakes."

I hoped I might shake him up with this approach. He had perceived me to be the most sympathetic on our side to his needs, partly because the Palestinians made me the public target of criticism so often and partly because he believed I had responded the most to his needs on having the summit. If even I was losing faith in him, maybe he would realize either he would have to reveal where he was going or he would have to permit his negotiators more room to maneuver. If that is what I wanted, I was not to get it in this meeting.

Instead, I got a repeat of why he could not move before Arafat did. He would not let Arafat pocket his moves. He had always talked about how the summit would create a pressure cooker and that would produce new moves. Now I asked what happened to the pressure cooker? What happened to his logic for the summit? Again, I asked, Why are we here? His response was that the pressure cooker had to work first on Arafat; then things would happen. If we would just get tougher with the Palestinians, if they would just see that we were not siding with their positions, then everything would change.

He wanted to discuss Jerusalem. What, he asked, did I think the Palestinians needed? I said, in addition to clear control of the Haram, they needed some sovereignty in a part of existing East Jerusalem. Al-Quds* could not simply be Abu Dis and the villages outside of the existing municipal boundaries of East Jerusalem.

Here again, he took a tough position. What he had signaled to the President on

---

*Literally, "the holy," is how the Arab world refers to Jerusalem.

Jerusalem he now seemed to walk back on, saying he could not give more than autonomy for the outer villages like Bayt Hanina and Shua'fat. When I pressed on this point given our earlier conversation, he said it simply was not possible to do more in the outer villages.

When I left the meeting, I said to Martin (who had joined me for the meeting), He is hardening but I think it is just tactics. He wants us to push the Palestinians and get Arafat to move before he will do anything. It is all part of his strategy to wait to move until we are all up against the wall, and he wants us to create that wall for Arafat. And our arguments to the contrary—like my asking him why we were here—are clearly not going to move him, at least for the time being. Martin agreed with my assessment, but wondered whether he might actually be hardening his positions, especially with the arrival at Camp David of Dan Meridor.*

Shortly afterward, I saw Sandy and Madeleine and briefed them on the meeting with Barak. Sandy was livid; we were at this summit because of Barak; he was going to guarantee failure; the President would have to pay for it; and we would have to say why we failed. He would see Barak and say all this to him. He was unmoved by my assessment of why Barak was doing what he was doing.

We then saw the President, and I briefed him on the meeting, but also gave him my assessment of Barak's strategy for the summit. Sandy put in his view and what he would say to Barak, and the President agreed he should do that. Now, however, it was time for us to have the President sit with the negotiators again and see what, if any, impact his meetings from the day before had had on their discussions.

The first meeting was with the territory, borders, and security group, and we did not have to wait long to find out. While Arafat had told President Clinton that he had given instructions for Abu Ala to proceed the way the President had asked, Abu Ala's approach remained unchanged. In response to an Israeli map that showed three different colors—brown for the Palestinian state, orange for the areas the Israelis would annex, and red for transitional areas—Abu Ala was not prepared to discuss Israeli needs unless the Israelis first accepted the principle of the territorial swap and reduced the areas they sought to annex.

The President at first tried to reason with Abu Ala, explaining that he could see "why this map is not acceptable to you. But you cannot say to them, not good enough, give me something more acceptable; that's not a negotiation. Why not say the orange area is too big, let's talk about your needs and see how we can reduce the orange area

---

*Dan arrived late to the summit; he was now in the Center Party with Amnon and serving as Minister Without Portfolio in Barak's government. Dan was more conservative at this stage on most of the core issues than the rest of the Israeli negotiating team.

and turn it into brown. If we focus on the security aspect and look at the Jordan Valley, we might discuss the security issues and see if we can reduce the orange area." Shlomo agreed with that approach—thereby signaling that he was open to reducing the orange area, which amounted to close to 14 percent of the total of the West Bank outside of Jerusalem.

Abu Ala continued to resist. As he did, and as he repeated old arguments about the settlements being illegal and the Palestinians needing the 1967 lines, the President's face began to turn red. Mohammad Rashid turned to me and said the President is getting upset, why don't we take a break? I thought that was a good idea, believing that a private meeting with the Palestinians might allow the President to tell Abu Ala and his colleagues that they were contradicting what he asked them to do and what Arafat agreed they would do—and he would not proceed in a situation where he was told one thing and they did another.

I went over and whispered to the President that it might make sense to take a break and deal alone with the Palestinians. He listened but did not respond. Instead, he proceeded to tell Abu Ala, "I don't see what you lose by assuming you will get a swap in the end or there won't be a deal. You can still discuss the orange areas in the Jordan Valley and in the corridor from Jerusalem to Jericho and see how you turn that to brown. Okay, you don't like this map, but it is an Israeli proposal and either you get specific about what you need to change or offer your own map."

Abu Ala said they did not want to present a map where they gave up their territory; if Israel wanted to justify modifications in the border, it needed to do so with a more reasonable map. I could see now that the President was livid. So I stood up and suggested we take a break.

But it was too late. The President had had enough, and he let it rip. He said this was an outrageous approach. He had risked a great deal in having this summit. He had been advised not to take this risk. He disregarded this advice because he felt it necessary to do all he could to reach an agreement. But this was an outrageous waste of his time and everyone else's time. He had offered a reasonable approach that did not compromise Palestinian interests. They lost nothing by trying it, and Abu Ala was simply not willing to negotiate. No one could accept what he was asking for. He would not be a part of something not serious, and this wasn't serious, it was a mockery. Arafat had given his agreement to what the President was asking for and now he comes to the meeting and finds an outrageous approach—and he repeated, shouting now, "an outrageous approach."

At that point, the President stood up and stalked out. Everyone was stunned. The Israelis got up and left. We were at Holly, and the next meeting was to be between Saeb and Gilad on Jerusalem. They were in the next room waiting. They had heard the President shouting, and saw him stalk out. I walked over to them and told them "the next meeting is canceled."

I waited outside Holly, and Mohammad Dahlan came out. He asked me what they should do. "Mohammad," I said, "you need to have us go to the President and say you will proceed either with your own map or you will take a blank map from us and draw in what you think is a reasonable way to respond to the Israeli needs as you understand them." He liked the latter option. Mohammad Rashid joined us, saying he understood the President was angry, was justified in being so, but it would have been much better if he had not blown up in front of the Israelis. Dahlan agreed.

"What did you expect?" I asked. "He lays out an approach, he gets Arafat's explicit okay, and then he hears the same bullshit. You guys are taking advantage of the President of the United States and he has had it." Dahlan said he would go to work on the blank map option.

They left and I went to lunch. Abu Ala was shaken. He told Gamal that he should leave; he could not be responsible for destroying Arafat's relationship with the President. When I sat next to him, he repeated maybe he should not negotiate, and then asked quite revealingly, Why are their tactics okay and mine are not? For Abu Ala, this was all about tactics. He was trying to get the best deal he could, and this was simply part of the game. Didn't the President understand that?

I told Abu Ala that the President's patience had run out. It was time to get past the games. We were running out of time, and it was time to get down to the real give-and-take. He repeated maybe he should go and not negotiate. While telling him that he and I were friends and that was not going to change, I made no effort to try to talk him out of that.

After I left the lunch, I went over Jon's draft. I worked on it for about an hour and a half, and was comfortable with it. But I wanted to see what was going on in the back channel, both because that might affect when we chose to present our proposal and I also wanted to be able to test certain ideas. At that point, I went looking for Yossi, and found him sitting with Amnon and Mohammad Rashid. They seemed glum. I asked what was going on, and they said they were trying to figure out what to do.

I said, Isn't the problem whether what the three of you are trying to do is something that your leaders can accept? Turning to Rashid, I asked, When you say 92 percent on the territory with a 2-to-3 percent swap, and when you say shared responsibilities and a kind of "B" in the Old City and sovereignty in all the remaining neighborhoods, do you really represent Arafat? Isn't that the crux of the problem?

His response surprised me. He said, "When I say these things, I am more representative of Arafat than they are of Barak." Neither Amnon nor Yossi contradicted him when I turned to them. Their expressions told the story that they could not work out anything with Rashid now. Notwithstanding their hopeful expressions of the night before about their discreet discussions with Mohammad Dahlan and Mohammad Rashid, they were now no longer sure they could deliver. Apparently, Barak's posture with me was also his posture with them. The back channel, which last night seemed so hopeful and which I was counting on, was clearly not going to be our salvation.

Before leaving them, I asked Yossi, "What do you suggest we do now?" He answered that the President should sit down with one person designated by each leader and see what was possible on each core issue. I had a different idea: Barak now knew that the President had exploded against the Palestinians, but Barak wasn't permitting any movement on his side. In light of that, the President should say, We are not going anywhere. We can lay down a paper which you, Mr. Prime Minister, won't like, especially on Jerusalem. If we cannot do that, I think we are out of business. The only other option I can think of is for me to ask you and Arafat to designate two on a side to sit through the night and try to come up with a package deal. By tomorrow at noon, I would ask the four to come and brief me on what they were able to produce.

I felt we needed to shake up the situation. We could do that with our paper, but I was not confident the President would present it if Barak opposed it. In addition, I feared that not having the back channel to help with it and, in effect, to vet it and lobby for it, we stood much less chance of having it succeed. I went to see the President. Sandy and Madeleine were sitting with him on the Aspen deck. I explained where things stood; the formal negotiations were going nowhere; the back channel was going nowhere. We could proceed with our paper, but the chances of it working without the input and promotion from the back channel were very limited, at least at this stage. I presented my idea; President Clinton liked it and went to see Barak. Barak asked to think about what the President had suggested, and asked him not to go to Arafat until he came back to the President.

I decided to do some conditioning of Gilad. At this point, I considered him to be more representative of Barak than anyone else on the Israeli team. I met him alone at Holly. It was around eight in the evening; the room was relatively dark, with the only available light coming from a low-wattage lamp situated between our two sofa chairs. It provided a somber, semi-mysterious cast to our meeting.

I told him I wanted to give "a little context" for the discussion that the President had just finished with "the PM." He told me he knew about the President's conversation with Barak and the two options he had raised, and was anxious to hear what I had to say. I told him that the President was serious about calling the summit off; neither side was doing anything. We could force the action with a paper, but Barak would not like the paper. Gilad wanted to know what we would propose if we presented a paper now. It was important to know this now because "it will be a heavy responsibility to decide whether to work through the night to do a deal—knowing we will be revealing our real positions"—and he wanted to weigh that against the alternative. He concluded, saying that quitting was not an option—so it was either our paper or doing something seriously on their own now.

I said, "Look, we have not shared this with anyone and we have not finalized the paper. The President will make the final call on the paper, so this is between you and me." He replied, "Understood." And I proceeded to describe the main elements:

—On territory, we won't try to finalize it now; instead, we will identify a range for the area to be annexed by Israel of 3 to 12 percent; we will make it clear that there will have to be "compensation" to the Palestinians for the area that becomes part of Israel. We will use that term to signal swaps, leaving only a little ambiguity since there could be other ways to compensate the Palestinians. But there will be little doubt about the signal;

—On refugees, we will tilt toward you, using the Beilin–Abu Mazen formulation on right of return (the Palestinians insist on it, Israel recognizes the human suffering and need to solve the problem), and we will emphasize the practical limitations on return;

—On Jerusalem, we will propose Palestinian sovereignty in the outer neighborhoods of Bayt Hanina and Shua'fat; for the inner neighborhoods, there will have to be real autonomy, meaning that they get planning and zoning; on the Old City, there will need to be shared responsibilities; and the Palestinians will get jurisdiction, not sovereignty, on the Temple Mount/Haram.

Gilad's facial reactions told a story: he grimaced as I went over the points on swaps and planning and zoning in the inner neighborhoods. He did not react to the points on refugees or those on sovereignty over Bayt Hanina and Shua'fat or the shared responsibilities in the Old City.

When I finished describing what would be in the paper, he asked if the range on territory could be 4 to 13 percent; I said, maybe 4 to 12 percent, but only so he understood where we would end up. He said, I know you want to end up at 8 percent, but it will help if the range is 4 to 13 percent. I said I would think about it. He asked, Do you really have to signal swaps now? I said we were not doing it definitively but how could we purport to present a paper that was credible as a bridge without signaling it?

Finally, he said planning and zoning in the inner neighborhoods is very difficult; he understood Palestinian needs but there could not be unlimited building in an area that also had some Israeli presence. I said we are talking about a borough system; there will probably have to be a master plan; but nothing will be changed from a Palestinian standpoint if they don't have planning and zoning. Remember, these neighborhoods are staying under your sovereignty—that's the big thing and there has to be some selling point for such an arrangement.

We parted, with my assuming that he would talk to Barak about the choices. At around 10 p.m., Barak asked to see the President, and I told the President I had briefed Gilad on the general points in our paper so he understood the choices of getting a paper now or working through the night to try to do a deal. I said I would not be surprised if Barak raised some of what I had told Gilad. The President nodded, and headed into what would turn out to be a difficult, albeit productive, one-on-one meeting with Barak.

The President's face was still red as he described the meeting when he returned to Laurel. Barak had been angry, complaining to the President that "you cannot go with a swap now or the villages now"—something the President interpreted as meaning Barak wanted to save these for the end—"otherwise, these will be the point of departure for Arafat. You cannot put down a paper that is so far out in front of me."

The President got angry in return, saying he had beaten up on the Palestinians today, but in truth Barak wasn't doing a thing in a summit he had insisted on having. If he did not want us to put the paper down with the two villages, then we would not include them in the paper, but Barak should know there would be no deal. If he did not want a credible U.S. paper, then he had to go and get serious. "Let your two guys work without constraints tonight and try to do a deal." Barak said "okay."

The President said he would see Arafat now. He asked Barak whom he would send to the meeting, and Barak told him it would be Shlomo and Gilad. In turn, Barak asked who we would ask for from Arafat, and the President said Mohammad Dahlan and Mohammad Rashid. Barak liked that.

The President saw Arafat with Gamal. Arafat agreed and said he would let us know shortly who his two would be. He asked who the two were on the Israeli side and the President told him. Arafat understood that this two-on-two meeting would be secret, it would not be disclosed to others, they would work through the night and report to the President by noon. Their purpose was *not* to engage in bargaining as usual, they were to try to cut a deal on the core issues. There was, as the President told him, no way we could continue as we had, and if a deal was not possible, it was better to know it now.

Within about ten minutes we got the word it would not be Dahlan and Rashid. Instead, Saeb Erekat would join Dahlan. Gamal said that this would be okay, because Mohammad Rashid could sit with Arafat and work him, repeating what Rashid had told Gamal he would do. I disagreed, saying it was a bad sign—maybe unavoidable because Gilad is representing the Israelis—because the most flexible person on the Palestinian side was not going to be in these talks.

The four came to see the President at around 12:30 a.m. and he gave them a pep talk, trying to inspire them on their task and what was at stake. He also said, To protect you, whatever you come up with I am prepared to present as ours; you have "immunity" for what you do because I will assume responsibility for whatever you do. As the four came out of Aspen, I saw very different looks on their faces: Shlomo and Gilad clearly saw this as an opportunity. But Saeb and Dahlan had a look of dread on their faces—suggesting they did not know whether Arafat would truly back them if they compromised on any of the core issues.

Day 6 had already begun. I had Beth Jones* arrange the details and management of their meeting. I told her the meeting should be in the President's office in Laurel. The four of them were to be sequestered. She was not to let them leave before morning; and others weren't to know what they were doing. Beth asked if they should come to my cabin at around six-thirty in the morning, and I said I don't want them moving around. Just guard the room and manage their departure.

Beth took this responsibility very seriously.

| DAY 6 |

At 3 a.m., Beth called to say that she had received a message that Barak wanted to speak to Shlomo, should she allow the call to go through? I replied, Yes, if a leader wants to speak to one of the negotiators we cannot say no.

At just before 7 a.m., Beth called and said Dahlan wanted to go take a shower and pray, was that permitted? I replied, Yes, we are not going to say no to prayer, especially when we may need it. But tell him he has to be back in thirty minutes. He was.

At ten-thirty, Beth called to say they were ready to break, was that all right, and I said yes. She then put Gilad on the phone and he reported the following: "We stretched very far, further than the PM's instructions, and, unfortunately, nothing changed; they simply listened, took notes, and asked questions. There were no responses." I asked, No responses? And he said, They only responded on Jerusalem. Saeb, he said, proposed that East Jerusalem be divided, with all the Arab neighborhoods becoming Palestinian and all the Jewish neighborhoods becoming Israeli.

---

*Beth was the logistics coordinator for Camp David.

Gilad went on to say that we went very far, frankly farther than your ideas on Jerusalem. We moved on territory very far, and we got nothing in return. "We cannot go on this way."

I then asked, "What do you think is the next step?" Paradoxically, he said, "I think we can do it." Now I was confused. But rather than continue, I suggested that they brief the President at noon. He asked if it could be one o'clock so they could sleep for an hour and also brief Barak. I agreed, and we contacted the Palestinians.

The four came back to Laurel to brief the President. It was clear that Shlomo and Gilad had made big moves:

—On Jerusalem, the northern Arab neighborhoods of Kafr Aqab, Kalandia, and Bayt Hanina would become sovereign; the inner neighborhoods (Shaykh Jarrah, Wadi al-Jawz) would have services provided by the Palestinian capital of Al-Quds while being under Israeli sovereignty; in the Old City, there would be a special regime in which there would be shared responsibilities in the Muslim and Christian Quarters— the special regime and the shared responsibilities would need to be worked out jointly;

—On territory, the Israelis would seek 10.5 percent of the territory for the blocs. On the eastern border, the Palestinians would have most of the border with Jordan; Israel would retain only a small segment.

There was little discussion of refugees. When Saeb spoke, he called attention to what he had proposed on Jerusalem, emphasizing that this was both a big move and a logical one. When I asked Saeb what he had said on territory, he replied that once the principle of swaps was accepted, then they could work out the modifications on the border. He added we recognize the Israelis have needs and we can address them once the principle of swaps is accepted. Dahlan said given the Israeli move on the border, he was now prepared to discuss security with the Israeli security experts.

Shlomo, in summing up, had said that he and Gilad had come in the spirit that the President had asked. They came to make a deal, stretching well beyond their instructions. Unfortunately, he said, their Palestinian friends had not come in such a spirit, but he hoped they would consider carefully everything he had suggested and respond in kind. Saeb responded, appreciating the seriousness of the discussion but also claiming that he had gone very far on Jerusalem. He was out on a limb, accepting Jewish neighborhoods in East Jerusalem that most Palestinians considered illegal. Now the two sides should continue their negotiations. Gilad got angry and said this is rock bottom for us. "You think you can just take this as a new floor and negotiate from there. We came to make a deal, not to go into the souk."

Barak had always sought to find the time, the environment, or the mechanism in which Arafat could not simply pocket what Israel offered. He wanted the pressure cooker to work on Arafat. But when we had come with two alternatives—we present a paper or you send your guys to do real business—Barak had finally relented and permitted Shlomo and Gilad to try to forge a package deal. But in Gilad's words, the Palestinians had come more to maneuver in the souk than to negotiate a deal.

Unfortunately for Gilad, the President's summary of the meeting was not going to be satisfying. Clinton told Gilad, Shlomo, Saeb, and Mohammad that they had all worked hard, we appreciated it, and we would now try to build on what they had done. I knew Shlomo and Gilad would not take this well, perceiving that the President had just let the Palestinians off the hook.

As I accompanied Shlomo and Gilad outside, Shlomo said to me, "If we had behaved in 1948 the way they do here, we would never have had a state." In our meeting with the President afterward, I said this is going to confirm Barak's worst fears: he moves in a big way, Arafat pockets it, and he is expected to move again in a way that will definitely go beyond his redlines.

I said that while Barak might have been angry last night about us getting out front of him on Jerusalem and swaps, his guys went beyond our ideas on sovereignty over the neighborhoods in East Jerusalem; they went very far on the Old City; and for the first time they gave most of the border with Jordan to the Palestinians. What did they get in return? I said Saeb's move on Jerusalem is something, but we have known about it for some time, and on territory what they got was a replay of Abu Ala's approach—the very approach you blew up over yesterday. The Palestinians did not do what you asked. We cannot ask Barak for anything more; the Palestinians have made that impossible. But understand that when you see Arafat he will devalue everything the Israelis did. You have to push him back hard and say they moved and you didn't. Enough is enough. You have to say I cannot get you anything else unless you move seriously.

Sandy said we have to get something from Arafat to bring to Barak. John Podesta said Arafat wants a swap, why not tell him you want me to try to get a swap, give me just under 10 percent on the territory and I will try to get you a swap. But I can't do better than that.

After some additional discussion, we agreed that the President should press for more than just Israel's territorial requirements. The President would press for those and for Israel's security needs in the Jordan Valley and for our needs on "end-of-conflict language." John pointed out that without "end-of-conflict language," the President would not be able to produce the American presence that Arafat sought as part of the security arrangements—"the Congress won't go for putting American troops there without explicit end-of-conflict language."

The President was worked up by the time he went to see Arafat, and he and Gamal came back saying that the meeting was the toughest ever. The President looked at me and said he pushed Arafat along the lines we had discussed, and Arafat responded predictably. He tried to belittle what was presented—89.5 percent of the territory, sovereignty in several outer neighborhoods of East Jerusalem, an independent border for the Palestinians with Jordan including almost the entirety of the Jordan River and Valley. Arafat suggested this was less than Rabin offered—saying his partner, Rabin, had promised him 90 percent. (In an earlier briefing I told the President that this was one of Arafat's mythologies; Rabin had never done that, and, in fact, Rabin had envisioned only going to between 70 and 80 percent.) When Arafat said this, the President responded by saying that Rabin never made that commitment and it is ridiculous that you keep repeating it. "We can all go home and I will say they seriously negotiated and you did not." Rob, who was the note-taker in the meeting, said Arafat was almost in tears and said to the President that their relationship meant everything to him and told him, "Who else can I talk to, you are the only one I can talk to."

After the blowup, the President, according to Rob, had softened and asked Arafat to come back with a response on the territory, security, or end of conflict. The President said I need a response I can work with on at least one of these. And Arafat promised to come back to him with a response.

In the meantime, Barak was livid, seeing everything in apocalyptic terms. After the President had gone to see Arafat, I saw Amnon and he told me Ehud had "hated" what Shlomo had done. Shlomo had gone too far and Ehud felt cornered. Little did I know how cornered until later when I heard from Martin, who had received a message from Barak for the President transmitted by Dani. Dani told Martin the Prime Minister had hoped the President would see this message before meeting with Arafat. That had not happened.

The message was stunning for its dark, foreboding overtones. To see just how stunning, it is worth quoting from it extensively:

> *I took the report of Shlomo Ben-Ami and Gilad Sher of last night's discussion very badly. This is not negotiations. This is a manipulative attempt to pull us to a position we will never be able to accept, without the Palestinians moving one inch. Yasir Arafat would not dare to do it without believing that in the U.S. delegation there is a strong bias amongst many of the American team for his positions. The President is of course objective but . . . the American team is not objective . . . I have taken upon myself unprecedented risks on the way to the summit and even the positions . . . presented by our people last night . . . which*

I heard about after the fact and even though they are not my positions, they
represent additional risks. There are people in my delegation who strongly oppose
these moves . . . There will not be another Israeli Prime Minister who is
prepared to do this only to find out that it is not a fair negotiation.

I do not intend to allow the Israeli state to fall apart physically or morally.
The state of Israel is the implementation of the dream of the Jewish people for
generation upon generation. We achieved it after enormous effort and the
expenditure of a great deal of blood and sweat. . . . There is no way that I will
preside in Camp David over the closing of this saga.

Since 1948, we have faced an attempt to force us to collapse. I will not
allow it to happen. This is an unusual moment of truth. Only a sharp shaking
of Arafat by the President will give a chance to the process. Only if Arafat comes
to understand that this is the moment of truth will he move. He has to see that
he has a chance to achieve an independent Palestinian state . . . or the
alternative of a tragedy where the U.S. will stand with Israel. Only if Arafat
understands this will there be a chance to save the summit.

It is my belief that it is now or never. I will not be able to live with the
situation that was created last night. . . . When the people of Israel will
understand how far we were ready to go we will have the power to stand together
unified in such a struggle, however tough it will become, even if we will be
forced to confront the entire world. There is no power in the world that can force
on us collective national suicide.

Peace will be achieved only if there is a real willingness to negotiate on both
sides. I am sure the people of Israel and the American people will understand it
when the details will be revealed.

I knew before reading this message that Barak felt cornered. I had no idea how dark his vision was. We had already decided to shake Arafat without having received this message. We, too, had had enough of the Palestinian unwillingness to negotiate. Perhaps if the President had read this message before seeing Arafat, he would not have softened at the end of his meeting with the Chairman, asking only for a response on one of the three points of territory, security, or end of conflict. Or perhaps he would have gone to see Barak first to affect the psychology of a leader who was seeing everything now in life-and-death terms.

I would have suggested that. Unfortunately, I still did not know of the full contents of the message until the President was already meeting with Arafat. Martin had summarized the message to Sandy, who offered his own summary to the President. The message made Sandy even more certain that we should not go back to Barak until we had something meaningful from Arafat.

I had argued for such a posture earlier, but that was before I knew how bleak Barak's mood was. Once Martin read me the note, I called Sandy. He told me he had tried to see Barak but had only been able to see Dani, and he told him how tough the President was going to be with Arafat.

Now I told Sandy that is not good enough. We cannot let Barak sink into a deeper funk. The President needs to meet with him and let him vent. Sandy agreed. Madeleine agreed too, but also felt that Barak owed us an apology for saying we were all Palestinian "symps."

While we waited for Arafat's reply to the President, I thought about Barak. He was a master manipulator, and we could not discount that his message was part manipulation. But it was so overwrought that I felt it had to be more than just an effort to manipulate us. Why was he in such a dark mood? Why did he see what had happened last night in such dire terms? After all, he was talking about collapse, ending the dream, and national suicide.

I decided that it had dawned on him that his conception of a deal was not going to work. The price he was going to have to pay for a deal was higher than he'd envisioned and it went against everything he had ever believed. He was, after all, a man who had been unhappy with Oslo; abstained on the Interim Agreement; and had never been a member of what Yossi Beilin had always called the "so-called peace mafia" in Israel. Although the price went against his very grain, he also realized the alternative to a deal—for him personally and for his country. Would he have to face the moment of truth he so often talked about? Would he survive politically after the summit? Would the high price of confrontation he had always talked about as the alternative to a summit now have to be paid?

The language of this message reflected a man not just anguished but in personal crisis. And yet at the end he spoke not only of a potential threat about the reaction of the American people—so you'd better be with me—but also of the need to shake Arafat in order to save the summit. He had not given up; he was trying to pressure us to pressure Arafat. It might not be a typical manipulation, but there was certainly an element of him trying to shock us into far more forceful threats against Arafat.

The President had shaken Arafat, but we did not yet have the response. Gamal said he was pushing for them to respond seriously. Dahlan had told Gamal he was pushing for 4 percent with a swap; Gamal had told him to make it 5 percent with a swap. I reacted angrily, saying that was nothing. In Eilat, Dahlan had offered 4 percent with a swap; 5 percent now with a swap was not a move at all. Rob and Yossi had told different Palestinians to make it 5 percent with no swap. I told each that was not good enough—not at this stage, not if we were to go back to Barak and then be able to move toward an agreement where each side would still have to give more.

The response from Arafat was clever. It came in the form of a letter from Arafat in Arabic transmitted by Saeb to Rob—Rob having been the note-taker in the President's meeting with Arafat. Gamal translated it. While not mentioning a percentage of territory for the settlement blocs, Arafat said, "I agree that the ratio of exchange will be in accordance with the agreed-upon size of the settlements. I will leave it up to you if we can guarantee a solution to East Jerusalem for you to determine the ratio." When Rob questioned Saeb on what this meant, Saeb replied, "We accept settlements, you know the sizes, the President can decide the ratio. If there is a trade-off between issues and Palestinian sovereignty over East Jerusalem, the President can determine the percentage of the land and the ratio."

In the most charitable interpretation of this, if the Palestinians got sovereignty over East Jerusalem, the President could determine the size of the area to be annexed for the settlement blocs and the amount of land to be swapped in return for that annexation. It was the most charitable interpretation because that is not what the letter said. I read Arafat's actual language—"the ratio of exchange will be in accordance with the agreed-upon size of the settlements"—as ambiguous. Arafat could say this meant that the Israeli annexation of territory for the settlement blocs must be matched by a swap of an equal territory for the Palestinians.

But we did not interpret it this way because when Rob brought the letter, he explained what Saeb said about the meaning of the key sentences. I was uneasy both because I did not know if we should be counting on Saeb's interpretation and because I was not sure what we had gotten even if we did. Even with the most favorable interpretation, we were being told, Give us sovereignty over East Jerusalem—effectively all of East Jerusalem including the Jewish neighborhoods—and then you can decide the annexation and the swap. We might be able to produce on borders and territory for Barak, but it would come at an unacceptable price to him.

Still, if we took the charitable interpretation—Saeb's interpretation—we could say we had gotten a serious counterproposal from the Palestinians. That was the most I wanted to say, but in this case my caution and misgivings were overruled: Everyone—the President, Sandy, Madeleine, Rob—wanted to cast this as a major move. Everyone wanted to portray it as a decision that was qualified but one that allowed us to decide the size of territorial annexation and the swap.

Again, I felt we needed to claim less, but three factors overrode my hesitancy. First, Barak's foreboding letter: he was so down that to go to him with less than a decisive answer on territory would change nothing. (In this case, if Barak was simply trying to shock us, he went overboard in a way that did not serve his interest.) Second, Saeb's interpretation: it seemed to be a clear-cut trade-off: give us what we want on Jerusalem and you get what you want on territory; it was close to what Shlomo had originally told Abu Ala and appeared to set up a negotiation in which each side's position could be refined. And third, Gamal reported a conversation he had with one of Arafat's bodyguards. According to this account, Arafat had blown up at Abu Mazen and Abed Rabbo when they suggested offering no more than 1 or 2 percent of the territory as the appropriate response to Clinton. Supposedly, Arafat shouted that "you will make me look ridiculous to both the American and Israeli sides." Taking all these factors together, we reached the conclusion that this was real and the President could now go to Barak with something meaningful in hand.

Given his nature, the President was not going to undersell what he had, and he didn't. The President wanted a deal—we all did. He told Barak that Arafat gave him the discretion to determine the territory and as a result "Arafat will come very close to meeting your territorial needs, by which I take it will be somewhere between 8 and 10 percent. He wants a swap, but only a symbolic one. He said if I think it is fair, he will think it is fair." The President noted other Arafat desiderata: not wanting the Israelis between his state and Jordan; being treated like other Arab leaders in terms of having independent borders with their neighbors; ending the conflict only after everything was implemented, not simply declared and agreed; and, a package that included an acceptable outcome on Jerusalem.

I was not with the President when he made this presentation to Barak; the model of his going alone with Bruce as the note-taker continued to be applied. I was troubled later when Bruce read me the notes, particularly because it left Barak with the impression that Arafat had agreed to no less than 8 percent annexation for the settlement blocs, and with little emphasis on the qualifiers that were applied to this figure. (And here I still had my doubts about how real Arafat's acceptance of 8 percent and our "discretion" was.) Upon hearing Bruce's readout, I knew that I should have objected more strenuously to portraying Arafat's response as meeting Barak on the territory, if for no other reason than to get the President to qualify what he would say to Barak.

There was another reason I felt this. There were few secrets between the Israelis and Palestinians at Camp David; both Dahlan and Rashid shared nearly everything with Yossi, and I did not think that Yossi held back much from them. Maybe they would keep their own ideas from other members of their delegations, but to think that they would not share an Arafat letter to the President was an illusion. Sooner or later Barak would know what Arafat had written. A verbal understanding was one thing; a letter another. When Barak saw it or had it described by Yossi, he would know the President was overselling what we had.

Maybe the tendency to focus on deal-making and the big picture is endemic to a presidential summit of this sort. But the risk of perpetuating the ambiguity that leads to misunderstanding—and even a sense of betrayal—accompanies such a focus. And that was my worry now.

But we were where we were. Even with the best reading of the Arafat letter, we stood no chance of producing the territorial outcome Barak wanted without an answer on Jerusalem. I turned my sights to resolving that. Here there was a brick wall.

While the President was with Barak, Martin and I sat with Amnon and Yossi. We told them there had been a response from Arafat on territory that was serious, but they would have to wait to hear it from Barak, who was hearing it from the President even as we met. But, of course, they knew we would not solve the territory if we could not solve Jerusalem.

They responded by saying they understood this and had spent the last two days working with Mohammad Dahlan and Mohammad Rashid on Jerusalem. They were stuck. The two Mohammads, who were the most aware of Israeli needs, simply, in Yossi's words, did "not understand how critical, how important Jerusalem is to us."

Yossi had mentioned to me earlier that he thought maybe if the Palestinians could gain sovereignty over the Muslim Quarter in the Old City, that could solve their problem. (Gilad had mentioned the same idea to Rob.) I now asked Amnon if he thought Israel could accept that. He said, "No, it won't work."

We left the meeting and I said to Martin, We'd better think of ways to compensate the Palestinians for what they won't be able to get from the Israelis on Jerusalem. I told him what occurs to me is that we could tell Arafat the American embassy will be built in the part of Abu Dis that extends into the current municipal boundaries of East Jerusalem.* That would be a big symbol for Arafat. I said in addition the President could lead an international delegation that Arafat could host and take to the Haram, again symbolizing for the world, especially the Arab world, Palestinian control.

Maybe, I went on, if you add that to Palestinian sovereignty in specified neighborhoods in East Jerusalem, functional autonomy in the inner neighborhoods, shared responsibilities in the Old City, an office for Arafat in the Old City, special sovereign corridors to the Old City, and jurisdiction over the Haram/Temple Mount, that will do it. But I still had my doubts, telling Martin as we decided to call it a night that if Israel

---

*Most of Abu Dis was outside the municipal boundaries of East Jerusalem, but there was a small corner of a few hundred meters that crossed the municipal border.

must retain exclusive sovereignty over the Temple Mount, I am afraid we need to come up with something else to add to the symbolic and legal weight of the Palestinians in the Old City and their holy sites.

Jon Schwartz and Gamal were about to do precisely that.

| DAY 7 |

Gamal came into my cabin at seven-thirty in the morning saying he could not sleep at night because Jon had come up with a possibility and he had thought about how it could be sold to the Palestinians. Jon had discovered that after the 1967 war the Israelis had offered to give UN personnel diplomatic status and immunities in the holy sites in Jerusalem. Jon's thought was to resurrect that idea and give the holy sites, under Palestinian jurisdiction, the status of a diplomatic mission or of a foreign embassy. Technically speaking, while the Israelis would retain sovereignty over the land, they could not enter these sites unless the Palestinians accepted their doing so. As with any foreign mission, the Palestinians would have a sovereign-like status that was inviolable, even while the Israelis preserved symbolic sovereignty.

Gamal suggested we take Jon's idea and have Israel confer this status on the five permanent members of the UN Security Council (the Perm 5) and have the Perm 5 then grant the Palestinians a permanent custodianship over the Haram. I liked the terminology, especially since it seemed to give the Palestinians the same status over the Haram as the Saudis had over the holy places of Mecca and Medina. Gamal was very enthusiastic, and certain we could sell this to the Palestinians. I agreed that it might just work, particularly if combined with other steps designed to create international recognition of the Palestinians in at least a part of East Jerusalem.

We met with the President at around nine-thirty in the morning. By that time, I had met with Jon and we had refined the idea. To make it work, we would need Israel to finalize a deal with the Perm 5 plus the Vatican and Morocco, the chair of the Jerusalem Committee of the Organization of the Islamic Conference (OIC).* This international committee would then confer the status of "permanent custodian" on the new Palestinian state.

Ironically, while we were developing this idea, several members of the Israeli team

---

*The Organization of the Islamic Conference joins all Muslim countries in a political coalition to advocate for Muslim interests in international organizations. The OIC is composed of several bodies, which include four standing committees devoted to Information and Cultural Affairs, Economic and Trade Cooperation, Scientific and Technological Affairs, and Jerusalem, Al-Quds.

had come up with a similar idea. They were looking to give the Palestinians a sovereign-like status in the Muslim Quarter for Arafat's office and they came up with the idea of it having the status of a diplomatic mission. Though similar as a principle, our idea was geared to the Temple Mount/Haram. I suggested to the President that he go first to Barak *not* to present the custodian idea but to see if he could sell Barak the rest of the package on Jerusalem: sovereignty in specified outer neighborhoods; functional autonomy in the inner neighborhoods to include planning and zoning and security; and shared responsibilities in the Old City. If he could, then we needed to develop a package we could present to Arafat. That package should initially be presented without the custodian idea. I wanted to hold back the custodian idea, believing that together with our embassy being in East Jerusalem and the President leading an international delegation to be hosted by Arafat, this might be the sweetener that would help close the deal at the end.

But first we needed to see if Barak would buy the rest of the Jerusalem ideas. And in his meeting with the President, he did not. Barak resisted planning and zoning and security in the inner neighborhoods; moreover, before we did any more on Jerusalem, Barak wanted to discuss the Jerusalem ideas with his team and come back to us. He saw me as he was leaving the meeting with the President and told me that he could not afford for us to make any further concessions to the Palestinians without getting something more from them.

I mentioned this to the President, and he felt we must wait for Barak to come back to us before proceeding with the Palestinians. Since President Clinton had not raised the custodian idea with Barak, I told him I would go to "his guys" and sell an idea that was close to what they were already considering.

Unfortunately, I could not have meetings with any Israelis as Barak brought his team together, making them unavailable. While we were informed their session would last for a few hours, the few hours stretched into all day. We were on hold. The President, taking Barak's admonition not to offer any further "concessions" to the Palestinians, felt we could not at this point go over new ideas with them. So we were meeting neither with Israelis nor Palestinians.

All told, we waited thirteen hours for the Israelis to come out of their meeting. While I had seen Shlomo when he came out briefly to get food, he was closemouthed, saying only that this was a "very high-quality meeting in which the whole team is expressing its views on everything." High-quality or not, Barak was acting as if no one else was at Camp David. We kept Arafat on hold, with the President preferring to postpone seeing him until he had something else to say. If we were going to sell Arafat a package on Jerusalem, we needed him to feel that we were not simply cooking it up with Barak. We needed not to play on his suspicions or make him feel as if he were being taken for granted. As usual, Barak was either underestimating or misreading the impact of his behavior on others.

Finally, around midnight, the President's anger and impatience reached a peak, and he insisted we break up the Israelis' meeting. We were then informed that Barak would come shortly to see the President. But then another thirty minutes went by, and we got word that a medic had gone to Dogwood, Barak's cabin. We learned that Barak had choked on a peanut and required the Heimlich maneuver to be able to resume breathing. Getting that word defused the President's anger—but not by much and not for long.

When Barak arrived, he brought Shlomo and Dani with him, and so Sandy, the Secretary, and I remained with the President. Barak presented us with a paper that he wanted us to present to the Palestinians as our own. Not only did it pose questions as if the Palestinians had a test they must pass, but it walked back some of the key moves Shlomo had made. Now, instead of 10.5 percent, the territory to be annexed was 11.3 percent; now, instead of at least three villages in the current municipal boundaries of East Jerusalem to become part of sovereign Al-Quds, it was one village. On almost every issue there was a retreat. This is what Barak had put us on hold for thirteen hours to do.

The President blew up. "You kept us and Arafat waiting all day and you want me to present something less than what Shlomo presented as our idea? I won't do it. I just won't do it. I would have no credibility. I can't go see Arafat with a retrenchment. You want to present these ideas directly to Arafat, to the Palestinians, you go ahead and see if you can sell it. There is no way I can. This is not real. This is not serious. I went to Shepherdstown and was told nothing by you for four days. I went to Geneva and felt like a wooden Indian doing your bidding." With his voice rising and his face red, he shouted, "I will not let it happen here. I will simply not do it."

Barak was initially very low-key in his response. He spoke in a very soft voice, saying that these decisions went to the very heart of Israel's well-being, its security, and its very life. He had a responsibility to be very careful and he could not continue to play Arafat's game of manipulation. As he went on, Barak became more and more emotional. He found the way the Palestinians negotiate to be completely outrageous; their behavior should not be tolerated. He said we would not tolerate such behavior in children.

It was now the President's turn to soften. He had sympathy for Barak's predicament, and conveyed that. (Clinton's anger never lasted for long; it was always genuine, not done for effect.)

We had talked before Barak's arrival for the meeting about the President not committing to what Barak wanted out of this meeting. We had anticipated that he would ask the President to sell some ideas to Arafat on Jerusalem; we did not know he wanted us to walk back on Shlomo's ideas. But in anticipation of being asked to sell Barak's

ideas as our own, we had persuaded the President to tell Barak he would need to caucus with his team and then get back to him.

In fact, after asking if I had some questions for Barak about the Israeli paper,
which I did, the President adjourned the meeting, telling Barak he would call him
when he had considered the best way to proceed. It was now about two-thirty in the
morning. After some venting on what Barak had asked us to do, we settled on the idea
of going to Arafat in the morning with questions we would pose to him on what he
could do on Jerusalem. At three-thirty, the President called Barak and he came back for
a meeting that he held one-on-one with note-takers on the back patio of Aspen. Sandy,
Madeleine, and I sat in the tent area across from the front of Aspen while we waited for
the meeting to finish. At about four-fifteen in the morning they got up, and then as
they walked toward us Barak took the President alone to the side for another fifteen
minutes. Madeleine, exasperated, asked what could he possibly be saying now? "Simple,"
I replied, "he saw us and is telling the President not to reveal what they have just decided."

We went inside with the President and he confirmed what I'd told Madeleine, by
noting that Barak had softened and did not require us to present his questions; we
could proceed however we felt best with Arafat, including asking hypothetical questions on Jerusalem—but he asked the President not to reveal their conversation to anyone. It was now after four-thirty in the morning, and the President asked me to draft
our impressions of what Barak could do on Jerusalem and some hypothetical questions
that he could use with Arafat later in the morning.

Since I felt we now had to lean forward, especially after having had Arafat cool his
heels for the entire preceding day, I drafted an approach to Arafat that went beyond the
package I had envisioned the night before. Now I posed the following question: If he
could get sovereignty over the outer neighborhoods, sovereignty over the Muslim
Quarter in the Old City, and the custodial role over the holy sites, would he be prepared to proceed on that basis? I did not mention the inner neighborhoods, but I was
now signaling that he could get sovereignty over one neighborhood in the Old City
and I was introducing the custodial idea. I was worried that we had lost a day, and we
had to bring things to a head, especially given Barak's mind-set. We needed to show
movement on Jerusalem or we were going nowhere. That was my thinking, and I
would present that to the President at ten in the morning—four hours from the time
I fell into bed to finish day 7.

| DAY 8 |

I went to breakfast before going to brief the President. I was uneasy. I believed we
had to go ahead with the hypothetical questions on Jerusalem to Arafat. But I knew

Arafat's tactic was working—we kept moving toward him without much movement from him. Barak kept becoming more suspicious of us. As Yossi joined me for breakfast, I asked whether it was possible to change the dynamic of the summit. I told Yossi I was concerned that neither Arafat nor Barak was engaging directly with each other or representatives of the other side. For Arafat, that meant never really understanding the limits of what Barak could do. For Barak, it meant being spared exposure to Palestinian concerns—instead he got them only indirectly either from us or from members of his team. In either case, he viewed what he was hearing as colored by our respective tendencies to be taken in by the Palestinian sense of victimhood.

Thinking out loud, I asked Yossi whether he thought it might help if he and Rashid were to go together to meet Barak and Arafat separately, spelling out clearly what was possible and impossible on each side. This would be one way for each leader to hear something from the other from a source he respected. If done right, it could also show Arafat was trying to meet Barak's needs but also had his own on Jerusalem and the other issues. Yossi shook his head, saying, "Dennis, it won't work. Ehud won't accept anything he does not hear directly from Arafat." But he won't meet Arafat, I replied, given his fear that Arafat will remain mute and he (Barak) will have his positions recorded and somehow made formal. Yossi shrugged, saying, "You are right."

That got me nowhere, but I still felt we needed to change the dynamic through a direct private exchange involving the two leaders. As I was still pondering this with Yossi, I got a message that the President was ready for me. I went to see the President, outlining my questions and hypothetical approach toward Arafat on Jerusalem. I told him, "This is very forward-leaning on Jerusalem, but I don't see us moving with less than this for Arafat and I don't see Barak responding if we don't have some sign that Arafat is prepared to meet him partway on Jerusalem."

The President accepted the questions, believing it was consistent with his understanding with Barak from their last meeting. We would now be introducing, as a hypothetical, sovereignty in at least one part of the Old City as well as the custodial idea. I was uneasy, knowing Arafat's tendency to pocket, but we were hitting the wall, and as Sandy kept reminding us, the President was scheduled to leave the next day.

Unfortunately, the President got nowhere with Arafat. Arafat would accept nothing but sovereignty for all of East Jerusalem. He could not be in a position where he transformed Israeli occupation of East Jerusalem and the Haram into Israeli sovereignty. He could not be seen as sanctioning this. Now it looked like we were stuck and would fail.

As the President briefed us on Arafat's reaction, he asked me was there anything else we could do. I could think of only one thing that might work, and that was, as I put it, some "shock treatment." I proposed that I go to the back channel representatives on each side and tell them that the President was fed up and ready to call it a day. I had some ideas that might save the summit if each could accept them, but if the President did not hear something new in the next two hours, he was ready to declare the summit over. Without even asking what I was going to tell each side, the President told me to go for it.

I went to Amnon's cabin, where Amnon, Shlomo, Yossi and the two Mohammads tended to hang out. I saw Amnon and Shlomo and told them we were at the end of the road. Nothing was working; Barak's performance yesterday made it much harder with Arafat because we kept him sitting around for thirteen hours. The meeting this morning had not gone well—no surprise. The President was now ready to declare the summit a failure. The only thing I could think to do was to suggest a package on Jerusalem and go for broke. This was my personal view and did not represent a U.S. position. I did not know if they could accept it, but the key elements were as follows:

—The outer neighborhoods would get Palestinian sovereignty;
—The inner neighborhoods would get meaningful self-government, including planning and zoning, security, and dispute resolution responsibility;
—In the Old City, the Palestinians would get sovereignty over the Muslim and Christian Quarters;
—On the Haram, the Palestinians would get custodianship.

I knew that neither Shlomo nor Amnon was too pleased with this because it went beyond what they thought it was possible to sell. (They had reluctantly accepted Palestinian sovereignty over the Muslim Quarter, something Yossi had raised, but even Yossi had not thought of going beyond that to include the Christian Quarter. My thinking was that the Christian and Muslim Quarters represented almost half of the Old City geographically, but were home to the vast majority of the Arab population—and Arafat was always talking about the Christian sites.) But rather than get into a debate over it, Amnon and Shlomo took the two-hour deadline seriously and went off to tell Barak. Just as they got up to leave, Mohammad Dahlan and Mohammad Rashid arrived with Yossi. I repeated what I had just told Amnon and Shlomo, emphasizing this was my personal view and did not represent a U.S. position. They, too, did not stay around to debate; they went off to see Arafat.

The next several hours were maddening. Neither side came back to us. But they did meet with each other. Shlomo tried out ideas that did not go as far as mine, but went further than what he had previously presented to the Palestinians. The main differences between the ideas I presented and his were that he did not give the Palestinians sovereignty over the Christian Quarter in the Old City and Palestinian responsibilities in the inner neighborhoods were a little more limited. I found this out when Shlomo called me and told me he had presented to the Palestinians ideas close to mine but more acceptable to Barak. I did not see why the Palestinians would accept something less than what I'd presented and told Shlomo so.

But, in truth, that did not matter. The Palestinians were tied completely in knots and at war with each other. Those who were negative throughout—Abed Rabbo and Arafat's advisor, Akram Haniya—opposed any compromise at this point. Dahlan and Rashid, with Hassan Asfour, apparently fought for at least a response. Others like Abu Mazen, Abu Ala, Saeb, and Nabil looked for where Arafat was coming from. And the Chairman remained mute. In the end, the Palestinians responded neither to Shlomo's ideas nor to mine.

Having tried to shock both sides and having only succeeded in tying the Palestinians in knots, we had two choices: tell both sides we were left with no choice but to call an end to the summit (and work with both on an appropriate statement announcing this—something that might yet move them to find a way out) or seek a more limited agreement and a more limited outcome to the summit. The latter was not necessarily inconsistent with the tactics of saying we were now calling an end to the summit.

The President saw Barak and presented him with the two choices. The more limited agreement would defer Jerusalem but seek agreement on everything else. Barak, of course, had originally preferred such an approach, but the more he focused on the "end of conflict," the more he became wedded to doing a full deal with no outstanding issues or claims.

Initially, Barak reacted to the President by saying it might work. But the more he thought about it, the more he felt that deferring Jerusalem would not work. He asked the President to give him a little more time to think about it. Clinton granted this.

An hour later, Barak called and asked to see the President alone. After the meeting, the President was clearly buoyant, but asked that only Sandy, Madeleine, John Podesta, and I remain in the room. He said, This is really sensitive, but I got a lot from Barak. Barak had finally presented his bottom lines, but he wanted the President to present these to Arafat as points he (the President) would try to get from Barak. On territory, he would go to 9 percent annexation in the West Bank with a 1 percent swap opposite Gaza; the Palestinians would get 85 percent of the border with Jordan. On Jerusalem, he would accept our idea of the Muslim and Christian Quarters being under Palestinian sovereignty, and seven out of eight or nine of the outer neighborhoods being under Palestinian sovereignty; the inner neighborhoods would have planning and zoning, security, and law enforcement powers. On the Haram, Arafat would get custodianship. On security, Israeli needs would be met, and there would be an international presence, and Israel would have control of the Jordan Valley for fewer than twelve years. Finally, on refugees, there would be a satisfactory solution for both sides.

The President finished and asked, What do you think? I said, He wants a deal. I went on to say, We smoked him out by saying the only choice now is to end the summit or settle for a lesser deal. The pressure cooker worked on him, but will it work on Arafat? Mr. President, I continued, you got what you are going to get out of Barak, now you have to produce Arafat. You have to sell this using all the drama you can muster. No note-taker with Arafat. This has to be you and him. These ideas represent the best you can do. You have to say you stretched farther than you ever thought you would, and Barak will hate these ideas. But you are prepared to press him to accept because ultimately you believe this is fair for both. This is a historic moment for Arafat; he must seize it. This moment won't come again with you; "there won't be a better president for Arafat and there won't be a better Israeli government for him—tell him he cannot afford to lose both of you."

The President listened to me and then simply said, "I got it." He asked to see Arafat alone. Gamal was there to interpret. Arafat came alone to Aspen. We retreated from the living room to the kitchen. Rob and Bruce joined us in the kitchen and then went into the pantry. From the pantry way they were able to listen through the crack in the swinging door that opened into the living room. Initially, I chose not to try to squeeze into that area with them. After about thirty minutes, Rob came in and gave a thumbs-down sign. But he said the President is really trying, leaning right up in Arafat's face, pointing, talking about what is at stake, the money we might be able to get for him, our relationship, what could be lost, etc.

I mused with John Podesta that Arafat may simply not be up to making a deal. He is a revolutionary; he has made being a victim an art form; he can't redefine himself into someone who must end all claims and truly end the conflict.

I finally decided to go and listen through the door as well. With Rob, Bruce, and me leaning up against the swinging door, I had the image of the Marx Brothers movie where people keep going into a tiny stateroom on a ship and suddenly the door crashes open and they all pour out of the room. I whispered this and we all smiled, straining not to laugh lest we make a sound. For whatever reason, at this point Arafat's mood seemed to change. He stopped resisting and said he would consider everything the President said and come back with an answer. The President had asked him to come back and tell him whether he would accept the President's ideas as "the basis to conclude a deal."

The President suggested that Arafat either come back to him directly or go through Gamal with his answer or with any questions. The President and Gamal walked Arafat out. Both the President and Gamal were hopeful. The President described the meeting, saying that when he first presented the ideas Arafat's initial reaction was to say these are "just ideas that Dennis Ross has cooked up with Barak." The President said he told him, "Like hell, I have worked very hard for this, you don't want it, you won't get anything close to it." The President then joked that he worked the custodian idea very hard and Gamal was so emotional trying to sell it, "that I was ready to sign up to custodianship myself."

It was now 1 a.m., and our mood had once again shifted from doom and gloom to hope. I decided that there was no point in staying up and waiting for the Palestinians to come with a response; instead, I went to bed, thinking it was better to get whatever sleep I could before being awakened. I did not expect to get much.

| DAY 9 |

As it happened, I was not awakened until 7:30 a.m.—with a call from Bruce saying the President was going to meet Arafat at nine, and we would have a prebrief in about a half hour. Bruce also told me that things had not gone well during the night. Summarizing, he said that the Palestinians had initially come back to Gamal with a number of questions, including what was the meaning of custodianship for the Haram, who would have sovereignty? Since the Palestinians would have sovereignty over 85 percent of the length of their border with Jordan, would Israel have control or sovereignty over the remaining 15 percent? What was meant by a satisfactory solution to the refugee problem? Why were only seven or eight of the outer neighborhoods going to get sovereignty and not all nine? What happened to the exchange in size and value in reference to the 9 percent annexation and the 1 percent swap? Gamal had gone back to the Palestinians with answers after Rob, he, and Sandy had worked them out. Then the Palestinians had come back and said since President Clinton needed to leave to go to Asia, we should take a two-week break during which Arafat could consult with Arab leaders. The Sandy-led group response was that there would be no break; we needed an answer on the U.S. ideas: Were they a basis for concluding an agreement, yes or no. The answer came back "no."

I was stunned that I had not been awakened. Neither had Madeleine. I called the Secretary to tell her what had happened so she would know before going to the meeting with the President. She was furious. That she had not been awakened made her angry. That I had not been awakened left her incredulous. How, she asked, could they develop any answers without going to you? I had no response.

I was angry, but also philosophical. I did not know that my responses would have

been different, especially because I knew Barak, having stretched so far, would probably pull everything off the table if he thought the Palestinians were once again taking a
bottom line and simply trying to get more out of him. Still, I thought, some of the
questions, even as Bruce described them, were interesting. Knowing that the Palestinians would be suspicious that anything we presented would have been cleared with
Barak—and knowing that they would want to put their own imprint on these ideas—
I suspected the questions could have been a tactic on the part of some in Arafat's delegation to try to get to "yes" or at least to give something other than a negative response.
Questions like, would Israel have sovereignty or control on the 15 percent of the border with Jordan that would not be Palestinian, or why wouldn't all the outer neighborhoods of Jerusalem become sovereign Palestinian territory, provided a possible basis for
discussion with the Palestinians. If they were part of a game to whittle down what we
had presented, we were not going anywhere. But if they were a clever approach to get
Arafat hooked on the ideas as the basis, we needed to explore this possibility. We could
tell Barak the Palestinians had questions and we were dealing with them—but would
only come back to him if the Palestinians had accepted these ideas as the basis of a settlement. Now, however, the possibility of testing the meaning of the Palestinian questions had apparently been lost, without my having a shot at it.

But there was no need for me to get angry with anyone, the Secretary's anger was
sufficient for both. She blew up at Sandy, whose response was that he assumed that with
Gamal involved, she and I had been kept informed. Gamal's explanation was that Sandy
had determined who was involved and Sandy wanted to work quickly and not expand
the circle. Rob simply apologized, saying he had known there would be a problem.

At this point, I was less concerned about being left out and more concerned with
the survival of the summit. However we had gotten here, the fact was that the Palestinians had turned down the package of ideas as the basis for a deal. I asked, as we gathered for the meeting, whether they had understood that a basis did not mean they had
to accept everything as is. And Gamal said he had spent a lot of time explaining what
was meant by basis—and they had still turned it down.

It was obvious that we were in serious trouble. In the 9 a.m. briefing with the President, Sandy took the lead and was backed by Madeleine in saying that Arafat was
blowing it and had to know that. Both said we must be very tough with Arafat now.

The President turned to me, looking for the words that might move Arafat now.
Arafat, I said, needs to know that you feel Barak has been prepared to move very far,
and he has not. While you had promised him that you would not blame anyone if the
summit did not succeed, that was based on the assumption of both sides making a
good-faith effort. You could not say that Arafat had done that. As such, if the summit
ends now, you will publicly have to put the onus on him.

Additionally, I suggested the President make one personal point and one larger historical point. Personally, "tell him you have done more for Arafat than anyone else internationally, and now stretched farther than you thought possible to produce a dignified deal for the Palestinians. You would make no more efforts for him."

Historically, you must put what was now happening in the larger context of Palestinians always rejecting what they should have accepted: "Tell Arafat that there is not a single member of his delegation who does not believe that saying 'no' in 1948 had not been a historic mistake for the Palestinians; Arafat himself has told us that he was prevented by the Syrians and the Soviets from accepting the original Camp David deal in 1978 when there were only 5,000 settlers in the West Bank and the Palestinians could have vetoed there being any more; don't have the next generation of Palestinians regret another historic 'no' that has left them much worse off." I concluded by saying, Mr. President, tell Arafat that in 1948 there was "nothing you could have done; in 1978, you were prevented from acting; today, this is your decision."

The President said he understood what he had to do. Sandy suggested that the Secretary join the President for the meeting with Arafat and that he and I go to see Barak in the meantime to brief him on what had happened.

With Barak, all the emotion of his meeting with Clinton the other night came pouring out: "Arafat was never serious, never a partner." Politically, in Israel, now he would have no choice but to go to a national unity government, though he might be too weak for that as he would be charged with jeopardizing the country with his concessions; if Arafat is not prepared to accept our ideas as the basis, then a confrontation is inevitable.

When I explored the possibility of a limited agreement consisting only of an agreement on statehood and then negotiating the rest of the issues—borders, settlements, security, refugees, and Jerusalem—as juridical equals, Barak was emphatic, saying, "No way." I could neither get him to consider an alternative to confrontation nor give me an explanation as to why he could not accept "a statehood for continuing negotiations outcome."

We regrouped at Aspen and heard about the President's meeting with Arafat. Arafat had not budged, and as the President told me, "he simply blew off the argument on 1948 and today." The President was not surprised by Barak's reaction—Clinton now felt that Barak was justified in feeling this way. Before deciding to call it quits, Clinton felt I should join Madeleine and take one more run at Arafat—either to see if we could move him on the President's ideas or at least get him to accept that we might forge agreement on all issues but defer Jerusalem.

In Arafat's cabin—with just Saeb and Nabil Abu Rudeina joining him—the Chairman said no to both. While telling him he had to find a way to say yes, I said,

"Let's be more precise. What if we can work out agreement on everything, including most of the Jerusalem issues, but defer only the Haram or the Old City? You would preserve your positions on these, not surrender your claims, and the negotiations could continue."

Again, he said no; when I asked him what he lost with such an approach, he got angry, saying these were not only his "claims, but Indonesia, Pakistan, Malaysia—" Madeleine cut him off, saying he was "blowing it," he had done nothing here to reach an agreement. In turn, Arafat got very emotional, asking her if she wanted to go to his funeral; what about her assurance letter at Sharm? She had not lived up to her assurances. This was a non sequitur, but he was angry now and so was the Secretary.

Saeb tried to intervene, saying enormous progress has been made, "let's keep negotiating. We need more time, have Dennis come out to the region for two weeks." Madeleine said, We are done playing your games, and she stalked out.

I followed Madeleine out of the room but didn't leave the cabin. Saeb came up to me and pleaded for us not to give up. In a tone of sorrow, not anger, I explained that the President had gone as far as he could; if the Palestinians were not prepared to accept what the President had presented as the basis, they could only save the summit by raising some new ideas directly with the Israelis. Absent that, "we are out of business."

I was not trying to manipulate Saeb. The summit was about to collapse. The President had made his best effort, and now so had Barak. Arafat had said no to everything. I was appealing to Saeb to save the situation by offering a new idea that would convince Barak—or at least those around him—that all was not lost.

Saeb asked, What about the close-in (Jerusalem) neighborhoods becoming A areas? Probing his thinking, I asked him why the Israelis would find this interesting, and he answered, Because for now it means that we get only "jurisdiction, not sovereignty." I suggested he try this on the Israelis. He listened and then asked if I had any other ideas. Saeb, I replied, the ball is in your court, not ours. The President won't accept any other ideas unless they come from you. He nodded, but again asked, "Do you have any ideas?" Like me, Saeb was grasping for any possibilities. So I told him, Why not try the following for the Haram and the close-in neighborhoods. For the Haram, have Palestinian sovereignty above ground and Israeli sovereignty below ground; you need sovereignty over the surface, they need it underground where the Temple was. For the close-in neighborhoods, why not have a referendum to determine their ultimate disposition, say ten or fifteen years down the road. That way the Israelis can say they preserved their sovereignty and yet Palestinians can feel they would eventually get it. Each of these ideas could meet both sides' essential needs, I said, but I offer these to you as possible ways out; don't present them as my ideas, the President has had it and isn't prepared for us to offer anything more.

Saeb listened but did not respond, and I left and returned to Aspen. The President was sitting around the table with Sandy, Madeleine, and John Podesta. I described my conversation with Saeb, mentioning his idea on the close-in neighborhoods and noting that indicated that the Palestinians did have some ideas.

I was not ready to give up. Quoting the President's words to Abu Ala earlier the week, "Let's satisfy ourselves that we did everything we could," I suggested that the President host one from each side, see if some new ideas could be put on the table that could be taken back to Barak, after which the President should bring Barak and Arafat together. Madeleine was the only one who supported this, feeling that we could not end the summit without the two leaders having a serious, substantive meeting.

The President said this made sense, but he wanted first to make calls to President Mubarak, Crown Prince Abdullah of Saudi Arabia, King Abdullah of Jordan, and President Ben Ali of Tunisia. He hoped they might move Arafat. Given Barak's sensitivities that we not expose what he had been prepared to accept, the President was not going to brief them on the ideas he had presented to Arafat. Rather, he was going to ask them to press Arafat to defer Jerusalem but try to resolve everything else. While I doubted this could work, Sandy thought this was the only way to rescue the summit.

The next several hours were spent largely sitting around Aspen waiting for the calls to be connected and conducted. While all the Arab heads of state said they would see what they could do, only King Abdullah and President Ben Ali were actually willing to be helpful. Each said they would call Arafat and urge him to accept deferral. Ben Ali told the President that Arafat was deeply afraid to make a decision and he might need more time. In fact, the Palestinian delegation seemed increasingly desperate and fearful at this point—wanting us to rescue them but not capable of doing anything on their own. The ideas I'd given Saeb were lifelines they could not grasp.

Yossi Ginossar went to Arafat's cabin and found him sitting alone, paralyzed and desperate. I reported this to the President, and it was decided that the President should go see Arafat and make one last effort to see if he would accept a deferral option. He did see him, but again got nowhere—indeed, this time he heard an outrageous new mythology, "Solomon's Temple was not in Jerusalem, but Nablus." Arafat was challenging the core of Jewish faith, and seeking to deny Israel any claim in the Old City.

We decided that the President should talk to Barak about not making a confrontation the inevitable course of action. There was obviously an option between total peace and total confrontation. We heard that Barak had gone to Laurel to eat and the Secretary and I headed down there. She sat with Barak and began to work on him, urging him to keep the process going and not bring it to a crashing end. Then the President arrived and sat alone with Barak for over half an hour. (Afterward the President told us he had said to Barak: "You are smarter than me and you are experienced in war and I am not. But I am more experienced than you in politics and there are several things I have learned. The most important is don't corner your adversaries and don't corner yourself; always leave yourself a way out. Don't lock yourself into a losing option.")

While the President was sitting with Barak, Hassan Asfour came to me with a complaint and a suggestion. First, Hassan told me what I had suspected: "You made a big mistake by not seizing our questions about what the President had presented to Arafat." You should have engaged us on the border, the number of Jerusalem neighborhoods to get sovereignty, your ideas on refugees. "We knew these were Israeli ideas and this was our way of proceeding with them. You know us, why didn't you understand this?" When I did not respond, he continued, saying, Okay, you did not pick up on our initial way of dealing with the ideas, here's another way to do so: let the international community deal with the sovereignty question on the Haram/Temple Mount and treat the rest of the ideas as a basis.

While close to the deferral option, it was actually more interesting. It preserved the whole package but internationalized the sovereignty question on the sensitive issue of the Haram/Temple Mount. I knew that Barak might resist it on the grounds that he was not getting what he needed on the Temple Mount but was making key concessions on everything else. Still, it was a creative way to defuse the hardest issue. I told Hassan I would see what I could do.

I told the President about the conversation after he finished talking to Barak. He agreed I should try it out on Barak, and I did so. Predictably, Barak did not like it; he was not ready to concede everything else if he did not have at least nominal sovereignty over the Temple Mount. Nonetheless, he said he would think about it.

Shortly after this conversation, he phoned the President and, as we were to find out later, suggested the following approach: both sides would remain at Camp David while the President went to Asia for the G-8 summit. There would be a one-on-one discussion to work out a formula on the Temple Mount/Haram; there would be only informal discussions between the two sides until such a formula was developed; once it was, there would be formal talks again with the President's ideas as the basis. The President agreed and said he would present this to Arafat.

This call took place while I was at Barak's cabin, talking with Amnon and Oded. None of us knew this call was going on, but both told me nearly the whole delegation had been working on Barak to stay at least another day. None wanted to race off to a confrontation.

I came back to report this conversation, and the President briefed our group in general terms on his talk with Barak. It was time to go see Arafat, but before we did

Sandy insisted that we needed Barak's promise to stay for the whole time the President was gone—"it would be a disaster for Barak to spend the night and leave after the President was gone." At Sandy's urging, the President called Barak and said he was about to go see Arafat but needed Barak's assurance that he would stay until the President returned. Barak agreed.

The President saw Arafat and told him that he had persuaded Barak to stay until he returned from Asia to attempt one-on-one discussions until a formula on the Haram was worked out. The President said the Israelis would be "tight" on everything unless there was such a formula. This was a loose way of describing what had been agreed with Barak, but was consistent with the way he had described his conversation to us.

Unfortunately, in describing his conversation this way, the President made no reference to his "ideas"—what he had presented to Arafat and the Palestinians had rejected—being the basis for everything but the Haram. I was in the Arafat meeting, but had no reason to refine what the President said. What was clear, however, was the palpable relief the Palestinians felt that the summit was not going to end.

During the course of the evening, everyone assumed that the summit was over. Barak had asked for the vans to be brought to ready the Israeli delegation's departure. When the Palestinians saw that, they did likewise. The vans sat packed outside Barak's and Arafat's cabins and opposite Aspen. But only the President was leaving this night. He would go to the G-8 summit in Okinawa and return in three days. We would all be staying. As Madeleine and I drove down with the President to his press conference to announce his departure and the continuation of the Camp David summit, I turned to the Secretary and said, "Beware of what you wish for."

| DAY 10 |

My foreboding turned out to be warranted. The President was gone but we had a problem. Barak and Arafat had completely different understandings of the basis on which the rest of us stayed.

Arafat felt there was no conditionality. Barak felt there was very clear conditionality. For Barak, the President's ideas provided the parameters for resolving all issues except the Haram/Temple Mount. Though he had told President Clinton that informal talks on the other issues could proceed, he was now not interested in pursuing a broader understanding until the formula on the Haram/Temple Mount was resolved—and he made this very clear to the Secretary and me.

When we saw Arafat, he explained he was ready to authorize formal or informal discussions between very small or larger groups. While Arafat made no mention of the

President's ideas, Nabil Sha'ath, Saeb, the two Mohammads, and even Abu Ala said they knew they had to respond because serious ideas were on the table.

In effect, they were acknowledging that they had not been serious yet and that the President's ideas were a basis—or rather a point of departure. Barak wanted them to be the basis for conclusion, meaning that some limited mutual changes might be possible for an agreement. Arafat's colleagues, however, were treating them as a starting point, meaning they all might be revised upward toward Palestinian needs.

Before seeing Barak again, we needed greater clarity on what the President and Barak had said to each other on the phone. Bruce had taken notes on the phone call. He went over his notes with us. Based on his record of the call, the President had agreed that his ideas were the basis for staying. But Barak agreed to accept informal discussions in parallel with the Haram talks, provided the President's ideas set the parameters for those discussions.

Recognizing the problem, Madeleine felt I should privately meet with Barak and try to persuade him of the value of having informal discussions on everything. I saw him alone and started by telling him that I understood that he had two concerns: first, that our ideas were his "roof," not his "ceiling," and, if anything, he wanted our ideas scaled back at least a little; and second, that he thought the process was unfair because "you feel you always have to give, and they don't." He nodded approvingly. I went on and said the problem now is that I believe the Palestinians are finally ready to do their part and you should see it in the discussions. I asked, "Why not test it?"

He said the test was their readiness to say yes or no to the President's ideas. If they cannot say yes, he said, "let the summit break over their no." He only listened when I replied that there is a chance to reach an agreement, but it will now require reconciling your need not to move further with their desire to talk and not feel they have been presented with a "take-it-or-leave-it proposition."

Barak was unmoved. A short while later, Shlomo, after speaking with Barak, reported that Barak was adamant that there be no discussions—informal or formal—lest Arafat once again wiggle out of a commitment he had made to Clinton.

We had spent the day going back and forth trying to start discussions, but this was bound to be a fruitless exercise. It was clear that Barak once again saw Arafat as acting in bad faith. We had to explain to him that there was a misunderstanding, and that Arafat had not been at fault, we were the ones who had been at fault. The Secretary told Barak this at 8 p.m. He was mortified.

He said he felt terrible. He did not want to put the Secretary in an embarrassing position. She said she would announce at dinner there had been some misunderstandings that were unfortunate, that informal discussions in the smallest possible groups should resume after dinner, but that for the duration of the President's absence the President's ideas would be off the table. She told the Prime Minister that way he would not have to feel bound by them. He nodded glumly, and we went off to dinner.

At dinner, Barak was extremely morose. He would not say a word, even when Dahlan tried to engage him in conversation. He told his delegation after dinner that he wanted there to be no discussion on Jerusalem and was against the security and border people meeting together. He was shutting down.

I talked to Shlomo and said it was ridiculous to re-create the circumstances that existed before Camp David when nothing could be discussed. They could not be here and not have discussions; he agreed and said nearly the whole Israeli team agreed with this. He would sit on his own with Saeb and Hassan. And that night other informal discussions began taking place.

| DAY 11 |

Ehud Barak remained closeted in his room, isolating himself from everyone, even those on his team. Dan Meridor and Shlomo told me they had never seen him so depressed. In talking with Martin, we surmised that he believed his tactics had failed, and now he understood that even further concessions would be necessary if there was to be an agreement. And that put him in a position where he might not be able to deliver what was agreed.

I was worried, but less so than Shlomo. He feared that Barak would walk away from everything that he had reluctantly been willing to accept. It was clear that little would be possible unless we could move the Palestinians to respond with something credible. Rob and I talked separately with Rashid and told him that it would now be impossible for us to move Barak any further; on the contrary, he might well retreat. We needed them to accept the President's ideas as the basis or it would be over.

Rashid told each of us that he was working on a letter from Arafat that would accept the President's ideas as a basis but would offer some modifications, like, for example, on land of 8 percent for the settlement blocs and 3 to 4 percent for the swap. But the letter never materialized and I set two tasks for us on this day. First, I asked the informal grouping of Amnon, Shlomo, and Mohammad Dahlan and Mohammad Rashid to try to come up with a package to save the day, and I gave them a paper that illustrated international precedents for finessing issues of sovereignty. Second, I directed our team to prepare fallback options that might be presented to the two sides. I asked Martin to outline our proposals on borders, security, and refugees, with either partial understandings on Jerusalem or a deferral of Jerusalem. I asked Aaron to do a general principles fallback—one in which the broad principles on each issue might be agreed but the specifics would still have to be negotiated. I was not optimistic but felt we had to try to produce whatever we could.

| DAY 12 |

The informal meetings between the two sides were continuing, and Amnon and Rashid, in particular, were talking about all issues. We were not a part of these discussions, believing that they might be more open with each other if they did not have an American "witness" present.

George Tenet arrived in the morning. George had been on standby, ready to come to Camp David if there was a point when we needed him. Both Dahlan and General Shlomo Yanai requested his presence, telling me they believed he could help resolve the security issues. I went down to brief him about where we were and what had been put on the table. He was astounded by what Barak had been willing to accept. He, too, wondered whether Barak could deliver what he had accepted, and asked incredulously, "Why hasn't Arafat accepted this?"

I said I was not sure, but there were several possibilities. The Haram was a genuine problem for Arafat and he really could not accept even nominal Israeli sovereignty over it. Or it could be a tactic, he is simply holding out to see what more he can get, and he will play this until he is convinced he has finally hit the wall; or, at the end of the day, he may not be up to it. He may not be able to accept anything less than getting everything. Ending the conflict may be too much for him. It requires too much personal redefinition. Indeed, I told George that Arafat has been defined by the image and reality of struggle. Could he really end grievances, end claims, and say it was now over? I had my doubts, particularly given his performance during the summit. "We never hear anything from him except old mythologies and now a new one. Did you know the Temple did not exist in Jerusalem but in Nablus?"

George just shook his head and asked, "What the hell do you want me to do with him?" I said the obvious point would be to focus on what he will lose. But I went on and said, I think we should try a little reverse psychology. "Time for a little jujitsu."

I suggested that George talk to Arafat about Barak's mood. Tell him the truth: that Barak thinks he has gone too far, and is probably now counting on Arafat to say no so he can back away from what he was willing to accept with the President. Say no now, and you let Barak off the hook. Say yes now, and you corner him. George said he would try it.

The plan for the day was now for George to see Arafat, after which the Secretary would take Arafat to her farm, located about twenty to twenty-five minutes away. The reason for taking Arafat outside was that Barak had indicated he wanted to visit the

Gettysburg battlefield.* Given the ground rules about the leaders not leaving, we could not let Barak leave unless Arafat was also allowed to leave Camp David for a period of time. Given Barak's mood, we felt it good for everyone to let him go.

In advance of that, we wanted to use George's presence to see if we could begin to re-engage Barak. Martin went to Barak's cabin to see if he could arrange a meeting for George with Barak. The answer was not immediately forthcoming—indeed Barak, as it turned out, would not see George until the evening. Martin did get to see Barak briefly, and Barak told him that we needed to tell Arafat that if he did not accept the President's ideas as the basis, we should tell him we would break relations with him. Martin had replied that doing so might not even be in Israel's interest. After all, if we did so, our ability then to affect Arafat would disappear. Martin asked, If there is a confrontation between the two of you, do you really want us to lose our ability to influence Arafat? Martin interpreted his response as indicating that this was more a tactic than a desired outcome on Barak's part. But the message Martin heard was one that Barak repeated to George when he saw him, and it was what he was conveying to others around the country in calls he was making. (We were now hearing back from people like Hillary Clinton and Bob Shrum, Gore's political advisor, who were receiving such calls from Barak.)

I was actually relieved to hear about these messages. It meant that he was reengaging, and he was playing his own game of tactics and manipulation.

I decided to try a new move. I asked the informal group of Amnon, Shlomo, Mohammad Dahlan, Mohammad Rashid, and Yossi Ginossar to join me at my cabin at 3 p.m. for an off-the-record discussion. I asked them to give me their impressions of where we were and what was possible before I offered any thoughts. Mohammad Dahlan spoke first, saying that the two key issues were territory and the Haram; Rashid said we have to find common ground, and he observed that even "God cannot create another Haram/Temple Mount." He talked of there being five options for resolving this, the most difficult of all issues: the Palestinians have sovereignty, the Israelis have it, neither has it, sovereignty is shared by the two, or a third party has it. Shlomo spoke of this "sacred mountain" and said there was a need to upgrade and legalize the control the Palestinians have today while also recognizing the Israeli "symbolic" connection to it. Amnon said he was not a religious person but even he felt that as an Israeli he could not be asked to "give up the dream" of the Temple. Because of that, he said, maybe it is best to defer the issue of the Haram/Temple Mount.

I asked whether deferral was an option, and Dahlan said that it was not. Quoting

*Camp David is situated in western Maryland, close to the state border with Pennsylvania, and less than an hour from Gettysburg.

what Rashid and Shlomo had said about it being a "sacred mountain," I asked what if we were to say this is a unique, sacred space, unlike any other in the world; as such, it should not be governed by traditional concepts of sovereignty. There would be local jurisdiction only.

No one grabbed this notion. So I tried another alternative: the Palestinians get religious and administrative sovereignty and Israel retains sovereignty in name only.

Here again, both sides were able to restrain their enthusiasm. We broke up at this point with all agreeing we would continue our discussion. Dahlan and Rashid left first. After they left, Amnon and Shlomo told me they were unhappy that I had tried out new ideas that went beyond the President's ideas. They felt I should not be doing so before we knew if the Palestinians were going to accept even those ideas.

I told them that it was clear that the President's idea of custodianship on the Haram would not work; it was clear we had to find a solution to that or we were going to fail. What I had done was consistent with the agreed idea of an informal way of exploring a possible formula for resolving the Haram/Temple Mount issue. That did not satisfy them, and they said they would not report this meeting to Barak. Later Yossi told me I had embarrassed his two friends by raising new ideas. Puzzled, I asked, "What's going on? How else are we going to overcome the difference now?"

Yossi explained that there had been "a story in the Israeli press today accusing Amnon and Shlomo of pressuring Ehud to make concessions on Jerusalem." I now understood that neither Amnon nor Shlomo needed more exposure on the issue, nor, since they assumed that Barak was behind the story, did they need to give Ehud ammunition against them.

Now, for the first time, there were fissures on the Israeli side as well. With Barak at Gettysburg, I decided it was time for a diversion. The Hawthorne "cabin" had a two-lane bowling alley and also a movie theater, in addition to a game room and a small pub. Aaron, Gamal, Rob, and I went bowling, with me impressing them all by scoring 163. After that we joined the Palestinians to see the movie showing that night, *Gladiator*. It was 2 a.m. when the movie ended, and I walked out with Abu Ala, Yasser, and Saeb, all feeling somehow that the movie was a metaphor for our efforts.

| DAY 13 |

With President Clinton due to return in the early evening, I began the day focusing on how to present refinements to our ideas. I knew from Shlomo and others on the Israeli team they could go the "extra mile" if they had some "ammunition" to justify doing so. The key was to get enough of a "yes" from Arafat to go back to Barak and say we were in business.

George Tenet had seen Arafat and felt that he had gotten a qualified yes from him on the President's ideas. But when he described what Arafat had said, I could see the "qualification," but had a harder time seeing the "yes." Arafat was saying yes provided he got several additions: the Armenian Quarter in the Old City and contiguity with sovereignty in all the inner neighborhoods. Barak would certainly interpret this as a "no."

But then Barak switched signals. He asked to see Madeleine and me, and told us that after much reflection he had to pull back. He felt he could not deliver what the President had previously suggested. He could provide more on sovereignty over the inner neighborhoods, but he could not provide anything other than a special regime on the Old City. In other words, sovereignty outside the walls of the Old City was salable; inside those walls it was not.

Suddenly we had two highly qualified "yes's," and no easy way to bridge them. Should we acknowledge failure or try a variant in the procedure? I decided on the latter, and proposed that each side send one or two negotiators to meet the President with the understanding that they would come without their redlines and their rhetoric and explore each issue. Such an approach would allow us to crystallize the core differences and identify ways to bridge each issue, putting each leader in a position to decide if he could accept the President's bridging ideas.

When we suggested this approach to each leader—even prior to the President's arrival—both readily accepted it. Barak's mood had lightened considerably, suggesting to me that he had now thought everything through and was comfortable with his new position.

We briefed the President on his return, and he liked the idea of sitting with a negotiator or two on each side and proceeding issue by issue. We had not been heavily involved in the security discussions until George arrived at Camp David. We decided to start with security, believing we might make progress and build some momentum.

Starting at 11:30 p.m., we made headway on the first set of security issues: Israeli early-warning stations in the West Bank, airspace—Israeli needs to be reconciled with Palestinian civilian air usage—and joint and cooperative responses to terrorism. On the second set of issues—demilitarization of the Palestinian state and an Israeli and international presence in the Jordan Valley—we had mixed results. Palestinians had more of a problem with the symbolism of not having an army than with the practicality of limiting their forces and the weapons they could possess. For their part, the Israelis required a presence in the Jordan Valley, but as Shlomo Yanai observed, this presence could be small and replaced by international forces after a decade. We did not resolve the differences on these issues, but we could see ways to overcome them and made some proposals for doing so. Finally, on the last set of issues—Israeli access routes in the West Bank in the event of a threat from the east and the management of Palestinian border crossings—we faced basic disagreements. In the event of emergency, the Israelis felt they must have unimpeded routes to the Jordan River, and also declared that they needed at least a limited presence at the border passages and crossings—but after much discussion they would accept an international or third-party presence to deal with the infiltration of terrorists and the smuggling of prohibited weapons and other contraband. While Abu Ala was open to this, Mohammad Dahlan was dead set against any Israeli or foreign presence on the border crossings and rejected the idea that the Israelis should have guaranteed access routes into the West Bank—"If they are going to do it, let them do it, but don't ask us to agree formally."*

We took a break at 3 a.m., asking the two sides to consult with their leaders on the areas where there were key differences. The President had gotten his second wind just as George and I were beginning to fade. But he was ebullient. He said this is working: we are really getting through the issues. I was less certain. I feared Arafat's answer on an Israeli presence in the Jordan Valley, and was uneasy about Dahlan's positions on border crossings and emergency Israeli deployment.

After an hour's break, both sides returned. My concerns proved well founded, with Arafat rejecting any Israeli presence in the Jordan Valley beyond the time of withdrawal, siding with Dahlan on the third-party presence on the border, and rejecting an idea we had proposed for having four-way patrols—Israeli, Palestinian, Jordanian, and American—on both sides of the Jordan River. We spent another hour and a half discussing these issues and possible solutions and finally broke at five-thirty in the morning.

| DAY 14 |

We resumed a little after ten-thirty to deal with the issue of refugees. But it quickly became apparent that neither side had come with the mind-set we wanted: no redlines and no rhetoric. At one point, Nabil Sha'ath created a possible opening, saying that Palestinians must not have the feeling that they were giving up any chance to return to Israel. I raised the possibility of allowing the Palestinian refugees the right to apply to go to Israel as one of their choices, provided it was understood that only Israel had the right to decide who could be admitted. Both sides wanted to think about how they might work with such a formulation, but little more was accomplished in this meeting.

The next meeting was to be with those working on territory and borders. The refugee meeting told me we had already lost the dramatic effect of having the President

---

*On the Israeli fear of infiltration of terrorists into the Palestinian state, the concern was that once in Palestine, a terrorist could make his way into Israel as Jerusalem was to be an open city, with no border and no checkpoints.

engage intensively and through the night with the negotiators. We were, unfortunately, back in the world of rhetoric and redlines—not bottom lines. Given that, I told the President he would do better to meet with the two sides separately—at least that way he might have more success drawing them out on what was possible and what was not.

He agreed and we started with Shlomo and Gilad. The President let me open the meeting by saying we were at the end of the line and this had to be a "no bullshit meeting." While I hoped for some shock effect in front of the President, it was not forthcoming. Shlomo and Gilad were clearly in no position to offer anything more. The same was true for the Palestinians. When Abu Ala and Hassan Asfour showed the President a map with 2 percent annexation, it was clear we had played out the string with the negotiators, and the President cut the meeting short.

We had tried everything. We had exhausted both sides and ourselves. I could think of only one other step to try. While the President took a nap, I suggested to Madeleine and Sandy the following: the President meets Arafat and says, Assuming we work out a satisfactory outcome on the Haram for both sides, here's what I can do and not do on Jerusalem. He would then spell out that Arafat would get sovereignty on eight of the nine outer neighborhoods; he would get sovereignty on one or two of the inner neighborhoods to ensure a link to the Haram; there would be a special regime in the Old City, with a sovereign Palestinian compound in the Muslim Quarter next to the Haram. The President would ask Arafat whether he could accept this. If so, we would then work to crack the other issues; if not, we would work for a "soft landing." Both Sandy and Madeleine felt it was worth a try.

At the same time that I was making this suggestion to them, Martin, meeting with Shlomo, told him we were about to collapse, and asked what could be done? Shlomo's advice was for the President to meet the two leaders and put his best possible bridging proposal on Jerusalem to them. For him, it was as follows: all the outer neighborhoods get sovereignty, there is "limited" sovereignty on the inner neighborhoods, there is a sovereign compound for the Palestinians in the Muslim Quarter and a special regime for the Old City as a whole, and "sovereign" is used as an adjective, not a noun, on the Temple Mount (meaning the Palestinians would have "sovereign jurisdiction" there).

Shlomo and I were not far apart in our thinking on the substance. On the procedure, Shlomo wanted the meeting to take place with both leaders, whereas I wanted to find out first whether there was any chance with Arafat. When the President awoke, he decided he liked the idea of going to Arafat first. He did not want to see Barak again without having anything from Arafat, feeling that doing so had cost him before.

A meeting with Arafat was set up in the President's cabin. I decided to stay out of the meeting for two reasons. First, I thought Arafat might use my presence as a diversion; if he did not like what the President was saying, he might focus on me as an excuse, repeating again his previous claim that I had cooked this idea up with Barak. Second, I feared that I might lose my cool with Arafat. I had had it with him. Unlike at Wye, when in private with the President he at least had raised some ideas, here at Camp David he had not presented a single idea or single serious comment in two weeks. If someone was going to blow, it needed to be the President, not me.

As it turned out, the meeting produced nothing. Arafat would not accept what the President could do, and the President did blow up, at one point yelling that Arafat had "been here fourteen days and said no to everything."

The summit was over; however, neither side wanted it to end just yet. Shlomo still wanted the President to meet the two leaders alone and present them with a final offer. Barak was against this. I suggested that one negotiator from each side meet briefly with the President to discuss our exit strategy. This was accepted and Shlomo came for the Israelis and Saeb for the Palestinians. I was with the President, and Bruce was there as the note-taker.

This brief meeting lasted two and a half hours, producing one last remarkably poignant search for a solution. Shlomo started by trying to put in perspective the summit, its meaning, and the moment we were all now facing. He spoke of how the discussions allowed each of us to discover things about the other; allowed us for the first time in history to "touch the permanent status issues deeply." While providing insight and hope, he was afraid that the moment of opportunity would be lost if an agreement was not achieved now. The exposure of the Israeli concessions at Camp David, without an agreement, would spell "the political end of the peace camp in Israel." Barak's government would fall, the Israeli concessions would be lost, and with President Clinton gone, time would run out.

The question, he said, boiled down to "whether leaders are able to assume a decision that is less than their dream." As he put it, the mythological part of the prospective deal was the hard part. The Israelis had tried to face up to their mythology on Jerusalem. Their slogan had been "No division of Jerusalem," but "leaders don't achieve greatness on the basis of slogans." They had been willing to take on their slogan by accepting Palestinian sovereignty in the outer neighborhoods of Jerusalem, by providing autonomy on the inner neighborhoods, by accepting my suggestion that the Muslim and Christian Quarters have Palestinian sovereignty, and by agreeing to Palestinian custodial responsibility for the Haram/Temple Mount. While "we would maintain soft, almost nonexistent sovereignty on the surface," he concluded wistfully, "you would be the custodian, the protector of billions of Muslims. . . ."

Saeb responded by noting that great progress had been made. He acknowledged the significance of the Israeli moves, but insisted that Arafat could not accept Israeli sovereignty—no matter how soft—on the Haram. He could not accept Israeli sovereignty over the inner neighborhoods around the Old City.

Now the President spoke. "Let's look at everything," he said, "and see if we can come up with a better answer." We spread a big map of Jerusalem on the table and Shlomo said, There are four parts to Jerusalem: outer neighborhoods, inner neighborhoods, the Old City, and the Temple Mount. He asked Saeb, "If I can solve the inner neighborhoods for you, can you get Arafat to accept a special regime for the Old City with a sovereign [Palestinian] compound in the Muslim Quarter adjacent to the Temple Mount?"

Saeb replied he could not accept that, but could Shlomo accept "sovereignty with arrangements" for the Old City? Shlomo said, I can only respond to your needs on the inner neighborhoods if you respond to us on the Old City and the Temple Mount.

Saeb's "sovereignty with arrangements" was another way of saying limited sovereignty; Shlomo was signaling that this could be accepted for the inner neighborhoods if there could be a special regime for the Old City. Now I decided to try an idea: If we put the issue of the Haram/Temple Mount to the side, would the powers and functions of the limited sovereignty for the inner neighborhoods be the same as those of the special regime in the Old City? Was it a label that would distinguish these two areas, but not a practical reality on the ground?

Shlomo nodded, but added that in the Old City there would basically be a sharing of responsibilities. Saeb said yes, but Israel will have the sovereignty. To which Shlomo replied that the very concept of a special regime meant that limitations would be applied to sovereignty—meaning, in effect, that it was sovereignty with arrangements for both sides—Saeb's very suggestion. Saeb did not respond.

President Clinton, realizing that Shlomo was redefining the very meaning of sovereignty on the Old City—the most sacred of issues for Israelis—now weighed in. Why not, he said, solve the Old City by saying there would be a special regime, refer to each side's "sovereign" powers in the regime, and, in effect, introduce the word but treat it as an adjective. The President was trying to preserve the symbolic value of each side being able to say that it had some kind of sovereignty while making it practically meaningless. Shlomo and Saeb looked uncertain, and so I added, "Look, maybe the list of powers or responsibilities should be applied to the inner neighborhoods, the Old City, and the Haram. For each, we would then decide if we could use 'sovereignty' as either a noun or an adjective in describing that power." Saeb asked, So how would you describe each side's power or responsibility on the Haram?

I said the Palestinians would have "custodial or religious sovereignty" and the Israelis would have the "remaining sovereignty." Saeb asked, Why not simply do away with sovereignty for either side?

But Shlomo said he could not give up or concede sovereignty. (This became another classic case of the parties being out of sync. In the coming weeks the Israelis were to see the value of no sovereignty for the Temple Mount and the Palestinians were no longer willing to accept this.)

With Shlomo's response, we went back to the idea of deferring all or part of the Jerusalem question and trying to resolve all other issues. Saeb was extremely candid: the Palestinians could not do that because they would lose all their leverage on the Jerusalem issue if they did so. Seeing this through the prism of their weakness, he was saying, in effect, that Israel would lose all incentive to respond to the Palestinians on Jerusalem if everything else was resolved. He went so far as to suggest, Why not resolve everything and defer both refugees and Jerusalem—leaving room for trade-offs between the remaining issues. Shlomo was incredulous, asking were "Palestinian refugees a favor to Israel?"

It was Shlomo's turn to look at Saeb's suggestion through the prism of Israeli fears: Israel would concede over 90 percent of the territory and in return the Palestinians would retain their animating grievances for the conflict—the refugees and Jerusalem. In Shlomo's eyes, Israel was giving up a great deal and getting nothing in return.

Sandy and Madeleine had joined us during the discussion on deferral. Sandy made an effort to persuade Saeb that deferring only the question of sovereignty on the Old City and the Haram could serve Palestinian interests, emphasizing they would achieve everything else and would still be able to assert their claims. Saeb, convinced that the Palestinians would come under pressure to simply settle later on, was having none of it.

It was now past midnight. We had been at it since 9:30 p.m. The President turned to Saeb and tried his version of a Hail Mary, go-for-broke idea, saying, "How about I try to get you the following: sovereignty in the outer neighborhoods; limited sovereignty in the inner neighborhoods." (Saeb interjected "sovereignty with arrangements," and I answered "limited sovereignty.") "Sovereignty in the Muslim and Christian Quarters, with custodial sovereignty over the Haram." Saeb wrote this down, and the President said, "I have no earthly idea whether Barak can accept this," to which I responded, "I do, and he won't." Clinton nodded, saying to Saeb, "That is probably true, but I will try anyway. Will you take this to the Chairman and come back to me with his answer?"

Feeling uneasy myself, trying to soften the impact on Shlomo, who was visibly unhappy, and at the same time signal to Saeb that we might try to walk the President back, I said, "Saeb, you have to present this as part of a discussion, not an idea with the same standing as the ideas that the President presented to the Chairman."

This did not satisfy Shlomo. Looking pained, he said, "This is too much. It goes beyond what Barak can accept on the Muslim and Christian Quarters, goes beyond what he can accept on the Temple Mount by giving now 'custodial sovereignty,' and goes beyond what he can accept on the inner neighborhoods by giving limited sovereignty."

Notwithstanding Shlomo's comments and mine, Saeb, who had written all this down, said he doubted that Arafat would accept it. Sandy said, Then present him with the deferral option too.

The President got up and left the table. It was now 12:40 a.m. Saeb said he would go to see the Chairman and come back with an answer.

We got our answer from Arafat via Saeb at three in the morning. In the interim, Gamal and Rob went to Arafat's cabin and argued and pleaded with those around Arafat to give the President a positive answer. Their effort was for naught. Arafat would not accept either option—not the President's last "idea" on Jerusalem, and not the deferral of any part of Jerusalem. Instead, he suggested continued negotiations.

I had not joined Gamal and Rob. We had done enough pleading with Arafat. We had continually moved toward him; while his negotiators moved, he had not moved at all.

While Gamal and Rob were making their last-minute pleadings, I went back to my cabin and briefed the others. It was now a little after 1 a.m. I asked Aaron to draft a one-page statement that we could issue in the morning emphasizing the unprecedented character of these negotiations, the absence of any alternative to negotiations, our opposition to unilateral actions or declarations by either side, and continuing U.S. support for those who were prepared to make decisions for peace. (Being "prepared to make decisions" was obviously a dig at Arafat.)

The President informed Barak of Arafat's answer around 3:15 a.m. At 3:45 Barak asked for me to come see him, and I went to his cabin. He was very somber. He felt there would be no choice but to go to a national unity government. He also felt the failure at Camp David would mark the end of twenty years of peacemaking and would lead to an immediate deterioration into conflict. He said he would need help and support from us and proceeded to list what was essential for him politically:

—a very clear statement by us that all ideas presented at Camp David were null and void;
—a new strategic upgrade in relations;
—a package of new bilateral support militarily;

—a readiness to move our embassy to Jerusalem to show Barak had gained on
Jerusalem, not lost;

—a commitment to fight a unilateral declaration of statehood by the Palestinians,
including a guarantee of opposition to admission of that state to the UN.

I told Barak we would look carefully at every request he was making, but that if he
went on the warpath in the aftermath of Camp David, our ability to respond to his
needs would go down, not up. As the responsible leader of a country, he could not
adopt a position with only two alternatives: peace or total war.

At this point, Dan Meridor joined us, and Barak left, whereupon I turned to Dan,
saying, "I know how you are feeling; I feel very much the same, but the world is not
black and white and the choices available cannot be war or peace. You and the Palestinians still have to live together." He nodded, saying, "Of course, of course. . . . I personally feel we are lucky Arafat did not agree because we were giving up too much. I
understand Barak feels let down and angry and we have to find a way to manage and
continue to negotiate. It will take time, particularly because the Palestinians must understand we cannot do everything that was raised here. That will be very hard for them.
Maybe we can find a way to talk about some of the issues here and put Jerusalem off
for some time. I don't know, but in the meantime Barak will need some help from
you"—he is vulnerable to the charge that he gave away the store and got nothing in return. (Dan recounted many of the points on Barak's list, acknowledging that we would
probably not move our embassy to Jerusalem but emphasizing that we must vigorously
oppose a unilateral declaration of Palestinian statehood.)

I appreciated his candor and told him so. It was now close to five in the morning.
The President had gone to sleep, with a wake-up call for eight-thirty. Sandy told me
that in the morning there would be a trilateral meeting with the leaders in which we
would agree on the general statement that I had asked Aaron to draft. Madeleine, feeling we could never explain having come to Camp David and never required a direct,
substantive discussion between Barak and Arafat, had pressed the President hard to
hold a trilateral meeting to conclude the summit with Barak and Arafat—and President Clinton had agreed.

Aaron was waiting in my cabin when I returned, and we went through his draft.
It was good; I would go over it with the President and show it to Barak. Would we also
have to show it to Arafat? he asked. I saw no point in doing so; after all, he was getting
what he wanted: a continuing process without any obligation on his part. The issue
was not whether Arafat would accept this statement, but whether Barak would go
along with it or simply declare that the effort at working with Arafat was over.

Aaron now was concerned about our acquiescing in Barak's going off the deep end and making us a party to a confrontation with Arafat. I was not sure, but felt that Barak's willingness to accept the statement would take care of Aaron's concern. Sure enough, Barak agreed with all the basic points of the statement: he only wanted one change. In the passage about there being "no alternative to negotiations" for resolving the conflict, he inserted the word "good-faith" before "negotiations."

In the trilateral meeting, Barak was extremely somber, expressing his deep disappointment. He declared that he had thought we would reach an agreement that would change the future; that would produce two states, Israel and Palestine side by side. Maybe it was "beyond our reach, but I still think it could have been achieved."

Arafat, knowing that (in the President's words) he was "the skunk at the party," was effusive in his praise of President Clinton and emotional in his call for peace. "Mr. President, we truly and genuinely appreciate all you have done and . . . will continue to do to continue the peace process, the process my old partner Rabin paid his life for. For the sake of our children, we know we must continue the peace process, in spite of all the difficulties. I am confident that the Israeli and Palestinian people want peace. . . . I am confident that with your great help and efforts we will overcome the difficulties . . . for the sake of all the children of Palestine, Israel, and the entire Middle East."

The President asked me for the draft declaration we would issue, and he read it aloud. Arafat, clearly relieved, said, "What you decide, we will agree to." Barak simply nodded. The President asked both to let him speak to the press first and they agreed.

The summit was over. The President would make his statement and meet the press back at the White House. We went over his press statement in his cabin before leaving.

Rob had written the press statement knowing that the President would want to praise Barak but not Arafat. It spoke of Barak's courage and simply said that Arafat had come to Camp David to pursue the peace process. I knew the contrast would be seen as implicit criticism of Arafat—something his performance at Camp David warranted.

The President's problem with the formulation was that it seemed like a non sequitur: "You got me praising Barak and saying Arafat showed up. It's apples and oranges." I told him that was true, but this was a way of drawing the distinction between the two without directly criticizing Arafat and yet still lauding Barak—something I felt Barak would need domestically. The President was very keen to help Barak, feeling that if we could shore him up politically now, we could keep the process alive.

This was uppermost in the President's mind when he spoke to the press at the White House. He went well beyond his press statement, explaining what Barak had done, how he was motivated by Israeli security needs throughout, how it took great courage to adopt positions, especially on Jerusalem, that were difficult but ultimately visionary in meeting Israeli needs and making peace possible.

As I watched in the pressroom, I marveled at his capacity to put the best face on what Barak had done. While he sought to address the American public as well as note the historic, indeed unprecedented, nature of the discussions that had taken place, his target audience was the Israeli public—a public that held him in extraordinarily high esteem. And his "pitch" was personal: he had enormous respect for what Barak had done, and the Israeli public could be proud of their Prime Minister, a statesman and a leader.

Of course, this tribute also made it hard for Barak to go back to the region and take the low road on Arafat. The President was making clear that the game was not over, just the summit.

The press conference shaped the assessment of the summit not only in Israel but here as well. While it was not portrayed as a success, it was also not seen as a failure; rather, it was considered a necessary step on the way to a solution. This, of course, suited the Palestinians. They sought to avoid blame, and notwithstanding Barak's desire to withdraw the ideas that had been put on the table, those ideas would become the new baseline.

For our part, the U.S. team, too, tended to believe that something profound had happened at Camp David. The taboos on serious discussion of the core issues like Jerusalem, borders, and refugees had been broken. Jerusalem, in particular, no longer had to be treated only as a slogan. It was demystified; it could be discussed. The reality that there were exclusively Arab neighborhoods that Israelis did not live in, and never went to, could be exposed, and created possibilities for solutions along the lines we had been exploring. Maybe we could take advantage of the taboos being broken; maybe the President was right that if we could help sustain Barak's position, we might yet produce a permanent peace deal in the remaining months of the Clinton administration.

In this respect, Clinton had a better feel for Israeli politics than Barak. While the "right" in Israel was outraged over the concessions that Barak was prepared to contemplate, it quickly became apparent that the rest of Israel was not. Not enthusiastic to be sure, but ready to live with what Barak contemplated if it produced an end-of-conflict peace.

The real question was on the Palestinian side. Was the summit transforming for Yasir Arafat? Were we witnessing a typically tactical set of moves by Arafat to improve the terms of what he could get, or were we seeing someone not capable of doing a deal to end the conflict? He, not Barak, would determine if a final peace agreement was possible in the next few months.

The Denouement—From Camp
David to the Intifada to the Clinton Ideas

FOLLOWING CAMP DAVID, I decided that I would leave my post as negotiator at the end of the Clinton administration. I shared this only with Madeleine, telling her that I knew that if we did not reach an agreement by the end of the term, the pendulum was going to swing away from reaching a solution back to crisis management. I was now too invested in a solution to return again to the role of the "fireman" constantly putting out the fires merely to keep the process going. I would not announce this decision until November 6, on the eve of the election. I certainly did not want anyone speculating that given my long tenure I would now be desperate to produce an agreement before I left. That was the last message I wanted the Palestinians to receive at this moment.

After all, Yasir Arafat had returned to Gaza after the summit and was greeted as a hero. He had defied the President and Barak. He had stood up for Palestinian rights and would not accept a diktat—or that was the image he and those around him sought to cultivate. Palestinians would always support the idea that they should not surrender their rights. Arafat, ever the symbol of defiance—a symbol that was so often the motivating force in the Palestinian movement—was comfortable in public but not so comfortable in private.

Notwithstanding the public appearance of defiance, I began getting calls from all those around Arafat—Rashid, Dahlan, Erekat, Abu Rudeina—telling me that the Chairman understood that great progress had been made and another summit would be needed. We should start to plan it now. When would I be coming to the region? We could begin the efforts as soon as I came.

I was not about to give this away. We might believe that we still had a chance to reach agreement, but I was convinced we must change our approach to the Palestinians. They must now prove they were up to the task of peacemaking. I told Rashid: "Tell the Chairman he is dreaming. We just shot our wad. We exposed the President before the world and produced nothing. We cannot invest the power and prestige of the presidency and of the United States in another high-level failure. The President is now convinced that the Chairman is not capable of making a decision to end the conflict. If you want to convince Clinton to have another summit, if you want to convince me to argue for it, Arafat must prove he is prepared to reach agreement, prove he will wrap everything up. Do it with the Israelis now so the agreement is there but simply needs to be formalized."

In the beginning of August, I did not find it difficult to keep the Palestinians at arm's length. The President was paying attention to the unfolding political developments at home: the Republican convention had been extraordinarily successful in promoting the image of George W. Bush as a "compassionate conservative"—in the mainstream of the country's attitudes—and a leader who was a straight shooter, who would "restore" honor to the office of the presidency, and who would end the Clinton era's poisonous politics. President Clinton was looking ahead to the Democratic convention, where, even though Vice President Gore did not want him to play a major role, he would have a chance to set the record straight about the success of his presidency. (Even prior to the Democratic convention, the Vice President succeeded in blunting Bush's momentum by showing he could do the unexpected—something that recast his image—when he selected Senator Joseph Lieberman, an Orthodox Jew, as his running mate.)

While I felt little pressure initially in August to be more responsive to the Palestinians, their pleas for me to visit the region began to escalate as some of the Israelis also began to press me to come. I held firm with them as well, particularly because I knew they had been and would be talking to the Palestinians. Even though most of the Israeli negotiators were angry at Arafat and wanted us to put pressure on him, they also felt a pressure on themselves—some because they believed that reaching an agreement with the Palestinians was the only way to preserve their government and others because they were convinced that the historic possibility to end the conflict would disappear if their government fell or was transformed.

Barak kept making noises that he would go to a national unity government with Ariel Sharon, a prospect driven by the reality that Barak's government had become a minority government when Shas left the cabinet in July. Sooner or later Barak would have to expand his government's base in order to ensure its survival, a process that required making common cause with those who were perceived to be unbending on the Palestinians and considered the peace process anathema.

The peace camp dominated Barak's current cabinet, and I feared its sense of desperation would be communicated to Arafat. If it were, Arafat would hold back, waiting once again for the Israelis or us to move further toward him. I wanted us to do nothing—so that Arafat would see that the next move was his to make.

On August 9, Arafat (doubtless prompted by those around him) sent the President a letter. In it, he said that he would be setting up a discreet channel with the Israelis to discuss Jerusalem and security. Only when these discussions reached the point where agreement was possible would he return to the President and ask for the President's intervention.

The discreet channel met almost daily throughout August and September, discussing a practical approach to every neighborhood in East Jerusalem and the Old City. Whose law would apply in what neighborhoods? How would security there be coordinated? How could the city remain united even as functional responsibilities in different neighborhoods were assumed? Gilad Sher and Israel Hasson (the deputy director of Shin Bet) for the Israelis, and Saeb Erekat and Mohammad Dahlan for the Palestinians addressed these and other questions systematically. On these practical questions of Jerusalem, they made real progress, but quickly became bogged down on security issues, disagreeing over what had been agreed at Camp David.

This led the Israelis to insist that we, as the keepers of the record, should sit down with both sides and serve as the judge in establishing the new baselines of Camp David. I was leery of doing this; it would relieve Arafat and his negotiators of the burden to act on their own.

Yet our general reluctance to say no to Israeli requests led the President, Madeleine, and Sandy to urge me to go to the area and participate in the private channel. Relenting, I made it clear that the most I would do in the meetings was summarize our understandings from Camp David—understandings that were not as forward-leaning as Gilad wanted them to be, but not as limited as Dahlan suggested.

I had another reason to go to the area. During the spring, Debbie and I had decided that in August we would take the family for a visit to Israel, to Jericho in the West Bank and to Gaza. All our tickets had been bought. All our special tours had been set up. We would forfeit several thousand dollars if we were to cancel the trip now—not to mention the price I would have paid with the family.

Not going was not an option. We were due to arrive in Israel on August 19. I decided to go to the area three days earlier than the rest of the family. I made it clear that while I would join the secret meetings during my trip, I would not be available every day.

To give the secret meetings cover—to establish a motive for my presence in the region—I also arranged to see both leaders. Not surprisingly, Arafat was eager to see me, and I went to see him first. That suited Ehud Barak, who wanted the onus to be on Arafat. Whether because he was feeling defensive or because he was trying to encourage me to see that an agreement was possible, he was very optimistic: Camp David had been a great success; more progress had been made there than at any time in the process; Barak, the man he had so often disparaged, he now praised for having gone "beyond my partner Rabin." (I told him "way beyond" Rabin, who would have found the ideas on the borders and Jerusalem almost impossible to stomach. I reminded Arafat that Leah Rabin was now criticizing Barak for what he had been willing to accept on Jerusalem, saying, "Yitzhak would never have accepted this.")

Then I met Barak and summarized the conversation. He was not impressed, saying, "Let them prove something in the private discussions." He was pleased to hear I was going to see Amre Moussa, the Egyptian Foreign Minister. Though he saw Moussa as a latter-day Nasserist, always looking to the lowest common denominator in the Arab world, he was convinced that joint American-Egyptian pressure on Arafat was probably the best way to move the Chairman.

The day before Debbie and the kids arrived in Jerusalem, I went by private plane to Alexandria and then was driven an hour to a beautiful resort area along the Mediterranean where Moussa had his vacation house. It had the look of any prosperous beach resort: condominiums, tennis courts away from the water, and more luxurious homes on the beach itself.

Gamal Helal brought his family to this resort every August; he greeted me on the outskirts of Moussa's house, looking tan and relaxed. "The Egyptians know there is a real opportunity and they are ready to do their part; they are talking to both Israelis and Palestinians, and Israel Hasson visited the Egyptians in the last few days," he told me.

Moussa's patio was on the beach, and we ate lunch under a blue awning whose colors were only slightly darker than the cloudless sky. I joked that this is where we should hold all our meetings. Then I briefed on the issues, what I felt each side could do, and the importance of finding a way to solve what remained the crux of the matter: the Haram/Temple Mount. Moussa spread out a large map of Jerusalem and we pored over it; I described the area around the Haram, the Mughrabi Gate leading into it from the Kotel area (the Wailing Wall and the vast plaza in front of it), the place just inside the Magribi Gate where the Israelis hoped Jews would be able to pray on a few religious holidays, areas where Arafat could have a separate entrance into the Haram, etc.

Moussa felt the Haram issue was the real sticking point with Arafat. At Camp David, we had never had a serious discussion of different options for the Haram/

Temple Mount. Since the summit, I had thought a lot about the different alternatives and I now presented them to Moussa:

—Remove sovereignty as an issue. In this unique space, sovereignty would either belong to God or simply not be relevant. The Palestinians would have responsibility for the area and would ensure there was no threat from the surface of the Haram to the plaza below where Jews would pray at the Wailing Wall. The Israelis would have responsibility for the Wailing Wall and the tunnels along the length of the Western Wall.

—Give Palestinians sovereignty over the mosques—the Dome of the Rock and Al-Aqsa—and the Israelis sovereignty over the Western Wall, with an international regime governing the issue of excavation either from the surface or from behind the wall. Each would get sovereignty only over the actual religious sites, not the broader areas of which they were a part. In this way the religious sites would be equated and each would have sovereignty over what was sacred to it.

—Come up with a term other than "sovereignty" to explain the relationship each side would have to their respective holy space. For example, we could say that the Palestinians would have jurisdiction over the Haram while the Israelis would have jurisdiction over the Western Wall and the holy space it was connected to.

Moussa felt that the Palestinians must be able to use the word "sovereign" as it applied to the Haram. He suggested that the Palestinians get "sovereign jurisdiction" over the Haram and the Israelis get "sovereign jurisdiction" over the Wailing Wall. I told him the Wailing Wall was only a small part of the retaining wall of the Temple and it was the Western Wall the Israelis would have to have. I raised one other possibility: What if we were silent on the wall but gave the Palestinians sovereignty or sovereign jurisdiction over the Haram and Israelis the equivalent over the Jewish Quarter and the Jewish holy places connected to the quarter? This formula would allow each side to claim that it had the sovereignty or jurisdiction it needed.

I was searching for an answer. Moussa was interested in only one option: the one he had raised. Again, I repeated it was a nonstarter unless it referred to the Western, not Wailing, Wall for the Israelis. He suggested that we write up these options. He preferred to present them first to Arafat to see what he might be willing to accept. But when I told him that we needed to provide the options to both sides simultaneously, he agreed and suggested that he present the options to Arafat and I present them to Barak.

I liked that approach. It invested Egypt in the process and gave them a responsibility to make it work. It would deny Arafat the argument that our options did not take account of the broader Arab and Islamic audiences that he must also address on Jerusalem. He could hardly claim that Egypt was insensitive on the broader religious concerns in the Islamic world, thus making it harder for Arafat to reject these options.

Upon completing our discussion on the Haram, Moussa gave me a paper he and his staff had produced on borders, refugees, and security. The paper was interesting in that it was an Egyptian effort to outline acceptable criteria for agreement on these issues. The Egyptians had been talking to Palestinians and Israelis. Significantly, in the three weeks since the summit a steady stream of Israelis had been coming to Egypt to see Mubarak, Moussa, Osama al-Baz, and Omar Suleiman, the Egyptian chief of intelligence.

Moussa told me the paper was the result of the conversations the Egyptians had been having with both sides. Since the Egyptians were putting criteria on paper, I did not expect them to depart very far from consensus positions in the Arab world on how to resolve the issues. Thus, I was not surprised to see that the Egyptian paper tilted toward the Palestinian positions. What I objected to, however, was that the paper tried to pocket the most advanced positions they had heard from individual Israelis—positions I said that we had never heard from Barak or any member of the Israeli negotiating team. For example, the paper asserted that an Israeli had said that Israel could withdraw from 94 percent of the territory and provide a swap on top of that. I knew what we had extracted at Camp David (91 percent of the territory and a 1 percent swap) and 94 percent plus a swap was not a baseline Israeli position—particularly because I knew this would be treated as a point of departure for the talks, not the end of the story.

While I did not see the Egyptian paper as something we could work with, there was clearly a newfound Egyptian readiness to play an active role—and Moussa and I concluded our discussion agreeing to speak on a daily basis for as long as I remained in the area.

| ARAFAT RESTRAINS HIS ENTHUSIASM |

Upon my return to Israel the evening before my family arrived, I saw Barak and reported on the discussion with Moussa. He categorically dismissed the prospect of withdrawal from 94 percent of the West Bank as impossible. On the options on the Haram/Temple Mount, he listened, then stressed that Israel could not surrender sovereignty over the Temple Mount to the Palestinians. That was an interesting formulation, implying that Israel might not demand exclusive sovereignty or even require sovereignty as an outcome.

I waited for two days to see Arafat, wanting to be sure that Moussa had conveyed the options to him. (As it turned out, Mubarak asked Arafat to come see him on August 21 and I would see Arafat later that evening.) I asked Gamal to join me for the meeting and not just to interpret. Since we would be discussing the options on the Haram, I anticipated that Arafat might well again declare that the Temple—the most sacred place in Jewish tradition—did not exist in Jerusalem but was in Nablus. I did not want to turn this issue into Arafat the Muslim debating me the Jew. I wanted Gamal, a Christian of Coptic origin who was originally from Egypt, to tell Arafat that this was an outrageous attempt to delegitimize the Israeli connection to Jerusalem. Gamal was happy to take on this role.

Whereas Arafat had been warm and effusive in our first meeting, I could tell from the moment I walked into the room that his mood was different this time. I knew Arafat had talked to Moussa earlier in the day, and I guessed he was anticipating that I would pressure him on the Haram, and signaling that he was not disposed to be flexible.

When I asked if the Egyptians had conveyed four options on the Haram, he acknowledged they had done so, noting they had been conveyed as my options. I responded that these were neither American nor Egyptian options; they simply reflected what Moussa and I thought were the real choices available. What was his reaction? He shrugged and said he had none. Did that mean he viewed them all equally? Again, he was nonresponsive, and now raised his new mythology, saying, "Of course, the Temple did not exist in Jerusalem, but in Nablus."

Gamal knew this was his cue. What ensued surprised even me. Gamal started very politely, suggesting to Arafat that whatever his personal views, the one core premise of any process must be that one side did not question the religious faith of the other side. But Arafat would not back down, telling Gamal that he knew nothing of religion, whereas he (the Chairman) was an expert on all religions, especially on Judaism, and the Temple did not exist in Jerusalem. They began to argue, and Gamal said if the Jews believe the Temple existed in Jerusalem, then for our purposes it existed in Jerusalem.

Finally, after nearly ten minutes of increasing invective, I intervened and said, "Mr. Chairman, regardless of what you think, the President of the United States *knows* that the Temple existed in Jerusalem. If he hears you denying its existence there, he will never again take you seriously. My advice to you is never raise this view again in his presence."

Arafat may not have been willing to engage on any of the four options on the Haram, but he stopped his argument with Gamal and never again raised his myth on the Temple in either the President's presence or mine. (Of course, that did not prevent him from raising it with countless others.)

With that issue sidelined, I told Arafat that he would be seeing the President again in New York on September 6 or 7 at the Millennium Summit and that this might well be his last chance to convince the President he was prepared to reach a deal. He needed to come to New York with a response on the Haram that the President would find credible. "Don't miss that opportunity," I admonished. He listened but said nothing.

The Millennium Summit had been designed to bring all the leaders of the world to the UN during September of 2000. This was the kind of event that Yasir Arafat lived for—to be seen on the world stage as a global leader. We needed to use this event to get Arafat to move. With President Clinton going to help broker an end to the conflict in the Congo during my vacation, I saw one additional opportunity to make the Egyptians an active partner in pressuring Arafat. I suggested that the President stop in Cairo to see Hosni Mubarak on his way back from Africa. I wanted President Clinton to encourage Mubarak to persist, especially on the issue of the Haram, even if Arafat was resisting. Leaving Debbie and the kids in Eilat, I went to Cairo and joined the President. The President's stopover was noteworthy for two reasons. First, the two Presidents agreed that the only hope for reaching an agreement was if it was clear that the Haram—the issue we felt was most likely to prevent agreement—could be settled. Both agreed that the meeting in New York was the point at which an understanding on it must be achieved—and that we would work together to achieve it. Second, in speaking with Osama al-Baz after the meeting, I reminded him of what he had told me prior to our going to Camp David—namely, that the Palestinian dream was to get 91 percent of the territory. "Well," I asked, "they were offered 92 percent. What happened?" His reply was simple: "They raised their expectations."

| MEETINGS IN NEW YORK AND A NEW U.S. INITIATIVE |

I was to hold several meetings with both sets of negotiators both before and after the Millennium Summit in New York. Getting around New York City at this time was no small feat. Streets were closed off; lockdowns would take place whenever the President or others were moving in motorcades around the city. It presented no real problem for me because I love to walk in New York—and we were staying in the Waldorf Towers. The Towers were only a few blocks away from the UN Plaza Hotel, where the Palestinians were staying. The Israelis were farther away at the Park Lane Hotel on Central Park South, but I was still able to walk there in fifteen minutes.

Prior to the Millennium Summit, I had a different purpose with the negotiators on each side. With the Israeli side I was trying to draw Shlomo and Gilad out on what Israel could accept if we were to make a proposal. They had become convinced that nothing was possible without a U.S. proposal. Barak, too, had changed in this regard, emphasizing with me before I left Israel in early September that he thought we would have to present a proposal if there was to be an agreement; naturally, he felt Israel was already at its redlines and wanted to reveal nothing more. Given that, I knew I would have to try a different technique if I was going to learn more from Shlomo and Gilad about the limits of what Israel could accept. In this case, I decided to tell them what I thought the Palestinians could ultimately live with—and test their response to my assessment.

They were all ears as I told them I believed that the Palestinians could accept 7 percent annexation in the West Bank but would need a 2 percent swap of territory in return. In other words, I felt that the Palestinians had to get a net 95 percent of the territory, not the 92 percent of Camp David. On Jerusalem, I said I thought the Palestinians would need to get the Arab neighborhoods—outer, inner, and in the Old City—under their sovereignty. On the Haram, I told them I was not sure but felt in the end the Palestinians would swallow one of the options I had developed with Moussa. On security, I said the Palestinians would accept a nonmilitarized state, provided they were permitted levels and categories of weapons that would provide them with credible means to deal with any internal threats to Arafat.

I ran through the remaining security issues—control of Palestinian airspace, Israeli redeployment to the Jordan River in a clear emergency, early-warning sites, international forces or presence in the Jordan Valley and at the Palestinian borders—and finally concluded on the refugee question. While not sure, I told them the Palestinians would probably try to hold out for a combination of the following on refugees:

—the right to apply to return to Israel;
—an agreed number on the refugees the Israelis would admit under a humanitarian rubric;
—and priority status for admission given to refugees in Lebanon, many of whom had extended families in northern Israel.

I could tell that Shlomo and Gilad were intrigued and encouraged. Interestingly, they did not question my assessment of the Palestinian bottom lines or near bottom lines. While raising two concerns on Jerusalem (e.g., retaining Israeli sovereignty over religiously significant or historic Jewish sites in Arab neighborhoods like the City of David in Silwan and the need for special arrangements in the Old City), it was only on refugees that Shlomo and Gilad argued that they could not accept what I was suggesting the Palestinians would require. Specifically, they resisted the idea that the Palestinian refugees would have a right to apply to return. Though acknowledging that Israel could veto any application—and there was no Palestinian right of return in this formulation—Gilad declared that if the Palestinians had the right to apply and were turned down by Israel, the onus would be on Israel and there would be a festering sore.

I explained that the Palestinians wanted to preserve at least the appearance of choice. Could, I asked, the international committee that would be established to help with re-settlement and rehabilitation of refugees also screen applicants and deny entry to those who did not fit the narrow criteria that Israel would establish?

Gilad felt that would only perpetuate the myth that they might still return to Israel. Shlomo agreed and persuasively argued it was time for both sides to give up their myths. Israel was giving up its myths: being in the Jordan Valley forever and dividing Jerusalem. These myths were as central to Israel's belief system as the right of return was to the Palestinians. It was time for both sides to accept reality and surrender their myths.

On the other issues, Shlomo and Gilad went through the motions emphasizing the difficulty they would have in accepting the other positions I had outlined. But it was clear to me that their real concern was less the substance of these positions and more the question of whether the Palestinians at the end of the day would actually ac-cept them.

This was a very legitimate concern, but initially with the Palestinians—Saeb Erekat and Mohammad Dahlan and Mohammad Rashid—I focused more on resolv-ing the Haram than on drawing them out on what they might be able to live with more generally. On the Haram, I told them Arafat either must accept one of the four options I presented or he must offer something new that is credible.

When Saeb tried out the idea of the Organization of the Islamic Conference (OIC) rather than the Palestinians holding the sovereignty over the Haram, I told him that was a worse outcome for the Israelis than the Palestinians holding sovereignty. With coun-tries like Iran, Iraq, and Libya as members of the OIC, Israel would have no explanation and no assurance about the protection of Israeli interests. Knowing Saeb, I suspected that this was probably Arafat's idea and he was hoping to condition us to it.

George Tenet had come to town to speak to Arafat and Dahlan on the security is-sues. I asked George to shoot the OIC idea down with Arafat when he met him the night before the President's meeting with the Chairman. Arafat did raise it with him, and George told him bluntly it was a nonstarter. He also told him it was his belief that if Arafat did not resolve the issue of the Haram with the President in their meeting, he saw little prospect of there being a summit or an agreement before the end of the Pres-ident's term.

I was hoping to convince Arafat that he had to make a decision on this now and at least communicate it privately to the President if he wanted our intervention. George did his job, but in this case the President did not do his. Notwithstanding our efforts to convince Arafat that he must be prepared to try to resolve the Haram issue if the President was to engage anymore, President Clinton did not convey that message in the meeting with Arafat. On the contrary, when Arafat predictably raised his idea of the OIC's sovereignty over the Haram, the President, while noting this would probably not work, suggested we could look at other options. Rather than telling Arafat that we had developed feasible options—options the Egyptians also found feasible—and the ball was in his court either to respond or to come up with something that was truly credible if the United States was to continue to make an effort, the President shied away from confronting Arafat.

Why? It was not because he had not been briefed. Together in the briefing before the President's meeting with Arafat, George and I told him that notwithstanding our efforts to preempt Arafat's OIC idea, he was still likely to raise it—and the President needed to tell him to forget it. President Clinton did not react with us and did not bluntly reject Arafat on this issue. Instead, he chose to soft-pedal it because he felt that if Arafat was raising an alternative to Palestinian sovereignty—even if it was not acceptable—we should treat this as an opening. Over time we could create some sort of international solution that Arafat and Barak would accept, and the President wanted to keep the ball in play until that moment.

Both George and I were unhappy with such an approach. Our experience with Arafat taught us that he would think he could obtain an unrealistic settlement for the Haram/Temple Mount. Moreover, the President as much as told him that the blunt talk he'd heard from George and me separately did not matter; indeed, that our threats about no longer intervening could safely be ignored.

Though he had been angry at Arafat at Camp David, President Clinton remained convinced that he could bring Arafat around and that it was a mistake to put him in a corner. Prior to Camp David, I was more open to approaching Arafat the President's way, especially given Barak's treatment of him. After Camp David, however, the Arafat who made decisions only when left with no choice, only when he saw the train was leaving without him, was back in sharp focus for me. I now believed that the only chance to move Arafat was to convince him he was about to lose his historic opportunity to end the conflict and create a viable independent state. For that, Arafat must see that we would simply walk away, and that the Israelis would not chase after him. In addition, Egypt needed to make clear to him that he was about to lose his moment—and would not be forgiven for having done so.

We worked on the Egyptians at a New York breakfast meeting between Secretary Albright and Foreign Minister Moussa later that month, a meeting in which Moussa told the Secretary that Egypt would "insist that Arafat accept an American proposal" if we made one. But it was clear that neither we nor the Israelis would demand of Arafat that he make a move or else see the process end for the Clinton administration.

Now, after the President's meeting, it was clear we were not going to pressure Arafat, at least not prior to presenting an American proposal. Perhaps the President was right. Perhaps the best time to pressure Arafat would be after we made the proposal and he inevitably dithered in his response.

Regardless, I knew now that my approach to the Palestinians had to be on determining what they could live with in a proposal and what they would not be able to accept. In my meetings with Saeb and the two Mohammads—sometimes together, sometimes not—I used the same approach I had with Shlomo and Gilad. Only now I was outlining what I thought the Israelis could accept in the end. Now I was trying to condition them to what would be required if there was to be a deal.

Naturally, I could not simply present the mirror image of what I had told Shlomo and Gilad about what I believed the Palestinians could ultimately accept. In some areas, like security, where I believed there was a great deal of convergence and the Palestinians knew they would have to concede, that would not be a problem. But in others, like territory, I had watched the Palestinian position go from 4 percent Israeli annexation with an equal swap in May to 2 percent with an equal swap at Camp David. In Osama al-Baz's words, they had raised their expectations. If I knew the Israelis could accept a net of 95 percent of the territory going to the Palestinians, I could not say that now, lest the Palestinians treat that as the new point of departure, not the end point.

Here I had to strike a delicate balance. If I simply repeated the positions that had been presented at Camp David on territory/borders and Jerusalem, the Palestinians would not take the effort seriously and would not provide greater insight into what they would ultimately accept. On these two issues, I decided to indicate what I thought was possible including the limits beyond what we had discussed at Camp David. On security, I decided to make the same presentation I had made to Shlomo and Gilad. And because we had never presented an idea on refugees, I decided to present basically what Shlomo and Gilad had told me.

Specifically, on territory I suggested that we might be able to get Israel to accept an 8 percent annexation at the end of the day and we would see if we could press them to go slightly beyond the 1 percent swap they had accepted at Camp David—meaning I was signaling that the Palestinians would get 93 to 93.5 percent of the territory as opposed to the 92 percent offered at Camp David. On Jerusalem, I said I thought the Israelis would have to accept Palestinian sovereignty in the Arab neighborhoods outside the Old City, meaning the inner municipal neighborhoods. This went beyond Camp David, where only the outer neighborhoods—those not near the walled Old City— would become sovereign Palestinian areas.

On the Haram, I said the ball is in your court—the OIC idea is a nonstarter. Finally, on refugees, I said the Israelis are not going to accept the "right of return" to Israel under any guise. Right of return to your state makes perfect sense; right of return to Israel means you do not believe in a two-state solution.

I added there were a number of steps we could take to give the Palestinians some cover on this issue. We could refer to UN General Assembly resolution 194—the Palestinian bible on the refugees—in the text. We could create a large international fund for compensation for refugees and to help with repatriation, resettlement, and rehabilitation. We could press the Israelis to accept a limited number of refugees on a humanitarian basis and make sure they gave priority for such admission to Palestinian refugees in Lebanon. But in the final analysis, the Palestinians were not going to have a right of return to Israel.

Initially, the going was not easy with Saeb or Mohammad Dahlan. They argued that I was describing Israeli bottom lines that ruled out a deal. I was in effect arguing for Israeli positions that would deny the Palestinians what they needed to sell a deal: clear independence, sovereignty over the Haram, and a just resolution of the refugee problem.

I was tough in response: They focused on their needs to the exclusion of the Israeli needs. They were hearing me go beyond Camp David; they could see on Jerusalem even something that went beyond Saeb's Camp David suggestion of "A" status for the inner neighborhoods. If they persisted in their positions, I saw little reason for us to make a proposal because there could not be an agreement.

Like Shlomo and Gilad, they wanted an American proposal. They could reach an agreement only if each side had to react to an American proposal.

If that's what is required, I told them, "help me construct one. It won't be everything you want, but it should respond to what each of you needs. If you tell me that what I have said makes it impossible for you, then I see no reason to continue with the effort."

At this point, they became more responsive. On territory, they argued that the key was to preserve the territorial integrity of the West Bank. Dahlan, in particular, argued that if you exceed 6 percent annexation you begin to break up the integrity of the territory; Saeb spoke of enlarging the size of the swap area adjacent to Gaza to relieve the terrible population density there.

Dahlan was especially poignant on this subject, observing that we were asking for 8 percent annexation of the West Bank to accommodate 80 percent of Israel's 200,000 Israeli settlers. He pointed out that they were asking us to increase the size of the swap area to relieve the pressure on 1.2 million Palestinians living in Gaza—an area roughly equal in size to the area we now said the Israelis would need to annex for the "comfort" of their settlers in the West Bank.

On refugees, they focused on the practical questions, not those of principle: Could we increase the numbers of "humanitarian" refugees the Israelis would admit? Could the numbers be skewed to permit most of those from Lebanon who would want to come? Could we come up with some categories like, for example, one in which those who had left in 1948 could choose to come back? (They believed that the number of those who'd fled in 1948 who were still alive and would actually want to return to Israel was very small.)

They were signaling what they might be able to live with. Ironically, I found Dahlan most resistant on the issue in which I expected the least problem—security. He was still resisting three points: Israeli control of airspace, Israeli right to redeploy in an emergency, and an international presence at all border and entry points. Yes, he understood that this was an area in which Israel needed the greatest reassurance. But don't, he argued, rob us of any appearance of independence.

I never believed in misleading those with whom I negotiated. While acknowledging his concern—and the fervency of it—I told him I did not believe an agreement was possible without accommodating the Israeli concerns in these three areas.

Before we concluded our meetings in New York, Rashid told me that this was hard for Mohammad Dahlan but in the end the Chairman would accept "what you are asking on security." By mid-September, when both sides had returned to the Middle East, I was confident that we could put together an acceptable proposal. Each would battle hard over it, but we could amend it to respond to what each could live with, even if they had to swallow hard to do so.

| READYING THE PROPOSAL, ONE LAST ROUND, AND SHARON GOES TO THE TEMPLE MOUNT |

To be sure, President Clinton still had to decide whether to present a comprehensive proposal. We would be breaking new ground. The United States, even at Camp David, had never adopted a position on all the final status issues. To go on record with firm positions on all the core issues was a historic step. Once taken, it would be hard to take it back.

Naturally, I wanted a thorough discussion with President Clinton of the ideas that might be presented. While the President was in favor of proceeding, Sandy preferred to have him read what I would present as our best judgment, and not engage in a discussion. There was thus no discussion with the President, but in my office I thrashed out the parameters with the members of the team—Aaron, Gamal, Jon, and Rob.

Our internal discussions were heated. Indeed, I would often say that if outside observers saw our discussions, they could easily conclude that we disliked each other.

They would have been dead wrong. Our passion for the issue—the desire for peace—was an extraordinary unifier. It was a bond that we shared. However, we also all felt the responsibility that came with putting an American proposal on the table. Suddenly our judgments about what would work also came into conflict with what we thought was right or just or fair.

Aaron was always arguing for a just and fair proposal. I was not against a fair proposal. But I felt the very concept of "fairness" was, by definition, subjective. Similarly, both Rob and Gamal believed that the Palestinians were entitled to 100 percent of the territory. Swaps should thus be equal. They believed this was a Palestinian right. Aaron tended to agree with them not on the basis of right, but on the basis that every other Arab negotiating partner had gotten 100 percent. Why should the Palestinians be different?

I disagreed. I was focused not on reconciling rights but on addressing needs. In negotiations, one side's principle or "right" is usually the other side's impossibility. Of course, there are irreducible rights. I wanted to address what each side needed, not what they wanted and not what they felt they were entitled to.

Our main disagreements were on the borders. I felt that the Israelis needed 6 to 7 percent of the territory for both security and political purposes. Having looked at maps with 8 percent given to Israeli settlement blocs, I believed it was possible for the Palestinians to have territorial contiguity and viability with 7 percent Israeli annexation. Gamal and Rob wanted no more than 3 to 4 percent annexation and wanted it compensated with an equivalent swap of territory. On refugees, we had no disagreement. Gamal was the most insistent on having the Palestinians face reality: there would be no right of return to Israel, and this was truly the measure of the Palestinian readiness to make peace with Israel.

On Jerusalem and security, our differences were generally minor. We drafted a proposal for the President to consider. I agreed to suggest a range on the territorial issue extending from 4 to 8 percent annexation and a 2 to 3 percent swap. While my colleagues were not happy, I said I would be sure that all views were aired before the President made a decision. In any case, I felt strongly about 6 to 7 percent annexation, and I was not prepared to lower the ceiling. Nor was I prepared to introduce the idea of an equivalent swap.

Of course, our internal discussions did not take place in a vacuum. Both sides were calling daily. When were we going to come with the ideas? Had the President decided yet? Did we need to have further discussions with them? Both sides exhibited anxiety: the Israelis out of fear we might get cold feet and not come with the ideas; the Palestinians out of concern about what the ideas might be.

Finally, in the third week of September, Gilad telephoned to tell me that he and

Saeb would place a joint call later that day and ask to have both sides come to Washington for one more round of discussions with us. Gilad said this was actually Saeb's request but he had accepted Saeb's plea to make this a joint request. When I asked specifically what they would be requesting, Gilad said it was not a request for trilateral discussions but rather for me again to work with each side separately to go over what each could ultimately accept. Gilad made it clear it was Saeb and his colleagues who wanted one last round before we made our proposals. When the joint call came later that day, I agreed.

Before the negotiators arrived in Washington, Arafat visited Barak at his home. Though the negotiators had met often, the leaders had not seen each other since Camp David. Gilad and Saeb (among others) hoped to warm the chilly relations between the two leaders. Both sides reported that the meeting was very warm; Barak and Arafat met alone for about forty-five minutes, then called President Clinton before concluding their evening, with Barak telling the President, "I will be a better partner with the Chairman than even Rabin."

It was in this seemingly hopeful setting that the negotiators arrived for three days of discussions starting September 26. To preserve discretion and to keep the negotiators away from the press, we had them stay at the Ritz-Carlton in Pentagon City. During the course of the three days, I probed to see where the real redlines were. On the Israeli side, I found it with Shlomo on refugees. Shlomo was normally mild-mannered and polite. He rarely if ever lost his temper, but at one point when I had just seen the Palestinians and was asking him how high the Israelis could go on admission of refugees, he lost his composure.

Believing that I would not be pressing for numbers on refugees if it were not for new Palestinian demands, he launched into a tirade. The Palestinian style of negotiation, he said, was to get what they could on every issue; once they had it, they would simply go on to the next issue. Israel was stretching to the maximum on borders and Jerusalem, and the Palestinian response was not to try to meet Israeli needs or produce a package with trade-offs but instead to see what they could get on refugees. He had had it. Enough was enough.

In this particular case, I told Shlomo, the request came from me, not from the Palestinians. "I am raising this because you want an American proposal and I am seeing what the limits are. You want to be mad at someone, be mad at me." He nodded, but I could see I had not persuaded him.

For once, there were no fireworks in the talks with the Palestinian delegation. They were all business. Saeb Erekat, Mohammad Dahlan, and even Akram Haniya (who I knew to have been a negative influence at Camp David), were focused on each issue, trying to explain what they thought they needed and the Israelis could accept.

Dahlan actually came with a new security proposal—one that addressed many of the Israeli concerns but drew the line on an Israeli right to redeploy forces in the event of an emergency. Saeb was determined to play the role of the statesman, being as reasonable and accommodating as he could.

Little did I know that these three days would mark probably the highest hopes for peace during my tenure—and that a descent into chaos and violence would soon follow. At the time, there was one development that Palestinians say transformed everything: Ariel Sharon's visit to the Haram/Temple Mount. Sharon, the leader of the Likud opposition visited the Temple Mount on September 28 with a large contingent of Israeli police providing security for him; both Likud Party politics and his desire to demonstrate that the Barak government could not surrender this sacred ground prompted his visit. On the twenty-seventh, the second day of our meetings, Saeb asked to see me alone during the afternoon. He said he had a personal request from Arafat for me: Might I be able to use our influence to stop Sharon from going to the Haram Al-Sharif the next day? I told Saeb that if we were to ask Sharon not to go, he would seize the U.S. request to make political hay with his right-wing base; he would castigate us and say he would not give in to pressure from any source—including the United States—on Israel's right to the Temple Mount. "We won't dissuade him," I said, "but we may incite him."

But I promised Saeb I would try to persuade Shlomo to limit or block the visit. Shlomo Ben-Ami wore two hats. He was acting Foreign Minister and he was also the Minister of Internal Security. In the past, interior ministers, including Likud ministers, would often cite security concerns to justify the prevention of provocative Israeli behavior in the Arab neighborhoods of East Jerusalem. With that in mind, I asked Shlomo if he could invoke security risks to prevent Sharon from going to the Temple Mount. He said he could not because Israeli intelligence assessed that there was no great risk of violence. Yet as I entered his room, he was on the phone with Jibril Rajoub—the head of Palestinian Preventive Security in the West Bank. He was coordinating with Rajoub, and Rajoub was asking only that Sharon not be allowed to enter the mosques—meaning he might walk around the Haram the next day but not do more than that. Much to Sharon's dislike, Shlomo invoked the security provision to prevent Sharon from entering the mosques but not the Haram grounds.*

Ironically, there was an incident on the twenty-seventh, the day before Sharon's

---

*Only later did I ask the question, If there really was no great concern about the visit provoking violence, why surround Sharon with a massive police presence?

visit. But this involved the killing of an Israeli soldier in an ambush in Gaza, an event the Israelis claim marked the real beginning of the Intifada. On the twenty-eighth, when Sharon went to the Haram, everything was quiet. All hell was to break loose on the twenty-ninth.

But on the twenty-eighth, the last day of our discussions, no one on either delegation acted as if this was a potentially catastrophic development. No one even raised it, even though Sharon—given the seven-hour time difference—had already completed his visit to the Haram before we began our last day's discussions. And our last day's discussions proved quite interesting—I summarized my impressions of where we were on each issue and what I expected the President to do. I told each side that I did not know for sure that the President would present a proposal, but my recommendation, particularly after these three days of separate discussions, was for him to do so. Without describing specifically what we would present, I gave each side a sense of direction on each issue. On borders, I said our proposal would be less than 9 percent annexation discussed at Camp David, but would be closer to that 9 percent than to the 2 percent the Palestinians had countered with at that time; on swaps, I said we would offer more than at Camp David but the swap would neither be equal to the Israeli annexation nor large; on security, I told each that the Dahlan approach on security was serious, but the right of reentry in clearly defined emergency circumstances was important; on refugees, I said there would be no right of return to Israel—telling the Palestinians that if they insisted on this we need not come with a proposal. But I also offered a new idea, explaining that there would be a right of return of Palestinians to the new state and to the "swapped" areas that would be incorporated into it—and in the swap areas that were currently part of Israel we would invest in development so that refugees might settle there. Finally, on Jerusalem, I said we would go beyond Camp David on the question of Palestinian sovereignty for Arab neighborhoods.

I was not asked about the Haram and did not offer anything new on it. In concluding, I said the President would still have to make his final decisions on whether he would come with a proposal and what it would be.

Both sides were optimistic after our final meetings. Notwithstanding the Sharon visit to the Haram, the mood among Erekat, Dahlan, and even Akram Haniya was good. This was not just my impression. Before he left that evening, Mohammad Dahlan phoned George Tenet and boldly declared: "There would be an agreement." (George in turn phoned me and asked, "What did you do with Mohammad? He is leaving here a happy man.")

The good mood did not last long. A new and awful reality was about to confront us and preempt the American proposal—at least for a few months.

| THE INTIFADA: ARAFAT CHOOSES TO RIDE THE WAVE |

I bid good-bye to the Palestinians at about 4 p.m. Two hours later Dani Yatom called me and said Israel had hard evidence that the Palestinian Authority was planning massive, violent demonstrations throughout the West Bank the next morning, Friday, September 29—ostensibly a response to the Sharon visit; Palestinian youth would pour out of the mosques after Friday prayers and go on a rampage.

Dani was very clear: This would be a disaster. The Prime Minister was ready to consider the far-reaching proposal we were preparing; he, too, saw hope in my discussions with the parties. But he could not be making historic concessions in the face of violence. Through their own channels, the Israelis had sent messages to Arafat about the planned violence and there had been no response; it was up to us to persuade Arafat to prevent the violence.

There was little time to act. I briefed the Secretary and then she called Arafat and told him what he must do and what was at stake. Arafat told the Secretary he would do all that he could.

We now know Arafat did not lift a finger to stop the demonstrations, which produced the second Intifada, the next day or in succeeding days. Why not? Some believe that after Camp David he concluded that he could not achieve what he wanted through negotiations and therefore resorted to violence. Certainly that is Ehud Barak's view today. Others believe he planned an escalation to violence all along—or at least after the Israeli withdrawal from Lebanon—in no small part because, in accordance with the "Palestinian narrative," he needed Palestinian independence to result from struggle.*

My view is different. Arafat never planned anything, but he also never foreclosed options. He always kept open the option of violence, believing he might need it at some point if the Israelis would not satisfy him. Sharon's visit gave him a perfect pretext to allow violence to erupt, and it also had the benefit of demonstrating that on the Haram his hands were tied—there could be no flexibility. In this sense, Arafat countenanced violence as a tactical move to gain advantage, but underestimated how uncontrollable the ensuing events might be.

Tragically, he did not appreciate that there was now an extremely combustible mixture. Shaul Mofaz, the Chief of Staff of the Israeli military, worried that the Israelis

---

*Imad Falouji, a Palestinian cabinet minister, declared that the Intifada "had been planned since Chairman Arafat's return from Camp David, when he turned the tables in the face of the former U.S. President and rejected the American conditions." "Palestinian Minister says Palestinian Uprising Was Planned," AP, March 2, 2001.

had largely lost their ability to deter Palestinian violence after the more than a week of violence back in May—when Fatah activists and Palestinian security forces had fired on the IDF but had been met with a relatively weak response. He vowed the IDF would be much stronger in response next time. If they were not, the Palestinians would lose all respect for the IDF and act accordingly. Mofaz told me that only an immediate, strong, and preemptory response would reestablish the Israeli deterrent.

Mofaz, of course, understood that there was anger on the Palestinian street, but felt this was why a political settlement was needed. However, in the meantime he felt there was great danger in letting Palestinians think they could get away with violence.

In the first few days of the violence, the Israeli response was very strong: fifty Palestinians were killed and hundreds wounded, compared with five Israeli civilian deaths.

During that first week—and even through the first two months—Arafat claimed that he was restraining his "soldiers," and the scarcity of IDF casualties was proof of it. But, in fact, there was little restraint on his side; Mofaz's preparation and use of overwhelming force accounted for the disparity in the casualties.

Several other factors, many not planned by either side, fueled the violence. In the initial confrontation on the Haram—when large stones were heaved over the wall onto the plaza below where Jewish worshipers were praying—the head of the Israeli police in Jerusalem was knocked unconscious. While he was still in command, the Israeli forces sought to contain the riot, without live ammunition. Once he was taken to the hospital, Israeli police began using live ammunition in addition to rubber bullets. Five Palestinians were killed, and word spread throughout the West Bank that the Israelis had perpetrated a massacre on the Haram, sparking violence throughout the territories.

Soon large crowds of Palestinians, most throwing stones but some armed with guns and grenades, began attacking Israeli military positions in both the West Bank and Gaza. The result: many more Palestinian casualties. The funerals for each fatality created waves of new emotion and triggered new attacks against the Israeli positions, bringing about more casualties.

During the first days of the violence, a horrifying event became an emblem in Palestinian and Arab eyes of Israeli brutality and indifference to Palestinian lives. Mohammed al-Durrah, a twelve-year-old boy, and his father were caught in the crossfire between IDF and Palestinian gunners at the Netzarim junction in Gaza; the sickening image of this little boy crouching next to his father and the father pleading for the shooting to stop, only to see the boy killed, created outrage among Palestinians. As Arab satellite television replayed the footage of this incident over and over, it became the enduring image of this new Intifada—one Palestinians now called the Al-Aqsa Intifada.

But there were horrifying televised images of Israeli suffering as well. Two Israeli reservists inadvertently took a wrong turn and drove into Ramallah in the initial weeks of the Intifada; they were arrested by the Palestinian police and taken to a police station. Word spread of their presence; a mob overwhelmed those in the police station and murdered the Israelis, throwing their mutilated bodies out of a second-story window in front of a crowd lusting for blood. Then the killers, with obvious pleasure, held up their own bloody hands to show the mob and the television cameras below their handiwork.

Like Palestinians, the Israeli public was outraged. Their anger was compounded by a sense of betrayal. To try to reduce friction in one sensitive area, the Israeli cabinet approved an agreement with the Palestinian security forces in which the Israeli soldiers guarding Joseph's Tomb in Nablus would leave there in return for Palestinian guarantees of this Jewish holy site. After the Israeli pullout, the token Palestinian security presence sent there was quickly overwhelmed by a Palestinian mob that ransacked and destroyed the synagogue at the site, burning its sacred texts and holy scrolls. When this, too, was seen on Israeli television, the Israeli public was outraged at the Palestinians and the Barak government alike, believing its readiness to make concessions was once again being exploited as a weakness.

What did our administration do to try to contain the violence that was rapidly taking on a life of its own? The President, the Secretary, George Tenet, and I were on the phone nearly nonstop with Barak and Arafat and those around them. Arafat portrayed himself and the Palestinians as innocent victims, while Barak saw Arafat as cynically manipulating the violence. We sought to get Barak to order the IDF both to exercise greater restraint in the use of live fire and to expose themselves less to Palestinians. With Arafat, we sought to get orders to interpose the Palestinian security forces between Palestinian rioters and the Israeli military checkpoints and positions in the West Bank and Gaza.

We were caught in a cycle of riots, Palestinian deaths, funerals for the victims, incitement at the funerals, and renewed riots directed at the Israeli military positions. None of the Israeli positions were in or near the center of the Palestinian cities or towns, requiring the Palestinian stone-throwers or gunners to go find them. The President's pleas to Arafat fell on deaf ears. Arafat pointed out that he had no rockets, no tanks, no Apache helicopters—only Israel did—and he asked for the Israelis to pull back their forces, exercise restraint, and get through one day without funerals. Yet he gave no orders to his own forces to stop the riots, much less stop taking part in them.

While Barak was emotional, declaring repeatedly to President Clinton that Arafat must choose between war and peace, Shlomo Ben-Ami looked for a way out and tried to find a way to get Israel to take a step back. He pulled Israeli police forces back in Jerusalem on the Friday after September 29 so as not to have their presence provoke trouble. He was the moving force behind the decision to pull Israeli troops out of the Joseph's Tomb area in Nablus. And he agreed with me that we could only break the escalating cycle if we created, in my words, enough "drama to give Arafat a ladder to climb down from the position he was in and an explanation for doing so."

In my view, Arafat, ever the tactician, was now trying to exploit the environment to reverse the international impression that had been created after Camp David—namely, that Barak wanted peace and Arafat did not. In the new Intifada, Arafat sought to reclaim his role as victim. Assuming the status of victim required the Israelis to make concessions, not the Palestinians. It meant that the international community or the United States should assume responsibility for resolving the conflict, and relieve him of it.

But as the victim, Arafat suddenly had less control than previously over forces building up from the Palestinian street. This was so because the different Palestinian forces—the Fatah activists, elements of the security forces, and Hamas—seemed to regard the new Intifada as an opportunity to gain greater power for themselves. Arafat, the master of maneuvering, would want to control the violence lest any one group become too powerful. At the same time, he would try to ride the emotional wave that the violence reflected in Palestinian society—pent-up anger over the failed promise of Oslo and genuine anger at Arafat himself for the corruption within the Palestinian Authority.

I now wanted an event that would give Arafat an excuse to reassert control and step back from the violence. Shlomo, having spoken with a number of European governments, suggested a meeting in Paris between Barak and Arafat and the Secretary. This would give the French a reason to be helpful, even if they would not be a direct part of the three-way meeting. I worried about President Chirac's propensity to grandstand in such a setting, but agreed that a meeting in Europe could be useful—especially if it provided a reason to try to cool passions in anticipation of what such a meeting might produce.

So we met in Paris: Barak, Arafat, Madeleine, George Tenet, and me. Going in, I had in mind a particular step that might satisfy Arafat's need to show he had produced something without violating Barak's need to show Arafat did not gain from the violence. My idea was to take advantage of the Hebron precedent of 1994. After Baruch Goldstein's killing spree in Hebron in 1994, Rabin accepted the creation and deployment of the TIPH—the Temporary International Presence in Hebron. The TIPH was small and symbolic, and led by the Norwegians. Why not create something similar now? Why not use them as monitors for what we would also reestablish—namely, buffer zones around all Israeli military postions?

| THE PARIS AND SHARM SUMMITS:
PROMISES MADE, PROMISES UNFULFILLED |

Both Arafat and Barak brought delegations to Paris on October 4, and our three delegations met at our ambassador's residence in Paris. The residence is spectacular; it has expansive grounds, imposingly large rooms conjuring up images of the Louis XIV era and is filled with tapestries and artwork worthy of the Louvre. Felix Rohatyn was our ambassador at the time, and he had spent a great deal of his own money to restore the grandeur of the residence—something the French appreciated.

The violence was in its sixth day and the irony of meeting in such a grand place to discuss a new Intifada was not lost on any of us. Arafat seemed relaxed; Barak was edgy, and clearly fearful of appearing to reward the violence. As I suspected, he was determined that Arafat not gain anything. Arafat, conversely, sought something to show his people that once again he had craftily produced for them.

We met with Barak and his delegation first, and we heard a tirade from him. When I tried my idea of a symbolic TIPH-like group of monitors on him, he rejected it categorically: "Arafat wants to internationalize the conflict; we will not do it." When I argued that he was not breaking new ground—Rabin had created the precedent and the monitors deployed at points of friction would serve Israel's interests—he was adamant: "No way."

Barak the purist, Barak the seeker of clarity, would not take advantage of the Rabin precedent because Arafat would appear to gain something from it. To be sure, Arafat wanted to gain an internationalized response to the violence—a point those around him argued for passionately in our meetings. More than a TIPH-type presence, they wanted a full-blown international force "to protect our people from the Israeli military." As Arafat sat silently, Nabil Sha'ath and Saeb Erekat argued emotionally that the Chairman "cannot leave here without producing at least a sign for his people that there will be protection from the Israelis."

Seeing that they could not persuade us on international forces or monitors, Nabil and Saeb—with Arafat joining the discussion on this—pressed for an inquiry commission. This would at least allow them to demonstrate to Palestinians that there would be some accountability or responsibility that might be assigned to the Israelis for Palestinian dead and wounded. Though not necessarily accepting this point, I felt there was merit in a fact-finding committee and did not mind if the Palestinians used it to provide themselves with cover or an explanation for calling off the violence. So I suggested a U.S.-led fact-finding committee to look into how the violence erupted, how and why it had intensified, and what lessons both sides could draw from it to avoid any repetition of it in the future.

In a three-way meeting, both Arafat and Barak were willing to accept such a formulation. They differed on the makeup of the fact-finding group. Barak wanted only Americans; Arafat wanted it to be international in composition and led by the UN.

Agreeing to come back to this, we turned our attention to the practical steps each side could take to make it easier for the other to step back from the abyss. During the early evening, Barak asked for a break to caucus with his delegation on possible moves.

After a delay of close to two hours—recalling the day we spent waiting at Camp David—Arafat got fed up with sitting around and stalked out, ordering his car to leave. As Madeleine literally ran after him, I interrupted the Israeli caucus, telling the Prime Minister that we were fed up; that Arafat felt like an underling waiting to be beckoned.

Madeleine, having persuaded Arafat to stay, also told Barak he could not treat the Palestinians this way. Barak, chagrined, came downstairs and apologized to Arafat, changing the mood and setting the stage for a good discussion on managing key points of friction. The Erez crossing in Gaza was one such point. The two sides quickly agreed on creation of a perimeter around it, with the Palestinians ensuring that the building next to the Israeli military position would not be used as a platform from which to shoot at the Israelis. We began going over what each side needed to do. The Israelis would give new orders to their forces, making sure they would only fire on Palestinians if their lives were endangered. The Palestinians would stop demonstrators and rioters from going to the Israeli checkpoints, and Arafat would give orders to the Palestinian security forces and the Tanzim, the Fatah activists, not to initiate violence—something Arafat did during this part of the discussion when he asked for a phone and called Gaza to give these orders. George Tenet, guiding the two sides, gradually developed a number of agreed points verbally.

George asked me to summarize for Arafat and Barak the points of agreement, and both leaders accepted my verbal summary. Barak then asked if I would put the agreed points in writing so both leaders could sign them. I asked Arafat if he was willing to have me put on paper what we had just agreed to and he nodded his approval. But he also said that French President Chirac had wanted to host the Prime Minister and him and it was impolite to keep him waiting any longer, so perhaps while I prepared the paper the Secretary, he, and Barak could go see Chirac.

Neither the verbal points nor my write-up included any reference to an international presence or monitors. This, it turned out, is why Arafat wanted to see Chirac at that point. When the Secretary and Barak began to describe the understanding I was now preparing, Chirac said that it was not acceptable without inclusion of an international presence. He, who had taken part in none of the day's discussion but had obviously been informed by the Palestinians in advance of the meeting, was taking the Palestinian side and insisting that the understanding we had painstakingly developed was incomplete. Both the Secretary and Barak felt set up. Arafat now had a reason not to sign a document that did not contain a reference to an international presence—or something that suggested at a minimum some international criticism of the Israeli use of force against the Palestinians.

On the issue of the fact-finding committee and its composition, which might have implied there could be some criticism of Israeli tactics, I had tried several compromises, including the suggestion that it would be American-led but with supporting staff to include Europeans. Barak was willing to accept that in the end; Arafat was not. In the paper I drafted I had incorporated all the points that had been agreed as well as a point on a fact-finding group, leaving the exact composition vague.

After the Chirac meeting, Arafat did not return to the residence, but to his hotel. In his stead, he sent Nabil Sha'ath and Saeb to the residence to negotiate the paper. This launched an all-night negotiation, with Nabil and Saeb challenging everything I had written. While not challenging the substance of the agreed points, they argued that Arafat needed cover in any signed document. He could not talk about groups on the Palestinian side as if they were responsible for the violence, and he was now giving orders to stop the violence. I tried to understand whether they were really walking away from the substance or simply looking for a different way to package what Arafat had accepted for the Palestinian street. The fact that they wanted the paper to start with Israeli, not Palestinian, responsibilities suggested this was more about form than substance. But the fact that Arafat had not returned suggested to me that he was looking for a way to avoid concluding the agreement—at least formally.

Both Nabil and Saeb denied that the Chairman was seeking to walk away from the agreement, but after much prodding, did admit that Mubarak had invited both Arafat and Barak to come see him tomorrow and that it would be best to conclude the agreement in Sharm al-Sheikh in Mubarak's presence.

That might have been fine, except that Barak was convinced that if he were to go to Egypt without the agreement signed, he would be subject to pressure from Mubarak to give more to Arafat. He feared, given the experience with Chirac, that Arafat would seek to corner him on the international presence or inquiry commission issues—either one of which he assumed Mubarak would back unconditionally. Moreover, he saw Arafat's reluctance to sign what he had agreed to verbally as an indication of bad faith on his part.

Though we literally worked through the night, speaking twice to Moussa to have him convey to both the Palestinian negotiators and Arafat that Egypt wanted them to come to Sharm al-Sheikh with the agreement already signed, Arafat would not authorize his negotiators to conclude the understandings. Barak, for his part, would not go to Egypt without a signed agreement.

There was thus no signed agreement, and Barak announced he was returning to Israel. We put the best face on the meeting and the all-night session, announcing that what was important was not a written piece of paper but the performance on the promises made. For a day the promises seemed to be holding. The Israelis showed greater restraint in response to Palestinian rioters, and in a number of places, Palestinian police made an effort to hold back demonstrators, physically blocking them from Israeli positions.

But this lasted only a day, at least on the Palestinian side. When we met Arafat with Mubarak later in Egypt, there was a clear signal from the Chairman that he was not going to do much the next day—Friday, the Muslim day of prayer. When, in front of Mubarak, I said it was very important to "keep things calm after tomorrow's Friday prayers," Arafat replied, "I am worried about what is going to happen tomorrow"—as if he were incapable of doing anything about it.

His answer indicated to me that he was not going to stop or contain the trouble, even though Shlomo was acting to keep the Israeli police out of sight in the Haram area, and in a low profile in and around the Old City.

That, of course, did not stop those bent on trouble the next day: an angry crowd of Palestinians simply attacked an Israeli police station near St. Stephens Gate near the Old City wall. Friday was a bad day and the next became worse when the Israelis pulled out of Joseph's Tomb only to see it ransacked a few hours later.

Barak had lived up to the promises of Paris; Arafat, past the first day, had not. Now Barak had reached his limit. Saturday evening, October 7, Barak announced a forty-eight-hour ultimatum: "If we don't see a change in the patterns of violence in the next two days, we will regard this as a cessation by Arafat of the peace process. And we will order the army . . . to use all means at their disposal to halt the violence."

That night the President spoke to Arafat, and I heard something different in Arafat's voice: he sounded afraid. I felt he took Barak's ultimatum seriously, and the President was effective in reinforcing it, particularly by emphasizing that there was nothing that he would be able to do if Arafat did not now give orders to the Tanzim to stop the violence. For the first time in their conversations since September 29, President Clinton was angry. Arafat seemed to understand, and told the President he would give orders to the Tanzim.

This might have been a genuine moment to stop the violence if Barak and our administration had stuck to their guns. But Barak came under pressure from his cabinet—dominated by the left—not to suspend the negotiations. Europe echoed this. For our part, though, the President had been tough with Arafat, he asked Barak if he really wanted to imprison himself with the ultimatum. Where would he be if Arafat did not respond? Under pressure from the Europeans—and at least implicitly us—at the end of the forty-eight hours Barak extended the deadline to give the international community time to work on Arafat to get him to perform.

Having declared an ultimatum, Barak should not have backed off. Arafat was scared and ready to perform. Barak no doubt had to be mindful of the politics of his cabinet and the politics of his country, and the two were not the same. Those who continued to believe a deal was possible with Arafat dominated his cabinet; they feared that once the negotiations were suspended, it would be difficult to resume them—the very objective of their opponents on the right. Yet the mood of the country had soured, particularly in the face of Palestinian violence and the perception that every act of Israeli restraint fed the violence.

Barak was torn, and tried to have it both ways, effectively ensuring that he would have neither. Meanwhile, with the heat off him, Arafat nonetheless did begin to perform, and for a few days the violence did taper off. Would it have continued without another event intervening? We will never know. Unfortunately, there was another event: The October 12 lynching in a Palestinian police station in Ramallah of two Israeli reserve soldiers took place.

This time Barak would not be restrained. We tried to reach him that morning and he would not take the President's calls. He was going to retaliate and hit the Palestinian Authority hard. Barak had helicopters destroy security offices adjacent to Arafat's compound in Gaza—with Arafat in the compound. The IDF destroyed several other police stations in Gaza City and in the West Bank, including the one where the soldiers were murdered. Beyond this, the Israelis tightened the siege around Gaza and the West Bank, making movement within and to the outside basically impossible. They closed the Gaza airport and the international passageways, and built barriers around the cities in the West Bank.

Now it was Arafat's turn to be defiant. While Israel had taken care to warn Palestinians to get out of these buildings before destroying them from the air, Palestinian cities were under attack even so. Moreover, Palestinians were effectively being quarantined—and their plight was televised around the world. Arafat made the most of this imagery and soon it appeared that events were spinning out of control again.

It was in this context that again I pushed for an event of greater drama. Now I felt there was little prospect of breaking an escalating cycle of violence, reprisal, anger, and grievance if we did not force both sides to take a step back and pause. I argued for the President to put together a summit in Egypt, hosted by President Mubarak, that would put pressure on both sides to agree to a practical set of steps designed to defuse the conflict.

Arafat, initially feeling that the mood internationally was swinging in his favor, resisted the idea of the summit. Before he would agree to the summit he sought Israeli withdrawal to military positions held prior to the Intifada; an end to the closure of the Gaza airport and the international passageways; and a commitment on an international fact-finding commission.

We worked for several days with President Mubarak, UN Secretary-General Kofi Annan—who happened to be in the region and was shuttling between Barak and Arafat—King Abdullah of Jordan, Crown Prince Abdullah of Saudi Arabia, and European leaders to get Arafat to understand that all the issues he was raising would be addressed in the summit. But there would be no preconditions for the summit. Arafat relented and we went to Sharm al-Sheikh for two days, October 16 and 17.

Sharm was co-chaired by President Clinton and President Mubarak; King Abdullah, Kofi Annan, and Javier Solana of Spain (representing the European Union) all participated. But the U.S. delegation ran the show. Though we initially tried to draft an agreed communiqué at the ministerial level, it became clear that this was mission impossible. The Palestinians insisted on Israeli mea culpas that were never going to be forthcoming. After several hours of trying to fashion a document, I suggested that the President meet with the leaders separately. In the meantime, George Tenet and Omar Suleiman—the head of Egyptian intelligence—began joint discussions with Israeli and Palestinian security officials.

By early evening, George called to tell me that they were making good progress toward an agreed security work plan—the essence of which was parallel declarations of a cease-fire, Palestinian orders to security forces and Tanzim to stop violence, Palestinian establishment of no-demonstration zones near Israeli positions, Israeli reopening of the Gaza airport and international passageways after forty-eight hours, and a gradual withdrawal by the IDF over the course of a week to the positions it held pre-September 29. This sequence began with common declarations but required two days of clear Palestinian performance before the Israelis would have to begin to reciprocate. It was to remain confidential. Of course, nothing ever came easily, and while the basic substance of this plan did not change, the wording and additional elements on no Palestinian incitement and Israeli restraint became a source of contention. In the end, Avi Dichter, the new Israeli head of Shin Bet, obtained Barak's approval, but Jibril Rajoub told George that we would have to get Arafat's explicit acceptance of the plan.

Close to midnight, George asked to convene a three-way meeting with Clinton, Mubarak, and Arafat to get the Chairman's approval. I accompanied the President and George to the meeting, and Suleiman and Osama al-Baz accompanied Mubarak. Rajoub and Abu Rudeina were with Arafat. Arafat listened as George presented the points of the work plan. Rajoub did not say a word. Arafat, his leg twitching, did not immediately respond.

I was familiar with this posture. Arafat used silence to create nervousness, to suggest opposition, and to indicate the need to be further satisfied. Both Mubarak and President Clinton tried to fill the vacuum created by Arafat's silence. Mubarak was trying to coax Arafat into accepting the work plan, saying that after it was accepted a political process would resume and "President Clinton will be able to help you." Clinton picked up on that theme, telling the Chairman that he was ready to help the Palestinians but he needed a calm environment to do so, and this work plan was the way to produce it.

Arafat referred to the need for international monitors or at least a commission again, as if he was reopening everything. I signaled to the President that I wanted to say something and he asked me to speak. "Mr. Chairman," I said, "we have a work plan developed by George Tenet and Omar Suleiman. Both men know your needs. What they have done requires both sides to move with very precise steps pegged to a timeline. Without the agreed approach on security, nothing is going to happen. There will be no U.S. proposal—though we have given a great deal of thought to one—there will be no easing of the conditions for your people, and you will lose the remaining time of the Clinton presidency. And you have told me repeatedly we can only resolve the conflict and make peace with President Clinton."

At this point, Arafat nodded, and President Clinton told him he needed his help to move things forward. Arafat agreed to the work plan, but of course we still needed to agree on what would be said at the end of the summit—and who would say it.

Based on the polemical discussions earlier over a communiqué, my recommendation was to have us issue a statement on behalf of the parties. This avoided the need for either side to sign the statement, but still required basic agreement on its content to ensure that neither side would contradict what we said. The President met with Arafat and Barak separately and alone first in the early hours of the morning and again prior to the issuance of the statement to garner their agreement.

We had three substantive parts to the statement: first, general steps that would be taken to restore security and end the violence—steps that embraced the outlines of the Tenet work plan without spelling out the timetable for the specific steps; second, the formation of a fact-finding committee based on the United States working with the Israelis and Palestinians—and "in consultation with the United Nations Secretary-General." The committee would have responsibility for assessing the facts "on the events of the past several weeks and how to prevent their recurrence"; third, the development of a pathway back to negotiations to result from our announcing that the United States would consult with the parties on how best to resume "efforts to reach a permanent status agreement."

It was not easy to produce the parts of the Statement addressing the fact-finding committee and the resumption of the peace process. Barak was determined to preserve a U.S.-led committee and to prevent an immediate resumption of peace negotiations before seeing that the violence had really stopped. Arafat continued to seek a UN-led fact-finding committee and wanted peace talks to resume the next day, either because he wanted to use this as cover for stopping the violence or because he wanted to use violence as a lever on the negotiations.

We bridged the differences by declaring that on the fact-finding committee we would consult with Kofi Annan on its formation and it would be led by Americans—eventually former senators George Mitchell and Warren Rudman—but would have European and Muslim representatives. On the peace talks, we announced that we would consult with the two sides for two weeks to determine how best "to move forward."

Arafat ultimately accepted the statement in a meeting with the President and Mubarak shortly before the President issued it. Until the end, Amre Moussa resisted it, arguing it was too general and that the Israelis needed to make gestures immediately in terms of lifting the siege of the Palestinians—something that was to take place over the course of a week, assuming that the Palestinians performed in the initial forty-eight hours. Mubarak not only overruled Moussa but also excluded him from the last meeting with Clinton and Arafat.*

In Arafat's private meeting with the President, the Chairman told Clinton he was ready to go to another summit but felt it was important for him and Barak to have separate meetings with the President first to pave the way. As a result, the President invited him to come to Washington.

Arafat got his invitation to Washington and we got our statement at the end of Sharm but once again Arafat failed in his performance. In the name of the Palestinian Authority a general statement calling for an end to violence was issued, but the buffer zones did not appear, the incitement did not end, and the violence continued. Thus, the Israelis, after making some initial moves, stopped their compliance. When George Tenet and I each made calls to Rajoub and Dahlan, we were told that the Chairman would fulfill his obligations but needed to wait until after an Arab summit to be held on October 21–22. It was the first summit of the Arab League in four years and the Chairman wanted to use it to justify the steps he would then take—or so we were told.

I saw it differently, and said so to the President and Vice President in an October 24 meeting in the Situation Room with the entire national security team. In my view, Arafat saw the Intifada as a vehicle to reestablish his leverage with Arab leaders for the first time in a decade. They had ignored him or thrown him crumbs throughout the

---

*Some believe that Moussa's behavior at Sharm led Mubarak to replace him as Foreign Minister six months later.

1990s. He was not a threat to them, and because the United States was managing the peace process, they felt able to turn their back on him. Now, with the Intifada playing day and night on Arab satellite TV, with anger welling up on the Arab street, with Arafat seen as fighting for Palestinian rights and Arab regimes under pressure to do something, it was Arafat these regimes needed to respond to. Arafat, regardless of "what he told you at Sharm," will keep milking this.

President Clinton replied, "Dennis, I always agree with your analysis and your recommendations, but I don't this time because it leaves Arafat with a complete dead end. He achieves nothing that endures. The Arab leaders won't in the end do anything for him. He will force Barak either to turn to Sharon or out of office, and he will have nothing."

The presumption that Arafat still wanted a deal led us to preserve his invitation to the White House on November 9—two days after the Bush-Gore election—even though Arafat did not fulfill his promises from Sharm al-Sheikh. Barak was to follow Arafat to Washington on Sunday, November 12.

| THE WHITE HOUSE MEETINGS AND A NEW BACK CHANNEL |

Unlike President Clinton, I doubted Arafat's purposes. Reestablishing his leverage on Arab leaders and building his stature in the Arab world superseded his interest in stopping the Intifada at this juncture. Was he ready at the very last moment, at the very last minute, to do a final peace deal with Israel? I remained uncertain, even if increasingly skeptical. If he retained an interest in doing a deal, I felt our only chance was to keep the pressure on him—and from that standpoint, we should have rescinded his invitation to the White House. But that was not in the cards, so I sought to use Arafat's prospective meeting with President Clinton—something he always wanted—as a lever on him to stop the violence. In the two-week period after the Arab summit, I told Arafat and those around him that it was hard to believe that the President would be willing to see him at the White House if the violence continued.

While the violence did not stop, it did abate in the week prior to the visit. In truth, it is highly unlikely that President Clinton would have canceled his meeting under any circumstances at this point. He was determined to try to transform the situation, his presidency was coming to a close, and he remained convinced that he could get something done. The messages he was receiving from Barak at this time were decidedly mixed. He wanted the President to be very tough on Arafat, to tell him that this was it and a failure to make meaningful concessions would expose the Chairman before the world as someone committed to conflict, not peace. In effect, Barak wanted the President to be tough on Arafat to soften him up—so that Arafat might then do a deal.

Barak had obviously not given up and—even with my doubts—neither had I. In light of my enduring question as to what Arafat would do at the moment of truth, I told the President that in the meeting he needed to test whether Arafat would do a deal. The President agreed: he would present the basic parameters within which a deal was possible and ask whether Arafat was prepared to accept them.

On territory and borders, the President would tell Arafat that the end result for the Palestinians would be "mid-90s." On security, the President would repeat what I had told the Palestinians in September on nonmilitarization, airspace, emergency re-deployment, early-warning stations, an international presence, and border controls. On East Jerusalem, in a move beyond Camp David and even what I had implied in September, he would speak of a broad principle: what was Arab would be Palestinian and what was Jewish would be Israeli; on the Haram, he would say that each side would have to control what was holy to them. And on refugees, his message would be blunt: there could not be a right of return to Israel, but there could be a large international fund for compensation.

The punch line at the end of the presentation: the President would need to know from Arafat if this was "in the ballpark" of what he could accept. If so, the President would work for agreement; if not, there was nothing more he could do.

As I entered the White House for the November 9 meeting, I was struck by the timing. We had just had a presidential election, and yet two days after it we did not know who Bill Clinton's successor was going to be. For Bill Clinton, maybe this was a time to be thinking even more of building his legacy, particularly if a disputed election might affect the authority of his successor. I told the President he should say something about the election—and how this changed nothing for him: he would be leaving office in two and a half months and needed to know now whether a deal was possible.

Clinton nodded his assent. He began the meeting by explaining the meaning of a U.S. election in which the outcome for president was still uncertain, saying, "The only thing that is certain is that I won't be President on January 20." Then he turned to the matter of Middle East peace, following his outline closely on all issues except refugees. On refugees, he was less blunt than planned, choosing a different way to explain why Israel could not be expected to accept the right of return as a principle: no Israeli prime minister could be expected to make gut-wrenching compromises on all issues and have an opening on refugees that, in his words, would produce "an elephant in his living room twenty years later," as the youthful Palestinian population returned en masse to Israel.

At this point, Arafat took an article from *Ha'aretz* out of his pocket. It reported that many of the Russians who had come to Israel were either not Jewish or not considered Jewish by the rabbinate in Israel. His point was that if the Israelis can let in these Russians, they can let in the Palestinians.*

Nonetheless, the President asked if the parameters for agreement that he had outlined were in the ballpark of what he could agree to. Arafat answered, "Yes!" Naturally, I wanted to be sure that he meant it—that he understood what the President was asking—so I interjected, "Mr. Chairman, the President needs to know that what he has just presented to you is basically acceptable to you; in the ballpark means that you basically accept it as the outlines of what you could live with on each issue in an agreement."

Arafat responded, "Yes, as principles it is acceptable." I asked, What about the details? Were they acceptable? He could not say. He was not agreeing to the details because he had not been presented with the details. The President said knowing that the general points he had presented were acceptable was what he needed to know at this time. Arafat again acknowledged they were.

In retrospect, perhaps we read too much into his answer. Perhaps he was going to say yes to this in the belief that it would create a new baseline in the negotiations that was sufficiently general that it would not bind him or make it possible for us to claim bad faith later on. But the President, Sandy, Madeleine, and I (and all the members of the team) took Arafat's yes to be a serious answer—one that meant that these parameters constituted an acceptable framework for him for the final deal. Arafat had never revealed anything meaningful to us on the outlines of a permanent status deal before. Here he seemed to be acknowledging basic compromises on all the core issues—and in effect confirming the view that at the last moment he was capable of deciding and making peace.

For our part, we were eager to tell Barak that Arafat would accept these parameters as the basis for a deal. But on November 12, when I joined the President for his private discussion with Barak over dinner in the President's small kitchen behind the Oval Office, Barak's response was a nonresponse. He simply listened to the parameters and to Arafat's acceptance of them "as being in the ballpark" and chose not to comment. Instead, he again focused on the violence, making clear he would have to toughen his policy if we did not toughen ours toward Arafat. Understandable at one level, but unlikely given what we had just reported to him.

With our dinner discussion going nowhere, I raised an idea I had broached to Arafat during his visit: Why not open a back channel between himself and Amnon Shahak first to defuse the violence and second to work on understandings on perma-

---

*This became Arafat's standard way of responding on the right of return issue; even throughout the first year of the Bush administration, he would show visiting groups this same article. Danny Rubenstein, "Arafat to PM: Time to make peace, not incite," *Ha'aretz,* June 24, 2001.

nent status? Arafat had agreed to this channel. Why don't you start it and see if it produces? I now asked Barak. Though hardly enthusiastic, Barak agreed.

As it turned out, Barak would not actually launch this channel for nearly two weeks. When he did, it almost immediately led to a further scaling back of the violence. Indeed, in the first meeting, Arafat surprised Shahak, by offering to take a step Amnon considered more difficult than the ones he was raising: sending Palestinian police to Beit Jala (next to Bethlehem) in order to stop Palestinian shooting into the Jerusalem neighborhood of Gilo. This was certain to be more meaningful to Israelis than stopping violence in Gaza.

Unfortunately, after this good start, there was an incident in Gaza in which one of the officers in Dahlan's Preventive Security Organization (PSO) killed an Israeli. Amnon canceled the next meeting, but as the violence diminished, Amnon agreed to resume the discussions with the permanent status issues now put on the table. In the subsequent meetings, Arafat requested that Gilad Sher and Saeb Erekat reengage on the details of the issues and they did so.

Conditions continued to improve. The riots and demonstrations had stopped during the month of November. But shooting incidents remained a problem, especially either in or from the West Bank against Israelis. Until the back channel began, there were over forty such incidents daily. Afterward, they dropped to six or seven a day. Both we and the Israelis now believed that Arafat was making a real effort to bring the situation under control. My conversations with Yossi Ginossar, Gilad, Amnon, Saeb, Mohammad Dahlan, and Mohammad Rashid indicated that progress was also being made on the permanent status discussions.

Both sides suggested that it would be a good time for me to see Arafat. I did not want to go to the area now because the Mitchell-led fact-finding committee was there on its initial trip—and for it to be seen as independent, it was important for me to keep my distance from this group. Instead, I suggested a meeting in Morocco, and Arafat quickly agreed.

| ARAFAT OFFERS NEW HOPE IN RABAT |

I could not go to Rabat to see Arafat without seeing the King first. King Mohammad of Morocco had inherited the throne at the time of his father's death in the summer of 1999. He was young, in his mid-thirties, with a delicate manner and appearance. He was intelligent and ready to reinforce my messages with Arafat, believing we were on the verge of losing a historic opportunity. I was pleased with his response, but also knew he did not have the clout or authority of his father. Having announced that I would be leaving as the U.S. negotiator at the end of the term in January, I now joked with my team after seeing the King that if I were doing a David Letterman Top Ten reasons for knowing when it was time to leave the peace process, I had just seen number one on the list: when you go from being younger than all the leaders you dealt with to be being much older. (I had just turned fifty-two, nearly twenty years older than this young King.)

Of course, I was not older than Arafat. But he was not showing his age in this meeting. We were now in the month of Ramadan. We began the meeting after the Iftar meal that breaks the fast at sundown. He was in a great mood. After Saeb briefed us on his meetings with Gilad, covering where they stood on security and Jerusalem in particular, I asked to see the Chairman alone.

I started our private meeting by reminding him that he had always said we would only reach agreement with President Clinton, and I agreed with his assessment. That was why I had decided to leave at the end of the administration—either we would reach agreement now or there would be a long hiatus. Though the battling in the courts had not yet been resolved between Bush and Gore, I told Arafat that I believed Bush would prevail and that the new Bush administration was unlikely to invest much in Middle East peace—particularly if President Clinton, after all his efforts, failed to achieve an agreement.

Arafat initially said, "I hope you will not leave. We need you. Both sides need you." We were sitting no more than three feet apart. I said, "I am leaving so let's try to finish this. Look, we have five weeks left. We don't have time to screw around. I am not going to fool you, and you are not going to fool me. Let's level with each other. You know what the Israelis can do on the issues. You are the only one on your side who knows what you can accept at the end of the day. You and I both know that no one on your side knows what you are going to decide. I need to know, is there a deal here?"

Arafat, looking intently at me, said, "Yes, there is." Why? I asked. "Because," Arafat replied, "I am serious and they are serious."

That was not enough for me. So I said, "You are talking about intentions, and I am asking about capabilities. I need to know if there is a deal based on what you know the Israelis can do. Is there?" Again, he said, "Yes," and again I asked why, and again he repeated, "Because I am serious and they are serious."

"Let's be more precise," I said. I am going to run through what I believe the Israelis can do at the end of the day, and you tell me whether you can accept it—only that is going to tell us whether there is a deal. He nodded. I said, You have heard from Saeb on security issues and what he briefed is what I think Israel will require. But on the other issues, here's my best judgment of what Barak can accept. On territory, he is "going to need 7 to 8 percent annexation and can live, in my judgment, with a 2 percent swap. You get 94 to 95 percent of the territory." On Jerusalem, he can ultimately accept "the principle of what is Arab is Palestinian and what is Jewish is Israeli," but he will need sovereignty over historic and religious sites like "the Jewish cemetery on the Mount of Olives, and the City of David in a part of the Silwan neighborhood," on the Old City, sovereignty will be based on the division of "what is Arab is yours and what is Jewish is his," but there will also have to be a special regime that governs the day-to-day reality. On the Haram, he can "live with your control over the surface as long as he has control over the subsurface." And on refugees, he cannot accept the right of return to Israel; he can "accept unlimited right of return to your state," and areas that are currently part of Israel that will become part of your state. He can "admit a very small number of refugees into Israel under the title of family reunification" and priority here can be given to refugees from Lebanon—but "I am talking about total numbers of a few thousand."

I paused and then said, That's the essence of what you can get from the Israelis. Now, "can you live with that? Can you do a deal based on that?"

"Yes," was his simple reply. I looked at him as his eyes remained fixed on me. He was not going to add to this reply, not to qualify it or to expand on it. He was not going to try to negotiate the issues or tell me he could do most of this but would need something more here or there. I had been blunt and this was his response. I asked him how he thought we should follow up on this conversation, and he suggested I get together with the negotiators. When I suggested we bring them to Washington to try to forge the agreement, he was enthusiastic.

As I bid him good-bye, I wondered what I had really gotten. Was he as ready as he seemed to do the deal? I decided to go to our embassy in Rabat and place secure calls to Madeleine to report on the meeting and to Martin so he could brief Barak.

Each was enthusiastic. Each asked me why I was less so. I told each I was not sure about Arafat. I was afraid that he thought both Barak and Clinton were so desperate for a deal that it did not matter what I said about bottom lines. But I agreed we had to test what he had told me by bringing the negotiators together in Washington.

Not surprisingly, Barak tried to reach me before I left Morocco the next morning to hear directly from me. Having a briefing from someone else was never as good as hearing it from the horse's mouth. I did speak to him later that day, but from an aristocratic mansion an hour outside of London.

If we were headed toward a deal, I wanted the Saudis to back it unequivocally. So I made arrangements to stop secretly to see Bandar at his country estate outside of London. When I briefed Bandar, he shared my doubts, but was willing to help and push Arafat as hard as he could to accept the deal that was in the offing. Bandar provided his elegant study for whatever calls I had to make. When I reached Barak, he wanted me to repeat carefully what I had told Arafat, how Arafat had responded, and how I assessed all of this. I told him honestly I was not sure, but we had to test it. He agreed, and I suggested that we bring the negotiators for one final round to Bolling Air Force Base just outside of Washington on December 19.

Calls made, I explained to Bandar that I had spoken to Barak and that he was hopeful and ready for one last round of negotiations based on what I had said to Arafat. It was a chilly December evening as we sat in front of Bandar's fireplace, and he said something I will never forget: "If Arafat does not accept what is available now, it won't be a tragedy, it will be a crime."

| ONE LAST ROUND PRODUCES THE CLINTON IDEAS |

Starting on December 19, each side sent delegations to Bolling Air Force Base. Though it was arranged on short notice, the Air Force made the base, its VIP center, and its row of condominiums available to the sizable delegations each had brought. By appearances, the small team of lawyers on each side suggested they were ready to draft.

I hosted a lunch to open the meetings. I told both teams that we were now facing the moment of truth. Either we would conclude an agreement now or we would probably lose the possibility—and face unknown consequences—for the foreseeable future. To facilitate their task I would narrow the bounds within which they would negotiate the remaining differences by presenting general parameters on each issue. Both sides listened to my presentation and seemed responsive.

Before leaving them at Bolling, with a plan to return anytime they needed me, I sat with each side separately. First, with the Israelis, Gilad Sher passed on a message from Barak: he could not go below 7 percent annexation in the West Bank. That was rock bottom. Barak would appreciate it if I would reinforce this position with the Palestinians. Gilad said the two sides would shortly sit together and see if they could hammer out agreements. When I saw Saeb Erekat and Mohammad Dahlan a little later before their first meetings, Dahlan raised the territorial issue, reminding me that in September he had said that 6 percent annexation would break up the integrity of the West Bank. Now he said the Palestinians could not accept more than 5 percent as the upper limit. I told him, "Mohammad, you know I have never misled you. I always tell you what I believe. I am quite certain the Israelis will not go below 7 percent annexation. You can get a net 95 percent of the territory with a 2 percent swap but you will not do better than that. Look for some other forms of compensation from the Israelis or from us."

Saeb said, "Dennis, listen to Mohammad, we will need more territory." To which I replied, Saeb, it is not going to happen, think about what else you can get on safe passage or use of Israeli ports or a Palestinian desalinization plant in Haifa. (I was suggesting additional nonterritorial forms of compensation to the Palestinians for the Israeli annexation.)

Neither Mohammad nor Saeb liked what I had to say, but they knew it was pointless to try to press for more from me. They went to meet their Israeli counterparts.

At Bolling it was easy for small groups of different Israelis and Palestinians to sit together. Gidi Grinstein, Israel Hasson, Mike Herzog, and others had come with Gilad and Shlomo. It was a large delegation and, I soon found out, not a unified one. That evening, Dahlan called Gamal and asked him to pass on to me word that the Israelis had accepted 5 percent annexation.

When Gamal told me this, I was stunned and angry. My initial instinct was to question this. But I also knew that Dahlan would be stupid to make it up, knowing I could easily check it.

I called Gilad and told him what I had been told. While it was clear he was unhappy, he did not deny this had been conveyed to the Palestinians. I was furious. What was the point of my conveying a tough posture on issues of supposed principle to the Israeli side if they were simply going to undercut me? "Don't ask me to convey any messages or reinforce your positions from now on," I told him. "I won't do it."

Over the next several days the talks between the two sides quickly became frozen again on the gaps that separated them on each position. Both sides again brought us back to the late September position of saying they could respond to us but not to each other. Could we break the logjam by making a proposal?

I checked with both leaders to see if this was, in fact, their position as well. It was. After spending another day going over with each set of negotiators what they could live with and what they could not, we proceeded to develop what became known as the Clinton ideas.

| SHAPING THE CLINTON IDEAS |

Given all the work we had done, it was not especially difficult to come up with ideas or a proposal that we felt met the essential needs of each side. After discussions with Madeleine and Sandy, I believed there were three important ways to qualify what we presented. First, we would present a comprehensive proposal on the core issues of Jerusalem, borders, security, and refugees. On borders, Jerusalem, and refugees, we would provide some very limited options from which to choose. (The thought was that these would be the two sides' decision to make and they could still negotiate them, but we were shrinking the gaps on each issue to very limited and inherently bridgeable choices.) Second, fearing the Arafat style of pocketing any advance and treating it as a point of departure and not the culmination of the effort, we would not present a formal piece of paper that would exist after the Clinton presidency ended, but would instead have President Clinton present the ideas informally and orally. And lastly, and very much related to the concern about pocketing, we would withdraw the ideas if they were not acceptable to either side. (In particular, we would tell Arafat that the ideas would "disappear when President Clinton leaves office.")

To add to the informality, I recommended that we present the Clinton ideas as "ideas," not as a proposal. The President accepted this approach, and I informed both sides that he would present his ideas on Saturday morning, December 23, at the White House. The Saturday presentation required the Israelis to move to a hotel near the White House before sundown on Friday so they could walk to the meeting without violating the Sabbath.

| DAHLAN'S MIDNIGHT PLEA |

My parting words to both sides on Friday afternoon, December 22, were that we had listened carefully to both sides and what the President would present would reflect his best judgment of what they each needed, not what they wanted. Late that night, Gamal called to tell me that Dahlan needed to come see me. "Is this really necessary?" I asked, and Gamal reported that Dahlan felt he "must see you." Gamal brought him to my house around midnight.

Mohammad Dahlan was the leader of the security forces in Gaza. His role had grown over the years beyond security, and Arafat, especially during the Netanyahu period, had begun to use him in all the sensitive negotiations. While thanking me for seeing him, now he wasted no time on pleasantries. Instead, he asked a direct question: "What are you going to make us eat in the morning?" I knew he was asking what they would have a hard time swallowing.

With the President set to present the ideas in less than ten hours, I saw no reason to hold back, at least in terms of what would be difficult for them. "Mohammad," I said, "I won't tell you all the ideas, but I will tell you what will be hard for you." He nodded, and I told him, You will have to accept that the Israelis will have a right to redeploy their forces to the Jordan River in an emergency; you will have to accept that there will be no right of return for refugees to Israel, even though we will give you some cover rhetorically; and while you will get sovereignty over the Haram, they will get sovereignty over the Western Wall and the space connected to it.

He grimaced and said, "Can't you do a little better for us?" I shook my head, saying, No way. While it may be hard for you, you know from what I have not said, it is going to be harder on Barak, and given the mood in Israel, "I am not even sure he can deliver what we are asking."

Dahlan did not respond, but left little doubt he was unhappy. At that moment, I decided both to test whether this was a show and, if it was not, to give him and us a way out. "Mohammad," I said, "there is no way for us to soften further what we are asking of you, but we have no interest in presenting ideas that you cannot accept and will have to reject. Personally, I also have no desire to see the last big act of the Clinton presidency fail. So if you tell me you cannot accept the ideas, I will tell President Clinton not to present them. You don't have to decide now, but I need to know by eight in the morning."

Dahlan was quiet for several minutes and then softly said, "Go ahead and present the ideas." Whatever his reservations, he chose not to take the out I was offering him. Rightly or wrongly, he believed that Arafat would accept them.

| PRESENTING THE IDEAS AND CALLING ARAB LEADERS |*

The plan was for the President to read the ideas to the Israeli and Palestinian negotiating teams in the Cabinet Room at the White House, then depart, leaving me behind to be sure the two sides recorded every word correctly. He would then call Mubarak, Crown Prince Abdullah of Saudi Arabia, and King Abdullah of Jordan to get their support for the ideas even before Arafat (who was in Gaza) received the ideas from his negotiators. It was not just that we wanted their support; we also did not want Arafat to present a misleading version of the President's ideas to them.

I left my meeting with President Clinton in the Oval Office in order to join the negotiators prior to the President's entry into the Cabinet Room. The negotiators would sit on the same side of the table, the President and our team on the other side. As he greeted both delegations, he was as stern as I had ever seen him. He told both sides he would read the points slowly so they could record them. Before reading, however, he told them that these ideas represented the culmination of our effort, not the beginning point of negotiations. Negotiations could take place within the parameters, but not on the parameters themselves. If either side could not accept the parameters, we would withdraw the ideas, and in any case they would no longer exist once he left office. Finally, he told each side they would have five days to respond with either a yes or a no. A nonanswer would be taken as a no. A maybe would be taken as a no.

---

*The full text of the Clinton ideas as presented by President Clinton to Arafat and Barak appears in the Appendix.

With that as his preamble, President Clinton proceeded to present his ideas. What follows is the essence of his presentation. On territory, there would be a range of 4 to 6 percent on annexation in the West Bank to accommodate 80 percent of the Israeli settlers in three settlement blocs. In partial compensation for the annexation, there would be a range of 1 to 3 percent swap of territory provided to the Palestinians, and nonterritorial compensation could include the creation of a permanent safe passage between the West Bank and Gaza. President Clinton emphasized that in drawing the borders, we would insist on contiguity of territory for the Palestinian state and on minimizing the number of Palestinians absorbed into the areas the Israelis annexed.

On security, the key would lie in an international presence that could be withdrawn only by mutual consent; it would monitor the implementation of the agreement. This security force would gradually take the place of the Israel Defense Forces, which would remain in the Jordan Valley for a period of up to six years. Israel would also retain three early-warning sites in the West Bank with a Palestinian liaison presence for as long as Israel deemed necessary. The Palestinian state would be nonmilitarized, with a strong Palestinian security force for internal security and with the international force providing border security and deterrence. Palestinians would have sovereignty over their airspace but would have to accommodate Israeli training and operational needs. And the IDF could redeploy to the Jordan River in the event of an external threat, constituting a "national state emergency" in Israel.

On refugees, the solution had to be consistent with the two-state approach. The formulation on "right of return" had to "make clear that there is no specific right of return to Israeli itself" while not negating "the aspiration of the Palestinian people to return to the area." With this in mind, two alternative formulations were proposed: both sides recognize the right of Palestinian refugees to return to historic Palestine, or alternatively both sides recognize the right of Palestinian refugees to return to their homeland.

Five possible homes for Palestinian refugees were identified: the state of Palestine; areas in Israel being transferred to Palestine in a land swap; rehabilitation in a host country; resettlement in a third country (like the United States, Canada, Australia, Great Britain, etc.); and admission to Israel.

The right of return would pertain only to the first two homes—meaning the new state of Palestine. Admission into Israel would be Israel's sovereign decision.

Priority should be given to the refugee population in Lebanon, and it would be agreed that this basic approach would constitute implementation of UN General Assembly resolution 194.

On Jerusalem, the principle of what is Arab is Palestinian and what is Jewish is Israeli would apply to the neighborhoods of East Jerusalem with contiguity for Israeli and Palestinian neighborhoods guiding the final arrangements. The same principle would apply in the Old City, along with special arrangements for governing this small area of one square kilometer. As for the Haram, the following alternatives were offered: (1) The Palestinians would gain sovereignty over the Haram and the Israelis would gain sovereignty over the Western Wall and either the Holy of Holies of which it is a part or the holy space of which it is a part; or (2) the Palestinians would gain sovereignty over the Haram and the Israelis sovereignty over the Western Wall and the two would share functional sovereignty over excavation.

I came up with the "Holy of Holies" or the "holy space" language as a way of addressing the existence of the Temple without mentioning it. According to Jewish tradition, the Ark of the Covenant, the place in the Temple where the Ten Commandants were kept, was in the Holy of Holies.

The last point in the President's presentation was on end of conflict. In his words, "The agreement clearly mark[s] the end of the conflict and its implementation put[s] an end to all claims."

Neither side said a word while President Clinton was speaking. When he was finished, he did not ask for questions. He stated that this was his best judgment of what it would take to produce an agreement. He could not do better, and we would not negotiate it. He would expect an answer in five days. He wished them luck and said good-bye.

As soon as he departed, I said I would go over his presentation word by word to be sure both sides had it correctly. Nearly as soon as I began going over the words, Saeb and Gilad—as if to show that they each had real problems—began to complain about specific formulations. I was past the point of playing games, and simply said: "You don't like it, we can stop now and we can withdraw the President's ideas." Both sides asked me to continue. As I did, both then sought to clarify particular points. Here Rob Malley interjected that the President had been clear, we had had sufficient consultations with both sides, they now had to transmit this to their leaders and decide.

Once I had finished going over the words, both sides left the White House and spent the rest of the day caucusing among themselves and calling various members of my team before returning home. I made it clear I would take no calls. We had done what we could do. Both sides had asked for an American proposal; they had gotten it. It was the best we could do. Now they both faced their moments of truth.

| BARAK SAYS YES; ARAFAT EQUIVOCATES |

Arafat was never good at facing moments of truth. They tended by definition to close doors, to foreclose options. Now, especially with the end of conflict as part of the President's ideas, he was on the spot.

Almost immediately he looked for ways to avoid an early decision. He wanted clarifications. When we communicated back that he must accept the President's ideas first before we would engage in any discussions, he sent Saeb to seek clarifications from Gilad. Not surprisingly, Saeb was not happy with what he heard from Gilad—who told him that the Israelis would like to lease an additional 1 percent of the territory from the Palestinians, and the lease would be for "999 years." Saeb then called me to explain that the Chairman was very concerned about what Gilad had said.

I was blunt in response: "Gilad does not speak for us, and these are the President's ideas, not Gilad's or Barak's. Like you, they will have to accept them by the twenty-seventh." Saeb pleaded with me to come and sit with him and Gilad. I said no, seeing this as an obvious ploy to turn the President's ideas into a new basis for negotiation, not the basis of conclusion. Meanwhile, Arafat persuaded President Mubarak to call President Clinton and ask for me to come and sit with Saeb and Gilad; this, despite Mubarak having told the President in their conversation on the twenty-third, that the Clinton ideas were historic and he would encourage Arafat to accept them. Now he would only say that "Arafat has questions." Mubarak was not about to assume a responsibility for the Palestinians. But we were not about to relieve Arafat of his need to make a decision.

However, he probed every possible out. Yossi Ginossar was at Sloan-Kettering in New York recuperating from cancer surgery. Amnon Shahak was also in New York at this time. Now Arafat sent Abu Ala and Mohammad Rashid to see them. Yossi called to tell me this, reporting that they were clearly trying to see if the Israelis would join them in redefining the Clinton ideas—or at least accepting a need for more time. I sensed that Yossi was also probing me to see if we were going to stand firm now. "Yossi," I said, "these are the President's ideas and he will not let me talk to anyone now. Both sides must first accept the ideas."

"That's what I told them," he answered. But he also added that, based on what we are hearing from Abu Ala, "I do not believe the old man is ready to make a decision."

Shortly after my conversation with Yossi, Abu Ala called me. He told me that "the Chairman has asked me to come see you." "Abu Ala," I said, "you are my friend and I will always want to see you, but when you come, I will not talk about the ideas. The President won't let me. We must have an acceptance first before I can talk about them."

He was clearly disappointed, saying there was little point in his coming under those circumstances. But Arafat was not giving up, especially knowing our relationship. Within a half hour Abu Ala called back, telling me that "Abu Ammar wants me to come even though you said you won't talk about the ideas." Fine, I said, you know I am always happy to see you.

Abu Ala would visit Washington on December 29, two days after answers were due. On the twenty-seventh, Barak convened his security cabinet in Jerusalem and they voted to accept the Clinton ideas with reservations. But the reservations were within the parameters, not outside them. Barak's government had now formally accepted ideas that would effectively divide East Jerusalem, end the IDF's presence in the Jordan Valley, and produce a Palestinian state in roughly 97 percent of the West Bank, and 100 percent of Gaza.

There were only mixed messages from the Palestinians on the twenty-seventh—some suggesting the ideas would be rejected, others suggesting that more talks were needed. Mubarak pleaded with us to give Arafat more time and not to treat his non-response as a no. President Clinton agreed to that, even as he called Arab leaders on a daily basis to have them pressure Arafat to say yes lest he miss a historic opportunity.

On December 29, Abu Ala arrived and Gamal joined me in meeting with him and Mohammad Rashid. They understood I would not talk about the ideas and limited themselves to explaining that Arafat was under a great deal of pressure to say no. Did they understand the consequences of that? I asked. They did. Was no one on their side arguing for the best deal they would ever get? There was, but they did not sound confident about the outcome. I asked to be alone with Abu Ala.

When we were alone, I told him, You are my friend and I don't want you coming back in three months and saying, "You never told me really what would happen if the Chairman says no." So let me tell you: "First, I will be gone. I may be the guy your colleagues love to hate, but I am also the one they all wake up at 3 a.m. when they have a problem. You know that I understand your problems, your needs, and your aspirations very well. You know that I often explain them better than any of you do. You won't have me anymore. Unfortunately, my absence will be the least of your worries. Far more important, Clinton is going to be gone. And he is going to be replaced by a new President who lost the popular vote. George W. Bush becomes President with almost no political capital. He has no interest in this issue. The people around him don't like the issue and think it is hopeless. Having watched Clinton invest the resources of the presidency in it and get stiffed by Arafat, they will want nothing to do with Arafat. They believe we indulged Arafat too much.

"Mark my words, they will disengage from the issue and they will do so at a time when you won't have Barak, or Amnon or Shlomo, but at a time when you will have Sharon as Prime Minister. He will be elected for sure if there is no deal, and your 97 percent will become 40 to 45 percent; your capital in East Jerusalem will be gone; the IDF out of the Jordan Valley will be gone; unlimited right of return for refugees to your state will be gone. Abu Ala, you know I am telling you the truth."

He looked at me sadly and with a note of complete resignation replied, "I am afraid it may take another fifty years to settle this now." As the meeting ended, I didn't know which of us was more depressed.

| ONE LAST GASP |

Following Arafat's meeting with President Ben Ali of Tunisia and Foreign Minister bin Yahya's call requesting that the President see Arafat, President Clinton invited Arafat to Washington for a meeting on January 2. Before seeing the President at the White House, Bandar and Egyptian ambassador Nabil Fahmy went to see Arafat at his Washington hotel. According to Mohammad Rashid, who was at the meeting, they pushed Arafat hard to accept the President's ideas, telling him it was his decision but he should understand this was the best deal he was going to get and the new Bush administration would in all likelihood disengage from the issue. At a minimum, it was in his interest to have the new administration see he had said yes. Bandar had lived up to his promise to me and brought the Egyptians into this as well.

Alas, Arafat was not up to peacemaking. After the meeting with President Clinton, it was clear: he was not up to ending the conflict, and already he had effectively rejected the President's ideas. His reservations were deal-killers, involving his actual rejection of the Western Wall part of the formula on the Haram, his rejection of the most basic elements of the Israeli security needs, and his dismissal of our refugee formula. All were deal-killers.

For me, there was no mistaking that this was the end of the road. However, because of the Israeli election, we tried one final gambit. With Barak pressing for the President to travel to the area, President Clinton was ready for one last roll of the dice. I thought this was crazy, but the President was unwilling to say no to Barak, and was willing even in the last two weeks of his presidency to fly to Israel and meet with Barak and Arafat. President Clinton found it difficult to give up, especially believing that Barak's certain defeat would spell the end of peacemaking in the Middle East for a long time to come. The President did not believe there would be a benign status quo in the absence of any hope for peace; instead he feared a deteriorating environment that imposed increasingly high costs on Palestinians and Israelis alike.

I shared his analysis, but felt our administration was past the point where it could make a difference. Still, I could not dissuade the President from going to the area by simply arguing against it, so I suggested one last test: the President should call Arafat and tell him he would come to the area to conclude an agreement, but only if Arafat first worked out a set of understandings with the Israelis on the core issues of Jerusalem, refugees, security, and borders. The President would ask Arafat to meet for twenty-four hours straight with Amnon Shahak and Shimon Peres, the two Israelis he trusted the most, in order to resolve everything or at least resolve how everything would be dealt with. If at the end of the twenty-four-hour period the two sides called the President jointly and reported that they had overcome their differences, the President would fly to the area and preside over the finalization of their agreement.

President Clinton liked this idea, ran it by Barak—who also liked it—and then called Arafat. Arafat acted like someone facing a visit to the dentist. He would like to do it, but he would not be available. He had to go see President Ben Ali of Tunisia. Standing by, I scribbled a note to the President saying you are offering him a historic opportunity, you are prepared to take this enormous leap, and he is too busy. What does that tell us?

The President pushed him, but the most that Arafat was willing to do was to have the negotiators get together again. "Saeb could meet Peres." He would join them after they met. This was another no. If Arafat was truly looking for a way to conclude an agreement—partial or complete—here was his opportunity, even timed to coincide dramatically with the end of the Clinton presidency.

How many times did Arafat have to tell us no before we heard "no"? How many times could excuses be made for him? Those who argue that we just ran out of time ignore the many opportunities Arafat had refused. They ignore that with the Clinton ideas practically on the table at the end of September, Arafat either let the Intifada begin or, as some argue, actually gave orders for it. They ignore his actual rejection of the specifics of the Clinton ideas. They ignore his extraordinary rebuff of the President's extraordinary offer to come to the area in his final days as President.

They even ignore a last-gasp effort on the part of the Israelis to produce a joint letter from Barak and Arafat that would summarize the areas of agreement and the baselines for the negotiations that could be sent to President Clinton as he left office. In early January, Gilad Sher came to Washington to work on this letter with us. He and his colleagues now understood that the election was a lost cause. Barak was going to lose. The letter was an effort to concretize points of agreements in a way that would tie Sharon's hands as Prime Minister. Even this Arafat was not prepared to do because it required him to acknowledge concessions on his side. Even creating new advantageous baselines for the Palestinians on all the core issues was not sufficient for Arafat, who was in the end unwilling to even appear to be conceding anything.

Yasir Arafat had definitively demonstrated that he could not end the conflict. We had made every conceivable effort to do what we now had to accept was impossible with Yasir Arafat.

During the first week of the Bush presidency, the negotiators on both sides went to Taba, Egypt. The real purpose was not to reach agreement, but on the Israeli side to try to constrain what Sharon could do and on the Palestinian side to try to get the Bush administration to buy into the Clinton ideas.

Neither was going to happen. Did we come close? Yes. Were the Palestinian negotiators ready to do the deal that was available? Yes. Did we ultimately fail because of the mistakes that Barak made and the mistakes that Clinton made? No, each, regardless of his tactical mistakes, was ready to confront history and mythology. Only one leader was unable or unwilling to confront history and mythology: Yasir Arafat.

Anwar Nusseibeh decried the Mufti of Jerusalem as someone who succeeded as a symbol and failed as a leader. Tragically, for Palestinians and Israelis alike, these words captured the essence of Arafat fifty-three years later.

Learning the Lessons of the Past and
Applying Them to the Future

SOME MAY LOOK AT the Middle East and draw only one lesson: Peace is not possible. Conflict is the norm. The decade of peacemaking efforts was noble, but futile.

I do not accept that. The peace process that began in Madrid in 1991 has altered the landscape of the Middle East. The idea of Arabs and Israelis talking to one another is no longer considered illegitimate. Even during the worst of the Israeli-Palestinian fighting of the last few years, Israelis and Palestinians have continued to talk to one another. Regular meetings between Israeli and Palestinian scholars, journalists, politicians, and officials have continued, and for the first time serious grassroots initiatives involving joint Israeli and Palestinian efforts have emerged in groups such as "One Voice" and the "People's Voice." Israelis (at least in small numbers) have also continued to travel to Egypt and Jordan—and in Jordan the economy has benefited significantly from Qualified Industrial Zones in which Israeli-Jordanian joint ventures produce goods that are exported duty-free to the United States. While Israel's relations with countries like Oman, Tunisia, Morocco, and Qatar have been frozen, they have not been broken, and quiet dealings and occasional public meetings continue to take place.

Mutual recognition of Arabs and Israelis proved to be irreversible. There has been no return to the mutual rejection and denial of the past. Moreover, a new consensus emerged among Israelis and Palestinians and internationally as well on the essential requirement for peace: two states, Israel and Palestine, coexisting and living in secure and recognized borders.

To be sure, there were reasons that peace has proved difficult to achieve. Translating general principles into concrete agreements has never been easy, particularly given the irreconcilability of objectives and the competing claims to the same territory. Too often that has reflected the reality that when one side was ready to make hard decisions the other was not. Here the historical pattern is striking. In the 1930s and 1940s, the Jews of Palestine were ready to find a compromise and the Arabs, rejecting the very idea of a Jewish state, were not. In the year following the first Arab-Israeli war, Syria's leader, Colonel Husni Zaim, was ready to reach a deal but the Israelis, given the price of Zaim's territorial demands, were not. After the 1967 war, Israel was ready to return nearly all the captured territories for peace, but the Arabs, guided by Nasser's "three no's," were not ready to accept Israel, much less negotiate with it. And when Anwar Sadat succeeded Nasser in 1970, his overtures were dismissed by the Israelis before the 1973 war.

Certainly in the decade of the 1990s—a decade in which the diplomacy of direct talks replaced the traditional diplomacy through denial—it is not surprising that the failure to end the conflict reflected an even more pronounced pattern of the Israelis and Syrians and the Israelis and Palestinians being out of sync. The historical reality of one being ready when the other was not was bound to be stronger at a time when negotiations had become legitimate but the stakes involved in ending the conflict became far greater.

In the case of the Israelis and Syrians, there were several key junctures at which the two sides may have thought they were in sync in their purposes but were not. Yitzhak Rabin in 1993 offered the Syrians full withdrawal, expecting an equally bold response. But Asad was only prepared to slowly grind out an agreement in a negotiation marked more by attrition than give-and-take. Similarly, Shimon Peres, after Rabin's assassination, offered to fly "high and fast" to an agreement, but Asad was ready to go only low and slow. With Barak, however, it was Asad who was anxious to move quickly in December–January of 1999–2000, and Barak who felt he could not.

Was it also a case of being out of sync in 1999–2000 between Israelis and Palestinians? The answer here may be more complicated. If Yasir Arafat, as it appears, has been simply incapable of making a permanent, comprehensive peace deal, the obvious approach should have been to do another, lesser deal. The problem, however, is that Barak wanted to end the conflict, seeing great political difficulty in doing partial deals in which Israel would give up more territory but receive nothing irrevocable from the Palestinians in return. Arafat claimed he wanted a permanent status deal, but proved unable to negotiate one. Was timing the issue or was Arafat incapable of transforming himself from a revolutionary into a statesman?

I came to believe the latter, but continue to ask myself whether the unilateral Israeli withdrawal from Lebanon might have made a difference. I doubt it, because I never saw any indication that Arafat was ready to surrender his mythologies or level with his public. However, there can be no denying that the success of the Hizbollah model—violence works, negotiations don't—probably had at least some effect on Arafat. It may well have raised the costs, in his eyes, of making fundamental concessions. It may have convinced him that pressuring the Israelis through violence would produce more for him. It may have altered his calculus so that waiting seemed the best option. If that is true, we have another instance of the parties being out of sync, with Barak ready to end the conflict and Arafat either believing it to be too costly or simply being incapable of doing it.

I suspect that being out of sync reflects a deeper reality. The costs of making peace have always been perceived as high, and it takes great courage or profound pressure for Middle Eastern leaders to make the leap. It takes little to dissuade them from doing so. If there are leaders who see themselves in historic terms—as Anwar Sadat and Menachem Begin did—the fact that one will take the leap is bound to leave the other feeling that he must also meet the challenge. More often there have been asymmetries in leaders: Rabin and Asad seemed alike in many respects. Both were cautious, prone to calculate carefully, disinclined to move in any but small steps, and highly suspicious. But Rabin, having been voted in as Prime Minister a second time, was poised for historic choices. Asad could not break the habit of a lifetime, finding it impossible not to haggle over every issue when Rabin was expecting boldness to be matched by boldness. Peres, by inclination, was a leader always looking for revolutionary, not evolutionary, moves. It was no surprise that Asad would not embrace the Peres approach, even if the Rabin assassination made him a more flexible negotiator. Later Asad, seeing succession as the overriding imperative, was ready to change his behavior for a short period during Barak's tenure. But peace was a derivative of the succession issue, and if he thought the pursuit of it would jeopardize his son's chances of succeeding him, he was bound to change directions.

And that is an essential point. Events *have* consistently undone opportunities. Violence has often reduced the ability and the willingness to make possible concessions for peace, and at times undercut those perceived as too accommodating. Four suicide bombings in nine days in 1996 changed the climate in Israel and elected Bibi Netanyahu. Without the suicide bombings in 1996, Peres (wearing the slain Rabin's mantle) would have won with an unprecedented mandate. Peres was already a man on a peace mission, and given the progress made at Wye, a deal with Asad probably would have been produced within a year or so. An Israeli-Syrian deal would have fundamentally altered the region. There would have been no Hizbollah model indicating that violence works. There would have been no base in Syria or Lebanon for militant rejectionists. There would have been pressure on Arafat to do a deal, not avoid one.

Why is the peace process so quick to come undone? One cannot ascribe this only to a lack of courageous leaders. Something more fundamental is at work here. As a rule, Arab leaders lack legitimacy. There is no sense of participation—politically or economically—among most Arab publics, and Arab leaders have traditionally been selected, not elected—or worse, they have seized power. So they are easily put on the defensive and fear being accused of conceding principles or perceived rights. Their sense of vulnerability makes them risk-averse, and events that heighten their perception of risks are bound to dissuade them from persevering.

Democratically elected Israeli leaders don't lack legitimacy. But they preside in a highly competitive political environment, with governments that are always based on coalitions of different parties. Their rivals can exploit acts of violence and terror, particularly because most Israelis continue to question whether the Arabs or the Palestinians are truly prepared to live with them. The inherent distrust of their neighbors' intentions makes it difficult for Israeli leaders to persevere in peacemaking in circumstances in which acts of terror take place. In such an environment, extremists on both sides have the capacity to undo moments of great promise.

For all that, peacemaking efforts have not died, even when moments of opportunity have been lost. That too reflects an important reality: There is an underlying desire for peace among both publics. There is an understanding among the mainstreams in the Arab world and in Israel that continuing conflict is ultimately not an acceptable alternative. But both sides will have to adjust their attitudes and behaviors if they are to make peace a reality. Here, too, lessons from the past provide a clear guide as to where each must change.

| ARABS MUST ACCEPT COMPROMISE; ISRAELIS MUST BE WILLING TO GIVE UP CONTROL |

The one unmistakable insight from the past about the Arabs is this: No Israeli concession can ever be too big.

During Barak's tenure, this basic Arab instinct was demonstrated vividly. When Israel unilaterally withdrew from Lebanon—and the UN confirmed that the withdrawal was in accordance with UN Security Council resolution 425—the Arab world welcomed this Israeli action. However, when Hizbollah, shortly after the Israeli withdrawal, claimed the Sheba farms area in Syria as Lebanese, Mubarak and other Arab leaders suggested that the Israelis withdraw from there as well. Similarly, when Barak was prepared to withdraw from all but 400 meters of the Golan Heights, Asad's rejection in Geneva militated against any Arab acknowledgment of the significance of the Israeli move. Finally, when, on December 23, 2000, President Clinton called Mubarak, King Abdullah of Jordan, and the Crown Prince of Saudi Arabia, they all felt that the ideas he had presented to the Israelis and Palestinians were historic. They all said they supported them and would press Arafat to accept them as well. However, when Arafat did not, they did not put pressure on him, privately or publicly, and did not publicly acknowledge the significance of the Israeli government's acceptance of the Clinton ideas.

In earlier periods, the same impulse governed the Egyptian efforts to work with the Labor Party in opposition to Likud-led governments. The pattern since at least 1989 is one of Egypt working with members of the Labor Party to adopt policies that would push Israel in a direction of greater compromise, without Egypt ever accepting Labor's view of Israel's substantive requirements.

The underlying reality has been that the Arab partner in a negotiation with Israel is always the arbiter of what is acceptable in the eyes of even moderate Arab leaders. Whether other leaders think the course taken is wise or not the decision belongs exclusively to those whose land is at stake. Few would question the logic of this in the Arab world; after all, the land is "theirs," and Israel is getting their acceptance in return. But the main lesson here is that it matters little how hard moves may be for Israel, it matters little what needs Israel may have. It will always be Israel's Arab partner, and not Israel, who decides if a deal can be done.

The kind of transformation that would make it possible for the Arab world to acknowledge that Israel has needs has yet to take place. Perhaps if the Arab world accepted Israel's moral legitimacy, Arab leaders could publicly accept that Israel has needs as well—justifying compromise and even pressure on the Arab side in the negotiation. But that has not happened yet.

As for the Israelis, genuine acceptance of their moral legitimacy could alter their continuing need for control. There are few in Israel who question the legitimacy of the Palestinian national movement. There are, however, many who question whether the Palestinians—or Arabs more generally—are truly willing to make peace with them. Surrendering control runs against the Israeli instinct. Partly it stems from the experience with the Arabs and Palestinians, and the related mistrust that convinces most Israelis that their security requires control. But partly it is also a matter of habit and an Israeli reluctance to give up territorial positions that are strategically beneficial to Israel—not to mention that the creation of nearly 150 settlements in the West Bank and Gaza has significantly raised the political costs of giving up control.

In the abstract, Israelis accept the need to surrender control and withdraw from the territory. And, certainly, having withdrawn from the whole of the Sinai Desert and parts of the West Bank and Gaza, they have demonstrated that they will reciprocate in exchange for real concessions on the part of the Arabs. But surrendering control and accepting genuine independence for the Palestinians does not come easily, and for the Israelis, it is the area where they must psychologically transform themselves.

To be sure, both Arabs and Israelis must transform basic attitudes. Some, like Walid al-Moualem, the former Syrian negotiator, used to argue that a transformation on the Arab side could only take place after their sense of grievance had first been removed. Ehud Barak at one point accepted this logic as it applied to the Palestinians, believing that it was more urgent to negotiate agreements than to try to transform psychology. In the absence of transformed attitudes, however, conflict-ending agreements proved difficult, even impossible, to reach. In the absence of transformed attitudes, mythologies were perpetuated, not challenged. Leveling with publics about compromise was avoided. The climate so necessary for rationalizing or explaining hard concessions was not created.

This was evident in both sets of negotiations. Between the Israelis and Syrians, it was more a case of Syrian resistance to any moves designed to transform the psychological climate. Israeli leaders from Rabin to Barak pressed for confidence-building measures; Asad consistently rejected them—seeing them not as building blocks of peace but rather as concessions to Israel. If Israeli leaders craved signs of acceptance, Asad wanted Israelis to pay for them. Asad resisted any outreach to the Israeli public on the grounds that it was a concession not to be given freely. Asad's view (as Barak was to recognize with regard to the Palestinians) was that transformation was for the period after peace was made—after he got his land back. As a result, he did not prepare his public, nor did he achieve what he might have during Rabin's time. Would Asad have engineered a real transformation of attitudes after Israeli withdrawal? Probably not; this would have been something for Syria's future leaders, not for him.

The logic of Oslo, as designed by the parties themselves, was completely different, at least in theory. Oslo was supposed to embody a process of living together. Israelis and Palestinians would build a web of cooperative relations; cooperation would take on a life of its own; warm peace would be the objective and the two sides would gain such a mutual stake in living together that existential issues would become far easier to resolve. Transformation defined the meaning of Oslo for both sides. However, neither side succeeded in transforming itself.

| UNDERSTANDING THE FAILURE OF OSLO |

Herein lies the main failure of Oslo: Transformation was required, but each side fell far short of what was required.

To be fair, the Israeli political leadership in 1993 made a psychological leap. Rabin described this transformation in revolutionary terms:

> As I have said, one does not make peace with one's friends. One makes peace with one's enemy.
>
> The world is turning upside-down before our eyes: the globes and atlases in your homes have become archaeological findings. Your geography books are about to become collectors' items. The most unlikely events are unfolding before our very eyes. Ideologies that moved hundreds of millions vanished without a trace: ideas which brought about the death of millions died themselves overnight. Borders were erased, or were moved. New States came into being, others fell. Heads of State left center-stage, while new leaders arose. Almost every day in recent years is more dramatic than the one before it. The great revolution in Moscow, and in Berlin, in Kiev and in Johannesburg, in Bucharest and in Tirana, is reaching Jerusalem, Tel-Aviv, Beer-Sheva and Tiberias. We are undergoing the revolution of peace.

But their rhetorical leap was not mirrored in the behaviors of those Israelis who ran the day-to-day policy for dealing with the Palestinians. The political decision was to devolve authority to the Palestinians and get Israel out of the business of running their lives. Yet the security officers, the civil administration, the Finance Ministry, and trade, agricultural, and customs officials who managed daily life with the Palestinians never internalized the spirit of that decision. Rather than turning over responsibility to Palestinians, too often the Israeli officials remained preoccupied with ensuring that the Palestinians could not do anything that might be damaging to Israeli interests.

Whether it was getting Palestinian goods through Israeli ports, exporting cut flowers to Europe, ending the indignities of Israeli checkpoints—even during extended periods when there were no acts of terror—denying Palestinians the right to import certain products from Jordan or the Arab world, or simply obtaining permits for building, Israeli officials continued to control most aspects of life for the Palestinians. If domestic Israeli politics dictated appeasing the settlers, settlement expansion continued along with Israelis building bypass roads that seemed to carve up the area the Palestinians perceived to be theirs. Whether it was preserving control or making unilateral decisions to meet perceived political needs, the Israelis acted as if all decisions should be informed by their needs, not by possible Palestinian needs or reactions. They would err on the side of Israeli needs, leaving the Palestinians chafing under continuing Israeli control. From a Palestinian standpoint, Oslo was a process that cemented Israeli control, not one that ended it.

On the other hand, the Palestinians failed not just to transform their day-to-day behavior. Their leader, Yasir Arafat, never went through any transformation at all. Israeli political leaders changed their words; Arafat did not.

Rabin and Peres had made a historic choice; Arafat made only a tactical move. He might say Oslo represented a strategic choice; in reality, for him it represented a strategic necessity. Arafat went to Oslo after the first Gulf War not because he made a choice but because he had no choice. He chose wrong in siding with Saddam Hussein, and his leadership was being challenged from within and without. Hundreds of thousands of Palestinians were expelled from the Gulf. The PLO was in deep financial crisis, having lost its financial base in the Gulf. Many in the Arab world were prepared to marginalize him, particularly as he seemed to have no answers. Oslo was his salvation. As such, it represented less a transformation than a transaction. Yes, he would begin to meet with Israelis. Yes, there was recognition, and—unlike with Asad—little resistance to meetings with Israelis at any level. But no, there was almost no conditioning of his public for peace. There was never talk of painful compromises for peace. On the contrary, Arafat was telling his public they would get everything, and give up nothing.

Even worse, he continued to promote hostility toward Israel. Thousands of Palestinian children went to summer camps where they were taught how to kidnap Israelis. Suicide bombers were called martyrs, even when Arafat would crack down on Hamas and Islamic Jihad. Violence as an instrument was never delegitimized nor given up as Arafat preserved his options. Israelis were held responsible for all ills—and the daily experience of Palestinians both confirmed these charges among the Palestinian public and gave Arafat an additional incentive to create an outlet for Palestinian anger.

The lack of a transformation made everything else harder. Negotiations were approached differently. Justification came easily for behaviors that were inconsistent with the spirit of peace but perceived to be necessary for internal political needs. Israelis would expand settlements, confiscate land, demolish houses, build bypass roads, and seize Jerusalem identity cards (effectively expelling Palestinians from their homes in Jerusalem) because they needed to do so in part because the Palestinians would not fulfill their responsibilities on security. Palestinians would hold back on security cooperation, engage in incitement to violence, promote grievances, and fail to fight terror acts against Israelis because the Israelis oppressed them and made them feel powerless. Notwithstanding limited agreements, the basic behaviors of each side did not change. Each new interim deal would thus produce more cynicism about the process than belief in it.

Without a transformation, the connections between the Israeli and Palestinian publics could not be developed. The capacity to learn to live together and see its value would not inform both publics. The stake in building their mutual relationship would not become compelling. Lesser agreements would neither build momentum nor create a new reality between both peoples. And yet a new reality was the key to being able to compromise on Jerusalem, refugees, and borders—the issues that went to the heart of self-definition and identity on both sides.

Ironically, Oslo was not a total bust. While it did not create connections between publics, it did create strong bonds between the negotiators. It legitimized negotiations even while it failed to break down the barriers between publics and societies. That explains why so much was done in the negotiations: why, in effect, Camp David and its aftermath did produce the intellectual infrastructure for settling Jerusalem, refugees, and borders; why we were able in the Clinton proposals to offer what will probably be the basic outlines of the eventual peace settlement between Israelis and Palestinians.

To be sure, I would not now be writing about the failings of Oslo if it had not been for Yasir Arafat. As one of the Palestinians at Camp David said to me, "We needed David Ben-Gurion, and we got Yasir Arafat." There was an agreement in hand; even with the limitations of Oslo and the absence of the envisioned transformation, there was a historic opportunity to be seized.

Had Nelson Mandela been the Palestinian leader and not Yasir Arafat, I would be writing now how, notwithstanding the limitations of the Oslo process, Israelis and Palestinians had succeeded in reaching an "end of conflict" agreement. In effect, Oslo might not have failed if Arafat had been prepared to be a leader and not just a symbol. As a symbol, he could not give up Palestinian myths. As a symbol, he could not compromise or concede in order to end the conflict. As a symbol, he had to remain a unifying figure even to those who rejected peace with Israel. And as a symbol, he could only engage in transactions with the Israelis, not generate a fundamental transformation.

| SHOULDN'T WE HAVE KNOWN ABOUT ARAFAT? |

In the prologue I posed the question: Shouldn't we have known that Arafat would not be up to the task of ending the conflict? Shouldn't we have avoided trying to resolve the conflict given the leader we were dealing with?

In retrospect, perhaps, but at the time there was good reason to believe that Arafat would do a permanent status deal. After all, he had crossed the threshold of recognizing Israel's right to exist in 1993 and in so doing had incurred the wrath of the secular and religious rejectionists (so much so that in 1994 the Israelis and we warned him of assassination plots against him). In addition, Arafat concluded five limited deals with the Israelis, characteristically following the same pattern on each one, holding out until the last possible moment before deciding and reaching agreement. Moreover, his negotiators actually did negotiate on permanent status issues at Camp David and afterward, making meaningful concessions on three settlement blocs in the West Bank, accepting that the Jewish neighborhoods of East Jerusalem would be Israeli, and agreeing to Israeli early-warning sites in the West Bank.

In describing Arafat earlier, I said he was a decision-avoider, not a decision-maker. Passivity was part of his avoidance. He never faced up to hard choices if he did not have to—even with himself. By never fully deciding, he avoided exposure and possible opposition, and he preempted his colleagues from revealing to people like me or to the Israelis what the ultimate concessions might be.

For Arafat, therefore, not revealing himself was tactically smart and psychologically necessary. But it made it very hard for us—or anyone—to guess what he would do in the end. Even those closest to him did not know. But they believed he would strike the deal. Moreover, they believed he was the only one who could make the necessary compromises on the existential questions.

Whenever my exasperation with Arafat was reaching its limits, Abu Mazen, Abu Ala, or Mohammad Dahlan (or Yossi Ginossar) would remind me that only Arafat had the moral authority among Palestinians to compromise on Jerusalem, refugees, and borders. Whatever his limitations—whatever his maddening qualities—they would say, "Remember, he is the only one who can concede on fundamental issues." Often Abu Mazen or Abu Ala or other Palestinian negotiators would tell me, "You prefer dealing with us because you see us as more moderate, but we cannot deliver, only he can."

Throughout, they remained convinced that he would do so in the end. Abu Mazen, who had been with Arafat since the mid-1960s, believed that having recognized Israel, having committed to Oslo, Arafat would decide finally to end the conflict. Abu Ala, who had been with Arafat since the late 1960s, strongly agreed.

If those closest to him were convinced he would close the deal, were we wrong to assume that as well? Perhaps Arafat himself did not know what he would do. Perhaps his habitual passivity led him to avoid considering in his own mind what it would be necessary for him to do.

I am convinced that one of the reasons Arafat never prepared his people for the hard compromises is that he never prepared himself. Our great failing was not in misreading Arafat. Our great failing was in not creating the earlier tests that would have either exposed Arafat's inability to ultimately make peace or forced him to prepare his people for compromise.

Arafat saw us as his equalizer with the Israelis. We should have made certain that he knew that we would not play that role, at least on permanent status, unless we saw him preparing his public for compromise on Jerusalem, land, and refugees. We should have made certain that he knew we would condition our involvement on his conditioning his public that they would not get 100 percent on Jerusalem or borders or refugees. His unwillingness to prepare his public would then have been a good indicator of his intentions and his capability.

But we did not impose on Arafat the need to prepare his public. Too often we were mindful of his being the weaker party and having few "cards" to play—a theme that Arafat and those around him constantly emphasized.

We did not impose on the Israelis either in this regard. However, there was one Israeli leader, Ehud Barak, who did engage in conditioning his public, if only indirectly through leaks to the press. Israelis were fed a steady diet of reports indicating that Israel would give up more than 90 percent of the territories, divide East Jerusalem, permit Palestinian refugees to return in at least small numbers, and accept international forces in place of the IDF in the Jordan Valley. Ironically, whatever Barak's fears about exposure of the concessions he'd made at Camp David, the Israeli public was largely passive in response. Because of the "conditioning," they were not surprised by the concessions, and if the Palestinians were ready to end the conflict, the Israeli public was prepared to accept these concessions.

While we could not have contrived a moment of truth—there either is such a moment or there is not—we could have created ground rules for our own involvement in the process. Our involvement, desired strongly by both sides, but especially by the Palestinians, should have been dependent on public conditioning for compromise, on each side fulfilling commitments and behaving in a way that fit the objectives of the negotiating process. Here, too, there are a number of lessons that stand out for making any future negotiating process successful.

| MAKING THE NEGOTIATING PROCESS SUCCESSFUL |

One critical lesson from the Oslo period is that no negotiation is likely to succeed if there is one environment at the negotiating table and another one on the street. Negotiations do not take place in a vacuum. They are affected by daily events and unpleasant realities. During the Oslo process, each side felt free to take steps that were bound to create problems for the other. Each preserved its political space while undercutting the space of the other. Israelis made Palestinians feel powerless with unilateral actions. The Palestinians' systemic incitement in their media, an educational system that bred hatred, and the glorification of violence made Israelis feel that their real purpose was not peace.

Negotiations between Israelis and Palestinians are bound to be difficult in any case. But the difficulty is certain to be compounded if each side feels it can engage in actions that either betray the purpose of the talks or ignore the effect on the other side. To avoid a replay of what happened in the Oslo process, it is essential to create a "code of conduct" for each side. The "code" would exclude bad behaviors, eliciting from each side what it would most like the other to avoid doing.

Ruling out the bad behaviors is not enough, however. To reinforce the negotiations and make it easier to transform attitudes, it is necessary to foster good behaviors. People-to-people programs that break down barriers between publics need to be promoted. Programs that bring together students, teachers, journalists, artists, and others in cooperative ventures are necessary for breeding greater familiarity, for making it harder to demonize, and for eroding stereotypes between the publics. All of us talked a good game when it came to people-to-people programs. Yet our investment in these programs in terms of time, money, and effort was far too limited. We focused far too much on the leaders and negotiators and far too little on the publics on each side.

To be sure, peace cannot be negotiated from the bottom up in these societies. But peace will not come only from the top down, either. Avoiding bad behaviors and promoting real ties, profitable ties, between publics is one of the most important lessons for negotiations that grows out of the Oslo period. Ironically, the near absence of diplomacy in the last few years has triggered the emergence of grassroots activity between Israelis and Palestinians for the first time. Perhaps in time, groups such as One Voice and the People's Voice can play a more significant role in convincing leaders that the potential costs of compromise are not prohibitive.

Oslo demonstrated something else about negotiations. The best plans and the best agreements mean little without implementation, and implemetation may be difficult to achieve without accountability for the commitments or obligations made or assumed. We were certainly guilty of not holding either side accountable.

One of the mythologies about Oslo is that it was only the Palestinians who failed to fulfill their commitments. Unfortunately, it was both sides. Arafat's track record on fulfilling commitments has always been abysmal. But from the very beginning of the implementation process, the Israelis felt no need to fulfill many of their obligations. That certainly made it easier for Arafat to ignore his commitments.

Throughout Oslo, neither side wanted to be singled out by us for nonperformance; each always wanted the onus to be on the other side.

Too often we shied away from putting the onus on one side or the other because we feared we would disrupt a process that had great promise. When, during Rabin's time, the military administration in the territories was supposed to be withdrawn and was not, we did not say so publicly out of concern that Rabin was already under a great deal of pressure from the right, and we did not need to compound his domestic difficulties. In Arafat's case, the security breaches, especially the releases from jail of those involved in terrorist activities, were handled in private for fear of giving those in the U.S. Congress and in Israel who sought to break ties with the PLO a basis on which to do so. At different points, either we sought to avoid a public row with Israel—especially during Netanyahu's time, given the potential political problems here—or we decided to cut Barak some slack because his commitment to making historic decisions was so clear. And at some points, when Israelis were not producing on their side, we shied away from forcing Arafat's hand out of fear that he was being weakened and believing it would be a mistake to push him too hard. Arafat has always been a master at turning weakness into strength, and we were too quick to believe in his weakness.

Whatever the reason, we could always convince ourselves that it was never the right time to disrupt the process. It was never the right time to insist on freezing all discussions until a breached commitment had been corrected. It was never the right time to go public and say clearly why we had a problem and who was responsible for it.

Every negotiating process has within it the seeds of its own justification. Often the process becomes self-sustaining and essentially an end in itself. That happened with Oslo, and we need to learn the lessons from it. By never holding either side accountable, by never being prepared to disrupt the process and put it on hold, we contributed to an environment in which commitments were rarely taken seriously by either side, knowing there would never be any real consequence. In the future, there must be a consequence for nonperformance—and to have real meaning, it must be publicly seen. When all sides have to explain publicly why a particular step has been taken, why they are being blamed, why they have not acted in accordance with an obligation, they will feel the consequence.

There are two last lessons on the negotiating process and the American role that bear mention. First, there can be no deal unless each side is prepared to respond to the essential needs of the other. Each has desires and wants, and slogans that encapsulate beliefs and mobilize domestic passions. But agreements are forged not on the basis of reconciling slogans or desires, but on the basis of reconciling needs—on the basis of reconciling the fundamentals each must have to preserve its identity, dignity, and political base. The Clinton ideas presented on December 23, 2000, did that between Israelis and Palestinians—at least in our best judgment. We never did the same on the Syrian track; the ideas presented on March 26, 2000, in Geneva were what Barak was prepared to have us convey to Asad. They were close to his bottom lines, but not his definitive bottom lines. Understanding the core needs on each side is a precondition for shaping an outcome to this conflict. We understood it on the Syrian track but wisely never presented our best judgment the way we did between Israelis and Palestinians.

I say wisely because the second lesson here is that the most important American role is not putting our best judgments on the table. Our most important role may be getting the sides to the negotiating table when the only dialogue they have is one of violence. The paradox of the American role is that it may be most important when an agreement is least likely. At that point, we may play a crucial role in getting the two to talk and not to shoot. Certainly, during the Netanyahu period my major role was forcing meetings and producing minimal understandings that preserved calm and continued a political dialogue. Had the Bush administration understood this at the outset of its tenure, the second Intifada might never have been transformed into a war. It might have been contained. Active American diplomacy might have prevented a bad situation from deteriorating to the point where both Israelis and Palestinians question the fundamental intentions of the other.

Almost by definition, the best measure of whether the parties are ready to conclude the conflict is whether they are prepared to make historic decisions. We can make those decisions easier. We can offer guarantees on security; financial assistance to demonstrate the material benefits of hard decisions; and political and international support to bolster the legitimacy of the decisions, all of which may be important in helping each side cross historic thresholds. But we cannot create the will for such decisions. And it is foolhardy to try to impose such decisions.

Imposed decisions will not endure. No agreement forced from the outside will ever have legitimacy. For Palestinians, an imposed solution may be appealing on a superficial level. But it, too, will generate opposition, particularly when, as is likely, the Palestinians have to surrender the right of return for refugees to Israel. No Palestinian leader, certainly not Arafat, will say he accepted such an imposed outcome. Rather, he will claim he had no choice but to acquiesce in it. He will neither defend it nor seek to legitimize it. And he and others will inevitably challenge it over time. Imposition for the Palestinians provides a convenient excuse not to end the conflict but to perpetuate it, not to assume responsibility but to avoid it, not to adjust to the new reality but to wait until the circumstances permit them again to try to alter it.

An imposed solution will thus be no solution at all. Ultimately, the United States may make its greatest contribution to peace by standing against efforts to impose solutions and standing for the principle that regional leaders must finally exercise their responsibilities to confront history and mythology. Only when they are prepared to do that will the peace agreements endure. Only then will agreements be seen for what they are—authentic and legitimate reflections of what Israelis, Palestinians, and Arabs have decided. We can help them make these decisions, but we cannot substitute our will for theirs.

| THE KEY TO PEACE: DEBUNKING MYTHOLOGIES
AND ACCEPTING REALITY |

I tell this story in much detail for a very basic reason: Peacemaking can never succeed in an environment dominated by mythologies and untruths. One can decide that peace is not possible because the gap between the two sides is simply too great to overcome. But efforts to promote peace should not falter because one side or the other believes in myths that bear no relationship to reality. If ever there was a regional conflict that has been sustained by mythologies, by avoiding the unpleasantness of reality, by ignoring the need to see the world as it is, it is the Middle East.

My purpose is to debunk mythologies. My purpose is to engage in truth-telling with an eye toward getting all parties to adjust to reality. Certainly, Arabs, Israelis, and Palestinians must face up to reality and not continue to deny it.

Arab leaders have long sought to use the cause of Palestine without ever thinking that it imposed a price on them. Of course, they understood that it has tremendous resonance with their publics; here was a grievance, an injustice, a wrong that must be righted. Here was a justification for anger that could be useful in diverting attention away from the failings of any regime. Here was imagery that could be used to build internal legitimacy for regimes that had little.

But it was their very lack of legitimacy that made Arab leaders reluctant to pressure Yasir Arafat to be responsible and to seize opportunities. No Arab leader ever wanted Arafat to say publicly that he, President Mubarak or Crown Prince Abdullah or King Abdullah, had pressured him to surrender Palestinian rights. Arab leaders may have used the cause of Palestine, but they also became trapped by it.

Throughout the 1990s, when the United States carried the burden of diplomacy, we effectively took the issue off their backs. Arab leaders sat on the sideline. In Secretary Baker's words, they were only too happy to "hold our coats." After our victory in the Gulf, the Saudis and others had no interest in dealing with Arafat. With Oslo, they needed, in their eyes, to do little, and unfortunately they did little. When the oil-rich states could have used their resources along with the rest of the world to help build an incipient state in Gaza and the West Bank, they did not. When they could have helped to build the benefits of peace and the stake that Palestinians had in Oslo, they did not. When we wanted them to stop the flow of "private monies" from Islamic charities to groups like Hamas, they did not. When they could have delegitimized terror by declaring that it endangered Palestinian goals, they were silent. When we wanted them to reach out to Israel to show the Israeli public that Arab attitudes had truly changed, they did the bare minimum. And, certainly, when they might have conditioned their publics for peace with Israel, they did not.

Their fundamental myth was that they could exploit the cause and never be threatened by it. But the combination of the Intifada and the emergence of Arab satellite television stations (such as Al-Jazeera) produced a combustible mixture. Though normalization with Israel had been deliberately limited, the peace process enabled the satellite stations to operate in the West Bank, Gaza, and Israel. But the access was not used to promote understanding. On the contrary, with the eruption of the Intifada, the stations competed to see who could bring more images of Israeli brutality against Palestinians into homes throughout the region. The result was anger that put pressure on Arab regimes to do something, anger that made Arab regimes vulnerable.

Has it produced a new sense of responsibility on the part of Arab regimes? Has it produced an understanding that they, and not only we, have a role to fulfill if the conflict is to be settled? Has it made them any more willing to play a different kind of public role with Palestinians and Israelis, encouraging compromise as a principle and rejecting these groups, who carry out terror?

Not yet. Like the Palestinians and the Israelis, they, too, will have to take difficult steps. They will have to operate in the open, putting pressure on the Palestinians and reaching out to Israelis. With Arafat or any Palestinian leader, they must separate support for the Palestinian cause from criticism of Palestinian behaviors that are irresponsible. They must say in public that particular actions by Arafat or others threaten the Palestinian cause; that suicide bombers are not martyrs; that there is a legitimate way to redress grievances and an illegitimate way to do so; that those who pursue the cause through illegitimate means are enemies of that cause. And with Israelis, Arab countries—including those that already have peace treaties (Egypt and Jordan) and those that don't—must be willing to reach out to the Israeli public.

Crossing these public thresholds would amount to a psychological revolution for Arab regimes. It would have a dramatic effect on peacemaking. Not surprisingly, it would also be a dramatic indicator that Arab leaders have made the decision to surrender their myths and adjust to reality.

Israelis have their own adjustments to make. Israelis must face the fact that Palestinians will require an independent state in both appearance and reality. Carving up the West Bank, preserving broad buffer zones, and maintaining an Israeli presence all around the perimeter of the Palestinian state will not produce a solution. During Barak's time that was understood. While Prime Minister Ariel Sharon has made important, unprecedented declarations regarding Palestinian statehood, withdrawal from Gaza and evacuation of settlements unilaterally, the unacceptability of continued Israeli occupation of the Palestinian people, and the need to disengage from Palestinians and divide the land, he has certainly also reestablished some of Israel's myths: that Israel could never surrender the Jordan Valley lest it give up its essential security border; that Israel must control the basic powers and functions of the Palestinian state lest it become a threat either on its own or through the means of others; that all of Jerusalem, including the exclusively Arab neighborhoods of Jerusalem, must remain Israeli lest the division of East Jerusalem rob Israel of its link to its Jewish heritage.

In the context of an ongoing war with the Palestinians, especially one abetted by Arafat after he had turned down a chance to end the conflict, who was going to question the value of reestablishing such positions? Palestinians did pose a threat. Palestinians needed to understand that the consequence of violence and terror would not be Israeli concessions but increasing Israeli demands. Israel did need confidence that its real security requirements would be met, and not made dependent on the good faith of the Palestinians.

But Israelis also need to understand the difference between posturing to disabuse the Palestinians of their illusions and reembracing positions that no Palestinians, even those most determined to live in peace with Israel, could accept at the end of the day.

For their part, the Palestinians, too, must give up the illusion that Arafat fostered: that they did not have to compromise on land or on refugees or on Jerusalem, and maybe most important, that they did not have to be responsible. Being a victim has never been compatible with responsibility. As victims, the Palestinians were owed something. Their rights and their needs had to come first, and it was too much to expect that they would take unpopular decisions that responded to Israeli needs and stand by them. As victims, Palestinians could not be expected to put responsibility over unity, taking on those in their society who rejected peaceful coexistence. Finally, it was unfair to expect Palestinians to acknowledge mistakes and learn from them.

Unfortunately, until the Palestinians are prepared to learn from the past and not simply deny it or reinvent it, they will not alter their behavior. Indeed, they will not alter their reality of always being victims. Being a victim has not just become the Palestinian condition; it has become a strategy. That is not to say that Palestinians have not been victimized. They surely have. They surely were betrayed in the past, and they surely have suffered.

But they have also helped to ensure their status as victims. Never seizing opportunities when they presented themselves. Blaming others for their predicament. Declaring unmistakable defeats as victories. Keeping refugee camps as a reminder of their grievances. Neglecting to examine how their own decisions have contributed to their problems. Fearing to ever delegitimize those who used violence to oppose the process. Refusing to make decisions and be accountable for them.

In the end, peace will not be possible until the Palestinians decide that being victims only guarantees that they will remain victims. Palestinians must be prepared to make their own decisions and stand by them. They must not seek the easy way out of having others decide for them. Arafat's desire to have an imposed solution is a device to avoid having to make difficult decisions. But decision avoidance is also responsibility avoidance. Decision avoidance means not having to explain why certain unpopular compromises are necessary.

So long as the Palestinian leadership does not have to level with its own public, little can change. So long as it can hide behind others, the leadership will signal to those who oppose peace that it is okay to do so—that in Palestinian terms the opposition must be right. Embracing peace means taking responsibility for the tough decisions and telling the public that Palestinians are deciding their own future—and that those prepared to use violence to frustrate that future are enemies of the Palestinian cause.

Arafat's greatest travesty as a leader is that he did nothing to delegitimize those who used violence against the Israelis. Never throughout the Oslo process did he declare that those carrying out terror and violence against Israelis were wrong, were illegitimate, were enemies of the Palestinian cause. He might arrest them from time to time; he might tell us he had "zero tolerance for terror." But the message for Palestinians was that he was under pressure from us or the Israelis and he had to do this—not that Palestinian aspirations were being threatened by violence and that Palestinian interests demanded it not be tolerated.

True, the Israelis should not have made Palestinians feel powerless. But nonviolent protest by Palestinians would have galvanized the Israeli public and made them a powerful partner for the Palestinian cause.

When there is a Palestinian leadership prepared to make clear that there is a legitimate way to pursue the Palestinian cause and an illegitimate way to do so—and violence is illegitimate—peace will no longer be a distant dream. At that moment, the myths on all sides will give way to reality. And even if the Israeli leadership of the time is not ready for the necessary compromises, the Israeli public will insist that they be made.

That is one of history's most powerful lessons. The Israeli people will demand that any government respond when they perceive they have a partner. They showed that with Sadat, and Menachem Begin proved to be up to the challenge; they showed that first by voting Yitzhak Shamir and later Bibi Netanyahu out of office and voting in Yitzhak Rabin and Ehud Barak on each occasion; and they showed it in their response to Camp David in 2000. Even after the summit's failure, the Israeli public still believed the Palestinians were a partner and that the failure was about bargaining, not about rejection. As a result, the Israeli public was prepared to accept previously unimaginable concessions, believing that an end-of-conflict deal remained possible. When the second Intifada signaled the opposite, the corollary to demanding a response to an Arab partner also became evident: turning to an Israeli leader who would demonstrate to the

Palestinians (and the Arabs) the consequences of not being a partner. That psychological imperative explains the landslide election of Ariel Sharon as Prime Minister in February 2001.

| ARE THERE ALTERNATIVES TO PEACE AGREEMENTS? |

If the story of peacemaking between Arabs and Israelis tells us anything, it is that there are no shortcuts to peace. There are no quick fixes, no imposed settlements. But it also tells us something else: It is important to recognize what is possible and what is not possible and shape objectives accordingly. If a solution is not possible at a given moment, then act in ways designed to defuse tensions and hostility. In circumstances in which formal or final agreements are not in the cards for political and psychological reasons, tacit understandings may transform the environment and make more formal agreements possible at a later point. In the year 2004, after three years of warfare between Israelis and Palestinians, that may be the situation in the Middle East. Certainly, many in Israel have come to this conclusion. They no longer believe there will be a responsible Palestinian partner any time soon; but they also think that there must be a more coherent defensive posture to ensure the security of Israelis; and they worry that demographic trends will make it impossible to preserve Israel as a Jewish state unless Israel withdraws from the bulk of the West Bank and Gaza. These sentiments have fed a movement for unilateral separation or disengagement from the territories.

Historically, Prime Minister Ariel Sharon opposed unilateral withdrawal and construction of a separation fence, particularly because it would mean Israeli "concessions" without quid pro quos from the Palestinians, and inevitably make it difficult to remain in those settlements on the "wrong" side of the fence. But after three years of Intifada and more than nine hundred Israeli dead, his position changed. That does not mean there is an Israeli consensus on the route of the separation fence or barrier in the West Bank, but there is a consensus that unilateral disengagement is necessary.

While unilateral Israeli withdrawal to new borders can be a possible step, it cannot produce a solution. It may create more defensible borders for the Israelis, at least in terms of ending the illogic of having large numbers of Israeli soldiers protecting small numbers of settlers. It may also greatly reduce the Israeli control of Palestinian life, something that is essential to defusing Palestinian anger and alienation. But Palestinians are likely to reject any borders that are imposed by Israel, even if they involve withdrawal from territories and some settlements. The Palestinians will accept what they get but insist that their land is still occupied, and the withdrawal line is likely to become the new line of confrontation.

To avoid that eventuality, Israeli separation or disengagement needs to be coordinated. If, as is likely, it is not possible for the Israelis and Palestinians to coordinate these steps directly, the United States should do so. With the Israelis, the United States would coordinate on the route of the security barrier to ensure that it makes infiltration into Israel difficult, minimizes the numbers of Palestinians Israel would absorb, imposes the fewest possible hardships on Palestinian villages affected by the barrier, and preserves the possibility of an eventual two-state solution in time. With the Palestinians, the United States would coordinate on the responsibilities the Palestinians would assume in the areas the Israelis evacuate. Palestinians would need to understand that recognition of Palestinian sovereignty in these areas would be withheld if the Palestinian Authority failed to prevent these territories from being used as a platform from which to carry out attacks against Israel.* American coordination should extend to providing the assistance the Palestinian Authority feels it needs to meet its security responsibilities and its immediate and longer term economic needs. Finally, American coordination with the international community would be necessary to legitimize what would be a new transitional phase, one in which coordinated disengagement (and tacit understandings) made it possible to end warfare and restore normal life for Israelis and Palestinians alike.

With the Syrians, tacit understandings that facilitate a final agreement on the Syrian track are less likely and perhaps less necessary. The Syrians will never accept partial withdrawals, except as part of a phased withdrawal. But crosscutting realities should always be recognized for their possible benefit in transforming the peacemaking possibilities. Take, for example, the American war on terror. The Bush administration has demanded that Syria close down the operations of Hamas and Islamic Jihad in Damascus and cut off Hizbollah in Lebanon. Syria has not done so. Perhaps Syrian behavior might change if it saw both what it would gain by ending its support for these groups and also what it might lose by not doing so. Apart from improving bilateral ties, the administration could offer to launch a serious, credible peace initiative between Syria and Israel. While making clear that this would necessarily involve Israeli withdrawal, the administration would also make clear that nothing was possible unless the Syrians unmistakably ended their support for all the rejectionist groups. To increase the Syrian incentive to act, the regime would be told quietly that if it did not choose peace over terror, it ran the risk of a tougher American policy toward Damascus, one designed to create greater isolation of the regime.

The point is that even when the conditions for Arab-Israeli peace may appear lacking, there may be steps taken or leverage that can be applied to restore a peace process. As much as I would like to see America act to promote Israeli-Syrian peace, we should

---

*Similarly, Palestinians should understand that if they don't fulfill their security responsibilities, the new Israeli security line—while not a border—could be there a long time.

not forget that the core of the Arab-Israeli conflict remains the conflict between Israelis and Palestinians. There is no escaping the need to address it.

Ultimately, one reality that cannot be ignored is that Israelis and Palestinians are destined to be neighbors. History and geography leave them no choice. Neither can wish the other away. Neither can forge an outcome in which the other does not exist.

Moreover, neither can impose an outcome on the other. The Israelis with all their military power cannot extinguish Palestinian aspirations. The Palestinians with all their anger and use of terror will not succeed in forcing the Israelis to submit through violence.

Like it or not, they must recognize that their fate is intertwined. Their choice is either to live in perpetual struggle, with endless victims, pain, sorrow, and destruction, or to live in peaceful coexistence. From all the efforts I made over the years, I am certain that the mainstreams of both sides understand that reality. However, translating that understanding from an abstraction into a practical reality has proven far more difficult than I had hoped. I have no doubts that it will come about eventually. It may come only after disengagement and separation. It may take a "divorce" before there can be reconciliation. For the sake of all who have suffered, for all our sakes, it is essential to shrink the time it takes to move from theory to reality. Unfortunately in the case of the Middle East, time does not stand still, and too often it is measured in blood.

Upon leaving the government, I knew that the situation between Israelis and Palestinians would worsen. I had warned Abu Ala about what to expect if Arafat said no to the Clinton ideas. Much of what I told him was unfortunately prophetic, but I did not expect the situation to deteriorate so dramatically. Catastrophic violence has become commonplace over the last three years. Four bombs in nine days shocked and traumatized Israelis in 1996 and cost Shimon Peres the election, but the traumatic has now become tragic routine for both Israelis and Palestinians.

The cost of not having a peace process has never been so clear. While American engagement in itself could provide no guarantee of success, one unmistakable lesson from the post-Clinton years is that U.S. disengagement is not the answer. With only very limited American diplomacy between Israelis and Palestinians, the Intifada was transformed into a war, with a vast escalation in the suffering on both sides. For Israelis and Palestinians alike, the price they paid for having no peace process was extraordinarily high.

To put this in perspective, forty-two Israelis were killed in the first four months of the Intifada (until the end of the Clinton Administration). By May 2004, more than 960 Israelis had been killed. Palestinian fatalities went from 350 to nearly 3000.* The wounded amount to ten to twenty times the numbers killed. The economies on both sides have also paid a severe price. While the Israeli economy is in crisis, having declined in absolute terms over the last three years, the Palestinian economy has been devastated. More than 60 percent of Palestinians are presently living below the poverty level, and 1.8 million in the West Bank and Gaza are now dependent on subsistence from the UN and other international agencies.†

---

*For further means of comparison, throughout the seven and a half years of Oslo, 250 Israelis and 1,100 Palestinians died.

†According to the State Department's 2003 Human Rights Report, 63 percent of Palestinian

But there has been another casualty as well: The psyches of both sides have been deeply wounded. Both Israeli and Palestinian publics have come to doubt whether they have a partner in peace on the other side. The problem is less a loss of confidence and more a loss of faith. And that faith cannot be restored overnight.

I did not believe it would come to this because I assumed that as the conflict escalated we would be driven to intervene to defuse it, much as we did during the Netanyahu period. I took as a given that our stakes in the Middle East would make it difficult for us to disengage from Arab-Israeli peacemaking. The United States had too many other concerns in the region that gave us a reason to act in a way that would at least limit the conflict.

| TERROR AND U.S. INTERESTS IN MIDDLE EAST PEACEMAKING |

Even before 9/11, the Middle East was the source of most of the world's terror. While the Arab-Israeli conflict, and its core struggle between Israelis and Palestinians, was not the cause of international terror and certainly was not the reason for 9/11, it has done more to poison the atmosphere in the region than any other factor. It has been a convenient excuse for Arab regimes to resist reform. It has served as a pretext to divert attention and anger away from internal failings and onto the United States and Israel. Indeed, the sole area in which the Arab media has been largely free and unrestricted has been in its ability to attack America and Israel and make them responsible for every conceivable ill.

In a culture that has been so heavily shaped by humiliation, the Palestinian cause has been and remains a constant reminder of a wrong not yet righted. Suicidal attacks that so betray the tenets of Islam became justified in the minds of many in the Arab world on the grounds that this was the only effective way to hit back at the powerful. Too often, suicidal terror has been lionized in the Arab world as the Palestinian "F-16." The credo of the powerless is to lash out, especially against those they are socialized to hate in mosques and schools, and who seem so indifferent to their rights and their needs.

Throughout the Middle East, America is accused of having a double standard. No doubt our support for Israel has been a part of that Arab perception. But so has the perception that we always use democracy as a weapon against those we don't like and never against those we do. Again, if there is one lesson from 9/11, it is that we can no longer

---

households live below the poverty line—54 percent of families in Gaza and 84 percent of families in the West Bank. In a May 23, 2003 speech, Prime Minister Sharon cited the figure of 1.8 million Palestinians currently depending on UN assistance.

be indifferent to how the Saudi regime or the Egyptian government treats its own people. The anger, the alienation, and the hopelessness have been a breeding ground for Bin Ladenism, and have made us a target.

Solving, or at least making the effort to defuse, the Arab-Israeli conflict would not make our problems in the Middle East disappear. It would not suddenly end terror as a phenomenon. It would not be the panacea that many seek. But it would remove a cause that remains more evocative than any other in the region, and it would undo or mitigate one of the greatest sources of resentment that is easily exploited by the radical Islamists. For that reason alone, the United States must deal with the conflict, even while it presses Arab regimes to assume their responsibilities on peacemaking and reforming.*

While many have argued that Arab regimes cannot take on the demands of peace and reform at the same time, the lessons of the past suggest exactly the opposite. Only Arab leaders who feel more legitimate can take risks for peace and assume their responsibilities. Only Arab leaders who become more legitimate won't fear delegitimizing those responsible for employing terror. So long as groups like Hamas or Hizbollah can never be criticized by name by Arab or Islamic authorities, their acts of terror will be seen as credible. Similarly, so long as their suicide bombers continue to be glorified as martyrs, terror as an instrument will remain acceptable—not just in the Middle East, but elsewhere as well.

As such, the U.S. agenda in the Middle East must promote peace and reform together as one part of our war on terror. Did I fully understand that connection before 9/11? No, I did not, believing that pursuing peace must take precedence over reform. With Arafat, I had believed that peace was possible even if democracy was not. But I understood that disengagement from Arab-Israeli peacemaking did not serve our interests of fostering greater stability in a region that every American President since Harry Truman considered vital. And, I believed that understanding would, as Israeli and Palestinian deaths mounted, also guide Bill Clinton's successor.

However, when George W. Bush's administration assumed office in January 2001, it looked at the Arab-Israeli conflict through a different lens and shifted direction dramatically. Whereas intensive involvement characterized the Clinton administration's Middle East diplomacy (and, for that matter, the first Bush administration's as well),

---

*Arab regimes must restore hope by opening up, ending corruption, fostering accountability, becoming more economically effective, and creating greater inclusion and political participation. Interestingly, small Arab countries with younger leaderships from Morocco to Jordan to Bahrain are experimenting with such reforms. To its credit, the Bush administration has made democratization and reform an essential pillar of its declaratory policy on the Middle East.

the new Bush administration made the decision to disengage. No longer would there be an envoy to the peace process. Even the words "peace process" were banned from the public and private lexicon in the first months of the administration.

Several critical assumptions seemed to guide the new approach: that the Clinton administration erred in wanting peace more than the parties, with the President excessively involved; that Yasir Arafat was indulged too much; that the newly elected Ariel Sharon–led government in Israel meant little would be possible diplomatically; and that American interests in the region were threatened much more by Iraq than by ongoing Israeli-Palestinian troubles. If anything, dealing with Iraq, as opposed to the Israeli-Palestinian conflict, was seen as far more likely to transform the landscape of the Middle East.

In fairness to the administration, President Bush and those around him were right to believe that we had indulged Arafat too much. If he wanted to be an honored guest at the White House, he needed to earn those invitations with his behavior. Maybe they were also right that the President needed to be less involved than Clinton had been, if for no other reason than to keep presidential currency from being devalued. One can even argue that raising the profile of U.S. efforts against Iraq might also have made sense so long as doing so was not an alternative to having a Middle East peace process.

Yet for all that, the administration's approach was mistaken from the start. Part of the administration's problem was that it tended to believe that nothing could be accomplished, and therefore the United States should make no effort. The fallacy here was thinking that if the conflict could not be ended, there was nothing to be done. But there *was* something to be done. It was essential to act to prevent the situation from deteriorating, from becoming a war, which would make it far more difficult to pursue peace at a later juncture. At Camp David, I told Ehud Barak that the only choices cannot be peace or war, for if peace is not now attainable, war is guaranteed. I was to make the same point to leading figures in the Bush transition team, but their assumptions precluded receptivity.

Because of these assumptions and the hesitancy to be involved, the administration missed two early opportunities for containing the Intifada and restoring a peacemaking path. The first was the release of the Mitchell Report. Under a mandate given by the Sharm al Sheikh Summit in the fall of 2000, former Senator George Mitchell headed an international commission that assessed the causes of the Intifada and made a series of recommendations for transforming the situation. The findings were privately conveyed to the administration on April 30, 2001, and released to the public on May 21. They specified steps that both Palestinians and Israelis needed to take: the Palestinians on security, including specific action against the groups and the infrastructure responsible for terror; and Israelis on restoring normal life to Palestinians, including the removal of barriers to Palestinian movement of people and goods and a freeze on settlement activity.

While hardly enthusiastic, neither Sharon nor Arafat wanted to be seen as opposing the Mitchell Report. That created an opening for creative diplomacy. At that moment, either the Secretary of State or a senior envoy should have gone to the area and shuttled back and forth between Israelis and Palestinians until there was an agreement on very precise and tangible steps for implementing the Mitchell recommendations (or some agreed-upon variation of them) on the ground. Or, if agreement was not possible, the administration's senior official should have remained on the scene until such time as to be able to credibly declare which leader was not, in fact, prepared to accept what was required for implementation.

Of course, to do either required an administration that was prepared not only to roll up its sleeves and conduct the hard work of diplomacy, but also to clearly invest itself in a way that conveyed seriousness to Israelis and Palestinians alike. That went too much against the Bush administration's initial assumptions, and led Secretary Powell to say that "shuttle diplomacy is not what we need right now. Unfortunately, that posture—and low-visibility U.S. involvement—sent the Israelis and Palestinians the signal that the United States was not serious about the Mitchell Report, and that therefore they need not worry about the consequences of not acting on it. And, of course, they did not.

Within a few weeks, there was a new and horrific development. A Palestinian suicide bomber walked into a crowded Tel Aviv night club, the Dolphinarium, and blew himself up, killing twenty-one Israeli teenagers. The bombing had a searing effect within Israel. Up to that point the suicide bombings had occurred only infrequently, and none had taken place in Tel Aviv since Ariel Sharon had become prime minister. Up to that point, Sharon, despite his dislike for Arafat, had been using Omri, his son, as a private channel to the Chairman, clearly indicating his readiness to do business with him. That stopped after the Dolphinarium incident. No more would Sharon have contact with Arafat. For Sharon, however, the closing of a private channel did little to relieve the public pressure on him to respond in a much tougher fashion against Palestinian terror.

To head off pressure on Sharon to use much more force against the Palestinian Authority and to respond to growing international demands for us to do something, the administration sent CIA director George Tenet to the area to work with both sides. George, a veteran of the Clinton-era diplomacy, conducted an intense shuttle over the course of a week and produced the Tenet Security Work Plan. It was a very clear timeline of steps that both sides committed to taking. Here was the kind of diplomacy that was required, but it failed for lack of implementation. As the Director of Central Intelligence, George Tenet could not remain in the area to hold each side's feet to the fire on the commitments they had made. But someone had to do so. Here again there was a moment; here again there was a reluctance to sustain public involvement that might have created accountability, and the Tenet Work Plan was never implemented.

| THE BUSH ADMINISTRATION BEGINS TO CHANGE |

Under growing pressure from Arab leaders, especially Crown Prince Abdullah of Saudi Arabia, the Bush administration decided to re-engage in Middle East diplomacy in August 2001. The President sent a private letter to the Crown Prince, establishing for the first time that U.S. policy henceforth would be to support a two-state solution to the Israeli-Palestinian conflict.* In addition, the Saudis and others were told that the President would have a brief meeting with Yasir Arafat on the margins of the United Nations General Assembly meetings in New York.

None of this was announced, and the events of September 11 interrupted the advent of a new diplomacy. The shock of the attack on the World Trade Center necessarily focused the administration on fashioning a strategy and a response against those who had killed more Americans in a single day than any previous enemy. Waging war against Osama Bin Laden and the Taliban in Afghanistan became our priority. Given the administration's understandable preoccupation with the war in Afghanistan, a new effort on Israeli-Palestinian diplomacy was put on the back burner.

In the late fall, with the Intifada's violence continuing unabated, Secretary Powell announced that retired General Anthony Zinni was being sent to the region to try to broker a ceasefire. His mandate was deliberately limited to security issues, and he was not to explore any political questions. While it was clearly more involved than previously, the administration's reluctance to seriously engage remained the guiding principle of its approach through the late fall and early winter of 2001–02. The hesitancy was reinforced by perceptions that Yasir Arafat was doing little to stop terror, that he had frustrated General Zinni's ceasefire negotiations, and that he had lied to the administration about the Palestinian Authority's attempt to smuggle a huge cache of Iranian arms into the territories using the ship the *Karine-A*.

---

*For details of the letter, see Robert Kaiser and David Ottaway, "Saudi Leader's Anger Revealed Shaky Ties; Bush's Response Eased a Deep Rift on Mideast Policy; Then Came Sept. 11," *The Washington Post*, February 10, 2002, p. A1. While the Clinton parameters presented to the two sides in December 2000 would have provided for an independent Palestinian state, the parameters represented ideas to resolve the differences between the two sides, were never stated as formal policy, and were withdrawn at the end of the administration.

Following the IDF's sweep of West Bank cities and a short, unproductive trip to the region by Secretary Powell in April 2002, the administration again came under increased international pressure to do something. The result was President Bush's speech of June 24, 2002, outlining his vision for peacemaking. He publicly called for a two-state solution to the conflict. However, by emphasizing a performance-based approach to peace, he in effect told the Palestinians that if they wanted a state, they would have to earn it. They must reform themselves, build credible institutions, end corruption, fight the terrorists, and create an alternative leadership untainted by terror. If the Palestinians did all this, he called on Israel to accept Palestinian statehood and "end the occupation that began in 1967."*

Though long on exhortation and short on plans, the President's speech was a historic statement. He was telling the Palestinians that they could not have a state built on a foundation of terror and corruption, but if they reformed themselves they would have a state based roughly on the 1967 borders—at least that is how the Arab world interpreted the reference to ending the occupation that began in 1967. If nothing else, President Bush created a new basis for the international community to address Middle East peace. Palestinian reform now became the focal point for activity, with emphasis on creating transparency and accountability in the Palestinian Authority. But translating this new emphasis into a new reality on the ground was bound to be difficult. There was nothing immediately practical in terms of what had been proposed. Reform as an objective was essential, but it was unlikely to be achievable unless the Israelis would relax their grip on the territories so reformers could move, meet, and plan. For its part, the Israeli government might support Palestinian reform, particularly if the reforms would sideline Yasir Arafat, but it was not inclined to relax its grip on the territories if the result of doing so would be fresh terror attacks in Israel. The stalemate held.

| THE ROADMAP TO PEACE:
TACTICAL OBJECTIVE, STRATEGIC CONSEQUENCE |

It was Arab leaders who initially raised the concept of a roadmap, notwithstanding their concern that the President's speech demanded too much from Palestinians

---

*"President Bush Calls for New Palestinian Leadership," The White House, June 24, 2002: http://www.whitehouse.gov/news/releases/2002/06/20020624-3.html. During the speech, President Bush defined the parameters of a two-state solution to mean "that the Israeli occupation that began in 1967 will be ended through a settlement negotiated between the parties, based on UN Resolutions 242 and 338, with Israeli withdrawal to secure and recognize borders."

and too little from Israelis. Desperate for the United States to intervene, they embraced the President's ultimate vision but called for a plan— a roadmap—to get there.*

Here again, the administration did not rush to develop such a plan. Arab leaders and Europeans were pleading for one that might put the President's words into action. Both argued that the U.S. position in the Middle East was being threatened by the administration's reluctance to defuse the Israeli-Palestinian war and by its apparent eagerness to go to war with Saddam Hussein. Faced with the uncertainty of who to deal with on the Palestinian side (given the call for an alternative leadership) and with the tactical need to gain support for or at least acquiescence in its Iraq policy, the administration agreed to work with the European Union (EU), the United Nations, and Russia in drafting a roadmap that might reflect the President's vision. While the United States would not let these other countries determine its response to Iraq, it would let them help shape the conduct of U.S. diplomacy between the Israelis and Palestinians, an unprecedented step in the U.S. approach to Arab-Israeli issues. Few things better indicate that the administration's real objective here had less to do with Middle East peace and much more to do with winning support for its Iraq policy. Arabs, Europeans, and others would find it easier to tolerate U.S. military action to bring down Saddam Hussein if the administration could point to its making a serious effort on Israeli-Palestinian peace—or so the thinking went.

This tactical objective led to a reversal of the traditional approach to Arab-Israeli diplomacy. Rather than working out understandings with the parties, the administration engaged in a negotiation with the other three members of the Quartet (the EU, the UN, and Russia). Consequently, the roadmap reflected agreement with parties that had no responsibility for carrying out even one of the steps they were calling for. Conversely, the roadmap was presented to the parties that would have to implement these steps after the Quartet had already agreed to it. They were each offered the opportunity to make comments, but not to engage in a negotiation about its content or how it

---

*Published on April 30, 2003, the roadmap called for a comprehensive solution to the Arab-Israeli conflict based on two states, Israel and Palestine. This was to be achieved in three phases. The first phase involved Palestinian security action and reform, and Israeli lifting of the siege. The second involved the creation of a Palestinian state with provisional borders. The third involved resolving all the permanent status issues. More broadly, the roadmap specified that "the settlement will resolve the Israel-Palestinian conflict, and end the occupation that began in 1967, based on the foundations of the Madrid Conference, the principle of land for peace UN Security Council Resolutions 242, 338, and 1397, agreements previously reached by the parties, and the initiative of Saudi Crown Prince Abdullah—endorsed by the Beirut Arab League Summit—calling for acceptance of Israel as a neighbor living in peace and security, in the context of a comprehensive settlement."

might actually be implemented. Such an approach had several advantages: it would avoid the prospect of difficult, grinding negotiations with the Israelis and Palestinians; sidestep the problem of dealing with Yasir Arafat; and build an international consensus that would be difficult to reverse and might actually influence the parties.

But it also had a fatal flaw: the roadmap could never be brought to life if it were based only on the understandings of outsiders. Indeed, it could only materialize with clear and unambiguous understandings between the parties themselves on what each side would actually do, when they would do it, where they would do it, and how they would do it. That, however, required not only making the effort to negotiate such understandings, but investing enough political capital in the effort to demonstrate that this mattered to us. Absent such diplomacy, it should have come as no surprise that the roadmap, once unveiled, could not be implemented. Though President Bush publicly announced the roadmap in March, before the beginning of the war in Iraq, and then went to summits in Sharm al Sheikh and Aqaba in June, it took several more weeks of negotiations after the summits to produce agreement on the initial steps that each side might take. Even these steps represented very few of the initial steps called for in the roadmap.

| THE IMPACT OF THE WAR IN IRAQ |

Ousting Saddam Hussein was never going to yield peace between Israel and the Palestinians. The conflict between two national movements with competing historic claims to the same territory had little to do with the issues of his dictatorship. But the war and the fall of Saddam's regime did have an impact on U.S. diplomacy and on the Israelis and Palestinians. Realizing as much, President Bush—as part of the effort to build support for the war—made promises to a number of leaders, including Arab leaders, that he would make a serious effort on Israeli-Palestinian peace once Saddam Hussein was vanquished. The more he repeated this privately, the more he became sincerely wedded to doing it, and to implementing the roadmap. Whatever the initial motives the administration had for the roadmap, it now became the President's avowed policy.

And neither the Israelis nor the Palestinians wanted to say no to President Bush, who appeared triumphant in the aftermath of Saddam's stunning defeat. Prime Minister Sharon, knowing that most Israelis believed the United States had removed a strategic threat to Israel, was not about to reject an initiative by the U.S. President. Similarly, neither Arafat nor Palestinian reformist leaders had any interest in denying a U.S. initiative at this point. On the contrary, Palestinians sought the intervention of the world's only superpower to transform the situation on the ground.

There is a big difference, however, between avoiding saying no, on the one hand,

and actually saying yes to specific American requests on the other. Saying yes might mean moving toward the difficult decisions involved in peacemaking. Saying yes requires a different mind-set, one in which there is a willingness to confront constituencies that resist compromise, and one in which leaders are prepared to think not only in terms of their own political needs but their counterpart's as well. While Saddam's defeat did not necessarily create these impulses on either side, it did suggest that change was possible and that the moment should be seized at least to produce relief for both sides.

In this sense, President Bush's readiness to involve himself for the first time by going to the region and holding summits came at a moment when both Israelis and Palestinians were ready to stop the day-to-day struggle that was imposing such pain on each of them. On this point, they basically agreed. Their "agreement" did not extend to the content of peace negotiations or even to the content of the roadmap, but it did reflect important developments within each society.

| NEW REALITIES |

Among Palestinians, support for violence had begun to wane in the period preceding the war in Iraq. Though a majority of Palestinians favored violence from the beginning of the Intifada, especially as a way to inflict pain on Israelis who were inflicting pain on them, this sentiment began to change in early 2003. In February, polls indicated that a slim majority now opposed the violence. By June, 73 percent of the Palestinians in the territories favored an end to it.* Palestinians were longing for a return to a more normal life, one in which the Israeli siege could be lifted and movement of people and goods could be restored. No end to the violence would mean no lifting of the checkpoints.

Under duress, Yasir Arafat appointed Mahmoud Abbas (Abu Mazen) as the first-ever prime minister of the Palestinian Authority. The Bush administration effectively used the Palestinian desire for U.S. intervention to pressure Arafat to make the appointment, saying it could only unveil the roadmap when there was a credible prime minister in place. But it was Palestinian reformers who had first raised the idea of a prime minister. Indeed, Palestinian pressure on Arafat for reform pre-dated President Bush's June 24 speech. It emerged following the Israeli operation "Defensive Shield," in which the IDF entered every Palestinian city in the West Bank except Jericho and

---

*A survey conducted by the Palestinian Center for Policy and Survey Research from June 19–22 found that 73 percent of Palestinians favored a *hudna,* a one-year voluntary cessation of violence against Israelis. Moreover, 80 percent of respondents favored a joint Israeli-Palestinian ceasefire of unlimited duration.

destroyed extensive parts of the casbahs of Jenin and Nablus as they sought to root out terrorist cells over a seven-week period in the spring of 2002. Unexpectedly, the overwhelming Palestinian desire after the Israelis withdrew was not for revenge but for reform. They knew they needed massive reconstruction, but they did not want to reconstruct the "rot" that had been Yasir Arafat's government.*

Palestinians were not prepared to unseat Arafat, who remained an icon. But they wanted him to share power, and the emergence of Abu Mazen as prime minister represented what they had sought. No one on the Palestinian side had more consistently opposed violence than Abu Mazen. At one point, he publicly challenged those, including Arafat, who argued for the Intifada, saying that it yielded the opposite of their stated goals: It extended Israeli occupation, tightened the Israeli control of East Jerusalem, and strengthened Prime Minister Sharon. To Abu Mazen, the continued violence was producing a disaster for Palestinians and threatening the cause itself.

Critical support for stopping the violence also came from some leaders of the Tanzim, the Fatah activists who control much of the grassroots organization, especially in the cities of the West Bank. Tanzim leaders produced the first Intifada from 1987–90 and have played an important role in the second one. As several of their leaders explained to me, they initially believed that this Intifada would prove to the Israelis that force would not work against the Palestinians. Instead, it was proving that force could not work on either side. Worse, as the Intifada continued, their agenda of a two-state solution, produced through negotiations, was being supplanted by the Hamas agenda of ongoing struggle. Without a break in the situation, they feared that the ability to produce a two-state solution could be lost.

The push for a ceasefire came strongly from the Tanzim and clearly also reflected the mood of the Palestinian public. In these circumstances, Hamas was not about to oppose a ceasefire, believing that it could use the respite to rebuild, and that sooner or later the Israelis would create a pretext for going back to the struggle.

In Israel, there was also a readiness to transform the situation. Certainly, the Israeli public was ready for it, with two-thirds opposing the resumption of targeted killings by

---

*A poll conducted by the Palestinian Center for Policy and Survey Research from May 15–18, 2000, found that 91 percent of Palestinians supported "fundamental reforms" in the Palestinian Authority. Equally noteworthy, respondents favored a number of specific actions by a wide majority— including 85 percent supporting unification of security services, 95 percent supporting the dismissal of ministers accused of mismanagement or corruption, 83 percent supporting holding elections, and 92 percent supporting the adoption of a basic law or constitution.

the IDF at this time.* But coupled with the desire to see the violence end was a feeling among Israelis that the Palestinians, having imposed the violence on Israel, must show they were serious about stopping it.

With the emergence of Abu Mazen as prime minister, the Israeli public and Prime Minister Sharon saw an opportunity. With President Bush's initiative, Sharon saw a need, but the ongoing economic crisis in Israel also motivated him. Sharon came to believe that Israel's economy could not recover unless the war with the Palestinians stopped, and for the first time he began to publicly say so. At the time the cabinet was voting on endorsing the roadmap, Sharon declared to his constituency, "the thought and idea that we can continue keeping under occupation—we might not like the word, but it is occupation—3.5 million Palestinians, is very bad for Israel, the Palestinians, and Israel's economy."

Together with the U.S. defeat of Saddam Hussein, exhaustion on both sides combined to create a very real moment to end the Israeli-Palestinian war and restore the possibility of peace. But to capitalize on that moment, the Bush administration would have to engage in an unprecedented way, sustain that engagement, and make clear that it would hold both sides accountable. Initially, that was the President's posture.

| NEW INVOLVEMENT BUT HESITANT DIPLOMACY |

President Bush was serious about promoting peace between Israelis and Palestinians after Saddam's fall. It was not only that he had promised to make a renewed effort; it was also that he believed that change in Iraq could usher in broader changes in the region. He had made the decision to go to war; he had been willing to go to war over the opposition of traditional U.S. allies France and Germany, and with the UN Security Council unwilling to vote a second resolution authorizing the war; and, at least in April and May of 2003, his decision appeared vindicated. This was a moment to make a push for the implementation of the roadmap, in part also because the advent of Abu Mazen as the Palestinian prime minister appeared to create a credible peace partner for the Israelis.

At the time, I believed that the administration should make a push. But I knew the key to near-term success was to work out very practical steps that each side would

---

*Following the failed IDF attack against Hamas leader Abdelaziz Al-Rantissi in June 2003, a poll published in the Israeli daily *Yediot Ahronot* found that 67 percent of Israelis opposed the recommencement of targeted killings. Within that group, 58 percent backed a temporary suspension of strikes against militant leaders in order to afford Abbas an opportunity to curb the activities of extremist groups. Only 9 percent of Israelis objected to the policy of targeted killings irrespective of circumstances ("Poll: Israelis Oppose Military Strikes," Associated Press, June 13, 2003). In April 2004, the Israelis succeeded in killing Rantissi.

take to produce real results on the ground. Both sides had to feel a new reality. Israelis had to stop fearing the next suicide bomb on a bus or in a restaurant. Palestinians had to see that the Israeli siege, with 160 checkpoints in the West Bank alone, would be lifted. The latter was essential in order to build Abu Mazen's authority.

Abu Mazen had no real following among the Palestinian public. Over the years Arafat had ensured that no other Palestinian ever gained much visibility with the Palestinian public. He would foster competition among those around him, and if someone like Abu Mazen or Abu Ala began to get too much attention, he would undermine them. The Palestinian public wanted change, and even if they did not know Abu Mazen well, polls showed that 75 percent of Palestinians in the West Bank and Gaza felt he should be given a chance. But he had to do something with the chance. He had to show that his way worked, that he could affect Israeli behavior, that the siege would end, and that life would get better. The more he succeeded along these lines, the more he would raise the costs to Arafat of trying to block him.

Given his opposition to Palestinian violence and his readiness to try to discredit it publicly, all those committed to Israeli-Palestinian peace had an interest in seeing Abu Mazen's authority grow. For his part, Abu Mazen knew that Arafat would try to create obstacles in his path—after all, his success would prove that Arafat was the problem. Abu Mazen counted on the international community, led by the United States, both to help him deliver and to pressure Arafat not to inhibit his efforts to fulfill Palestinian responsibilities.

The administration seemed to understand this at one level, but ultimately failed to act in a way that made it possible for Abu Mazen to succeed. This is not to say it was solely within the administration's power to ensure his success. The Israelis had to help. Abu Mazen also had to be more assertive, and obviously overcoming Arafat was never going to be easy.

Still, the key was actively working to get the two sides to take the right steps on the ground. When the President made the decision to travel to the Middle East and take part in two summits in early June, one in Sharm al-Sheikh and one in Aqaba, he was signaling that after two years in office his administration was going to take a new and determined interest in the peace process. His words reflected that. He spoke of creating real accountability, even while helping to build Abu Mazen's standing by showing that he could command a position internationally (and, by implication, Arafat could not). This was the point of having a summit in Sharm with President Mubarak, Crown Prince Abdullah, King Abdullah, and Prime Minister Abu Mazen, followed by a summit hosted by King Abdullah in Aqaba with Prime Ministers Sharon and Abu Mazen. President Bush was there to demonstrate that we would act to foster real change, and that Abu Mazen was our partner in that effort.

Unfortunately, the moment of maximum American leverage provided by President Bush's visit to the area was largely wasted on declarations. No matter how good the words, they were bound to ring hollow with Israelis and Palestinians alike if nothing changed on the ground, if their day-to-day reality remained unchanged. And, as if to show that very little was going to change for the better, twenty-three Israelis were killed by terrorists in the week after the Aqaba summit.

The mistake was not the decision to send President Bush to the summits. The mistake was to send the President to the area without specific understandings worked out on what each side was actually going to do on the ground. At that moment, President Bush had enormous leverage. Given their defensiveness about their ties to the United States following the U.S. invasion of Iraq, President Mubarak and Crown Prince Abdullah had a special interest in showing that America would now bring its weight to bear on solving the Israeli-Palestinian conflict. And both Mubarak and Abdullah could have used their leverage with Abu Mazen and Arafat to press for acceptance of an agreement on mutual steps that we could have brokered at that time. And, certainly Prime Minister Sharon would have found it difficult to resist if the Palestinians were prepared to take steps on security.

Instead of steps, however, there were positive declarations, and these, ironically, damaged Abu Mazen. He was attacked for addressing Israeli concerns on security but appearing to ignore traditional Palestinian demands on refugees and full Israeli withdrawal. Had he been able to point immediately to Israeli pull-backs from Palestinian cities, Arafat could not have orchestrated such attacks against him.

Even worse, the summits produced conflicting expectations. I was in the Middle East shortly after President Bush left the area, and I saw Abu Mazen in Ramallah a few days after the Aqaba summit. He believed that President Bush accepted that it would take him time to be able to organize the Palestinian security forces, and until then he would not have to take any steps on security. I was sure that was not what President Bush had meant to convey. The problem, I told Abu Mazen, was that if he was not acting to rein in Hamas and Islamic Jihad until he developed more capability, I doubted the Israelis would pull back or lift any checkpoints. There was, I said, a built-in paradox: "You want the Israelis to lift the siege, but they won't do it unless they see you acting on security, and if they don't lift the siege, you don't believe you will have the credibility to act on security." Abu Mazen nodded, but was counting on the United States to move the Israelis. As I expected, however, the Israelis believed they did not have to do anything on pull-backs until they saw demonstrative Palestinian action on arrests of Hamas and Islamic Jihad operatives.

The President had announced that we would be monitoring what each side would now do and would be sending an envoy, John Wolf, to help ensure accountability. The instinct was right. But there had to be clear understandings on what each was expected to do, and, in this case, there were none.

It was almost as if the administration felt that the roadmap to peace would be self-implementing. How could it be? It had not been negotiated with the parties. It had fifty-two paragraphs, and each side interpreted each one differently. The Israelis had a very expansive definition of Palestinian responsibilities to dismantle terrorist infrastructure under the terms of the roadmap; the Palestinians had a minimalist definition. Similarly, the Palestinians had a maximal definition of Israeli responsibilities to restore normal life and freeze all settlement activity, including natural growth; the Israelis had a minimalist one. And we offered neither bridging proposals on what each obligation meant nor our own definition for what we felt would constitute performance. Without that, what were we monitoring?

Three weeks after Aqaba the Israelis and Palestinians negotiated a limited understanding that provided for an Israeli lifting of checkpoints in Gaza and a pull-out from Bethlehem and Palestinian security steps in those areas. This was a far cry from what the roadmap called for in the first phase: the Palestinians making arrests, collecting illegal weapons, actively working to prevent acts of terror, and dismantling the terrorist infrastructure; and the Israelis facilitating a return to normal life, lifting checkpoints, dismantling all unauthorized settler outposts, and freezing settlement activity. Nonetheless, the agreement was useful. Had it been a first step implemented immediately after Aqaba and succeeded by subsequent steps, the administration might have presided over the end of the day-to-day war and the re-establishment of a real peace process.

But it had not happened immediately after Aqaba, and it was not succeeded by other steps. Instead, the Palestinians had worked out an internal truce, *hudna,* that obligated Hamas, Islamic Jihad, and the al Aqsa Martyrs' Brigades to cease attacks on Israelis for three months. Clearly, Abu Mazen hoped to use a period of calm to get the Israelis to stop targeted killings of Palestinians and to lift the siege. He could use the time to build his authority and leverage against these groups, hoping to keep them from reverting to terror attacks at the end of the three-month period.

In fact, there was a lull of nearly six weeks in suicide bomb attacks. The Israelis, however, were not a party to the *hudna,* and during these weeks their intelligence covertly saw Hamas and Islamic Jihad using the ceasefire to rebuild, smuggle in new arms and explosives, test longer-range Qassem rockets, and plan for subsequent attacks—all without any hint of disruption or threat from the Palestinian Authority. Consequently, Israel continued to make arrests in the West Bank, and in early August two Hamas and Islamic Jihad operatives were killed when they resisted arrests. A suicide bomb attack at the entrance of the settlement at Ariel shook the general ceasefire between the Israelis and Palestinians on August 12, but on August 19 it was literally blown apart. On that day, a suicide bomber blew himself up on a Jerusalem bus, killing 23 and wounding more than 130.

Throughout this period, the administration had John Wolf present in the area. He sought to reinforce the reciprocal obligations from the limited agreement and to build on them. He was supposedly there to produce accountability. Yet while the President may have spoken of creating accountability, the administration was not prepared to act that way. The proof: Wolf's mission was to have no visibility. Pressure on each side was to remain purely private. But there is no such thing as private accountability. Neither Israelis nor Palestinians will ever believe there are any consequences if everything is to remain private. So long as an envoy—especially one who is seen as being relatively low level—is the only one applying pressure, there is no fear of the onus being put on either side.

To make matters worse, by keeping Wolf's mission invisible, the administration made it impossible for Abu Mazen to act. For while there were no public U.S. demands on the Palestinians to close down the smuggling tunnels or secure certain areas in Gaza with arrests and seizure of weapons or have Palestinian police assume control of particular West Bank areas, there were public demands by Israeli Prime Minister Sharon to do so. So Abu Mazen could not act without appearing in Palestinian eyes as if he was giving into Sharon's diktat. Under these circumstances, it was only a matter of time before Abu Mazen would fail.

When I saw him in June 2003 in Ramallah, I asked him how much time he had to show his way worked, to show that he could produce before Arafat would subvert him. He parried my question, asking me how much time I thought he had. My answer was four to five months. He said, "I have four months." We were both wrong. With the collapse of the ceasefire, and Arafat's blockage of Abu Mazen's attempt to finally go after Hamas and Islamic Jihad, Abu Mazen resigned after three months.

The resignation of Abu Mazen marked a turning point. Even though Arafat was to appoint Abu Ala as the new prime minister, he blocked Abu Ala from acting on security—retaining complete control over the Palestinian security organizations. Unlike Abu Mazen, who believed he could overcome Arafat, Abu Ala hoped merely to co-opt him. He felt if he could get the Israelis to permit Arafat to travel again, leaving the virtual prison of his headquarters, and could get the U.S. administration to support new elections for the Arafat position (something Arafat would see as re-legitimizing him internationally), he could in exchange convince Arafat to accept the enforcement of a real ceasefire. But neither the Israelis nor the administration were ready to agree to these steps, particularly before seeing that Abu Ala could produce anything on his end.

At the time of this writing, both the Sharon government and the Bush administration believe that Abu Ala is completely hamstrung by Arafat, making it difficult for him to be a partner. Worse, chaos in the Palestinian areas has been growing, and the impulse toward unilateralism has taken on a new life in Israel.

Sooner or later, unilateralism on the Israeli side was an inevitability if there was little prospect of agreement with the Palestinians. It was only a matter of time before the demographic trends, combined with the absence of any real change in the security situation, were going to force a different path in Israel. The overriding issue on which Israelis agree is that Israel must remain a Jewish and democratic state. Given demographic trends that indicate that as early as the year 2010, and certainly not later than 2015, there will be more Arabs than Jews between the Mediterranean Sea and the Jordan River, Israel cannot remain in the West Bank and Gaza and retain its Jewish, democratic character. While this understanding was latent for a very long time, it has now become a very public issue in Israel. Ehud Olmert, one of the former princes of Likud and Sharon's Deputy Prime Minister, declared in December 2003 that Israel could not remain in the territories lest it lose its moral grounding and find its Jewish supporters internationally unable to defend an apartheid reality.

Partition was bound to happen at some point. For Yitzhak Rabin, who understood both the demographic and security arguments for partition, his preference was to produce it through agreement with the Palestinians. But he was prepared to "separate" from the Palestinians if agreement was not possible. Prime Minister Sharon, though a pronounced opponent of building a separation fence when Yitzhak Rabin first proposed it in 1995 and Ehud Barak reintroduced it after the outbreak of the Intifada, has now become a proponent of both the fence and the concept of disengagement. Partly, he has been driven by the security reality: The fence around Gaza has proven effective in preventing suicide attacks into Israel from Gaza in the last three years. Small wonder, therefore, that 83 percent of the Israeli public favors the building of a comparable fence or barrier on the West Bank.*

For Sharon and other leaders in Likud such as Bibi Netanyahu, the issue is no longer whether to build the fence, but where to do so. They understand well that the settlers, the core of the traditional Likud constituency, fear being on the "wrong" side of the fence. The fence inevitably will create a new security line. Protecting Israelis to the west of the line will become easier for the IDF if they do not have to be dispersed, protecting outlying settlements and the roads that lead to them. From that standpoint alone, the Israeli military would have a more coherent defense posture. Inherently, unless Sharon builds a fence in both the eastern and the western side of the West Bank,

---

*Palestinians refer to the fence as a wall, playing up the imaging of an apartheid wall. In truth, approximately five percent of the barrier is a wall. David Makovsky, *The Defensible Fence: Fighting Terror and Enabling a Two-State Solution,* The Washington Institute for Near East Policy, 2004.

settlers who are east of the fence will be more vulnerable and ultimately not in a sustainable position.

That is why Ehud Olmert has spoken about withdrawing from 80–85 percent of the West Bank unilaterally. The fact that most of the settlers—though not most of the settlements—are in the area closest to the "green line" also makes it possible to absorb more than three-fourths of the settlers in the 15 percent of the area that Olmert would have Israel hold on to. At Camp David and again in the Clinton ideas we spoke of three settlement blocs that could accommodate 80 percent of the settlers. But we were focused on an agreement that would annex these areas to Israel and for which there would be some territorial compensation to the Palestinians.

While Ariel Sharon's approach to unilateral withdrawal has been far more circumscribed than Ehud Olmert's, at least as applied to the West Bank, he also declared his commitment to disengagement in December of 2003. A short time later, he announced that he would withdraw from Gaza, declaring that he was "working on the assumption that in the future there will be no Jews in Gaza." This was a stunning turnaround for the architect of the settler movement and a leader who as prime minister in 2002 had declared that Netzarim (a settlement in Gaza) was as important to Israel as Tel Aviv. Demographic realities, an ongoing and unacceptable security situation, and the emergence of the Geneva accords all put pressure on Sharon to show he had a policy and not simply a posture that offered no change and no possibilities.*

Even before his public declaration on Gaza, Sharon had approached the Bush administration to explain what he intended and to seek certain assurances from the United States. Apart from wanting U.S. backing for his step on the international stage, Sharon also believed that to overcome resistance to his plan within his government and party, he needed to show he was gaining something for Israel. Among other things, he sought U.S. asssurances on Israel not being forced back to the June 4, 1967 lines, recognition of Israel's large settlement blocs in the West bank, and rejection of the principle of right of return for Palestinian refugees to Israel in any eventual peace settlement. With such assurances in hand, he could, he believed, easily overcome the opposition within his government. That turned out to be a miscalculation.†

None of the assurances Sharon sought were necessarily inconsistant with the Clinton ideas. But, of course, they were being sought in a very different context. There was

---

*The Geneva Accords were negotiated by delegations of quasi-official Palestinians and Israelis outside the government. They produced a detailed peace agreement; they borrowed liberally from the Clinton ideas but went beyond them on both borders and refugees. Sharon declared the Accords suicidal for Israel, but clearly felt the need to have an answer to them and not just a critique.

†While Sharon was undoubtedly correct that the assurances from the U.S. would mean a great deal to the majority of Israelis, Sharon overestimated the affect the assurances would have on his own Likud

no end game for negotiations—indeed, there were no negotiations at all between Israelis and Palestinians—and Sharon was declaring a unilateral approach precisely because he saw no Palestinian partner and no prospect of having one any time soon. The Bush administration shared his view of the Palestinians, and, after overcoming its instinctive reluctance to be more heavily involved, it did engage in a two-month process of consultations with Sharon over the assurances he sought. In the end, Sharon received assurances that were far less explicit than he sought, but the harsh Palestinian reaction to them and their claims that the U.S. had prejudged what could be done in negotiations, fostered the impression that historic thresholds had been crossed.

The Bush administration might have tempered the Palestinian response, which, of course, also set a tone for Arab leaders, had it held parallel talks with the Palestinians, Egyptians, Jordanians, and Europeans while it was consulting with Israel. There was nothing wrong with working out understandings with the Israelis, especially because it was Sharon who was taking the initiative. But by doing this in a very public process, and by excluding the Palestinians, the administration made its task of building on the Sharon initiative of withdrawing from Gaza and pulling back partially in the West Bank more difficult than it had to be.

And it is essential to build on the Sharon initiative. It can, assuming it is implemented, provide a basis on which to unfreeze the situation. But it must be done the right way. If done in isolation, it could result in Hamas gaining control over Gaza and chaos in the West Bank. But withdrawals that are coordinated so that the Palestinian Authority understands when the Israelis will pull back; what the United States and others (the Europeans, the Russians, and the Arabs) expect the PA will do in terms of security and reform as withdrawal approaches and unfolds; how hand-offs of settlements could be given to the PA and not to Hamas; and how security and economic assistance could be provided if the Palestinians will assume their responsibilities could all be part of an active diplomatic effort to manage the Israeli decision to pull back.

Only the United States has the wherewithal to lead such an effort. Here is the meaning of American engagement. Obviously, I am a believer in U.S. engagement in Middle East peacemaking. But not all engagement makes sense. The United States cannot impose peace, and is unlikely ever to assume a mandate or trusteeship over the Palestinian people. But the United States can and must fashion diplomacy that meets

party. With 70 percent of Israelis supporting his initiative, he believed he would be certain to win a referendum held only in the Likud party, and that such a win would marginalize the right wing. Unfortunately, Sharon underestimated the possible backlash and organizational skills of Likud party activists, and he lost the vote decisively. With the majority of Israelis favoring the Sharon plan, Likud's referendum victory could portray it as an extreme, not mainstream, party and could come back to haunt the party.

the requirements and possibilities of the time. We can coordinate with the Israelis so they build a fence that responds to the security, demographic, humanitarian, and political criteria, that serves Israel's needs, and that preserves an eventual two-state solution. We can deal with the Palestinian prime minister and legislative council, emphasizing our readiness to recognize Palestinian sovereignty in the areas from which Israel withdraws, provided the Palestinians assume their responsibilities. We can encourage the Europeans to offer material assistance—and make clear we will do so as well—if the EU will also work with the Palestinians on assuming those responsibilities. (We can even join with the Europeans and others in offering an international security presence and assistance to reinforce, but not take the place of, Palestinian efforts). We can press the Egyptians, who after all border Gaza and therefore have a stake in its stability, to work with the Palestinian Authority and the Israelis should the Israelis implement the Sharon declaration of a Gaza first withdrawal.

As difficult as the period since 2001 has been for Israelis and Palestinians, as much as they have suffered and bear the scars and the legacy from the last three years, the situation is hopeless only if we make it so. After all, notwithstanding Sharon's political and legal difficulties, Israel is still likely to evacuate settlements in Palestinian areas for the first time (or, should Sharon prove unable to deliver, to take some other step designed to unfreeze the situation and create a basis for a Palestinian response in the coming year or so). When the withdrawal (or some other step) takes place, an opening will be created. To be sure, if the time prior to the Israeli withdrawal is lengthly and filled with violence, the opening will quickly close. That is certainly possible. But it is equally possible that the reality of Israel leaving Gaza will raise the stakes for Palestinian reformers, make them more assertive, induce them to show the world that Palestinians can govern themselves and be responsible free of Israeli control, and, therein, raise the costs to Arafat of appearing to block Palestinian gains.

Regardless, there is room for creative diplomacy. Every moment that is lost in the Middle East tends to make the task of peacemaking more difficult. Let us hope that the moment that is likely to be created by the Israeli decision to withdraw at least partially is not one more lost opportunity. Peace may not be just around the corner, but it is not beyond our grasp to produce a way-station to it. Coordinated unilateralism, tacit understandings, or a limited bilateral agreement could re-create an environment that makes peace possible again. It could, if intensively shaped, restore Israeli and Palestinian faith in peacemaking, mitigating the omnipresent Israeli fear of Palestinian terror and the Palestinian conviction that Israel will never surrender its control over them. In any case, a way-station is necessary to change the climate and make it possible to get beyond Yasir Arafat and the dysfunction he cultivated. When that happens, the peace may no longer be missing.

Appendix

President Clinton's Parameters as Presented by Him to the Israeli and Palestinian Negotiators on December 23, 2000.

On Wednesday, I went over general parameters to help focus your negotiations and gave you specific tasks. I know you have been working hard. I have heard reports from Madeleine and Dennis, and frankly, I believe that at this rate you will not get there. We are running out of time and cannot afford to lose this opportunity.

I believe it is my responsibility to give you my best judgment of what it will take to narrow your differences on key issues so that leaders can take final decisions. Obviously, you will have to resolve other issues; but if you can resolve these core ones, I believe you will reach a deal.

I want to make clear this is not a U.S. proposal. Rather, it reflects my best judgment of what it will take to conclude an agreement in the next two weeks. If these ideas are not accepted by either side, they will be off the table and have no standing in the future.

I ask you to take these ideas back to your leaders. I am prepared to meet with them separately to further refine them and plan for a summit to conclude an agreement. But it should be clear to them that they should not come here to renegotiate these ideas. They should come here to try to refine them within the boundaries I will set forth. I would like to know by Wednesday if they are prepared to come on that basis.

TERRITORY

You heard from me last time that I believe the solution will need to provide for Palestinian sovereignty over somewhere between 90 and 100 percent of West Bank territory, and that there will need to be swaps and other territorial arrangements to compensate for the land Israel annexes for its settlement blocs.

Based on what I have heard since we last met, I believe the solution should be in the mid-90 percents; I believe you should work on the basis of a solution that provides between 94 and 96 percent of West Bank territory to the Palestinian state with a land swap of 1 to 3 percent; you will need to work out other territorial arrangements such as permanent Safe Passage. As you work out the territorial arrangements, you might also consider the swap of leased land to meet your respective needs.

Given these parameters, you should lose no time in developing final maps consistent with the criteria I laid out last time (e.g., 80 percent of the settlers in blocs, contiguity of territory for each side, minimize annexation and the number of Palestinians affected).

SECURITY

As I said on security the last time, the challenge is to address legitimate Israeli security concerns while respecting Palestinian sovereignty. The key lies in an international presence that can only be withdrawn by the agreement of both sides. My best judgment is that Israeli withdrawal should be phased over thirty-six months while the international force is gradually introduced into the area. At the end of this period, a small Israeli presence in fixed locations would remain in the Jordan Valley under the authority of the international force for another thirty-six months. This period could be reduced in the event of favorable regional developments that diminish the threats to Israel.

On early-warning stations, I believe that Israel should maintain three facilities on the West Bank with a Palestinian liaison presence; the stations would be subject to review after three years, with any change in status to be mutually agreed.

On the emergency deployments, I understand you still have work to do on developing maps of the relevant areas and routes. In defining what would constitute an "emergency," I suggest you think about formulations that refer to "an imminent and demonstrable threat to Israel's national security that requires Israel to declare a national state of emergency." Of course, the international forces would need to be notified of any such determination.

On airspace, I suggest that the state of Palestine will have sovereignty over its airspace but that the two sides should work out special arrangements for Israeli training and operational needs.

I understand that the Israeli position is that Palestine should be defined as a "demilitarized state," while the Palestinian side has proposed "a state of limited arms." As a possible compromise formula I suggest you think in terms of a "non-militarized state." This would be consistent with the fact that, as well as a strong Palestinian security force, Palestine will have an international force for border security and deterrence purposes. Whatever the terminology, you need to work out specific understandings on the parameters of the Palestinian security forces.

JERUSALEM AND REFUGEES

I am acutely aware how difficult the Jerusalem and refugee issues are to both sides. My sense, however, is that the remaining gaps are more in formulations than in the practical realties.

JERUSALEM

On Jerusalem, as I said last time the most promising approach is to follow the general principle that what is Arab in the City should be Palestinian and what is Jewish should be Israeli; this would apply to the Old City as well. I urge you to work on maps to create maximum contiguity for both sides within this framework.

We have all spent a lot of energy trying to solve the issue of the Haram/Temple Mount. One thing seems clear to me—the gap does not relate to practical administration of the area but to symbolic issues of sovereignty and finding a way to accord respect to the religious beliefs of both sides. This is nevertheless clearly one of your most sensitive issues and concerns the interests of religious communities beyond Israel and Palestine.

I know you have been speaking about a number of formulations. Perhaps you can agree on one. But I want to suggest two additional approaches that I believe would formalize Palestinian de facto control over the Haram while respecting the convictions of the Jewish people. Under each, there could be an international monitoring system to provide mutual confidence.

1. Your agreement could provide for Palestinian sovereignty over the Haram, and for Israeli sovereignty over either "the Western Wall and the space sacred to Judaism of which it is a part" or "the Western Wall and the holy of holies of which it is a part." There would be a firm commitment by both not to excavate beneath the Haram or behind the Western Wall.
2. Alternatively, the agreement could provide for Palestinian sovereignty over the Haram and Israeli sovereignty over the Western Wall and for "shared functional sovereignty over the issue of excavation under the Haram or behind the Western Wall." That way, mutual consent would be required before any excavation takes place in these areas.

One of these formulations should be acceptable to you both.

REFUGEES

The issue of Palestinian refugees is no less sensitive than Jerusalem. But here again my sense is that your differences are focused mostly on how to formulate your solutions, not on what will happen on the practical level.

I believe Israel is prepared to acknowledge the moral and material suffering caused to the Palestinian people as a result of the 1948 War and the need to assist the international community in addressing the problem. I also believe the Palestinian side is prepared to join in such an international solution and that we have a pretty good idea of what it would involve.

The fundamental gap seems to be how to handle the concept of the right of return. I know the history and how hard it would be for the Palestinian leadership to appear to be abandoning this principle. At the same time, I know the Israeli side cannot accept any reference to a right of return that would imply a right to immigrate to Israel in defiance of Israel's sovereign policies on admission or that would threaten the Jewish character of the State.

Any solution will have to address both of these needs. It will also have to be consistent with the two-state approach that both sides have accepted as the way to end the Israeli-Palestinian conflict. A new State of Palestine is about to be created as the homeland of the Palestinian people, just as Israel was established as the homeland of the Jewish people. Under this two-state solution, our guiding principle has to be that the Palestinian state will be the focal point for the Palestinians who choose to return to the area, without ruling out that Israel will accept some of these refugees.

I believe you need to adopt a formulation on the right of return that will make clear there is no specific right of return to Israel, itself, but that does not negate the aspirations of Palestinian refugees to return to the area. I propose two alternatives:

Both sides recognize the right of Palestinian refugees to return to historic Palestine.
Both sides recognize the right of Palestinian refugees to a homeland.

The agreement would define the implementation of this general right in a way that is consistent with the two-state solution. It would list the five possible homes for refugees: 1) The State of Palestine; 2) Areas in Israel being transferred to Palestine in the land swap; 3) Rehabilitation in host country; 4) Resettlement in third country; 5) Admission to Israel.

In listing these five options, you would make clear that return to the West Bank, Gaza, or the areas acquired through the land swap would be a right for all Palestinian refugees, while rehabilitation in their host countries, resettlement in third countries, or absorption into Israel would depend upon the policies of those countries. Israel could indicate in the agreement that it intended to establish a policy so that some of the refugees could be absorbed into Israel, consistent with Israel's sovereign decision.

I believe that priority should be given to the refugee population in Lebanon. Taken together the parties would agree that these steps implement Resolution 194.

END OF CONFLICT

I propose that the agreement clearly mark the end of the conflict and its implementation put an end to all claims. This could be implemented through a UN Security Council Resolution that notes that resolutions 242 and 338 have been implemented and through the final release of Palestinian prisoners.

WRAP-UP

I believe this is the outline of a fair and lasting agreement. It gives the Palestinian people the ability to determine their future on their own land, a sovereign and viable state recognized by the international community, al-Quds as its capital, sovereignty over the Haram, and new lives for the refugees.

It gives the people of Israel a genuine end to the conflict, real security, the preservation of sacred religious ties, the incorporation of 80 percent of the settlers into Israel, and the largest Jewish Jerusalem in history, recognized by all as your capital.

This is the best I can do. I would ask you to brief your leaders and let me know if they are prepared to come for discussions based on these ideas. I want to be very clear on one thing. These are my ideas. If they are not accepted they are not just off the table. They go with me when I leave office.

Notes

Chapter 1: Why Israelis, Arabs, and Palestinians See the World the Way They Do

16   The effect on world Jewry: Martin Gilbert, *Israel: A History* (New York: William Morrow, 1998), pp. 34–35.

17   But only the Hebrew people: quoted in Gilbert, pp. 34–35.

18   Arab resistance to Jewish immigration: Tom Segev, *One Palestine Complete: Jews and Arabs Under the Mandate* (New York: Metropolitan Books, 2000), pp. 273–83.

19   "A partial Jewish state . . .": quoted in Segev, p. 403.

22   "We are waiting for . . .": Yitzhak Rabin quoted Dayan in a major policy address focused on peace negotiations. "Statement in the Knesset by Prime Minister Rabin," October 3, 1994, in *Israel's Foreign Relations: Selected Documents, 1992–1994*, vol. 14 (Jerusalem: Ministry of Foreign Affairs, 1995), p. 800.

26   Resolution 242 established the principles: Arthur Goldberg, the U.S. Ambassador to the UN at the time, deliberately excluded the article "the" from the language of the resolution, which allowed us to interpret the resolution as not necessarily meaning withdrawal from all the territories captured in 1967. Given linguistic differences in the translation, others, including the French, maintained a different interpretation. For a complete discussion of the resolution and its interpretations, see *UN Security Council Resolution 242: The Building Block of Peacemaking* (Washington, D.C.: The Washington Institute for Near East Policy, 1993).

29   Those Israelis: Begin speech at the Hebrew University in September 1972 that I attended, HU, 1972.

29   George Antonius's historic work: George Antonius, *The Arab Awakening: The Story of the Arab National Movement* (London: Hamish Hamilton, 1938).

30   Rather that the numbers: Adeed Dawisha, *Arab Nationalism in the Twentieth Century: From Triumph to Despair* (Princeton: Princeton University Press, 2003); see chapter 2.

30   The arrival and competitive impulses: Antonius, pp. 40–45.

30   But C. Ernest Dawn: Rashid Khalidi, Lisa Anderson, Muhammad Muslih, and Reeva S. Simon, eds., *The Origins of Arab Nationalism* (New York: Columbia University Press, 1991), p. ix. See also C. Ernest Dawn, "The Origins of Arab Nationalism," in the same volume. Dawn concludes that Arab nationalism arose not in response to Western and Christian influences but as an outgrowth of "Islamic modernism" and a power struggle by the elite in Ottoman society to remain politically relevant.

31   He replied sharply: "The Sharif Husain's Second Note to Sir Henry McMahon," September 9, 1915; printed in Antonius, p. 417.

31   "any concession designed": "The Sharif Husain's Fourth Note to Sir Henry McMahon," January 1, 1916; printed in Antonius, p. 425.

32   Bin Laden: Quoted in John F. Burns, "The Wanted Man," *The New York Times,* October 8, 2001.

33   But the assembly: Segev, p. 106.

33   kill "an entire nation . . .": quoted in Segev, pp. 107–8.

34   "Make the enemy . . .": William A. Eddy, *FDR Meets Ibn Saud* (New York: American Friends of the Middle East, 1954), p. 34.

35   It was the Arabs: Antonius, p. 391.

35   "Obviously, they thought": quoted in Segev, p. 510

35   "I underestimated the strength": quoted in Segev, p. 510.

36   Their cause was used: Fawaz Turki, *The Disinherited* (New York: Monthly Review Press, 1972).

36   Middle-class nationalists: Fouad Ajami, *The Arab Predicament: Arab Political Thought and Practice Since 1967* (Cambridge, Cambridge University Press, 1981), p. 12.

37   For many Arab intellectuals: Ajami and William B. Quandt, Fuad Jabber, and Ann Mosely Lesch, *The Politics of Palestinian Nationalism* (Berkeley: University of California Press, 1973).

38   The "enervating and degrading existence": Turki, pp. 37–38.

39   The "dominant Arab order": Fouad Ajami, pp. 141–49.

41   Strikes and stone-throwing: The origins of the first Intifada are chronicled in Ze'ev Schiff and Ehud Yaari, *Intifada: The Palestinian Uprising—Israel's Third Front* (New York: Simon and Schuster, 1989).

42   In 1990: For a good analysis of the impact of Palestinian support for Iraq and Saddam Hussein, see Judith Miller, "Nowhere to Go: The Palestinians After the War," *New York Times Magazine*, July 21, 1991.

Chapter 2: The Road to Madrid

47   By the mid-1980s: *Sunday Times* (London), June 15, 1969.

48   During President Asad's trip: George Breslauer, *Soviet Strategy in the Middle East* (Boston: Unwin Hyman, 1990), esp. Galia Golan chapter, pp. 160, 164.

61   "It is not up to Egypt": "Arafat, Mubarak Speak After Meeting," MENA, November 2, 1989, FBIS-NES-89-212.

67   In the Arab Middle East: Steven Walt, *The Origins of Alliances* (Ithaca, N.Y.: Cornell University Press, 1987).

73   "The land is important": James A. Baker III, *The Politics of Diplomacy* (New York: G. P. Putnam's Sons, 1995), p. 456.

Chapter 3: Rabin, Presidential Transition, the Syrian Pocket, and Oslo

90   "Taciturn, shy, reflective . . .": Henry Kissinger, *White House Years* (Boston: Little, Brown, 1979), p. 355.

92   "What can we do?": quoted in Elli Wohlgelernter, "War Hero and Peacemaker," *Jerusalem Post*, November 5, 1995, p. 1.

94   "Jewish independence will not endure": quoted in Martin Gilbert, *Israel: A History* (New York: William Morrow, 1998), p. 211.

101   Yossi approved the idea: David Makovsky, *Making Peace with the PLO* (Boulder, Colo.: Westview Press, 1996), pp. 21–22.

102   In the first round: Makovsky, p. 23.

107   The depth of withdrawal: See Itamar Rabinovich, *The Brink of Peace* (Princeton: Princeton University Press, 1998), p. 83.

111   He would be prepared to commit: This was a conditioned commitment, not a hypothetical, as some in Israel later described it. For one such description, see Rabinovich, pp. 104–6.

120   I believe that it was Carter's urging: Others on Clinton's political staff later described rehearsing the handshake in advance. See, for example, George Stephanopoulos, *All Too Human* (New York: Little Brown, 1999).

Chapter 7: The Interim Agreement

192   Regardless of whether it was Peres's or Arafat's idea: Uri, in his book, recounts that after the Nobel ceremony in Oslo, Abu Ala met him in Jerusalem and said, "We must save the process," and that Arafat was now suspicious of the Peres proposal. Uri Savir, *The Process: 1,110 Days That Changed the Middle East* (New York: Random House, 1998), p. 158.

195   "Thereafter, a 'further redeployment' . . .": Savir, p. 172.

198   In area B: "Israeli-Palestinian Interim Agreement on the West Bank and the Gaza Strip," September 28, 1995. Full text available at www.state.gov/p/nea/rls/22678.htm.

199   They were deliberately going slow: Abderrahman al-Rashed, "Asharq al-Aswat," see *Mideast Mirror*, August 7, 1995: p. 9.

199   Palestinians increasingly complained: editorial in the East Jerusalem newspaper *An-Nahar*, see *Mideast Mirror*, August 7, 1995, pp. 9–10.

Chapter 10: Could the Peace Process Be Saved?

248–49 The summit's declaration: "Press Conference with Presidents Clinton and Mubarak, Sharm el-Sheikh, 13 March 1996, including the Joint Statement of the Summit of the Peacemakers," in *Israel's Foreign Relations: Selected Documents, 1992–1994*, vol. 15 (Jerusalem: Ministry of Foreign Affairs, 1995), pp. 444–51.

Chapter 11: Bibi Wins, Will Peace Lose?

267   "I would ask you": Michael Dobbs and Nora Boustany, "Summit Concludes with Little Progress," *Washington Post*, October 3, 1996: p. A1.

Chapter 15: The 13 Percent Solution

353   He was tough on terror: Israel TV Channel 1, "Netanyahu interview on peace process, other issues," BBC Summary of World Broadcasts, posted July 30, 1997.

354   "Let me be clear": Madeleine Albright, "The Israeli-Palestinian Peace Process," speech given to the National Press Club, Washington, D.C., August 6, 1997.

356   "we cannot give in to terror": press statement by Secretary of State Madeleine Albright, September 4, 1997, Department of State.

365   "all the security steps": The Israeli newspaper *Yidiot Aharonot* published the security memorandum on December 24, 1997. For a translation, see "Israeli paper publishes translation of Israeli-PNA security memorandum," in BBC Summary of World Broadcasts, December 29, 1997.

Chapter 20: "Syria's My Priority"

510   He got Barak to refer to Asad's legacy: Patrick Seale, *Al-Hayat* (London), June 23, 1999. Translated in BBC Summary of World Broadcasts, June 29, 1999.

Chapter 22: The Rise and Fall of the Israeli-Syrian Deal

571   The author, Amos Oz: Quoted in "It's Assad's Move," *The Jerusalem Post*, January 14, 2000; p. 8.

Chapter 25: The Denouement—From Camp David to the Intifada to the Clinton Ideas

737   Saturday evening, October 7: Lee Hockstader, "Middle East Conflict Widens; Clashes Rock Lebanese Border; Barak Gives Arafat Ultimatum," *The Washington Post*, October 8, 2000.

740   We had three: "Remarks by the President and President Hosni Murbarak of Egyptian delivery of joint statements at the Conclusion of the Middle East Peace Summit," The White House, Office of the Press Secretary, October 17, 2000.

757   as some argue, actually gave orders for it: See, for example, Ehud Ya'ari, "The Israeli-Palestinian Confrontation: Toward a Divorce," Jerusalem Issue Brief, Vol. 2, No. 2, June 30, 2002.

Chapter 26: Learning the Lessons of the Past and Applying Them to the Future

765   "As I have said . . .": Yitzhak Rabin, *The Rabin Memoirs,* Second Edition (Tel Aviv: Steimatzky House, 1994), p. III. This passage was added to Rabin's mem-

oirs in their second edition and comes from an introductory essay, "On the Road to Peace."

Epilogue

785   "shuttle diplomacy . . .": Secretary Colin L. Powell, "Remarks on the Sharm al-Sheikh Fact-Finding Committee," Washington, D.C., May 21, 2001.

792   "the thought and idea . . .": BBC Worldwide Monitoring translation of Voice of Israel broadcast of Sharon speech. "Sharon tells Likud of Need for Political Deal with the Palestinians," May 26, 2003.

798   "working on the assumption . . .": James Bennet, "Angering Settlers, Sharon Says Most May Have to Leave Gaza," *The New York Times,* February 3, 2003.

Acknowledgments

The foundation of this book is a working record that I kept during my time as envoy. It was at the suggestion of Tom Friedman of *The New York Times*, who knows the value of first-hand experience, that I began to keep such a record: writing about my expectations before each trip and negotiating session, and writing afterward to describe what had actually happened—often in the middle of the night between rounds of negotiations. I would note where what I heard matched my expectations, and I would try to account for the areas where it did not. In less stressful times, I would review the record, while constantly adding to it. Those with whom I dealt were struck by how I seemed to know every detail and was always able to quote what they had said back to them. And so the record became a useful tool in diplomacy; moreover, the act of writing it often gave me additional perspective and at times was a way for me to try to shape the day-to-day strategy.

The book, like the peace process itself, also reflects the unflagging efforts of many people. I owe a great deal to those who were my closest working companions. Aaron Miller, Gamal Helal, Nick Rasmussen, and John Schwartz worked from an extraordinary sense of commitment and belief—no trip was too hard, no work too demanding, no disruptions of their personal plans unacceptable.

Martin Indyk, too, was a kindred spirit throughout the process, and was particularly helpful during his tenures as U.S. Ambassador to Israel. Jill Indyk constantly had to accommodate our demands to use their residence for meetings, dinners, and late-night talks. Unfailingly, she did so with warmth and grace. Others like Toni Verstandig joined the team later, but energetically and selflessly contributed to our efforts.

Naturally, I owe a great deal to those who placed me in a position to shape and conduct our peace process diplomacy: President George H. W. Bush, Secretary James A. Baker, President Bill Clinton, Secretary Warren Christopher, and Secretary Madeleine Albright. All of them did what they could to achieve Arab-Israeli peace, and all of them gave me the mandate that a negotiator needs. It was a privilege to work with them, and a stirring reminder of how leaders can be driven by a profound sense of purpose.

Over the years many others in the State Department and in our embassies throughout the Middle East and Europe helped facilitate our efforts. I shall always be grateful to countless other colleagues, too numerous to mention, who, no matter the time of day or night and no matter the need, lent their support to the diplomacy. Their work is often unseen and anonymous, and I thank them.

For support during the writing of the book, I owe a great deal to the Washington Institute for Near East Policy and its president, Fred Lafer, who welcomed me upon my departure from the government. No one could have designed a place with more support, collegiality, and intellectual stimulation from which to write. I am especially indebted to Robert Satloff and Patrick Clawson, the director and deputy director, for their support. David Makovsky, my Institute colleague and friend, also offered many constructive comments. At the Institute, a large number of research assistants and summer interns assisted in research and fact checking at different stages of this project, and I owe them all a debt of gratitude. In particular, I want to thank Jacqueline Kaufmann, who helped as I was organizing the book and its content; she worked tirelessly to both provide assistance on research and to manage many of the demands on my time in the early stages of the writing. Eran Benedek, Evan Langenhahn, and Michael Bergman picked up the work Jacqueline had done and organized the fact-checking effort, responding with skill and talent to any and all needs.

Ben Fishman, my research assistant, took on the onerous task of transforming a draft text into something like a final document: providing thoughtful comments, raising questions, helping with the editing and footnoting, arranging for maps to be made, and meticulously fact-checking the whole.

I am also very grateful to Marguerite Dale, my executive assistant. In the last two years when, during Rob Satloff's sojourn to Morocco, I served as the director of the Washington Institute, Marguerite juggled my various responsibilities there, at the Kennedy School and Brandeis, and on the road—managing to magically set aside time for me to write.

Jamie Rubin, who has an innate ability to get to the essence of an issue, made a number of extremely useful substantive and stylistic suggestions on an early draft. Robert Danin and Ken Stein also offered helpful comments. Two younger scholars, Leonard Wood and Eitan Goldstein, suggested sensible changes in the narratives chapter. And Issa Kassissich, one of my students at the Kennedy School, corrected a number of mistakes in the text.

It is my good fortune that Esther Newberg of ICM was a believer in this book from the beginning; she gave me an invaluable tutorial about the book publishing world, and was a constant source of support and sage advice.

Jonathan Galassi, publisher of Farrar, Straus and Giroux, was also an enthusiast for this project from the outset. He encouraged me to offer a historical context, not only to ground the story but to offer a broader perspective about what it reveals.

As the manuscript underwent revision, Paul Elie, senior editor at Farrar, Straus and Giroux, was as much a partner as an editor, tightening the narrative without doing damage to the story and its lessons. Best of all, he was a pleasure to work with. So was Paul's assistant, Kathryn Lewis, who worked diligently to transform the final manuscript into a book.

Above all, I thank my family. After the Hebron agreement, Bibi Netanyahu wrote a letter thanking me for my efforts and offering additional thanks "to your long-suffering family." The book and the process it describes have been an odyssey not only for me, but for Debbie, Gabe, Rachel, and Ilana. Not only were they understanding of my absences and preoccupations, they, too, became deep believers in the quest for Middle East peace. It became as much their effort as mine, and, more than they will ever know or believe, they sustained me when I needed it—and then sustained me all over again as I wrote about it. Rachel and Ilana particularly helped their technically challenged father with computer-related needs, and Debbie and Gabe offered valuable comments and editorial suggestions.

Through it all, Debbie always kept me grounded with her honesty, support, and love. I could not have done it without her.

Index